P9-CAO-513

www.wadsworth.com

wadsworth.com is the World Wide Web site for Wadsworth and is your direct source to dozens of online resources.

At *wadsworth.com* you can find out about supplements, demonstration software, and student resources. You can also send e-mail to many of our authors and preview new publications and exciting new technologies.

wadsworth.com
Changing the way the world learns®

MORAL ISSUES IN BUSINESS

Ninth Edition

William H. Shaw
San Jose State University

Vincent Barry
Bakersfield College

THOMSON

™

WADSWORTH

Australia • Canada • Mexico • Singapore • Spain
United Kingdom • United States

THOMSON

WADSWORTH

Publisher: Holly J. Allen
Philosophy Editor: Steve Wainwright
Assistant Editors: Lee McCracken, Anna Lustig
Editorial Assistant: Anna Lustig
Marketing Manager: Worth Hawes
Marketing Assistant: Kristi Bostock
Advertising Project Manager: Bryan Vann
Print/Media Buyer: Rebecca Cross
Composition Buyer: Ben Schroeter

Permissions Editor: Bob Kauser
Production Service: Penmarin Books
Text Designer: Harry Voigt
Copy Editor: Adrienne Armstrong
Cover Designer: Ross Carron
Cover Image: Photodisc Blue Collection, Getty Images
Cover Printer: Phoenix Color
Compositor: Thompson Type
Printer: Maple-Vail Book Manufacturing Group

Copyright © 2004 Wadsworth, a division of Thomson Learning, Inc. Thomson Learning™ is a trademark used herein under license.

ALL RIGHTS RESERVED. No part of this work covered by the copyright hereon may be reproduced or used in any form or by any means—graphic, electronic, or mechanical, including but not limited to photocopying, recording, taping, Web distribution,information networks, or information storage and retrieval systems—without the written permission of the publisher.

Printed in the United States of America
2 3 4 5 6 7 06 05 04

For more information about our products, contact us at:
Thomson Learning Academic Resource Center
1-800-423-0563

For permission to use material from this text, contact us by:
Phone: 1-800-730-2214 **Fax:** 1-800-730-2215
Web: http://www.thomsonrights.com

Library of Congress Conrol Number: 2003104087

Student Edition: ISBN 0-534-53654-9
Instructor's Edition: ISBN 0-534-53664-6

Wadsworth/Thomson Learning
10 Davis Drive
Belmont, CA 94002-3098
USA

Asia
Thomson Learning
5 Shenton Way #01-01
UIC Building
Singapore 068808

Australia
Nelson Thomson Learning
102 Dodds Street
South Melbourne, Victoria 3205
Australia

Canada
Nelson Thomson Learning
1120 Birchmount Road
Toronto, Ontario M1K 5G4
Canada

Europe/Middle East/Africa
Thomson Learning
High Holborn House
50/51 Bedford Row
London WC1R 4LR
United Kingdom

Latin America
Thomson Learning
Seneca, 53
Colonia Polanco
11560 Mexico D.F.
Mexico

Spain
Paraninfo Thomson Learning
Calle Magallanes, 25
28015 Madrid
Spain

Brief Contents ━━━━━━━━━━━━━━━■

Contents ━━━━━━━━━━━━━━━━━━━━━━━━━━━━━━━━ ■

Preface ■

As *Moral Issues in Business* enters its ninth edition, business ethics is now a well-established academic subject. Most colleges and universities offer courses in it, and scholarly interest in the field continues to grow. This is all to the good: It is difficult to imagine an area of study that has greater importance to society or greater relevance to students.

Yet some people still scoff at the idea of business ethics, jesting that the very concept is an oxymoron. To be sure, recent years have seen the newspapers filled with lurid stories of corporate misconduct and felonious behavior by individual businesspeople. And many suspect that what the newspapers report represents only the tip of the proverbial iceberg. Yet these reports should push the reflective person, not to make fun of business ethics, but rather to think more deeply about the nature and purpose of business in our society and about the ethical choices individuals must inevitably make in their business and professional lives.

Business ethics has an interdisciplinary character. Questions of economic policy and business practice intertwine with issues in politics, sociology, and organizational theory. Although business ethics remains anchored in philosophy, even here abstract questions in normative ethics and political philosophy mingle with analysis of practical problems and concrete moral dilemmas. Furthermore, business ethics is not just an academic study but also an invitation to reflect on our own values and on our own responses to the difficult moral choices that the world of business can pose. Accordingly, this book sticks to the four main objectives of previous editions: to expose students to the important moral issues that arise in various business contexts; to provide students with an understanding of the moral, social, and economic environments within which those problems occur; to introduce students to the ethical concepts that are relevant for resolving those moral problems; and to assist students in developing the necessary reasoning and analytical skills for doing so. Although the book's primary emphasis is on business, its scope extends to related moral issues in other organizational and professional contexts.

Moral Issues in Business has four parts. Part One, "Moral Philosophy and Business," discusses the nature of morality and presents the main theories of normative ethics and the leading approaches to questions of economic justice. Part Two, "American Business and Its Basis," examines the institutional foundations of business, focusing on capitalism as an economic system and the nature and role of corporations in our society. Part Three, "The Organization and the People in It," identifies a variety of ethical issues and moral challenges that arise out of the interplay of employers and employees within an organization, including the problem of discrimination. Part Four, "Business and Society," concerns moral problems involving business, consumers, and the natural environment.

CHANGES IN THIS EDITION

Although instructors who have used the previous edition will find the organization and content of the book familiar, we have revised *Moral Issues in Business* with thoroughness. We have updated material throughout and tried to enhance the clarity of our discussions and the accuracy of our treatment of both philosophical and empirical issues. We remain committed to providing students with a textbook that they will find clear, understandable, and engaging. This edition, like its predecessor, gives expanded treatment to the many ethical issues facing real people in the world of work: civil liberties on the job, personnel policies and procedures, union issues, drug testing, job satisfaction, downsizing, AIDS in the workplace, conflicts of interest, worker participation, day care and maternity leave, the "mommy track," and employee health and safety, among other topics.

The case studies now number forty-nine, four of them new, many others revised or updated. The case studies vary in kind and in length, but they are designed to enable instructors and students to pursue further some of the issues discussed in the text and to analyze them in more specific contexts. The case studies should provide a lively springboard for classroom discussion and the application of ethical concepts.

There are thirty-two supplementary readings, nine of them new. These essays address both theoretical topics and applied issues such as drug testing, sexual harassment, animal rights, downsizing, whistle blowing, advertising, discrimination, multinational corporations, the ethics of sales, and much more. These readings are intended to augment the text by permitting selected topics to be studied in more detail and by exposing students to alternative perspectives and analysis. In selecting and editing the readings, we have sought to provide philosophically interesting essays that will engage students and lend themselves well to class discussion.

WAYS OF USING THE BOOK

A course in business ethics can be taught in a variety of ways. Instructors have different approaches to the subject, different intellectual and pedagogical goals, and different classroom styles. They emphasize different themes and start at different places. No textbook can be all things to all instructors. In any case, were a textbook to succeed in this goal, it would lose its individual voice. Nevertheless, because of the range of topics covered, because of the three types of material in the book—text, cases, and readings—and because of the amount of material we have provided, teachers have great flexibility in how they use *Moral Issues in Business* and in how they organize their courses.

Naturally, the book can be taught cover to cover just as it is, but in a semester course this will require a brisk pace. Many instructors will wish to linger on certain topics, touch briefly on others, and skip some altogether. Assigning all the cases and extra readings as well as the text of a chapter obviously provides for the greatest depth of coverage, but the text can easily be taught by itself or with only some of the cases or readings. The book readily permits topics to be dealt with briefly by assigning only selections from the case studies, the readings, or the text itself, instead of the chapter as a whole. Depending on the instructor's approach, it is even possible to focus the course on the case studies themselves or the readings, with the text assigned only as background.

The chapters themselves are relatively self-contained, allowing them to be taught in various orders without loss of coherence. Instructors eager to get to the more specific moral issues discussed in later chapters could skip Parts One and Two (perhaps assigning only Solomon's "It's Good Business") and begin with the topics that interest them. Other instructors may choose to start with the analysis of capitalism in Chapter 4 or with the discussion of corporate responsibility in Chapter 5, then spend the bulk of the term on the chapters devoted to particular moral topics in business, returning later to some of the issues of Part One. Still other teachers may wish to devote much of a semester to the foundational concerns of Parts One and Two and deal more briefly and selectively with later matters.

ACKNOWLEDGMENTS

We wish to acknowledge our great debt to the many people whose ideas and writings have influenced us over the years. Philosophy is widely recognized to involve a process of ongoing dialogue. This is nowhere more evident than in the writing of textbooks, whose authors can rarely claim that the ideas being synthesized, organized, and presented are theirs alone. Without our colleagues, without our students, and without a larger philosophical community concerned with business and ethics, this book would not have been possible. We would especially like to thank the reviewers of this and the previous three editions of *Moral Issues in Business* for their thoughtful criticisms and helpful suggestions: Thomas Adajian, North Carolina State University; Chris Boorse, University of Delaware; Scott Calef, Xavier University of Louisiana; Herbert Cassel, University of Indianapolis; Michael Clifford, Mississippi State University; John Corvino, Wayne State University; Daniel Dombrowski, Seattle University; Julia Driver, Brooklyn College; Janice Loutzenhiser, California State University, San Bernardino; Krishna Mallick, Bentley College; Mark Michael, Austin Peay State University; Glenn Moots, Northwood University; Thomas O'Brochta, Loyola University of Chicago; Keith Price, DePaul University; Nancy Snow, Marquette University; and Robert T. Sweet, Clark State Community College.

Part One

Moral Philosophy
and Business

1

The Nature of Morality

Sometimes the rich and mighty fall. Ask Kenneth Lay, chairman and CEO of Enron until that once mighty company nose-dived and crashed. Founded in the 1980s, Enron soon became a dominant player in the field of energy trading, growing rapidly to become America's seventh-biggest company. Wall Street loves growth, and Enron was its darling, admired as dynamic, innovative, and—of course—profitable. The fact that nobody could quite understand exactly how the company made its money didn't hurt, either. In 1998 the value of Enron stock increased 40 percent. The next year it shot up 58 percent, and in 2000 it went up an unbelievable 89 percent.

After *Fortune* magazine voted it "the most innovative company of the year" in 2000, Enron proudly took to calling itself not just "the world's leading energy company" but "the world's leading company." But when Enron was forced to declare bankruptcy in December 2001—the largest Chapter 11 filing in U.S. history—the world learned that its legendary financial prowess was illusory and the company's success built on the sands of hype. And the hype continued to the end. Even with the company's financial demise fast approaching, Kenneth Lay was still recommending the company's stock to its employees—at the same time that he and other executives were cashing in their shares and bailing out.

Enron's crash cost the retirement accounts of its employees more than a billion dollars as the company's stock fell from the stratosphere to only a few pennies a share. Outside investors lost even more. The reason Enron's collapse caught investors by surprise—the company's market value was $28 billion in October 2001, just two months before its bankruptcy—was that Enron had always made its financial records and accounts as opaque as possible. It did this by creating a Byzantine financial structure of off-balance-sheet special-purpose entities—reportedly as many as 9,000—that were supposed to be separate and independent from the main company. Enron's board of directors condoned these and other dubious accounting practices and voted twice to permit executives to pursue personal interests that ran contrary to those of the company. When Enron was obliged to redo its financial statements for 1997–2000, its profits dropped $600 million and its debts increased $630 million.

Still, Enron's financial auditors should have spotted these and other problems. After all, the shell game Enron was playing is an old one, and months before the company ran aground, Enron Vice President Sherron Watkins had warned Lay that the company could soon "implode in a wave of accounting scandals." Yet both Arthur Andersen, Enron's longtime outside auditing firm, and Vinson & Elkins, the company's law firm, had routinely put together and signed off on various dubious financial deals, and in doing so made large profits for themselves. Arthur Andersen, in particular, was supposed to make sure that the company's public records reflected financial reality, but Andersen was more worried about its auditing and consulting fees than its fiduciary responsibilities. Even worse, when the scandal began to break, a partner at Andersen organized the shredding of incriminating Enron documents before investigators could lay their hands on them. As a result, the eighty-nine-year-old accounting firm was convicted of obstructing justice, and it went out of business. (This was not the first time Andersen had been in trouble, by the way. The year before the Securities and Exchange Commission had fined it $7 million for approving misleading accounts at Waste Management, and it also had to pay $110 million to settle a lawsuit for auditing work it did for Sunbeam before it, too, filed for bankruptcy.)

Enron's fall also revealed the conflicts of interest that threaten the credibility of Wall Street's analysts—analysts who get compensated based on their ability to bring in and support investment banking deals. Enron was known in the industry as the "deal machine" because it generated so much investment banking business—limited partnerships, loans, and derivatives. This may explain why, only days before Enron filed bankruptcy, just two of the sixteen Wall Street analysts who covered the company recommended that clients sell the stock.[1] But the rot doesn't stop there. Enron and Andersen enjoyed extensive political connections, which had helped over the years to ensure the passage of a series of deregulatory measures favorable to the energy company. Of the 248 members of Congress sitting on the eleven House and Senate committees charged with investigating Enron's collapse, 212 had received money from Enron or its accounting firm.

Stories of business corruption and of greed and wrongdoing in high places have always fascinated the popular press, and media interest in business ethics has never been higher. But one

should not be misled by the headlines and news reports. Not all moral issues in business involve giant corporations and their well-heeled executives, and few cases of business ethics are widely publicized. The vast majority of them involve the mundane, uncelebrated moral challenges that working men and women meet daily.

Although the financial shenanigans at Enron were complicated, once their basic outline is sketched, the wrongdoing is pretty easy to see: deception, dishonesty, fraud, disregarding one's professional responsibilities, and unfairly injuring others for one's own gain. But many of the moral issues that arise in business are complex and difficult to answer. The topic of business ethics includes not just the question of the moral or immoral motivations of businesspeople, but also a whole range of problems that arise in the context of business. These issues are too numerous to compile, but consider these typical questions:

Is passing a personality or honesty test a justifiable preemployment condition? Are drug tests? What rights do employees have on the job? How should business respond to employees who have AIDS? What, if anything, must it do to improve work conditions?

Should manufacturers reveal all product defects? At what point does acceptable exaggeration become lying about a product or service? When does aggressive marketing become consumer manipulation?

What are businesses' environmental responsibilities? Is a corporation obliged to help combat social problems such as poverty, pollution, and urban decay? Must business fight sexism and racism? How far must it go to ensure equality of opportunity? How should organizations respond to the problem of sexual harassment?

May employees ever use their positions inside an organization to advance their own interests? Is insider trading or the use of privileged information immoral? How much loyalty do workers owe their companies? What say should a business have over the off-the-job activities of its employees?

What obligations does a worker have to outside parties, such as customers, competitors, or society generally? When, if ever, is an employee morally required to blow the whistle?

These questions typify business issues with moral significance. The answers we give are determined largely by our moral standards, principles, and values. What these standards and principles are, where they come from, and how they can be assessed are some of the concerns of this opening chapter. In particular, you will encounter the following topics:

1. The nature, scope, and purpose of business ethics
2. The distinguishing features of morality and how it differs from etiquette, law, and professional codes of conduct
3. The relationship between morality and religion
4. The doctrine of ethical relativism and its difficulties
5. What it means to have moral principles, the nature of conscience, and the relationship between morality and self-interest
6. The place of values and ideals in a person's life
7. The social and psychological factors that sometimes jeopardize an individual's integrity
8. The characteristics of sound moral reasoning

ETHICS

"The word *ethics* comes from the Greek word *ethos,* meaning character or custom," writes philosophy professor Robert C. Solomon.[2] Today we use the word *ethos* to refer to the distinguishing disposition, character, or attitude of a specific people, culture, or group (as in, for example, "the American ethos" or "the business ethos"). According to Solomon, the etymology of *ethics* suggests its basic concerns: (1) individual

character, including what it means to be "a good person," and (2) the social rules that govern and limit our conduct, especially the ultimate rules concerning right and wrong, which we call *morality.*

Philosophers generally distinguish ethics from morality. "Morality" refers to a person or group's standards of right and wrong or good and bad, and "ethics" refers to the study and assessment of those standards. Thus, when we reflect critically on our own moral standards or the moral values of the society around us, we are beginning to do ethics. Few people, however, would distinguish a person's "morals" from his or her "ethics," and almost everyone uses "ethical" and "moral" interchangeably to describe people we consider good and actions we consider right, and "unethical" and "immoral" to designate bad people and wrong actions. This book follows that common usage.

Business and Organizational Ethics

The primary focus of this book is ethics as it applies to business. *Business ethics* is the study of what constitutes right and wrong, or good and bad, human conduct in a business context. For example, would it be right for a store manager to break a promise to a customer and sell some hard-to-find merchandise to someone else, whose need for it is greater? What, if anything, should a moral employee do when his or her superiors refuse to look into apparent wrongdoing in a branch office? If you innocently came across secret information about a competitor, would it be permissible for you to use it for your own advantage?

"Business" and "businessperson" are broad terms. "Business" may denote a corner hamburger stand or a multinational corporation that does business in several countries. A "businessperson" may be a gardener engaged in a one-person operation or a company president responsible for thousands of workers and enormous corporate investments. Accordingly, the word *business* will be used here simply to mean any organization whose objective is to provide goods or services for profit. *Businesspeople* are those who participate in planning, organizing, or directing the work of business.

But this book takes a broader view as well. It is concerned with moral issues that arise anywhere that employers and employees come together. That is, it is as much about organizational ethics as business ethics. An *organization* is a group of people working together to achieve a common purpose. The purpose may be to offer a product or service primarily for profit, as in business. But the purpose may also be health care, as in medical organizations; public safety and order, as in law-enforcement organizations; education, as in academic organizations; and so on. The cases and illustrations presented in this book deal with moral issues and dilemmas in both business and nonbusiness organizational settings.

People occasionally poke fun at the idea of business ethics, declaring that the term is a contradiction or that business has no ethics. Such people take themselves to be worldly and realistic. They think they have a down-to-earth idea of how things really work. In fact, despite its pretense of sophistication, this attitude is embarrassingly naive. People who express it have little grasp of the nature of ethics and only a superficial understanding of the real world of business. After you have read this book, you will perhaps see the truth of this judgment.

Personal and Business Ethics

Because the study of business and organizational ethics is part of the broader study of ethics, this book discusses basic ethical concepts and general theories of right and wrong. To discover guidelines for moral decision making within an organization, we must first explore guidelines for making moral decisions generally. The intimacy between ethics in general and ethics as applied to business contexts implies that one's personal ethics cannot be neatly divorced from one's organizational ethics. In fact, it is safe to say that

those who have studied and thought seriously about ethics in general and about their own values in particular have a better basis for making moral decisions in an organizational setting than those who have not.

Perhaps an appreciation of this point was what prompted a number of executives at top U.S. companies and the deans and alumni of several prestigious business schools to suggest in an important study that the ideal MBA program should include a sound grounding in ethics. In the words of the study's conductor: "Today's marketplace calls for a business executive who is bold enough to build his or her reputation on integrity and who has a keen sensitivity to the ethical ramifications of his or her decision making."[3] However, if people within business and nonbusiness organizations are to build their reputations on integrity and have a keen sensitivity to the ethical dimensions of their decisions, they must be guided by sound moral standards. Moral standards are the basis of ethical conduct and differ significantly from nonmoral standards.

MORAL VERSUS NONMORAL STANDARDS

Moral questions differ from other kinds of questions. Whether your office computer can download a copyrighted album from the Web is a factual question, not a moral question. On the other hand, whether you should download the album is a moral question. When we answer a moral question or make a moral judgment, we appeal to moral standards. These standards differ from other kinds of standards.

Wearing shorts to a formal dinner party is boorish behavior. Murdering the King's English with double negatives violates the basic conventions of proper language usage. Photographing the finish of a horse race with low-speed film is poor photographic technique. In each case a standard is violated—fashion, grammatical, technical—but the violation does not pose a serious threat to human well-being.

Moral standards are different because they concern behavior that is of serious consequence to human welfare, that can profoundly injure or benefit people.[4] The conventional moral norms against lying, stealing, and murdering deal with actions that can hurt people. And the moral principle that human beings should be treated with dignity and respect uplifts the human personality. Whether products are healthful or harmful, work conditions safe or dangerous, personnel procedures biased or fair, privacy respected or invaded are also matters that seriously affect human well-being. The standards that govern our conduct in these matters are moral standards.

A second characteristic follows from the first. Moral standards take priority over other standards, including self-interest. Something that morality condemns—for instance, the burglary of your neighbor's home—cannot be justified on the nonmoral grounds that it would be a thrill to do it or that it would pay off handsomely. We take moral standards to be more important than other considerations in guiding our actions.

A third characteristic of moral standards is that their soundness depends on the adequacy of the reasons that support or justify them. For the most part, fashion standards are set by clothing designers, merchandisers, and consumers; grammatical standards by grammarians and students of language; technical standards by practitioners and experts in the field. Legislators make laws, boards of directors make organizational policy, and licensing boards establish standards for professionals. In every case, some authoritative body is the ultimate validating source of the standards and thus can change the standards if it wishes. Moral standards are not made by such bodies, although they are often endorsed or rejected by them. More precisely, the validity of moral standards depends not on authoritative fiat but rather on the quality of the arguments or the reasoning that supports them. Precisely what constitutes adequate grounds or justification for a moral standard is a debated question, which, as we will see in the next chap-

ter, underlies disagreement among philosophers over which specific moral principles are best.

Although these three characteristics set moral standards apart from others, it is useful to discuss more specifically how morality differs from three things with which it is sometimes confused: etiquette, law, and professional codes of ethics.

Morality and Etiquette

Etiquette refers to the norms of correct conduct in polite society or, more generally, to any special code of social behavior or courtesy. In our society, for example, it is considered bad etiquette to chew with your mouth open or to pick your nose when talking to someone; it is considered good etiquette to say "please" when requesting and "thank you" when receiving and to hold a door open for someone entering immediately behind you. Good business etiquette typically calls for writing follow-up letters after meetings, returning phone calls, and dressing appropriately. It is commonplace to judge people's manners as "good" or "bad" and the conduct that reflects them as "right" or "wrong." "Good," "bad," "right," and "wrong" here simply mean socially appropriate or socially inappropriate. In these contexts, such words express judgments about manners, not ethics.

So-called rules of etiquette that you might learn in an etiquette book are prescriptions for socially acceptable behavior. If you want to fit in, get along with others, and be thought well of by them, you should observe common rules of etiquette. If you violate the rules, then you're rightly considered ill-mannered, impolite, or even uncivilized, but not necessarily immoral.

Rules of etiquette are generally nonmoral in character: "Say 'congratulations' to the groom but 'best wishes' to the bride"; "Push your chair back into place upon leaving a dinner table." But violations of etiquette can have moral implications. The male boss who refers to female subordinates as "honey" or "doll" shows bad manners. If such epithets diminish the worth of female employees or perpetuate sexism, then they also raise moral issues concerning equal treatment and denial of dignity to human beings.

Scrupulous observance of rules of etiquette does not make one moral. In fact, it can camouflage moral issues. A few decades ago in some parts of the United States, it was considered bad manners for blacks and whites to eat together. Those who obeyed the convention and were thus judged well-mannered certainly had no grounds for feeling moral. The only way to dramatize the injustice underlying this practice was to violate the rule and be judged ill-mannered. For those in the civil rights movement of the 1960s, being considered boorish was a small price to pay for exposing the unequal treatment and human degradation that underlay this rule of etiquette.

Morality and Law

Before distinguishing between morality and law, one should understand the term *law.* Basically, there are four kinds of law: statutes, regulations, common law, and constitutional law.

Statutes are laws enacted by legislative bodies. The law that prohibits theft is a statute. Congress and state legislatures enact statutes. (Laws enacted by local governing bodies such as city councils usually are termed *ordinances.*) Statutes make up a large part of the law and are what many of us mean when we speak of laws.

Limited in their knowledge, legislatures often set up boards or agencies whose functions include issuing detailed regulations of certain kinds of conduct—*administrative regulations.* For example, state legislatures establish licensing boards to formulate regulations for the licensing of physicians and nurses. As long as these regulations do not exceed the board's statutory powers and do not conflict with other kinds of law, they are legally binding.

Common law refers to laws applied in the English-speaking world when there were few statutes. Courts frequently wrote opinions explaining the bases of their decisions in specific cases, including the legal principles they deemed appropriate. Each of these opinions became a precedent for later decisions in similar cases. The massive body of legal principles that accumulated over the years is collectively referred to as common law. Like administrative regulations, common law is valid if it harmonizes with statutory law and with still another kind, constitutional law.

Constitutional law refers to court rulings on the requirements of the Constitution and the constitutionality of legislation. The U.S. Constitution empowers the courts to decide whether laws are compatible with the Constitution. State courts may also rule on the constitutionality of state laws under state constitutions. Although the courts cannot make laws, they have far-reaching powers to rule on the constitutionality of laws and to declare them invalid. The U.S. Supreme Court has the greatest judiciary power and rules on an array of cases, some of which bear directly on the study of business ethics.

People sometimes confuse legality and morality, but they are different things. On one hand, breaking the law is not always or necessarily immoral. On the other hand, the legality of an action does not guarantee that it is morally right. Let's consider these points further.

1. *An action can be illegal but morally right.* For example, helping a Jewish family to hide from the Nazis was against German law in 1939, but it would have been a morally admirable thing to have done. Of course, the Nazi regime was vicious and evil. By contrast, in a democratic society with a basically just legal order, the fact that something is illegal provides a moral consideration against doing it. For example, one moral reason for not burning trash in your back yard is that it violates an ordinance that your community has voted in favor of. Some philosophers believe that sometimes the illegality of an action can make it morally wrong, even if the action would otherwise have been morally acceptable. But even if they are right about this, the fact that something is illegal does not trump all other moral considerations. Nonconformity to law is not always immoral, even in a democratic society. There can be circumstances where, all things considered, violating the law is morally permissible, perhaps even morally required.

Probably no one in the modern era has expressed this point more eloquently than Dr. Martin Luther King, Jr. Confined in the Birmingham, Alabama, city jail on charges of parading without a permit, King penned his now famous "Letter from Birmingham Jail" to eight of his fellow clergymen who had published a statement attacking King's unauthorized protest of racial segregation as unwise and untimely. King wrote:

> All segregation statutes are unjust because segregation distorts the soul and damages the personality. It gives the segregator a false sense of superiority and the segregated a false sense of inferiority. Segregation, to use the terminology of the Jewish philosopher Martin Buber, substitutes an "I-it" relationship for an "I-thou" relationship and ends up relegating persons to the status of things. Hence segregation is not only politically, economically, and sociologically unsound, it is morally wrong and sinful. . . . Thus it is that I can urge men to obey the 1954 decision of the Supreme Court,* for it is morally right; and I can urge them to disobey segregation ordinances, for they are morally wrong.[5]

2. *An action that is legal can be morally wrong.* For example, it may have been perfectly legal for the chairman of a profitable company to lay off 125 workers and use three-quarters of the money saved to boost his pay and that of the company's other top manager,[6] but the morality of his doing so is open to debate.

Or, to take another example, suppose that you're driving to work one day and see an accident victim sitting on the side of the road, clearly in shock and needing medical assistance. Because you know first aid and are

in no great hurry to get to your destination, you could easily stop and assist the person. Legally speaking, though, you are not obligated to stop and render aid. Under common law, the prudent thing would be to drive on, because by stopping you would bind yourself to use reasonable care and thus incur legal liability if you fail to do so and the victim thereby suffers injury. Many states have enacted so-called Good Samaritan laws to provide immunity from damages to those rendering aid (except for gross negligence or serious misconduct). But in most states the law does not oblige people to give such aid or even to call an ambulance. Moral theorists would agree, however, that if you sped away without rendering aid or even calling for help, your action might be perfectly legal but would be morally suspect. Regardless of the law, such conduct would almost certainly be wrong.

What then may we say about the relationship between law and morality? To a significant extent, law codifies a society's customs, ideals, norms, and moral values. Changes in law tend to reflect changes in what a society takes to be right and wrong, but sometimes changes in the law can alter people's ideas about the rightness or wrongness of conduct. However, even if a society's laws are sensible and morally sound, it is a mistake to see them as sufficient to establish the moral standards that should guide us. The law cannot cover the wide variety of possible individual and group conduct, and in many situations it is too blunt an instrument to provide adequate moral guidance. The law generally prohibits egregious affronts to a society's moral standards and in that sense is the "floor" of moral conduct, but breaches of moral conduct can slip through cracks in that floor.

Professional Codes

Somewhere between etiquette and law lie *professional codes of ethics.* These are the rules that are supposed to govern the conduct of members of a given profession. Generally speaking, the members of a profession are understood to have

---

*In *Brown v. Board of Education of Topeka* (1954), the Supreme Court struck down the half-century-old "separate but equal doctrine," which permitted racially segregated schools as long as comparable quality was maintained.

agreed to abide by those rules as a condition of their engaging in that profession. Violation of the professional code may result in the disapproval of one's professional peers and, in serious cases, loss of one's license to practice that profession. Sometimes these codes are unwritten and are part of the common understanding of members of a profession—for example, that professors should not date their students. In other instances, these codes or portions of them may be written down by an authoritative body so they may be better taught and more efficiently enforced.

These written rules are sometimes so vague and general as to be of little value, and often they amount to little more than self-promotion by the professional organization. The same is frequently true when industries or corporations publish statements of their ethical standards. In other cases—for example, with attorneys—professional codes can be very specific and detailed. It is difficult to generalize about the content of professional codes of ethics, however, because they frequently involve a mix of purely moral rules (for example, client confidentiality), of professional etiquette (for example, the billing of services to other professionals), and of restrictions intended to benefit the group's economic interests (for example, limitations on price competition).

Given their nature, professional codes of ethics are neither a complete nor a completely reliable guide to one's moral obligations. First, not all the rules of a professional code are purely moral in character, and even when they are, the fact that a rule is officially enshrined as part of the code of a profession does not guarantee that it is a sound moral principle. As a professional, you must take seriously the injunctions of your profession, but you still have the responsibility to critically assess those rules for yourself.

Regarding those parts of the code that concern etiquette or financial matters, bear in mind that by joining a profession you are probably agreeing, explicitly or implicitly, to abide by those standards. Assuming that those rules don't require morally impermissible conduct, then consenting to them gives you some moral obligation to follow them. In addition, for many, living up to the standards of one's chosen profession is an important source of personal satisfaction. Still, you must be alert to situations in which professional standards or customary professional practice conflicts with the ordinary demands of morality. Adherence to a professional code does not exempt your conduct from scrutiny from the broader perspective of morality.

Where Do Moral Standards Come From?

So far you have seen how moral standards are different from various nonmoral standards, but you probably wonder about the source of those moral standards. Most, if not all, people have certain moral principles or a moral code that they explicitly or implicitly accept. Because the moral principles of different people in the same society overlap, at least in part, we can also talk about the moral code of a society, meaning the moral standards shared in common by its members. How do we come to have certain moral principles and not others? Obviously, many things influence us in the moral principles we accept: our early upbringing, the behavior of those around us, the explicit and implicit standards of our culture, our own experiences, and our critical reflections on those experiences.

For philosophers, though, the important question is not how in fact we came to have the particular principles we have. The philosophical issue is whether the principles we have can be justified. Do we simply take for granted the values of those around us? Or, like Martin Luther King, Jr., are we able to think independently about moral matters? By analogy, we pick up our nonmoral beliefs from all sorts of sources: books, conversations with friends, movies, various experiences we've had. The philosopher's concern is not so much with how we actually got the beliefs we have, but whether or to what extent those beliefs—for example, that women are more emotional than men or that telekinesis is possible—can withstand critical scrutiny. Likewise, ethical theories attempt to justify moral standards and ethical beliefs. The next chapter examines some of the major theories of normative ethics. That is, it looks at what some of the major thinkers in human history have argued are the best-justified standards of right and wrong.

But first we need to consider the relationship between morality and religion on the one hand and that between morality and society on the other. Some people maintain that morality just boils down to religion. Others have argued for the doctrine of *ethical relativism,* which says that right and wrong are only a function of what a particular society takes to be right and wrong. Both these views are mistaken.

RELIGION AND MORALITY

Any religion provides its believers with a world-view, part of which involves certain moral instructions, values, and commitments. The Jewish and Christian traditions, to name just two, offer a view of humans as unique products of a divine intervention that has endowed them with consciousness and an ability to love. Both these traditions posit creatures who stand midway between nature and spirit. On one hand, we are finite and bound to earth, not only capable of wrongdoing but born morally flawed (original sin). On the other, we can transcend nature and realize infinite possibilities.

Primarily because of the influence of Western religion, many Americans and others view themselves as beings with a supernatural destiny, as possessing a life after death, as being immortal. One's purpose in life is found in serving and loving God. For the Christian, the way to serve and love God is by emulating the life of Jesus of Nazareth. In the life of Jesus, Christians find an expression of the highest virtue—love. They love when they perform selfless acts, develop a keen social conscience, and realize that human beings are creatures of God and therefore intrinsically worthwhile. For the Jew, one serves and loves God chiefly through expressions of justice and righteousness. Jews also develop a sense of honor derived from a commitment to truth, humility, fidelity, and kind-ness. This commitment hones their sense of responsibility to family and community.

Religion, then, involves not only a formal system of worship but also prescriptions for social relationships. One example is the mandate "Do unto others as you would have them do unto you." Termed the "Golden Rule," this injunction represents one of humankind's highest moral ideals and can be found in essence in all the great religions of the world:

> Good people proceed while considering that what is best for others is best for themselves. (*Hitopadesa,* Hinduism)
>
> Thou shalt love thy neighbor as thyself. (*Leviticus* 19:18, Judaism)
>
> Therefore all things whatsoever ye would that men should do to you, do ye even so to them. (*Matthew* 7:12, Christianity)
>
> Hurt not others with that which pains yourself. (*Udanavarga* 5:18, Buddhism)
>
> What you do not want done to yourself, do not do to others. (*Analects* 15:23, Confucianism)
>
> No one of you is a believer until he loves for his brother what he loves for himself. (*Traditions,* Islam)

Although inspiring, such religious ideals are very general and can be difficult to translate into precise policy injunctions. Religious bodies, nevertheless, occasionally articulate positions on more specific political, educational, economic, and medical issues, which help mold public opinion on matters as diverse as abortion, euthanasia, nuclear weapons, and national defense. Roman Catholicism has a rich tradition of formally applying its core values to the moral aspects of industrial relations. Pope John Paul II's encyclical *Centesimus Annus,* the Pontifical Council for Social Communication's 1997 report on advertising and its 2002 report on ethics and the Internet, and the National Conference of Catholic Bishops' pastoral letter *Economic Justice for All,* on Catholic social teaching and the U.S. economy, stand in this tradition. Having gone through several drafts over more than two years before its final approval by the Conference, and then revised and expanded ten years later, the pastoral letter is really a book-length reflection on the moral dimensions and human consequences of American economic life. It examines specific policy questions and is intended to help shape a national discussion of these issues.

Morality Needn't Rest on Religion

Many people believe that morality must be based on religion, either in the sense that without religion people would have no incentive to be moral or in the sense that only religion can provide moral guidance. Others contend that morality is based on the commands of God. None of these claims is very plausible.

First, although a desire to avoid hell and to go to heaven may prompt some of us to act morally, this is not the only reason or even the most common reason that people behave morally. Often we act morally out of habit or simply because that is the kind of person we are. It would just not occur to most of us to swipe an elderly lady's purse, and if the idea did occur to us, we wouldn't do it because such an act simply doesn't fit with our personal standards or with our concept of ourselves. We are often motivated to do what is morally right out of concern for others or just because it is right. In addition, the approval of our peers, the need to appease our conscience, and the desire to avoid earthly punishment may all motivate us to act morally. Furthermore, atheists generally live lives as moral and upright as those of believers.

Second, the moral instructions of the world's great religions are general and imprecise: They do not relieve us of the necessity to engage in moral reasoning ourselves. For example, the Bible says, "Thou shall not kill." Yet Christians disagree among themselves over the morality of fighting in wars, of capital punishment, of killing in self-defense, of slaughtering animals, of abortion and euthanasia, and of allowing foreigners to die from famine because we have not provided them with as much food as we might

have. The Bible does not give unambiguous answers to these moral problems, so even believers must engage in moral philosophy if they are to have intelligent answers. On the other hand, there are lots of reasons for believing that, say, a cold-blooded murder motivated by greed is immoral; one need not believe in a religion to figure that out.

Third, although some theologians have advocated the *divine command theory*—that if something is wrong (like killing an innocent person for fun), then the only reason it is wrong is that God commands us not to do it—many theologians and certainly most philosophers would reject this view. They would contend that if God commands human beings not to do something, such as commit rape, it is because God sees that rape is wrong, but it is not God's forbidding rape that makes it wrong. The fact that rape is wrong is independent of God's decrees.

Most believers think not only that God gives us moral instructions or rules but also that God has moral reasons for giving them to us. According to the divine command theory, this would make no sense. In this view, there is no reason that something is right or wrong, other than the fact that it is God's will. All believers, of course, believe that God is good and that He commands us to do what is right and forbids us to do what is wrong. But this doesn't mean, say critics of the divine command theory, that God's saying so makes a thing wrong, any more than your mother's telling you not to steal makes it wrong to steal.

All this is simply to argue that morality is not necessarily based on religion in any of these three senses. That religion influences the moral standards and values of most of us is beyond doubt. But given that religions differ in their moral principles and that even members of the same faith often disagree on moral matters, you cannot justify a moral principle simply by appealing to religion—for that will only persuade those who already agree with your particular interpretation of your particular religion. Besides, most religions hold that human reason is capable of understanding what is right and wrong, so it is human reason to which you will have to appeal in order to support your ethical principle.

ETHICAL RELATIVISM

Some people do not believe that morality boils down to religion but rather that it is just a function of what a particular society happens to believe. This view is called *ethical relativism,* the theory that what is right is determined by what a culture or society says is right. What is right in one place may be wrong in another, because the only criterion for distinguishing right from wrong—and so the only ethical standard for judging an action—is the moral system of the society in which the act occurs.

Abortion, for example, is condemned as immoral in Catholic Ireland but is practiced as a morally neutral form of birth control in Japan. According to the ethical relativist, then, abortion is wrong in Ireland but morally permissible in Japan. The relativist is not saying merely that the Irish believe abortion is abominable and the Japanese do not; that is acknowledged by everyone. Rather, the ethical relativist contends that abortion is immoral in Ireland because the Irish believe it to be immoral and that it is morally permissible in Japan because the Japanese believe it to be so. Thus, for the ethical relativist there is no absolute ethical standard independent of cultural context, no criterion of right and wrong by which to judge other than that of particular societies. In short, what morality requires is relative to society.

Those who endorse ethical relativism point to the apparent diversity of human values and the multiformity of moral codes to support their case. From our own cultural perspective, some seemingly immoral moralities have been adopted; polygamy, pedophilia, stealing, slavery, infanticide, and cannibalism have all been tolerated or even encouraged by the moral system of one society or another. In light of this fact, the ethical relativist believes that there can be no nonethnocentric standard by which to judge actions.

Some thinkers believe that the moral differences between societies are smaller and less significant than they appear. They contend that variations in moral standards reflect differing factual beliefs and differing circumstances rather than fundamental differences in values. But suppose they are wrong about this matter. The relativist's conclusion still does not follow. As Allan Bloom writes, "The fact that there have been different opinions about good and bad in different times and places in no way proves that none is true or superior to others. To say that it does so prove is as absurd as to say that the diversity of points of view expressed in a college bull session proves there is no truth."[7] Disagreement in ethical matters does not imply that all opinions are equally correct.

Moreover, ethical relativism has some unpleasant implications. First, it undermines any moral criticism of the practices of other societies as long as their actions conform to their own standards. We cannot say that slavery in a slave society like that of the American South 150 years ago was immoral and unjust as long as that society held it to be morally permissible.

Second, and closely related, is the fact that for the relativist there is no such thing as ethical progress. Although moralities may change, they cannot get better or worse. Thus, we cannot say that our moral standards today are any more enlightened than they were in the Middle Ages.

Third, it makes no sense from the relativist's point of view for people to criticize principles or practices accepted by their own society. People can be censured for not living up to their society's moral code, but that is all. The moral code itself cannot be criticized because whatever a society takes to be right really is right for it. Reformers who identify injustices in their society and campaign against them are only encouraging people to be immoral—that is, to depart from the moral standards of their society—unless or until the majority of the society agrees with the reformers. The minority can never be right in moral matters; to be right it must become the majority.

The ethical relativist is right to emphasize that in viewing other cultures we should keep an open mind and not simply dismiss alien social practices on the basis of our own cultural prejudices. But the relativist's theory of morality doesn't hold up. The more carefully we examine it, the less plausible it becomes. There is no good reason for saying that the majority view on moral issues is automatically right, and the belief that it is automatically right has unacceptable consequences.

Relativism and the "Game" of Business

In his well-known and influential essay "Is Business Bluffing Ethical?" Albert Carr argues that business, as practiced by individuals as well as by corporations, has the impersonal character of a game—a game that demands both special strategy and an understanding of its special ethical standards.[8] Business has its own norms and rules that differ from those of the rest of society. Thus, according to Carr, a number of things that we normally think of as wrong are really permissible in a business context. His examples include conscious misstatement and concealment of pertinent facts in negotiation, lying about one's age on a résumé, deceptive packaging, automobile companies' neglect of car safety, and utility companies' manipulation of regulators and overcharging of electricity users. He draws an analogy with poker:

> Poker's own brand of ethics is different from the ethical ideals of civilized human relationships. The game calls for distrust of the other fellow. It ignores the claim of friendship. Cunning deception and concealment of one's strength and intentions, not kindness and openheartedness, are vital in poker. No one thinks any the worse of poker on that account. And no one should think any the worse of the game of business because its standards of right and wrong differ from the prevailing traditions of morality in our society.[9]

What Carr is defending here is a kind of ethical relativism: Business has its own moral standards, and business actions should be evaluated only by those standards.

One can argue whether Carr has accurately identified the implicit rules of the business world (for example, is misrepresentation on one's résumé really a permissible move in the business game?), but let's put that issue aside. The basic question is whether business is a separate world to which ordinary moral standards don't apply. Carr's thesis implies that any special activity following its own rules is exempt from external moral evaluation, but as a general proposition this is unacceptable. The Mafia, for example, has an elaborate code of conduct, accepted by the members of the rival "families." For them, gunning down a competitor or terrorizing a local shopkeeper may be strategic moves in a competitive environment. Yet we rightly refuse to say that gangsters cannot be criticized for following their own standards. Normal business activity is a world away from gangsterism, but the point still holds. Any specialized activity or practice will have its own distinctive rules and procedures, but the morality of those rules and procedures can still be evaluated.

Moreover, Carr's poker analogy is itself weak. For one thing, business activity can affect others—such as consumers—who have not consciously and freely chosen to play the "game." Business is indeed an activity involving distinctive rules and customary ways of doing things, but it is not really a game. It is the economic basis of our society, and we all have an interest in the goals of business (in productivity and consumer satisfaction, for instance) and in the rules business follows. Why should these be exempt from public evaluation and assessment? Later chapters return to the question of what these goals and rules should be. But to take one simple point, note that a business/economic system that permits, encourages, or tolerates deception will be less efficient (that is, work less well) than one in which the participants have fuller knowledge of the goods and services being exchanged.

In sum, by divorcing business from morality, Carr misrepresents both. He incorrectly treats the standards and rules of everyday business activity as if they had nothing to do with the standards and rules of ordinary morality, and he treats morality as something that we give lip service to on Sundays but that otherwise has no influence on our lives.

HAVING MORAL PRINCIPLES

Most people at some time in their lives pause to reflect on what moral principles they have or should have and on what moral standards are the best justified. (Moral philosophers themselves have defended different moral standards; Chapter 2 discusses these various theories.) When a person accepts a moral principle, when that principle is part of his or her personal moral code, then naturally the person believes the principle is important and well justified. But there is more to moral principles than that, as Professor Richard Brandt (1910–1997) of the University of Michigan emphasized. When a principle is part of a person's moral code, that person is strongly motivated toward the conduct required by the principle, and against behavior that conflicts with that principle. The person will tend to feel guilty when his or her own conduct violates that principle and to disapprove of others whose behavior conflicts with it. Likewise, the person will tend to hold in esteem those whose conduct shows an abundance of the motivation required by the principle.[10]

Other philosophers have, in different ways, reinforced Brandt's point. To accept a moral principle is not a purely intellectual act like accepting a scientific hypothesis or a mathematical theorem. Rather, it also involves a desire to follow that principle for its own sake, the likelihood of feeling guilty about not doing so, and a tendency to evaluate the conduct of others according to the principle in question. We would find it very strange, for example, if Sally claimed to be morally opposed to cruelty to animals yet abused her own pets and felt no inclination to protest when some ruffians down the street set a cat on fire.

Conscience

People can, and unfortunately sometimes do, go against their moral principles, but we would doubt that they sincerely held the principle in question if violating it did not bother their conscience. We have all felt the pangs of conscience, but what exactly is conscience and how reliable a guide is it? Our conscience, of course, is not literally a little voice inside of us. To oversimplify a complex piece of developmental psychology, our conscience evolved as we internalized the moral instructions of the parents or other authority figures who raised us as children.

When you were very young, you were probably told to tell the truth and to return something you filched to its proper owner. If you were caught lying or being dishonest, you were probably punished—scolded, spanked, sent to bed without dinner, denied a privilege. On the other hand, truth telling and kindness to your siblings were probably rewarded—with approval, praise, maybe even hugs or candy. Seeking reward and avoiding punishment motivate small children to do what is expected of them. Gradually, children come to internalize those parental commands. Thus, they feel vaguely that their parents know what they are doing even when the parents are not around. When children do something forbidden, they experience the same feelings as when scolded by their parents—the first stirrings of guilt. By the same token, even in the absence of explicit parental reward, children feel a sense of self-approval about having done what they were supposed to have done.

As we grow older, of course, our motivations are not so simple and our self-understanding is greater. We are able to reflect on and understand the moral lessons we were taught, as well as to refine and modify those principles. As adults we are morally independent agents. Yet however much our conscience has evolved and however much our adult moral code differs from the moral perspective of our childhood, those pangs of guilt we occasionally feel still stem from that early internalization of parental demands.

The Limits of Conscience

How reliable a guide is conscience? People often say, "Follow your conscience" or "You should never go against your conscience," but not only is such advice not very helpful, it may sometimes be bad advice. First, when we are genuinely perplexed over what we ought to do, we are trying to figure out what our conscience ought to be saying to us. When it is not possible to do both, should we keep our promise to a colleague or come to the aid of an old friend? To be told that we should follow our conscience is no help at all.

Second, it may not always be good for us to follow our conscience. It all depends on what our conscience says. Our conscience might reflect moral motivations that cannot withstand critical scrutiny. Consider an episode in Chapter 16 of Mark Twain's *The Adventures of Huckleberry Finn.* Huck has taken off down the Mississippi on a raft with his friend, the runaway slave Jim, but as they get nearer to the place where Jim will become legally free, Huck starts feeling guilty about helping him run away:

> It hadn't ever come home to me before, what this thing was that I was doing. But now it did; and it stayed with me, and scorched me more and more. I tried to make out to myself that *I* warn't to blame, because *I* didn't run Jim off from his rightful owner; but it warn't no use, conscience up and says, every time: "But you knowed he was running for his freedom, and you could a paddled ashore and told somebody." That was so—I couldn't get around that, no way. That was where it pinched. Conscience says to me: "What had poor Miss Watson done to you, that you could see her nigger go off right under your eyes and never say one single word? What did that poor old woman do to you, that you could treat her so mean? . . ." I got to feeling so mean and miserable I most wished I was dead.

Here Huck is feeling guilty about doing what we would all agree is the morally right thing to do. But Huck is only a boy, and his pangs of conscience reflect the principles that he has picked up uncritically from the slave-owning society around him. Unable to think independently about matters of right and wrong, Huck in the end decides to disregard his conscience. He follows his instincts and sticks by his friend Jim.

The point here is not that you should ignore your conscience but that the voice of conscience is itself something that can be critically examined. A pang of conscience is like a warning. When you feel one, you should definitely stop and reflect on the rightness of what you are doing. On the other hand, you cannot justify your actions simply by saying you were following your conscience. Terrible crimes have occasionally been committed in the name of conscience.

Moral Principles and Self-Interest

Sometimes doing what you believe would be morally right and doing what would best satisfy your own interests may be two different things. Imagine that you are in your car hurrying home along a quiet road, trying hard to get there in time to see the kickoff of an important football game. You pass an acquaintance who is having car trouble. He doesn't recognize you. As a dedicated fan, you would much prefer to keep on going than to stop and help him, thus missing at least part of the game. You might rationalize that someone else will eventually come along and help him if you don't, but deep down you know that you really ought to stop. On the other hand, self-interest seems to say, "Keep going."

Consider another example.[11] You have applied for a new job, and if you land it, it will be an enormous break for you: It is exactly the kind of position you want and have been trying to get for some time. It pays well and will settle you into a desirable career for the rest of your life. The competition has come down to just you and one other person, and you believe correctly that she has a slight edge on you. Now imagine that you could spread a nasty rumor about her that would guarantee that she wouldn't get the job, and that you could do this in a way that wouldn't come back to you. Presumably, circulating this lie would violate your moral code; on the other hand, doing it would clearly be to your benefit.

Some people argue that moral action and self-interest can never genuinely be in conflict, and some philosophers have gone to great lengths to try to prove this, but they are almost certainly mistaken. They maintain that if you do the wrong thing, then you will be caught, your conscience will bother you, or in some way "what goes around comes around," so that your misdeed will come back to haunt you. This is often correct. But unfortunate as it may be, sometimes—viewed just in terms of personal self-interest—it may pay off for you to do what you know to be wrong. People sometimes get away with their wrongdoings, and if their conscience bothers them at all, it may not bother them that much. To believe otherwise not only is wishful thinking but also shows a lack of understanding of morality.

Morality serves to restrain our purely self-interested desires so we can all live together. The moral standards of a society provide the basic guidelines for cooperative social existence and allow conflicts to be resolved by appeal to shared principles of justification. If our interests never came into conflict—that is, if it were never advantageous for one person to deceive or cheat another—then there would be little need for morality. We would already be in heaven. Both a system of law that punishes people for hurting others and a system of morality that encourages people to refrain from pursuing their self-interest at a great expense to others help to make social existence possible.

Usually, following our moral principles is in our best interest. This idea is particularly worth noting in the business context. Several recent writers have argued persuasively not only that moral behavior is consistent with profitability but also that the most morally responsible companies are among the most profitable.[12] Apparently, respecting the rights of employees, treating suppliers fairly, and being straightforward with customers pay off.

But notice one thing. If you do the right thing only because you think it will pay off, you are not really motivated by moral concerns. Having a moral principle involves having a desire to follow the principle for its own sake—just because it is the right thing to do. If you do the right thing only because you believe it will pay off, you might just as easily not do it if it looks as if it is not going to pay off.

In addition, there is no guarantee that moral behavior will always pay off in strictly selfish terms. As argued earlier, there will be exceptions. From the moral point of view, you ought to stop and help your acquaintance, and you shouldn't lie about competitors. From the selfish point of view, you should do exactly the opposite. Should you follow your self-interest or your moral principles? There's no final answer to this question. From the moral point of view, you should, of course, follow your moral principles. But from the selfish point of view, you should look out solely for "number one."

Which option you choose will depend on the strength of your self-interested or self-regarding desires in comparison with the strength of your other-regarding desires (that is, your moral motivations and your concern for others). In other words, your choice will depend on the kind of person you are, which depends in large part on how you were raised. A person who is basically selfish will pass by the acquaintance in distress and will spread the rumor, whereas a person who has a stronger concern for others, or a stronger desire to do what is right just because it is right, will not.

Although it may be impossible to prove to selfish persons that they should not do the thing that best advances their self-interest (since, if they are selfish, that is all they care about), there are considerations that suggest it is not in a person's overall self-interest to be a selfish person. People who are exclusively concerned with their own interests tend to have less happy and less satisfying lives than those whose desires extend beyond themselves. This is sometimes called the *paradox of hedonism.* Individuals who care only about their own happiness will generally be less happy than those who care about others. Moreover, people often find greater satisfaction in a life lived according to moral principle, and in being the kind of person that entails, than in a life devoted solely to immediate self-interest. Thus, or so many philosophers have argued, people have self-interested reasons not to be so self-interested. How do selfish people make themselves less so? Not overnight, obviously, but by involving themselves in the concerns and cares of others, they can in time come to care sincerely about those persons.

MORALITY AND PERSONAL VALUES

Some philosophers distinguish between morality in a narrow sense and morality in a broad sense. In a narrow sense, morality is the moral code of an individual or a society (insofar as the moral codes of the individuals making up that society overlap). Although the principles that make up our code may not be explicitly formulated, as laws are, they do guide us in our conduct. They function as internal monitors of our own behavior and as a basis for assessing the actions of others. Morality in the narrow sense concerns the principles that do or should regulate people's conduct and relations with others. These principles can be debated, however. (Take, for example, John Stuart Mill's contention that society ought not to interfere with people's liberty when their actions affect only themselves.) And a large part of moral philosophy involves assessing rival moral principles. This discussion is part of the ongoing development in our moral culture. What is at stake are the basic standards that ought to govern our behavior—that is, the basic framework or ground rules that make coexistence possible. If there were not already fairly widespread agreement about these principles, our social order would not be possible.

But in addition we can talk about our morality in a broader sense, meaning not just the principles of conduct that we embrace but also the values, ideals, and aspirations that shape our lives. Many different ways of living our lives would meet our basic moral obligations. The type of life each of us seeks to live reflects our individual values—whether following a profession, devoting ourselves to community service,

raising a family, seeking solitude, pursuing scientific truth, striving for athletic excellence, amassing political power, cultivating glamorous people as friends, or some combination of these and many other possible ways of living. The life that each of us forges and the way we understand that life are part of our morality in the broad sense of the term.

It is important to bear this in mind throughout your study of business ethics. Although the usual concern is with the principles that ought to govern conduct in certain situations—for example, whether a hiring officer may take an applicant's race into account, whether employees may be forced to take an AIDS test, or whether corporate bribery is permissible in countries where people turn a blind eye to it—your choices in the business world will also reflect your other values and ideals—or in other words, the kind of person you are striving to be. What sort of ideal do you have of yourself as a businessperson? How much weight do you put on profitability, for instance, as against the quality of your product or the socially beneficial character of your service?

The decisions you make in your career and much of the way you shape your working life will depend not just on your moral code but also on the understanding you have of yourself in certain roles and relationships. Your morality—in the sense of your ideals, values, and aspirations—involves, among other things, your understanding of human nature, tradition, and society; of one's proper relationship to the natural environment; and of an individual's place in the cosmos. Professionals in various fields, for example, will invariably be guided not just by rules but also by their understanding of what being a professional involves, and a businessperson's conception of the ideal or model relationship to have with clients will greatly influence his or her day-to-day conduct.

There is more to living a morally good life, of course, than being a good businessperson or being good at your job, as Aristotle (384–322 B.C.E.) argued long ago. He underscored the necessity of our trying to achieve virtue or excellence, not just in some particular field of endeavor but as human beings. Aristotle thought that things have functions. The function of a piano, for instance, is to make certain sounds, and a piano that performs this function well is a good or excellent piano. Likewise, we have an idea of what it is for a person to be an excellent athlete, an excellent manager, or an excellent professor—it is to do well the types of things that athletes, managers, or professors are supposed to do.

But Aristotle also thought that, just as there is an ideal of excellence for any particular craft or occupation, similarly there must be an excellence that we can achieve simply as human beings. That is, he thought that we can live our lives as a whole in such a way that they can be judged not just as excellent in this respect or in that occupation, but as excellent, period. Aristotle thought that only when we develop our truly human capacities sufficiently to achieve this human excellence will we have lives blessed with happiness. Philosophers since Aristotle's time have been skeptical of his apparent belief that this human excellence would come in just one form, but many would underscore the importance of developing our various potential capacities and striving to achieve a kind of excellence in our lives. How we understand this excellence is a function of our values, ideals, and worldview—our morality in a broad sense.

INDIVIDUAL INTEGRITY AND RESPONSIBILITY

Previous sections discussed what it is for a person to have a moral code, as well as the sometimes conflicting pulls of moral conscience and self-interest. In addition, we have seen that people have values and ideals above and beyond their moral principles, narrowly understood, that also influence the lives they lead. And we have seen the importance of reflecting critically on both moral principles and moral ideals and val-

ues as we seek to live morally good and worthwhile lives. None of us, however, lives in a vacuum, and social pressures of various sorts always affect us. Sometimes these pressures make it difficult to stick with our principles and to be the kind of person we wish to be. Corporations are a particularly relevant example of an environment that can potentially damage individual integrity and responsibility.

The Individual Inside the Corporation

Corporations exact a price for the many benefits they offer their members—jobs, status, money, friendship, personal fulfillment. Sometimes the price of corporate membership amounts to individual conscience, as the experience of David A. Frew, professor of behavioral science, indicates.[13]

Frew interviewed a number of workers at various levels of a corporation known to be a substantial polluter. He discovered that although each person recognized and deplored the organization's polluting activities, each was willing to continue daily activities that contributed to the problem. One respondent even volunteered that it wouldn't be long before the company despoiled the surrounding area. When pressed further about his feelings, he said that he could do nothing but move to a cleaner environment.

Frew was frightened by the "ecologically schizophrenic" behavior he witnessed. But this schizophrenia goes beyond ecological issues. On many fronts—marketing, pricing, competition, contract fulfillment, management practices—the man or woman inside the organization can find it difficult, at times perhaps impossible, to reconcile the dictates of conscience with organizational policy.

One need not study the corporate scene long before observing the bind that people can experience from trying to reconcile two basic roles. The first role is that of the private individual: a decent, responsible person who readily admits the need for moral principles. The second role is that of the organization member: a human being who rarely exhibits, or is expected or encouraged to exhibit, any of the moral sensitivity of the private person. These Jekyll-and-Hyde personalities share little moral ground, and Hyde can often brutalize Jekyll when personal and organizational values collide.

About a century ago, Dan Drew, church builder and founder of Drew Theological Seminary, made a distinction between one's private life and one's business life that can be viewed as a defense of the subordination of the individual to organizational interests. Addressing a group of businessmen, Drew said:

> Sentiment is all right up in that part of the city where your home is. But downtown, no. Down there the dog that snaps the quickest gets the bone. Friendship is very nice for a Sunday afternoon when you're sitting around the dinner table with your relations, talking about the sermon that morning. But nine o'clock Monday morning, [such] notions should be brushed aside like cobwebs from a machine. I never took any stock in a man who mixed up business with anything else. He can go into other things outside of business hours, but when he's in the office he ought not to have a relation in the world—and least of all a poor relation.[14]

The many recent cases of corporate misconduct suggest that corporate organizations have frequently embraced Drew's exhortation. While "downtown," the dominant businessperson personality (Mr. Hyde) often is expected to repress the values that the private individual (Dr. Jekyll) lives by at home. In conflicts, the decent personality is to be sacrificed on the altar of expedience with a prayerful "that's business."

But don't assume that members of corporations would prefer things that way. A basic assumption of this book is that people would rather be Dr. Jekyll than Mr. Hyde, would rather be morally responsible individuals than conscienceless "team players." And yet the structure and function of organizations in general, and corporate organizations in particular, require

that their members adhere to organizational norms and, in fact, force commitment and conformity to them.

Organizational Norms

One of the major characteristics of an organization, indeed of any group, is the shared acceptance of organizational rules by its members. Acceptance can take different forms; it can be conscious or unconscious, overt or subtle, but it is almost always present, because an organization can survive only if it holds its members together. Group cohesiveness requires that individual members "commit" themselves—that is, relinquish some of their personal freedom in order to further organizational goals. One's degree of commitment—the extent to which one accepts group norms and subordinates self to organizational goals—is a measure of one's loyalty to the "team."

The corporation's goal is profit. To achieve this goal, top management sets goals for return on equity, sales, market share, and so forth. For the most part the norms or rules that govern corporate existence are derived from these goals. But clearly there's nothing in either the norms or goals that necessarily encourages moral behavior; indeed, they may discourage it.

Mounting evidence suggests that most managers experience role conflicts between what is expected of them as efficient, profit-minded members of an organization and what is expected of them as ethical persons. In a series of in-depth interviews with recent graduates of the Harvard MBA program, researchers Joseph L. Badaracco, Jr., and Allen P. Webb found that these young managers frequently received explicit instructions or felt strong organizational pressure to do things they believed to be sleazy, unethical, or even illegal.[15] Another survey found that managers at all levels experience role conflicts because of "pressure from the top" to meet corporate goals and comply with corporate norms. Of the managers interviewed, 50 percent of top managers, 65 percent of middle managers, and 84 percent of lower managers agreed that "managers today feel under pressure to compromise personal standards to achieve company goals."[16]

The young managers interviewed by Badaracco and Webb identified four powerful organizational "commandments" as responsible for the pressure they felt to compromise their integrity:

> First, performance is what really counts, so make your numbers. Second, be loyal and show us that you're a team player. Third, don't break the law. Fourth, don't overinvest in ethical behavior.[17]

Although most corporate goals and norms are not objectionable when viewed by themselves, they frequently put the people who must implement them into a moral pressure cooker. The need to meet corporate objectives, to be a team player, and to conform to organizational norms can lead otherwise honorable individuals to engage in unethical conduct.

Conformity

It is no secret that organizations exert pressure on their members to conform to norms and goals. What may not be so widely known is how easily individuals can be induced to behave as those around them do. A dramatic example is provided in the early conformity studies by social psychologist Solomon Asch.[18]

In a classic experiment, Asch asked groups of seven to nine college students to say which of three lines on a card (right, below) matched the length of a standard line on a second card (left, below):

Only one of the subjects in each group was "naive," or unaware of the nature of the experiment. The others were stooges of the experimenter, who had instructed them to make incorrect judgments in about two-thirds of the cases and in this way to pressure the naive subjects to alter their correct judgments.

The results were revealing. When the subjects were not exposed to pressure, they invariably judged correctly, but when the stooges gave false answers, the subjects changed their responses to conform with the unanimous majority judgments. When one stooge differed from the majority and gave the correct answer, naive subjects maintained their position three-fourths of the time. However, when the honest stooge switched to the majority view in later trials, the errors made by naive subjects rose to about the same level as that of subjects who stood alone against a unanimous majority.

Why did they yield? Some respondents said they didn't want to seem different, even though they continued to believe their judgments were correct. Others said that although their perceptions seemed correct, the majority couldn't be wrong. Still other subjects didn't even seem aware that they had caved in to group pressure. Even those who held their ground tended to be profoundly disturbed by being out of step with the majority and confessed to being sorely tempted to alter their judgments. Indeed, a subsequent study found that students who stood firm in their judgments suffered more anxiety than those who switched. One student with the strength of his correct convictions was literally dripping with perspiration by the end of the experiment.[19]

In these experiments, which cumulatively included several hundred students, the subjects were not exposed to the authority symbols that people inside an organization face: bosses, boards, presidents, professional peers, established policy, and so on. Nor would their responses entail the serious long-range impact that bucking the system can carry for members of an organization: being transferred, dismissed, frozen in a position, or made an organizational

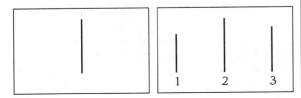

1   2   3

pariah. And of course the students did not bring to these experiments the financial, educational, and other personal investments that individuals bring to their jobs. In comparison, men and women within an organization are under greater pressures to conform than the students in Asch's studies. Unfortunately, conformity can mean the surrender of moral autonomy. It can also result in *bystander apathy* and *groupthink.*

Bystander Apathy. Back in the 1960s a tragic event leaped off the front pages of the newspapers. A young woman named Kitty Genovese was stabbed to death in New York City. The murder was not in itself so unusual. What was particularly distressing was that thirty-eight of Kitty Genovese's neighbors witnessed her brutal slaying. In answer to her pitiful screams of terror at 3 A.M., they came to their windows and remained there for the 30 minutes it took her assailant to brutalize her. Of the thirty-eight, not one attempted to intervene in any way; no one even phoned the police.

Why didn't Kitty Genovese's neighbors help her? One reason, many social psychologists believe, is that an individual's sense of personal responsibility is inversely proportional to the number of people witnessing the event. Thus, the more people who are observing an event, the less likely any of them will feel obliged to do anything. In emergency situations, we seem naturally to let the behavior of those around us dictate our response. This diffusion of responsibility can lead to bystander apathy. Submerged in the group or the crowd, the individual can lose any sense of individuality. Feeling anonymous and thus not responsible, the individual may not even question the morality of his or her actions.

Groupthink. A related phenomenon is what social psychologists call "groupthink." Groupthink happens when pressure for unanimity within a highly cohesive group overwhelms its members' desire or ability to appraise the situation realistically and consider alternative courses of action. Members of the group close their eyes to nega-

tive information, ignore warnings that the group may be mistaken, and discount outside ideas that might contradict the thinking or decisions of the group. Group members may have the illusion that the group is invulnerable or that because the group is good or right, whatever it does is permissible. Individuals in the group tend to self-censor thoughts that go against the group's ideas and rationalize away conflicting evidence, and the group as a whole implicitly or explicitly pressures potential dissenters to conform. Groupthink thus leads to irrational, sometimes disastrous decisions, and it has enormous potential for doing moral damage.

Is there anything about the corporate organization that encourages bystander apathy, groupthink, and, more generally, the surrender of individual moral autonomy? Viewed as a massive group, corporations certainly encourage these phenomena as much as, and perhaps more than, most groups. Moreover, organizational pressure to produce, make profit, and conform can cultivate, or at least do nothing to inhibit, these propensities. Beyond this, many corporations fail to institutionalize ethics. They don't articulate or communicate ethical standards to their members; they don't actively enforce them; and they retain structures and policies that thwart individual integrity.

Although what is expected of members of a corporation sometimes clashes with their own moral values, they are rarely encouraged to deal with the conflict in an open, mature way. In fact, the more one suppresses individual moral urges in the cause of organizational interests, the more "mature," committed, and loyal one is considered to be. Conversely, the less willing the individual, the less "mature" and the more suspect. For example, when a Beech-Nut employee expressed concerns about the fact that the concentrate the company was producing for its "100% pure" apple juice contained nothing more than sugar water and chemicals, his annual performance review described his judgment as "colored by naïveté and impractical ideals."[20] Employees frequently have to fight hard to maintain their moral integrity in a show-down with organizational priorities.

Often, however, the problem facing us is not that of doing what we know to be right but rather of deciding what the right thing to do is. In business and organizational contexts, many difficult and puzzling moral questions need to be answered. How do we go about doing that? Is there some reliable procedure or method for answering moral questions? In science, the scientific method tells us what steps to take if we seek to answer a scientific question, but there is no comparable moral method for engaging moral questions. There is, however, general agreement about what constitutes good moral reasoning.

MORAL REASONING

It is useful to view moral reasoning at first in the context of *argument*. An argument is a group of statements, one of which (called the *conclusion*) is claimed to follow from the others (called the *premises*). Here's an example of an argument:

Argument 1

If a person is a mother, the person is a female.

Fran is a mother.

Therefore, Fran is a female.

The first two statements (the premises) of this argument happen to entail the third (the conclusion), which means that if I accept the first two as true, then I must accept the third as also true. Not to accept the conclusion while accepting the premises would result in a contradiction—holding two beliefs that cannot both be true at the same time. In other words, if I believe that all mothers are females and Fran is a mother (the premises), then I cannot deny that Fran is a female (the conclusion) without contradicting myself. An argument like this one, whose premises logically entail its conclusion, is termed *valid*.

An *invalid* argument is one whose premises do not entail its conclusion. In an invalid argu-

ment, I can accept the premises as true and reject the conclusion without any contradiction. Thus:

Argument 2

If a person is a mother, the person is a female.

Fran is a female.

Therefore, Fran is a mother.

The conclusion of this argument does not necessarily follow from the true premises. I can believe that every mother is a female and that Fran is a female and deny that Fran is a mother without contradicting myself.

One way to show this is by means of a *counterexample,* an example that is consistent with the premises but is inconsistent with the conclusion. Let's suppose Fran is a two-year-old, a premise that is perfectly consistent with the two stated premises. If she is, she can't possibly be a mother. Or let's suppose Fran is an adult female who happens to be childless, another premise that is perfectly consistent with the stated premises but obviously at odds with the conclusion. If an argument is valid (such as Argument 1), then no counterexamples are possible.

A valid argument can have untrue premises, as in the following:

Argument 3

If a person is a female, she must be a mother.

Fran is a female.

Therefore, Fran must be a mother.

Like Argument 1, this one is valid. If I accept its premises as true, I must accept its conclusion as true; otherwise I will contradict myself. Although valid, this argument is unsound because one of its premises is false—namely, "If a person is a female, she must be a mother." Realizing the patent absurdity of one of its premises, no sensible person would accept this argument's conclusion. But notice why the argument is unsound—not because the reasoning procedure is invalid but because one of the premises is false. *Sound arguments,* such as Argument 1, have true premises and valid reasoning. *Unsound arguments* have at least one false premise, as in Argument 3, or invalid reasoning, as in Argument 2.

Now let's consider some *moral arguments,* which can be defined simply as arguments whose conclusions are moral judgments, assertions about the moral worth of a person, action, activity, policy, or organization. Here are some examples that deal with affirmative action for women and minorities in the workplace:

Argument 4

If an action violates the law, it is morally wrong.

Affirmative action on behalf of women and minorities in personnel matters violates the law.

Therefore, affirmative action on behalf of women and minorities in personnel matters is morally wrong.

Argument 5

If an action violates the will of the majority, it is morally wrong.

Affirmative action on behalf of women and minorities in personnel matters violates the will of the majority.

Therefore, affirmative action on behalf of women and minorities in personnel matters is morally wrong.

Argument 6

If an action redresses past injuries that have disadvantaged a group, it is morally permissible.

Affirmative action on behalf of women and minorities in personnel matters redresses injuries that have disadvantaged these groups.

Therefore, affirmative action on behalf of women and minorities in personnel matters is morally permissible.

Argument 7

If an action is the only practical way to remedy a social problem, then it is morally permissible.

Affirmative action on behalf of women and minorities in personnel matters is the only practical way to remedy the social problem of unequal employment opportunity.

Therefore, affirmative action on behalf of women and minorities in personnel matters is morally permissible.

The first premise in each of these arguments is a moral standard, the second an alleged fact, and the conclusion a moral judgment. *Moral reasoning* or argument typically moves from a moral standard, through one or more factual judgments about some person, action, or policy related to that standard, to a moral judgment about that person, action, or policy. Good moral reasoning will frequently be more complicated than these examples; often it will involve an appeal to more than one standard as well as to various appropriate factual claims. Still, these examples illustrate its most basic form.

Defensible Moral Judgments

If a moral judgment or conclusion is defensible, then it must be supportable by a defensible moral standard, together with relevant facts. A moral standard supports a moral judgment if the standard, taken together with the relevant facts, logically entails the moral judgment and if the moral standard itself is a sound standard. If someone argues that affirmative action for minorities and women is right (or wrong) but cannot produce a supporting principle when asked, then the person's position is considerably weakened. And if the person does not see any need to support the judgment by appeal to a moral standard, then he or she simply does not understand how moral concepts are used or is using moral words like "right" or "wrong" differently from the way they are commonly used.

Keeping this in mind—that moral judgments must be supportable by moral standards and facts—will aid your understanding of moral discourse, which can be highly complex and sophisticated. It will also sharpen your own critical faculties and improve your moral reasoning and ability to formulate relevant moral arguments.

Patterns of Defense and Challenge

In assessing arguments, one must be careful to clarify the meanings of their key terms and phrases. Often premises can be understood in more than one way, and this ambiguity may lead people to accept (or reject) arguments that they shouldn't. For example, "affirmative action" seems to mean different things to different people (see Chapter 9 on job discrimination). Before we can profitably assess Arguments 4 through 7, we have to agree on how we understand "affirmative action." Similarly, Argument 5 relies on the idea of "violating the will of the majority," but this notion has to be clarified before we can evaluate either the moral principle that it is wrong to violate the will of the majority or the factual claim that affirmative action does violate the majority's will.

Assuming that the arguments are logically valid in their form (as Arguments 4 through 7 are) and that their terms have been clarified and possible ambiguities eliminated, then we must turn our attention to assessing the premises of the arguments. Should we accept or reject their premises? Remember that if an argument is valid and you accept the premises, you must accept the conclusion.

Let's look at some further aspects of this assessment process:

1. *Evaluating the factual claims.* If the parties to an ethical discussion are willing to accept the moral standard (or standards) in question, then they can concentrate on the factual claims. Thus, for example, in Argument 4 they will focus on whether affirmative action on behalf of women and minorities is in fact illegal. In Argument 7 they will need to determine whether affirmative action is really the only practical way to remedy the social problem of unequal employment opportunity. Analogous questions can be asked about the factual claims of Arguments 5 and 6. Answering them in the affirmative would require considerable supporting data.

2. *Challenging the moral standard.* Moral arguments generally involve more than factual disputes. The moral standards they appeal to may be controversial. One party might challenge the moral standard on which the argument relies, contending that it is not a plausible one and that we should not accept it. The critic might do this in several different ways—for example, by showing that there are exceptions to the standard, that the standard leads to unacceptable consequences, or that it is inconsistent with the arguer's other moral beliefs.

In the following dialogue, for example, Lynn is attacking Sam's advocacy of the standard "If an action redresses past injuries that have disadvantaged a group, it is morally permissible."

Lynn: What would you think of affirmative action for Jews in the workplace?
Sam: I'd be against it.
Lynn: What about Catholics?
Sam: No.
Lynn: People of Irish extraction?
Sam: They should be treated the same as anybody else.
Lynn: But each of these groups and more I could mention were victimized in the past by unfair discrimination and probably in some cases continue to be.
Sam: So?
Lynn: So the standard you're defending leads to a judgment you reject: namely, that Jews, Catholics, and Irish should be compensated by affirmative action for having been disadvantaged. How do you account for this inconsistency?

At this point Sam, or any rational person in a similar position, has three alternatives: abandon or modify the standard, alter his moral judgment, or show how women and minorities fit the original principle even though the other groups do not.

3. *Defending the moral standard.* When the standard is criticized, then its advocate must defend it. Often this requires invoking an even more general principle. A defender of Argument 6, for example, might defend the redress principle by appealing to some more general conception of social justice. Or defenders might try to show how the standard in question entails other moral judgments that both the critic and the defender accept, thereby enhancing the plausibility of the standard. In the following exchange, Lynn is defending the standard of Argument 5: "If an action violates the will of the majority, it is morally wrong":

Lynn: Okay, do you think the government should impose a national religion on all Americans?
Sam: Of course not.
Lynn: What about requiring people to register their handguns?
Sam: I'm all for it.
Lynn: And using kids in pornography?
Sam: There rightly are laws against it.
Lynn: But the principle you're objecting to— that an action violating the will of the majority is wrong—leads to these judgments that you accept.

Of course, Lynn's argument is by no means a conclusive defense for her moral standard. Other moral standards could just as easily entail the judgments she cites, as Sam is quick to point out:

Sam: Now wait a minute. I oppose a state religion on constitutional grounds, not because it violates majority will. As for gun control, I'm for it because I think it will reduce violent crimes. And using kids in pornography is wrong because it exploits and endangers children.

Although Lynn's strategy for defending the standard about majority rule proved inconclusive, it does illustrate a common and often persuasive way of arguing for a moral principle.

4. *Revising and modifying the argument.* Arguments 4 through 7 are only illustrations, and all the moral principles they mention are very simple—too simple to accept without qualification. (The principle that it is immoral to break the law in all circumstances, for example, is implausible. Nazi Germany furnishes an obvious counterexample to it.) But once the standard has been effectively challenged, the defender of the argument, rather than abandon the argument altogether, might try to reformulate it. For instance, the defender might replace the original, contested premise with a better and more plausible one that still supports the conclusion. For example, Premise 1 of Argument 4 might be replaced by: "If an action violates a law that is democratically decided and that is not morally unjust, then the action is immoral." Or the defender might revise the conclusion of his or her argument, perhaps by restricting its scope. A more modest, less sweeping conclusion will often be easier to defend.

In this way, the discussion continues, the arguments on both sides of an issue improve, and we make progress in the analysis and resolution of ethical issues. In general, in philosophy we study logic and criticize arguments not in order to be able to score quick debating points but rather to be able to think better and more deeply about moral and other problems. Our goal as moral philosophers is not to "win" arguments but to arrive at the truth—or, put less grandly, to find the most reasonable answer to an ethical question.

Requirements for Moral Judgments

Moral discussion and the analysis of ethical issues can take various, often complicated, paths. Nevertheless, the preceding discussion implies certain minimum adequacy requirements for moral judgments. Although there is no complete list of adequacy criteria, moral judgments should be (1) logical, (2) based on facts, and (3) based on sound or defensible moral principles. A moral judgment that is weak on any of these grounds is open to criticism.

Moral Judgments Should Be Logical. To say that moral judgments should be logical implies several things. First, as indicated in the discussion of moral reasoning, our moral judgments should follow logically from their premises. The connection between (1) the standard, (2) the conduct or policy, and (3) the moral judgment should be such that 1 and 2 logically entail 3. Our goal is to be able to support our moral judgments with reasons and evidence, rather than basing them solely on emotion, sentiment, or social or personal preference.

Forming logical moral judgments also means ensuring that any particular moral judgment of ours is compatible with our other moral and nonmoral beliefs. We must avoid inconsistency. Most philosophers agree that if we make a moral judgment—for example, that it was wrong of Smith to alter the figures she gave to the outside auditors—then we must be willing to make the same judgment in any similar set of circumstances—that is, if our friend Brown, our spouse, or our father had altered the figures. In particular, we cannot make an exception for ourselves, judging something permissible for us to do while condemning others for doing the very same thing.

Moral Judgments Should Be Based on Facts. Adequate moral judgments cannot be made in a vacuum. We must gather as much relevant information as possible before making them. For example, an intelligent assessment of the morality of insider trading would require an understanding of, among other things, the different circumstances in which it can occur and the effects it has on the market and on other traders. The information supporting a moral judgment, the facts, should be relevant—that is, the information should actually relate to the judgment; it should be complete, or inclusive of all significant data; and it should be accurate or true.

Moral Judgments Should Be Based on Acceptable Moral Principles. We know that moral judgments are based on moral standards. At the highest level of moral reasoning, these standards embody and express very general moral principles. Reliable moral judgments must be based on sound moral principles—principles that can withstand critical scrutiny and rational criticism. What, precisely, makes a moral principle sound or acceptable is one of the most difficult questions that the study of ethics raises and is beyond the scope of this book. But one criterion is worth mentioning, what philosophers call our "considered moral beliefs."

These beliefs contrast with our gut responses, with beliefs based on ignorance or prejudice, and with beliefs we just happen to hold without having thought them through. As philosophy professor Tom Regan explains, our considered beliefs are those moral beliefs "we hold *after* we have made a conscientious effort . . . to think about our beliefs coolly, rationally, impartially, with conceptual clarity, and with as much relevant information as we can reasonably acquire."[21] We have grounds to doubt a moral principle when it clashes with such beliefs. Conversely, conformity with our considered moral judgments is good reason for regarding it as provisionally established.

This does not mean that conformity with our considered beliefs is the sole or even basic test of a moral principle, any more than conformity with well-established beliefs is the exclusive or even fundamental test of a scientific hypothesis. (Copernicus's heliocentric hypothesis, for example, did not conform with what passed in the medieval world as a well-considered belief, the Ptolemaic view that the earth was the center of the universe.) But conformity with our considered beliefs seemingly must play some part in evaluating the many alternative moral principles that are explored in the next chapter.

SUMMARY

1. Ethics deals with individual character and the moral rules that govern and limit our conduct. It investigates questions of moral right and wrong, duty and obligation, and moral responsibility.

2. Business ethics is the study of what constitutes right and wrong (or good and bad) human conduct in a business context. Closely related moral questions arise in other organizational contexts.

3. Moral standards concern behavior that has serious consequences for human well-being, and they take priority over other standards, including self-interest. Their soundness depends on the adequacy of the reasons that support or justify them.

4. Morality must be distinguished from etiquette (which concerns rules for well-mannered behavior), from law (statutes, regulations, common law, and constitutional law), and from professional codes of ethics (which are the special rules governing the members of a profession).

5. Morality is not necessarily based on religion. Although we draw our moral beliefs from many sources, for philosophers the issue is whether those beliefs can be justified.

6. Ethical relativism is the theory that right and wrong are determined by what one's society says is right and wrong. There are many problems with this theory. Also dubious is the theory that business has its own morality, divorced from ordinary ideas of right and wrong.

7. Accepting a moral principle involves a motivation to conform one's conduct to that principle. Violating the principle will bother one's conscience, but conscience is not a perfectly reliable guide to right and wrong.

8. Part of the point of morality is to make social existence possible by restraining self-interested behavior. Sometimes doing what is morally right can conflict with one's personal interests. In general, though, following your moral principles will enable you to live a more satisfying life.

9. Morality as a code of conduct can be distinguished from morality in the broader sense of the values, ideals, and aspirations that shape a person's life.

10. Several aspects of corporate structure and function work to undermine individual moral responsibility. Organizational norms, group commitment, and pressure to conform (sometimes leading to bystander apathy or groupthink) can all make the exercise of individual integrity difficult.

11. Moral reasoning consists of forming moral judgments, assessments of the moral worth of persons, actions, activities, policies, or organizations. Moral reasoning and argument typically appeal both to moral standards and to relevant facts. Moral judgments should be entailed by the relevant moral standards and the facts, and they should not contradict our other beliefs. Both standards and facts must be assessed when moral arguments are being evaluated.

12. Philosophical discussion generally involves the revision and modification of arguments; in this way progress is made in the analysis and resolution of moral and other issues.

13. Conformity with our considered moral beliefs is an important consideration in evaluating moral principles. A considered moral belief is one held only after we have made a conscientious effort to be conceptually clear, to acquire all relevant information, and to think rationally, impartially, and dispassionately about the belief and its implications. We should doubt any moral principle that clashes with many of our considered beliefs.

CASE 1.1

Made in the U.S.A.—Dumped in Brazil, Africa, Iraq . . .

When it comes to the safety of young children, fire is a parent's nightmare. Just the thought of their young ones trapped in their cribs and beds by a raging nocturnal blaze is enough to make most mothers and fathers take every precaution to ensure their children's safety. Little wonder that when fire-retardant children's pajamas first hit the market, they proved an overnight success. Within a few short years more than 200 million pairs were sold, and the sales of millions more were all but guaranteed. For their manufacturers, the future could not have been brighter. Then, like a bolt from the blue, came word that the pajamas were killers. The U.S. Consumer Product Safety Commission (CPSC) moved quickly to ban their sale and recall millions of pairs. Reason: The pajamas contained the flame-retardant chemical Tris (2,3-dibromoprophyl), which had been found to cause kidney cancer in children.

Whereas just months earlier the 100 medium and small garment manufacturers of the Tris-impregnated pajamas couldn't fill orders fast enough, suddenly they were worrying about how to get rid of the millions of pairs now sitting in warehouses. Because of its toxicity, the sleepwear couldn't even be thrown away, let alone sold. Indeed, the CPSC left no doubt about how the pajamas were to be disposed of—buried or burned or used as industrial wiping cloths. All meant millions of dollars in losses for manufacturers.

The companies affected—mostly small, family-run operations employing fewer than 100 workers—immediately attempted to shift blame to the mills that made the cloth. When that attempt failed, they tried to get the big department stores that sold the pajamas and the chemical companies that produced Tris to share the financial losses. Again, no sale. Finally, in desperation, the companies lobbied in Washington for a bill making the federal government partially responsible for the losses. It was the government, they argued, that originally had required

the companies to add Tris to pajamas and then had prohibited their sale. Congress was sympathetic; it passed a bill granting companies relief, but the bill was vetoed.

While the small firms were waging their political battle in the halls of Congress, ads began appearing in the classified pages of *Women's Wear Daily*. "Tris-Tris-Tris . . . We will buy any fabric containing Tris," read one. Another said, "Tris—we will purchase any large quantities of garments containing Tris."[22] The ads had been placed by exporters, who began buying up the pajamas, usually at 10 to 30 percent of the normal wholesale price. Their intent was clear: to dump° the carcinogenic pajamas on overseas markets.[23]

Tris is not the only example of dumping. There were the 450,000 baby pacifiers, of the type known to have caused choking deaths, that were exported for sale overseas, and the 400 Iraqis who died and the 5,000 who were hospitalized after eating wheat and barley treated with a U.S.-banned organic mercury fungicide. Winstrol, a synthetic male hormone that had been found to stunt the growth of American children, was made available in Brazil as an appetite stimulant for children. DowElanco sold its weed killer Galant in Costa Rica, although the Environmental Protection Agency (EPA) forbade its sale to U.S. farmers because Galant may cause cancer. After the U.S. Food and Drug Administration (FDA) banned the painkiller dipyrone because it can cause a fatal blood disorder, Winthrop Products continued to sell dipyrone in Mexico City.

Manufacturers that dump products abroad clearly are motivated by profit, or at least by the hope of avoiding financial losses resulting from hav-

---

°Dumping is a term apparently coined by *Mother Jones* magazine to refer to the practice of exporting to other countries products that have been banned or declared hazardous in the United States.

ing to withdraw a product from the U.S. market. For government and health agencies that cooperate in the exporting of dangerous products, sometimes the motives are more complex.

For example, when researchers documented the dangers of the Dalkon Shield intrauterine device—among the adverse reactions were pelvic inflammation, blood poisoning, tubal pregnancies, and uterine perforations—its manufacturer, A. H. Robins Co., began losing its domestic market.[24] As a result, the company worked out a deal with the Office of Population within the U.S. Agency for International Development (AID), whereby AID bought thousands of the devices at a reduced price for use in population-control programs in forty-two countries.

Why do governmental and population-control agencies approve for sale and use overseas a birth control device proved dangerous in the United States? They say their motives are humanitarian. Because the rate of dying in childbirth is high in Third World countries, almost any birth control device is preferable to none. Analogous arguments are used to defend the export of pesticides and other products judged too dangerous for use in the United States: Foreign countries should be free to decide for themselves whether the benefits of those products are worth their risks. In line with this, some Third World government officials insist that denying their countries access to these products is tantamount to violating their countries' national sovereignty.

This reasoning has found a sympathetic ear in Washington, for it turns up in the "notification" system that regulates the export of banned or dangerous products overseas. Based on the principles of national sovereignty, self-determination, and free trade, the notification system requires that foreign governments be notified whenever a product is banned, deregulated, suspended, or canceled by a U.S. regulatory agency. The State Department, which implements the system, has a policy statement on the subject that reads in part: "No country should establish itself as the arbiter of others' health and safety standards. Individual governments are generally in the best position to establish standards of public health and safety."

Critics of the system claim that notifying foreign health officials is virtually useless. For one thing, other governments rarely can establish health standards or even control imports into their countries. Indeed, most of the Third World countries where banned or dangerous products are dumped lack regulatory agencies, adequate testing facilities, and well-staffed customs departments.

Then there's the problem of getting the word out about hazardous products. In theory, when a government agency such as the EPA or the FDA finds a product hazardous, it is supposed to inform the State Department, which is to notify local health officials. But agencies often fail to inform the State Department of the product they have banned or found harmful, and when it is notified, its communiqués typically go no further than U.S. embassies abroad. One embassy official even told the General Accounting Office that he "did not routinely forward notification of chemicals not registered in the host country because it may adversely affect U.S. exporting." When foreign officials are notified by U.S. embassies, they sometimes find the communiqués vague or ambiguous or too technical to understand.

But even if communication procedures were improved or the export of dangerous products forbidden, there are ways that companies can circumvent these threats to their profits—for example, by simply changing the name of the product or by exporting the individual ingredients of a product to a plant in a foreign country. Once there, the ingredients can be reassembled and the product dumped.[25] The United States does prohibit its pharmaceutical companies from exporting drugs banned in this country, but sidestepping the law is not that difficult. "Unless the package bursts open on the dock," one drug company executive observes, "you have no chance of being caught."

Unfortunately for us, in the case of pesticides, the effects of overseas dumping are now coming home. In the United States, the EPA bans all crop uses of DDT and dieldrin, which kill fish, cause tumors in animals, and build up in the fatty tissue of humans. It also bans heptachlor, chlordane, leptophos, endrin, and many other pesticides, including 2,4,5-T (which contains the deadly poison dioxin, the active ingredient in Agent Orange, the notorious defoliant used in Vietnam) because they are dangerous to human beings. No law, however, prohibits the sale of DDT and these other U.S.-banned pesticides overseas, where thanks to corporate dumping they are routinely used in agriculture. In one recent three-month period, for example, U.S. chemical companies exported 3.9 million pounds of banned and withdrawn pesticides. The FDA now estimates, through spot checks, that 10 percent of our imported food is contaminated with residues of banned pesticides. And the FDA's most commonly used testing procedure does not even check for 70 percent of the pesticides known to cause cancer. With the doubling of exports of Mexican produce to the United States since the signing of the North American Free Trade Agreement (NAFTA), the problem of pesticide-laced food has only grown worse.[26]

Discussion Questions

1. Do you think dumping involves any moral issues? What are they?

2. Complete the following statements by filling in the blanks with either "moral" or "nonmoral":

   a. Whether or not dumping should be permitted is a _____ question.

   b. "Are dangerous products of any use in the Third World?" is a _____ question.

   c. "Is it proper for the U.S. government to sponsor the export of dangerous products overseas?" is a _____ question.

   d. Whether or not the notification system will protect the health and safety of people in foreign lands is a _____ question.

3. Can a moral argument be made in favor of dumping, when doing so does not violate U.S. law? Do any moral considerations support illegal dumping? Speculate on why dumpers dump. Do you think they believe that what they are doing is morally permissible?

4. Defend or challenge the present notification system by appeal to moral principles and facts.

5. What moral arguments can be made against legal and illegal dumping? Should we have laws prohibiting more types of dumping? What is your position on dumping, and what principles and values do you base it on?

CASE 1.2

The A7D Affair

Kermit Vandivier could not have predicted the impact on his life of purchase order P-237138, issued by LTV Aerospace Corporation.[27] The order was for 202 brake assemblies for a new Air Force light attack plane, the A7D, and news of the LTV contract was cause for uncorking the champagne at the B. F. Goodrich plant in Troy, Ohio, where Vandivier worked. Everyone agreed, including Vandivier, that Goodrich had carried off a real coup. Although the LTV order was a small one, it signaled that Goodrich was back in LTV's good graces after living under a cloud of disrepute. Ten years earlier, Goodrich had built a brake for LTV that, to put it kindly, hadn't met expectations. As a result, LTV had written off Goodrich as a reliable source of brakes. So although modest, the LTV contract was a chance for Goodrich to redeem itself, one that the people at the Troy plant were determined to make good.

LTV's unexpected change of heart after ten years was easily explained. Goodrich made LTV an offer it couldn't refuse—a ridiculously low bid for making the four-disk brakes. Had Goodrich taken leave of its financial senses? Hardly. Because aircraft brakes are custom made for a particular aircraft, only the brakes' manufacturer has replacement parts. Thus, even if it took a loss on the job, Goodrich figured it could more than make up for it in the sale of replacement parts. Of course, if Goodrich bungled the job, there wouldn't be a third chance.

John Warren, a seven-year veteran and one of Goodrich's most capable engineers, was made project engineer and lost no time in working up a preliminary design for the brake. Perhaps because the design was faultless or perhaps because Warren was given to temper tantrums when criticized, coworkers accepted the engineer's plan without question. So there was no reason to suspect that young Searle Lawson, one year out of college and six months with Goodrich, would come to think Warren's design was fundamentally flawed.

Lawson was assigned by Warren to produce the final production design. He had to determine the best materials for brake linings and identify any needed adjustments in the brake design. This process called for extensive testing to meet military specifications. If the brakes passed the grueling tests, they would then be flight-tested by the Air Force.

Lawson was under pressure to meet LTV's target date for flight tests, so he lost no time in getting down to work. Because he hadn't received the brake housing and some other parts yet, he used a housing from a brake similar to the A7D's and built a prototype of the four-disk design. What Lawson particularly wanted to learn was whether the brake could withstand the extreme internal temperatures, in excess of 1000 degrees F, when the aircraft landed.

When the brake linings disintegrated in the first test, Lawson thought the problem might be defective parts or an unsuitable lining. But after two more consecutive failures, he decided the problem lay in the design: The four-disk design was simply too small to stop the aircraft without generating so much heat that the brake linings melted. In Lawson's view, a larger, five-disk brake was needed.

Lawson knew well the implications of his conclusion. The four-disk brake assemblies that were arriving at the plant would have to be junked, and more tests would have to be conducted. The accompanying delays would preclude on-time delivery of the production brakes to LTV.

Lawson reported his findings and recommendations to John Warren. Going to a five-disk design was impossible, Warren told him. Officials at Goodrich were already boasting to LTV about how well the tests were going. Besides, Warren was confident that the problem lay not in the four-disk design but in the brake linings themselves.

Unconvinced, Lawson went to Robert Sink, who supervised engineers on projects. Sink was in a tight spot. If he agreed with Lawson, he would be indicting his own professional judgment: He was the man who had assigned Warren to the job. What's more, he had accepted Warren's design without reservation and had assured LTV more than once that there was little left to do but ship them the brakes. To recant now would mean explaining the reversal not only to LTV but also to the Goodrich hierarchy. In the end, Sink, who was not an engineer, deferred to the seasoned judgment of Warren and instructed Lawson to continue the tests.

His own professional judgment overridden, Lawson could do little but bash on with the tests. Because all the parts for the brake had by this time arrived, he was able to build a production model of the brake with new linings and subject it to the rigorous qualification tests. Thirteen more tests were conducted, and thirteen more failures resulted. It was at this point that data analyst and technical writer Kermit Vandivier entered the picture.

Vandivier was looking over the data of the latest A7D test when he noticed an irregularity: The instrument recording some of the stops had been deliberately miscalibrated to indicate that less pressure was required to stop the aircraft than actually was the case. Vandivier immediately showed the test logs to test lab supervisor Ralph Gretzinger, who said he'd learned from the technician who miscalibrated the instrument that Lawson had requested the miscalibration. Later, while confirming this account, Lawson said he was simply following the orders of Sink and Russell Van Horn, manager of the design engineering section, who according to Lawson were intent on qualifying the brakes at whatever cost. For his part, Gretzinger vowed he would never permit deliberately falsified data or reports to leave his lab.

A month later, the brake was again tested, and again it failed. Nevertheless, Lawson asked Vandivier to start preparing the various graph and chart displays for qualification. Vandivier refused and told Gretzinger what he'd been asked to do. Gretzinger was livid. He again vowed that his lab would not be part of a conspiracy to defraud. Then, bent on getting to the bottom of the matter, Gretzinger rushed off to see Russell Line, manager of the Goodrich Technical Services Section.

An hour later, Gretzinger returned to his desk looking like a beaten man. He knew he had only two choices: defy his superiors or do their bidding.

"You know," he said to Vandivier, "I've been an engineer for a long time, and I've always believed that ethics and integrity were every bit as important as theorems and formulas, and never once has anything happened to change my beliefs. Now this. . . . Hell, I've got two sons I've got to put through school and I just . . ." When his voice trailed off, it was clear that he would in fact knuckle under. He and Vandivier would prepare the qualifying data, then someone "upstairs" would actually write the report. Their part, Gretzinger rationalized, wasn't really so bad. "After all," he said, "we're just drawing some curves, and what happens to them after they leave here—well, we're not responsible for that." Vandivier knew Gretzinger didn't believe what he was saying about not being responsible. Both of them knew that they were about to become principal characters in a plot to defraud.

Unwilling to play his part, Vandivier decided that he, too, would confer with Line. Line was sympathetic; he said he understood what Vandivier was going through. But in the end he said he would not refer the matter to chief engineer H. C. "Bud" Sunderman, as Vandivier had suggested. Why not? Vandivier wanted to know.

"Because it's none of my business, and it's none of yours," Line told him. "I learned a long time ago not to worry about things over which I had no control. I have no control over this."

Vandivier pressed the point. What about the test pilots who might get injured because of the faulty brakes? Didn't their uncertain fate prick Line's conscience?

"Look," said Line, growing impatient with Vandivier's moral needling, "I just told you I have no control over this thing. Why should my conscience bother me?" Then he added, "You're just getting all upset over this thing for nothing. I just do as I'm told, and I'd advise you to do the same."

Vandivier made his decision that night. He knew, of course, he was on the horns of a dilemma. If he wrote the report, he would save his job at the expense of his conscience. If he refused, he would honor his moral code and, he was convinced, lose his job—an ugly prospect for anyone, let alone a forty-two-year-old man with a wife and seven children. The next day, Vandivier phoned Lawson and told him he was ready to begin on the qualification report.

Lawson shot over to Vandivier's office with all the speed of one who knows that, swallowed fast, a bitter pill doesn't taste so bad. Before they started on the report, though, Vandivier, still uneasy with his decision, asked Lawson if he fully understood what they were about to do.

"Yeah," Lawson said acidly, "we're going to screw LTV. And speaking of screwing," he continued, "I know now how a whore feels, because that's exactly what I've become, an engineering whore. I've sold myself. It's all I can do to look at myself in the mirror when I shave. I make me sick."

For someone like Vandivier, who had written dozens of them, the qualification report was a snap. It took about a month, during which time the brake failed still another final qualification test, and the two men talked almost exclusively about the enormity of what they were doing. In the Nuremberg trials they found a historical analogy to their own complicity and culpability in the A7D affair. More than once, Lawson opined that the brakes were downright dangerous, that anything could happen during the flight tests. His opinion proved prophetic.

When the report was finished, copies were sent to the Air Force and LTV. Within a week test flights were begun at Edwards Air Force Base in California. Goodrich dispatched Lawson to Edwards as its representative, but he wasn't there long. Several "unusual incidents" brought the flight tests literally to a screeching halt. Lawson returned to the Troy plant, full of talk about several near crashes caused by brake trouble during landings. That was enough to send Vandivier to his attorney, to whom he told the whole sorry tale.

Although the attorney didn't think Vandivier was guilty of fraud, he was convinced that the analyst/writer was guilty of participating in a conspiracy to defraud. Vandivier's only hope, the attorney counseled, was to make a clean breast of the matter to the FBI. Vandivier did. Evidently the FBI informed the Air Force of Vandivier's disclosure, for within days the Air Force, which had previously accepted the qualification report, demanded to see some of the raw data compiled during the tests.

At this point both Lawson and Vandivier decided to resign from Goodrich. In his letter of resignation, addressed to Russell Line, Vandivier cited the A7D report and stated: "As you are aware, this report contains numerous deliberate and willful misrepresentations which, according to legal counsel, constitute fraud and expose both myself and others to criminal charges of conspiracy to defraud. . . . The events of the past seven months have created an atmosphere of deceit and distrust in which it is impossible to work. . . ."

Vandivier was soon summoned to the office of Bud Sunderman, who scolded him mercilessly. Among other things, Sunderman accused Vandivier of making irresponsible charges and of arch disloyalty. It would be best, said Sunderman, if Vandivier cleared out immediately. Within minutes, Vandivier had cleaned out his desk and left the plant.

Two days later Goodrich announced it was recalling the qualification report and replacing the old brake with a new five-disk brake at no cost to LTV.

Aftermath:

- A year later, a congressional committee reviewed the A7D affair. Vandivier and Lawson testified as government witnesses, together with Air Force officers and a General Accounting Office team. All testified that the brake was dangerous.

- Robert Sink, representing the Troy plant, depicted Vandivier as a mere high school graduate with no technical training, who preferred to follow his own lights rather than organizational guidance. R. G. Jeter, vice president and general counsel of Goodrich, dismissed as ludicrous even the possibility that some thirty engineers at the Troy plant would stand idly by and see reports changed and falsified.

- The congressional committee adjourned after four hours with no real conclusion. The following day the Department of Defense, citing the

A7D episode, made major changes in its inspection, testing, and reporting procedures.

- The A7D eventually went into service with the Goodrich-made five-disk brake.
- Searle Lawson went to work as an engineer for LTV assigned to the A7D project.
- Russell Line was promoted to production superintendent.
- Robert Sink moved up into Line's old job.
- Kermit Vandivier became a newspaper reporter for the *Daily News* in Troy, Ohio.

Discussion Questions

1. To what extent did Lawson, Vandivier, and Gretzinger consider the relevant moral issues before deciding to participate in the fraud? What was their reasoning? What led Vandivier to seek legal counsel and then to become a government witness?

2. How did Sink and Line look at the matter? How would you evaluate their conduct?

3. Do you think Vandivier was wrong to work up the qualification report? What moral principle or principles underlie your judgment?

4. Do you think Vandivier was right in "blowing the whistle"? Was he morally required to do so? Again, explain the moral principles on which your judgment is based.

5. Identify and discuss the pressure to conform evident in the A7D episode. Explain the effect of diffusion of responsibility in this case.

6. Do you think the existence of a corporate ethical code, a high-ranking ethics committee, or in-house ethical training might have altered events? What steps could Goodrich take to ensure more ethical behavior in the future?

7. In your opinion, can Goodrich in any way be held morally responsible for the A7D affair, or does the responsibility fall solely on individuals?

Notes to Chapter 1

1. Arthur Levitt, Jr., "Legacy of Hype," *San Jose Mercury News,* January 27, 2002, 5C.

2. Robert C. Solomon, *Morality and the Good Life* (New York: McGraw-Hill, 1984), 3.

3. Beverly T. Watkins, "Business Schools Told They Should Produce Generalists, Not Specialists," *Chronicle of Higher Education,* April 25, 1984, 13.

4. On characteristics of moral standards, see Manuel G. Velasquez, *Business Ethics,* 5th ed. (Upper Saddle River, N.J.: Prentice Hall, 2001), 9–11.

5. Martin Luther King, Jr., "Letter from Birmingham Jail," in *Why We Can't Wait* (New York: Harper & Row, 1963), 85.

6. *Newsweek,* May 26, 1997, 54.

7. Allan Bloom, *The Closing of the American Mind* (New York: Simon & Schuster, 1987), 39.

8. Albert Z. Carr, "Is Business Bluffing Ethical?" *Harvard Business Review* 46 (January–February 1968).

9. Ibid., 145.

10. Richard B. Brandt, *A Theory of the Good and the Right* (New York: Oxford University Press, 1979), 165–170.

11. Baruch Brody, *Beginning Philosophy* (Englewood Cliffs, N.J.: Prentice Hall, 1977), 33.

12. See Tad Tuleja, *Beyond the Bottom Line* (New York: Penguin Books, 1987); Curtis C. Vershoor, "Corporate Performance Is Closely Linked to a Strong Ethical Commitment," *Business and Society Review* 104 (Winter 1999); James E. Post, Anne T. Lawrence, and James Weber, *Business and Society: Corporate Strategy, Public Policy, and Ethics,* 10th ed. (New York: McGraw-Hill, 2002), 104–105; and "The Best Corporate Citizens Perform Better Financially," *Business Ethics,* March/April 2002, 13.

13. See David A. Frew, "Pollution: Can the People Be Innocent While Their Systems Are Guilty?" *Academy of Management Review,* March 1973.

14. Quoted in Robert Bartels, ed., *Ethics in Business* (Columbus: Ohio State University Press, 1963), 35.

15. Joseph L. Badaracco, Jr., and Allen P. Webb, "Business Ethics: A View from the Trenches," *California Management Review* 37 (Winter 1995): 8.

16. See Milton Snoeyenbos, Robert Almeder, and James Humber, eds., *Business Ethics*, 3rd ed. (Buffalo, N.Y.: Prometheus Books, 2001), 136.

17. Badaracco and Webb, "Business Ethics," 10.

18. See Solomon E. Asch, "Opinion and Social Pressure," *Scientific American*, November 1955, 31–35.

19. M. D. Bogdanoff et al., "The Modifying Effect of Conforming Behavior Upon Lipid Responses Accompanying CNS Arousal," *Clinical Research* 9 (1961): 135.

20. Lynn Sharp Paine, "Managing for Organizational Integrity," *Harvard Business Review* 72 (March–April 1994): 108.

21. Tom Regan, *Defending Animal Rights* (Urbana: University of Illinois Press, 2001), 45.

22. Mark Hosenball, "Karl Marx and the Pajama Game," *Mother Jones*, November 1979, 47.

23. Unless otherwise noted, the facts and quotations reported in this case are based on Mark Dowie, "The Corporate Crime of the Century," *Mother Jones*, November 1979, and Russell Mokhiber, *Corporate Crime and Violence* (San Francisco: Sierra Club Books, 1988), 181–195. See also Jane Kay, "Global Dumping of U.S. Toxics Is Big Business," *San Francisco Examiner*, September 23, 1990, A2, and Christopher Scanlan, "Danger for Sale," *San Jose Mercury News*, May 19, 1991, 9A, and May 20, 1991, 3A.

24. See Mark Dowie and Tracy Johnston, "A Case of Corporate Malpractice," *Mother Jones*, November 1976.

25. Mark Dowie, "A Dumper's Guide to Tricks of the Trade," *Mother Jones*, November 1979, 25.

26. Bernard Gavzer, "We Can Make Our Food Safer," *Parade Magazine*, October 19, 1997, 5–6.

27. The material for this case has been drawn from Kermit Vandivier, "Why Should My Conscience Bother Me?" in Robert Heilbroner, ed., *In the Name of Profit* (New York: Doubleday, 1972). For a discussion skeptical of Vandivier's version of these events, see John H. Fielder, "Give Goodrich a Break," *Business and Professional Ethics Journal* 7 (Spring 1988).

Reading ■

IT'S GOOD BUSINESS

ROBERT C. SOLOMON

Robert C. Solomon argues for the immediate, practical relevance of ethics for our business lives. He debunks the idea that business is fundamentally amoral or immoral. Business is not a blind scramble for profits and survival, but rather an established practice with firmly fixed rules and expectations, and people in business are professionals. Although unethical business, like crime, sometimes pays, there is no conflict between ethical business behavior and success. Solomon concludes with eight crucial rules for ethical thinking in business.

WHY ETHICS?

Seminars in business ethics . . . almost always begin with and are periodically brought back around to

Reprinted by permission from *The New World of Business* by Robert C. Solomon. Copyright © 1994 by Rowman and Littlefield Publishers, Inc.

such practical questions as "What does this have to do with my job?" or "Will understanding ethics help me do my job better?"

Such questions deserve and demand three immediate, practical answers.

1. *Ethical errors end careers more quickly and more definitively than any other mistake in judgment or accounting.* To err is human, perhaps, but to be caught lying, cheating, stealing, or reneging on contracts is not easily forgotten or forgiven in the business world. And for good reason: Such actions undermine the ethical foundation on which the business world thrives. Almost everyone can have compassion for someone caught in an ethical dilemma. No one can excuse immorality.

For every glaring case of known unethical conduct that goes unpunished, a dozen once-promising careers silently hit a dead end or quietly go down the tubes. On relatively rare occasions, an unhappy executive or employee is singled out and forced to pay public penance for conduct that everyone knows—he or she and the attorney will loudly protest—"goes on all the time." But much more often, unethical behavior, though unearthed, will go unannounced; indeed, the executive or employee in question will keep his or her job and may not even find out that he or she has been found out—may never even realize the unethical nature of his or her behavior. A career will just go nowhere. Responsibilities will remain routine, promotions elusive.

What makes such career calamities so pathetic is that they are not the product of greed or immorality or wickedness. They are the result of ethical naiveté.

They happen because an employee unthinkingly "did what he was told to do"—and became the scapegoat as well.

They happen because a casual public comment was ill-considered and had clearly unethical implications—though nothing of the kind may have been intended.

They happen because a middle manager, pressed from above for results, tragically believed the adolescent clichés that pervade the mid-regions of the business world, such as "In business, you do whatever you have to do to survive." (It is both revealing and instructive that although we often hear such sentiments expressed in seminars for middle managers, we virtually never hear them in similar seminars for upper-level executives.)

They happen because upper management wasn't clear about standards, priorities, and limits, or wasn't reasonable in its expectations, or wasn't available for appeal at the critical moment.

They happen because an anonymous employee or middle manager hidden in the complexity of a large organization foolishly believed that such safe anonymity would continue, whatever his or her behavior.

They happen, most of all, because a person in business is typically trained and pressured to "think business," without regard for the larger context in which business decisions are made and legitimized.

Unethical thinking isn't just "bad business"; it is an invitation to disaster in business, however rarely (it might sometimes seem) unethical behavior is actually found out and punished. . . .

2. *Ethics provides the broader framework within which business life must be understood.*

There may be a few people for whom business is all of life, for whom family and friendship are irrelevant, for whom money means only more investment potential and has nothing to do with respect or status or enjoying the good life. But most successful executives understand that *business is part of life.* Corporations are part of a society that consists of something more than a market. Executives and employees do not disappear into their jobs as if into a well, only to reappear in "real life" at the end of the business day.

Successful managers, we now all know, stay close to their subordinates—and not just as subordinates. The best corporations in their "search for excellence" begin and remain close to their customers, and not just in their narrowest role as consumers. Money may be a scorecard, a measure of status and accomplishment, but it is not the ultimate end. Business success, like happiness, often comes most readily to those who do not aim at it directly.

Executives are most effective and successful when they retain their "real life" view of themselves, their position, and the human world outside as well as inside the corporation. Business ethics, ultimately, is just business in its larger human context. . . .

3. *Nothing is more dangerous to a business— or to business in general—than a tarnished public image.* A few years ago, *Business and Society Review* reported the results of a Harris Poll—one among many—that showed that public confidence in the executives running major corporations had declined "drastically" . . . ; 87% of the respondents in a parallel poll agreed that most businessmen were more interested in profits than in the public interest. Whether or not such suspicions seriously affect sales, they indisputably hurt the bottom line in a dozen other hurtful ways—not least among them the pressure for government regulation. The fact is that a tarnished image has direct consequences, for sales, for profits, for morale, for the day-to-day running of the business. Distrust of an industry ("big oil," "the insurance racket") can hurt every company, and distrust of an individual company can quickly drive it to bankruptcy. . . .

THE MYTH OF AMORAL BUSINESS

Business people have not always been their own best friends. John D. Rockefeller once boasted that he was quite willing to pay a man an annual salary of a million dollars, if the man had certain qualities:

> [He] must know how to glide over every moral restraint with almost childlike disregard . . . [and have], besides other positive qualities, no scruples whatsoever, and [be] ready to kill off thousands of victims—without a murmur.
> Robert Warshow, *Jay Gould* (1928)

Such talk is unusually ruthless, but it exemplifies horribly a myth that has often clouded business thinking—what University of Kansas business ethicist Richard De George calls the "myth of amoral business." According to the myth, business and ethics don't mix. People in business are concerned with profits, with producing goods and services, with buying and selling. They may not be immoral, but they are amoral—that is, not concerned with morals. Moralizing is out of place in business. Indeed, even good acts are to be praised not in moral terms but only in the cost/benefit language of "good business."

The myth of amoral business has a macho, mock-heroic corollary that makes ethical paralysis almost inevitable. It is the dog-eat-dog rhetoric of the Darwinian jungle—"survival of the fittest." In fact, almost everybody and most companies manage to survive without being the "fittest." The anxiety of switching jobs, of not getting promotions, of losing an investment, or of going bankrupt, however upsetting, is rarely a "matter of life and death." In *The Right Stuff,* Tom Wolfe sympathetically quotes the wife of one of the Air Force test pilots. She mentions a friend's complaint about her husband's dog-eat-dog existence on Madison Avenue and reflects, "What if her husband went into a meeting with a one-in-four chance of survival?"

If the myth of amoral business and its Darwinian corollary were nothing but a way of talking on the way to the office, it would not be worth attention or criticism. But the fact is that it does enter into business thinking, and often at exactly the critical moment when an ethical decision is to be made. Worse, the amoral rhetoric of business quickly feeds public suspicion of business and eas-ily becomes part of the condemnation of business. A handful of scandals and accidents that might otherwise be viewed as the unfortunate byproducts of any enterprise become "proof" of what the businessmen themselves have been saying all along—that there is no interest in ethics in business, only the pursuit of profits. . . .

Business people who do not talk about ethics often complain a great deal about "regulation" without realizing that the two are intimately connected. Legal regulation is the natural response of both society and government to the practice of amorality, however nobly that practice is couched in the rhetoric of "free enterprise." If a business scandal or tragedy is quickly and convincingly chastized by business people, there is neither time nor pressure for regulation. But when scandal and tragedy are at the same time surrounded by ethical neglect or silence or, worse, yet another appeal to "the market" as the long-term corrective, government regulation becomes inevitable. In case anyone still wants to ask why ethics should be relevant to the bottom line, one might simply reply that regulation is the price business pays for bad ethical strategy. . . .

THE THREE Cs OF BUSINESS ETHICS

. . . Business ethics is not an attack on business but rather its first line of defense. Adam Smith knew this well enough: Business has prospered because business has dramatically improved the quality of life for all of us. Moreover, the emphasis on freedom and individuality in a business society has done more than any conceivable socialist revolution to break down traditional inequities in power and wealth, even if it inevitably creates some inequities of its own. Business ethics begins with consumer demand and productivity, with the freedom to engage in business as one wishes, and with the hope—inconceivable in most parts of the world—that one can better one's life considerably through one's own hard work and intelligence. These are the values of business ethics, and the whole point of business ethics is to define and defend the basic goals of prosperity, freedom, fairness, and individual dignity.

Many critics of business are trained in the rhetoric of ethics, but most business people are not. Those in business naturally prefer to stick with what they know and sidestep the ethical issues—which is ruinous. It is one thing to know that product Z costs $0.14 to make and retails for $1.59, that raising the price to $1.79 would increase profits and not dampen demand, that cheaper materials or foreign labor could lower the cost of manufacturing to $0.09, although sales would eventually diminish as consumer expectations went unsatisfied. But it is something more to think about the quality of product Z, the contribution it makes to American life (even if only by way of amusement or novelty). Not incidentally, these ethical virtues may be essential to the bottom line as well.

Business ethics is nothing less than the full awareness of what one is doing, its consequences and complications. Thinking about ethics in business is no more than acknowledging that one has taken these into account and is willing to be responsible for them. It is being aware of

1. the need for *compliance* with the rules, including the laws of the land, the principles of morality, the customs and expectations of the community, the policies of the company, and such general concerns as fairness;

2. the *contributions* business can make to society, through the value and quality of one's products or services, by way of the jobs one provides for workers and managers, through the prosperity and usefulness of one's activities to the surrounding community;

3. the *consequences* of business activity, both inside and outside the company, both intended and unintended, including the reputation of one's own company and industry. . . .

Part of the problem for business ethics is the image of business as "big" business, as a world of impersonal corporations in which the individual is submerged and ethics is inevitably sacrificed to bureaucratic objectives. To set the image straight, therefore, let us remind ourselves of a single vital statistic: Half of American business is family business; 50% of the GNP; 50% of the employees. Some of these family businesses are among the Fortune 500. Others are Mom and Pop groceries and Sally and Lou's Restaurant. But it is essential to remember that however much our focus may be on corporations and corporate life, business in America is not a monolithic, inhuman enterprise. As the great French philosopher Rousseau once said of society, we might say of American business life that its origins are in the family, that its "natural" model *is* the family. Business is ultimately about relationships between people—our compliance with the rules we all form together, our contributions to the well-being of others as well as to our own, the consequences of our activities, for good and otherwise. There is nothing amoral or unethical about it. . . .

BUSINESS SCUM

The most powerful argument for ethics in business is success. Ethical businesses are successful businesses; excellence is also ethical. But ethics is no guarantee of success. To say so on our part would be—unethical. The fact is that there are, as we all know, business scum—those shifty, snatch-a-buck operations that give business a bad name. And some of them, ethics be damned, are profitable.

Brake Breakers, Inc., is a small franchise in the Midwest that specializes in brake, suspension, and wheel repairs. Company policy includes hiring men with little education and working them long hours at a single semiskilled job. Wages are accordingly minimal, and employee turnover is more often a matter of burnout than of leaving for another job. (This saves a lot on fringe benefits and pensions; no one has ever collected on them.)

Foremost among the employees' skills, however, is the delivery of a prepackaged sermon designed to convince all but the most cautious customer that the $149.25 brake-rebuilding special is far preferable to the mere replacement of the brake shoes, which is all that is usually required (and often all that is actually done).

Managers are rewarded on the basis of the success of these little speeches by their employees. Their job is first and foremost to make sure that the minimum is never enough—not hard given the level of mechanical know-how of most of the customers.

But even with the $149.25 special, extra costs are almost always included, sometimes for some other (unnecessary) part but more often than not because of the "unexpected difficulty" of this particular repair. When a customer insists on the minimum repair, it is up to the manager to see to it that more absolutely necessary work is "discovered" in the middle of the job. (This is called the "step method.") Few customers are in a position to do more than complain and curse for the moment, but no one ever expects them to come back anyway.

Managers are expected to keep actual costs down. Used parts are sold in place of new parts. (Sometimes, the car's original part is cleaned or polished and simply reinstalled.) A few miles down the road, who can tell?

Within the company, employees are reminded daily, "There are fifty people waiting for your job." Everyone is hired with the promise "Within three years, you can work up to a managerial position." In fact, managers are always hired from outside—typically friends of the boss. (It is understood that they will supplement their salaries by skimming within the shop.) Managerial turnover, accordingly, is low. Brake Breakers is not the sort of company that can afford to have a disgruntled manager quit in disgust, although any charges he might bring against the company could dependably be turned against him as well.

Brake Breakers, Inc., is everyone's stereotypical image of unethical business in action. Its people sell a shoddy product to customers who don't need it, and they don't always sell what they say they are selling. Employees are treated like serfs, and accounting procedures at every level of the company are, to put it politely, suspect. The customer is virtually never satisfied, but it is the nature of the business that people who need brake repairs need them fast and do not know what has to be done or how much it should cost. They are ripe for the taking, and they are taken. The price is still low enough and the job near enough adequate that no one sues. The "lifetime guarantee" isn't worth the paper it's printed on, but it is a fact about brake jobs that there is only so much that can go wrong, and a disgruntled customer usually doesn't bother coming back anyway. It's a perfect setup. At least half

of the profits, even on a modest system of objective ethical accounting, are obtained by cheating the customer and the employees.

How does Brake Breakers, Inc., stack up according to our three Cs of business ethics? Not very well.

Compliance: Minimal; just enough to avoid legal penalties and major lawsuits but far below the level of concern for ethics that we all expect of every business.

Contributions: Well, they do fix brakes, even if some of them aren't broken. But a dozen more dependable businesses—both national franchises and local service stations—would do a better job with less flimflam. To provide a service is not in itself a contribution. We also want to know if it is a service that would otherwise be performed as well and as cheaply by other firms.

Consequences: Disgruntled customers, hesitation among motorists to have their brakes checked when they ought to, occasional accidents, a notoriously bad reputation for car-repair shops in general (hurting those that do good, honest work), and an exemplary case of unethical business to turn consumers and congressional investigators against business in general.

It is too often supposed that the business of business ethics is to prove to the management of such unethical enterprises as Brake Breakers, Inc., that crime does not pay. That is too much to ask for.

- Show them, perhaps, that they are setting themselves up for lawsuits.

  In fact, it just hasn't happened.

- Show them, then, that they are losing customers.

  In fact, it is a business with a regular supply of customers, no repeat customers in any case and little dependence on word of mouth. (In fact, they depend on the absence of word of mouth, since people are often too ashamed at having been "taken" to tell their friends about it.)

- Show them how well Midas and Meineke have been doing because of their reputation for dependability.

  But, the manager at Brake Breakers tells us with a laugh, "We ain't Midas."

- Argue, then, that unethical business practices cannot possibly pay off in the long run.

    "In the long run," the amused manager tells us, unknowingly echoing the economist John Maynard Keynes, "we're all dead."

The fact—sad, perhaps—is that unethical business, like crime, sometimes pays. In any system based on trust, a few deceivers will prosper. There is no guarantee that ethics is good for the bottom line. There is no guarantee that those who do wrong will get caught or feel guilty. There is no guarantee—in business or elsewhere—that the wicked will suffer and the virtuous will be rewarded (at least, not in this life). But, that said, we can nonetheless insist without apology that good ethics is good business. Where immorality is so easily identified, we can be sure that morality is the general rule, not merely an accessory or an exception. The *point* of doing business is to do well by providing the best service or product at a reasonable cost. Those businesses that exploit the *possibility* of getting away with less are merely parasitic on the overwhelming number of businesses that are doing what they are supposed to.

PRACTICES MAKE PERFECT: A BETTER WAY TO LOOK AT BUSINESS

> A practice is any association of definitely patterned human behavior wherein the description and meaning of kinds of behavior involved and the kinds of expectations involved are dependent upon those rules which define the practice.
>
> John Rawls
> (professor of philosophy, Harvard University)

Business is not a scramble for profits and survival. It is a way of life, an established and proven *practice* whose prosperity and survival depend on the participation of its practitioners. Business ethics is not ethics applied to business. It is the foundation of business. Business life thrives on competition, but it survives on the basis of its ethics.

Business is first of all a cooperative enterprise with firmly fixed rules and expectations. A view from a visitors' gallery down to the floor of the New York Stock Exchange may not look very much like a cooperative enterprise with fixed rules and expectations, but beneath the apparent chaos is a carefully orchestrated set of agreements and rituals without which the Exchange could not operate at all. There can be no bogus orders, and bid ranges are carefully controlled. The use of information is restricted, but traders trade information as well as securities. The rules of the Exchange, contrary to superficial appearances, are uncompromising. Break them and you're off the floor for good. Right there at the busy heart of capitalism, there is no question that *business is a practice,* and people in business are *professionals.*

In business ethics, it is often profitable to compare business with a game. Games are also practices. Baseball, for instance, is a practice. It has its own language, its own gestures with their own meanings, its own way of giving significance to activities that, apart from the game, might very well mean nothing at all. (Imagine a person who suddenly runs and slides into a canvas bag filled with sand on the sidewalk, declaring himself "safe" as he does so.) The practice is defined by certain sorts of behavior—"pitching" the ball in a certain way (if, that is, the practice designates you as the "pitcher"), trying to hit the ball with a certain well-defined implement (the "bat"), running a certain sequence of "bases" in a certain order subject to certain complex restrictions (one of which is that one not be "tagged" by another person holding the ball). Anyone who has tried to explain what is happening in a baseball game to a visitor from another country with a different "national pastime" can attest to the complexity of these rules and definitions, though most Americans feel quite familiar with them and can focus their attention—as players or as spectators—on such simple-sounding concerns as "Who's up?" and "Who's on first?"

Business is like baseball in that it is a practice. A day at the stock exchange makes it quite clear just how many rituals, rules, and restrictions are involved in every buy-and-sell transaction. . . . The business world is far more open to extra "players" and to alternative courses of action than is baseball, but within the institutions that make up the practice of business, roles and alternatives are clearly specified—as "jobs" and "positions," as obligations and options. Strategic ethics begins by emphasizing business as a practice with strict rules and expectations that acceptable players honor implicitly—*or they are out of the game.* To throw out players who cheat is as important to a healthy enterprise as is the inevitable exit of players who can't play well. Bad business is much more damaging to business than are badly run businesses.

Business, like baseball, is defined by its rules. Some of these have to do with the nature of contracts. Many have to do with *fairness* in dealing with employees, customers, and government agents (hence the existence of such policing bodies as the IRS, the SEC, the FDA, etc., etc.). Indeed, the notion of fairness in exchanges is more central to business than to any other practice—whether in terms of work and salary, price and product, or public services and subsidies. Without fairness as the central expectation, there are few people who would enter into the market at all. (Consider the chill on the market following dramatic "insider trading" cases.) Without the recognition of fair play, the phrase "free enterprise" would be something of a joke. The rules of business, accordingly, have mainly to do with fairness. Some of these rules ensure that the market will remain open to everyone. Some of the rules protect those who are not players in the practice but whose health, jobs, or careers are affected by it. Some of the rules have to do with serving the needs or wishes of the community (the law of supply and demand can be interpreted not only as an economic mechanism but as an ethical imperative). Some have to do with "impact"—the effects of a business on its surrounding communities and environment. If business had no effects on the surrounding community but was rather a self-enclosed game, there would be no more public cry for business ethics than for "hopscotch ethics" (which is not to say that there is no ethics to hopscotch).

It is within this description of a practice that we can also define the terms "virtue" and "vice" in business ethics. Some virtues and vices go far beyond the bounds of business, of course; they are matters of morality (honesty, for instance). But in business ethics there are virtues and vices that are particular to business and to certain business roles.

Close accounting and "watching every penny" are virtues in a shipping clerk but not in someone who is entertaining a client. Keeping a polite distance is a virtue in a stockholder but not in a general manager. Tenaciousness may be a virtue in a salesman but not in a consultant. Outspokenness may be a virtue in a board member but not in the assistant to the president. Being tough-minded is a virtue in some managerial roles but not in others.

In general, we can say this: A virtue sustains and improves a practice. A virtue in business is an ethical trait that makes business in general possible, and this necessarily includes such virtues as respect for contracts as well as concern for product quality, consumer satisfaction, and the bottom line. A vice, on the other hand, degrades and undermines the practice. Shady dealing and reneging on contracts are vices and unethical not because of an absolute moral law but because they undermine the very practice that makes doing business possible.

Thinking about business as a practice and business people as professionals gives us a set of persuasive responses to the Brake Breakers case:

1. Business in general depends on the acceptance of rules and expectations, on mutual trust and a sense of fairness, even if—as in any such practice—a few unscrupulous participants can take advantage of that trust and betray that concern for fairness.

2. Brake Breakers, Inc., can continue to prosper in their scummy ways only so long as they remain relatively insignificant, with a small enough market share not to bring down the wrath of major competitors and sufficiently little publicity not to inspire a class-action suit. Unethical behavior may bring profits, but only limited profits.

3. It is clearly in the interest of business in general and other firms in that particular industry to warn consumers about Brake Breakers, even to put them out of business. The success and strength of a profession and its independence from externally imposed regulations depends on the internal "policing" of unethical behavior. Doctors have never doubted this; lawyers are learning. But so long as business thinks of itself as unregulated competition where "anything goes" rather than as a profession to be protected from abuse, this vital policing for

survival will go unattended, or it will be attended to by the government.

4. The practice of business is a small world. Fly-by-Night Enterprises Ltd. and Brake Breakers, Inc., may succeed for a while, but, in general, people catch on—fast. Irate customers tell their friends—and their lawyers. They also get even. They sue, for triple damages. They write the newspapers, or "60 Minutes." They drop a note to the IRS, or they call the Better Business Bureau. The banker's kid who was cheated on the job complains to his father the month before the lease has to be renewed. Or the victim happens to be a litigious lawyer with time on his hands. But the effects of unethical business practices are not always so obvious as a dip in the bottom line or a subpoena waiting at the office. They are often slow and insidious, the bottom of a career eaten out from under, or a company that is doing "OK" but could and should be doing much better. There are no guarantees that unethical behavior will be punished, but the odds are pretty impressive.

5. In any profession, it's hard to get clean again. Suppliers tighten their terms; priority status disappears. The hardheaded businessman is supposed to say "Who cares?" But if so, there are few hardheaded businessmen, only a small number of bottom-line-minded sociopaths. Character is who you are, the thing you are trying to prove by making money in the first place. One of the classic movie lines is "My money's as good as anyone else's." Perhaps. But are *you* as good? That isn't just a matter of money.

Why should Brake Breakers, Inc., get ethical? Let's ask another question: How would you feel about yourself if you spent your working days as a manager of Brake Breakers? What would you tell your kids? . . .

THINKING ETHICS: THE RULES OF THE GAME

Ethics is, first of all, a way of thinking.

Being ethical is also—of course—*doing* the right thing, but what one does is hardly separable from how one thinks. Most people in business who do

wrong do so not because they are wicked but because they think they are trapped and do not even consider the ethical significance or implications of their actions.

What is thinking ethically? It is thinking in terms of *compliance* with the rules, implicit as well as explicit, thinking in terms of the *contributions* one can make as well as one's own possible gains, thinking in terms of avoiding harmful *consequences* to others as well as to oneself. Accordingly, [here are] eight crucial rules for ethical thinking in business.

Rule No. 1: Consider other people's well-being, including the well-being of nonparticipants. In virtually every major religion this is the golden rule: "Do unto others as you would have them do unto you"; or, negatively, "Do not do unto others as you would not have them do unto you." Ideally, this might mean that one should try to maximize everyone's interests, but this is unreasonable. First of all, no one really expects that a businessman (or anyone else) would or should sacrifice his own interests for everyone else's. Second, it is impossible to take everyone into account; indeed, for any major transaction, the number of people who will be affected—some unpredictably—may run into the tens or hundreds of thousands. But we can readily accept a minimum version of this rule, which is to make a *contribution* where it is reasonable to do so and to avoid *consequences* that are harmful to others. There is nothing in the golden rule that demands that one deny one's own interests or make sacrifices to the public good. It says only that one must take into account human effects beyond one's own bottom line and weigh one's own gain against the losses of others.

Rule No. 2: Think as a member of the business community and not as an isolated individual. Business has its own rules of propriety and fairness. These are not just matters of courtesy and protocol; they are the conditions that make business possible. Respect for contracts, paying one's debts, and selling decent products at a reasonable price are not only to one's own advantage; they are necessary for the very existence of the business community.

Rule No. 3: Obey, but do not depend solely on, the law. It goes without saying, as a matter of prudence if not of morality, that businesses and business people ought to obey the law—the most obvious meaning of *compliance.* But what needs to be added is that ethical thinking is not limited to legal obedience. There is much unethical behavior that is not illegal, and the question of what is right is not always defined by the law. The fact is that many things that are not immoral or illegal are repulsive, disgusting, unfair, and unethical—belching aloud in elevators, throwing a disappointing dish at one's host at dinner, paying debts only after the "final notice" and the threat of a lawsuit arrives, fleecing the feebleminded, taking advantage of trust and good faith, selling faulty if not dangerous merchandise under the rubric "Buyer beware." Check the law—but don't stop there.

Rule No. 4: Think of yourself—and your company—as part of society. Business people and businesses are citizens in society. They share the fabric of feelings that make up society and, in fact, contribute much of that feeling themselves. Business is not a closed community. It exists and thrives because it serves and does not harm society. It is sometimes suggested that business has its own ethical rules and that they are decidedly different from those of the larger society. Several years ago business writer Albert Carr raised a major storm in the *Harvard Business Review* by arguing that business, like poker, had its own rules and that these were not to be confused with the moral rules of the larger society. The comparison with poker has its own problems, but, leaving those aside for now, we can see how such a view not only invites but *demands* the most rigorous regulation of business. Business is subject to the same ethical rules as everyone else because businessmen do *not* think of themselves as separate from society. A few years ago, the then chairman of the Ford Foundation put it bluntly: "Either we have a social fabric that embraces us all, or we're in real trouble." So too with ethics.

Rule No. 5: Obey moral rules. This is the most obvious and unavoidable rule of ethical thinking and the most important single sense of *compliance.* There may be room for debate about whether a moral rule applies. There may be questions of in-

terpretation. But there can be no excuse of ignorance ("Oh, I didn't know that one isn't supposed to lie and cheat"), and there can be no unexcused exceptions ("Well, it would be all right to steal in *this* case"). The German philosopher Immanuel Kant called moral rules "categorical imperatives," meaning that they are absolute and unqualified commands for everyone, in every walk of life, without exception, not even for harried executives. This is, perhaps, too extreme to be practical, but moral rules are the heart of ethics, and there can be no ethics—and no business—without them.

Rule No. 6: Think objectively. Ethics is not a science, but it does have one feature in common with science: The rules apply equally to everyone, and being able to be "disinterested"—that is, to think for a moment from other people's perspectives—is essential. Whether an action is *right* is a matter quite distinct from whether or not it is in *your* interest. For that matter, it is quite independent of your personal opinions as well.

Rule No. 7: Ask the question "What sort of person would do such a thing?" Our word "ethics" comes from the Greek word *ethos,* meaning "character." Accordingly, ethics is not just obedience to rules so much as it is the concern for your personal (and company) character—your reputation and "good name"—and, more important, how you feel about yourself. Peter Drucker summarizes the whole of business ethics as "being able to look at your face in the mirror in the morning."

Rule No. 8: Respect the customs of others, but not at the expense of your own ethics. The most difficult kind of ethical thinking that people in business have to do concerns not a conflict between ethics and profits but rather the conflict between two ethical systems. In general, it is an apt rule of thumb that one should follow the customs and ethics of the community. But suppose there is a conflict not only of mores but of morals, as in the apartheid policies of South Africa. Then the rule to obey (and support) one's own moral principles takes priority. What is even more difficult is what one should do when the moral issue is not clear and moral categories vary from culture to culture. A much debated example is the question of giving money to expedite a transaction in many third-world countries. It is "bribery" in our system, "supporting public servants" in theirs. Bribery is illegal and unethical here because it contradicts our notion of a free and open market. But does the same apply in the third world, where business (and social life) have very different presuppositions?

Ethical thinking is ultimately no more than considering oneself and one's company as citizens of the business community and of the larger society, with some concern for the well-being of others and—the mirror image of this—respect for oneself and one's character. Nothing in ethics excludes financially sound thinking, and there is nothing about ethics that requires sacrificing the bottom line. In both the long and the short run, ethical thinking is essential to strategic planning. There is nothing unethical about making money, but money is not the currency of ethical thinking in business.

Review and Discussion Questions

1. Solomon describes the view that business and ethics don't mix as the "myth of amoral business." Why does he think it is a myth? Do you agree?

2. Do most businesspeople respect the "Three Cs"? In your experience, how much unethical behavior is there in business today? What happens to companies like Brake Breakers? Can they be successful?

3. Does the existence of "business scum" undermine Solomon's claim that businesspeople are professionals and that business is a practice with definite rules?

4. What are the "rules of the game" in business today? Should those rules be changed in any way?

5. Assess Solomon's claim that "there is nothing about ethics that requires sacrificing the bottom line" (p. 44). Is it compatible with his statement that "there is no guarantee that ethics is good for the bottom line" (p. 40)?

Reading ━━━━━━━━━━ ■

MORAL RESPONSIBILITY IN THE AGE OF BUREAUCRACY

DAVID LUBAN, ALAN STRUDLER, AND DAVID WASSERMAN

Large bureaucratic organizations frequently dilute an individual's sense of moral responsibility, and members of such organizations are all too likely to acquiesce in organizational misconduct. One reason for this is that inside the organization knowledge can be so fragmented that an individual may be partially or wholly ignorant of what the organization is doing. David Luban, Alan Strudler, and David Wasserman examine this problem. Whereas most moral theories presuppose that the moral agent knows that a decision must be made and what choices are available, these authors explore the moral responsibilities of individuals in organizational situations in which they lack this knowledge.

BACKGROUND OF THE PROBLEM

The bureaucratic fragmentation of knowledge and dilution of responsibility are pervasive phenomena in modern society. To set the stage for our analysis, we first describe the scope of the problem and briefly review some of the research, commentary, and debate it has provoked. We conclude this background section by discussing the research most relevant to our own concerns, the Milgram studies of destructive obedience to authority.

The Collectivization of the Workplace

Most work in modern society is done by organizations: corporations, governments, hospitals, foundations, universities, accounting firms, armies. Even

Excerpted by permission from David Luban, Alan Strudler, and David Wasserman, "Moral Responsibility in the Age of Bureaucracy," *Michigan Law Review* 90 (August 1992). © 1992 Michigan Law Review Association.

such supposedly independent professionals as physicians and lawyers practice in large organizations to an ever-increasing extent. The HMO has replaced the family physician, and the new graduates of today's law schools join firms, of which the largest now employ over a thousand lawyers, rather than hanging out a shingle. The problems of professional and business ethics have thus become the problems of supervisors and subordinates in organizational settings. Indeed, in a culture such as ours, where our first question to each other is often not "How do you do?" but "What do you do?" the ethics of the workplace has enormous impact on how we think of morality in general. To a great extent, ethics in the organizational setting has come to define ethics as a whole. We speak of team players and loose cannons, leaders and followers, as categories of moral judgment and not simply of social description.

The Organization Man and the Other-Directed Society

The transformation of the workplace appears to have wrought a transformation in values, replacing individual responsibility and internal norms with group identification and external norms. As the postwar American economy assumed its contemporary form, several leading social scientists and commentators explored the psychology of "The Organization Man," in the famous title of William H. Whyte's book. Whyte used this term to describe "the ones of our middle class who have left home, spiritually as well as physically, to take the vows of organization life."[1] He ascribed to them the "Social Ethic," which includes "a belief in the group as the source of creativity" as well as "a belief in 'belongingness' as the ultimate need of the individual."[2]

David Riesman described middle-class Americans as a "Lonely Crowd," and elaborated a famous typology of characters. In Riesman's scheme, people of premodern societies were *tradition-directed,* and the sanction for deviation was *shame*; in early modern societies people were *inner-directed,* guided by an internal moral compass, acquired in childhood, which induces *guilt* when one deviates. In contemporary society, however, we have become *other-directed:* our "contemporaries are the source of direction for the individual. . . . [T]he process of paying close attention to the signals from others . . . remain[s] unaltered throughout life."[3] For other-directed individuals, the sanction for deviance has changed: "As against guilt-and-shame controls, though of course these survive, one prime psychological lever of the other-directed person is a diffuse *anxiety.*"[4] Sociologist Robert Jackall conducted interviews with 143 managers in sev-eral contemporary American corporations. In the anxiety-ridden world of middle management, "[m]anagers have a myriad of aphorisms that refer to how the power of CEOs, magnified through the zealous efforts of subordinates, affects them. . . . [One such maxim is] 'When he sneezes, we all catch colds'. . . ."[5] Jackall comments:

> As a result, independent morally evaluative judgments get subordinated to the social intricacies of the bureau-cratic workplace. Notions of morality that one might hold and indeed practice outside the workplace . . . become ir-relevant. . . . Under certain conditions, such notions may even become dangerous. For the most part, then, they remain unarticulated lest one risk damaging crucial rela-tionships with significant individuals or groups.[6]

Historical Perspective

The collectivization of the workplace and the threat it poses to traditional moral values are hardly new phenomena; they have been recognized, and lamented, for the past 150 years. The erosion of in-dividual responsibility and the evils of bureaucracy have engaged conservative writers since the advent of the industrial revolution. Over a century ago, Karl Marx likewise criticized what he called "the real mindlessness of the state." "The bureaucracy is a circle from which no one can escape," Marx contended. "The highest point entrusts the under-standing of particulars to the lower echelons, whereas these, on the other hand, credit the high-est with an understanding in regard to the univer-sal; and thus they deceive one another."[7] In 1932, Reinhold Niebuhr wrote his classic treatise *Moral Man and Immoral Society,* in which he argued that

> [i]ndividual men may be moral. . . . They are endowed by nature with a measure of sympathy and consideration for their kind, the breadth of which may be extended by an astute social pedagogy. . . . But all these achievements

are more difficult, if not impossible, for human societies and social groups. In every human group there is less reason to guide and to check impulse, less capacity for self-transcendence, less ability to comprehend the needs of others and therefore more unrestrained egoism than the individuals, who compose the group, reveal in their personal relationships.[8]

Niebuhr's argument recognizes that the increasing organization of society will be accompanied by a di-lution of morality.

. . . [T]he problems Marx and Niebuhr discussed in a theoretical vein came to life in the most horrible way possible during World War II, where ostensibly civilized human beings tortured and slaughtered twelve million men, women, and children in exter-mination camps. The names of the camps—Auschwitz, Treblinka, Majdanek—have become synonymous with the incomprehensible willingness of ordinary human beings to do anything, no matter how atrocious, when ordered to do so by those in au-thority. Here, again, an explanation may be offered in terms of the division of responsibility within groups. Consider a historian's description of the euthanasia program Hitler ordered to eliminate mentally retarded, handicapped, or genetically ill Germans (individuals Hitler called "useless eaters"):

> The euthanasia program . . . demonstrated how, through fragmentation of authority and tasks, it was possible to fashion a murder machine. Hitler had enunciated an off-hand, extra-legal decree, and had not wanted to be both-ered about it again. Brandt had ordered the "scientific" implementation of the program and, like Hitler, wished to hear no complaints. The directors and personnel of institu-tions rationalized that matters were out of their hands and that they were just filling out questionnaires . . . , though in reality each form was the equivalent of a death warrant. . . . The personnel at the end of the line excused themselves on the basis that they were under compulsion, had no power of decision, and were merely performing a function. Thousands of people were involved, but each considered himself nothing but a cog in the machine and reasoned that it was the machine, not he, that was responsible.[9]

The horrors of Nazism are without parallel, but the bureaucratic pattern of organization that fragments the knowledge required for moral decisionmaking is common to large institutions throughout contem-porary society. Jackall describes the typical corpo-rate structure in terms not unlike those Marx used to characterize "the real mindlessness of the state":

Power is concentrated at the top in the person of the chief executive officer (CEO) and is simultaneously decentralized; that is, responsibility for decisions and profits is pushed as far down the organizational line as possible.

. . . [P]ushing details down protects the privilege of authority to declare that a mistake has been made. . . . Moreover, pushing down details relieves superiors of the burden of too much knowledge, particularly guilty knowledge.

. . . [Middle managers] become the "point men" of a given strategy and the potential "fall guys" when things go wrong.[10]

Hannah Arendt described the bureaucratic phenomenon as a novel form of governance appearing alongside the classical distinction among rule by one (monarchy), rule by "the best" (aristocracy), rule by the few (oligarchy), and rule by the many (democracy). She wrote of

the latest and perhaps most formidable form of . . . dominion: bureaucracy or the rule of an intricate system of bureaus in which no men, neither one nor the best, neither the few nor the many, can be held responsible, and which could be properly called rule by Nobody. (If, in accord with traditional political thought, we identify tyranny as government that is not held to give account of itself, rule by Nobody is clearly the most tyrannical of all, since there is no one left who could even be asked to answer for what is being done. It is . . . impossible to localize responsibility and to identify the enemy. . . .)[11]

Such rumors of the demise of responsibility may be exaggerated; yet Arendt's description has the ring of familiarity. A graphic contemporary analogue appeared in litigation surrounding the Dalkon Shield. In his opinion, Federal Judge Frank Theis angrily noted:

The project manager for Dalkon Shield explains that a particular question should have gone to the medical department, the medical department representative explains that the question was really the bailiwick of the quality control department, and the quality control department representative explains that the project manager was the one with the authority to make a decision on that question. . . . [I]t is not at all unusual for the hard questions posed in Dalkon Shield cases to be unanswerable by anyone from Robins [the manufacturer].[12]

One must not be naive, of course: often the defense of fragmented knowledge will be entered falsely and cynically, as a form of liability screening. Executives in the hot seat should be treated with the same skepticism that greeted German officials who "didn't know." Despite this healthy skepticism, however, we remain convinced that fragmented knowledge is a genuine phenomenon that we cannot simply dismiss as a lame excuse.

The Psychology of Destructive Obedience

Social scientists have labored to understand the Holocaust and to answer the all-important question whether it could occur in other settings. Stanley Milgram conducted perhaps the most significant—and certainly the most famous—experimental studies to address this issue. Milgram's experiments underscore our thesis because they illustrate the ways in which social and institutional pressures to obey reinforce, and are reinforced by, the fragmentation of knowledge in modern bureaucracies and other large organizations.

In Milgram's experiments, volunteers in a Yale University experiment were ordered by the experimenter to administer gradually increasing electric shocks to another "subject" (actually a confederate of the experimenter), ostensibly to study the effect of punishment on learning. As the "shocks" increased in intensity, the confederate displayed increasing discomfort, demanded that the experiment stop, screamed with pain, complained of a heart condition, and finally fell silent as if he were unconscious.[13] In this original experiment, sixty-five percent of the subjects went all the way, administering the highest possible, potentially lethal, level of shock. Those subjects who administered the maximum shock expressed great discomfort at the cruel task they were assigned; many of them berated the experimenter, protested, or insisted that they would not proceed with the experiment—all the while continuing to flip the switches.

Milgram conducted a number of important variations on the original experiment, several of which suggest the role that incomplete and fragmented knowledge may play in facilitating destructive obedience and the abdication of individual responsibility. In one version, the experiment was removed from the anxiety-relieving auspices of Yale to a seedy-looking storefront operation in nearby Bridgeport. Less able to reassure themselves that the experimenters knew what they were doing, fifty-three percent of the subjects refused to go all the way. This suggests that compliant subordinates often believe that their qualms are merely the result of incomplete understanding, and assume that those in charge have good reasons for what they are doing.

The rate of compliance also declined when the subject could see the victim, and declined even further when the subject was actually required to hold the victim's hand on the contact-plate. In this latter version of the experiment, seventy percent of the subjects stopped before administering the maximum level of shock. . . .

Another form of ignorance that appears to have played a significant role in Milgram's experiments was the absence of a clear-cut moment of decision. Few subjects would have hesitated to give a mild, tingling shock; most probably would have refused to give an initial shock of maximum voltage. The gradual escalation of voltage was insidious because it deprived subjects of an obvious stopping point, encouraging them to defer resistance until they saw themselves as committed, or as compromised. This kind of slippery slope may characterize many of the decisions made in contemporary organizations.

Another variant of the Milgram experiments, however, provides some encouragement that resistance and reform may be possible in organizational settings. In this study, the subject was assigned to a team administering the shocks, while the other team members were really confederates of the experimenter. Milgram discovered that compliance was extraordinarily sensitive to peer pressure. When the other team members refused to proceed with the experiment, only ten percent of the subjects remained obedient to the experimenter and "went all the way." Conversely, when a teammate rather than the subject took charge of physically administering the shock, 92.5% of the subjects went along with the experiment up to the maximum shock. In Niebuhr's terms, we may think of moral man made *less* moral by an immoral society, but *more* moral by a society of his betters. . . .

The Milgram studies, then, suggest the role of imperfect and fragmented knowledge in organizational misconduct. The less individuals appreciate the consequences of their acts, the need to decide, and the available alternatives, the easier it will be for them to engage in destructive obedience. Milgram's experiments suggest that the fragmentation of knowledge promotes organizational wrongdoing by blunting the edge of moral conflict.

Although Milgram's research focused on subordinates, parallel problems arise for supervisors. As we have seen, bureaucratic structures serve to deny supervisors knowledge of operational details, blunt their awareness of harsh consequences, and help them rationalize what they cannot ignore. The result is the deep paradox of the "rule by Nobody": when neither superiors nor subordinates may be held responsible, we face an uncanny situation in which responsibility has seemingly been conjured out of existence.

The Inadequacy of Ethical Tradition and Philosophical Theory

. . . We believe that the specter of fragmented knowledge, divided responsibility, ambiguous orders, and unknown consequences is inadequately addressed in the moral discourse of Western societies. Virtually every approach to normative ethics, from the Ten Commandments to the latest wrinkles in philosophy journals, focuses primary attention on moral problems in which four *knowledge conditions* are satisfied—knowledge conditions that are frequently absent in individual decisionmaking and almost never found in organizational settings.

First, the decisionmaker recognizes that he or she has come to a fork in the road: The decisionmaker knows *that* a decision must be made. Do I or don't I cheat on the examination? Do I or don't I protest when I hear an acquaintance tell an anti-Semitic joke? Situations such as these are readily identifiable as moral decisions. Typically, when we face one of these questions, we know that we face it.

Second, the decisionmaker recognizes that he or she must make the choice in a fairly short, distinct period of time: The decisionmaker knows *when* a decision must be made, or at least *by* when it must be made. The examination is tomorrow; I must confront the acquaintance about his anti-Semitic joke now or never.

Third, the decisionmaker confronts a small number of well-defined options: The decisionmaker knows *what choices* are available. For example, a lawyer, learning that her client is using her services to perpetrate a fraud, can quickly catalogue her options: do what the client asks, try to talk the client out of the plan, blow the whistle on the client, or resign.

Fourth, the decisionmaker has the information needed to make the decision: The decisionmaker knows *what is needed* to make the choice. Even in situations of radically incomplete information, theories of rational decisionmaking under uncertainty allow us to assign probability-estimates to these various outcomes in order to generate a recommendation, though that recommendation may be merely to flip a coin.

These, then, are the four knowledge conditions of moral decisionmaking: we know *that* a decision must be made, *when* a decision must be made, *what choices* are available, and *what is needed* to make the choice. From the Biblical "Thou shalt not steal" and the Golden Rule, to Kant's categorical imperative and the utilitarian injunction to achieve the greatest good for the greatest number, the core precepts of the major systems of ethical thought are directed to agents who satisfy the knowledge conditions. If the conditions are not satisfied, ethical systems generally respond with mitigation or even immunity: forgiving those who "know not what they do" is basic to Western understandings of moral responsibility.

Ignorance can, of course, be culpable; but most philosophers and legal theorists who acknowledge the phenomenon of culpable ignorance have implicitly confined it to a small range of exceptional cases: conspirators who attempt to preserve their deniability, or drunks who have willfully stupefied themselves. The possibility that the modern workplace may place millions of ordinary individuals in a state of culpable ignorance throughout their careers has never, to our knowledge, been explicitly addressed in moral theory.

In an organizational setting, one or more of the four knowledge conditions typically fails at a critical juncture. As the Milgram experiments illustrated, individuals in bureaucratic settings may not fully ap-

preciate that a decision must be made, understand when it should be made, realize what choices are open to them, and comprehend what the consequences of different choices will be. A law firm associate asked to research a small point of law or a junior architect asked to design a detail may have no idea that the project as a whole raises deep questions of professional ethics. Even if they have their suspicions, it is often impossible to pinpoint a moment of truth when the decision must be made. No clear list of options, or even clear understanding of who to speak with, may exist, and the subordinate may never believe she has sufficient information to fashion a solution.

The failure of these knowledge conditions is created or maintained by organizational structure. Typically, supervisors parcel out subtasks to a number of subordinate employees. None of the subordinates may have more than the most general idea of what the entire project is about, while the supervisor may know nothing about the details of each subordinate's subtasks. No member of the organization might recognize a moral problem, because the problem arises not from what any *one* member of the team is doing, but rather from all their actions put together. The fact that each is merely a member of a team lulls them into a sense of security, so that they feel no pressing need to find out more about what is going on. Though they may resolve not to be "good Germans" at the moment of truth, the moment of truth never arrives.

This, then, is the central philosophical question that the problem of fragmented knowledge raises: *Is it possible to formulate satisfactory principles of individual responsibility when any or all of the four knowledge conditions presupposed by standard moral theories fail?*

RESPONSIBILITY WITHOUT KNOWLEDGE

. . . At bottom, four approaches exist to the problem of "deeds without doers." First, we can simply accept as a tragic fact of modern existence that organizational wrongs may be committed for which no one—neither individuals nor the organization—can rightly be held responsible. More optimistically, we can either hold the organization itself morally responsible for the wrongdoing or hold all the individuals affiliated with the organization strictly liable. Finally, we can extend standard principles of culpable ignorance to explain why individuals in organizations may be held responsible for their actions even though the knowledge conditions fail. This is the approach we will defend. . . .

Extending Individual Responsibility

The simplest way of extending the concept of culpable ignorance to situations in which the knowledge conditions fail is to invoke an analogy to drunk driving. By the time a driver has had six drinks, he may no longer have the reflexes or judgment to avoid an accident, and thus in one sense he is not responsible for what he does behind the wheel. Obviously, though, we *do* hold him responsible. Why? The answer seems simple enough: although we agree that once he became drunk he lost effective control of his actions, we blame him for becoming drunk in the first place. Though he was not fully responsible at the time of the accident, it was his own fault that he was not responsible. In Aristotle's words, "when one has once let go of a stone, it is too late to get it back—but the agent was responsible for throwing it, because the origin of the action was in himself."[14]

Analogously, we may agree that individuals in organizational settings often do not know enough to be held responsible for organizational wrongdoings and yet we insist that they should have known. They were willfully blind. Thus, for example, if an SS officer claimed that he did not know about the SS's murderous activities, we may wish to insist that his ignorance is blameworthy. He should have known what he was joining.

The drunk driving analogy suggests that we can hold people responsible for getting into the very predicament that at first glance seems to relieve them of responsibility. If we focus on the act of drinking, this suggests that an employee is responsible for the predicament he gets into by joining an organization that fragments relevant knowledge. Except in the case of outlaw groups like the SS, however, we do not want to treat the act of joining an organization, like the act of heavy drinking, as suspect or presumptively wrong.

We would do better to focus on the driving aspect of the drunk driving analogy. Driving is a valuable activity, and our licensing procedures are designed to make it widely available. Because of the lethal potential of the automobile, however, the privilege of driving hinges on an exercise of alertness, caution, and self-restraint that we do not require of pedestrians or passengers. We allow pedestrians and passengers to impair their reflexes and judgment with alcohol, but we treat it as a legal and moral offense for a driver or prospective driver to do so.

Analogously, because of the great potential for harm arising from the division of labor and fragmentation of knowledge in a corporate or bureaucratic organization, employees may acquire duties far more demanding than doing no evil. They must look and listen for evil and attempt to thwart it if they discover it. These duties, however, are not as limited and well-defined as those imposed on the driver. We expect prospective drivers to "just say no," but we cannot expect organizational employees to know everything about the operation in which they are involved. While drinking is a gratuitous impediment to driving, fragmented knowledge inheres in the structure of the organization itself. We are left with a question that does not arise in the context of drunk driving: What and how much precaution do we require of the individual employee?

We cannot answer this question definitively, but we can begin by suggesting several obligations that arise from the specific risk of organizational enterprise: the risk that an individual will do or contribute to great harm without knowing it.

1. *Obligations of investigation.* The first, most obvious, possibility is to hold individuals in organizational settings morally responsible for discerning the nature of their own projects and for discovering what other employees are doing with their work products. The idea is obvious because it remedies the absence of knowledge in the most straightforward way: by demanding that individuals do their best to acquire the knowledge they lack.

2. *Obligations of communication.* A second possibility is to hold individuals who possess

troublesome knowledge morally responsible for communicating it to others in the organization. Obviously, communication may be a risky course of action: supervisors treasure their "deniability," and shooting the messenger is often their knee-jerk response. Yet riskiness does not distinguish this from other moral responsibilities: we often believe that people have moral obligations to act against their self-interest.

3. *Obligations of protection.* The previous suggestions imply that supervisors may have moral obligations to protect their subordinates from adverse consequences of investigation and communication. For example, they may be morally responsible for protecting whistleblowers from retaliation.

4. *Obligations of prevention.* Those in management positions may have moral obligations to forestall wrongdoing by setting up structures that avoid the problems we have been examining. Such preventive mechanisms might include ombudsmen, incentive structures that reward moral action, channels for anonymous information about problems, and so on. Interestingly, the American Bar Association's 1983 ethics code requires supervisors in law firms to take measures that ensure that their subordinates behave ethically.

5. *Obligations of precaution.* In some cases, we may be able to analogize the act of joining an organization to the act of heavy drinking: the individual knows or should know that once she becomes involved, her discretion and knowledge will be so constricted that she cannot be held responsible for wrongdoing that, in broad outline, she can reasonably anticipate. The fatal misstep is involving herself in the first place. More often than not, would-be employees of organizations have some prior sense of the organization's values and culture. We may therefore hold individuals responsible for joining the organization in the first place, as we might hold an individual German responsible for joining the SS.

That individuals in an organization have obligations like these, and that their breach provides a basis for assigning the individuals responsibility for wrongs done in ignorance, seems plausible. But

this approach to extending individual responsibility for organizational wrongdoing raises two critical questions. First, how demanding are these obligations? . . . Second, how much vigilance is enough? . . .

As we have described them, the moral obligations of the individual employee seem to fall somewhere between *perfect* duties like not killing, with fairly precise boundaries, and *imperfect* duties like charity or self-improvement, that require only some indeterminate effort. If we attempt to make these duties perfect, through more precise formulation, we risk defining them too narrowly; if we attempt to make them imperfect, by demanding a "reasonable" effort, we risk making them too vague. . . .

What is an individual responsible for in failing to fulfill these *preemptive duties,* as we shall call the obligations of investigation, communication, protection, prevention, and precaution? Should we blame her only for the breach of the preemptive duty, or should we blame her for the resulting offense as if she had known all the relevant facts (and thus hold her immune from censure if no harm results)? Is the employee responsible just for failing to investigate (at the time she fails to do so), or does she lose her excuse of ignorance with respect to any facts the investigation would have yielded?

Neither approach seems fully satisfactory. In limiting responsibility to the breach of preemptive duties, we impose the same blame or punishment regardless of what wrongs result; in withholding the excuse of ignorance for the offense, we treat a negligent employee as if she were responsible for intentional wrongdoing. And if we assign responsibility *only* when a wrong is actually done, we fail to censure those lucky enough to ignore their special obligations without adverse effect. . . .

Paul Robinson has argued that the law can recognize a person's responsibility for getting into a predicament without denying her the excuse created by that predicament.[15] The critical inquiry is whether, in acting in a way that creates an excuse, the individual is at fault for the offense excused.

To return to the drunk driving analogy, a driver who drank until he was no longer able to appreciate the hazards of the road would not lose the excuse of ignorance if an accident occurred, as if he had knowingly caused the accident. Rather, he would be guilty of reckless homicide for disregarding the risk of a fatal accident; if he should have known of the risk but remained ignorant (e.g., because he did not bother to find out that the punch he was drinking was highly alcoholic), he would be guilty of negligent homicide.[16]

Applied to organizational wrongdoing, an approach like Robinson's would ground the employee's responsibility for the harm in her preemptive duties to investigate, prevent, and so forth. By breaching these duties, the employee has played a role in causing or contributing to the commission of the offense. The key question would not be whether the employee deliberately, recklessly, or negligently breached her duty but whether, by failing to perform it, she intentionally, recklessly, or negligently facilitated the wrongdoing.

Thus, if an employee should have known that by investigating a new project before it commenced, she could ascertain whether it involved exporting toxic substances, and there was some reason to suspect that it might, she would be responsible for negligently exporting those substances, even if, by the time she exported them, the most diligent inquiry would not have revealed their toxic character. Had she actually known that an investigation could have revealed that information, but failed to investigate, she would be responsible for recklessly exporting toxic substances, even if, by the time she exported them, she was no longer able to ascertain their toxic character.

In some cases, this approach may lead us to hold employees who act in ignorance responsible for intentional wrongdoing. If the employee deliberately insulated herself from knowledge about the exports, intending to export toxic substances without being told that specific exports were toxic, she would be responsible for their intentional export despite her ignorance at the time she exported them. But if she deliberately insulated herself from such knowledge only because she hated confrontations, she would be responsible for no more than reckless export, since she did not know the character of the substances or intend or hope that they might be toxic. This approach, then, avoids the harshness of denying an employee an excuse for or-

ganizational wrongdoing if she has any fault for creating the excuse. It treats her as responsible for wrongdoing only to the extent that she is at fault for excusing or justifying its commission. . . .

CONCLUSION

The preemptive obligations we are proposing have in recent years become widely accepted in both public and private bureaucracies. Governmental agencies typically have ombudsmen, and state and federal governments have enacted protections for whistleblowers. In the wake of several incidents, the Exxon Corporation has enacted regulations requiring employees who notice possible misconduct or dangerous situations to notify their superiors in writing; the superiors, in turn, are required to respond in writing, and if no written response is forthcoming, the employee must jump the chain of command and inform higher-level executives.

Regarded as public policy proposals, our preemptive obligations are already found in corporate manuals and memoranda. We are not offering a proposal for regulations whose time has come, however, but an account of individual moral responsibility. That is, we argue not only that bureaucratic organizations should institute policies along the lines we have suggested, but also that individual executives within the organizations are morally blameworthy for failing to implement such policies and that individual employees and executives are morally blameworthy for violating preemptive obligations *even in the absence of policies implementing them.*

Notes

1. William H. Whyte, Jr., *The Organization Man* 3 (1956).
2. *Id.* at 7.
3. David Riesman, *The Lonely Crowd* 22 (1950) (emphasis omitted).
4. *Id.* at 26.
5. Robert Jackall, *Moral Mazes: The World of Corporate Managers* 22 (1988).
6. *Id.* at 105.
7. Karl Marx, *Critique of Hegel's "Philosophy of Right"* 46–47 (Joseph O'Malley, ed., 1970).

8. Reinhold Niebuhr, *Moral Man and Immoral Society* xi–xii (rev. ed. 1960).

9. Robert E. Conot, *Justice at Nuremberg* 210–211 (1983).

10. Jackall, *supra* note 5, at 17, 20–21.

11. Hannah Arendt, *On Violence* 38–39 (1970).

12. *In re* A. H. Robins Co. "Dalkon Shield" IUD Prods. Liab. Litig., 575 F. Supp. 718, 724 (D. Kan. 1983).

13. See Stanley Milgram, *Obedience to Authority: An Experimental View* 3–4 (1974).

14. Aristotle, *Nichomachean Ethics* bk. III, ch. V, 1114a, at 124 (J. A. K. Thomson trans., rev. ed. 1976). . . .

15. Paul H. Robinson, "Causing the Conditions of One's Own Defense: A Study in the Limits of Theory in Criminal Law Doctrine," 71 *Va. L. Rev.* 1 (1985).

16. Similarly, if a person negligently provoked another to use deadly force, he would not lose his right to kill in self-defense. If he exercised that right, however, he would be guilty of negligent homicide for creating the need for self-defense. If he provoked another in order to give himself a legal justification for killing that person, he would be guilty of intentional homicide.

   To bear any responsibility for the ultimate offense, the agent must be at fault for creating the specific excusing or justifying condition he relies on. If he negligently provoked someone without reason to expect that she would resort to deadly force, he would not be guilty of homicide in creating the need for self-defense. He would be responsible at most for negligent provocation and the use of nondeadly defensive force.

Review and Discussion Questions

1. In the modern world, most individuals work in organizations. Describe how this can affect people's sense of responsibility and the morality of their conduct.

2. Describe Stanley Milgram's famous experiment. What are its most significant implications?

3. What four knowledge conditions are presupposed by the standard theories of moral decision making? Are the authors correct to assert that "in an organizational setting, one or more of the four knowledge conditions typically fails at a critical juncture"?

4. What do the authors mean by the problem of "deeds without doers"? What general approach to this problem do they take, and what are the three rival approaches that they put aside?

5. According to the authors, what five obligations do individuals inside an organization have? Do you agree? Do you think that the authors demand too much of the individual? Suppose an individual neglects to fulfill one of these duties. To what extent are we justified in blaming the person for any subsequent organizational misconduct?

Further Reading for Chapter 1

On Ethics

John Arthur, ed., *Morality and Moral Controversies,* 5th ed. (Upper Saddle River, N.J.: Prentice Hall, 1999) and **William H. Shaw**, ed., *Social and Personal Ethics,* 4th ed. (Belmont, Calif.: Wadsworth, 2002) contain essays in both theoretical and applied ethics.

James Rachels, *The Elements of Moral Philosophy,* 3rd ed. (New York: McGraw-Hill, 1999) is an excellent, clear introduction.

George Sher, ed., *Moral Philosophy,* 2nd ed. (San Diego: Harcourt Brace Jovanovich, 1998) and **Louis P. Pojman**, ed., *Ethical Theory,* 3rd ed. (Belmont, Calif.: Wadsworth, 1998) offer more advanced readings on various topics in moral philosophy.

Moral Reasoning

Patrick Hurley, *A Concise Introduction to Logic,* 7th ed. (Belmont, Calif.: Wadsworth, 2000) is a good introduction to all the main areas of logic.

 InfoTrac® College Edition: For further information or to conduct research, please go to www.infotrac-college.com.

Joel Rudinow and **Vincent Barry,** *Invitation to Critical Thinking,* 4th ed. (Fort Worth, Texas: Harcourt Brace, 1999) provides a guide to argument assessment.

Business and Morality

Both **Richard T. De George**, *Business Ethics,* 5th ed. (New York: Macmillan, 1999) and **Manuel G. Velasquez**, *Business Ethics,* 5th ed. (Upper Saddle River, N.J.: Prentice Hall, 2002) contain useful introductions to moral philosophy in relation to business. **Robert E. Frederick,** ed., *A Companion to Business Ethics* (Malden, Mass.: Blackwell, 1999) is a collection of essays by different authors on all aspects of business ethics. Two pertinent discussions of moral conduct in business are **Glenn Martin,** "Once Again: Why Should Business Be Ethical?" *Business and Professional Ethics Journal* 17 (Winter 1998) and **Kevin Gibson,** "Excuses, Excuses: Moral Slippage in the Workplace," *Business Horizons* 43 (November–December 2000).

Three good sources of advanced work in business ethics are the *Business and Professional Ethics Journal,* the *Business Ethics Quarterly,* and the *Journal of Business Ethics.*

2

Normative Theories of Ethics

In an award-winning television drama, police captain Frank Furillo firmly believes that the two toughs just brought in by his officers are guilty of the rape-murder of a nun earlier that morning inside the parish church. But the evidence is only circumstantial. As word of the crime spreads, the community is aghast and angry. From all sides—the press, local citizens, city hall, the police commissioner—pressure mounts on Furillo and his department for a speedy resolution of the matter. On the street outside Furillo's office, a mob is growing frenzied, hoping to get their hands on the two young men and administer "street justice" to them. One of the crowd has even taken a shot at the suspects inside the police station!

The police, however, have only enough evidence to arraign the suspects on the relatively minor charge of being in possession of goods stolen from the church. Furillo and his colleagues could demand a high bail, thus keeping the defendants in custody while the police try to turn up evidence that will convict the men of murder. But in a surprise move at the arraignment, the district attorney, acting in conjunction with Furillo, declines to ask the judge for bail. The men are free to go, but they and their outraged public defender, Joyce Davenport, know that their lives will be worthless once they hit the streets: Community members have sworn to avenge the much-loved sister if the police are unable to do

their job. To remain in police custody, and thus safe, their only choice is to confess to murder. So the two men confess.

Davenport argues passionately but unsuccessfully against what she considers to be a police-state tactic. Anyone in that circumstance, guilty or innocent, would confess. It is an affront to the very idea of the rule of law, she contends: police coercion by way of mob pressure. No system of justice can permit such conduct from its public officials. Yet the confession allows the police to locate the murder weapon, thus bringing independent confirmation of the culprits' guilt. Furillo's tactic, nevertheless, does not rest easily on his own conscience, and the screenplay closes with him entering the church confessional later that night: "Forgive me, Father, for I have sinned. . . ."

Furillo is understandably worried about whether he did the morally right thing. His action was successful, and it was for a good cause. But does the end always justify the means? Did the police and district attorney behave in a way that accords with due process and the rights of defendants? Should community pressure influence one's professional decisions? Did Furillo act in accordance with some principle that he could defend publicly? In a tough and controversial situation like this, the issue does not concern the moral sincerity of either Furillo or Davenport. Both can be assumed to want to do what is right, but what exactly is the morally justified thing to do? How are we to judge Furillo's tactics?

Chapter 1 noted that a defensible moral judgment must be supportable by a sound moral principle. Moral principles provide the confirmatory standard for moral judgments. The use of these principles, however, is not a mechanical process in which one cranks in data and out pops an automatic moral judgment. Rather, the principles provide a conceptual framework that guides us in making moral decisions. Careful thought and open-minded reflection are always necessary to work from one's moral principles to a considered moral judgment.

But what are the appropriate principles to rely on when making moral judgments? The truth is that there is no consensus among people who have studied ethics and reflected on these matters. Different theories exist as to the proper standard of right and wrong. As Professor Bernard Williams has put it, we are heirs to a rich and complex ethical tradition, in which a variety of different moral principles and ethical considerations intertwine and sometimes compete.[1]

This chapter discusses the different normative perspectives and rival ethical principles that are our heritage. After distinguishing between what are called consequentialist and nonconsequentialist normative theories, it looks in detail at several ethical approaches, discussing their pros and cons and their relevance to moral decision making in an organizational context:

1. Egoism, both as an ethical theory and as a psychological theory

2. Utilitarianism, the theory that the morally right action is the one that achieves the greatest total amount of happiness for everyone concerned

3. Kant's ethics, with his categorical imperative and his emphasis on moral motivation and respect for persons

4. Other nonconsequentialist normative themes: duties, moral rights, and prima facie principles

The chapter concludes with an attempt to tie together the major concerns of the different normative theories and suggests a general way of approaching moral decision making.

CONSEQUENTIALIST AND NONCONSEQUENTIALIST THEORIES

In ethics, *normative theories* propose some principle or principles for distinguishing right actions from wrong actions. These theories can, for convenience, be divided into two kinds: consequentialist and nonconsequentialist.

Many philosophers have argued that the moral rightness of an action is determined solely by its results. If its consequences are good, then the act is right; if they are bad, the act is wrong. Moral theorists who adopt this approach are therefore called *consequentialists.* They determine what is right by weighing the ratio of good to bad that an action will produce. The right act is the one that produces (or will probably produce) at least as great a ratio of good to evil as any other course of action.

One question that arises here is, Consequences for whom? Should one consider the consequences only for oneself? Or the consequences for everyone affected? The two most important consequentialist theories, *egoism* and *utilitarianism,* are distinguished by their different answers to this question. Egoism advocates individual self-interest as its guiding principle, whereas utilitarianism holds that one must take into account everyone affected by the action. But both theories agree that rightness and wrongness are solely a function of an action's results.

By contrast, *nonconsequentialist* (or *deontological*) theories contend that right and wrong are determined by more than the likely consequences of an action. Nonconsequentialists do not necessarily deny that consequences are morally significant, but they believe that other factors are also relevant to the moral assessment of an action. For example, a nonconsequentialist would hold that for Kevin to break his promise to Cindy is wrong not simply because it has bad results (Cindy's hurt feelings, Kevin's damaged reputation, and so on) but because of the inherent character of the act itself. Even if more good than bad were to come from Kevin's breaking the promise, a nonconsequentialist might still view it as wrong. What matters is the nature of the act in question, not just its results. This concept will become clearer later in the chapter as we look at some specific nonconsequentialist principles and theories.

EGOISM

In the late summer of 2000, a dismayed American public learned that the Firestone tires on Ford Explorers, one of the country's most popular vehicles, were dangerously prone to split apart on the road, causing the SUVs to roll over and crash. When officials began demanding a recall, the controversy was reminiscent of an earlier one involving Firestone's "500" steel-belted radials, which a House subcommittee had implicated in at least fifteen deaths. When Firestone announced that it was discontinuing the controversial "500," newspapers at the time interpreted this to mean that Firestone would immediately remove the tires from the market. In fact, Firestone intended only a "rolling phaseout" and continued to manufacture the tire. When a Firestone spokesperson was later asked why the company had not corrected the media's misinterpretation of its intent, the spokesperson said that Firestone's policy was to ask for corrections only when it was beneficial to the company to do so—in other words, only when it was in the company's self-interest.

The view that identifies morality with self-interest is referred to as *egoism*. Egoism contends that an act is morally right if and only if it best promotes an agent's long-term interests. (Here an "agent" can be a single person or, as in the Firestone example, an organization.) Egoists use their best long-term advantage as the standard for measuring an action's rightness. If an action produces or will probably produce for the agent a greater ratio of good to evil in the long run than any other alternative, then

that action is the right one to perform, and the agent should take that course to be moral.

Moral philosophers distinguish between two kinds of egoism: personal and impersonal. Personal egoists claim they should pursue their own best long-term interests, but they do not say what others should do. Impersonal egoists claim that everyone should follow his or her best long-term interests.

Misconceptions about Egoism

Several misconceptions haunt both versions of egoism. One is that egoists do only what they like, that they believe in "eat, drink, and be merry." Not so. Undergoing unpleasant, even painful experience meshes with egoism, provided such temporary sacrifice is necessary for the advancement of one's long-term interests.

Another misconception is that all egoists endorse *hedonism,* the view that only pleasure (or happiness) is of intrinsic value, the only good in life worth pursuing. Although some egoists are hedonistic—as was the ancient Greek philosopher Epicurus (341–270 B.C.E.)—other egoists have a broader view of what constitutes self-interest. They identify the good with knowledge, power, or what some modern psychologists call self-actualization. Egoists may, in fact, hold any theory of what is good.

A final but very important misconception is that egoists cannot act honestly, be gracious and helpful, or otherwise promote other people's interests. Egoism, however, requires us to do whatever will best further our own interests, and doing this sometimes requires us to advance the interests of others. In particular, egoism tells us to benefit others when we expect that our doing so will be reciprocated or when the act will bring us pleasure or in some way promote our own good. For example, egoism might discourage a shopkeeper from trying to cheat customers because it is likely to hurt business in the long run. Or egoism might recommend to the chair of the board that she hire as a vice president her nephew, who is not the best candidate for the job but of whom she is very fond. Hiring the nephew might bring her more satisfaction than any other course of action, even if the nephew doesn't perform his job as well as someone else might.

Psychological Egoism

So egoism does not preach that we should never assist others but rather that we have no basic moral duty to do so. The only moral obligation we have is to ourselves. Although you and I are not required to act in the interests of others, we should if that is the best way to promote our own self-interest. In short: Always look out for "number one."

Proponents of the ethical theory of egoism generally attempt to derive their basic moral principle from the alleged fact that human beings are by nature selfish creatures. According to this doctrine, termed *psychological egoism,* people are, as a matter of fact, so constructed that they must behave selfishly. Psychological egoism asserts that all actions are in fact selfishly motivated and that truly unselfish actions are therefore impossible. Even such apparently self-sacrificial acts as giving up one's own life to save the lives of one's children or blowing the whistle on one's organization's misdeeds at great personal expense are, according to psychological egoism, done to satisfy the person's own self-interested desires. For example, the parent may seek to perpetuate the family line or to avoid guilt, and the worker may be after fame or revenge.

Problems with Egoism

Although egoism as an ethical doctrine has always had its adherents, the theory is open to very strong objections. It is safe to say that few, if any, philosophers today would advocate it as either a personal or an organizational morality. Consider these objections:

1. *Psychological egoism is not a sound theory.* Of course, self-interest motivates all of us to some extent, and we all know of situations in which someone pretended to be acting altruistically or morally but was really only motivated by self-interest. The theory of psychological egoism contends, however, that self-interest is the only thing that ever motivates anyone.

Now this claim seems open to many counterexamples. Take the actual case of a man who, while driving a company truck, spotted smoke coming from inside a parked car and a child trying to escape from the vehicle. The man quickly made a U-turn, drove up to the burning vehicle, and found a one-year-old girl trapped in the back seat, restrained by a seat belt. Flames raged in the front seat as heavy smoke billowed from the car. Disregarding his own safety, the man entered the car and removed the infant, who authorities said otherwise would have died from the poisonous fumes and the flames.

Or take a more mundane example. It's Saturday, and you feel like having a beer with a couple of pals and watching the ball game. On the other hand, you believe you ought to take your two children to the zoo, as you had earlier suggested to them you might. Going to the zoo would bring them a lot of pleasure—and besides, you haven't done much with them recently. Of course, you love your children and it will bring you some pleasure to go to the zoo with them, but—let's face it—they've been rather cranky lately and you'd prefer to watch the ball game. Nonetheless, you feel an obligation and so you go to the zoo.

These appear to be cases in which people are acting for reasons that are not self-interested. Of course, the reasons that lead you to take your children to the zoo—a sense of obligation, a desire to promote their happiness—are your reasons, but that by itself does not make them self-interested reasons. Still less does it show that you are selfish. Anything that you do is a result of your desires, but that fact doesn't establish what the believer in psychological egoism claims—namely, that the only desires you have, or the only desires that ultimately move you, are self-interested desires.

Psychological egoists (that is, advocates of the theory of psychological egoism) will claim that deep down both the heroic man who saved the girl and the unheroic parent who took the children to the zoo were really motivated by self-interest in some way or another. Maybe the hero was hoping to win praise or the parent to advance his or her own pleasure by enhancing the children's affection for the parent. Or maybe some other self-interested consideration motivated them. Psychological egoists can always claim that some yet-to-be-identified subconscious egoistic motivation is the main impulse behind any action.

At this point, though, the psychological egoists' claims sound a little far-fetched, and we may suspect them of trying to make their theory true by definition. Whatever example we come up with, they will simply claim that the person is really motivated by self-interest. One may well wonder how scientific this theory is, or how much content it has, when both the hero and the coward, both the parent who goes to the zoo and the parent who stays home, are equally selfish in their motivations.

A defender of egoism as an ethical doctrine could concede that people are not fully egoistic by nature and yet continue to insist that people ought morally to pursue only their own interests. Yet without the doctrine of psychological egoism, the ethical thesis of egoism becomes less attractive. Other types of ethical principles are possible. We all care about ourselves, but how much sense does it make to see self-interest as the basis of right and wrong? Do we really want to say that someone acting altruistically is behaving immorally?

2. *Ethical egoism is not really a moral theory at all.* Many critics of egoism as an ethical standard contend that it misunderstands the nature and point of morality. As Chapter 1 explained, morality serves to restrain our purely self-interested desires so we can all live together. If our interests never came into conflict—that is, if it were never advantageous for one person to deceive or cheat another—then we would have no need for morality. The moral standards of a society provide the basic guidelines for cooperative social existence and allow us to re-solve conflicts by appeal to shared principles of justification.

It is difficult to see how ethical egoism could perform this function. In a society of egoists, people might publicly agree to follow certain rules so their lives would run more smoothly. But it would be a very unstable world, because people would not hesitate to break the rules if they thought they could get away with it. Nor can egoism provide a means for settling conflicts and disputes, because it simply tells each party to do whatever is necessary to promote effectively his or her interests.

Many moral theorists maintain that moral principles apply equally to the conduct of all persons and that their application requires us to be objective and impartial. Moral agents are seen as those who, despite their own involvement in an issue, can be reasonably disinterested and objective—those who try to see all sides of an issue without being committed to the interests of a particular individual or group, including themselves. If we accept this attitude of detachment and impartiality as at least part of what it means to take a moral point of view, then we must look for it in any proposed moral principle.

Those who make egoism their moral standard are anything but objective, for they seek to guide themselves by their own best interests, regardless of the issue or circumstances. They do not even attempt to be impartial, except insofar as impartiality furthers their own interests. And, according to their theory, any third party offering advice should simply represent his or her own interest.

3. *Ethical egoism ignores blatant wrongs.* The most common objection to egoism as an ethical doctrine is that by reducing everything to the standard of best long-term self-interest, egoism takes no stand against seemingly outrageous acts like stealing, murder, racial and sexual discrimination, deliberately false advertising, and wanton pollution. All such actions are morally neutral until the test of self-interest is applied.

Of course, the egoist might argue that this objection begs the question by assuming that such acts are immoral and then repudiating egoism on this basis when, in fact, their morality is the very issue that moral principles such as egoism are meant to resolve. Still, egoism must respond to the widely observed human desire to be fair or just, a desire that at least sometimes seems stronger than competing selfish desires. A moral principle that allows the possibility of murder in the cause of self-interest offends our basic intuitions about right and wrong; it clashes with many of our considered moral beliefs.

UTILITARIANISM

Utilitarianism is the moral doctrine that we should always act to produce the greatest possible balance of good over bad for everyone affected by our action. By "good," utilitarians understand happiness or pleasure. Thus, the greatest happiness of all constitutes the standard that determines whether an action is right or wrong. Although the basic theme of utilitarianism is present in the writings of many earlier thinkers, Jeremy Bentham (1748–1832) and John Stuart Mill (1806–1873) were the first to develop the theory explicitly and in detail. Both Bentham and Mill were philosophers with a strong interest in legal and social reform. They used the utilitarian standard to evaluate and criticize the social and political institutions of their day—for example, the prison system. As a result, utilitarianism has long been associated with social improvement.

Bentham viewed a community as no more than the individual persons who compose it. The interests of the community are simply the sum of the interests of its members. An action promotes the interests of an individual when it adds to the individual's pleasure or diminishes the person's pain. Correspondingly, an action augments the happiness of a community only insofar as it increases the total amount of individual happiness. In this way, Bentham argued for the utilitarian principle that actions are right if they promote the greatest human welfare, wrong if they do not.

For Bentham, pleasure and pain are merely types of sensations, which differ only in number, intensity, and duration. He offered a "hedonic calculus" of six criteria for evaluating pleasure and pain exclusively by their quantitative differences. This calculus, he believed, makes possible an objective determination of the morality of anyone's conduct, individual or collective, on any occasion.

Bentham rejected any distinctions based on quality of pleasure except insofar as they might indicate differences in quantity. Thus, whenever equal amounts of pleasure are involved, throwing darts is as good as writing poetry and baking a cake as good as composing a symphony; reading Stephen King is of no less value than reading Shakespeare. Although he himself was an intelligent, cultivated man, Bentham maintained there is nothing intrinsically better about cultivated and intellectual pleasures than about crude and prosaic ones. The only issue is which yields the greater amount of enjoyment.

John Stuart Mill thought Bentham's concept of pleasure was too simple. He viewed human beings as having elevated faculties that allow them to pursue various kinds of pleasure. The pleasures of the intellect and imagination, in particular, have a higher value than those of mere sensation. Thus, for Mill the utility principle allows consideration of the relative quality of pleasure and pain.

Although Bentham and Mill had different conceptions of pleasure, both men identified pleasure and happiness and considered pleasure the ultimate value. In this sense they are hedonists: Pleasure, in their view, is the one thing that is intrinsically good or worthwhile. Anything that is good is good only because it brings about pleasure (or happiness), directly or indirectly. Take education, for example. The learning process itself might be pleasurable to us; reflecting on or working with what we have learned might bring us satisfaction at some later time; or by making possible a career and life that we could not have had otherwise, education might bring us happiness indirectly. By contrast, critics of Bentham and Mill contend that things other than happiness are also inherently good—for example, knowledge, friendship, and aesthetic satisfaction. The implication is that these things are valuable even if they do not lead to happiness.

Some moral theorists have modified utilitarianism so that it aims at other consequences in addition to happiness. Other utilitarians, wary of trying to compare one person's happiness with another's, have interpreted their theory as requiring us not to maximize happiness but rather to maximize the satisfaction of people's desires or preferences. The focus here will be utilitarianism in its standard form, in which the good to be aimed at is human happiness or welfare, but what will be said about standard or classical utilitarianism applies, with the appropriate modifications, to other versions as well.

Although this chapter will also consider another form of utilitarianism, known as *rule utilitarianism,* utilitarianism in its most basic version, often called *act utilitarianism,* states that we must ask ourselves what the consequences of a particular act in a particular situation will be for all those affected. If its consequences bring more total good than those of any alternative course of action, then this action is the right one and the one we should perform. Thus a utilitarian could defend Frank Furillo's decision not to request bail, thereby coercing a confession from the suspects.

Consider another example: In a famous case, medical researchers initiated a long-range study of viral hepatitis at Willowbrook State Hospital, a New York institution for mentally retarded children. The researchers were interested in understanding the pathogenesis of viral hepatitis and the effectiveness of gamma globulin as an agent for inoculating people against hepatitis. Willowbrook seemed like a good choice for the investigation because the disease was rampant there. To get the kind of precise data they considered most useful, the researchers decided to deliberately infect some of the incoming children with the strain of hepatitis virus epidemic at the institution.

The value of the Willowbrook research is well documented. As a direct result, we increased our scientific understanding of viral hepatitis and how to treat it. But nagging moral questions persist. Should retarded children have been used as subjects in experiments that were not directly therapeutic? Supporters of the research insist that the consent of the children's parents was obtained. But even if the facts warranted another conclusion, some people would still defend the Willowbrook experiments on the grounds that they produced the most good for the whole society. In other words, the suffering of some individuals was justified because it maximized the total happiness produced.

Six Points about Utilitarianism

Before evaluating utilitarianism, one should understand some points that might lead to confusion and misapplication. First, when deciding which action will produce the greatest happiness, we must consider unhappiness or pain as well as happiness. Suppose, for example, that an action produces eight units of happiness and four units of unhappiness. Its net worth is four units of happiness. Suppose also that an opposed action produces ten units of happiness and seven units of unhappiness; its net worth is three units. In this case we should choose the first action over the second. In the event that both lead not to happiness but to unhappiness, and there is no third option, we should choose the one that brings fewer units of unhappiness.

Second, actions affect people to different degrees. Your playing your radio loudly might enhance two persons' pleasure a little, cause significant discomfort to two others, and leave a fifth person indifferent. The utilitarian theory is not that each person votes on the basis of his or her pleasure or pain, with the majority ruling, but rather that we add up the various pleasures and pains, however large or small, and go with the action that brings about the greatest net amount of happiness.

Third, because utilitarians evaluate actions according to their consequences, and actions produce different results in different circumstances, almost anything might, in principle, be morally right in some particular circumstance. For example, whereas breaking a promise generally produces unhappiness, there can be circumstances in which, on balance, more happiness would be produced by breaking a promise than by keeping it. In those circumstances, utilitarianism would require us to break the promise.

Fourth, utilitarians wish to maximize happiness not simply immediately but in the long run as well. All the indirect ramifications of an act have to be taken into account. Lying might seem a good way out of a tough situation, but if and when the people we deceive find out, not only will they be unhappy, but our reputations and our relationships with them will be damaged. This is a serious risk that a utilitarian cannot ignore.

Fifth, utilitarians acknowledge that we often do not know with certainty what the future consequences of our actions will be. Accordingly, we must act so that the expected or likely happiness is as great as possible. If I take my friend's money, unbeknownst to him, and buy lottery tickets with it, there is a chance that we will end up millionaires and that my action will have maximized happiness all around. But the odds are definitely against it; the most likely result is loss of money (and probably of a friendship, too). Therefore, no utilitarian could justify gambling with purloined funds on the grounds that it might maximize happiness.

Sometimes it is difficult to determine the likely results of alternative actions, and no modern utilitarian really believes that we can assign precise units of happiness and unhappiness to people. But as Mill reminds us, we really do have quite a lot of experience as to what typically makes people happy or unhappy. In any case, as utilitarians our duty is to strive to maximize total happiness, even when it may seem difficult to know what action is likely to promote the good effectively.

Finally, when choosing among possible actions, utilitarianism does not require us to disregard our own pleasure. Nor should we give it added weight. Rather, our own pleasure and pain enter into the calculus equally with the pleasures and pains of others. Even if we are sincere in our utilitarianism, we must guard against the possibility of being biased in our calculations when our own interests are at stake. For this reason, and because it would be time consuming to do a utilitarian calculation before every action, utilitarians encourage us to rely on rules of thumb in ordinary moral circumstances. We can make it a rule of thumb, for example, to tell the truth and keep our promises, rather than to calculate possible pleasures and pains in every routine case, because we know that in general telling the truth and keeping promises result in more happiness than lying and breaking promises.

Utilitarianism in an Organizational Context

Several features about utilitarianism make it appealing as a standard for moral decisions in business and nonbusiness organizations.

First, utilitarianism provides a clear and straightforward basis for formulating and testing policies. By utilitarian standards, an organizational policy, decision, or action is good if it promotes the general welfare more than any other alternative. A policy is considered wrong (or in need of modification) if it does not promote total utility as well as some alternative would. Utilitarians do not ask us to accept rules, policies, or principles blindly. Rather, they require us to test their worth against the standard of utility.

Second, utilitarianism provides an objective and attractive way of resolving conflicts of self-interest. This feature of utilitarianism dramatically contrasts with egoism, which seems incapable of resolving such conflicts. By proposing a standard outside self-interest, utilitarianism greatly minimizes and may actually eliminate such disputes. Thus, individuals within organizations make moral decisions and evaluate their actions by appealing to a uniform standard: the general good.

Third, utilitarianism provides a flexible, result-oriented approach to moral decision making. By recognizing no actions of a general kind as inherently right or wrong, utilitarianism encourages organizations to focus on the results of their actions and policies, and it allows them to tailor their decisions to suit the complexities of their situations. This facet of utilitarianism enables organizations to make realistic and workable moral decisions.

Critical Inquiries of Utilitarianism

1. *Is utilitarianism really workable?* Utilitarianism instructs us to maximize happiness, but in difficult cases we may be very uncertain about the likely results of the alternative courses of action open to us. Furthermore, comparing your level of happiness or unhappiness with mine is at best tricky, at worst impossible—and when many people are involved, the matter may get hopelessly complex. Even if we assume that it is possible to make comparisons and to calculate the various possible results of each course of action that a person might take (and the odds of each happening), is it realistic to expect people to take the time to make those calculations and, if they do, to make them accurately? Some critics of act utilitarianism have contended that teaching people to follow the basic utilitarian principle would not in fact promote happiness because of the difficulties in applying utilitarianism accurately.

2. *Are some actions wrong, even if they produce good?* Like egoism, utilitarianism focuses on the results of an action, not on the character of the action itself. For utilitarians, no action is in itself objectionable. It is objectionable only when it leads to a lesser amount of total good than could otherwise have been brought about. Critics of utilitarianism, by contrast, contend that some actions can be immoral and thus things we must not do, even if doing them would maximize happiness.

Suppose a dying woman has asked you to promise to send the $25,000 under her bed to her nephew in another part of the country. She dies without anyone else's knowing of the money or of the promise that you made. Now suppose, too, that you know the nephew is a spendthrift and a drunkard and, were the money delivered to him, it would be wasted in a week of outrageous partying. On the other hand, a very fine orphanage in your town needs such a sum to improve and expand its recreational facilities, something that would provide happiness to many children for years to come. It seems clear that on utilitarian grounds you should give the money to the orphanage, because this action would result in more total happiness.

Many people would balk at this conclusion, contending that it would be wrong to break your promise, even if doing so would bring about more good than keeping it. Having made a promise, you have an obligation to keep it, and a deathbed promise is particularly serious. Furthermore, the deceased woman had a right to do with her money as she wished; it is not for you to decide how to spend it. Likewise, having been bequeathed the money, the nephew has a right to it, regardless of how wisely or foolishly he might spend it. Defenders of utilitarianism, however, would insist that promoting happiness is all that really matters and warn you not to be blinded by moral prejudice.

Critics of utilitarianism, on the other hand, maintain that utilitarianism is morally blind in not just permitting, but requiring, immoral actions in order to maximize happiness. Philosopher Richard Brandt states the case against act utilitarianism this way:

> Act-utilitarianism . . . implies that if you have employed a boy to mow your lawn and he has finished the job and asks for his pay, you should pay him what you promised only if you cannot find a better use for your money. . . . It implies that if your father is ill and has no prospect of good in his life, and maintaining him is a drain on the energy and enjoyments of others, then, if you can end his life without provoking any public scandal or setting a bad example, it is your positive duty to take matters into your own hands and bring his life to a close.[2]

In the same vein, ethicist A. C. Ewing concludes that "[act] utilitarian principles, logically carried out, would result in far more cheating, lying and unfair action than any good man would tolerate."[3]

Defenders of act utilitarianism would reply that these charges are exaggerated. Although it is theoretically possible, for example, that not paying the boy for his work might maximize happiness, this is extremely unlikely. Utilitarians contend that only in very unusual circumstances will pursuit of the good conflict with our ordinary ideas of right and wrong, and in those cases—like the deathbed promise—we should put aside those ordinary ideas. The antiutilitarian replies that the theoretical possibility that utilitarianism may require immoral conduct shows it to be an unsatisfactory moral theory.

3. *Is utilitarianism unjust?* Utilitarianism concerns itself with the sum total of happiness produced, not with how that happiness is distributed. If policy X brings two units of happiness to each of five people and policy Y brings nine units of happiness to one person, one unit each to two others, and none to the remaining two, then Y is to be preferred (eleven units of happiness versus ten), even though it distributes that happiness very unequally.

Worse still from the critic's point of view, utilitarianism may even require that some people's happiness be sacrificed in order to achieve the greatest overall amount of happiness. Sometimes the general utility may be served only at the expense of a single individual or group. Under the right of eminent domain, for example, the government may appropriate private property for public use, usually with compensation to the owner. Thus, the government may legally purchase your house from you to widen a highway—even if you don't want to sell the house or want more money than the government is willing to pay. The public interest is served at your private expense. Is this just?

Or consider the Dan River experiment, part of the long-running controversy over the cause of brown lung disease. Claiming that the disease is caused by the inhalation of microscopic fibers in cotton dust, textile unions fought for years for tough regulations to protect their workers. The Occupational Safety and Health Administration (OSHA) responded by proposing cotton dust standards, which would require many firms to install expensive new equipment. A few months before the deadline for installing the equipment, officials at Dan River textile plants in Virginia asked the state to waive the requirements for a time so the company could conduct an experiment to determine the precise cause of brown lung disease. Both the state and the Department of Labor allowed the extension. In response, the Amalgamated Clothing and Textile Workers Union asked OSHA to stop the proposed project, charging, "It is simply unconscionable to allow hundreds of cotton mill workers to continue to face a high risk of developing brown lung disease."[4]

Suppose that the Dan River project does expose workers to a "high risk" of contracting lung disease. If so, then a small group of individuals—633 textile workers at ten locations in Danville, Virginia—are being compelled to carry the burden of isolating the cause of brown lung disease. Is this just?

Although their critics would say no, utilitarians would respond that it is, if the experiment maximizes the total good of society. Does it? If the project succeeds in identifying the exact cause of the disease, then thousands of textile workers across the country and perhaps around the world will benefit. Researchers might also discover a more economical way to ensure worker safety, which in turn would yield a consumer benefit: more economical textiles than the ones produced if the industry installs expensive new equipment. Certainly, utilitarians would introduce the potential negative impact on workers at Dan River, but merely as one effect among many others. After the interests of all affected parties are equally weighed, if extending the deadline would likely yield the greatest net utility, then doing so is just—despite the fact that workers may be injured. (This discussion is not intended to justify the project or to foreclose a fuller utilitarian analysis of the case but merely to illustrate generally the utilitarian approach.)

The Interplay Between Self-Interest and Utility

Both self-interest and utility play important roles in organizational decisions, and the views of many businesspeople blend these two theories. To the extent that each business pursues its own interests and each businessperson tries to maximize personal success, business practice can be called egoistic. But business practice is also utilitarian in that pursuing self-interest is thought to maximize the total good, and playing by the established rules of the competitive game is seen as advancing the good of society as a whole. The classical capitalist economist Adam Smith (1723–1790) held such a view. He argued that if business is left to pursue its self-interest, the good of society will be served. Indeed, Smith believed that only through egoistic pursuits could the greatest economic good for the whole society be produced. The essence of Smith's position can be seen in the following passage from *The Wealth of Nations* (1776), in which Smith underscores the interplay between self-interest and the social good and between egoism and utilitarianism:

> Every individual is continually exerting himself to find out the most advantageous employment for whatever capital he can command. It is his own advantage, indeed, and not that of the society, which he has in view. But the study of his own advantage, naturally, or rather necessarily, leads him to prefer that employment which is most advantageous to the society. . . .
>
> As every individual, therefore, endeavours as much as he can . . . to employ his capital . . . [so] that its produce may be of the greatest value, every individual necessarily labors to render the annual revenue of the society as great as he can. He generally, indeed, neither intends to promote the public interest, nor knows how much he is promoting it. . . . He intends only his own security; and by directing that industry in such a manner as its product may be of the greatest value, he intends only his own gain, and he is in this, as in many other cases, led by an invisible hand to promote an end which was no part of his intention. Nor is it always the worse for the society that it was no part of it. By pursuing his own interest he frequently promotes that of the society more effectually than when he really intends to promote it. I

have never known much good done by those who affected to trade for the public good. It is an affectation, indeed, not very common among merchants, and very few words need be employed in dissuading them from it.[5]

Many today would agree with Smith,* conceding that business is part of a social system, that cooperation is necessary, and that certain competitive ground rules are needed and should be followed. At the same time, they would argue that the social system is best served by the active pursuit of self-interest within the context of established rules. Thus, the position these individuals recommend has been dubbed the ethics of "restrained egoism." It is egoistic because it recommends the pursuit of self-interest; it is restrained because it permits pursuit of self-interest only within the rules of business practice.[6]

KANT'S ETHICS

Most of us find the ideal of promoting human happiness and well-being an attractive one and, as a result, admire greatly people like Mother Teresa (1910–1997), who devoted her life to working with the poor. Despite the attractiveness of this ideal, many moral philosophers are critical of utilitarianism—particularly because, like egoism, it reduces all morality to a concern with consequences. Although nonconsequentialist normative theories vary significantly, adopting different approaches and stressing different themes, the writings of the preeminent German philosopher Immanuel Kant (1724–1804) provide an excellent example of a thoroughly nonconsequentialist approach to ethics. Perhaps few thinkers today would endorse Kant's theory on every point, but his work has greatly influenced subsequent philosophers and has helped shape our general moral culture.

Kant sought moral principles that do not rest on contingencies and that define actions as inherently right or wrong apart from any particular circumstances. He believed that moral rules can,

---

*Chapter 4 examines Smith's position in more detail.

in principle, be known as a result of reason alone and are not based on observation (as are, for example, scientific judgments). In contrast to utilitarianism and other consequentialist doctrines, Kant's ethical theory holds that we do not have to know anything about the likely results of, say, my telling a lie to my boss in order to know that it is immoral. "The basis of obligation," Kant wrote, "must not be sought in human nature, [nor] in the circumstances of the world." Rather it is *a priori,* by which he meant that moral reasoning is not based on factual knowledge and that reason by itself can reveal the basic principles of morality.

Good Will

Chapter 1 mentioned Good Samaritan laws, which shield from lawsuits those rendering emergency aid. Such laws, in effect, give legal protection to the humanitarian impulse behind emergency interventions. They formally recognize that the interventionist's heart was in the right place, that the person's intention was irreproachable. And because the person acted from right intention, he or she should not be held liable for any inadvertent harm except in cases of extreme negligence. The widely observable human tendency to introduce a person's intentions in assigning blame or praise is a good springboard for engaging Kant's ethics.

Nothing, said Kant, is good in itself except a good will. This does not mean that intelligence, courage, self-control, health, happiness, and other things are not good and desirable. But Kant believed that their goodness depends on the will that makes use of them. Intelligence, for instance, is not good when used by an evil person.

By *will* Kant meant the uniquely human capacity to act from principle. Contained in the notion of good will is the concept of duty: Only when we act from duty does our action have moral worth. When we act only out of feeling, inclination, or self-interest, our actions— although they may be otherwise identical with ones that spring from the sense of duty—have no true moral worth.

Suppose that you're a clerk in a small stop-and-go store. Late one night a customer pays for his five-dollar purchase with a twenty-dollar bill, which you mistake for a ten. It's only after the customer leaves that you realize you short-changed him. You race out the front door and find him lingering by a vending machine. You give him the ten dollars with your apologies, and he thanks you profusely.

Can we say with certainty that you acted from a good will? Not necessarily. You may have acted from a desire to promote business or to avoid legal entanglement. If so, you would have acted in accordance with, but not from, duty. Your apparently virtuous gesture just happened to coincide with duty. According to Kant, if you do not will the action from a sense of your duty to be fair and honest, your action does not have true moral worth. Actions have true moral worth only when they spring from a recognition of duty and a choice to discharge it.

But then what determines our duty? How do we know what morality requires of us? Kant answered these questions by formulating what he called the "categorical imperative." This extraordinarily significant moral concept is the linchpin of Kant's ethics.

The Categorical Imperative

We have seen that egoists and utilitarians allow factual circumstances or empirical data to determine moral judgments. In contrast, Kant believed that reason alone can yield a moral law. We need not rely on empirical evidence relating to consequences and to similar situations. Just as we know, seemingly through reason alone, such abstract truths as "Every change must have a cause," so we can arrive at absolute moral truth through nonempirical reasoning, and thereby discover our duty.

For Kant, an absolute moral truth must be logically consistent, free from internal contradiction. For example, it is a contradiction to say that an effect does not have a cause. Kant aimed to ensure that his absolute moral law would avoid such contradictions. If he could formulate such a rule, he maintained, everyone would be obliged to follow it without exception.

Kant believed that there is just one command (imperative) that is categorical—that is necessarily binding on all rational agents, regardless of any other considerations. From this one categorical imperative, this universal command, we can derive all commands of duty. Kant's *categorical imperative* says that we should always act in such a way that we can will the maxim of our action to become a universal law. So Kant's answer to the question "What determines whether an act is right?" is that an act is morally right if and only if we can will it to become a universal law of conduct.

The obvious and crucial question that arises here is, "When are we justified in saying that the maxim of our action can become a universal law of conduct?"

By *maxim,* Kant meant the subjective principle of an action, the principle (or rule) that people in effect formulate in determining their conduct. For example, suppose building contractor Martin promises to install a sprinkler system in a project but is willing to break that promise to suit his purposes. His maxim can be expressed this way: "I'll make promises that I'll break whenever keeping them no longer suits my purposes." This is the subjective principle, the maxim, that directs his action.

Kant insisted that the morality of any maxim depends on whether we can logically will it to become a universal law. Could Martin's maxim be universally acted on? That depends on whether the maxim as law would involve a contradiction. The maxim "I'll make promises that I'll break whenever keeping them no longer suits my purposes" could not be universally acted on because it involves a contradiction of will. On the one hand, Martin is willing that it be possible to make promises and have them honored. On the other, if everyone intended to break promises when they so desired, then promises would not be honored in the first place, because it is in the nature of promises that they be believed. A law that allowed promise breaking would contradict the very nature of a promise.

Similarly, a law that allowed lying would contradict the very nature of serious communication, for the activity of serious communication (as opposed to joking) requires that participants intend to speak the truth. I cannot, without contradiction, will both serious conversation and lying. By contrast, there is no problem, Kant thinks, in willing promise keeping or truth telling to be universal laws.

Consider, as another example, Kant's account of a man who, in despair after suffering a series of major setbacks, contemplates suicide. While still rational, the man asks whether it would be contrary to his duty to take his own life. Could the maxim of his action become a universal law of nature? Kant thinks not:

> His maxim is this: From self-love I make it my principle to shorten my life when its continued duration threatens more evil than it promises satisfaction. There only remains the question whether this principle of self-love can become a universal law of nature. One sees at once a contradiction in a system of nature whose law would destroy life by means of the very same feeling that acts so as to stimulate the furtherance of life. . . . Therefore, such a maxim cannot possibly hold as a universal law of nature and is, consequently, wholly inconsistent with the supreme principle of all duty.[7]

When Kant insists that a moral rule be consistently universalizable, he is saying that moral rules prescribe categorically, not hypothetically. A hypothetical prescription tells us what to do if we desire a particular outcome. Thus, "If I want people to like me, I should be nice to them" and "If you want to go to medical school, you must take biology" are hypothetical imperatives. They tell us what we must do on the assumption that we have some particular goal. If that is what we want, then this is what we must do. On the other hand, if we don't want to go to medical school, then the command to take biology does not apply to us. In contrast, Kant's imperative is categorical—it commands unconditionally. That is, it is necessarily binding on everyone, regardless of his or her specific goals or desires, regardless of consequences. A categorical imperative takes the form of "Do this" or "Don't do that"—no ifs, ands, or buts.

Universal Acceptability. There is another way of looking at the categorical imperative. Each person, through his or her own acts of will, legislates the moral law. The moral rules that we obey are not imposed on us from the outside. They are self-imposed and self-recognized, fully internalized principles. The sense of duty that we obey comes from within; it is an expression of our own higher selves.

Thus, moral beings give themselves the moral law and accept its demands on themselves. But that is not to say we can prescribe anything we want, for we are bound by reason and its demands. Because reason is the same for all rational beings, we all give ourselves the same moral law. In other words, when you answer the question "What should I do?" you must consider what all rational beings should do. If the moral law is valid for you, it must be valid for all other rational beings.

To see whether a rule or principle is a moral law, we can thus ask if what the rule commands would be acceptable to all rational beings acting rationally. In considering lying, theft, or murder, for example, you must consider the act not only from your own viewpoint but from the perspective of the person lied to, robbed, or murdered. Presumably, rational beings do not want to be lied to, robbed, or murdered. The test of the morality of a rule, then, is not whether people in fact accept it but whether all rational beings thinking rationally would accept it regardless of whether they are the doers or the receivers of the actions. This is an important moral insight, and most philosophers see it as implicit in Kant's discussion of the categorical imperative, even though Kant (whose writings are difficult to understand) did not make the point in this form.

The principle of universal acceptability has important applications. Suppose a man advocates a hiring policy that discriminates against women. For this rule to be universally acceptable, the man would have to be willing to accept it if he were a woman, something he would presumably be unwilling to do. Or suppose the manufacturer of a product decides to market it even though the manufacturer knows that the product is unsafe when used in a certain common way and that consumers are ignorant of this fact. Applying the universal acceptability principle, the company's decision makers would have to be willing to advocate marketing the product even if they were themselves in the position of uninformed consumers. Presumably they would be unwilling to do this. So the rule that would allow the product to be marketed would fail the test of universal acceptability.

Humanity as an End, Never as Merely a Means. In addition to the principle of universal acceptability, Kant explicitly offered another, very famous way of formulating the core idea of his categorical imperative. According to this formulation, rational creatures should always treat other rational creatures as ends in themselves and never as only means to ends. This formulation underscores Kant's belief that every human being has an inherent worth resulting from the sheer possession of rationality. We must always act in a way that respects this humanity in others and in ourselves.

As rational beings, humans would act inconsistently if they did not treat everyone else the way they themselves would want to be treated. Here we see shades of the Golden Rule. Indeed, Kant's moral philosophy can be viewed as a profound reconsideration of this basic nonconsequentialist principle. Because rational beings recognize their own inner worth, they would never wish to be used as entities possessing worth only as means to an end.

Thus, when brokers at the Dallas office of Prudential Securities encouraged unnecessary buying and selling of stocks in order to reap a commission (a practice called "churning"), they were treating their clients simply as a means and not respecting them as persons, as ends in themselves.[8] Likewise, Kant would object to using patients as subjects in a medical experiment without their consent. Even though great social benefit might result, the researchers would intentionally be using the patients solely as a means to the researchers' own goals and thus would be failing to respect the patients' basic humanity.

Kant maintained, as explained first, that an action is morally right if and only if we can will it to be a universal law. We now have two ways of reformulating his categorical imperative that may be easier to grasp and apply:

First reformulation: An action is only right if the agent would be willing to be so treated were the positions of the parties reversed.

Second reformulation: One must always act so as to treat other people as ends in themselves.

Kant in an Organizational Context

Like utilitarianism, Kant's moral theory has application for organizations.

First, the categorical imperative gives us firm rules to follow in moral decision making, rules that do not depend on circumstances or results and that do not permit individual exceptions. No matter what the consequences may be or who does it, some actions are always wrong. Lying is an example: No matter how much good may come from misrepresenting a product, such deliberate misrepresentation is always wrong. Similarly, one cannot justify exposing uninformed children to the risk of hepatitis on the grounds that it advances medical knowledge.

Second, Kant introduces an important humanistic dimension into business decisions. One of the principal objections to egoism and utilitarianism is that they permit us to treat humans as means to ends. Kant's principles clearly forbid this. Many would say that respect for the inherent worth and dignity of human beings is much needed today in business, in which encroaching technology and computerization tend to dehumanize people under the guise of efficiency. Kant's theory puts the emphasis of organizational decision making where it belongs: on individuals. Organizations, after all, involve human beings working in concert to provide goods and services for other human beings. The primacy Kant gives the individual reflects this essential aspect of business.

Third, Kant stresses the importance of motivation and of acting on principle. According to Kant, it is not enough just to do the right thing; an action has moral worth only if it is done from a sense of duty—that is, from a desire to do the right thing for its own sake. The importance of this point is too often forgotten. Sometimes when individuals and organizations believe that an action promotes the interests of everyone, they are actually rationalizing—doing what is best for themselves and only imagining that somehow it will also benefit others. Worse still, they may defend their actions as morally praiseworthy when, in fact, they are only behaving egoistically. They wouldn't do the morally justifiable thing if they didn't think it would pay off for them. By stressing the importance of motivation, a Kantian approach serves as a corrective to this. Even an action that helps others has moral value for Kant only if the person doing it is morally motivated—that is, acting on principle or out of moral conviction.

Critical Inquiries of Kant's Ethics

1. *What has moral worth?* According to Kant, the clerk who returns the ten dollars to the customer is doing the right thing. But if his action is motivated by self-interest (perhaps he wants to get a reputation for honesty), then it does not have moral worth. That seems plausible. But Kant also held that if the clerk does the right thing out of instinct, habit, or sympathy for the other person, then the act still does not have moral worth. Only if it is done out of a sense of duty does the clerk's action have moral value. Many moral theorists have felt that Kant was too severe on this point. Do we really want to say that giving money to famine relief efforts has no moral worth if one is emotionally moved to do so by pictures of starving children rather than by a sense of duty? We might, to the contrary, find a person with strong human sympathies no less worthy or admirable than the person who gives solely out of an abstract sense of duty.

2. *Is the categorical imperative an adequate test of right?* Kant said that a moral rule must function without exception. Critics wonder why the prohibition against such actions as lying, promise breaking, suicide, and so on must be exceptionless. They say that Kant failed to distinguish between saying that a person should not except himself or herself from a rule and that the rule itself has no exceptions.

If stealing is wrong, it's wrong for me as well as for you. "Stealing is wrong, except if I do it" is not universalizable, for then stealing would be right for all to do, which contradicts the assertion that stealing is wrong. But just because no one may make of oneself an exception to a rule, it does not follow that the rule itself has no exceptions.

Suppose, for example, that we decide that stealing is sometimes right, perhaps in the case of a person who is starving. Thus, the rule becomes "Never steal except when starving." This rule seems just as universalizable as "Never steal." The phrase "except . . ." can be viewed not as justifying a violation of the rule but as building a qualification into it. Critics in effect are asking why a qualified rule is not just as good as an unqualified one. If it is, then we no longer need to state rules in the simple, direct, unqualified manner that Kant did.

In fairness to Kant, it could be argued that his universalization formula can be interpreted flexibly enough to meet commonsense objections. For example, perhaps we could universalize the principle that individuals should steal rather than starve to death or that it is permissible to take one's own life to extinguish unspeakable pain. And yet to qualify the rules against stealing, lying, and taking one's life seems to invite a non-Kantian analysis to justify the exceptions. One could, it seems, universalize more than one moral rule in a given situation: "Do not lie unless a life is at stake" versus "Lying is wrong unless necessary to avoid the suffering of innocent people." If so, then the categorical imperative would supply at best a necessary, but not a sufficient, test of right. But once we start choosing among various alternative rules, then we are

adopting an approach to ethics that Kant would have rejected.

3. *What does it mean to treat people as means?* Kant's mandate that individuals must always be considered as ends in themselves and never merely as means expresses our sense of the intrinsic value of the human spirit and has profound moral appeal. Yet it is not always clear when people are being treated as ends and when merely as means. For example, Kant believed that prostitution is immoral because, by selling their sexual services, prostitutes allow themselves to be treated as means. Prostitutes, however, are not the only ones to sell their services. Anyone who works for a wage does so. Does that mean that we are all being treated immorally, because our employers are presumably hiring us as a means to advance their own ends? Presumably not, because we freely agreed to do the work. But then the prostitute might have freely chosen that line of work, too.

OTHER NONCONSEQUENTIALIST PERSPECTIVES

For Kant, the categorical imperative provided the basic test of right and wrong, and he was resolutely nonconsequentialist in his application of it. You know now what he would say about the case of the deathbed promise: The maxim permitting you to break your promise cannot be universalized, and hence it would be immoral of you to give the money to the orphanage, despite the happiness that doing so would bring. But nonconsequentialists are not necessarily Kantians, and several different nonutilitarian moral concerns emerged in the discussion of the deathbed promise example.

Critics of act utilitarianism believe that it is faulty for maintaining that we have one and only one moral duty. A utilitarian might follow various principles as rules of thumb, but they are only calculation substitutes. All that matters morally to utilitarians is the maximization of happiness. Yet this idea, many philosophers think, fails to do justice to the richness and complexity of our moral lives.

Prima Facie Principles

One influential philosopher who argued this way was the British scholar W. D. Ross (1877–1971).[9] Ross rejected utilitarianism as too simple and as untrue to the way we ordinarily think about morality and about our moral obligations. We see ourselves, Ross and like-minded thinkers contend, as being under various moral duties that cannot be reduced to the single obligation to maximize happiness. Often these obligations grow out of special relationships into which we enter or out of determinate roles that we undertake. Our lives are intertwined with other people's in particular ways, and we have, as a result, certain specific moral obligations.

For example, as a professor, Rodriguez is obligated to assist her students in the learning process and to evaluate their work in a fair and educationally productive way—obligations to the specific people in her classroom that she does not have to other people. As a spouse, Rodriguez must maintain a certain emotional and sexual fidelity to her partner. As a parent, she must provide for the individual human beings who are her children. As a friend to Smith, she may have a moral responsibility to help him out in a time of crisis. Having borrowed money from Chang, Rodriguez is morally obligated to pay it back. Thus, different relationships and different circumstances generate a variety of specific moral obligations.

In addition, we have moral duties that do not arise from our unique interactions and relationships with other people. For example, we ought to treat all people fairly, do what we can to remedy injustices, and make an effort to promote human welfare generally. The latter obligation is important, but for a nonconsequentialist like Ross it is only one among various obligations that people have.

At any given time, we are likely to be under more than one obligation, and sometimes these obligations can conflict. That is, we may have an obligation to do *A* and an obligation to do *B*, where it is not possible for us to do both *A* and *B*. For example, I promise to meet a friend on an urgent matter, and now, as I am hurrying there, I pass an injured person who is obviously in need of assistance. Stopping to aid the person will make it impossible for me to fulfill my promise. What should I do? For moral philosophers like Ross, there is no single answer for all cases. What I ought to do will depend on the circumstances and relative importance of the conflicting obligations. I have an obligation to keep my promise, and I have an obligation to assist people in distress. What I must decide is which of these obligations is, in the given circumstance, the more important. I must weigh the moral significance of the promise against the comparative moral urgency of assisting the injured person.

Ross and many contemporary philosophers believe that all (or at least most) of our moral obligations are prima facie ones. A *prima facie obligation* is an obligation that can be overridden by a more important obligation. For instance, we take the keeping of promises seriously, but almost everyone would agree that in some circumstances—for example, when a life is at stake—it would be not only morally permissible, but morally required, to break a promise. Our obligation to keep a promise is a real one, and if there is no conflicting obligation, then we must keep the promise. But that obligation is not absolute or categorical; it could in principle be outweighed by a more stringent moral obligation. The idea that our obligations are prima facie is foreign to Kant's way of looking at things.

Consider an example that Kant himself discussed.[10] Imagine that a murderer comes to your door, wanting to know where your friend is so that he can kill her. Your friend is in fact hiding in your bedroom closet. Most people would probably agree that your obligation to your friend overrides your general obligation to tell the truth and that the right thing to do would be to lie to the murderer to throw him off your friend's trail. Although you have a genuine obligation to tell the truth, it is a prima facie obligation, one that other moral considerations can outweigh. Kant disagreed. He maintained that you must always tell the truth—that is, in all circumstances and without exception. For him, telling the truth is an absolute or categorical obligation, not a prima facie one.

Ross thought that our various prima facie obligations could be divided into seven basic types: duties of fidelity (that is, to respect explicit and implicit promises), duties of reparation (for previous wrongful acts), duties of gratitude, duties of justice, duties of beneficence (that is, to make the condition of others better), duties of self-improvement, and duties not to injure others.[11] Unlike utilitarianism, Ross's ethical perspective is pluralistic in recognizing a variety of genuine obligations. But contrary to Kant, Ross does not see these obligations as absolute and exceptionless. On both points, Ross contended that his view of morality more closely fits with our actual moral experience and the way we view our moral obligations.

Ross also saw himself as siding with common-sense morality in maintaining that our prima facie obligations are obvious. He believed that the basic principles of duty are as self-evident as the simplest rules of arithmetic and that any person who has reached the age of reason can discern that it is wrong to lie, to break promises, and to injure people needlessly. However, what we should do, all things considered, when two or more prima facie obligations conflict is often difficult to judge. In deciding what to do in any concrete situation, Ross thought, we are always "taking a moral risk."[12] Even after the fullest reflection, judgments about which of these self-evident rules should govern our conduct are only "more or less probable opinions which are not logically justified conclusions from the general principles that are recognised as self-evident."[13]

Assisting Others

Nonconsequentialists believe that utilitarianism presents too simple a picture of our moral world. In addition, they worry that utilitarianism risks making us all slaves to the maximization of total happiness. Stop and think about it: Isn't there something that you could be doing—for instance, volunteering at the local hospital or orphanage, collecting money for Third World development, helping the homeless—that would do more for the general good than what you are doing now or are planning to do tonight or tomorrow? Sure, working with the homeless might not bring you quite as much pleasure as what you would otherwise be doing, but if it would nonetheless maximize total happiness, then you are morally required to do it. However, by following this reasoning, you could end up working around the clock, sacrificing yourself for the greater good. This notion seems mistaken.

Most nonutilitarian philosophers, like Ross, believe that we have some obligation to promote the general welfare, but they typically view this obligation as less stringent than, for example, the obligation not to injure people. They see us as having a much stronger obligation to refrain from violating people's rights than to promote their happiness or well-being.

From this perspective, a manufacturing company's obligation not to violate OSHA regulations and thereby endanger the safety of its employees is stronger than its obligation to open up daycare facilities for their children, even though the cost of both is the same. The company, in other words, has a stronger duty to respect its contractual and legal employment-related obligations than to promote its employees' happiness in other ways. Likewise, for a company to violate people's rights by despoiling the environment through the discharge of pollutants would be morally worse than for it to decide not to expand a job training program in the inner city, even if expanding the program would bring about more total good.

Different nonutilitarian philosophers may weight these particular obligations differently, depending on their particular moral theory. But they typically believe that we have a stronger duty not to violate people's rights or in some other way injure them than we do to assist people or otherwise promote their well-being.

A utilitarian, concerned solely with what will maximize happiness, is less inclined to draw such a distinction.

Many moral philosophers draw a related distinction between actions that are morally required and charitable or *supererogatory* actions—that is, actions that it would be good to do but not immoral not to do. Act utilitarianism does not make this distinction. While we admire Mother Teresa and Albert Schweitzer for devoting their lives to doing good works among the poor, we see them as acting above and beyond the call of duty; we do not expect so much from ordinary people. Yet people who are not moral heroes or who fall short of sainthood may nonetheless be living morally satisfactory lives.

Nonutilitarian theorists see the distinction between morally obligatory actions and supererogatory actions not so much as a realistic concession to human weakness but as a necessary demarcation if we are to avoid becoming enslaved to the maximization of the general welfare. The idea here is that each of us should have a sphere in which to pursue our own plans and goals, to carve out a distinctive life plan. These plans and goals are limited by various moral obligations, in particular by other people's rights, but the demands of morality are not all-encompassing.

Moral Rights

What, then, are rights, and what rights do people have? Broadly defined, a *right* is an entitlement to act or have others act in a certain way. The connection between rights and duties is that, generally speaking, if you have a right to do something, then someone else has a correlative duty to act in a certain way. For example, if you claim a "right" to drive, you mean that you are entitled to drive or that others should—that is, have a duty to—permit you to drive. Your right to drive under certain conditions is derived from our legal system and is thus considered a *legal right*.

In addition to rights that are derived from some specific legal system, we also have *moral rights*. Some of these moral rights derive from special relationships, roles, or circumstances in which we happen to be. For example, if Tom has an obligation to return Bob's car to him on Saturday morning, then Bob has a right to have Tom return his car. If I have agreed to water your plants while you are on vacation, you have a right to expect me to look after them in your absence. As a student, you have a right to be graded fairly, and so on.

Even more important are rights that do not rest on special relationships, roles, or situations. For example, the rights to life, free speech, and unhampered religious affiliation are widely accepted, not just as the entitlements of some specific political or legal system but as fundamental moral rights. More controversial, but often championed as moral rights, are the rights to medical care, decent housing, education, and work. Moral rights that are not the result of particular roles, special relationships, or specific circumstances are called *human rights*. They have several important characteristics.

First, human rights are universal. For instance, if the right to life is a human right, as most of us believe it is, then everyone, everywhere, and at all times, has that right. By contrast, there is nothing universal about your right that I keep my promise to help you move or about my right to drive 65 miles per hour on certain roads.

Second, and closely related, human rights are equal rights. If the right to free speech is a human right, then everyone has this right equally. No one has a greater right to free speech than anyone else. In contrast, your daughter has a greater right than do the daughters of other people to your emotional and financial support.

Third, human rights are not transferable, nor can they be relinquished. If we have a fundamental human right, we cannot give, lend, or sell it to someone else. We cannot waive it, and no one can take it from us. That is what is meant in the Declaration of Independence when certain rights—namely, life, liberty, and the pursuit of happiness—are described as "unalienable." By comparison, legal rights can be renounced or transferred, as when one party sells another a house or a business.

Fourth, human rights are natural rights, not in the sense that they can be derived from a study of human nature, but in the sense that they do not depend on human institutions the way legal rights do. If people have human rights, they have these rights simply because they are human beings. They do not have them because they live under a certain legal system. Human rights rest on the assumption that people have certain basic moral entitlements merely on the basis of their humanity. No authoritative body assigns them human rights. The law may attempt to protect human rights, to make them explicit and safe through codification, but the law is not their source.

Rights, and in particular human rights, can be divided into two broad categories: negative rights and positive rights. *Negative rights* reflect the vital interests that human beings have in being free from outside interference. The rights guaranteed in the Bill of Rights—freedom of speech, assembly, religion, and so on—fall within this category, as do the rights to freedom from injury and to privacy. Correlating with these are duties that we all have not to interfere with others' pursuit of these interests and activities. *Positive rights* reflect the vital interests that human beings have in receiving certain benefits. They are rights to have others provide us with certain goods, services, or opportunities. Today, positive rights often are taken to include the rights to education, medical care, a decent neighborhood, equal job opportunity, comparable pay, and so on. Correlating with these are positive duties for appropriate parties to assist individuals in their pursuit of these interests.

Thus a child's right to education implies not just that no one should interfere with the child's education but also that the necessary resources for that education ought to be provided. In the case of some positive rights—for example, the right to a decent standard of living, as proclaimed by the United Nations' 1948 Human Rights Charter—who exactly has the duty to provide the goods and services required to fulfill

those rights is unclear. Also, interpreting a right as negative or positive is sometimes controversial. For example, is my right to liberty simply the right not to be interfered with as I live my own life, or does it also imply a duty on the part of others to provide me with the means to make the exercise of that liberty meaningful?

The significance of positing moral rights is that they provide grounds for making moral judgments that differ radically from utilitarianism's grounds. Once moral rights are asserted, the locus of moral judgment becomes the individual, not society. For example, if every potential human research subject has a moral right to be fully informed about the nature of a medical experiment and the moral right to decide freely for himself or herself whether to participate, then it is wrong to violate these rights—even if, by so doing, the common good would be served. Again, if workers have a right to compensation equal to what others receive for doing comparable work, then they cannot be paid less on the grounds that this will maximize total well-being. And if everyone has a right to equal consideration for a job regardless of color or sex, then sex and color cannot be introduced merely because so doing will result in greater net utility.

Utilitarianism, in effect, treats all such entitlements as subordinate to the general welfare. Thus, individuals are entitled to act in a certain way and entitled to have others allow or aid them to so act only insofar as acknowledging this right or entitlement achieves the greatest good. The assertion of moral rights, therefore, decisively sets nonconsequentialists apart from utilitarians.

Nonconsequentialism in an Organizational Context

We have already looked at Kant's ethics in an organizational context, but the themes of the other nonconsequentialist approaches also have important implications for moral decision making in business and nonbusiness organizations.

First, in its non-Kantian forms nonconsequentialism stresses that moral decision making involves the weighing of different moral factors and considerations. Unlike utilitarianism, nonconsequentialism does not reduce morality solely to the calculation of consequences; rather, it recognizes that an organization must usually take into account other equally important moral concerns. Theorists like Ross emphasize that, contrary to what Kant believed, there can often be rival and even conflicting obligations on an organization. For example, obligations to employees, stockholders, and consumers may pull the corporation in different directions, and determining the organization's proper moral course may not be easy.

Second, nonconsequentialism acknowledges that the organization has its own legitimate goals to pursue. There are limits to the demands of morality, and an organization that fulfills its moral obligations and respects the relevant rights of individuals is morally free to advance whatever (morally permissible) ends it has—public service, profit, government administration, and so on. Contrary to utilitarianism, organizations and the people in them need not see themselves as under an overarching obligation to seek continually to enhance the general welfare.

Third, nonconsequentialism stresses the importance of moral rights. Moral rights, and in particular human rights, are a crucial factor in most moral deliberations, including those of organizations. Before it acts, any morally responsible business or nonbusiness organization must consider carefully how its actions will impinge on the rights of individuals—not just the rights of its members, such as stockholders and employees, but also the rights of others, such as consumers. Moral rights place distinct and firm constraints on what sorts of things an organization can do to fulfill its own ends.

Critical Inquiries of Nonconsequentialism

1. *How well justified are these nonconsequentialist principles and moral rights?* Ross maintained that we have immediate intuitive knowledge of the basic prima facie moral principles, and indeed it would seem absurd to try to deny that it is wrong to cause needless suffering or that making a promise imposes some obligation to keep it. Only someone the moral equivalent of colorblind could fail to see the truth of these statements; to reject them would seem as preposterous as denying some obvious fact of arithmetic—for example, that $12 + 4 = 16$. Likewise, it appears obvious—indeed, as Thomas Jefferson wrote, "self-evident"—that human beings have certain basic and inalienable rights, unconditional rights that do not depend on the decrees of any particular government.

Yet we must be careful. What seems obvious, even self-evident, to one culture or at one time in human history may turn out to be not only not self-evident but actually false. That the earth is flat and that heavier objects fall faster than lighter ones were two "truths" taken as obvious in former centuries. Likewise, the inferiority of women and of various nonwhite races was long taken for granted; this supposed fact was so obvious that it was hardly even commented on. The idea that people have a right to practice a religion that the majority "knows" to be false—or, indeed, to practice no religion whatsoever—would have seemed morally scandalous to many of our forebears and is still not embraced in all countries today. Today, many vegetarians eschew meat eating on moral grounds and contend that future generations will consider our treatment of animals, factory farming in particular, to be as morally benighted as slavery. So what seems obvious, self-evident, or simple common sense may not be the most reliable guide to morally sound principles.

2. *Can nonconsequentialists satisfactorily handle conflicting rights and principles?* People today disagree among themselves about the correctness of certain moral principles. Claims of right, as we have seen, are often controversial. For example, do employees have a moral right to their jobs—an entitlement to be fired only with just cause? To some of us, it may seem obvious that they do; to others, perhaps not. And how are we to settle various conflicting claims of right? Jones, for instance, claims a right to her property, which she has acquired honestly through her labors; that is, she claims a right to do with it as she wishes. Smith is ill and claims adequate medical care as a human right. Because he cannot afford the care himself, acknowledging his right will probably involve taxing people like Jones and thus limiting their property rights.

To sum up these two points: First, even the deliverances of moral common sense have to be examined critically; and second, nonconsequentialists should not rest content until they find a way of resolving disputes among conflicting prima facie principles or rights. This is not to suggest that nonconsequentialists cannot find deeper and theoretically more satisfactory ways of grounding moral claims and of handling disputes between them. The point to be underscored here is simply the necessity of doing so.

UTILITARIANISM ONCE MORE

Until now, the discussion of utilitarianism has focused on its most classic and straightforward form, called act utilitarianism. According to act utilitarianism, we have one and only one moral obligation, the maximization of happiness for everyone concerned, and every action is to be judged according to how well it lives up to this principle. But a different utilitarian approach, called rule utilitarianism, is relevant to the discussion of the moral concerns characteristic of nonconsequentialism—in particular, relevant to the nonconsequentialist's criticisms of act utilitarianism. The rule utilitarian would, in fact, agree with many of these criticisms. (Rule utilitarianism has been formulated in different ways, but this discussion follows the version defended by Richard Brandt.)

Rule utilitarianism maintains that the utilitarian standard should be applied not to individual actions but to moral codes as a whole. The rule utilitarian asks what moral code (that is, what

set of moral rules) a society should adopt to maximize happiness. The principles that make up that code would then be the basis for distinguishing right actions from wrong actions. As Brandt explains:

> A rule-utilitarian thinks that right actions are the kind permitted by the moral code optimal for the society of which the agent is a member. An optimal code is one designed to maximize welfare or what is good (thus, utility). This leaves open the possibility that a particular right act by itself may not maximize benefit. . . . On the rule-utilitarian view, then, to find what is morally right or wrong we need to find which actions would be permitted by a moral system that is "optimal" for the agent's society.[14]

The "optimal" moral code does not refer to the set of rules that would do the most good if everyone conformed to them all the time. The meaning is more complex. The optimal moral code must take into account what rules can reasonably be taught and obeyed, as well as the costs of inculcating those rules in people. Recall from Chapter 1 that if a principle or rule is part of a person's moral code, then it will influence the person's behavior. The person will tend to follow that principle, to feel guilty when he or she does not follow it, and to disapprove of others who fail to conform to it. Rule utilitarians must consider not just the benefits of having people motivated to act in certain ways but also the costs of instilling those motivations in them. As Brandt writes:

> The more intense and widespread an aversion to a certain sort of behavior, the less frequent the behavior is apt to be. But the more intense and widespread, the greater the cost of teaching the rule and keeping it alive, the greater the burden on the individual, and so on.[15]

Thus, the "optimality" of a moral code encompasses both the benefits of reduced objectionable behavior and the long-term costs. Perfect compliance is not a realistic goal. "Like the law,"

Brandt continues, "the optimal moral code normally will not produce 100 percent compliance with all its rules; that would be too costly."[16]

Elements of the rule-utilitarian approach were clearly suggested by Mill himself, although he did not draw the distinction between act and rule utilitarianism. According to the rule-utilitarian perspective, we should apply the utilitarian standard only to the assessment of alternative moral codes; we should not try to apply it to individual actions. That is, we should seek to determine the specific set of principles that would in fact best promote total happiness for society. Those are the rules we should promulgate, instill in ourselves, and teach to the next generation.

What Will the Optimal Code Look Like?

Rule utilitarians such as Brandt argue strenuously that the ideal or optimal moral code for a society will not be the single act-utilitarian command to maximize happiness. They contend that teaching people that their only obligation is to maximize happiness would not in fact maximize happiness.

First, people will make mistakes if they always try to promote total happiness. Second, if all of us were act utilitarians, such practices as keeping promises and telling the truth would be rather shaky, because we would expect others to keep promises or tell the truth only when they believed that doing so would maximize happiness. Third, the act-utilitarian principle is too demanding, because it seems to imply that each person should continually be striving to promote total well-being.

For these reasons, rule utilitarians believe that more happiness will come from instilling in people a pluralistic moral code, one with a number of different principles. By analogy, imagine a traffic system with just one rule: Drive your car in a way that maximizes happiness. Such a system would be counterproductive; we do much better in terms of total human well-being to have a variety of traffic regulations—for example, obey stop signs, yield to the right, and pass only on the left. In such a pluralistic system we

cannot justify cruising through a red light with the argument that doing so maximizes total happiness by getting us home more quickly.

The principles of the optimal code would presumably be prima facie in Ross's sense—that is, capable of being overridden by other principles. Different principles would also have different moral weights. It would make sense, for example, to instill in people an aversion to killing that is stronger than the aversion to telling white lies. In addition, the ideal code would acknowledge moral rights. Teaching people to respect moral rights maximizes human welfare in the long run.

The rules of the optimal code provide the sole basis for determining right and wrong. An action is not necessarily wrong if it fails to maximize happiness; it is wrong only if it conflicts with the ideal moral code. Rule utilitarianism thus gets around many of the problems that plague act utilitarianism. At the same time, it provides a plausible basis for deciding which moral principles and rights we should acknowledge and how much weight we should attach to them. We try to determine those principles and rights that, generally adhered to, would best promote human happiness.

Still, rule utilitarianism has its critics. There are two common objections. First, act utilitarians maintain that a utilitarian who cares about happiness should be willing to violate rules in order to maximize happiness. Why make a fetish out of the rules?

Second, nonconsequentialists, while presumably viewing rule utilitarianism more favorably than act utilitarianism, still balk at seeing moral principles determined by their consequences. They contend, in particular, that rule utilitarians ultimately subordinate rights to utilitarian calculation and therefore fail to treat rights as fundamental and independent moral factors.

MORAL DECISION MAKING: TOWARD A SYNTHESIS

Theoretical controversies permeate the subject of ethics, and as we have seen, philosophers have proposed rival ways of understanding right and wrong. These philosophical differences of perspective, emphasis, and theory are significant and can have profound practical consequences. This chapter has surveyed some of these issues, but obviously it cannot settle all of the questions that divide moral philosophers. Fortunately, however, many problems of business and organizational ethics can be intelligently discussed and even resolved by people whose fundamental moral theories differ (or who have not yet worked out their own moral ideas in some systematic way). This section discusses some important points to keep in mind when analyzing and discussing business ethics and offers, as a kind of model, one possible procedure for making moral decisions.

In the abstract, it might seem impossible for people to reach agreement on controversial ethical issues, given that ethical theories differ so much and that people themselves place moral value on different things. Yet in practice moral problems are rarely so intractable that open-minded and thoughtful people cannot, by discussing matters calmly, rationally, and thoroughly, make significant progress toward resolving them. Chapter 1 stressed that moral judgments should be logical, should be based on facts, and should appeal to sound moral principles. Bearing this in mind can often help, especially when various people are discussing an issue and proposing rival answers.

First, in any moral discussion, make sure participants agree about the relevant facts. Often moral disputes hinge not on matters of moral principle but on differing assessments of what the facts of the situation are, what alternatives are open, and what the probable results of different courses of action will be. For instance, the directors of an international firm might acrimoniously dispute the moral permissibility of a new overseas investment. The conflict might appear to involve some fundamental clash of moral principles and perspectives and yet, in fact, be the result of some underlying disagreement about what effects the proposed investment will have on the lives of the local population. Until

this factual disagreement is acknowledged and dealt with, little is apt to be resolved.

Second, once there is general agreement on factual matters, try to spell out the moral principles to which different people are, at least implicitly, appealing. Seeking to determine these principles will often help people clarify their own thinking enough to reach a solution. Sometimes they will agree on what moral principles are relevant and yet disagree over how to balance them; identifying this discrepancy can itself be useful. Bear in mind, too, that skepticism is in order when someone's moral stance on an issue appears to rest simply on a hunch or intuition and cannot be related to some more general moral principle. As moral decision makers, we are seeking not just an answer to a moral issue but an answer that can be publicly defended, and the public defense of a moral judgment usually requires an appeal to general principle. By analogy, judges do not hand down judgments based simply on what strikes them as fair in a particular case. They must relate their decisions to general legal principles or statutes.

A reluctance to defend our moral decisions in public is almost always a warning sign. If we are unwilling to account for our actions publicly, chances are that we are doing something we cannot really justify morally. In addition, Kant's point that we must be willing to universalize our moral judgments is relevant here. We cannot sincerely endorse a principle if we are not willing to see it applied generally. Unfortunately, we occasionally do make judgments—for example, that Alfred's being late to work is a satisfactory reason for firing him—that rest on a principle we would be unwilling to apply to our own situations; hence, the moral relevance of the familiar question: "How would you like it if . . . ?" Looking at an issue from the other person's point of view can cure moral myopia.

Obligations, Ideals, Effects

As a practical basis for discussing moral issues in organizations, it is useful to try to approach those issues in a way that is acceptable to individuals of diverse moral viewpoints. We want to avoid as much as possible presupposing the truth of one particular theoretical perspective. By emphasizing factors that are relevant to various theories, both consequentialist and nonconsequentialist, we can find some common ground on which moral decision making can proceed. Moral dialogue can thus take place in an objective and analytical way, even if the participants do not fully agree on all philosophical issues.

What concerns, then, seem common to most ethical systems? Following Professor V. R. Ruggiero, three common concerns suggest themselves.[17] A first concern is with *obligations*. Every significant human action—personal and professional—arises in the context of human relationships. These relationships can be the source of specific duties and rights. In addition, we are obligated to respect people's human rights. Obligations bind us. In their presence, morality requires us, at least prima facie, to do certain things and to avoid doing others.

A second concern common to most ethical systems is the impact of our actions on important *ideals*. An ideal is some morally important goal, virtue, or notion of excellence worth striving for. Clearly, different cultures impart different ideals and, equally important, different ways of pursuing them. Our culture respects virtues like tolerance, compassion, and loyalty, as well as more abstract ideals like peace, justice, fairness, and respect for persons. In addition to these moral ideals, there are institutional or organizational ideals: efficiency, productivity, quality, stability, and so forth. Does a particular act serve or violate these ideals? Both consequentialists and nonconsequentialists can agree that this is an important concern in determining the moral quality of actions.

A third common consideration regards the *effects* of actions. When reflecting on a possible course of action, one needs to take into account its likely results. Although nonconsequentialists maintain that things other than consequences or results can affect the rightness or wrongness of actions, few if any of them would ignore consequences entirely. Almost all nonconsequentialist theories place some moral weight on the results of our actions.

Ruggiero isolated, then, three concerns common to almost all ethical systems: obligations, ideals, and effects. In so doing he provided a kind of practical synthesis of consequentialist and nonconsequentialist thought, which seems appropriate for our purposes. A useful approach to moral questions in an organizational context will therefore reflect these considerations: the obligations that derive from organizational relationships or are affected by organizational conduct, the ideals at stake, and the effects or consequences of alternative courses of action. Any action that honors obligations while respecting ideals and benefiting people can be presumed to be moral. An action that does not pass scrutiny in these respects will be morally suspect.

This view leads to what is essentially a two-step procedure for evaluating actions and choices. The first step is to identify the important considerations involved: obligations, ideals, and effects. Accordingly, we should ask if any basic obligations are involved. If so, what are they and who has them? What ideals does the action respect or promote? What ideals does it neglect or thwart? Who is affected by the action and how? How do these effects compare with those of the alternatives open to us? The second step is to decide which of these considerations deserves emphasis. Sometimes the issue may be largely a matter of obligations; other times, some ideal may predominate; still other times, consideration of effects may be the overriding concern.

Keep the following rough guidelines in mind when handling cases of conflicting obligations, ideals, and effects:

1. When two or more moral obligations conflict, choose the stronger one.
2. When two or more ideals conflict, or when ideals conflict with obligations, honor the more important one.
3. When rival actions will have different results, choose the action that produces the greater good or the lesser harm.

These guidelines imply that we know (1) which one of the conflicting obligations is greater, (2) which of the competing ideals is higher, and (3) which of the actions will achieve the greater good or the lesser harm. They also suggest that we have some definite way of balancing obligations, ideals, and effects when these considerations pull in different directions.

The fact is that we have no sure procedure for making such comparative determinations, which involve assessing worth and assigning relative priorities to our assessments. In large part, the chapters that follow attempt to sort out the values and principles embedded in the tangled web of frequently subtle, ill-defined problems we meet in business and organizational life. It is hoped that examining these issues will help you (1) identify the obligations, ideals, and effects involved in specific moral issues and (2) decide where the emphasis should lie among the competing considerations.

SUMMARY

1. Consequentialist moral theories see the moral rightness or wrongness of actions as a function of their results. If the consequences are good, the action is right; if they are bad, the action is wrong. Nonconsequentialist theories see other factors as also relevant to the determination of right and wrong.

2. Egoism is the consequentialist theory that an action is right when it promotes the individual's best interests. Proponents of this theory base their view on the alleged fact that human beings are, by nature, selfish (the doctrine of psychological egoism). Critics of egoism argue that (a) psychological egoism is implausible, (b) egoism is not really a moral principle, and (c) egoism ignores blatant wrongs.

3. Utilitarianism, another consequentialist theory, maintains that the morally right action is the one that provides the greatest happiness for all those affected. In an organizational context, utilitarianism provides an objective way to resolve conflicts of self-interest and encourages a realistic and result-oriented approach to moral decision making. But critics contend that (a) utilitarianism is not really workable, (b) some actions are wrong even if they produce good results, and (c) utilitarianism incorrectly overlooks considerations of justice and the distribution of happiness.

4. Kant's theory is an important example of a purely nonconsequentialist approach to ethics. Kant held that only when we act from duty does our action have moral worth. Good will is the only thing that is good in itself.

5. Kant's categorical imperative states that an action is morally right if and only if we can will that the maxim (or principle) represented by the action be a universal law. For example, a person making a promise with no intention of keeping it cannot universalize the maxim governing his action, because if everyone followed this principle, promising would make no sense. Kant believed that the categorical imperative is binding on all rational creatures, regardless of their specific goals or desires and regardless of the consequences.

6. There are two alternative formulations of the categorical imperative. The first is that an act is right only if the actor would be willing to be so treated if the positions of the parties were reversed. The second is that one must always act so as to treat other people as ends, never merely as means.

7. Kant's ethics gives us firm standards that do not depend on results; it injects a humanistic element into moral decision making and stresses the importance of acting on principle and from a sense of duty. Critics, however, worry that (a) Kant's view of moral worth is too restrictive, (b) the categorical imperative is not a sufficient test of right and wrong, and (c) distinguishing between treating people as means and respecting them as ends in themselves may be difficult in practice.

8. Other nonconsequentialist theories stress other moral themes. Philosophers such as

Ross argue, against both Kant and consequentialists, that we are under a variety of distinct moral obligations. These are prima facie, meaning that any one of them may be outweighed in some circumstances by other, more important moral considerations. Nonconsequentialists believe that a duty to assist others and to promote total happiness is only one of a number of duties incumbent on us.

9. Nonconsequentialists typically emphasize moral rights—entitlements to act in a certain way or to have others act in a certain way. These rights can rest on special relationships and roles, or they can be general human rights. Rights can be negative, protecting us from outside interference, or they can be positive, requiring others to provide us with certain benefits or opportunities.

10. In an organizational context, nonconsequentialism (in its non-Kantian forms) stresses the plurality of moral considerations to be weighed. While emphasizing the importance of respecting moral rights, it acknowledges that morality has limits and that organizations have legitimate goals to pursue. Critics question whether (a) nonconsequentialist principles are adequately justified and whether (b) nonconsequentialism can satisfactorily handle conflicting rights and principles.

11. Rule utilitarianism is a hybrid theory. It maintains that the proper principles of right and wrong are those that would maximize happiness if society adopted them. Thus, the utilitarian standard does not apply directly to individual actions but rather to the adoption of the moral principles that guide individual action. Rule utilitarianism avoids many of the standard criticisms of act utilitarianism.

12. Despite disagreements on controversial theoretical issues, people can make significant progress in resolving practical moral problems through open-minded and reflective discussion. One useful approach is to identify the (possibly conflicting) obligations, ideals, and effects in a given situation and then to identify where the emphasis should lie among these different considerations.

Baby M

One of the most controversial cases of our times began when Mary Beth Whitehead of Brick Town, New Jersey, agreed to be impregnated by artificial insemination with the sperm of a stranger and to carry his child. In other words, she agreed, like hundreds of other women in the past twenty years, to be a "surrogate mother." She was twenty-nine years old, happily married, with a son and a daughter of her own. Why did she decide to do it? Mary Beth called it "the most loving gift of happiness," but she also saw the practical side. The $10,000 she would earn would help pay for her children's education.[18]

The man who was to become the sperm-donating father of the child was William Stern, a forty-year-old biochemist. Both he and his wife, Elizabeth, a pediatrician, longed to have children of their own, but Elizabeth was diagnosed as having a mild form of multiple sclerosis, and pregnancy was felt to be risky for her. Not only is there a shortage of healthy, white babies available for adoption, but also the couple was too old to be acceptable to most adoption agencies. In any case, Stern wanted a child that was his own flesh and blood. Noel Keane, a Dearborn, Michigan, lawyer specializing in surrogacy cases, brought the Sterns together with Whitehead and her husband. They signed a contract, which Keane had drawn up.

The six-page contract was strictly business. In addition to Whitehead's fee, which was put in escrow until Stern received the baby, the Sterns paid over $10,000 in nonrefundable fees and expenses to Keane. In the contract Stern agreed to assume all legal responsibility for the baby, even if it was born with serious defects. For her part, Whitehead was required to undergo amniocentesis; if the test indicated problems, she agreed to have an abortion if Stern requested it. In the contract Mary Beth Whitehead acknowledged that the child would be conceived "for the sole purpose of giving said child to William Stern."

Noel Keane's law firm and the Infertility Center of New York (which he partly owns) have arranged hundreds of commercial surrogate births. Whitehead later claimed that Keane did not give her proper counseling, whereas he maintains that the standard psychological tests she took gave little reason to anticipate any special problems. In only two cases handled by Keane had the surrogate mothers changed their minds. This was to be the third time.

After Mary Beth Whitehead gave birth to a healthy, blond, blue-eyed little girl—called Sara by her, Melissa by the Sterns, and "Baby M" by the courts—she was overwhelmed with intense emotion. "Seeing her, holding her. She was my child," Whitehead remembers. "It overpowered me. I had no control. I had to keep her."

Whitehead gave the child to the Sterns as agreed, but her first night without the baby was miserable. The next day she begged the Sterns to let her have the child for just one week. They agreed, but at the end of the week, Whitehead didn't want to return the child. She asked if the Sterns would agree to let her have the child one weekend a month and two weeks during the summer. They insisted on the original contract and went to court to enforce it. The money due Whitehead was still in the escrow account. Six weeks later, a family court judge awarded the Sterns temporary custody, but the next day the Whiteheads ran off with the baby. The Sterns paid more than $20,000 for a private investigator, who spent three months tracing the Whiteheads to the home of Mary Beth's mother in Florida. He and the FBI visited the home, grabbed the baby, and took her away, returning her to the Sterns.

Four days after Baby M's first birthday, New Jersey Judge Harvey Sorkow called Mary Beth Whitehead a "woman without empathy," and most of the world agreed that she was an unfit mother when it learned of a tape recording that Bill Stern had secretly made of a desperate phone call from her when she was on the run. "I'd rather see me and her dead before you can get her," Mary Beth had said. "I gave her life and I can take her life away."

Ruling that the Sterns were better able, emotionally and financially, to be Baby M's parents, Judge Sorkow awarded the child to them and performed an adoption ceremony in his chambers that made Elizabeth Stern the legal mother of Melissa.

A three-judge panel upheld Sorkow's decision, but Whitehead promised to continue the legal battle, claiming that she didn't mean what she had said on the phone. "It was such a stressful time. It was like they were crucifying me. I felt like Jesus Christ, I really did. I would never have hurt Melissa." Months went by. Finally, the New Jersey Supreme Court ruled that the surrogacy agreement was "illegal, perhaps criminal, and potentially degrading to women." William Stern retained custody, but Whitehead won maternal visitation rights, and adoption by Mrs. Stern (who has no parental rights) was voided.

The court's decision, however, is binding only in New Jersey. Immediately after the Baby M case, measures addressing surrogacy were introduced in every state legislature, but few were adopted. Michigan and Florida now forbid paid surrogacy arrangements, and five other states have deemed surrogacy contracts legally unenforceable. Meanwhile, technology has given a new twist to the continuing moral and legal controversy.

Not long after the Baby M case was resolved, California Superior Court Judge Richard Parslow denied parental rights to a surrogate mother named Anna L. Johnson, an Orange County nurse. In this case, however, Johnson had no genetic connection to the baby boy she carried in her womb and gave birth to. He had been conceived by in vitro (or laboratory) fertilization from the sperm and egg of Mark and Crispina Calvert and then implanted in Johnson's womb. The Calverts hired Johnson's services for $10,000 because they were eager to produce their own genetic offspring, even though a hysterectomy prevented Crispina from carrying a baby (but not from producing fertile eggs). After the baby was born, Anna Johnson, just like Mary Beth Whitehead before her, changed her mind and sought to keep the baby. In his decision, Judge Parslow declined to follow California law, which defined the mother as the woman who gives birth to the child. Instead, he ruled, in effect, that genes make the mom: Anna Johnson's womb was little more than a home in which she had sheltered and fed the legal offspring of the genetic parents.

A few days later, newspapers reported that medical researchers had succeeded in making six prematurely menopausal women pregnant by implanting them with donated eggs fertilized in vitro with their husband's sperm. In these cases, though, it was the donor of the fertilized egg—the genetic mother—who relinquished her claim to motherhood, not the gestational mother.

The contradiction between these cases and Judge Parslow's decision was eventually addressed by the California Supreme Court. It upheld Judge Parslow's decision, ruling that Anna Johnson has no maternal rights to Chris Calvert, the boy she gave birth to. For the high court, though, the crucial factor in determining maternity is intent: "We conclude that . . . she who intended to procreate the child—that is, she who intended to bring about the birth of a child that she intended to raise as her own—is the natural mother under California law." However, Justice Joyce L. Kennard, the only woman on the high court, dissented, criticizing the court for relying on the "intent" of the genetic and birth mothers to break the "tie" over who should get the baby. "A pregnant woman intending to bring a child into the world is more than a mere container or breeding animal," Justice Kennard wrote. "She is a conscious agent of creation no less than the genetic mother, and her humanity is implicated on a deep level. Her role should not be devalued." In Justice Kennard's view, the primary factor in deciding custody should be neither genes nor contractual intent, but what is in the best interests of the child.

Discussion Questions

1. Is the Baby M case a case of "baby selling," as critics charge, or are surrogacy agencies correct to claim that they are simply selling a woman's services? Under either description, is there anything morally questionable about surrogate-mother agreements? How would such agreements be analyzed from the point of view of each of the major theories discussed in this chapter?

2. Discuss the motivations of the various parties to this dispute. To what moral principle(s) could Mary Beth Whitehead appeal to justify her subsequent actions? How could the Sterns defend their response?

3. Lawyers such as Noel Keane are in the business of arranging surrogate births. How should their role be morally evaluated?

4. Who should keep Baby M? In your opinion, did the New Jersey Supreme Court make the right decision? Identify and weigh the relevant moral principles.

5. Is genetic motherhood relevant to your assessment of the Baby M case? Was Mary Beth Whitehead's situation significantly different from Anna L. Johnson's? Should Johnson have been granted visitation rights?

6. Assess the reasoning of the California Supreme Court. Should "intent" determine motherhood?

7. Should surrogate motherhood be legal? If so, how (if at all) should the law regulate it? What legislative provisions would be best?

CASE 2.2

The Ford Pinto

There was a time when the "made in Japan" label brought a predictable smirk of superiority to the face of most Americans. The quality of most Japanese products usually was as low as their price. In fact, few imports could match their domestic counterparts, the proud products of Yankee know-how. But by the late 1960s, an invasion of foreign-made goods chiseled a few worry lines into the countenance of U.S. industry. In Detroit, worry was fast fading to panic as the Japanese, not to mention the Germans, began to gobble up more and more of the subcompact auto market.

Never one to take a back seat to the competition, Ford Motor Company decided to meet the threat from abroad head-on. In 1968, Ford executives decided to produce the Pinto. Known inside the company as "Lee's car," after Ford president Lee Iacocca, the Pinto was to weigh no more than 2,000 pounds and cost no more than $2,000.[19]

Eager to have its subcompact ready for the 1971 model year, Ford decided to compress the normal drafting-board-to-showroom time of about three-and-a-half years into two. The compressed schedule meant that any design changes typically made before production-line tooling would have to be made during it.

Before producing the Pinto, Ford crash-tested various prototypes, in part to learn whether they met a safety standard proposed by the National Highway Traffic Safety Administration (NHTSA) to reduce fires from traffic collisions. This standard would have required that by 1972 all new autos be able to withstand a rear-end impact of 20 mph without fuel loss, and that by 1973 they be able to withstand an impact of 30 mph. The prototypes all failed the 20-mph test. In 1970 Ford crash-tested the Pinto itself, and the result was the same: ruptured gas tanks and dangerous leaks. The only Pintos to pass the test had been modified in some way—for example, with a rubber bladder in the gas tank or a piece of steel between the tank and the rear bumper.

Thus, Ford knew that the Pinto represented a serious fire hazard when struck from the rear, even in low-speed collisions. Ford officials faced a decision. Should they go ahead with the existing design, thereby meeting the production timetable but possibly jeopardizing consumer safety? Or should they delay production of the Pinto by redesigning the gas tank to make it safer and thus concede another year of subcompact dominance to foreign companies? Ford not only pushed ahead with the original design but stuck to it for the next six years.

What explains Ford's decision? The evidence suggests that Ford relied, at least in part, on cost-benefit reasoning, which is an analysis in monetary terms of the expected costs and benefits of doing something. There were various ways of making the Pinto's gas tank safer. Although the estimated price of these safety improvements ranged from only $5 to $8 per vehicle, Ford evidently reasoned that the increased cost outweighed the benefits of a new tank design.

How exactly did Ford reach that conclusion? We don't know for sure, but an internal report, "Fatalities Associated with Crash-Induced Fuel Leakage and Fires," reveals the cost-benefit reasoning that the company used in cases like this. This report was not written with the Pinto in mind; rather, it concerns fuel leakage in rollover accidents (not rear-end collisions), and its computations applied to all Ford vehicles, not just the Pinto. Nevertheless, it illustrates the type of reasoning that was probably used in the Pinto case.

In the "Fatalities" report, Ford engineers estimated the cost of technical improvements that would prevent gas tanks from leaking in rollover accidents to be $11 per vehicle. The authors go on to discuss various estimates of the number of people killed by fires from car rollovers before settling on the relatively low figure of 180 deaths per year. But given that number, how can the value of those individuals' lives be gauged? Can a dollars-and-cents figure be assigned to a human being? NHTSA thought so. In 1972, it estimated that society loses $200,725 every time a person is killed in an auto accident (adjusted for inflation, today's figure would, of course, be considerably higher). It broke down the costs as follows:

Future productivity losses	
Direct	$132,000
Indirect	41,300
Medical costs	
Hospital	700
Other	425
Property damage	1,500
Insurance administration	4,700
Legal and court expenses	3,000
Employer losses	1,000
Victim's pain and suffering	10,000
Funeral	900
Assets (lost consumption)	5,000
Miscellaneous accident costs	200
Total per fatality	**$200,725**

Putting the NHTSA figures together with other statistical studies, the Ford report arrives at the following overall assessment of costs and benefits:

Benefits

Savings:	180 burn deaths, 180 serious burn injuries, 2,100 burned vehicles
Unit cost:	$200,000 per death, $67,000 per injury, $700 per vehicle
Total benefit:	$(180 \times \$200,000) + (180 \times \$67,000) + (2,100 \times \$700) =$ $49.5 million

Costs

Sales:	11 million cars, 1.5 million light trucks
Unit cost:	$11 per car, $11 per truck
Total cost:	$12.5 \text{ million} \times \$11 = \$137.5$ million

Thus, the costs of the suggested safety improvements outweigh their benefits, and the "Fatalities" report accordingly recommends against any improvements—a recommendation that Ford followed.

Likewise in the Pinto case, Ford's management, whatever its exact reasoning, decided to stick with the original design and not upgrade the Pinto's fuel tank, despite the test results reported by its engineers. Here is the aftermath of Ford's decision:

- Between 1971 and 1978, the Pinto was responsible for a number of fire-related deaths. Ford puts the figure at 23; its critics say the figure is closer to 500. According to the sworn testimony of Ford engineers, 95 percent of the fatalities would have survived if Ford had located the fuel tank over the axle (as it had done on its Capri automobiles).

- NHTSA finally adopted a 30-mph collision standard in 1976. The Pinto then acquired a rupture-proof fuel tank. In 1978 Ford was obliged to recall all 1971–1976 Pintos for fuel-tank modifications.

- Between 1971 and 1978, approximately fifty lawsuits were brought against Ford in connection with rear-end accidents in the Pinto. In the Richard Grimshaw case, in addition to awarding over $3 million in compensatory damages to the victims of a Pinto crash, the jury awarded a landmark $125 million in punitive damages against Ford. The judge reduced punitive damages to $3.5 million.

- On August 10, 1978, eighteen-year-old Judy Ulrich, her sixteen-year-old sister Lynn, and their eighteen-year-old cousin Donna, in their 1973 Ford Pinto, were struck from the rear by a van near Elkhart, Indiana. The gas tank of the Pinto exploded on impact. In the fire that resulted, the three teenagers were burned to death. Ford was charged with criminal homicide. The judge in the case advised jurors that Ford should be convicted if it had clearly disregarded the harm that might result from its actions, and that disregard represented a substantial deviation from acceptable standards of conduct. On March 13, 1980, the jury found Ford not guilty of criminal homicide.

For its part, Ford has always denied that the Pinto is unsafe compared with other cars of its type and era. The company also points out that in every model year the Pinto met or surpassed the government's own standards. But what the company doesn't say is that successful lobbying by it and its industry associates was responsible for delaying for seven years the adoption of any NHTSA crash standard. Furthermore, Ford's critics claim that there were more than forty European and Japanese models in the Pinto price and weight range with safer gas-tank position. "Ford made an extremely irresponsible decision," concludes auto safety expert Byron Bloch, "when they placed such a weak tank in such a ridiculous location in such a soft rear end."

Has the automobile industry learned a lesson from Ford's experience with the Pinto? Some observers thought not when, in February 1993, an Atlanta jury held the General Motors Corporation responsible for the death of a Georgia teenager in the fiery crash of one of its pickup trucks. At the trial, General Motors contended in its defense that when a drunk driver struck seventeen-year-old Shannon Moseley's truck in the side, it was the impact of the high-speed crash that killed Moseley. However, the jury was persuaded that Moseley survived the collision only to be consumed by a fire caused by his truck's defective fuel-tank design. Finding that the company had known that its "side-saddle" gas tanks, which are mounted outside the rails of the truck's frame, are dangerously prone to rupture, the jury awarded $4.2 million in actual damages and $101 million in punitive damages to Moseley's parents.

What undoubtedly swayed the jury was the testimony of former GM safety engineer Ronald E. Elwell. Although Elwell had testified in more than fifteen previous cases that the pickups were safe, this time he switched sides and told the jury that the company had known for years that the side-saddle design was defective but had intentionally hidden its knowledge and had not attempted to correct the problem. At the trial, company officials attempted to paint Elwell as a disgruntled employee, but his testimony was supported by videotapes of General Motors' own crash tests. After the verdict, General Motors said that it still stood behind the safety of its trucks and contended "that a full examination by the National Highway Traffic Safety Administration of the technical issues in this matter will bear out our contention that the . . . pickup trucks do not have a safety related defect."

Since then, however, the Department of Transportation has determined that GM pickups of the style Shannon Moseley drove do pose a fire hazard and that they are more prone than competitors' pickups to catch fire when struck from the side. Still, GM has rejected requests to recall the pickups and repair them. Meanwhile, the Georgia Court of Appeals threw out the jury's verdict in the Shannon Moseley case on a legal technicality— despite ruling that the evidence submitted in the case showed that GM was aware that the gas tanks were hazardous but did not try to make them safer to save the expense involved.

Discussion Questions

1. What moral issues does the Pinto case raise?

2. Suppose Ford officials were asked to justify their decision. What moral principles do you think they would invoke? Assess Ford's handling of the Pinto from the perspective of each of the moral theories discussed in this chapter.

3. Utilitarians would say that jeopardizing motorists does not by itself make Ford's action morally objectionable. The only morally relevant matter is whether Ford gave equal consideration to the interests of each affected party. Do you think Ford did this?

4. Is cost-benefit analysis a legitimate tool? What role, if any, should it play in moral deliberation? Critically assess the example of cost-benefit analysis given in the case study. Is there anything unsatisfactory about it? Could it have been improved upon in some way?

5. Speculate about Kant's response to the NHTSA's placing a monetary value on a human life.

6. What responsibilities to its customers do you think Ford had? What are the most important moral rights, if any, operating in the Pinto case?

7. Would it have made a moral difference if the savings resulting from not improving the Pinto gas tank had been passed on to Ford's customers? Could a rational customer have chosen to save a few dollars and risk having the more dangerous gas tank? What if Ford had told potential customers about its decision?

8. Is it wrong for business to sell a product that is not as safe as it could be, given current technology? Is it wrong to sell a product that is less safe than competing products on the market?

9. The maxim of Ford's action might be stated: "When it would cost more to make a safety improvement than not, it's all right not to make it." Can this maxim be universalized? Does it treat humans as ends in themselves? Would manufacturers be willing to abide by it if the positions were reversed and they were in the role of consumers?

10. Should Ford have been found guilty of criminal homicide in the Ulrich case?

11. Was GM responsible for Shannon Moseley's death? Compare that case with Ford and the Pinto.

CASE 2.3

Blood for Sale

Sol Levin was a successful stockbroker in Tampa, Florida, when he recognized the potentially profitable market for safe and uncontaminated blood and, with some colleagues, founded Plasma International. Not everybody is willing to make money by selling his or her own blood, and in the beginning Plasma International bought blood from people addicted to drugs and alcohol. Although innovative marketing increased Plasma International's sales dramatically, several cases of hepatitis were reported in recipients. The company then began looking for new sources of blood.[20]

Plasma International searched worldwide and, with the advice of a qualified team of medical consultants, did extensive testing. Eventually they found that the blood profiles of several rural West African tribes made them ideal prospective donors. After negotiations with the local government, Plasma International signed an agreement with several tribal chieftains to purchase blood.

Business went smoothly and profitably for Plasma International until a Tampa paper charged that Plasma was purchasing blood for as little as fifteen cents a pint and then reselling it to hospitals in the United States and South America for $25 per pint. In one recent disaster, the newspaper alleged, Plasma International had sold 10,000 pints, netting nearly a quarter of a million dollars.

The newspaper story stirred up controversy in Tampa, but the existence of commercialized blood marketing systems in the United States is nothing new. Approximately half the blood and plasma obtained in the United States is bought and sold like any other commodity. About 40 percent is given to avoid having to pay for blood received or to build up credit so blood will be available without charge if the donor needs it. By contrast, the National Health Service in Great Britain relies entirely on a voluntary system of blood donation. Blood is neither bought nor sold. It is available to anyone who needs it without charge or obligation, and donors gain no preference over nondonors.

In an important study, economist Richard Titmuss showed that the British system works better than the American one in terms of economic and administrative efficiency, price, and blood quality. The commercialized blood market, Titmuss argued, is wasteful of blood and plagued by shortages. In the United States, bureaucratization, paperwork, and administrative overhead result in a cost per unit of blood that is five to fifteen times higher than in Great Britain. Hemophiliacs, in particular, are disadvantaged by the U.S. system and have enormous bills to pay. In addition, commercial markets are much more likely to distribute contaminated blood.

Titmuss also argued that the existence of a commercialized system discourages voluntary donors. People are less apt to give blood if they know that others are selling it. Philosopher Peter Singer has elaborated on this point:

If blood is a commodity with a price, to give blood means merely to save someone money. Blood has a cash value of a certain number of dollars, and the importance of the gift will vary with the wealth of the recipient. If blood cannot be bought, however, the gift's value depends upon the need of the recipient. Often, it will be worth life itself. Under these circumstances blood becomes a very special kind of gift, and giving it means providing for strangers, without hope of reward, something they cannot buy and without which they may die. The gift relates strangers in a manner that is not possible when blood is a commodity.

This may sound like a philosopher's abstraction, far removed from the thoughts of ordinary people. On the contrary, it is an idea spontaneously expressed by British donors in response to Titmuss's questionnaire. As one woman, a machine operator, wrote in reply to the question why she first decided to become a blood donor: "You can't get blood from supermarkets and chain stores. People themselves must come forward; sick people can't get out of bed to ask you for a pint to save their life, so I came forward in hopes to help somebody who needs blood."

The implication of this answer, and others like it, is that even if the formal right to give blood can coexist with commercialized blood banks, the respondent's action would have lost much of its significance to her, and the blood would probably not have been given at all. When blood is a commodity, and can be purchased if it is not given, altruism becomes unnecessary, and so loosens the bonds that can otherwise exist between strangers in a community. The existence of a market in blood does not threaten the formal right to give blood, but it does away with the right to give blood which cannot be bought, has no cash value, and must be given freely if it is to be obtained at all. If there is such a right, it is incompatible with the right to sell blood, and we cannot avoid violating one of these rights when we grant the other.[21]

Both Titmuss and Singer believe that the weakening of the spirit of altruism in this sphere has important repercussions. It marks, they think, the increasing commercialization of our lives and makes similar changes in attitude, motive, and relationships more likely in other fields.

Discussion Questions

1. Is Sol Levin running a business "just like any other business," or is his company open to moral criticism? Defend your answer by appeal to moral principle.

2. What are the contrasting ideals of the British and U.S. blood systems? Which system, in your opinion, best promotes human freedom and respect for people?

3. Examine the pros and cons of commercial transactions in blood from the egoistic, the utilitarian, and the Kantian perspectives.

4. Are Titmuss and Singer right to suggest that the buying and selling of blood reduces altruism? Does knowing that you can sell your blood (and that others are selling theirs) make you less inclined to donate your blood? Do we have a right to give blood that cannot be bought?

5. Many believe that commercialization is increasing in all areas of modern life. If this is so, is it something to be applauded or condemned? Is it wrong to treat certain things—such as human organs—as commodities?

6. Did Plasma International strike a fair bargain with the West Africans who supplied their blood to the company? Or is Plasma guilty of exploiting them in some way? Explain your answer.

7. Do you believe that we have a moral duty to donate blood? If so, why and under what circumstances? If not, why not?

Notes to Chapter 2

1. Bernard Williams, *Ethics and the Limits of Philosophy* (Cambridge, Mass.: Harvard University Press, 1985), 16.

2. Richard B. Brandt, "Toward a Credible Form of Utilitarianism," in Hector-Neri Castañeda and George Nakhnikian, eds., *Morality and the Language of Conduct* (Detroit: Wayne State University Press, 1963), 109–110.

3. A. C. Ewing, *Ethics* (New York: Free Press, 1965), 40.

4. Molly Moore, "Did the Experts Really Approve the 'Brown Lung' Experiment?" *Washington Post National Weekly Edition,* June 4, 1984, 31.

5. Adam Smith, *The Wealth of Nations* (New York: Modern Library, 1985), 223–225.

6. Tom L. Beauchamp and Norman E. Bowie, eds., *Ethical Theory and Business,* 6th ed. (Upper Saddle River, N.J.: Prentice Hall, 2001), 16.

7. Immanuel Kant, *Grounding for the Metaphysics of Morals* (Indianapolis: Hackett, 1988), 30–31 (translation modified).

8. Kurt Eichenwald, "Commissions Are Many, Profits Few," *New York Times,* May 24, 1993, C1.

9. See, in particular, W. D. Ross, *The Right and the Good* (London: Oxford University Press, 1930).

10. Immanuel Kant, *Practical Philosophy,* ed. M. J. Gregor (Cambridge: Cambridge University Press, 1996), 611–615.

11. Ross, *The Right and the Good,* 21.

12. Ibid., 30.

13. Ibid., 31.

14. Richard B. Brandt, "The Real and Alleged Problems of Utilitarianism," *Hastings Center Report,* April 1983, 38.

15. Ibid., 42.

16. Ibid., 42.

17. Vincent Ryan Ruggiero, *The Moral Imperative* (Port Washington, N.Y.: Alfred Publishers, 1973).

18. The facts of this case are based on articles in *Newsweek,* January 19 and April 13, 1987; *Economist,* March 21, 1987; *Los Angeles Times,* March 6, 1989; *New York Times,* November 4, 1990; *Nation,* December 31, 1990; and *San Jose Mercury News,* May 21, 1993.

19. This case study is based on Douglas Birsch and John H. Fielder, eds., *The Ford Pinto Case* (Albany, N.Y.: State University of New York Press, 1994); "G.M. Is Held Liable Over Fuel Tanks in Pickup Trucks," *New York Times,* February 5, 1993,

A1; and "Federal Study Finds Danger of Fire in G.M. Pickup Trucks," *New York Times,* October 18, 1994, A1.

20. This and the following three paragraphs are based on a case created by T. W. Zimmerer and P. L. Preston in R. D. Hay, E. R. Gray, and J. E. Gates, eds., *Business and Society* (Cincinnati: South-Western, 1976). The remainder of the case draws on Peter Singer, "Rights and the Market," in John Arthur and William H. Shaw, eds., *Justice and Economic Distribution,* 2nd ed. (Englewood Cliffs, N.J.: Prentice Hall, 1991), and Richard M. Titmuss, *The Gift Relationship* (London: George Allen & Unwin, 1972).

21. Singer, "Rights and the Market." Reprinted by permission of the author. See also "Blood Donation—Altruism or Profit?" *British Medical Journal,* May 4, 1996, 1114.

Reading ■

WHAT WOULD A SATISFACTORY MORAL THEORY BE LIKE?

JAMES RACHELS

After studying various moral theories, one is bound to be left wondering what to believe. In this selection from The Elements of Moral Philosophy, *James Rachels sketches what he thinks would be a satisfactory ethical theory. Although his theory has much in common with utilitarianism, it takes seriously people's right to choose and the moral importance of treating people as they deserve to be treated. In this way Rachels follows Kant's emphasis on respect for persons.*

Some people believe that there cannot be progress in Ethics, since everything has already been said. . . . I believe the opposite. . . . Compared with the other sciences, Non-Religious Ethics is the youngest and least advanced.
Derek Parfit, *Reasons and Persons* (1984)

MORALITY WITHOUT HUBRIS

Moral philosophy has a rich and fascinating history. A great many thinkers have approached the subject from a wide variety of perspectives and have produced theories that both attract and repel the thoughtful reader. Almost all the classical theories contain plausible elements, which is hardly surprising, considering that they were devised by philosophers of undoubted genius. Yet the various theories are not consistent with one another, and most are vulnerable to crippling objections. After reviewing them, one is left wondering what to believe. What, in the final analysis, is the truth? Of course, different philosophers would answer this question in different ways. Some might refuse to answer at all, on the grounds that we do not yet know enough to have reached the "final analysis." (In this, moral philosophy is not much worse off than any other subject of human inquiry—we do not know the final truth about almost anything.) But we do know a lot, and it may not be unduly rash to venture a guess as to what a satisfactory moral theory might be like.

From *The Elements of Moral Philosophy,* 2nd ed., by James Rachels. Copyright © 1993 by Random House, Inc. Reprinted by permission of Mcraw-Hill, Inc. Some section headings added.

A Modest Conception of Human Beings

A satisfactory theory would, first of all, be sensitive to the facts about human nature, and it would be appropriately modest about the place of human beings in the scheme of things. The universe is some 18 billion years old—that is the time elapsed since the "big bang"—and the earth itself was formed about 4.6 billion years ago. The evolution of life on the planet was a slow process, guided not by design but (largely) by random mutation and natural selection. The first humans appeared quite recently. The extinction of the great dinosaurs 65 million years ago (possibly as the result of a catastrophic collision between the earth and an asteroid) left ecological room for the evolution of the few little mammals that were about, and after 63 or 64 *more* years, one line of that evolution finally produced us. In geological time, we arrived only yesterday.

But no sooner did our ancestors arrive than they began to think of themselves as the most important things in all creation. Some of them even imagined that the whole universe had been made for their benefit. Thus, when they began to develop theories of right and wrong, they had held that the protection of their own interests had a kind of ultimate and objective value. The rest of creation, they reasoned, was intended for their use. We now know better. We now know that we exist by evolutionary accident, as one species among many, on a small and insignificant world in one little corner of the cosmos.

How Reason Gives Rise to Ethics

Hume, who knew only a little of this story, nevertheless realized that human *hubris* is largely unjustified. "The life of a man," he wrote, "is of no greater importance to the universe than that of an oyster." But he also recognized that our lives are important to *us*. We are creatures with desires, needs, plans, and hopes; and even if "the universe" does not care about those things, we do. Our theory of morality may begin from this point. In order to have a convenient name for it, let us call this theory *Morality Without Hubris*—or *MWH* for short. MWH incorporates some elements of the various classical theories while rejecting others.

Human *hubris* is largely unjustified, but it is not *entirely* unjustified. Compared to the other creatures on earth, we do have impressive intellectual capacities. We have evolved as rational beings. This fact gives some point to our inflated opinion of ourselves; and, as it turns out, it is also what makes us capable of having a morality. Because we are rational, we are able to take some facts as *reasons* for behaving one way rather than another. We can articulate those reasons and think about them. Thus we take the fact that an action would help satisfy our desires, needs, and so on—in short, the fact that an action would *promote our interests*—as a reason in favor of doing that action. And of course we take the fact that an action would frustrate our interests as a reason against doing it.

The origin of our concept of "ought" may be found in these facts. If we were not capable of considering reasons for and against actions, we would have no use for such a notion. Like the lower animals, we would simply act from impulse or habit, or as Kant put it, from "inclination." But the consideration of reasons introduces a new factor. Now we find ourselves impelled to act in certain ways as a result of deliberation, as a result of thinking about our behavior and its consequences. We use the word "ought" to mark this new element of the situation: we *ought* to do the act supported by the weightiest reasons.

Once we consider morality as a matter of acting on reason, another important point emerges. In reasoning about what to do, we can be consistent or inconsistent. One way of being inconsistent is to accept a fact as a reason for action on one occasion, while refusing to accept a similar fact as a reason on another occasion, even though there is no difference between the two occasions that would justify distinguishing them. (This is the legitimate point made by Kant's Categorical Imperative. . . .) This happens, for example, when a person unjustifiably places the interests of his own race or social group above the comparable interests of other races and social groups. Racism means counting the interests of the members of the other races as less important than the interests of the members of one's own race, despite the fact that there is no general difference between the races that would justify it. It is an offense against morality because it is first an offense against reason. Similar remarks could be made about other doctrines that divide humanity into the morally favored and disfavored, such as egoism, sexism, and (some forms of) nationalism. The upshot is that reason requires impartiality: we ought to act so as to promote the interests of everyone alike.

If Psychological Egoism were true, this would mean that reason demands more of us than we can manage. But Psychological Egoism is not true; it gives an altogether false picture of human nature and the human condition. We have evolved as social creatures, living together in groups, wanting one another's company, needing one another's cooperation, and capable of caring about one another's welfare. So there is a pleasing theoretical "fit" between (a) what reason requires, namely impartiality; (b) the requirements of social living, namely adherence to a set of rules that, if fairly applied, would serve everyone's interests; and (c) our natural inclination to care about others, at least to a modest degree. All three work together to make morality not only possible, but in an important sense natural, for us.

Responsibility and Desert

So far, MWH sounds very much like Utilitarianism. However, there is one other fact about human beings that must be taken into account, and doing so will give the theory a decidedly nonutilitarian twist. As rational agents, humans have the power of choice: they may choose to do what they see to be right, or they may choose to do wrong. Thus they are *responsible* for their freely chosen actions, and they are judged morally good if they choose well or wicked if they choose badly. This, I think, has two consequences. First, it helps to explain why freedom is among the most cherished human values. A person who is denied the right to choose his or her own actions is thereby denied the possibility of achieving any kind of personal moral worth. Second, the way a person may be treated by others depends, to some extent, on the way he or she has chosen to treat them. One who treats others well deserves to be treated well in return, while one

who treats others badly deserves to be treated badly in return.

This last point is liable to sound a little strange, so let me elaborate it just a bit. Suppose Smith has always been generous to others, helping them whenever he could; now he is in trouble and needs help in return. There is now a *special* reason *he* should be helped, above the general obligation we have to promote the interests of everyone alike. He is not just another member of the crowd. He is a particular person who, by his own previous conduct, has *earned* our respect and gratitude. But now consider someone with the opposite history: suppose Jones is your neighbor, and he has always *refused* to help you when you needed it. One day your car wouldn't start, for example, and Jones wouldn't give you a lift to work—he had no particular excuse, he just wouldn't be bothered. Imagine that, after this episode, Jones has car trouble and he has the nerve to ask you for a ride. Perhaps you think you should help him anyway, despite his own lack of helpfulness. (You might think that this will teach him generosity.) Nevertheless, if we concentrate on what he *deserves*, we must conclude that he deserves to be left to fend for himself.

Adjusting our treatment of individuals to match how they themselves have chosen to treat others is not just a matter of rewarding friends and holding grudges against enemies. It is a matter of treating people as *responsible agents,* who by their own choices show themselves to be deserving of particular responses, and toward whom such emotions as gratitude and resentment are appropriate. There is an important difference between Smith and Jones; why shouldn't that be reflected in the way we respond to them? What would it be like if we did *not* tailor our responses to people in this way? For one thing, we would be denying people (including ourselves) the ability to earn good treatment at the hands of others. Morally speaking, we would all become simply members of the great crowd of humanity, rather than individuals with particular personalities and deserts. Respecting people's right to choose their own conduct, and then adjusting our treatment of them according to how they choose, is ultimately a matter of "respect for persons" in a sense somewhat like Kant's.

We are now in a position to summarize the outline of what, in my judgment, a satisfactory moral theory would be like. Such a theory would see morality as based on facts about our nature and interests, rather than on some exaggerated conception of our "importance." As for the principles on which we ought to act, the theory is a combination of two ideas: first, that *we ought to act so as to promote the interests of everyone alike;* and second, that *we should treat people as they deserve to be treated, considering how they have themselves chosen to behave.*

But now the key question is: How are these two ideas related? How do they fit together to form a unified principle of conduct? They are not to be understood as entirely independent of one another. The first establishes a general presumption in favor of promoting everyone's interests, impartially; and the second specifies grounds on which this presumption may be overridden. Thus the second thought functions as a qualification to the first; it specifies that we may sometimes *depart from* a policy of "equal treatment" on the grounds that a person has shown by his past behavior that he deserves some particular response. We may therefore combine them into a single principle. The primary rule of morality, according to MWH, is:

> We ought to act so as to promote impartially the interests of everyone alike, except when individuals deserve particular responses as a result of their own past behavior.

This principle combines the best elements of both Utilitarianism and Kantian "respect for persons," but it is not produced simply by stitching those two philosophies together. Rather, it springs naturally from a consideration of the main facts of the human condition—that we are perishable beings with interests that may be promoted or frustrated, and that we are rational beings responsible for our conduct. Although more needs to be said about the theoretical basis of this view, I will say no more about it here. Instead I will turn to some of its practical implications. Like every moral theory, MWH implies that we should behave in certain ways; and in some cases, it implies that commonly accepted patterns of behavior are wrong and should be changed. The plausibility of the theory will depend in part on how successful it is

in convincing us that our behavior should conform to its directives.

THE MORAL COMMUNITY

When we are deciding what to do, whose interests should we take into account? People have answered this question in different ways at different times: egoists have said that one's own interests are all-important; racists have restricted moral concern to their own race; and nationalists have held that moral concern stops at the borders of one's country. The answer given by MWH is that *we ought to give equal consideration to the interests of everyone who will be affected by our conduct.* In principle, the community with which we should be concerned is limited only by the number of individuals who have interests, and that, as we shall see, is a very large number indeed.

This may seem a pious platitude, but in reality it can be a hard doctrine. As this is being written, for example, there is famine in Ethiopia and millions of people are starving. People in the affluent countries have not responded very well. There has been some aid given, but relatively few people have felt personally obligated to help by sending contributions to famine-relief agencies. People would no doubt feel a greater sense of obligation if it were their neighbors starving, rather than strangers in a foreign country. But on the theory we are considering, the location of the starving people makes no difference; *everyone* is included in the community of moral concern. This has radical consequences: for example, when a person is faced with the choice between spending ten dollars on a trip to the movies or contributing it for famine relief, he should ask himself which action would most effectively promote human welfare, with each person's interests counted as equally important. Would he benefit more from seeing the movie than a starving person would from getting food? Clearly, he would not. So he should contribute the money for famine relief. If this sort of reasoning were taken seriously, it would make an enormous difference in our responses to such emergencies.

If the moral community is not limited to people in one place, neither is it limited to people at any one *time.* Whether people will be affected by our actions now or in the distant future makes no difference. Our obligation is to consider all their interests equally. This is an important point because, with the development of nuclear weapons, we now have the capacity to alter the course of history in an especially dramatic way. Some argue that a full-scale nuclear exchange . . . would result in the extinction of the human race. The prediction of "nuclear winter" supports this conclusion. The idea is that the detonation of so many nuclear devices would send millions of tons of dust and ash into the stratosphere, where it would block the sun's rays. The surface of the earth would become cold. This condition would persist for years, and the ecology would collapse. Those who were "lucky" enough to escape death earlier would nevertheless perish in the nuclear winter. Other theorists contend that this estimate is too pessimistic. Civilization might come to an end, they say, and most people might die, but a few will survive, and the long upward struggle will begin again.

Considering this, it is difficult to imagine *any* circumstances in which the large-scale use of nuclear weapons would be morally justified. . . . Suppose a situation arises in which [a country], despite America's nuclear strength, acts against the very interests our arsenal is supposed to protect. Would we then be justified in using our strategic weapons? Suppose we did. In executing a policy designed to protect our interests, we would not only have destroyed ourselves; we would have violated the interests of all the people yet to come (assuming, of course, that there were at least some survivors who could try to rebuild civilization). In the larger historical context, our interests are of only passing importance, certainly not worth the price of condemning countless future generations to the miseries of a post–nuclear war age. History would not judge the Nazis to have been the pre-eminent villains of our time. That distinction would be reserved for us.

There is one other way in which our conception of the moral community must be expanded. Humans, as we have noted, are only one species of animal inhabiting this planet. Like humans, the other animals also have interests that are affected by what we do. When we kill or torture them, they are harmed, just as humans are harmed when treated in those ways. The utilitarians were right to insist that the interests of nonhuman animals must be given weight in our moral calculations. As Bentham pointed out, excluding creatures from moral consideration because of their species is no more justified than excluding them because of race, nationality, or sex. . . . Impartiality requires the expansion of the moral community—not only across space and time but across the boundaries of species as well.

JUSTICE AND FAIRNESS

MWH has much in common with Utilitarianism, especially in what I called MWH's "first idea." But . . . Utilitarianism has been severely criticized for failing to account for the values of justice and fairness. Can MWH do any better in this regard? It does, because it makes a person's past behavior relevant to how he or she should be treated. This introduces into the theory an acknowledgment of personal merit that is lacking in unqualified Utilitarianism. . . .

Questions of justice arise any time one person is treated differently from another. Suppose an employer must choose which of two employees to promote, when he can promote only one of them. The first candidate has worked hard for the company, taking on extra work when it was needed, giving up her vacation to help out, and so on. The second candidate, on the other hand, has always done only the minimum required of him. (And we will assume he has no excuse; he has simply *chosen* not to work very hard for the company.) Obviously, the two employees will be treated very differently: one will get the promotion; the other will not. But this is all right, according to our theory, because the first employee deserves to be advanced over the second, considering the past performance of each. The first employee has earned the promotion, the second has not.

This is an easy case, in that it is obvious what the employer should do. But it illustrates an important difference between our theory and Utilitarianism. Utilitarians might argue that their theory also yields the right decision in this case. They might observe that it promotes the general welfare for companies to reward hard work; therefore the Principle of

Utility, unsupplemented by any further consideration, would also say that the first employee, but not
the second, should be promoted. Perhaps this is so.
Nevertheless, this is unsatisfactory because it has
the first employee being promoted for the *wrong
reason.* She has a claim on the promotion because
of her own hard work, and not simply because
promoting her would be better for us all. MWH ac-
commodates this vital point, whereas Utilitarianism does not.

MWH holds that a person's voluntary actions
can justify departures from the basic policy of
"equal treatment," but *nothing else can.* This goes
against a common view of the matter. Often, people think it is right for individuals to be rewarded
for physical beauty, superior intelligence, or other
native endowments. (In practice, people often get
better jobs and a greater share of life's good things
just because they were born with greater natural
gifts.) But on reflection, this does not seem right.
People do not deserve their native endowments;
they have them as a result of what John Rawls has
called "the natural lottery." Suppose the first employee in our example was passed over for the promotion, despite her hard work, because the second
employee had some native talent that was more
useful in the new position. Even if the employer
could justify this decision in terms of the company's
needs, the first employee would rightly feel that
there is something unfair going on. She has worked
harder, yet he is now getting the promotion, and
the benefits that go with it, because of something
he did nothing to merit. That is not fair. A just society, according to MWH, would be one in which
people may improve their positions through work
(with the opportunity for work available to everyone), but they would not enjoy superior positions
simply because they were born lucky. . . .

As I said at the outset, MWH represents my best
guess about what an ultimately satisfactory moral
theory might be like. I say "guess" not to indicate
any lack of confidence; in my opinion, MWH *is* a
satisfactory moral theory. However, it is instructive
to remember that a great many thinkers have tried
to devise such a theory, and history has judged
them to have been only partially successful. This
suggests that it would be wise not to make too
grandiose a claim for one's own view. Moreover, as
the Oxford philosopher Derek Parfit has observed,
the earth will remain habitable for another billion
years, and civilization is now only a few thousand
years old. If we do not destroy ourselves, moral philosophy, along with all the other human inquiries,
may yet have a long way to go.

Review and Discussion Questions

1. Why does Rachels call his theory *Morality
    Without Hubris*?

2. According to him, what important implications
    does the fact of human rationality have for
    ethics?

3. How and why does Rachels modify the utilitar-
    ian approach? Would you agree that Rachels
    successfully combines the best elements of
    utilitarianism and Kantianism?

4. According to Rachels, who is in "the moral
    community"? How would adopting his
    perspective cause people to change their moral
    attitudes and conduct? In your view, do the
    practical implications of his theory make it
    more plausible or less?

Reading ━━━━━━━━━━━━━━ ■

VIRTUES AND BUSINESS ETHICS

JOSEPH R. DESJARDINS

Philosophers concerned with business ethics have generally followed the strategy of identifying and defending certain general principles of ethics and then applying them to specific situations in business. DesJardins is skeptical of this approach on both practical and theoretical grounds. Drawing on Aristotle and the contemporary philosopher Alasdair MacIntyre, DesJardins recommends an alternative approach to business ethics, one that focuses on moral virtue and being a good person rather than on formal ethical principles.

Much of the work done by philosophers in business ethics has been structured by an overly narrow understanding of ethical theory. This understanding is characterized by an almost total reliance upon moral rules and principles and an almost total disregard of virtues and the ethics of character. As understood by many philosophers working in business ethics, the goal of ethical theory is to identify and defend some fundamental principle that can serve as the foundation for all morality. Such a principle will provide this foundation if it can, first, be defended as categorically binding on all rational agents and, second, be capable of moving such agents to specific acts that are required by the principle. Generally, this second goal is achieved if the principle can function as a major premise from which specific practical conclusions can be deduced.

Much of the first-order writing done by philosophers in business ethics has involved the second goal: applying general ethical principles to specific situations in business and from these principles deriving what one ought to do in that situation. Moral philosophers less interested in "applied ethics" have

been content in pursuing the first goal. Thus, moral philosophy today is often divided into two areas: Those working in ethical theory are charged with justifying certain principles (for example, utility, the categorical imperative) as binding on all persons, while those working in applied ethics attempt to show how these principles commit one to accepting certain specific conclusions about whistle-blowing, employee rights, and so on. Thus applied ethics stands in the same relationship to ethical theory as engineering stands to physics. The theorist defends the general principle while the practitioner applies that principle to solve particular practical problems.

Given this principle-based understanding of ethical theory, the means for institutionalizing ethical responsibility within corporations is clear. The task is to get the corporation to accept some ethical principle as the guide for the activities of its members. A number of different strategies have been proposed to meet this goal. Milton Friedman, for example, suggests that corporations ought to adopt the principle of profit maximization as their guide. This principle, through the functioning of a free and competitive market, will lead the corporation to fulfill its social responsibility. Others have argued for a utilitarian principle broader than profit maximization, claiming that corporations ought to be guided by a more general understanding of social goods and by the recognition of a responsibility to bring about such goods.

Still others argue for nonutilitarian principles. Tom Donaldson, for example, defends a version of social contract theory of corporate social responsibility.[1] In this view, a corporation institutionalizes its ethical responsibility by obeying the implicit contract that exists between it and society.

These and many other similar strategies share a belief that the road to ethical responsibility lies with the internalization of some independently justified principle. In what follows, I suggest that there are good reasons for thinking that any such approach will fail. I then go on to consider an alternative strategy for institutionalizing ethical behavior.

THE FLAW IN PRINCIPLE-BASED ETHICS

What, then, is wrong with principle-based ethics? Why do I suppose that attempts to institutionalize

Reprinted by permission of the publisher from W. Michael Hoffman, Jennifer Mills Moore, and David A. Fredo, eds., *Corporate Governance and Institutionalizing Ethics.* Copyright © 1984 by D. C. Heath and Company.

ethical responsibility within corporations that rely upon principles will fail? There are both practical and theoretical reasons for this skepticism.

First, we should take seriously the fact that in practice, ethical principles seldom give any unambiguous practical advice. Adopting a principle-based approach in business ethics leads to numerous practical difficulties. A seemingly endless series of problems arises when one attempts to derive from such principles as the categorical imperative or the principle of utility, solutions to ethical problems faced by businesspeople. Hopeless ambiguity in application, apparent counterexamples, ad hoc rebuttals, counterintuitive conclusions, and apparently contradictory prescriptions create an overwhelming morass in the discussion of particular moral situations. The confusion is compounded even further when recommendations from competing principles are added to the discussion. Those of us who have tried to teach business ethics in this way can attest that ethics is not engineering: Unambiguously correct or even generally accepted answers occur very seldom. This radical inconclusiveness of ethical debates should at least suggest that something is wrong with our approaches to moral problems.

Beyond these practical problems, and partly explaining them, lie additional conceptual difficulties. By far the most significant is the fact that no ethical principle has yet been established in any plausible fashion as categorically binding upon all people. Philosophers have simply failed to justify the principles they apply in business ethics. Principle-based ethical theories are committed to the view that without the prior independent justification of the principle, attempts to institutionalize ethical responsibility by appeal to a principle will fail. Since we must admit the outright failure of the project of justifying moral principles, we should be skeptical of attempts to ground business responsibility upon moral principles.

Two further problems with the emphasis upon principles can lead us into a discussion of the alternative approach. First, principle-based ethics tends to identify particular actions as the core of morality and tends to ignore the character of the person who performs those acts. Ethical principles, whether they be called rules, maxims, laws, or action guides,

inevitably conceive of moral judgments in terms of the question What should I do? and disregard the equally practical question of What [kind of person] should I be? Consequently, business ethics often labors under the inadequate assumption that every particular act can, once and for all, be determined as obligatory, prohibited, or permissible. . . .

Of course, this conviction can be seriously questioned. Why should we assume that the moral world is unambiguous? In light of the vast number of experiences that have given rise to the rapid recent growth of applied ethics, should we not assume just the opposite? I suggest that we recognize the moral life to be often fundamentally ambiguous. Ethics is not like problem solving in science or technology: There just may not *be* clear moral answers "out there" waiting to be discovered if only we use the right method. Principle-based ethics encourages us to think that there are such answers. If only we apply the right principle carefully enough, we can determine the moral status of each individual action.

A second, not unrelated, problem concerns the impersonal nature of principles. Principles are distinct from the people who are to use them: They are external rules to be internalized, adopted, accepted as one's own, and applied. This creates a gap between person and principle, a gap that underlies some of the most serious problems in ethics. Even if moral principles were plausibly justified as binding on all rational agents (a goal that, I suggested above, has yet to be approached), the motivation question remains. Why should I do what is required by this principle? As a motivational question, this remains open. Even if the principle could give us unambiguous advice, we can (and do) sensibly ask Why should *I* do this? Principle-based ethics leaves us with an unbridgeable motivational gap between the applied principle and the action. (On the face of it, it seems that the closer a principle comes to the goal of being rationally justified—for example, the categorical imperative—the more formal it is and the more empty it is of motivational content. On the other hand, the closer a principle is to providing a motive to act—for example, the utilitarian happiness principles—the farther it is from being rationally binding on all rational agents.)

AN ALTERNATIVE APPROACH

Let us suppose that, unlike technical or scientific problems, moral problems have no answers or solutions just waiting to be discovered. What if there were no single right answer to many of the moral problems confronting us? Besides despair, is any alternative open to us? I would like to suggest that there is, and that we can be guided to this alternative by Aristotle.

The Aristotelian Good

Aristotle characterizes good acts as those acts performed by the good man. Although this often is thought to be circular, it seems to me to contain a wealth of truth. Imagine that you are lost deep in a jungle. There is no *one* way out of this predicament and indeed you may never get out. What would you hope for? I would want neither a map nor a survival handbook. Since I don't know where I am to begin with, a map will be of little help. Since the handbook cannot hope to cover every situation that might be encountered, it can be only marginally helpful. Rather, I would like a person who is experienced in the ways of the jungle to act as my guide. I think that Aristotle saw moral problems in much the same way. Deciding how we should live our lives is like deciding what to do in the jungle. Principles and rules will be of little help since, like maps, they can be helpful only when you already know where you are (have already established that the rule is morally justified) and, like handbooks, they cannot hope to cover all situations. What we need is a person experienced in the ways of life.

Accordingly, the Aristotelian good world is not one that conforms to some preestablished principle. Rather, it is a world populated by good people. I suggest that the good business also is not one that conforms to some preestablished principle, but one that is populated by good people. A morally responsible business is not one that measures its actions against some external principle, but is one in which good people are making the decisions.

Such a good person would be a person of character, disciplined to avoid the temptations of immediate, short-term pleasures. She would recognize that much of what is worthwhile in life is not easily and immediately achievable. This person would not be overcommitted to rules and regulations; she would have the courage to be creative, to encourage and entertain new ideas, to sometimes go on intuition. (The good person certainly would not be a bureaucrat!) The good person would also enjoy others, recognizing that solitude in a social world will result in the loss of great good. This might imply that the good person have a sense of humor. The good person would also foster her intellectual abilities. Reason and intelligence can contribute much (but not all) to the good life. Above all else, the good person possesses *phronesis,* or practical wisdom. Following Aristotle, since ethics is not a demonstrative science and since there are no unambiguous answers in ethics, a type of reasoning different from scientific reasoning will be required of the good person. The ability to make reasonable decisions in situations in which there is no right answer is the mark of phronesis: It is to possess practical wisdom.

It is the nature of phronesis that one cannot specify, a priori, what it will amount to in practice. In general, it is the ability to apply lessons learned in the past to new situations in the present. It is to be able to make appropriate adjustments so that general lessons fit the specific situation. Phronesis requires us to fit our reasoning to the situation and to avoid forcing present situations into preconceived categories. In this sense, phronesis is the antithesis of bureaucratic reasoning. It is the ability to adapt to changing situations without losing sight of one's ultimate goal. A business seeking to foster the development of good persons will be well advised to encourage the development of phronesis.[2]

The Nature of Virtues

I would now like to pursue some suggestions about the nature of the virtues that are found in Alasdair MacIntyre's book *After Virtue.*

Traditionally, the virtues have been conceptually tied to some *telos,* or some "good life" for man. The virtues were those character traits that promoted the attainment of the good life. The good man, in turn, was that person who possessed these virtues. The history of moral philosophy from at least the seventeenth century essentially ignores the role of the virtues in ethical theory. At best, the virtues were given a position alongside sentiments and feelings as being part of the noncognitive, and therefore arbitrary and subjective, side of morality. The most compelling explanation for this view centers on the fact that modern philosophy has, by and large, rejected the notion that there is any single, nonarbitrary telos for man. Some writers would trace this to the individualism of post-Hobbesian liberalism. The focus of that liberalism is upon man as atomistic individual and away from man as social. Since individual men have different ends, it becomes folly to try to identify some one end for all men. Other writers of a Marxist bent trace this loss of a human telos to the alienation that results from the modern industrial-capitalist society. Still other commentators trace the rejection of a human telos to the rejection of teleology in general during the scientific revolution that took place during the sixteenth and seventeenth centuries. Whatever the cause, the lack of some one telos for all people prevented the development of anything but a subjective, variable account of virtues.

I am not prepared to defend some conception of the good life for man. Nevertheless, some suggestions we find in MacIntyre might start us in the right direction. In regard to the good life, MacIntyre says:

> To ask "What is the good for me?" is to ask how best I might live out that unity [of an individual life] and bring it to completion. To ask "What is the good life for man?" is to ask what all answers to the former question must have in common.[3]

What all answers to the first question have in common involves what is necessary to live a unified, whole life. The unity of a life can emerge only when that life is situated in a social and historical context, a "narrative" in MacIntyre's phrase, that gives meaning to that life. Individuals do not exist as solipsists, our every action—indeed, our every thought—can be meaningful only within a complex social, historical, and linguistic context. Thus, to try and live our life in isolation from others will undermine the very context that gives meaning to and ultimately unifies our lives. It will effectively prevent us from attaining our own good, the fulfillment of our life story or narrative.

What does this have to do with business ethics? It seems to me that there are two ways in which the roles people play in business can be understood. Only one of these will contribute to that unity of the human life by situating the person within a social and historical context.

In what I call the *instrumental view,* individuals fill roles that are simply means to some other end (profit for the employer, wages for the employee). In this view, an individual fills a position in much the same way that components are plugged into a stereo system. Individuals are interchangeable parts, and as such they are denied any intrinsic value or meaning of their own. This essentially is the bureaucratic view of business in which an organizational chart gives meaning to each position. The position itself and the individual who fills it have value only so long as they are efficient means to some external end. In this view, individuals are encouraged to think of themselves as role-players. Like the manager in Albert Carr's "Business Bluffing" article, individuals play a variety of roles: managers, spouses, parents, religious believers, political constituents. When stripped of these roles, however, the individual means little or nothing. As a result, individuals are denied the unity of life that is essential to the pursuit of their good life.

On the other hand, there is what I call the *professional view* in which the positions individuals occupy are valuable in themselves and not just as means to some other end. Like the medical or teaching profession, these positions derive their value from those goods (what MacIntyre calls "internal goods") that can be achieved only through the practice of that activity. Individuals occupying these positions derive meaning and value from the pursuit and attainment of goods that are internal to those positions. These goods are essentially social, having developed during a long social history and, in turn, contributing to the future good of that society. As such, these positions are more likely to foster the unity (or integrity) that is necessary to live out one's life and bring it to completion. Unlike jobs, professions do not ask the individual participant to suspend the pursuit of the good life while at work.

In the instrumental view, work is what one does to earn the money needed to pursue what is valuable. Since value is therefore determined by money, the individual is left to assign her own value to anything at all. In the professional view, one pursues what has been established as valuable in itself by the social history of that profession. This pursuit of the objective social good is an intrinsic part of the profession. I would suggest that we develop the professional conception of business management by recognizing the intrinsic value of business as the supplier of goods and services. In this view the function of business (indeed, its social responsibility) is to produce goods and services that contribute to the good of society. Moral philosophers are encouraged to examine the character traits necessary to attain these goods in the attempt to describe the virtues of business management.

Tying some of these suggestions together, let us say that the "good life" for man lies in the pursuit of excellence. Let us say that excellence for business is the pursuit of goods and services that contribute to and advance the social good. This social good, ultimately, is a decision that should be made in the political arena. (This calls for an approach to business ethics in terms of social and political philosophy rather than in terms of ethical theory.) Nevertheless, we can say that a business can institutionalize ethics by fostering the development of good people within its ranks. Ways of doing this include closely identifying employee positions with the pursuit of business excellence. In part, this requires avoiding the instrumental view of employee roles. It would also include the encouragement of phronesis as its decision procedure and the avoidance of bureaucratic formalism.

Notes

1. See his *Corporations and Morality* (Englewood Cliffs, N.J.: Prentice Hall, 1981).
2. For an interesting parallel to this account of phronesis in business, see *In Search of Excellence* by Thomas Peters and Robert Waterman (New York: Harper & Row, 1982).
3. Alasdair MacIntyre, *After Virtue* (Notre Dame, Ind.: University of Notre Dame Press, 1981), 203.

Review and Discussion Questions

1. What does DesJardins mean by "principle-based ethics"? Explain what he sees as its practical and theoretical problems. Do you agree with DesJardins's criticisms? Can we do without principle-based ethics?

2. Explain the significance of Aristotle's concept of *phronesis*. How does Aristotle's approach to ethics differ from those described in this chapter and from that developed by James Rachels in the previous essay?

3. What implications does MacIntyre's discussion of virtues and the good life have for business ethics? Explain the difference between the "instrumental" and the "professional" view of the roles people play in business.

4. What do you think is the best way of doing business ethics? Why? Is it possible to combine principle-based ethics with the approach recommended by DesJardins?

Further Reading for Chapter 2

Tom L. Beauchamp, *Philosophical Ethics,* 3rd ed. (New York: McGraw-Hill, 2000) is an introductory text with selected readings covering classical ethical theories, rights, and the nature of morality.

William H. Shaw, *Contemporary Ethics: Taking Account of Utilitarianism* (Oxford: Blackwell, 1999) sympathetically examines the utilitarian approach to ethics.

   InfoTrac College Edition: For further information or to conduct research, please go to www.infotrac-college.com.

Peter Singer, ed., *A Companion to Ethics* (Oxford: Blackwell, 1991) is a comprehensive reference work with survey essays by many individual authors.

Christina Hoff Sommers, ed., *Right and Wrong* (New York: Harcourt Brace Jovanovich, 1986), **Judith A. Boss,** ed., *Perspectives on Ethics,* 2nd ed. (New York: McGraw-Hill, 2003), and **Mark Timmons**, ed., *Conduct and Character,* 4th ed. (Belmont, Calif.: Wadsworth, 2003) provide good selections of readings on egoism, relativism, utilitarianism, Kantianism, and other normative theories.

(See also the readings suggested at the end of Chapter 1.)

3

Justice and Economic Distribution

It seems strange to recall that until the early years of the twentieth century, there was no federal tax on personal income. Only with the passing of the Sixteenth Amendment to the U.S. Constitution in 1913 was Congress granted the right to collect tax on the income of its citizens. Since then, the income tax laws have grown enormously complex. Lawyers study for years to master the intricacies of the system, and most people with middle incomes or better require professional assistance to file their annual tax forms. Because the tax rules do so much to shape the character of our economy and the distribution of income and wealth across the country, their fairness is something that concerns most Americans.

Fairness was a theme when both George Bush and his Democratic opponent, Al Gore, campaigned for president in 2000 by promising tax reductions. And, indeed, one of the first things President Bush did, once in office, was to push a sheaf of income tax cuts through Congress. True, his predecessor, Bill Clinton, had raised the federal income tax, but only on individuals with a taxable income over $115,000. They saw their income tax rate increase from 31 percent to 36 percent. Clinton also slapped a 10 percent surcharge on those with incomes above $240,000. However, until Ronald Reagan lowered it, the tax rate for the wealthiest individuals had been 63 percent (indeed, until 1960 it had been 91 percent). When President Reagan reduced taxes on the wealthy, he also eliminated some important tax loopholes. But the most significant feature of his tax policy was its rejection of the principle of "progressivity"—namely, that the wealthy ought to pay taxes at a higher rate than the poor.

Although recent tax cuts mostly benefit the well-to-do, our wealthier citizens still, of course, pay the bulk of the nation's income taxes—for the simple reason that most of the nation's income goes to them. Indeed, in recent years wealthier Americans have been getting more and more, as the distribution of national income has grown increasingly unequal. Since 1977, after-tax incomes for the bottom 60 percent of Americans have declined 12 percent, while the top 1 percent have seen their incomes double.[1] The disproportionate gains of the well-to-do mean that they are getting a larger share of the pie than before. According to the U.S. Census Bureau, as Table 3.1 shows, over recent decades the nation's total income has been getting divided in an increasingly unequal way, with those who are already very well off securing a steadily growing share of aggregate family income. The flip side, of course, is that the bottom 60 percent are now receiving a smaller share than before.

Table 3.1 Share of Aggregate Family Income[2]

	1970	1980	1990	2001
Best-off fifth	40.9%	41.1%	44.3%	47.7%
Second fifth	23.8%	24.4%	23.8%	22.9%
Middle fifth	17.6%	17.6%	16.6%	15.4%
Fourth fifth	12.2%	11.6%	10.8%	9.7%
Poorest fifth	5.4%	5.3%	4.6%	4.3%
Top 5%	15.6%	14.6%	17.4%	21.0%

The gap between the wealthiest 10 percent and the poorest 10 percent is greater in the United States than in any industrialized country except Russia.[3] Moreover, for the last three decades, median family income, measured in constant dollars, has gone up only because wives are working more than before. Although real wages for production and nonsupervisory workers grew by 75 percent from 1947 to 1973, since then wages have declined and remain below their 1973 peak.[4]

By contrast, middle-level managers have fared much better, and top executives have done spectacularly well. In 2002 *Business Week*'s annual survey of the two highest-paid executives at America's largest companies showed their average total pay (salary, bonuses, and long-term compensation) to be $11 million. Among the highest paid were Steve Jobs of Apple Computer and Timothy Koogle of Yahoo!, who took home $84 million and $64 million, respectively. But even their pay appears modest compared with that of Josef Straus of JDS Uniphase ($150.8 million) and Howard Solomon of Forest Laboratories ($148.5 million)—not to mention the whopping $706.1 million pocketed by Lawrence Ellison of Oracle, which broke all previous records for CEO compensation.[5]

The United States leads the world in executive pay.[6] Japan's CEOs, for example, earn a salary of only $300,000 to $500,000 a year, with far fewer bonuses and stock options than their American counterparts.[7] As a result of the stock market slump, average pay for American CEOs has declined slightly since 2000. Nevertheless, since 1980 the compensation of CEOs has grown from 42 times that of a production worker to 531 times greater.[8] Since 1990, CEO pay has gone up 571 percent. In comparison, corporate profits have grown by a relatively modest 114 percent, and the average worker's pay by a mere 37 percent (which is just above inflation at 32 percent).[9] A schoolteacher who made $31,166 in 1990 would now make $177,958 if teachers' salaries had grown at the same rate as CEO pay. The median weekly salary for all workers is $597.[10] If the average CEO works 60 hours a week, 52 weeks a year, then he or she earns that much every 10 minutes.

Our well-heeled CEOs symbolize the well-documented increase in income inequality in the United States. This chapter will not speculate on the causes of this income shift, but we can see the evidence of it all around us—for example, in corporate America's two-tiered marketing. Instead of aiming their products and services at a mass middle-class market, companies must now position their offerings as either upscale or downscale, tailoring them either to affluent professionals or to low-wage earners.[11] Our economy has created millions of new jobs in the last twenty years, but these have been predominantly in low-income sectors of the economy, such as the fast-food industry. Good, well-paying middle-income jobs—especially in industries such as steel, automotives, and machine tools—are scarcer than ever. More and more families require two incomes just to get by; those with only one income frequently find themselves unable to sustain a middle-class lifestyle.

Not only is income inequality increasing in our society and the middle class shrinking (from 61 percent of families in 1969 to 50 percent today), but also workers at the bottom are less likely to move up in their lifetimes. The United States has always prided itself on being a land of opportunity and upward mobility, but recent evidence suggests that the economy is becoming more rigid and class bound. "You can't take solace anymore in the American dream of working hard and migrating up through society," says William J. McDonough, president of the Federal Reserve Bank of New York. In fact, today there is significantly less upward mobility for low-wage earners in the United States than there is in Europe.[12]

These trends are even more alarming when set against the background of the extremely unequal distribution of wealth in this country. Not only do the top 1 percent receive a disproportionate share of the total income, but they already own nearly 40 percent of the nation's total net worth—more than is owned by the entire bottom 90 percent of U.S. households. The economic elite own half of all stocks, mutual funds, financial securities, and trusts, two-thirds of all business equity, and 36 percent of nonresidential real estate.[13] It would, for example, take a city of more than a quarter-million average Americans—the size of Rochester, New York—to equal the net worth of Bill Gates alone.

There is nothing inevitable about such great inequalities in income and wealth. The distribution of income in Japan and Germany is far more equal than in the United States, and both nations are just as thoroughly capitalist as we are. In fact, the United States is the most unequal industrialized nation in the world in terms of income and wealth.[14] Although it has the highest child poverty rate of any industrial country, with more than 21 percent of its children growing up poor, the United States chooses to spend only 0.6 percent of its gross national product on basic income support for children; Canada spends 1.6 percent.[15] Inequality of income is not some brute fact of nature, even in market-oriented societies. Rather, political choices determine how income is ultimately distributed. How much inequality a society is willing to accept reflects both its moral values and the relative strength of its contending social and political forces.

Arguments can be made for and against different degrees of income inequality, for and against progressivity in taxation, and for and against more specific tax regulations. But whatever one's position on these issues, it probably relies on some theory of economic justice for evaluating a particular tax regulation, the tax system as a whole, or even the society's economic system. The topic of economic justice deals with that constellation of moral issues raised by a society's distribution of wealth, income, status, and power.

Ethical questions arise daily about how wealth and goods should be allocated. Given the relative scarcity of a society's resources, deciding how these resources should be distributed is an important moral task. Should everyone receive roughly the same amount? Or should people be rewarded according to how hard they work or how much they contribute to society? To what extent should economic distribution take need into account? For example, with modern technology at their disposal, today's hospitals are able to perform life-prolonging feats of medicine that were undreamed of only a couple of decades ago, but these services are often extraordinarily costly. Who, then, should have access to them? Those who can afford them? Any who need them? Those who are most likely to benefit?

Chapter 2 discussed several basic moral theories and the general principles of right and wrong associated with them. This chapter focuses on the more specific topic of justice and economic distribution—that is, on the principles that are relevant to the moral assessment of society's distribution of economic goods and services. Although the topic is an abstract one, it is particularly relevant to the study of business ethics, because it concerns the moral standards to be used in evaluating the institutional frameworks within which both business and nonbusiness organizations operate. Specifically, this chapter will examine:

1. The concept of justice, its relation to fairness, equality, rights, or what people deserve, and some rival principles of economic distribution

2. The utilitarian approach to justice in general and economic justice in particular

3. The libertarian theory, which places a moral priority on liberty and free exchange

4. The contractarian and egalitarian theory of John Rawls

THE NATURE OF JUSTICE

Justice is an old concept with a rich history, a concept that is fundamental to any discussion of how society ought to be organized. Philosophical concern with justice goes back at least to ancient Greece. For Plato and some of his contemporaries, justice seems to have been the paramount virtue or, more precisely, the sum of virtue with regard to our relations with others. Philosophers today, however, generally distinguish justice from the whole of morality. The complaint that something is "unjust" is more specific than that it is "bad" or "immoral." What, then, makes an act, policy, or institution unjust? Unfortunately, the terms *just* and *unjust* are vague, and different people use them in different ways. Still, talk of justice or injustice typically focuses on at least one of several related ideas—fairness, equality, desert, or rights.

First, justice is often used to mean *fairness.* Justice frequently concerns the fair treatment of members of groups of people or else looks backwards to the fair compensation of prior injuries. Exactly what fairness requires is difficult to say, and different standards may be pertinent in different cases. If corporate manager Smith commits bribery, he is justly punished under our laws. If other managers commit equally serious crimes but are allowed to escape punishment, then Smith suffers a comparative injustice because he was unfairly singled out. On the other hand, Smith and other white-collar criminals are treated unfairly and thus unjustly, although this time for the opposite reason, if stiffer sentences are meted out to common criminals for less grave offenses.

One way unfairness creates injustice is when like cases are not treated in the same fashion. Following Aristotle, most philosophers believe that we are required, as a formal priniciple of justice, to treat similar cases alike except where there is some relevant difference. This principle emphasizes the role of impartiality and consistency in justice, but it is a purely formal principle because it is silent about which differences are relevant and which are not. Furthermore, satisfying this formal requirement does not guarantee that justice is done. For example, a judge who treats similar cases alike can succeed in administering fairly and nonarbitrarily a law that is itself unjust (like a statute requiring racial segregation).

Related to Aristotle's fairness requirement is a second idea commonly bound up with the concept of justice, namely, that of *equality.* Justice is frequently held to require that our treatment of people reflect their fundamental moral equality. While Aristotle's formal principle of justice does not say whether we are to assume equality of treatment until some difference between cases is shown or to assume the opposite until some relevant similarities are demonstrated, a claim of injustice based on equality is meant to place the burden of proof on those who would endorse unequal treatment. Still, the premise that all persons are equal does not establish a direct relationship between justice and economic distribution. We all believe that some differences in the treatment of persons are consistent with equality (punishment, for example), and neither respect for equality nor a commitment to equal treatment necessarily implies an equal distribution of economic goods.

Despite equality, then, individual circumstances—in particular, what a person has done—make a difference. We think it is unjust, for example, when a guilty person goes free or an innocent person hangs, regardless of how others have been treated. This suggests that justice sometimes involves, as a third aspect, something in addition to equal or impartial treatment. Justice also requires that people get what they *deserve* or, as a number of ancient moralists put it, that each receive his or her due.

This is closely related to a fourth and final idea, namely, that one is treated unjustly when one's moral *rights* are violated. John Stuart Mill, in fact, made this the defining characteristic of injustice. In his view, what distinguishes injustice from other types of wrongful behavior is that it involves a violation of the rights of some identifiable person:

> Whether the injustice consists in depriving a person of a possession, or in breaking faith with him, or in treating him worse than he deserves, or worse than other people who have no greater claims—in each case the supposition implies two things: a wrong done, and some assignable person who is

wronged. . . . It seems to me that this feature in the case—a right in some person, correlative to the moral obligation—constitutes the specific difference between justice and generosity or beneficence. Justice implies something which it is not only right to do, and wrong not to do, but which some individual person can claim from us as a moral right.[16]

Rival Principles of Distribution

Justice, then, is an important subclass of morality in general, a subclass that generally involves appeals to the overlapping notions of fairness, equality, desert, and rights. Turning to the topic of distributive justice—that is, to the proper distribution of social benefits and burdens (in particular, economic benefits and burdens)—a number of rival principles have been proposed. Among the principles most frequently recommended as a basis of distribution are: to each an equal share, to each according to individual need, to each according to personal effort, to each according to social contribution, and to each according to merit. Every one of these principles has its advocates, and each seems plausible in some circumstances. But only in some. There are problems with each. For example, if equality of income were guaranteed, then the lazy would receive as much as the industrious. On the other hand, effort is hard to measure and compare, and what one is able to contribute to society may depend on one's luck in being at the right place at the right time. And so on. No single principle seems to work in enough circumstances to be defended successfully as the sole principle of justice in distribution.

It often seems that we simply employ different principles of distributive justice in different circumstances. For example, corporations in certain industries may be granted tax breaks because of their social contribution; welfare programs operate on the basis of need; and business firms award promotions for meritorious performance. Moreover, multiple principles may often be relevant to a single situation. Sometimes they may pull in the same direction, as when wealthy professionals such as doctors defend their high incomes simultaneously on grounds of superior effort, merit, social contribution, and even (because of the high cost of malpractice insurance) need. Or the principles may pull in different directions, as when a teacher must balance effort against performance in assigning grades to pupils. Some philosophers are content to leave the situation here. As they see it, there are various equally valid, prima facie principles of just distribution—equality, need, effort, and so on—and one must try to find the principle that best applies in the given circumstances. If several principles seem to apply, then one must simply weigh them the best one can.

In his book *Spheres of Justice,* Michael Walzer pursues a more sophisticated version of this pluralistic approach.[17] Skeptical of the assumption that justice requires us to implement (in different contexts) some basic principle or set of principles, Walzer argues

> that different goods ought to be distributed for different reasons, in accordance with different procedures, by different agents; and that all these differences derive from different understandings of the social goods themselves—the inevitable product of historical and cultural particularism.[18]

Different norms and principles govern different distributive spheres, and these norms and principles are shaped by the implicit social meanings of the goods in question. He continues:

> Every social good or set of goods constitutes, as it were, a distributive sphere within which only certain criteria and arrangements are appropriate. Money is inappropriate in the sphere of ecclesiastical office. . . . There is no single standard [against which all distributions are to be measured]. But there are standards (roughly knowable even when they are also controversial) for every social good and every distributive sphere in every particular society.[19]

As Walzer sees it, distributive criteria are determined by the particular, historically shaped social meanings of the goods in question. The philosophical task is to tease out the inner logic of each type of good, thus revealing the tacit, socially shared values that govern (or should govern) its distribution.

Walzer's historically informed discussion of topics like medical care or dirty and degrading work are rich and intriguing, but his view implies that when it comes to issues of distributive justice, the best philosophers can do is to try to unravel the implicit, socially specific norms that govern the distribution of different goods in a particular society. Many contemporary philosophers disagree. They believe that we should step further back than Walzer does from existing norms and social arrangements and seek some general theory of justice in economic distribution, on the basis of which we can assess current social practices. Three such theories are the utilitarian, the libertarian, and the Rawlsian (egalitarian).

THE UTILITARIAN VIEW

For utilitarians, as Chapter 2 explained, happiness is the overarching value. Whether one assesses the rightness and wrongness of actions in terms of how much happiness they produce, as an act utilitarian does, or uses happiness as the standard for deciding what moral principles a society should accept as the basis for determining right and wrong, as a rule utilitarian does, happiness is the only thing that is good in and of itself. On that utilitarians are agreed.

Earlier we considered John Stuart Mill's idea that injustice involves the violation of the rights of some identifiable person. This is what distinguishes it from other types of immoral behavior. But if injustice involves the violation of moral rights, the question arises of how a utilitarian like Mill understands talk of rights. Mill's position was that saying I have a right to something is saying I have a valid claim on society to protect me in the possession of that thing, either by the force of law or through education and opinion. And I have that valid claim in the first place because society's protection of my possession of that thing is warranted on utilitarian grounds. "To have a right, then, is . . . to have something

which society ought to defend me in the possession of. If the objector goes on to ask why it ought, I can give him no other reason than general utility."[20] What utilitarianism identifies as rights are certain moral rules, the observance of which is of the utmost importance for the long-run, overall maximization of happiness.

Accordingly, Mill summed up his view of justice as follows:

> Justice is a name for certain classes of moral rules which concern the essentials of human well-being more nearly, and are therefore of more absolute obligation, than any other rules for the guidance of life; and the notion which we have found to be of the essence of the idea of justice—that of a right residing in an individual—implies and testifies to this more binding obligation.
> The moral rules which forbid mankind to hurt one another (in which we must never forget to include wrongful interference with each other's freedom) are more vital to human well-being than any maxims, however important, which only point out the best mode of managing some department of human affairs.[21]

Although justice for Mill was ultimately a matter of promoting social well-being, not every issue of social utility was a matter of justice. The concept of justice identifies certain important social utilities, that is, certain rules or rights, the upholding of which is crucial for social well-being.

For utilitarians, then, justice is not an independent moral standard, distinct from their general principle. Rather, the maximization of happiness ultimately determines what is just and unjust. Critics of utilitarianism contend that knowing what will promote happiness is always difficult. People are bound to estimate consequences differently, thus making the standard of utility an inexact and unreliable principle for determining what is just. Mill, however, did not see much merit in this criticism. For one thing, it presupposes that we all agree about what the principles of justice are and how to apply them. This is far from the case, Mill argued. Indeed, without utilitarianism to provide a determinate standard of justice, one is always left with a plethora of competing principles, all of which seem to have some plausibility but are mutually incompatible.

As an example, Mill pointed to the conflict between two principles of justice that occurs in the realm of economic distribution. Is it just or not, he asked, that more talented workers should receive a greater remuneration? There are two possible answers to this question:

> On the negative side of the question it is argued that whoever does the best he can deserves equally well, and ought not in justice to be put in a position of inferiority for no fault of his own; that superior abilities have already advantages more than enough . . . without adding to these a superior share of the world's goods; and that society is bound in justice rather to make compensation to the less favored for this unmerited inequality of advantages than to aggravate it.[22]

This argument sounds plausible, but then so does the alternative answer:

> On the contrary side it is contended that society receives more from the more efficient laborer; that, his services being more useful, society owes him a larger return for them; that a greater share of the joint result is actually his work, and not to allow his claim to it is a kind of robbery; that, if he is only to receive as much as others, he can only be justly required to produce as much.[23]

Here we have two conflicting principles of justice. How are we to decide between them? The problem, Mill said, is that both principles seem plausible:

> Justice has in this case two sides to it, which it is impossible to bring into harmony, and the two disputants have chosen opposite sides; the one looks to what it is just that the individual should receive, the other to what it is just that the community should give.[24]

Each disputant is, from his or her own point of view, unanswerable. "Any choice between them, on grounds of justice," Mill continued, "must be perfectly arbitrary." What, then, is the solution? For Mill, the utilitarian, it was straightforward: "Social utility alone can decide the preference."[25] The utilitarian standard must be the ultimate court of appeal in such cases. Only the utilitarian standard can provide an intelligent and satisfactory way of handling controversial questions of justice and of resolving conflicts between two competing principles of justice.

Utilitarianism and Economic Distribution

The utilitarian theory of justice ties the question of economic distribution to the promotion of social well-being or happiness. Utilitarians want an economic system that will bring more good to society than any other system. But what system is that? Utilitarianism itself, as a normative theory, provides no answer. The answer depends on the relevant social, economic, and political facts. A utilitarian must understand the various possibilities, determine their consequences, and assess the available options. Obviously, this is not a simple task. Deciding what sort of economic arrangements would best promote human happiness requires the utilitarian to consider many things, including (1) the type of economic ownership (private, public, mixed); (2) the way of organizing production and distribution in general (pure laissez faire, markets with government planning and regulation, fully centralized planning); (3) the type of authority arrangements within the units of production (worker control versus managerial prerogative); (4) the range and character of material incentives; and (5) the nature and extent of social security and welfare provisions.

As a matter of historical fact, utilitarians in the early nineteenth century tended to favor free trade and the laissez-faire view of Adam Smith that unregulated market relations and free competition best promote the total social good.[26] Today it is probably fair to say that few, if any, utilitarians believe happiness would be maximized by a pure nineteenth-century-style capitalism, without any welfare arrangements. However, they are not in agreement on the question of what economic arrangements would in fact maximize happiness. Nonetheless, many utilitarians would favorably view increased worker participation in industrial life and more equal distribution of income.

Worker Participation. In his *Principles of Political Economy*, originally published in 1848, Mill argued for the desirability of breaking down the sharp and hostile division between the producers, or workers, on the one hand, and the capitalists, or owners, on the other. Not only would this be a good thing, it was also something that the advance of civilization was tending naturally to bring about: "The relation of masters and workpeople will be gradually superseded by partnership, in one or two forms: in some cases, association of the labourers with the capitalist; in others, and perhaps finally in all, association of labourers among themselves."[27] These developments would not only enhance productivity but—more importantly—promote the fuller development and well-being of the people involved. The aim, Mill thought, should be to enable people "to work with or for one another in relations not involving dependence."[28]

By the association of labor and capital, Mill had in mind different schemes of profit sharing. For example, "in the American ships trading to China, it has long been the custom for every sailor to have an interest in the profits of the voyage; and to this has been ascribed the general good conduct of those seamen."[29] This sort of association, however, would eventually give way to a more complete system of worker cooperatives:

> The form of association, however, which if mankind continue to improve, must be expected in the end to predominate, is not that which can exist between a capitalist as chief, and workpeople without a voice in the management, but the association of the labourers themselves on terms of equality, collectively owning the capital with which they carry on their operations, and working under managers elected and removable by themselves.[30]

In *Principles* Mill discussed several examples of successful cooperative associations and viewed optimistically the future of the cooperative movement:

> Eventually, and in perhaps a less remote future than may be supposed, we may, through the cooperative principle, see our way to a change in society, which would combine the freedom and independence of the individual, with the moral, intellectual, and economical advantages of aggregate production; and which . . . would realize, at least in the industrial department, the best aspirations of the democratic spirit.[31]

What that transformation implied for Mill was nothing less than "the nearest approach to social justice, and the most beneficial ordering of industrial affairs for the universal good, which it is possible at present to foresee."[32]

Greater Equality of Income. Utilitarians are likely to be sympathetic to the argument that steps should be taken to reduce the great disparities in income that characterize our society. That is, they are likely to believe that making the distribution of income more equal is a good strategy for maximizing happiness. The reason for this goes back to what economists would call "the declining marginal utility of money." This phrase simply means that successive additions to one's income produce, on average, less happiness or welfare than did earlier additions.

The declining utility of money follows from the fact, as Professor Richard Brandt explains it, that the outcomes we want are preferentially ordered, some being more strongly wanted than others:

> So a person, when deciding how to spend his resources, picks a basket of groceries which is at least as appealing as any other he can purchase with the money he has. The things he does not buy are omitted because other things are wanted more. If we double a person's income, he will spend the extra money on items he wants less (some special cases aside), and which will give less enjoyment than will the original income. The more one's income, the fewer preferred items one buys and the more preferred items one already has. On the whole, then, when the necessities of life have been purchased and the individual is spending on luxury items, he is buying items which will give less enjoy-

ment. . . . This conclusion corresponds well with common-sense reflection and practice.[33]

The obvious implication is that a more egalitarian allocation of income—that is, an allocation that increases the income of those who now earn less—would boost total happiness. Brandt, for one, therefore defends equality of after-tax income on utilitarian grounds, subject to the following exceptions: supplements to meet special needs, supplements necessary for incentives or to allocate resources efficiently, and variations to achieve other socially desirable ends, such as population control.[34] Brandt states that this guiding principle of distribution is of only prima facie force and may have to be balanced against other principles and considerations. Still, it illustrates the point that utilitarians today are likely to advocate increased economic equality.

THE LIBERTARIAN APPROACH

Whereas utilitarians associate justice with social utility, philosophers who endorse what is called *libertarianism* identify justice with an ideal of liberty. For them, liberty is the prime value, and justice consists in permitting each person to live as he or she pleases, free from the interference of others. Accordingly, one libertarian asserts: "We are concerned with the condition of men in which coercion of some by others is reduced as much as possible in society."[35] Another maintains that libertarianism is "a philosophy of personal liberty—the liberty of each person to live according to his own choices, provided he does not attempt to coerce others and thus prevent them from living according to their choices."[36] Such views show clearly the libertarian's association of justice with liberty and of liberty itself with the absence of interference by other persons.

Libertarians firmly reject utilitarianism's concern for total social well-being. Utilitarians are willing to restrict the liberty of some, to interfere with their choices, if doing so will promote greater net happiness than not doing so. Libertarians cannot stomach this approach. As long as you are not doing something that interferes

with anyone else's liberty, then no person, group, or government should disturb you in living the life you choose—not even if its doing so would maximize social happiness.

Although individual liberty is something that all of us value, it may not be the only thing we value. For the libertarian, however, liberty takes priority over other moral concerns. In particular, justice consists solely of respect for individual liberty. A libertarian world, with a complete commitment to individual liberty, would be a very different world from the one we now live in. Consider the following: In the case of *Bowers v. Hardwick*, the U.S. Supreme Court upheld a Georgia law forbidding sodomy between consenting male homosexuals; the government registers young men for military service and can, if it chooses, draft them; laws prevent adults from ingesting substances that the legislature deems harmful or immoral (such as marijuana and cocaine); and the state imposes taxes on our income to—among many other things—support needy citizens, provide loans to college students, and fund various projects for the common good. From a libertarian perspective, none of these policies is just.

Given the assumption that liberty means noninterference, libertarians generally agree that liberty allows only a minimal or "nightwatchman" state. Such a state is limited to the narrow functions of protecting its citizens against force, theft, and fraud; enforcing contracts; and performing other such basic maintenance functions. In this view, a more extensive state—in particular, one that taxes its better-off citizens to support the less fortunate ones—violates the liberty of individuals by forcing them to support projects, policies, or persons they have not freely chosen to support.

Nozick's Theory of Justice

Although libertarians differ in how they formulate their theory, the late Harvard professor Robert Nozick's *Anarchy, State, and Utopia* is a very influential statement of the libertarian case.[37] Nozick's challenging and powerful advocacy of libertarianism has stimulated much debate, obliging philosophers of all political persuasions to take the libertarian theory seriously. His views are thus worth presenting in detail.

Nozick begins from the premise that people have certain basic moral rights, which he calls "Lockean rights." By alluding to the political philosophy of John Locke (1632–1704), Nozick wishes to underscore that these rights are both negative and natural. They are negative because they require only that people forbear from acting in certain ways—in particular, that we refrain from interfering with others. Beyond this, we are not obliged to do anything positive for anyone else, nor is anyone required to do anything positive for us. We have no right, for example, to be provided with satisfying work or with any material goods that we might need. These negative rights, according to Nozick, are natural in the sense that we possess them independently of any social or political institutions.

These individual rights impose firm, virtually absolute restrictions (or, in Nozick's phrase, "side constraints") on how we may act. We cannot morally infringe on someone's rights for any purpose. Not only are we forbidden to interfere with a person's liberty in order to promote the general good, we are prohibited from doing so even if violating that individual's rights would somehow prevent other individuals' rights from being violated. Each individual is autonomous and responsible, and should be left to fashion his or her own life free from the interference of others—as long as doing so is compatible with the rights of others to do the same. Only an acknowledgment of this almost absolute right to be free from coercion, Nozick argues, fully respects the distinctiveness of individuals, each with a unique life to lead.

A belief in these rights shapes Nozick's theory of economic justice, which he calls the "entitlement theory." Essentially, Nozick maintains that people are entitled to their holdings (that is, goods, money, and property) as long as they have acquired them fairly. Stated another way, if you have obtained your possessions without vio-lating other people's Lockean rights, then you are entitled to them and may dispose of them as you choose. No one else has a legitimate claim on them. If you have secured a vast fortune without injuring other people, defrauding them, or otherwise violating their rights, then you are morally permitted to do with your fortune whatever you wish—bequeath it to a relative, endow a university, or squander it in riotous living. Even though other people may be going hungry, justice imposes no obligation on you to help them.

The first principle of Nozick's entitlement theory concerns the original acquisition of holdings—that is, the appropriation of unheld goods or the creation of new goods. If a person acquires a holding in accordance with this principle, then he or she is entitled to it. If, for example, you retrieve minerals from the wilderness or make something out of materials you already legitimately possess, then you have justly acquired this new holding. Nozick does not spell out this principle or specify fully what constitutes a just original acquisition, but the basic idea is clear and reflects the thinking of John Locke.

Property is a moral right, said Locke, because individuals are morally entitled to the products of their labor. When they mix their labor with the natural world, they are entitled to the resulting product. Thus, if a man works the land, then he is entitled to the land and its products because through his labor he has put something of himself into them. This investment of self through labor is the moral basis of ownership, Locke wrote, but there are limits to this right:

> In the beginning . . . men had a right to appropriate, by their labour, each one of himself, as much of the things of nature, as he could use. . . . Whatsoever he tilled and reaped, laid up and made use of, before it spoiled, that was his peculiar right; whatsoever he enclosed, and could feed, and make use of, the cattle and product was also his. But if either the grass of his inclosure rotted on the ground, or the fruit of his planting perished without gathering, and laying up,

this part of the earth . . . was still to be looked on as waste, and might be the possession of any other.[38]

In this early "state of nature" prior to the formation of government, property rights were limited not only by the requirement that one not waste what one claimed, but also by the restriction that "enough and as good" be left for others—that is, that one's appropriation not make others worse off. Later, however, with the introduction of money, Locke thought that both these restrictions were overcome. You can pile up money beyond your needs without its spoiling; and if your property is used productively and the proceeds offered for sale, then your appropriation leaves others no worse off than before.

Nozick's second principle concerns transfers of already-owned goods from one person to another: how people may legitimately transfer holdings and how they may legitimately get holdings from others. If a person possesses a holding because of a legitimate transfer, then he or she is entitled to it. Again, Nozick does not work out the details, but it is clear that acquiring something by purchase, as a gift, or through exchange would constitute a legitimate acquisition. Gaining it through theft, force, or fraud would violate the principle of justice in transfer.

Nozick's third and final principle states that one can justly acquire a holding only in accord with the two principles just discussed. If you come by a holding in some other way, you are not entitled to it. Nozick sums up his theory this way:

1. A person who acquires a holding in accordance with the principle of justice in acquisition is entitled to that holding.

2. A person who acquires a holding in accordance with the principle of justice in transfer, from someone else entitled to the holding, is entitled to the holding.

3. No one is entitled to a holding except by (repeated) applications of 1 and 2.

In short, the distribution of goods in a society is just if and only if all are entitled to the holdings they possess. Nozick calls his entitlement theory "historical" because what matters is how people come to have what they have. If people are entitled to their possessions, then the distribution of economic holdings is just, regardless of what the actual distribution happens to look like (for instance, how far people are above or below the average income) or what its consequences are.

The Wilt Chamberlain Example

Nozick argues that respect for liberty inescapably leads one to repudiate other conceptions of economic justice in favor of his entitlement approach. One of his most ingenious examples features Wilt Chamberlain, the late basketball star. Suppose, Nozick says, that things are distributed according to your favorite nonentitlement theory, whatever it is. (He calls this distribution D_1.) Now imagine that Wilt Chamberlain signs a contract with a team that guarantees him $5 from the price of each ticket. Whenever people buy a ticket to a game, they drop $5 into a special box with Chamberlain's name on it. To them it is worth it to see him play. Imagine then that in the course of a season 1 million people attend his games and Chamberlain ends up with far more than the average income—far more, indeed, than anyone else in the society earns. This result (D_2) upsets the initial distributional pattern (D_1).

Can the proponent of D_1 complain? Nozick thinks not:

> Is [Chamberlain] entitled to this income? Is this new distribution, D_2, unjust? If so, why? There is *no* question about whether each of the people was entitled to the control over the resources they held in D_1; because that was the distribution (your favorite) that (for the purposes of the argument) we assumed was acceptable. Each of these persons *chose* to give [$5] of their money to Chamberlain. . . . If D_1 was a just distribution, and people voluntarily moved from it to D_2, transferring parts of their shares they were given under D_1 . . . isn't D_2 also just? If the people were entitled to dispose of the resources to which they were

entitled (under D_1), didn't this include their being entitled to give it to, or exchange it with, Wilt Chamberlain? Can anyone else complain on grounds of justice?[39]

Having defended the legitimacy of Chamberlain's new wealth, Nozick pushes his case further, arguing that any effort to maintain some initial distributional arrangement like D_1 will interfere with people's liberty to use their resources as they wish. To preserve this original distribution, he writes, society would have to "forbid capitalist acts between consenting adults":

> The general point illustrated by the Wilt Chamberlain example . . . is that no [nonentitlement] principle of justice can be continuously realized without continuous interference with people's lives. Any favored pattern would be transformed into one unfavored by the principle, by people choosing to act in various ways; for example, by people exchanging goods and services with other people, or giving things to other people. . . . To maintain a pattern one must either continually interfere to stop people from transferring resources as they wish to, or continually (or periodically) interfere to take from some persons resources that others for some reason chose to transfer to them.[40]

The Libertarian View of Liberty

Libertarianism clearly involves a commitment to leaving market relations—buying, selling, and other exchanges—totally unrestricted.* Force and fraud are forbidden, of course, but there should be no interference with the uncoerced exchanges of consenting individuals. Not only is the market morally legitimate, but any attempt to interfere with consenting and nonfraudulent transactions between adults will be unacceptable. Thus, libertarians are for economic laissez faire and against any governmental economic activity that interferes with the marketplace, even if the point of the interference is to enhance the performance of the economy.

---

*Chapter 4 examines the nature of market economies in general and capitalism in particular.

It is important to emphasize that libertarianism's enthusiasm for the market rests on this commitment to liberty. By contrast, utilitarian defenders of the market defend it on the ground that an unregulated market works better than either a planned, socialist economy or the sort of regulated capitalism with some welfare benefits that we in fact have in the United States. That is, if a utilitarian defends laissez faire, he or she does so because of its consequences. Convince a utilitarian that some other form of economic organization better promotes human well-being, and the utilitarian will advocate that instead. With libertarians this is definitely not the case. As a matter of fact, libertarians typically agree with Adam Smith that unregulated capitalist behavior best promotes everyone's interests. But even if, hypothetically, someone like Nozick were convinced that some sort of socialism or welfare capitalism outperformed laissez-faire capitalism economically—greater productivity, shorter working day, higher standard of living—he or she would still reject this alternative as morally unacceptable. To tinker with the market, however beneficial it might be, would involve violating someone's liberty.

Libertarians say that their commitment to an unrestricted market reflects the priority of liberty over other values. However, libertarians do not value liberty in the mundane sense of people's freedom to do what they want to do. Rather, libertarians understand freedom in terms of their theory of rights, thus building a commitment to private property into their concept of liberty. According to them, being able to do what you want does not automatically represent an increase in your liberty. It does so only if you remain within the boundaries set by the Lockean rights of others. Likewise, one is unfree or coerced only when one's rights are infringed.

Imagine, for example, that having purchased the forest in which I occasionally stroll, the new owner bars my access to it. It would seem that my freedom has been reduced because I can no longer ramble where I wish. But libertarians deny that this is a restriction of my liberty. My liberty is restricted if and only if someone violates my

Lockean rights, which no one has done. Suppose that I go for a hike in the forest anyway. If the sheriff's deputies arrest me, they prevent me from doing what I want to do. But according to libertarianism, they do not restrict my liberty, nor do they coerce me. Why not? Because my hiking in the forest violates the landowner's rights.

Here libertarians seem driven to an unusual use of familiar terminology, but they have no choice. They cannot admit that abridging the landowner's freedom to do as he wants with his property would expand my freedom. If they did, then their theory would be in jeopardy. They would have to acknowledge that restricting the liberty or property rights of some could enhance the liberty of others. In other words, if their theory committed them simply to promoting as much as possible the goal of people doing what they want to do, then libertarians would be in the position of balancing the freedom of some against the freedom of others. But this sort of balancing and trading off is just what libertarians dislike about utilitarianism.

If liberty means being free to do what you want, it's not true that libertarians value it above everything else. What they value are Lockean property rights, which then set the parameters of liberty. Libertarians frequently contend (1) that private property is necessary for freedom and (2) that any society that doesn't respect private property rights is coercive. But libertarianism makes 1 true by definition, and 2 is incorrect. Any system of property (whether Lockean, socialist, or something in between) necessarily puts restrictions on people's conduct; its rules are coercive. What one system of property permits, another forbids. Society X prevents me from hiking in your woods, whereas society Y prevents you from stopping me. Both systems of rules are coercive. Both grant some freedoms and withhold others.

Markets and Free Exchange

Libertarians defend market relations, then, as necessary to respect human liberty (as their theory understands liberty). However, in doing so,

libertarians do not assert that, morally speaking, people deserve what they receive from others through gift or exchange, only that they are entitled to whatever they receive. The market tends generally, libertarians believe, to reward people for skill, diligence, and successful performance. Yet luck plays a role, too. Jack makes a fortune from having been in the right place at the right time with his beanie babies, while Jill loses her investment because the market for bottled water collapses. The libertarian position is not that Jack deserves to be wealthy and Jill does not; rather, it is that Jack is entitled to his holdings if he has acquired them in accordance with the principles of justice.

The same point comes up with regard to gifts and inheritance. Inheritance strikes many people as patently unfair. How can it be just, they ask, that one child inherits a vast fortune, the best schooling, and social, political, and business connections that will ensure his or her future, while another child inherits indigence, inferior schooling, and connections with crime? At birth neither youngster deserves anything—a fact suggesting, perhaps, that an equal division of holdings and opportunities would be the only fair allocation. For his part, Nozick contends that deserving has no bearing on the justice of inherited wealth; people are simply entitled to it as long as it is not ill gotten. Or looking at it the other way, if one is entitled to one's holdings, then one has a right to do with them as one wishes, including using them to benefit one's children.

According to libertarians, a totally free market is necessary for people to exercise their fundamental rights. Sometimes, however, unregulated market transactions can lead to disastrous results. Unfortunately, this is more than just a theoretical possibility. Amartya Sen, the Nobel Prize–winning economist, has shown how in certain circumstances changing market entitlements have led to mass starvation. Although the average person thinks of famine as caused simply by a shortage of food, Sen and other experts have established that famines are frequently accompanied by no shortfall of food in absolute terms. Indeed, even more food may be available during a famine than in nonfamine years—if one has the money to buy it. Famine occurs because large numbers of people lack the financial wherewithal to obtain the necessary food.[41]

For example, drought may cause food output in one area to decline and the peasants in that area to starve because they lack the means to buy food from elsewhere, even though there is no dearth of food in the country as a whole (Ethiopia in 1973). Or famine may result when the purchasing power of one occupational group shoots up, ruining the chances of other groups, whose nominal incomes have not changed, to buy food (Bengal in 1943). A reduction of food output because of potato blight triggered the great Irish famine of the 1840s, which killed a higher proportion of the population than any other famine in recorded history. But if one looks at the United Kingdom as a whole, there was no shortage of food. Food could certainly have moved from Britain to Ireland if the Irish could have afforded to purchase it. As it was, at the height of the famine, food was exported from Ireland to England because the prosperous English could pay a higher price for it.[42]

Libertarians would find it immoral and unjust to force people to aid the starving or to tax the affluent in order to set up programs to relieve hunger or prevent famines in the first place. Nor does justice require that a wealthy merchant assist the hungry children in his community to stay alive. And it would certainly violate the merchant's property rights for the children to help themselves to his excess food. Nevertheless, although justice does not require that one assist those in need, libertarians would generally acknowledge that we have some humanitarian obligations toward others. Accordingly, they would not only permit but also presumably encourage people to voluntarily assist others. Justice does not require the merchant to donate, and it forbids us from forcing him to do so, but charity on his part would be a good thing. This reflects the libertarian's firm commitment to property rights: What you have legitimately acquired is yours to do with as you will.

Property Rights

Nozick's theory makes property rights virtually sacrosanct. From the perspective of libertarianism, property rights grow out of one's basic moral rights, either reflecting one's initial creation or appropriation of the product, some sort of exchange or transfer between consenting persons, or a combination of these. Property rights exist prior to any social arrangements and are morally antecedent to any legislative decisions that a society might make. However, Nozick's critics argue that it is a mistake to think of property as a simple, pre-social relation between a person and a physical thing.

First, property is not restricted to material objects like cars, watches, or houses. In developed societies, it may include more abstract goods, interests, and claims. For instance, property may include the right to pay debts with the balance in a bank account, the right to dividends from a corporate investment, and the right to collect from a pension plan one has joined. In fact, the courts have counted as property a wide range of items such as new life forms, an original idea, pension payments, the news, or a place on the welfare rolls.[43]

Second, property ownership involves a bundle of different rights—for instance, to possess, use, manage, dispose of, or restrict others' access to something in certain specified ways. The nature of this bundle differs among societies, as do the types of things that can be owned. In any society, property ownership is structured by the various implicit or explicit rules and regulations governing the legitimate acquisition and transfer of various types of goods, interests, and claims. Not only do property rights differ between societies, but the nature of ownership can also change over time in any given society. As a general trend, the social restrictions on property ownership in the United States have increased dramatically during our history (much to the displeasure of libertarians).

For these reasons, most nonlibertarian social and political theorists view property rights as a function of the particular institutions of a given society. This is not to say that a society's property arrangements cannot be criticized. On the contrary, their morality can be assessed just as the morality of any other institution can.

RAWLS'S THEORY OF JUSTICE

A Theory of Justice by Harvard University's John Rawls is generally thought to be the single most influential work of the post–World War II period in social and political philosophy, at least in the English language.[44] Not only has Rawls's elegant theory touched a responsive chord in many readers, but also his book has helped rejuvenate serious work in normative theory. Even those who are not persuaded by Rawls find themselves obliged to come to terms with his thinking. Although Rawls's basic approach is not difficult to explain (and Rawls himself had sketched out his key concepts in earlier articles), *A Theory of Justice* elaborates his ideas with such painstaking care and philosophical thoroughness that even vigorous critics of the book (such as his colleague Robert Nozick) pay sincere tribute to its many virtues.

By his own account, Rawls presents his theory as a modern alternative to utilitarianism, one that he hopes will be compatible with the belief that justice must be associated with fairness and the moral equality of persons. Rawls firmly wishes to avoid reducing justice to a matter of society utility. At the same time, his approach differs fundamentally from Nozick's. Rawls conceives of society as a cooperative venture among its members, and he elaborates a conception of justice that is thoroughly social. He does not base his theory, as Nozick does, on the postulate that individuals possess certain natural rights prior to any political or social organization.

Two main features of Rawls's theory are particularly important: his hypothetical-contract approach and the principles of justice that he derives with it. Rawls's strategy is to ask what we would choose as the fundamental principles to govern society if, hypothetically, we were to meet for this purpose in what he calls the "original position." He then elaborates the nature of this original position, the constraints on the choice facing us, and the reasoning that he thinks people in the original position would follow. In this way, Rawls offers a modern variant of social contract theory, in the tradition of Hobbes, Locke, Rousseau, and other earlier philosophers. Rawls argues that people in the original position would agree on two principles as the basic governing principles of their society, and that these principles are, accordingly, the principles of justice. These principles are examined at some length in a later section. But briefly, the first is a guarantee of certain familiar and fundamental liberties to each person, and the second—more controversial—holds in part that social and economic inequalities are justified only if those inequalities benefit the least advantaged members of society.

The Original Position

Various principles of economic justice have been proposed, but an important question for philosophers is whether, and how, any such principles can be justified. Thinking of possible principles of economic distribution is not all that difficult, but proving the soundness of such a principle, or at least showing it to be more plausible than its rivals, is a challenging task. After all, people seem to differ in their intuitions about what is just and unjust, and their sentiments are bound to be influenced by their social position. Nozick's entitlement theory, for example, with its priority on property rights, is bound to seem more plausible to a corporate executive than to a migrant farm worker. The justice of a world in which some children are born into wealth while other children struggle by on welfare is unlikely to seem as obvious to the poor as it may to the well-to-do.

The strategy Rawls employs to identify and justify some basic principles of justice is to imagine that people come together for the purpose of deciding on the ground rules for their society, in particular on the rules governing economic distribution. Although in the past groups of people have written down constitutions and similar political documents, never have the members of a society decided from scratch on the basic principles of justice that should govern them. Nor is it even remotely likely that people will do this in the future. What Rawls imagines is a thought experiment. The question is hypothetical: What principles would people choose in this sort of original position? If we can identify these principles, Rawls contends, then we will have identified the principles of justice just because they are the principles that we would all have agreed to.

The Nature of the Choice. On what basis are we to choose these principles? The most obvious answer is that we should select principles that strike us as just. But this won't work. Even if we are all agreed on what is just and unjust, we would be relying on our already existing ideas about justice as a basis for choosing the principles to govern our society. Philosophically, this approach doesn't accomplish anything. We would simply be going in a circle, using our existing conception of justice to prove the principles of justice.

Rawls suggests instead that we imagine people in the original position choosing solely on the basis of self-interest. That is, each individual chooses the set of principles for governing society that will be best for himself or herself (and loved ones). We don't have to imagine that people are antagonistic or that outside of the original position they are selfish; we just imagine that they hope to get the group to choose those principles that will, more than any other possible principles, benefit them. If people in the original position can agree on some governing principles on the basis of mutual self-interest, then these principles will be, Rawls thinks, the principles of justice. Why? Because the principles are agreed to under conditions of equality and free choice. By analogy, if we make up a game and all agree ahead of time, freely and equally, on how the game is to be played, nobody can later complain that the rules are unfair.

The Veil of Ignorance. If people in the original position are supposed to choose principles on the basis of self-interest, agreement seems unlikely. If Carolyn has vast real estate holdings, she will certainly want rules that guarantee her extensive property rights, while her tenants are likely to support rules that permit rent control. Likewise, the wealthy will tend to advocate rules rather like Nozick's entitlement theory, while those without property will, on the basis of their self-interest, desire a redistribution of property. Conflicts of self-interest seem bound to create totally irreconcilable demands. For instance, artists may contend that they should be rewarded more than professional people, men that they should earn more than women, and laborers that they merit more than people with desk jobs.

Agreement seems unlikely, given that some rules would benefit one group while other rules would benefit another. As a way around this problem, Rawls asks us to imagine that people in the original position do not know what social position or status they hold in society. They do not know whether they are rich or poor, and they do not know their personal talents and characteristics—whether, for example, they are athletic or sedentary, artistic or tone deaf, intelligent or not very bright, physically sound or handicapped in some way. They do not know their race or even their sex. Behind what Rawls calls the "veil of ignorance," people in the original position know nothing about themselves personally or about what their individual situation will be once the rules are chosen and the veil is lifted. They do, however, have a general knowledge of history, sociology, and psychology—although no specific information about the society they will be in once the veil is lifted.

Under the veil of ignorance, the people in Rawls's original position have no knowledge about themselves or their situation that would lead them to argue from a partial or biased point of view. No individual is likely to argue that some particular group—such as white men, property owners, star athletes, philosophers—should receive special social and economic privileges when, for all that individual knows, he or she will be nonwhite, propertyless, unathletic, and bored by philosophy when the veil is lifted. Because individuals in the original position are all equally ignorant of their personal predicament and they are all trying to advance their self-interest, agreement is possible. The reasoning of any one person will be the same as the reasoning of each of the others, for each is in identical circumstances and each has the same motivation. As a result, no actual group has to perform Rawls's thought experiment. People who read Rawls's book can imagine that they are in the original position and then decide whether they would choose the principles Rawls thinks they would.

The veil of ignorance, in effect, forces people in the original position to be objective and impartial and makes agreement possible. Also, according to Rawls, the fact that people have no special knowledge that would allow them to argue in a biased way accords with our sense of fairness. The circumstances of the original position are genuinely equal and fair, and because of this, the principles agreed to under these conditions have a good claim to be considered the principles of justice.

Choosing the Principles

Although people in the original position are ignorant of their individual circumstances, they know that whatever their particular goals, interests, and talents turn out to be, they will want more, rather than less, of what Rawls calls the "primary social goods." These include not just income and wealth but also rights, liberties, opportunities, status, and self-respect. Of course, once the veil of ignorance is lifted, people will have more specific ideas about what is good for them—they may choose a life built around religion, one spent in commerce and industry, or one devoted to academic study. But whatever these particular individual goals, interests, and plans turn out to be, they will almost certainly be furthered, and definitely never limited, by the

fact that people in the original position secured for themselves more rather than less in the way of primary goods.

How, then, will people in the original position choose their principles? *A Theory of Justice* explores in depth the reasoning that Rawls thinks would guide their choice. At the heart of Rawls's argument is the contention that people in the original position will be conservative, in the sense that they will not wish to gamble with their future. In setting up the ground rules for their society, they are determining their own fate and that of their children. This exercise is not something to be taken lightly, a game to be played and replayed. Rather, with so much at stake, people will reason cautiously.

Consider, for example, the possibility that people in the original position will set up a feudal society: 10 percent of the population will be nobles, living a life of incredible wealth, privilege, and leisure; the other 90 percent will be serfs, toiling away long hours to support the extravagant lifestyles of the aristocracy. Perhaps some people would consider the joy of being a pampered noble so great that they would vote for such an arrangement behind the veil of ignorance, but they would be banking on a long shot. When the veil of ignorance is lifted, the odds are nine to one that they will be poor and miserable serfs, not lords. Rawls thinks that people in the original position will not, in fact, gamble with their futures. They will not agree to rules that make it overwhelmingly likely that they will have to face a grim life of hardship.

Rawls argues that for similar reasons people in the original position will not adopt the utilitarian standard to govern their society, because the utilitarian principle might sacrifice the well-being of some to enhance society's total happiness. People in the original position, Rawls argues, will not be willing to risk sacrificing their own happiness, once the veil of ignorance is lifted, for the greater good.

What people in the original position would actually do, Rawls believes, is follow what game strategists call the *maximin rule* for making decisions. This rule says that you should select the alternative under which the worst that could happen to you is better than the worst that could happen to you under any other alternative; that is, you should try to *maxi*mize the *mini*mum that you will receive. This rule makes sense when you care much more about avoiding an unacceptable or disastrous result (such as being a serf) than about getting the best possible result (being a noble) and when you have no real idea what odds you are facing. It is a conservative decision principle, but Rawls thinks that people in the original position will find it a rational and appropriate guideline for their deliberations.

Rawls's Two Principles

Rawls argues that people in the original position considering various alternatives will eventually endorse two principles as the most basic governing principles of their society. These principles, because they are agreed to in an initial situation of equality and fairness, will be the principles of justice. Once these two principles of justice have been decided, the people in the original position can gradually be given more information about their specific society. They can then go on to design their basic social and political institutions in more detail.

Rawls states the two basic principles of justice as follows:

1. Each person is to have an equal right to the most extensive total system of equal basic liberties compatible with a similar system of liberty for all.[45]

2. Social and economic inequalities are to satisfy two conditions: First, they are to be attached to positions and offices open to all under conditions of fair equality of opportunity; and second, they are to be to the greatest expected benefit of the least advantaged members of society.[46]

According to Rawls, the first principle takes priority over the second, at least for societies that have attained a moderate level of affluence. The liberties Rawls has in mind are the traditional democratic ones of freedom of thought, conscience, and religious worship, as well as freedom of the person and political liberty. Explicitly absent are "the right to own certain kinds of property (e.g., means of production), and freedom of contract as understood by the doctrine of laissez-faire." The first principle guarantees not only equal liberty to individuals but also as much liberty to individuals as possible, compatible with others having the same amount of liberty. There is no reason why people in the original position would settle for anything less.

All regulations could be seen as infringing on personal liberty, because they limit what a person may do. The law that requires you to drive on the right-hand side of the road denies you the freedom to drive on either side whenever you wish. Some would argue that justice requires only an equal liberty. For example, as long as every motorist is required to drive on the right-hand side of the road, justice is being served; or if everyone in a dictatorial society is forbidden to criticize the leader's decisions, then all are equal in their liberty. But Rawls argues that if a more extensive liberty were possible, without inhibiting the liberty of others, then it would be irrational to settle for a lesser degree of liberty. In the case of driving, permitting me to drive on either side of the road would only interfere with the liberty of others to drive efficiently to their various destinations, but introducing right-turn-on-red laws enhances everyone's liberty. In the dictatorship example, free speech could be more extensive without limiting anyone's liberty.

The second principle concerns social and economic inequalities. Regarding inequalities, Rawls writes:

> It is best to understand not *any* differences between offices and positions, but differences in the benefits and burdens attached to them either directly or indirectly, such as prestige and wealth, or liability to taxation and compulsory services. Players in a game do not protest against there being different positions, such as batter, pitcher, catcher, and the like, nor to there being various privi-

leges and powers as specified by the rules; nor do the citizens of a country object to there being the different offices of government such as president, senator, governor, judge, and so on, each with their special rights and duties.[47]

Rather, at issue are differences in wealth and power, honors and rewards, privileges and salaries that attach to different roles in society.

Rawls's second principle states that insofar as inequalities are permitted—that is, insofar as it is compatible with justice for some jobs or positions to bring greater rewards than others—these positions must be open to all. In other words, there must be meaningful equality of opportunity in the competition among individuals for those positions in society that bring greater economic and social rewards. This, of course, is a familiar ideal, but what exactly a society must do to achieve not just legal but full and fair equality of opportunity will be a matter of debate.

The other part of the second principle is less familiar and more controversial. Called the *difference principle*, it is the distinctive core of Rawls's theory. It states that inequalities are justified only if they work to the benefit of the least advantaged group in society. By "least advantaged," Rawls simply means those who are least well off. But what does it mean to require that inequalities work to the benefit of this group?

Imagine that we are back in the original position. We wish to make sure that under the principles we choose, the worst that can happen to us once the veil of ignorance is lifted is still better than the worst that might have happened under some other arrangement. We might, therefore, choose strict social and economic equality. With an equal division of goods, there's no risk of doing worse than anyone else, no danger of being sacrificed to increase the total happiness of society. In the case of liberty, people in the original position do insist on full equality, but with social and economic inequality, the matter is a little different.

Suppose, for instance, that as a result of dividing things up equally, people lack an incen-

tive to undertake some of the more difficult work that society needs done. It might then be the case that allowing certain inequalities—for example, paying people more for being particularly productive or for undertaking the necessary training to perform some socially useful task—would work to everyone's benefit, including those who would be earning less. If so, then why not permit those inequalities? Compare the two diagrams:

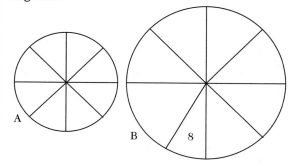

Each pie represents a possible social and economic distribution among eight basic groups (the number eight is arbitrary) in society. In Figure A, things are divided equally; in Figure B, unequally. Imagine that if a society permits inequalities as an incentive to get people to work harder or to do work that they would not have wanted to do otherwise, then the overall amount to be distributed among its members will be greater. That is, the economic pie will increase in size from A to B, and the people with the thinnest slice of B will be better off than they would have been with an equal slice of A.

Which society will people in the original position prefer? Obviously the one represented by Figure B, because the minimum they can attain in B (the slice labeled 8) is bigger than any of the eight equal slices in A. People in the original position do not care about equality of distribution as a value in and of itself; they want the social and economic arrangement that will provide them with the highest minimum.

Rawls is not trying to prove that economic inequalities will always, or even usually, trickle down to the least advantaged (although, of course, some people believe that). Rather, his point is simply that people in the original position would not insist on social and economic equality at all costs. If permitting some people to be better off than the average resulted in the least-well-off segment of society being better off than it would have been under a strictly equal division, then this is what people in the original position will want. Rawls's difference principle is intended to capture this idea. Rawls's principles permit economic inequalities only if they do in fact benefit the least advantaged.

Consider the recurrent proposal to further lower or even eliminate the income tax on capital gains (that is, on personal income from the sale of assets like stocks, bonds, and real estate). Proponents claim that the tax break will spur trading in financial assets, which will in turn lead to growth in tax revenues, and that the cut will trigger more long-term investment, helping revitalize the economy. Critics of the proposal contest both claims. Still, everyone agrees that the tax break would certainly increase the income of the rich because the wealthiest 1.4 percent of households receive 73.2 percent of all capital-gains income.[48] Will lowering taxes on the rich benefit the least advantaged members of society more in the long run than any alternative tax policy?

This question illustrates the application of Rawls's difference principle in a practical context, but we must remember that Rawls intends his principles to be used not as a direct guide to day-to-day policy decisions but rather as the basis for determining what form society's primary social, political, and economic institutions should take in the first place. What will these institutions look like? More specifically, what sort of economic system will best satisfy Rawls's difference principle? Rawls does not answer this question. He sees it as primarily a question for economists and other social scientists, whereas the task of philosophers like himself is the preliminary one of working out a satisfactory conception of justice. Rawls does appear to believe, however, that a liberal form of capitalism, with sufficient welfare provisions, would satisfy his principles, but he does not rule

out the possibility that a democratic socialist system could as well.

Fairness and the Basic Structure

Rawls intends his theory as a fundamental alternative to utilitarianism, which he rejects on the grounds that maximizing the total well-being of society could permit an unfair distribution of burdens and benefits. Utilitarianism, in Rawls's view, treats people's pleasures and pains as completely interchangeable: A decrease of happiness here is justified by greater happiness there. Within a person's own life, such trade-offs are sensible. An increase of pain now (as the dentist fills a cavity in my tooth) is justified in terms of greater happiness later (no painful, rotted tooth). But between individuals, as when Jack's happiness is decreased to provide Jill with a more-than-compensating gain, such trade-offs are morally problematic.

Thus Rawls stresses that, in his view,

each person possesses an inviolability founded on justice that even the welfare of society as a whole cannot override. . . . Therefore . . . the rights secured by justice are not subject to political bargaining or to the calculus of social interests.[49]

And he emphasizes that the difference principle

excludes, therefore, the justification of inequalities on the grounds that the disadvantages of those in one position are outweighed by the greater advantages of those in another position. This rather simple restriction is the main modification I wish to make in the utilitarian principle as usually understood.[50]

On the other hand, Rawls is equally unsympathetic to the approach adopted by Nozick. Contrary to the entitlement theory, he argues that the primary subject of justice is not, in the first instance, transactions between individuals but rather "the basic structure, the fundamental social institutions and their arrangement into one scheme." Why? As Rawls explains:

Suppose we begin with the initially attractive idea that the social circumstances and people's relationships to one another should develop over time in accordance with free agreements fairly arrived at and fully honored. Straightaway we need an account of when agreements are free and the social circumstances under which they are reached are fair. In addition, while these conditions may be fair at an earlier time, the accumulated results of many separate and ostensibly fair agreements . . . are likely in the course of time to alter citizens' relationships and opportunities so that the conditions for free and fair agreements no longer hold. The role of the institutions that belong to the basic structure is to secure just background conditions against which the actions of the individuals and associations take place. Unless this structure is appropriately regulated and adjusted, an initially just social process will eventually cease to be just, however free and fair particular transactions may look when viewed by themselves.[51]

Additional considerations support taking the basic structure of society as the primary subject of justice—in particular, the fact that the basic structure shapes the wants, desires, hopes, and ambitions of individuals. Thus, Rawls continues:

Everyone recognizes that the institutional form of society affects its members and determines in large part the kind of person they want to be as well as the kind of person they are. The social structure also limits people's ambitions and hopes in different ways. . . . So an economic regime, say, is not only an institutional scheme for satisfying existing wants but a way of fashioning desires and aspirations in the future.[52]

Rawls stresses that because the basic structure is the proper focus of a theory of justice, we cannot expect the principles that apply to it to be simply an extension of the principles that govern everyday individual transactions:

The justice of the basic structure is, then, of predominant importance. The first problem of justice is to determine the principles to regulate inequalities and to adjust the profound and long-lasting effects of social, natural, and historical contingencies, partic-

ularly since these contingencies combined with inequalities generate tendencies that, when left to themselves, are sharply at odds with the freedom and equality appropriate for a well-ordered society. In view of the special role of the basic structure, we cannot assume that the principles suitable to it are natural applications, or even extensions, of the familiar principles governing the actions of individuals and associations in everyday life which take place within its framework. Most likely we shall have to loosen ourselves from our ordinary perspective and take a more comprehensive viewpoint.[53]

Benefits and Burdens

The passages quoted here touch on a theme that is central to Rawls's theory. Inevitably, there will be natural differences among human beings—in terms of physical prowess, mental agility, and so on—but there is nothing natural or inevitable about the weight attached by society to those differences. For Rawls, a desirable feature of any account of justice is that it strives to minimize the social consequences of purely arbitrary, natural differences. He stresses that no one deserves his or her particular natural characteristics. We cannot say that Robert Redford deserves to be handsome or that Albert Einstein deserved to be blessed with an excellent mind any more than we can say that Fred merits his shortness or Pamela her nearsightedness. Their attributes are simply the result of a genetic lottery. But Rawls goes beyond this to argue that even personal characteristics like diligence and perseverance reflect the environment in which one was raised:

It seems to be one of the fixed points of our considered judgments that no one deserves his place in the distribution of native endowments, any more than one deserves one's initial starting place in society. The assertion that a man deserves the superior character that enables him to make the effort to cultivate his abilities is equally problematic; for his character depends in large part upon fortunate family and social circumstances for which he can claim no credit. The notion of desert seems not to apply to these cases.[54]

Accordingly, Rawls thinks we cannot really claim moral credit for our special talents or even our virtuous character. In Rawls's view, then, if our personal characteristics are not something that we deserve, we have no strong claim to the economic rewards they might bring. On the contrary, justice requires that the social and economic consequences of these arbitrarily distributed assets be minimized.

> We see then that the difference principle represents, in effect, an agreement to regard the distribution of natural talents as a common asset and to share in the benefits of this distribution whatever it turns out to be. Those who have been favored by nature, whoever they are, may gain from their good fortune only on terms that improve the situation of those who have lost out. The naturally advantaged are not to gain merely because they are more gifted, but only to cover the costs of training and education and for using their endowments in ways that help the less fortunate as well. No one deserves his greater natural capacity nor merits a more favorable starting place in society. But it does not follow that one should eliminate these distinctions. There is another way to deal with them. The basic structure can be arranged so that these contingencies work for the good of the least fortunate. Thus we are led to the difference principle if we wish to set up the social system so that no one gains or loses from his arbitrary place in the distribution of natural assets or his initial position in society without giving or receiving compensating advantages in return.[55]

This important passage from *A Theory of Justice* reflects well Rawls's vision of society as a cooperative project for mutual benefit.

SUMMARY

1. Justice is one important aspect of morality. Talk of justice and injustice generally involves appeals to the related notions of fairness, equality, desert, and rights. Economic or distributive justice concerns the principles appropriate for assessing society's distribution of social benefits and burdens, particularly wealth, income, status, and power.

2. Economic distribution might be based on pure equality, need, effort, social contribution, or merit. Each of these principles is plausible in some circumstances but not in others. In some situations, the principles pull us in different directions. Dissatisfied with a pluralistic approach, some moral philosophers have sought to develop more general theories of justice.

3. Utilitarianism holds that the maximization of happiness ultimately determines what is just and unjust. Mill contended, more specifically, that the concept of justice identifies certain very important social utilities and that injustice involves the violation of the rights of some specific individual.

4. Utilitarians must examine a number of factual issues in order to determine for themselves which economic system and principles will best promote social well-being or happiness. Many utilitarians favor increased worker participation and a more equal distribution of income.

5. The libertarian theory identifies justice with liberty, which libertarians understand as living according to our own choices, free from the interference of others. They reject utilitarianism's concern for total social well-being.

6. The libertarian philosopher Robert Nozick defends the entitlement theory. His theory holds that the distribution of goods, money, and property is just if people are entitled to what they have—that is, if they have acquired their possessions without violating the rights of anyone else.

7. In the Wilt Chamberlain example, Nozick argues that theories of economic justice not in accord with his inevitably fail to respect people's liberty.

8. Libertarians operate with a distinctive concept of liberty, defend free exchange and

laissez-faire markets without regard to results, put a priority on freedom over all other values, and see property rights as existing prior to any social arrangements. Critics contest each of these features of libertarianism.

9. John Rawls's approach lies within the social-contract tradition. He asks us to imagine people meeting in the "original position" to choose the basic principles that are to govern their society. Although in this original position people choose on the basis of self-interest, we are to imagine that they are behind a veil of ignorance, with no personal information about themselves. Rawls contends that any principles agreed to under these circumstances have a strong claim to be considered the principles of justice.

10. Rawls argues that people in the original position would follow the maximin rule for making decisions. They would choose principles guaranteeing that the worst that could happen to them is better than the worst that could happen to them under any

rival principles. Rawls argues that they would agree on two principles. The first states that each person has a right to the most extensive scheme of liberties compatible with others having the same amount of liberty. The second principle states that to be justified, any inequalities must be to the greatest expected benefit of the least advantaged and open to all under conditions of fair equality of opportunity.

11. Rawls rejects utilitarianism because it might permit an unfair distribution of burdens and benefits. Contrary to the entitlement theory, he argues that the primary focus of justice should be the basic social structure, not transactions between individuals. He contends that society is a cooperative project for mutual benefit and that justice requires us to reduce the social and economic consequences of arbitrary natural differences among people.

CASE 3.1

Whatever Happened to the Steel Industry?

Steel was the core of U.S. industry, the heavy metal basis for a productive system that was the envy of the world. Pittsburgh, Youngstown, and other communities in our industrial heartland symbolized that productive system. Built around the steel industry, they were hard working, tough, proud, and patriotic—the home turf of great athletes, including Joe Namath and Stan Musial. Steel was good for those cities, the people who made it, and the country.

For generations, an implicit social contract had existed in those steel towns. Since the early 1940s, the companies had recognized the union; the union had left investment decisions to the companies; and steelworker families had bought homes, sent chil-

dren to college for the first time, and retired on pensions.[56] But now, sadly, that world has come to an end. The steel industry has collapsed.

Not so very long ago, Youngstown, Ohio, and neighboring Pittsburgh, Pennsylvania, employed more than 100,000 steelworkers, but by the late 1980s little or no steel was being made in either community. (Nationwide, 483,000 steel jobs disappeared.[57]) The steel communities were traumatized; their life-support system had been ripped out. As one local union president remarked, "You felt as if the mill would always be there." But now it was all over. The vice president of another local union said: "Most people couldn't believe it. It was so huge and had operated so long and so many people depended on it for their livelihood." More than one steelworker in Youngstown indicated that the only similar upheaval they had experienced was Pearl Harbor.

For years the steel companies had presented an unchanging public message: They were eager to modernize their mills and continue making steel. But they lacked capital. Through no fault of their own, the steel companies claimed, but as the result of restrictive environmental regulation, high union wages and benefits, and unfair dumping in U.S. markets of foreign, government-subsidized steel, they found themselves unable to make steel profitably. They were therefore unable to accumulate the necessary capital for updating U.S. steel mills.

Initially, communities such as Youngstown and Pittsburgh accepted this message and threw their political support behind the companies. When the first major mill closed, union leaders petitioned Congress to impose emergency quotas on foreign steel. But the attitude of the communities and the workers gradually changed. A string of broken promises led them to doubt the sincerity of the steel industry's claim that it sought to invest in steel. As lawyer and community activist Staughton Lynd reported:

> Painfully it was learned that the problem went beyond the companies' lack of commitment to existing mills. The companies were not even committed to steel. They would "flow" investment capital to whatever investment opportunity was most profitable. They would take money created by steelworkers and use it to buy real estate, chemical companies, savings and loan associations, insurance companies and oil fields.

The steel companies were abandoning steel. Symbolically, U.S. Steel changed its name to USX. It was getting out of the steel business.

In the fight against the plant shutdowns that were destroying their communities, local activists and union members came to two conclusions. First, because the steel industry was basing its investment decisions on the effort to maximize profits in the short run, steel companies were postponing needed modernization; they were investing outside the steel industry, where the rate of profit was higher. Second, because of its capital-intensive character, the steel business would probably continue to yield a lower rate of profit than other investment opportunities. Tinkering with external factors (environmental regulation, depreciation allowances, import quotas, currency exchange rates, and so on) to induce the steel companies to make a socially desirable investment in steel was a policy that had failed.

Lots of new, even radical, ideas began to circulate in the traditionally conservative steel towns. One response was the emergence of the idea of eminent domain, championed by Lynd and others. Legally, *eminent domain* is the sovereign's power to take private property for public use against the owner's will, subject to the constitutional requirement that just compensation be paid. Applied to the crisis in steel, a state or local government could take, or threaten to take, a closed or closing plant from the company that owned it and then operate the plant or sell it to a new owner. In effect, the community says, "If USX (or whatever company) still wants to run the Homestead Works (or whatever facility is threatened with closure), God bless it. But if it refuses to run it any longer, then we, the people, will have to find another way."

This thinking led nine municipalities in the Monongahela Valley to join together to incorporate the Steel Valley Authority (SVA), a regional development agency organized under the Pennsylvania Municipal Authorities Act. The SVA has the power to take property by eminent domain for the purpose of retaining and developing existing industries. Armed with eminent domain power, a community could acquire an abandoned steel mill without the consent of its owner and so bring about its continued use. Underlying this, Lynd suggested, is the concept of a generalized trust that a community extends to enterprises within its borders to operate for the common good. As long as the enterprise exercises such stewardship, it can and should remain in private hands. But if the enterprise is permitted to stand idle, or if capital earned there is taken out of the community for other purposes, then the community can rightfully intervene by eminent domain.

Update:

Communities like Youngstown will never be what they once were, and the United States still imports most of its steel from overseas. But in the 1990s the U.S. steel industry began making a comeback. Led by so-called mini-mills—small, technologically advanced operators that turn out small batches of steel from scrap—some of the large mills were once again cranking out millions of tons of steel. In 1996, for instance, Bethlehem Steel hired its first new production workers since 1979, and at the end of 2001 the U.S. Steel Corporation was reborn when USX became Marathon Oil and spun off its steelmaking subsidiary as a separate company. Still, the big steel companies remain as reluctant as ever to make the investments necessary to keep up with new technologies introduced elsewhere. Thus, when the market price of steel, relatively high as recently as 2000, began falling, the big steelmakers were in trouble. Instead of modernizing, however, or tightening their belts, they began calling, yet again, for protection from foreign competition. Their call was heard by President Bush, who in March 2002 slapped tariffs of up to 30 percent on selected steel imports. As a result, the steel industry gets more "breathing space" to overhaul itself, and Americans get to pay higher prices for autos, appliances, and other consumer goods.[58]

Discussion Questions

1. The steel companies blame the decline of their industry on restrictive environmental regulations, high wages, and unfair foreign competition. Steelworkers argue that the companies were too absorbed with short-run profits, that they failed to anticipate and respond to foreign competition, and that they lacked a sense of social responsibility. Evaluate these claims and counterclaims.

2. What social obligation, if any, does a company have to continue producing an important commodity when it can invest more profitably elsewhere? Union members and activists believe that renewed investment in steel is socially desirable. Assess that contention.

3. Can the steel companies be accused of acting unjustly? What responsibilities, if any, does a company have to the community and to its workforce to continue operating?

4. Does justice require that companies exercise a kind of stewardship for the common good, as Lynd suggested?

5. Assess the idea of eminent domain as a response to the crisis in the steel industry. Is it morally defensible?

6. How would the utilitarian, libertarian, and Rawlsian theories of justice evaluate the use of eminent domain, both in general and in this particular case?

CASE 3.2

Battling over Bottled Water

Water is the lifeblood of the earth, but by 2025, according to the U.N., two-thirds of the world's population could face chronic shortages of water. In fact, some countries are already importing huge supertankers of freshwater from other countries. But one place that's definitely not short of water is the state of Michigan, which has 11,000 lakes and is surrounded by Lakes Michigan, Huron, Superior, and Erie. So it came as a surprise to some that the Nestlé company's new Ice Mountain bottled-water plant in Mecosta County, Michigan, dredged up so much controversy when it began pumping water from a local spring.[59]

Nestlé's willingness to invest $100 million to build a new 410,000-square-foot bottling plant in Mecosta reflects the fact that bottled water is big business, with annual sales of $6 billion (up 35 percent since 1997). Many county residents, in fact, are thrilled about Nestlé's being there. The Ice Mountain plant employs about a hundred people at $12 to $23 per hour, significantly more than many local jobs pay. And the company shells out hundreds of thousands of dollars in local taxes. Township supervisor Maxine McClellan says, "This is probably the best project we've ever brought into Mecosta County." She adds that she wants "a diversified economy where our kids don't have to move away to find jobs."

The problem, as some local residents see it, is that Nestlé has also built a 12-mile stainless steel pipeline from the plant to Sanctuary Spring, which sits on an 850-acre private deer-hunting ranch, and plans to pump as much as 262 million gallons a year from the spring, which is part of the headwaters of the Little Muskegon River, which flows into the Muskegon and then into Lake Michigan. But whose water is Nestlé pumping? That's the question being asked by Michigan Citizens for Water Conservation (MCWC), a local Mecosta group that has filed suit contesting Nestlé's right to the spring's waters. Although the company has a ninety-nine-year lease on the land, MCWC contends that the water itself is a public resource. As Jim Olson, MCWC's lawyer, explains it, under the doctrine of "reasonable use" the owners of a stream can use its water for drinking, boating, swimming, or anything else "as long as it's in connection with their land." But, he argues, "this does not include the right to transport water to some distant land for [some other] use. We're arguing that the same is true with groundwater—you can't sever it from the estate."

Michigan State Senator Ken Sikkema, who chaired a task force on Michigan water issues, rejects that argument: "A farmer pumps water out of the ground, waters potatoes, and sends the potatoes to Illinois—there's no real difference. The water in those potatoes is gone." This reasoning hasn't assuaged the fears of three American Indian tribes who have joined the fray. Citing an 1836 treaty that protects their fishing and hunting rights in the Great Lakes region, they have brought a federal lawsuit against Nestlé and Michigan Governor John Engler to stop what they see as a massive water grab. "Our fear," says a spokesperson for the Little Traverse Bay Bands of Odawa Indians, "is that the export could significantly and permanently damage the fishery."

However, David K. Ladd, head of the Office of Great Lakes and an appointee of Governor Engler, argues that bottled water is a special case. Legally, he contends, it's a "food," regulated by the Food and Drug Administration. "There's no difference between Perrier bottling water, Gerber making baby food, or Miller brewing beer. When you incorporate water from the basin into a product, it's no longer water per se." And Brendan O'Rourke, an Ice Mountain plant manager, adds that the 262 million gallons it pumps are less than 1 percent of the annual recharge rate of the local watershed, equivalent to just 14 minutes of evaporation from the surface of Lake Michigan.

Discussion Questions

1. Should people in Michigan be concerned about how, and by whom, the state's ground-water gets used? In your view, what issues of justice does this case raise?

2. Does Nestlé's pumping 262 million gallons of water per year from Sanctuary Spring consti-tute "reasonable use"? Is the company treating either local residents or the Native American tribes unfairly, or would it be unfair to restrict Nestlé's use of water from the spring?

3. Is groundwater a public resource, the use of which is appropriate for society to regulate? Or is it the property of those who own the land to use as they see fit? Who has the strongest claim on groundwater—the owners of the land from which it is pumped, the original inhabitants of the area (that is, the local Indian tribes), local residents, citizens of the whole Great Lakes region, or all Americans?

4. Assess this case from the perspective of the utilitarian, libertarian, and Rawlsian theories of justice. How would each address the case? Which theory's approach do you find the most helpful or illuminating?

CASE 3.3

Poverty in America

In recent years the U.S. Census Bureau has brought some glad tidings: The median income of American households has been increasing. Mean-while, the number of families with incomes below the poverty line—defined as $17,960 for a family of four—has declined, and overall the poverty rate has fallen to 11.3 percent, about what it had been back in the 1970s. Still, despite the long economic boom of the 1990s, 32.3 million Americans con-tinue to live in poverty, a third of them children. That's more than one out of every nine people.[60] Moreover, the average adult American has a 60 percent chance of living at least one year below the poverty line and a 33 percent chance of experienc-ing dire poverty.[61]

Most people think that those described as "poor" in the United States are pretty well off by world stan-dards. The truth is, in life expectancy twenty-year-old U.S. males rank thirty-sixth among the world's nations, and twenty-year-old U.S. females rank twenty-first. Our infant mortality rate is worse than that in twenty-one other Western nations. Moreover, millions of Americans endure hunger. According to the U.S. Department of Agriculture, 31 million Americans lack "food security," and in 3 million American households one or more persons go hungry during the year.[62] Figures from the Food Research and Action Center are even more alarm-ing; it reports that 5 million children under age twelve go hungry each month.[63] In addition, one out of every four Americans lives in substandard housing, and in most cities one sees people roam-ing the streets in tattered clothing, picking their food out of garbage cans. Homeless people—many of them former mental patients released from state hospitals, others jobless individuals and families unable to afford housing—live in aban-doned cars and shacks or simply sleep in doorways and on subway grates. Precise figures are impossi-ble to obtain. One recent survey found 280,000 people homeless,[64] but other experts estimate that 600,000–700,000 Americans are homeless on any given night and that 3 to 12 million Americans are homeless sometime during the year.[65]

People in different walks of life and in different circumstances experience poverty. Many others live on the edge of poverty and are in continual danger of falling into it through illness, job loss, or other misfortune. In the United States today, the "working poor"—that is, those who work full time, year around, while earning an income below the poverty line—number 2.8 million. They represent a higher percentage of the workforce than in the 1970s as well-paid unionized manufacturing jobs have been replaced by nonunion service jobs.[66] In 1997, the minimum wage was increased to $5.15 per hour, but it is still less in real terms than it was in 1969. Someone working forty hours a week, every week, for that wage cannot raise his or her family out of poverty. In fact, according to a housing advocacy group, a minimum-wage earner can't afford to rent a two-bedroom home anywhere in the United States.[67]

Many poor people are unable to work and depend on outside assistance. Recent legislative efforts to reform the welfare system rely on certain myths about welfare recipients. Investigation shows, for instance, that most people do not stay on the welfare rolls for years. They move on and off, and less than 1 percent remain on welfare for ten years. Contrary to popular mythology, the majority of those who receive welfare are young children whose mothers must remain at home. They are not able-bodied adults who are unwilling to work. Nor do welfare mothers differ from non-welfare mothers in the number of children they have. About 70 percent of welfare families have only one or two children, and there is little financial incentive to have more. Half of the families who receive welfare include an adult who works full or part time, and research consistently demonstrates that poor people have the same strong desire to work that the rest of the population does.[68] Two-thirds of the mothers on welfare did not grow up in families that received welfare—contrary to the stereotype of intergenerational welfare dependency—and only 7.6 percent of them are under eighteen and unmarried.[69]

There has never been a way to live well on welfare. Under the old system of AFDC (Aid to Families with Dependent Children), by 1996 welfare benefits had fallen, in real terms, to 51 percent of what they had been in 1971.[70] With annual cash allowances for a family on AFDC ranging from $1,416 in Mississippi to $6,780 in New York, even in the most generous states stipends were never enough to allow a family to escape from poverty.[71] In 1996 Congress replaced AFDC with TANF (Temporary Assistance to Needy Families). Under the new system, the entitlement of poor people to support has been replaced by block grants to the states to run their own welfare programs. The grants are limited to a certain amount of money; if they run out, the states are not required to make additional expenditures. Welfare recipients are required to work for pay or to enroll in training programs, and financial support is limited to a lifetime maximum of five years. This shift in policy has been controversial. Since the TANF system began, the number of people receiving welfare benefits has declined, but experts disagree about the reasons: Is it a growing economy offering more opportunities, the success of the new approach in encouraging welfare recipients to make themselves employable, or simply people who are not able to take care of themselves being denied support?[72]

One thing that is clear is the large number of women living in poverty. This includes women with inadequate income following divorce, widowhood, or retirement, as well as women raising children alone. Wage discrimination against women is one factor. Women who work full time, year round earn only about two-thirds of what men earn. And millions of women hold full-time jobs that pay wages near or below the poverty line.

Women's responsibilities for child rearing are another important factor. Despite many changes in recent years, women continue to have primary responsibility in this area. When marriages break up, mothers typically take custody and bear the major financial burden. Fewer than half the women raising children alone are awarded child support, and fewer than half of those entitled to it receive the full amount. Of family households headed by women, 52 percent have incomes below $25,000 and 19.7 percent have incomes below $10,000.[73]

Most poor people in our nation—about two-thirds of them—are white, but blacks are about three times more likely to be poor. Whereas fewer than one out of every ten white Americans is poor, more than one of every five African Americans and Hispanics are below the poverty line. Many members of the minority communities have succeeded in moving up the economic ladder, but the overall picture is bleak. African-American family income, for instance, is only 62 percent that of white family income.[74]

Discussion Questions

1. Does the existence of poverty imply that our socioeconomic system is unjust? Does the concentration of poverty in certain groups make it more unjust than it would be otherwise?

2. Surveys show that Americans, even poor Americans, favor individualistic explanations of poverty (such as lack of effort or ability, poor morals, poor work skills) over structural explanations (such as inadequate schooling, low wages, lack of jobs), whereas Europeans favor structural explanations of poverty over individualistic explanations.[75] What are the causes of poverty? How is one's answer to this question likely to affect one's view of the justice or injustice of poverty?

3. What moral obligation, if any, do we have individually and as a society to reduce poverty? What steps could be taken? What role should business play?

4. How would a utilitarian view the facts about poverty? What are the implications for our society of the concept of the declining utility of money?

5. How would a libertarian like Nozick view poverty in the United States? How plausible do you find the libertarian's preference for private charity over public welfare?

6. How would our economy be assessed from the point of view of Rawls's difference principle? Can it be plausibly maintained that, despite poverty, our system works to "the greatest expected benefit of the least advantaged"? Is this an appropriate standard?

Notes to Chapter 3

1. Laura D'Andrea Tyson, "Tax Cuts for the Rich Are Even More Wrong Today," *Business Week,* July 8, 2002, 26. See also Andrew Hacker, *Money: Who Has How Much and Why* (New York: Simon & Schuster, 1997), 10.

2. U.S. Bureau of the Census, *Statistical Abstract of the United States 2001* (Washington, D.C.: U.S. Government Printing Office, 2002), Table 670, and "Historical Income Data: Current Population Survey Tables (Families)" at *www.census.gov.*

3. David Wallechinsky, "Are We Still Number 1?" *Parade Magazine,* April 13, 1997; Hacker, *Money,* 54; John Isbister, *Capitalism and Justice: Envisioning Social and Economic Fairness* (Bloomfield, Conn.: Kumarian Press, 2001), 55.

4. Lester C. Thurow, "The Boom That Wasn't," *New York Times,* January 18, 1999, 17; Edward N. Wolff, "The Stagnating Fortunes of the Middle Class," *Social Philosophy and Policy* 19 (Winter 2002): 55, 58.

5. "Executive Pay," *Business Week,* April 15, 2002, 80.

6. "American Pay Rattles Foreign Partners," *New York Times,* January 17, 1999, sec. 4, 1.

7. "Learning How to Talk About Salary in Japan," *New York Times,* April 7, 2002, sec. 3, 12.

8. "Suite Deals," *U.S. News & World Report,* April 29, 2002, 32.

9. "Suite Deals," 33.

10. Lynn Brenner, "How Did You Do?" *Parade Magazine,* March 3, 2002, 4.

11. "Two-Tier Marketing," *Business Week,* March 17, 1997, 82–90.

12. "Is America Becoming More of a Class Society?" *Business Week,* February 26, 1996. See also "Widening Income Gap Divides America," *USA Today,* September 20, 1996, 1B.

13. Edward N. Wolff, *Top Heavy: The Increasing Inequality of Wealth in America and What Can Be Done About It,* rev. ed. (New York: New Press, 2002), 8, 27.

14. "Gap in U.S. Called Widest," *New York Times,* April 17, 1995, A1.

15. Leonard Silk, "Rich-Poor Gap Gets Wider in U.S.," *San Francisco Chronicle,* May 12, 1989, C5; John Marshall, "Child Poverty Is Abundant," *San Francisco Chronicle,* October 7, 1996, B2; Catholic Campaign for Human Development, "Poverty Facts," June 2002 (available at *www.usccb.org/cchd/povertyusa*).

16. John Stuart Mill, *Utilitarianism* (Indianapolis: Bobbs-Merrill, 1957), 71.

17. Michael Walzer, *Spheres of Justice* (New York: Basic Books, 1983). See also Jon Elster, *Local Justice: How Institutions Allocate Scarce Goods and Necessary Burdens* (New York: Russell Sage, 1992).

18. Walzer, *Spheres of Justice,* 6.

19. Ibid., 10.

20. Mill, *Utilitarianism,* 66.

21. Ibid., 73.

22. Ibid., 71.

23. Ibid.

24. Ibid.

25. Ibid.

26. Smith's ideas are discussed further in Chapter 4.

27. John Stuart Mill, *Principles of Political Economy,* edited by Donald Winch (Harmondsworth, Middlesex: Penguin, 1970), 129.

28. Ibid., 128.

29. Ibid., 129.

30. Ibid., 133.

31. Ibid., 139–140.

32. Ibid., 140–141.

33. Richard B. Brandt, *A Theory of the Good and the Right* (New York: Oxford University Press, 1979), 312–313.

34. Ibid., 310.

35. F. A. Hayek, *The Constitution of Liberty* (Chicago: University of Chicago Press, 1960), 11.

36. John Hospers, *Libertarianism* (Los Angeles: Nash, 1971), 5.

37. Robert Nozick, *Anarchy, State, and Utopia* (New York: Basic Books, 1974).

38. John Locke, *Second Treatise of Government* (Indianapolis: Hackett Publishing, 1980), 23–24.

39. Nozick, *Anarchy, State, and Utopia,* 161.

40. Ibid., 163.

41. Amartya Sen, *Development as Freedom* (New Delhi: Oxford University Press, 1999), Chapter 7. See also Amartya Sen, *Poverty and Famines* (New York: Oxford University Press, 1981), and Jean Drèze and Amartya Sen, *Hunger and Public Action* (Oxford: Oxford University Press, 1989).

42. Sen, *Development as Freedom,* 167, 170–171.

43. Lawrence C. Becker and Kenneth Kipnis, eds., *Property: Cases, Concepts, Critiques* (Englewood Cliffs, N.J.: Prentice Hall, 1984), 3–5.

44. John Rawls, *A Theory of Justice* (Cambridge: Harvard University Press, 1971). For subsequent developments in Rawls's thinking, see John Rawls, *Political Liberalism* (New York: Columbia University Press, 1993).

45. Rawls, *A Theory of Justice,* 302; cf. *Political Liberalism,* 291.

46. Rawls, *Political Liberalism,* 6; cf. *A Theory of Justice,* 60, 83, 302.

47. John Rawls, "Justice as Fairness," *Philosophical Review* 67 (April 1958): 167.

48. Arthur MacEwan, "Ask Mr. Dollar," *Dollars & Sense,* November–December 1997, 39; Michelle Cottle, "The Real Class War," *Washington Monthly,* July–August 1997, 12.

49. Rawls, *A Theory of Justice,* 4.

50. Rawls, "Justice as Fairness," 168.

51. *Political Liberalism,* 265–266.

52. Ibid., 269.

53. Rawls, "A Kantian Conception of Equality," *Cambridge Review* 96 (February 1975): 95.

54. *A Theory of Justice,* 104.

55. Ibid., 101–102.

56. See Staughton Lynd, "Towards a Not-for-Profit Economy," *Harvard Civil Rights–Civil Liberties Law Review* (Winter 1987), from which this case study is drawn.

57. Barnaby J. Feder, "Survival: A Struggle in a Town that Steel Forgot," *New York Times,* April 27, 1993, C1.

58. Robert J. Barro, "Big Steel Doesn't Need Any More Propping Up," *Business Week,* April 1, 2002, 24.

59. This case study is based on "Where They're Boiling over Water," *Business Week,* May 27, 2002, 24E6–24E9.

60. U.S. Bureau of the Census, *Statistical Abstract of the United States 2001* (Washington, D.C.: U.S. Government Printing Office, 2002), Tables 664, 679, 680.

61. Mark R. Rank and Thomas A. Hirschl, "The Likelihood of Poverty Across the American Adult Life Span," *Social Work* 44 (May 1999): 205.

62. Mark Andrews et al., "Household Food Security in the United States 1999" (U.S. Department of Agriculture: Fall 2000).

63. Colin Greer, "Something Is Robbing Our Children of Their Future," *Parade Magazine,* March 5, 1995, 4.

64. "Census Releases Count of Homeless at Shelters," *San Jose Mercury News,* October 31, 2001, C-3.

65. Ellen L. Bassuk, Angela Browne, and John C. Buckner, "Single Mothers and Welfare," *Scientific American,* October 1996, 66; National Coalition for the Homeless, "How Many People Experience Homelessness?" February 1999 (available at *www.nationalhomeless.org/numbers.html*).

66. "Working Full Time Is No Longer Enough," *Wall Street Journal,* June 29, 2000, A2.

67. *Wall Street Journal,* September 19, 2002, A1.

68. See Bob Herbert, "Scapegoat Time," *New York Times,* November 16, 1994, A19, and Ruth Sidel, "The Welfare Scam," *Nation,* December 12, 1994, 712.

69. Bassuk, Browne, and Buckner, "Single Mothers and Welfare," 66–67.

70. Robert Pear, "Welfare Buying Power Wanes, Report Says," *San Francisco Chronicle,* November 19, 1996, A9.

71. U.S. Bureau of the Census, *Statistical Abstract of the United States 1998* (Washington, D.C.: U.S. Government Printing Office, 1999), 390.

72. John Isbister, *Capitalism and Justice: Envisioning Social and Economic Fairness* (Bloomfield, Conn.: Kumarian Press, 2001), 118; cf. "A Howl from the States," *Economist,* May 25, 2002.

73. *Statistical Abstract of the United States 2001,* Table 671.

74. Ibid., Tables 668, 669.

75. William Julius Wilson, *When Work Disappears* (New York: Random House, 1996), 159–160, 179–181.

Reading ━━━━━ ■

INCOME
DISTRIBUTION

JOHN ISBISTER

The distribution of income in the United States is strikingly unequal. Taking as his starting point Plato's suggestion that in a just society the rich should possess no more than four times as much as the poor, economics professor John Isbister explores what limits there should be to inequality and what a just distribution of income would look like. He explains why perfect equality of income would be inefficient and argues that pay differentials are necessary to compensate for training, as incentives for hard work, and to acknowledge status differences. However, a wage differential ratio of eight to one would probably be sufficient for these purposes, and with this in mind, he sketches a model of what a just income range would be for a country like the United States.

People living in capitalist countries may have equal moral standing, but they do not have equal access to the goods and services provided by their economies. Their incomes are vastly unequal.

A good way of looking at the income distribution in a country is to compare the portion of total national income going to the poorest 20 percent of

Reprinted by permission from John Isbister, *Capitalism and Justice: Envisioning Social and Economic Fairness.* Copyright © 2001 Kumarian Press. Some notes omitted.

the population with the portion going to the richest 20 percent. Each group of 20 percent is called a "quintile." According to calculations by the World Bank, in fifteen industrialized countries, including much of western Europe plus Canada, the United States, and Australia, the bottom quintile of households earns an average of about 8 percent of the national income, while the top quintile earns around 39 percent.[1] Of those countries, the United States has the most skewed distribution of incomes, with the lowest and highest quintiles earning 5 percent and 45 percent, respectively. In the United States, the most prosperous one-tenth of the population earn 29 percent of total income. As far as one can tell (data from before the 1970s are skimpy on this topic), the income distribution in the United States became more equal throughout the twentieth century until about 1973, and the proportion of people living in poverty fell. After 1973, however, incomes became less equal, and the proportion of people in poverty fluctuated without a trend. The huge increases in national income since 1973 have gone overwhelmingly to the rich, while the incomes of most Americans, when corrected for inflation, have fallen.[2] Some evidence exists that the poorest began to benefit from the long economic expansion at the end of the 1990s.[3]

Uneven as these figures for household income are, they are egalitarian compared to the figures for the distribution of wealth in the United States (income is what you earn, while wealth is what you own). According to data compiled by Edward N. Wolff, the share of wealth held by the top quintile was 85 percent at last count.[4]

The average pay of a CEO in a major corporation was $11.9 million in 2000.[5] The latest estimates are that the poverty line is about $20,000 for a family of four in the United States, and almost 17 percent of families fall below that threshold. The ratio of these two figures—11.9 million divided by 20,000—is almost 600, and this of course understates the ratio between the richest and the poorest American, since some earned much more than $11.9 million and many took in less than the poverty threshold. To avoid being accused of alarmism, however, let us take this as the ratio between the "typical" rich and poor families in the United States: 600:1.

What spread of incomes is consistent with social justice? This chapter proposes an answer. . . . The reasoning supporting my answer is, I hope, defensible, but in some respects it is unavoidably intuitive. I will try to be explicit about the intuitions; readers with different intuitions may wish to adjust my conclusions. . . .

PLATO'S COLONY

Economists are typically reluctant to say just what distribution of incomes is morally justified; it all depends, they say, on one's values and assumptions. We do, however, have one carefully thought out and precise recommendation. It comes from Plato's *Laws,* written in the fourth century B.C., a dialogue on the principles to govern a new colony. In book 5 of *Laws,* Plato says that the colony should consist of 5,040 households, each household given a lot of equal size. The purpose of the laws in the new society is "that our people should be supremely happy and devotedly attached to one another, but citizens will never be thus attached where there are many suits at law between them, and numerous wrongs committed, but where both are rarest and of least consequence." This leads him, a few sentences later, to consider the optimal income distribution. . . . Plato is clear: no hiding behind the veil of value-neutrality for him. Each man shall have at a minimum a lot of equal size and equal opportunity. Because of different personal characteristics, some will earn more than this. Because of equal opportunity, men may move up and down the income ladder. The maximum allowable is four times the value of the lot, because anything higher will induce jealousy, crime, strife, and conflict. Any income or property earned above this limit is forfeit to the state or to the gods.

It is a good answer. . . . Equality of opportunity—which we have taken to be the most basic meaning of equality in justice—is provided for. Citizens have a guaranteed income, so they will not fall into dire poverty. They have the right to be rewarded for their hard work and talents, but not so much that they will induce envy, which would rupture the attachment of one citizen to another. It is a reasonable balancing act between different components of justice.

Classical Greece was a different world from today's advanced capitalism. Is it possible that 4:1 is no longer the right ratio and that it should be replaced by something like 600:1?

WHAT DIFFERENCES IN LABOR INCOMES ARE NEEDED FOR EFFICIENCY?

. . . Since we are of equal moral worth, our incomes should be as equal as possible—not because justice requires equality of outcomes but because if incomes vary from family to family, the children in our families will have unequal opportunities. Let us begin the discussion of an optimal income distribution, therefore, by assuming a utopian society in which all incomes are equal and no barriers of class, race, gender, sexual preference, nationality, or anything else impede equality of opportunity.

Such a society would, unfortunately, be inefficient, because people would have no financial incentive to be productive. Their incomes, being equal, would be unrelated to their contributions to society. People are motivated by many factors, not just money, but money matters. Efficiency, therefore, conflicts with equality, and we must compromise. We should ask what are the *minimum departures from equality* necessary to bring about the efficiency that we really need. The departures should be minimal because every concession to income differences in support of efficiency will take us further down the road of unequal opportunity for children.

People get their income from different sources, principal among them wages and salaries from labor, rents from land and improvements on the land, interest and dividends from investments, profits from entrepreneurship, transfers from the government, and gifts and inheritances. The most important source is wages and salaries, which account for over two-thirds of personal income in the United States. We begin, therefore, by thinking about the relationship between employees' incomes and efficiency. Why might we want firms and other organizations to pay people at unequal rates?

Many of the wage differences that exist in the real world are obviously unjust. Differences caused by discrimination based on race, gender, or other personal characteristics, or by family connections or monopoly power, have no place in a just world. Some of the existing wage differences cannot be so easily dismissed, however, because they are signals that lead to the efficient employment of labor.

Take a simple example. A society has just two jobs, server at a fast-food establishment and high-tech engineer, each with its own employer. It has two workers, Mary and George. Mary is technically adept while George is inept in most pursuits. Both employers would prefer to hire Mary. If the wages in both positions were equal, Mary might choose the less-demanding job of food server, leaving George to take the engineering post, and that would be an inefficient allocation of labor. If, however, the employers are allowed to set their own rates of pay, the high-tech employer will likely raise Mary's rate to such a level that she chooses the engineering job. The fast-food employer will not be able to match the offer, although she would like to hire Mary, because Mary, although she is worth more behind the counter than George is, is not worth as much behind the counter as she is in the lab. The high-tech employer will be able to outbid the fast-food employer for Mary's services. The resulting allocation of labor will be efficient: Mary in the engineering job and George behind the food counter. The story shows that sometimes, not always, wages are an indicator of productivity. When wages differ, and when people try to get jobs with the highest possible wages, they may sort themselves out among the available jobs in such a way as to promote efficiency.

What departures from equal wages should we want, on grounds of efficiency? We probably have different answers—depending upon the weights we give to equality and efficiency—but we can narrow our disagreement by identifying some of the specific reasons for thinking that inequality promotes efficiency.

The first efficiency-related justification for unequal wages is to persuade some people to undertake education, apprenticeships, and training programs so that they will enhance their skills. Consider an eighteen-year-old who has just graduated from high school and is choosing between two careers, one as a clerk, a job she can start immediately, the other as a doctor. In the just world of equal opportunity that we are assuming, she has not already been tracked by her race or class or by her high school counselor into choosing one or the other career; she can make an autonomous choice. If she chooses the medical career, she faces twelve more years of training—four years of college, four years of medical school, and four years of residency—during all of which time, let us assume, she will earn no income at all, before she can start earning a doctor's income. (This is an oversimplification, since residents typically earn a low salary.) If the society wants some doctors, it may have to pay her an income, once she finishes her residency, sufficient to persuade her that she was right to give up the clerical job. How much more does she need to earn?

She expects to retire at age sixty-five, so if she chooses to be a clerk she will have forty-seven years of income-earning work, and if she chooses the medical career she will have thirty-five years. She may reason that she needs to make at least as much during her thirty-five years of doctoring as she would have during her forty-seven years of clerking. On these grounds, the annual income of a doctor would need to be 34 percent above that of a clerk; that is, the ratio of incomes would be 1.34:1. One way to think of this is that she would go in debt for the first twelve years, by the amount of the clerical salary forgone each year, then would pay off the debt during her earning years and still have the same income during those years, net of debt repayments, as the clerk. The two lifetime incomes would be the same, just arranged differently over time.

Actually the ratio would have to be higher than 1.34:1 because of time preference and the interest rate. For a variety of reasons, people prefer to have their income earlier rather than later. Perhaps it is a fear of death, a fear that they may not be around to enjoy the later income, or perhaps it is a failure of imagination, a failure to understand that they will want income as much in the future as they do now. Whatever the reason, it is normal for people to prefer income earlier rather than later. Put differently, if they are going to have to put off their income, they need to be compensated for the wait, by earning interest. So part of the dilemma facing our high school graduate is that if she chooses a clerical career, she will begin earning income now, when she most wants it. To persuade her to choose medicine, a career whose rewards will come later, we will need to sweeten the pot. By how much? Suppose her rate of time preference is 5 percent a year—that is, she would be indifferent between receiving $100 today and $105 a year from now; and suppose also that 5 percent is the interest rate she would have to pay on funds that she borrows while she is in her twelve years of medical education. Under these circumstances, a calculation discounting future income at a 5 percent annual rate demonstrates that the doctor's annual pay rate would have to be roughly double that of the clerk's, or a ratio of 2:1.

It was not by chance that a doctor's career was used in this example, but because medicine has the longest training period of any profession. Even the longest training period can justify an earnings ratio in the neighborhood of only 2:1. In a way, of course, there is no income difference in this example. Thought of in terms of lifetime earnings or, more accurately, in terms of the present value of lifetime earnings when discounted for time preference, the two earnings figures are the same.

A second reason for thinking that earnings differences promote efficiency is that many people need the prospect of higher earnings, or the fear of lower earnings, as an incentive to work hard and effectively. A good deal of evidence on this subject comes from the experience of agricultural communes in communist China and the former Soviet Union. They were very large farms, sometimes with a membership of tens of thousands of workers. In many cases, each worker was paid the same amount, calculated as a portion of the earnings of the commune. When the commune did well, earnings rose, and vice versa. The contribution that any one worker made to the success of the overall operation was too small to be noticed and had no perceptible effect on that worker's compensation. Agricultural economist D. Gale Johnson, writing about the Soviet communes in 1983, said, "The farm worker sees little or no relationship between his or her work and the pay received. Consequently there is little incentive to do any particular job well, to work hard, or to work long hours during busy seasons of the year."[6] . . .

We know, therefore, that equal wages, unrelated to a worker's effort, cause major problems in overall efficiency. When we try to quantify the effect of merit pay on actual performance, however, we find conflicting evidence. Some studies show a substantial impact, others only a weak one. The difference in findings may be related to the difficulty that organizations have in assessing meritorious performance. In any case, many organizations establish a salary range for each position and attempt to locate people within that range according to their performance. The range varies from position to position and from organization to organization, but it seldom exceeds 50 percent of the base pay for the position.[7]

I have personal experience, however, of a merit range of approximately 100 percent. On the university campus where I teach, tenured full professors are typically promoted to that rank in their early forties and can look forward to twenty to twenty-five more working years before retirement. Since they are in the privileged position of holding tenure, they are in no danger of being fired. What keeps them working hard—and most of them do work hard—over those twenty-five years? Part of the answer is pride in their work. Beyond that, material incentives are provided. Approximately every three years, each professor goes through a rigorous peer review. Success in one of these merit reviews normally results in a pay increase of about 5 percent; there are a number of cases, however, of no increase, on the one hand, or 10 percent or even greater increases, on the other. The net result of all these personnel actions is that, at any time, the gap between the highest and lowest paid full professor is about 2:1. I can report, from many years of having been subject to this system of merit pay and having helped to administer it, that the professors take it very seriously. The increments provide not only income but, equally if not more importantly, recognition of the value of their work.

This is just one observation, and it probably lies at the extreme range of what is needed to keep people working effectively. People with less job security, who face the prospect of being fired if their performance is unsatisfactory, probably need less incentive pay: hence the more typical range of 50 percent or less. In a few cases, the ratio may need to be as high as 2:1.

A third connection between wage inequality and efficiency comes from organizational hierarchies. Most of us work in organizations with many layers of status and function. From the president at the top through all the vice presidents and assistant vice presidents to the section chiefs and the assistant chiefs, the professionals and the quasi professionals, the technicians and the clericals, the custodians and the cleaners, the number of layers is often quite large in big organizations. It seems to be important that each superior layer in the organization carry a higher rate of pay than the layer below it, since most people find it hard to supervise people with higher salaries or to be supervised by people with lower. This is not a universal phenomenon; for example, some professional sports stars play under coaches who earn lower salaries. Still, it is the convention that a higher rank carry higher compensation, and probably for good reason. How much total differential is required? In the real world, the gap between the top and the bottom is often enormous, reflecting a significant difference between each separate position. In a just world that honored the goal of equality as well as efficiency, the gap would not have to be as great. A ratio of 2:1 between top and bottom, for example, would allow for at least twenty separate gradations of 5 percent or fifty gradations of 2 percent.

Some people think the gap needs to be greater; not surprisingly, they tend disproportionately to be people with higher incomes.[8] The *New York Times* records a conversation between its reporter and several top corporate executives, including L. Dennis Kozlowski, CEO of Tyco International.

> Q. It's often said that at a certain level it no longer matters how much any of you make, that you would be doing just as good a job for $100 million less or $20 million less.
>
> Kozlowski: Yeah, all my meals are paid for, for as long as I'm around. So, I'm not working for that any longer. But it does make a difference in the charities I ultimately leave monies behind to, and it's a way of keeping score.[9]

It does not take an overly active imagination to think of better ways of funding charities and cheaper ways of keeping score.

Combining the reasons for pay differences among employees that we have discussed so far—compensation for training, incentives for hard work, and status differences in the hierarchy—and assuming that the reasons for pay differences are completely independent one from another, we come up with a maximum ratio between the top and the bottom of the labor force of 8:1, that is, $2 \times 2 \times 2$.

Factors exist that could reduce or increase this ratio. There are at least two reasons for reducing it. First, the justifications for pay differentials sometimes overlap. A person who is highly trained is likely to qualify for a more senior position in the hierarchy. One way a person is rewarded for good job performance is often by being promoted to a job at the next status level. To a certain extent, therefore—not totally—the three categories collapse into a single category.

Second, the discussion so far has taken no account of what is sometimes called "psychic income." In a free labor market, people get to choose their jobs, at least to a certain extent, and they often choose them because they like them. The young woman who was deciding between a clerical and a medical career might have had a strong preference for medicine. She might have chosen to be a doctor even if it paid less over her lifetime than a clerical job; the difference is her psychic income. Suppose Michael Jordan—who became the world's greatest and highest-paid basketball player—had figured out at the age of eighteen that he could have had a clerical career paying $30,000 a year or a basketball career paying $20,000. There is a good chance he would have chosen basketball, because he loved it. The same sort of reasoning is true of the other categories. Many of my professor colleagues work hard because they enjoy research and teaching; money is not the main issue. . . . In organizational hierarchies, many people simply want to be boss; the fact that the next position up comes with a higher salary is an added bonus, but it is not the only incentive. In other words, the added psychic income that usually attaches to higher-status positions reduces although it does not eliminate the need for pay differentials.

On the other side, an argument for increasing the ratio is that we have not exhausted the reasons for thinking that pay differentials signal an efficient allocation of labor. In the first example, both employers preferred Mary over George, not necessarily because she was more highly trained or because she was a more conscientious worker—she may not have been—but because she was more skilled and effective.

In the real world, the gap in effectiveness between some of the most-skilled people like Mary and some of the least-skilled people like George is enormous. Think, for example, about the difference between a Nobel Prize–winning scientist and a typical high school dropout—or, along a different dimension of competency, about the difference between Michael Jordan and an athletic klutz like, say, me. If compensation packages are kept within a ratio of about 8:1, they may be insufficient, in some cases, to direct people to their most efficient employment. In fact, any restriction on the spread of incomes is likely to have some negative effect on efficiency. We must arrive at a compromise, therefore, achieving neither as much equality as we would like nor as much efficiency. If we opt for complete equality, our productive system will collapse. If we opt for the most efficient possible system, we will suffer from extreme inequality, as we do now.

A salary ratio of 8:1 is a good compromise. A range between, say, $20,000 and $160,000 a year would provide a great deal of room for wages to be related to effectiveness. It would probably constrain some labor contracts that would otherwise

be efficient, but surely not many, particularly in view of the points made above about the narrowing effects of both psychic income and the overlapping of categories. Moreover, since equality is so important, I think the distribution of labor incomes should be bell-shaped, with many more people in the middle than at the extremes. . . .

DIFFERENCES IN NONLABOR INCOMES

What about nonlabor income, including interest, dividends, rent, profits, and appreciation in the value of assets? Much of this is income earned by people in return for providing capital. Capital is defined as a means of production that has itself been produced: for the most part, although not entirely, buildings, plant, and equipment. It is essential to the production process, so a way must be found of providing it.

. . . In capitalism, the capital is owned privately. Suppose we start with a situation of absolutely equal distribution of income. Some people consume all their income and have nothing left at the end of the year. Others consume only half their income, save the rest, and purchase capital with it. In each successive year they do the same. Essentially they are postponing their consumption in the hope of increasing it in the long run. In the first year, they consume only half the goods they might have. In each successive year, though, their income grows if their investments turn out successfully, because they earn increasing amounts of capital income as the capital stock they own grows. Eventually their income is so large, because of the capital income they are adding each year, that not only their income but their consumption exceeds that of their nonsaving neighbors. They save a portion of their income each year and create capital with it because they expect they will be compensated with capital income in the future. If they did not expect this capital income, they would not continue to save. In a capitalist system, therefore, a limit on the income that can be earned from capital will likely reduce the amount of capital available to the society. The citizens may decide that this is a worthwhile limit to impose, but they will have to reckon with the loss in efficiency.

In a noncapitalist society, the answer may be different. If savings were made from the profits of firms structured as worker cooperatives, say, or from the profits of state-owned enterprises, or from the excess of a government's tax receipts over its expenditures, capital would not be in individual hands and the income accruing to capital could be shared in any way. The world in which we live is, however, capitalist.

Profits can be thought of as the return to entrepreneurship, to organization, or, if you will, to risk taking. A person, a group, or a company with a new idea invests some money in developing that idea in the hope that it will be commercially successful. If they fail, they lose their money and time; if they succeed, they reap profits. The prospect of profits is, therefore, an engine of growth. If profits are restricted in a capitalist society, there is a chance that risk taking, innovation, and growth will be reduced.

FREEDOM, EFFICIENCY, AND INCOMES

We have uncovered problems with a strict income ratio of 8:1. This sort of spread, or less, is all that is required to compensate us for our merits and to provide most of the incentives that are needed for efficiency. Neither this limit nor any limit, however, will allow us the most efficient possible economy. Some unusual people are so productive that virtually any restriction on their labor income will lead to the possibility that they will not be employed in the most efficient way. Limits on the incomes of capital owners and entrepreneurs may induce some of them to reduce their contributions to economic growth.

A second sort of problem inheres in any limit on incomes. If the limit is applied rigidly, it may violate the norm of freedom, and freedom is an important component of justice. . . . Freedom requires not just the absence of constraints. In its broadest sense, it moves us toward a fairly egalitarian income distribution, so that everyone can have an equal capacity to do what she wants to do. Therefore, in the name of freedom, one can justify taking some resources from people with means in order to redistribute them to people without. The high-income earners among us do not deserve to keep all their income, as a matter of freedom, be-cause they depend upon so many other people in the earning of it. They do, however, deserve to keep some of it. Confiscation of all their income, or all their income over a fixed limit, would violate their freedom. The concept of freedom surely includes a certain security, a right to be free from arbitrary seizure of one's property. One does not have to go as far as the libertarian philosopher Robert Nozick, who claims that virtually any taxation of one's wealth is a violation of justice, to assert that people have the right to hold on to *some* of what they have created and earned.

It follows that a binding limit on the top incomes that people can earn will create problems of either efficiency or freedom. Consider the example of Bill Gates, who amassed the world's greatest fortune by innovating in microelectronics. Confronted by the news that he would have to forfeit all his annual income above $160,000, he could take one of two steps: he could stop innovating or he could continue. If he stopped, the society would become less efficient. The products he has developed have, after all, improved the productivity and increased the enjoyment of millions of people. We may not care much what income he takes home to his family, but we do care about continued improvements in the quality of our lives. If, on the other hand, he continued to innovate, and thereby earned income above the $160,000 limit only to see all of it confiscated by the tax collector, his freedom to at least some security in his holdings would be violated.

AN ETHICALLY DEFENSIBLE DISTRIBUTION OF INCOMES

Let's summarize where we have gotten so far. The idea of equal incomes is initially attractive because it would ensure equal opportunity for succeeding generations. Completely equal incomes would, however, lead to a society that most of us would not be willing to tolerate. We would not be compensated for the autonomous use of our will, we would have no financial incentive to work efficiently, we would suffer from a shortage of capital and entrepreneurship, and our right to some security in our possessions would be violated. So we must retreat from complete equality. We should not, however, retreat as far as the inequality in, for example, the current American economy. The inequality in such a society egregiously violates the standards of both equal opportunity and equal freedom. For almost all of us, a ratio of something like 8:1 in earned incomes should be more than sufficient to recognize the differences in desert among us and to persuade us to work efficiently. Most of us need only a 2:1 ratio. The criteria of equality, freedom, and efficiency conflict, and we should try to arrive at a compromise that honors all of them as much as possible, but none of them completely. In a small number of cases, I think we will want to permit incomes to rise above the 8:1 limit, in the interests of both freedom and efficiency.

So we will have to abandon Plato's idea that we can specify an exact ratio between the highest and lowest incomes that is compatible with justice. Fortunately we have another measure, the share of total personal incomes accruing to different percentiles of the population. Some of the current data were given at the beginning of this [reading]. The latest figures for the United States show the lowest 20 percent of the population receiving 5 percent of the income, and the highest 20 percent 45 percent.

No overall distribution of incomes guarantees social justice, of course, since what looks like a defensible array of incomes may hide individual injustices. We can speculate, however, about what the distribution of incomes might look like if justice were achieved.

Begin with an average family income of about $90,000, which is the range that existed in the United States at the end of the twentieth century. This may seem high to readers, but remember it is the average income per family, not per person. The median family income in the United States—the income below which half the families are found—is about half the average, approximately $45,000.[10] The gap between the median and the average is a measure of how skewed the current distribution is, with a small number of exceptionally rich people pulling the average above the median. If the population were concentrated near the center of the income distribution, with symmetrical tails on either side, the median and average would roughly coincide.

Table 1 Hypothetical Income Distribution for a Country of 1,000 People

Annual Income (in $ Thousands)	Average Income of Families in Range (in $ Thousands)	Number of Families	Income Earned by Group (in $ Thousands)
20	20	100	2,000
20–40	30	50	1,500
40–60	50	50	2,500
60–80	70	220	15,400
80–100	90	310	27,900
100–120	110	220	24,200
120–140	130	40	5,200
140–160	150	9	1,350
over 160	300	1	300
Total		1,000	80,350

A just distribution of family incomes would, I think, follow these principles. First, no family would fall below the poverty line, no matter what the contribution of its members to overall production. . . . In a world of justice, no child suffers the disadvantage of growing up poor. The figure of $20,000 is the poverty cutoff for a family of four; we simplify the discussion by taking $20,000 as the cutoff for all families. Second, most families would be within a 2:1 ratio of incomes. This is sufficient to provide most of the incentives needed for economic efficiency. Third, except for a small number of people, the maximum ratio of incomes would be 8:1. Fourth, a few incomes would rise above the 8:1 ratio.

One expression of these principles is in Table 1, which shows 75 percent of the families within a 2:1 ratio, earning between $60,000 and $120,000 a year. Another 10 percent are right at the poverty line of $20,000; most of these are families whose adult members either cannot or choose not to earn the subsistence level of income, and they are brought up to this level by transfers from the government. Ten percent are above the poverty line but below the middle-income range, and 5 percent are above the middle-income range. Among the latter group, 0.1 percent of the families in the country earn incomes above the 8:1 ratio.

In Table 1, total personal income is $80,350,000, so with 1,000 families, the average personal income is $80,350, a little below the actual figure in the United States in recent years and well within the range of average incomes in most advanced capitalist countries. The median income is close to the average, a result of the facts that families are bunched near the center of the distribution and that incomes are not severely skewed at either end. The bottom 20 percent of the population earn 7.5 percent of the income while the top 20 percent earn 29 percent of the income, both figures indicating a more egalitarian distribution than currently exists in the United States.

This is not the only array of incomes consistent with justice—for example, the portion of the population just at the poverty line might be lower. It is, however, a fair array, allowing as it does considerable differences in personal incomes to reflect differences in accomplishments and incentives, while responding to the fact of moral equality by restricting most incomes within a narrow 2:1 band.

Notes

1. World Bank, *World Development Report 1999/2000* (New York: Oxford University Press, 1999).

2. Frank Levy, *The New Dollars and Dreams* (New York: Russell Sage Foundation, 1998).

3. Jeff Madrick, "How New Is the New Economy?" *New York Review of Books* 46 (September 23, 1999): 42–50.

4. Edward N. Wolff, *Top Heavy: The Increasing Inequality of Wealth in America and What Can Be Done about It* (New York: New Press, 1996).

5. David Leonhardt, "Executive Pay Drops Off the Political Radar," *New York Times,* April 16, 2000, Week in Review, 5.

6. D. Gale Johnson and Karen McConnell Brooks, *Prospects for Soviet Agriculture in the 1980s* (Bloomington: Indiana University Press, 1983), 199.

7. Frederick W. Cook, "Merit Pay and Performance Appraisal," in *The Compensation Handbook: A State-of-the-Art Guide to Compensation Strategy and Design,* ed. Milton L. Rock and Lance A. Berger (New York: McGraw-Hill, 1991), 542–66.

8. Alan Wolfe, "The Pursuit of Autonomy," *New York Times Magazine,* May 7, 2000, 53–56.

9. Reed Abelson, "A Leader's-Eye View of Leadership," *New York Times,* October 10, 1999, sec. 3, 1.

10. The figures in this paragraph may be found in or calculated from United States Census Bureau, *Statistical Abstract of the United States: 1999,* 119th ed. (Washington, D.C.: 1999), Tables 70, 732, and 750.

Review and Discussion Questions

1. Inequality of income is greater in the United States than in other capitalist countries. What do you think explains this? Is there something unjust about extreme inequality?

2. Why does Plato wish to limit inequality? Does inequality of income have negative social consequences?

3. Restate and critically assess the three efficiency-related justifications for unequal wages that Isbister presents. Explain "psychic income" and the other factors that could reduce or increase the 8:1 ratio that Isbister comes up with.

4. Isbister's Table 1 outlines what he takes to be an ethically defensible distribution of income. Assess his proposed distribution from the point of view of utilitarianism, libertarianism, and Rawls's theory of justice.

5. Does justice require our society to attempt to move toward a more equal distribution of income? How might it attempt to do so? How equal should the distribution of income be? Does respect for freedom limit the pursuit of equality?

Reading ──────────────■

IS INHERITANCE JUSTIFIED?

D. W. HASLETT

Many people support inheritance because they believe it is an essential and necessary feature of capitalism. After reviewing some facts about wealth distribution and inheritance in the United States today, D. W. Haslett argues against this view. He contends not only that inheritance is not essential to capitalism, but that it is inconsistent with the fundamental values underlying capitalism. In particular, inheritance violates the capitalistic ideals of "distribution according to productivity," "equal opportunity," and "freedom." Haslett maintains, accordingly, that the practice of inheritance, as it exists today, should be abolished.

I. BACKGROUND INFORMATION

Family income in the United States today is not distributed very evenly. The top fifth of American families receives 57.3 percent of all family income, while the bottom fifth receives only 7.2 percent.

But, for obvious reasons, a family's financial well-being does not depend upon its income nearly as much as it does upon its wealth, just as the strength of an army does not depend upon how many people joined it during the year as much as it does upon how many people are in it altogether. So if we really want to know how unevenly economic well-being is distributed in the United States today, we must look at the distribution not of income, but of wealth.

Although—quite surprisingly—the government does not regularly collect information on the distribution of wealth, it has occasionally done so. The results are startling. One to two percent of American families own from around 20 to 30 percent of

the (net) family wealth in the United States; 5 to 10 percent own from around 40 to 60 percent. The top fifth owns almost 80 percent of the wealth, while the bottom fifth owns only 0.2 percent. So while the top fifth has, as we saw, about eight times the income of the bottom fifth, it has about 400 times the wealth. Whether deliberately or not, by regularly gathering monumental amounts of information on the distribution of income, but not on the distribution of wealth, the government succeeds in directing attention away from how enormously unequal the distribution of wealth is, and directing it instead upon the less unequal distribution of income. But two things are clear: wealth is distributed far more unequally in the United States today than is income, and this inequality in the distribution of wealth is enormous. These are the first two things to keep in mind throughout our discussion of inheritance.

The next thing to keep in mind is that, although estate and gift taxes in the United States are supposed to redistribute wealth, and thereby lessen this inequality, they do not do so. Before 1981 estates were taxed, on an average, at a rate of only 0.2 percent—0.8 percent for estates over $500,000—hardly an amount sufficient to cause any significant redistribution of wealth. And, incredibly, the Economic Recovery Act of 1981 *lowered* estate and gift taxes.

Of course the top rate at which estates and gifts are *allegedly* taxed is far greater than the 0.2 percent rate, on the average, at which they are *really* taxed. Prior to 1981, the top rate was 70 percent, which in 1981 was lowered to 50 percent. Because of this relatively high top rate, the average person is led to believe that estate and gift taxes succeed in breaking up the huge financial empires of the very rich, thereby distributing wealth more evenly. What the average person fails to realize is that what the government takes with one hand, through high nominal rates, it gives back with the other hand, through loopholes in the law. . . . Indeed, as George Cooper shows, estate and gift taxes can, with the help of a good attorney, be avoided so easily they amount to little more than "voluntary" taxes.[1] As such, it is not surprising that, contrary to popular opinion, these taxes do virtually nothing to reduce

D. W. Haslett, "Is Inheritance Justified?" *Philosophy and Public Affairs* 15 (Spring 1986). Copyright © 1986 by Princeton University Press. Reprinted by permission of Princeton University Press. Some notes omitted, and some section titles added.

the vast inequality in the distribution of wealth that exists today.

Once we know that estate and gift taxes do virtually nothing to reduce this vast inequality, what I am about to say next should come as no surprise. This vast inequality in the distribution of wealth is (according to the best estimates) due at least as much to inheritance as to any other factor. Once again, because of the surprising lack of information about these matters, the extent to which this inequality is due to inheritance is not known exactly. One estimate, based upon a series of articles appearing in *Fortune* magazine, is that 50 percent of the large fortunes in the United States were derived basically from inheritance. But by far the most careful and thorough study of this matter to date is that of John A. Brittain. Brittain shows that the estimate based upon the *Fortune* articles actually is too low,[2] that a more accurate estimate of the amount contributed by inheritance to the wealth of "ultrarich" males is 67 percent.[3] In any case, it is clear that, in the United States today, inheritance plays a large role indeed in perpetuating a vastly unequal distribution of wealth. This is the final thing to keep in mind throughout the discussion which follows.

II. INHERITANCE AND CAPITALISM

Capitalism (roughly speaking) is an economic system where (1) what to produce, and in what quantities, is determined essentially by supply and demand—that is, by people's "dollar votes"—rather than by central planning, and (2) capital goods are, for the most part, privately owned. In the minds of many today, capitalism goes hand in hand with the practice of inheritance; capitalism without inheritance, they would say, is absurd. But, if I am right, the exact opposite is closer to the truth. Since, as I shall try to show in this section, the practice of inheritance is incompatible with basic values or ideals that underlie capitalism, what is absurd, if anything, is capitalism *with* inheritance. . . .

I do not try to show here that the ideals underlying capitalism are worthy of support; I only try to show that inheritance is contrary to these ideals. And if it is, then from this it follows that, *if* these

ideals are worthy of support (as, incidentally, I think they are), then we have prima facie reason for concluding that inheritance is unjustified. What then are these ideals? For an answer, we can do no better than turn to one of capitalism's most eloquent and uncompromising defenders: Milton Friedman.

Distribution According to Productivity

The point of any economic system is, of course, to produce goods and services. But, as Friedman tells us, society cannot very well *compel* people to be productive and, even if it could, out of respect for personal freedom, probably it should not do so. Therefore, he concludes, in order to get people to be productive, society needs instead to *entice* them to produce, and the most effective way of enticing people to produce is to distribute income and wealth according to productivity. Thus we arrive at the first ideal underlying capitalism: "To each according to what he and the instruments he owns produces."[4]

Obviously, inheritance contravenes this ideal. For certain purposes, this ideal would require further interpretation; we would need to know more about what was meant by "productivity." For our purposes, no further clarification is necessary. According to *any* reasonable interpretation of "productivity," the wealth people get through inheritance has nothing to do with their productivity. And one need not be an adherent of this ideal of distribution to be moved by the apparent injustice of one person working eight hours a day all his life at a miserable job, and accumulating nothing, while another person does little more all his life than enjoy his parents' wealth, and inherits a fortune.

Equal Opportunity

But for people to be productive it is necessary not just that they be *motivated* to be productive, but that they have the *opportunity* to be productive. This brings us to the second ideal underlying capitalism: equal opportunity—that is, equal opportunity for all to pursue, successfully, the occupation of their choice. According to capitalist ethic, it is OK if, in the economic game, there are winners and losers, provided everyone has an "equal start." As Friedman puts it, the ideal of equality compatible with capitalism is not equality of outcome, which would *discourage* people from realizing their full productive potential, but equality of opportunity, which *encourages* people to do so.[5]

Naturally this ideal, like the others we are considering, neither could, nor should, be realized fully; to do so would require, among other things, no less than abolishing the family and engaging in extensive genetic engineering. But the fact that this ideal cannot and should not be realized fully in no way detracts from its importance. Not only is equal opportunity itself an elementary requirement of justice but, significantly, progress in realizing this ideal could bring with it progress in at least two other crucial areas as well: those of productivity and income distribution. First, the closer we come to equal opportunity for all, the more people there will be who, as a result of increased opportunity, will come to realize their productive potential. And, of course, the more people there are who come to realize their productive potential, the greater overall productivity will be. Second, the closer we come to equal opportunity for all, the more people there will be with an excellent opportunity to become something other than an ordinary worker, to become a professional or an entrepreneur of sorts. And the more people there are with an excellent opportunity to become something other than an ordinary worker, the more people there will be who in fact become something other than an ordinary worker or, in other words, the less people there will be available for doing ordinary work. As elementary economic theory tells us, with a decrease in the supply of something comes an increase in the demand for it, and with an increase in the demand for it comes an increase in the price paid for it. An increase in the price paid for it would, in this case, mean an increase in the income of the ordinary worker vis-à-vis that of the professional and the entrepreneur, which, surely, would be a step in the direction of income being distributed more justly.

And here I mean "more justly" even according to the ideals of capitalism itself. As we have seen, the capitalist ideal of distributive justice is "to each according to his or her productivity." But, under capitalism, we can say a person's income from some occupation reflects his or her productivity only to the extent there are no unnecessary limitations upon people's opportunity to pursue, successfully, this occupation—and by "unnecessary limitations" I mean ones that either *cannot* or (because doing so would cause more harm than good) *should not* be removed. According to the law of supply and demand, the more limited the supply of people in some occupation, then (assuming a healthy demand to begin with) the higher will be the income of those pursuing the occupation. Now if the limited supply of people in some high-paying occupation . . . is the result of unnecessary limitations upon people's opportunity to pursue that occupation, then the scarcity is an "artificial" one, and the high pay can by no means be said to reflect productivity. The remedy is to remove these limitations; in other words, to increase equality of opportunity. To what extent the relative scarcity of professionals and entrepreneurs in capitalist countries today is due to natural scarcity, and to what extent to artificial scarcity, no one really knows. I strongly suspect, however, that a dramatic increase in equality of opportunity will reveal that the scarcity is far more artificial than most professionals and entrepreneurs today care to think—*far* more artificial. . . .

That inheritance violates the (crucial) second ideal of capitalism, equal opportunity, is, once again, obvious. Wealth *is* opportunity, and inheritance distributes it very unevenly indeed. Wealth is opportunity for realizing one's potential, for a career, for success, for income. There are few, if any, desirable occupations that great wealth does not, in one way or another, increase—sometimes dramatically—one's chances of being able to pursue, and to pursue successfully. And to the extent that one's success is to be measured in terms of one's income, nothing else, neither intelligence, nor education, nor skills, provides a more secure opportunity for "success" than does wealth. Say one inherits a million dollars. All one then need do is purchase long-term bonds yielding a guaranteed interest of ten percent and (presto!) one has a yearly income of $100,000, an income far greater than anyone who toils eight hours a day in a factory will probably ever have. If working in the factory pays, relatively, so little, then why, it might be asked, do not all these workers become big-time investors themselves? The answer is that they are, their entire lives, barred from doing so by a lack of initial capital which others, through inheritance, are simply handed. With inheritance, the old adage is only too true: "The rich get richer, and the poor get poorer." Without inheritance, the vast fortunes in America today, these enormous concentrations of economic power, would be broken up, allowing wealth, and therefore opportunity, to become distributed far more evenly.

Freedom

But so far I have not mentioned what many, including no doubt Friedman himself, consider to be the most important ideal underlying capitalism: that of liberty or, in other words, freedom. This ideal, however, takes different forms. One form it takes for Friedman is that of being able to engage in economic transactions free from governmental or other types of human coercion. The rationale for this conception of freedom—let us call it freedom in the "narrow" sense—is clear. As Friedman explains it, assuming only that people are informed about what is good for them, this form of freedom guarantees that ". . . no exchange will take place unless both parties benefit from it."[6] If at least the parties themselves benefit from the transaction, and it does not harm anyone, then, it is fair to say, the transaction has been socially valuable. So people with freedom of exchange will, in doing what is in their own best interests, generally be doing what is socially valuable as well. In other words, with this form of freedom, the fabled "invisible hand" actually works.

All of this is a great oversimplification. For one thing, a transaction that benefits both parties may have side effects, such as pollution, which harm others and, therefore, the transaction may not be socially valuable after all. So freedom, in the narrow sense, should certainly not be absolute. But the fact that freedom, in this sense, should not be absolute does not prevent it from serving as a useful ideal. . . .

There are [those] whose conception of freedom is that of not being subject to any governmental co-ercion (or other forms of human coercion) for any purposes whatsoever—a conception sometimes referred to as "negative" freedom. It is true that governmental (or other) coercion for purposes of enforcing the abolition of inheritance violates this ideal, but then, of course, so does any such coercion for purposes of *maintaining* inheritance. So this "anticoercion" ideal . . . neither supports nor opposes the practice of inheritance, and therefore this conception of freedom need not concern us further here. . . .

A very popular variation of the anticoercion conception of freedom is one where freedom is, once again, the absence of all governmental (or other human) coercion, *except for any coercion necessary for enforcing our fundamental rights.* Prominent among our fundamental rights, most of those who espouse such a conception of freedom will tell us, is our right to property. So whether this conception of freedom supports the practice of inheritance depends entirely upon whether our "right to property" should be viewed as incorporating the practice of inheritance. But whether our right to property should be viewed as incorporating the practice of inheritance is just another way of stating the very point at issue in this investigation. . . . Consequently, this popular conception of freedom cannot be used here in support of the practice of inheritance without begging the question.

But there is still another conception of freedom espoused by many: that which we might call freedom in the "broad" sense. According to this conception of freedom, to be free means to have the ability, or the opportunity, to do what one wants. For example, according to this conception of freedom, rich people are, other things being equal, freer than poor people, since their wealth provides them with opportunities to do things that the poor can only dream about. . . .

Let us now see whether inheritance and freedom are inconsistent. Consider, first, freedom in the narrow sense. Although inheritance may not be inconsistent with this ideal, neither is the *abolishment* of inheritance. This ideal forbids governmental interference with free exchanges between people; it does not necessarily forbid governmental interference with *gifts* or *bequests* (which, of course, are not *exchanges*). Remember, Friedman's rationale for this ideal is, as we saw, that free exchange promotes the "invisible hand"; that is, it promotes the healthy functioning of supply and demand, which is at the very heart of capitalism. Supply and demand hardly require gifts, as opposed to exchanges, in order to function well.

If anything, gifts and bequests, and the enormous concentrations of economic power resulting from them, hinder the healthy functioning of supply and demand. First of all, gifts and bequests, and the enormous concentrations of economic power resulting from them, create such great differences in people's "dollar votes" that the economy's demand curves do not accurately reflect the needs of the population as a whole, but are distorted in favor of the "votes" of the rich. And inheritance hinders the healthy functioning of supply and demand even more, perhaps, by interfering with supply. As we have seen, inheritance (which, as I am using the term, encompasses large gifts) is responsible for some starting out in life with a vast advantage over others; it is, in other words, a major source of unequal opportunity. As we have also seen, the further we are from equal opportunity, the less people there will be who come to realize their productive potential. And, of course, the less people there are who come to realize their productive potential, the less overall productivity there will be or, in other words, the less healthy will be the economy's *supply* curves. So, while inheritance may not be *literally* inconsistent with freedom in the narrow sense, it does, by hindering indirectly both supply and demand, appear to be inconsistent with the "spirit" of this ideal. . . .

So we may conclude that, at best, inheritance receives no support from freedom in the narrow sense. But it remains for us to consider whether inheritance receives any support from the other relevant ideal of freedom, an ideal many, including myself, would consider to be the more fundamental of the two: freedom in the broad sense—being able to do, or having the opportunity to do, what one wants. So we must now ask whether, everything considered, there is more overall opportunity throughout the country for people to do what they want with inheritance, or without it.

On the one hand, without inheritance people are no longer free to leave their fortunes to whomever they want and, of course, those who otherwise would have received these fortunes are, without them, less free to do what they want also.

But to offset these losses in freedom are at least the following gains in freedom. First, as is well known, wealth has, generally speaking, a diminishing marginal utility. What this means is that, generally speaking, the more wealth one already has, the less urgent are the needs which any given increment of wealth will go to satisfy and, therefore, the less utility the additional wealth will have for one. This, in turn, means that the more evenly wealth is distributed, the more overall utility it will have.* And since we may assume that, generally speaking, the more utility some amount of wealth has for someone, the more freedom in the broad sense it allows that person to enjoy, we may conclude that the more evenly wealth is distributed, the more overall freedom to which it will give rise. Now assuming that abolishing inheritance would not lessen *overall* wealth . . . and that it would indeed distribute wealth more evenly, it follows that, by abolishing inheritance, there would be some gain in freedom in the broad sense attributable to the diminishing marginal utility of wealth. Next, abolishing inheritance would also increase freedom by increasing equality of opportunity. Certainly those who do not start life having inherited significant funds (through either gift or bequest) start life, relative to those who do, with what amounts to a significant handicap. Abolishing inheritance, and thereby starting everyone at a more equal level, would obviously leave those who otherwise would have suffered this handicap (which would be the great majority of people) more free in the broad sense.

I, for one, believe these gains in freedom—that is, those attributable to the diminishing marginal

---

*The more evenly wealth is distributed, the more overall utility it will have since any wealth that "goes" from the rich to the poor, thereby making the distribution more even, will (given the diminishing marginal utility of wealth) have more utility for these poor than it would have had for the rich, thus increasing overall utility.

utility of wealth and more equality of opportunity—would *more* than offset the loss in freedom resulting from the inability to give one's fortune to whom one wants. Abolishing inheritance is, I suggest, analogous to abolishing discrimination against blacks in restaurants and other commercial establishments. By abolishing discrimination, the owners of these establishments lose the freedom to choose the skin color of the people they do business with, but the gain in freedom for blacks is obviously greater and more significant than this loss. Likewise, by abolishing inheritance the gain in freedom for the poor is greater and more significant than the loss in freedom for the rich. So to the list of ideals that inheritance is inconsistent with, we can, if I am right, add freedom in the broad sense.

To recapitulate: three ideals that underlie capitalism are "distribution according to productivity," "equal opportunity," and "freedom," the latter being, for our purposes, subject to either a narrow or a broad interpretation. I do not claim these are the *only* ideals that may be said to underlie capitalism; I do claim, however, that they are among the most important. Inheritance is inconsistent with both "distribution according to productivity," and "equal opportunity." Perhaps it is not, strictly speaking, inconsistent with the ideal of freedom in the narrow sense, but neither is the abolishment of inheritance. On the other hand, it probably *is* inconsistent with what many would take to be the more fundamental of the two relevant ideals of freedom: freedom in the broad sense. Since these are among the most important ideals that underlie capitalism, I conclude that inheritance not only is not essential to capitalism, but is probably inconsistent with it. . . .

III. A PROPOSAL FOR ABOLISHING INHERITANCE

First, my proposal for abolishing inheritance includes the abolishment of all large gifts as well—gifts of the sort, that is, which might serve as alternatives to bequests. Obviously, if such gifts were not abolished as well, any law abolishing inheritance could be avoided all too easily.

Of course we would not want to abolish along with these large gifts such harmless gifts as ordinary birthday and Christmas presents. This, however, raises the problem of where to draw the line. I do not know the best solution to this problem. The amount that current law allows a person to give each year tax free ($10,000) is too large a figure at which to draw the line for purposes of a law abolishing inheritance. We might experiment with drawing the line, in part at least, by means of the distinction between, on the one hand, consumer goods that can be expected to be, within ten years, either consumed or worth less than half their current value and, on the other hand, all other goods. We can be more lenient in allowing gifts of goods falling within the former category since, as they are consumed or quickly lose their value, they cannot, themselves, become part of a large, unearned fortune. The same can be said about gifts of services. But we need not pursue these technicalities further here. The general point is simply that, so as to avoid an obvious loophole, gifts (other than ordinary birthday presents, etc.) are to be abolished along with bequests.

Next, according to my proposal, a person's estate would pass to the government, to be used for the general welfare. If, however, the government were to take over people's property upon their death then, obviously, after just a few generations the government would own virtually everything—which would certainly not be very compatible with capitalism. Since this proposal for abolishing inheritance *is* supposed to be compatible with capitalism, it must therefore include a requirement that the government sell on the open market, to the highest bidder, any real property, including any shares in a corporation, that it receives from anyone's estate, and that it do so within a certain period of time, within, say, one year from the decedent's death. This requirement is, however, to be subject to one qualification: any person specified by the decedent in his will shall be given a chance to *buy* any property specified by the decedent in his will before it is put on the market (a qualification designed to alleviate slightly the family heirloom/business/farm problem . . .). The price to be paid by this person shall be whatever the property is worth (as determined by governmental appraisers, subject to appeal) and any credit terms shall be rather lenient (perhaps 10 percent down, with the balance, plus interest, due over the next 30 years).

Finally, the abolishment of inheritance proposed here is to be subject to three important exceptions. First, there shall be no limitations at all upon the amount a person can leave to his or her spouse. A marriage, it seems to me, should be viewed as a joint venture in which both members, whether or not one stays home tending to children while the other earns money, have an *equally* important role to play; and neither, therefore, should be deprived of enjoying fully any of the material rewards of this venture by having them taken away at the spouse's death. And unlimited inheritance between spouses eliminates one serious objection to abolishing inheritance: namely, that it is not right for a person suddenly to be deprived, not only of his or her spouse, but also of most of the wealth upon which he or she has come to depend—especially in those cases where the spouse has, for the sake of the marriage, given up, once and for all, any realistic prospects of a career.

The second exception to be built into this proposal is one for children who are orphaned, and any other people who have been genuinely dependent upon the decedent, such as any who are mentally incompetent, or too elderly to have any significant earning power of their own. A person shall be able to leave funds (perhaps in the form of a trust) sufficient to take care of such dependents. These funds should be used only for the dependent's living expenses, which would include any educational or institutional expenses no matter how much. They should not, of course, be used to provide children with a "nest egg" of the sort others are prohibited from leaving their children. And at a certain age, say twenty-one (if the child's formal education has been completed), or upon removal of whatever disability has caused dependency, the funds should cease. This exception eliminates another objection to abolishing inheritance—the objection that it would leave orphaned children, and other dependents, without the support they needed.

The third and final exception to be built into this proposal is one for charitable organizations—ones created not for purposes of making a profit, but for charitable, religious, scientific, or educational pur-poses. And, in order to prevent these organizations from eventually controlling the economy, they must, generally, be under the same constraint as is the government with respect to any real property they are given, such as an operating factory: they must, generally, sell it on the open market within a year. . . .

IV. AN OBJECTION

We turn next to what is, I suppose, the most common objection to abolishing inheritance: the objection that, if people were not allowed to leave their wealth to their children, they would lose their incentive to continue working hard, and national productivity would therefore fall. In spite of the popularity of this objection, all the available evidence seems to indicate the contrary. For example, people who do not intend to have children, and therefore are obviously not motivated by the desire to leave their children a fortune, do not seem to work any less hard than anyone else. And evidence of a more technical nature leads to the same conclusion: people, typically, do not need to be motivated by a desire to leave their children (or someone else) great wealth in order to be motivated to work hard.[7]

Common sense tells us the same thing. The prospect of being able to leave one's fortune to one's children is, no doubt, for some people one factor motivating them to be productive. But even for these people, this is only *one* factor; there are usually other factors motivating them as well, and motivating them to such an extent that, even if inheritance were abolished, their productivity would be unaffected. Take, for example, professional athletes. If inheritance were abolished, would they try any less hard to win? I doubt it. For one thing, abolishing inheritance would not, in any way, affect the amount of money they would be able to earn for use during their lives. So they would still have the prospect of a large income to motivate them. But there is something else which motivates them to do their best that is, I think, even more important, and is not dependent on money: the desire to win or, in other words, to achieve that which entitles them to the respect of their colleagues, the general public, and themselves. Because of the desire to win, amateur athletes compete just as fiercely as professionals. Abolishing inheritance would in no way affect this reason for doing one's best either. Athletes would still have the prospect of winning to motivate them. Businessmen, doctors, lawyers, engineers, artists, researchers—in general, those who contribute most to society—are not, with respect to what in the most general sense motivates them, really very different from professional athletes. Without inheritance, these people would still be motivated by the prospect of a sizable income for themselves and, probably even more so, by the prospect of "winning"; that is, by the prospect of achieving, or continuing to achieve, that which entitles them to the respect of their colleagues, the general public, and themselves.

Notes

1. George A. Cooper, *A Voluntary Tax? New Perspectives on Sophisticated Estate Tax Avoidance* (Washington, D.C.: Brookings Institution, 1979).

2. John A. Brittain, *Inheritance and the Inequality of National Wealth* (Washington, D.C.: Brookings Institution, 1978), pp. 14–16.

3. Ibid., p. 99.

4. Milton Friedman, *Capitalism & Freedom* (Chicago: University of Chicago Press, 1962), pp. 161–162.

5. Milton & Rose Friedman, *Freedom to Choose* (New York: Harcourt Brace Jovanovich, 1979), pp. 131–140. . . .

6. Friedman, *Capitalism & Freedom*, p. 13.

7. See, for example, D. C. McClelland, *The Achieving Society* (Princeton: Van Nostrand, 1961), pp. 234–235; and Seymour Fiekowsky, *On the Economic Effects of Death Taxation in the United States* (unpublished doctoral dissertation, Harvard University, 1959), pp. 370–371.

Review and Discussion Questions

1. Has Haslett correctly identified the fundamental ideals underlying capitalism? Would you agree that inheritance is contrary to capitalism's fundamental values?

2. Distinguish freedom in the narrow sense from freedom in the broad sense. Which is the more useful concept? How would the abolition of inheritance affect freedom (in both senses)?

3. How would a utilitarian, a libertarian, and a Rawlsian evaluate inheritance?

4. How feasible do you find Haslett's proposal for abolishing inheritance? Would it be just?

Further Reading for Chapter 3

John Arthur and **William H. Shaw**, eds., *Justice and Economic Distribution*, 2nd ed. (Englewood Cliffs, N.J.: Prentice Hall, 1991) contains substantial extracts from Rawls's *A Theory of Justice* and Nozick's *Anarchy, State, and Utopia*, contemporary presentations of the utilitarian approach, and various recent essays discussing the topic of economic justice.

Joel Feinberg, *Social Philosophy* (Englewood Cliffs, N.J.: Prentice Hall, 1973), Chapter 7, discusses the different types of justice and injustice.

John Isbister, *Capitalism and Justice: Envisioning Social and Economic Fairness* (Bloomfield, Conn.: Kumarian Press, 2001)

InfoTrac College Edition: For further information or to conduct research, please go to www.infotrac-college.com.

discusses a number of questions of justice in the real world, such as income distribution, taxation, welfare, and foreign aid, in a readable but thoughtful way.

Will Kymlicka, *Contemporary Political Philosophy*, 2nd ed. (Oxford: Oxford University Press, 2001) covers the major schools of contemporary political thought and their competing views of justice and community.

Robert M. Stewart, ed., *Readings in Social and Political Philosophy*, 2nd ed. (New York: Oxford University Press, 1996), Part III, provides a number of important essays on justice and equality, including contributions from Rawls and Nozick.

Various authors discuss economic inequality in the United States in *Social Philosophy and Policy* 19 (Winter 2002): "Should Differences in Income and Wealth Matter?" and *Daedalus* (Winter 2002): "On Inequality."

Part Two

American Business
and Its Basis

4

The Nature of Capitalism

In March 1996 the U.S. Department of Labor issued a report that most Americans took to be very good news, indeed: After months of concern about layoffs and declining economic prospects, the economy had added 700,000 jobs the previous month—more jobs than in any month since 1983. Further, the unemployment rate had fallen from 5.8 percent to 5.5 percent. This report wasn't considered good news, however, at the New York Stock Exchange, the heart of American capitalism. The day the report was issued, the Dow Jones industrial average plunged over 171 points, its third largest point decline ever. Why? The reason is complicated. Although economic expansion and increased employment are good for ordinary people, they also raise the specter of inflation. Wall Street traders had been counting on the Federal Reserve Board to lower short-term interest rates and thus add fuel to a bull market, but any hint of inflation, traders feared, would prevent the Fed from doing so.

As it turned out, the sharp drop in the stock market that day was only a minor dip in the upward growth of a long bull market that still had four more years to run. And the brief pain investors felt then was nothing compared to the pain they were to feel in the early years of the present century as the air leaked gradually, but inexorably, out of what, by the end of the 1990s, had clearly become a speculative bubble in the stock market. High-flying dot-com and other technology stocks suffered the most as the laws of capitalist reality—which many pundits thought had been suspended as the United States was supposedly leading the world into a "new economy"—reasserted themselves, reducing the nominal value of American stocks by trillions of dollars. Experts disagree on the exact causes of the long run-up in stock prices (the Dow Jones industrial average had grown from 875 in 1982 to 11,497 in early 2000, and the technology heavy NASDAQ index from 196 to 4,069). They also disagree on the causes of the stock market's subsequent decline. But they agree that Wall Street's troubles have reverberated around the globe, with stocks suffering in markets as far away as London, Tokyo, Johannesburg, and Hong Kong.

That is not surprising. Capitalism is a worldwide system, multinational firms operate without regard for traditional political boundaries, and the economies of capitalist nations are intricately interconnected. But what exactly is the nature of the economic system called capitalism? What is its underlying economic philosophy? What has it accomplished and what are its prospects for the future? This chapter examines these and related questions.

Looking back in history, one must definitely credit capitalism with helping break the constraints of medieval feudalism, which had severely limited individual possibilities for improvement. In place of a stifling economic system, capitalism offered opportunities for those blessed with imagination, an ability to plan, and a willingness to work. Capitalism must also be credited with enhancing the abundance and diversity of consumer goods beyond Adam Smith's wildest dreams. It has increased our material wealth and our standard of living and has converted our cities from modest bazaars into treasure troves of dazzling merchandise.

In the light of such accomplishments and the acculturation process that tends to glorify them, it is possible to overlook capitalism's theoretical and operational problems, which have serious moral import. This chapter attempts to identify some of these problems and their moral implications. It provides some basic historical and conceptual categories for understanding the socioeconomic framework within which business transactions occur and moral issues arise. In particular, this chapter addresses the following topics:

1. The definition of capitalism and its major historical stages

2. Four of the key features of capitalism: companies, profit motive, competition, and private property

3. Two classical moral justifications of capitalism—the first based on the right to property, the second on Adam Smith's concept of the "invisible hand"

4. Fundamental criticisms of capitalism—in particular, the persistence of inequality and poverty, capitalism's implicit view of human nature, the rise of economic oligarchies, the shortcomings of competition, and the employee's experience of alienation and exploitation on the job

5. The problems facing capitalism in the United States today—in particular, slow growth in productivity, declining interest in the actual manufacturing of goods, and our changing attitudes toward work

CAPITALISM

Capitalism can be defined ideally as an economic system in which the major portion of production and distribution is in private hands, operating under what is termed a profit or market system. The U.S. economy is the world's leading capitalistic economy. All manufacturing firms are privately owned, including those that produce military hardware for the government. The same applies to banks, insurance companies, and most transportation companies. All businesses—small, medium, and large—are also privately owned, as are power companies. With the exception of government expenditures for such things as health, education, welfare, highways, and military equipment, no central governing body dictates to these private owners what or how much of anything will be produced. For example, officials at Ford, Chrysler, and General Motors design their products and set their own production goals according to anticipated consumer demand.

The private ownership and market aspects of capitalism contrast with its polar opposite, socialism. Ideally, *socialism* is an economic system characterized by public ownership of property and a planned economy. Under socialism, a society's productive equipment is not owned by individuals (capitalists) but by public bodies. Socialism depends primarily on centralized planning rather than on the market system for both its overall allocation of resources and its distribution of income; crucial economic decisions are made not by individuals but by government. In the former Soviet Union, for example, government agencies decided the number of automobiles—including models, styles, and colors—to be produced each year. Top levels of government formulated production and cost objectives, which were then converted to specific production quotas and budgets that individual plant managers had to follow.

A hybrid economic system advocated by some socialists (and once approximated by Yugoslavia) is *worker control socialism.*[1] Individual firms respond to a market in acquiring the necessary factors of production and in deciding what to produce. The workforce of each enterprise controls the enterprise (although it may elect or hire managers to oversee day-to-day operations), and the profits accrue to the workers as a group to divide in whatever manner they agree on. However, although the workers manage their factories, the capital assets of each enterprise are owned by society as a whole and not by private individuals.

Historical Background of Capitalism

What we call capitalism did not fully emerge until the Renaissance in Europe during the fifteenth and sixteenth centuries. Before the Renaissance, business exchanges in medieval Europe were organized through guilds, which were associations of individuals of the same trade.

Today if you want a pair of shoes, you head for a shoe store, where you find an array of shoes. If nothing strikes your fancy, you set out for another shop, and perhaps another, until at last you find what you want. Or, if still disappointed, you might ask the store clerk to order a pair in your size from the manufacturer or its distributor. You certainly wouldn't ask the clerk to have someone make you a pair of shoes. Under the guild organization, shoemakers, who were also shoe sellers, made shoes only to fill orders. If they had no orders, they made no shoes. The shoemaker's sole economic function was to make shoes for people when they wanted them. His labor allowed him to maintain himself, not advance his station in life. When the shoemaker died, his business went with him—unless he had a son to inherit and carry on the enterprise. As for shoe quality and cost, the medieval shopper could generally count on getting a good pair of shoes at a fair price because the cobblers' guild strictly controlled quality and price.

Weaving was another big medieval trade. In fact, in the fourteenth century weaving was the leading industry in the German town of Augsburg. Little wonder, then, that an enterprising young man named Hans Fugger became a weaver when he settled there in 1367. But young Hans had ambitions that stretched far beyond the limits of the weaving trade and the handicraft guild system. And they were grandly realized, for within three short generations a family of simple weavers was transformed into a great German banking dynasty.[2]

Not content with being a weaver, Hans Fugger began collecting and selling the products of other weavers. Soon he was employing lots of weavers, paying them for their labor, and selling their products as his own. His son, Jacob Fugger, continued the business, which was expanded by Jacob Fugger II, the foremost capitalist of the Renaissance. Under his direction, the family's interests expanded into metals and textiles. Jacob Fugger II also lent large sums of money to the Hapsburg emperors to finance their wars, among other things. In return, he obtained monopoly rights on silver and copper ores, which he then traded. When Fugger bought the mines themselves, he had acquired all the components necessary to erect an extraordinary financial dynasty.

Like latter-day titans of American industry, Fugger employed thousands of workers and paid them wages, controlled all his products from raw material to market, set his own quality standards, and charged whatever the traffic would bear. In one brief century, what was once a handicraft inseparable from the craftsperson had become a company that existed outside any family members. What had once motivated Hans Fugger—maintenance of his station in life—had given way to gain for gain's sake, the so-called *profit motive.* Under Jacob Fugger II, the company amassed profits, a novel concept, that well exceeded the needs of the Fuggers. And the profits were measured not in goods or in land but in money.

Capitalism has undergone changes since then.[3] For example, the kind of capitalism that emerged in the Fuggers' time is often termed *mercantile capitalism,* because it was based on mutual dependence between state and commercial interests. Implicit in mercantile capitalism are the beliefs that national wealth and power are best served by increasing exports and collecting precious metals in return, and that the role of government is to provide laws and economic policies designed to encourage production for foreign trade, keep out imports, and promote national supremacy.

In the United States in the period after the Civil War, *industrial capitalism* emerged, which is associated with the development of large-scale industry. The confluence of many postwar factors produced industrial expansion in America, including a sound financial base, the technology for mass production, expanding markets for cheaply manufactured goods, and a large and willing labor force. Exploiting these fortuitous conditions was a group of hard-driving, visionary entrepreneurs called robber barons by their critics and captains of industry by their supporters: Cornelius Vanderbilt, Cyrus McCormick, Andrew Carnegie, John D. Rockefeller, John Gates, and others.

As industrialization increased, so did the size and power of business. The private fortunes of a few individuals could no longer underwrite the accelerated growth of business activity. The large sums of capital necessary could be raised only through a corporate form of business, in which risk and potential profit were distributed among numerous investors.

As competition intensified, an industry's survival came to depend on its financial strength to reduce prices and either eliminate or absorb competition. To shore up their assets, industries engaged in *financial capitalism,* characterized by pools, trusts, holding companies, and an interpenetration of banking, insurance, and industrial interests. Hand in hand with this development, the trend continued toward larger and larger corporations, controlling more and more of the country's economic capacity.

The economic and political challenges of the Great Depression of the 1930s helped usher in still another phase of capitalism, often called *state welfare capitalism,* in which government plays an active role in regulating economic activities in an effort to smooth out the boom-and-bust pattern of the business cycle. In addition, government programs like Social Security and unemployment insurance seek to enhance the welfare of the workforce, and legislation legitimizes the existence of trade unions. Today state

welfare capitalism prevails. Conservative politicians sometimes advocate less government control of business, but in reality the governments of all capitalist countries are deeply involved in the management of their economies.

Even though the study of capitalism's evolution is best left to economic historians, it is important to keep in mind capitalism's dynamic nature. There is nothing fixed and immutable about this or any other economic system; it is as susceptible to the social forces of change as any other institution. Nevertheless, the capitalism we know does have some prominent features that were evident in the earliest capitalistic businesses.

KEY FEATURES OF CAPITALISM

Complete coverage of capitalism's features has filled many a book. Four features of particular significance—the existence of companies, profit motive, competition, and private property—will be discussed briefly here.

Companies

Chapter 2 mentioned the Firestone case, in which a media misrepresentation was left uncorrected. When asked why Firestone officials had not corrected the error, a Firestone spokesperson said that Firestone's policy was to ask for corrections only when it was beneficial to the company to do so. Expressions like "Firestone's policy" and "beneficial to the company" reflect one key feature of capitalism: the existence of companies or business firms separate from the human beings who work for and within them.

"It's not in the company's interests," "The company thinks that," "From the company's viewpoint," "As far as the company is concerned"—all of us have heard, perhaps even used, expressions that treat a business organization like a person or at least like a separate and distinct entity. Such personifications are not mere lapses into the figurative but bespeak a basic characteristic of capitalism: Capitalism permits the creation of companies or business organizations that exist separately from the people associated with them.

Today the big companies we're familiar with—General Electric, AT&T, Ford, IBM—are, in fact, incorporated businesses, or corporations. Chapter 5 discusses the nature of the modern corporation, including its historical evolution and its social responsibilities. Here it's enough to observe that, in the nineteenth century, Chief Justice John Marshall defined a *corporation* as "an artificial being, invisible, intangible, and existing only in the contemplation of law." Although a corporation is not something that can be seen or touched, it does have prescribed rights and legal obligations within the community. Like you or me, a corporation may enter into contracts and may sue or be sued in courts of law. It may even do things that the corporation's members disapprove of. The corporations that loom large on our economic landscape harken back to a feature of capitalism evident as early as the Fugger dynasty: the existence of the company.

Profit Motive

A second characteristic of capitalism lies in the motive of the company: to make profit. As dollar-directed and gain-motivated as our society is, most of us take for granted that the human being is by nature an acquisitive creature who, left to his or her own devices, will pursue profit with all the instinctual vigor of a cat chasing a mouse. However, as economist Robert Heilbroner points out, the "profit motive, as we understand it, is a very recent phenomenon. It was foreign to the lower and middle classes of Egyptian, Greek, Roman, and medieval cultures, only scattered throughout the Renaissance times, and largely absent in most Eastern civilizations." The medieval church taught that no Christian ought to be a merchant. "Even to our Pilgrim forefathers," Heilbroner writes, "the idea that gain ought to be a tolerable—even a useful—goal in life would have appeared as nothing short of a doctrine of the devil." Heilbroner concludes: "As a ubiquitous characteristic of society, the profit motive is·as modern an invention as printing."[4]

Modern or not, profit in the form of money is the lifeblood of the capitalist system. Companies and capitalists alike are motivated by a robust appetite for money profit. Indeed, the profit motive implies and reflects a critical assumption about human nature: that human beings are basically economic creatures, who recognize and are motivated by their own economic self-interests.

Competition

If self-interest and an appetite for money profit drive individuals and companies, then what stops them short of holding up society for exorbitant ransom? What stops capitalists from bleeding society dry?

Adam Smith provided an answer in his monumental treatise on commercial capitalism, *An Inquiry into the Nature and Causes of the Wealth of Nations* (1776). Free competition, said Smith, is the regulator that keeps a community activated only by self-interest from degenerating into a mob of ruthless profiteers. When traditional restraints are removed from the sale of goods and from wages and when all individuals have equal access to raw materials and markets (the doctrine of *laissez faire,* from the French meaning "to let [people] do [as they choose]"), we are all free to pursue our own interests. In pursuing our own interests, however, we come smack up against others similarly motivated. If any of us allow blind self-interest to dictate our actions—for example, by price gouging or employee exploitation—we will quickly find ourselves beaten out by a competitor who, let's say, charges less and pays a better wage. Competition thus regulates individual economic activity.

To sample the flavor of Smith's argument, imagine an acquisitive young woman in a far-away place who wants to pile up as much wealth as possible. She looks about her and sees that people need and want strong twilled cotton trousers, so she takes her investment capital and sets up a jeans factory. She charges $45 for a pair of jeans and soon realizes handsome profits. The woman's success is not lost on other business minds, especially manufacturers of formal slacks and dresses, who observe a sharp decline in those markets. Wanting a piece of the jeans action, numerous enterprises start up jeans factories. Many of these start selling jeans for $40 a pair. No longer alone in the market, our hypothetical businesswoman must either check her appetite for profit by lowering her price or risk folding. As the number of jeans on the market increases, their supply eventually overtakes demand, and the price of jeans declines further and further. Inefficient manufacturers start dropping like flies. As the competition thins out, the demand for jeans slowly balances with the supply, and the price regulates itself. Ultimately, an equilibrium is reached between supply and demand, and the price of jeans stabilizes, yielding a normal profit to the efficient producer.

In much this way, Adam Smith tried to explain how economic competition steers individuals pursuing self-interest in a socially beneficial direction. By appealing to their self-interest, society can induce producers to provide it with what it wants—just as manufacturers of formal slacks and dresses were enticed into jeans production. But competition keeps prices for desired goods from escalating; high prices are self-correcting because they call forth an increased supply.

Private Property

In its discussion of the libertarian theory of justice, Chapter 3 emphasized that property should not be identified only with physical objects like houses, cars, and video recorders. Nor should ownership be thought of as a simple relationship between the owner and the thing owned. First, one can have property rights over things that are not simple physical objects, as when one owns stock in a company. Second, property ownership involves a generally complex bundle of rights and rules governing how, under what circumstances, and in what ways both the owner and others can use, possess, dispose of, and have access to the thing in question.

Private property is central to capitalism. To put it another way, capitalism as a socio-

economic system is a specific form of private property. What matters for capitalism is not private property simply in the sense of personal possessions, because a socialist society can certainly permit people to own houses, television sets, and jogging shoes. Rather, capitalism requires private ownership of the major means of production and distribution. The means of production and distribution include factories, warehouses, offices, machines, computer systems, trucking fleets, agricultural land, and whatever else makes up the economic resources of a nation. Under capitalism, private hands control these basic economic assets and productive resources. Thus, the major economic decisions are made by individuals or groups acting on their own in pursuit of profit. These decisions are not directly coordinated with those of other producers, nor are they the result of some overall plan. Any profits (or losses) that result from these decisions about production are those of the owners.

Capital, as an economic concept, is closely related to private property. Putting it simply, capital is money that is invested for the purpose of making more money. Individuals or corporations purchase various means of production or other related assets and use them to produce goods or provide services, which are then sold. They do this not for the purpose of being nice or of helping people out but rather to make money—more money, hopefully, than they spent to make the goods or provide the services in the first place. Using money to make money is at the heart of the definition of capitalism.

MORAL JUSTIFICATIONS OF CAPITALISM

People tend to take for granted the desirability and moral legitimacy of the political and economic system within which they live. Americans are no exception. We are raised in a society that encourages individual competition, praises capitalism, promotes the acquisition of material goods, and worships economic wealth. Newspapers, television, recordings, movies, and other forms of popular culture celebrate these values, and rarely are we presented with fundamental criticisms of or possible alternatives to our socioeconomic order. Small wonder, then, that most of us blithely assume, without ever bothering to question, that our capitalist economic system is a morally justifiable one.

Yet as thinking people and moral agents, it is important that we reflect on the nature and justifiability of our social institutions. The proposition that capitalism is a morally acceptable system is very much open to debate. Whether we decide that capitalism is morally justified will depend, at least in part, on which general theory of justice turns out to be the soundest. Chapter 3 explored in detail the utilitarian approach, the libertarian alternative, and the theory of John Rawls. Now, against that background, this chapter looks at two basic ways defenders of capitalism have sought to justify their system: first, the argument that the moral right to property guarantees the legitimacy of capitalism and, second, the utilitarian-based economic argument of Adam Smith. The chapter then considers some criticisms of capitalism.

The Natural Right to Property

As Americans, we live in a socioeconomic system that guarantees us certain property rights. Although we are no longer permitted to own other people, we are certainly free to own a variety of other things, from livestock to stock certificates, from our own homes to whole blocks of apartment buildings. A common defense of capitalism is the argument that people have a fundamental moral right to property and that our capitalist system is simply the outcome of this natural right.

In Chapter 3, we saw how Locke attempted to base the right to property in human labor. When individuals mix their labor with the natural world, they are entitled to the results. This idea seems plausible in many cases. For example, if Carl diligently harvests coconuts on the island he shares with Adam, while Adam himself idles away his days, then most of us would agree that Carl has an entitlement to those coconuts that

Adam lacks. But property ownership as it actually exists in the real world today is a very complex, socially shaped phenomenon. This is especially true in the case of sophisticated forms of corporate and financial property—for example, bonds or stock options.

One could, of course, reject the whole idea of a natural right to property as a fiction, as, for example, utilitarians do. In their view, although various property systems exist, there is no natural right that things be owned privately, collectively, or in any particular way whatsoever. The moral task is to find that property system, that way of organizing production and distribution, with the greatest utility. Yet even if one believes that there is a natural right to property, at least under some circumstances, one need not believe that this right leads to capitalism or that it is a right to have a system of property rules and regulations just like the one we now have in the United States. That is, even if Carl has a natural right to his coconuts, there may still be moral limits on how many coconuts he can rightfully amass and what he can use them for. When he takes his coconuts to the coconut bank and receives further coconuts as interest, his newly acquired coconuts are not the result of any new labor on his part. When we look at capitalistic property—that is, at socioeconomic environments in which people profit from ownership alone—then we have left Locke's world far behind.

A defender of capitalism may reply, "Certainly, there's nothing unfair about Carl's accruing these extra coconuts through his investment; after all, he could have eaten his original coconuts instead." And, indeed, within our system this reasoning seems perfectly correct. It is the way things work in our society. But this fact doesn't prove that Carl has some natural right to use his coconuts to make more coconuts—that is, that it would be unfair or unjust to set up a different economic system (for example, one in which he had a right to consume his coconuts but no right to use them to earn more coconuts). The argument here is simply that the issue is not an all-or-nothing one. There may be certain fundamental moral rights to property, but those rights need not be unlimited nor guarantee capitalism as we know it.

Adam Smith's Concept of the Invisible Hand

Relying on the idea of a natural right to property is not the only way and probably not the best way to defend capitalism. Another, very important argument defends capitalism in terms of the many economic benefits the system brings, claiming that a free and unrestrained market system, which exists under capitalism, is more efficient and more productive than any other possible system and is thus to be preferred on moral grounds. Essentially, this is a utilitarian argument, but one doesn't have to be a utilitarian to take it seriously. As mentioned in Chapter 2, almost every normative theory puts some moral weight on the consequences of actions. Thus if capitalism does indeed work better than other ways of organizing economic life, then this will be a very relevant moral fact—one that will be important, for instance, for Rawlsians.

This section sketches Adam Smith's economic case for capitalism, as presented in *The Wealth of Nations.* Smith argues that when people are left to pursue their own interests, they will, without intending it, produce the greatest good for all. Each person's individual and private pursuit of wealth results—as if, in Smith's famous phrase, "an invisible hand" were at work—in the most beneficial overall organization and distribution of economic resources. Although the academic study of economics has developed greatly since Smith's times, his classic arguments remain extraordinarily influential.

Smith took it for granted that human beings are acquisitive creatures. Self-interest and personal advantage, specifically in an economic sense, may not be all that motivate people, but they do seem to motivate most people much of the time. At any rate, they are powerful enough forces that any successful economic system must strive to harness them. We are, Smith thought, strongly inclined to act so as to acquire more and more wealth.

In addition, humans have a natural propensity for trading—"to truck, barter, and exchange." Unlike other species, we have an almost constant need for the assistance of others. Yet because people are creatures of self-interest, it is folly for us to expect others to act altruistically toward us. We can secure what we need from others only by offering them something they need from us:

> Whoever offers to another a bargain of any kind, proposes to do this. Give me that which I want, and you shall have this which you want, is the meaning of every such offer; and it is in this manner that we obtain from one another the far greater part of those good offices which we stand in need of. It is not from the benevolence of the butcher, the brewer, or the baker that we expect our dinner, but from their regard to their own interest. We address ourselves, not to their humanity but to their self love, and never talk to them of our own necessities but of their advantages.[5]

This disposition to trade, said Smith, leads to the division of labor—dividing the labor and production process into areas of specialization, which is the prime means of increasing economic productivity.

Thus, Smith reasoned that the greatest utility will result from unfettered pursuit of self-interest. Individuals should be allowed unrestricted access to raw materials, markets, and labor. Government interference in private enterprise should be eliminated, free competition encouraged, and economic self-interest made the rule of the day. Because human beings are acquisitive creatures, we will, if left free, engage in labor and exchange goods in a way that results in the greatest benefit to society. In our efforts to advance our own economic interests, we inevitably act to promote the economic well-being of society generally:

> Every individual is continually exerting himself to find the most advantageous employment for whatever capital he can command. It is his own advantage, indeed, and not that of the society, which he has in view. . . . [But] by directing that industry in such a manner

as its produce may be of the greatest value, he [is] . . . led by an invisible hand to promote an end that was no part of his intention. . . . By pursuing his own interest he frequently promotes that of society more effectually than when he really intends to promote it.[6]

To explain why pursuit of self-interest necessarily leads to the greatest social benefit, Smith invoked the law of supply and demand, which was alluded to in discussing competition. The law of supply and demand tempers the pursuit of self-interest exactly as competition keeps the enterprising capitalist from becoming a ruthless profiteer. The law of supply and demand similarly solves the problems of adequate goods and fair prices.

Some think the law of supply and demand even solves the problem of fair wages, for labor is another commodity up for sale like shoes or jeans. Just as the price of a new product at first is high, like the jeans in the hypothetical example, so, too, are the wages of labor in a new field. But as labor becomes more plentiful, wages decline. Eventually they fall to a point at which inefficient laborers are eliminated and forced to seek other work, just as the inefficient manufacturers of jeans were forced out of that business and into others. And like the price of jeans, the price of labor then stabilizes at a fair level. As for the inefficient laborers, they find work and a living wage elsewhere. In seeking new fields of labor, they help maximize the majority's opportunities to enjoy the necessities, conveniences, and trifles of human life.

Some modern capitalists claim that capitalism operates as Smith envisioned and can be justified on the same utilitarian grounds. But not everyone agrees.

CRITICISMS OF CAPITALISM

The two major defenses of capitalism have not persuaded critics that it is a morally justifiable system. Their objections to capitalism are both theoretical and operational. Theoretical criticisms challenge capitalism's fundamental values, basic assumptions, or inherent economic tendencies. Operational criticisms focus more on capitalism's alleged deficiencies in actual practice (as opposed to theory)—in particular, on its failure to live up to its own economic ideals.

The following criticisms are a mix of both theoretical and operational concerns. They raise political, economic, and philosophical issues that cannot be fully assessed here. The debate over capitalism is a large and important one; the presentation that follows should be viewed as a stimulus to further discussion and not as the last word on the pros and cons of capitalism.

Inequality

Chapter 3 and Case 3.3 documented the profound economic inequality that exists in our capitalist society. The disparity in personal incomes is enormous; a tiny minority of the population owns the vast majority of the country's productive assets; and at the beginning of the twenty-first century, our society continues to be marred by poverty and homelessness. With divisions of social and economic class comes inequality of opportunity. A child born to a working-class family, let alone to an unwed teenager in an inner-city ghetto, has life prospects and possibilities that pale beside those of children born to wealthy, stock-owning parents. This reality challenges capitalism's claim of fairness, and the persistence of poverty and economic misfortune provides the basis for a utilitarian objection to it.

Few doubt that poverty and inequality are bad things, but defenders of capitalism make several responses to those who criticize it on these grounds:

1. A few extreme supporters of capitalism simply deny that it is responsible for poverty and inequality. Rather, they say, government interference with the market causes these problems. Left to itself, the market would eliminate unemployment and poverty while ultimately lessening inequality. But neither theoretical economics nor the study of history supports this reply. Most economists and social theorists would agree that in the past seventy years or so activist government policies have done much, in all the Western capitalist countries, to reduce poverty and (to a lesser extent) inequality.

2. More moderate defenders of capitalism concede that, in its pure laissez-faire form, capitalism does nothing to prevent and may even foster inequality and poverty. However, they argue that the system can be modified or its inherent tendencies corrected by political action, so that inequality and poverty are reduced or even eliminated. Critics of capitalism reply that the policies necessary to seriously reduce inequality and poverty are either impossible within a basically capitalist economic framework or unlikely to be carried out in any political system based on capitalism.

3. Finally, defenders of capitalism argue that the benefits of the system outweigh this weak point. Inequality is not so important if living standards are rising and even the poor have better lives than they did in previous times. This contention rests on an implicit comparison with what things would be like if society were organized differently and is, accordingly, difficult to assess. Naturally, it seems more plausible to those who are relatively favored by, and content with, the present economic system than it does to those who feel disadvantaged by it.

Some critics of capitalism go on to maintain that, aside from inequalities of income and ownership, the inequality inherent in the worker-capitalist relationship is itself morally undesirable. John Stuart Mill found capitalism inferior in this respect to more cooperative and egalitarian economic arrangements. "To work at the bidding and for the profit of another," he wrote, "is not . . . a satisfactory state to human beings of educated intelligence, who have ceased to think themselves inferior to those whom they serve."[7] The ideal of escaping from a system of "superiors" and "subordinates" was well expressed by the great German playwright

and poet Bertolt Brecht when he wrote that "He wants no servants under him/And no boss over his head."[8]

Human Nature and Capitalism

The theory of capitalism rests on a view of human beings as rational economic creatures, individuals who recognize and are motivated largely by their own economic self-interests. Adam Smith's defense of capitalism, for instance, assumes that consumers have full knowledge of the diverse choices available to them in the marketplace. They are supposed to know the price structures of similar products, to be fully aware of product differences, and to be able to make the optimal choice regarding price and quality.

But the key choices facing today's consumers are rarely simple. From foods to drugs, automobiles to appliances, fertilizers to air conditioners, the modern marketplace is a cornucopia of products whose nature and nuances require a high level of consumer literacy. Even with government agencies and public interest groups to aid them, today's consumers are rarely an equal match for powerful industries that can influence prices and create and shape markets. The effectiveness of advertising, in particular, is difficult to reconcile with the picture of consumers as the autonomous, rational, and perfectly informed economic maximizers that economics textbooks presuppose when they attempt to demonstrate the benefits of capitalism. Consumers frequently seem to be pawns of social and economic forces beyond their control.

According to some critics of capitalism, however, what is objectionable about capitalism's view of human beings as essentially economic creatures is not this gap between theory and reality but rather the fact that it presents little in the way of an ideal to which either individuals or societies may aspire. As George Soros puts it, "Humans are capable of transcending the pursuit of narrow self-interest. Indeed, they cannot live without some sense of morality. It is market fundamentalism, which holds that the social good is best served by allowing people to pursue their self-interest without any thought for the social good . . . that is a perversion of human nature."[9] Not only does capitalism rest on the premise that people are basically acquisitive, individualistic, and materialistic, but in practice capitalism strongly reinforces those human tendencies. Capitalism, its critics charge, presents no higher sense of human mission or purpose, whereas other views of society and human nature do.

Christianity, for example, has long aspired to the ideal of a truly religious community united in *agape,* selfless love. And socialism, because it views human nature as malleable, hopes to see people transformed from the "competitive, acquisitive beings that they are (and that they are *encouraged* to be) under all property-dominated, market-oriented systems." In the more "benign environment of a propertyless, non-market social system," socialists believe that more cooperative and less selfish human beings will emerge.[10] Such positive ideals and aspirations are lacking in capitalism—or so its critics charge.

Competition Isn't What It's Cracked Up to Be

As we have seen, one of the key features of capitalism is competition. Unfettered competition supposedly serves the collective interest while offering rich opportunities for the individual. But competition is one of the targets of capitalism's critics. They contend that capitalism breeds oligopolies that eliminate competition and concentrate economic power, that a system of corporate welfare protects many businesses from true marketplace competition, and finally that competition is neither generally beneficial nor desirable in itself.

Capitalism Breeds Oligopolies. As early as the middle of the nineteenth century, the German philosopher and political economist Karl Marx (1818–1883) argued that capitalism leads to a concentration of property and resources, and thus economic power, in the hands of a few. High costs, complex and expensive machinery, intense competition, and the advantages of large-scale production all work against the survival of small firms, said Marx. Many see proof of Marx's argument in today's economy.

Before the Industrial Revolution, capitalism was characterized by comparatively free and open competition among a large number of small firms. Since then the economy has come to be dominated by a relatively small number of enormous companies that can, to a distressing extent, conspire to set prices, eliminate competition, and monopolize an industry. The food industry is a perfect example, with four or fewer firms controlling the vast majority of sales of almost any given product.[11]

Antitrust actions have sometimes fostered competition and broken up monopolies, as in the cases of such corporate behemoths as Standard Oil and AT&T. And recently the government has gone after Microsoft for "exclusionary and predatory" business practices. On the whole, however, such actions have proved ineffectual in halting the concentration of economic power in large oligopolistic firms. Increasingly multinational in character, these giant corporations frequently do business around the globe, disavowing allegiance to any particular nation. Today more than a quarter of the world's economic activity comes from the 200 largest corporations.[12]

Robert Heilbroner suggests that the rise of such giant enterprises has changed the face of capitalism as they attempt to alter the market setting through a system of public and private planning. This planning assumes many guises, from union contracts that eliminate uncertainties in the labor market to sophisticated advertising calculated to foster dependable product markets; from tacit price-fixing within an industry to cozy relationships with government intended to create programs that will ensure continuing high levels of demand. "At its worst," he writes, "we find it in the military-industrial complex—the very epitome of the new symbiotic business-government relations."[13]

Business professor Robert B. Carson concurs that in terms of competition, our present-day economic system differs from the textbook model of capitalism. He writes:

> In surveying the American business system it is obvious that competition still exists; however, it is not a perfect competition. Often it is not price competition at all. With the possible exception of some farm markets where there are still large numbers of producers of similar and undifferentiated products (wheat, for instance), virtually every producer of goods and services has some control over price. The degree of control varies from industry to industry and between firms within an industry. Nevertheless, it does exist and it amounts to an important modification in our model of a free-enterprise economy.[14]

Corporate Welfare Programs Protect Businesses. In March 2002 President Bush slapped tariffs ranging from 8 percent to 30 percent on imported steel, continuing a thirty-year tradition of cosseting the steel industry with various subsidies and protections that has cost users $120 billion. The tariffs were held to be necessary because of a surge of imported steel, even though foreign steel imports had declined 27.5 percent in the preceding four years.[15] In June 2002, Congress passed a farm bill that dramatically increased subsidies on large staple crops like lentils and peanuts, and reinstated subsidies that had previously been eliminated on crops like honey, wool, and mohair. Overall, the bill increases agricultural subsidies by 80 percent and will cost the government $180 to $190 billion over ten years.[16] Nationally, farm subsidies already total about $20 billion a year— which doesn't include the higher prices that consumers pay. Most of the money goes to the largest and wealthiest farmers, a secret that the Environment Working Group made public for the first time when, thanks to the Freedom of Information Act, it posted on its Web site a listing of every farm subsidy received by every farmer since 1996.

Subsidies for farmers and tariffs for the steel industry are just the most blatant examples of the way corporate welfare programs assist business and protect it from competition. Thanks to duties, fees, and restrictions on imported products, American consumers pay at least $75 billion a year more for goods than they otherwise would.[17] And this, of course, is in addition to what corporate subsidies cost them as taxpayers.

For example, the Agriculture Department's Market Access Program funds both generic and brand-name advertising abroad for American agricultural products. The program paid $450,000 to Campbell Soup Company to help it entice Japanese, Koreans, and Argentineans to drink V-8 juice, and it also laid out $1 million to M&M Mars to improve consumer recognition of its product; $1.5 million to push sales of mink coats; $6.6 million to promote Sunkist oranges; and $4.9 million to Ernest and Julio Gallo to market its wines internationally.[18] The program's annual price tag is $85 million, which is less than what it costs for the U.S. Forest Service to build roads and subsidize logging in national forests for the benefit of private timber companies.[19] Other government-sponsored corporate welfare programs include the Export Enhancement Program ($1 billion a year), the Export-Import Bank ($742 million), the credit programs of the Overseas Private Investment Corporation ($68 million), and the Foreign Military Financing Program, which spends around $3.3 billion each year assisting foreign countries to purchase U.S. military products.[20] The Department of Commerce's Advanced Technology Program supports high-tech research. In practice, this has meant payments of $14.5 million to General Electric, $34 million to AT&T, and a whopping $50.9 million to Boeing.[21]

The list goes on and on.[22] Every year the federal government doles out an estimated $85 billion to private business in direct subsidy programs. In addition, the government spent an estimated $200 billion over a ten-year period bailing out the savings and loan industry. Some put total federal spending for corporate welfare at over $167 billion a year, which is far more than combined state and federal spending on social welfare programs for the poor.[23]

Competition Is Not a Good. Because the profit motive governs capitalism, it should not be surprising that even those companies that preach the doctrine of free competition are willing to shelve it when collusion with other firms, or government tariffs and subsidies, make higher profits possible. How else to explain the fact that the United States forbids foreign companies from owning airlines in America and prevents foreign airlines from picking up passengers at more than one American city? In these ways, capitalism fails to live up to its own ideal. But some critics of capitalism repudiate the ideal of competition, arguing that competition is neither beneficial in general nor desirable in itself.

The critics point to empirical studies establishing that in business environments there is frequently a negative correlation between performance and individual competitiveness.[24] In other words, it is often cooperation, rather than competitiveness, that best enhances both individual and group achievement. According to Alfie Kohn, the reason is simple: "Trying to do well and trying to beat others are two different things."[25] Competition is an extrinsic motivator; not only does it not produce the kind of results that flow from enjoying the activity itself, but also the use of extrinsic motivators can undermine intrinsic motivation and thus adversely affect performance in the long run. The unpleasantness of competition can also diminish people's performance.

The critics also contend that competition often precludes the more efficient use of resources that cooperation allows. When people work together, coordination of effort and an efficient division of labor are possible. By contrast, competition can inhibit economic coordination, cause needless duplication of services, retard the exchange of information, foster copious litigation, and lead to socially detrimental or counterproductive results such as business failures, mediocre products, unsafe working conditions, and environmental neglect. When presented with examples of the beneficial results of com-petition, the critics argue that on closer inspection the supposed advantages turn out to be short lived, illusory, or isolated instances.

Exploitation and Alienation

Marx argued that as the means of production become concentrated in the hands of the few, the balance of power between capitalists (bourgeoisie) and laborers (proletariat) tips further in favor of the bourgeoisie. Because workers have nothing to sell but their labor, said Marx, the bourgeoisie is able to exploit them by paying them less than the true value created by their labor. In fact, Marx thought, it is only through such an exploitative arrangement that capitalists make a profit and increase their capital. And the more capital they accumulate, the more they can exploit workers. Marx predicted that eventually workers would revolt. Unwilling to be exploited further, they would rise and overthrow their oppressors and set up an economic system that would truly benefit all.

The development of capitalist systems since Marx's time belies his forecast. Legal, political, and economic changes have tempered many of the greedy, exploitative dispositions of early capitalism. The twentieth century witnessed legislation curbing egregious worker abuse, guaranteeing a minimum wage, and ensuring a safer and more healthful work environment. The emergence of labor unions and their subsequent victories significantly enlarged the worker's share of the economic pie. Indeed, many of the specific measures proposed by Marx and his collaborator Friedrich Engels in the *Communist Manifesto* (1848) have been implemented in capitalist countries: a program of graduated income tax, free education for all children in public schools, investiture of significant economic control in the state, and so on.

Still, many would say that although democratic institutions may have curbed the excesses of capitalism, they can do nothing to prevent the alienation of workers that results from having to do unfulfilling work. Again, because of the unequal positions of capitalist and worker, laborers must work for someone else—they must do work imposed on them as a means of satisfying the needs of others. As a result, they must eventually feel exploited and debased. And this is true, critics of capitalism claim, not just of manual laborers, but also of white-collar workers, many of whom identify with the cubicle dwellers of the cartoon strip *Dilbert.*

But what about workers who are paid handsomely for their efforts? They, too, said Marx, remain alienated, for as the fruits of their labor are enjoyed by someone else, their work ultimately proves meaningless to them. The following selection from Marx's "Economic and Philosophic Manuscripts" (1844) summarizes his notion of alienation as the separation of individuals from the objects they create, which in turn results in one's separation from other people, from oneself, and ultimately from one's human nature:

> The worker is related to the *product of his labor* as to an *alien* object. For it is clear . . . that the more the worker expends himself in work the more powerful becomes the world of objects which he creates in face of himself, the poorer he becomes in his inner life, and the less he belongs to himself. . . . The worker puts his life into the object, and his life then belongs no longer to himself but to the object. . . . What is embodied in the product of his labor is no longer his own. The greater this product is, therefore, the more he is diminished. The *alienation* of the worker in his product means not only that his labor becomes an object, assumes an *external* existence, but that it exists independently, *outside himself,* and alien to him, and that it stands opposed to him as an autonomous power. . . .
>
> What constitutes the alienation of labor? First, that the work is *external* to the worker, that it is not part of his nature; and that, consequently, he does not fulfill himself in his work but denies himself. . . . His work is not voluntary but imposed, *forced labor.* It is not the satisfaction of a need, but only a *means* for satisfying other needs. Its alien character is clearly shown by the fact that as soon as there is no physical or other compulsion it is avoided like the plague. External labor, labor

> in which man alienates himself, is a labor of self-sacrifice. . . . Finally, the external character of work for the worker is shown by the fact that it is not his own work but work for someone else, that in work he does not belong to himself but to another person. . . .
>
> We have now considered the act of alienation of practical human activity, labor, from two aspects: (1) the relationship of the worker to the *product of labor* as an alien object which dominates him . . . [and] (2) the relationship of labor to the *act of production* within *labor.* This is the relationship of the worker to his own activity as something alien and not belonging to him. . . . This is *self-alienation* as against the above-mentioned alienation of the *thing.*[26]

In Marx's view, when workers are alienated they cannot be truly free. They may have the political and social freedoms of speech, religion, and governance, but even with these rights, individuals still are not fully free. Freedom from government interference and persecution does not necessarily guarantee freedom from economic exploitation and alienation, and it is for this kind of freedom that Marx and Engels felt such passion.

Some would say that one need not wade through Marxist philosophy to get a feel for what he and others mean by worker alienation. Just talk to workers themselves, as writer Studs Terkel did. In different ways the hundreds of workers from diverse occupations that Terkel interviewed speak of the same thing: dehumanization.

> Mike Fitzgerald . . . is a laborer in a steel mill. "I feel like the guys who built the pyramids. Somebody built 'em. Somebody built the Empire State Building, too. There's hard work behind it. I would like to see a building, say the Empire State, with a footwide strip from top to bottom and the name of every bricklayer on it, the name of every electrician. So when a guy walked by, he could take his son and say, 'See, that's me over there on the 45th floor. I put that steel beam in.' . . . Everybody should have something to point to."

Sharon Atkins is 24 years old. She's been to college and acidly observes, "The first myth that blew up in my face is that a college education will get you a worthwhile job." For the last two years she's been a receptionist at an advertising agency. "I didn't look at myself as 'just a dumb broad' at the front desk, who took phone calls and messages. I thought I was something else. The office taught me differently."

. . . Harry Stallings, 27, is a spot welder on the assembly line at an auto plant. "They'll give better care to that machine than they will to you. If it breaks down, there's somebody out there to fix it right away. If I break down, I'm just pushed over to the other side till another man takes my place. The only thing the company has in mind is to keep that machine running. A man would be more eager to do a better job if he were given proper respect and the time to do it."[27]

TODAY'S ECONOMIC CHALLENGES

Capitalism faces a number of important critical questions, both theoretical and operational. These criticisms are a powerful challenge, especially to capitalism in its pure laissez-faire form. But, as we have seen, today's capitalism is a long way from the laissez-faire model. Corporate behemoths able to control markets and sway governments have replaced the small-scale entrepreneurs and free-wheeling competition of an earlier day. And governments in all capitalist countries actively intervene in the economic realm; they endeavor to assist or modify the so-called invisible hand; and over the years they have reformed or supplemented capitalism with programs intended to enhance the security of the workforce and increase the welfare of their citizens.

This reality complicates the debate over capitalism. Its defenders may be advocating either the pure laissez-faire ideal or the modified state welfare capitalism that we in fact have. Likewise, those who attack the laissez-faire ideal may do so on behalf of a modified, welfarist capitalism, or they may criticize both forms of capi-

talism and defend some kind of socialism, in which private property and the pursuit of profit are no longer governing economic principles. We thus have a three-way debate over the respective strengths and weaknesses of laissez-faire capitalism, state welfare capitalism, and socialism.

The rest of this chapter leaves this fundamental debate behind. Instead of looking at criticisms of capitalism in general and at issues relevant to any capitalist society, it examines some of the more specific socioeconomic challenges facing the United States today. These problems include slow growth in productivity, business's obsession with short-term results and its declining interest in production, and our changing attitudes toward work.

Slow Growth in Productivity

At the beginning of Chapter 3, the trend toward an increasingly inequitable distribution of national income was discussed. At the very least, this problem is aggravated by a persistently weak rate of growth in the country's gross domestic product. In the hundred years before 1973, the American economy grew at an annual rate of 3.4 percent; since then it has been growing at an average of only 2.4 percent per year.[28] It might seem that a mere 1 percent drop in the rate of economic growth is nothing to worry about, but, as one economist writes, "the damage done by slow growth accumulates the way interest does in a savings account."[29] The 1 percent yearly reduction in growth has meant a loss of goods and services since 1973 of over $12 trillion, equivalent to a $50,000 loss in earnings for the typical American family. Additional capital would also have been available for investment because of higher individual savings and increased corporate profits.[30]

To most experts, this slowdown in economic growth reflects a declining rate of growth in productivity. From 1973 until the mid-1990s average annual productivity grew by only 1.1 percent a year, far below its 1960–1973 rate of nearly 3 percent a year.[31] In recent years the rate of productivity growth has increased, but whether that growth can sustain itself, now that the '90s economic boom is over, remains to be seen. Wrapped up with the question of productivity growth is the problem of adequate capital formation, that is, with investment in new factories and equipment—an area where America has frequently fallen behind its economic rivals. For instance, plant and equipment investment per U.S. labor force member has typically been half that of Germany, and one-third that of Japan.[32] In turn, their growth in productivity has been two to three times the U.S. rate.[33] "America's chances of owning the twenty-first century," writes Lester C. Thurow, dean of MIT's Sloan School of Management, "depend upon the answer to a simple question: Can it get its productivity growth rate up to the standards of its chief rivals?"[34]

"Productivity isn't everything," writes MIT economist Paul Krugman, "but in the long run it is almost everything."[35] If strong, consistent productivity growth is not maintained, our standard of living will stagnate. According to some economic measures, this is already happening. Adjusted for inflation, wages of nonsupervisory workers—some four-fifths of the workforce—have decreased since their peak in 1972.[36] Although median family income has increased in recent years, in real terms it is not that much higher than thirty years ago despite the fact that far more families now have two wage-earners.[37] Although in the past the United States led the world in terms of the standard of living we provide our workers, today we are in thirteenth place—far behind in wages, benefits, health care, pensions, paid vacation days, and educational opportunities.[38]

To make matters worse, in the past quarter century the United States has been steadily losing its share of both foreign and domestic markets. In 1970, 64 of the world's 100 largest industrial corporations were American. Today the figure is around 40.[39] The nation's huge balance of trade deficit is only the most visible sign of this relative decline. After having shrunk in the early 1990s from its 1987 peak, the trade deficit rose to over $400 billion in 2002—the highest level in American history. The United States hasn't posted a trade surplus since 1975.

Exclusive Focus on Short Term

For a number of years now, observers of the business scene have charged that U.S. companies are preoccupied with short-term performance at the expense of long-term strategies, and that this strategic myopia is an important part of the story behind America's declining rate of productivity. According to the critics, their short-term orientation has made U.S. corporations unimaginative, inflexible, and uncompetitive. The critics take as their classic example the failure of Detroit to respond to increasing foreign competition in the 1960s, with the consequent loss of U.S. dominance of the auto industry. These business strategists have urged U.S. companies to become more visionary, arguing that they must define long-term goals and be willing to stick to them even at the expense of short-term profit. Some businesspeople have accepted this advice, as evidenced by the willingness of Amazon and other dot-com companies to lose money for years as they attempt to build market share.

By a number of measures, U.S. companies have in recent years become more competitive—certainly by comparison with their sluggish performance in the 1970s and 1980s. Today, they are producing better-quality products and doing so more flexibly and innovatively than ever. Yet American companies frequently appear less willing than many foreign rivals to gamble on long-term research and development or to sacrifice current profits for benefits ten or fifteen years into the future.[40] By comparison with countries such as Germany and Japan, established U.S. corporations continue to be obsessed with their stock market performance and to govern themselves far more by short-term indicators such as share price and quarterly profits. As a result, write management consultants Adrian Slywotsky and Richard Wise, "many [American] companies with apparently strong growth records in recent years have achieved them through relatively short-term, unsustainable tactics—acquisitions, international expansion, price increases, or accounting gimmicks."[41]

There's no question that corporate America's obsession with short-term performance—when coupled with what Federal Reserve Chairman Alan Greenspan has called "infectious greed"[42]—has created a high-pressure economic environment conducive to fraudulent behavior. Since the exposure of criminal conduct at Enron in late 2001, a long list of companies—including Adelphia Communications, Computer Associates, Dynegy, Global Crossing, Qwest, Rite Aid, Tyco International, WorldCom, and Xerox, just to name the best-known cases—have been found to have manipulated financial data or committed outright fraud so as to appear to meet their short-term financial goals. These and other revelations of unethical conduct have, in turn, weakened the trust necessary for the efficient functioning of our economic system. This is why President Bush has stated that "at this moment, America's greatest economic need is higher ethical standards." Although it's true, as he has also said, that "in the long run, there's no capitalism without conscience; there is no wealth without character," he may have neglected the extent to which a relentless emphasis on short-term results has pressured some of the nation's most prominent business leaders to do things they wouldn't normally do.[43] As one business ethicist writes:

> Managing a corporation with the single measure of share price is like flying a 747 for maximum speed. You can shake the thing apart in the process. It's like a farmer forcing more and more of a crop to grow, until the soil is depleted and nothing will grow. Or like an athlete using steroids to develop muscle mass, until the body's health is damaged.
>
> Enron's problem was not a lack of focus on shareholder value. The problem was a lack of accountability to anything except share value. This contributed to a mania, a detachment from reality. And it led to a culture of getting the numbers by any means necessary.[44]

Declining Interest in Production

Traditionally, capitalists have made money by producing goods. Manufacturing was the backbone of the American economy and the basis of our prosperity. In industry after industry, however, U.S. companies have conceded manufacturing dominance to foreign competitors. Today, for example, one can't buy a television made in the United States; Wal-Mart employs more people than the Big Three automakers do; and as of 1992, for the first time, more Americans work in government than in manufacturing.

"Hollow Corporations" Since the 1980s, many U.S. manufacturers have been closing up shop or curtailing their operations and becoming marketing organizations for other producers, usually foreign. The result is the evolution of a new kind of company: manufacturers that do little or no manufacturing. They may perform a host of profit-making functions—from design to distribution—but they lack their own production base. Companies long identified with making goods of all sorts now often produce only the package and the label. In contrast to traditional manufacturers, they have become "hollow" or "weightless."

Many U.S. manufacturers are now pursuing a strategy of "outsourcing"—that is, buying parts or whole products from other producers, both at home and abroad. The manufacturer's traditional vertical structure, in which it makes virtually all crucial parts, is thereby being replaced by a network of small suppliers. Proponents of the new system describe it as flexible and efficient, a logical outcome of the drive to lower the costs of doing business. But critics point to the problems outsourcing can create for the companies that do it.[45] Moreover, they worry about whether the United States can prosper without a strong manufacturing base. As Tsutomu Ohshima, a senior manufacturing director of Toyota Motor Corporation, puts it: "You can't survive with just a service industry."[46] In terms of wages, productivity, and innovation, the service sector fails to compare with basic industry. Nor can the service economy thrive if manufacturing is allowed to wither.

Mergers and Takeovers Also reflective of American business's declining interest in production is the increase in corporate mergers and acquisitions. Takeovers and the extensive corporate restructuring that accompanied them emerged as an important economic trend in the 1980s and have continued to the present day. In fact, since the mid-1990s mergers and acquisition activity has grown sevenfold to around $1.5 trillion annually.[47] Recently, for example, Exxon took over Mobil, Travelers Group acquired Citicorp, and NationsBank merged with BankAmerica, smashing all records for merger and acquisition in a single year. Yet, much of this merger and takeover activity is directed toward making money through the manipulation of existing assets rather than through the production of new or better goods. Many U.S. entrepreneurs and capitalists seem to have found better and easier ways to make profit than the time-honored technique of competing in the production of goods and services.

Changing Attitudes Toward Work

Some commentators believe that the decline in U.S. productivity growth is related not just to takeovers, outsourcing, and a short-term performance mentality, but also to our changing attitudes toward government, social institutions, business, and especially work. Whether or not these pundits are correct, there is little question that people's ideas about the value of work and the role it should play in their lives are continually changing. Coming to grips with these shifting attitudes is one of the challenges facing our socioeconomic system at the beginning of the twenty-first century. In particular, the fabled American work ethic seems to be fading away. Or is it?

The so-called work ethic values work for its own sake, seeing it as something necessary for every person. It also emphasizes the belief that hard work pays off in the end and is thus part and parcel of the American Dream. "If you work hard enough," the expression goes, "you'll make it." Today, however, only one in three people believes this, down from 60 percent in a 1960 survey.[48] In addition, some experts believe that as people become less optimistic about the future and begin to doubt that their efforts will pay off, they become less interested in work than in looking out for themselves. Paul Kostek, a career development expert, contends that "people more so than ever are looking out for themselves and focus on what they want out of their career as the old social contract is broken." "I see more of a 'me-first' attitude," adds management professor Abigail Hubbard.[49]

In addition, with increased education, people are rearranging their ideas about what's important in life and about what they want out of it. The evidence can be seen in the workplace itself. For example, it is not uncommon for operative workers to balk at doing the monotonous tasks their ancestors once accepted, albeit grudgingly. Loyalty to employers seems on the decline, and loyalty to fellow workers seems on the rise. Turnover rates in many industries are enough to make discontinuity an expensive problem. Organizational plans, schedules, and demands no longer carry the authoritative clout they once did; workers today often subordinate them to personal needs, which results in rampant absenteeism. Moreover, employee sabotage and violence, once unheard of, occur frequently enough today to worry management. Adding to industry's woes, drug use at the office is increasingly the cause of employee theft, absenteeism, and low productivity.

According to an international survey about what matters most to different cultures, Americans place work eighth in importance behind values such as their children's education and a satisfactory love life. (In Japan, by contrast, work ranks second only to good health.)[50] Another survey reveals that more and more Americans—both men and women—are shelving job success to be with their families.[51] Although it is impossible to pin down workers' attitudes toward work today, basically they seem willing to work hard on a job they find interesting and rewarding as long as they have the freedom to influence the nature of their jobs and pursue their own lifestyles. They have a growing expectation that work should provide self-respect, nonmaterial rewards, and substantial opportunities for personal growth. And they have a growing willingness to demand individual rights, justice, and equality on the job.[52]

If industry is to improve productive capacity and be competitive, it must seriously confront these changing social attitudes. As Paul Bernstein argues, it is counterproductive to compare today's worker with an idealized worker of yesteryear. Rather, we must acknowledge that we have a new work ethic, which in Bernstein's words

> is part and parcel of the individual desire for meaningful and challenging labor in which some autonomy is an integral feature. An increasingly professionalized work force will not accept a golden embrace unless it is accompanied by fulfilling jobs that have been designed for a labor force that sees work in relation to family, friends, leisure and self-development. Work, for most of us, continues as an important part of our lives, but only in relation to our total experience.[53]

SUMMARY

1. Capitalism is an economic system in which the major portion of production and distribution is in private hands, operating under a profit or market system. Socialism is an economic system characterized by public ownership of property and a planned economy.

2. Capitalism has gone through several stages: mercantile, industrial, financial, and state welfare.

3. Four key features of capitalism are the existence of companies, profit motive, competition, and private property.

4. One basic defense of capitalism rests on a supposed natural moral right to property. Utilitarians deny the existence of such rights; other critics doubt that this right entitles one to have a system of property rules and regulations identical to the one we now have in the United States.

5. Utilitarian defense of capitalism is associated with the classical economic arguments of Adam Smith. Smith believed that human beings are acquisitive and that they have a natural propensity for trading, and he insisted that when people are left free to pursue their own economic interests, they will, without intending it, produce the greatest good for all.

6. Critics question the basic assumptions of capitalism (theoretical challenges) and whether it has delivered on its promises (operational challenges). Specifically, they raise the following issues: Can capitalism eliminate poverty and reduce inequality? Are humans basically economic creatures? Does capitalism breed oligopolies that thwart competition? Is competition valuable? Does capitalism exploit and alienate?

7. As the twenty-first century begins, our capitalist socioeconomic system faces a number of challenges. Among the problems that must be overcome are slow productivity growth, an excessive concern with short-term performance, and a lack of interest in the actual manufacturing of goods. In addition, we must come to grips with our society's changing attitudes toward work.

CASE 4.1

The Downsizing of America

When General Motors decided to close its Willow Run assembly plant in Ypsilanti, Michigan, the company didn't know that Ypsilanti would fight back—which it did by filing suit against GM. In court, Douglas Winters, the attorney for Ypsilanti Township, argued that GM should be required to keep the plant open because it had promised to maintain jobs there in exchange for tax abatements totaling $14 million. Otherwise, Winters contended, GM should return the $14 million and pay damages. To the surprise of GM officials, Michigan Circuit Court Judge Donald Shelton bought Winters's argument, issuing an order preventing GM from closing its Ypsilanti plant and shifting the work elsewhere. Unfortunately for Ypsilanti, though, a higher court later overturned Judge Shelton's ruling, freeing GM to transfer production of large rear-wheel-drive cars from Ypsilanti to Arlington, Texas.[54]

For its part, GM said that closing Willow Run was simply part of a plan to shrink its production facilities to match a smaller market share. In this respect, GM's decision to shut down its Ypsilanti operation reflects a larger trend. Industrial manufacturing is declining in the United States as plants have been closing with alarming frequency in the industrial heartland of America. Old industrial cities, their economies intertwined with the economic health of aging manufacturing plants, are ailing as those plants are being forced to close, cut back, or relocate to remote locales.

Today, sadly, the decline of smokestack America and the pain it has meant for many blue-collar workers and their communities are already old news. The closing of old factories has been pushed out of the headlines by a flood of white-collar layoffs, the result of restructuring and cost cutting in a wide range of industries—not just in manufacturing, but also in banking and finance, communication services, and high technology, among others. In recent years, older, better-educated, and better-paid workers have been more likely to be axed than have blue-collar workers. Take Steven A. Holthau-

sen, for example. For two decades he was a loan officer with a salary of $1,000 a week. He survived three bank mergers only to learn when he returned from a family vacation that he no longer had a job. For a year Holthausen scraped by on commissions earned as a freelance mortgage broker, supplemented by severance pay and unemployment insurance. For a while he pumped gas at a station owned by a former bank customer. His wife left him. Now he earns $1,000 a month—a quarter of his former salary—as a tour guide.

Or meet James E. Sharlow. The same age as Holthausen, Sharlow was laid off by Eastman Kodak after twenty-six years when the company shut down the plant he managed. Over a three-year period, Sharlow sent out over two thousand résumés, but the market for white-collar positions is glutted with job-seekers, and Sharlow landed only ten interviews. He was one of two finalists for a job managing a plant in Southern California, for which 3,000 people had applied. He didn't get the position. Today he works as a consultant in the electronics department of a local college for less than a quarter of the $130,000 he used to make.

Holthausen and Sharlow are among those caught up in a tidal wave of layoffs—layoffs that are no longer concentrated among blue-collar workers in old and uncompetitive manufacturing firms in the industrial heartland. Since 1979 more than 43 million people have been thrown out of work, as companies have sought to modernize their operations, reduce labor costs, and increase their global competitiveness. One-third of all households have seen a family member lose a job, and nearly 40 percent more know a relative, friend, or neighbor who has been laid off. Layoffs affect 3 million people every year, and one is far more likely to be laid off than to be the victim of a violent crime.

The large and established *Fortune* 500 companies have been setting the pace: 50,000 jobs cut at Sears, Roebuck and Company; 16,800 at Eastman Kodak; 18,000 at Delta Airlines; 123,300 at AT&T;

and 175,000 at IBM. American firms sacked 677,795 people in 1998 alone,[55] but the layoffs are still going strong. For example, Lucent Technologies cut 29,000 jobs in 2001 and a further 27,000 in 2002; during the same time period DaimlerChrysler cut 26,000, SBC Communications 31,000, Verizon 15,000, Procter & Gamble 9,600, and AT&T a further 23,000.[56] Fortunately, the number of new jobs created since 1979 has been more than enough to absorb both laid-off workers and new people beginning their careers. However, the new jobs that discharged employees eventually get tend to pay less; only a third of them end up in equally remunerative or better-paying jobs. Sometimes, they are even re-hired by their original employers at a lower wage or as "independent contractors" without fringe benefits. This disturbing trend has been called the "Downsizing of America," and its human costs are only now beginning to be explored.[57]

Some commentators believe that downsizing is exaggerated, that it barely exceeds the usual turnover in jobs that is characteristic of any capitalist economy.[58] Others challenge the widespread belief that downsizing has meant that U.S. corporations have become less bureaucratic by shedding managerial jobs. Economist David Gordon contends not only that, compared with others nations, U.S. companies are still top-heavy with management and administration, but also that this "bureaucratic burden" has continued to increase.[59]

Nevertheless, employees, including managers, are more fearful than ever of losing their jobs. Job security seems to be a thing of the past. "No one is immune from the job-cutting ax," says James Challenger, a Chicago outplacement authority. "One day you are a member of a team and the next day your entire division is being dismantled."[60] At the workplace, fear of unemployment can easily create suspicion, dampen employee loyalty, and reduce innovation, creativity, and risk taking. Employees complain about managing the orphaned workloads of downsized colleagues and fight for high-profile posts so that if the ax falls, it won't fall on them.[61]

Critics also charge that many companies have downsized blindly, saving money through layoffs that have meant reduced output, poorer-quality products, and frayed relations with customers. For example, after Delta Airlines eliminated more than 10,000 positions, its on-time performance fell to the bottom of the list for major airlines. With airline agents, baggage handlers, and maintenance workers in short supply, customer service deteriorated, and complaints to the Department of Transportation soared. Studies by the American Management Association have found that fewer than half the firms that have cut their workforces since 1990 have succeeded in raising their profits, and only a third increased productivity.[62]

What is even more worrisome to many is that layoffs occur even when companies are doing well. For example, AT&T announced that it was laying off 40,000 employees at a time when it was making record profits and its chairman, Robert E. Allen, was pulling in an annual salary of $14 million. Likewise, BankAmerica decided to lay off 4 percent of its workforce after its stock had risen 50 percent that year and its profits reached an all-time high. Some observers fear that downsizing and widespread fear of unemployment, when coupled with increasing economic inequality, growing poverty, and a stagnating standard of living for the majority, signal the fraying of our social fabric. Princeton University political theorist Alan Ryan writes:

> When we reach a situation in which the bottom 80 percent—not the underclass, but most of the population—sees itself struggling to make ends meet, sees no gains from increased productivity, and sees an elite creaming [off] all the benefits of a transformed economy, trouble looms.[63]

This is a serious concern. History shows that economic fears, class tensions, and social distress can cause social instability. At a time when some business experts are predicting that 90 percent of white-collar jobs in the U.S. will be destroyed beyond recognition in the next ten to fifteen years,[64] one can only hope, then, that downsizing does not become the "capsizing of America."

Discussion Questions

1. Have you or a family member experienced layoffs, downsizing, or corporate restructuring? Do you know anyone who has?

2. What is causing downsizing? Is it inevitable? Is it economically necessary? What effects are downsizing and the fear of layoffs having on our society?

3. Some would argue that economic change always brings social dislocation and that we should simply accept the current wave of layoffs as one result of automation, international competition, and the workings of a free market. Do you agree?

4. Do corporations have a moral obligation to avoid laying off longtime employees like Steven Holthausen and James Sharlow? Do layoffs ever violate the rights of workers? Should layoffs, plant closures, and outsourcing be regulated in some way?

5. The CEOs who have laid off thousands of workers have often seen their own compensation skyrocket at the same time. Is there anything unjust about this? Does a CEO have an obligation to share the pain? If layoffs increase the company's profits, is the CEO entitled to a boost in pay?

6. What, if anything, does downsizing reveal about the attitudes of corporations toward their employees? Do you find anything in the current plight of America's workers, both blue- and white-collar, that confirms the Marxist view of capitalism?

7. What is your assessment of the future of American manufacturing? What about America's capitalist system in general?

CASE 4.2

Hucksters in the Classroom

Increased student loads, myriad professional obligations, and shrinking school budgets have sent many public school teachers scurrying for teaching materials to facilitate their teaching.

They don't have to look far. Into the breach has stepped business, which is ready, willing, and able to provide current print and audiovisual materials for classroom use.[65] These industry-supplied teaching aids are advertised in educational journals, distributed directly to schools, and showcased at educational conventions. Clearasil, for example, distributes a teaching aid and color poster called "A Day in the Life of Your Skin." Its message is hard to miss: Clearasil is the way to clear up your pimples. Domino's Pizza supplies a handout that is supposed to help kids learn to count by tabulating the number of pepperoni wheels on one of the company's pizzas. Chef Boyardee sponsors a study program on sharks based on its "fun pasta," which is shaped like sharks and pictured everywhere on its educational materials.

The list goes on. General Mills supplies educational pamphlets on Earth's "great geothermic 'gushers'" along with the company's "Gushers" snack (a candy filled with liquid). The pamphlets recommend that teachers pass the "Gushers" around and then ask the students as they bite the candy, "How does this process differ from that which produces erupting geothermic phenomena?" In an elementary school in Texas, teachers use a reading program called "Read-A-Logo." Put out by Teacher Support Software, it encourages students to use familiar corporate names such as McDonald's, Hi-C, Coca-Cola, or Cap'n Crunch to create elementary sentences, such as, "I had a hamburger and a Pepsi at McDonald's." Courtesy of literature from the Pacific Lumber Company, students in California learn about forests; they also get Pacific Lumber's defense of its forest-clearing activities: "The Great American Forest . . . is renewable forever." At Pembroke Lakes elementary school in Broward County, Florida, ten-year-olds learned how to design a McDonald's restaurant, and how to apply and interview for a job at McDonald's, thanks to a seven-week company-sponsored class intended to teach them about the real world of work.

"It's a corporate takeover of our schools," says Nelson Canton of the National Education Association. "It has nothing to do with education and everything to do with corporations making profits and hooking kids early on their products." "I call it the phantom curriculum," adds Arnold Fege of the National PTA, "because the teachers are often unaware that there's subtle product placement." There's nothing subtle, however, about the product placement in *Mathematics Applications and Connections,* a textbook used by many sixth graders. It begins its discussion of the coordinate system with an advertisement for Walt Disney: "Have you ever wanted to be the star of a movie? If you visit Walt Disney-MGM Studios Theme Park, you could become one." Other math books are equally blatant. They use brand-name products like M&Ms, Nike shoes, and Kellogg's Cocoa Frosted Flakes as examples when discussing surface area, fractions, decimals, and other concepts.

All this is fine with Lifetime Learning Systems, a marketing firm that specializes in pitching to students the products of its corporate customers. "[Students] are ready to spend and we reach them," the company brags, touting its "custom-made learning materials created with your [company's] specific marketing objectives in mind." Today's 43 million schoolchildren have tremendous buying power. Elementary schoolchildren spend $15 billion a year and influence another $160 billion in spending by parents. Teenagers spend $57 billion of their own money and $36 billion of their families' money. It's not surprising, then, that many corporations clearly see education marketing as a cost-effective way to build brand loyalty.

Both Gillette and Schick provide in-school programs to introduce young people to their razors; other companies sponsor school contests that offer prizes for buying their products. In exchange for 5,125 soup labels, for example, Campbell Soup Company furnishes schools with a filmstrip, "The Boyhood of Abraham Lincoln." Orville Redenbacher's Popcorn offers schools ten cents for every label they collect, and Hershey's a nickel for every wrapper. With many schools facing economic hardship and rising enrollments, *Retailing* is fast becoming the fourth R of public education.

Corporate America's most dramatic venture in the classroom, however, began in 1990, when Whittle Communications started beaming into classrooms around the country its controversial Channel One, a television newscast for middle and high school students. The broadcasts are twelve minutes long—ten minutes of news digest with slick graphics and two minutes of commercials for Levi's jeans, Gillette razor blades, Head & Shoulders shampoo, Snickers candy bars, and other familiar products. Although a handful of states have banned Channel One, it is seen by 8 million young people every school day—a teen audience fifty times larger than that of MTV.

Kohlberg Kravis Roberts & Co., which now owns Channel One, provides cash-hungry schools with thousands of dollars worth of electronic gadgetry, including TV monitors, satellite dishes, and video recorders, if the schools agree to show the broadcasts. In return, the schools are contractually obliged to broadcast the program in its entirety to all students at a single time on 90 to 95 percent of the days that school is in session. The show cannot be interrupted, and teachers do not have the right to turn it off.

For their part, students seem to like Channel One's fast-paced MTV-like newscasts. "It was very interesting and it appeals to our age group," says student Angelique Williams. "One thing I really like was the reporters were our own age. They kept our attention." But educators wonder how much students really learn. A University of Michigan study found that students who watched Channel One scored only 3.3 percent better on a thirty-question test of current events than did students in schools without Channel One. Although researchers called this gain so small as to be educationally unimportant, they noted that all the Channel One students remembered the commercials. That, of course, is good news for Kohlberg Kravis Roberts, which charges advertisers $157,000 for a thirty-second spot. That price sounds high, but companies are willing to pay it because Channel One delivers a captive, narrowly targeted audience.

That captive audience is just what worries the critics. Peggy Charren of Action for Children's Television calls the project a "great big, gorgeous Trojan horse. . . . You're selling the children to the advertisers. You might as well auction off the rest of the school day to the highest bidders." On the other hand, Principal Rex Stooksbury of Central High School in Knoxville, which receives Channel One, takes a different view. "This is something we see as very, very positive for the school," he says. And as student Danny Diaz adds, "We're always watching commercials" anyway.

Discussion Questions

1. What explains industry's thrust into education? Is it consistent with the basic features of capitalism?

2. Have you had any personal experience with industry-sponsored educational materials? What moral issues, if any, are involved in the affiliation between education and commercial interests?

3. Do you think students have a "moral right" to an education free of commercial indoctrination?

4. If you were a member of a school board contemplating the use of either industry-sponsored materials or Channel One, what would you recommend?

5. Do you think industry in general and Channel One in particular are intentionally using teachers and students as a means to profit? Or do they have a genuine concern for the education process? On the other hand, if teachers and students benefit from these educational materials or from viewing Channel One, is there any ground for concern?

CASE 4.3

Licensing and Laissez Faire

The United States is a capitalist country, and our system of medical care is, to a significant extent, organized for profit. True, many hospitals are nonprofit, but the same cannot be said of doctors, who, judged as a whole, form an extremely affluent and privileged occupational group.

Sometimes physicians themselves seem a little uncomfortable about the business aspect of their professional lives or worry that outsiders will misinterpret their attention to economic matters. For example, the professional journal *Medical Economics*, which discusses such pocketbook issues as malpractice insurance, taxes, fees, and money management (a recent cover story was titled "Are You Overpaying Your Staff?"), works hard at not being available to the general public. When a subscriber left his copy on a commercial airliner, another reader found it and sent the mailing label to the magazine; the magazine's editor sent a cautionary note to the subscriber. The editor advises readers to "do your part by restricting access to your personal copies of the magazine. Don't put them in the waiting room, don't leave them lying about in the examination rooms, and don't abandon them in public places."[66]

Medical Economics probably suspects that even in our capitalist society many people, including probably most doctors, would not like to think of physicians simply as medical entrepreneurs who are in it for the money. And, indeed, many people here and many more in other countries criticize our medical system for being profit oriented. They think medical care should be based on need and that ability to pay should not affect the quality of medical treatment one receives. Interestingly, though, some people criticize medical practice in the United States as being insufficiently market oriented; University of Chicago professor of economics Milton Friedman is one of them.

Friedman has been a longstanding critic of occupational licensure in all fields. His reasoning is straightforward: Licensure—the requirement that one obtain a license from a recognized authority in order to engage in an occupation—restricts entry into the field. Licensure thus permits the occupational or professional group to enjoy a monopoly in the provision of services. In Friedman's view, this contravenes the principles of a free market to the disadvantage of us all.

Friedman has no objection to certification; that is, to public or private agencies certifying that an individual has certain skills. But he rejects the policy of preventing people who do not have such a certificate from practicing the occupation of their choice. Such a policy restricts freedom and keeps the price of the services in question artificially high. When one reads the long lists of occupations for which some states require a license—librarians, tree surgeons, pest controllers, well diggers, barbers, even potato growers, among many others—Friedman's case gains plausibility. But Friedman pushes his argument to include all occupations and professions.

Does this mean we should let incompetent physicians practice? Friedman's answer is yes.[67] In his view the American Medical Association (AMA) is simply a trade union, though probably the strongest one in the United States. It keeps the wages of its members high by restricting the number of those who can practice medicine.

The AMA does this not just through licensure but also, even more effectively, through controlling the number of medical schools and the number of students admitted to them. Today, for instance, over 45,000 applicants vie every year for roughly 16,000 medical school vacancies.[68] The medical profession, Friedman charges, limits entry into the field both by turning down applicants to medical school and by making standards for admission and licensure so difficult as to discourage many young people from ever trying to gain admission.

Viewed as a trade union, the AMA has been singularly effective. As recently as the 1920s, physicians were far down the list of professionals in terms of income; the average doctor made less than the average accountant. Today, physicians constitute the profession that arguably has the highest status and the best pay in the country. Although physicians' incomes vary widely depending on their medical specialty, today the average doctor earns $199,000 a year, more than five times the income of the average full-time worker.[69] Still, the medical establishment remains worried. It believes that there are too many doctors in the United States, and that "this surplus breeds inefficiency and drives up costs."[70]

The economic logic behind this proposition is murky. An increase in the supply of barbers, plumbers, or taxi drivers does not drive up the cost of getting a haircut, having your pipes fixed, or taking a cab. Why should it be different with doctors? Critics of the medical profession believe that its real worry is the prospect of stabilizing or even declining incomes. In any case, the doctors have written two prescriptions.

The first is to reduce the number of medical students by closing down some medical schools; the second is to make it more difficult for foreign doctors to practice here. Although the medical establishment has often expressed concern about the quality of foreign medical training, today the worry is strictly a matter of quantity. "We've got to stop the pipeline of foreign medical graduates," says Dr. Ed O'Neil of the Center for the Health Professions at the University of California, San Francisco. "They are a big chunk of physician oversupply. . . . We're just trying to be rational."[71] As for home-grown doctors, Congress is following medical advice and trying to stem the supposed glut. In 1997, it decided to pay hospitals around the country hundreds of millions of dollars to decrease the number of physicians they train. It turns out, however, that the United States has fewer doctors per 1,000 than do Germany, Sweden, France, and many other developed countries.[72] In fact, the United States is now predicted to have a shortage of 200,000 physicians by 2020.[73]

Medical licensure restricts the freedom of people to practice medicine and prevents the public from buying the medical care it wants. Nonetheless, most people would probably defend the principle of licensure on the grounds that it raises the standards of competence and the quality of care. Friedman contests this. By reducing the amount of care available, he contends, licensure also reduces the average quality of care people receive. (By analogy, suppose that automobile manufacturers were forbidden to sell any car that did not have the quality of a Mercedes Benz. As a result, people who owned cars would have cars of higher average quality than they do now. But because fewer people could afford cars and more of them would, therefore, have to walk or ride bicycles, such a regulation would not raise the quality of transportation enjoyed by the average person.) Friedman charges, furthermore, that the monopoly created by the licensing of physicians has reduced the incentive for research, development, and experimentation, both in medicine and in the organization and provision of services.

Since Friedman initially presented his argument forty years ago, some of the alternatives to traditional practice that he proposed have come to pass; prepaid services have emerged, and group and clinic-based practices are on the increase. But what about his main contention that instead of licensure we should allow the marketplace to sort out the competent from the incompetent providers of medical services?

Friedman's critics contend that even if the licensing of professionals "involves violating a moral rule" against restricting individuals' "freedom of opportunity," it is still immoral to allow an unqualified person to engage in potentially harmful activities without having subjected the person to adequate tests of competence.[74] Despite the appeal of Friedman's arguments on behalf of free choice, the danger still remains, they say, that people will be victimized by the incompetent.

Consider, for example, the quack remedies and treatments peddled to AIDS patients here and abroad. Bottles of processed pond scum and concoctions of herbs, injections of hydrogen peroxide or of cells from the glands of unborn calves, the eating of bee pollen and garlic, $800 pills containing substances from mice inoculated with the AIDS virus, and even whacking the thymus gland of patients to stimulate the body's immune system—all

these are among the treatments offered to desperate people by the unscrupulous and eccentric.[75] Deregulation of the medical field seems most unlikely to diminish such exploitation.

Discussion Questions

1. What explains the fact that licenses are required for so many occupations? What do you see as the pros and cons of occupational licensure in general? Does it have benefits that Friedman has overlooked?

2. Do you believe that licensure in medicine or any other field is desirable? In which fields and under what circumstances? What standards would you use to determine where licensure is needed?

3. Is occupational licensure consistent with the basic principles and values of capitalism? Is it a violation of the free-market ideal? How would you respond to the argument that licensure illegitimately restricts individual freedom to pursue a career or a trade?

4. Does licensure make the market work more or less effectively? Would you agree that as long as consumers are provided accurate information, then they should be permitted to make their own choices with regard to the services and products they purchase—even when it comes to medical care? Or is licensing necessary to protect them from making incorrect choices?

5. Friedman and others view the AMA as a trade union, and they believe that the high incomes of doctors are due more to artificial restrictions on the free market than to the inherent value of their services. Is this an accurate or fair picture of the medical profession?

6. Is licensing an all-or-nothing issue, or is it possible that although there are certain services that we should permit only licensed practitioners to perform, there are other services now monopolized by the same practitioners that could be performed less expensively but equally competently by paraprofessionals or laypersons?

CASE 4.4

An Internet Parasite

When you're cruising the Web, do those little pop-up ads bother you? If so, one of the companies you have to thank is Gator Corp., an Internet advertising firm. It makes software that monitors what you do online and then displays those ads when you visit certain Web sites. Gator has cut deals with various software makers to have them include its software on their programs. As a result, millions of computer owners have Gator's software on their PCs. Gator also gives away "e-wallet" software, which helps you fill out forms on Web sites, but this free software comes with Gator's "spy-ware" built in.[76]

Gator sells those pop-up ads to advertisers, who want to reach people who visit certain Web sites, but without paying the fees that the owners of those Web sites would charge. Gator calls what it does "behavioral marketing." Its critics call the company a "parasite" because it siphons ad money from Web sites that others have constructed. Not only does Gator need other people's Web sites to exist, but also its program threatens the existence of those sites by taking away some of the income they need to keep running. Gator's critics accuse it of unfair competition, and several large American publishing companies with Web sites have filed suit against Gator to protect their online business interests. Ironically, one of the companies joining the lawsuit is the *New York Times,* which once used Gator's services to sell subscriptions to people who visited the Web sites of its competitors.

Although his employer is one of the companies suing Gator, *Wall Street Journal* columnist Lee Gomes worries that the publishers' lawsuit may impinge on your right to control what you do with your computer and to use it to interact with the Internet in the way you choose. "The publishers," he says, "seem to be saying that you should look at their Web sites only the way they say you should. They say you can't have someone else's pop-up ad on top of their sites." If the publishers win, he rea-

sons, this will be another setback for the concept of "fair use"—the idea that people who use copyrighted material have certain rights, too (for example, to record a copyrighted television program for their own use later).

Instead, Gomes thinks the publishers should try persuasion instead of litigation, free speech instead of legal coercion. In particular, the publishers claim that most Gator users don't realize that they have it on their computers or, at least, don't understand how it tracks their Web-surfing habits. Gator denies this, but in any case the publishers could, Gomes says, inform their Web site visitors that there are programs like Ad-aware that allow PC owners to check whether their computers have Gator or other sorts of "adware" on them and then, if they want, to delete those programs. The publishers could also point out that Microsoft, Yahoo!, and others provide "e-wallet" software without any Gator-like tracking built in. This, Gomes argues, is the right way to respond to the challenge of Gator—by giving computer users more choice, not less.

Discussion Questions

1. Is Gator a threat to the business interests of the publishers and other Web site owners? If so, do they have a legitimate complaint against Gator? Or is this a case of big companies' ganging up to thwart a smaller business rival?

2. Is Gator guilty of unfair competition? Has it violated the implicit rules of a free-market, capitalistic system? Is it a parasite that should be put out of business or a legitimate business operation?

3. What, if anything, should the publishers do about Gator? Is Gomes's "free speech" strategy likely to work? How would you deal with Gator

if you owned a popular, expensive-to-run Web site?

4. Does Gator's software violate the right to privacy of PC owners? If the lawsuit succeeds in stopping Gator, would this be a setback for the idea of "fair use"? Would it violate the rights of PC owners?

5. Is your view of this case affected by whether you personally find pop-up ads annoying?

CASE 4.5

A New Work Ethic?

You would think that employees would do something if they discovered that a customer had died on the premises. But that's not necessarily so, according to the Associated Press, which reported that police discovered the body of a trucker in a tractor trailer rig that had sat—with its engine running—in the parking lot of a fast-food restaurant for nine days. Employees swept the parking lot around the truck but ignored the situation for over a week until the stench got so bad that someone finally called the police.

That lack of response doesn't surprise James Sheehy, a human resources manager in Houston, who spent his summer vacation working undercover at a fast-food restaurant owned by a relative.[77] Introduced to coworkers as a management trainee from another franchise location who was being brought in to learn the ropes, Sheehy was initially viewed with some suspicion, but by the third day the group had accepted him as just another employee. Sheehy started out as a maintenance person and gradually rotated through various cooking and cleaning assignments before ending up as a cashier behind the front counter.

Most of Sheehy's fellow employees were teenagers and college students who were home for the summer and earning additional spending money. Almost half came from upper-income families and the rest from middle-income neighborhoods. More than half were women, and a third were minorities. What Sheehy reports is a whole generation of workers with a frightening new work ethic: contempt for customers, indifference to quality and service, unrealistic expectations about the world of work, and a get-away-with-what-you-can attitude.

A recent survey shows that employee theft accounts for 50 percent more revenue loss for retailers than shoplifting.[78] Sheehy's experience was in line with this. He writes that the basic work ethic at his place of employment was a type of gamesmanship that focused on milking the place dry. Theft was rampant, and younger employees were subject to peer pressure to steal as a way of becoming part of the group. "It don't mean nothing," he says, was the basic rationale for dishonesty. "Getting on with getting mine" was another common phrase, as coworkers carefully avoided hard work or dragged out tasks like sweeping to avoid additional assignments.

All that customer service meant, on the other hand, was getting rid of people as fast as possible and with the least possible effort. Sometimes, however, service was deliberately slowed or drive-through orders intentionally switched in order to cause customers to demand to see a manager. This was called "baiting the man," or purposely trying to provoke a response from management. In fact, the general attitude toward managers was one of disdain and contempt. In the eyes of the employees, supervisors were only paper-pushing functionaries who got in the way.

Sheehy's coworkers rejected the very idea of hard work and long hours. "Scamming" was their ideal. Treated as a kind of art form and as an accepted way of doing business, scamming meant taking shortcuts or getting something done without much effort, usually by having someone else do it. "You only put in the time and effort for the big score" is how one fellow worker characterized the work ethic he shared with his peers. "You got to just cruise through the job stuff and wait to make the big score," said another. "Then you can hustle. The office stuff is for buying time or paying for the groceries."

By contrast, they looked forward to working "at a real job where you don't have to put up with hassles." "Get out of school and you can leave this to the real dummies." "Get an office and a computer and a secretary and you can scam your way through anything." On the other hand, these young employees believed that most jobs were like the fast-food industry: automated, boring, undemanding and unsatisfying, and dominated by difficult people. Still, they dreamed of an action-packed business world, an image shaped by a culture of video games and action movies. The college students in particular, reports Sheehy, identified with the Michael Douglas character in the movie *Wall Street* and believed that a no-holds-barred, trample-over-anybody, get-what-you-want approach is the necessary and glamorous road to success.

Discussion Questions

1. How typical are the attitudes that Sheehy reports? Does his description of a new work ethic tally with your own experiences?

2. What are the implications for the future of American business of the work ethic Sheehy describes?

3. Some might discount Sheehy's experiences either as being the product of one particular industry or as simply reflecting the immaturity of young employees. Would you agree?

4. Is it reasonable to expect workers, especially in a capitalist society, to be more devoted to their jobs, more concerned with quality and customer service, than Sheehy's coworkers were? What explains employee theft?

5. In what ways does the culture of our capitalist society encourage attitudes like those Sheehy describes?

Notes to Chapter 4

1. See David Schweickart, *Against Capitalism* (Boulder, Colo.: Westview, 1996).

2. For a succinct treatment of the rise of the Fugger dynasty, see Ned M. Cross, Robert C. Lamm, and Rudy H. Turk, *The Search for Personal Freedom* (Dubuque, Iowa: William C. Brown Company, 1972), 12.

3. Ibid., 13. See also Robert B. Carson, *Business Issues Today: Alternative Perspectives* (New York: St. Martin's Press, 1982), 3–30.

4. Robert Heilbroner, *The Worldly Philosophers*, 5th ed. (New York: Simon & Schuster, 1980), 22–23.

5. Adam Smith, *The Wealth of Nations* (New York: Modern Library, 1985), 16.

6. Ibid., 223–225.

7. As quoted by G. A. Cohen, *History, Labour, and Freedom* (Oxford: Oxford University Press, 1988), 273.

8. Ibid., 265.

9. Quoted by Joseph E. Stiglitz, "A Fair Deal for the World," *New York Review of Books,* May 23, 2002, 28.

10. Robert Heilbroner, *The Economic Problem* (Englewood Cliffs, N.J.: Prentice-Hall, 1972), 725.

11. Jim Hightower, "Food Monopoly: Who's Who in the Thanksgiving Business?" *Texas Observer,* November 17, 1978. For a study of oligopoly in the breakfast cereal industry, see Deborah Baldwin, "The Cornflake Cartel," *Common Cause Magazine,* Summer 1993.

12. Richard J. Barnet, "Lords of the Global Economy," *Nation,* December 19, 1994, 754.

13. Heilbroner, *Worldly Philosophers,* 302.

14. Carson, *Business Issues Today,* 29.

15. For details, see David E. Sanger, "Bush Puts Tariffs of as Much as 30% on Steel Imports," *New York Times,* March 6, 2002, A1; "Rust Never Sleeps," *Economist,* March 9, 2002, 61; and "So Far, Steel Tariffs Do Little," *Wall Street Journal,* September 13, 2002, A1.

16. Laura D'Andrea Tyson, "The Farm Bill Is a $200 Billion Disaster," *Business Week,* June 3, 2002, 26.

17. Keith Bradsher, "As U.S. Urges Free Markets, Its Trade Barriers Are Many," *New York Times,* February 7, 1992, A1.

18. Thomas A. Hemphill, "Confronting Corporate Welfare," *Business Horizons* 40 (Nov.–Dec. 1997): 5.

19. Timothy Taylor, "Corporate 'Welfare' Is Tricky," *San Jose Mercury News,* September 21, 1995, 7F.

20. Stephen Moore, "Corporate Welfare Queens," *National Review,* May 19, 1997, 27–28; Ralph Nader, "Investments in Corporate Welfare Pay Off," *San Jose Mercury News,* January 7, 1996, 7C.

21. Moore, "Corporate Welfare Queens."

22. See Donald L. Barlett and James B. Steele, "How the Little Guy Gets Crunched," *Time,* February 7, 2000, 34–38; Timothy W. Maier, "Business Fares Well with Welfare," *Insight on the News,* December 29, 1997, 12; Hemphill, "Confronting Corporate Welfare"; Moore, "Corporate Welfare Queens."

23. Paulette Olson and Dell Champlin, "Ending Corporate Welfare As We Know It," *Journal of Economic Issues* 32 (September 1998): 759; Donald L. Barlett and James B. Steele, "Corporate Welfare," *Time,* November 9, 1998, 38; Hemphill, "Confronting Corporate Welfare," 2.

24. Alfie Kohn, *No Contest: The Case Against Competition* (Boston: Houghton Mifflin, 1986), 46–55. This paragraph and the next are based on Chapter 3, "Is Competition More Productive?"

25. Ibid., 55.

26. This extract is from *Karl Marx: Early Writings,* translated by T. B. Bottomore, 1963. Used with permission of McGraw-Hill Book Company.

27. Studs Terkel, "How I Am a Worker," in Leonard Silk, ed., *Capitalism: The Moving Target* (New York: Quadrangle, 1974), 68–69.

28. Jeff Madrick, "The End of Affluence," *New York Review of Books,* September 21, 1995, 13, and "Computers: Waiting for the Revolution," *New York Review of Books,* March 26, 1998, 29. See also Simon Head, "The New, Ruthless Economy," *New York Review of Books,* February 29, 1996, and "We Are All Fine-Tuners Now," *Economist,* May 17, 1997, 81.

29. Madrick, "The End of Affluence," 13.

30. Ibid.

31. "A Working Hypothesis," *Economist,* May 11, 1996, 74; Paul Krugman, "How Fast Can the U.S. Economy Grow?" *Harvard Business Review* 75 (July–August 1997): 126; and Federal Reserve Bank of Cleveland, "U.S. Productivity Growth" at *www.clev.frb.org/research/Et97/0397/USprod.htm.*

32. Lester C. Thurow, "Who Owns the Twenty-First Century?" *Sloan Management Review* 33 (Spring 1992): 11.

33. *Economist,* May 11, 1996, 18, 74.

34. Thurow, "Who Owns," 11.

35. Paul Krugman, *The Age of Diminished Expectations,* rev. ed. (Cambridge, Mass.: MIT Press, 1994), 13.

36. David M. Gordon, *Fat and Mean: The Corporate Squeeze of Working Americans and the Myth of Managerial "Downsizing"* (New York: Free Press, 1996), 19–20, and "Working Harder for Less," *Economist,* September 7, 1996, 28.

37. "All Boats Rising," *Economist,* September 30, 2000, 67; U.S. Bureau of the Census, *Statistical Abstract of the United States 2000* (Washington, D.C.: U.S. Government Printing Office, 2001), Table 737.

38. Bernard Sanders, "Clinton Must Go to the People," *Nation,* June 21, 1993; Gordon, *Fat and Mean,* 27–29; but cf. *Fortune,* April 18, 1994, 54.

39. Robert Heilbroner, "We Have Met the Enemy," *Nation,* May 11, 1992, 634; "The Global 500," *Fortune,* July 22, 2002.

40. See William Beaver, "Corporations' Misguided Obsession with Shareholder Wealth," *Business and Society Review* 95 (1996).

41. Adrian Slywotsky and Richard Wise, "Resist the Urge to Merge," *Wall Street Journal,* July 16, 2002, B2.

42. "Greenspan Issues Hopeful Outlook as Stocks Sink," *Wall Street Journal,* July 17, 2002, A1.

43. "Excerpts from President's Speech," *Wall Street Journal,* July 10, 2002, A8; Bill Straub, "A Matter of Greed," *Rocky Mountain News,* July 5, 2002, 3B.

44. Marjorie Kelly, "Waving Goodbye to the Invisible Hand," *Business Ethics,* March/April 2002, 5.

45. "Has Outsourcing Gone Too Far?" *Business Week,* April 1, 1996; "The Outing of Outsourcing," *Economist,* November 25, 1995.

46. Norman Jonas, "The Hollow Corporation," *Business Week,* March 3, 1986. For a contrasting perspective, see "The Next Society: A Survey of the Near Future," *Economist,* November 3, 2001, 11–13.

47. Slywotsky and Wise, "Resist the Urge to Merge."

48. A. Alvarez, "Learning from Las Vegas," *New York Review of Books,* January 11, 1996, 16.

49. Sherwood Ross, "Workers Fearful of Being Laid Off," *San Jose Mercury News,* December 17, 1995, 2PC.

50. *New York Times,* May 14, 1989, sec. 3, 1.

51. *Chicago Tribune,* October 29, 1995, sec. 1, 17.

52. Thomas A. Kochan, Harry C. Katz, and Robert B. McKersie, *The Transformation of American Industrial Relations* (New York: Basic Books, 1986), 209; Ian I. Mitcoff and Elizabeth A. Denton, "A Study of Spirituality in the Workplace," *Sloan Management Review* 40 (Summer 1999): 83–92.

53. Paul Bernstein, "The Work Ethic that Never Was," *Wharton Magazine* 4 (Spring 1980): 19–25.

54. See "Waiting for Verdict on GM Plant, Town" and "Court OKs GM Plan to Close Michigan Plant," *Chicago Tribune,* August 3 and 5, 1993.

55. "Overworked and Overpaid," *Economist,* January 30, 1999, 55.

56. "An Alternative to Cocker Spaniels," *Economist,* August 29, 2001, 49; "After the Boom . . . the Bust," *New York Times,* June 26, 2002, B1.

57. See *The Downsizing of America* (New York: Random House, 1996). Except as otherwise noted, this *New York Times* report is the source of the information in this case study. But see also "The Year Downsizing Grew Up," *Economist,* December 21, 1996.

58. John Cassidy, "All Worked Up," *New Yorker,* April 22, 1996.

59. Gordon, *Fat and Mean,* Chapter 2.

60. Ross, "Workers Fearful," 1PC. See also "Despite Humming Economy, Workers Sweat Job Security," *USA Today,* March 2, 1999, 1A.

61. "The Big Squeeze on Workers," *Business Week,* May 13, 2002, 96.

62. Roger E. Alcaly, "Reinventing the Corporation," *New York Review of Books,* April 10, 1997, 38–40. See also "Understaffing Is Becoming a Problem," *USA Today Magazine,* January 1998, 9.

63. Alan Ryan, "Too Nice to Win," *New York Review of Books,* March 21, 1996, 11.

64. Tom Peters, "What Will We Do for Work?" *Time,* May 29, 2000, 50.

65. This case study draws on "Gripes Grow Over Rampant Textbook Ads," *San Francisco Chronicle,* June 26, 1999, A1; "Knowing the Score," *California Educator,* December 1998; "This Lesson Is Brought to You by . . . ," *Business Week,* June 30, 1997; "This Lesson Is Brought to You by . . . ," *Good Housekeeping,* February 1996; and Alex Molnar, "Learning to Ad," *New Republic,* March 22, 1993. "Mixed Reviews on Classroom Commercials," *San Francisco Chronicle,* March 8, 1989, is the source of the quotations in the final two paragraphs.

66. "Memo from the Editor," *Medical Economics,* November 7, 1988.

67. See the chapter entitled "Occupational Licensure" in Milton Friedman, *Capitalism and Freedom* (Chicago: University of Chicago Press, 1962); in particular, 149.

68. "Medical Schools Are Urged to Cut Admissions by 20%," *New York Times,* November 17, 1995, C2.

69. Peter Kilborn, "Doctors' Pay Regains Ground," *New York Times,* April 22, 1998, A20.

70. "Competition and Cutbacks Hurt Foreign Doctors in U.S.," *New York Times,* November 7, 1995, B15.

71. Ibid.

72. "Casualty," *Economist,* April 13, 2002, 56.

73. Jay Greene, "Now Forecast Is for Shortage of Physicians," *amednews.com,* January 21, 2002.

74. Bernard Gert, "Licensing Professions," *Business and Professional Ethics Journal* 1 (Summer 1982): 52; Donald Weinert, "Commentary," *Business and Professional Ethics Journal* 1 (Summer 1982): 62.

75. "Preying on AIDS Patients," *Newsweek,* June 1, 1987; Marian Segal, "Quackery and AIDS" at *www.thebody.com/fda/quackery.html* (June 2002).

76. This case study is based on Lee Gomes's *Boomtown* column, "In Attacking 'Parasite,' Publishers' Lawsuit May Hurt Your Rights," *Wall Street Journal,* July 15, 2002, B1.

77. James W. Sheehy, "New Work Ethic Is Frightening," *Personnel Journal,* June 1990, is the source of this case.

78. Adam Geller, "Amid the Recession, More Employees Are Stealing from Work," *Santa Cruz Sentinel,* March 24, 2002, D1.

Reading ─────────────────────■

BUDDHIST ECONOMICS

E. F. SCHUMACHER

When thinking about economic matters, people in our society make a number of assumptions. These assumptions have important theoretical and practical consequences, but we simply take their truth for granted. Author and economist E. F. Schumacher exposes several of these implicit dogmas simply by showing how the thinking of a Buddhist economist would differ from that of a modern Western economist on some basic issues: the nature of work, the benefits of mechanization, the relation between material wealth and human well-being, and the use of natural resources.

"Right Livelihood" is one of the requirements of the Buddha's Noble Eightfold Path. It is clear, therefore, that there must be such a thing as Buddhist economics.

Buddhist countries have often stated that they wish to remain faithful to their heritage. So Burma: "The New Burma sees no conflict between religious values and economic progress. Spiritual health and material well-being are not enemies: they are natural allies." Or: "We can blend successfully the religious and spiritual values of our heritage with the benefits of modern technology." Or: "We Burmans have a sacred duty to conform both our dreams and our acts to our faith. This we shall ever do."

All the same, such countries invariably assume that they can model their economic development plans in accordance with modern economics, and they call upon modern economists from so-called advanced countries to advise them, to formulate the policies to be pursued, and to construct the grand design for development, the Five-Year Plan

Excerpt from "Buddhist Economics" from *Small Is Beautiful: Economics as if People Mattered*, by E. F. Schumacher. Copyright © 1973 by E. F. Schumacher. Reprinted by permission of HarperCollins Publishers, Inc. Footnotes omitted.

or whatever it may be called. No one seems to think that a Buddhist way of life would call for Buddhist economics, just as the modern materialist way of life has brought forth modern economics.

Economists themselves, like most specialists, normally suffer from a kind of metaphysical blindness, assuming that theirs is a science of absolute and invariable truths, without any presuppositions. Some go as far as to claim that economic laws are as free from "metaphysics" or "values" as the law of gravitation. We need not, however, get involved in arguments of methodology. Instead, let us take some fundamentals and see what they look like when viewed by a modern economist and a Buddhist economist.

There is universal agreement that a fundamental source of wealth is human labour. Now, the modern economist has been brought up to consider "labour" or work as little more than a necessary evil. From the point of view of the employer, it is in any case simply an item of cost, to be reduced to a minimum if it cannot be eliminated altogether, say, by automation. From the point of view of the workman, it is a "disutility"; to work is to make a sacrifice of one's leisure and comfort, and wages are a kind of compensation for the sacrifice. Hence the ideal from the point of view of the employer is to have output without employees, and the ideal from the point of view of the employee is to have income without employment.

The consequences of these attitudes both in theory and in practice are, of course, extremely far-reaching. If the ideal with regard to work is to get rid of it, every method that "reduces the work load" is a good thing. The most potent method, short of automation, is the so-called division of labour and the classical example is the pin factory eulogised in Adam Smith's *Wealth of Nations*. Here it is not a matter of ordinary specialisation, which mankind has practised from time immemorial, but of dividing up every complete process of production into minute parts, so that the final product can be produced at great speed without anyone having had to contribute more than a totally insignificant and, in most cases, unskilled movement of his limbs.

The Buddhist point of view takes the function of work to be at least threefold: to give a man a chance to utilise and develop his faculties; to enable him to overcome his ego-centredness by joining with other people in a common task; and to bring forth the goods and services needed for a becoming existence. Again, the consequences that flow from this view are endless. To organise work in such a manner that it becomes meaningless, boring, stultifying, or nerve-racking for the worker would be little short of criminal; it would indicate a greater concern with goods than with people, an evil lack of compassion, and a soul-destroying degree of attachment to the most primitive side of this worldly existence. Equally, to strive for leisure as an alternative to work would be considered a complete misunderstanding of one of the basic truths of human existence, namely that work and leisure are complementary parts of the same living process and cannot be separated without destroying the joy of work and the bliss of leisure.

From the Buddhist point of view, there are therefore two types of mechanisation which must be clearly distinguished: one that enhances a man's skill and power and one that turns the work of man over to a mechanical slave, leaving man in a position of having to serve the slave. How to tell the one from the other? "The craftsman himself," says Ananda Coomaraswamy, a man equally competent to talk about the modern west as the ancient east, "can always, if allowed to, draw the delicate distinction between the machine and the tool. The carpet loom is a tool, a contrivance for holding warp threads at a stretch for the pile to be woven round them by the craftsmen's fingers; but the power loom is a machine, and its significance as a destroyer of culture lies in the fact that it does the essentially human part of the work." It is clear, therefore, that Buddhist economics must be very different from the economics of modern materialism, since the Buddhist sees the essence of civilisation not in a multiplication of wants but in the purification of human character. Character, at the same time, is formed primarily by a man's work. And work, properly conducted in conditions of human dignity and freedom, blesses those who do it and equally their products. The Indian philosopher and economist J. C. Kumarappa sums the matter up as follows:

If the nature of the work is properly appreciated and applied, it will stand in the same relation to the higher faculties as food is to the physical body. It nourishes and enlivens the higher man and urges him to produce the best he is capable of. It directs his free will along the proper course and disciplines the animal in him into progressive channels. It furnishes an excellent background for man to display his scale of values and develop his personality.

If a man has no chance of obtaining work he is in a desperate position, not simply because he lacks an income but because he lacks this nourishing and enlivening factor of disciplined work which nothing can replace. A modern economist may engage in highly sophisticated calculations on whether full employment "pays" or whether it might be more "economic" to run an economy at less than full employment so as to ensure a greater mobility of labour, a better stability of wages, and so forth. His fundamental criterion of success is simply the total quantity of goods produced during a given period of time. "If the marginal urgency of goods is low," says Professor Galbraith in *The Affluent Society*, "then so is the urgency of employing the last man or the last million men in the labour force." And again: "If . . . we can afford some unemployment in the interest of stability—a proposition, incidentally, of impeccably conservative antecedents—then we can afford to give those who are unemployed the goods that enable them to sustain their accustomed standard of living."

From a Buddhist point of view, this is standing the truth on its head by considering goods as more important than people and consumption as more important than creative activity. It means shifting the emphasis from the worker to the product of work, that is, from the human to the subhuman, a surrender to the forces of evil. The very start of Buddhist economic planning would be a planning for full employment, and the primary purpose of this would in fact be employment for everyone who needs an "outside" job: it would not be the maximisation of employment nor the maximisation of production. Women, on the whole, do not need an "outside" job, and the large-scale employment of women in offices or factories would be considered a sign of serious economic failure. In particular, to let mothers of young children work in factories while the children run wild would be as uneconomic in the eyes of a Buddhist economist as the employment of a skilled worker as a soldier in the eyes of a modern economist.

While the materialist is mainly interested in goods, the Buddhist is mainly interested in liberation. But Buddhism is "The Middle Way" and therefore in no way antagonistic to physical well-being. It is not wealth that stands in the way of liberation but the attachment to wealth; not the enjoyment of pleasurable things but the craving for them. The keynote of Buddhist economics, therefore, is simplicity and non-violence. From an economist's point of view, the marvel of the Buddhist way of life is the utter rationality of its pattern—amazingly small means leading to extraordinarily satisfactory results.

For the modern economist this is very difficult to understand. He is used to measuring the "standard of living" by the amount of annual consumption, assuming all the time that a man who consumes more is "better off" than a man who consumes less. A Buddhist economist would consider this approach excessively irrational: since consumption is merely a means to human well-being, the aim should be to obtain the maximum of well-being with the minimum of consumption. Thus, if the purpose of clothing is a certain amount of temperature comfort and an attractive appearance, the task is to attain this purpose with the smallest possible effort, that is, with the smallest annual destruction of cloth and with the help of designs that involve the smallest possible input of toil. The less toil there is, the more time and strength is left for artistic creativity. It would be highly uneconomic, for instance, to go in for complicated tailoring, like the modern west, when a much more beautiful effect can be achieved by the skillful draping of uncut material. It would be the height of folly to make material so that it should wear out quickly and the height of barbarity to make anything ugly, shabby or mean. What has just been said about clothing applies equally to all other human requirements. The ownership and the consumption of goods is a means to an end, and Buddhist economics is the systematic study of how to attain given ends with the minimum means.

Modern economics, on the other hand, considers consumption to be the sole end and purpose of all economic activity, taking the factors of production—land, labour, and capital—as the means. The former, in short, tries to maximise human satisfactions by the optimal pattern of consumption, while the latter tries to maximise consumption by the optimal pattern of productive effort. It is easy to see that the effort needed to sustain a way of life which seeks to attain the optimal pattern of consumption is likely to be much smaller than the effort needed to sustain a drive for maximum consumption. We need not be surprised, therefore, that the pressure and strain of living is very much less in, say, Burma than it is in the United States, in spite of the fact that the amount of labour-saving machinery used in the former country is only a minute fraction of the amount used in the latter.

Simplicity and non-violence are obviously closely related. The optimal pattern of consumption, producing a high degree of human satisfaction by means of a relatively low rate of consumption, allows people to live without great pressure and strain and to fulfill the primary injunction of Buddhist teaching: "Cease to do evil; try to do good." As physical resources are everywhere limited, people satisfying their needs by means of a modest use of resources are obviously less likely to be at each other's throats than people depending upon a high rate of use. Equally, people who live in highly self-sufficient local communities are less likely to get involved in large-scale violence than people whose existence depends on world-wide systems of trade.

From the point of view of Buddhist economics, therefore, production from local resources for local needs is the most rational way of economic life, while dependence on imports from afar and the consequent need to produce for export to unknown and distant peoples is highly uneconomic and justifiable only in exceptional cases and on a small scale. Just as the modern economist would admit that a high rate of consumption of transport services between a man's home and his place of work signifies a misfortune and not a high standard of life, so the Buddhist economist would hold that to satisfy human wants from faraway sources rather than from sources nearby signifies failure rather than success. The former tends to take statistics showing an increase in the number of ton/miles per head of the population carried by a country's transport system as proof of economic progress, while to the latter—the Buddhist economist—the same statistics would indicate a highly undesirable deterioration in the *pattern* of consumption.

Another striking difference between modern economics and Buddhist economics arises over the use of natural resources. Bertrand de Jouvenel, the eminent French political philosopher, has characterised "western man" in words which may be taken as a fair description of the modern economist:

> He tends to count nothing as an expenditure, other than human effort; he does not seem to mind how much mineral matter he wastes and, far worse, how much living matter he destroys. He does not seem to realise at all that human life is a dependent part of an ecosystem of many different forms of life. As the world is ruled from towns where men are cut off from any form of life other than human, the feeling of belonging to an ecosystem is not revived. This results in a harsh and improvident treatment of things upon which we ultimately depend, such as water and trees.

The teaching of the Buddha, on the other hand, enjoins a reverent and non-violent attitude not only to all sentient beings but also, with great emphasis, to trees. Every follower of the Buddha ought to plant a tree every few years and look after it until it is safely established, and the Buddhist economist can demonstrate without difficulty that the universal observation of this rule would result in a high rate of genuine economic development independent of any foreign aid. Much of the economic decay of south-east Asia (as of many other parts of the world) is undoubtedly due to a heedless and shameful neglect of trees.

Modern economics does not distinguish between renewable and non-renewable materials, as its very method is to equalise and quantify everything by means of a money price. Thus, taking various alternative fuels, like coal, oil, wood, or water-power: the only difference between them recognised by modern economics is relative cost per equivalent unit. The cheapest is automatically the one to be preferred, as to do otherwise would be irrational and "uneconomic." From a Buddhist point of view, of course, this will not do; the essential difference between non-renewable fuels like coal and oil on the one hand and renewable fuels like wood and water-power on the other cannot be simply overlooked. Non-renewable goods must be used only if they are indispensable, and then only with the greatest care and the most meticulous concern for conservation. To use them heedlessly or extravagantly is an act of violence, and while complete non-violence may not be attainable on this earth, there is nonetheless an ineluctable duty on man to aim at the ideal of non-violence in all he does.

Just as a modern European economist would not consider it a great economic achievement if all European art treasures were sold to America at attractive prices, so the Buddhist economist would insist that a population basing its economic life on non-renewable fuels is living parasitically, on capital instead of income. Such a way of life could have no permanence and could therefore be justified only as a purely temporary expedient. As the world's resources of non-renewable fuels—coal, oil, and natural gas—are exceedingly unevenly distributed over the globe and undoubtedly limited in quantity, it is clear that their exploitation at an ever-increasing rate is an act of violence against nature which must almost inevitably lead to violence between men.

This fact alone might give food for thought even to those people in Buddhist countries who care nothing for the religious and spiritual values of their heritage and ardently desire to embrace the materialism of modern economics at the fastest possible speed. Before they dismiss Buddhist economics as nothing better than a nostalgic dream, they might wish to consider whether the path of economic development outlined by modern economics is likely to lead them to places where they really want to be. Towards the end of his courageous book *The Challenge of Man's Future*, Professor Harrison Brown of the California Institute of Technology gives the following appraisal:

> Thus we see that, just as industrial society is fundamentally unstable and subject to reversion to agrarian existence, so within it the conditions which offer individual freedom are unstable in their ability to avoid the conditions which impose rigid organisation and totalitarian

control. Indeed, when we examine all of the foreseeable difficulties which threaten the survival of industrial civilisation, it is difficult to see how the achievement of stability and the maintenance of individual liberty can be made compatible.

Even if this were dismissed as a long-term view there is the immediate question of whether "modernisation," as currently practised without regard to religious and spiritual values, is actually producing agreeable results. As far as the masses are concerned, the results appear to be disastrous—a collapse of the rural economy, a rising tide of unemployment in town and country, and the growth of a city proletariat without nourishment for either body or soul.

It is in the light of both immediate experience and long-term prospects that the study of Buddhist economics could be recommended even to those who believe that economic growth is more important than any spiritual or religious values. For it is not a question of choosing between "modern growth" and "traditional stagnation." It is a question of finding the right path of development, the Middle Way between materialist heedlessness and traditionalist immobility, in short, of finding "Right Livelihood."

Review and Discussion Questions

1. From the Buddhist point of view, what is the function of work? What do you see as the main social and economic implications of the Buddhist perspective?

2. Schumacher sees simplicity as a keynote of Buddhist economics. What's the connection between simplicity and nonviolence? Why does Buddhism value simplicity? Does capitalism promote needless complexity?

3. How do Buddhism and capitalism differ in their understanding of the nature and purpose of human existence? Is the Buddhist view of the role of women sexist?

4. What distinguishes Buddhist economics from modern economics in its approach to material wealth? To natural resources? With which approach are you more sympathetic and why?

5. Is a capitalist economic system compatible with a Buddhist perspective? Is any other economic system?

6. Would you agree that Buddhism has something to teach us about economics?

Reading ————————————— ■

MARKETS AND THE ROLE OF ETHICS IN CAPITALISM

AMARTYA SEN

In this extract from his book, Development as Freedom, *Amartya Sen, winner of the Nobel Prize in economics, discusses the advantages and limitations of markets and the important, but overlooked, role of business ethics in the successful functioning of a capitalist system. Like other economists, Sen appreciates the beneficial results of markets, but he also emphasizes the importance of the freedom they provide. Interest groups that attempt to restrict market competition for their own benefit should be resisted, but Sen acknowledges that markets do have shortcomings, which may justify our interfering with their operation. This is particularly true with respect to issues of equity, public goods, and other cases where the private pursuit of gain runs counter to social interests. In the final sections of the reading, Sen goes on to argue that for its successful operation capitalism requires more than self-interested, profit-maximizing behavior. Rather, it depends on mutual trust and adherence to certain norms—that is, on business ethics.*

MARKETS, LIBERTY AND LABOR

Even though the merits of the market mechanism are now very widely acknowledged, the *reasons* for wanting markets are often not fully appreciated. . . . In recent discussions, the focus in assessing the market mechanism has tended to be on the *results* it ultimately generates, such as the incomes or the utilities yielded by the markets. This is not a negligible issue, and I shall come to it presently. But the more immediate case for the freedom of market transaction lies in the basic importance of that free-

From Amartya Sen, *Development as Freedom*. Copyright © 1999 Amartya Sen. Used by permission of Alfred A. Knopf, a division of Random House, Inc. Notes omitted.

dom itself. We have good reasons to buy and sell, to exchange, and to seek lives that can flourish on the basis of transactions. To deny that freedom in general would be in itself a major failing of a society. This fundamental recognition is *prior* to any theorem . . . showing . . . the . . . outcomes of markets . . . in terms of incomes, utilities and so on.

The ubiquitous role of transactions in modern living is often overlooked precisely because we take them for granted. There is an analogy here with the rather underrecognized—and often unnoticed—role of certain behavioral rules (such as basic business ethics) in developed capitalist economies (with attention being focused only on aberrations when they occur). But when these values are not yet developed, their general presence or absence can make a crucial difference. In the analysis of development, the role of elementary business ethics thus has to be moved out of its obscure presence to a manifest recognition. Similarly, the absence of the freedom to transact can be a major issue in itself in many contexts.

This is, of course, particularly so when the freedom of labor markets is denied by laws, regulations or convention. Even though African American slaves in the pre–Civil War South may have had pecuniary incomes as large as (or even larger than) those of wage laborers elsewhere and may even have lived longer than the urban workers in the North, there was still a fundamental deprivation in the fact of slavery itself (no matter what incomes or utilities it might or might not have generated). The loss of freedom in the absence of employment choice and in the tyrannical form of work can itself be a major deprivation.

The development of free markets in general and of free seeking of employment in particular is a much appreciated fact in historical studies. Even that great critic of capitalism Karl Marx saw the emergence of freedom of employment as momentous progress. . . . But this issue concerns not just history but the present as well, since this freedom is critically important right now in many parts of the world. Let me illustrate this point with four quite different examples.

First, various forms of labor bondage can be found in many countries in Asia and Africa, and there are persistent denials of basic freedom to seek wage employment away from one's traditional bosses. . . . The situation has been more studied in India than elsewhere . . . , but there is enough evidence that similar problems are present in several other countries as well.

Second (to turn now to a very different illustration), the failure of bureaucratic socialism in Eastern Europe and the Soviet Union cannot be fully grasped merely in terms of the economic problems in generating incomes or other results, such as life expectancies. Indeed, in terms of life expectancies, the communist countries often did quite well, relatively speaking (as is readily checked from the demographic statistics of the Soviet Union, pre-reform China, Vietnam and Cuba, among others). In fact, several of the ex-communist countries now are in a significantly *worse* position than they were under communist rule—perhaps nowhere more so than in Russia itself (where the life expectancy at birth of Russian men has dropped now to about fifty-eight years—considerably below those in India or Pakistan). And yet the population is unwilling to vote to return to the previous arrangements. . . .

In assessing what happened, the economic inefficiency of the communist system must, of course, be recognized. But there is also the more immediate issue of the denial of freedom in a system where markets were simply ruled out in many fields. . . .

Third, . . . in the distressing subject of child labor (as prevalent, for example, in Pakistan, or India, or Bangladesh), there is an embedded issue of slavery and bondage, since many of the children working in exacting tasks are forced to perform them. The roots of such servitude may go back to the economic deprivation of the families from which they come—sometimes the parents are themselves under some kind of bondage vis-à-vis the employers—and on top of the nasty issue of laboring children, there is also the barbarity of children being *forced* to do things. The freedom to go to school, in particular, is hampered not only by the weakness of primary educational programs in these regions, but in some cases also by the lack of any choice that the children (and often their parents) have in deciding what they want to do.

The issue of child labor tends to divide South Asian economists. Some have argued that merely abolishing child labor without doing anything to enhance the economic circumstances of the families involved may not serve the interest of the children themselves. There is certainly a debatable issue here, but the frequent congruence of child labor with what effectively is slavery does make it, in those cases, a simpler choice. The starkness of slavery yields a forceful case for more vigorous enforcement of antislavery as well as anti-child-labor legislation. The system of child labor—bad enough on its own—is made much beastlier still through its congruence with bondage and effective slavery.

Fourth, the freedom of women to seek employment outside the family is a major issue in many third world countries. This freedom is systematically denied in many cultures, and this in itself is a serious violation of women's liberty and gender equity. The absence of this freedom militates against the economic empowerment of women, and also has many other consequences. Aside from the direct effects of market employment in adding to the economic independence of women, outside work is also causally important in making women have a better "deal" in intrahousehold distributions. Needless to say, women's work at home can be backbreaking, but it is rarely honored or even recognized (and certainly not remunerated), and the denial of the right to work outside the home is a rather momentous violation of women's liberty.

The prohibition of outside employment for women can sometimes be brutally executed in an explicit and fierce way (as, for example, in . . . Afghanistan [under the Taliban]). In other cases, the prohibition may work more implicitly through the power of convention and conformity. Sometimes there may not even be, in any clear sense, a ban on women's seeking employment, and yet women reared with traditional values may be quite afraid to break with the tradition and to shock others. The prevailing perceptions of "normality" and "appropriateness" are quite central to this question. . . .

MARKETS AND EFFICIENCY

The labor market can be a liberator in many different contexts, and the basic freedom of transaction can be of central importance, quite aside from

P 188

whatever the market mechanism may or may not achieve in terms of incomes or utilities or other results. But it is important also to examine those consequential results, and I turn now to that—rather different—issue.

In assessing the market mechanism, it is important to take note of the forms of the markets: whether they are competitive or monopolistic (or otherwise uncompetitive), whether some markets may be missing (in ways that are not easily remediable) and so on. Also, the nature of factual circumstances (such as the availability or absence of particular kinds of information, the presence or absence of economies of large scale) may influence the actual possibilities and impose real limitations on what can be achieved through various institutional forms of the market mechanism.

In the absence of such imperfections (including the nonmarketability of some goods and services), classical models of general equilibrium have been used to demonstrate the merits of the market mechanism in achieving economic efficiency. This is standardly defined in terms of what economists call "Pareto optimality": a situation in which the utility (or welfare) of no one can be raised without reducing the utility (or welfare) of someone else. This efficiency achievement—the so-called Arrow-Debreu theorem . . .—is of real importance despite the simplifying assumptions.

The Arrow-Debreu results show, inter alia, that—given some preconditions—the results of the market mechanism are not improvable in ways that would enhance everyone's utility (or enhance the utility of some without reducing the utility of anyone else). . . .

These efficiency results do not say anything about the equity of outcomes, or about the equity in the distribution of freedoms. A situation can be efficient in the sense that no one's utility or substantive freedom can be enhanced without cutting into the utility or freedom of someone else, and yet there could be enormous inequalities in the distribution of utilities and of freedoms.

The problem of inequality, in fact, gets magnified as the attention is shifted from income inequality to the inequality in the *distribution of substantive freedoms and capabilities*. This is mainly because of the possibility of some "coupling" of income inequality, on the one hand, with unequal advantages in converting incomes into capabilities, on the other. The latter tends to intensify the inequality problem already reflected in income inequality. For example, a person who is disabled, or ill, or old, or otherwise handicapped may, on the one hand, have problems in *earning* a decent income, and on the other, also face greater difficulties in *converting* income into capabilities and into living well. The very factors that may make a person unable to find a good job and a good income (such as a disability) may put the person at a disadvantage in achieving a good quality of life even with the same job and with the same income. This relationship between income-*earning* ability and income-*using* ability is a well-known empirical phenomenon in poverty studies. The interpersonal income inequality in the market outcomes may tend to be magnified by this "coupling" of low incomes with handicaps in the conversion of incomes into capabilities.

The freedom-efficiency of the market mechanism, on the one hand, and the seriousness of freedom-inequality problems, on the other hand, are worth considering *simultaneously*. The equity problems have to be addressed, especially in dealing with serious deprivations and poverty, and in that context, social intervention including governmental support may well have an important role. To a great extent, this is exactly what the social security systems in welfare states try to achieve, through a variety of programs including social provision of health care, public support of the unemployed and the indigent and so on. But the need to pay attention *simultaneously* to efficiency and equity aspects of the problem remains, since equity-motivated interference with the working of the market mechanism can weaken efficiency achievements even as it promotes equity. It is important to be clear about the need for simultaneity in considering the different aspects of social evaluation and justice. . . .

MARKETS AND INTEREST GROUPS

The role that markets play must depend not only on what they can do, but also on what they are allowed to do. There are many people whose interests are well served by the smooth functioning of markets, but there are also groups whose established interests may be hurt by such functioning. If the latter groups are politically more powerful and influential, then they can try to see that markets are not given adequate room in the economy. This can be a particularly serious problem when monopolistic production units flourish—despite inefficiency and various types of ineptitude—thanks to insulation from competition, domestic or foreign. The high product-prices or the low product-qualities that are involved in such artificially propped-up production may impose significant sacrifice on the population at large, but an organized and politically influential group of "industrialists" can make sure that their profits are well protected. . . .

It is one of the ironies of the history of ideas that some who advocate radical politics today often fall for old economic positions that were so unequivocally rejected by Smith, Ricardo and Marx. . . . It is not surprising that the protected bourgeoisie often do their best to encourage and support the illusion of radicalism and modernity in dusting up generically anti-market positions from the distant past.

It is important to join these arguments through open-minded criticisms of the claims made in favor of general restriction of competition. This is not to deny that attention must also be paid to the political power of those groups that obtain substantial material benefits from restricting trade and exchange. Many authors have pointed out, with good reason, that the advocacies involved must be judged by identifying the vested interests involved, and by taking note of the influence of "rent-seeking activities" implicit in keeping competition away. As Vilfredo Pareto pointed out, in a famous passage, if "a certain measure A is the case of the loss of one franc to each of a thousand persons, and of a thousand franc gain to one individual, the latter will expend a great deal of energy, whereas the former will resist weakly; and it is likely that, in the end, the person who is attempting to secure the thousand francs via A will be successful." Political influence in search of economic gain is a very real phenomenon in the world in which we live.

Confronting such influences has to occur not merely through resisting—and perhaps even "ex-

posing" (to use an old-fashioned word)—the seekers of profit from captive markets, but also from taking on their intellectual arguments as proper subjects of scrutiny. Economics does have a long tradition in that critical direction, going back at least to Adam Smith himself, who simultaneously pointed his accusing finger at the perpetrators, and went on to debunk their claims in favor of the thesis of social benefits from disallowing competition. Smith argued that the vested interests tend to win because of their "better knowledge of their own interest" (*not* "their knowledge of publick interest"). He wrote:

> The interest of the dealers, however, in any particular branch of trade or manufactures, is always in some respects different from, and even opposite to that of the publick. To widen the market and to narrow the competition, is always the interest of the dealers. To widen the market may frequently be agreeable enough to the interest of the publick; but to narrow the competition must always be against it, and can serve only to enable the dealers, by raising their profits above what they naturally would be, to levy for their own benefit, an absurd tax upon the rest of their fellow-citizens. The proposal of any new law or regulation of commerce which comes from this order, ought always to be listened to with great precaution, and ought never to be adopted till after having been long and carefully examined, not only with the most scrupulous, but with the most suspicious attention.

There is no reason why vested interests must win if open arguments are permitted and promoted. . . . This is an ideal field for more public discussion of the claims and counterclaims on the different sides, and in the test of open democracy, public interest may well have excellent prospects of winning against the spirited advocacy of the small coterie of vested interests. . . .

NEED FOR CRITICAL SCRUTINY OF THE ROLE OF MARKETS

Indeed, critical public discussion is an inescapably important requirement of good public policy since the appropriate role and reach of markets cannot be predetermined on the basis of some grand, general formula—or some all-encompassing attitude—either in favor of placing everything under the market, or of denying everything to the market. Even Adam Smith, while firmly advocating the use of markets where it could work well (and denying the merits of any *general* rejection of trade and exchange), did not hesitate to investigate economic circumstances in which particular restrictions may be sensibly proposed, or economic fields in which nonmarket institutions would be badly needed to supplement what the markets can do.

It must not be presumed that Smith's critique of the market mechanism was always gentle, or, for that matter, that he got his critical points invariably right. Consider, for example, his advocacy of legal restriction on usury. Smith was, of course, opposed to any kind of general ban on charging interest on loans (as some antimarket thinkers had advocated). However, he wanted to have legal restrictions imposed by the state on the maximum rates of interest that could be charged:

> In countries where interest is permitted, the law, in order to prevent the extortion of usury, generally fixes the highest rate which can be taken without incurring a penalty. . . .
>
> The legal rate, it is to be observed, though it ought to be somewhat above, ought not to be much above the lowest market rate. If the legal rate of interest in Great Britain, for example, was fixed so high as eight or ten per cent, the greater part of the money which was to be lent, would be lent to prodigals and projectors, who alone would be willing to give this high interest. Sober people, who will give for the use of money no more than a part of what they are likely to make by the use of it, would not venture into the competition. A great part of the capital of the country would thus be kept out of the hands which were most likely to make a profitable and advantageous use of it, and thrown into those which were most likely to waste and destroy it.

In Smith's interventionist logic the underlying argument is that market signals can be misleading, and the consequences of the free market may be much waste of capital, resulting from private pursuit of misguided or myopic enterprises, or private waste of social resources. . . .

It is not particularly important to assess these specific arguments of Smith, but it is important to see what his general concerns are. What he is considering is the possibility of social loss in the narrowly motivated pursuit of private gains. This is the opposite case to the more famous remark of Smith: "It is not from the benevolence of the butcher, the brewer, or the baker that we expect our dinner, but from their regard to their own interest. We address ourselves, not to their humanity but to their self-love. . . ." If the butcher-brewer-baker example draws our attention to the mutually beneficial role of trade based on self-interest, the prodigal-projector argument points to the possibility that under certain circumstances private profit motives may indeed run counter to social interests. It is this general concern that remains relevant today. . . .

The lesson to draw from Smith's analysis of the market mechanism is not any massive strategy of jumping to policy conclusions from some general "pro" or "anti" attitude to markets. After acknowledging the role of trade and exchange in human living, we still have to examine what the other consequences of market transactions actually are. We have to evaluate the actual possibilities critically, with adequate attention being paid to the contingent circumstances that may be relevant in assessing all the results of encouraging markets, or of restraining their operation. If the butcher-brewer-baker example points to a very common circumstance in which our complementary interests are mutually promoted by exchange, the prodigal-projector example illustrates the possibility that this may not work in quite that way in every case. There is no escape from the necessity of critical scrutiny. . . .

Those who have tended to take the market mechanism to be the best solution of every economic problem may want to inquire what the limits of that mechanism may be. I have already commented on issues of equity and the need to go beyond efficiency considerations. . . . But even in achieving efficiency, the market mechanism may sometimes be less than effective, particularly in the presence of what are called "public goods."

One of the assumptions standardly made to show the efficiency of the market mechanism is that every commodity—and more generally everything on which our welfares depend—can be bought and sold in the market. It can all be marketed (if we want to place it there), and there is no "nonmarketable" but significant influence on our welfare. In fact, however, some of the most important contributors to human capability may be hard to sell exclusively to one person at a time. This is especially so when we consider the so-called public goods, which people consume *together* rather than separately.

This applies particularly in such fields as environmental preservation, and also epidemiology and public health care. I may be willing to pay my share in a social program of malaria eradication, but I cannot buy my part of that protection in the form of "private good" (like an apple or a shirt). It is a "public good"—malaria-free surroundings—which we have to consume together. Indeed, if I do manage somehow to organize a malaria-free environment where I live, my neighbor too will have that malaria-free environment, without having to "buy" it from anywhere.

The rationale of the market mechanism is geared to private goods (like apples and shirts), rather than to public goods (like the malaria-free environment), and it can be shown that there may be a good case for the provisioning of public goods, going beyond what the private markets would foster. Exactly similar arguments regarding the limited reach of the market mechanism apply to several other important fields as well, where too the provision involved may take the form of a public good. Defense, policing and environmental protection are some of the fields in which this kind of reasoning applies.

There are also rather mixed cases. For example, given the shared communal benefits of basic education, which may transcend the gains of the person being educated, basic education may have a public-good component as well (and can be seen as a semipublic good). The persons receiving education do, of course, benefit from it, but in addition a general expansion of education and literacy in a region can facilitate social change (even the reduction of fertility and mortality . . .) and also help to enhance economic progress from which others too benefit. The effective reach of these services may require cooperative activities and provisioning by the state or the local authorities. Indeed, the state has typically played a major role in the expansion of basic education across the world. The rapid spread of literacy in the past history of the rich countries of today (both in the West and in Japan and the rest of East Asia) has drawn on the low cost of public education combined with its shared public benefits.

It is in this context rather remarkable that some market enthusiasts recommend now to the developing countries that they should rely fully on the free market even for basic education—thereby withholding from them the very process of educational expansion that was crucial in rapidly spreading literacy in Europe, North America, Japan, and East Asia in the past. The alleged followers of Adam Smith can learn something from his writings on this subject, including his frustration at the parsimony of public expenditure in the field of education:

> For a very small expence the publick can facilitate, can encourage, and can even impose upon almost the whole body of the people, the necessity of acquiring those most essential parts of education.

The "public goods" argument for going beyond the market mechanism supplements the case for social provisioning that arises from the need of basic capabilities, such as elementary health care and basic educational opportunities. Efficiency considerations thus supplement the argument for equity in supporting public assistance in providing basic education, health facilities and other public (or semipublic) goods. . . .

While capitalism is often seen as an arrangement that works only on the basis of the greed of everyone, the efficient working of the capitalist economy is, in fact, dependent on powerful systems of values and norms. Indeed, to see capitalism as nothing other than a system based on a conglomeration of greedy behavior is to underestimate vastly the ethics of capitalism, which has richly contributed to its redoubtable achievements.

The use of formal economic models to understand the operation of market mechanisms, as is the standard practice in economic theory, is to some extent a double-edged sword. The models can give insight into the way the real world operates. On the other hand, the structure of the model can conceal some implicit assumptions that produce the regular relations that the models build on. Successful markets operate the way they do not just on the basis of exchanges being "allowed," but also on the solid foundation of institutions (such as effective legal structures that support the rights ensuing from contracts) and behavioral ethics (which makes the negotiated contracts viable without the need for constant litigation to achieve compliance). The development and use of trust in one another's words and promises can be a very important ingredient of market success. . . .

Despite its effectiveness, capitalist ethics is, in fact, deeply limited in some respects, dealing particularly with issues of economic inequality, environmental protection and the need for cooperation of different kinds that operate outside the market. But within its domain, capitalism works effectively through a system of ethics that provides the vision and the trust needed for successful use of the market mechanism and related institutions.

BUSINESS ETHICS, TRUST AND CONTRACTS

Successful operation of an exchange economy depends on mutual trust and the use of norms—explicit and implicit. When these behavioral modes are plentiful, it is easy to overlook their role. But when they have to be cultivated, that lacuna can be a major barrier to economic success. There are plenty of examples of the problems faced in precapitalist economies because of the underdevelopment of capitalist virtues. Capitalism's need for motivational structures that are more complex than pure profit maximization has been acknowledged in various forms, over a long time, by many leading social scientists, such as Marx, Weber, Tawney and others. That nonprofit motives have a role in the success of capitalism is not a new point, even though the wealth of historical evidence and conceptual arguments in that direction is often neglected in contemporary professional economics.

A basic code of good business behavior is a bit like oxygen: we take an interest in its presence only when it is absent. . . . What may not cause wonder or surprise in Zurich or London or Paris may, however, be quite problematic in Cairo or Bombay or Lagos (or Moscow), in their challenging struggle to

establish the norms and institutions of a functioning market economy. Even the problem of political and economic corruption in Italy, which has been much discussed in recent years (and has also led to radical changes in the political equilibrium in Italy), relates a good deal to the somewhat dualist nature of the Italian economy, with elements of "underdevelopment" in some parts of the economy and the most dynamic capitalism elsewhere in the same economy.

In the economic difficulties experienced in the former Soviet Union and countries in Eastern Europe, the absence of institutional structures and behavioral codes that are central to successful capitalism has been particularly important. There is need for the development of an alternative system of institutions and codes with its own logic and loyalties that may be quite standard in the evolved capitalist economies, but that are relatively hard to install suddenly as a part of "planned capitalism." Such changes can take quite some time to function—a lesson that is currently being learned rather painfully in the former Soviet Union and in parts of Eastern Europe. The importance of institutions and behavioral experiences was rather eclipsed there in the first flush of enthusiasm about the magic of allegedly automatic market processes.

The need for institutional developments has some clear connection with the role of codes of behavior, since institutions based on interpersonal arrangements and shared understandings operate on the basis of common behavior patterns, mutual trust and confidence in the other party's ethics. The reliance on rules of behavior may typically be implicit rather than explicit—indeed so implicit that its importance can be easily overlooked in situations where such confidence is not problematic. But wherever it *is* problematic, overlooking the need for it can be quite disastrous. . . .

VARIATIONS OF NORMS AND INSTITUTIONS WITHIN THE MARKET ECONOMY

Behavioral codes vary even among the developed capitalist economies, and so does their effectiveness in promoting economic performance. While capitalism has been very successful in radically enhancing output and raising productivity in the modern world, it is still the case that the experiences of different countries are quite diverse. The successes of East Asian economies (in recent decades), and most notably of Japan (stretching further back), raise important questions about the modeling of capitalism in traditional economic theory. To see capitalism as a system of pure profit maximization based on individual ownership of capital is to leave out much that has made the system so successful in raising output and in generating income.

Japan has frequently been seen as the greatest example of successful capitalism, and despite the longish period of recent recession and financial turmoil, this diagnosis is unlikely to be completely washed away. However, the motivation pattern that dominates Japanese business has much more content than would be provided by pure profit maximization. Different commentators have emphasized distinct motivational features in Japan. Michio Morishima has outlined the special characteristics of the "Japanese ethos" as emerging from particular features of the history of Japan and its tendency toward rule-based behavior patterns. Ronald Dore and Robert Wade have identified the influence of "Confucian ethics.". . .

Indeed, there is some truth even in the apparently puzzling claim made in *The Wall Street Journal* that Japan is "the only communist nation that works." That enigmatic remark points to the non-profit motivations underlying many economic and business activities in Japan. We have to understand and interpret the peculiar fact that one of the most successful capitalist nations in the world flourishes economically with a motivation structure that departs, in some significant spheres, from the simple pursuit of self-interest, which—we have been told—is the bedrock of capitalism.

Japan does not, by any means, provide the only example of a special business ethics in promoting capitalist success. The merits of selfless work and devotion to enterprise in raising productivity have been seen as important for economic achievements in many countries in the world, and there are many variations in these behavioral codes even among the most developed industrial nations.

INSTITUTIONS AND BEHAVIORAL NORMS

To conclude the discussion of different aspects of the role of values in capitalist success, we must see the system of ethics underlying capitalism as involving a good deal more than sanctifying greed and admiring cupidity. The success of capitalism in transforming the general level of economic prosperity in the world has drawn on morals and codes of behavior that have made market transactions economical and effective. In making use of the opportunities offered by the market mechanism and greater use of trade and exchange, the developing countries have to pay attention not only to the virtues of prudential behavior, but also to the role of complementary values, such as the making and sustaining of trust, avoiding the temptations of pervasive corruption, and making assurance a workable substitute for punitive legal enforcement. In the history of capitalism there have been significant variations within the basic capitalist behavioral codes, with divergent achievements and experiences, and there are things to be learned there as well.

The big challenges that capitalism now faces in the contemporary world include issues of inequality (especially that of grinding poverty in a world of unprecedented prosperity) and of "public goods" (that is, goods that people share together, such as the environment). The solution to these problems will almost certainly call for institutions that take us beyond the capitalist market economy. But the reach of the capitalist market economy itself is, in many ways, extendable by an appropriate development of ethics sensitive to these concerns. The compatibility of the market mechanism with a wide range of values is an important question, and it has to be faced along with exploring the extension of institutional arrangements beyond the limits of the pure market mechanism.

Review and Discussion Questions

1. Sen believes that the market is valuable both for the freedom it provides and for the results it delivers. Give examples of each. Which is the more important rationale for capitalism—freedom or efficiency?

2. Give your own examples of the efforts of interest groups to restrict market competition for their own benefit. What point does Vilfredo Pareto make in this context? What factors determine whether an interest group succeeds in protecting itself from competition?

3. Why did Adam Smith advocate legal restrictions on usury? What lesson does Sen draw from this example?

4. What are "public goods"? Give some examples. How do they show the limits of the market mechanism? Is education a public good? Explain why or why not.

5. What does Sen mean when he writes that capitalism needs "motivational structures that are more complex than pure profit maximization"? Why does capitalism require business ethics for its successful operation? In your view, what values and motivational structures are the most important for capitalism's functioning?

Reading ■

THE GREAT NON-DEBATE OVER INTERNATIONAL SWEATSHOPS

IAN MAITLAND

These days, contractors in Third World countries like Indonesia and China manufacture most of the shoes, shirts, and other clothing that large American footwear and apparel companies sell. Because working conditions in these factories are poor and the wages they pay are exceedingly low, critics call them "sweatshops" and condemn American companies like Nike and Levi Strauss for using them. Although these critics believe that international sweatshops represent capitalism at its worse, Ian Maitland, a management professor at the University of Minnesota, defends them against the charge of exploitation on both factual and ethical grounds. He examines and rejects the idea that sweatshops pay unconscionable wages, that they impoverish local workers and widen the gap between rich

and poor, and that American companies collude with repressive regimes that stifle dissent and repress workers. Arguing that interfering with the market can have terrible results, he concludes not only that paying market wages in developing countries is morally permissible, but also that it may be morally wrong for companies to pay wages that exceed market levels.

In recent years, there has been a dramatic growth in the contracting out of production by companies in the industrialized countries to suppliers in developing countries. This globalization of production has led to an emerging international division of labor in footwear and apparel in which companies like Nike and Reebok concentrate on product design and marketing but rely on a network of contractors in Indonesia, China, Central America, etc., to build shoes or sew shirts according to exact specifications and deliver a high quality good according to precise delivery schedules. As Nike's vice president for Asia has put it, "We don't know the first thing about manufacturing. We are marketers and designers."

The contracting arrangements have drawn intense fire from critics—usually labor and human rights activists. The "critics" (as I will refer to them) have charged that the companies are (by proxy) exploiting workers in the plants (which I will call "international sweatshops") of their suppliers. Specifically, the companies stand accused of chasing cheap labor around the globe, failing to pay

Reprinted by permission of the author from the *British Academy of Management Annual Conference Proceedings*, September 1997. Some notes omitted.

their workers living wages, using child labor, turning a blind eye to abuses of human rights, and being complicit with repressive regimes in denying workers the right to join unions and failing to enforce minimum labor standards in the workplace, and so on.

The campaign against international sweatshops has largely unfolded on television and, to a lesser extent, in the print media. What seems like no more than a handful of critics has mounted an aggressive, media-savvy campaign that has put the publicity-shy retail giants on the defensive. The critics have orchestrated a series of sensational "disclosures" on prime time television exposing the terrible pay and working conditions in factories making jeans for Levi's or sneakers for Nike or Pocahontas shirts for Disney. . . .

Major U.S. retailers have responded by adopting codes of conduct on human and labor rights in their international operations. Levi Strauss, Nike, Sears, JCPenney, Wal-Mart, Home Depot, Philips Van-Heusen now have such codes. . . . Peter Jacobi, President of Global Sourcing for Levi Strauss, has advised: "If your company owns a popular brand, protect this priceless asset at all costs. Highly visible companies have any number of reasons to conduct their business not just responsibly but also in ways that cannot be portrayed as unfair, illegal, or unethical. This sets an extremely high standard since it must be applied to both company-owned businesses and contractors. . . ."[1] And according to another Levi Strauss spokesman, "In many respects, we're protecting our single largest asset: our brand image and corporate reputation.". . .

OBJECTIVE OF THIS ESSAY

In this confrontation between the companies and their critics, neither side seems to have judged it to be in its interest to seriously engage the issue at the heart of this controversy, namely: What are appropriate wages and labor standards in international sweatshops? As we have seen, the companies have treated the charges about sweatshops as a public relations problem to be managed so as to minimize harm to their public images. The critics have apparently judged that the best way to keep public in-

dignation at boiling point is to oversimplify the issue and treat it as a morality play featuring heartless exploiters and victimized third world workers. The result has been a great non-debate over international sweatshops. . . .

This essay takes up the issue of what are appropriate wages and labor standards in international sweatshops. Critics charge that the present arrangements are exploitative. I proceed by examining the specific charges of exploitation from the standpoints of both (a) their factual and (b) their ethical sufficiency. . . .

WHAT ARE ETHICALLY APPROPRIATE LABOR STANDARDS IN INTERNATIONAL SWEATSHOPS?

What are ethically acceptable or appropriate levels of wages and labor standards in international sweatshops? The following four possibilities just about run the gamut of standards or principles that have been seriously proposed to regulate such policies.

1. *Home-country standards:* It might be argued (and in rare cases has been) that international corporations have an ethical duty to pay the same wages and provide the same labor standards regardless of where they operate. However, the view that home-country standards should apply in host countries is rejected by most business ethicists and (officially at least) by the critics of international sweatshops. Thus, Thomas Donaldson argues that "[b]y arbitrarily establishing U.S. wage levels as the bench mark for fairness one eliminates the role of the international market in establishing salary levels, and this in turn eliminates the incentive U.S. corporations have to hire foreign workers."[2] Richard De George makes much the same argument: If there were a rule that said "that American MNCs [multinational corporations] that wish to be ethical must pay the same wages abroad as they do at home. . . . [then] MNCs would have little incentive to move their manufacturing abroad; and if they did move abroad they would disrupt the local labor market with artificially high wages that bore no relation to the local standard or cost of living."[3]

2. *"Living wage" standard:* It has been proposed that an international corporation should, at a minimum, pay a "living wage." Thus, De George says that corporations should pay a living wage "even when this is not paid by local firms."[4] However, it is hard to pin down what this means operationally. According to De George, a living wage should "allow the worker to live in dignity as a human being." In order to respect the human rights of its workers, he says, a corporation must pay "at least subsistence wages and as much above that as workers and their dependents need to live with reasonable dignity, given the general state of development of the society." As we shall see, the living wage standard has become a rallying cry of the critics of international sweatshops. Apparently, De George believes that it is preferable for a corporation to provide no job at all than to offer one that pays less than a living wage.

3. *Donaldson's test:* Thomas Donaldson believes that "it is irrelevant whether the standards of the host country comply or fail to comply with home country standards; what is relevant is whether they meet a universal, objective minimum." He tries to specify "a moral minimum for the behavior of all international economic agents."[5] However, he concedes . . . that "many rights . . . are dependent for their specification on the level of economic development of the country in question."[6] Accordingly, he proposes a test to determine when deviations from home-country standards are unethical. That test provides as follows: "The practice is permissible if and only if the members of the home country would, under conditions of economic development relevantly similar to those of the host country, regard the practice as permissible."[7] Donaldson's test is vulnerable to Bernard Shaw's objection to the Golden Rule, namely that we should not do unto others as we would they do unto us, because their tastes may be different. The test also complicates matters by introducing counterfactuals and hypotheticals (if I were in their place [which I'm not] what would I want?). This indeterminacy is a serious weakness in an ethical code: It is likely to confuse managers who want to act ethically and to provide loopholes for those who don't.

4. *Classical liberal standard:* Finally, there is what I will call the classical liberal standard. According to this standard a practice (wage or labor practice) is ethically acceptable if it is freely chosen by informed workers. For example, in a recent report the World Bank invoked this standard in connection with workplace safety. It said: "The appropriate level is therefore that at which the costs are commensurate with the value that informed workers place on improved working conditions and reduced risk."[8] Most business ethicists reject this standard on the grounds that there is some sort of market failure or the "background conditions" are lacking for markets to work effectively. Thus, for Donaldson full (or near-full) employment is a prerequisite if workers are to make sound choices regarding workplace safety: "The average level of unemployment in the developing countries today exceeds 40 percent, a figure that has frustrated the application of neoclassical economic principles to the international economy on a score of issues. With full employment, and all other things being equal, market forces will encourage workers to make trade-offs between job opportunities using safety as a variable. But with massive unemployment, market forces in developing countries drive the unemployed to the jobs they are lucky enough to land, regardless of the safety."[9] . . . De George, too, believes that the necessary conditions are lacking for market forces to operate benignly. Without what he calls "background institutions" to protect the workers and the resources of the developing country (e.g., enforceable minimum wages) and/or greater equality of bargaining power exploitation is the most likely result.[10]. . .

THE CASE AGAINST INTERNATIONAL SWEATSHOPS

To many of their critics, international sweatshops exemplify the way in which the greater openness of the world economy is hurting workers. According to one critic, "as it is now constituted, the world trading system discriminates against workers, especially those in the Third World." Globalization means a transition from (more or less) regulated domestic economies to an unregulated world economy. The superior mobility of capital, and the essentially fixed, immobile nature of world labor, means a fundamental shift in bargaining power in favor of large international corporations. Their global reach permits them to shift production almost costlessly from one location to another. As a consequence, instead of being able to exercise some degree of control over companies operating within their borders, governments are now locked in a bidding war with one another to attract and retain the business of large multinational companies.

The critics allege that international companies are using the threat of withdrawal or withholding of investment to pressure governments and workers to grant concessions. "Today [multinational companies] choose between workers in developing countries that compete against each other to depress wages to attract foreign investment." The result is a race for the bottom—a "destructive downward bidding spiral of the labor conditions and wages of workers throughout the world. . . ." Thus, critics charge that in Indonesia wages are deliberately held below the poverty level or subsistence in order to make the country a desirable location. The results of this competitive dismantling of worker protections, living standards and worker rights are predictable: deteriorating work conditions, declining real incomes for workers, and a widening gap between rich and poor in developing countries. I turn next to the specific charges made by the critics of international sweatshops.

Unconscionable Wages

Critics charge that the companies, by their proxies, are paying "starvation wages" and "slave wages." They are far from clear about what wage level they consider to be appropriate. But they generally demand that companies pay a "living wage." . . . According to Tim Smith, wage levels should be "fair, decent or a living wage for an employee and his or her family." He has said that wages in the maquiladoras of Mexico averaged $35 to $55 a week (in or near 1993) which he calls a "shockingly substandard wage," apparently on the grounds that it "clearly does not allow an employee to feed and care for a family adequately."[11] In 1992, Nike came

in for harsh criticism when a magazine published the pay stub of a worker at one of its Indonesian suppliers. It showed that the worker was paid at the rate of $1.03 per day which was reportedly less than the Indonesian government's figure for "minimum physical need."

Immiserization Thesis

Former Labor Secretary Robert Reich has proposed as a test of the fairness of development policies that "[l]ow-wage workers should become better off, not worse off, as trade and investment boost national income." He has written that "[i]f a country pursues policies that . . . limit to a narrow elite the benefits of trade, the promise of open commerce is perverted and drained of its rationale.[12] A key claim of the activists is that companies actually impoverish or immiserize developing country workers. They experience an absolute decline in living standards. This thesis follows from the claim that the bidding war among developing countries is depressing wages. . . .

Widening Gap Between Rich and Poor

A related charge is that international sweatshops are contributing to the increasing gap between rich and poor. Not only are the poor being absolutely impoverished, but trade is generating greater inequality within developing countries. Another test that Reich has proposed to establish the fairness of international trade is that "the gap between rich and poor should tend to narrow with development, not widen." Critics charge that international sweatshops flunk that test. They say that the increasing GNPs of some developing countries simply mask a widening gap between rich and poor. "Across the world, both local and foreign elites are getting richer from the exploitation of the most vulnerable." And, "The major adverse consequence of quickening global economic integration has been widening income disparity within almost all nations. . . ." There appears to be a tacit alliance between the elites of both first and third world to exploit the most vulnerable, to regiment and control and conscript them so that they can create the material conditions for the elites' extravagant lifestyles.

Collusion with Repressive Regimes

Critics charge that, in their zeal to make their countries safe for foreign investment, third world regimes, notably China and Indonesia, have stepped up their repression. Not only have these countries failed to enforce even the minimal labor rules on the books, but they have also used their military and police to break strikes and repress independent unions. They have stifled political dissent, both to retain their hold on political power and to avoid any instability that might scare off foreign investors. Consequently, critics charge, companies such as Nike are profiting from political repression. "As unions spread in [Korea and Taiwan], Nike shifted its suppliers primarily to Indonesia, China and Thailand, where they could depend on governments to suppress independent union-organizing efforts."

EVALUATION OF THE CHARGES AGAINST INTERNATIONAL SWEATSHOPS

The critics' charges are undoubtedly accurate on a number of points: (1) There is no doubt that international companies are chasing cheap labor. (2) The wages paid by the international sweatshops are—by American standards—shockingly low. (3) Some developing country governments have tightly controlled or repressed organized labor in order to prevent it from disturbing the flow of foreign investment. Thus, in Indonesia, independent unions have been suppressed. (4) It is not unusual in developing countries for minimum wage levels to be lower than the official poverty level. (5) Developing country governments have winked at violations of minimum wage laws and labor rules. However, most jobs are in the informal sector and so largely, outside the scope of government supervision. (6) Some suppliers have employed children or have subcontracted work to other producers who have done so. (7) Some developing country governments deny their people basic political rights. China is the

obvious example; Indonesia's record is pretty horrible but had shown steady improvement until the last two years. But on many of the other counts, the critics' charges appear to be seriously inaccurate. And, even where the charges are accurate, it is not self-evident that the practices in question are improper or unethical, as we see next.

Wages and Conditions

Even the critics of international sweatshops do not dispute that the wages they pay are generally higher than—or at least equal to—comparable wages in the labor markets where they operate. According to the International Labor Organization (ILO), multinational companies often apply standards relating to wages, benefits, conditions of work, and occupational safety and health that both exceed statutory requirements and those practised by local firms. The ILO also says that wages and working conditions in so-called Export Processing Zones (EPZs) are often equal to or higher than jobs outside.[13] The World Bank says that the poorest workers in developing countries work in the informal sector where they often earn less than half what a formal sector employee earns. Moreover, "informal and rural workers often must work under more hazardous and insecure conditions than their formal sector counterparts."[14]

The same appears to hold true for the international sweatshops. In 1996, young women working in the plant of a Nike supplier in Serang, Indonesia, were earning the Indonesian legal minimum wage of 5,200 rupiahs or about $2.28 each day. As a report in the *Washington Post* pointed out, just earning the minimum wage put these workers among higher-paid Indonesians: "In Indonesia, less than half the working population earns the minimum wage, since about half of all adults here are in farming, and the typical farmer would make only about 2,000 rupiahs each day."[15]. . . Also in 1996, a Nike spokeswoman estimated that an entry-level factory worker in the plant of a Nike supplier made five times what a farmer makes. Nike's chairman, Phil Knight, likes to teasingly remind critics that the average worker in one of Nike's Chinese factories is paid more than a professor at Beijing University. There is also plentiful anecdotal evidence from non-Nike sources. A worker at the Taiwanese-owned King Star Garment Assembly plant in Honduras told a reporter that he was earning seven times what he earned in the countryside.[16] In Bangladesh, the country's fledgling garment industry was paying women who had never worked before between $40 and $55 a month in 1991. That compared with a national per capital income of about $200 and the approximately $1 a day earned by many of these women's husbands as day laborers or richshaw drivers.[17] . . .

There is also the mute testimony of the lines of job applicants outside the sweatshops in Guatemala and Honduras. According to Lucy Martinez-Mont, in Guatemala the sweatshops are conspicuous for the long lines of young people waiting to be interviewed for a job.[18] Outside the gates of an industrial park in Honduras . . . "anxious onlookers are always waiting, hoping for a chance at least to fill out a job application [for employment at one of the apparel plants]."[19]

The critics of sweatshops acknowledge that workers have voluntarily taken their jobs, consider themselves lucky to have them, and want to keep them. . . . But they go on to discount the workers' views as the product of confusion or ignorance, and/or they just argue that the workers' views are beside the point. Thus, while "it is undoubtedly true" that Nike has given jobs to thousands of people who wouldn't be working otherwise, they say that "neatly skirts the fundamental human-rights issue raised by these production arrangements that are now spreading all across the world." Similarly, Charles Kernaghan says that "[w]hether workers think they are better off in the assembly plants than elsewhere is not the real issue." Kernaghan, and Jeff Ballinger of the AFL-CIO, concede that the workers desperately need these jobs. But "[t]hey say they're not asking that U.S. companies stop operating in these countries. They're asking that workers be paid a living wage and treated like human beings."[20] Apparently these workers are victims of what Marx called false consciousness, or else they would grasp that they are being exploited. According to Barnet and Cavanagh, "For many workers . . . exploitation is not a concept easily comprehended because the alternative prospects for earning a living are so bleak."[21]

Immiserization and Inequality

The critics' claim that the countries that host international sweatshops are marked by growing poverty and inequality is flatly contradicted by the record. In fact, many of those countries have experienced sharp increases in living standards—for all strata of society. In trying to attract investment in simple manufacturing, Malaysia and Indonesia and, now, Vietnam and China are retracing the industrialization path already successfully taken by East Asian countries such as Taiwan, Korea, Singapore, and Hong Kong. These four countries got their start by producing labor-intensive manufactured goods (often electrical and electronic components, shoes, and garments) for export markets. Over time they graduated to the export of higher value-added items that are skill-intensive and require a relatively developed industrial base.

As is well known, these East Asian countries have achieved growth rates exceeding eight percent for a quarter-century. . . . The workers in these economies were not impoverished by growth. The benefits of growth were widely diffused: These economies achieved essentially full employment in the 1960s. Real wages rose by as much as a factor of four. Absolute poverty fell. And income inequality remained at low to moderate levels. It is true that in the initial stages the rapid growth generated only moderate increases in wages. But once essentially full employment was reached, . . . the increased demand for labor resulted in the bidding up of wages as firms competed for a scarce labor supply.

Interestingly, given its historic mission as a watchdog for international labor standards, the ILO has embraced this development model. It recently noted that the most successful developing economies, in terms of output and employment growth, have been "those who best exploited emerging opportunities in the global economy."[22] An "export-oriented policy is vital in countries that are starting on the industrialization path and have large surpluses of cheap labour." Countries that have succeeded in attracting foreign direct investment (FDI) have experienced rapid growth in manufacturing output and exports. The successful attraction of foreign investment in plant and equipment "can be a powerful spur to rapid industrialization and employment creation.". . .

According to the World Bank, the rapidly growing Asian economies (including Indonesia) "have also been unusually successful at sharing the fruits of their growth."[23] In fact, while inequality in the West has been growing, it has been shrinking in the Asian economies. They are the only economies in the world to have experienced high growth *and* declining inequality, and they also show shrinking gender gaps in education. . . .

Profiting from Repression?

What about the charge that international sweatshops are profiting from repression? It is undeniable that there is repression in many of the countries where sweatshops are located. But economic development appears to be relaxing that repression rather than strengthening its grip. The companies are supposed to benefit from government policies (e.g., repression of unions) that hold down labor costs. However, as we have seen, the wages paid by the international sweatshops already match or exceed the prevailing local wages. Not only that, but incomes in the East Asian economies, and in Indonesia, have risen rapidly. Moreover, even the sweatshops' critics admit that the main factor restraining wages in countries like Indonesia is the state of the labor market. . . . The high rate of unemployment and underemployment acts as a brake on wages: Only about 55 percent of the Indonesian labor force can find more than thirty-five hours of work each week, and about two million workers are unemployed.

The critics, however, are right in saying that the Indonesian government has opposed independent unions in the sweatshops out of fear they would lead to higher wages and labor unrest. But the government's fear clearly is that unions might drive wages in the modern industrial sector *above* market-clearing levels—or, more exactly, farther above market. . . . I think we can safely take at face value its claims that its policies are genuinely in-

tended to help the economy create jobs to absorb the massive numbers of unemployed and underemployed.

LABOR STANDARDS IN INTERNATIONAL SWEATSHOPS: PAINFUL TRADE–OFFS

Who but the grinch could grudge paying a few additional pennies to some of the world's poorest workers? There is no doubt that the rhetorical force of the critics' case against international sweatshops rests on this apparently self-evident proposition. However, higher wages and improved labor standards are not free. After all, the critics themselves attack companies for chasing cheap labor. It follows that, if labor in developing countries is made more expensive (say, as the result of pressure by the critics), then those countries will receive less foreign investment, and fewer jobs will be created there. Imposing higher wages may deprive these countries of the one comparative advantage they enjoy, namely low-cost labor. . . .

By itself that may or may not be ethically objectionable. But these higher wages come at the expense of the incomes and the job opportunities of much poorer workers. As economists explain, higher wages in the formal sector reduce employment there and (by increasing the supply of labor) depress incomes in the informal sector. The case against requiring above-market wages for international sweatshop workers is essentially the same as the case against other measures that artificially raise labor costs, such as the minimum wage. In Jagdish Bhagwati's words: "Requiring a minimum wage in an overpopulated, developing country, as is done in a developed country, may actually be morally wicked. A minimum wage might help the unionized, industrial proletariat, while limiting the ability to save and invest rapidly which is necessary to draw more of the unemployed and nonunionized rural poor into gainful employment and income."[24] The World Bank makes the same point: "Minimum wages may help the most poverty-stricken workers in industrial countries, but they clearly do not in developing nations. . . . The workers whom minimum wage legislation tries to protect—urban formal workers—already earn much more than the less favored majority. . . . And inasmuch as minimum wage and other regulations discourage formal employment by increasing wage and nonwage costs, they hurt the poor who aspire to formal employment."[25]

The story is no different when it comes to labor standards other than wages. If standards are set too high they will hurt investment and employment. The World Bank report points out that "[r]educing hazards in the workplace is costly, and typically the greater the reduction the more it costs. Moreover, the costs of compliance often fall largely on employees through lower wages or reduced employment. As a result, setting standards too high can actually lower workers' welfare. . . ." Perversely, if the higher standards advocated by critics retard the growth of formal sector jobs, then that will trap more informal and rural workers in jobs that are far more hazardous and insecure than those of their formal sector counterparts. . . .

Of course it might be objected that trading off workers' rights for more jobs is unethical. But, so far as I can determine, the critics have not made this argument. Although they sometimes implicitly accept the existence of the trade-off (we saw that they attack Nike for chasing cheap labor), their public statements are silent on the lost or forgone jobs from higher wages and better labor standards. At other times, they imply or claim that improvements in workers' wages and conditions are essentially free: According to Kernaghan, "Companies could easily double their employees' wages, and it would be nothing."

In summary, the result of the ostensibly humanitarian changes urged by critics are likely to be (1) reduced employment in the formal or modern sector of the economy, (2) lower incomes in the informal sector, (3) less investment and so slower economic growth, (4) reduced exports, (5) greater inequality and poverty. . . .

CONCLUSION: THE CASE FOR NOT EXCEEDING MARKET STANDARDS

. . . The business ethicists whose views I summarized at the beginning of this essay—Thomas Donaldson and Richard De George—objected to letting the market alone determine wages and labor standards in multinational companies. Both of them proposed criteria for setting wages that might occasionally "improve" on the outcomes of the market.

Their reasons for rejecting market determination of wages were similar. They both cited conditions that allegedly prevent international markets from generating ethically acceptable results. Donaldson argued that neoclassical economic principles are not applicable to international business because of high unemployment rates in developing countries. And De George argued that, in an unregulated international market, the gross inequality of bargaining power between workers and companies would lead to exploitation.

But this essay has shown that attempts to improve on market outcomes may have unforeseen tragic consequences. We saw how raising the wages of workers in international sweatshops might wind up penalizing the most vulnerable workers (those in the informal sectors of developing countries) by depressing their wages and reducing their job opportunities in the formal sector. . . . As we have seen, above-market wages paid to sweatshop workers may discourage further investment and so perpetuate high unemployment. In turn, the higher unemployment may weaken the bargaining power of workers vis-à-vis employers. Thus, such market imperfections seem to call for more reliance on market forces rather than less. Likewise, the experience of the newly industrialized East Asian economies suggests that the best cure for the ills of sweatshops is more sweatshops. But most of the well-intentioned policies proposed by critics and business ethicists are likely to have the opposite effect.

Where does this leave the international manager? If the preceding analysis is correct, then it follows that it is ethically acceptable to pay market wage rates in developing countries (and to provide employment conditions appropriate for the level of development). That holds true even if the wages pay less than so-called living wages or subsistence or even (conceivably) the local minimum wage. The appropriate test is not whether the wage reaches some predetermined standard but whether it is freely accepted by (reasonably) informed workers. The workers themselves are in the best position to judge whether the wages offered are superior to their next-best alternatives. (The same logic applies *mutatis mutandis* to workplace labor standards.)

Indeed, not only is it ethically acceptable for a company to pay market wages, but it may be ethically unacceptable for it to pay wages that exceed market levels. That will be the case if the company's above-market wages set precedents for other international companies that raise labor costs to the point of discouraging foreign investment. Furthermore, companies may have a social responsibility to transcend their own narrow concern with protecting their brand image and to publicly defend a system that has improved the lot of millions of workers in developing countries.

Notes

1. Peter Jacobi in Martha Nichols, "Third-world families at work: Child labor or child care," *Harvard Business Review* (Jan.–Feb. 1993).

2. Thomas Donaldson, *Ethics of International Business* (New York: Oxford University Press, 1989), 98.

3. Richard De George, *Competing with Integrity in International Business* (New York: Oxford University Press, 1993), 79.

4. De George, *Competing with Integrity*, 356–57.

5. Donaldson, *Ethics of International Business*, 145.

6. Ibid., 101.

7. Ibid., 103.

8. World Bank, *World Development Report 1995. "Workers in an Integrating World Economy"* (New York: Oxford University Press, 1995), 77.

9. Donaldson, *Ethics of International Business*, 115.

10. De George, *Competing with Integrity*, 48.

11. Tim Smith, "The power of business for human rights," *Business & Society Review* (January 1994): 36.

12. Robert B. Reich, "Escape from the global sweatshop: Capitalism's stake in uniting the workers of the world," *Washington Post*, May 22, 1994. Reich's test is intended to apply in developing countries "where democratic institutions are weak or absent."

13. International Labor Organization, *World Employment 1995* (Geneva: ILO, 1995), 73.

14. World Bank, *Workers in an Integrating World Economy*, 5.

15. Keith B. Richburg and Anne Swardson, "U.S. industry overseas: Sweatshop or job source? Indonesians praise work at Nike factory," *Washington Post*, July 28, 1996.

16. Larry Rohter, "To U.S. critics, a sweatshop; for Hondurans, a better life," *New York Times*, July 18, 1996.

17. Marcus Brauchli, "Garment industry booms in Bangladesh," *Wall Street Journal*, August 6, 1991.

18. Lucy Martinez-Mont, "Sweatshops are better than no shops," *Wall Street Journal*, June 25, 1996.

19. Rohter, "To U.S. critics, a sweatshop."

20. William B. Falk, "Dirty little secrets," *Newsday*, June 16, 1996.

21. Richard J. Barnet and John Cavanagh, "Just undo it: Nike's exploited workers," *New York Times*, February 13, 1994.

22. ILO, *World Employment 1995*, 75.

23. World Bank, *The East Asian Miracle* (New York: Oxford University Press, 1993), 2.

24. Jagdish Bhagwati and Robert E. Hudec, eds., *Fair Trade and Harmonization* (Cambridge: MIT Press, 1996), vol. 1, p. 2.

25. World Bank, *Workers in an Integrating World Economy*, 75.

Review and Discussion Questions

1. Explain why you agree or disagree with Maitland's characterization of the controversy over sweatshops as a "non-debate." If the use of international sweatshops is legitimate capitalist behavior, why do the big companies that use them typically avoid debating the issue? What does this fact tell us about global capitalism?

2. What are the four different standards that have been proposed for setting wages and labor standards in international sweatshops? Critically assess each standard. Are you persuaded by Maitland's criticism of Donaldson's test? Why do Donaldson and De George believe the classical liberal standard is inapplicable to poor, developing countries? Explain why you agree or disagree with their arguments.

3. By American standards, wages in international sweatshops are very low, and working conditions appear terrible. Does the fact that foreign workers are eager to take these jobs establish that those wages and conditions are morally acceptable?

4. Critics of international sweatshops believe that their wages and working conditions are morally inadequate, that international sweatshops impoverish local workers and increase inequality

between rich and poor, and that the companies that use them end up colluding with repressive regimes. Maitland disputes each of these points. With regard to each point, with whom do you agree and why?

5. Business ethicists like Donaldson and De George believe that multinational companies operating in the Third World should not leave it to the market alone to determine wages and working conditions. Maitland, to the contrary,

argues that interfering with the market may have tragic consequences. With whom do you agree and why?

6. Maitland believes that international managers act rightly by paying market wages in developing countries and that it may even be wrong for them to pay wages that exceed market levels. What would you do if you were an international manager?

Further Reading for Chapter 4

"Globalisation and Its Critics: A Survey of Globalisation" in *The Economist,* September 29, 2001, is an intelligent, balanced discussion of the world capitalist system.

Robert L. Heilbroner and **Lester C. Thurow**, *Economics Explained,* rev. ed. (New York: Simon & Schuster, 1994) is two respected economists' analysis of how our economy works, what its current difficulties are, and where it is headed.

Paul Krugman, *The Age of Diminished Expectations,* rev. ed. (Cambridge, Mass.: MIT Press, 1994) provides an insightful analysis of today's important economic issues.

Tibor R. Machan, ed., *The Main Debate: Communism Versus Capitalism* (New York: Random House, 1986) is a collection of accessible essays that debate the relative merits of capitalism and socialism.

David Schweickart, *After Capitalism* (Lanham, Md.: Rowman & Littlefield, 2002) is an argument for worker control socialism.

 InfoTrac College Edition: For further information or to conduct research, please go to www.infotrac-college.com.

5

Corporations

Nearly fifty years ago the vice president of Ford Motor Company described the modern business corporation as the dominant institution of American society. Today few observers would disagree. As one of them puts it, "The modern corporation is *the* central institution of contemporary society."[1] As an aggregate, corporations wield awesome economic clout, and the 500 largest U.S. companies constitute at least three-quarters of the American economy. But the dominant role of corporations in our society extends well beyond that. Not only do they produce almost all of the goods and services we buy, but also they and their ethos permeate everything from politics and communications to athletics and religion. And their influence is growing relentlessly around the world—even if the reach of multinational corporations and the negative consequences of globalization are sometimes exaggerated.[2]

By any measure, the biggest corporations are colossi that dominate the earth. Many of them employ tens of thousands of people, and the largest have hundreds of thousands in their ranks. PepsiCo, for example, has about 116,000 employees worldwide, a figure that pales beside General Electric's approximately 340,000 and General Motors's 388,000—not to mention the 1.2 million people who work for Wal-Mart, the world's largest private-sector employer. And their revenues are dazzling. In 2002, for example, General Motors took in more than $177 billion,

Wal-Mart $220 billion, Ford $162 billion, and IBM $86 billion. By comparison, the gross domestic product (GDP) of Norway (that is, the total market value of all the goods and services produced there) was around $37 billion; that of Portugal $44 billion. The state of California, which has far and away the largest annual revenue of any U.S. state, makes about what General Motors makes. But Kansas takes in only around $12.8 billion and Vermont less than a third of that.

And corporations are growing larger and wealthier every year. For example, in 1989 Time Inc. merged with Warner Communications to form Time Warner. Seven years later Time Warner combined with Turner Broadcasting. Then in January 2001, in a move that shook up Wall Street, Time Warner and America Online merged. At a stroke, the new company they created was valued at $350 billion. What does $350 billion mean? It is equivalent to the GDP of India, the fifteenth highest in the world. It is more than the combined GDPs of Hungary, Ukraine, the Czech Republic, New Zealand, Peru, and Pakistan. And it is more than the industrial output of the United Kingdom or the manufacturing output of China.

Like any other modern corporation, in principle AOL Time Warner is a three-part organization, made up of stockholders, who provide the capital, own the corporation, and enjoy liability limited to the amount of their investments; managers, who run the business operations; and employees, who produce the goods and services. However, a corporate giant like AOL Time Warner is less like a single company and more like "a fabulously wealthy investment club with a limited portfolio." Such companies invest in subsidiaries, whose heads, writes business analyst Anthony J. Parisi, "oversee their territories like provincial governors, sovereigns in their own lands but with an authority stemming from the power center. . . . The management committee exacts its tribute (the affiliate's profits from current operations) and issues doles (the money needed to sustain and expand those operations)."[3] In the best-run organizations the management system is highly structured and impersonal. It provides the corporation's overall framework, the formal chain of command, that ensures that the company's profit objectives are pursued.

The emergence of corporate behemoths like AOL Time Warner is one of the more intriguing chapters in the evolution of capitalism. Certainly the political theory of John Locke and the economic theory of Adam Smith admitted no such conglomerates of capital as those that originated in the nineteenth century—as late as 1832 hardly any private firms had ten or more employees[4]—and today dominate America's, even the world's, economic, political, and social life. This book isn't the place to analyze why a people committed to an individualistic social philosophy and a free-competition market economy allowed vast oligopolistic organizations to develop. Rather, the concern here is with the problem of applying moral standards to corporate organizations and with understanding their social responsibilities. After a brief review of the history of the corporation, this chapter looks at the following specific topics:

1. The meaning of *responsibility* and the debate over whether corporations can be meaningfully said to have moral responsibility

2. The controversy between the narrow and the broad views of corporate social responsibility

3. Four key arguments in this debate: the invisible-hand argument, the hand-of-government argument, the inept-custodian argument, and the materialization-of-society argument

4. The importance of institutionalizing ethics within corporations and how this may be done

THE LIMITED–LIABILITY COMPANY

If you ask a lawyer for a definition of *corporation*, you will probably get something like the following: A corporation is a thing that can endure beyond the natural lives of its members and that has incorporators who may sue and be sued as a unit and who are able to consign part of their property to the corporation for ventures of limited liability.[5] *Limited liability* is a key feature of the modern corporation. It means that the members of the corporation are financially liable for corporate debts only up to the extent of their investments.

In addition, limited-liability companies, or corporations, differ from partnerships and other forms of business association in two ways. First, a corporation is not formed simply by an agreement entered into among its first members. It becomes incorporated by being publicly registered or in some other way having its existence officially acknowledged by the law. Second, although a partner is automatically entitled to his or her share of the profits as soon as they are ascertained, the shareholder in a corporation is entitled to a dividend from the company's profits only when it has been "declared." Under U.S. law, dividends are usually declared by the directors of a corporation.

When we think of corporations, we naturally think of giants such as General Motors, Exxon-Mobil, AT&T, General Electric, and IBM, which exert enormous influence over our economy and society. But the local independently owned convenience store may be a corporation, and historically the concept of a corporation has been broad enough to encompass churches, trade guilds, and local governments. Corporations may be either *for* profit or *non*profit-making. Princeton

University, for example, is a nonprofit corporation. Companies like Eastman Kodak, by contrast, aim to make money for shareholders. Corporations may be privately owned or owned (in part or whole) by the government. U.S. corporations are almost entirely privately owned, but Renault of France, for example, was once a publicly owned corporation. A small group of investors may own all the outstanding shares of a privately owned, profit-making corporation (a "privately held" corporation), or its stock may be traded among the general public (a "publicly held" corporation). All companies whose stocks are listed on the New York and other stock exchanges are publicly held corporations.

Several stages mark the evolution of the corporation. The corporate form itself developed during the early Middle Ages, and the first corporations were towns, universities, and ecclesiastical orders. They were chartered by government and regulated by public statute. As corporate bodies, they existed independently of the particular individuals who constituted their membership at any given time. By the fifteenth century, the courts of England had evolved the principle of limited liability—thus setting limits, for example, on how much an alderman of the Liverpool Corporation might be required to pay if the city went bankrupt. During the medieval period, however, the law did not grant corporate status to purely profit-making associations. In those days, something besides economic self-interest had to be seen as uniting the members of the corporation: religion, a trade, shared political responsibilities.

This state of affairs changed during the Elizabethan era, as the actual incorporation of business enterprises began. European entrepreneurs were busy organizing trading voyages to the East and to North America. The East India Company, which epitomizes the great trading companies of this period, was formed in 1600, when Queen Elizabeth I granted to a group of merchants the right to be "one body corporate" and bestowed on it a trading monopoly to the East Indies. In the following decades, numerous other incorporated firms were granted trading monopolies and colonial charters. Much of North America's settlement, in fact, was initially underwritten as a business venture.

Although the earliest corporations typically held special trading rights from the government, their members did not pool capital. Rather, they individually financed voyages using the corporate name and absorbed the loss individually if a vessel sank or was robbed by pirates. But as ships became larger and more expensive, no single buyer could afford to purchase and outfit one, and the loss of a ship would have been ruinous to any one individual. The solution was to pool capital and share liability. Thus emerged the prototype of today's corporations.[6]

The first instance of the corporate organization of a manufacturing enterprise in the United States occurred in 1813, but only after the Civil War did the movement toward the corporate organization of business really begin.[7] The loosening of government restrictions on corporate chartering procedures in the nineteenth century marks this final stage of corporate evolution. Until the mid-1800s, prospective corporations had to apply for charters—in England to the Crown, and in the United States to state governments. Government officials carefully studied applications, rejecting some and burdening others with special conditions (for example, limits on the amount of property that might be owned or restrictions on where it might be held) in order to promote the public good. Critics of the incorporation system charged that it really promoted favoritism, corruption, and unfair monopolies. Gradually, the old system of incorporation was replaced by the system we know today, in which corporate status is granted essentially to any organization that fills out the forms and pays the fees.

Lurking behind this change were two important theoretical shifts. First, underlying the old system was the mercantilist idea that a corporation's activities should advance some specific public purpose. But Adam Smith and, following him, Alexander Hamilton, the first U.S. Secretary of the Treasury, challenged the desirability of a direct tie between business enterprise and public policy. Their idea was that businesspeople should be encouraged to explore their own avenues of enterprise. The "invisible hand" of the market would direct their activities in a socially beneficial direction more effectively than any public official could.

Second, when nineteenth-century reformers argued for changes in incorporation procedures, they talked not only about government favoritism and the advantages of a laissez-faire approach but also about the principle of a corporation's right to exist.[8] Any petitioning body with the minimal qualifications, they asserted, has the right to receive a corporate charter. By contrast, the early Crown-chartered corporations were clearly creations of the state, in accordance with the legal-political doctrine that all corporate status was a privilege bestowed by the state as it saw fit. According to the reformers, however, incorporation is a by-product of the people's right of association, not a gift from the state.

Even though the right of association supports relaxed incorporation procedures, the state must still incorporate companies and guarantee their legal status. Corporations must be recognized by the law as a single agent in order for them to enjoy their rights and privileges. To a large extent, then, the corporation remains, as Chief Justice John Marshall put it in 1819, "an artificial being, invisible, intangible, and existing only in the contemplation of the law."[9]

Corporations are clearly legal agents. But are they also moral agents? And whereas corporations have definite legal responsibilities, what, if any, social and moral responsibilities do they have?

CORPORATE MORAL AGENCY

Some time ago, the citizens of Massachusetts were asked in a referendum whether they wanted to amend the state constitution to allow the legislature to enact a graduated personal income tax. Predictably enough, they said no.

What made an otherwise unremarkable exercise of the initiative process noteworthy was that the First National Bank of Boston and four other businesses in the state wanted to spend money to express opposition to the referendum. The Massachusetts Supreme Judicial Court said they could not, that banks and business corporations are prohibited by law from spending corporate funds to publicize political views that do not materially affect their property, business, or assets. However, the U.S. Supreme Court in a 5 to 4 decision (*First National Bank of Boston v. Bellotti*)[10] struck down the Massachusetts court's decision and thereby defined the free-speech rights of corporations for the first time.

Writing for the majority, Justice Lewis Powell said: "If the speakers here were not corporations, no one would suggest that the state could silence their proposed speech. It is the type of speech indispensable to decision making in a democracy, and this is no less true because the speech comes from a corporation rather than from an individual." In a dissenting opinion, however, Justice Byron R. White said that states should be permitted to distinguish between individuals and corporations. "Ideas which were not a product of individual choice," said White, "are entitled to less First Amendment protection."

Some view the *Bellotti* decision as a blow to consumers and citizens, but the Supreme Court has reaffirmed its position in a number of subsequent cases, most recently in 1999 when it unanimously overturned a federal ban on broadcast advertising of casino gambling. In holding that the First Amendment protects corporations, the Court has blurred the distinction between individuals and corporations. However, in doing so, it has laid a basis for claiming not only that corporations enjoy the same moral and political rights as citizens but also that, because of this, corporations bear the same responsibilities that individual human beings do. In other words, if corporations have the same rights that moral agents have, then, like individuals, they can and should be held morally responsible for their actions.

The problem, of course, is that corporations are not human beings but artificial "persons" created by the law. They are collections of different, changing individuals who set goals and policies and perform specific actions. Given that corporations are not actual persons, in what sense can they be held morally responsible for their actions? Or as Lord Thurlow, an eighteenth-century lawyer, put it, how can you "expect a corporation to have a conscience, when it has no soul to be damned and no body to be kicked?"[11]

At this point, it may help to understand what is meant by "moral responsibility." Often, of course, people are simply said to have a moral responsibility to do whatever it is that morality requires of them. Thus, I may have a moral responsibility to help my neighbor, to keep my promise to Peter, to tell the truth to my colleagues, and to return a misplaced squash racquet to its rightful owner. But reference to an individual's moral responsibility may also have other meanings. Three further senses of "moral responsibility" (or "morally responsible") are relevant here.

Meanings of "Moral Responsibility"

In the first sense, "moral responsibility" refers to holding people morally accountable for some past action. If you leap into a river and rescue a drowning child, you are responsible for the child's being saved and deserve to be praised. If you are playing with your car's radio while you drive and, as a result, cruise through a stop sign, you are responsible for the accident that results; you deserve to be blamed. On the other hand, if the accident resulted from your having suffered a heart attack, you would not be seen as morally responsible (as opposed to legally liable) for it. Morally speaking, the accident was not your fault; we would not criticize you for it. Responsibility in this sense of accountability for actions, therefore, refers to people's meriting blame or praise for particular actions they have performed. Determining responsibility in this sense requires an assessment of causes and various moral considerations.

In the second sense, "moral responsibility" refers to one's accountability, not for a particular past action, but for the care, welfare, or treatment of others as derived from the specific social role that one plays. Thus, parents are responsible for seeing that their children go to school; teachers are responsible for what occurs in their classrooms; doctors are responsible for the treatment of their hospital patients. These specific role responsibilities are typically set by social or organizational conventions.

The third sense of "moral responsibility" refers to one's capacity for making moral or rational decisions on one's own. When parents hire a babysitter for their young children, they implicitly recognize that their children lack the mental and emotional maturity to make competent, informed decisions. Likewise, when the law grants parents almost complete legal control over their young children, it implicitly asserts that children cannot be trusted to make important decisions regarding their own welfare. They are not yet mature enough to be deemed fully responsible for their actions. On the other hand, the babysitter and the parents presumably are morally responsible agents. They have the capacity to make autonomous, informed, and rational moral decisions.

If a person is not morally responsible in the third sense, he or she cannot be considered morally responsible in either of the other two senses. People who cannot make rational or moral decisions on their own cannot be held accountable for their actions or for the welfare of anyone else. On the other hand, if they can make such decisions, then in theory they can be held accountable for their actions and for the welfare of others. The relationship between the third sense of "morally responsible" and the other two, then, is that it is a necessary, although not a sufficient, condition for the others.

The importance of recognizing the logical priority of moral responsibility in the third sense is that once it is established, it is theoretically possible to hold the agent responsible in the other senses. This in turn simplifies the issue of corporate moral responsibility. If corporations, like individuals, can make rational and moral decisions on their own—if they are moral agents—then in theory they can have genuine moral responsibilities to others and can be praised or blamed for their actions.

Although this point seems simple, the task of determining whether corporations can make such decisions remains anything but simple. Immediately, we must ponder whether it makes sense to say that any entity other than individual persons can make decisions in the first place, moral or otherwise.

Can Corporations Make Moral Decisions?

Corporate internal decision (CID) structures amount to established procedures for accomplishing specific goals. For example, consider ExxonMobil's system, as depicted by Anthony J. Parisi:

> All through the Exxon system, checks and balances are built in. Each fall, the presidents of the 13 affiliates take their plan for the coming year and beyond to New York for review at a meeting with the management committee and the staff vice presidents. The goal is to get a perfect corporate fit. Some imaginary examples: The committee might decide that Exxon is becoming too concentrated in Australia and recommend that Esso Eastern move more slowly on that continent. Or it might conclude that if the affiliates were to build all the refineries they are proposing, they would create more capacity than the company could profitably use. One of the affiliates would be asked to hold off, even though, from its particular point of view, a new refinery was needed to serve its market.[12]

The implication here is that any decisions coming out of ExxonMobil's annual sessions are formed and shaped to effect corporate goals, "to get a perfect corporate fit." Metaphorically, all data pass through the filter of corporate procedures and objectives. The remaining distillation constitutes the decision. Certainly the participants actively engage in decision making. But in addition to individual persons, the other major component of corporate decision making consists of the framework in which policies and activities are determined.

The CID structure lays out lines of authority and stipulates under what conditions personal actions become official corporate actions. Some philosophers have compared the corporation to a machine or have argued that because of its structure it is bound to pursue its profit goals single-mindedly. As a result, they claim, it is a mistake to see a corporation as being morally responsible or to expect it to display such moral characteristics as honesty, considerateness, and sympathy. Only the individuals within a corporation can act morally or immorally; only they can be held responsible for what it does.[13]

Others have argued the contrary. The CID structure, like an individual person, collects data about the impact of its actions. It monitors work conditions, employee efficiency and productivity, and environmental impacts. Professors Kenneth E. Goodpaster and John B. Matthews argue that as a result, there is no reason a corporation cannot show the same kind of rationality and respect for persons that individual human beings can. By analogy, they contend, it makes just as much sense to speak of corporate moral responsibility as it does to speak of individual moral responsibility.[14] Thomas Donaldson agrees. He argues that a corporation can be a moral agent if moral reasons enter into its decision making and if its decision-making process controls not just the company's actions but also its structure of policies and rules.[15]

Philosopher Peter French arrives at the same conclusion in a slightly different way.[16] The CID structure, says French, in effect absorbs the intentions and acts of individual persons into a "corporate decision." Perhaps no corporate official intended the course or objective charted by the CID structure, but, French contends, the corporation did. And he believes that these corporate intentions are enough to make corporate acts "intentional" and thus make corporations "morally responsible."

Professor of philosophy Manuel Velasquez demurs. An act is intentional, says Velasquez, only if the entity that formed the intention brings about the act through its bodily movements. "The intentions French attributes to corporations, then, do not mark out corporate acts as intentional because the intentions are attributed to one entity (the corporation) whereas the acts are carried out by another entity (the corporate members)."[17] In Velasquez's view, then, the corporation's members and not the corporation bring about the acts of the corporation. Velasquez concludes that only corporate members, not the corporation itself, can be held morally responsible.

Vanishing Individual Responsibility

Some might argue that whether or not corporations as artificial entities can properly be held morally responsible, the nature and structure of modern corporate organizations allow virtually everyone to share moral accountability for an action—"moral responsibility" in the first sense. But in practice this diffusion of responsibility can mean that no particular person or persons are held morally responsible. This masking of moral accountability may not seem so unusual: Inside and outside corporations, assigning praise and blame can be problematic. But the masking phenomenon does appear to reflect the troubling possibility that the impersonality of the corporate entity so envelops its members that they in effect lose their moral agency. It may be that, for all practical purposes, members of corporate organizations cannot be considered capable of making moral decisions ("moral responsibility" in the third sense) in a corporate context. A case in point is National Semiconductor Corporation.

National Semiconductor, a large California manufacturer of microelectronic circuits, pleaded guilty to a forty-count indictment and was fined $1.75 million for selling parts that were not subjected to the tests prescribed by the contracting party, the Defense Department. In response, the Pentagon proposed suspending National Semiconductor from military sales, a ban that it subsequently lifted after the company promised to conduct such tests in the future. What really rankled the defense agency was that National Semiconductor refused to identify the company employees responsible for the incomplete testing. Why the refusal? National Semiconductor

president Charles Sporck said that no individuals should be singled out for punishment because the incomplete testing was "an industry pattern beyond any one individual's responsibility."[18]

This incident points up the inherent difficulties of assigning personal responsibility to members of corporations. For argument's sake, assume that Sporck is correct: It's virtually impossible to assign moral responsibility to any single individual for the incomplete testing. But why couldn't we rightly expect the appropriate parties to have acted differently? Because, says Sporck, an industrywide pattern placed the acts of noncompliance outside the realm of personal responsibility. If he's right, then CIDs not only gave rise to the industry pattern but effectively paralyzed, if not usurped, the moral agency of corporate members. From here it is an easy step to the conclusion that not only does it make no sense to speak of corporate moral agency, it is equally vacuous to speak of individual moral agency in a corporate context. This conclusion in turn raises the specter of actions without actors in any moral sense—of flouted contracts, as in the case of National Semiconductor, without any morally responsible parties.

There are at least two ways to escape the intellectual discomfort posed by morally actorless actions. One would be to attribute moral agency to corporations and assign responsibilities to them just as we do to individual persons. The other choice, not necessarily incompatible with the first, is to conclude that explanations like Sporck's are nothing but lame excuses to protect blameworthy individuals. It may well be that cases like National Semiconductor really dramatize how easy and automatic it has become to conveniently submerge personal responsibility in the protoplasmic CID structures of modern corporate organizations. Perhaps until CID structures are reconstituted to deal explicitly with noneconomic matters, we can expect more of the same evasion of personal responsibility.

The issue of corporate moral agency undoubtedly will continue to exercise scholars. Meanwhile, the inescapable fact is that corporations are increasingly being accorded the status of biological persons, with all the rights and responsibilities implied by that status. Before it was gobbled up by another corporation, the Continental Oil Company expressed in an in-house booklet the public perception and its implications as follows:

> No one can deny that in the public's mind a corporation can break the law and be guilty of unethical and amoral conduct. Events . . . such as corporate violation of federal laws and failure of full disclosure [have] confirmed that both our government and our citizenry expect *corporations* to act lawfully, ethically, and responsibly.
>
> Perhaps it is then appropriate in today's context to think of Conoco as a *living corporation*; a sentient being whose conduct and personality are the collective effort and responsibility of its employees, officers, directors, and shareholders.[19]

Today, many companies and many of the people inside them accept without hesitation the idea that corporations are moral agents with genuinely moral, not just legal, responsibilities. This point was illustrated recently when Colonial Pipeline of Atlanta published full-page advertisements in several newspapers headlined "We Apologize." The company used the ads to take responsibility for having spilled oil into the Reedy River of South Carolina three years before. True, the ads were part of a plea agreement with the Justice Department for having violated the Clean Water Act (the company also agreed to pay a $7 million fine). Yet the company's words had ethical overtones. As Laura Nash of the Harvard Divinity School comments, they put "moral emotion into what is essentially a legal statement" because "the word 'apologize' . . . admits a sense of shame and humility."[20]

If, then, it makes sense to talk about the social and moral responsibilities of corporations, either in a literal sense or as a shorthand way of referring to the obligations of the individuals that make up the corporation, what are these responsibilities?

CORPORATE RESPONSIBILITY

In 1963 Tennessee Iron & Steel, a subsidiary of United States Steel, was by far the largest employer, purchaser, and taxpayer in Birmingham, Alabama. In the same city at the same time, racial tensions exploded in the bombing of an African-American church, killing four black children. The ugly incident led some to blame U.S. Steel for not doing more to improve race relations, but Roger Blough, chairman of U.S. Steel, defended his company:

> I do not either believe that it would be a wise thing for United States Steel to be other than a good citizen in a community, or to attempt to have its ideas of what is right for the community enforced upon the community by some sort of economic means. . . .
>
> When we as individuals are citizens in a community we can exercise what small influence we may have as citizens, but for a corporation to attempt to exert any kind of economic compulsion to achieve a particular end in the racial area seems to me quite beyond what a corporation can do.[21]

Not long afterward, Sol M. Linowitz, chairman of the board of Xerox Corporation, declared in an address to the National Industrial Conference Board: "To realize its full promise in the world of tomorrow, American business and industry—or, at least, the vast portion of it—will have to make social goals as central to its decisions as economic goals; and leadership in our corporations will increasingly recognize this responsibility and accept it."[22] Thus, the issue of business's corporate responsibility was joined. Just what responsibilities does a corporation have? Is its responsibility to be construed narrowly as merely profit making? Or more broadly to include refraining from harming society and even contributing actively and directly to the public good?

Narrow View: Profit Maximization

As it happened, the year preceding the Birmingham incident had seen the publication of *Capitalism and Freedom*, in which author Milton

Friedman forcefully argued that business has no social responsibilities other than to maximize profits:

> The view has been gaining widespread acceptance that corporate officials and labor leaders have a social responsibility that goes beyond serving the interest of their stockholders or their members. This view shows a fundamental misconception of the character and nature of a free economy. In such an economy, there is one and only one social responsibility of business—to use its resources and engage in activities designed to increase its profits so long as it stays within the rules of the game, which is to say, engages in open and free competition, without deception or fraud. . . . Few trends could so thoroughly undermine the very foundations of our free society as the acceptance by corporate officials of a social responsibility other than to make as much money for their stockholders as possible.[23]

Although from Friedman's perspective the only responsibility of business is to make money for its owners, obviously a business may not do literally anything whatsoever to increase its profits. Gangsters pursue profit maximization when they ruthlessly rub out their rivals, but such activity falls outside what Friedman referred to as "the rules of the game." Harvard professor Theodore Levitt echoed this point when he wrote, "In the end business has only two responsibilities—to obey the elementary canons of face-to-face civility (honesty, good faith, and so on) and to seek material gain."[24]

What, then, are the rules of the game? Obviously, elementary morality rules out deception, force, and fraud, and the rules of the game are intended to promote open and free competition. The system of rules in which business is to pursue profit is, in Friedman's view, one that is conducive to the laissez-faire operation of Adam Smith's "invisible hand" (which was discussed in Chapter 4). Friedman is a conservative economist who believes that by allowing the market to operate with only the minimal restrictions necessary to prevent fraud and force, society will maximize its overall economic well-being. Pursuit of profit is what makes our system go. Anything that dampens this incentive or inhibits its operation will weaken the ability of Smith's "invisible hand" to deliver the economic goods.

Because the function of a business organization is to make money, the owners of corporations employ executives to accomplish this goal, thereby obligating these managers always to act in the interests of the owners. According to Friedman, to say that executives have social responsibilities means that at least sometimes they must subordinate owner interests to some social objective, such as controlling pollution or fighting inflation. They must then spend stockholder money for general social interests—in effect, taxing the owners and spending these taxes on social causes. But taxation is a function of government, not private enterprise; executives are not public employees but employees of private enterprise. The doctrine of social responsibility thus transforms executives into civil servants and business corporations into government agencies, thereby diverting business from its proper function in the social system.

Friedman is critical of those who would impose on business any duty other than that of making money, and he is particularly harsh with those business leaders who themselves take a broader view of their social responsibilities. They may believe that they are defending the free-enterprise system when they give speeches proclaiming that profit isn't the only goal of business or affirming that business has a social conscience and takes seriously its responsibility to provide employment, refrain from polluting, eliminate discrimination, and so on. But these business leaders are shortsighted; they are helping to undermine capitalism by implicitly reinforcing the view that the pursuit of profit is wicked and must be regulated by external forces.[25]

Friedman acknowledges that often corporate activities are described as an exercise of "social responsibility" when, in fact, they are intended simply to advance the company's self-interest. For example, it might be in the long-term self-interest of a corporation that is a major employer in a small town to spend money to enhance the local community by helping to improve its schools, parks, roads, or social services, thereby attracting good employees to the area, reducing the company's wage bill, or improving worker morale and productivity. By portraying its actions as dictated by a sense of social responsibility, the corporation can generate good will as a by-product of expenditures that are entirely justified by self-interest. Friedman has no problem with a company pursuing its self-interest by these means, but he rues the fact that "the attitudes of the public make it in the self-interest [of corporations] to cloak their actions in this way."[26] Friedman's bottom line is that the bottom line is all that counts, and he firmly rejects any notion of corporate social responsibility that would hinder a corporation's profit maximization.

The Broader View of Corporate Social Responsibility

The rival position to that of Friedman and Levitt is simply that business has other obligations in addition to pursuing profits. The phrase *in addition to* is important. Critics of the narrow view do not as a rule believe there is anything wrong with corporate profit. They maintain, rather, that corporations have other responsibilities as well—to consumers, to their employees, and to society at large. If the adherents of the broader view share one belief, it is that corporations have responsibilities beyond simply enhancing their profits because, as a matter of fact, they have such great social and economic power in our society. With that power must come social responsibility. As professor of business administration Keith Davis puts it:

> One basic proposition is that *social responsibility arises from social power*. Modern business has immense social power in such areas as minority employment and environmental pollution. If business has the power, then a just relationship demands that business also bear responsibility for its actions in these areas. Social responsibility arises

from concern about the consequences of business's acts as they affect the interests of others. Business decisions do have social consequences. Businessmen cannot make decisions that are solely economic decisions, because they are interrelated with the whole social system. This situation requires that businessmen's thinking be broadened beyond the company gate to the whole social system. Systems thinking is required.

> Social responsibility implies that a business decision maker in the process of serving his own business interests is obliged to take actions that also protect and enhance society's interests. The net effect is to improve the quality of life in the broadest possible way, however quality of life is defined by society. In this manner, harmony is achieved between business's actions and the larger social system. The businessman becomes concerned with social as well as economic outputs and with the total effect of his institutional actions on society.[27]

Adherents of the broader view, like Davis, stress that modern business is intimately integrated with the rest of society. Business is not some self-enclosed world, like a private poker party. Rather, business activities have profound ramifications throughout society. As a result, although society expects business to pursue its economic interests, business has other responsibilities as well.

Melvin Anshen has cast the case for the broader view in a historical perspective.[28] He maintains that there is always a kind of "social contract" between business and society. This contract is, of course, only implicit, but it represents a tacit understanding within society about the proper goals and responsibilities of business. In effect, in Anshen's view, society always structures the guidelines within which business is permitted to operate in order to derive certain benefits from business activity. For instance, in the nineteenth century society's prime interest was rapid economic growth, which was viewed as the source of all progress, and the engine of economic growth was identified as the drive for profits by unfettered, competitive, private enterprise. This attitude was reflected in the then-existing social contract.

Today, however, society has concerns and interests other than rapid economic growth—in particular, a concern for the quality of life and for the preservation of the environment. Accordingly, the social contract is in the process of being modified. In particular, Anshen writes, "it will no longer be acceptable for corporations to manage their affairs solely in terms of the traditional internal costs of doing business, while thrusting external costs on the public."

In recent years we have grown more aware of the possible deleterious side effects of business activity, or what economists call *externalities*. Externalities are the unintended negative (or in some cases positive) consequences that an economic transaction between two parties can have on some third party. Industrial pollution provides the clearest illustration. Suppose, for example, that a factory makes widgets and sells them to your firm. A by-product of this economic transaction is the waste that the rains wash from the factory yard into the local river, waste that damages recreational and commercial fishing interests downstream. This damage to third parties is an unintended side effect of the economic transaction between the seller and buyer of widgets.

Defenders of the new social contract, like Anshen, maintain that externalities should no longer be overlooked. In the jargon of economists, externalities must be "internalized." That is, the factory should be made to absorb the cost, either by disposing of its waste in an environmentally safe (and presumably more expensive) way or by paying for the damage the waste does downstream. On one hand, basic fairness requires that the factory's waste no longer be dumped onto third parties. On the other hand, from the economic point of view, requiring the factory to internalize the externalities makes sense, for only when it does so will the price of the widgets it sells reflect their true social cost. The real production cost of the widgets includes not just labor, raw materials, machinery, and so

on but also the damage done to the fisheries downstream. Unless the price of widgets is raised sufficiently to reimburse the fisheries for their losses or to dispose of the waste in some other way, then the buyer of widgets is paying less than their true cost. Part of the cost is being paid by the fishing interests downstream.

Some advocates of the broader view go beyond requiring business to internalize its externalities in a narrow economic sense. Keith Davis maintains that in addition to considering potential profitability, a business must weigh the long-range social costs of its activities as well. Only if the overall benefit to society is positive should business act:

> For example, a firm that builds row upon row of look-alike houses may be saving $5,000 on each house and passing along $4,000 of the saving to each buyer, thus serving consumer interests. In the long run, however, this kind of construction may encourage the rapid development of a city slum. In this instance, the lack of long-range outlook may result in serious social costs. . . .

> In sum, the expectation of the social responsibility model is that a detailed cost/benefit analysis will be made prior to determining whether to proceed with an activity and that social costs will be given significant weight in the decision-making process. Almost any business action will entail some social costs. The basic question is whether the benefits outweigh the costs so that there is a net social benefit. Many questions of judgment arise, and there are no precise mathematical measures in the social field, but rational and wise judgments can be made if the issues are first thoroughly explored.[29]

Corporations, Stockholders, and the Promissory Relationship

When asked, most Americans say that a corporation's top obligation is to its employees; others say it is to the community or nation. Only 17 percent think stockholders deserve the highest priority.[30] The advocates of the narrow view argue that the majority's attitude reflects a widespread misunderstanding of the proper relationship between management and the owners (or stockholders) of a corporation. This relationship is a *promissory* relationship, and it imposes an obligation on management that is inconsistent with any social responsibility other than profit maximization. In effect, management agrees to maximize stockholder wealth in return for specific compensation. It's as if you turned $10,000 over to an investment manager and told her: "Make me as much money with this as you can. In return, I'll give you 10 percent of the earnings." If the consultant agrees to the terms, then you would properly consider any whimsical investment of your capital immoral and probably illegal. Of course, she could refuse your offer, thus precluding any such obligation.

Law professor Christopher D. Stone, however, has argued that the relationship between corporate management and its shareholders is not the same as between you and an investment adviser.[31] For one thing, rarely if ever is the purchase of stock in a corporation couched in such explicitly promissory terms. Would-be investors pick companies that look profitable or are likely to grow or whose policies appeal to them, and they buy shares in those firms. Or they ask their stockbrokers simply to purchase what "looks good." Either way, shares are purchased through a broker from current shareholders, who have acquired their shares the same way. Very few investors put their money directly into a corporation; rather, they buy shares that were initially issued years ago.

Other factors further weaken the analogy between holding stock and entrusting money to a financial manager: (1) Most shareholders aren't even aware who the managers of "their" corporations are; (2) most shareholders never have direct contact with management; (3) the complexity of management systems in most modern corporations makes it impossible to pinpoint a single manager or group of managers directly responsible for keeping the promise; (4) the managers were never given a choice, as your adviser was, of refusing to maximize your profits as a shareholder.

But even if a promissory agreement exists between shareholder and management obligating management to make the most possible money for shareholders, must such a promise always be kept? Promises create obligations, but few people would claim that the existence of a promise automatically settles all the moral issues. For example, if I promise to meet you for lunch, I have an obligation to keep that promise. But that obligation is not absolute. We wouldn't regard the promise to meet at a certain time and place as justification for refusing to give cardiopulmonary resuscitation to a heart attack victim. Better to break the promise and save a life than keep the promise and lose a life. The point is that, even if a promise to maximize profits runs from management to shareholders, it's doubtful that the typical shareholder interprets this promise as a mandate for management to maximize profits at all social costs.

Even if such a promise is so construed, we can still ask: Is such an agreement morally binding? After all, a contract to do evil—for example, to kill someone—is invalid. By the same token, a promise that requires management to subordinate all moral considerations— for example, a healthful environment or safe products—to the end of stockholder profits would be immoral. Management, therefore, would not be obliged to honor it and, in fact, should break it.

But then precisely what is the nature of and the basis for the relationship between shareholder and corporate executive? For whom are managers working, and to whom are they responsible: shareholders, society, employees? Friedman argues:

> The whole justification for permitting the corporate executive to be selected by the shareholders is that the executive is an agent serving the interest of his principal. This justification disappears when the corporate executive imposes taxes and spends the proceeds for "social" purposes. He becomes

in effect a public employee, a civil servant, even though he remains in name an employee of a private enterprise.[32]

But is it true that stockholders actually select corporate executives? As long ago as 1932 Adolf Berle and Gardiner Means showed that because stock ownership in large corporations is so dispersed, actual control of the corporation has passed to management.[33] Today, as most business observers acknowledge, management handpicks the board of directors, thus controlling the body that is supposed to police it. "The CEO puts up the candidates; no one runs against them, and management counts the votes," says Nell Minow of the Corporate Library, a corporate watchdog Web site. "We wouldn't deign to call this an election in a third-world country."[34] Even in those rare cases when shareholders put up their own candidates, such proxy fights are expensive, and the incumbent management has the corporate coffers at its disposal to fight them.

As a result, the board of directors typically rubber-stamps the policies and recommendations of management. That's why it's not surprising that in 2000 the directors of Enron ignored shareholder interests and approved paying out $750 million in executive compensation—$140 million of it to its chairman—when the company's entire net income was only $975 million. And how else to explain the lavish retirement packages that boards lavish on former CEOs; these often include a million-dollar annual pension, an expensive apartment, a car and driver, and free use of the company aircraft.[35] True, in the past couple of decades, institutional investors like pension funds and large mutual funds have increased their sway over corporate policies, but it's still exceedingly difficult for shareholders to change policies they don't like because the voting rules are rigged in management's favor.[36]

But even if stockholders did select corporate executives, it wouldn't follow that the executives are therefore bound to act solely in the interest of stockholder profits. Some stockholders, for example, might expect executives to act in an environmentally responsible manner, even if

that means less profit. And why shouldn't stockholders who want to expand the notion of corporate responsibility fight for just that? Friedman dismisses such cases as "some stockholders trying to get other stockholders . . . to contribute against their will to 'social' causes. . . ." But why couldn't it be a case of the activists trying to open debate about the nature of their corporation's social responsibility? Besides, if activist stockholders wish to make their corporations more socially responsible, why don't they have a right to do that as owners?

Friedman believes that if executives "impose taxes on stockholders and spend the proceeds for 'social' purposes, they then become 'civil servants,' and thus should be selected through a political process." He considers such a proposition absurd, or at best socialistic. And yet others contend that corporations are too focused on profits and fear the damage to society when firms are willing to sacrifice all other values on the altar of the bottom line. They don't think it absurd at all that corporations should take a broader view of their social role and responsibilities. They see nothing in the management-stockholder relationship that would morally forbid corporations from doing so.

Even if Friedman's critics are correct and broadening the notion of corporate social responsibility does not violate a promissory relationship between stockholder and management, the discussion is not over. We must still ask: Should the notion of corporate responsibility be broadened?

SHOULD CORPORATE RESPONSIBILITY BE BROADENED?

Four important arguments against broadening corporate responsibility can be conveniently termed the invisible-hand argument, the hand-of-government argument, the inept-custodian argument, and the materialization-of-society argument.[37] Advocates of broadened corporate responsibility base their case in part on a rejection of these arguments.

The Invisible-Hand Argument

Adam Smith claimed that when each of us acts in a free-market environment to promote our own economic interests we are led by an "invisible hand" to promote the general good. Like-minded contemporary thinkers such as Friedman agree. They point out that corporations, in fact, were chartered by states precisely with utility in mind. If businesses are permitted to seek self-interest, their activities will inevitably yield the greatest good for society as a whole. To invite corporations to base their policies and activities on anything other than profit making is to politicize business's unique economic function and to hamper its ability to satisfy our material needs. Accordingly, corporations should not be invited to fight racial injustice, poverty, or pollution, to broaden competition, or to help reduce prices or increase accessibility to products, except insofar as these activities enhance corporate profits.

Yet this argument allows that corporations may still be held accountable for their actions. To the degree that they fulfill or fail to fulfill their economic role, they can be praised or blamed. And they can rightly be criticized for breaking the law or violating the rules of the game, for example, by shady accounting practices that mislead investors about company assets. But corporations should not be held morally responsible for noneconomic matters; to do so would distort the economic mission of business in society and undermine the foundations of the free-enterprise system.

Perhaps within a restricted area of economic exchange, when the parties to the exchange are roughly equal, then each pursuing self-interest can result in the greatest net good. But in the real world of large corporations, the concept of an invisible hand orchestrating the common good often stretches credulity. For example, California deregulated its electricity market to promote competition and give the invisible hand room to operate. But the result was a disaster. Instead of cheaper energy, the state got power blackouts and soaring prices as energy companies adroitly and greedily manipulated the market. Each time the state tried to make the market work better, energy sellers devised new ways to exploit the system. The state government only stanched the crisis by a costly intervention that has basically put it in the power business.[38]

Modern corporations bear about as much resemblance to Smith's self-sufficient farmers and craftspersons as today's military complex bears to the Continental militia. Given the sway they have over our economy and society, large corporations are more like public enterprises than private ones. They also have enormous influence over the lives of their millions of employees. As Professor Virginia Held reminds us, today's modern corporation is "an almost feudal structure in its hierarchical structure and lack of democratic organization."[39] And if an invisible hand has been operating, its movements have been decidedly clumsy. The United States has seen its standard of living stagnate. For many American workers, unemployment is as great a threat as ever. Poverty and hunger persist, and the disparity between rich and poor has yet to narrow.

The Hand-of-Government Argument

Others, such as economist and social critic John Kenneth Galbraith, agree that business's social role is purely economic and that corporations should not be considered moral agents.[40] However, these critics reject the assumption that Smith's "invisible hand" will have the effect of moralizing corporate activities. Left to their own self-serving devices, they warn, modern corporations will enrich themselves while impoverishing society. They will pollute, allow racial and sexual inequalities to fester, deceive consumers, and strive to eliminate competition and keep prices high through oligopolistic practices. They will do these things, the argument continues, because as economic institutions they are quite naturally and properly profit motivated. But what is profitable is not necessarily socially useful or desirable; and what is socially useful and desirable is not always profitable.

Then how is the corporation's natural and insatiable appetite for profit to be controlled? Through government regulation. The strong hand of government, through a system of laws and incentives, can and should bring corporations to heel.

"Do not blame corporations and their top executives" for things like layoffs or urge them to acknowledge obligations beyond the bottom line, writes Robert Reich, Secretary of Labor under President Clinton. "They are behaving exactly as they are organized to behave." He pooh-poohs moral appeals and rejects the idea that CEOs should seek to balance the interests of shareholders against those of employees and their communities. Rather, Reich says, "if we want corporations to take more responsibility" for the economic well-being of Americans, then government "will have to provide the proper incentives."[41]

This advice sounds realistic and is intended to be practical, but it rejects the notion of broadening corporate social responsibility just as firmly as the invisible-hand argument does. That argument puts the focus on the market. Galbraith's and Reich's argument puts it on the visible hand of government. Both positions agree, however, in thinking it misguided to expect or demand that business firms do anything other than pursue profit.

Critics of the hand-of-government view contend that it is a blueprint for big, intrusive government. Moreover, they doubt that government can control any but the most egregious corporate immorality. They fear that many questionable activities will be overlooked, safely hidden within the labyrinth of the corporate structure. Lacking intimate knowledge of the goals and subgoals of specific corporations, as well as of their daily operations, government simply can't anticipate a specific corporation's moral challenges. Rather, it can prescribe behavior only for broad, cross-sectional issues, such as bribery, price-fixing, unfair competition, and the like.

Finally, is government a credible custodian of morality? If recent experience has taught anything, it is that government officials are not always paragons of virtue. Looked at as another organization, government manifests many of the same structural characteristics that test moral behavior inside the corporation. Furthermore, given the awesome clout of corporate lobbyists, one wonders whether, as moral police, government officials will do anything more than impose the values and interests of their most generous financiers. Can we seriously expect politicians to bite the hand that feeds them?

The Inept-Custodian Argument

Some who argue against broadening corporate responsibility say that corporate executives lack the moral and social expertise to make other than economic decisions. To charge them with noneconomic responsibilities would be to put social welfare in the hands of inept custodians. Thus, business analyst Walter Goodman writes: "I don't know of any investment adviser whom I would care to act in my behalf in any matter except turning a profit. . . . The value of these specialists . . . lies in their limitations; they ought not allow themselves to see so much of the world that they become distracted."[42]

It may be true, as Goodman suggests, that corporate members lack the moral or social expertise that a broader view of corporate responsibility would seem to require of them. But more or less the same can be said of most people in organizations: They are not trained moral philosophers or social scientists. And yet we don't ordinarily restrict the activities of these parties, individually or collectively, to carefully circumscribed organizational goals. Physicians, for example, are to provide health care. Is it therefore objectionable for them as physicians to campaign against nuclear arms—indeed, to conceive of their social responsibility in such terms? Is it beyond the role of pediatricians to publicly support legislation requiring the use of seat belts in automobiles? Again, every year the Committee on Public Doublespeak of the National Council of Teachers of English gives a "Doublespeak Award," usually to a business or political leader, for flagrant use of language that pretends to communicate but really does not. Should the committee's members, all of whom are teachers of English, confine their language instruction to the classroom and avoid trying to attract public attention to good, clear, solid language usage?

Of course, the analogy between physicians and English teachers on the one hand and corporate executives on the other is imperfect. For one thing, English teachers know proper language usage, and physicians are qualified to address the health aspects of nuclear war and the health hazards of driving without restraining devices. Furthermore, the social activism of these professionals does not threaten the earnings of their employers. Nevertheless, such comparisons do make the larger point that responsibility is not always limited to narrow professional or occupational concerns. If we consider physician and teacher activities like the aforementioned defensible, then it seems fair to ask: What, if anything, makes the social role of the corporation unique, so that its responsibility and that of those it employs should be confined solely to profit making?

The Materialization-of-Society Argument

Related to the inept-custodian argument is one expressing the fear that if permitted to stray from strictly economic matters, corporate officials will impose their materialistic values on all of society. Thus, broadening corporate responsibility will "materialize" society instead of "moralizing" corporate activity.

More than forty-five years ago, Harvard professor Theodore Levitt expressed this concern:

The danger is that all these things [resulting from having business pursue social goals other than profit making] will turn the corporation into a twentieth century equivalent of the medieval church. . . . For while the corporation also transforms itself in the process, at bottom its outlook will always remain materialistic. What we have then is the frightening spectacle of a powerful economic functional group whose future and perception are shaped in a tight materialistic context of money and things but which imposes its narrow ideas about a broad spectrum of unrelated noneconomic subjects on the mass of man and society. Even if its outlook were the purest kind of good will, that would not recommend the corporation as an arbiter of our lives.[43]

This argument seems to assume that corporations do not already exercise enormous discretionary power over us. But as Keith Davis points out, business already has immense social power. "Society has entrusted to business large amounts of society's resources," says Davis, "and business is expected to manage these resources as a wise trustee for society. In addition to the traditional role of economic entrepreneurship, business now has a new social role of trusteeship. As trustee for society's resources, it serves the interests of all claimants on the organization, rather than only those of owners, or consumers, or labor."[44]

As Paul Camenisch notes, business is already using its privileged position to propagate, consciously or unconsciously, a view of humanity and the good life.[45] Implicit in the barrage of advertisements to which we are subjected daily are assumptions about happiness, success, and human fulfillment. In addition, corporations or industry groups sometimes speak out in unvarnished terms about social and economic issues. For example, ExxonMobil publishes editorial-style advertisements in the newspaper criticizing the Clean Air Act Amendments or arguing against using economic sanctions to promote American foreign policy goals; Philip Morris campaigns publicly for the cigarette legislation it favors; and drug companies such as Eli Lilly, Procter & Gamble, and Bristol-Myers Squibb contribute to conservative think tanks that seek to reduce the regulatory powers of the Food and Drug Administration.[46]

The point here is that business already promotes consumerism and materialistic values. It doesn't hesitate to use its resources to express its views and influence our political system on issues that affect its economic interests. If corporations take a broader view of their social responsibilities, are they really likely to have a more materialistic effect on society, as Levitt suggests, than they do now? It's hard to believe they could. Levitt's view implies that there is some threat to society's values when corporations engage in philanthropy or use their economic and political muscle for other than purely self-interested ends. But society's values are not endangered when Sara Lee donates 2 percent of its pretax profits (nearly $13 million) to charitable causes, mostly cultural institutions and organizations serving disadvantaged people,[47] or when General Mills gives away 3 percent of its domestic pretax earnings ($45 million) to community organizations, donates food to people in need, and helps inner-city companies to get up and running.[48] And where is the "materialization of society" if, instead of advertising on a silly situation comedy that reaches a large audience, a corporation spends the same amount underwriting a science program with fewer viewers solely out of a sense of social responsibility?

INSTITUTIONALIZING ETHICS WITHIN CORPORATIONS

The criticisms of these four arguments against broadening corporate responsibility have led many people inside and outside business to adopt the broader view of corporate responsibility—that the obligations of the modern business corporation extend beyond simply making money for itself. Society grants corporations the right to exist, gives them legal status as separate entities, and permits them to use natural resources. It does this not to indulge the profit appetites of owners and managers but, as Camenisch says, because it needs "the available raw materials transformed into needed goods and services, and because business in its contemporary form has been conspicuously successful in doing just that."[49] In return for its sufferance of corporations, society has the right to expect corporations not to cause harm, to take into account the external effects of their activities, and whenever possible to act for the betterment of society.

The list of corporate responsibilities goes beyond such negative injunctions as "Don't pollute," "Don't misrepresent products," and "Don't

bribe." Included also are affirmative duties like "See that your product or service makes a positive contribution to society," "Improve the skills of your employees," "Seek to hire the disabled," "Give special consideration to the needs of historically disadvantaged groups," "Contribute to the arts and education," "Locate plants in economically depressed areas," and "Improve working conditions." This class of affirmative responsibilities includes activities that are not intrinsically related to the operations of the corporation— responsibilities that each of us, whether individuals or institutions, has simply by virtue of our being members of society.[50] Precisely how far each of us must go to meet these responsibilities depends largely on our capacity to fulfill them, which, of course, varies from person to person, institution to institution. But given their considerable power and resources, large corporations seem better able to promote the common good than individuals or small businesses.

How corporations are to promote the common good cannot be answered very specifically; methods will depend on the type of firm and its particular circumstances. Proponents of broadening corporate responsibility probably would agree that the first step is to create an ethical atmosphere within the corporation. This means making ethical behavior a high priority. How to do this? At least four actions seem called for:

1. Corporations should acknowledge the importance, even necessity, of conducting business morally. Their commitment to ethical behavior should be unequivocal and highly visible, from top management down.

2. Corporations should make a real effort to encourage their members to take moral responsibilities seriously. This commitment would mean ending all forms of retaliation against those who buck the system and rewarding employees for evaluating corporate decisions in their broader social and moral contexts.

3. Corporations should end their defensiveness in the face of public discussion and criticism. Instead, they should actively solicit the views of stockholders, managers, employees, suppli-

ers, customers, and society as a whole. Corporations should invite outside opinions and conduct a candid ethical audit of their organizational policies, priorities, and practices.

4. Corporations must recognize the pluralistic nature of the social system of which they are a part. Society consists of diverse, interlocked groups, all vying to maintain their autonomy and advance their interests. These groups are so related that the actions of one inevitably affect the standing of another on a variety of levels: economic, political, educational, cultural. As part of society, corporations affect many groups, and these groups affect corporations. Failing to realize this, corporations can lose sight of the social framework that governs their relationship with the external environment.

Undoubtedly, other general directives could be added to this list. Still, if corporate responsibility should be expanded, then something like the preceding approach seems basic.

Limits to What the Law Can Do

Critics of the hand-of-government argument question Galbraith's and Reich's view that society should not expect business to behave morally but rather should simply use government to direct business's pursuit of profit in socially acceptable directions. This issue is worth returning to in the present context. All defenders of the broad view of corporate social responsibility believe that more than laissez faire is necessary to ensure that business behavior is socially and morally acceptable. Yet there is a tendency to believe that law is a fully adequate vehicle for this purpose.

Law professor Christopher Stone has argued, however, that there are limits on what the law can be expected to achieve.[51] Three of his points are particularly important. First, many laws, like controls on the disposal of toxic waste, are passed only after there is general awareness of the problem; in the meantime, damage has already been done. The proverbial barn door has been shut only after the horse has left.

Second, formulating appropriate laws and designing effective regulations are difficult. It is hard to achieve consensus on the relevant facts, to determine what remedies will work, and to decide how to weigh conflicting values. In addition, our political system gives corporations and their lobbyists significant input into the writing of laws. Not only that, but the specific working regulations and day-to-day interpretation of the law require the continual input of industry experts. This is not a conspiracy but a fact of life. Government bureaus generally have limited time, staffing, and expertise, so they must rely on the cooperation and assistance of those they regulate.

Third, enforcing the law is often cumbersome. Legal actions against corporations are expensive and can drag on for years, and the judicial process is often too blunt an instrument to use as a way of managing complex social and business issues. In fact, recourse to the courts can be counterproductive, and Stone argues that sometimes the benefits of doing so may not be worth the costs. Legal action may simply make corporations more furtive, breeding distrust, destruction of documents, and an attitude that "I won't do anything more than I am absolutely required to do."

What conclusion should be drawn? Stone's argument is not intended to show that regulation of business is hopeless. Rather, what he wants to stress is that the law cannot do it alone. We do not want a system in which businesspeople believe that their only obligation is to obey the law and that it is morally permissible for them to do anything not (yet) illegal. With that attitude, disaster is just around the corner. More socially responsible business behavior requires, instead, that corporations and the people within them not just respond to the requirements of the law but hold high moral standards—and that they themselves monitor their own behavior.

Ethical Codes and Economic Efficiency

It is, therefore, important that corporations examine their own implicit and explicit codes of conduct and the moral standards that are being propagated to their employees. Yet ethical behavior in the business world is often assumed to come at the expense of economic efficiency. Defenders of the broader view, like Anshen, as well as defenders of the narrow view, like Friedman, seem to make this assumption. Anshen believes that other values should take priority over economic efficiency, whereas Friedman contends business should concern itself only with profit and, in this way, maximize economic well-being. In his important essay "Social Responsibility and Economic Efficiency," Nobel Prize–winning economist Kenneth Arrow has challenged this assumption.[52]

First, any kind of settled economic life requires a certain degree of ethical behavior, some element of trust and confidence. Much business, for instance, is conducted on the basis of oral agreements. In addition, says Arrow, "there are two types of situation in which the simple rule of maximizing profits is socially inefficient: the case in which costs are not paid for, as in pollution, and the case in which the seller has considerably more knowledge about his product than the buyer."

The first type of situation relates to the demand that corporations "internalize their externalities." In the second situation, in which the buyer lacks the expertise and knowledge of the seller, an effective moral code, either requiring full disclosure or setting minimal standards of performance (for example, the braking ability of a new automobile), enhances rather than diminishes economic efficiency. Without such a code, buyers may purchase products or services they don't need. Or because they don't trust the seller, they may refrain from purchasing products and services they do need. Either way, from the economist's point of view the situation is inefficient.

An effective professional or business moral code—as well as the public's awareness of this code—is good for business. Most of us, for example, have little medical knowledge and are thus at the mercy of doctors. Over hundreds of years, however, a firm code of ethical conduct has developed in the medical profession. As a result, people generally presume that their

physician will perform with their welfare in mind. They rarely worry that their doctor might be taking advantage of them or exploiting them with unnecessary treatment. By contrast, used-car dealers have historically suffered from a lack of public trust.

For a code to be effective it must be realistic, Arrow argues, in the sense of connecting with the collective self-interest of business. And it must become part of the corporate culture, "accepted by the significant operating institutions and transmitted from one generation of executives to the next through standard operating procedures [and] through education in business schools."

For both Arrow and Stone, then, the development of feasible and effective business and professional codes of ethics must be a central focus of any effort to enhance or expand corporate responsibility. The question is how to create a corporate atmosphere conducive to moral decision making.

Corporate Moral Codes

What can be done to improve the organizational climate so individual members can reasonably be expected to act ethically? If those inside the corporation are to behave morally, they need clearly stated and communicated ethical standards that are equitable and enforced. This development seems possible only if the standards of expected behavior are institutionalized—that is, only if they become a fixture in the corporate organization. To institutionalize ethics within corporations, professor Milton Snoeyenbos suggests that top management should (1) articulate the firm's values and goals, (2) adopt an ethical code applicable to all members of the company, (3) set up a high-ranking ethics committee to oversee, develop, and enforce the code, and (4) incorporate ethics training into all employee-development programs.[53]

The company's code of ethics should not be window dressing or so general as to be useless. It should set reasonable goals and subgoals, with an eye on blunting unethical pressures on subordinates. In formulating the code, the top-level ethics committee should solicit the views of corporate members at all levels regarding goals and subgoals, so that the final product articulates "a fine-grained ethical code that addresses ethical issues likely to arise at the level of subgoals."[54] Moreover, the committee should have full authority and responsibility to communicate the code and decisions based on it to all corporate members, clarify and interpret the code when the need arises, facilitate the code's use, investigate grievances and violations of the code, discipline violators and reward compliance, and review, update, and upgrade the code.

To help employees in ethically difficult situations, a good corporate ethics program must be user friendly. It should provide a support system with a variety of entry points, one that employees feel confident about using.[55] In addition, part of all employee-training programs should be devoted to ethics. At a minimum, this should include study of the code, review of the company's procedures for handling ethical problems, and discussion of employer and employee responsibilities and expectations. Snoeyenbos and others believe that institutionalizing ethics within the corporation in these ways, when supplemented by the development of industrywide codes of ethics to address issues beyond a particular firm, will go far toward establishing a corporate climate conducive to individual moral decision making.

Corporate Culture

During the past two decades, organizational theorists and writers on business management have increasingly emphasized "corporate culture" as the factor that makes one company succeed while another languishes. Although intangible in comparison with things like sales revenue and profit margin, corporate culture is often the key to a firm's success.

What is corporate culture? One writer describes it as "the shared beliefs top managers have in a company about how they should manage themselves and other employees, and how they should conduct their business(es). These beliefs are often invisible to the top managers but have a major impact on their thoughts and actions."[56] Another writer puts it this way: "Culture is the pattern of shared values and beliefs that gives members of an institution meaning and provides them with rules for behavior in their organization."[57] W. Brooke Tunstall, an assistant vice president of AT&T, provides a fuller definition. He describes corporate culture as "a general constellation of beliefs, mores, customs, value systems and behavioral norms, and ways of doing business that are unique to each corporation, that set a pattern for corporate activities and actions, and that describe the implicit and emergent patterns of behavior and emotions characterizing life in the organization."[58]

Corporate culture may be both explicit and implicit. The formal culture of a corporation, as expressed in idealized statements of values and norms, should also be distinguished from the informal culture that shapes beliefs, values, and behavior. In addition, there may be multiple and overlapping cultures within an organization because employees have different backgrounds, work in different divisions of the organization, and may be subject to different systems of rewards and sanctions.[59]

Organizational theorists emphasize the importance of monitoring and managing corporate culture—beginning with an attempt to understand each corporation's distinctive culture—to prevent dysfunctional behavior and processes. As one consultant puts it, "A corporation's culture is what determines how people behave when they are not being watched."[60] If management does not make explicit the values and behavior it desires, the culture will typically develop its own norms, usually based on the types of behavior that lead to success within the organization. Thus, the desired values must be communicated and transmitted throughout the organization. Conduct congruent with them must be rewarded and conduct inconsistent with them sanctioned. Overlooking behavior that contradicts the desired norms can have the effect of encouraging and even rewarding it.

These points are crucial when it comes to corporate social responsibility. Management needs to understand the real dynamics of its own organization. At Sears, for example, new minimum work quotas and productivity incentives at its auto centers created a high-pressure environment that led employees to mislead customers and sell them unnecessary parts and services, from brake jobs to front-end alignments.[61] Thus, it is necessary for socially responsible executives to ask: How do people get ahead in the company? What conduct is actually rewarded, what values are really being instilled in employees? Andrew C. Sigler, chairman of Champion International, stresses this point: "Sitting up here in Stamford, there's no way I can affect what an employee is doing today in Texas, Montana, or Maine. Making speeches and sending letters just doesn't do it. You need a culture and peer pressure that spells out what is acceptable and isn't and why. It involves training, education, and follow-up."[62]

Internal or external corporate responsibility audits can help close the gap between stated values, goals, and mission, on the one hand, and reality on the other.[63] Another aspect of follow-up is strict enforcement. Chemical Bank, for instance, has fired employees for violations of the company's code of ethics even when nothing illegal was done. Xerox has dismissed people for minor manipulation of records and the padding of expense accounts. (By contrast, some of the nation's most prestigious stock brokerage firms employ salespeople with long records of violating securities laws.[64]) Executives at both Xerox and General Mills also emphasize that civic involvement is a crucial part of corporate ethics. As one General Mills executive puts it: "It's hard to imagine that a person who reads to the blind at night would cheat. . . ."[65]

Johnson & Johnson is widely seen as a model of corporate responsibility, especially because of its decisive handling of the Tylenol crisis of 1982, when seven people in the Chicago area died from cyanide-laced Extra-Strength Tylenol capsules. The company immediately recalled 31 million bottles of Tylenol from store shelves across the nation and notified 500,000 doctors and hospitals about the contaminated capsules. A toll-free consumer hotline was set up the first week of the crisis, and consumers were offered the opportunity to replace Tylenol capsules with a free bottle of Tylenol tablets. Johnson & Johnson was also open with the public instead of being defensive about the deaths. Accurate information was promptly released, and domestic employees and retirees were kept updated on developments. The chairman of the company appeared on the talk show *Donahue* and on *60 Minutes* to answer questions about the crisis, and other executives were interviewed by *Fortune* and *The Wall Street Journal.*

Despite the setback—the recall alone cost Johnson & Johnson $50 million after taxes—Tylenol rebounded within a year, in large part because the public never lost faith in Johnson & Johnson. The company itself credits its sixty-year-old, one-page statement of values, known as the Credo, with enabling it to build the employee trust necessary for maintaining a firm corporate value system. The Credo acknowledges the company's need to make a sound profit while addressing its obligations to provide a quality product, to treat its employees fairly and with respect, and to be a good corporate citizen, supporting the community of which it is a member.

The Credo is "the most important thing we have in this company," says chairman Ralph Larsen. But creating and maintaining a morally sound corporate culture is an ongoing task, and Johnson & Johnson hasn't always been able to live up to its own values. In 1995, for instance, the company agreed to pay $7.5 million in fines and costs after admitting that wayward employees had shredded papers to hinder a federal probe into the marketing of an acne cream. "There was no excuse," admits Larsen. "But it is a huge undertaking to spread our values around the world."[66]

SUMMARY

1. What we know as the modern business corporation has evolved over several centuries,

and incorporation is no longer the special privilege it once was.

2. Corporations are legal entities, with legal rights and responsibilities similar but not identical to those enjoyed by individuals. Business corporations are limited-liability companies—that is, their owners or stockholders are liable for corporate debts only up to the extent of their investments.

3. The question of corporate moral agency is whether corporations are the kind of entity that can have moral responsibilities. There are at least three senses of "morally responsible." If corporations can make rational and moral decisions, then they can be held morally blameworthy or praiseworthy for their actions. Philosophers disagree about whether the corporate internal decision (CID) structure makes it reasonable to assign moral responsibility to corporations.

4. This problem is compounded by the difficulty of assigning moral responsibility to individuals inside corporations.

5. Despite these controversies, the courts and the general public find the notion of corporate responsibility useful and intelligible—either in a literal sense or as shorthand for the obligations of individuals in the corporation.

6. The debate over corporate responsibility is whether it should be construed narrowly to cover only profit maximization or more broadly to include refraining from socially undesirable behavior and contributing actively and directly to the public good.

7. Proponents of the narrow view, such as Milton Friedman, contend that diverting corporations from the pursuit of profit makes our economic system less efficient. Business's only social responsibility is to make money within the rules of the game. Private enterprise should not be forced to undertake public responsibilities that properly belong to government.

8. Defenders of the broader view maintain that corporations have additional responsibilities because of their great social and economic power. Business is governed by an implicit social contract, which requires it to operate in ways that benefit society. In particular, corporations must take responsibility for the unintended side effects of their business transactions (externalities) and weigh the full social costs of their activities.

9. Advocates of the narrow view stress that management has a promissory relation with the owners (stockholders) of a corporation, which obligates it to focus on profit maximization alone. Critics challenge this argument.

10. Should corporate responsibility be broadened? Four arguments against doing so are the invisible-hand argument, the hand-of-government argument, the inept-custodian argument, and the materialization-of-society argument. Finding flaws with each of these arguments, critics claim there is no solid basis for restricting corporate responsibility to profit making.

11. Those proposing broader corporate responsibilities see the creation of an ethical atmosphere within the corporation as an important first step. Essential to this atmosphere are acknowledgment of the critical importance of ethics, encouragement of morally responsible conduct by all employees, openness to public discussion and review, and recognition of the pluralistic nature of our social system.

12. Corporations and the people who make them up must have high moral standards and monitor their own behavior because there are limits to what the law can do to ensure that business behavior is socially and morally acceptable.

13. All settled economic life requires trust and confidence. The adoption of realistic and workable codes of ethics in the business world can actually enhance business efficiency. This is particularly true when there

is an imbalance of knowledge between the buyer and the seller.

14. To improve the organizational climate so individuals can reasonably be expected to act ethically, corporations should adopt an ethical code, set up a high-ranking ethics committee, and include ethics training in their employee-development programs. Attention to corporate culture is also crucial to the successful institutionalization of ethics inside an organization.

CASE 5.1

Exxon and Captain Hazelwood

On the dark night of March 23–24, 1989, an Exxon Corporation supertanker, named the *Exxon Valdez*, ran aground on Bligh Reef in Alaska's Prince William Sound. It ruptured and began emptying 10.8 million gallons of crude oil into the sea, despoiling a coastline the length of California's and creating the worst oil spill the nation has ever seen. More than 2,800 sea otters; 250,000 seabirds; 22 killer whales; and many other species of wildlife died as a result.[67]

Many of the *Exxon Valdez*'s crew members that night were exhausted from working an average of 140 hours of overtime a month, a routine experience on Exxon ships. The ship itself carried a crew of only twenty, a third smaller than on older tankers. The Coast Guard had approved this reduction after oil companies convinced it that ships in the class of the *Exxon Valdez* did not need larger crews. Still, modern instruments did not prevent the crew and officers from going long stretches with little or no sleep and from working extensive overtime.

Exxon policy and federal regulations forbid officers from drinking any alcoholic beverage within four hours of embarking or from having drugs or alcohol on board. Exxon relies on the captains of its ships to enforce these regulations, but the captain of the *Exxon Valdez*, Joseph J. Hazelwood, may not have been the best person for this job. He was treated for alcohol abuse in 1985, and he was not licensed to drive a car in his home state of New York because of a conviction for drunken driving. Witnesses report his drinking on voyages. And before the ship departed late on March 23, Captain Hazelwood and several of the ship's officers allegedly spent much of the day boozing in town. Hazelwood and the ship's chief engineer admit to having drinks up until an hour and a half before departure, and Hazelwood failed an initial blood-alcohol test given him by the Coast Guard after the spill. (A year later, however, an Anchorage, Alaska, jury acquitted Hazelwood of the criminal charge of operating a watercraft while under the influence of alcohol. But he was convicted of a misdemeanor—negligent discharge of oil—although he unsuccessfully appealed the verdict for years. Since 1999, he has been obliged to spend 200 hours each summer for five years in a community service program, picking up trash off the streets of Anchorage.)

The *Exxon Valdez* departed at 11:06 P.M. It was initially under the command of an independent harbor pilot, Captain William Murphy. His job done, he left the ship at 11:24 P.M., returning control of it to Hazelwood. He later said that he smelled liquor on Captain Hazelwood's breath, but Murphy did not report it. Hazelwood took command and radioed the Coast Guard that he was turning southeast into the incoming shipping lane to avoid ice.

The ship was then put on automatic pilot, something that Coast Guard regulations and Exxon policy say should be done only in the open sea.

A little later, after Third Mate Gregory T. Cousins plotted the ship's course, Hazelwood ordered him to change direction, take the ship off automatic pilot, and steer it due south through the incoming shipping lane into the shallower waters around Busby Island (a few miles before Bligh Reef). When the ship neared a lighted buoy by the island, Cousins was then to turn it back into the inbound shipping lane. The Coast Guard was not notified of this change in course. Meanwhile, Coast Guard radar, although capable of tracking the ship that far, lost touch with the ship when it temporarily went off the screen. With that visual link cut, the Exxon crew and the Coast Guard failed to stay in radio contact.

At this point, half an hour before the ship ran aground, Hazelwood went to his cabin, turning the *Exxon Valdez* over to the third mate. Cousins did not have a license to pilot the tanker, but turning the wheel over to unqualified officers appears to have been a common practice on Exxon tankers. Third Mate Cousins later testified that he ordered the ship to turn in the area of the buoy, as instructed by Hazelwood, at 11:55 P.M. However, the ship's recorder shows that the turn was not made until about six minutes later, around the time that a lookout (posted on the bridge instead of 800 feet farther forward on the bow) reported a flashing light. That was the light marking Bligh Reef. Cousins ordered a hard right rudder to avoid the reef, but it was too late. At 12:04 A.M., the *Exxon Valdez* ran aground.

Nearly a quarter of our domestic oil comes through the glaciers surrounding Prince William Sound, but twelve uneventful years of tanker traffic had numbed state regulators, oil company executives, and federal officials to the possibility of an environmental disaster at the edge of the last American wilderness. The Alyeska Pipeline Service Company, a consortium of seven oil companies that includes Exxon, had estimated that a spill of this magnitude could happen only once every twenty-four years. In 1981, the consortium dismissed its oil-spill response team, the only unit set up exclusively to clean up spills in Prince William Sound. Since 1984, the Coast Guard, which watches over marine traffic carrying oil, had also been scaling back. For instance, as a result of budget cuts, its 100,000-watt radar had been replaced with a 50,000-watt unit.

Alyeska was obligated to have a specific amount of cleanup equipment at the dock and to have any large spill contained within five hours of the accident. But it took fourteen hours for a barge carrying cleanup equipment to arrive at the accident site, and even then an Exxon official turned down a request to circle the tanker with a containment boom. Exxon's elaborate oil-spill response plan is twenty-eight volumes thick, but Dennis Kelso, Alaska's environment commissioner, calls this document "the biggest piece of maritime fiction since *Moby Dick.*" Yet it was Kelso's office that had approved it.

Instead of attempting, during the calm weather of the first two days, to encircle the oil with booms and scoop it up with skimmers (as called for in its plan), Exxon decided to use chemical dispersants to break the oil into tiny droplets that would easily dissolve. But it was very slow in doing so. Later, the chairman of Exxon, Lawrence Rawl, contended that the company was not granted permission to use the dispersants during the first two days, when up to half of the spilled oil could have been taken care of. But Exxon never had an adequate supply of chemicals on hand in Alaska; only 69 barrels were available for a job that called for nearly 10,000, and even six days after the spill Exxon still had only a fraction of the number of barrels needed. And contrary to Rawl's claim that the government had failed to approve the deployment of these chemicals, the records and testimony at a federal inquiry establish that their use had, in fact, been approved in advance.

In retrospect, some critics thought that Exxon should have used double-hulled tankers, as had been proposed in the 1970s as a safeguard in the initial planning of the Alaska pipeline. Double-hulled tankers lower the risk of a spill, but there are trade-offs. They are more expensive to build and carry only 60 percent as much oil as single-hulled tankers. That means more tanker traffic, more docking facilities, and more opportunity for human error.[68]

In October 1991, two-and-a-half years after the spill, Exxon pled guilty to three misdemeanors and agreed to pay $900 million in civil damages and a $125-million criminal fine to settle federal and state charges against it. The settlement with the state of Alaska and the federal government called for Exxon, which had an annual revenue of over $100 billion and annual profits of around $6 billion, to make payments over a ten-year period. In addition, Exxon had by then also spent an estimated $2.5 billion on cleanup efforts. "We believe that Exxon's response to that spill was a unique show of corporate responsibility," says Exxon attorney Pat Lynch.[69]

Not everyone agrees. Local fishermen complain that Prince William Sound is still not what it once was. In 1994, an Alaska jury sided with them, ordering Exxon to pay the fishermen $287 million. It also hit Exxon with an astounding $5 billion in punitive damages for the company's recklessness in causing the spill. But the story doesn't end there. In 1996, it came to light that in 1991 Exxon had struck a secret settlement deal with seven seafood processors, in which they promised to turn over to Exxon any money they received from awards of punitive damages. Exxon's new chief, Lee Raymond, lied about this in court. This news sent Federal Judge H. Russell Holland through the roof. He criticized Exxon for its "Jekyll and Hyde" conduct—for "behaving laudably in public and deplorably in private":

> Had the jury been told the whole story, and learned that Exxon had arranged a secret deal to capture nearly 15 percent of the punitive damages, the jury may very well have increased the punitive damages by 15 percent. . . . Public policy will not allow Exxon to use a secret deal to undercut the jury system, the court's numerous orders upholding the punitive ver-

dict, and society's goal in punishing Exxon's recklessness.[70]

Meanwhile, the company has yet to pay any of the 1994 judgment, having challenged it in an appeals process that has dragged on for years.

Discussion Questions

1. Describe the actions, decisions, and policies that contributed to the *Exxon Valdez*'s despoiling of Alaska's coastline. How would you compare the roles played by Captain Hazelwood and by Chairman Rawl?

2. Is Exxon as a corporate agent morally responsible for what happened, or are individuals inside the company responsible? Should a specific person or persons be singled out for blame, or should the entire organization be held accountable?

3. Who or what, in your view, bears prime responsibility for this disaster?

4. What, if anything, does this episode reveal about Exxon's sense of social responsibility? Do you think the company has a narrow or a broad view of its corporate responsibility?

5. Are there specific organizational policies, attitudes, goals, or norms at Exxon that may have contributed to this disaster? If you were the CEO at Exxon, what changes, if any, would you make?

6. How might such environmental catastrophes be avoided in the future? Is greater government regulation called for?

7. Assess Exxon's response to the oil spill. In your view, what should Exxon pay for the damage it caused? How could a fair legal settlement be determined? Should the corporation or its officers be subject to criminal punishment?

CASE 5.2

Living and Dying
with Asbestos

Asbestos is a fibrous mineral used for fireproofing, electrical insulation, building materials, brake linings, and chemical filters. If exposed long enough to asbestos particles—usually ten or more years—people can develop a chronic lung inflammation called asbestosis, which makes breathing difficult and infection easy. Also linked to asbestos exposure is mesothelioma, a cancer of the chest lining that sometimes doesn't develop until forty years after the first exposure. Although the first major scientific conference on the dangers of asbestos was not held until 1964, the asbestos industry knew of its hazards more than sixty years ago.[71]

As early as 1932, the British documented the occupational hazards of asbestos dust inhalation. Indeed, on September 25, 1935, the editors of the trade journal *Asbestos* wrote to Sumner Simpson, president of Raybestos-Manhattan, a leading asbestos company, asking permission to publish an article on the dangers of asbestos. Simpson refused and later praised the magazine for not printing the article. In a letter to Vandivar Brown, secretary of Johns-Manville, another asbestos manufacturer, Simpson observed: "The less said about asbestosis the better off we are." Brown agreed, adding that any article on asbestosis should reflect American, not English, data.

In fact, American data were available, and Brown, as one of the editors of the journal, knew it. Working on behalf of Raybestos-Manhattan and Johns-Manville and their insurance carrier, Metropolitan Life Insurance Company, Anthony Lanza had conducted research between 1929 and 1931 on 126 workers with three or more years of asbestos exposure. But Brown and others were not pleased with the paper Lanza submitted to them for editorial review. Lanza, said Brown, had failed to portray asbestosis as milder than silicosis, a lung disease caused by long-term inhalation of silica dust and resulting in chronic shortness of breath.

Under the then-pending Workmen's Compensation law, silicosis was categorized as a compensable disease. If asbestosis was worse than silicosis or indistinguishable from it, then it, too, would have to be covered. Apparently Brown didn't want this and thus requested that Lanza depict asbestosis as less serious than silicosis. Lanza complied and also omitted from his published report the fact that more than half the workers examined—67 of 126—were suffering from asbestosis.

Meanwhile, Sumner Simpson was writing F. H. Schulter, president of Thermoid Rubber Company, to suggest that several manufacturers sponsor additional asbestos experiments. The sponsors, said Simpson, could exercise oversight prerogatives; they "could determine from time to time after the findings are made whether we wish any publication or not." Added Simpson: "It would be a good idea to distribute the information to the medical fraternity, providing it is of the right type and would not injure our companies." Lest there be any question about the arbiter of publication, Brown wrote to officials at the laboratory conducting the tests:

> It is our further understanding that the results obtained will be considered the property of those who are advancing the required funds, who will determine whether, to what extent and in what manner they shall be made public. In the event it is deemed desirable that the results be made public, the manuscript of your study will be submitted to us for approval prior to publication.

Industry officials were concerned with more than controlling public information flow. They also sought to deny workers early evidence of their asbestosis. Dr. Kenneth Smith, medical director of a Johns-Manville plant in Canada, explained why seven workers he found to have asbestosis should not be informed of their disease:

It must be remembered that although these men have the X-ray evidence of asbestosis, they are working today and definitely are not disabled from asbestosis. They have not been told of this diagnosis, for it is felt that as long as the man feels well, is happy at home and at work, and his physical condition remains good, nothing should be said. When he becomes disabled and sick, then the diagnosis should be made and the claim submitted *by the Company.* The fibrosis of this disease is irreversible and permanent so that eventually compensation will be paid to each of these men. But as long as the man is not disabled, it is felt that he should not be told of his condition so that he can live and work in peace and the Company can benefit by his many years of experience. Should the man be told of his condition today there is a very definite possibility that he would become mentally and physically ill, simply through the knowledge that he has asbestosis.

When lawsuits filed by asbestos workers who had developed cancer reached the industry in the 1950s, Dr. Smith suggested that the industry retain the Industrial Health Foundation to conduct a cancer study that would, in effect, squelch the asbestos–cancer connection. The asbestos companies refused, claiming that such a study would only bring further unfavorable publicity to the industry and that there wasn't enough evidence linking asbestos and cancer industrywide to warrant it.

Shortly before his death in 1977, Dr. Smith was asked whether he had ever recommended to Johns-Manville officials that warning labels be placed on insulation products containing asbestos. He testified as follows:

The reasons why the caution labels were not implemented immediately, it was a business decision as far as I could understand. Here was a recommendation, the corporation is in business to make, to provide jobs for people and make money for stockholders and they had to take into consideration the effects of everything they did, and if the application of a caution label identifying a product as hazardous would cut out sales, there would be serious financial implications. And the powers that be had to make some effort to judge the necessity of the label vs. the consequences of placing the label on the product.

Dr. Smith's testimony and related documents have figured prominently in hundreds of asbestos-related lawsuits. In the 1980s these lawsuits swamped Manville (as Johns-Manville is now called) and forced the company into bankruptcy. A trust fund valued at $2.5 billion was set up to pay Manville's asbestos claimants. To fund the trust, shareholders were required to surrender half the value of their stock, and the company had to give up much of its projected earnings over the next twenty-five years. Claims, however, soon overwhelmed the trust, which ran out of money in 1990. After various legal delays, the trust fund's stake in Manville was increased to 80 percent, and Manville was required to pay it an additional $300 million in dividends. The trust fund itself was restructured to pay the most seriously ill victims first, but average payments to victims were lowered significantly—from $145,000 to $43,000.[72]

Meanwhile, in 1997 the U.S. Supreme Court struck down a landmark $1.3-billion class-action settlement between some twenty former asbestos producers and their injured workers. A few years earlier, the companies involved had approached the workers' lawyers and agreed to settle thousands of existing health complaints, in a deal that netted the lawyers millions of dollars in fees. Then the lawyers and companies devised a settlement agreement involving people who had not filed claims against the company by a specified date. It was this aspect of the settlement that was the main sticking point. Although a lower court had praised the settlement for "forging a solution to a major social problem," the Supreme Court balked at the fact that future claimants were not allowed to opt out of the agreement. A class-action agreement, the Court said, was not the best way to resolve thousands of different claims involving different factual and legal issues.[73] In 1999, the Court rejected a second proposed settlement. As a result, thousands of lawsuits that would have been settled by the agreements continue to clog federal dockets.

The situation is made worse by the fact that in the last few years asbestos-related litigation has expanded exponentially—spun out of control, some would say—as workers who did not make asbestos, but only handled it every now and then or worked in the vicinity of those who did, are suing companies that never made the stuff but only used it. Altogether more than 200,000 cases are pending nationwide against more than 1,000 companies.[74] In fact, of the 91,000 cases filed in 2001, only 6 percent of the plaintiffs have actually suffered from asbestos-related diseases. Almost all of the other claimants are seeking compensation for anxiety they have experienced over the risk that they might have asbestosis.[75]

Discussion Questions

1. How is this case relevant to the debate over corporate social responsibility? Assess the actions of the asbestos companies from the perspective of both the narrow and the broad views of corporate social responsibility.

2. Should the asbestos companies be seen as moral agents capable of making moral decisions and deserving of praise or blame? Or should only the individual people involved be considered morally responsible agents?

3. Simpson and Brown presumably acted in what they thought were the best financial interests of their companies. Nothing they did was illegal. On what grounds, if any, are their actions open to criticism?

4. If you were a stockholder in Raybestos-Manhattan or Johns-Manville, would you have approved of Simpson's and Brown's conduct? If not, why not?

5. Hand-of-government proponents would say that it's the responsibility of government, not the asbestos industry, to ensure health and safety with respect to asbestos—that in the absence of appropriate government regulations, asbestos manufacturers have no responsibility other than to operate efficiently and profitably. Do you agree?

6. Assess Dr. Smith's decision to conceal from workers the nature of their health problems. Did he do all he was morally obliged to do as an employee of an asbestos company? What about Lanza's suppression of data in his report?

7. Do you think a corporate ethical code, together with an industrywide code, a corporate ethics committee, and training in ethics for management personnel, would have made a difference in this case?

8. What responsibilities do asbestos manufacturers now have to their injured workers? How should society respond to these workers' claims for restitution? Is our legal system adequate for handling this problem? Should the asbestos companies be punished in some way, or is their liability to civil lawsuits sufficient?

9. Do you see any parallels between this case and the tobacco industry's response to the health risks of smoking?

CASE 5.3

Selling Infant Formula Abroad

In the mid-1860s Henri Nestlé developed infant formula to save the life of an infant who couldn't be breast fed. According to officials at Nestlé—a Swiss-based corporation that is now the world's third largest food company, with annual sales of nearly $39 billion—the Frenchman's concoction has been saving lives ever since, especially in developing countries. They point to relief organizations such as the International Red Cross, which has used the formula to feed thousands of starving infants in refugee camps, for example. Without its infant formula, the Nestlé people say, Third World mothers considering use of a breast-milk substitute would use less nutritious local alternatives. Maybe so. But a hundred years after it was first developed, Henri Nestlé's sweet idea turned sour, threatening the Nestlé Corporation's dominant share of the $5–$6 billion international market for infant formula.[76]

The infant formula controversy began to heat up in 1970 at a United Nations–sponsored meeting on infant feeding in Bogotá, Colombia. Meeting to discuss different aspects of world hunger, the Protein Advisory Group (PAG)—made up of nutritionists, pediatricians, and food-industry representatives—hammered out a broad framework for cooperation among business, health care, and government. They were especially concerned about the worldwide decline in breast feeding, despite the demonstrated superiority of mother's milk over infant formula. But some PAG members bristled at what they thought was PAG's failure to engage a critical issue: the implications of marketing infant formula in Third World countries.

Straightaway the media began reporting some of the common marketing practices of infant-formula companies:

Item—Dressed as health care professionals, representatives of formula companies visited villages to promote the use of infant formula.

Item—While interned in clinics and hospitals, new mothers were given free samples of infant formula.

Item—Free or low-cost supplies of infant formula were given to health institutions, thus routinizing bottle feeding within hospitals and discouraging breast feeding.

Item—Product labels failed to warn of potential dangers from incorrect use of infant formula.

Most damaging from the industry's viewpoint was infant formula's alleged complicity in the death of Third World infants. Dr. Derrick B. Jelliffe, then director of the Caribbean Food and Nutrition Institute, claimed that millions of infants suffered and died as a result of bottle feeding. A major reason was that Third World mothers could not take sterilization and storage precautions commonplace in homes with modern kitchens.

Outraged by these allegations, the Infant Formula Action Coalition (INFACT) was formed in 1977. It focused its indignation on Nestlé, the largest producer of infant formula worldwide. Chaired by Douglas A. Johnson and joined by a hundred other religious and health organizations, INFACT instituted an international boycott against the Nestlé Company, charging it with aggressive marketing tactics designed to pressure mothers in underdeveloped countries to switch from breast feeding to bottle feeding, thus contributing to high infant-mortality rates.

INFACT's and Jelliffe's bold charges were weakened by a shortage of reliable information—as Nestlé's defenders were quick to point out. Was breast feeding really decreasing in developing nations? Were infant morbidity and mortality in fact increasing? No one really knew. And even if bottle feeding was increasing and even if there was a connection between it and increased infant mortality, no one could claim for certain that Nestlé's promotional practices had much, if anything, to do with it. Also overlooked was the fact that Third World mothers who cannot nurse are also more likely to be subject to the economic factors that make bottle feeding risky.[77]

In May 1981, the World Health Organization (WHO) adopted a "Code of Marketing of Breast-milk Substitutes," which called on governments to prohibit advertising of infant formula that discourages breast feeding. The code would prohibit, for example, sending women dressed as nurses to rural villages or paying local health workers to push infant formula. Of the 119 WHO members who voted, 118 voted for adoption. The sole opposition vote was cast by the United States, which invoked the principles of free trade and free speech. The United States said that WHO had no business telling private business how to sell its products and that it didn't want to make WHO an international Federal Trade Commission.

Speaking in his capacity as president of the International Council of Infant Food Industries, E. W. Saunders, a Nestlé vice president, branded the code unacceptably ambiguous. Nevertheless, Nestlé officials announced that Nestlé would support it. INFACT and others identified four areas for Nestlé to review: educational materials dealing with infant formula, hazard warnings and labels, gifts to health professionals, and free supplies to hospitals. Until Nestlé complied, INFACT threatened to pursue its campaign against the company. Nestlé said it already was complying and that the charges of noncompliance were based on subjective interpretations of the code. To safeguard its reputation as well as its infant-formula market, Nestlé dipped into its war chest to fight the boycott—to the tune, some say, of $40 million.

While on one front Nestlé was waging a battle to preserve its reputation, on another it was moving toward a more constructive resolution to the problem. Because WHO had no enforcement authority, there was no neutral party to monitor compliance with its "Code of Marketing of Breastmilk Substitutes." So Nestlé formed the Nestlé Infant Formula Audit Commission (NIFAC). NIFAC, which was chaired by former Senator Edmund S. Muskie, was asked to review Nestlé's instructions to field personnel to see

if they could be improved. This novel approach to the seemingly intractable situation was like hiring a private judge to arbitrate a personal dispute. At the same time, Nestlé continued to meet with officials at WHO and the United Nations International Children's Emergency Fund (UNICEF) to obtain the most accurate interpretation of the code.

NIFAC labored for eighteen months, issuing quarterly reports to the public and requesting from WHO/UNICEF several clarifications of the code. Its efforts eventually bore fruit. On January 26, 1984, the international boycott against Nestlé was suspended when Nestlé developed procedures for dealing with the four specific points of the code in dispute.

Regarding educational material, Nestlé agreed to include in all materials dealing with the feeding of infants information on (1) the benefits and superiority of breast feeding, (2) maternal nutrition and preparation for maintenance of breast feeding, (3) the negative effect on breast feeding of introducing partial bottle feeding, (4) the difficulty of reversing the decision not to breast-feed, (5) possible health hazards of inappropriate food or feeding methods, and (6) the social and financial consequences of the decision to use infant formula.

Regarding hazard warning labels, Nestlé agreed to test different statements in Third World countries, with the help of specialized consultants recommended by WHO and UNICEF. It specifically promised to ensure that product users fully understood the consequences of inappropriate or incorrect use arising from unclean water, dirty utensils, improper dilution, and storage of prepared foods without refrigeration.

Regarding gifts to health professionals, Nestlé agreed not to give gifts such as chocolate, key rings, and pens to health professionals. It also agreed to avoid product advertising in technical and scientific publications.

Regarding low-cost supplies of infant formula to health institutions, Nestlé recognized that this might inadvertently discourage breast feeding. Accordingly, it agreed to restrict the distribution of supplies to situations in which infants had to be fed on breast-milk substitutes and to help specify the conditions that would warrant such substitutes.

In announcing that a truce had been reached, Nestlé officials and protesters literally broke candy together—Nestlé chocolate, naturally—to celebrate the end of the six-and-a-half-year conflict. Douglas A. Johnson praised Nestlé for moving forward to become a model for the entire industry. The WHO code, said Johnson, has changed from "an urgent moral mandate to the accepted business practice of the largest and singly most important factor in the world." Nestlé officials viewed the settlement as "proof that its efforts" to comply with the WHO code "have finally been recognized." They boasted that Nestlé was the first company to "unilaterally apply the code in developing countries" and to "submit its activities in this area to examination by an independent commission. . . . The time has now come for all interested parties to concentrate their effort on solutions to the fundamental cause of infant mortality and malnutrition in the Third World."[78]

After a verification period of eight months, boycott leaders were satisfied that Nestlé had begun to put into place the agreed-on changes, and the "suspended" boycott was officially ended. Unfortunately, the story of Nestlé and infant formula does not come to a happy end there. Four years later, in October 1988, Douglas A. Johnson and his Minneapolis-based organization Action for Corporate Accountability charged Nestlé with noncompliance. They urged a resumption of the boycott against Nestlé as well as an expansion of the boycott to include American Home Products (AHP), the second-largest distributor of infant formula in developing nations. Nestlé's Taster's Choice Instant Coffee and Carnation Coffeemate became targets of the boycott, along with AHP's Anacin and Advil pain relievers. Action for Corporate Accountability accused both companies of violating at least the spirit—and, according to Johnson, also the letter—of the WHO code.

Specifically, Nestlé and AHP were accused of continuing to dump free supplies of formula on hospitals to induce mothers to bottle-feed their infants. The code permits donations of formula for infants needing breast-milk substitutes, but it prohibits distributing free formula solely for sales promotion. The effectiveness of free samples is well known in the advertising world. Mothers who receive free samples are far more likely to bottle-feed than those who do not. By the time the mother and baby have been discharged from the hospital, the mother's milk will have begun to dry up. She and the baby will have become hooked on the formula, Action for Corporate Accountability argued, just when the companies' donations stop and profit making begins.

Thad Jackson, a Washington spokesperson for Nestlé, insisted that the company was in "total compliance" with national and international codes. He also said that the company never gave the product directly to mothers. "We do not dump supplies in hospitals," he stated. Carol Emerling, an official of AHP, also challenged the boycott. "This whole activity is based on allegations that we violate the WHO code—and we flat out deny that."[79]

Monitoring by the United Methodist Church, however, concluded that the industry continued to violate restrictions on supplies to hospitals. One study of forty-five hospitals in four Asian countries found that Nestlé was supplying formula to 80 percent of them—in enough quantity to feed over 110 percent of their infants. AHP supplied formula to 64 percent of the hospitals. Moreover, the companies' own data suggested that the practice was designed to produce sales. In Brazil, for instance, where Nestlé had a monopoly on infant formula, it distributed no free supplies to hospitals. When the government of the Ivory Coast conducted a campaign to promote breast feeding, Nestlé stepped up its donations of formula to that nation's hospitals.[80]

Boycotts are difficult to organize and sustain, and Johnson's efforts to mount a second one against Nestlé had little effect. But there was some progress. In March 1992, UNICEF and WHO joined forces to launch a new "Baby-Friendly Hospital Initiative." Nestlé is one of the parties that pledged to coordinate efforts on behalf of this initiative, designed to encourage breast feeding and halt the distribution of free or low-cost samples of infant formula to hospitals in developing nations.

Unfortunately, though, the problem is not limited to the Third World. To secure a contract allowing it to be the only company to provide free formula samples to all mothers giving birth in New York City hospitals, AHP paid $1 million to the New York City Health and Hospital Corporation. New York's plan was to spend the entire sum on promoting breast feeding. Would this counteract the influence of those free samples to mothers? AHP was willing to gamble $1 million that it wouldn't.[81]

Update:

UNICEF estimates that 1.5 million babies die each year because they are not breast fed. And over twenty years after WHO adopted a code of conduct for the marketing of infant formula, International Baby Food Action Network and affiliated organizations like Baby Milk Action continue to campaign against Nestlé and other infant-formula companies, charging that they violate the code by marketing their product aggressively to young mothers and pregnant women in the Third World.[82] For its part, Nestlé insists that it markets infant formula only as a supplement to breast feeding.

Discussion Questions

1. What moral issues are raised by the controversy over infant formula? Do you find anything objectionable in the marketing techniques used to sell infant formula? What moral rights, if any, are at stake in this controversy? How would you respond to the argument that all Nestlé was doing was selling a high-quality product at its normal price to willing buyers?

2. In light of this case, do you think it makes sense to talk of a corporation like Nestlé as a moral agent, or is it only the people in it who can be properly described as having moral responsibility?

3. Identify the views of corporate social responsibility held by the different actors and organizations in this case. In what ways does this case raise questions about the social and moral responsibility of corporations?

4. Appraise Nestlé's actions from the perspective of both the narrow and the broader view of corporate social responsibility.

5. How would you assess Nestlé's conduct throughout the whole controversy? Has Nestlé acted in good faith? Do you think it is sincerely concerned about the drawbacks and dangers of using infant formula?

6. Throughout the dispute, Nestlé has insisted that the WHO code is ambiguous and that the company's critics are holding Nestlé accountable to their own subjective interpretation of the code. Does this point have merit? How might the problem be dealt with?

7. Can boycotts be effective in pressuring corporations to exercise social responsibility? When, if ever, does an individual have a moral obligation to participate in a corporate boycott?

CASE 5.4

Levi Strauss at Home and Abroad

Juvenile Manufacturing of San Antonio, Texas, began making infants' and children's garments in a plant on South Zarzamora Street in 1923; in the 1930s, the company switched to boys' and men's clothing and changed its name to Santone Industries. During the 1970s, Santone manufactured sports jackets for Levi Strauss & Co., which eventually decided to buy out the company. In 1981, Levi Strauss paid $10 million and took over operations on South Zarzamora Street.[83]

Although the garment industry had been struggling in some parts of the country, it had prospered in San Antonio—not least on South Zarzamora Street. One of three Levi's plants in the city, the plant was slowly converted in the late 1980s from making sports jackets to manufacturing the company's popular Dockers trousers, which had surpassed Levi's 501 jeans as the firm's top-selling line. And despite the sweatshop image that the industry brings to people's minds, many of San Antonio's semiskilled workers were happy to be employed at Levi Strauss. They thought that pay at the plant—which averaged about $11,480 per year—was good, and the company gave them a turkey every Thanksgiving and a small gift every Christmas. Benefits were respectable, too: paid maternity leave for qualified employees, health insurance, and ten days of paid vacation at Christmas and ten during the summer.

Then in 1990, Levi Strauss decided to close the plant—the largest layoff in San Antonio's history—and move its operations to Costa Rica and the Dominican Republic. This was the course of action that had been recommended the previous year by Bruce Stallworth, the firm's operations controller. Closing the plant would cost $13.5 million, Stallworth calculated, but transferring its production abroad would "achieve significant cost savings," enabling the company to recover its closing costs within two years. In 1989, it cost $6.70 to make a pair of Dockers at the South Zarzamora plant. Plant management had hoped to reduce that to $6.39 per unit in 1990, but even that would be significantly higher than the per unit cost of $5.88 at the Dockers plant in Powell, Tennessee—not to mention the $3.76 per unit cost Levi Strauss could get by using Third World contractors.

Stallworth attributed the San Antonio plant's high costs to workers' compensation expenses, to a less-than-full-capacity plant operation, and to the fact that "conversion from sports coats to Dockers has not been totally successful." Retraining workers who have spent years sewing jackets to sew trousers, it seems, is not that easy. Furthermore, running the San Antonio plant efficiently would mean running it at full capacity, but operating at full capacity on South Zarzamora Street with 1,115 workers—compared with 366 and 746 employees, respectively, at the company's other two U.S. Dockers plants—meant too many pairs of trousers produced by high-priced American labor. Workers at San Antonio averaged six dollars an hour, which is about a day's pay in the Caribbean and Central America for workers with the same level of skill.

Bob Dunn, Levi Strauss vice president of community affairs and corporate communications, denies that the company did anything it shouldn't have done with regard to closing the plant. "We didn't see any way to bring costs in line." And he adds: "As much as people like Dockers, our research shows people are not willing to pay $5 or $10 more for a pair of pants just because the label says 'Made in the U.S.A.'"

Closing plants is nothing new for Levi Strauss. Before closing South Zarzamora Street, it had already closed twenty-five plants and shifted the work overseas, either to its foreign production plants or to overseas contractors. Using overseas contractors saves the firm even more money, because in addition to lower wages the company avoids paying directly for benefits like health insurance and workers' compensation. This time, though, the company's decision to close a domestic plant and move its production abroad prompted local labor activists to fight back. They filed a class-action lawsuit and organized a boycott of Levi's products.

Despite an annual Thanksgiving hunger strike by protesters at Levi Strauss headquarters in San Francisco, the boycott gained little publicity outside San Antonio, and the lawsuit fizzled out. Neither seems to have dampened sales, but they embarrassed the company, which donated nearly $100,000 to help local agencies retrain its former employees and gave San Antonio an additional $340,000 to provide them with extra job counseling and training services.

Most politicians kept a low profile on the issue, praising Levi Strauss for offering its workers more than was legally required and promising to try to recruit a new company to use the empty factory. U.S. Representative Henry B. Gonzales, however, spoke out harshly: "When a company is so irresponsible— a company that has been making money and then willy-nilly removes a plant to get further profit based on greed and cheaper labor costs in the Caribbean— I say you have a bad citizen for a company."

To this, Bob Dunn responded, "Our sense is we do more than anyone in our industry and more than almost anyone in American industry." He was proud of the way Levi Strauss treated people when it closed plants. "We try to stress the right values," he said. "It's not easy. There isn't always one right answer."

Dunn's emphasis on values reflects the thinking of Levi Strauss's Robert D. Haas, CEO until 1999, now chairman of its board. Ever since he organized a successful leveraged buyout of the company, Haas has tried to create a more values-centered management at Levi Strauss by emphasizing social responsibility and employee rights. A year after the closure on South Zarzamora Street, the company's values-centered management received a second blow when a contractor in the U.S. territory of Saipan was accused of virtually enslaving some of its Chinese workers. When the company learned the contractor was not paying the island's legal minimum wage, it fired him and formed a top-management committee to monitor its overseas contractors. Levi Strauss

then went on to become the first multinational to adopt guidelines for its hired factories. The first part of its "Global Sourcing Guidelines" covers the treatment of workers and the environmental impact of production; the second part sets out the company's standards for choosing the countries in which it will do business.

As a result of its guidelines, Levi Strauss stopped all production in China because of human rights abuses and systemic mistreatment of labor. For instance, in a factory in Shenzhen, women sew for twelve hours a day plus overtime and receive only two days off a month. They have no health care and no compensation for injury (although Chinese legislation requires this). Their pay is often below the legal minimum of twelve cents an hour. Back home in San Francisco, the decision to pull out of China caused a fiery debate within the company. Because Chinese labor is so cheap, a committee had recommended that the company stay in China and work to make things better, but Haas decided to withdraw from China altogether. With an annual revenue of $6.5 billion, Levi Strauss is the largest clothing company in the world, and because it has no direct investment in China, it could afford to pull out. But some business analysts worried that in the long run the company could be sacrificing a great deal by leaving China. China is the world's fastest-growing economy, and some predict that it will be the world's largest economy in twenty years.

Many people praised Levi Strauss's decision, but it dumbfounded some companies. At Nike, one executive said, "I can't figure it out. I have no idea what Levi's is doing." Nike was still having trouble figuring it out when the cartoon strip *Doonesbury* began pummeling the athletic footwear company for having its products made in sweatshops in Vietnam. Cheap Asian labor is a high priority for Nike's top executive Philip Knight, and his company has long favored places like Indonesia and China, where pay is poor and labor unions are suppressed. In Indonesia, the women who work at the sweatshops of Nike contractors make $2.20 a day, and it took four years of violent struggle to get the minimum wage raised that high. Now Nike has moved into Vietnam, where labor costs are cheaper yet. At one Nike plant in Vietnam, investigators found that employees worked sixty-five hours a week—more than Vietnamese law allows—for a weekly wage of ten dollars and that 77 percent of them suffered respiratory problems from breathing chemical fumes at work.

By contrast, Levi Strauss believes that a growing number of its customers shun products made in sweatshops. Consumers "don't want to buy a shirt made by children in Bangladesh or forced labor in China," says one industry observer. The firm's top management also believes that Levi Strauss is emblematic of American culture and that its mildly anti-establishment image must be guarded. "Anyone seeking to protect their brand and company reputation will realize these policies make sense," says Bob Dunn, who helped design the company's overseas guidelines. For this reason, some critics do not charge that Levi Strauss was foolish to leave China, but rather that its decision was dictated only by bottom-line profitability—that it was a publicity stunt aimed at attracting more customers.

But the team of inspectors that Levi Strauss has monitoring its contractors is a reality, not a publicity stunt. They regularly visit factories and are prepared to fire violators of the company's guidelines—such as the factory operator who was strip-searching female workers to determine whether they were, as they claimed, menstruating and thus, according to local Muslim law, entitled to a day off with pay. The firm has also pulled out of Myanmar because of human rights abuses in that country. The company is sensitive to local mores, however, and its first goal is not to boycott countries or cancel contracts. In Bangladesh, its inspectors discovered that a contractor was employing children under the age of fourteen—something that is legal there, but contrary to Levi Strauss guidelines. The company didn't want the children discharged, which would hurt the families who are often dependent on their income, but it didn't want the children working, either. So Levi Strauss devised a solution: Younger children would be paid while attending school and would be offered full-time jobs when they turned fourteen.

Update:
Six years after withdrawing from China because of human rights violations, Levi Strauss reported in April 1998 that it would resume manufacturing its clothing there. The company denied, however, that its decision was related to its having just closed several U.S. plants, but the reversal of its China policy provoked an outcry among human rights groups, who accused Levi Strauss of putting profits before its self-proclaimed concern for workers. The company's critics pointed to a National Labor Committee report that found gross labor violations in twenty-one Chinese factories. These include forced overtime (sometimes amounting to a work week of ninety-six hours), wages as low as thirteen cents per hour, and restrictions on workers' freedom to assemble. And the U.S. State Department declared that it had not detected any "appreciable" improvement in China's human rights record during that period. Executives at Levi Strauss responded, however, that it is now possible for the company to operate in China while adhering to its corporate code of conduct. Unlike before, it now has contracting partners who are willing and able to adhere to its code, and improvements in the company's monitoring system enable it to prevent abuses at its own factories.

For its part, Nike has begun to see the light of social responsibility. Bowing to pressure from its critics, the company has now pledged to root out underage workers and to require overseas manufacturers of its wares to meet strict U.S. health and safety standards. It also agreed to allow outsiders from labor and human rights groups to join the auditors who inspect Nike's Asian factories—a demand the company had long resisted. Nike CEO Knight acknowledged the public-relations problem facing his company, which stood accused, he said, of having "singlehandedly lowered the human rights standard for the sole purpose of maximizing profits." Nike had "become synonymous with slave wages, forced overtime and arbitrary abuse." But, Knight continued, "I believe that the American consumer does not want to buy products made in abusive conditions." He did not, however, pledge to increase wages.

Meanwhile, Levi Strauss has closed twenty-four North American plants since 1997 and laid off 13,000 employees. In 2002 it announced that it would close six more U.S. factories, including the ninety-six-year-old San Francisco factory that makes the company's

501 jeans. The latest closing will leave the company with only two American plants: a sewing plant and a finishing center, both in San Antonio. (At its peak in the early 1980s, the company had fifty plants.) "We can't swim against the tide," said Levi's Robert Haas. The company had invested tens of millions of dollars in automated equipment, training, and incentives, trying to keep domestic plants competitive enough to offset the overseas wage differential, but it hasn't been enough, he stated. "Today's announcement is just facing the realities."

However, to help its displaced workers, Levi Strauss was prepared to provide them with three weeks' severance pay per year of service and was giving them eight months' notice of the layoff, instead of the two months required by law. Levi Strauss also offered displaced workers up to $6,000 each to help them make the transition into new fields. The money could be used for job training, community college education, English-language lessons, moving expenses, or setting up a small business. "We can't ignore the fact that certain jobs are not going to be sustainable in North America," said Haas. "They're done better in other countries. But companies . . . must be sensitive to [the workers'] circumstances and help move [them] into the next stage of their lives."

Discussion Questions

1. Evaluate the pros and cons of Levi Strauss's decision to close its South Zarzamora Street plant. Was it a sound business decision? Was it a socially responsible decision? Could the company have reasonably been expected to keep the plant running?

2. Having decided to close the plant, was there more that Levi Strauss could and should have done for its laid-off workers?

3. How, if at all, is your assessment of Levi Strauss's responsibilities affected by the fact that the company bought the plant and then closed it nine years later?

4. Should consumers avoid products that are made by sweatshops? Should they shun companies that lay workers off needlessly? Are consumer boycotts ever justified? When are such boycotts likely to be effective? Under what circumstances would you participate in a consumer boycott?

5. How would you feel if you had been an employee at the plant? Bob Dunn said, "My hope is that as time passes and people have a chance to reflect on what we've done, [people who have lost jobs] will judge us to have been responsible and fair." Do you think Levi Strauss's former employees will judge it that way?

6. With regard to Levi Strauss's conduct both at home and abroad, does it make sense to talk about the company as a morally responsible agent whose actions can be critically assessed, or can we assess only the actions and decisions of individual human beings inside the company?

7. Do corporations have a responsibility to monitor the conduct of the companies they do business with—in particular, their contractors and suppliers? Do they have a responsibility to avoid doing business in countries that are undemocratic, violate human rights, or permit exploitative work conditions? Compare and critically assess the conduct of Levi Strauss and Nike in this respect.

8. Should Levi Strauss have resumed its manufacturing operations in China? Should it have pulled out in the first place?

9. Is Levi Strauss sincere in its professed concern for foreign workers? Is Nike?

10. American consumers say that they don't like having their clothes made by exploited workers in foreign sweatshops. Is consumer pressure sufficient to get American companies to improve the pay and working conditions of foreign factory workers?

11. Some pessimists say that because most companies don't make social welfare a priority, competition will ultimately undermine the efforts of companies like Levi Strauss to establish standards. Assess this argument.

CASE 5.5

Charity to Scouts?

"I don't care what BankAmerica does," fumed Lynn Martin at a meeting of the board of directors of Baytown Company, a San Francisco Bay Area firm that runs four different family-oriented restaurants and owns a string of six popular fast-food take-out establishments (called "Tip-Top"). "We took a principled stand at the time," she continued, "and I don't think there's enough evidence to justify changing our minds now."

Like a lot of local companies, Baytown supports various charitable causes in the Bay Area. The company has always figured that it had an obligation to give more back to the community than good food; besides, people in the Bay Area expect local companies to display a sense of social responsibility. Among the groups that Baytown has always helped support is the regional Boy Scouts district. Not only did Baytown think the Scouts worthy of its corporate help but giving to the organization seemed to fit well with Tip-Top's all-American theme and with the family character of Baytown's other restaurants.

A simple thing suddenly got complicated, however, when the San Francisco Bay Area United Way decided to pull $1 million in annual funding for the Scouts because of the group's refusal to admit gays. Soon after that, BankAmerica, Wells Fargo Bank, and Levi Strauss & Co. also decided to stop funding the Boy Scouts. A month later, Baytown's directors resolved to follow suit.

"We were pretty clear at the time," continued Martin, "that we didn't have any business supporting an organization that was perceived as discriminatory."

"Not me," said Tom Boyd. "I always thought that since the Boy Scouts are a private group, they can do whatever they want."

"Well, maybe they have a right to discriminate if they want, but that's not the point," said Ed Framers. "The rest of us agreed with Lynn that as a company we shouldn't be helping a group that discriminates. Of course, that was before everybody around the country started making such a fuss about companies stopping their funding of the Scouts. We all know about those antigay groups demonstrating against the United Way and threatening to boycott the bank."

"Those groups hardly represent thinking in the Bay Area," Lynn Martin shot back.

"That's true," agreed Scott Arming, "but still we run a family-oriented business."

"What's that supposed to mean? Do you think gays and lesbians don't come to our restaurants? Do you think they don't have families? Do you think—"

"O.K., O.K.," Arming interjected.

"Lynn's right about that," Ed Framers said. "In fact, as far as I know, our customers never said much about it, one way or the other."

Executive Director Susan Lee then spoke up: "Well, I got a few phone calls about it, but there weren't really complaints. It was more people wanting to get more information about the situation. Of course, you always get a few cranks. . . ."

"Ain't that the truth," murmured Boyd to Framers.

"Anyway," Lee continued, "things are different now. BankAmerica has reversed its decision and is resuming funding to the Boy Scouts because the Scouts have lifted their ban on gays."

"That's what the bank says," said Lynn Martin. "But the whole thing is pretty murky if you ask me. Here, look at the newspaper story. The article reports company spokesman Peter Magnani as explaining that

> the bank had first interpreted the Scouts membership policy as banning gay members. But after consulting with Boy Scouts national President John Clendenin, the organization clarified its policy and 'made it clear' that membership is open to all boys who subscribe to Scouting oaths and laws.
>
> 'We take that to mean all boys, regardless of their sexual orientation,' said Magnani.[84]

"But then," Martin continued, "the newspaper goes on to quote a spokesperson for the Boy Scouts of America as saying that there has been 'absolutely no change in our policy. We do not believe that homosexuals provide positive role models.' What are we supposed to make of that? It looks as if the bank is trying to wriggle out of a stand that turned out not to be as popular as it thought it would be."

"That sounds pretty cynical," Ed Framers said. "The bank says here that its decision 'was based solely on the Scouts' clarification of its policy,' and the Scouts' national president is quoted as saying that the organization is 'open to all boys as long as they subscribe to the Boy Scouts Oath and Law.' You weren't a Scout, Lynn, but I was, and the oath and law are only basic stuff about trustworthiness and honesty; there's nothing about sexuality. Besides we're talking about boys, not adults. I think the whole thing has been blown out of proportion."

Martin quickly responded, "Don't you think boys have sexual feelings? Come on, Ed, give me a break. And besides, if there is nothing in the Scout oath or whatever it is about sexuality, why does the organization have to take a stand one way or the other?"

"Maybe the Scouts shouldn't have taken a stand," Susan Lee inserted, "but at this point it looks as if we have to. When we stopped giving to the Scouts, that sent one message; if we reverse our decision now, that sends another. Frankly, I don't like being in the position of having to impose our values, one way or the other."

"Yes, but you yourself said that there's no way to avoid it," Lynn Martin shot back. "So we should at least stand behind the right values."

"And what are those?" asked Lee.

"I don't have the slightest idea myself," Tom Boyd whispered to Scott Arming.

Arming ignored him as he turned to the group: "You know, I think we are and should continue to be a socially responsible company. But maybe we should reconsider whether being socially responsible means giving to charitable causes in the first place. Is that something we are truly obligated to do, or are we just following a fad? I mean, I hate to bring up the bottom line, but every dollar we give to the Boy Scouts or anybody else is one less dollar for the company and its stockholders."

"Come on, Scott, you know it's not as simple as that," responded Susan Lee. "Charitable contributions bring us good will, and it's the kind of thing the community expects an enlightened company to do."

"You may not be persuaded, Scott," Ed Framers added, "but I think what Susan says is right. In any case, we don't need a debate about general principles. We need to figure out what we are going to do about the Boy Scouts."

The meeting continued. . . .

Discussion Questions

1. What do you think Baytown should do? Explain your reasoning. What business factors are relevant to your decision? What moral factors?

2. Are Baytown's directors operating with a broad or a narrow conception of corporate social responsibility?

3. Were Baytown and the other companies right to have withdrawn their support from the Boy Scouts? Is there anything wrong with companies attempting to influence the policies of an organization like the Scouts?

4. What do you think explains BankAmerica's policy reversal? Is Lynn Martin's cynicism warranted?

5. Scott Arming doubts that businesses have an obligation to support charitable organizations. Do they?

Notes to Chapter 5

1. John McDermott, *Corporate Society: Class, Property, and Contemporary Capitalism* (Boulder, Colo.: Westview, 1991), 4.

2. "Foreign Friends," *Economist,* January 8, 2000, 87–88.

3. Anthony J. Parisi, "How Exxon Rules Its Great Empire," *San Francisco Chronicle,* August 5, 1980, 27. For an update, see "Inside the Empire of Exxon the Unloved," *Economist,* March 15, 1994.

4. "The Next Society: A Suvey of the Near Future," *Economist,* November 3, 2001, 16.

5. Thomas Donaldson, *Corporations and Morality* (Englewood Cliffs, N.J.: Prentice-Hall, 1982), 2.

6. Ibid., 4.

7. David E. Schrader, "The Oddness of Corporate Ownership," *Journal of Social Philosophy* 27 (Fall 1996): 106.

8. Donaldson, *Corporations and Morality,* 5.

9. Ibid., 3.

10. 435 U.S. 765 (1978).

11. "Prosecutor's Dilemma," *Economist,* June 15, 2002, 76.

12. Parisi, "How Exxon Rules," 38.

13. See John R. Danley, "Corporate Moral Agency: The Case for Anthropological Bigotry," in W. Michael Hoffman and Jennifer M. Moore, eds., *Business Ethics: Readings and Cases in Corporate Morality* (New York: McGraw-Hill, 1984); and John Ladd, "Morality and the Ideal of Rationality in Formal Organizations," in Thomas Donaldson and Patricia Werhane, eds., *Ethical Issues in Business: A Philosophical Approach,* 2nd ed. (Englewood Cliffs, N.J.: Prentice-Hall, 1983).

14. See Kenneth Goodpaster and John B. Matthews, Jr., "Can a Corporation Have a Conscience?" *Harvard Business Review* 60 (January–February 1982):132–141.

15. Donaldson, *Corporations and Morality,* 10.

16. See Peter French, "The Corporation as a Moral Person," *American Philosophical Quarterly* 16 (July 1979): 207–215. J. Angelo Corlett, "Corporate Responsibility and Punishment," *Public Affairs Quarterly* 2 (January 1988) criticizes French's theory.

17. Manuel G. Velasquez, "Why Corporations Are Not Morally Responsible for Anything They Do," *Business and Professional Ethics Journal* 2 (Spring 1983): 8. See also Christopher McMahon, "The Political Theory of Organizations and Business Ethics," *Philosophy and Public Affairs* 24 (Fall 1995): 303.

18. Paul Richter, "Pentagon Lifts Threat to Ban National Semi," *Los Angeles Times,* August 8, 1984, IV-1.

19. "The Conoco Conscience," Continental Oil Company, quoted in Goodpaster and Matthews, "Can a Corporation Have a Conscience?" 141.

20. Jeffrey L. Seglin, "A Safer World for Mea Culpas," *New York Times,* March 21, 1999, sec. 3, 4.

21. Quoted in Clarence C. Walton, *Corporate Social Responsibilities* (Belmont, Calif.: Wadsworth, 1967), 169–170.

22. Quoted in Bernard D. Nossiter, *The Mythmakers: An Essay on Power and Wealth* (Boston: Houghton Mifflin, 1964), 100.

23. Milton Friedman, *Capitalism and Freedom* (Chicago: University of Chicago Press, 1962), 133.

24. Theodore Levitt, "The Dangers of Social Responsibility," *Harvard Business Review* 36 (September–October 1958).

25. Milton Friedman, "The Social Responsibility of Business Is to Increase Its Profits," *New York Times Magazine,* September 13, 1970, 33, 126.

26. Ibid., 124.

27. Reprinted from Keith Davis, "Five Propositions for Social Responsibility," *Business Horizons* 18 (June 1975): 20. Copyright © 1975 by the Foundation for the School of Business at Indiana University. Used with permission.

28. Melvin Anshen, "Changing the Social Contract: A Role for Business," *Columbia Journal of World Business* 5 (November–December 1970). See also James E. Post, Anne T. Lawrence, and James Weber, *Business and Society: Corporate Strategy, Public Policy, Ethics,* 10th ed. (New York: McGraw-Hill, 2002), 16–17.

29. Davis, "Five Propositions for Social Responsibility," 22 (figures altered).

30. "Work Week," *Wall Street Journal,* May 21, 1996, A1.

31. See Christopher D. Stone, *Where the Law Ends* (New York: Harper & Row, 1975), 80–87.

32. Friedman, "The Social Responsibility of Business," 122.

33. Adolf A. Berle, Jr., and Gardiner C. Means, *The Modern Corporation and Private Property* (New York: Macmillan, 1932).

34. "Design by Committee," *Economist,* June 15, 2002, 71; see also Alan Murray, "Political Capital," *Wall Street Journal,* July 16, 2002, A4.

35. Joann S. Lublin, "How CEOs Retire in Style," *Wall Street Journal,* September 13, 2002, B1.

36. Louis Lavelle, "How Shareholder Votes Are Legally Rigged," *Business Week,* May 20, 2002, 48.

37. See Goodpaster and Matthews, "Can a Corporation Have a Conscience?" 136.

38. "As California Starved for Energy, U.S. Businesses Had a Feast," *Wall Street Journal,* September 16, 2002, A1.

39. Virginia Held, *Property, Profits, and Economic Justice* (Belmont, Calif.: Wadsworth, 1980), 11.

40. Goodpaster and Matthews, "Can a Corporation Have a Conscience?" 137.

41. Robert B. Reich, "How to Avoid These Layoffs," *New York Times*, January 4, 1996, A13. See also George F. Will, "A Capable Candidate in Waiting," *San Jose Mercury News,* February 10, 2002, 7P.

42. Walter Goodman, "Stocks Without Sin," *Harper's*, August 1971, 66.

43. Levitt, "The Dangers of Social Responsibility," 44. See also George G. Brenkert, "Private Corporations and Public Welfare," *Public Affairs Quarterly* 6 (April 1992): 155–168.

44. Davis, "Five Propositions for Social Responsibility," 20.

45. Paul F. Camenisch, "Business Ethics: On Getting to the Heart of the Matter," *Business and Professional Ethics Journal* 1 (Fall 1981). Reprinted at the end of this chapter.

46. See *New York Times*, March 2, 1995, A17; November 28, 1995, C5; and July 30, 1998, A23; *San Jose Mercury News*, May 17, 1996, 13A; and *San Francisco Chronicle*, July 24, 1996.

47. "The Cecil Rhodes of Chocolate-Chip Cookies," *Economist,* May 25, 1996, 74.

48. "Good Citizens of the Community," *Business Ethics,* March/April 2002, 9.

49. Camenisch, "Business Ethics."

50. See Robert C. Solomon, *Above the Bottom Line: An Introduction to Business Ethics*, 2nd ed. (Fort Worth, Tex.: Harcourt Brace, 1994), 282.

51. See Stone, *Where the Law Ends*, Chapter 11.

52. Kenneth J. Arrow, "Social Responsibility and Economic Efficiency," *Public Policy* 21 (Summer 1973).

53. Milton Snoeyenbos and Barbara Caley, "Managing Ethics," in Milton Snoeyenbos, Robert Almeder, and James Humber, eds., *Business Ethics*, 3rd ed. (Buffalo, N.Y.: Prometheus, 2001), 143.

54. Snoeyenbos and Caley, "Managing Ethics," 141.

55. Gillian Flynn, "Make Employee Ethics Your Business," *Personnel Journal*, June 1995.

56. Jay W. Lorsch, "Managing Culture: The Invisible Barrier to Strategic Change," *California Management Review* 28 (Winter 1986). Quoted by Donald P. Robin and R. Eric Reidenbach, *Business Ethics: Where Profits Meet Value Systems* (Englewood Cliffs, N.J.: Prentice-Hall, 1989), 59.

57. Alyse Lynn Booth, "Who Are We?" *Public Relations Journal* (July 1985). Quoted by Robin and Reidenbach, *Business Ethics*, 59.

58. W. Brooke Tunstall, "Cultural Transition at AT&T," *Sloan Management Review* (Fall 1983). Quoted by Robin and Reidenbach, *Business Ethics*, 59.

59. Robin and Reidenbach, *Business Ethics*, Chapter 4.

60. "When Something Is Rotten, *Economist,* July 27, 2002, 53.

61. Lynn Sharp Paine, "Managing for Organizational Integrity," *Harvard Business Review* 72 (March–April 1994): 107–108.

62. "Businesses Are Signing Up for Ethics 101," *Business Week*, February 15, 1988, 56.

63. Sandra Waddock and Neil Smith, "Corporate Responsibility Audits: Doing Well by Doing Good," *Sloan Management Review* 41 (Winter 2000): 75–83.

64. Scot J. Paltrow, "Brokers Who Break the Rules," *Los Angeles Times,* July 1, 1992, A1.

65. "Businesses Are Signing Up," 56.

66. *Economist,* April 8, 1995, 57, and August 19, 1995, 56.

67. This case study is based on Timothy Egan, "Elements of Alaska Oil Spill Disaster," *New York Times*, May 22, 1989, A10. See also Robert F. Hartley, *Business Ethics: Violations of the Public Trust* (New York: John Wiley & Sons, 1993), Chapter 16, and the tenth anniversary reports in the *New York Times,* March 6, 1999, A1, and *San Francisco Chronicle,* March 24, 1999, A1.

68. Hartley, *Business Ethics*, 231.

69. "Jury Rules Exxon Must Pay," *USA Today*, August 12, 1994, 3A.

70. "Exxon Is Accused of 'Astonishing Ruse' in Oil-Spill Trial," *New York Times*, June 14, 1996, D4.

71. Samuel S. Epstein, "The Asbestos 'Pentagon Papers,'" in Mark Green and Robert Massie, Jr., eds., *The Big Business Reader: Essays on Corporate America* (New York: Pilgrim Press, 1980), is the primary source of the facts and quotations reported here.

72. See "Asbestos Claims to Be Reduced under New Plan," *Wall Street Journal*, November 20, 1990, A4, and "Court Rejection of Asbestos Trust Means More Delay," *Santa Cruz Sentinel*, December 8, 1992, B4.

73. "Asbestos Settlement Tossed," *San Jose Mercury News*, May 11, 1996, 1D; "Voiding of Class-Action Asbestos Settlement Upheld," *New York Times,* June 26, 1997, C25.

74. "The $200 Billion Miscarriage of Justice," *Fortune,* March 4, 2002, 155.

75. "Outlandish Claims," *Economist,* May 25, 2002, 75; "Spreading Out of Control," *Economist,* September 21, 2002, 71–72; Susan Warren, "High Court to Weigh Two Key Issues of Asbestos Litigation," *Wall Street Journal,* November 6, 2002, B1.

76. For further, more detailed discussions of the marketing of infant formula, see Lisa H. Newton and David P. Schmidt, *Wake-Up Calls: Classic Cases in Business Ethics* (Belmont, Calif.: Wadsworth, 1996), Chapter 3, and Hartley, *Business Ethics*, Chapter 10.

77. Newton and Schmidt, *Wake-Up Calls*, 65–67.

78. "Boycott Against Nestlé over Infant Formula to End Next Month," *Wall Street Journal*, January 27, 1984, 1.

79. "New Boycott Plea in Infant Formula Fight," *San Francisco Chronicle*, October 5, 1988, A9.

80. Carol-Linnea Salmon, "Milking Deadly Dollars from the Third World," *Business and Society* 68 (Winter 1989).

81. Salmon, "Milking Deadly Dollars."

82. See, in particular, *www.babymilkaction.org*.

83. The first part of this case study is based on Jeannie Kever, "What Price Layoffs?" *San Francisco Examiner,* November 18, 1990, D1. The second part is based on G. Pascal Zachary, "Exporting Rights," *Wall Street Journal,* July 28, 1994, A1; William Beaver, "Levi's Is Leaving China," *Business Horizon* 38 (March–April 1995), 35–40; Kevin Donaher, "Niketown—Just Don't Do It," *San Francisco Chronicle,* February 20, 1997, A23; Bob Herbert, "Nike's Bad Neighborhood," *New York Times,* June 14, 1996, A29, and "Mr. Young Gets It Wrong," June 27, 1997, A21; and Steven Greenhouse, "Nike Shoe Plant in Vietnam Is Called Unsafe for Workers," *New York Times,* November 8, 1997, A1. The Update is based on reports in the *San Francisco Chronicle,* November 12, 1997, April 9, 1998, and February 29, 1999; *New York Times,* April 9 and May 13, 1998; and *San Jose Mercury News,* April 9, 2002.

84. Fernando Quintero, "B of A Will Now Fund Boy Scouts," *San Jose Mercury News,* August 19, 1992, B3.

Reading ————————————— ■

THE GREED CYCLE: HOW CORPORATE AMERICA WENT OUT OF CONTROL

JOHN CASSIDY

In this essay, John Cassidy, author of Dot.Con *and a staff writer for* The New Yorker, *tells the story of how the stock market boom of the 1990s collapsed amid the debris of business failures and corporate scandals. Since the emergence of the modern publicly held corporation in the nineteenth century, there has been a "principal-agent" problem—namely, how to ensure that managers act in the interest of the shareholders. An attempt to deal with this problem, the stockholder-value movement led to the 1980s wave of leveraged buyouts and then in the 1990s to the increased use of stock options as executive compensation. This, however, created an environment in which CEOs had an incentive to mislead investors, and thus keep stock prices high, by inflating corporate earnings through accounting skullduggery that exaggerated revenues and understated costs.*

There are many ways to take the measure of what has happened to corporate America in recent years.

Reprinted by permission. © 2002 John Cassidy. Originally in *The New Yorker.*

As good a way as any is to flip through some back copies of the *Financial Times,* which recently published a remarkable series of articles on what it termed the "barons of bankruptcy—a privileged group of top business people who made extraordinary personal fortunes even as their companies were heading for disaster." The *F.T.* examined the twenty-five biggest business collapses since the start of [2001]. From the beginning of 1999 to the end of 2001, senior executives and directors of these doomed companies walked away with some $3.3 billion in salary, bonuses, and the proceeds from sales of stock and stock options. Some of the names on the list were familiar to anybody who reads the papers: Global Crossing's Gary Winnick ($512.4 million); Enron's Kenneth Lay ($246.7 million); and WorldCom's Scott Sullivan ($49.4 million). However, there were also many names that haven't received much public attention, such as Clark McLeod and Richard Lumpkin, the former chairman and the former vice-chairman, respectively, of McLeodUSA, a telecommunications company based in Cedar Rapids, Iowa. These two corporate philanthropists cashed in stock worth ninety-nine million dollars and a hundred and sixteen million dollars, respectively, before the rest of the stockholders were wiped out.

Even veteran observers have been taken aback by recent events. "It became a competitive game to see how much money you could get," Paul Volcker, the former chairman of the Federal Reserve Board, told me when I visited him at his office in Rockefeller Center . . . Earlier . . . Volcker [had] tried and failed to rescue Arthur Andersen, Enron's accounting firm, which ended up going out of business. "Corporate greed exploded beyond anything that could have been imagined in 1990," Volcker went on. "Traditional norms didn't exist. You had this whole culture where the only sign of worth was how much money you made."

Economists from Adam Smith to Milton Friedman have seen greed as an inevitable and, in some ways, desirable feature of capitalism. In a well-regulated and well-balanced economy, greed helps to keep the system expanding. But it is also kept in check, lest it undermine public faith in the entire enterprise. The extraordinary thing about the last few years is not the mere presence of greed but the way it was systematically encouraged and then allowed to career out of control. Kenneth Lay, in quietly selling stock and exercising stock options worth more than two hundred million dollars shortly before Enron collapsed, wasn't just being a selfish, unscrupulous individual: he was defying the social contract that underpins a system, which, despite its faults, has lasted almost two hundred years.

In 1814, Francis Cabot Lowell, a Boston merchant, founded the first public company, when he built a textile factory on the banks of the Charles River in Waltham, Massachusetts, and called it the Boston Manufacturing Company. Lowell had smuggled a plan of a power loom out of England, and he intended to compete with the Lancashire mills. But he couldn't afford to pay for the construction and installation of expensive machinery by himself, so he sold stock in his company to ten associates. Within seven years, these stockholders had received a cumulative return of more than a hundred per cent, and Lowell had established a new business model. Under its auspices, mankind has invented cures for deadly diseases, extracted minerals from ocean floors, extended commerce to all corners of the earth, and generated unprecedented rates of economic expansion.

Initially, most economists were skeptical of Lowell's innovation. At the heart of any public company there is an implicit bargain: the managers promise to run the company in the owners' interest, and the stockholders agree to hand over day-to-day control of the business to the managers. Unfortunately, there is no easy way to make sure that the managers don't slack off, or divert some of the stockholders' money into their own pockets. Adam Smith was among the first to identify this problem. "The directors of such companies . . . being the managers rather of other people's money than of their own, it cannot well be expected that they should watch over it with the same anxious vigilance with which the partners in a private [company] frequently watch over their own," Smith wrote in "The Wealth of Nations." And he went on, "Negligence and profusion, therefore, must always prevail, more or less, in the management of the affairs of such a company."

Smith thought that private companies would remain the normal way of doing business, but technological change and financial necessity proved him wrong. With the development of the railroads, for example, companies like the New York Central and the Union Pacific needed to raise tens of millions of dollars from outside investors to lay track and buy rolling stock. And because the administrative complexity of the railroads was too much for a single entrepreneur to handle, a new class of full-time executives . . . emerged to run them. Though the emerging industry attracted dubious financiers like Jay Gould, most of the professional managers were content to collect generous salaries and pensions rather than habitually attempt to rob the stockholders and bondholders. . . .

Alas, by the late nineteen-twenties it was clear that corporate perfidy was prospering in an impressive variety of forms, most of them involving insiders exploiting their position to fleece outsiders. After the stock-market crash of 1929, congressional investigators uncovered widespread insider trading, stock-price manipulation, and diversion of corporate funds to personal use. Then, as now, the revelations of corporate wrongdoing prompted the federal government to respond. The Securities Act of 1933 imposed extensive disclosure requirements on any company wanting to issue stock, and outlawed insider dealing and other attempts to manipulate the market. In 1934, the Securities and Exchange Commission was set up to enforce the new regulations.

Public confidence in business eventually recovered, but the potential conflict of interest at the heart of public companies was never fully resolved. During the nineteen-sixties and early seventies, corporate managers were often cavalier about the interests of stockholders. Back then, the chief executive's compensation was usually linked to the size of the firm he ran—the bigger the company, the bigger the paycheck. This encouraged business leaders to build sprawling empires rather than focus on their firms' profitability and stock price. Many of them spent heavily on perquisites of office, such as lavish headquarters and corporate retreats, and they kept on spending even when their companies ran into trouble.

In theory, the stockholders could have joined together to force out managers, but organizing such a collective effort was costly and time consuming, and it rarely happened. Nor was managerial waste constrained by competition from rival firms that didn't splurge on pink marble for the office bathrooms. Companies like General Motors saw their businesses decimated by foreign competition, but C.E.O.s, such as G.M.'s Roger Smith, rarely suffered. From a stockholder's perspective, something more potent was required to get those who ran the companies to serve the interests of those who owned the companies. When the solution materialized, it would turn out to be more potent than anybody had imagined.

Thirty years ago, two obscure young financial economists provided the spark for reform. Michael Jensen and William Meckling had graduate degrees from the University of Chicago. . . . They began with the supposition that senior managers, faced with competition from other firms, would do the best they could for their stockholders, by cutting costs and trying to make as big a profit as possible. "But the more we thought about it the more we realized that what we had been taught in Chicago and believed most of our lives wasn't true," Jensen recalled recently. "It wasn't automatically true that corporations would maximize value."

Jensen and Meckling . . . planted the idea that the most important people in any company are not the employees or the managers but the owners— the stockholders and bondholders. This model provided an intellectual rationale, of sorts, for the controversial explosion in C.E.O. pay that began in the nineteen-eighties; and it justified the widespread adoption of executive stock options.

Jensen and Meckling analyzed the relationship between stockholders and managers as a "principal-agent problem"—a dilemma that arises whenever one party (the principal) employs another (the agent) to do a job for him. It might be a family hiring a contractor to renovate its house, a company hiring a brokerage firm to manage its retirement fund, or even an electorate choosing a government. In all these cases, the same issue arises: How can the principal insure that the agent acts in his or her interest? As anybody who has dealt with a contractor knows, there is no simple solution. One option is to design a contract that rewards the contractor for doing the job well. Municipal-construction projects, for example, have a chronic tendency to overrun, snarling traffic and infuriating the public. So when the City of New York, say, puts out tenders for roadwork, its contracts often include financial incentives for finishing the work early and penalties for being late.

Jensen and Meckling were the first economists to apply this idea to corporations. They argued that there was no perfect way to align the interests of the owners and the managers. In any firm that relied on outsiders for financing, the senior executives would make some damaging decisions. If the firm issued stock, they would waste some of the proceeds on perks like corporate jets. If the firm issued debt, the managers, knowing that the bondholders would be the main losers if anything went wrong, would make too many risky investments. The "agency costs" that the business incurred as a result of these actions were unavoidable. It didn't matter whether the firm was a cosseted monopoly or a company facing extensive competition: managers would destroy value.

. . . Eventually . . . most economists accepted Jensen and Meckling's logic, and they began to ask more questions: How should the performances of senior executives be measured? Was it better to give them money, in the form of salaries or bonuses, or company stock? If some managerial inefficiency was inevitable, how could it be minimized? Principal-agent theory provided a clear answer to these questions: treat chief executives just like plumbers, contractors, or any other truculent agent, and reward them for acting in the best interest of the principal—i.e., the stockholders.

At the time, many chief executives saw their main task as overseeing the welfare of their employees and customers. As long as the firm made a decent profit every year and raised the dividend it paid its stockholders, this was considered good enough. But, once C.E.O.s were viewed as merely the agents of the firm's owners, they were urged to live by a new, simpler credo: shareholder value. Henceforth, economists and management gurus agreed, their overriding aim should be to maximize the value of the firm, as it was determined in the stock market.

The shareholder-value movement soon attracted rich and aggressive investors who used the economists' arguments to justify attacks on corporate America. During the hostile-takeover wave of the nineteen-eighties, controversial figures like T. Boone Pickens and Carl Icahn bought stakes in public companies they considered undervalued and, claiming to represent the ordinary stockholder, often tried to seize control. Since the corporate raiders financed their attacks with borrowed money, their takeovers became known as "leveraged buyouts," or LBOs. In a typical LBO, the acquirer would buy out the public stockholders and run the company as a private concern, slashing costs and slimming it down. The ultimate aim was to refloat the company on the stock market at a higher valuation. Individual raiders weren't the only force behind LBOs. Wall Street firms like Kohlberg Kravis Roberts and Hicks, Muse also got in on the game. Nearly half of all major public corporations received a takeover offer in the eighties. Many companies were forced to lay off workers and sell off underperforming divisions in order to boost their stock price and fend off potential bidders. Raiders were popularly denounced as speculators and predators, which, of course, most of them were. . . .

Still, many economists defended LBOs as an effective way to overcome the agency problems that Jensen and Meckling had identified. The stock-

holders who sold out often made considerable profits, and the managers of bought-out companies were usually given large chunks of equity. Senior executives would be forced to run the firms more efficiently, it was argued, because of all the debt that had been taken on, and, if they boosted the value of the firm, they should make a lot of money themselves.

. . . When the economy went into a recession during the early nineteen-nineties, many of the firms that had gone private, such as Macy's and Revco, couldn't keep up their interest payments, and the resulting wave of bankruptcies discredited the LBO as a business model. Far from creating value, many LBOs had ended up wiping out the investors and bondholders who financed them. The only people who consistently made money were the stockholders and senior managers who sold out early on. The enduring economic lesson of the LBO era was that unleashing greed wasn't enough to raise efficiency. But the message that corporate America took from its ordeal was quite different: senior executives who converted to the new religion of shareholder value tended to get very rich, while those who argued that corporations ought to consider their employees and customers as well as their stockholders often ended up without a job.

At the same time, corporations came to realize that leveraged buyouts weren't the only way to align the interests of managers and shareholders. There was a much simpler tool available, which didn't involve going to all the trouble of a multibillion-dollar takeover: the executive stock option. Once endowed with a generous grant of these magical instruments, a senior executive would no longer think of himself as a mere hired hand but as a proprietor who had the long-term health of the firm at heart. That was the theory, anyway.

An executive stock option is a legal contract that grants its owner the right to buy a stock in his or her company at a certain price (the "strike price") on a certain date in the future. Take a company with a stock price of fifty dollars that grants its chief executive the right to buy a million shares three years hence at the current market price. Assume the stock price rises by ten per cent year year, so that after three years it is trading at about sixty-six dollars and fifty cents. At that point, the chief executive can "exercise" his option and make the company sell him a million shares at fifty dollars. Then he can sell the shares in the open market, and clear a profit of sixteen and a half million dollars. . . .

In 1980, fewer than a third of chief executives of public companies were granted stock options. Most firms still depended on bonuses and profit sharing to motivate and reward their senior managers. As the nineteen-eighties progressed, and the Dow tripled, stock options began to look much less risky. Thanks to the startling growth of firms that used them heavily, such as Microsoft and Intel, they also became fashionable. . . . Yet the real benefit of granting stock options—or so economists insisted—was that they solved the problem of providing incentives to senior executives. . . .

By 1994, seven in ten chief executives received option grants, and stock options made up about half of their average take-home pay. In the second half of the nineties, so-called "mega-options"—options grants worth at least ten million dollars—became the norm. In 1997, according to the executive-compensation consulting firm Pearl Meyer & Partners, ninety-two of America's top two hundred chief executives received mega-options, with an average value of thirty-one million dollars. A year later, two Harvard economists, Brian J. Hall and Jeffrey Liebman, took another look at managerial pay and confirmed what anybody who followed the financial pages already knew: C.E.O.s weren't paid anything like bureaucrats. They were paid more like rock stars.

Wittingly and unwittingly, Washington encouraged the great giveaway. During the 1992 election campaign, Bill Clinton and Al Gore made a political issue out of lavish C.E.O. pay. A year later, the new Administration limited to a million dollars the tax deductions that corporations could take for executive salaries. The reform turned out to be counterproductive. Since executive stock options weren't counted as regular compensation, corporations had yet another reason to pay their senior managers less in salary and more in options. In 1994, the Financial Accounting Standards Board (F.A.S.B.), the descendant of the Accounting Principles Board, set out to force companies to deduct the value of the stock options they granted from their earnings. Following an intense lobbying campaign by Silicon Valley companies, several leading members of Congress, including Joseph Lieberman and Dianne Feinstein, threatened to put the F.A.S.B. out of business if it went ahead with the change. The board backed down, and the latest official attempt to control corporate avarice came to an end.

The rise of the stock option revolutionized the culture of corporate America. The chief executives of blue-chip companies, who in the nineteen-eighties had portrayed Icahn, Pickens, and their ilk as corporate vandals, now embraced the values of the raiders as their own. For decades, the Business Roundtable, a lobbying group that represents the C.E.O.s of dozens of major companies, had stressed the social role that corporations played in their communities, as well as the financial obligations they owed their stockholders. In 1997, the Business Roundtable changed its position statement to read, "The paramount duty of management and board is to the shareholder."

In many cases, the C.E.O.s turned into corporate raiders themselves, albeit internal raiders. Companies like I.B.M., Xerox, and Procter & Gamble, acting on their own volition, fired tens of thousands of workers. Their chief executives insisted that the "downsizing" was necessary to compete effectively, and that was sometimes true. But once the C.E.O.s were in possession of mega-options, they had another motivating factor: an enormous vested interest in boosting their firms' stock price. For the first time, they had an opportunity to create fortunes on a scale hitherto reserved for industrial pioneers like Rockefeller, Morgan, and Gates. In 1997, Michael Eisner, the chairman and chief executive of Walt Disney, earned five hundred and seventy million dollars. A year later, Mel Karmazin, the chief executive of CBS, exercised options worth almost two hundred million dollars.

The scattered protests at these startling payouts notwithstanding, many economists credited the doctrine of shareholder value for reinvigorating

American business. In spite of fears that downsizing would devastate communities, the economy thrived, and the total number of jobs in the country increased. Far from being pilloried, ruthless businessmen ended up being lauded. . . .

As long as the economy kept expanding and the stock market kept going up, most Americans were content to avert their eyes from the lopsided manner in which the rewards of the long boom were being distributed. For those who looked closely, though, there was already evidence that executive stock options were sometimes being abused. . . .

As the Nasdaq headed for 5,000, even some leading advocates of the shareholder-value movement called for changes in the design of stock options. In early 1999, Alfred Rappaport, a consultant who wrote the management text "Creating Shareholder Value," published an article in the *Harvard Business Review* in which he pointed out, "Under current compensation schemes, senior managers are rewarded even when their companies underperform." The vertiginous rise in the Nasdaq and the Dow meant that nearly anybody who was lucky enough to be in charge of a public company stood to get very rich, however lacklustre his performance. Rappaport proposed indexing the strike price of executive stock options to the Dow or the Nasdaq. This way, he explained, the options would rise in value only if the stock outperformed the market, and chief executives would have to earn their fortunes.

Despite the eminent sense of this proposal, nobody in corporate America paid any heed to it. Under the nonsensical accounting rules covering options, the value of indexed options had to be deducted from earnings, whereas the value of ordinary options didn't. Businesses weren't willing to reduce their earnings by making the switch. . . .

Worse still, many companies repriced their senior executives' stock options at a lower level whenever the stock price fell. The chip company Advanced Micro Devices, for example, repriced the options of its founder, Jerry Sanders III, no fewer than six times, allowing him to make untold millions of dollars while his firm's stock performed modestly. The software company Oracle followed the same practice. In 2000, Larry Ellison, Oracle's already wealthy founder, made seven hundred million dollars by cashing in some low-priced options shortly before his firm's stock price collapsed.

It is hard to think of a better example of what is wrong with corporate America. When the firm's stock price does well, the people in charge make out like lottery winners. When the stock price plummets, they get another set of chances to win. The scheme, in its audacity, and its logic, is almost beautiful. Graef Crystal, an expert on executive pay, who wrote the book "In Search of Excess: The Overcompensation of American Executives," told me recently that if you combine a volatile stock with a willingness to reprice the stock options "then you have created a money machine, an antigravity device, which guarantees that the senior executives will get super-rich."

The most insidious aspect of executive stock options is that—especially in tough times—they give senior managers a strong incentive to mislead investors about the true condition of their companies. Even before the current raft of financial scandals, more and more firms were resorting to accounting skullduggery, exaggerating their revenues and understating their costs.

Economists like Michael Jensen largely ignored this disturbing development, but inside the accounting world it was well known. Under the American system of corporate governance, which hasn't changed much since the nineteen-thirties, public companies provide an earnings update every quarter, and release a more detailed, audited report every twelve months. In preparing their financial results, firms rely on the Generally Accepted Accounting Principles, a lengthy set of rules that the S.E.C. and the big accounting firms agree upon. The rules are designed to provide a fair picture of how much money a company is making after subtracting its expenses from its revenues, but a determined management can interpret them in many different ways.

In 1993, Howard Schilit, a professor of accounting at American University, in Washington, D.C., published a book about the tricks that companies use to boost their earnings. Back then, most people who weren't C.P.A.s assumed that (outside Hollywood, anyway) accounting standards were clear and exacting, but Schilit had uncovered dozens of ways in which firms can manipulate their results. His book, "Financial Shenanigans: How to Detect Accounting Gimmicks and Fraud in Financial Reports," identified seven accounting dodges ranging from sleight of hand to outright fraud: (1) recording revenue too soon or of questionable quality; (2) recording bogus revenue; (3) boosting income with one time gains; (4) shifting current expenses to a later or an earlier period; (5) failing to record liabilities or improperly reducing them; (6) shifting current revenue to a later period; (7) shifting future expenses to the current period as a special charge.

The following year, Schilit founded the Center for Financial Research & Analysis, a company that monitors corporate financial statements and issues warnings to its clientele of institutional investors. As the decade progressed, the number of warnings increased. "The accounting problems didn't suddenly happen in the last six months or twelve months," Schilit told me not long ago. "They were horrendous in the period from 1997 onward." Schilit and his colleagues often received a hostile reaction when they publicly questioned a company's earnings. "People got very angry," Schilit recalled. "The amount of money that C.E.O.s were making from out-of-control option plans was astounding, but everybody who was around them was happy, because they were also getting rich. They didn't want somebody raising questions." . . .

Cendant was a major financial scandal. Almost twenty billion dollars of shareholder value was wiped out, and the company ended up paying $2.8 billion to settle shareholder suits, but the story rarely made it out of the business section. Schilit told me, "When a bull market is raging, investors lose a lot of money on Cendant, and the advisers, the investment bankers, say, 'O.K., Joe. Fraud can happen. But you made a lot of money on the previous five deals I brought you.' Investors tend to grit their teeth and say, 'Yes, I got nailed on this one, but I did make money on the five other deals.'"

Around the time that the truth about Cendant emerged, an accounting scandal forced Al Dunlap to resign from Sunbeam, the appliance maker. . . . Dunlap denied any wrongdoing, but in 2001 the S.E.C. charged him and four of his former colleagues with fraud, claiming that they had given a false impression of Sunbeam's business by inflating its "stock price and thus improving its value as an acquisition target." Sunbeam eventually filed for bankruptcy, and its stockholders . . . ended up with nothing.

The frauds at Cendant and Sunbeam were dwarfed by an even bigger accounting scandal, at Waste Management, the largest trash-hauling company in the country. . . . The S.E.C. launched an investigation, which discovered that between 1992 and 1996 Waste Management had exaggerated its profits by $1.43 billion.

Cendant and Waste Management were both scrappy firms trying to crash their way into the financial establishment. Lucent Technologies, the former equipment-making division of A.T.&T., was the bluest of blue chips. Lucent went public in April, 1996; within three years its stock had risen eightfold, and it had become the most widely held stock in America. In 1998, Lucent generated about a billion dollars in net income. Investors were expecting the firm's rapid growth to continue over the next year, and the company was doing nothing to dispel the idea that it would. But in reality Lucent's sales were slowing, and its inventories were rising. The company included in its earnings gains from its corporate pension plan (shenanigan No. 3), started capitalizing software expenditures (shenanigan No. 4), and created new reserves related to acquisitions (shenanigan No. 7). In February and May of 1999, the Center for Financial Research & Analysis issued two warnings about Lucent's financial condition. "There wasn't one thing that leaped out at you," Howard Schilit recalled. "There was just a whole series of little tricks here and there."

As usual, investors didn't pay much attention. That November, Lucent's stock hit eighty dollars. On January 6, 2000, Schilit and his colleagues issued a third warning, detailing how Lucent had artificially boosted its earnings by reversing a previous restructuring charge. A week later, Lucent announced that it would miss Wall Street's earnings estimates for the last quarter of 1999, and its stock fell sharply. Two and a half years later, it is trading below two dollars.

"What Lucent taught a lot of people, me included, was that this could happen anywhere,"

Schilit said. "These blue-chip companies were just as susceptible to accounting trickery as the small ones."

If investors had been paying more attention, they would have seen that Schilit wasn't the only one warning that something was wrong with the upbeat figures corporate America was releasing. Between the fourth quarter of 1996 and the fourth quarter of 2000, the firms in the S. & P. 500 reported that their earnings per share had increased from $38.73 to $54.78, with not a single down quarter. Even at the end of 2000, most big companies were predicting further rises in profits. But according to the Commerce Department, which measures the gross domestic product and its components, corporate profits peaked in 1997, at close to eight hundred billion dollars. Thereafter, they fell sharply, to just above seven hundred and twenty billion dollars in 1998. Profits didn't recover their 1997 level until 2000, whereupon they slumped again in 2001.

There are two possible ways to explain the glaring difference between the Commerce Department's numbers and corporate America's. The government calculates profits from corporate tax filings, which often contain lower estimates of earnings than the filings that firms present to Wall Street. (For some reason, firms feel no urge to exaggerate their profits to the I.R.S.) Moreover, the government gathers numbers from all types of enterprises, big and small, whereas the S. & P. 500 is composed of the largest corporations in the country. It is at least conceivable that the decline in profitability that the Commerce Depatment detected was concentrated among tax avoiders and small firms. But a far more convincing explanation is that the vast majority of major corporations were artificially inflating their profits. Instead of admitting that rising wages and intense competition were corroding their earnings, they were resorting to subterfuge.

The men heading these companies faced an unenviable dilemma. At the stock market's peak, many of them had options worth tens of millions of dollars. But this wealth was alarmingly evanescent: with a plunge in the company's stock price, their options would be rendered worthless. In these circumstances, it would have taken a brave man to tell the truth about what was happening to corporate earnings. Such corporate statesmen were in short supply. Far more common were senior executives, who, in Alan Greenspan's words, sought to "harvest" some of their stock-market gains before it was too late.

Even Michael Jensen, the great defender of big payouts for C.E.O.s, now concedes that the design of enormous stock-options packages had a disastrous effect on corporate ethics. If he had his way, Jensen told me recently, every standard executive stock option would be scrapped. Instead, managers would receive options with a strike price that went up every year. "I was a defender of the move toward stock options and more liberal rewards for C.E.O.s. But I'm now a critic of where we got to," Jensen said. "For a long time now, we've had a situation in which the stock prices of many firms have been too high," he explained. "That is to managers what heroin is to a drug addict." When stock prices are overvalued, managers get into an elaborate game with Wall Street to try and justify them. "But if they are too high you can't possibly justify them. So you keep struggling for ways to get the earnings up, to generate the reports that the market is expecting to see." Whenever a company does admit that its earnings aren't growing as rapidly as investors are expecting, its stock price gets crushed and its management gets pilloried. "Once you train managers by penalizing them for telling the truth and rewarding them for lying, then that kind of unethical behavior gets extended to all sorts of things," Jensen said.

Jensen's discovery that executive stock options can have perverse results is rather belated, but his analysis of the last few years is hard to fault. Stock options, instead of spurring corporate leaders to build businesses that would create wealth for decades to come, encouraged them to manage for the short term, tailoring their actions to the demands of Wall Street stock analysts; and, in all too many cases, the practice turned them into crooks. WorldCom, for example, the second-biggest long-distance phone company in the country, classed billions of dollars in routine expenditures, such as payments the firm made to other telephone companies for connecting calls, as capital investments, which made it look a lot more profitable than it really was. Global Crossing, a startup company that built a transatlantic communications network, swapped fibre-optic capacity with other telecommunications companies in order to create fake revenues. Dynegy, an energy-trading firm, recorded phantom trades to do the same thing. Xerox, Qwest, and Rite Aid are all accused of inflating their revenues.

None of these accounting shenanigans emerged until after the Nasdaq crashed, in April, 2000, but they were all similar to the ones Schilit had identified in the nineties. At Enron, the finagling was more complicated. The wrongdoing appears to have begun in earnest toward the end of 1997, when the credit-rating agencies (Moody's and Standard & Poor's) became increasingly concerned about the debt that Enron had taken on as it expanded from a gas-pipeline company into areas like energy trading and online commerce. If the credit-rating agencies had downgraded Enron's debt, its stock price would have fallen, which would have had a disastrous impact on the massive stock-option packages that virtually all the firm's senior executives owned. In order to forestall this eventuality, Andrew Fastow, Enron's chief financial officer, set up a series of investment partnerships, with names like Chewco and LJM1, which were used to reduce Enron's debt and disguise its losses on new ventures. An investigative committee appointed by Enron's board later concluded that "the transactions between Enron and the LJM partnerships resulted in Enron increasing its reported financial results by more than a billion dollars, and enriching Fastow and his co-investors by tens of millions of dollars at Enron's expense." Just as important, the partnerships helped to maintain Enron's stock price long enough for the firm's senior management to cash in hundreds of millions of dollars of stock options.

Jensen has been looking closely at Enron. In a recent working paper, he and another economist, Joseph Fuller, pointed out that "Enron was in many ways an extraordinary company. It boasted significant global assets, true achievements, dramatic innovations, and a promising long-run future." The firm's one big problem was its outsize stock-market valuation, which in August, 2001, reached almost seventy billion dollars. In order to justify this outlandish figure, Wall Street analysts were demanding higher earnings, and Enron's top executives were casting around for ways to meet these demands. "If Enron's management had confronted the analysts with courage and conviction and resisted their relentless focus on outsize earnings growth, the company could have avoided questionable actions taken to please the analysts and the markets," Jensen and Fuller conclude. "The result could well have been a lower-valued but stable and profitable company."

A corollary of this argument is that Kenneth Lay and his colleagues were not necessarily deceitful or venal people; nor were the heads at WorldCom, Dynegy, and Global Crossing: they were all victims of circumstance. "It is important to recognize that this doesn't come about as a result of crooks," Jensen insisted. "This comes about as a result of honest people being subjected to forces that they don't understand. The forces are very strong, and this evolves over a period of time. You end up with highly moral, honest people doing dishonest things. It wasn't as if the Mafia had taken over corporate America. We are too quick to say—and the media feed this—that if a bad thing happens it's because a bad person did it, and that person had evil intentions. It is much more likely that there were some bad systems in place."

What Jensen doesn't say, of course, is that he and other economists were at least partly responsible for the compensation systems that unleashed an orgy of self-enrichment. In retrospect, Jensen and his colleagues were hopelessly naïve in assuming that executive stock options wouldn't be abused. If the past thirty years have demonstrated anything, it is that the avarice of America's corporate leaders is practically unlimited, and so is their power to run companies in their own interest. "When I did my first study, in 1973, the average C.E.O. of a major company was making about forty-five times the average pay of the workers," Graef Crystal reminded me recently. "When I wrote my book, in 1991, the pay ratio was a hundred and forty. Now it's five hundred." Under the light-handed regulation of public companies that has been fashionable since the Reagan era, the onus has fallen on auditors, boards of directors, and outside stockholders to restrain the selfishness of senior executives, but none of these groups have proved up to the task.

Even before the Enron scandal, it was clear that many auditors were not doing their jobs properly. In the case of Waste Management, for example, Arthur Andersen complained about many of the bookkeeping ruses that the senior managers were using, but it approved the company's financial statements nonetheless. Had Andersen done otherwise, it would have risked losing a lucrative client. Between 1991 and 1997, Andersen billed Waste Management $7.5 million in audit fees and $11.8 million in fees for other services, such as work on tax and regulatory issues. Meanwhile, Andersen Consulting billed Waste Management six million dollars, $3.7 million of which was related to a strategic review designed to "increase shareholder value."

Boards of directors often end up as patsies for the senior managers they are supposed to be monitoring. As Graef Crystal has been pointing out for years, the typical American board is composed of ten friends of the chairman, a token woman, and a token representative of a minority group. All too often, chief executives largely determined their own compensation arrangements, and the board rubber-stamped them.

"I think there were some people who were greedy, and who felt nobody was watching and they could get away with anything," Carl McCall, the state comptroller of New York, said when I spoke to him last month. McCall recently served on a New York Stock Exchange panel that recommended a set of reforms for companies wanting to list themselves on the Exchange. After the reforms are adopted, every company on the N.Y.S.E. must have a majority of independent directors on its board, and three of the company's committees— the audit committee, the compensation committee, and the nominating and governance committee— must be made up solely of independent directors. (At the moment, members of the audit committee

have to be independent, but companies are not even required to have compensation, nominating, or governance committees.)

These are worthwhile reforms, but, as Paul Volcker points out, "There's a limit on the supervisory, skeptical role that you can expect a board of directors to provide. In a successful company, the directors are going to have a collegial feeling. They have been appointed by the C.E.O. They are going to be heavily influenced by what he says. They are going to give him the benefit of the doubt." Moreover, a management team that is determined to act crookedly can often hide its fraud. At Enron, the outside directors included a former accounting professor and a former federal energy regulator, but neither of them was aware of the extent of what had been happening to the company until they read it in the newspapers.

Of course, senior executives are ultimately responsible to the owners of the company: the stockholders. But it was the weakness of the stockholders that justified the use of executive stock options to begin with, and little has changed in this regard. Most investors will simply sell their stock in a company if they see something they don't like. During the nineteen-nineties, there was another reason that investors were reluctant to police rapacious executives: most were too greedy themselves to question the startling earnings growth that supported the bull market. They gleefully accepted the optimistic line that Wall Street and corporate America fed to them, pausing only to inspect their monthly statements from Fidelity and Charles Schwab. It was only after the bubble burst that they were shocked to discover that many of the schemes they had been sold were illusory, and that some senior executives were dishonest.

. . . There are at least two ways that C.E.O.s could be reined in. In Germany, most big firms have two boards: an operating board, which deals with the day-to-day running of the company, and a supervisory board, which oversees the actions of the senior managers. The chief executive doesn't even have a seat on the supervisory board. In Britain, the post of chairman and chief executive is often split, so the company has two powerful figures at the top, who can keep an eye on each other. Americans often presume that their system of corporate governance is the best in the world, but there are things to be learned from practices elsewhere. Above all, it is time to downsize the myth of the all-powerful C.E.O. Effective leadership is one aspect of corporate success, but it is by no means the only one. History, competition, and luck also play crucial roles. And most C.E.O.s are eminently replaceable.

In recent weeks, senior executives of WorldCom and Adelphia Communications have been paraded before the cameras in handcuffs. . . . These pictures . . . sent a salutary message to other senior executives: public companies are social organizations with social responsibilities. Unless this message is heeded, the furor over Kenneth Lay and his fellow corporate scoundrels will gradually fade. And, once the economy and the stock market revive, the greed cycle will start up again.

Review and Discussion Questions

1. What is a publicly held corporation, and how does it differ from a private company? Why did publicly held corporations eventually replace private companies as the dominant form of capitalist economic organization?

2. What is the principal-agent problem, and how does it apply to corporate managers?

3. What are leveraged buyouts? What economic benefit are they supposed to bring, and what negative effects do they have?

4. What factors encouraged the rapid expansion of stock options as a form of executive compensation? How did they lead to both the financial boom of the 1990s and its collapse?

5. Do the issues discussed by Cassidy denote deep, permanent flaws in our corporate system, or are they only transient problems? What future do you foresee for corporate America? Are there ways in which our corporate system can and should be reformed?

6. What effect has the "greed cycle" discussed by Cassidy had on the rest of the economy and on our society generally? Can we avoid future greed cycles or are they an inevitable part of our system?

Reading ────────────■

THE ETHICS OF CORPORATE DOWNSIZING

JOHN ORLANDO

In recent years corporations have been downsizing their workforces at an unprecedented rate. Although this business trend may have benefited the economy overall, its human price has been high as hardworking employees suffer the emotional and financial repercussions of losing their jobs. In this essay John Orlando argues that downsizing is often morally wrong. He begins by challenging the assumption that the interests of shareholders take priority over those of employees, arguing instead for their moral equality. This equality implies that for downsizing to be permissible it must be justifiable from a utilitarian perspective, which takes into account the interests of both shareholders and workers. However, Orlando argues that the utilitarian case for downsizing is unproved and that there are at least three moral arguments against it. Although downsizing may be justified in extreme cases, for example, if it is necessary to save the corporation, Orlando concludes that downsizing merely to increase profit will usually be wrong.

I. THE ISSUE

A survey of contemporary business ethics literature leads one to believe that the primary ethical questions facing businesses today concern topics such as affirmative action, sexual harassment, and the environment. While these are without a doubt weighty concerns, many workers, especially manufacturing workers, would place corporate downsizing—the closing of whole plants or divisions in order to increase profits—at the head of their list of ethically contentious business practices. Though

From *Business Ethics Quarterly* 9 (April 1999). Copyright © 1999 The Society for Business Ethics. Reprinted by permission. Some notes omitted.

the issue has provoked considerable debate in the popular press, the philosophical community has largely ignored it.

This oversight is curious given that downsizing is arguably the major business trend of our era. . . . The statistics on downsizing's human costs are sobering. One study found that 15 percent of downsized workers lost their homes, and another that the suicide rate among laid-off workers is thirty times the national average.[1] Despite the rosy picture of the economy painted by the popular media, where attention is constantly drawn to the growth of the stock market, evidence suggests that trends such as downsizing have led to a general decline in employee earnings, as well as a widening of the gulf between rich and poor in America.[2] Added to this is the fact that since the loss of jobs is concentrated in a relatively small geographic area, these closings affect the entire community. Businesses that rely upon workers' spending will feel the pinch, often leading to secondary layoffs. Consequently, communities as a whole have been devastated by such closings.[3] Downsizing also carries with it serious nonquantifiable harms. News of mass layoffs sends psychological tremors across the nation, leading to general worker apprehension about job security and less job satisfaction.[4] Worse yet, the anxiety of unemployment often leads to psychological symptoms such as depression, or expresses itself through a variety of unpleasant behaviors: i.e., crime, domestic violence, child abuse, and alcohol and drug abuse.[5] . . .

I will argue that acts of downsizing are very often morally wrong. I will begin by demonstrating that the business ethics literature has yet to identify a morally relevant distinction between the situation of the shareholder and that of the worker in relation to the corporation. This means that the corporate manager has no naturally greater duty to shareholders than to workers. I will make my case by examining, and dismissing, the various arguments advanced for privileging the interests of shareholders above all other parties. I then advance arguments against the moral permissibility of acts of downsizing. I will finish with a few words about how the concerns I raise might [guide corporate managers and] provide direction for future investigations into the ethical status of [downsizing in particular business circumstances] . . .

II. THE MORAL EQUALITY OF WORKERS AND SHAREHOLDERS

Property Rights

First, it must be understood that one cannot justify the position that shareholder concerns take precedence over all other groups simply by appeal to the fact that the shareholders are the legal owners of the corporation. In that case, all one has done is provide a definition of the term *shareholder;* one has yet to provide a morally relevant reason for privileging the interests of that group. This is analogous to arguing that abortion is impermissible after viability because that is the point where the fetus could survive outside of the womb.

The natural tack at this point is to assert that a legal owner has property rights that allow her to dispose of her property in any manner she sees fit. But this justification skews the issue in the shareholder's favor by appealing to a paradigm that does not apply in the case of corporate ownership. The term *property rights* conjures up images of property for personal *use,* not *profit.* For instance, property rights advocates normally worry about laws that place restrictions on the use of one's homestead, such as laws regulating the appearance of one's home. . . . We may harbor a deep-seated intuition that property is sacred, but that intuition is tied to property with which we are in some respect intimately connected, such as a home.

To avoid glossing over the distinction between property for private use and property for profit, we will need to narrow our inquiry to an example of property for profit. Imagine that I own an apartment which I have rented to a couple for ten or fifteen years (think Fred and Ethel from "I Love Lucy"). I discover that I can make more money by dividing up the apartment and renting it to college students. My intuition is that I have a responsibility to the people who rent from me. At the very least, I should assure the couple, who might be frightened about the prospect of being thrown into the street, that I will not have them leave until they have procured similar housing elsewhere at a similar cost. I would

also feel obligated to ensure that their transition is as easy as possible by, for instance, helping them move. Moreover, the purpose of the money will have a bearing on the moral status of the act. The act is far easier to justify if it is needed to pay for my wife's extended medical care, than if it merely allows me to buy a longer sailboat. Thus, the general appeal to property rights breaks down when the property in question is for profit, and when we turn to scenarios closer to the practice of downsizing itself.

Fiduciary Duties

Many theorists and business managers defend the moral superiority of shareholders on grounds that corporate managers are bound by a fiduciary duty to their shareholders that trumps any competing duties. The burden of proof is then taken to fall on the shoulders of those arguing against this position to demonstrate that the manager has equally strong duties to others as well. . . .

But this characterization of the issue misconstrues the lines of justification for the duties of an agent in a fiduciary relationship. The fiduciary duty does not establish the obligations of the agent; it is rather prior considerations pertaining to the nature of the relationship that determine the parameters of that duty. For instance, the fiduciary duty of a lawyer to her client is not the same as that of a realtor to his client. Thus, the fiduciary duty itself cannot establish the agent's obligations, since the obligations differ in the two cases. This means that we must look to the particularities of the relationship to identify the contours of the manager's duty to her shareholders. The term *fiduciary duty* is merely a label for whatever obligations the manager owes to the shareholder; it does not create those duties, and thus cannot justify them. . . .

There is considerable evidence that the fiduciary duty of a corporate manager has been historically justified as a means of protecting the owner from that manager. The legal justification of this duty can be traced to the 1741 court ruling in *The Charitable Corporation v. Sir Robert Sutton*, where the court ruled that managers of corporations were "most properly agents of those who employ them." Interestingly, the suit was brought against the managers of The Charitable Corporation for "self-dealing by executives, theft, failure of inventory control, and a huge unmet financial commitment." Notice that the neglect of managerial duty cited involved not benevolent contributions to others, but rather acting in their *own* interest. . . .

Hence, there is good reason to believe that the legal basis of fiduciary duties of corporate managers to shareholders has been construed as the obligation to not advance their own interests against those of the shareholders. Adopting this view of the fiduciary relationship would mean that when a corporate manager takes into account the interests of stakeholders, even where that comes at the expense of profits, this does not conflict with a manager's fiduciary duty to shareholders.

Risk

Ian Maitland provides two justifications for the position that corporate managers have duties to shareholders over those to other parties. The first appeals to the fact that shareholders have invested capital in the corporation. Why is this fact morally relevant? According to Maitland, shareholders have taken a risk in placing their money in the hands of the corporation, and are thereby due compensation in the form of having their interests given privilege over those of other parties. Maitland states that:

> As a practical matter, no stakeholder is likely to agree to bear the risk associated with the corporation's activities unless it gets the commitment that the corporation will be managed for its benefit. That is logical because the stockholder alone stands to absorb any costs of mismanagement.[6]

It is strange, however, to think that the worker who loses his job has not absorbed any costs of mismanagement. Maitland's point must be that while workers stand to lose their jobs due to corporate mismanagement, they only lose future potential earnings, whereas shareholders lose something they have placed into the corporation. However, workers too have placed something at risk when accepting a job. At the very least, the worker has bypassed other possible job opportunities, opportunities that may have turned out to be financially more rewarding. Also, some have gone to school in the hopes of pursuing a career in the field, thereby investing substantial sums of money (or accruing substantial debt) in the process. Even more importantly, many workers have purchased homes in the expectation of a steady income, and in this manner have risked their homes on the corporation. We can also add to our list the various ways in which workers plant roots in the community which are disrupted when they are forced to relocate, such as placing their children in local schools or having their spouses accept jobs. While the worker's investment in a corporation is not of the same sort as the shareholder's, it constitutes a risk nevertheless, and so the worker's position is not dissimilar to that of the shareholder. The only difference between the risks taken by the two parties is one of degree, and the degree of that risk will depend upon the particular situation of each individual.

Contracts

Maitland's second argument is that corporations are fundamentally a "freely chosen . . . nexus . . . of contracts" between its stakeholders, which establish both the "rights" and the "obligations" of each party.[7] These contracts stipulate that the worker will give the corporation her labor in return for a fixed wage, while the shareholder will receive all of the profits of the corporation in return for investing capital in it. When third parties tinker with that arrangement, they violate the right of self-determination of the members of the contract, who have determined the terms of the contracts under "free," "voluntary," and "uncoerced" bargaining circumstances.[8] . . .

However, Maitland's picture of the corporation simply does not square with reality. It turns out that most shareholders expect corporate managers to take into account the interests of other constituencies when making decisions about the welfare of the corporation.[9] More importantly, shareholders tend to think of themselves not as owners of the corporation, but rather as investors in it. . . . For the vast majority of shareholders, dabbling in the stock market is thought of as one means among many of investing one's money, something chosen for its high rate of return, not in order to become a corporate owner. Thus, it is hard to understand how the investor can be acting under the assumption of an unstated contract between himself, management, and the company's employees. On the other side, employees have traditionally assumed that taking a job meant having it for life as long as they perform their duties well. Given these considerations, if we are basing such contracts on the implicit understandings and expectations of the parties involved, the evidence actually points in the very opposite direction to which Maitland argues.

Finally, one can raise serious doubts about the assertion that the worker/manager/shareholder relationship has been established under "free, voluntary, and uncoerced" circumstances. For one, the parties are by no means in an equal bargaining position. Despite Maitland's insistence that the disgruntled employee can always "fire his boss by resigning," employees often find that they have very few job options given their skills, the labor market, and the costs of moving to another area. Shareholders, however, have thousands of companies from which to choose, and a variety of mechanisms specifically designed to make movement in and out of the stock market as easy as possible. . . .

Other People's Money

Milton Friedman also advances two arguments against the position that corporations have a responsibility to parties other than shareholders. Friedman's first objection is that "the corporation is an instrument of the stockholders who own it," meaning that the manager is acting with other people's money, and thus serving the public interest at the expense of profits is an impermissible use of that money.[10] Another way to put it is that any action that diminishes profits to aid other parties constitutes a "tax" on the shareholders' income.

However, such a use of the shareholders' income is only impermissible if it is unauthorized, and as I have noted, most shareholders expect managers to take into account considerations beyond maximizing profits. Moreover, shareholders in a modern corporation can withdraw their money from that corporation with a simple phone call, and thus the manager who announces his intention to act for the public good gives shareholders plenty of time to remove

their money before such a "tax" is levied. More importantly, it is a generally accepted principle that moral duties "transfer through" from principal to agent, such that if it is morally forbidden for me to do something, then it is forbidden for me to enlist an agent to act on my behalf. Thus, an act of downsizing cannot be morally justified in virtue of the fact that it is done in the interests of the shareholders of the corporation, since if it is wrong for the shareholder to perform that act, then it is equally wrong for the manager to do so for them. The fact that a manager is an agent of others cannot itself make the action morally right, and therefore the moral status of the act will turn on other considerations.

Private vs. Public

Friedman's second objection is that requiring corporations to act in the social interest disrupts the private/public distinction which is at the heart of the free market system. Care for the public welfare, the objection goes, is properly the function of the state acting through officers specifically appointed for the task, not of businesspersons trained in other fields. Note that Friedman need not be against public welfare measures in principle, only those that place the burden of caring for the public welfare on the shoulders of corporations.

But this point can be met with at least two responses. First, one might argue . . . that corporations are best thought of as entities permitted to exist by the state because they serve the public good, not because individuals have a right to enrich themselves through them. Of course, corporate activities can end up doing both, but the issue concerns what justifies their existence, and in fact there is considerable historical evidence that corporations were originally conceived as a means of advancing the public good. Thus, the objection requires a defense of the position that corporations must only be run for the private good of their owners. Second, the objection cannot be applied to the case at hand. Downsizing concerns a corporation terminating the employment of its workers. Thus, unlike providing food and shelter to those in need, there is no public sector analogue to the service being demanded of corporations. . . .

I have argued that no philosophically sound argument has yet been advanced for privileging the interests of shareholders over those of workers simply by virtue of the fact that they are shareholders. This is not to say that no such argument may someday appear, but rather that in the absence of compelling reasons to the contrary, we must assume that the worker has an equal moral standing as the shareholder since they are, after all, both humans. Cast in this manner, the burden of proof in the debate runs contrary to what has been up to now believed by its participants. It has been tacitly assumed that it is the job of those arguing for the moral status of nonshareholders to establish their position, perhaps due to the earlier-mentioned view of fiduciary duties. But one of our most deeply felt convictions is that two human beings have equal moral status until morally relevant considerations can distinguish between them. Thus, it is really on the shoulders of those arguing for privileging the interests of the shareholders to make their case. This, I have argued, they have yet to do, leaving us to default to the presumption of equality.

The Utilitarian Argument

I now wish to examine the utilitarian defense of downsizing. It seems to me that once the moral equality of workers and shareholders has been granted, the only considerations that could justify acts of downsizing would be consequentialist in nature. At the very least, arguments currently advanced to justify acts of downsizing, when they do not rely upon the premise of a moral superiority of shareholders, have been utilitarian. Thus, if I can establish that the utilitarian case has yet to be made, I will have demonstrated that we have yet to find an adequate defense of downsizing.

. . . Utilitarianism is generally construed as the principle that the act that maximizes total utility is morally right. Thus, one could argue that downsizing benefits the majority of the population, and though it leaves some individuals by the wayside, the benefit to the whole outweighs the harm to the few. The entire economy, it might be argued, is becoming more efficient. Moreover, the stock market has skyrocketed, benefiting all those who have investments in mutual funds.

But there is reason to doubt whether downsizing has generated a net gain in utility. A group of researchers recently concluded a fifteen-year study which found that when acts of downsizing are not accompanied by careful restructuring of the corporation—in other words, when people are simply laid off in order to lower costs of production without thought of how the remaining employees will sustain levels of productivity—downsizing has always hurt the corporation in the long run.[11] Reich also notes that the downsizing trend has caused a general drop in employee loyalty in the United States.[12] Workers are far less likely to go the extra mile for firms who treat them as disposable cogs in the corporate machine. While loyalty is not easily quantifiable, and thus does not show up in a corporate ledger, it will affect the company's overall performance. . . .

But even if the case could be made that downsizing improves the overall health of the economy, there would still be a gap between this fact and the conclusion that overall utility has risen. If the argument were to terminate at this point, it would be assuming that one can equate well-being with financial gain; however, far more things go into determining one's well-being. For instance, it is indisputable that the anxiety from job loss has a profoundly negative influence upon one's psychic health. The harm of unemployment cannot simply be measured by the total loss of income; it produces fear for one's own well-being as well as the well-being of one's family, not to mention the anxiety experienced by those other groups themselves. When these factors are taken into account, it becomes clear that utilitarian considerations do not clearly point in favor of downsizing. It might in fact be determined that downsizing improves net utility in the long run, but the empirical evidence is inconclusive. Our position on the issue, therefore, will need to be informed by other considerations.

III. ARGUMENTS AGAINST DOWNSIZING

Harming Some to Benefit Others

Up to this point I have argued only that defenders of downsizing have failed to establish that downsizing is morally permissible. Here I will present reasons for thinking that downsizing is often morally wrong. The first argument appeals to the widely held intuition . . . that causing a great harm for a lesser benefit, even to a great number of people, cannot be morally justified. Most people would even consider it wrong to incur a great harm to a few in order to produce a great benefit to the many, such as removing the eyes from a sighted man and implanting them in two blind persons so that they can now see (with only a drop off in peripheral vision and depth perception distinguishing them from those with two eyes). There are even some who believe that no amount of harm to an individual can be justified on grounds that it will benefit others, since harms and benefits are incommensurable commodities. Given that statistics demonstrate that downsizing often leads to the loss of home and even suicide, it seems hard to deny that at least some downsized workers incur a significant harm from the practice. On the other side, since investors in a large corporation tend to diversify their assets, they incur only a minor benefit when any one stock price rises. Thus, if the act of downsizing is not done as a means of saving the corporation—preventing more workers from losing their jobs—but rather to increase profits, it involves causing a great harm for a minor benefit.

We can also draw a distinction within the practice of downsizing which will serve to amplify its wrongfulness in certain circumstances. Ask yourself if there is a difference in the moral status of the following two acts: First, a country involved in a just war bombs the other side's munitions factory in order to end the war, knowing that the bombing will also destroy a grade school bordering the factory and thus killing ten children. Second, a country in a just war bombs the school where the leaders of the opposing country send their kids in order to get them to end the war (accidentally destroying the neighboring munitions factory in the process). Most people would agree that the latter act is far worse than the former. The best way to explain this intuition is that in the latter act, the death of the children is a means to ending the war, while in the former it is an unfortunate byproduct of that means. The children in the second act are being *used* in a way that they are not being used in the former act.

Now consider the case where a CEO downsizes under the knowledge that the mere news of these layoffs will be greeted favorably by the stock market, and thus cause stock prices to rise . . . as opposed to the case where downsizing will improve profits by increasing productivity. Here the very act that harms the workers—the loss of their jobs—itself produces the benefit to shareholders. Harm is not a simple byproduct of an act which independently brings benefit, but rather is the means to that benefit. This grates even more deeply against our intuitions that it is wrong to use individuals for others' benefit.

Legitimate Expectations

We might also approach the issue from the perspective of the legitimate expectations of the individuals involved. To illustrate this notion, consider the possibility that the federal government repeals the home interest tax break without any other modifications in the tax code. While I see no reason why homeowners, and not renters, deserve such a break, one could question the action on grounds that homeowners have made plans under the assumption that this break would continue. Those who lose their homes because of the change in the tax laws would have a legitimate complaint, even though there was never a written guarantee that current tax laws would remain forever unchanged. Similarly, workers have made plans under the assumption of a continued source of income. These are not simply plans for leisure activities such as vacations, but rather plans that impinge upon their fundamental well-being as well as the well-being of their families. There are, however, no similar expectations on the part of the shareholder. For one, shareholders know that stock prices are volatile and that they take a risk when entering the market. Thus, no reasonable investor backs her home on the future performance of her securities. Investors may expect a certain average rate of return, but this is over the long term and they budget accordingly. They do not bank important items such as their homes on the assumption of the continued unprecedented rates of return seen in the past few years. Surely, these returns are treated as "icing on the cake," and thus if preserving jobs will diminish returns to the levels historically expected from the market, no critical expectations are thwarted. Also, as mentioned earlier, shareholders tend to consider the companies in which they invest to have obligations to parties other than themselves. Hence, one cannot plead that shareholders entered the market expecting that the company would be run solely for their own benefit.

Fairness

We may also appeal to the work of John Rawls to provide critical perspective on the issue. . . . I will draw upon what I consider his more central intuition: that the arbitrary conditions of one's situation ought not to count against one's life prospects. The idea here is that the individual does not deserve the rewards or punishments that come via things for which she is not responsible. At the very least, these factors include genetic endowments and the social institutions of the society in which she lives. . . .

To apply the principle here, we would first note that the worker who loses his job does so through no fault of his own. Someone fired due to incompetence is not downsized. Downsizing does not involve a surgical removal of all employees in a firm whose work is not up to snuff; instead, whole divisions are removed by virtue of their overall profitability, with no effort made to determine if individual members of those divisions are at fault. In fact, if a division or plant is unprofitable it is most likely due to mismanagement on the part of those running the corporation. This is perhaps one of the reasons why downsized workers feel betrayed, as no attempt is made by management to judge their actual job performance. Downsized workers find themselves harmed due to forces outside of their control. Moreover, these forces have conspired to selectively harm them since upper management tends to be insulated from these harms, by devices such as receiving a sizable "golden parachute" when dismissed. True, there are a variety of ways in which natural and social forces reward and punish arbitrarily but this does not make those harms permissible or release us from obligations to mitigate them.

On the other side, shareholders have done nothing to merit the sharp gains that downsizing produces. Perhaps they are owed good faith efforts at sound management by the corporation in virtue of their investment, but they cannot claim to deserve the special increases in the value of their investments due solely to laying off workers. The fact that we happen to live in a world where canning large numbers of workers is a quick means of increasing profits is not any of their doing. Note also that those shareholders who have invested through mutual funds have not themselves chosen to invest in this particular firm. These investors most likely have little idea as to which stocks their mutual funds actually hold, since one of the appeals of these funds is that they allow individuals to enter the market without the need to concern themselves with the intricacies of investing, or the day-to-day fluctuations of the market. . . .

IV. APPLYING THE RESULTS AND RELATED CONCERNS

. . . Business managers will need to examine the actual situations of their shareholders and workers, as well as that of the company, in order to ascertain if a decision to downsize is morally permissible. While this grants that some acts of downsizing may be morally permissible, simply establishing that corporate managers cannot lay claim to a special duty to shareholders that trumps any competing duties cuts against the grain of much of corporate America's current philosophy. For instance, in a speech to business representatives, David Rockefeller argued that corporations "have a responsibility to society beyond that of maximizing profits for shareholders." Yet he quickly qualified this position by stating that "let me add, before they come to retract my Chicago degree, that making profits must come first." While many business persons would agree that corporations have some obligations to persons besides shareholders, all but the most socially conscious would likely consider anathema the position that these obligations stand on equal footing with obligations to shareholders. . . .

How might the corporate manager apply the insights gathered here to a particular situation? First and foremost, an act of downsizing that prevents the collapse of the corporation can be justified on grounds that the organism is saved by amputating a limb. However, we must keep in mind that bankruptcy does not always mean the complete shutting down of shop. Bankruptcy courts make every effort to find a way of restructuring the debts of the corporation to keep it in business. In fact, corporations have been known to use bankruptcy as a means of avoiding a court settlement. But an act of downsizing that merely increases profits, which seems increasingly the case, requires a careful analysis of the harms and benefits it will incur to the parties involved. For a small firm, such as a fast-food franchise with a single proprietor, the owner may be at greater risk than her employees. The owner most likely has a large percentage of her personal fortune wrapped up in the company, whereas the workers are usually (but not always) high school students just earning extra spending money. However, with a large corporation, the results are likely to be quite different. It bears mention that the corporate entity is grounded in the principle that a separation exists between the corporation and the personal finances of its owners, a device created specifically to minimize the risk to shareholders. Thus, the owner of a corporation is not personally liable for its debts; if IBM dissolves, shareholders need not fear that IBM's creditors will come knocking at their doors. Legal protection to the shareholder is built into the corporation's charter. More importantly, since investors tend not to risk money that is required for their sustenance, their losses do not normally affect their immediate well-being. By contrast, the worker who banks his home on his job places his immediate well-being, as well as the well-being of his family, in far greater peril. Finally, investors today diversify their assets through mutual funds which own shares in thousands of corporations. Thus, losses from one stock create only a minor shift in the fund's overall value. This means that acts of downsizing can cause great harm to a few for a minor benefit to the many, something that I have argued is not morally permissible. Also, one can argue that the sole proprietor who has nursed the business from the ground up merits greater consideration than the mutual fund investor who may not even know that he or she owns shares in the corporation. Moreover, the worker who has purchased a home, and started a family, based on the assumption of the continued source of income, is deserving of greater consideration than the investor who finds that unprecedented gains in the stock market allow him to extend his vacation to Aruba by a week. . . .

Notes

1. Richard L. Bunning, "The Dynamics of Downsizing," *Personnel Journal* 69, no. 9 (Sept. 1990): 69.

2. Interview with Secretary of Labor Robert Reich in *Challenge*, July/August 1996, 4. Reich notes that while the *average* wage is up, the *median* wage (the wage of the individual in the middle) is down. The discrepancy is due to the unprecedented rise in compensation for top executives during the 1980s and 1990s.

3. Downsizing by the auto industry in the 1970s and 1980s caused Flint, Michigan's unemployment rate to climb to the highest in the United States, and its crime rate to rise accordingly. *Facts About the Cities,* ed. Allan Carpenter (New York: H. W. Wilson Co., 1992).

4. Harvey M. Brenner, *Mental Illness and the Economy* (Cambridge: Harvard University Press, 1973); Ralph Catalano and David Dooley, "Economic Predictors of Depressed Mood and Stressful Life Events in a Metropolitan Community," *Journal of Health and Social Behavior* 18 (1977): 292–307; Jean Hartley, Dan Jacobson, Bert Klandermans, and Tinka van Vuuren, *Job Insecurity: Coping With Jobs at Risk* (Newbury Park: Sage, 1991); and John R. Reynolds, "The Effects of Industrial Employment Conditions on Job-Related Distress," *Journal of Health and Social Behavior* (June 1977): 105–18.

5. David Dooley, Ralph Catalano, and Karen S. Rook, "Personal and Aggregate Unemployment and Psychological Symptoms," *Journal of Social Issues* 44 (1988): 107–23; David Dooley, Ralph Catalano, and Georjeanna Wilson, "Depression and Unemployment: Panel Findings from the Epidemiologic Catchment Area Study," *American Journal of Community Health* 22 (1994): 745–65.

6. Ian Maitland, "The Morality of the Corporation: An Empirical or Normative Disagreement?" *Business Ethics Quarterly* 4, no. 4 (1994): 445–57.

7. Maitland, op. cit., 449.

8. Maitland, op. cit., 450.

9. Larry D. Sonderquist and Robert P. Vecchio, "Reconciling Shareholders' Rights and Corporate Responsibility: New Guidelines for Management," *Duke Law Journal* (1978): 840; reproduced in John R. Boatright, "Fiduciary Duties and the Shareholder-Management Relation: Or, What's So Special About Shareholders?" *Business Ethics Quarterly* 4, no. 4 (October 1994): 398.

10. Friedman, "The Social Responsibility of Business Is to Increase Its Profits," *New York Times Magazine,* Septem-

ber 1970, reprinted in *Ethical Theory and Business,* ed. Tom L. Beauchamp and Norman E. Bowie (Englewood Cliffs, NJ: Prentice-Hall, 1979), 136–38.

11. Wayne F. Cascio, interview on National Public Radio, November 14, 1997.

12. Reich, op. cit.

Review and Discussion Questions

1. Orlando discusses six arguments intended to show that the interests of shareholders take priority over those of other groups. State each of these six arguments in one or two sentences, and then critically assess Orlando's responses to them. Which of the arguments are the strongest? Which do you see as the weakest? Do you agree that there is moral equality between workers and shareholders? If so, what implications does this have?

2. Can downsizing be supported on utilitarian grounds? Explain why or why not.

3. Is downsizing wrong because it is an instance of "harming some to benefit others," as Orlando argues?

4. Orlando's "legitimate expectations" argument against downsizing rests on the premise that "workers have made plans under the assumption of a continued source of income." Is that premise true and, if so, was it reasonable for workers to make this assumption?

5. Orlando argues that downsizing is unfair by appealing to the principle that people do not deserve rewards or punishments for things for which they are not responsible. Do you accept Orlando's principle? If so, does it show that downsizing is wrong?

Reading ———————————————■

ETHICAL DILEMMAS FOR MULTINATIONAL ENTERPRISE: A PHILOSOPHICAL OVERVIEW

RICHARD T. DE GEORGE

Corporations today are increasingly multinational in their business activities. This fact has stirred up controversy about the effects of those activities on foreign countries and about what sort of moral responsibilities multi-national corporations have. In this essay, Professor De George clarifies these issues by explaining and defending five basic theses, which provide a useful framework for discussing the moral dilemmas that multinationals can face. While De George defends multinationals against some of their critics, he maintains that there are definite moral standards to which they must adhere.

Reprinted by permission of the publisher from W. Michael Hoffman, Ann E. Lange, and David A. Fredo, *Ethics and the Multinational Enterprise* (Lanham, Md.: University Press of America, 1986). Copyright © 1986 by University Press of America. Some notes omitted.

First World multinational corporations (MNCs) are both the hope of the Third World and the scourge of the Third World. The working out of this paradox poses moral dilemmas for many MNCs. I shall focus on some of the moral dilemmas that many American MNCs face.

Third World countries frequently seek to attract American multinationals for the jobs they provide and for the technological transfers they promise. Yet when American MNCs locate in Third World countries, many Americans condemn them for exploiting the resources and workers of the Third World. While MNCs are a means for improving the standard of living of the underdeveloped countries, MNCs are blamed for the poverty and starvation such countries suffer. Although MNCs provide jobs in the Third World, many criticize them for transferring these jobs from the United States. American MNCs usually pay at least as high wages as local industries, yet critics blame them for paying the workers in underdeveloped countries less than they pay American workers for comparable work. When American MNCs pay higher than local wages, local companies criticize them for skimming off all the best workers and for creating an internal brain-drain. Multinationals are presently the most effective vehicle available for the development of the Third World. At the same time, critics complain that the MNCs are destroying the local cultures and substituting for them the tinsel of American life and the worst aspects of its culture. American MNCs seek to protect the interests of their shareholders by locating in an environment in which their enterprise will be safe from destruction by revolutions and confiscation by socialist regimes. When they do so, critics complain that the MNCs thrive in countries with strong, often right-wing, governments.[1]

The dilemmas the American MNCs face arise from conflicting demands made from opposing, often ideologically based, points of view. Not all of the demands that lead to these dilemmas are equally justifiable, nor are they all morally mandatory. We can separate the MNCs that behave immorally and reprehensibly from those that do not by clarifying the true moral responsibility of MNCs in the Third World. To help do so, I shall state and briefly defend five theses.

Thesis 1: Many of the moral dilemmas MNCs face are false dilemmas which arise from equating United States standards with morally necessary standards.

Many American critics argue that American multinationals should live up to and implement the same standards abroad that they do in the United States and that United States mandated norms should be followed.* This broad claim confuses morally nec-

---

*The position I advocate does not entail moral relativism, as my third thesis shows. The point is that although moral norms apply uniformly across cultures, U.S. standards are not the same as moral standards, should themselves be morally evaluated, and are relative to American conditions, standard of living, interests, and history.

essary ways of conducting a firm with United States government regulations. The FDA sets high standards that may be admirable. But they are not necessarily morally required. OSHA specifies a large number of rules which in general have as their aim the protection of the worker. However, these should not be equated with morally mandatory rules. United States wages are the highest in the world. These also should not be thought to be the morally necessary norms for the whole world or for United States firms abroad. Morally mandatory standards that no corporation—United States or other—should violate, and moral minima below which no firm can morally go, should not be confused either with standards appropriate to the United States or with standards set by the United States government. Some of the dilemmas of United States multinationals come from critics making such false equations.

This is true with respect to drugs and FDA standards, with respect to hazardous occupations and OSHA standards, with respect to pay, with respect to internalizing the costs of externalities, and with respect to foreign corrupt practices. By using United States standards as moral standards, critics pose false dilemmas for American MNCs. These false dilemmas in turn obfuscate the real moral responsibilities of MNCs.

Thesis 2: Despite differences among nations in culture and values, which should be respected, there are moral norms that can be applied to multinationals.

I shall suggest seven moral guidelines that apply in general to any multinational operating in Third World countries and that can be used in morally evaluating the actions of MNCs. MNCs that respect these moral norms would escape the legitimate criticisms contained in the dilemmas they are said to face.

1. *MNCs should do no intentional direct harm.* This injunction is clearly not peculiar to multinational corporations. Yet it is a basic norm that can be usefully applied in evaluating the conduct of MNCs. Any company that does produce intentional direct harm clearly violates a basic moral norm.

2. *MNCs should produce more good than bad for the host country.*

This is an implementation of a general utilitarian principle. But this norm restricts the extent of that principle by the corollary that, in general, more good will be done by helping those in most need, rather than by helping those in less need at the expense of those in greater need. Thus the utilitarian analysis in this case does not consider that more harm than good might justifiably be done to the host country if the harm is offset by greater benefits to others in developed countries. MNCs will do more good only if they help the host country more than they harm it.

3. *MNCs should contribute by their activities to the host country's development.*

If the presence of an MNC does not help the host country's development, the MNC can be correctly charged with exploitation, or using the host country for its own purposes at the expense of the host country.

4. *MNCs should respect the human rights of their employees.*

MNCs should do so whether or not local companies respect those rights. This injunction will preclude gross exploitation of workers, set minimum standards for pay, and prescribe minimum standards for health and safety measures.

5. *MNCs should pay their fair share of taxes.*

Transfer pricing has as its aim taking advantage of different tax laws in different countries. To the extent that it involves deception, it is itself immoral. To the extent that it is engaged in to avoid legitimate taxes, it exploits the host country, and the MNC does not bear its fair share of the burden of operating in that country.

6. *To the extent that local culture does not violate moral norms, MNCs should respect the local culture and work with it, not against it.*

MNCs cannot help but produce some changes in the cultures in which they operate. Yet, rather than simply transferring American ways into other lands, they can consider changes in operating procedures, plant planning, and the like, which take into account local needs and customs.

7. *MNCs should cooperate with the local government in the development and enforcement of just background institutions.*

Instead of fighting a tax system that aims at appropriate redistribution of incomes, instead of preventing the organization of labor, and instead of resisting attempts at improving the health and safety standards of the host country, MNCs should be supportive of such measures.

Thesis 3: Wholesale attacks on multinationals are most often overgeneralizations. Valid moral evaluations can be best made by using the above moral criteria for context-and-corporation-specific studies and analysis.

Broadside claims, such that all multinationals exploit underdeveloped countries or destroy their culture, are too vague to determine their accuracy. United States multinationals have in the past engaged—and some continue to engage—in immoral practices. A case by case study is the fairest way to make moral assessments. Yet we can distinguish five types of business operations that raise very different sorts of moral issues: (1) banks and financial institutions; (2) agricultural enterprises; (3) drug companies and hazardous industries; (4) extractive industries; and (5) other manufacturing and service industries.

If we were to apply our seven general criteria in each type of case, we would see some of the differences among them. Financial institutions do not generally employ many people. Their function is to provide loans for various types of development. In the case of South Africa they [did] not do much—if anything—to undermine apartheid, and by lending to the government they usually strengthen[ed] the government's policy of apartheid. In this case, an argument can be made that they [did] more harm than good. . . . Financial institutions can help and have helped development tremendously. Yet the servicing of debts that many Third World countries face condemns them to impoverishment for the foreseeable future. The role of financial institutions in this situation is crucial and raises special and difficult moral problems, if not dilemmas.

Agricultural enterprises face other demands. If agricultural multinationals buy the best lands and use them for export crops while insufficient arable land is left for the local population to grow enough to feed itself, then MNCs do more harm than good to the host country—a violation of one of the norms I suggested above.

Drug companies and dangerous industries pose different and special problems. I have suggested that FDA standards are not morally mandatory standards. This should not be taken to mean that drug companies are bound only to local laws, for the local laws may require less than morality requires in the way of supplying adequate information and of not producing intentional, direct harm. The same type of observation applies to hazardous industries. While an asbestos company will probably not be morally required to take all the measures mandated by OSHA regulations, it cannot morally leave its workers completely unprotected.

Extractive industries, such as mining, which remove minerals from a country, are correctly open to the charge of exploitation unless they can show that they do more good than harm to the host country and that they do not benefit only either themselves or a repressive elite in the host country.

Other manufacturing industries vary greatly, but as a group they have come in for sustained charges of exploitation of workers and the undermining of the host country's culture. The above guidelines can serve as a means of sifting the valid from the invalid charges.

Thesis 4: On the international level and on the national level in many Third World countries the lack of adequate just background institutions makes the use of clear moral norms all the more necessary.

American multinational corporations operating in Germany and Japan, and German and Japanese multinational corporations operating in the United States, pose no special moral problems. Nor do the operations of Brazilian multinational corporations in the United States or Germany. Yet First World multinationals operating in Third World countries have come in for serious and sustained moral criticism. Why?

A major reason is that in the Third World the First World's MNCs operate without the types of constraints and in societies that do not have the same kinds of redistributive mechanisms as in the developed countries. There is no special difficulty in United States multinationals operating in other First World countries because in general these countries *do* have appropriate background institutions.[2]

More and more Third World countries are developing controls on multinationals that insure the companies do more good for the country than harm. Authoritarian regimes that care more for their own wealth than for the good of their people pose difficult moral conditions under which to operate. In such instances, the guidelines above may prove helpful.

Just as in the nations of the developed, industrial world the labor movement serves as a counter to the dominance of big business, consumerism serves as a watchdog on practices harmful to the consumer, and big government serves as a restraint on each of the vested interest groups, so international structures are necessary to provide the proper background constraints on international corporations.

The existence of MNCs is a step forward in the unification of mankind and in the formation of a global community. They provide the economic base and substructure on which true international cooperation can be built. Because of their special position and the special opportunities they enjoy, they have a special responsibility to promote the cooperation that only they are able to accomplish in the present world.

Just background institutions would preclude any company's gaining a competitive advantage by engaging in immoral practices. This suggests that MNCs have more to gain than to lose by helping formulate voluntary, UN (such as the code governing infant formulae),[3] and similar codes governing the conduct of all multinationals. A case can also be made that they have the moral obligation to do so.

Thesis 5: The moral burdens of MNCs do not exonerate local governments from responsibility for what happens in and to their country. Since responsibility is linked to ownership, governments that insist on part or majority ownership incur part or majority responsibility.

The attempts by many underdeveloped countries to limit multinationals have shown that at least some governments have come to see that they can use multinationals to their own advantage. This may be done by restricting entry to those companies that produce only for local consumption, or that bring desired technology transfers with them. Some countries demand majority control and restrict the export of money from the country. Nonetheless, many MNCs have found it profitable to engage in production under the terms specified by the host country.

What host countries cannot expect is that they can demand control without accepting correlative responsibility. In general, majority control implies majority responsibility. An American MNC, such as Union Carbide, which had majority ownership of its Indian Bhopal plant, should have had primary control of the plant. Union Carbide, Inc. can be held liable for the damage the Bhopal plant caused because Union Carbide, Inc. did have majority ownership.[4] If Union Carbide did not have effective control, it is not relieved of its responsibility. If it could not exercise the control that its responsibility demanded, it should have withdrawn or sold off part of its holdings in that plant. If India had had majority ownership, then it would have had primary responsibility for the safe operation of the plant.

This is compatible with maintaining that if a company builds a hazardous plant, it has an obligation to make sure that the plant is safe and that those who run it are properly trained to run it safely. MNCs cannot simply transfer dangerous technologies without consideration of the people who will run them, the local culture, and similar factors. Unless MNCs can be reasonably sure that the plants they build will be run safely, they cannot morally build them. To do so would be to will intentional, direct harm.

The theses and guidelines that I have proposed are not a panacea. But they suggest how moral norms can be brought to bear on the dilemmas American multinationals face and they suggest ways out of apparent or false dilemmas. If MNCs observed those norms, they could properly avoid the moral sting of their critics' charges, even if their critics continued to level charges against them.

Notes

1. The literature attacking American MNCs is extensive. Many of the charges mentioned in this essay are found in Richard J. Barnet and Ronald E. Muller, *Global Reach: The Power of the Multinational Corporations*, New York: Simon & Schuster, 1974, and in Pierre Jalee, *The Pillage of the Third World*, translated from the French by Mary Klopper, New York and London: Modern Reader Paperbacks, 1968.

2. This position is consistent with that developed by John Rawls in his *A Theory of Justice*, Cambridge, Mass.: Harvard University Press, 1971, even though Rawls does not extend his analysis to the international realm. The thesis does not deny that United States, German, or Japanese policies on trade restrictions, tariff levels, and the like can be morally evaluated.

3. For a general discussion of UN codes, see Wolfgang Fikentscher, "United Nations Codes of Conduct: New Paths in International Law," *The American Journal of Comparative Law* 30 (1980), pp. 577–604.

4. The official Indian Government report on the Bhopal tragedy has not yet appeared. The Union Carbide report was partially reprinted in the *New York Times*, March 21, 1985, p. 48. The major *New York Times* reports appeared on December 9, 1984, January 28, 30, and 31, and February 3, 1985.

Review and Discussion Questions

1. Explain each of De George's five theses in your own words. Do you agree with them? Are any open to doubt or possible objection? Explain.

2. What do you see as the most important moral dilemmas that face American MNCs operating overseas? With regard to the five types of business operations distinguished by De George (in his discussion of Thesis 3), do you think that MNCs operating in Third World countries do more good than harm?

3. De George offers seven moral guidelines for multinationals operating in the Third World. Do you agree with them? What would a proponent of the narrow view of corporate responsibility say about them? Has De George overlooked any other responsibilities that multinationals have?

4. De George denies that American MNCs should live up to and implement the same standards abroad as they do at home. Do you agree? Does De George's position imply some kind of ethical relativism?

Reading——————————————■

BUSINESS ETHICS: ON GETTING TO THE HEART OF THE MATTER

PAUL F. CAMENISCH

It is common in discussions of business ethics to make one of two assumptions. The first is that business ethics is essentially the prevailing moral code of the society applied to business. The second is that business ethics is essentially a matter of applying certain standards of social responsibility to corporations. Paul F. Camenisch argues in the following essay that neither approach gets to the heart of business ethics. To do this, we must inquire about the fundamental nature of business—what it is, what it claims to do, and what distinctive functions it performs.

Camenisch keys on two essential elements of business: profit and the provision of goods and services. By Milton Friedman's account, the profit goal takes precedence over the other: If business makes a profit, it meets its responsibility to society. Camenisch demurs; whereas profit may be an adequate criterion for assessing a business undertaking, he says it is an inadequate ethical ideal. Camenisch goes on to argue that the business activity itself must be scrutinized according to how it affects "human flourishing directly through the kind of products or services it provides, and through the responsible or irresponsible use of limited and often nonrenewable resources."

THE HEART OF BUSINESS ETHICS

Many current discussions of business ethics seem in the end to locate the ethical concern some distance from the central and essential activity of business. One way this is done is to assume that the content of business ethics is no more and no less than the prevailing moral code of the society as applied to business activities. Business persons and institutions, like all other citizens, are expected to refrain from murder, from fraud, and from polluting the environment. But we cannot limit business ethics to such matters. In fact, perhaps we ought not even call this *business* ethics for the same reasons that we do not say that parental ethics prohibits my brutalizing my children. This is not parental ethics but just ethics plain and simple. This constraint arises from what it means to be a decent human being, not from what it means to be a parent. Similarly, the prohibition upon murdering to eliminate a business competitor is not part of a *business* ethic, for it does not arise from what it means to be engaged in business, nor does it apply to one simply because one is engaged in business. It too arises from what it means to be a decent, moral human being.

The second way of moving ethical issues to the edge of business's activities usually occurs under the rubric of "business's social responsibilities." The most remote of the issues raised here involve the question of whether corporations should devote any of their profits to philanthropic, educational and other sorts of humanitarian undertakings. This is a controversial issue which will not be easily resolved, but even if we concluded that this was a social responsibility of business, it would again fail to be business ethics in any specific and distinctive sense. It would simply be the application to this corporate member of a general societal expectation that members of a society existing in extensive interdependence with and benefitting from that society ought, if able, to contribute some portion of their wealth to such worthy causes. It should in passing be noted that there are persuasive grounds for rejecting this form of social responsibility for business.

Another class of social responsibilities urged upon business is somewhat closer to business activity as such since they can be fulfilled in the course of business's central activity of producing and marketing goods and services. These are the negative duties of neither creating nor aggravating social ills

Paul F. Camenisch, "Business Ethics: On Getting to the Heart of the Matter," *Business and Professional Ethics Journal* 1 (Fall 1981): 59–69. Reprinted by permission of the author. Section titles added.

which might arise from business activity such as discriminatory employment, advancement and remuneration along racial, sexual, or other irrelevant lines, dangerous working conditions, and avoidable unemployment or worker dislocation.

Still we have not yet reached the heart of business ethics because we have said nothing of the ethics which come to bear on business *as business*, on business at its very heart and essence. But what is this "heart" of the business enterprise, and how and why are business ethics to be grounded in it?

Imagine a corporation which observes all the moral claims already noted—it does not commit fraud or murder, it freely contributes from its profits to various community "charities," its employment practices are above reproach, and it sells quality products at a fair and competitive price while securing for its investors a reasonable return on their investment. So far so good. Its moral record is impeccable. But imagine that the only conceivable use of its products is for human torture. Can we say that here there are no moral or ethical judgments to be made? That the kind of service or product which is at the heart of the enterprise is entirely inconsequential in any and all moral assessments of that enterprise? I do not see how morally sensitive persons or societies can set aside their moral perceptions at this point.

Of course one good reason for resisting this suggestion is the great difficulty in making such assessments of goods and services. *Whose* assessments will prevail? We might get general agreement on instruments of human torture—although even here I would not expect unanimity. But what of other goods such as napalm, Saturday-night specials, pornographic materials, junk foods, tobacco, liquors, etc., and services such as prostitution, the training of military mercenaries, or even the provision of such, or the training of the armed forces of repressive regimes, offensive-oriented "survival" courses, the construction of the usually redundant fast-food outlets along suburban slurp strips? In addition to these items in which virtually everyone should be able to see some detrimental elements, there is an additional class of items which some would list here because of their use of limited, even

nonrenewable, resources for no purpose beyond momentarily satisfying the whimsey of the indiscriminate wealthy, the bored, the vain, or of increasing corporate profits. . . .

But how do we carry business ethics to the very heart of the business enterprise? I would argue that we can begin by asking the question of what the business sector is and claims to do, what its distinctive function is in the larger society of which it is a part. The norms, both moral and otherwise, for the conduct of an agent, whether individual or corporate,* can be determined only after we have established what that agent's relations are to other agents in the moral community, what role the agent plays in relation to them, what the agent's activities in the context of that community aim at. . . .

TWO ESSENTIAL ELEMENTS OF BUSINESS

In looking for the essential or definitive element in business I would suggest that it is necessary and helpful to see business as one form of that activity by which humans have from the beginning sought to secure and/or produce the material means of sustaining and then of enhancing life. It is plausible to assume that in earlier times individuals and small groups did this for themselves in immediate and direct ways such as gathering, hunting and fishing, farming, producing simple tools and weapons, etc. With the passage of time developments such as co-operative efforts, barter and monetary exchange modified this simple and idyllic situation. Business, I would suggest, enters this picture as that form of such activities in which the exchanges engaged in are no longer motivated entirely by

---

*I am not prepared to enter here into the current debate concerning the existence and/or nature of corporate moral agency. For my present point it is sufficient to note that the moral stances, decisions and actions of various persons engaged in business and working together, as or through a corporation, do have impacts on the life of society and of its members of the sort I here have in mind. Whether these impacts are to be credited to those individual persons or to the corporation seems to make little difference in the present analysis.

the intention of all participants to secure goods or services immediately needed to sustain and/or enhance their own lives, but by the design of at least some of the participants to make a profit, i.e., to obtain some value in excess of what they had before the exchange which is sufficiently flexible that it can be put to uses other than the immediate satisfaction of the recipient's own needs and desires. It should be noted that this last point is as much or more a matter of defining business, as it is of charting its historical emergence.

In the above statement I am suggesting that there are two essential elements in any adequate definition of business, the *provision of goods and services*, and the fact that this is done with the intention of making a *profit*. The first of these shows business's continuity with the various other human activities just noted by which life has been sustained and enhanced throughout the ages and enables us to understand business in relation to the larger society. The second is a more specific characteristic and sets business off from these other activities by revealing its distinctive internal dynamic. But this element does *not* sever business's connection with those predecessors. The crucial moral points to be made here are that moral/ethical issues arise around both of these elements and that the most important ones concern the "goods and services" element, i.e., the connection between business and the larger society of which it is part.

This appears to put me in definite tension with Milton Friedman who attempts to ground business ethics, or at least that portion of it which he calls the social responsibility of business, in the profit element only: "In . . . [a free] economy, there is one and only one social responsibility of business—to use its resources and engage in activities designed to increase its profits so long as it stays within the rules of the game, which is to say, engages in open and free competition, without deception or fraud."[1]

Of course it is unfair to Friedman to say that for him the maximization of profit is business's only moral duty since he may assume that playing by the rules of the game and that even conducting oneself so as to make a profit in such a "game" would bring additional restraints to bear on business, restraints

which many of us would consider to be *moral* restraints. Nevertheless, Friedman's statement does seem to put undue emphasis on business's profit-making function in answering the question of its social and/or moral responsibility.

But however one interprets Friedman's statement, we do here encounter a question fundamental to our present point. This is the question of whether, in defining business and understanding it as a moral reality, we should focus primarily on its goal of producing goods and services or of generating a profit. One can attempt to resolve this question in several ways. There is the rather common sense way of looking at the way most persons generally apply the label "business." A producer of goods and services intending to make a profit but failing to do so is still, by most accounts, engaged in business. Of course some might respond that the concept of profit is still crucial to this activity's being considered business even though here it is present in intention only. But consider the other side. What if profit is present but the provision of goods and services is entirely absent as in a bank robbery? Most, I take it, would deny that here we have just another instance of business, or even an instance of business of a rather unusual sort. Most would simply want to deny that the bank robber was engaged in business at all. Of course one might salvage the position that business is defined by profit-making and yet avoid having to consider the bank robber a businessman by arguing that profit is not just any kind of gain at all, but is a particular sort of gain or is gain realized only under certain circumstances. But even this move would tend to support my position that a single simple concept of profit is not by itself sufficient to define what we mean by business. Whether these additional defining characteristics are written into a more complex definition of profit or are seen as additional to profit is a matter of indifference in terms of the present argument.

Secondly, one could take a more reflective, analytical approach and ask what the relation between these two elements—providing goods and services and profit-making—is, to see if that relation grants a kind of priority to either of them. I would argue, consistent with the above scenario of the emergence of business, that business's primary function, like that of the activities it supplants, is the producing of goods and services to sustain and enhance human existence. Profit then, given the way business functions in the marketplace, becomes one of the necessary means by which business enables itself to continue supplying such goods and services. This would mean that the goods and services element must be given priority in our understanding of business as a social reality and in our moral/ethical response to it. For in the absence of goods and services which are really *goods* and *services*, the making of a profit is at best morally irrelevant. In the absence of the end sought, the means for achieving it are otiose. . . .

Finally, in trying to settle the question of the relation between profits on the one hand and goods and services on the other, one might look at business in terms of its social function and ask why societies have generated and now support and sustain business. Surely it is not for business's own sake, nor for the sake of the few who own and manage businesses so that they can make a profit. Society has no need for profit-making as such. But rather, societies generate, encourage and sustain business because societies need the available raw materials transformed into needed goods and services, and because business in its contemporary form has been conspicuously successful in doing just that. In fact, in the current setting it may be that only business has the resources and the know-how to do that job on the needed scale.

All three of these ways of addressing the relation between these two elements would seem to confirm my position that the provision of goods and services can, perhaps must, be given priority over the profit element in our understanding of business. The major implication of this position for the resulting business ethics would be that the assessment of business as such and of specific business enterprises would begin with the question of whether the goods and services produced thereby serve to enhance or detract from the human condition, whether they contribute to or obstruct human flourishing. Implicit here is the suggestion that businesses engaged in producing goods and ser-vices which do not contribute to human flourishing are engaged in a morally questionable enterprise, and those engaged in producing goods and services inimical to human flourishing are engaged in immoral activity. . . .

ASSESSING BUSINESS'S CONTRIBUTION TO HUMAN FLOURISHING

Of course this suggestion concerning the heart of business ethics is rife with problems. Chief among them is the question of how we define the human flourishing which business is to serve. While we cannot resolve this question here, raising it at least serves to demonstrate that business ethics, like any serious ethics, will need to develop a philosophical or theological anthropology, a view of humanity and what its proper pursuit, its appropriate fulfillment is.

Some, of course, will argue that the only proper answers to such questions are the ones given by consumers in the marketplace as they use their purchasing power to vote for or against the various answers business implicitly offers in the form of diverse goods and services. While this may be an acceptable answer when one focuses exclusively on the relation between the individual consumer and the marketplace, it is clearly inadequate when we focus on the marketplace in relation to the total society, its present condition and needs and its future prospects. And clearly it is unrealistic, even irresponsible, to attempt to view an enterprise as large and as extensively intertwined with the total fabric of the society as is business only in its relation to individual consumers and their choices. Furthermore, the "marketplace as voting booth" answer to these questions is a costly trial and error method. And given advertising and other forms of demand formation, the significance of consumer "votes" is very unclear. Yet to have such judgments made by any agency outside the marketplace has serious implications for citizen-consumer freedom and rights in a free society.

In light of these difficult problems it might be tempting to give up the search for criteria by which to assess the performance of business at the level of its central function. And yet there are at least three important reasons for attempting this assessment in spite of the obvious problems. As we become increasingly aware of the limits of the earth and its resources within which all of humanity both present and future must live, and of the fact that in our present setting only business has the means and the know-how to transform those resources on any significant scale into the needed goods and services, it becomes increasingly clear that the total society has a crucial stake in, and should therefore have a say about, what business does with this our common legacy. As Keith Davis has suggested, ". . . business now has a new social role of . . . trustee for society's resources. . . ."[2] The knowing use of nonrenewable resources to make products of little or no human value and/or with short useful life solely for the sake of an immediate profit thus becomes a serious disservice to the larger society. An ethic of the sort here proposed provides a framework within which we could raise the question of how this trusteeship can best be exercised.

Secondly, this enterprise of assessing business in terms of its contribution to human flourishing is called for and legitimated by the fact that business in its various activities is already propagating, whether consciously or not, a view of humanity and of what human flourishing consequently means, views which of course assign a major role to the consumption of the goods and services business produces.[3] Even if this view of humanity is only implicit or perhaps especially if it is implicit, its content and potential impact call for assessment by parties outside the business sector.

Finally, the difficult task of responding to business on these central issues is worth undertaking because of the role business plays in contemporary America and similar societies. In observing the role of business and related economic matters in contemporary America one might almost suggest that we have moved from a sacralized society dominated by religious concerns, through a secularized one in which various major sectors attained considerable autonomy in their own spheres, to a commercialized or an economized culture in which the common denominators which unify and dominate all areas of activity are business related or business grounded considerations such as dollar-value, profitability, marketability, efficiency, contribution to

the gross national product, etc. And as Thomas Donaldson and Patricia Werhane have written:

> There may be nothing inherently evil about the goals of economic growth, technological advance, and a higher material standard of living; but critics such as Galbraith have argued that when these become the primary goals of a nation there is a significant lowering in the quality of human life. Economic goals are able to distract attention from crucial human issues, and freedom, individuality, and creativity are lost in a society dominated by large corporations and economic goals.[4]

If the above is a plausible interpretation of the role of business, broadly understood, in contemporary America, and of some of its implications for human flourishing, then it should be obvious that we have need for an ethic which responds to the central activity of business, since the crucial human implications of such cultural domination by business arise from this central function and not from the less central concerns often raised in business ethics. . . .

But why should business submit to the scrutiny and recommendations of an ethic such as is proposed here? One answer would be because such an ethic is predicated on what business *is*—one important part of society's efforts to enable its members to flourish, specifically that part which deals with the provision of the material means for sustaining and enhancing life.

"Of course," the critic might respond, "this answer works *if* we agree on what you say business is. But if we maintain that business must be defined and understood in terms of its own internal dynamics and goals, e.g., profit-making, rather than in terms of society's needs and goals, then the answer falls apart." True enough. But given business's extensive interdependence with society—its reliance on society's educational system to provide educated workers, on society's maintenance of transportation systems, of a stable social and political setting in which to do business, of a legal system by which business can adjudicate its disputes with competitors and customers, of what E. F. Schumacher has called the "infrastructure"[5]—it is naive to suggest that business is a self-sufficient and self-contained entity which can define its own goals and functions entirely independently of the society's goals and needs. As Robert A. Dahl has written:

Today it is absurd to regard the corporation simply as an enterprise established for the sole purpose of allowing profit making. We the citizens give them special rights, powers, and privileges, protection, and benefits on the understanding that their activities will fulfill purposes. Corporations exist only as they continue to benefit us. . . . Every corporation should be thought of as a social enterprise whose existence and decisions can be justified only insofar as they serve public or social purposes.[6]

Furthermore, anyone who argues that business should be permitted to define its own goals and purposes and thus its own ethics independently of societal interests will have to explain why business should be granted latitude at this point that is denied to other major sectors of societal activity such as politics, education, or the traditional professions such as law and medicine. . . .

There are numerous varied matters which are legitimately included in any adequate definition of business ethics. In fact, in a nascent field such as this it is as yet impossible to say with any certainty what is within and what is without its borders. But it does seem clear that any business ethic that does not respond first and foremost to business's contribution to or detraction from human flourishing through its essential and definitive activity of generating life sustaining and enhancing goods and services will have failed to lay a foundation from which to address all other questions for it will not yet have gotten to the heart of the matter.

Notes

1. Milton Friedman, *Capitalism and Freedom* (Chicago: University of Chicago Press, 1962), 133.

2. Keith Davis, "Five Propositions for Social Responsibility," in Tom L. Beauchamp and Norman E. Bowie, eds., *Ethical Theory and Business* (Englewood Cliffs, N.J.: Prentice-Hall, 1979), 170.

3. For one interpretation of the understanding of human flourishing assumed and propagated by much of business in a consumer society, see Edward Stevens, *Business Ethics* (New York: Paulist Press, 1979), 205–211.

4. Thomas Donaldson and Patricia H. Werhane, eds., *Ethical Issues in Business* (Englewood Cliffs, N.J.: Prentice-Hall, 1979), 330.

5. E. F. Schumacher, *Small Is Beautiful* (New York: Harper & Row, 1975), 273–274.

6. Robert A. Dahl, "A Prelude to Corporate Reform," in Robert L. Heilbroner and Paul London, eds., *Corporate Social Policy* (Reading, Mass.: Addison-Wesley Publishing Company, 1975), 18–19, as cited in Norman E. Bowie, "Changing the Rules," in Tom L. Beauchamp and Norman E. Bowie, eds., *Ethical Theory and Business* (Englewood Cliffs, N.J.: Prentice-Hall, 1979), 148.

Review and Discussion Questions

1. Could a company that makes products for human torture be a "socially responsible" company? Explain your answer. What about companies that make cigarettes, cheap guns, pornographic movies, or junk food?

2. What are Camenisch's three reasons for maintaining that the business goal of providing goods and services takes priority over making a profit? Do you agree with them?

3. Camenisch argues that business should promote "human flourishing." What does that mean to you? Do you think that there is any means other than the marketplace itself to decide what goods and services promote human flourishing?

4. Why does Camenisch believe that it is justified and important to develop criteria for assessing business in terms of human flourishing?

5. Would you agree that Camenisch has taken us to the "heart" of business ethics? What practical implications does his approach have?

Further Reading for Chapter 5

John R. Danley, "Corporate Moral Agency," in Robert E. Frederick, ed., *A Companion to Business Ethics* (Malden, Mass.: Blackwell, 1999) reviews the philosophical literature on this difficult topic with particular attention to the influential views of Peter French.

Thomas Donaldson, *Corporations and Morality* (Englewood Cliffs, N.J.: Prentice-Hall, 1982) discusses the moral status of corporations, arguments for and against corporate social responsibility, and the idea of a social contract for business, among other issues.

Peter A. French, *Collective and Corporate Responsibility* (New York: Columbia University Press, 1984) analyzes the philosophical issues involved in assigning moral responsibility to corporations and other collectivities, whereas his *Corporate Ethics* (Ft. Worth, Tex.: Harcourt Brace, 1996) looks at a wider range of moral issues involving corporations.

 InfoTrac College Edition: For further information or to conduct research, please go to www.infotrac-college.com.

Thomas M. Jones, Andrew C. Wicks, and **R. Edward Freeman,** "Stakeholder Theory: The State of the Art," in Norman E. Bowie, ed., *The Blackwell Guide to Business Ethics* (Malden, Mass.: Blackwell, 2002) discusses one influential way of thinking about the obligations of managers to stockholders and other stakeholders.

John McDermott, *Corporate Society: Class, Property, and Contemporary Capitalism* (Boulder, Colo.: Westview, 1991) analyzes the modern business corporation's impact on society.

David E. Schrader, "The Oddness of Corporate Ownership," *Journal of Social Philosophy* 27 (Fall 1996) argues that stockholders do not own the corporation.

Thomas I. White, ed., *Business Ethics: A Philosophical Reader* (New York: Macmillan, 1993) contains useful essays on corporate personhood and responsibility in Chapter 6 and on the punishing of corporations in Chapter 7.

Part Three

The Organization
and the People in It

6

The Workplace (1): Basic Issues

Scientists first described acquired immune deficiency syndrome, commonly known as AIDS, in 1981. Apparently the result of a new infection of human beings, AIDS probably stems originally from central or west Africa, where several subspecies of chimpanzees carry a closely related virus. Within three years scientists in the United States and France had isolated human T-lymphotropic virus III, now known as HIV, for "human immunodeficiency virus." HIV is the parent virus of AIDS and a couple of related diseases. To be infected with the virus is not automatically to have AIDS, but most of those infected go on to develop AIDS symptoms and often die from them. After identifying the virus, scientists quickly developed blood tests for its presence. As of this writing, the scientific race to develop a vaccine is on, and the stakes are high. AIDS is the leading cause of death of Americans between the ages of twenty-five and forty-four. Approximately 800,000 people in the United States are infected, and over 450,000 have already died. Researchers estimate that there are 40,000 new infections nationally each year.[1]

No one today can doubt the seriousness of AIDS. Media attention has ensured that the public is aware of its deadliness and the threat it poses, and this is a good thing. But when fear of danger combines with ignorance about a disease's nature and causes, panic is often the result. This has sadly been the case with AIDS—not least in the workplace.

Take what is, unfortunately, a typical case. John L. is a white-collar employee, working in the downtown branch of a firm operating in a middle-sized West Coast city. He had been feeling generally run-down and complained of various small ailments to his physician. When a routine checkup didn't reveal anything specific, John's doctor encouraged him to undergo a blood test for AIDS. He tested positive, which means that the antibodies for HIV are present in his body. Their presence means that he is infected by the virus and that it is probable, given his symptoms, that he has AIDS.

A few of John's friends in the office know of his recent ill health, and gradually word of his test results has circulated. And now problems have begun—not just for John but also for his coworkers and for management. John's colleagues feel uneasy around him; they're not sure what to do or to say, and some of them are very worried about possible contagion. A few coworkers feel strongly that John should not be permitted to go on working there. The boss is concerned not just with the prospect of declining work performance from John but with the effects of his presence on office morale. She may herself also have doubts about the wisdom or even the safety of allowing John to continue to interact with the public, which is part of his job.

The myriad problems, doubts, tensions, possibly even mild hysteria that the mere presence of John L. can create in a business or other organization are easy to imagine, but sorting out the morally relevant factors and deciding how the situation ought to be dealt with is less easy. What are John's rights and interests? How are these to be weighed against the interests and rights of both his coworkers and the organization itself? What responsibilities does an organization have to one of its members who may be facing a terminal illness? Given the size and organizational structure of John's workplace and the type of work in question, how—morally speaking—should management respond?

These are questions that more and more firms must answer. Reliable figures are difficult to come by, but given the nationwide statistics, virtually every large company can be assumed to have had cases of AIDS among its employees or their dependents. Half of all American workers consider AIDS their chief health concern. For the foreseeable future, the problems posed by AIDS in the workplace can only continue to increase. Yet nationwide only a small percentage of firms have or are planning to formulate a policy on AIDS.[2]

Traditionally, the obligations between a business organization and its employees could be boiled down to "A fair wage for an honest day's work." Business's primary, if not sole, obligation to its employees was to pay a decent wage. In return, employees were expected to work efficiently and to be loyal and obedient to their employer. This model of employer-employee relations is obviously too simple and fails to come to terms not just with the dilemmas facing John's office but also with many other major moral issues that arise in today's workplace. This chapter looks at some of these issues, in particular:

1. The state of civil liberties in the workplace

2. The efforts of some successful companies to respect the rights and moral dignity of their employees

3. Moral issues that arise with respect to personnel matters—namely, hiring, promotions, discipline and discharge, and wages

4. The role and history of unions in our economic system, their ideals and achievements, and the moral issues they raise

CIVIL LIBERTIES IN THE WORKPLACE

Employees have all sorts of job-related concerns. Generally speaking, they want to do well at their assignments, to get along with their colleagues, and to have their contributions to the organization recognized. Their job tasks, working conditions, wages, and the possibility of promotion are among the many things that occupy their day-to-day thoughts. Aside from the actual work that they are expected to perform, employees, being human, are naturally concerned about the way their organizations treat them. Frequently they find that treatment to be morally deficient and complain that the organizations for which they work violate their moral rights and civil liberties.

Consider the case of Louis V. MacIntire, who worked for the DuPont Company in Orange, Texas, for sixteen years. As a chemical engineer he was well paid, and during the course of his career at DuPont he received several promotions. MacIntire also had literary ambitions and wrote a novel, *Scientists and Engineers: The Professionals Who Are Not.* Several characters in the novel inveigh against various management abuses at the novel's fictional Logan Chemical Company and argue for a union for technical employees. Logan Chemical at least superficially resembles MacIntire's real-life employer, DuPont, and some of MacIntire's supervisors were unhappy with his thinly veiled criticisms. He was fired. MacIntire sued DuPont, claiming that his constitutional right of free speech had been violated. A Texas district judge threw that charge out of court.[3]

MacIntire's case illuminates what many see as the widespread absence of civil liberties in the workplace. David W. Ewing, former editor of the *Harvard Business Review,* is one of those writers. He sees the corporate invasion of employees' civil liberties as rampant and attacks it in scathing terms:

> In most . . . [corporate] organizations, during working hours, civil liberties are a will-o'-the-wisp. The Constitutional rights that employees have grown accustomed to in family, school, and church life generally must be left outdoors, like cars in the parking lot. As in totalitarian countries, from time to time a benevolent chief executive or department head may encourage speech, conscience, and privacy, but these scarcely can be called rights, for management can take them away at will. . . . It is fair to say that an enormous corporate archipelago has grown which, in terms of civil liberties, is as different from the rest of America as day is from night. In this archipelago . . . the system comes first, the individual second.[4]

Two historical factors, in Ewing's view, lie behind the absence of civil liberties and the prevalence of authoritarianism in the workplace. One of these factors was the rise of professional management and personnel engineering at the turn of the twentieth century, following the emergence of large corporations. This shaped the attitudes of companies toward their employees in a way hardly conducive to respecting their rights. As Frederick Winslow Taylor, generally identified as the founder of "scientific management," bluntly put it, "In the past, the man has been first. In the future, the system must be first."

The second historical factor is that the law has traditionally given the employer a free hand in hiring and firing employees. A century ago, a Tennessee court expressed this doctrine in memorable form. Employers, the court held, "may dismiss their employees at will . . . for good cause, for no cause, or even for cause morally wrong, without thereby being guilty of legal wrong." Similarly, a California court upheld this traditional rule shortly before World War I, observing that the "arbitrary right of the employer to employ or discharge labor, with or without

regard to actuating motives" is a proposition "settled beyond peradventure." And in 1975 a U.S. district court in Missouri upheld the traditional position in ruling against a whistle-blowing engineer at General Motors.[5]

In addition, common law requires that an employee be loyal to an employer, acting solely for the employer's benefit in matters connected to work. The employee is also duty bound "not to act or speak disloyally," except in pursuit of his own interests outside work. It's no wonder, then, that traditional employer-employee law has hardly been supportive of the idea of freedom of speech and expression for employees. Against that background, DuPont's treatment of MacIntire and the court's refusal to see a First Amendment issue in his case are not surprising.

According to common law, then, unless there is an explicit contractual provision to the contrary—and only around 10 percent of American workers have such contracts[6]—every employment is employment "at will," and either side is free to terminate it at any time without advance notice or reason. The common law, however, has been modified in important ways by congressional and state statutory provisions. The Wagner Act of 1935 was, in this respect, a watershed. It prohibited firing workers because of union membership or union activities. The Civil Rights Act of 1964 and subsequent legislation prohibit discrimination on the basis of race, creed, nationality, sex, or age. Equally important, employees in the public sector—that is, in federal, state, and local government—enjoy certain constitutional protections on the job and can be fired only "for cause." And many workers are protected by their union contracts from unjust dismissals.

Thus, today working people have protection against some forms of unjust termination, and many of them enjoy the assurance that they can expect due process and that at least some of their civil liberties and other moral rights will be respected on the job. "But," writes Clyde Summers in the *Harvard Business Review,* "random individuals who are unjustly terminated are isolated and without organizational or political voice. For them the harsh common law rule remains."[7]

Companies That Look Beyond the Bottom Line

The law is not static, however, and some courts have been willing in specific cases to break with tradition to protect employees' rights of speech, privacy, and conscience. The U.S. Supreme Court, for instance, has ruled that a state cannot deny unemployment benefits to employees who are fired because they refuse to work on their Sabbath day, even if they aren't members of an organized religion.[8] And in 1987 Montana became the first and so far the only state in the nation to enact legislation that workers cannot be fired without "good cause." Even without explicit legislation, wrongfully dismissed employees frequently have legal recourse. Thus, for example, a federal jury held that Mobil Chemical Company had wrongfully dismissed one of its top environmental officials after he refused to perform acts that would have violated federal and state environmental laws. The jury ordered Mobil to pay $375,000 in compensatory damages and $1 million in punitive damages. On the other hand, when Daniel Foley, district manager for Interactive Data Corporation, accurately reported to his employer that his new boss was under investigation by the FBI for embezzling funds on a former job, he was dismissed for "inadequate performance" three months later, despite a seven-year record of positive work reviews and a recent $6,700 bonus. He sued Interactive Data for wrongful termination, but the California Supreme Court decided that his dismissal did not violate the "public interest" and rejected his suit.

Thus, although the law seems to be gradually changing, leaving the common-law heritage of employer-employee doctrine behind, recent legal developments are complicated and not entirely consistent. The results not only depend on the details of each case but also vary from jurisdiction to jurisdiction and from court to court. As argued in Chapter 1, however, our moral obligations extend beyond merely keeping within the law. Thus, it is particularly significant that more corporations are coming to acknowledge, and to design institutional procedures that respect, the rights of their employees. Moreover, the firms taking the lead in this regard are often among the most successful companies in the country.

This fact cuts against the old argument that corporate efficiency requires employees to sacrifice their civil liberties and other rights between 9 and 5. Without strict discipline and the firm maintenance of management prerogatives, it has been claimed, our economic system would come apart at the seams. An increasing body of evidence, however, suggests just the opposite. As Ewing writes:

> Civil liberties are far less of a threat to the requirements of effective management than are collective bargaining, labor-management committees, job enrichment, work participation, and a number of other schemes that industry takes for granted. Moreover, the companies that lead in encouraging rights—organizations such as Polaroid, IBM, Donnelly Mirrors, and Delta Airlines—have healthier-looking bottom lines than the average corporation does.[9]

Although under no legal compulsion to do so, a small but growing number of companies encourage employee questions and criticisms about company policies affecting the welfare of employees and the community. Some companies foster open communication through regular, informal exchanges between management and other employees. Others, such as Delta Air Lines, have top officials answer questions submitted anonymously by employees—in the absence of supervisors. Still others, such as General Electric and New England Telephone, have a hotline for questions, worries, and reports of wrongdoing. Finally, some, like Dow Chemical, open the pages of company publications to employee questions and criticisms.

Union contracts frequently require companies to set up grievance procedures and otherwise attempt to see that their members are guaranteed due process on the job. Some enlightened nonunionized companies have done the same. Polaroid, for instance, has a well-institutionalized committee whose job it is to represent an employee with a grievance. The committee members are elected from the ranks, and reportedly a fair number of management decisions are overruled in the hearings. If the decision goes against the aggrieved employee, he or she is entitled by company rules to submit the case to an outside arbitrator.

Some companies—including Johnson Wax, Donnelly, Procter & Gamble, and Aetna Life and Casualty—go further. These companies have long followed no-layoff policies.[10] So do Lincoln Electric and Russell Corporation, the sweatshirt and athletic-wear manufacturer. Another example is Hewlett-Packard. A recession once reduced orders so much that HP management was considering a 10 percent cut in the workforce. Because laying off people was anathema, HP went a different route. It set up a working schedule of nine days out of ten for everybody in the company, from the CEO on down. The program stayed in place for six months, when orders picked up, and the full ten-day schedule returned. "The net result of this program," said William Hewlett, "was that effectively all shared the burden of the recession, good people were not turned out on a very tough job market, and, I might observe, the company benefited by having in place a highly qualified work force when business returned."[11]

Not only, then, is it a moral duty of companies to respect the rights and dignity of their employees, in particular by acknowledging their civil liberties and guaranteeing them due process, but doing so can also work to the company's benefit by enhancing employee morale and, thus, the company's competitive performance. Hence, there is little basis for the widespread belief that efficient management is incompatible with a fair workplace environment.

"What I absolutely believe is that honoring the people who do the work can produce stunning results for the company," says Sidney Harmon, CEO of Harmon International Industries. "If the people in the factory believe there's a real

effort to help improve their skills, provide opportunities for advancement and job security, they can do things that will blow your mind."[12] Some business writers push this point even further. For example, Robert Levering and Milton Moskowitz argue that:

> The authoritarian work style—long the standard operating procedure in business—has failed. That failure is at the root of the poor performance of U.S. companies and massive layoffs in the '80s and '90s. When management is disconnected from the people who work in the company, it becomes easy to fire those people. And when workers are disconnected from what they do, it becomes easy not to care about the product or service.[13]

Of course, a company that does not sincerely consider employee rights of inherent moral importance is not likely to reap the benefits of enhanced business performance. Trust, as more and more management theorists are saying,[14] is the key here, and employees can tell the difference between a company that has a genuine regard for their welfare and a company that only pretends to have moral concern.[15]

An example is Pacific Bell, which has won high marks for its humane response to the AIDS problem. With its strong emphasis on two-way commitment and loyalty, Pacific Bell has never considered revoking the medical coverage of employees with AIDS, as some companies have done. (The lifetime cost of medical treatment for an AIDS patient can easily run to six digits.) Pacific Bell has committed itself to keeping employees with AIDS on the job. "They need to keep working," says Pacific Bell's Tim O'Hara. "It gives them a reason to stay alive." The company's executive director of human resources, Jim Henderson, says bluntly, "People with AIDS are sick. We don't fire sick people." The company has also been visible in various AIDS initiatives and innovative in its AIDS education efforts.[16]

So far this chapter has affirmed that the workplace should provide an environment in which employees are treated fairly and their inherent dignity respected, and it has argued that doing so can be perfectly compatible with a firm's business goals. Although important, these points are generalities. They do not provide much guidance for dealing with the specific moral issues and dilemmas that arise day in and day out on the job. The remainder of this chapter and the chapter that follows take a closer look at some of these issues.

PERSONNEL POLICIES AND PROCEDURES

People make up organizations, and how an organization impinges on the lives of its own members is a morally important matter. One obvious and very important way organizational conduct affects the welfare and rights of employees and potential employees is through personnel policies and procedures—that is, how the organization handles the hiring, firing, paying, and promoting of the people who work for it. These procedures and policies structure an organization's basic relationship with its employees. This section looks at some of the morally relevant concerns to which any organization must be sensitive.

Hiring

A basic task of the employer or personnel manager is hiring. Employers generally seek to hire people who will enable the organization to produce the products or services it seeks to provide or to promote its other goals. Furthermore, the courts have used the principle of negligent hiring to broaden the liability of an employer for damage or injury caused by its employees—even after regular hours and away from the job site. For instance, Avis Rent-A-Car was required to pay $800,000 after a male employee raped a female employee; the jury found that the company had been negligent in hiring the man without thoroughly investigating his background.[17] In making hiring decisions, though, employers must be careful to treat job applicants fairly. As one might imagine, determining the fair thing

to do is not always easy. One useful way to approach some of the moral aspects of hiring is to examine the principal steps involved in the process: screening, testing, and interviewing.

Screening. When firms recruit employees, they attempt to screen them—that is, to attract applicants who have a good chance of qualifying for the job and to weed out applicants or potential applicants who are unlikely to succeed at the job. When done properly, screening ensures a pool of competent candidates and guarantees that everyone has been dealt with fairly; when done improperly, it undermines effective recruitment and invites injustices into the hiring process.

Screening begins with a job description and specification. A *job description* lists all pertinent details about a job, including its duties, responsibilities, working conditions, and physical requirements. A *job specification* describes the qualifications an employee needs, such as skills, educational experience, appearance, and physical attributes. Job descriptions and specifications must be complete and accurate. Otherwise, job candidates lack the necessary information for making informed decisions and can waste time and money pursuing jobs they are not suited for. In addition, disappointment and unfairness can result if a position is inaccurately described or wrongly classified. For example, some businesses intentionally misclassify hourly workers as salaried employees in order to avoid paying them overtime—Taco Bell, U-Haul, Farmer's Insurance, and General Dynamics are among the companies that have been accused of this.[18]

Since Congress passed the Americans with Disabilities Act (ADA), which became effective for all firms with fifteen or more employees in July 1994, employers must be careful not to screen out disabled applicants who have the capacity to carry out the job. The ADA is intended, among other things, to protect the rights of people with disabilities to obtain gainful employment, and it forbids employers from discriminating against employees or job applicants with disabilities when making employment decisions. Employers must also make "reasonable accommodations" for an employee or job applicant with a disability as long as this doesn't inflict "undue hardship" on the business.

In addition, of course, for several decades the law has forbidden discrimination against individuals on the basis of age, race, national origin, religion, or sex, and these are items that generally should never appear in job specifications or recruitment advertisements, nor should they figure in hiring. Consideration of such factors typically excludes job candidates on non-job-related grounds. Firms must be careful about job specifications that discriminate subtly —for example, "young person preferred" or "excellent opportunity for college student." Employers should eliminate such specifications from advertisements, not only because they are probably illegal, but also because they discourage qualified applicants from applying. Most organizations these days try to avoid gender-linked job terminology as well. The terms "salesperson," "mail carrier," and "bartender" are more inclusive than "salesman," "mailman," and "barman." An alternative is to use terms denoting both sexes ("waiter/waitress").

Bona fide occupational qualifications, or BFOQs, are job specifications to which the civil rights law does not apply. But BFOQs are very limited in scope. There are no BFOQs for race or color, and in the case of sex, BFOQs exist only to allow for authenticity (a male model) and modesty (a woman for a women's locker room attendant). In line with this, the Equal Employment Opportunity Commission (EEOC) filed a sex discrimination lawsuit against the restaurant chain Hooters, well known for its buxom "Hooter Girl" waitresses, for hiring only women as servers. Hooters resisted the decision, claiming that the job position is legitimately defined as one that makes sex relevant. After some unfavorable publicity (for one thing, no men had complained of discrimination), the EEOC quietly dropped the suit.

In validating job specifications, firms are not permitted to rely on the preferences of their customers as a reason for discriminatory employment practices. For example, the fact that for decades airline passengers were accustomed to being attended to by young female flight attendants and may even have preferred them could

not legally justify excluding men from this occupation. Similarly, a court has ruled that the fact that 20 percent of Domino's customers have a negative reaction to pizza deliverymen with beards does not constitute a substantial business justification for the company's no-beards rule. The EEOC holds that such rules discriminate against black men, who sometimes suffer from a genetic skin disorder that makes shaving difficult and painful.

Bilingual ability (English-Spanish, English-Vietnamese) may be a justifiable job specification in some areas of the country, where such skills can be essential for successful job performance. But employers need to be aware of the danger of creating unnecessary specifications for a position, especially if they unfairly discriminate on the basis of national origin. The ability to communicate effectively in English is a common workplace requirement, but it can seriously impede the employment prospects of some workers—Hispanics, in particular. As a result, the EEOC closely scrutinizes employers' language requirements to see if there is a nondiscriminatory business reason for them.

In addition, the EEOC has ruled in several cases that disqualifying a job applicant because the applicant has a pronounced foreign accent is unlawful national origin bias unless it can be proved that the accent would hinder the jobseeker's ability to perform the job.[19] On the other hand, the U.S. Court of Appeals in San Francisco determined that a heavy Filipino accent was a legitimate basis for rejecting an applicant for a job at a state department of motor vehicles office that required dealing with the public, even though the plaintiff had scored higher than all other candidates on a written examination. And in a Texas case, a Vietnamese immigrant was lawfully rejected for the position of energy conservation inspector because of an inadequate oral command of English. The job involved explaining local law to building owners, evaluating their use of light, air, and water, and helping them devise an acceptable conservation plan. The position required constant dialogue with various people, many of whom, in the court's words, were "unaccustomed to the peculiarities of the plaintiff's speech."[20]

In a handful of American cities local ordinances prohibit discrimination against those who are short or overweight. On this basis, Jennifer Portnick brought a case against a San Francisco franchise of Jazzercise, a dance-fitness company. Portnick, who is 5 feet 8 inches tall and weighs 240 pounds, had applied for a job as an aerobics instructor, but Jazzercise rejected her application because it required instructors to have a "fit appearance." After the city of San Francisco sided with Portnick in 2002, Jazzercise revised its job criteria and now agrees that "it may be possible for people of varying weights to be fit."[21]

Some employers wade into morally troubling waters by screening job applicants on the basis of lifestyle. For example, Multi-Developers Inc., a Georgia-based real estate company, won't hire anyone who engages in recreational activities that are "high risk"—like motorcycling, sky diving, motor racing, mountain climbing, or flying one's own plane. In Indianapolis, Best Lock Corporation won't employ anyone who admits to taking even an occasional alcoholic drink. Other companies, such as Turner Broadcasting System, flatly refuse to hire smokers.[22]

Ill-considered educational requirements are also potentially objectionable. Requiring more formal education than a job demands is not fair to candidates or the firm. If the education requirement exceeds job demands, candidates who don't meet it are denied equal consideration. Moreover, one of them may be the best person for the job. Thus, the firm, as well as the less-educated applicant, stands to lose. The other side of the coin is to deny an applicant job consideration because he or she is overqualified in terms of education or experience. To avoid the personal and organizational frustrations that can result from hiring overqualified people, companies are justified in raising the issue. But raising the issue is different from assuming that because on paper an applicant appears overqualified the applicant necessarily spells trouble for the company. The fact is that the employment ranks are filled with people successfully doing jobs for which they are technically overqualified.

One additional matter. As traditional gender roles change, more and more men are leaving the work world for personal reasons, such as to help raise children while their wives complete professional training. These men often face obstacles when they return to work. Employers assume that, because the man once quit work for personal reasons, he may very well do so again. Thus, discontinuity of employment is cutting some men off from job consideration, as it traditionally has for women.

"The hurdles men face returning to the job market are about three times greater" than those faced by women, says Charles Arons, president and chief executive officer for Casco Industries, a Los Angeles–based employment and recruiting firm. "There isn't a male I know of in an executive position who would accept raising kids as a legitimate excuse for not working for three years."

Thomas Schumann, director of selection and placement for Dayton-based Mead Corporation, agrees. "If other qualified candidates are available," he says, "my guess is that a personnel manager would go with somebody who doesn't raise that question."[23]

Certainly, employers in highly technical, rapidly changing fields are warranted in suspecting that an individual's career interruption may have left him (or her) out of touch. But to automatically disqualify a candidate because of this raises a question of fairness.

Tests. Testing is an integral part of the hiring process, especially with large firms. Tests are generally designed to measure the applicant's verbal, quantitative, and logical skills. Aptitude tests help determine an applicant's suitability for a job; skill tests measure the applicant's proficiency in specific areas, such as typing, shorthand, or arithmetic; personality tests help determine the applicant's maturity and sociability. In addition, some firms engaged in the design and assembly of precision equipment administer dexterity tests to determine how nimbly applicants can use their hands and fingers.

To be successful, a test must be valid. *Validity* refers to whether test scores correlate with performance in some other activity—that is, whether the test measures the skill or ability it is intended to measure. Just as important, tests must also be reliable. *Reliability* means that a subject's scores will remain relatively consistent from test to test (so that a test-taker won't score high one day and low the next). Clearly, not all tests are both valid and reliable. Many tests are not able to measure desired qualities, and others exhibit a woefully low level of forecast accuracy. Some companies use tests that haven't been designed for the company's particular situation. Legitimizing tests can be an expensive and time-consuming project, but if tests are used, the companies using them are obliged to ensure their validity and reliability. Otherwise, companies risk injuring applicants, stockholders, and even the general public. At the same time, companies must be cautious about the importance they place on such tests, because a test is only one measure in an overall evaluative process.

Even when tests are valid and reliable, they can be unfair—for example, if the tests are culturally biased or are irrelevant to job performance. The U.S. Supreme Court took a stand on this issue in the famous case of *Griggs v. Duke Power Company*.[24] The case involved thirteen African-American laborers who were denied promotions because they scored low on a company-sponsored intelligence test involving verbal and mathematical puzzles. In its decision, the Court found that the Civil Rights Act prohibits employers from requiring a high school education or the passing of a general intelligence test as a prerequisite for employment or promotion without demonstrating that the associated skills relate directly to job performance. The *Griggs* decision makes it clear that, if an employment practice like testing has an adverse impact (or unequal effect) on minority groups, then the burden of proof is on the employer to show the job-relatedness or business necessity of the test or other procedure. Duke Power Company couldn't do this.

In the aftermath of *Griggs* and other cases, many U.S. firms retreated from administering preemployment tests because of doubts about their legal validity. In recent years, though, testing has made a comeback in both the public and private sectors. Today, millions of job applicants are putting pencil to paper on skills tests, leadership tests, personality tests, loyalty tests, and tests to determine accident proneness—even tests to predict what an applicant's coworkers will think of him or her after a year on the job.[25] Management, of course, is seeking through testing to gain a potentially more productive group of workers whose skills match more closely the requirements of their jobs. In addition, many applicants prefer the objectivity of tests to the subjectivity of job interviews. Still, most experts believe that even the best tests cannot be a substitute for face-to-face interviews.

Interviews. When moral issues arise in interviewing, they almost always relate to the manner in which the interview was conducted. Human-resource experts rightly caution against rudeness, coarseness, hostility, and condescension in interviewing job applicants. In guarding against these qualities, personnel managers would do well to focus on the humanity of the individuals who sit across the desk from them, mindful of the very human need that has brought those people into the office. This is especially true when the interviewer might not otherwise identify closely with the person being interviewed because of cultural or other differences. Interviewers must exercise care to avoid thoughtless comments that may hurt or insult the person being interviewed—for instance, a passing remark about a person's physical disability or personal situation (a single parent, for instance). A comment that an unthinking interviewer might consider innocent or even friendly could be distressing to the person sitting across the table.

Roland Wall, a job placement counselor for individuals with disabilities, describes taking a developmentally disabled client, with an I.Q. of about 70, for a job interview. The personnel manager emerged from the room in which Wall's client was taking an initial test along with several other job applicants. The personnel manager asked Wall where his client was and was amazed to learn that she had gone in along with the others for testing. "Really?" he said. "I didn't see one in there." This personnel manager is probably more sensitive about people with disabilities than many employers, given his willingness to interview Wall's client, yet he assumed that because she was mentally retarded, the applicant would look a certain way—would look like "one."[26]

Even though everyone suffers from conscious and unconscious biases and stereotypes, interviewers should strive to free themselves as much as possible from these "idols of the mind," as the English philosopher Francis Bacon (1561–1626) called them. As Bacon put it: "The human understanding is like a false mirror, which, receiving rays irregularly, distorts and discolors the nature of things by mingling its own nature with it."[27] In short, we view things, people included, through the lens of our own preconceptions. Interviewers need to keep this fact in mind. Panel interviews with a uniform list of questions for all applicants can also help increase objectivity.

Promotions

It's no secret that factors besides job qualifications often determine promotions. How long you've been with a firm, how well you're liked, whom you know, even when you were last promoted—all these influence promotions in the real business world. As with hiring, the key moral ideal here is fairness. Nobody would seriously argue that promoting the unqualified is fair or justifiable. It's a breach of duty to owners, employees, and ultimately the general public. But many reasonable people debate whether promoting by job qualification alone is the fairest thing to do. Are other criteria admissible? If so, when, and how much weight should those criteria carry? These are tough questions with no easy answers. To highlight the problem we consider seniority, inbreeding, and nepotism, three factors that sometimes serve as bases for promotions.

Seniority. *Seniority* refers to longevity on a job or with a firm. Frequently job transfers or promotions are made strictly on the basis of seniority, but problems can occur with this promotion method. Imagine that personnel manager Manuel Rodriguez needs to fill the job of quality-control supervisor. Carol Martin seems slightly better qualified for the job than Jim Turner, except in one respect: Turner has been on the job for three years longer than Martin. Whom should Rodriguez promote to quality-control supervisor?

The answer isn't easy. Those who'd argue for Carol Martin—opponents of seniority—would undoubtedly claim that the firm has an obligation to fill the job with the most qualified person. In this way, the firm is best served and the most qualified are rewarded. Those advancing Turner's promotion—proponents of seniority—would contend that the company should be loyal to its senior employees, that it should reward them for faithful service. In this way, employees have an incentive to work hard and to remain with the firm.

When company policies indicate what part seniority should play in promotions and job transfers, the problem abates but does not vanish. We can still wonder about the morality of the policy itself. In cases in which no clear policy exists, the problem begs for an answer.

The difficulty of the question is compounded by the fact that seniority in itself does not necessarily indicate competence or loyalty. Just because Jim Turner has been on the job three years longer than Carol Martin does not necessarily mean he is more competent or more loyal. Of course, in some instances seniority may be a real indicator of job qualifications. A pilot who has logged hundreds of hours of flying time with an airline is more qualified for captaincy than one who hasn't.

Then there's the question of employee expectations. If employees expect seniority to count substantially, management can injure morale and productivity by overlooking it. True, worker morale might suffer equally should seniority alone determine promotions. Ambitious and competent workers might see little point in refining skills and developing talents when positions are doled out strictly on the basis of longevity.

It seems impossible, then, to say precisely what part, if any, seniority ought to play in promotions—all the more reason, therefore, for management to consider carefully its seniority policies. Of paramount importance in any decision is that management remember its twin responsibilities of promoting on the basis of qualifications and of recognizing prolonged and constructive contributions to the firm. A policy that provides for promotions strictly on the basis of qualifications seems heartless, whereas one that promotes by seniority alone seems mindless. The challenge for management is how to merge these dual responsibilities in a way that is beneficial to the firm and fair to all concerned.

Inbreeding. All the cautions about seniority apply with equal force to *inbreeding,* the practice of promoting exclusively from within the firm. In theory, whenever managers must fill positions they should look only to competence. The most competent, whether within or outside the firm, should receive the position. In this way responsibilities to owners are best served.

In practice, however, managers must seriously consider the impact of outside recruitment on in-house morale. Years of loyal service, often at great personal expense, invariably create a unique relationship between employer and employee and, with it, unique obligations of gratitude. The eighteen years that Becky Thompson has worked for National Textile create a relationship between her and the firm that does not exist between the firm and an outsider it may wish to hire for the job Thompson seeks. Some would argue that management has a moral obligation to remember this loyalty when determining promotions, especially when outside recruitment departs from established policy.

Nepotism. *Nepotism* is the practice of showing favoritism to relatives and close friends. Suppose a manager promoted a relative strictly be-

cause of the relationship between them. Such an action would raise a number of moral concerns, chief among them disregard of managerial responsibilities to the organization and of fairness to other employees.

Not all instances of nepotism raise serious moral concerns. For example, when a firm is strictly a family operation and has as its purpose providing work for family members, nepotistic practices are generally justified. Many people believe that it is unfair to exclude a person from consideration for a job just because he or she is a relative or friend of someone in the company. In fact, Advest Group, a brokerage firm, traditionally brings sons and daughters into the organization. "Good work ethics seem to run throughout families," says senior vice president Robert Rulevich.[28] But that is probably a minority view. Today, it is more common for companies to prohibit the employment of relatives, or at least to restrict such employment to avoid situations in which one relative is supervising another.

Even when a relative of someone in management is qualified for a position or deserving of promotion, one must consider the impact of the decision within the company. Will the selection breed resentment and jealousy among other employees? Will it discourage qualified outsiders from seeking employment with the firm? Will it create problems in future placement, scheduling, or dismissal of the relative? Will it make the person an object of distrust and hostility within the organization?

Discipline and Discharge

For an organization to function in an orderly, efficient, and productive way, managers and personnel departments establish guidelines for behavior based on such factors as appearance, punctuality, dependability, efficiency, and cooperation. This is not the place to examine the morality of specific rules and regulations, only the organization's treatment of employees when infractions occur.

For example, it's one thing to speak with a person privately about some infraction and quite another to chastise or punish the person publicly. Also, trying to correct someone's behavior on a graduated basis, from verbal warning to dismissal, is different from firing someone for a first infraction. The point is that discipline, although desirable and necessary, raises concerns about fairness, noninjury, and respect for persons in the way it's administered. To create an atmosphere of fairness, one in which rules and standards are equally applied, the principles of just cause and due process must operate.

Just cause requires that reasons for discipline or discharge deal directly with job performance. AIC Securities in Chicago, for example, lacked just cause for terminating with one day's notice an experienced employee with a good record because he had been diagnosed as having brain cancer.[29] And it's difficult to see why smoking in your car on company property is just cause for dismissal, even though you can be fired for it at two Motorola plants in Illinois.[30] Of course, distinguishing between a job-related and non-related issue is not always easy and can be controversial.

In addition, how a person behaves outside work is often incompatible with the image a company wishes to project. Does the organization have a right to discipline its employees for off-the-job conduct—for example, the doctor who was fired by his HMO for criticizing it on a talk show and at an industry conference?[31] The answer depends largely on the legitimate extent of organizational influence over individual lives—that is, on where precisely the company's legitimate interests stop and one's private life begins. Such concerns raise complex questions about privacy that are explored further in Chapter 7.

The second principle related to fair worker discipline and discharge is *due process,* which refers to the fairness of the procedures an organization uses to impose sanctions on employees. Of particular importance is that the rules be clear and specific, that they be administered consistently and without discrimination or favoritism, and that workers who have violated them be given a fair and impartial hearing. Due process requires both the hearing of grievances and the setting up of a step-by-step procedure by which an employee can appeal a managerial decision.

It is useful to distinguish among four types of discharge. *Firing* is for-cause dismissal—the result of employee theft, gross insubordination, release of proprietary information, and so on. *Termination* results from an employee's poor performance—that is, from his or her failure to fulfill expectations. *Layoff* usually refers to hourly employees and implies that they are "subject to recall," whereas *position elimination* designates the permanent elimination of a job as a result of workforce reduction, plant closing, or departmental consolidation.

Before dismissing an employee, it is important that management analyze carefully the reasons leading to this decision. The frequent success of wrongful termination lawsuits highlights the need for a rational and unbiased decision-making process. The organization must ask itself if its treatment of the employee follows the appropriate procedures for that type of discharge, as those procedures are outlined in the employee handbook, collective bargaining agreement, or corporate policy statement. In addition, the company must guard against preferential treatment. Have there been employees who behaved in the same way but were not let go?

Even-handedness and strict compliance with established procedures may not guarantee fairness. For example, unless it is stated in the contract or employees have union representation, a company may not (depending on the type of case and where it occurs) be legally obligated to give reasons for firing an employee, and it may not be legally obligated to give advance notice. When employers terminate someone without notice or cause, they may have been strictly faithful to contractual agreement or established practice, but have they been just? Have they acted morally?

In answering this question, it's helpful to distinguish between two employer responsibilities. Employers bear the responsibility of terminating the employment of workers who fail to fulfill their contractual obligations, but they are also obliged to terminate these workers as painlessly as possible. In other words, although employers have the right to fire, this does not mean they have the right to fire an employee in whatever way they choose. Because firing can be so materially and psychologically destructive to employees, management should take steps to ease its effects. Moreover, crass firings hurt a company's reputation and impair its ability to attract top-notch employees.[32]

The literature on personnel management provides many suggestions for handling the discharge of employees more compassionately and humanely, ranging from the recommendation not to notify employees of termination on Fridays, birthdays, wedding anniversaries, or the day before a holiday, to various steps to respect the terminated employee's privacy and dignity.[33] A company should not give a longtime employee a pink slip, as General Dynamics did, on the day he returns to work after burying his six-year-old son.[34] And, certainly, no employer should do what John Patterson, former head of NCR, a computer company, once did. He fired an underperforming executive by taking his desk and chair outside, dousing it with kerosene and setting it on fire in front of the poor man.[35] Even when an employee is fired for misconduct, the company must be careful not to defame the person—or risk paying the legal price.[36]

One obvious thing employers can do to ease the trauma of firing is to provide sufficient notice. Although federal law requires companies to give sixty days' advance notice of plant closings, many companies ignore this legal obligation.[37] Morally speaking, what constitutes sufficient notice of termination or discharge depends primarily on the nature of the job, the type of skill involved, the availability of similar jobs, and the employee's length of service. Whenever employers have reason to suspect that employees will react to notice of their terminations in a hostile,

destructive way, sufficient notice might merely take the form of severance pay. Ideally, the length of notice should be spelled out in a work contract.

For most people who have to do it, firing a worker is painfully difficult, at times impossible. In part to help managers perform the dirty job of terminating, enlightened organizations sometimes enlist the services of displacement companies. For a fee, the displacement company sends in a counselor who assists the displaced employee to assess personal strengths and weaknesses, analyze the causes of the dismissal, and start planning a job search. This makes the distasteful task of firing a little more palatable than it would otherwise be. And to be sure, it protects the company from being sued by the seasoned, middle-aged executive who may feel trifled with. Self-serving interests notwithstanding, companies using displacement experts deserve recognition for their attempt to ease the anguish of those who must fire and to help those terminated salvage both their interrupted careers and their self-respect.

Today—with frequent plant shutdowns and relocations, sizable layoffs and downsizing, and increased automation—moral management requires careful study of responsibilities to workers in times of job elimination. It's debatable whether Valiant Networks, a consulting company, did this. After laying off nearly 100 workers, it asked them to return half of the bonuses they'd received six months earlier. Those bonuses were contingent on the employees staying with the company for a year—which the axed employees hadn't done.[38] When weighing their responsibilities to terminated employees, companies need to remember that termination of employment affects not only workers but their families and the larger community as well. It is impossible here to specify further what measures can or should be taken to ease the effects of displacement. Different circumstances suggest different approaches. In some instances, job retraining might be appropriate, together with adequate notice and sufficient severance pay. When mergers are involved, firms probably should notify workers well in advance and provide them with alternatives. Whatever the approach, the point remains that when firms terminate workers, serious moral questions regarding fair treatment arise.

Wages

Every employer faces the problem of setting wage rates and establishing salaries. From the moral point of view, it is very easy to say that firms should pay a fair and just wage, but what constitutes such a wage? So many variables are involved that no one can say with mathematical precision what a person should be paid for a job. The contribution to the firm, the market for labor and products, the competitive position of the company, the bargaining power of the firm and unions, seasonal labor fluctuations, and individual needs all conspire to make a simple answer impossible. The issue is further complicated by the fact that remuneration can also include health care, retirement programs, perquisites like tips or a company car, and bonuses, commissions, and other incentive awards.

Still, the issue of a fair wage is not as morally insoluble as it might appear. As a general matter, in an ethical organization the basis of remuneration should be distributive justice, with a wage and salary system that centers on the employee's value to the business—his or her contribution to the organization—and not on extrinsic, non-job-related considerations like being a single parent or a relative of the CEO.[39] In addition, salary judgments should be made on criteria that are clear and publicly available and that are impersonally or objectively applied. Consideration of the following more specific factors can provide the well-intentioned business manager with some ethical guidelines and help minimize the chances of setting unfair wages and salaries:

1. *What is the law?* Federal law requires that businesses pay at least the minimum wage, and many cities or counties have enacted "living wage" ordinances that raise this minimum by up to several dollars an hour.[40] Although this is a clear legal and moral mandate, the Department of Labor estimates that

half of the nation's garment sewing shops violate the federal minimum-wage law.[41] An organization can, of course, satisfy the minimum requirements of the law and still not act morally. When setting pay scales, employers must consider all factors involved, not just legislative guidelines.

2. *What is the prevailing wage in the industry?* Although this factor is not foolproof, or even a moral barometer, the salaries given for similar positions in the industry can provide some direction for arriving at a fair wage.

3. *What is the community wage level?* This point recognizes that some communities have a higher cost of living than others. For example, it is more expensive to live in New York City than in Little Rock. The cost of living relates to basic maintenance needs and must be considered very seriously in establishing a wage. To ignore the cost of living would be to jeopardize worker welfare.

4. *What is the nature of the job itself?* Some jobs require more training, experience, and education than others. Some are physically or emotionally more demanding. Some jobs are downright dangerous, others socially undesirable. Risky or unskilled jobs often attract the least educated and the most desperate for work, thus leading to worker exploitation. Although it is impossible to draw a precise correlation between the nature of the job and what someone should be paid, a relationship exists that must be taken into account.

5. *Is the job secure? What are its prospects?* Employment that promises little or no security fails to fulfill a basic need of employees. In such cases employers should seek to compensate workers for this deprivation through higher pay, better fringe benefits, or both. On the other hand, a secure job with a guarantee of regular work and excellent retirement benefits (such as a civil service position) may justify a more moderate wage. In addition, a relatively low salary may be acceptable for a job that is understood to be a stepping stone to better positions inside the organization.

6. *What are the employer's financial capabilities?* What can the organization afford to pay? A start-up company with minimal cash flow and a narrow profit margin may be unable to pay more than a minimum wage. A mature company with a secure market position might easily afford to pay better wages.

7. *What are other employees inside the organization earning for comparable work?* To avoid discrimination and unfairness in setting wage rates, it is important to look at what the organization is already paying its present employees for work of a similar nature. Gross salary disparities that are not warranted by the nature of the work, the experience required, or other objective considerations can also hurt employee morale.

Guidelines 6 and 7 have recently come to the fore as both employees and stockholders have begun scrutinizing the benefits and perks paid to top management. Studies have found that huge salary imbalances between those at the top and their employees create resentment: The greater the differential grows, the more employee loyalty declines and the more turnover increases.[42] That information will come as no surprise to employees of ITT, who saw the company lavish $10.4 million on Chairman Rand Araskog and $5.3 million on President Bob Rowman the very same year that it fired 125 of the 200 workers at company headquarters in order to save $20 million.[43] At the same time, many stockholders are getting tired of seeing company profits going to its executives and not to them; hence, the uproar when the Walt Disney Company awarded CEO Michael Eisner a ten-year pay package that could yield him around $771 million. Eisner's handsome reward came only two months after the company had granted Michael Ovitz a severance package of $38.9 million in cash plus options on 3 million shares worth $54 million—for having served as Disney's president for fourteen months.[44]

Two final factors are of equal importance with Guidelines 1 through 7. The first is job performance. Some people work harder or are more talented, and thus accomplish more for the organization. Most businesses rightly seek to recognize and award achievement. As with an employee's base salary, however, bonuses and other awards must relate to business performance and be a function of criteria that are measurable and objectively applied. The second factor is how the wage agreement was arrived at. A fair wage presupposes a fair work contract, and the fairness of a work contract requires free negotiation and the informed and mutual consent of both employer and employee.

Employees are motivated by many things. One of the most important of these is the desire to be treated fairly. Feeling that they have been reasonably rewarded for their efforts is crucial to people's self-esteem.[45] Establishing fair wages can thus enhance the work environment, remove a potential source of job dissatisfaction, and help management discharge one of its prime responsibilities to employees.

UNIONS

This chapter and Chapter 7 are concerned with a number of moral issues that arise in the workplace between employer and employees, but no discussion of the workplace should overlook one of the basic institutions structuring employer-employee relations, determining the terms and conditions of employment, and shaping the environment in which people work—namely, labor unions. Accordingly, this section briefly examines the history and economic role of unions, the ideals that motivate them, and some of the moral dilemmas they raise.

History of the Union Movement

In a famous remark, Franklin D. Roosevelt said that free and independent labor unions are characteristic of a free and democratic modern nation. Many economists and students of the union movement go on to give it primary credit for raising the standard of living and increasing the security of working people in the United States. They argue that almost all the benefits enjoyed by employees today, whether they happen to be in unions or not, can be traced to union victories or to union-backed legislation. At the same time, the higher wages, paid vacations, health benefits, retirement pensions, and increased job security that unions have brought have, in turn, contributed to social stability in the country and, through enhanced demand, to economic growth itself. Yet as the history of the labor movement reveals, employers have opposed unionization and union demands at almost every step of the way—often with violence.

Just as the roots of capitalism can be traced to the handicraft guilds, so the earliest efforts of American unionism can be found in the craft unions of the eighteenth century.[46] At that time, groups of skilled artisans—carpenters, shoemakers, tailors, and the like—formed secret societies for two basic reasons: to equalize their relationship with their employers and to professionalize their crafts. They agreed on acceptable wages and working hours and pledged not to work for any employer who didn't provide them, and they set minimal admission standards for their crafts. They also agreed to keep their allegiance secret—and for good reason. If found out they would be fired, and if discovered trying to cause a strike they could be jailed.

Labor historians generally consider the Knights of Labor (K of L), established in 1869, the first truly national trade union. What distinguished the K of L from previous craft unions was that it assembled in one labor organization both skilled and unskilled workers from an industry. Although this arrangement gave the organization the strength of numbers, it also created resentment among the skilled workers, who viewed the unskilled as inferior and therefore unworthy of their association. Friction and destructive rivalries also broke out between the organization's more radical national leadership and its more conservative local directors. Public sentiment, although never wildly supportive, turned sharply against unions in the wake of the Chicago Haymarket Riot in 1886, in which a bomb was lobbed into a group of police trying to halt a labor rally. Compounding the fledgling union's problems was a sour national economy that left workers fearing for their jobs and avoiding any entanglements that might land them among the growing ranks of the unemployed. In any event, between 1885 and 1890 K of L membership plummeted from 700,000 to 100,000.

But while the K of L was tottering, a new union was being born. In 1886 the American Federation of Labor (AFL) was founded. Within seven years, under the astute and temperate leadership of Samuel Gompers, it built a membership of 500,000, which increased to about 2 million by 1917. Curiously, the survival and prosperity of the AFL must be attributed in no small measure to business itself. Fearing the radical and revolutionary tendencies of the Industrial Workers of the World (the "Wobblies"), business embraced the AFL as the lesser of the evils.

The cause of unionism was significantly advanced in 1935 with the passage of the National Labor Relations Act (also called the Wagner Act). This legislation prohibited employers from interfering with employees trying to organize unions, from attempting to gain control over labor unions, from treating union workers differently from nonunion workers, and from refusing to bargain with union representatives. The act helped increase union membership to almost 12 million by the end of World War II in 1945. Most of these members belonged to the Congress of Industrial Organizations (CIO), an offshoot of the AFL that brought together various workers—auto, sheet metal, steel, and so on—into industrywide unions. The distinct advantage of the CIO over the AFL was that its unions could call a firm's entire workforce out on strike, rather than just its skilled workers.

But increasing union strength also brought public suspicions and fears of union power. Many businesspeople and political critics encouraged these worries and quickly pointed to the wave of strikes after World War II as evidence of union abuse of power. In 1947 a newly elected Republican Congress passed the Taft-Hartley Act, which amended the National Labor Relations Act. The new act outlawed the closed shop (in which a person must be a member of the union before being hired); Section 14(b) permitted individual states to outlaw union shops (in which a person must join the union within a specified time after being hired). Today, twenty-two states, mostly in the South and West, are so-called right-to-work states, with *open shop* laws on their books. These laws prohibit union contracts requiring all employees on a job site to pay union dues or their equivalent, once hired. The Taft-Hartley Act also prohibits various labor practices designated as unfair, such as sympathy strikes and secondary boycotts.

Since the merging of the AFL and CIO in 1955, unions have attempted to increase membership by recruiting outside basic industry—for example, in education, government, white-collar professions, and service jobs. But they have been only moderately successful. For the past twenty years, union membership has been falling, both absolutely and as a percentage of the workforce. Whereas in the 1950s unions represented 36 percent of the private-sector workforce, today union members constitute only 9.5 percent (or approximately 10 million workers plus an additional 6 million government workers). Union membership as a percentage of the workforce is substantially lower in the United States than it is in most Western nations—for instance, Australia, Belgium, France, Germany, Japan, the Netherlands, and the United Kingdom. This fact may explain why hourly compensation for production workers in manufacturing is less in the United States than in those countries; in fact, American workers make only 92 percent of what their Japanese counterparts earn and only 74 percent of what German workers make.[47]

In recent years, unions have been more and more on the defensive, as the industries in which they have been traditionally based have declined. The number of days lost to strikes, for instance, has been at a record low, and in the past two decades many unions have been forced to go along with decreases in wages and benefits. Many corporate managements have become increasingly and aggressively antiunion. They

fire workers who support unions and conduct illegal antiunion campaigns with near impunity.[48] Frank Lorenzo's conduct at Continental Airlines exemplifies these bare-knuckle tactics. The company voluntarily filed for bankruptcy, reneged on its labor contracts, sliced its pay scales in half, and then kept on flying.[49]

The general political and legal climate has been unfavorable to labor in recent years. President Reagan set the antiunion tone of the 1980s when he fired nearly 12,000 striking air traffic controllers and broke their union. The union had been considered powerful, but it was soundly defeated. President Reagan prevailed because the controllers are federal employees and are forbidden by law from striking. More recently, the U.S. Supreme Court has allowed private employers to "replace permanently" workers who strike, despite the fact that the 1935 Wagner Act makes it illegal for employers to punish workers who go on strike by "firing" them.

Whatever the terminology, if workers risk losing their jobs because of a strike, then the balance of power in collective bargaining is dramatically altered. Instead of negotiating in good faith, a company can now provoke a strike, hire new workers to replace the pickets, and cut costs. And management has done exactly this in strikes at Phelps Dodge, International Paper, Greyhound, and the *New York Daily News.* In the latter case, the Tribune Company, which then owned the *Daily News* and had earlier broken three unions in a strike at the *Chicago Tribune,* spent a year preparing for a strike in New York. The company retained a Nashville law firm renowned for its union-busting activities, recruited and trained nonunion workers to produce a strike-breaking newspaper, and then forced the unions at the *Daily News* into calling a strike by locking out the paper's unionized delivery truck drivers.[50]

In the 1980s, Richard Edwards and Michael Podgursky described labor's situation in words that still hold true today:

> Bargaining structures built up over many years are crumbling and collapsing. . . . Rising product market competition, deregulation, and technological changes; adverse

labor force dynamics; worsening public policy; and the legacy of the long stagnation have thrust the labor movement into a qualitatively new stage. This new period is characterized . . . by: (a) greater corporate mobility, power, and militancy; (b) ineffective labor law and a growing indifference, and in some cases, outright opposition of the government towards organized labor and collective bargaining; and (c) a waning belief in unions as the agents of working class interests. In these hostile circumstances, American unions face a difficult and troubling future.[51]

Union Ideals

From the beginning, unions have been driven by an attempt to protect workers from abuses of power at the hands of employers. This effort is based on the indisputable premise that employers have tremendous power over individual workers. They can hire and fire, relocate and reassign, set work hours and wages, create rules and work conditions. Acting individually, a worker rarely is an employer's equal in negotiating any of these items. The position of most workers acting independently is further weakened by their lack of capital, occupational limitations, and personal and family needs. Furthermore, whereas employers obviously need workers, they rarely need any particular worker. They can, generally speaking, select whomever they want, for whatever reasons they choose.

Interestingly, Adam Smith himself recognized this fundamental imbalance in his classic *The Wealth of Nations.* Regarding the respective bargaining power of workers and their "masters," or employers, he wrote that "upon all ordinary occasions" employers "have the advantage in the dispute, and force the other into a compliance with their terms."

> The masters, being fewer in number, can combine much more easily. . . . We have no acts of parliament against combining to lower the price of work; but many against combining to raise it. In all such disputes the masters can hold out much longer. . . .

> Though they did not employ a single workman, [employers] could generally live a year or two upon the stocks which they have already acquired. Many workmen could not subsist a week, few could subsist a month, and scarce any a year without employment. In the long run the workman may be as necessary to his master as his master is to him, but the necessity is not so immediate.[52]

In an attempt, then, to redress the balance of power in their dealings with employers, workers band together. In acting as a single body, a union, workers in effect make employers dependent on them in a way that no individual worker can. The result is a rough equality or mutual dependence, which serves as the basis for collective bargaining—negotiations between the representatives of organized workers and their employers over things such as wages, hours, rules, work conditions, and, increasingly, participation in decisions affecting the workplace. As the World Bank and others have recognized, by giving workers a collective voice, unions do not just push up wages. They can also improve productivity and efficiency, promote stability in the workforce, and make government less likely to meddle in the labor market.[53]

Certainly no one can object to unionism's initial and overriding impulse: to protect workers from abuse and give them a voice in matters that affect their lives. Indeed, these two purposes are specifications of two lofty moral ideals: noninjury and autonomy. Ironically, it is out of respect for these ideals that some individuals criticize modern unions.

The critics argue that union shops infringe on the autonomy and right of association of individual workers. Even if workers are not required to join the union but only to pay some equivalent to union dues, the critics contend that this still infringes on their freedom. In addition, evidence suggests that companies in alliance with unions sometimes treat nonunion personnel less favorably than union members. Some workers have gone to court to argue that favoritism to union members is discriminatory and unlawful (see Case 6.4). Whether or not it is, it certainly raises a moral question about the right to determine for oneself organizational membership and participation.

Taking the union's viewpoint reveals competing ideals and other consequences that must be considered. First, there is organized labor's ideal of solidarity, which is vital to collective bargaining and to winning worker equality. Union proponents point to the fact that unionized workers earn more than other workers and that per capita personal income is higher in states with free collective bargaining than in right-to-work states. For instance, of the twenty-two right-to-work states, only Nevada and Virginia have personal incomes above the national average. Practically speaking, if workers receive union benefits without having to belong or pay dues, then they lack an incentive to join the union, which greatly weakens the union's ability to improve wages and strengthen workers' rights.

Second, there is a question of fairness. Is it fair for a nonunion worker to enjoy the benefits won by union members—often at great personal and organizational expense? This question arises most forcefully when unions are attempting to establish an *agency shop,* in which all employees must pay union dues but are not required to join the union. The agency shop is designed to eliminate free riders while respecting the individual worker's freedom of choice. Opponents claim that an agency shop does not so much eliminate free riders as create forced passengers.

Union Tactics

The tactics unions use to try to get management to accept their demands also raise moral issues.

Direct Strikes. The legal right to strike is labor's most potent tool in labor-management negotiations. A strike occurs when an organized body of workers withholds its labor to force the employer to comply with its demands. Because strikes can cause financial injuries to both employer and employee, inconvenience and perhaps worse to consumers, and economic dislocations in society, they always raise serious moral questions. On the other hand, sometimes workers cannot obtain justice and fair play in the workplace in any other way. Austin Fagothey and Milton A. Gonsalves suggest the following conditions of a justified strike:[54]

1. *Just cause.* "Just cause" refers to job-related matters. Certainly, inadequate pay, excessive hours, and dangerous and unhealthful working conditions are legitimate worker grievances and provide just cause for a strike. Revenge, personal ambition, petty jealousies, and the like do not constitute just cause and thus cannot justify a strike.

2. *Proper authorization.* For a strike to be legitimate it must be duly authorized. This means, first, that workers themselves must freely reach the decision without coercion and intimidation. Second, if the workers are organized, then the proposed strike must receive union backing (although this condition becomes difficult to apply when the local union chapter and the national organization don't see eye-to-eye).

3. *Last resort.* To be justified a strike must come as a last resort. This condition acknowledges the serious potential harm of strikes. A basic moral principle is that we should always use the least injurious means available to accomplish the good we desire. Since there is an array of less drastic collective-bargaining tactics that can and usually do achieve worker objectives, all these should be exhausted before a strike is called.

Even when a strike is warranted, however, not every means of implementing it is morally justified. Peaceful picketing and an attempt by striking workers to publicize their cause and peacefully persuade others not to cross the picket line are typically considered moral means of striking. Physical violence, threats, intimidation, and sabotage are not. More controversially, Fagothey and Gonsalves argue that if workers have the right to withhold their labor and strike, then employers have a right to fill their jobs with other workers but not with professional strikebreakers, whose presence incites violence and whose function extends beyond doing work to denying strikers justice and the right to organize.

The preceding discussion deals with direct strikes—that is, cessation of work by employees with the same industrial grievance. There is, however, another kind of strike, far more controversial than the direct strike: the sympathetic strike.

Sympathetic Strikes. A sympathetic strike occurs when workers who have no particular grievance of their own and who may or may not have the same employer decide to strike in support of others. The bigger unions become and the more diverse the workers they count among their members, the more likely are sympathetic strikes aimed at different employers. Indeed, the sympathetic strike can take on global proportions, as when American dockside workers refused to unload freighters from the Soviet Union to show support of the Solidarity movement in Poland.

Sometimes the sympathetic strike involves several groups of workers belonging to different unions but employed by the same company. Acting on a grievance, one group strikes. But because it is so small, it enlists the aid of the other groups; it asks them to engage in a sympathetic strike. Cases like these do not seem to differ in any morally significant way from direct strikes. Indeed, it could be argued that the affiliated groups have obligations of loyalty and beneficence to join the strike. It is true, of course, that the sympathetic strikers do not have personal grievances, but they do have the same unjust employer, and they are in a unique position to help remedy that injustice by withholding their labor.[55]

Sympathetic strikes involving groups of employees working for different employers differ significantly from direct strikes or sympathetic strikes against the same employer. For one thing, the employers being struck out of sympathy may be perfectly innocent victims whose treatment of workers is beyond reproach. They have lived up to their end of the work contract, only to have their workers break it.

On the other hand, such sympathetic strikes can be very effective. J.P. Stevens & Co., the second-largest company in the U.S. textile industry, fought unionization for decades. The company engaged in a variety of flagrantly unfair labor practices and refused to recognize or bargain collectively with the union, despite various court orders to do so.[56] During the boycott of J.P. Stevens products, United Auto Workers members at a General Motors plant in Canada refused to install J.P. Stevens carpeting in the cars they were producing, thus shutting down the assembly line. In less than half a day, J.P. Stevens carpeting was gone from the plant. Had U.S. workers done something similar, both they and the textile workers union would have been subject to legal action, but J.P. Stevens would not have been able to refuse to bargain as long as it did.

Boycotts and Corporate Campaigns. Besides strikes, unions also use boycotts to support their demands. A primary boycott occurs when union members and their supporters refuse to buy products from a company being struck. A secondary boycott occurs when people refuse to patronize companies that handle products of struck companies. Although the Taft-Hartley Act prohibits secondary boycotts, they still occur when unions urge shoppers not to buy from stores that purchase products from companies being struck.

The express purpose of any boycott is the same as a strike: to hurt the employer or company financially and thus strengthen the union's bargaining position. In general, a boycott is justifiable when it meets the same conditions as a strike. In the case of the secondary boycott, which is like a sympathetic strike, the damage is extended to those whose only offense may be that they are handling the products of the unjust employer—and perhaps they are handling them out of financial necessity. In such cases, Fagothey and Gonsalves reject secondary boycotts. But this assessment seems too automatic and doesn't allow us to weigh the likely harms and benefits in particular cases.[57]

A relatively new pressure tactic is the so-called corporate campaign, in which unions enlist the cooperation of a company's creditors to pressure the company to unionize or comply with union demands. The tactic first gained national recognition after it was successfully used to help the Amalgamated Clothing & Textile Workers Union win contracts with Farah Manufacturing Company, a Texas-based men's garment maker. Union representatives persuaded retailers in Birmingham, Alabama, to stop selling Farah slacks by threatening them with a consumer boycott and then persuaded Farah's major creditors to help mediate the dispute.

In another labor conflict, several unions united to mount a corporate campaign to force Washington Gas Company to settle a dispute with the International Union of Gasworkers. The Teamsters, the Service Employees International Union, the Laborers' International Union, and the Communications Workers of America joined forces with several local unions to pressure Crestar Bank—where Washington Gas has a line of credit—to intervene on the union side. To lean on Crestar, the unions had at their disposal pension funds, payroll accounts, normal operating capital for their organizations, and even the mortgages on their buildings. Crestar complained that it was only caught in the middle. "We are not a party to the dispute," said spokesman Barry Koling. "We are neutral with respect to the issues between them." But union spokesman Jorge Rivera responded, "We judge our business partners by their actions concerning workers."[58]

At the heart of the corporate campaign is the issue of corporate governance. In pressuring financial institutions with mass withdrawals and cancellations of policies, unions and administrators of public-employee pension funds are trying to influence those institutions' policies and business relationships. And when the financial institutions accede to union demands, they in turn pressure the recalcitrant company to change its business policies. The harshest critics of the corporate campaign call it corporate blackmail. Its champions view it as an effective way to get financial institutions and companies to become good corporate citizens. Such tactics, they say,

are necessary at a time when union wages are stagnating and when management has been so successful at exploiting labor laws and regulations to undermine unions and thwart their recruitment efforts.

SUMMARY

1. Writers like David Ewing believe that too many corporations routinely violate the civil liberties of their employees. Historically, this authoritarianism stems from (a) the rise of professional management and personnel engineering and (b) the common-law doctrine that employees can be discharged without cause.

2. Some very successful companies have taken the lead in respecting employees' rights and human dignity. Corporate profits and efficient management are compatible with a fair workplace environment.

3. Fairness in personnel matters requires, at least, that policies, standards, and decisions affecting workers be directly job-related, based on clear and available criteria, and applied equally.

4. Incomplete or nonspecific job descriptions can injure applicants by denying them information they need to reach informed occupational decisions.

5. Ordinarily, questions of sex, age, race, national origin, and religion are non-job-related and thus should not enter into personnel decisions. Lifestyle and ill-considered educational requirements may also be unfair. Discrimination against the disabled is now expressly forbidden by law.

6. A test is valid if it measures precisely what it is designed to determine and reliable when it provides reasonably consistent results. Tests that lack validity or reliability are unfair. Tests may also be unfair if they are culturally biased or if the performance they measure does not relate directly to job performance.

7. Most moral concerns in interviewing relate to how the interview is conducted. Interviewers should focus on the humanity of the candidate and avoid allowing their personal biases to color their evaluations.

8. A key issue in promotions is whether job qualification alone should determine who gets promoted. Seniority, or longevity on the job, is not necessarily a measure of either competency or loyalty. The challenge for management is to accommodate its twin responsibilities of promoting on the basis of qualifications and recognizing long-term contributions to the company.

9. Inbreeding, or promoting exclusively within the organization, presents challenges similar to those presented by seniority. Nepotism—showing favoritism to relatives or close friends—is not always objectionable, but it may overlook managerial responsibilities to the organization and may result in unfair treatment of other employees.

10. Most moral issues in employee discipline and discharge concern how management carries out these unpleasant tasks. Due process and just cause must operate if treatment is to be fair. Due process requires that there be procedures for workers to appeal discipline and discharge. To ease the trauma associated with discharge, employers should provide sufficient warning, severance pay, and perhaps displacement counseling.

11. The factors that bear on the fairness of wages include the law, the prevailing wage in the industry, the community wage level, the nature of the job, the security of the job, the company's financial capabilities, and the wages it is paying other employees for comparable work. Also important are job performance and the manner in which the wage is established. Fairness requires a legitimate work contract, one arrived at through free negotiation and informed and mutual consent.

12. Unions attempt to protect workers from abuse and give them a voice in matters that affect their lives. Critics charge that forcing workers to join unions infringes on autonomy and the right of association. They allege that union workers receive discriminatory and unlawful favoritism.

13. A direct strike is justified, argue some moral theorists, when there is just cause and proper authorization and when it is called as a last resort.

14. Sympathetic strikes involve the cessation of work in support of other workers with a grievance. When the companies involved are different, questions arise concerning possible injury and injustice to innocent employers, consumers, and workers.

15. Primary boycotts—refusing to patronize companies being struck—seem morally comparable to direct strikes. Secondary boycotts—refusing to patronize companies handling products of struck companies—are morally analogous to sympathetic strikes. In corporate campaigns, unions enlist the cooperation of a company's creditors to pressure the company to permit unionization or to comply with union demands.

CASE 6.1

Burger Beefs

When seventeen-year-old Wendy Hamburger (her real name) applied for a summer job at a Wendy's Old Fashioned Hamburgers outlet near her Barrington, Illinois, home, she hoped to earn some money for college. But after working there for only three months, she quit when a manager threatened to fire her if she refused to work an extra shift on a holiday.

Wendy wasn't too upset about losing her job. "It seemed like the job cost me more than I made," she says. She does concede, however, that Wendy's International did pay her a little attention during her brief connection with the company. It used her to get a lot of free publicity in Chicago-area newspapers, and its president and founder, R. David Thomas, mailed her an autographed photograph of himself, which presumably she didn't have to return when she quit.[59]

Actually, there's nothing atypical about Wendy's experience. Rock-bottom pay, unpleasant working conditions, and bossy bosses—all are familiar to the millions of teenage employees in the fast-food industry. Little wonder the average teenage worker quits in disgust within four months of being hired.

Such rapid turnover would disembowel most businesses. Not so for those that peddle billions of burgers, fries, and shakes a year. For them, frequent turnover is the rank fodder for their multimillion-dollar operations, at least according to critics. Instead of relying upon a small, stable workforce of well-paid and well-trained employees, the fast-food industry seeks out part-time, unskilled workers who are willing to accept low pay. Teenagers, of course, fit this bill perfectly. These days the nation's approximately 3.5 million fast-food workers are the largest group of minimum-wage earners in the country—only migrant farm workers consistently earn a lower hourly wage—and two-thirds of them are less than twenty years old.

"The whole system is designed to have turnover," says Robert Harbrant, secretary-treasurer for the AFL-CIO Food and Beverage Trades Department in Washington, D.C. That way the industry averts pay increases and thwarts union efforts to organize workers. Moreover, the fast-food chains work hard at making their machines and operating systems as foolproof as possible. That way their jobs require no skills, and any individual worker can be quickly replaced.

Industry executives deny such nefarious motives. They point out, correctly, that for most youngsters a fast-food job is their first work experience. Such unseasoned workers usually are undisciplined and unreliable. No sooner are they trained, say fast-food executives, than they up and leave.

Harlow E. White, president of Systems for Human Resources, Inc., thinks otherwise. He publicly wonders whether the 300 percent annual turnover of fast-food workers is the cause or effect of industry operations. He suspects that "the industry has managed to manufacture a self-fulfilling prophecy: 'We're going to have turnover. And by God, we do.'" While admitting that the teenage part-timer is crucial to fast-food success, industry officials insist that they do not purposely encourage turnover. "Turnover costs us money," asserts a spokesperson for Burger King, even while conceding that it takes little time to train a new worker.

Despite the industry's declared good intentions, discontent among fast-food workers is widespread. That's not surprising given that the vast majority of them are paid an hourly wage, provided no benefits, and scheduled to work only as needed. If the restaurant's busy, they're kept longer than usual. If business is slow, they're sent home early. For example, one teenage part-timer at a New York McDonald's shop says management there routinely has workers appear up to an hour ahead of work time and then "wait in the back room and punch in later when they need you." (A McDonald's official insists that this is an isolated case, that McDonald's does not condone such a policy.) And a teenage waitress in an Atlanta Steak n' Shake complains that she is scheduled for a two-hour workday, although it takes her that much time to make a round-trip from home to work. (A company official says this is a management problem, that the policy of Steak n' Shake is to pay workers for a minimum of three hours.)

Some believe that the companies' insistence that such problems lie with local management, not the home office, is buck passing. Richard Gilber, a compliance officer in the U.S. Labor Department's wage and hour division, places the blame squarely on the store-manager training programs conducted by the home offices. He says, "We find in many cases that the 20-year-old managers are sales oriented and cleanliness oriented. But they aren't taught much about employee relations. And the Wage Hour Law is just another three pages in the operating manual."

Wendy Hamburger agrees. "I went through three managers in the short time I was at Wendy's," she recalls. "They needed managers so badly they hired anyone. They got a lot of young guys in there who think they're Mr. Macho and want to exercise their power. They don't know anything."

A Burger King official conceded that much of the criticism is warranted. The industry, he says, has put people in their early twenties in charge of a million-dollar restaurant and sometimes forty employees under age eighteen and expects them to function like professionals. The results are often less than ideal. "You can train someone to fix a piece of equipment a lot easier than you can to deal with people," he says.

To be sure, a manager's job is no bowl of cherries. Ask the young woman who is paid not much more than minimum wage to run a McDonald's outlet that grosses $750,000 annually. "They don't pay managers enough," she complains. "I'm on my feet from 6 A.M. to 6 P.M. Often I don't have time to eat all day. On days off I come in a couple of hours or call in to check on my assistant managers. And I have to take work home, like weekly scheduling."

Low pay is the chronic complaint of fast-food employees. Most chains come under minimum-wage and overtime-pay laws, but they don't always abide by them. Although enforcement of the laws is often lax, fast-food franchises across the country have been found guilty of underpaying their workers and not keeping proper wage reports. In 1997, for example, a Washington State jury found that Taco Bell had systematically coerced employees into working off the clock in order to avoid paying them overtime. In addition, the industry routinely ignores child-labor laws that restrict the hours that young teenagers can work. A few years ago the Labor Department fined Burger King $500,000—the largest child-labor penalty in history—for letting fourteen- and fifteen-year olds work late into the night on school nights.

Over at Starbucks Coffee, things are a little different. In contrast to the giant fast-food chains, Starbucks recently became the first U.S. company to give its part-time, hourly employees full health care benefits and stock options—even though, like the burger chains, part-time workers make up most of the company's workforce. "It's not viewed as a professional job in America to work behind a counter," says the owner of Starbucks, Howard Schultz. "We don't believe that. We want to provide our people with dignity and self-esteem, and we can't do that with lip service. So we offer tangible benefits."

Discussion Questions

1. Do you think the fast-food industry dislikes turnover? Do you think it encourages turnover?

2. Are wages in the fast-food industry fair? Does the industry exploit teenage workers? Compare the attitude of Starbucks to its workers with that of the fast-food industry.

3. How would you evaluate personnel procedures and working conditions in the fast-food industry? Are they reasonable? Could they be improved?

4. If you were an executive of a fast-food company like McDonald's or Burger King, what steps, if any, would you take to address the complaints of your workers?

5. Do you think fast-food companies have responsibilities for how local licensees conduct their operations?

6. At home in the United States, McDonald's is a low-wage, nonunion employer, but when it does business in countries such as Germany, Great Britain, and Australia, it is obliged to permit its workers to unionize. Discuss the merits and liabilities of unionizing fast-food workers.

7. Do you think conditions in the fast-food industry support or belie the laissez-faire assumption that the natural interplay between

employer and employee will produce a fair wage and hospitable working conditions?

8. Rapid turnover in the fast-food industry, some would argue, just goes to show that young people today lack loyalty, industry, and perseverance—in short, that they really don't want to work. Would you agree?

CASE 6.2

AIDS in the Workplace

Carla Lombard always worked well with people. So when she opened her bagel shop Better Bagels seven years ago, she anticipated that managing her employees would be the easy part. She had worked for enough different bosses herself, she thought, to know what it took to be a good employer. Whether she was up to the financial side of running a business was her worry. As it turned out, however, Better Bagels flourished. Not only had Carla gone on to open three smaller branches of Better Bagels, but her bakery also made daily wholesale deliveries to dozens of coffee shops and restaurants around the city. No, the business was prospering. It was just that the personnel issues were more difficult than she had ever expected. Take this week, for example.

On Tuesday, Carla was in the main bagel shop when around noon Tom Walters's ex-wife, Frances, came in. Tom oversaw a lot of the early morning baking at that shop, and like most of Carla's employees put in his share of time working the sales counter. He was a good worker, and Carla had been considering promoting him next month to manager of one of the branch shops. After ordering a bagel, Frances took Carla aside. She beat around the bush for a few minutes before she got to her point, because she was there to tell Carla that Tom had AIDS. Frances said she was telling Carla because she "always liked her and thought she was entitled

to know because she was Tom's employer." Carla barely knew Frances, and she was so taken aback that she was at a loss for words. She was shocked and embarrassed and didn't know whether she should even discuss Tom with Frances. While Carla was still trying to recover herself, Frances took her bagel and left.

Carla was still concerned and upset when she saw Tom the next day. Perhaps he had been thinner and looked tired more often the last few months, Carla thought to herself. But she couldn't be sure, and Tom seemed to be his usual upbeat self. Carla wanted to discuss Frances's visit with Tom, but she couldn't bring herself to mention it. She had always liked Tom, but—face it, she thought—he's my employee, not my friend. And it's his business. If I were an employee, I wouldn't want my boss asking me about my health.

Later, however, she began to wonder if it wasn't her business after all. She overheard some customers saying that people were staying away from the local Denny's franchise because one of its cooks was reported to have AIDS. The rumor was that some of his fellow employees had even circulated a petition saying that the cook should go, but a local AIDS support group had intervened, threatening legal action. So the cook was staying, but the customers weren't. Carla knew something about

AIDS and thought some of what her customers were saying was bigoted and ill informed. She was pretty sure that you couldn't transmit HIV through food—including bagel—preparation, but she thought that maybe she should double-check her information. But what was really beginning to worry her were the business implications. She didn't want a Denny's-like situation at Better Bagels, but in her customers' comments she could see the possibility of something like that happening once the word got out about Tom, especially if she made him a manager. Carla was running a business, and even if her customers' fears might be irrational or exaggerated, she couldn't force them to visit her shops or eat her bagels.

Carla knew it was illegal to fire Tom for having AIDS, and in any case that's not the kind of person she was. But she couldn't afford to skirt the whole problem, she realized, as some large companies do, by simply sending the employee home at full pay. To be sure, doing that deprives the employee of meaningful work, but it removes any difficulties in the workplace, and the employee has no legal grounds for complaint if he or she is left on the payroll. And then, of course, there was always the question of Tom's future work performance. Putting the question of promotion aside, if he really was ill, as Frances had said, his work performance would probably decline, she thought. Shouldn't she begin developing some plan for dealing with that?

Discussion Questions

1. What are the moral issues in this case? What ideals, obligations, and consequences must Carla Lombard consider? What rights, if any, are at stake? Will it make a difference whether Carla adopts a Kantian approach or a utilitarian approach to this situation?

2. Would it be wrong of Carla to ask Tom Walters about his health? Why or why not? Defend your answer by appeal to moral principle.

3. Suppose Tom has AIDS; what should Carla do? Is an employee's HIV status a job-related issue? In particular, is it a factor Carla should consider in deciding whether to promote Tom? What part, if any, should the attitudes of Tom's coworkers play in Carla's decision?

4. How should companies address the problem of public fear and prejudice when employees with AIDS have direct contact with customers?

5. Should companies develop programs or policies that deal specifically with AIDS? If so, what characteristics should they have? Or should they deal with the problem only on a case-by-case basis? Should large corporations develop AIDS-awareness programs? Or should AIDS be treated no differently than any other disease?

CASE 6.3

Speaking Out About Malt

When Mary Davis, associate vice president for plant management at Whitewater Brewing Company, wrote an article for a large metropolitan newspaper in her state, she hadn't realized where it would lead. At first she was thrilled to see her words published. Then she was just worried about keeping her job.

It all started when her husband, Bob, who was working on his MBA, talked her into taking an evening class with him. She did, and to her surprise really got into the course, spending most of her weekends that semester working on her term project—a study of wine and beer marketing. Among other things her essay discussed those respectable wine companies like E. & J. Gallo (the nation's largest) that market cheap, fortified wines such as Thunderbird and Night Train Express. With an alcohol content 50 percent greater than regular wine and selling for around $1.75 a pint, these screw-top wines are seldom advertised and rarely seen outside poor neighborhoods, but they represent a $125-million-a-year industry. Skid-row winos are their major consumers, a fact that evidently embarrasses Gallo, because it doesn't even put its company name on the label.[60]

Mary's essay went on to raise some moral questions about the marketing of malt liquor, a beer brewed with sugar for an extra punch of alcohol. It has been around for about thirty years; what is relatively new is the larger size of the container. A few years ago, the industry introduced malt liquor in 40-ounce bottles that sell for about two dollars. Packing an alcohol content roughly equivalent to six 12-ounce beers or five cocktails, 40s quickly became the favorite high of many inner-city teenagers. Ads for competing brands stress potency—"It's got more" or "The Real Power"—and often use gang slang. Get "your girl in the mood quicker and get your jimmy thicker," raps Ice Cube in a commercial for St. Ides malt liquor. Like baggy pants and baseball caps turned backward, 40s soon moved from the inner city to the suburbs. Teenage drinkers like the quick drunk, and this worries drug counselors. They call 40s "liquid crack" and "date rape brew."[61]

Mary's instructor liked her article and encouraged her to rewrite it for the newspaper. The problem was that Whitewater also brews a malt liquor, called Rafter, that it had recently started offering in a 40-ounce bottle. True, Mary's article mentioned Whitewater's brand only in passing, but top management was distressed by her criticisms of the whole industry, which, they thought, damaged its image and increased the likelihood of further state and federal regulation. The board of directors thought Mary had acted irresponsibly, and Ralph Jenkins, the CEO, had written her a memo on the board's behalf instructing her not to comment publicly about malt liquor without first clearing her remarks with him. Mary was hurt and angry.

"I admit that the way the newspaper edited my essay and played up the malt liquor aspect made it more sensationalistic," Mary explained to her colleague Susan Watts, "but everything I said was true."

"I'm sure it was factual," replied Susan, "but the company thought the slant was negative. I mean, lots of ordinary people drink Rafter."

"I know that. Bob even drinks it sometimes. I don't know why they are so upset about my article. I barely mentioned Rafter. Anyway, it's not like Rafter is a big moneymaker. Most of our other beers outsell it."

"Well," continued Susan, "the company is really touchy about the whole issue. They think the product is under political attack these days and that you were disloyal."

"That's not true," Mary replied. "I'm no troublemaker, and I have always worked hard for Whitewater. But I do think they and the other companies are wrong to market malt liquor the way they do. It only makes a bad situation worse."

The next day Mary met with Ralph Jenkins and told him that she felt Whitewater was "invading," as she put it, her rights as a citizen. In fact, she had been invited to speak about wine and beer marketing at a local high school as part of its antidrug campaign. She intended to keep her speaking engagement and would not subject her remarks to company censorship.

Jenkins listened but didn't say much, simply repeating what he had already written in his memo. But two days later Mary received what was, in effect, an ultimatum. She must either conform with his original order or submit her resignation.

Discussion Questions

1. Do you think Mary Davis acted irresponsibly or disloyally? Does Whitewater have a legitimate concern about her speaking out on this issue? Does the company have a right to abridge her freedom of expression?

2. Is your answer to Question 1 affected by whether you agree or disagree with the views Mary Davis expressed?

3. Should there be any limits on an employee's freedom of expression? If not, why not? If so, under what circumstances is a company justified in restricting an employee's right to speak out? Does it make a difference what position the employee holds? What policy would you recommend that companies follow?

4. What do you think Mary Davis ought to do? What obligations, ideals, and consequences need to be weighed?

5. Assume that a CEO like Ralph Jenkins is legitimately worried that an employee is making damaging statements about the company. How should the CEO handle the situation? Is discharge or some sort of discipline called for?

CASE 6.4

Union Discrimination?

The National Right to Work Legal Defense Foundation is one of several antiunion organizations that have been active in recent years. The "right to work," in this context, means the alleged right of an individual to work without being obliged to join a union. To put it the other way around, it means that companies cannot sign contracts with unions agreeing to hire only workers who are willing to join the union.

What follows is one of the Foundation's advertisements, titled "Job Discrimination . . . It Still Exists":[62]

Paul Robertson is not a member of a persecuted minority. But he has experienced blatant discrimination all the same because he has chosen not to join a union.

Paul Robertson is a working man, a skilled licensed electrician with more than 20 years

experience. He found out the hard way how a big company and a big union can discriminate on the job.

Paul was hired by the Bechtel Power Corporation to work on their Jim Bridger Power Plant project in the Rock Springs, Wyoming, area. Only three months later, he was fired, supposedly because of a reduction in force.

But during the week preceding his discharge, Bechtel hired at least 19 union electricians referred by the local union and retained at least 65 unlicensed electricians.

A determined Paul Robertson filed unfair labor practice charges against the company and the union.

An administrative law judge ruled and was upheld by the full National Labor Relations Board that the union and the employer had indeed discriminated. The judge ordered that Robertson and seven other electricians be given the back pay they would have earned if they had been treated fairly.

The NLRB later reversed part of its decision, but Paul Robertson did not give up. With the help of the National Right to Work Legal Defense Foundation, he appealed the Board's decision to the U.S. Court of Appeals, arguing that hiring hall favoritism is discriminatory and unlawful.

Paul Robertson was fortunate. He found experienced legal help—all important because the case dragged on for nearly four years in the courts and the union still refused to obey the NLRB's backpay order.

The National Right to Work Legal Defense Foundation is helping everyone it can—currently in more than 75 cases involving academic and political freedom, protection from union violence, and other fundamental rights. But it would like to do even more.

If you'd like to help workers like Paul Robertson write: The National Right to Work Legal Defense Foundation. . . .

Discussion Questions

1. Assuming the Foundation's description of the case is accurate, was Paul Robertson treated unfairly? Was this a case of discrimination? If Robertson was an "at-will" employee, does he have any legitimate grounds for complaint?

2. Does it make a difference to your assessment of the case whether someone like Robertson knows, when he accepts a job, that he must join the union or that nonunion employees will be the first to be laid off?

3. If union employees negotiate a contract with management, part of which specifies that management will not hire nonunion employees, does this violate anyone's rights? Would a libertarian agree that the resulting union shop was perfectly acceptable?

4. Presumably Paul Robertson could have joined the union, but he chose not to. What principle, if any, do you think he was fighting for? Assess the union charge that people like Paul Robertson are "free riders" who want the benefits and wages that unionization has brought but try to avoid paying the dues that make those benefits and wages possible.

5. What do you see as the likely motivations of Bechtel Power and the union? How would they justify their conduct?

6. Why did the Foundation run this ad? Is the ad antiunion propaganda? Do you think the Foundation is sincerely interested in the rights of individual workers? Or is it simply interested in weakening unions vis-à-vis management?

7. Assess union shops and agency shops from the moral point of view. What conflicting rights, interests, and ideals are at stake? What are the positive and negative consequences of permitting union shops?

CASE 6.5

Old Smoke

The last thing Darlene Lambert felt like doing the first thing Monday morning was inhaling the stench of old cigarette smoke. Darlene wasn't crazy about the smell of cigarettes under the best of circumstances, but today she felt under the weather and the very thought of cigarette fumes made her feel slightly nauseated.

Darlene worked with one other person, a nonsmoker, in a small office of the personnel department at Redwood Associates, but her job sometimes required her to spend extended periods in the main files room, where Frank and Alice worked and smoked. They didn't smoke when Darlene or another nonsmoker had to use their room, and they were always careful to open the windows and air it out ahead of time. But the smell of cigarettes still permeated the room, Darlene thought. Alice and Frank were nice people and sympathetic to her feelings. But Alice had hinted that she thought Darlene was oversensitive to smoke, and Frank sometimes joked about smokers being persecuted these days for their habit.

At 9:05 A.M., Darlene marched into the office of her supervisor, Charles Renford, and told him that she couldn't work in the files room that day because of the odor of smoke. Renford was caught off guard and more than a little put out by Darlene's announcement because top management was suddenly requesting a report—"due yesterday"—and he needed Darlene to begin assembling the data in the files room. He reminded her that Redwood Associates made an effort to accommodate nonsmokers by guaranteeing that certain areas of the building be smoke free, but it wasn't prepared to ban smoking altogether. Not only do smokers have rights, Charles said, it would hurt productivity and morale to make employees leave the building to smoke. "They should quit smoking," Darlene rejoined. "It would be for their own good." "Maybe it would," said Charles, "but the company shouldn't force them to quit. Besides, it is easy for you, who's never smoked, to talk about quitting. I know, I used to smoke myself."

Renford brought the conversation back around to the required report and its importance. Darlene simply said, "I'm sorry, Charles, but if it means going into that room—and it does—then I'm simply not going to do it." And then she got up and returned to her office, leaving Charles Renford trying to figure out what he was going to do.

Discussion Questions

1. Would Charles Renford be within his rights to discipline Darlene Lambert for insubordination? Should he order Frank and Alice to stop smoking in their office altogether, or is Darlene oversensitive? How would you handle this situation if you were Charles? Is it possible for employers to find some compromise between smokers and nonsmokers?

2. Do Frank and Alice have a right to smoke in their office if no one is there? Should companies make an effort to accommodate the needs of smokers? What policy on smoking would you recommend to Redwood Associates? Is it appropriate for employers to ban smoking altogether inside their facilities? What about smoking outside but on company grounds?

3. Do employees have a right to a smokefree workplace? If so, does this right justify Darlene's refusing to do the report? Does it make a difference how important the report is, or how much her refusal inconveniences her employer?

4. In 1914 Thomas Edison had a policy of employing "no person who smoked cigarettes." Is such a policy discriminatory? Is it reasonable?

Notes to Chapter 6

1. "U.S. Rise in HIV Catches the Least Aware," *Wall Street Journal,* July 8, 2002, A17, and the Centers for Disease Control and Prevention at *www.cdc.gov/hiv.stats.htm.*

2. Al Gini and Michael Davis, "AIDS in the Workplace: Options and Responsibilities," in Thomas Donaldson and Al Gini, eds., *Case Studies in Business Ethics,* 4th ed. (Upper Saddle River, N.J.: Prentice-Hall, 1996), 121; Alan Miller, Thomas E. Backer, and Everett M. Rogers, "Business Education and the AIDS Epidemic: Responding in the Workplace," *Business Horizons* 40 (July–August 1997): 78.

3. See David W. Ewing, "Civil Liberties in the Corporation," in Tom L. Beauchamp and Norman E. Bowie, eds., *Ethical Theory and Business,* 2nd ed. (Englewood Cliffs, N.J.: Prentice-Hall, 1983), 141.

4. Ibid., 139–140.

5. Ibid., 140–141.

6. "Women in Suits," *Economist,* March 2, 2002, 61.

7. Clyde W. Summers, "Protecting All Employees Against Unjust Dismissal," *Harvard Business Review* 58 (January–February 1980); but see also "Business for Lawyers," *Economist,* January 23, 1988.

8. Stephen Wermiel, "High Court Backs Refusal to Work on Sabbath Day," *Wall Street Journal,* March 30, 1989, B8.

9. Ewing, "Civil Liberties," 148.

10. See Tad Tuleja, *Beyond the Bottom Line* (New York: Penguin, 1987), Chapter 5, and Jeffrey Pfeffer, "Practices of Successful Organizations: Employment Security," in Joseph R. DesJardins and John J. McCall, eds., *Contemporary Issues in Business Ethics,* 4th ed. (Belmont, Calif.: Wadsworth, 2000).

11. Tuleja, *Beyond the Bottom Line.*

12. Richard W. Stevenson, "Do People and Profits Go Hand in Hand?" *New York Times,* May 9, 1996, C1.

13. "The Work Place 100," *USA Weekend,* January 22–24, 1993, 4.

14. See "Trust in Me," *Economist,* December 16, 1995, 61.

15. Sue Shellenbarger, "Workers Leave If Firms Don't Stick to Values," *San Francisco Sunday Examiner & Chronicle,* June 27, 1999, CL31.

16. David L. Kirp, "Uncommon Decency: Pacific Bell Responds to AIDS," *Harvard Business Review* 67 (May–June 1989): 142.

17. See Marian M. Extejt and William N. Bockanic, "Issues Surrounding the Theories of Negligent Hiring and Failure to Fire," *Business and Professional Ethics Journal* 8 (Winter 1989).

18. "The Big Squeeze on Workers," *Business Week,* May 13, 2002, 96–97.

19. Eric Matusewitch, "Language Rules Can Violate Title VII," *Personnel Journal,* October 1990.

20. Ibid., 100. See also "Firms Can Insist on English," *San Jose Mercury News,* July 17, 1993, 9D.

21. "Instructor Wins Weight-Bias Case," *San Jose Mercury News,* May 7, 2002, 1B.

22. "If You Light Up on Sunday, Don't Come in on Monday," *Business Week,* August 26, 1991, 68–70; "Fight over Hiring Bans Reaches Law Makers," *San Jose Mercury News,* April 28, 1994, 1E; "One Whiff of Smoke and You're Out," *San Francisco Chronicle,* January 25, 1997, D2; and "At Risk from Smoking: Your Job," *Business Week,* April 15, 2002, 12.

23. Dean Rotbart, "Father Quit His Job for the Family's Sake; Now Hirers Shun Him," *Wall Street Journal,* April 13, 1981, 1. See also Martha Groves, "Letting Down Their Corporate Shields," *Los Angeles Times,* August 12, 1996, Business Part II, 7.

24. 401 U.S. 424 (1971).

25. "Employers Score New Hires," *USA Today,* July 9, 1997, 1B; "Put Applicants' Skills to the Test," *HR Magazine,* January 2000, 75–80.

26. Roland Wall, "Discovering Prejudice Against the Disabled," *ETC* 44 (Fall 1987): 236.

27. Francis Bacon, *The New Organon* (New York: Bobbs-Merrill, 1960), 48.

28. "Work Week," *Wall Street Journal,* May 21, 1996, A1.

29. "Disability Act's First Lawsuit," *San Jose Mercury News,* November 8, 1992, 3C.

30. *San Francisco Chronicle,* July 3, 1996, B5.

31. *Santa Cruz Sentinel,* December 27, 1995, B5.

32. "An Alternative to Cocker Spaniels," *Economist,* August 25, 2001, 49.

33. See, for example, "Termination with Dignity," *Business Horizons* 43 (September–October 2000): 4–10, and Jathan W. Janove, "Don't Add Insult to Injury," *HR Magazine,* May 2002, 113–120.

34. "Waging War in the Workplace," *Newsweek,* July 19, 1993.

35. "Special Report: Corporate Governance," *Economist,* June 15, 2002, 70.

36. Gabriella Stern, "Companies Discover That Some Firings Backfire into Costly Defamation Suits," *Wall Street Journal,* May 5, 1993, B1. See also "Executions Corporate Style," *HR Magazine,* January 2000, 118–127.

37. "Proper Warning of Layoffs Often Lacking," *San Jose Mercury News,* February 22, 1993, 8A, and "It's Legal, but . . . ," *San Jose Mercury News,* November 15, 1993, 1D.

38. "Axed Workers Asked to Return Bonuses," *San Jose Mercury News,* November 6, 2001, 1C.

39. Elizabeth Vallance, *Business Ethics at Work* (Cambridge: Cambridge University Press, 1995), 71.

40. See "The Case for Living Wage Laws," *Business Week,* April 22, 2002, 26.

41. "Garment Industry Turns to Self-Policing," *San Jose Mercury News,* May 6, 1996, 8E. See also "Dress Code," *Economist,* April 19, 1997, 28.

42. "High CEO Pay Can Damage Workers' Morale, Report Says," *San Francisco Examiner,* May 4, 1997, CL11.

43. "Zapping the Little Folks," *Newsweek,* May 26, 1997.

44. "Eisner's Pay Package Incites Protest by Disney Stockholders," *San Francisco Chronicle,* February 24, 1997, D6. See also "Who Profits If the Boss Is Overfed?" *New York Times,* June 20, 1999, sec. 3, 9.

45. Vallance, *Business Ethics,* 71.

46. The historical sketch that follows is based on Robert B. Carson, *Business Issues Today: Alternative Perspectives* (New York: St. Martin's Press, 1984), 139–142.

47. U.S. Bureau of the Census, *Statistical Abstract of the United States 2000* (Washington, D.C.: U.S. Government Printing Office, 2001), Tables 712, 1385.

48. Robert Kuttner, "Labor and Management—Will They Ever Wise Up?" *Business Week,* May 9, 1994, 16.

49. Although the U.S. Supreme Court upheld this maneuver in a similar case in 1984, Congress has since revised the bankruptcy law.

50. *San Francisco Chronicle,* March 2, 1991, A5; *Economist,* November 3, 1990, 35; "Union-Busting Owners Force Strike on Daily News Workers," *Guardian* (New York), November 7, 1990.

51. "Labor Unions: Context and Crisis" in R. C. Edwards, M. Reich, and T. E. Weisskopf, eds., *The Capitalist System,* 3rd ed. (Englewood Cliffs, N.J.: Prentice-Hall, 1986), 165.

52. Adam Smith, *An Inquiry into the Nature and Causes of the Wealth of Nations* (New York: Modern Library, 1985), 68.

53. See "The Future of Unions" and "Unions for the Poor," *Economist,* July 1, 1995, 16, 56.

54. Austin Fagothey and Milton A. Gonsalves, *Right and Reason: Ethics in Theory and Practice* (St. Louis: Mosby, 1981), 428–429.

55. Ibid., 429.

56. See Chapter 4 of Mary Gibson, *Workers' Rights* (Totowa, N.J.: Rowman & Allanheld, 1983). The film *Norma Rae* portrays the dogged resistance of a company like J.P. Stevens to unionization.

57. Fagothey and Gonsalves, *Right and Reason,* 428–429.

58. "Unions Threaten Huge Bank Withdrawal," *San Jose Mercury News,* April 10, 1996, 1C.

59. This case study is based on Jim Montgomery, "Burger Blues," *Wall Street Journal,* March 15, 1979, and Eric Schlosser, *Fast Food Nation* (New York: HarperCollins, 2002).

60. David Dietz, "The Bottom of the Barrel," *San Francisco Chronicle,* July 7, 1996, in "Sunday," 1.

61. "The Drink of Choice," *Santa Cruz Sentinel,* May 26, 1996, D1.

62. Reprinted by permission of the National Right to Work Legal Defense Foundation, Inc., 8001 Braddock Road, Suite 600, Springfield, VA 22160.

Reading ─────────■

AN EMPLOYEES'
BILL OF RIGHTS

DAVID W. EWING

In this selection from his book Freedom Inside the Organization, *David Ewing presents a nine-point bill of rights for employees. Any bill of rights, Ewing suggests, should take the form of succinct, practical injunctions, injunctions that are negative in form ("Thou shalt not . . .") and that can be readily understood by ordinary people. A bill of rights should also be enforceable, not just a statement of ideals. Ewing emphasizes that his bill of rights is a "working proposal" for further discussion.*

The bill of rights that follows is one person's proposal, a "working paper" for discussion, not a platform worked out in committee. . . .

1. *No organization or manager shall discharge, demote, or in other ways discriminate against any employee who criticizes, in speech or press, the ethics, legality, or social responsibility of management actions.*

Comment: This right is intended to extend the U.S. Supreme Court's approach in the *Pickering* case* to all employees in business, government, education, and public service organizations.

What this right does not say is as important as what it does say. Protection does not extend to employees who make nuisances of themselves or who balk, argue, or contest managerial decisions on normal operating and planning matters, such as the choice of inventory accounting method, whether to diversify the product line or concentrate it, whether to rotate workers on a certain job or spe-

cialize them, and so forth. "Committing the truth," as Ernest Fitzgerald called it, is protected only for speaking out on issues where we consider an average citizen's judgment to be as valid as an expert's— truth in advertising, public safety standards, questions of fair disclosure, ethical practices, and so forth.

Nor does the protection extend to employees who malign the organization. We don't protect individuals who go around ruining other people's reputations, and neither should we protect those who vindictively impugn their employers.

Note, too, that this proposed right does not authorize an employee to disclose to outsiders information that is confidential.

This right puts publications of nonunionized employees on the same basis as union newspapers and journals, which are free to criticize an organization. Can a free press be justified for one group but not for the other? More to the point still, in a country that practices democratic rites, can the necessity of an "underground press" be justified in any socially important organization?

2. *No employee shall be penalized for engaging in outside activities of his or her choice after working hours, whether political, economic, civic, or cultural, nor for buying products and services of his or her choice for personal use, nor for expressing or encouraging views contrary to top management's on political, economic, and social issues.*

Comment: Many companies encourage employees to participate in outside activities, and some states have committed this right to legislation. Freedom of choice of products and services for personal use is also authorized in various state statutes as well as in arbitrators' decisions. The third part of the statement extends the protection of the First Amendment to the employee whose ideas about government, economic policy, religion, and society do not conform with the boss's. It would also protect the schoolteacher who allows the student newspaper to espouse a view on sex education that is rejected by the principal, the staff psychologist who endorses a book on a subject considered taboo in the board room, and other independent spirits.

Reprinted by permission of Dutton Signet, a division of Penguin Books, USA Inc., from David Ewing, *Freedom Inside the Organization* (New York: Dutton, 1977). © 1977 by David W. Ewing.

*[eds.] In this important 1968 case, the Supreme Court found in favor of a public schoolteacher who had been fired for criticizing the policies of the school board in the local newspaper.

Note that this provision does not authorize an employee to come to work "beat" in the morning because he or she has been moonlighting. Participation in outside activities should enrich employees' lives, not debilitate them; if on-the-job performance suffers, the usual penalties may have to be paid.

3. *No organization or manager shall penalize an employee for refusing to carry out a directive that violates common norms of morality.*

Comment: The purpose of this right is to . . . afford job security (not just unemployment compensation) to subordinates who cannot perform an action because they consider it unethical or illegal. It is important that the conscientious objector in such a case hold to a view that has some public acceptance. Fad moralities—messages from flying saucers, mores of occult religious sects, and so on—do not justify refusal to carry out an order. Nor in any case is the employee entitled to interfere with the boss's finding another person to do the job requested.

4. *No organization shall allow audio or visual recordings of an employee's conversation or actions to be made without his or her prior knowledge and consent. Nor may an organization require an employee or applicant to take personality tests, polygraph examinations, or other tests that constitute, in his opinion, an invasion of privacy.*

Comment: This right is based on policies that some leading organizations have already put into practice. If an employee doesn't want his working life monitored, that is his privilege so long as he demonstrates (or, if an applicant, is willing to demonstrate) competence to do a job well.

5. *No employee's desk, files, or locker may be examined in his or her absence by anyone but a senior manager who has sound reason to believe that the files contain information needed for a management decision that must be made in the employee's absence.*

Comment: The intent of this right is to grant people a privacy right as employees similar to that which they enjoy as political and social citizens under the "searches and seizures" guarantee of the Bill of Rights (Fourth Amendment to the Constitu-

tion). Many leading organizations in business and government have respected the principle of this rule for some time.

6. *No employer organization may collect and keep on file information about an employee that is not relevant and necessary for efficient management. Every employee shall have the right to inspect his or her personnel file and challenge the accuracy, relevance, or necessity of data in it, except for personal evaluations and comments by other employees which could not reasonably be obtained if confidentiality were not promised. Access to an employee's file by outside individuals and organizations shall be limited to inquiries about the essential facts of employment.*

Comment: This right is important if employees are to be masters of their employment track records instead of possible victims of them. It will help to eliminate surprises, secrets, and skeletons in the clerical closet.

7. *No manager may communicate to prospective employers of an employee who is about to be or has been discharged gratuitous opinions that might hamper the individual in obtaining a new position.*

Comment: The intent of this right is to stop blacklisting. The courts have already given some support for it.

8. *An employee who is discharged, demoted, or transferred to a less desirable job is entitled to a written statement from management of its reasons for the penalty.*

Comment: The aim of this provision is to encourage a manager to give the same reasons in a hearing, arbitration, or court trial that he or she gives the employee when the cutdown happens. The written statement need not be given unless requested; often it is so clear to all parties why an action is being taken that no document is necessary.

9. *Every employee who feels that he or she has been penalized for asserting any right described in this bill shall be entitled to a fair hearing before an impartial official, board, or arbitrator. The findings and conclusions of the hearing shall be delivered in writing to the employee and management.*

Comment: This very important right is the organizational equivalent of due process of law as we know it in political and community life. Without due process in a company or agency, the rights in this bill would all have to be enforced by outside courts and tribunals, which is expensive for society as well as time-consuming for the employees who are required to appear as complainants and witnesses. The nature of a "fair hearing" is purposely left undefined here so that different approaches can be tried, expanded, and adapted to changing needs and conditions.

Note that the findings of the investigating official or group are not binding on top management. This would put an unfair burden on an ombudsperson or "expedited arbitrator," if one of them is the investigator. Yet the employee is protected. If management rejects a finding of unfair treatment and then the employee goes to court, the investigator's statement will weigh against management in the trial. As a practical matter, therefore, employers will not want to buck the investigator-referee unless they fervently disagree with the findings.

In Sweden, perhaps the world's leading practitioner of due process in organizations, [the] law . . . goes a little farther than the right proposed here. . . . Swedish law states that except in unusual circumstances a worker who disputes a dismissal notice can keep his or her job until the dispute has been decided by a court.

Every sizable organization, whether in business, government, health, or another field, should have a bill of rights for employees. Only small organizations need not have such a statement—personal contact and oral communications meet the need for them. However, companies and agencies need not have identical bills of rights. Industry custom, culture, past history with employee unions and associations, and other considerations can be taken into account in the wording and emphasis given to different provisions.

Review and Discussion Questions

1. What are the pros and cons of each of Ewing's nine points? Examine each point for any potential problems in enacting, interpreting, or enforcing it.

2. Are there any rights that you would add to Ewing's list? Are there any that you would delete?

3. Do you see any point in proposing and discussing a possible employees' bill of rights? Do you think employees would benefit from a bill of rights? Should each company adopt its own bill of rights or should a general bill of rights be enacted by law?

4. Some might argue that, instead of a bill of rights, it is up to individual employees, or their union, to negotiate their employment terms. Would you agree?

Reading ━━━━━━━━ ■

EMPLOYMENT AT WILL AND DUE PROCESS

PATRICIA H. WERHANE AND TARA J. RADIN

According to the common-law principle of employment at will (EAW), an employer may hire, fire, promote, or demote any employee (not covered by contract or statute) when and for whatever reason the employer wishes. Unlike public-sector employees, most workers in the private sector are "at will" employees and thus have no right to appeal employment decisions. Werhane and Radin critically assess several justifications for the principle of EAW. Urging that the right to procedural and substantive due process be extended to all employees, they argue that even if the principle of EAW is justified, it does not condone arbitrary employment decisions. They argue, further, that the distinction between public and private institutions is not sufficiently clear-cut to justify the denial of constitutional guarantees to employees in the private sector.

. . . The principle of EAW is a common-law doctrine that states that, in the absence of law or contract, employers have the right to hire, promote, demote, and fire whomever and whenever they please. . . .

In the United States, EAW has been interpreted as the rule that, when employees are not specifically covered by union agreement, legal statute, public policy, or contract, employers "may dismiss their employees at will . . . for good cause, for no cause, *or even for causes morally wrong*, without being thereby guilty of legal wrong."[1] At the same time, "at will" employees enjoy rights parallel to employer prerogatives, because employees may quit their jobs for any reason whatsoever (or no reason) without having to give any notice to their em-

Copyright © 1995 Patricia H. Werhane and Tara J. Radin. Reprinted by permission from Thomas Donaldson and Patricia H. Werhane, eds., *Ethical Issues in Business: A Philosophical Approach*, 5th ed. (1996). Some notes omitted.

ployers. "At will" employees range from part-time contract workers to CEOs, including all those workers and managers in the private sector of the economy not covered by agreements, statutes, or contracts. Today at least 60% of all employees in the private sector in the United States are "at will" employees. These employees have no rights to due process or to appeal employment decisions, and the employer does not have any obligation to give reasons for demotions, transfers, or dismissals. Interestingly, while employees in the *private* sector of the economy tend to be regarded as "at will" employees, *public*-sector employees have guaranteed rights, including due process, and are protected from demotion, transfer, or firing without cause.

Due process is a means by which a person can appeal a decision in order to get an explanation of that action and an opportunity to argue against it. Procedural due process is the right to a hearing, trial, grievance procedure, or appeal when a decision is made concerning oneself. Due process is also substantive. It is the demand for rationality and fairness: for good reasons for decisions. EAW has been widely interpreted as allowing employees to be demoted, transferred or dismissed without due process, that is, without having a hearing and without requirement of good reasons or "cause" for the employment decision. This is not to say that employers do not have reasons, usually good reasons, for their decisions. But there is no moral or legal obligation to state or defend them. EAW thus sidesteps the requirement of procedural and substantive due process in the workplace, but it does not preclude the institution of such procedures or the existence of good reasons for employment decisions.

EAW is still upheld in the state and federal courts of this country . . . , although exceptions are made when violations of public policy and law are at issue. . . .

During the last ten years, a number of positive trends have become apparent in employment practices and in state and federal court adjudications of employment disputes. Shortages of skilled managers, fear of legal repercussions, and a more genuine interest in employee rights claims and reciprocal obligations have resulted in a more careful spelling out of employment contracts, the development of elaborate grievance procedures, and in general less arbitrariness in employee treatment.[2] While there has not been a universal revolution in thinking about employee rights, an increasing number of companies have qualified their EAW prerogatives with restrictions in firing without cause. Many companies have developed grievance procedures and other means for employee complaint and redress. . . .

These are all positive developments. At the same time, there has been neither an across-the-board institution of due process procedures in all corporations nor any direct challenges to the *principle* (although there have been challenges to the practice) of EAW as a justifiable and legitimate approach to employment practices. Moreover, as a result of mergers, downsizing, and restructuring, hundreds of thousands of employees have been laid off summarily without being able to appeal those decisions.

"At will" employees, then, have no rights to demand an appeal to such employment decisions except through the court system. In addition, no form of due process is a requirement preceding any of these actions. Moreover, unless public policy is violated, the law has traditionally protected employers from employee retaliation in such actions. It is true that the scope of what is defined as "public policy" has been enlarged so that "at will" dismissals without good reason are greatly reduced. It is also true that many companies have grievance procedures in place for "at will" employees. But such procedures are voluntary, procedural due process is not *required,* and companies need not give any reasons for their employment decisions.

In what follows we shall present a series of arguments defending the claim that the right to procedural and substantive due process should be extended to all employees in the private sector of the economy. We will defend the claim partly on the basis of human rights. We shall also argue that the public/private distinction that precludes the application of constitutional guarantees in the private sector has sufficiently broken down so that the absence of a due process requirement in the workplace is an anomaly.

EMPLOYMENT AT WILL

EAW is often justified for one or more of the following reasons:

1. The proprietary rights of employers guarantee that they may employ or dismiss whomever and whenever they wish.

2. EAW defends employee and employer rights equally, in particular the right to freedom of contract, because an employee voluntarily contracts to be hired and can quit at any time.

3. In choosing to take a job, an employee voluntarily commits herself to certain responsibilities and company loyalty, including the knowledge that she is an "at will" employee.

4. Extending due process rights in the workplace often interferes with the efficiency and productivity of the business organization.

5. Legislation and/or regulation of employment relationships further undermine an already overregulated economy.

Let us examine each of these arguments in more detail. The principle of EAW is sometimes maintained purely on the basis of proprietary rights of employers and corporations. In dismissing or demoting employees, the employer is not denying rights to *persons.* Rather, the employer is simply excluding that person's *labor* from the organization. . . .

In dismissing an employee, a well-intentioned employer aims to rid the corporation of the costs of generating that employee's work products. In ordinary employment situations, however, terminating that cost entails terminating that employee. In those cases the justification for the "at will" firing is presumably proprietary. But treating an employee "at will" is analogous to considering her a piece of property at the disposal of the employer or corporation. Arbitrary firings treat people as things. When I "fire" a robot, I do not have to give reasons, because a robot is not a rational being. It has no use for reasons. On the other hand, if I fire a person arbitrarily, I am making the assumption that she does not need reasons either. If I have hired people, then, in firing them, I should treat them as such, with respect, throughout the termination process. This does not preclude firing. It merely asks employers to give reasons for their actions, because reasons are appropriate when people are dealing with other people.

This reasoning leads to a second defense and critique of EAW. It is contended that EAW defends employee and employer rights equally. An employer's right to hire and fire "at will" is balanced by a worker's right to accept or reject employment. The institution of any employee right that restricts "at will" hiring and firing would be unfair unless this restriction were balanced by a similar restriction controlling employee job choice in the workplace. Either program would do irreparable damage by preventing both employees and employers from continuing in voluntary employment arrangements. These arrangements are guaranteed by "freedom of contract," the right of persons or organizations to enter into any voluntary agreement with which all parties of the agreement are in accord.[3] Limiting EAW practices or requiring due process would negatively affect freedom of contract. Both are thus clearly coercive, because in either case persons and organizations are forced to accept behavioral restraints that place unnecessary constraints on voluntary employment agreements.[4]

This second line of reasoning defending EAW, like the first, presents some solid arguments. A basic presupposition upon which EAW is grounded is that of protecting equal freedoms of both employees and employers. The purpose of EAW is to provide a guaranteed balance of these freedoms. But arbitrary treatment of employees extends prerogatives to managers that are not equally available to employees, and such treatment may unduly interfere with a fired employee's prospects for future employment if that employee has no avenue for defense or appeal. This is also sometimes true when an employee quits without notice or good reason. Arbitrary treatment of employees *or* employers therefore violates the spirit of EAW—that of protecting the freedoms of both employees and employers.

The third justification of EAW defends the voluntariness of employment contracts. If these are agreements between moral agents, however, such agreements imply reciprocal obligations between the parties in question for which both are accountable. It is obvious that, in an employment contract, people are rewarded for their performance. What is seldom noticed is that, if part of the employment contract is an expectation of loyalty, trust, and respect on the part of an employee, the employer must, in return, treat the employee with respect as well. The obligations required by employment agreements, if these are free and noncoercive agreements, must be equally obligatory and mutually restrictive on both parties. Otherwise one party cannot expect—morally expect—loyalty, trust, or respect from the other.

EAW is most often defended on practical grounds. From a utilitarian perspective, hiring and firing "at will" is deemed necessary in productive organizations to ensure maximum efficiency and productivity, the goals of such organizations. In the absence of EAW unproductive employees, workers who are no longer needed, and even troublemakers, would be able to keep their jobs. Even if a business *could* rid itself of undesirable employees, the lengthy procedure of due process required by an extension of employee rights would be costly and time-consuming, and would likely prove distracting to other employees. This would likely slow production and, more likely than not, prove harmful to the morale of other employees. . . .

Such an argument assumes that due process increases costs and reduces efficiency, a contention that is not documented by the many corporations that have grievance procedures. . . . Procedural due process demands a means of appeal, and substantive due process demands good reasons, both of which are requirements for other managerial decisions and judgments. Neither demands benevolence, lifetime employment, or prevents dismissals. In fact, having good reasons gives an employer a justification for getting rid of poor employees.

In summary, arbitrariness, although not prohibited by EAW, violates the managerial ideal of rationality and consistency. These are independent grounds for not abusing EAW. Even if EAW itself is justifiable, the practice of EAW, when interpreted as condoning arbitrary employment decisions, is not justifiable. Both procedural and substantive due process are consistent with, and a moral requirement of, EAW. The former is part of recognizing obligations implied by freedom of contract, and the latter, substantive due process, conforms with the ideal of managerial rationality that is implied by a consistent application of this common law principle.

EMPLOYMENT AT WILL, DUE PROCESS, AND THE PUBLIC/PRIVATE DISTINCTION

The strongest reasons for allowing abuses of EAW and for not instituting a full set of employee rights in the workplace, at least in the private sector of the economy, have to do with the nature of business in a free society. Businesses are privately owned voluntary organizations of all sizes from small entrepreneurships to large corporations. As such, they are not subject to the restrictions governing public and political institutions. Political procedures such as due process, needed to safeguard the public against the arbitrary exercise of power by the state, do not apply to private organizations. Guaranteeing such rights in the workplace would require restrictive legislation and regulation. Voluntary market arrangements, so vital to free enterprise and guaranteed by freedom of contract, would be sacrificed for the alleged public interest of employee claims. . . .

Due process is . . . guaranteed for permanent full-time workers in the public sector of the economy, that is, for workers in local, state and national government positions. The Fifth and Fourteenth Amendments protect liberty and property rights such that any alleged violations or deprivation of those rights may be challenged by some form of due process. According to recent Supreme Court decisions, when a state worker is a permanent employee, he has a property interest in his employment. Because a person's productivity contributes to the place of employment, a public worker is entitled to his job unless there is good reason to question it, such as poor work habits, habitual absences, and the like. Moreover, if a discharge would prevent him from obtaining other employment, which often is the case with state employees who, if fired, cannot find further government employment, that employee has a right to due process before being terminated.

This justification for extending due process protections to public employees is grounded in the public employee's proprietary interest in his job. If that argument makes sense, it is curious that private employees do not have similar rights. The basis for this distinction stems from a tradition in Western thinking that distinguishes between the public and private spheres of life. The public sphere contains that part of a person's life that lies within the bounds of government regulation, whereas the private sphere contains that part of a person's life that lies outside those bounds. The argument is that the portion of a person's life that influences only that person should remain private and outside the purview of law and regulation, while the portion that influences the public welfare should be subject to the authority of the law. . . .

The public/private distinction was originally developed to distinguish individuals from the state and to protect individuals and private property from public—i.e., governmental—intrusion. . . . There are some questions, however, with the justification of the absence of due process with regard to the public/private distinction. Our economic system is allegedly based on private property, but it is unclear where "private" property and ownership end and "public" property and ownership begin. In the workplace, ownership and control is often divided. Corporate assets are held by an ever-changing group of individual and institutional shareholders. It is no longer true that owners exercise any real sense of control over their property and its management. Some do, but many do not. Moreover, such complex property relationships are spelled out and guaranteed by the state. This has prompted at least one thinker to argue that "private property" should be defined as "certain patterns of human interaction underwritten by public power."[5]

This fuzziness about the "privacy" of property becomes exacerbated by the way we use the term "public" in analyzing the status of businesses and in particular corporations. For example, we distinguish between privately owned business corporations and government-owned or -controlled public institutions. Among those companies that are not government owned, we distinguish between regulated "public" utilities whose stock is owned by private individuals and institutions; "publicly held" corporations whose stock is traded publicly, who are governed by special SEC regulations, and whose financial statements are public knowledge; and privately held corporations and entrepreneurships, companies and smaller businesses that are owned by an individual or group of individuals and not available for public stock purchase.

There are similarities between government-owned, public institutions and privately owned organizations. When the air controllers went on strike in the 1980s, Ronald Reagan fired them, and declared that, as public employees, they could not strike because it jeopardized the public safety. Nevertheless, both private and public institutions run transportation, control banks, and own property. While the goals of private and public institutions differ in that public institutions are allegedly supposed to place the public good ahead of profitability, the simultaneous call for businesses to become socially responsible and the demand for governmental organizations to become efficient and accountable further question the dichotomy between "public" and "private."

Many business situations reinforce the view that the traditional public/private dichotomy has been eroded, if not entirely, at least in large part. For example, in 1981, General Motors (GM) wanted to expand by building a plant in what is called the "Poletown" area of Detroit. Poletown is an old Detroit Polish neighborhood. The site was favorable because it was near transportation facilities and there was a good supply of labor. To build the plant, however, GM had to displace residents in a nine-block area. The Poletown Neighborhood Council objected, but the Supreme Court of Michigan decided in favor of GM and held that the state could condemn property for private use, with proper compensation to owners, when it was in the public good. What is particularly interesting about this case is that GM is not a government-owned corporation; its primary goal is *profitability*, not the common good. The Supreme Court nevertheless decided that it was in the *public* interest for Detroit to use its authority to allow a company to take over property despite the protesting of the property owners. In this case the public/private distinction was thoroughly scrambled.

The overlap between private enterprise and public interests is such that at least one legal scholar argues that "developments in the twentieth century have significantly undermined the "privateness' of modern business corporations, with the result that the traditional bases for distinguishing them from public corporations have largely disappeared."[6] Nevertheless, despite the blurring of the public and private in terms of property rights and the status and functions of corporations, the subject of employee rights appears to remain immune from conflation.

The expansion of employee protections to what we would consider just claims to due process gives to the state and the courts more opportunity to interfere with the private economy and might thus further skew what is seen by some as a precarious but delicate balance between the private economic sector and public policy. We agree. But if the distinction between public and private institutions is no longer clear-cut, and the traditional separation of the public and private spheres is no longer in place, might it not then be better to recognize and extend constitutional guarantees so as to protect all citizens equally? If due process is crucial to political relationships between the individual and the state, why is it not central in relationships between employees and corporations since at least some of the companies in question are as large and powerful as small nations? Is it not in fact inconsistent with our democratic tradition *not* to mandate such rights?

The philosopher T. M. Scanlon summarizes our intuitions about due process. Scanlon says,

> The requirement of due process is one of the conditions of the moral acceptability of those institutions that give some people power to control or intervene in the lives of others.[7]

The institution of due process in the workplace is a moral requirement consistent with rationality and consistency expected in management decision-making. It is not precluded by EAW, and it is compatible with the overlap between the public and private sectors of the economy. Convincing business of the moral necessity of due process, however, is a task yet to be completed.

Notes

1. Lawrence E. Blades, "Employment at Will versus Individual Freedom: On Limiting the Abusive Exercise of Employer Power," *Columbia Law Review*, 67 (1967), p. 1405, quoted from *Payne* v. *Western*, 81 Tenn. 507 (1884), and *Hutton* v. *Watters*, 132 Tenn. 527, S.W. 134 (1915).

2. See David Ewing, *Justice on the Job: Resolving Grievances in the Nonunion Workplace* (Boston: Harvard Business School Press, 1989).

3. See *Lockner* v. *New York*, 198 U.S. (1905), and Adina Schwartz, "Autonomy in the Workplace," in Tom Regan, ed., *Just Business* (New York: Random House, 1984), pp. 129–40.

4. Eric Mack, "Natural and Contractual Rights," *Ethics*, 87 (1977), pp. 153–59.

5. Morris Cohen, "Dialogue on Private Property," *Rutgers Law Review* 9 (1954), p. 357. See also *Law and the Social Order* (1933) and Robert Hale, "Coercion and Distribution in a Supposedly Non-Coercive State," *Political Science Quarterly,* 38 (1923), p. 470; John Brest, "State Action and Liberal Theory," *University of Pennsylvania Law Review* (1982), pp. 1296–1329.

6. Gerald Frug, "The City As a Legal Concept," *Harvard Law Review*, 93 (1980), p. 1129.

7. T. M. Scanlon, "Due Process," in J. Roland Pennock and John W. Chapman, eds., *Nomos XVIII: Due Process* (New York: New York University Press, 1977), p. 94.

Review and Discussion Questions

1. What is the principle of employment at will? Why do you think the law has upheld it so long? What are the two aspects of due process? What is the current legal situation with respect to due process at work?

2. Examine and critically assess each of the five justifications for EAW, as stated on page 312. Which of these arguments is the strongest? How persuasive are Werhane and Radin's rejoinders to them? Are there arguments for EAW that the authors have overlooked or not answered adequately?

3. The authors contend that due process is both "consistent with, and a moral requirement of, EAW." Assess both aspects of this assertion.

4. How is the public/private distinction relevant to the debate over EAW and due process? Why do the authors believe that the distinction is blurred? Do you agree? Should constitutional rights be extended to private-sector employees?

Reading ──────────■

THE LIBERTARIAN CRITIQUE OF LABOR UNIONS

PETER LEVINE

*Perhaps because of their individualism, many Americans
tend to be skeptical of, or even opposed to, labor unions.
At the more philosophical level, this sentiment is reflected
in the libertarian critique of unions. Libertarians contend
that unions violate individual rights, restrict people's freedom, and harm outsiders. In this essay, however, Peter
Levine argues that unions have the potential to safeguard
freedom and due process and even to protect the property
interests of workers in their jobs. Although the purely economic effects of unions are open to debate, unions make
an important contribution to civic society—a contribution
that libertarians in particular, with their enthusiasm for
nongovernmental associations, should appreciate.*

Many Americans, including some who would benefit economically from union membership, view
unions with ambivalence or even hostility. Fewer
than half of respondents to a poll recently conducted by Fox News thought that unions were
good for the country. This skepticism may reflect
disapproval with the alienating style and performance of the AFL-CIO in modern times. But
American individualism also plays a role. Americans tend to distrust organizations that seem to put
solidarity, security, and fraternity above personal
liberty, innovation, and competition. Therefore, despite generations of struggle, labor unions remain
cultural anomalies. Labor lawyer Thomas Geoghegan describes union meetings as events at which
"paunchy, middle-aged men, slugging down cans of
beer, come to hold hands, touch each other, and
sing 'Solidarity Forever.' O.K., that hardly ever
happens, but most people in this business, some-

Reprinted by permission of the author. Copyright © 2001 Peter
Levine. References omitted.

where, at some point, see it once, and it is the
damnedest un-American thing you will ever see."

Most prominent union supporters take for
granted that the labor movement benefits workers.
They often assume that opponents have selfish economic motives, while anti-union workers must be
victims of coercion of misinformation. This attitude
ignores the possibility that moral values (such as liberty, self-reliance, and efficiency) motivate distrust
of unions. Meanwhile, public figures on the other
side of the debate generally assume that unions are
harmful and talk darkly about bosses, strike-related
violence, and rent-seeking bureaucracies.

To their credit, libertarians approach the question with less partisanship. While they are receptive to unions as non-governmental associations,
they are also skeptical of institutions that interfere
with "free" markets. Since the libertarian position
captures certain widespread American attitudes in
a refined (and radical) form, it is a good starting
point for philosophical analysis. If libertarian arguments against unions are strong, then maybe public skepticism is justified. If, however, libertarians
employ flawed arguments, then perhaps the widespread distrust of unions is misguided.

UNIONS AGAINST INDIVIDUAL RIGHTS

Libertarians strongly defend freedom of choice and
association. Thus, when workers choose to act collectively, negotiate together, or voluntarily walk
off the job, libertarians have no reasonable complaint—even if other people are harmed—because
they support the right to make and exit voluntary
partnerships.

But unions gain strength by overriding private
rights. They routinely block anyone from working
under a non-union contract, and they prevent employers from making offers—even advantageous
ones—to individual workers unless the union is informed and consents. Unions declare strikes and establish picket lines to prevent customers and
workers from entering company property; they may
fine employees who cross these lines. They also extract fees from all workers who are covered by their
contracts. Although covered workers may avoid paying for certain union functions (such as lobbying)

that are not germane to contract issues, they must pay for strikes and other activities that some of them oppose.

The great libertarian theorist Friedrich Hayek concluded that unions "are the one institution where government has signally failed in its first task, that of preventing coercion of men by other men—and by coercion I do not mean primarily the coercion of employers but the coercion of workers by their fellow workers." Hayek may have been thinking mainly of corrupt and unaccountable union leaders. But even a completely democratic union sometimes supplants private rights. As libertarians like Morgan O. Reynolds point out, majorities within a union are able to ignore minorities' preferences.

Libertarians are especially critical of "closed shop" contracts (which require businesses to hire only union members) and "union shop" contracts (which require all employees to join a specified union after they are hired). Libertarians see such arrangements as state-sanctioned violations of private contract rights. Both closed shops and genuine union shops are now illegal in the United States, but if libertarian arguments are flawed, then perhaps these institutions deserve reconsideration.

In any case, "agency shops" remain in the 29 states that have not passed so called "right-to-work" legislation that bans this kind of contract. In an agency shop, the union negotiates one collective-bargaining agreement that covers a whole class of employees. Workers do not have to join the union, but they must pay dues and work under the union contract. Proponents argue that employees ought to pay fees for a service (union representation) that benefits them tangibly, just as they may be required to pay for food in the company canteen. But this also means that workers in agency shops cannot avoid their union's jurisdiction.

Although organized labor is popular among covered workers—only 8 percent would vote to "get rid of" their unions—libertarians insist that if even *one person* pays dues but opposes the existence of her union, then she is not a member of a voluntary association. As Senator Barry Goldwater (R-AZ) told the union leader Walter Reuther in 1953: "There is only one question in this whole field in my mind. What about the man who does not want to belong to the union?" Goldwater spoke in the days of the "closed shop," when union membership could be compulsory. But more recently, Representative Ron Goodlatte (R-VA) claimed that even an "agency shop" violates individual rights, because "compelling a man or woman to pay fees to a union in order to work violates the very principle of individual liberty upon which this nation was founded."

At times, unions have overridden some of their own members' economic interests. In one important case, African American workers, dissatisfied by their union's efforts to end discrimination at a department store, attempted to picket without the union's approval. The Supreme court ruled 8-1 (in a decision written by Justice Thurgood Marshall) that only the union could take such actions, because the principles of *organized* labor and *collective* bargaining implied that unions were entitled to gain power from disciplined action.

Unions have also abridged their members' individual freedom of conscience. Justice Potter Stewart once noted that a worker's "moral or religious views about the desirability of abortion may not square with the union's policy in negotiating a medical benefits plan. One person might disapprove of unions negotiating limits on the right to strike, believing that such policies guarantee the serfdom of the working class, while another person might object to unions on purely economic grounds."

Unions can harm outsiders, too, including the customers, managers, and owners of any company involved in a labor dispute. In general, libertarians believe that non-governmental organizations should be able to act freely in the marketplace, even if their behavior imposes costs on others. For instance, firms are within their rights to run competitors out of business or to lay off their employees. By the same token, it would seem that unions should not be stopped just because their tactics cost other people money. However, American unions owe some of their power to government recognition, so libertarians view any harms that they cause as impermissible violations of liberty. In particular, the libertarian economist Milton Friedman complains that unions raise labor costs and thus increase unemployment, to the detriment of poor people who are not their members. He insists that unions have "made the incomes of the working class more unequal by reducing the opportunities available to the most disadvantaged workers." Although unions often strive to protect poor people in order to narrow the pay differential between their own members and the rest of the workforce, Friedman's hypothesis is true in some cases.

UNIONS IN DEFENSE OF RIGHTS

Libertarians cite natural or individual rights, such as freedom of property and choice, that militate against unions. But unions also have the potential to *safeguard* freedom and due process. Some workers may see the job market as a "state of nature," a ruthless competition that endangers legitimate individual rights, and they may believe that a lone individual cannot secure through her own efforts a living wage, job tenure, freedom to criticize and dissent, and some measure of self-rule. Such workers may view their employer as a despot with absolute and arbitrary power. Although one way to guarantee rights is to pass and enforce appropriate legislation, employees may trust another strategy: unionization. A worker who is treated unfairly cannot expect her fellow workers to take effective action in defense of her (and their) rights unless they are organized into a disciplined organization such as a union.

This argument hinges on the notion that employers are "despots," since their power to discipline and fire workers is comparable to the police powers of a state. Charles E. Lindblom, a Yale professor of economics and political science, writes that the "mere threat of termination can be as constraining, as coercive, as menacing as an authoritative governmental command." Losing one's livelihood, especially through layoff or demotion, can be catastrophic and arbitrary, entirely lacking in due process or rational justification. Thus, unskilled workers in a glutted labor market may need a union to give them any semblance of rights. But workers who command a high price in the market may feel that they are more free without a union—which will impose its own rules, officials, and bureaucracies.

In addition to the balance of power between labor and capital, a second factor is also relevant: the degree to which supervisors act in the overall interest of their companies. Assume that you can trust your boss to help maximize the firm's profits. Then you may be happy without a union if your skills give you some leverage in contract negotiations. But your own supervisor may not be competent or responsible. He may be lazy, arbitrary, discriminatory, or motivated by completely selfish goals (as in cases of sexual harassment). Since it is dangerous to challenge a supervisor directly and difficult to change jobs, even workers with high market value may want enforceable and inflexible rules to govern salaries, promotion prospects, grievance procedures, and job descriptions. For people who distrust managers, a union is not an unwelcome bureaucracy but an independent institution to which they can appeal in defense of their rights.

Although unions support due process, fair treatment, and other rights for workers, they are typically seen as the enemy of *property* rights. However, some have argued that jobs should be seen as the property of workers, since their labor creates value. Late in the nineteenth century, political economist Henry C. Adams contended that, in appropriate circumstances, employees should "be given tenure of employment," so that they "cannot be discharged except for cause that satisfies a commission of arbitrators." Further, he believed that workers ought to be "consulted whether hours of work or the numbers employed shall be reduced," and given preference over those outside the industry. These steps would make jobs into "workmen's property." Adams added that the state could not be trusted to intervene fairly and, consequently, unions were the best means to redefine property.

As Adams (among others) realized, "property" admits of no universal, self-evident definition. Some have claimed that a class of objects should be defined as property because doing so encourages such positive consequences as increased investment and effort, or the efficient use and distribution of goods. At present, jobs are considered the alienable property of employers, who use them to maximize profits. If instead jobs were seen as the (non-transferable) property of workers, then although investment and innovation might suffer, employees might also feel deep satisfaction when positions became *theirs* because of their work. In short, Adams' proposal has both positive and negative implications, and the net change would be difficult to assess.

In my view, only the state has the authority to decide what is the best system of ownership in the labor market. The marketplace itself cannot make such decisions, because any market presupposes the existing system of property. Nor should we allow unions to determine property rights unilaterally, since they do not allow outsiders to vote. But elected legislatures could decide that jobs shall become workers' property under certain circumstances, and an appropriate means to that end would be to strengthen unions. After all, if investors can create entities such as corporations, with a well-defined set of property rights, then perhaps workers ought to be able to form entities such as bargaining units, with similar claims to property.

UNIONS AND COMPETITIVE MARKETS

Mainstream economic theory contends that a competitive market generally produces the greatest possible quantity and desired goods and services; in this sense, it is efficient. However, unions reduce competition in labor markets by preventing employers from firing unionized employees and by blocking job-seekers from accepting offers below the union rate. They may thus protect unproductive workers, raise costs, distort incentives, and frustrate entrepreneurship. Furthermore, organized labor is specifically exempted from antitrust laws whose general goal is to promote competition. Judge Richard A. Posner (who is often called a libertarian, although his views are idiosyncratic) concludes that American labor law is a device to promote the "cartelization of the labor supply by unions." Because it confers power on unions, the law "is founded on a policy that is the opposite of the policies of competition and economic efficiency that most economists support."

One economist has calculated that unions cost the country 4.9 percent of GDP annually. Other estimates are much lower, and some cite evidence that unions are good for the economy—boosting

morale and trust, reducing turnover, offering senior workers incentives to share knowledge with novices, and improving the flow of information between workers and managers. One recent study by Sandra E. Black and Lisa M. Lynch found that productivity in unionized firms was ten percent higher than in comparable non-unionized firms. Still, unions must at least sometimes reduce the nation's supply of goods and services. Of course, the same could be said of many private activities (smoking, gambling, early retirement) that libertarians consider well within the bounds of personal liberty. But Hayek distinguished between harms—which free people inevitably cause as they pursue their own interests—and coercion, which is impermissible. Hayek thought that unions acted coercively, so whenever they caused economic damage, they also violated rights and freedoms.

Contrary to what libertarians assume, freedom is not just a matter of selecting among choices in a marketplace. Imagine that workers have won some leverage over an employer because of a union. As a result, they can lay claim to a larger portion of the profits that their work generates. Now they must decide how tough to be in contract negotiations (considering possible damage to the company) and how seriously to risk a strike. They must also decide whether they want to use their collective muscle to pursue salary increases, equity among their membership, additional leisure time, job security, or insurance against catastrophic losses that would only affect their least fortunate members. This type of political deliberation and self-government is a form of freedom that is impossible without the union.

Libertarians sometimes argue that unions damage people's interests in a different way: by diminishing wealth or the supply of consumer goods and services. As economists David G. Blanchflower and Andrew J. Oswald note, "The idea that income buys happiness is one of the assumptions—made without evidence but rather for deductive reasons—in microeconomics textbooks." However, actual data reveal that, while money has a positive effect on happiness, its impact is "not as large as some would expect." Other variables—such as marriage, employment, and race—have more powerful effects. Indeed, while Americans have grown much wealthier in the aggregate since 1945, according to political scientist Robert Putnam, we have also seen a tenfold increase in the depression rate, a quadrupling of the teenage suicide rate, and dramatic increases in "headaches, indigestion, and sleeplessness" among younger people, even affluent ones.

Putnam argues these maladies can be traced to a decline in social connectedness. Interpreting data on self-reported happiness, he finds that "getting married is the 'happiness equivalent' of quadrupling your income" and that "regular club attendance, volunteering, entertaining, or church attendance is the happiness equivalent of getting a college degree or more than doubling your income." If the goal is the maximization of happiness or welfare, then one should strongly favor unions—even if they reduce aggregate money income—because they provide civic connections, which "rival marriage and affluence as predictors of life happiness."

UNIONS AS PARTS OF CIVIL SOCIETY

Unions are more than economic actors that negotiate with employers; they are also communities of workers, forums for debate, and lobbying organizations. They can thus be described as parts of "civil society," a social sector that enjoys strong support from libertarians—and most other ideological groups as well. However, this terminology raises a new set of questions about the proper role and scope of civil society.

Libertarians believe that civil society should consist of institutions that people can join and exit freely depending on their values and preferences. But Americans usually join unions because the company where they want to work happens to be unionized—not because they support the labor movement or want to frequent the union hall. Quitting the union would then mean waiving their right to vote without escaping the obligation to pay dues and to work under the union contract. Therefore, unions serve the goal of free association less well than other organizations do.

However, libertarians' equation of civil society with freedom of association overlooks some of its most attractive features. For instance, some people

argue that the purpose of civil society is to offer the moral and psychological advantages of *community,* which are missing in a competitive market. Unions commonly meet political theorist Thomas Bender's definition of a "community," which involves a limited number of people in a restricted social space who are "held together by shared understandings and a sense of obligation." Bender observes that relationships are "close, often intimate, and usually face to face," with individuals bound together by emotional ties rather than individual self-interest. He concludes that "there is a 'we-ness' in a community; one is a member." As philosopher Richard Rorty notes, "You would never guess, from William Bennett's and Robert Bork's speeches about the need to overcome liberal individualism, that the labor unions provide by far the best examples in America's history of the virtues these writers claim we must recapture. The history of the unions provides the best examples of comradeship, loyalty, and self-sacrifice."

Rorty is right: cultural conservatives should concede that unions exemplify some of their favorite virtues. Nevertheless, conservatives may reasonably prefer *other* institutions that promote different virtues as well—such as religious faith, military discipline, and individual initiative and responsibility. It is not obvious that unions are especially good at generating the most valuable virtues as ranked by conservatives, by liberals, or (least of all) by libertarians. However, perhaps unions generate virtues that are particularly neglected in our culture.

A third understanding of "civil society" views this sector as the source of "social capital." Robert Putnam and his colleagues use this phrase to refer to habits, skills, and attitudes—especially trust and a propensity to join organizations—that expedite collective action and lessen the burdens on government.

Union members have much more social capital than those who belong to no groups at all. According to the General Social Survey, union members are 10 percent more likely to trust other people, 19 percent more likely to express an interest in politics, 16 percent more likely to vote, 17 percent more likely to influence others about elections, and 22 percent more likely to talk to several people about important issues—a pattern that remains even when one controls for income, education, and employment status. Further, large numbers of union members report having contacted the government (18.3 percent), attended conferences (56.5 percent), or served as committee members (49 percent) and officers (36.8 percent) as a result of their membership.

However, union members are not very active in civil society compared to people who belong to at least one association, but not to a union. Union members perform at least five percent worse than these other participants on all the measures listed above except "influencing people about elections" (where union members are more active than other members). It seems, then, that unions boost civic participation, but to a lesser extent than the average association. Union membership is also a weak predictor of overall associational membership—unionized workers are not avid joiners the way that Rotarians and PTA volunteers are. Thus, although unions contribute to civil society and cultivate civic behavior, they are not outstanding contributors of civic life.

A fourth theory views "civil society" as the domain of interest groups, political factions, or lobbies. This definition clearly covers unions, since they lobby government officials, litigate, communicate to their own members about elections and issues, spend money on grassroots political campaigns, buy advertising, make endorsements, and donate to candidates and parties. Especially in recent decades (and especially in the United States), these political activities have been much more effective than such traditional tactics of labor unions as organizing workers, bargaining with employers, and striking.

One could object that unions do not "speak" for all their members, since they often take one public position instead of reflecting the diverse views of their members. Further, although unions are generally popular with their own rank-and-file, they score the lowest levels of support for their "positions on national issues" and their "endorsements of candidates in political campaigns." In a series of cases since 1977, the Supreme Court has ruled that union members may resign without penalty and that non-members who are required to pay dues

need not pay for lobbying or organizing efforts. These rulings have not gone far enough for libertarians, who worry about the status of workers who want to retain their union memberships (so that they can vote on bargaining issues) and yet disagree with the union's political agenda. Libertarians also complain that dissenting dues-payers must seek refunds instead of receiving automatic exemptions from the costs of political speech.

On the other hand, supporters of organized labor argue that the Court is overly concerned about dissenters' rights, especially since corporations are not similarly regulated. For instance, owners of companies are free to take a position on any issue and fire workers who disagree. And majorities of stockholders can dictate policies that minorities abhor. The right not to speak would be protected if *all* organizations were prohibited from lobbying, but this approach would undermine rights of association and petition. And allowing corporations to lobby while banning political action by unions would be discriminatory and arbitrary. Thus the current treatment of union lobbying seems defensible.

Indeed, unions often enhance public deliberation about national priorities by adding a disciplined, well-funded alternative to the influential views of corporations. In some cases, speech is a public good that cannot be produced by uncoordinated, individual action. Since many employees may be tempted to act as free riders, relying on others to speak for the interests of workers as a class, the few who do speak (or voluntarily pay for speech) will see weak results from their efforts. But if workers form a union for collective-bargaining purposes, and if it can *compel* everyone to pay for political activities, then all workers will gain a strong voice at a small cost to each. In many poor communities, unions are among the only institutions that have the power to fund themselves without outside assistance from either government or philanthropy. The benefit to the larger community is robust public debate, which libertarians prize. . . .

Unions also force other institutions, such as the mass media and legislatures, to debate issues that may otherwise be ignored. And by protecting freedom of association and criticism inside the workplace, unions give workers a means to *act* on their deliberate beliefs in ways that influence the wider society. As scholar-activists Harry Boyte and Nanci Kari argue in *Building America,* many "deliberative theorists put citizens in the role of judicious audience." That is, they assume a distinction between judgment—the citizens' role—and work or action, which is what rulers do. But when union members debate a contract, decide to strike, and then provide food and childcare for their fellow strikers, they fruitfully combine judgment, work, and action.

CONCLUSION

These arguments will not satisfy pure libertarians, but they do suggest that unions are compatible with personal liberty. To be sure, the powers and prerogatives of unions must be balanced against individual rights. Workers should be free to avoid union membership and dues beyond those necessary for contract negotiations, and all members ought to have enforceable rights against discrimination by their unions. But these qualifications (which are enshrined in current law) would not prevent strong unions from forming.

Unfortunately, the actual rate of union membership—15 percent of all employees; less in the private sector—is much lower than in other democracies and below half the level reached in America around 1950. About one third of non-unionized American workers believe that, "were an election held tomorrow, workers at their firm would support a union," but they are unlikely ever to have the opportunity to cast a vote.

Congress could respond to the current situation by legalizing "agency shops" nationwide. Research by economist David T. Ellwood and lawyer Glenn Fine suggests that this reform would allow about five percent of the population in current "right-to-work" states to join unions, for a total increase of millions of members.

Federal law could also approach corporate resistance differently. Companies typically rely on illegal tactics to stop an organizing drive by, for instance, intimidating union supporters and firing employees involved in organizing the union. Although federal judges may declare automatic certification of a union if they believe that laws have been broken, in practice, unions arising in this way are weak from the start and managers feel free not to make them serious contract offers. A better solution is to recognize a union as the sole legitimate bargaining agent of a workforce as soon as a majority of the covered workers signs a petition to unionize. Then employees would be spared a struggle against management intimidation, and neither side would know how deeply the rank-and-file was committed to the union or how well the union could weather a strike. This uncertainty would encourage management to negotiate seriously with the union leadership, which (for its part) would have dues money and other resources to use during the bargaining process.

Since this reform is untested in the U.S., one can only speculate on the results. But the proposal is consistent with the philosophical considerations explored in this article. As labor lawyer Thomas Geoghegan observes, "I can think of nothing, no law, no civil rights act, that would radicalize this country more, democratize it more . . . , than to make this one tiny change in the law: to let people join unions if they like, freely and without coercion, without threat of being fired, just as people are permitted to do in Europe and in Canada."

Review and Discussion Questions

1. In your experience, are Americans supportive of, hostile to, or indifferent to labor unions? Why are unions weaker in the United States than in other developed countries?

2. On what grounds are libertarians critical of labor unions? Do unions infringe on people's rights or do they safeguard those rights?

3. Do unions interfere with the right to property as libertarians believe? Assess the idea that jobs are the property of employees. What are its implications?

4. In your view, do unions have on balance positive or negative economic effects? Do they have positive or negative social effects? Do you agree with Levine that unions make an important contribution to civic society? Explain why or why not.

5. Today unions represent a smaller percentage of the workforce than they have in the past. Is this a good thing—for workers, the economy, or society as a whole? Should unions be supported by laws (a) making it easier for employees to establish unions, (b) outlawing companies from permanently replacing workers who go on strike, or (c) legalizing "agency shops" nationwide (that is, eliminating state "right-to-work" laws)? Assess each of these proposals.

Further Reading for Chapter 6

Ronald Duska, "Employee Rights," in Robert E. Frederick, ed., *A Companion to Business Ethics* (Malden, Mass.: Blackwell, 1999) discusses the nature of rights in general and the specific rights claimed for employees in recent times.

Thomas Geoghegan, *Which Side Are You On? Trying to Be for Labor When It's Flat on Its Back* (New York: Penguin, 1992) is the insightful and entertaining memoir of a labor lawyer.

Mary Gibson, *Workers' Rights* (Totowa, N.J.: Rowman & Allanheld, 1983) is rich in factual background and actual cases.

Reed Larson and **William L. Clay** debate right-to-work laws in "Does America Need a National Right-to-Work Law?" *Insight on the News* 14 (August 17, 1998).

Richard L. Lippke, *Radical Business Ethics* (Lanham, Md.: Rowman & Littlefield, 1995), Chapter 6, discusses the right to freedom of speech and conscience in the workplace.

Patricia Werhane, "Individual Rights in Business," in Tom Regan, ed., *Just Business: New Introductory Essays in Business Ethics* (New York: Random House, 1984), provides a useful overview of many basic moral issues in the workplace.

Michael T. Zugelder and **Steven D. Mauer,** "Small Business and the Americans with Disabilities Act," *Business Horizons* 41 (July–August 1998) discusses the rights and responsibilities of employers under the ADA.

InfoTrac College Edition: For further information or to conduct research, please go to www.infotrac-college.com.

7

The Workplace (2): Today's Challenges

It was a routine business day for Eastern Airlines—until it received an anonymous tip that some of its baggage handlers at Miami International Airport were using drugs. Eastern quickly sprang into action, ordering security guards to round up the ten employees then at work in the airport's plane-loading area. The employees were marched between two rows of guards and into waiting vans—"like terrorists," a lawsuit later claimed—all in full view of other employees and passengers. After questioning the workers, suspicious supervisors put them on board a bus, once again in front of onlookers, and took them to a hospital. There the employees were given an ultimatum: Either take a urine test or be fired on the spot.[1]

The baggage handlers were union members, but they caved in and took the test. All ten of them tested negative (that is, free of drugs), but they weren't happy about what they'd been through. Not long afterward, they filed suit against the airline in federal court, seeking damages of $30,000 each on charges of invasion of privacy, defamation, and intentional infliction of emotional distress. Eastern has since gone out of business, but the case represents in dramatic form one of the major issues dividing employers and employees today: privacy. Companies are delving further into employees' personal lives than ever before, claiming the need to monitor their behavior and probe into their health and habits. Workers are resisting ever more adamantly, fighting back for the right to be left alone.

In 1928, U.S. Supreme Court Justice Louis D. Brandeis described the right to privacy, or "the right to be let alone," as "the right most valued by civilized men." He was referring to the Fourth Amendment's guarantee that citizens are protected against illegal searches and seizures by government. Today many Americans are resisting invasions of their privacy not just by government agencies but also by intrusive employers. And not without reason: One survey shows that American bosses tend to be less respectful of employees' rights to privacy than their counterparts are in Europe and Canada.[2]

Businesses and other organizations frequently argue that they have a compelling need to know about the personal lives and conduct of their employees, while those employees firmly assert their right to a personal sphere not subject to the needs, interests, or curiosity of their employers. "I don't think politicians and corporate executives realize how strongly Americans feel about it," says a San Francisco lawyer who specializes in employee lawsuits. "It's not a liberal or a conservative issue, and the fear of abuse doesn't emanate from personnel policies. It's coming out of the larger, impersonal notion that workers are fungible, expendable items."[3]

Chapter 6 examined personnel policies and procedures, trade unions, the state of civil liberties on the job, and the efforts of some successful companies to respect the rights, dignity, and moral integrity of their workers. This chapter also focuses on moral issues that emerge in the workplace. It looks in detail at one crucial civil liberty—the right to privacy—and at the ethical choices it poses inside the organization. The remainder of the chapter examines several other topics that are stirring up controversy in today's workplace. More specifically, this chapter explores the following:

1. The nature of privacy and the problems of organizational influence over private decisions

2. The moral issues raised by the use of polygraph and personality tests, employee monitoring, and drug testing in the workplace

3. Working conditions—in particular, health and safety, styles of management, and provision of day-care facilities and maternity leave

4. Job satisfaction and dissatisfaction and the prospects for enhancing the quality of work life

ORGANIZATIONAL INFLUENCE IN PRIVATE LIVES

Privacy is widely acknowledged today to be a fundamental right, yet corporate behavior and policies often threaten privacy, especially in the case of employees. One way this happens is through the release of personal information about employees. The data banks and personnel files of business and nonbusiness organizations contain an immense amount of private information, the disclosure of which can seriously violate employees' rights. Most firms guard their files closely and restrict the type of material that they can contain in the first place, but the potential for abuse is still great. Although a complicated set of laws and court rulings limits access to such information, a wide range of snoops still manage, legitimately or illegitimately, to get their hands on it.

As a related matter, more employees are successfully suing their former bosses for passing on damaging information to prospective employers. The courts have traditionally considered this sort of information exchange between employers to be "privileged," but companies can lose this protection by giving information to too many people or by making false reports. Through fear of defamation suits, in fact, many organizations now refuse to reveal anything about former employees except their dates of employment. Such reticence obviously makes it more difficult for companies to screen job applicants.[4]

More significant are the threats to privacy that can arise on the job itself. For example, some bosses unhesitatingly rummage through the files of their workers, even when they are marked "private." Some companies routinely eavesdrop on their employees' phone calls, and many of them read their employees' email or peek at their instant messages. Voice mail isn't safe, either, as Michael Huttcut, a manager of a McDonald's outlet in St. Louis, learned the hard way. He was having an affair with a coworker, and the romantic voice-mail messages he sent her were retrieved and played by his boss. When Huttcut complained, he was fired.[5] Other companies secretly quiz managers—or even call in private investigators—to gain knowledge about the personal habits and behavior of workers who call in sick.[6]

Equally important is the way organizations attempt to influence behavior that ought properly to be left to the discretion of their employees—in particular, efforts to impose their own values on their workers. For example, Wal-Mart fired Lauren Allen, who was married but separated from her husband, for dating a coworker, who was single. Wal-Mart says that it "strongly believes in and supports the 'family unit'" and that the conduct of Allen and her coworker violated the company's rules.[7] Or consider those corporations who hit up their employees for political contributions. By bundling these individual contributions together as one gift, companies circumvent the ban on corporate campaign giving. Some people think IBM crossed the line in 1994 by urging its employees to work to defeat the health care bill then before Congress.[8]

There is, however, no consensus among philosophers or lawyers about how to define privacy, how far the right to privacy extends, or how to balance a concern for privacy against other moral considerations. All of us would agree, nonetheless, that we have a clear right to keep private certain areas of our lives and that we need to have our privacy respected if we are to function as complete, self-governing agents. Particularly important is our right to make personal decisions autonomously, free from the illegitimate influence of our employers.

Even when a genuine privacy right is identified, the strength of that right depends on circumstances—in particular, on competing rights and interests. Privacy is not an absolute value. Corporations and other organizations often have legitimate interests that may conflict with the privacy concerns of employees. Determining when organizational infringement on a person's private sphere is morally justifiable is, of course, precisely the question at issue.

Consider the case of Virginia Rulon-Miller, a marketing manager in IBM's office products division. She made the mistake of falling in love. A week after receiving a 13.3 percent pay raise, she was called on the carpet for dating Matt Blum, a former IBM account manager who had gone to a competitor. She and Blum had begun dating when Blum was at IBM, and he still played on the IBM softball team. IBM told Rulon-Miller to give up Blum or be demoted. "I was so steeped in IBM culture," she says, "that I was going to break up with Matt." But the next day, before she had a chance to do anything, she was dismissed. Even though IBM's decision was based on written policy governing conflicts of interest, a California jury decided that Rulon-Miller's privacy had been invaded. It awarded her $300,000.

On the other hand, a year later the Oregon Supreme Court upheld J. C. Penney's firing of a merchandising manager for dating another employee. He claimed that his right to privacy had been violated. Although it may seem harsh to fire an employee on the basis of personal lifestyle, the court said, private firms aren't barred from discriminating against workers for their choice of mates. And a federal district court permitted the firing of a New Mexico employee with an excellent work record because she was married to a worker at a competing supermarket.[9]

As a general rule, whenever an organization infringes on what would normally be considered the personal sphere of an individual, it bears the burden of establishing the legitimacy of that infringement. The fact that a firm thinks an action or policy is justifiable does not, of course, prove that it is. The firm must establish both that it has some legitimate interest at stake and that the steps it is taking to protect that interest are reasonable and morally permissible. But what are the areas of legitimate organizational influence over the individual?

Legitimate and Illegitimate Influence

The work contract; the firm's responsibilities to owners, consumers, and society at large; and the purpose of the firm itself all support the proposition that the firm is legitimately interested in whatever significantly influences work performance. What constitutes a significant influence on work performance, however, eludes precise definition because the connection between an act or policy and the job is often fuzzy. Take, for example, the area of dress. Ace Construction seems to have a legitimate interest in the kind of shoes Doug Bell wears while framing its houses because the quality of the shoes could affect his safety and job performance as well as the firm's liability. On the other hand, whether American Airlines was legitimately pursuing a genuine corporate interest when it forbade a black employee from wearing her hair in corn rows because the style clashed with the company's corporate image is more debatable. Or consider the ticket agent who was fired by another airline for refusing to wear makeup. Perhaps this was a legitimate demand in the name of good public relations, but maybe it was arbitrary and narrow minded.[10]

An employer's concern with dress can interfere with an employee's personal choices in other ways. Consider the case of Margaret Hasselman, who worked as a lobby attendant in a New York City high rise. Wearing the new uniform provided by her employer—a poncho with large openings under the arms, dancer's underpants, and white pumps—she repeatedly encountered sexual harassment. She complained about the outfit to her boss, but to no avail. When she eventually refused to wear it, she was fired. Issues of morality, of course, differ from questions of legality. But it is interesting that when Hasselman filed suit, the court ruled that no employer has the right to force workers to wear revealing or sexually provocative clothing. In contrast, in a subsequent case the Equal Employment Opportunity Commission (EEOC) upheld an employer's firing of several female employees who refused to wear swimsuits as part of a swimsuit promotion. The EEOC agreed that the swimsuits were revealing but found no reason to expect that the women would encounter sexual harassment.[11]

The general proposition that a firm has a legitimate interest only in employee behavior that significantly influences work performance applies equally to off-the-job conduct. BankAmerica probably fell afoul of this guideline when it fired Michael Thomasson, a legal secretary, for working as a gay stripper during his off-hours. After a coworker read a personal letter Thomasson had written on a company computer that mentioned his job as an exotic dancer, a group of bank employees, including several of Thomasson's supervisors, went to see him perform. Two weeks later he was dismissed—despite a record of positive job evaluations and a recent merit raise.[12]

Determining when conduct is significantly related to job performance can be difficult. For example, how would you decide the following case? In an off-the-job fight, a plant guard drew his gun on his antagonist. Although no one was injured, the guard's employer viewed the incident as grounds for dismissal. The employer reasoned that such an action indicated a lack of judgment on the part of the guard. Do you think the employer had a right to fire the guard under these circumstances? The courts did. By contrast, consider the employee who sold a small amount of marijuana to an undercover agent, or the employee who made obscene phone calls to the teenage daughter of a client. Their employers fired them, but the employees were reinstated by an arbitrator or the court.

Then there's the amorphous area of company image and the question of whether it can be affected by off-the-job conduct. The political activities of a corporate executive, for example, could significantly affect the image a firm wishes to project, whereas what an obscure worker on the firm's assembly line does politically might have a comparatively insignificant impact on the company's image. Companies and other organizations have an interest in protecting their good names. The off-duty conduct of employees might damage an organization's reputation, but in practice damage is often difficult to establish. For example, two IRS agents were suspended for "mooning" a group of women after leaving a bar. Would you agree with their suspension? An arbitrator didn't and revoked it. He couldn't see that their conduct damaged the IRS's reputation.[13]

Obviously we can't spell out exactly when off-duty conduct affects company image in some material way, any more than we can say precisely what constitutes a significant influence on job performance. But that doesn't prevent us from being able to judge that in many cases organizations step beyond legitimate boundaries and interfere with what should properly be personal decisions by their employees. This interference can take many forms, but three—one traditional, the other two modern—are worth discussing.

Involvement in Civic Activities. Business and other organizations have traditionally encouraged or pressured employees to participate in public-spirited activities off the job—presumably, to enhance the image of the company. Sometimes, for instance, organizations urge employees to participate in civic activities such as running for the local school board or heading up a commission on the arts. At other times business will encourage employees to join civic service organizations, such as Kiwanis, Lions, or Rotary. Still other times, firms may encourage and even compel employees to contribute to charities. Not too long ago a newspaper reported that an office worker was fired for not contributing more than $10 to the United Way. Such a modest contribution violated the firm's policy of requiring each employee to give the equivalent of an hour's pay each month. In this case the firm compelled workers to contribute; in other instances organizational recommendations or suggestions can have the impact of orders.

Members of the Army Band, however, won a suit claiming that the posting of soldiers' names who had not contributed to the United Way constituted coercion. The federal judge who heard the case barred all federal departments from setting 100 percent participation goals, holding group meetings to raise money, or using supervisors as fund collectors. His ruling also prohibited making noncontributors return their payroll-deduction cards and restricted the cards of contributors to personnel use. So far, though, this ruling has not limited the scope of fund-raising practices in other organizations.

Attempts by companies to influence off-the-job behavior often constitute invasions of privacy, specifically the privacy of personal decisions. By explicitly or implicitly requiring employees to associate themselves with a particular activity, group, or cause, firms are telling workers what to believe, what values to support, and what goals to promote outside work.

Health Programs. Sometimes organizations pressure employees in certain directions for "their own good." Consider the aggressive "wellness" programs that some companies are mounting to push employees toward healthier lifestyles. These paternalistic programs are aimed at helping employees live longer and improve their health and productivity. The programs teach employees about nutrition, exercise, stress, and heart disease and encourage them to give up smoking, eat more healthfully, moderate their drinking, and work out in the company gym or join a company sports team after work.[14]

Wellness programs try to make fitness part of the corporate culture, and that seems innocent enough. But some companies are making employees pay more for their health care benefits if they are overweight, have high blood pressure, or don't exercise.[15] And employees have been fired for smoking or taking a drink at home.[16] "I think employers are going to get deeper and deeper into the wellness business," says Professor Alan F. Westin of Columbia University. "This is going to throw up a series of profound ethical and legal dilemmas about how they should do it and what we don't want them to do."[17]

Intensive Group Experience. In recent years company interference has taken a more subtle form. Modern psychology has made us aware that most people never realize their potential for perceiving, thinking, feeling, creating, and experiencing. Attempts to enlarge the potential for personal growth have resulted in the human potential movement. The focus of this movement is on developing ways to help people lower their defenses, remove their masks, become more aware and open to experience, feel more deeply, express themselves more effectively, be more creative, and become everything they can be.

Intensive group experience goes by various names, such as sensitivity training groups, encounter groups, T-groups, awareness groups, creativity groups, and workshops. Industry frequently uses a form of intensive group experience called team-building groups to facilitate the attainment of production and related goals as well as to provide opportunities for improved human relations and personal growth. In a work context, the intensive group experience brings employees together and through various exercises attempts to enable them to realize their abilities, clarify and strengthen their motivations, and improve their capacity to work with others.

The potential benefits of such experiences in the workplace are exciting, for they can not only boost productivity but also help people meet their higher-level needs. Nevertheless, such group encounters can pose a threat to psychic privacy, especially when groups lay bare a participant's innermost feelings. Although this doesn't always occur, it can. When it does, privacy can be violated.

As with health programs and civic activities, the issue of voluntary participation is crucial. When employees are genuinely free to participate or not, then such group sessions are (optional) opportunities for job enrichment and function as legitimate vehicles for increasing employees' work performance and satisfaction. But when coercion infringes on personal decision making—even in a subtle form, as when participation in such groups becomes an unwritten prerequisite for job promotion—this raises moral concerns.

OBTAINING INFORMATION

It's no secret that firms frequently seek, store, and communicate information about employees without their consent. A firm may bug employee lounges, hoping to discover who's responsible for pilfering. Another firm may use a managerial grapevine, with supervisors meeting once a month to exchange anecdotal material about employees, some of it obtained in confidence, all of it gathered with the hope of anticipating potential troublemakers. Still another company may keep detailed files on the personal lives of its employees to ensure compatibility with organizational image and reputation.

Of special interest here are two common practices organizations engage in: subjecting employees to various tests and monitoring employees on the job to discover sundry information. Before beginning the discussion, however, we need to take a brief look at the concept of

informed consent and how it connects with these topics.

Informed Consent

Certainly no employee is ever compelled to take a lie-detector, personality, or genetic screening test in the sense that someone puts a loaded revolver to the person's head and says, "Take the test or else." But compulsion, like freedom, comes in degrees. Although an employee may not be compelled to take a test in the same way that a prisoner of war, for example, is compelled to cooperate with a captor, enough coercion may be present to significantly diminish the worker's capacity to consent freely to privacy-invading procedures.

Obviously if workers submit to an honesty exam or to a test for genetic disorders, they agree to do so. But was their consent valid and legitimate? Was it informed consent? That's the issue, and it is an altogether reasonable issue to raise, because information collected on workers is often intimately personal and private and, when used carelessly, can injure them.

Informed consent implies deliberation and free choice. Workers must understand what they are agreeing to, including its full ramifications, and must voluntarily choose it. Deliberation requires not only the availability of facts but also a full understanding of them. Workers must be allowed to deliberate on the basis of enough usable information, information that they can understand. But usable information is not of itself enough to guarantee informed consent. Free choice is also important—the *consent* part is as significant as the *informed* part of informed consent.

Everyone agrees that for consent to be legitimate, it must be voluntary. Workers must willingly agree to the privacy-invading procedure. They must also be in a position to act voluntarily. One big factor that affects the voluntariness of consent is the pressures, expressed and implied, exerted on employees to conform to organizational policy. Especially when these pressures to conform are reinforced with implicit reprisals, they can effectively undercut the voluntariness of consent. Thus, employers who ignore organizational pressures on workers to comply with privacy-invading procedures can misinterpret consent to a test as voluntary when it is not.

Polygraph Tests

When an individual is disturbed by a question, certain detectable physiological changes occur. The person's heart may begin to race, blood pressure may rise, respiration may increase. The polygraph simultaneously records changes in these physiological processes and, thus, is often used in lie detection.

Businesses cite several reasons for using polygraph tests. First, the polygraph is a fast and economical way to verify information provided by a job applicant and to screen candidates for employment. So used, it can help reveal personal philosophy, behavioral patterns, and character traits incompatible with the organization's purpose, function, and image.

Second, the polygraph allows employers to identify dishonest employees or job candidates, at a time when many companies are suffering staggering annual losses through in-house theft. Third, companies argue that the use of polygraphs permits business to abolish audits and oppressive controls. They say the use of polygraphs actually increases workers' freedom.

Those who defend the use of polygraphs rely on three assumptions that are open to question.[18] The first assumption is that lying triggers an involuntary, distinctive response that truth telling does not. But this is not necessarily the case. What the polygraph can do is record that the respondent was more disturbed by one question than by another, but it cannot determine why the person was disturbed. Perhaps the question made the person feel guilty or angry or frightened, but deception does not necessarily lurk behind the emotional response.

A classic case that makes the point involved Floyd Fay of Toledo, Ohio, who was sentenced to life imprisonment for murder, in part on the basis of having failed two polygraph tests. The tests included control questions, such as "Before the age of twenty-five, did you ever think of hurting someone for revenge?" Because Fay's heart beat faster and his palms perspired more when he was asked about the crime than when asked about the control questions, he was regarded as deceptive. Fay spent two years in jail before the real killers confessed.

Second, it is assumed that polygraphs are extraordinarily accurate. Lynn March, president of the American Polygraph Association, says that "when administered correctly by qualified operators, the tests are accurate more than 90 percent of the time."[19] But David T. Lykken, a psychiatry professor, claims that these boasts are not borne out by three scientifically credible studies of the accuracy of polygraphs used on actual criminal suspects. The accuracies obtained by qualified operators in these experiments were 63 percent, 39 percent, and 55 percent.[20] Whether the polygraph is accurate 90 percent of the time or less, the conclusion is the same: It cannot reveal with certainty that a person is or is not telling the truth.

The third major assumption about polygraphs is that they cannot be beaten. Lykken, for one, suggests otherwise. The easiest way to beat the polygraph, the psychiatrist claims, is by augmenting your response to the control question by some form of covert self-stimulation, like biting your tongue. He claims that Fay taught some augmenting techniques to twenty-seven fellow inmates who were charged with smuggling drugs and that twenty-three of them subsequently beat the lie detector. Not everybody believes this. Defenders of the polygraph contend that liars can't fool skilled operators of the machine. But even if the polygraph generally catches the guilty, it will also generate a disturbing number of "false positives"—that is, it will falsely identify as liars people who are telling the truth.

To see this, imagine that the polygraph is 95 percent accurate and suppose, for the sake of illustration, that at a large corporation with an in-house theft problem one out of every fifty employees is stealing from their employer. If the corporation has a thousand employees, then twenty will be crooks and 980 will be honest. If every employee is tested, then the test, being only 95 percent accurate, will identify nineteen of the twenty crooks; one will escape detection. But the test will also identify as liars 5 percent of the company's 980 innocent employees; that is, forty-nine people will be falsely accused. By firing all those who fail the polygraph, a company might well succeed in weeding out the guilty, but it would also seriously harm many innocent employees.

In addition to these considerations, polygraphs infringe on privacy. As professor of politics Christopher Pyle says, they violate "the privacy of beliefs and associations, the freedom from unreasonable searches, the privilege against self-accusation, and the presumption of innocence."[21] That is not to say employers never have the right to abridge privacy or employees never have an obligation to reveal themselves. In important cases of in-house theft, employers may be justified in using a polygraph as a last resort. But the threat to privacy remains.

The moral concerns embedded in the use of polygraphs suggest three points—in addition to the question of informed consent—to consider in evaluating their use in the workplace:

1. The information the organization seeks should be clearly and significantly related to the job. This caveat harks back to a determination of the legitimate areas of organizational influence over the individual.

2. Because the polygraph intrudes on psychic freedom, those administering it should consider whether they have compelling job-related reasons for doing so. Some persons contend that among the reasons must be the fact that the polygraph is the only way the organization can get information about a significant job-related matter. They believe that a firm should not subject employees to polygraph tests without having first exhausted all other means of preventing pilferage.

3. We must be concerned with how the polygraph is being used, what information it's gathering, who has access to this information, and how it will be disposed of.

Responding to moral concerns about polygraphs as well as to their practical and statistical limitations, Congress has passed the Employee Polygraph Protection Act. It prohibits most private employers from using lie detectors in "preemployment testing." Private security firms are exempted from the law, along with drug companies, contractors with certain government agencies, and selected others. The law permits the use of polygraphs in "ongoing investigations of economic loss or injury," but it provides a number of procedural safeguards. For instance, the employer must explain the test's purpose to the employee and the reason why he or she was selected to take it. The worker also has a right to consult with someone who will explain the workings and limitations of the machine. Ultimately, the worker retains the option not to submit to the test, and no one can be fired on the basis of a lie-detector test "without other supporting evidence."

Personality Tests

Companies often wish to determine whether prospective employees are emotionally mature, get along well with others, and have a good work ethic, and whether they would fit in with the organization, so they sometimes administer personality tests. These tests can reveal highly personal information, and they often intrude into areas of our lives and thoughts that we normally consider private. Consent is usually less than fully voluntary because personality tests are generally part of a battery of tests that job applicants must take if they wish to be considered for a position.

Used properly, personality tests serve two purposes in the workplace. First, they help screen applicants for jobs by indicating areas of adequacy and inadequacy. Second, in theory they simplify the complexities of business life by reducing the amount of decision making involved in determining whether an individual has the personal characteristics appropriate for a given job. For example, if a firm knows that Wendy Constantine is an introvert, it would hardly place her in public relations.

But one key premise underlying such tests is questionable. That premise is that all individuals can usefully and validly be placed into a relatively small number of categories in terms of personality types and character traits. In fact, test designers typically believe that one's overall personality is shaped by only three to five factors and that these factors, which they seek to measure, account for "99 percent of the differences in human behavior."[22] However, people rarely represent pure personality types, such as the classic introvert or extrovert. Nor is the possession of a character trait an all-or-nothing thing. Most of us possess a variety of personality traits in various degrees, and social circumstances often influence the characteristics we display and the talents we develop. When organizations attempt to categorize employees, they oversimplify both human nature and their employees' potential and force people into artificial arrangements that may do justice neither to employees nor to the firms they work for.

Personality tests also screen for organizational compatibility, sometimes functioning to eliminate prospective employees whose individuality or creativity may be exactly what the firm needs. Some companies, for example, seek employees who are extremely submissive to authority. Thus, when writer Barbara Ehrenreich submitted to a personality test for a job at Wal-Mart, she was reprimanded for getting the "wrong" answer when she agreed only "strongly" with the proposition, "All rules have to be followed to the letter at all times." The correct answer was "totally agree."[23] When used this way, personality tests raise a pressing moral issue in the employer-employee relationship: conformity of the individual to organizational ideals. Organizations by nature represent a dan-

ger to individual freedom and independence. When personality tests are used to screen for conformity to organizational values, goals, and philosophy, they can catalyze this natural tendency into a full-blown assault.

Then, of course, there's the intrusive nature of the questions. Questions like "Does driving give you a sense of power?" "Do you like a lot of excitement in your life?" or "If you could, would you work as an entertainer in Las Vegas?" may seem innocuous, but what about a personality test that delves into your love life or that asks men, "Was there ever a time in your life when you liked to play with dolls?" One disgruntled test-taker complains about "questions you wouldn't even answer for your own mother, if she asked you."[24] Worse, many of the tests asking these questions have little or no research to back them up or have not been validated for use in preemployment situations. Even those who favor testing admit as much. John Kamp, an industrial psychologist, points out that even intelligent businesspeople can be swayed by a good marketing pitch from the companies that peddle invalid or unreliable tests. "That's the unfortunate thing," he says. "A person with a slick pitch and no real research behind their tests can have a good business."[25]

Monitoring Employees on the Job

In the past decade, most major employers have gained the technical ability to monitor the performance of their employees through the computers and telephones they use. In businesses with phone-in customers, the practice is especially prevalent as a way of ensuring better and more efficient service. The Electronic Communications Privacy Act of 1986 restricts the government from eavesdropping on your cellular car phone, email, computer-to-computer transmissions, or private video conferences, but it permits employers to intercept employee communications if one of the parties involved agrees. The party "involved" is the employer.[26] Workers don't necessarily resent this monitoring, if it is in the open. "I don't think people mind having their work checked," says Morton Bahr, president of the Communications Workers of America. "It's the secretiveness of it" that bothers employees.[27]

According to the American Management Association, three-quarters of employers record employees' voice mail, email, or phone calls; review their computer files; or even videotape them—often without their knowledge.[28] Overseeing customer service is not the only reason companies monitor their employees. Some companies, for example, check employees' computers to see whether they exceed the allotted time for lunch or work breaks; others listen in on phone conversations and examine email messages to catch employees conducting personal business on company time. "What are they going to think up to do to us next?" wonders one employee. "It's scary. I'll bet no one monitors the phones or email of CEOs or other top executives."[29]

When in-house theft, sabotage, or other threatening conduct occurs, organizations frequently install monitoring devices—mirrors, cameras, and electronic recorders—to apprehend the employees who are responsible. But monitoring suspected trouble spots or private acts can create moral problems. Consider the two male employees of Boston Sheraton Hotel who were secretly videotaped changing clothes in the locker room during a hunt for a drug dealer. They weren't suspects, just bystanders.[30]

As with personality and polygraph tests, monitoring can gather information about employees without their informed consent. Organizations frequently confuse notification of such practices with employee consent, but notification does not constitute consent. When employee restrooms, dressing rooms, locker rooms, and other private places are bugged, an obvious and serious threat to privacy exists—posted notices notwithstanding. It's true that in some cases surveillance devices may be the only way to apprehend the guilty. Nevertheless, they can often do more harm than good by violating the privacy of the vast majority of innocent employees. Obviously, even more serious moral questions arise when monitoring devices are not used exclusively for the purposes intended but also for cajoling, harassing, or snooping on employees.

Drug Testing

Drug testing first became a live issue for some sports fans when the National Collegiate Athletic Association (NCAA) began banning college football players from postseason bowl competition based on the results of steroid testing. But for some years now, political and legal battles have been raging in all states over the drug testing of employees. Many companies have warmly embraced testing. Commonwealth Edison, for example, now routinely screens prospective employees for drug use. Its policy won support from a study published in the *Journal of the American Medical Association,* which showed that postal workers who tested positive for drug use in a preemployment urine test were at least 50 percent more likely to be fired, injured, disciplined, or absent than those who tested negative. Other companies, however, such as BankAmerica and AT&T, remain skeptical of the benefits of testing either current employees or job applicants.[31]

In principle, testing employees to determine whether they are using illegal drugs raises the same questions that other tests raise: Is there informed consent? How reliable are the tests? Is testing really pertinent to the job in question? Are the interests of the firm significant enough to justify encroaching on the privacy of the individual? But rather than reiterate these issues, all of which are important and relevant, this section limits itself to four additional remarks:

1. The issue of drug testing by corporations and other organizations arises in the broader context of the drug-abuse problem in America today (which includes the abuse not just of illegal street drugs but of alcohol and prescription medicines as well). To discuss this problem intelligently, one needs good information, reliable statistics, and sociological insight, yet these are difficult to come by. Popular newsmagazines run frequent and

alarming cover stories on drugs, and hours of television news are given over to sensationalistic drug-related stories. Likewise, many politicians find it advantageous to portray themselves as battling courageously against a rising flood of drugs. Yet most of this media coverage and political hoopla is at best superficial, at worst misleading and even hysterical. This is not to minimize the problems that alcohol and drug abuse can pose for businesses and other oganizations. Such problems are real and serious even though the use of illegal drugs, at least, appears to have dropped by half among workers since the mid-1980s.[32] Rather, the point is that excessive media attention and political posturing can create a false sense of crisis, leading people perhaps to advocate extreme or unnecessary measures.

2. Drugs differ, so one must carefully consider both what drugs one is testing for and why. Steroids, for instance, are a problem for the NCAA but not for IBM. And it is difficult to believe that Ford Meter Box was warranted in urine testing employees for nicotine in order to root out smokers.[33] To be defensible, drug testing must be pertinent to employee performance and there must be a lot at stake. Testing airline pilots for alcohol consumption is one thing; testing the baggage handlers is something else. To go on a fishing trip in search of possible employee drug abuse, when there is no evidence of a problem or of significant danger, seems unreasonable.

3. Drug abuse by an individual is a serious problem, generally calling for medical and psychological assistance rather than punitive action. The moral assessment of any program of drug testing must rest in part on the potential consequences for those taking the test: Will they face immediate dismissal and potential criminal proceedings, or therapy and a chance to retain their positions? To put the issue another way, when an organization initiates a testing program, does it approach this as a kind of police function? Or is it responsive to the needs and problems of individual employees? Some business writers argue that voluntary, nonpunitive drug-assistance programs are far more cost effective for companies, in any case, than testing initiatives.[34]

4. Any drug-testing program, assuming it is warranted, must be careful to respect the dignity and rights of the persons to be tested. Some alternatives to body fluid testing are less invasive of employee privacy. Due process must also be followed, including advance notification of testing as well as procedures for retesting and appealing test results. All possible steps should be taken to ensure individual privacy.

WORKING CONDITIONS

In a broad sense, the conditions under which people work include personnel policies and procedures, as well as the extent to which an organization is committed to respecting the rights and privacy of its employees. This section, however, examines three other aspects of working conditions: health and safety on the job, styles of management, and the organization's maternity and day-care arrangements.

Health and Safety

A Galveston grain elevator explodes, maiming a dozen workers; a southern poultry plant fire kills twenty-five workers; a methane explosion at a Kentucky mine leaves ten dead. These are dramatic episodes, and they gained national media coverage. By contrast, there was less publicity when Dennis Claypool, twenty-one, and Mark DeMoss, eighteen, suffocated as they cleaned a tanker trailer at a trucking company outside Chicago. The two didn't know that the tanker had recently been cleaned with nitrogen, which removes oxygen from the air. A freak accident? Experts say some 300 workers a year die in such "confined space" incidents.[35]

Industrial accidents don't just happen. They are caused—by inadequate worker training, lack of understanding of the job, improper tools and equipment, hazardous work environments, poor equipment maintenance, and overly tight scheduling.[36] Many experts believe that workplace injuries are related to behavior, not to shortcomings in technology. The key to a safer workplace, says one risk management consultant, is not engineering, but changing the company's "hidden culture"—the "unspoken rules that are adhered to"—to one that is proactively oriented toward safety.[37]

Employees in fact have a legal right to refuse work when it exposes them to imminent danger, and their employers are forbidden to reprimand or otherwise retaliate against them for doing so. The U.S. Supreme Court made this clear, when it upheld a lower court ruling in favor of two employees of the Whirlpool Corporation who had refused to follow their foreman's order to undertake maintenance activities they considered unsafe.[38] Although a number of states require companies to inform workers in writing of any life-threatening hazards, employees are often unaware of the dangers they face, many of which may be long-term, rather than imminent, hazards. Take the electronics industry, for example. It may look safe in comparison with many other occupations, but behind its clean, high-tech image lurk health hazards for workers—in particular, the chemical toxins that are indispensable to the manufacture of computer chips.[39]

Despite legislation, the scope of occupational hazards remains awesome and generally unrecognized. According to the Census Bureau, in a given year more than 5,000 workers are killed on the job.[40] The director of the Occupational Safety and Health Administration (OSHA) puts the figure higher. He says an average of thirty-two workers are killed on the job each day of the year in the United States.[41] Deaths are just part of the problem. Census Bureau statistics reveal that although the rate of industrial injury has been declining since 1960, the absolute number of workers disabled at work every year—approximately 3.8 million men and women—is greater than ever. Job-related injuries and illnesses cost the nation $65 billion a year—$171 billion when indirect costs such as lost wages

are included.[42] And when we take into account health problems that stem not from specific, identifiable events on the job but rather from years of labor or from long-term exposure to hazardous substances, then the problem escapes reliable measurement.

OSHA. With the 1970 Occupational Safety and Health Act the prime responsibility for regulating working conditions passed from the states to the federal government. The thrust of the act is "to ensure so far as possible every working man and woman in the nation safe and healthful working conditions," and it places a duty on employers to provide a workplace "free from recognized hazards that are causing or are likely to cause death or serious injury." In its early years, OSHA, created by the act, added to its own troubles by promulgating some rules that seemed trivial and nitpicking—for example, detailed guidelines regulating toilet seats and the belts to be worn by telephone line workers.[43] Fortunately, most of these rules have been repealed, but controversies have raged over how far OSHA should go in the cause of safety. The organization seeks to require only safeguards that are feasible; it has, for example, never attempted to entirely eliminate toxins in the workplace. But is "feasibility" to be understood in a broad economic and technological sense, or must the gains in safety outweigh the costs that particular companies must bear? And how are those costs and gains to be measured?

In any case, with limited resources and only a few thousand inspectors to monitor millions of workplaces, OSHA has always faced a daunting task, and its performance has been spotty. Worse, the relationship between OSHA and the businesses and industries it regulates has often been too cozy. Consider the case of Stephen Golab, a fifty-nine-year-old immigrant from Poland who worked for a year stirring tanks of sodium cyanide at the Film Recovery Services plant in Elk Grove, Illinois. One day he became dizzy from the cyanide fumes, went into convulsions, and died. OSHA then inspected the plant and fined Film Recovery Services $4,855 for twenty safety violations. OSHA subsequently cut the fine in half. In contrast, the state attorney general for Cook County filed criminal charges. Three company officials were convicted of murder and fourteen counts of reckless conduct. The company itself was also convicted of manslaughter and reckless conduct and was fined $24,000.

Since the Golab case, budget cuts have shrunk OSHA's staff further, and inspections and citations have dropped. At the same time Congress has pushed the agency from rule-making and enforcement to helping businesses comply with federal requirements. Critics call OSHA a "toothless tiger," which has moved from "beat cop to social worker."[44]

New Health Challenges. One problem that both OSHA and business will have to address in the future is the epidemic of occupational injury and illness known as musculoskeletal disorders. In offices and factories across the country, millions of workers suffer from aching backs, crippled fingers, sore wrists, and other problems caused or aggravated by their jobs. Carpal tunnel syndrome, low back pain, sciatica, tendinitis, and other musculoskeletal disorders account for one-third of all serious workplace injuries and cause more than 640,000 workers a year to miss time on the job.[45]

Telephone operators, court stenographers, and supermarket checkout clerks are just a few of the workers who must live with numb fingers, swollen knuckles, and aching wrists from the constant repetition of awkward hand and arm movements. The ailments in question may sound like minor complaints, but they are anything but trivial to those who suffer from them. Ask Janie Jue of San Francisco. For seventeen years she keyed in up to 48,000 strokes a day on an automatic letter-sorting machine for the post office. Today, just picking up a book or coffee pot sends bolts of pain tearing up her hand and arm. "I wish I could work," she says, "but it hurts from my elbow to my fingertips."[46] "For many years," remarks one expert, "it was just considered a cost of doing business. If you did certain jobs,

you would end up with hands crippled at the end of your career. That's not acceptable in this country any more."[47]

The breaking up of jobs into smaller and smaller units, with each worker performing fewer tasks but repeating them thousands of times a day, has contributed to the problem in manufacturing industries. Garment workers, meat packers, and others in hand-intensive jobs used to be able to recover at night from the cumulative stress on their bodies, but increased assembly-line speed and piecework rates now make it more difficult for their bodies to bounce back the next day. Moreover, musculoskeletal disorders are rampant among white-collar office workers, who are supposedly in safe office jobs. Those who spend all day at the video display terminal risk developing tendinitis, carpal tunnel syndrome, and other hand, neck, or back ailments.

The redesign of jobs, adjustable chairs, training in the proper use of video display terminals, and other preventive measures can often reduce the problem. In the meantime, it is not only the employees who are suffering. Musculoskeletal disorders decrease productivity and dampen morale, and having a skilled worker go out on long-term disability and vocational rehabilitation can cost a company a small fortune.[48]

One aspect of work life over which OSHA exercises little direct control is the shifts people work. Yet a team of scientists from Harvard and Stanford universities believes that the health and productivity of 25 million Americans whose work hours change regularly can be measurably improved if employers schedule shift changes to conform with the body's natural and adjustable sleep cycles. This is particularly important given that sleep deprivation and fatigue are prime causes of industrial accidents.[49] According to one expert, they cost Americans $100 billion a year in lost production, illnesses, absences, accidents, and death.[50] This fact makes worrisome the current trend in factory work toward shorter work weeks with longer weekdays (for example, four twelve-hour workdays, followed by three days off, then three twelve-hour workdays on followed by four days off), with employees alternating from day shifts one month to night shifts the next.[51]

Related to fatigue is an aspect of work life we have only recently begun to appreciate fully—the health implications of stress. Three-quarters of Americans say their jobs cause them stress.[52] One reason may be that the average American worker is logging more overtime and working more hours per week than at any time since the 1950s.[53] In fact, Americans put in longer hours on the job than do the workers of any other major industrialized nation.[54] And many of us complain about the pressure of excessive workloads.[55] Stressful job conditions diminish mental health and damage physical functioning as much as smoking does.[56] Revamping work environments that produce stress and helping employees learn to cope with stress are among the major health challenges facing American business now and in the years to come.

Management Styles

How managers conduct themselves on the job can do more to enhance or diminish the work environment than any other single facet of employer-employee relations. In survey after survey, employees rank honest company communications, personal recognition, and respectful treatment as more important than good pay. Unfortunately, according to a Columbia University psychologist, millions of workers suffer from bosses who are abusive, dictatorial, devious, dishonest, manipulative, and inhumane.[57]

This workplace reality runs contrary to the teachings of almost all management theorists. For example, in his classic work *The Human Side of Enterprise,* Douglas McGregor formulated Theory X to describe the management style premised on the belief that workers dislike work and will do everything they can to avoid it.[58] These managers insist that the average person wishes to avoid responsibility, lacks ambition, and values security over everything else. Accordingly, he or she must be coerced and bullied into conformity with organizational objec-

tives. McGregor advocated Theory Y, which assumes that employees basically like work and view it as something natural and potentially enjoyable. Workers are seen as motivated as much by pride and a desire for self-fulfillment as by money and job security. They don't dodge responsibility but accept it and even seek it out.

Since McGregor's book, other management writers have pursued this line of thought and recommended countless other management styles—including Theory Z, which touts Japanese-style respect for workers. More recently, some theorists have advocated an alternative management style that eschews a masculine, hierarchical, aggressive, analytic, winner-take-all approach in favor of a more personal, empathetic, and collaborative style, thought to be characteristic of, and more congenial to, women. This is not the place to discuss different theories of management, but clearly the management styles recommended by different writers, as well as the management styles actually adopted by different bosses, rest on implicit or explicit assumptions about human nature.

However, no set of assumptions about human nature is absolutely correct or incorrect, nor is there one perfectly right way to manage. But that's precisely the point. Moral problems inevitably arise when managers routinize their leadership style, regardless of the needs, abilities, and predilections of their particular employees. When managers ignore individual differences, they risk creating a work atmosphere that's distressing to workers and less productive than it might be. Moreover, implicit assumptions about human nature can easily become self-reinforcing because people tend to behave as they are treated. Thus, managers who treat employees as if they were incapable of taking initiative will probably end up with employees who don't take initiative. As a result managers must carefully examine their preconceptions when determining the most appropriate leadership style to adopt in their workplace.

Critics frequently charge that U.S. corporations are too bureaucratic—the United States has more managers per employee than any other industrial nation[59]—and that their managerial style is too conservative, traditional, and inflexible. Too many managers, it is alleged, put their personal ambition ahead of everything else. One such critic is H. Ross Perot. Perot became the largest shareholder in General Motors and a member of its corporate board when he sold his computer services company, Electronic Data Systems Corporation, to GM for $2.5 billion. Two years later GM ousted Perot from the board, buying back his GM stock for $700 million.

Why the buyback? Observers agree that the fiery Perot was more than GM could handle. Perot dared to question longstanding management practices; he talked to workers on the factory floor about new ideas; he shopped anonymously at GM dealerships, trying to evaluate customer service. All that was too much for GM. Under the buyback agreement, Perot isn't supposed to make negative comments about GM, but he does say the corporation is beset by power-hungry executives who spend all their time trying to move up the corporate ladder and care little about their product. "Corporate infighting," "management power struggles," "maneuvering and politics and power-grabbing," and "Machiavellian intrigues" are his phrases to describe the reality of corporate life today.[60]

We must be careful about generalizing from the experiences of one person in one company, but Perot's reports tally with too many others' to ignore what he says. Managers who devote their energies to corporate infighting and personal advancement and corporations that are too tradition-bound to handle strong criticism, even inside the boardroom itself, are real problems. Dealing with them is part of the economic challenge facing America today, as discussed in Chapter 4. But problems of management style also unfavorably affect employees' working conditions.

Day Care and Maternity Leave

One often overlooked area in discussions of working conditions is the provision of maternity/paternity leave and child-care services for workers with children. The need for day-care services is clearly growing, yet the United States falls behind many other industrialized nations in the provision of such services. The situation is even more striking with respect to maternity leave. At least 117 other countries provide paid maternity leave, but only since 1993 has federal legislation required employers to provide unpaid leave and reinstatement of pregnant employees.

Today women constitute about 46 percent of the paid labor force, a higher figure than at any time in history. In 1960 only 18.6 percent of married women with children under age six were in the paid labor force, but this number had grown to 45 percent by 1980. Today, nearly two-thirds of all married women with children under six work.[61] The rise in the employment participation rates of women with small children is expected to continue. Experts anticipate that for the foreseeable future two-thirds of all new workers will be women.

Given that women in our society continue to bear the primary responsibility for child rearing, their increasing participation in the paid workforce represents a growing demand for reasonable maternity-leave policies and affordable child-care services. Nor is this demand likely to diminish. Many families are unable to make satisfactory child-care arrangements, either because the services are unavailable or for the simple reason that the parents cannot afford them. An estimated 5 million children are thus left alone without any supervision while their parents work. The need for child-care services is particularly acute among single-parent families, 91 percent of which are headed by women. Single mothers have a higher rate of participation in the labor force than do married mothers. Nevertheless, many of them are too poor to pay for satisfactory child-care services.

Some companies try hard to help with employee child care.[62] Campbell Soup Co., for example, offers on-site day care, spending over $200,000 annually to subsidize 50 percent of tuition costs at the child-care center for the children of employees at corporate headquarters. Procter & Gamble holds priority rights for 75 percent of the spaces in two off-site centers near its Cincinnati headquarters. It also provides a day-care resource and referral service for the entire community. IBM provides a free nationwide referral system for its 267,000 employees and has helped develop child-care services where they have been deficient or lacking. Polaroid Corporation provides assistance with child-care costs for permanent employees earning less than $30,000. Because its employees work at all hours, America West Airlines provides 24-hour child care with a sliding scale subsidy to make it affordable. Goldman, Sachs, and Company, Time Warner, and Chase Manhattan Bank have opened child-care centers for employees whose regular child-care arrangements are temporarily disrupted. Despite these examples, the overall corporate record on child care is not as good as it could be.

Employers are in a good position to assist in the provision of child-care services, especially in light of cutbacks in federal funding. Few if any employers, however, currently feel obligated to offer child-care services, primarily because initiating and maintaining such programs cost money. Yet viewed from a broader perspective, day-care arrangements set up by companies themselves or by several companies together in the same area are socially cost-effective. With in-house day-care arrangements, parents need not make special trips to pick up and drop off their children. Because the parents are not far away, they can have more interaction with their children. Depending on the specific organization of work and the firm's flexibility, parents could share in the actual running of the child-care facility at assigned intervals during the course of their working day. Hewlett-Packard took an innovative step in this regard when, in conjunction with the local school district, it set up kindergarten and first-grade classes on company grounds for the children of employees. Other companies are now doing the same thing.[63]

Some business writers have argued, moreover, that offering child care as a fringe benefit and dealing as flexibly as possible with employees' family needs can prove advantageous for most employers. Such policies can be cost-effective in the narrower sense by decreasing absenteeism, boosting morale and loyalty to the firm, and enhancing productivity. This is an important consideration.

Even more important are the underlying moral issues. First, women have a right to compete on an equal terrain with men. The legal requirement that firms with fifty or more workers provide at least unpaid maternity leave and reinstatement respects this right. Whether firms should also provide paid maternity leave is more controversial, although one might argue that paid leave is necessary to give substance to this right. Or one might defend such a policy on the utilitarian ground that it would enhance total social welfare. In fact, many organizations find it in their self-interest to provide paid leave so they can attract better and more talented employees.

Second, from various ethical perspectives, the development of our potential capacities is a moral ideal—perhaps even a human right. For this reason, or from the point of view of promoting human well-being, many theorists would contend that women should not be forced to choose between childbearing and the successful pursuit of their careers. Nor should they be forced to reduce the quality of their commitment either to their children or to their careers. If employment circumstances force them to do so, and if those circumstances could reasonably be changed, then we have not lived up to the ideal of treating those women as persons whose goals are worthy of respect.

Third, although the past two or so decades have seen many criticisms of, and attempts to move beyond, the traditional male-female division of labor within the family, there can be little doubt that the world of work tends to reproduce those patterns. For instance, as mentioned in Chapter 6, men who leave work to help raise children often face enormous hurdles when returning to the job market. It seems clear that many fathers today feel hampered by work arrangements that pit meaningful career advancement against a fully developed family life.[64] Enhanced opportunities for part-time employment and job sharing, along with generous parental leave arrangements and flexible, afford-able, and accessible firm-sponsored child-care facilities, could enable both fathers and mothers to achieve a more personally desirable balance between paid work and family relations.

The moral value here is not to promote any single vision of the good life but rather to permit individuals, couples, and families as much au-tonomy as possible, given other social goals. They should be able to define the good life for themselves and to seek the arrangement of work and personal relations that makes that life possible. Firm-affiliated child-care services and other institutional arrangements that accommo-date parental needs can clearly play a key role in the overall redesigning of work to enhance workers' well-being.

REDESIGNING WORK

Chapter 4 looked at alienation under capitalism and changing attitudes toward work in America. It remains true that many, perhaps even most, employees are dissatisfied with their jobs to some extent. Any investigation of the moral is-sues arising around the workplace and any dis-cussion of the challenges facing business today must confront this basic problem and consider ways of improving the quality of work life.

Dissatisfaction on the Job

In the early 1970s the federal government con-ducted a major study of work in America, the basic findings of which are still relevant today.[65] The study identified three chief sources of worker dissatisfaction. The first concerned in-dustry's preoccupation with quantity, not quality; the rigidity of rules and regulations; and the fracturing of work into the smallest possible tasks, together with the monotonous repetition of these tasks. The second source of dissatisfac-tion concerned the lack of opportunities to be one's own boss. The third source of dissatisfac-tion concerned "bigness": More people work for large corporations now than ever before. Other studies since then have cited workers' feelings of powerlessness, meaninglessness, isolation, and self-estrangement or depersonalization.

The *Work in America* survey reported similar feelings in the managerial ranks. One out of three middle managers at that time was willing to join a union. Moreover, just as industrial workers voiced general complaints about work, so did middle managers. Some objected to the little in-fluence they had in their organizations, and oth-ers objected to the organization's goals, policies, and ways of operating. Still other managers com-plained about tension, frustration, and infighting that intraorganizational competition can breed. Beyond these complaints, the *Work in America* survey reported that many managers felt like cogs in a machine, like parts that could and would be replaced when a better part came along.

Other studies confirm that workers at all occu-pational levels express dissatisfaction with em-ployer policies and practices and with the behavior of top management.[66] If industry is to improve productive capacity and be more com-petitive, it must seriously confront these attitudes and the sources of employee dissatisfaction. It must devise ways to make work more satisfying and to improve the quality of work life.

As early as the 1920s, researchers began to realize that workers would be more productive if management met those needs that money can-not buy. Managers at the Hawthorne factory of Western Electric Company were conducting ex-periments to determine the effect of the work environment on worker productivity. In the liter-ature of work motivation, these studies have be-come known as the Hawthorne studies. What they discovered has been termed the "Haw-thorne effect."

Researchers in the Hawthorne studies chose a few employees to work in an experimental area, apart from the thousands of employees in the rest of the factory. Every effort was made to improve working conditions, from painting walls a cheer-ful color to making lights brighter. Worker pro-ductivity increased with each improvement. Then the experimenters decided to reverse the process. For example, lights were made dimmer. To every-one's surprise, productivity continued to increase.

The conclusion the researchers drew was that workers were producing more because they were receiving attention. Instead of feeling that they were spokes in an organizational wheel, they felt important and recognized. The attention had the effect of heightening their sense of personal identity and feeling of control over their work environment. Recognition of this effect can help management increase worker motivation and job satisfaction and also increase the organization's productivity.

Subsequent research corroborates and deepens the Hawthorne results.[67] In an important study conducted to shed light on the problem of poor worker motivation, Frederick Herzberg discovered that factors producing job satisfaction differed from those producing job dissatisfaction. Herzberg found that although job dissatisfaction frequently arises from extrinsic problems (such as pay, supervision, working conditions, and leadership styles), resolving those extrinsic problems does not necessarily produce satisfied workers. They can still express little or no job satisfaction. The reason, Herzberg contends, is that worker satisfaction depends on such factors as a sense of accomplishment, responsibility, recognition, self-development, and self-expression.

Other surveys lend credence to Herzberg's findings. When 1,533 workers at all occupational levels were asked to rank in order of importance to them some twenty-five aspects of work, they listed interesting work; sufficient help, support, and information to accomplish the job; enough authority to carry out the work; good pay; the opportunity to develop special skills; job security; and a chance to see the results of their work.[68]

In studying a cross-section of American workers, the Institute of Social Research found numerous mental health problems directly attributable to lack of job satisfaction. These problems included psychosomatic diseases such as ulcers and hypertension, low self-esteem, anxiety, and impaired interpersonal relations.[69] In general, studies indicate that greater mental health problems occur in low-status, boring, unchallenging jobs that offer little autonomy. Furthermore, such jobs tend to inhibit intellectual growth and the pursuit of richer, more fulfilling activities outside work.[70] Even worse, researchers have found that workers in boring, passive jobs are 33 to 35 percent more likely to die prematurely than workers in active jobs. Stressful work that offers little decision-making opportunity (like assembly-line work) makes an untimely demise even more likely.[71] These findings are of particular relevance to today's workforce, in which many persons of relatively high educational achievement occupy comparatively low-status jobs.

One of the most intriguing studies not only suggests a correlation between longevity and job satisfaction but also contends that job satisfaction is the strongest predictor of longevity.[72] The second major factor for longevity is happiness. Both of these factors predict longevity better than either the physical health or genetic inheritance of individuals.

Because the design of work materially affects the total well-being of workers, work content and job satisfaction are paramount moral concerns. But if we also assume that a happier, more contented worker is generally a more productive one, then it follows that business has an economic reason as well as a moral obligation to devise ways, in concert with labor and perhaps even government, to improve the quality of work life (QWL).

Quality of Work Life (QWL)

This book isn't the place for determining precisely what QWL measures firms should take. For some firms QWL may mean providing workers with less supervision and more autonomy. For others it may mean providing work opportunities to develop and refine skills. Still other firms might try to provide workers with greater participation in the conception, design, and execution of their work—that is, with greater responsibility and a deeper sense of achievement. Perhaps all companies ought to examine the impact of technology on job satisfaction. While typically increasing the efficiency of operations and eliminating the physical drudgery that plagued yesterday's workers, today's technology sometimes results in repetitive and boring tasks that, in the long run, may destroy job satisfaction and diminish productivity.

QWL programs can thaw the antagonistic worker-boss climate that exists in many plants, but the only way management can implement such programs is with the full cooperation of workers and their representatives, and some union members are a little wary. "The largest loss is the union's autonomy," says one.[73] "We become one with the corporate agenda. It's an unnatural place for the union to be." Investigators believe that the success of QWL programs and other workplace reform efforts depends on the ability of the organization to reinforce high levels of trust. To the extent that it does so, organizational performance can improve. But, warns William Cooke, professor at Wayne State University and author of a book on workplace reform, "if [workers] perceive management as doing this without due consideration for the welfare of employees . . . it will have the potential of destroying the efforts altogether."[74]

Granting workers new responsibilities and respect can benefit the entire organization. Randy Pennington, vice president of Performance Systems Corporation, tells of a friend who showed an ad for a new American car to a Japanese businessperson. The ad said that the car "set a new standard for quality because it was examined by 34 different quality inspectors." "Now, *this*," he said to his Japanese colleague, "is what we need to compete with you. Imagine: 34 quality inspectors!" The Japanese looked at the ad, smiled, and said, "You don't need 34 inspectors to get quality. You just need everyone who works on the car to be proud of the work. Then you'll need only one inspector."[75]

Today, closer union-management relations characterize many GM plants. Mike Spitzley, manager of GM's 5,300-worker car-truck plant in Janesville, Wisconsin, for example, says "most of the things we talk about, it's 'we.' It's not us versus them. We've pretty much realized that our goals are the same" as the union's. Mike O'Brien, president of the local chapter of the United Auto Workers, agrees. "There's something different going on," he says. "Years ago, it wasn't any of our business what went on in the business." The most striking example is GM's Saturn Corporation, where union and management share all big decisions, from choosing suppliers to picking the company's advertising agency.[76]

At GM, the ideals of improved job atmosphere, employee participation, and worker job security have meshed nicely with the goal of increased productivity. Studies provide evidence of this compatibility in many other cases, too. Not only is productivity 5 to 10 percent higher in companies with profit sharing, but productivity is also consistently higher in enterprises with an organized program of worker participation.[77] In the car industry, the key to success has been shown to be people, not robots or high-tech automation.[78] At United Airlines, cooperation, efficiency, and market share increased when employees bought 55 percent of the company.[79] In fact, compensation for top executives at the airline is now tied to worker satisfaction as measured by an outside survey firm.[80] This is in line with the views of many experts, who insist that worker-friendly companies outperform traditional command-and-control employers. They argue that new organizational structures and work practices that put a premium on collaboration and cooperation are fundamental to the nation's future economic success.[81]

Although a range of social and economic research supports this conclusion, there is no water-tight guarantee that worker participation and an improved quality of work life will always boost productivity; sometimes an apparent QWL improvement can lead to a decrease in productivity. For example, although diversifying tasks may make work more satisfying, it might hurt productivity or quality. Japanese carmakers, to cite one case, have effectively reduced the number of rejects on their assembly line, not by diversifying, but by standardizing the cars produced. Again, Volkswagen has found that its productivity and quality were higher when production consisted solely of the standard Rabbit than when other models were introduced.

Job-enlargement programs, by definition, add to the variety of tasks the worker is assigned; job-enrichment programs add some planning, designing, and scheduling to the operative worker's tasks. Both programs can tax the abilities of workers and in some cases may slow output and bruise quality. Worker involvement in production management may not fit well, some argue, with the two other ingredients that managers and management consultants see as essential for manufacturing reform: a just-in-time approach to eliminating waste and rigorous statistical process control to improve quality.[82]

On the other hand, employee involvement is essential to work elimination programs—programs that eliminate wasteful and unnecessary tasks, thus enhancing job satisfaction while making the organization leaner and more productive.[83] This is particularly important as competition pressures manufacturers in the car industry and elsewhere to move to smaller, more flexible factories.[84] Still, the possibility of a conflict between the obligation to make work more satisfying and the goal of increasing productivity will likely be at the heart of moral decisions in this area for years to come. To resolve them will require a cooperative effort by labor and management, rooted in the recognition that trade-offs are inevitable.

SUMMARY

1. Individuals have a right to privacy, in particular a right to make personal decisions autonomously, free from illegitimate influence. Whenever an organization infringes on an individual's personal sphere, it must justify that infringement.

2. A firm is legitimately interested in whatever significantly influences job performance, but there is no precise definition of "significant influence." Organizations may be invading privacy when they coerce employees to contribute to charities or to participate in wellness programs or in so-called intensive group experiences.

3. Information-gathering on employees can be highly personal and subject to abuse. The critical issue here is *informed consent,* which implies deliberation and free choice. Deliberation requires that employees be provided all significant facts concerning the information-gathering procedure and understand their consequences. Free choice means that the decision to participate must be voluntary and uncoerced.

4. Polygraph tests, personality tests, drug tests, and the monitoring of employees on the job can intrude into employee privacy. The exact character of these devices, the rationale for using them to gather information in specific circumstances, and the moral costs of doing so must always be carefully evaluated.

5. Health and safety remain of foremost moral concern in the workplace. The scope of occupational hazards, including shift work and stress, and the number of employees harmed by work-related injuries and diseases are greater than many people think. Enforcement of existing regulations has too often been lax.

6. Management style greatly affects the work environment. Managers who operate with rigid assumptions about human nature or who devote themselves to infighting and political maneuvering damage employees' interests.

7. Day-care services and reasonable parental-leave policies also affect working conditions. Despite the genuine need for and the ethical importance of both day care and flexible work arrangements for parents, only a handful of companies makes serious efforts to provide them.

8. Studies report extensive job dissatisfaction at all levels. Various factors influence satisfaction and dissatisfaction on the job. Redesigning the work process can enhance the quality of work life, the well-being of workers, and even productivity.

CASE 7.1

Unprofessional Conduct?

Teaching retarded elementary schoolchildren requires skill, patience, and devotion, and those who undertake this task are among the unsung heroes of our society. Their difficult and challenging work rarely brings the prestige or financial rewards it deserves. Mrs. Pettit was one of those dedicated teachers. Licensed to teach in California, she had been working with retarded children for over thirteen years when her career came to an abrupt end. Throughout that career, her competence was never questioned, and the evaluations of her school principal were always positive.

Teaching was not Pettit's only interest, however. She and her husband viewed with favor various "nonconventional sexual lifestyles," including "wife swapping," and they discussed their ideas on two local television shows. Although they wore disguises, at least one fellow teacher recognized them and discussed Mrs. Pettit's views with colleagues. A year later Pettit, then forty-eight years old, and her husband joined "The Swingers," a private club in Los Angeles that sponsored parties intended to promote diverse sexual activities among its members. An undercover police officer, Sergeant Berk, visited one of those parties at a private residence. Amid a welter of sexual activity, he observed Mrs. Pettit commit three separate acts of oral copulation with three different men in a one-hour period.

Pettit was arrested and charged with oral copulation. After a plea bargain was arranged, she pleaded guilty to the misdemeanor of outraging public decency and paid a fine. The school district renewed her teaching contract the next academic year, but two years later, disciplinary proceedings were initiated against her. The State Board of Education found no reason to complain about her services as a teacher, and it conceded that she was unlikely to repeat her sexual misconduct. But the Board revoked her elementary school life diploma—that is, her license to teach—on the ground that by engaging in immoral and unprofessional conduct at the party, she had demonstrated that she was unfit to teach.

Pettit fought the loss of her license all the way to the California Supreme Court, which upheld the decision of the Board of Education.[85] In an earlier case, the court had reversed the firing of a public schoolteacher for unspecified homosexual conduct, concluding that a teacher's actions could not constitute "immoral or unprofessional conduct" or "moral turpitude" unless there was clear evidence of unfitness to teach. But Pettit's case was different, the court hastened to explain.

The conduct in the earlier case had not been criminal, oral copulation had not been involved, and it had been private. Further, in that case the Board had acted with insufficient evidence of unfitness to teach; by contrast, three school administrators had testified that in their opinion, Pettit's conduct proved her unfit to teach. These experts worried that she would inject her views of sexual morality into the classroom, and they doubted that she could act as a moral example to the children she taught. Yet teachers, the court reaffirmed, are supposed to serve as exemplars, and the Education Code makes it a statutory duty of teachers to "endeavor to impress upon the minds of the pupils the principles of morality . . . and to instruct them in manners and morals."

In a vigorous dissent, Justice Tobringer rejected the opinion of the majority, arguing that no evidence had established that Pettit was not fit to teach. The three experts didn't consider her record; they couldn't point to any past misconduct with students, nor did they suggest any reason to anticipate future problems. They simply assumed that the fact of her sexual acts at the "swingers" party itself demonstrated that she would be unable to set a proper example or to teach her pupils moral principles.

Such an attitude is unrealistic, Tobringer argued, when studies show that 75 to 80 percent of the women of Pettit's educational level and age range engage in oral copulation. The majority opinion "is blind to the reality of sexual behavior" and unrealistically assumes that "teachers in their private lives should exemplify Victorian principles of sexual morality." Her actions were private and could not have affected her teaching ability. Had there not been clandestine surveillance of the party, the whole issue would never have arisen.

Discussion Questions

1. In concerning itself with Pettit's off-the-job conduct, did the Board of Education violate her right to privacy? Or was its concern with her lifestyle legitimate and employment related?

2. Was Pettit's behavior "unprofessional"? Was it "immoral"? Did it show a "lack of fitness" to teach? Explain how you understand the terms in quotation marks.

3. Was the Board of Education justified in firing Pettit? Explain.

4. Was the court's verdict consistent with its earlier handling of the case of the homosexual teacher?

5. If teachers perform competently in the classroom, should they also be required to be moral exemplars in their private lives? Are employees in other occupations expected to provide a moral example—either on or off the job?

6. Which of the following would, in your view, show unprofessional conduct, immorality, or lack of fitness to teach: drunken driving, smoking marijuana, advocating the use of marijuana, forging a check, resisting arrest for disorderly conduct and assaulting a police officer, being discovered in a compromising position with a student, propositioning a student, cheating on income tax, leading an openly homosexual lifestyle?

7. Under what conditions do employers have a legitimate interest in their employees' off-the-job conduct?

CASE 7.2

Testing for Honesty

"Charity begins at home." If you don't think so, ask the Salvation Army. Some years ago, one of the Army's local branches discovered that it had a problem with theft among its kettle workers, the people who collect money for the Army during the Christmas season. Some of the Army's kettlers were helping themselves to the Army's loot before the organization had a chance to dole it out. To put a stop to the problem, Army officials sought the assistance of Dr. John Jones, director of research for London House Management Consultants.

London House is one of several companies that market honesty tests for prospective employees. Some of these tests, such as London House's Personnel Selection Inventory (PSI), also measure the applicant's tendency toward drug use and violence.

All three categories—honesty, drugs, and violence—play a major part in company losses, according to the makers of these tests.

The company losses in question are astronomical. The U.S. Chamber of Commerce estimates that employee theft costs U.S. companies $40 billion annually; some unofficial estimates run three times as high. Moreover, 20 percent of the businesses that fail do so because of employee crime.[86] Compounding the problem is the cost of employee drug use in terms of absenteeism, lost initiative, inattentiveness, accidents, and diminished productivity. Employee violence also costs companies millions of dollars in damage, lost productivity, and lawsuits.

Honesty-test makers say that the only way to deal with these problems is before workers are hired, not after—by subjecting them to a preemployment psychological test that will identify those prospective employees who will be likely to steal, who have a history of violence or emotional instability, or who have used illegal drugs on a regular basis.

James Walls, one of the founders of Stanton Corporation, which has offered written honesty tests for twenty-five years, says that dishonest job applicants are clever at hoodwinking potential employers in a job interview. "They have a way of conducting themselves that is probably superior to the low-risk person. They have learned what it takes to be accepted and how to overcome the normal interview strategy," he says. "The high-risk person will get hired unless there is a way to screen him." For this reason, Walls maintains, written, objective tests are needed to weed out the crooks.[87]

Millions of written honesty tests are given annually. Since 1988 demand has been booming as a result of congressional restrictions on polygraph testing, which prohibit about 85 percent of applicant and employee polygraph testing in the United States. As a result, purveyors of written tests have also been in high demand: The British Maxwell Communication Corporation, for instance, spent $17.4 million to acquire London House; Business Risk International took over the Stanton Corporation; and Wackenhut Corporation of Coral Gables, Florida, acquired marketing rights to the Phase II Profile, a widely used honesty test.[88]

In addition to being legal, honesty tests are also more economical than polygraph tests. They cost between $7 and $14 per test, compared with $90 or so for a polygraph. Furthermore, the tests are easily administered at the workplace by a staff member to any category of worker, are easily and quickly evaluated by the test maker, and assess the applicant's overall answers rather than a few isolated responses. The tests are also nondiscriminatory. The Equal Employment Opportunity Commission's "Uniform Guidelines on Employee Selection Procedures" (1978) permits tests that measure psychological traits because the race, gender, or ethnicity of applicants has no significant impact on scores.[89]

A typical test begins with some cautionary remarks. Test-takers are told to be truthful because dishonesty can be detected, and they are warned that incomplete answers will be considered incorrect, as will any unanswered questions. Then applicants ordinarily sign a waiver permitting the results to be known to their prospective employer and authorizing the testing agency to check out their answers. Sometimes, however, prospective employees are not told that they are being tested for honesty, only that they are being asked questions about their background. James Walls justifies this less-than-frank explanation by saying that within a few questions it is obvious that the test deals with attitudes toward honesty. "The test is very transparent, it's not subtle."[90]

Some questions do indeed seem transparent—for example, "If you found $100 that was lost by a bank truck on the street yesterday, would you turn the money over to the bank, even though you knew for sure there was no reward?" But other questions are more controversial: "Have you ever had an argument with someone and later wished you had said something else?" If you were to answer no, you would be on your way to failing. Other questions that may face the test-taker are: "How strong is your conscience?" "How often do you feel guilty?" "Do you always tell the truth?" "Do you occasionally have thoughts you wouldn't want made public?" "Does everyone steal a little?" "Do you enjoy stories of successful crimes?" "Have you ever been so intrigued by the cleverness of a thief that you hoped the person would escape detection?" Or consider questions like "Is an employee who takes it easy at work cheating his employer?" or "Do you think a person should be fired by a company if it is found that he helped employees cheat the company out of overtime once in a while?" These ask you for your reaction to hypothetical dishonest situations. "If you are a particularly kind-hearted person who isn't sufficiently punitive, you fail," says Lewis Maltby, director of the workplace rights office at the American Civil Liberties Union. "Mother Teresa would never pass some of these tests."[91]

A big part of some tests is a behavioral history of the applicant. Applicants are asked to reveal the nature, frequency, and quantity of specific drug use, if any. They also must indicate if they have ever engaged in drunk driving, illegal gambling, traffic violations, forgery, vandalism, and a host of other unseemly behaviors. They must also state their opinions about the social acceptability of drinking alcohol and using other drugs.

Some testing companies go further in this direction. Instead of honesty exams, they offer tests designed to draw a general psychological profile of the applicant, claiming that this sort of analysis can predict more accurately than either the polygraph or the typical honesty test how the person will perform on the job. Keith M. Halperin, a psychologist with Personnel Decision, Inc. (PDI), a company that offers such tests, complains that most paper-and-pencil honesty tests are simply written equivalents of the polygraph. They ask applicants whether they have stolen from their employers, how much they have taken, and other questions directly related to honesty. But why, asks Halperin, "would an applicant who is dishonest enough to steal from an employer be honest enough to admit it on a written test?" It is more difficult for applicants to fake their responses to PDI's tests, Halperin contends.[92]

Not everyone is persuaded. Phyllis Bassett, vice-president of James Bassett Company of Cincinnati, believes tests developed by psychologists that do not ask directly about the applicant's past honesty are poor predictors of future trustworthiness.[93] This may be because, as some psychologists report, "it is very difficult for dishonest people to fake honesty." One reason is that thieves tend to believe that "everybody does it" and that therefore it would be implausible for them to deny stealing.[94] In general, those who market honesty exams boast of their validity and reliability, as established by field studies. They insist that the tests do make a difference, that they enable employers to ferret out potential troublemakers—as in the Salvation Army case.

Dr. Jones administered London House's PSI to eighty kettler applicants, which happened to be the number that the particular theft-ridden center needed. The PSIs were not scored, and the eighty applicants were hired with no screening. Throughout the fund-raising month between Thanksgiving and Christmas, the center kept a record of each kettler's daily receipts. After the Christmas season, the tests were scored and divided into "recommended" and "not recommended" for employ-

ment. After accounting for the peculiarities of each collection neighborhood, Jones discovered that those kettlers the PSI had not recommended turned in on the average $17 per day less than those the PSI had recommended. Based on this analysis, he estimated the center's loss to employee theft during the fund drive at $20,000.

The list of psychological-test enthusiasts is growing by leaps and bounds, but the tests have plenty of detractors. Many psychologists have voiced concern over the lack of standards governing the tests; the American Psychological Association favors the establishment of federal standards for written honesty exams. But the chief critics of honesty and other psychological exams are the people who have to take them. They complain about having to reveal some of the most intimate details of their lives and opinions.

For example, until an employee filed suit, Rent-A-Center, a Texas corporation, asked both job applicants and employees being considered for promotion true-false questions like these: "I have never indulged in any unusual sex practices," "I am very strongly attracted by members of my own sex," "I go to church almost every week," and "I have difficulty in starting or holding my bowel movements." A manager who was fired for complaining about the test says, "It was ridiculous. The test asked if I loved tall women. How was I supposed to answer that? My wife is 5 feet 3 inches." A spokesman for Rent-A-Center argues that its questionnaire is not unusual and that many other firms use it.[95]

Firms who use tests like Rent-A-Center's believe that no one's privacy is being invaded because employees and job applicants can always refuse to take the test. Critics disagree. "Given the unequal bargaining power," says former ACLU official Kathleen Bailey, "the ability to refuse to take a test is one of theory rather than choice—if one really wants the job."[96]

Discussion Questions

1. Describe how you'd feel having to take a psychological test or an honesty test either as an employee or as a precondition for employ-

ment. Under what conditions, if any, would you take such a test?

2. How useful do you think such tests are? Assuming that tests like those described are valid and reliable, are they fair? Explain.

3. Do you think tests like these invade privacy? Explain why or why not.

4. What ideals, obligations, and effects must be considered in using psychological tests as pre-employment screens? In your view, which is the most important consideration?

5. If you were an employer, would you require either employees or job applicants to pass an honesty exam? Explain the moral principles that support your position.

6. What do you think a business's reaction would be if the government required its executive officers to submit to a personality test as a precondition for the company's getting a government

contract? The tests would probe attitudes about questionable business practices, such as bribery, product misrepresentation, unfair competition, and so forth. If, in your opinion, the business would object, does it have any moral grounds for subjecting workers to comparable tests?

7. Utilitarians would not find anything inherently objectionable about psychological tests as long as the interests of all parties are taken into account and given equal consideration before such tests are made a preemployment screen. Do you think this is generally the case?

8. Should there be a law prohibiting or regulating psychological tests as a preemployment screen? Should a decision to use these tests be made jointly by management and labor, or is testing for employment an exclusive employer right?

CASE 7.3

She Snoops to Conquer

Jean Fanuchi, manager of a moderately large department store, was worried. Shrinkage in the costume jewelry department had continued to rise for the third consecutive month. In fact, this time it had nearly wiped out the department's net profit in sales. Worse, it couldn't be attributed to damage or improper handling of markdowns or even to shoplifting. The only other possibility was in-house theft.

Fanuchi ordered chief of security Matt Katwalski to instruct his security people to keep a special eye on jewelry department employees as they went about their business. She also instructed that packages, purses, and other containers employees carried with them be searched when workers left the store. When these measures failed to turn up any leads, Katwalski suggested they hire

a couple of plainclothes officers to observe the store's guards. Fanuchi agreed. But still nothing turned up.

"We're going to have to install a hidden camera at the checkout station in the jewelry department," Katwalski informed the manager.

"I don't know," Fanuchi replied.

"Of course," said Katwalski, "it won't be cheap. But you don't want this problem spreading to other departments, do you?" Fanuchi didn't.

"One other thing," Katwalski said. "I think we should install some microphones in the restroom, stockroom, and employee lounge."

"You mean snoop on our own employees?" Fanuchi asked, surprised.

"We could pick up something that could crack this thing wide open," Katwalski explained.

"But what if our employees found out? How would they feel, being spied on? And then there's the public to consider. Who knows how they'd react? Why, they'd probably think that if we are spying on our own workers, we were surely spying on them. No, Matt," Fanuchi decided. "Frankly, this whole approach troubles me."

"Okay, Ms. Fanuchi, but if it was my store . . ." Fanuchi cut in, "No."

"You're the boss," said Katwalski.

When the shrinkage continued, Fanuchi finally gave in. She ordered Katwalski to have the camera and microphones installed. Within ten days the camera had nabbed the culprit.

The microphones contributed nothing to the apprehension of the thief. But because of them Fanuchi and Katwalski learned that at least one store employee was selling marijuana and perhaps hard drugs, that one was planning to quit without notice, that three were taking food stamps fraudulently, and that one buyer was out to discredit Fanuchi. In solving their shrinkage problem, the pair had unwittingly raised another: What should they do with the information they had gathered while catching the thief?[97]

Discussion Questions

1. If you were Jean Fanuchi, how would you feel about your decision to order the installation of the viewing and listening devices? What other options did she have? Did she overlook any moral considerations or possible consequences?

2. Do employees have a right not to be spied on? If you were an employee at Fanuchi's store, would you think your privacy had been wrongly invaded?

3. How would you assess Fanuchi's actions if you were the owner of the store? Whose interests are more important in this case—the employer's or the employees'?

4. Do you think Fanuchi acted immorally? Why or why not? Evaluate her action by appeal to ethical principles.

5. How should Fanuchi and Katwalski handle the information they've gathered about their employees? Explain by appealing to relevant ideals, obligations, and effects.

CASE 7.4

Protecting the
Unborn at Work

The unobtrusive factory sits behind a hillside shopping center in the small college town of Bennington, Vermont. The workers there make lead automobile batteries for Sears, Goodyear, and other companies. Of the 280 workers employed there a decade or so ago, only twelve were women, none of whom was able to have children. The company, Johnson Controls, Inc., refused to hire any who could.[98]

Why? Because tiny toxic particles of lead and lead oxide fill the air inside the plant. According to the company, the levels of lead are low enough for adults, but too high for children and fetuses. Numerous scientific studies have shown that lead can damage the brain and central nervous system of a fetus; moreover, lead lingers in the bloodstream, which means that fetuses can be affected by it even if a woman limits her exposure to lead once she learns she is pregnant. Because of this, Johnson Controls decided that it would exclude women at all fourteen of its factories from jobs that entail high exposure to lead—unless they could prove that they couldn't become pregnant. The company made no exceptions for celibate women or women who used contraceptives. The company's position was simple: "The issue is protecting the health of unborn children."

Johnson Controls's stance was in line with the National Centers for Disease Control's recommendation that women of childbearing age be excluded from jobs involving significant lead exposure. Because by law its standards must be "feasible," Occupational Safety and Health Administration (OSHA) regulations permit chemicals in the workplace that are known to cause harm both to fetuses and to some adult employees. But OSHA holds that employers have a general duty to reduce the hazards of the workplace as far as possible. On this basis, employers such as Olin Corporation, American Cyanamid, General Motors, Monsanto, Allied Chemical, Gulf Oil, and B. F. Goodrich also adopted policies excluding women from chemical plant jobs judged to be hazardous to their potential offspring.

Scientific studies of the effect of exposure to toxic manufacturing chemicals on workers' reproductive health are, unfortunately, few. Only a small percentage of the workplace chemicals with a potential for damaging reproduction have been evaluated, and each year many new chemicals are introduced into factories. Although employers are obviously dealing with many unknowns, no one doubts that they have a moral and legal obligation to control and limit these risks as best they can. Lawsuits and even criminal sanctions have battered companies that have managed hazardous chemicals irresponsibly. Monsanto Chemical Company, for example, agreed to pay $1.5 million to six employees because exposure to a chemical additive used for rubber production allegedly gave them bladder cancer. Fetal protection policies aren't just dictated by management, though. "Women who become pregnant," the *New York Times* reports, "are beginning to demand the right to transfer out of jobs they believe to be hazardous, even when there is only sketchy scientific evidence of any hazard."

But many women were unhappy about the decision of Johnson Controls. They worried that fetal protection policies would be used to exclude women from more and more workplaces on the grounds that different chemical substances or certain tasks such as heavy lifting might be potential causes of miscarriage and fetal injury. In line with this, the United Automobile Workers, which represents many of the Johnson employees, sought to overturn the U.S. Court of Appeals decision that judged Johnson's policy to be "reasonably necessary to the industrial safety-based concern of protecting the unborn child from lead exposure." The union contends, to the contrary, that the policy discriminates against women, jeopardizing their hard-won gains in male-dominated industries.

Many women's advocates see the issue in slightly different terms. They believe policies like that of Johnson Controls challenge a woman's right not only to control her fetus, but to control her unfertilized eggs as well. In addition, such policies infringe on privacy: By taking a job at Johnson, a woman was in effect telling the world that she was sterile. And there is also the fundamental question of who knows what is best for a woman.

After bearing two children, Cheryl Chalifoux had a doctor block her fallopian tubes so that she couldn't become pregnant again. Although career advancement wasn't the reason she made her decision, it did enable her to switch from a factory job paying $6.34 an hour to one at Johnson's Bennington plant paying $15 an hour. Still, she says that the policy was unfair and degrading. "It's your body," she complains. "They're implying they're doing it for your own good." Cheryl Cook, also a mother of two who had surgery for the same reason, joined Chalifoux in leaving the other company to work for Johnson Controls. She says, "I work right in the lead. I make the oxide. But you should choose for yourself. Myself, I wouldn't go in there if I could get pregnant. But they don't trust you."

Isabelle Katz Pizler, director of women's rights at the American Civil Liberties Union, agrees. "Since time immemorial," she says, "the excuse for keeping women in their place has been because of their role in producing the next generation. The attitude of Johnson Controls is: 'We know better than you. We can't allow women to make this decision. We have to make it for them.'" And the ACLU has argued in court that "since no activity is risk-free, deference to an employer's analysis of fetal risk could limit women's participation in nearly every area of economic life."

To this the company responded that it has a moral obligation to the parties that cannot participate in the woman's decisions—namely, the unfertilized ovum and the fetus. In addition, the company has an obligation to stockholders, who would bear the brunt of lawsuits brought by employees' children born with retardation, nervous system disorders, or other disorders that lead can cause.

Joseph A. Kinney, executive director of the National Safe Workplace Institute in Chicago, sides with Johnson Controls, but only because he believes that letting women assume the burden of their safety undermines OSHA's responsibility to mandate workplace safety rules. "The discrimination side of the issue needs to be resolved," Kinney says. "But the ideal thing is to regulate lead out of the workplace and any other toxin that poses fetal damage."

However, the U.S. Supreme Court has ruled unanimously that the fetal protection policy at Johnson Controls violated the Civil Rights Act of 1964, which prohibits sex discrimination in employment.[99] Pointing to evidence that lead affects sperm and can thus harm the offspring of men exposed to it at the time of conception, the Court stated:

> Respondent does not seek to protect the unconceived children of all its employees. Despite evidence in the record about the debilitating effect of lead exposure on the male reproductive system, Johnson Controls is concerned only with the harms that may befall the unborn offspring of its female employees. . . . [The company's policy is] discriminatory because it requires only a female employee to produce proof that she is not capable of reproducing.

On the other hand, the Court was divided over whether fetal protection policies could ever be legally justified. Justice Harry A. Blackmun, writing for a majority of the Court, declared that they could not, that the Civil Rights Act prohibited all such policies:

> Decisions about the welfare of future children must be left to the parents who conceive, bear, support and raise them rather than to the employers who hire those parents. Women as capable of doing their jobs as their male counterparts may not be forced to choose between having a child and having a job.

Referring to the Pregnancy Discrimination Act of 1978, which amended the 1964 Civil Rights Act and prohibits employment discrimination on the basis of pregnancy or potential pregnancy, Blackmun added:

> Employment late in pregnancy often imposes risks on the unborn child, but Congress indicated that the employer may take into account only the woman's ability to get her job done.

A minority of the justices, however, were unwilling to go so far, and in a concurring opinion, Justice Byron R. White wrote that "common sense tells us that it is part of the normal operation of business concerns to avoid causing injury to third parties as well as to employees." But he added that, in his view, a fetal protection policy would not be defensible unless an employer also addressed other known occupational health risks.

Discussion Questions

1. Do you agree that Johnson Controls's fetal protection policy discriminated against women? Do pregnant women have a moral—not just a legal—right to work with lead?

2. Suppose exposure to lead did not affect sperm or the male reproductive system. Would Johnson's policy still have been discriminatory? Would it hamper women's efforts to win equality in the workplace?

3. Can there be a nondiscriminatory fetal protection policy? Is Justice White correct in arguing that companies have an obligation to avoid causing injury to fetuses just as they do other "third parties"?

4. Suppose a company forbids any employee capable of reproducing from working with lead. Would such a policy wrongly interfere with employees' freedom of choice? Would it be an invasion of their privacy? Would it be fair to employees who are fertile but plan to have no children?

5. Evaluate fetal protection policies from the egoistic, utilitarian, and Kantian perspectives. What rights are involved? What are the likely benefits and harms of such policies?

6. Assuming they are fully informed, do employees with a certain medical condition have a right to work at jobs that can be hazardous to the health of people in their condition? Or can company policy or OSHA regulations justifiably prevent them from doing so for their own good?

7. Would you agree with Joseph Kinney that the real issue is to remove toxins from the workplace? Is this a realistic goal?

CASE 7.5

The Mommy Track

"The cost of employing women in management is greater than the cost of employing men. This is a jarring statement, partly because it is true, but mostly because it is something people are reluctant to talk about."So begins a provocative article by Felice N. Schwartz.[100] Schwartz goes on to contend that the rate of turnover in management positions is two-and-a-half times higher among top-performing women than it is among men. Moreover, one-half of the women who take maternity leave return to their jobs late or not at all. "We know that women also have a greater tendency to plateau or to interrupt their careers," she writes. "But we have become so sensitive to charges of sexism and so afraid of confrontation, even litigation, that we rarely say what we know to be true."

Schwartz's article exploded like a bombshell. What really upset her critics was the distinction Schwartz drew between two types of women: the career-primary woman and the career-and-family woman.[101] Those in the first category put their careers first. They remain single or childless, or if they do have children, they are satisfied to have others raise them. The automatic association of all women with babies is unfair to these women, according to Schwartz—after all, some 90 percent of executive men but only 35 percent of executive women have children by age forty. "The secret to dealing with such women," Schwartz writes, "is to recognize them early, accept them, and clear artificial barriers from their path to the top."

The majority of women fall into Schwartz's second category. They want to pursue genuine careers while participating actively in the rearing of their children. Most of them, Schwartz contends, are willing to trade some career growth and compensation for freedom from the constant pressure to work long hours and weekends. By forcing these women to choose between family and career, companies lose a valuable resource and a competitive advantage. Instead, firms must plan for and manage maternity, they must provide the flexibility to help career-and-family women be maximally productive, and they must take an active role in providing family support and in making high-quality, affordable child care available to all women.

Schwartz's various suggestions of ways for organizations to serve the needs of working mothers and benefit from their expertise seem humane and practical. But her feminist critics see her as distinguishing between the strivers and the breeders, between women who should be treated as honorary males and those who should be shunted onto a special lower-paid, low-pressure career track—the now-notorious "mommy track." Former congresswoman Patricia Schroeder of Colorado says that Schwartz actually "reinforces the idea that you can either have a family or a career, but not both, if you're a woman."[102] And other women worry that Schwartz's article will encourage corporations to reduce pay and withhold promotions in exchange for the parental leave, flextime, and child care that they will sooner or later have to provide as they become more and more dependent on female talent.[103]

Barbara Ehrenreich and Deirdre English challenge Schwartz's data and call her article "a tortured muddle of feminist perceptions and sexist assumptions, good intentions and dangerous suggestions—unsupported by any acceptable evidence at all." What they resent is that Schwartz makes no mention of fathers or of shared parental responsibility for child raising. Schwartz is also accused of assuming that mothers don't need top-flight careers and of taking for granted the existing values, structures, and biases of a corporate world that is still male-dominated.

"Bumping women—or just fertile women, or married women, or whomever—off the fast track may sound smart to cost-conscious CEOs," they write. "But eventually it is the corporate culture itself that needs to slow down to a human pace . . . [and end] work loads that are incompatible with family life."[104]

"What's so disturbing about Felice Schwartz's article," adds Fran Rodgers, president of Work-Family Directions, a Massachusetts research and referral group, "is that it is devoted to fitting women into the existing culture, instead of finding ways to change that culture." And Rodgers rejects the idea of "dividing women into two groups, but completely ignoring the diversity among men."[105]

Other observers fear that men will simply leave the mommy trackers in the dust. "In most organizations, the mommy track is a millstone around your neck," says Richard Belous, an economist at the National Planning Association. "CEOs and rainmakers don't come out of the mommy track," he warns. "If you go part-time, you're signaling to your employer you're on the B-team."[106] Traditionally, men who make it to the upper ranks have relied on their wives to raise the kids and to take full responsibility at home. A fast-track woman who wants children, however, gets caught in a time and energy squeeze, even if her husband is an equal partner at home. And even though more men today are willing to share child-raising responsibilities, most still seem hesitant about making significant career sacrifices for spouse and family. There's no analogous "daddy track," it seems.

In fact, the evidence points to what's been called a "daddy penalty"—at least for dads in dual-career families. Two recent studies have shown that male managers whose wives stay home to care for their children earn more than their counterparts with working wives. Even when differences in the numbers of hours worked, years of experience, field of employment, and career interruptions are taken into account, men who are the sole breadwinners for their families enjoy incomes that are 20 to 25 percent higher than married men with children whose wives have careers.[107] Why? No one knows for sure. Some observers suggest that men who are the sole income earners work more, produce more, and push harder for raises and promotions. Others suggest that having a wife at home is a significant career resource, allowing the man to perform more effectively in his job. Yet others speculate that men who are strongly career oriented choose wives who support that choice in the first place, whereas men who want more balance between work and family are more likely to marry women who want to work. And, finally, there are those who believe that the data reflect a corporate prejudice in favor of traditional families.

Discussion Questions

1. Do you think Schwartz is correct to assert that the cost of employing women in management is greater than that of employing men? If you agree, what are the implications for corporate policy?

2. Can working women accurately be divided into Schwartz's two categories? Is it desirable for companies to distinguish the different types of career paths followed by female employees?

3. Do you think there already is such a thing as a mommy track? Is the idea of a mommy track a good one? Is it somehow discriminatory against women? Against men?

4. Should special organizational arrangements be made for workers who wish to combine career and child raising? Identify the steps that companies can take to accommodate parental needs more effectively.

5. Does a firm have an obligation to give employees the flexibility to work out the particular balance of career and family that is right for them? Or does this go beyond the social responsibilities of business?

Notes to Chapter 7

1. The facts reported here are from "Privacy," *Newsweek,* March 28, 1988, 61–68.

2. "Don't Pry," *Economist,* October 6, 1990, 18.

3. Quoted in "Privacy."

4. See Jeffrey L. Seglin, "Too Much Ado about Giving References," *New York Times,* February 21, 1999, sec. 3, 4. See also David W. Arnesen, C. Patrick Fleenor, and Martin Blizinsky, "Name, Rank, and Serial Number? The Dilemma of Reference Checks," *Business Horizons* 41 (July–August 1998): 71–78.

5. "Is Office Voice Mail Private?" *Wall Street Journal,* February 28, 1995, B1.

6. "As Abuse of Sick Leave Increases, Crackdown Raises Issues of Privacy," *New York Times,* November 30, 1992, A1.

7. Charles Reich, "The Corporate Control of Big Government," *Business and Society Review* 95 (1996): 61.

8. "How Would You Have Reacted to IBM's E-mail Health Care Plea?" *San Jose Mercury News,* August 27, 1994, 10D.

9. "Firms Find It Tougher to Dismiss Employees for Off-Duty Conduct," *Wall Street Journal,* March 29, 1988, 31.

10. *Dollars and Sense,* April 1989, 4; *San Francisco Examiner,* May 12, 1994, A14.

11. *Dollars and Sense,* 4.

12. "Legal Secretary Fired over Gay Stripper Job," *Santa Cruz Sentinel,* June 7, 1992, A10.

13. Terry L. Leap, "When Can You Fire for Off-Duty Conduct?" *Harvard Business Review* 66 (January–February 1988): 36.

14. See Scott Campbell, "Better Than the Company Gym," *HR Magazine,* June 1995, and "Wellness Becomes an Issue in the Workplace," *Santa Cruz Sentinel,* April 28, 2002, D-1.

15. Greg Jaffe, "Weighty Matters," *San Francisco Examiner,* February 22, 1998, J1.

16. "Shape Up—Or Else," *Newsweek,* July 1, 1991, 42; "If You Light Up on Sunday, Don't Come In on Monday," *Business Week,* August 26, 1991, 68–70.

17. "Privacy," 68.

18. See David T. Lykken, "Three Big Lies about the Polygraph," *USA Today,* February 17, 1983, 10A. See also William A. Nowlin and Robert Barbato, "The Truth about Lie Detectors," *Business and Society Review* 66 (Summer 1988), and "Scientists Say Lie Detector Doesn't Always Tell Truth," *Wall Street Journal,* October 9, 2002, B1.

19. Lynn March, "Lie Detectors Are Accurate and Useful," *USA Today,* February 17, 1983, 10A.

20. Lykken, "Three Big Lies."

21. Christopher H. Pyle, "These Tests Are Meant to Scare People," *USA Today,* February 17, 1983, 10A.

22. "Personality Counts," *HR Magazine,* February 2002, 30–31.

23. Barbara Ehrenreich, "Two-Tiered Morality," *New York Times,* June 30, 2002, sec. 4, 15.

24. "Trying to Get a Job? Check Yes or No," *New York Times,* November 28, 1997, B1.

25. Ibid.

26. Carol Kleiman, "The Boss May Be Listening," *San Jose Mercury News,* February 25, 1996, IPC.

27. "Privacy," 68.

28. See "2001 AMA Survey: Workplace Monitoring and Surveillance" at *www.amanet.org.*

29. Kleiman, "The Boss May Be Listening."

30. "What the Boss Knows about You," *Fortune,* August 9, 1993.

31. "Study May Spur Job-Applicant Drug Screening," *Wall Street Journal,* November 28, 1990, B1. See also *New York Times,* November 29, 1990, A17.

32. "Workers' Drug Use Drops 50%," *San Jose Mercury News,* April 13, 1996, 1D.

33. "If You Light Up on Sunday," 68.

34. James T. Wrich, "Beyond Testing: Coping with Drugs at Work," *Harvard Business Review* 66 (January–February 1988).

35. William Serrin, "The Wages of Work," *Nation,* January 28, 1991, 80–82; "Grain-Elevator Explosions Continue to Threaten Workers and Property," *Wall Street Journal,* July 21, 1981, sec. 2, 29; and "Top Executives Are More Liable to Be Held Liable," *Business Ethics,* January–February 1993, 10.

36. Myron I. Peskin and Francis J. McGrath, "Industrial Safety: Who Is Responsible and Who Benefits?" *Business Horizons* 35 (May–June 1992).

37. Beth Rogers, "Creating a Culture of Safety," *HR Magazine* (February 1995), 85. See also James Reason, "Achieving a Safe Culture: Theory and Practice," *Work & Stress* 12 (July–September 1998): 293–306.

38. *Whirlpool Corporation v. Marshall,* 445 U.S. 1 (1980).

39. See Joseph LaDoc, "The Not-So-Clean Business of Making Chips," *Technological Review* 87 (May–June 1984), and "Chip Makers Promise Action on Toxics," *San Jose Mercury News,* December 4, 1992, 1A.

40. U.S. Bureau of the Census, *Statistical Abstract of the United States 2000* (Washington, D.C.: U.S. Government Printing Office, 2001), Table 705.

41. "OSHA Vows to Make Workplace Safer," *San Jose Mercury News,* April 3, 1994, 1PC.

42. "Job Injuries, Illnesses Cost the U.S. as Much as Heart Disease, Study Says," *San Francisco Chronicle,* July 28, 1997, A5.

43. Archie B. Carroll, *Business and Society,* 2nd ed. (Cincinnati: SouthWestern, 1993), 453–454.

44. Dana Wilkie, "The Uphill Struggle for Workplace Health," *State Legislatures* 23 (June 2, 1997): 27–32.

45. "U.S. Acts to Cut Aches on the Job," *New York Times,* February 20, 1999, A1; Jennifer Powell, "A New Pain in the Neck," *PC/Computing,* April 2000, 44; and "New Ballgame for Repetitive-Stress Ailments," *Wall Street Journal,* April 28, 2002, D-6.

46. David Tuller, "The '90s 'Occupational Epidemic,'" *San Francisco Chronicle,* June 12, 1989, C1.

47. "U.S. Acts to Cut Aches," A8.

48. "Make Ergonomics," *HR Magazine,* April 2000, 37–42.

49. See "Fatigue: The Hidden Culprit," *USA Weekend,* January 29–31, 1993, and "Worker Fatigue Can Be Deadly," *San Jose Mercury News,* March 3, 1996.

50. Dorothy Foltz-Gray, "Sheepless Nights," *American Way,* May 1, 1999, 72.

51. "In Their Quest for Efficiency, Factories Scrap the 5-Day Week," *New York Times,* June 4, 1996, A1.

52. "Stress on the Job," *Newsweek,* April 25, 1988; see also "Stress: The Test Americans Are Failing," *Business Week,* April 18, 1988, and "Fear and Stress in Office Take Toll," *Wall Street Journal,* November 6, 1990, B1.

53. "If Workplace Is Stressful, There's a Way to Calm Down," *San Jose Mercury News,* April 4, 1993, 2PC; "Workaholics Anonymous," *Economist,* October 22, 1994, 20.

54. "Yes, American Workers Are Putting in Longer Hours," *San Francisco Examiner,* March 28, 1999, J-5.

55. Sue Shellenbarger, "Work and Family," *San Francisco Examiner,* March 21, 1999, CL 29.

56. Yawen Cheng et al., "Association Between Psychosocial Work Characteristics and Health Functioning in American Women," *British Medical Journal* 30 (May 27, 2000): 1432–1436.

57. Harvey Hornstein, *Brutal Bosses and Their Prey* (New York: Putnam, 1996).

58. Douglas McGregor, *The Human Side of Enterprise* (New York: McGraw-Hill, 1960).

59. David M. Gordon, *Fat and Mean: The Corporate Squeeze of Working Americans and the Myth of Managerial "Downsizing"* (New York: Free Press, 1996), 43; "The Glut of Managers," *Business Week,* March 25, 2002, 26.

60. "For Ross Perot, GM Ouster Still Rankles," *International Herald Tribune,* November 19, 1987.

61. *Statistical Abstract of the United States 2000,* Table 653.

62. See Bonnie Harris, "Child Care Comes to Work," *Los Angeles Times,* November 19, 2000, W1.

63. "Kids Go to School at H-P Work Site," *San Jose Mercury News,* February 10, 1993, 1A; "Companies Providing Schools for Workers' Children," *San Jose Mercury News,* July 28, 1996, 1PC.

64. In connection with this, see "Men Behaving Daddily," *Economist,* February 16, 2000, 110.

65. *Work in America: Report of a Special Task Force to the Secretary of Health, Education, and Welfare* (Cambridge: MIT Press, 1972).

66. Thomas A. Kochan, Harry C. Katz, and Robert B. McKersie, *The Transformation of American Industrial Relations* (New York: Basic Books, 1986), 224; see also Carlos Tejada, "Work Week," *Wall Street Journal,* August 21, 2002, B2.

67. But for a criticism of the original study, see "Scientific Myths That Are Too Good to Die," *New York Times,* December 9, 1998, sec. 4, 2.

68. Survey Research Center, *Survey of Working Conditions* (Ann Arbor: University of Michigan Press, 1970). See also Glenn Bassett, "The Case Against Job Satisfaction," *Business Horizons* 37 (May–June 1994).

69. H. Sheppard and N. Herrick, *Where Have All the Robots Gone?* (New York: Free Press, 1972).

70. A. R. Gini and T. J. Sullivan, *It Comes with the Territory* (New York: Random House, 1989), 27–29.

71. "Bored to Death at Work—Literally," *Business Week,* July 1, 2002, 16.

72. E. Palmore, "Predicting Longevity: A Follow-Up Controlling for Age," *Gerontologist* 9 (1969): 247–250.

73. Sharon Cohen, "Management, Unions Join Forces," *San Francisco Examiner,* December 9, 1990, D3.

74. Cohen, "Management, Unions."

75. Randy Pennington, "Collaborative Labor Relations: The First Line Is the Bottom Line," *Personnel,* March 1989, 78.

76. Cohen, "Management, Unions." See also "Japanese Plants in the U.S. Lose Edge to the Big Three," *International Herald Tribune,* June 17–18, 2000, 14, and "The NUMMI Road to Japan," *San Jose Mercury News,* May 18, 2002, 1C.

77. Alan S. Blinder, "Want to Boost Productivity? Try Giving Workers a Say," *Business Week,* April 17, 1989, 10; "A Firm of Their Own," *Economist,* June 11, 1994, 59.

78. "When GM's Robots Ran Amok," *Economist,* August 10, 1991, 64–65.

79. "United We Own," *Business Week,* March 18, 1996, 96.

80. "UAL: Labor Is My Co-Pilot," *Business Week,* March 1, 1999, 38.

81. See Roger E. Alcaly, "Reinventing the Corporation," *New York Review of Books,* April 10, 1997.

82. On this problem, see Janice A. Klein, "The Human Costs of Manufacturing Reform," *Harvard Business Review* 67 (March–April 1989).

83. D. Keith Denton, "!°#@#! I Hate This Job," *Business Horizons* 37 (January–February 1994).

84. "Special Report: Car Manufacturing," *Economist,* February 23, 2002, 72.

85. 109 Cal. Rptr. 665 (1973).

86. Samuel Greengard, "Theft Control Starts with HR Strategies," *Personnel Journal,* April 1993, 81–88; "The Thief on the Payroll," *San Jose Mercury News,* April 14, 1996, 1PC. See also "Taking at the Office Reaches New Heights," *New York Times,* July 12, 2000, C8, and "Amid the Recession, More Employees Are Stealing from Work," *Santa Cruz Sentinel,* March 24, 2002, D1.

87. Judith Crossen, "Job Applicants Would Disappoint Diogenes," *San Francisco Examiner,* December18, 1988, D15.

88. "Honest Answers—Postpolygraph," *Personnel,* April 1988, 8.

89. Susan Tempor, "More Employers Attempt to Catch a Thief by Giving Job Applicants 'Honesty' Exams," *Wall Street Journal,* August 3, 1981.

90. Crossen, "Job Applicants."

91. "Trying to Get a Job? Check Yes or No," *New York Times,* November 28, 1997, B1.

92. "Honest Answers," 10.

93. Ibid.

94. "Searching for Integrity," *Fortune,* March 8, 1993, 140.

95. "Texas Company Settles over Nosy Questions to Employees," *San Francisco Chronicle,* July 8, 2000, A3.

96. Tempor, "More Employers Attempt to Catch a Thief," 15.

97. This case study is based on a case reported in Thomas Garrett et al., *Cases in Business Ethics* (Englewood Cliffs, N.J.: Prentice Hall, 1968), 9–10.

98. Peter T. Kilborn, "Who Decides Who Works at Jobs Imperiling Fetuses?" *New York Times,* September 2, 1990, 1, is the main source for this case study.

99. *New York Times,* March 21, 1991, A1. Excerpts from *Automobile Workers v. Johnson Controls* quoted in the following paragraphs are from page A14.

100. Felice N. Schwartz, "Management Women and the New Facts of Life," *Harvard Business Review* 67 (January–February 1989): 65.

101. Ibid., 69.

102. Tamar Lewin, "New Look at Working Moms," *San Francisco Chronicle,* March 8, 1989, A1.

103. Barbara Ehrenreich and Deirdre English, "Blowing the Whistle on the 'Mommy Track,'" *Ms.,* July–August 1989, 56.

104. Ibid., 58.

105. Lewin, "New Look at Working Moms."

106. "The Mommy Track," *Newsweek,* March 20, 1989, 132.

107. "Men Whose Wives Work Earn Less, Studies Show," *New York Times,* October 11, 1994, A1; see also "Marriage's 'Unique Effect,'" *Business Week,* May 13, 2002, 32.

Reading ──────■

DRUG TESTING IN EMPLOYMENT

JOSEPH R. DESJARDINS
AND RONALD DUSKA

If drug testing of employees is not to violate privacy, the information it seeks must be relevant to the employment contract. DesJardins and Duska examine two arguments used to establish that knowledge of drug use is job-relevant information: first, that drug use adversely affects job performance and, second, that it can harm the employer, other employees, and the public. Although they reject the first argument, they grant that the second can, in certain limited circumstances, justify drug testing. But even in these cases, strict procedural limitations should be placed on drug testing—despite the fact that drug use itself is illegal. They conclude by raising the question of whether employee consent to drug testing is voluntary.

We take privacy to be an "employee right," by which we mean a presumptive moral entitlement to receive certain goods or be protected from certain harms in the workplace.[1] Such a right creates a prima facie obligation on the part of the employer to provide the relevant goods or, as in this case, refrain from the relevant harmful treatment. These rights prevent employees from being placed in the fundamentally coercive position where they must choose between their jobs and other basic human goods.

Further, we view the employer-employee relationship as essentially contractual. The employer-employee relationship is an economic one and, unlike relationships such as those between a government and its citizens or a parent and a child, exists primarily as a means for satisfying the economic interests of the contracting parties. The obligations that each party incurs are only those that it voluntarily takes on. Given such a contractual relationship, certain areas of the employee's life remain his or her own private concern, and no employer has a right to invade them. On these presumptions we maintain that certain information about an employee is rightfully private, in other words, that the employee has a right to privacy.

THE RIGHT TO PRIVACY

George Brenkert has described the right to privacy as involving a three-place relation between a person A, some information X, and another person B. The right to privacy is violated only when B deliberately comes to possess information X about A and no relationship between A and B exists that would justify B's coming to know X about A.[2] Thus, for example, the relationship one has with a mortgage company would justify that company's coming to know about one's salary, but the relationship one has with a neighbor does not justify the neighbor's coming to know that information.

Hence, an employee's right to privacy is violated whenever personal information is requested, collected, or used by an employer in a way or for any purpose that is *irrelevant to* or *in violation of* the contractual relationship that exists between employer and employee.

Since drug testing is a means for obtaining information, the information sought must be relevant to the contract if the drug testing is not to violate privacy. Hence, we must first decide whether knowledge of drug use obtained by drug testing is job relevant. In cases in which the knowledge of drug use is *not* relevant, there appears to be no justification for subjecting employees to drug tests. In cases in which information of drug use is job relevant, we need to consider if, when, and under what conditions using a means such as drug testing to obtain that knowledge is justified.

IS KNOWLEDGE OF DRUG USE JOB-RELEVANT INFORMATION?

Two arguments are used to establish that knowledge of drug use is job-relevant information. The

Reprinted by permission from Joseph R. DesJardins and John J. McCall, eds., *Contemporary Issues in Business Ethics,* 4th ed. (Belmont, Calif.: Wadsworth, 2000). Notes abridged.

first argument claims that drug use adversely affects job performance, thereby leading to lower productivity, higher costs, and consequently lower profits. Drug testing is seen as a way of avoiding these adverse effects. According to some estimates $25 billion are lost each year in the United States through loss in productivity, theft, higher rates in health and liability insurance, and similar costs incurred because of drug use.[3] Since employers are contracting with an employee for the performance of specific tasks, employers seem to have a legitimate claim upon whatever personal information is relevant to an employee's ability to do the job.

The second argument claims that drug use has been and can be responsible for considerable harm to individual employees, to their fellow employees, and to the employer, and third parties, including consumers. In this case drug testing is defended because it is seen as a way of preventing possible harm. Further, since employers can be held liable for harms done to employees and customers, knowledge of employee drug use is needed so that employers can protect themselves from risks related to such liability. But how good are these arguments?

THE FIRST ARGUMENT: JOB PERFORMANCE AND KNOWLEDGE OF DRUG USE

The first argument holds that drug use lowers productivity and that, consequently, an awareness of drug use obtained through drug testing will allow an employer to maintain or increase productivity. It is generally assumed that the performance of people using certain drugs is detrimentally affected by such use, and any use of drugs that reduces productivity is consequently job relevant. If knowledge of such drug use allows the employer to eliminate production losses, such knowledge is job relevant.

On the surface this argument seems reasonable. Obviously some drug use, in lowering the level of performance, can decrease productivity. Since the employer is entitled to a certain level of performance and drug use adversely affects performance, knowledge of that use seems job relevant.

But this formulation of the argument leaves an important question unanswered. To what level of performance are employers entitled? Optimal performance, or some lower level? If some lower level, what? Employers have a valid claim upon some *certain level* of performance, such that a failure to perform at this level would give the employer a justification for disciplining, firing, or at least finding fault with the employee. But that does not necessarily mean that the employer has a right to a maximum or optimal level of performance, a level above and beyond a certain level of acceptability. It might be nice if the employee gives an employer a maximum effort or optimal performance, but that is above and beyond the call of the employee's duty and the employer can hardly claim a right at all times to the highest level of performance of which an employee is capable. . . .

If the person is producing what is expected, knowledge of drug use on the grounds of production is irrelevant since, by this hypothesis, the production is satisfactory. If, on the other hand, the performance suffers, then to the extent that it slips below the level justifiably expected, the employer has preliminary grounds for warning, disciplining, or releasing the employee. But the justification for this action is the person's unsatisfactory performance, not the person's use of drugs. Accordingly, drug use information is either unnecessary or irrelevant and consequently there are not sufficient grounds to override the right of privacy. Thus, unless we can argue that an employer is entitled to optimal performance, the argument fails.

This counterargument should make it clear that the information that is job relevant, and consequently is not rightfully private, is information about an employee's level of performance and not information about the underlying causes of that level. The fallacy of the argument that promotes drug testing in the name of increased productivity is the assumption that each employee is obliged to perform at an optimal or at least quite high level. But this is required under few if any contracts. What is required contractually is meeting the normally expected levels of production or performing the tasks in the job description adequately (not optimally). If one can do that under the influence of drugs, then on the grounds of job performance at least, drug use is rightfully private. An employee who cannot perform the task adequately is not fulfilling the contract, and knowledge of the cause of the failure to perform is irrelevant on the contractual model.

Of course, if the employer suspects drug use or abuse as the cause of the unsatisfactory performance, then she might choose to help the person with counseling or rehabilitation. However, this does not seem to be something morally required of the employer. Rather, in the case of unsatisfactory performance, the employer has a prima facie justification for dismissing or disciplining the employee. . . .

THE SECOND ARGUMENT: HARM AND THE KNOWLEDGE OF DRUG USE TO PREVENT HARM

The performance argument is inadequate, but there is an argument that seems somewhat stronger. This is an argument that takes into account the fact that drug use often leads to harm. Using a variant of the Millian argument, which allows interference with a person's rights in order to prevent harm, we could argue that drug testing might be justified if such testing led to knowledge that would enable an employer to prevent harm.

Drug use certainly can lead to harming others. Consequently, if knowledge of such drug use can prevent harm, then knowing whether or not an employee uses drugs might be a legitimate concern of an employer in certain circumstances. This second argument claims that knowledge of the employee's drug use is job relevant because employees who are under the influence of drugs can pose a threat to the health and safety of themselves and others, and an employer who knows of that drug use and the harm it can cause has a responsibility to prevent it.

Employers have both a general duty to prevent harm and the specific responsibility for harms done by their employees. Such responsibilities are sufficient reason for any employer to claim that information about an employee's drug use is relevant if that knowledge can prevent harm by giving the employer grounds for dismissing the employee or not allowing him or her to perform potentially harmful tasks. Employers might even claim a right to reduce unreasonable risks, in this case the risks involving legal and economic liability for harms caused by employees under the influence of drugs, as further justification for knowing about employee drug use.

This second argument differs from the first, in which only a lowered job performance was relevant information. In this case, even to allow the performance is problematic, for the performance itself, more than being inadequate, can hurt people. We cannot be as sanguine about the prevention of harm as we can about inadequate production. Where drug use may cause serious harm, knowledge of that use becomes relevant if the knowledge of such use can lead to the prevention of harm and drug testing becomes justified as a means for obtaining that knowledge.

Jobs with Potential to Cause Harm

In the first place, it is not clear that every job has a potential to cause harm—at least, not a potential to cause harm sufficient to override a prima facie right to privacy. To say that employers can use drug testing where that can prevent harm is not to say that every employer has the right to know about the drug use of every employee. Not every job poses a threat serious enough to justify an employer coming to know this information.

In deciding which jobs pose serious-enough threats, certain guidelines should be followed. First the potential for harm should be *clear* and *present*. Perhaps all jobs in some extended way pose potential threats to human well-being. We suppose an accountant's error could pose a threat of harm to someone somewhere. But some jobs—like those of airline pilots, school bus drivers, public transit drivers, and surgeons—are jobs in which unsatisfactory performance poses a clear and present danger to others. It would be much harder to make an argument that job performances by auditors, secretaries, executive vice-presidents for public relations, college teachers, professional athletes, and the like could cause harm if those performances were carried on under the influence of drugs. They would cause harm only in exceptional cases.[4]

Not Every Person Is to Be Tested

But, even if we can make a case that a particular job involves a clear and present danger for causing harm if performed under the influence of drugs, it is not appropriate to treat everyone holding such a job the same. Not every jobholder is equally threatening. There is less reason to investigate an airline pilot for drug use if that pilot has a twenty-year record of exceptional service than there is to investigate a pilot whose behavior has become erratic and unreliable recently, or one who reports to work smelling of alcohol and slurring his words. Presuming that every airline pilot is equally threatening is to deny individuals the respect that they deserve as autonomous, rational agents. It is to ignore their history and the significant differences between them. It is also probably inefficient and leads to the lowering of morale. It is the likelihood of causing harm, and not the fact of being an airline pilot per se, that is relevant in deciding which employees in critical jobs to test.

So, even if knowledge of drug use is justifiable to prevent harm, we must be careful to limit this justification to a range of jobs and people where the potential for harm is clear and present. The jobs must be jobs that clearly can cause harm, and the specific employee should not be someone who has a history of reliability. Finally, the drugs being tested should be those drugs that have genuine potential for harm if used in the jobs in question.

LIMITATIONS ON DRUG-TESTING POLICIES

Even when we identify those situations in which knowledge of drug use would be job relevant, we still need to examine whether some procedural limitations should not be placed upon the employer's testing for drugs. We have said when a real threat of harm exists and when evidence exists suggesting that a particular employee poses such a threat, an employer could be justified in knowing about drug use in order to prevent the potential harm. But we need to recognize that so long as the employer has the discretion for deciding when the potential for harm is clear and present, and for deciding which employees pose the threat of harm, the possibility

of abuse is great. Thus, some policy limiting the employer's power is called for.

Just as criminal law imposes numerous restrictions protecting individual dignity and liberty on the state's pursuit of its goals, so we should expect that some restrictions be placed on employers to protect innocent employees from harm (including loss of job and damage to one's personal and professional reputation). Thus, some system of checks upon an employer's discretion in these matters seems advisable.

A drug-testing policy that requires all employees to submit to a drug test or to jeopardize their jobs would seem coercive and therefore unacceptable. Being placed in such a fundamentally coercive position of having to choose between one's job and one's privacy does not provide the conditions for a truly free consent. Policies that are unilaterally established by employers would likewise be unacceptable. Working with employees to develop company policy seems the only way to ensure that the policy will be fair to both parties. Prior notice of testing would also be required in order to give employees the option of freely refraining from drug use. Preventing drug use is morally preferable to punishing users after the fact, because this approach treats employees as capable of making rational and informed decisions.

Further procedural limitations seem advisable as well. Employees should be notified of the results of the test, they should be entitled to appeal the results (perhaps through further tests by an independent laboratory), and the information obtained through tests ought to be kept confidential. In summary, limitations upon employer discretion for administering drug tests can be derived from the nature of the employment contract and from the recognition that drug testing is justified by the desire to prevent harm, not the desire to punish wrongdoing.

THE ILLEGALITY CONTENTION

At this point critics might note that the behavior which testing would try to deter is, after all, illegal. Surely this excuses any responsible employer from being overprotective of an employee's rights. The fact that an employee is doing something illegal should give the employer a right to that information about his or her private life. Thus, it is not simply that drug use might pose a threat of harm to others, but that it is an *illegal* activity that threatens others. But again, we would argue that illegal activity itself is irrelevant to job performance. At best, *conviction* records might be relevant, but since drug tests are administered by private employers we are not only ignoring the question of conviction, we are also ignoring the fact that the employee has not even been arrested for the alleged illegal activity.

Further, even if the due process protections and the establishment of guilt are acknowledged, it still does not follow that employers have a claim to know about all illegal activity on the part of their employees.

Consider the following example: Suppose you were hiring an auditor whose job required certifying the integrity of your firm's tax and financial records. Certainly, the personal integrity of this employee is vital to adequate job performance. Would we allow the employer to conduct, with or without the employee's consent, an audit of the employee's own personal tax return? Certainly if we discover that this person has cheated on a personal tax return we will have evidence of illegal activity that is relevant to this person's ability to do the job. Given one's own legal liability for filing falsified statements, the employee's illegal activity also poses a threat to others. But surely, allowing private individuals to audit an employee's tax returns is too intrusive a means for discovering information about that employee's integrity. The government certainly would never allow this violation of an employee's privacy. It ought not to allow drug testing on the same grounds. Why tax returns should be protected in ways that urine, for example, is not, raises interesting questions of fairness. Unfortunately, this question would take us beyond the scope of this paper.

VOLUNTARINESS

A final problem that we also leave undeveloped concerns the voluntariness of employee consent. For most employees, being given the choice between submitting to a drug test and risking one's job by refusing an employer's request is not much of a decision at all. We believe that such decisions are less than voluntary and thereby hold that employers cannot escape our criticisms simply by including within the employment contract a drug-testing clause. Furthermore, there is reason to believe that those most in need of job security will be those most likely to be subjected to drug testing. Highly skilled, professional employees with high job mobility and security will be in a stronger position to resist such intrusions than will less skilled, easily replaced workers. This is why we should not anticipate surgeons and airline pilots being tested and should not be surprised when public transit and factory workers are. A serious question of fairness arises here as well.

Drug use and drug testing seem to be our most recent social "crisis." Politicians, the media, and employers expend a great deal of time and effort addressing this crisis. Yet, unquestionably, more lives, health, and money are lost each year to alcohol abuse than to marijuana, cocaine, and other controlled substances. We are well advised to be careful in considering issues that arise from such selective social concern. We will let other social commentators speculate on the reasons why drug use has received scrutiny while other white-collar crimes and alcohol abuse are ignored. Our only concern at this point is that such selective prosecution suggests an arbitrariness that should alert us to questions of fairness and justice.

In summary, then, we have seen that drug use is not always job relevant, and if drug use is not job relevant, information about it is certainly not job relevant. In the case of performance it may be a cause of some decreased performance, but it is the performance itself that is relevant to an employee's position, not what prohibits or enables that employee to do the job. In the case of potential harm being done by an employee under the influence of drugs, the drug use seems job relevant, and in this case drug testing to prevent harm might be legitimate. But how this is practicable is another question. It would seem that standard motor dexterity or mental dexterity tests given immediately prior to job performance are more effective in preventing harm, unless one concludes that drug use invariably and necessarily leads to harm. One must trust the individuals in any system for that system to work. One cannot police everything. Random testing might enable an employer to find drug users and to weed out the few to forestall possible future harm, but are the harms prevented sufficient to override the rights of privacy of the people who are innocent and to overcome the possible abuses we have mentioned? It seems not.

Clearly, a better method is to develop safety checks immediately prior to the performance of a job. Have a surgeon or a pilot or a bus driver pass a few reasoning and motor-skill tests before work. The cause of the lack of a skill, which lack might lead to harm, is really a secondary issue.

Notes

1. "A Defense of Employee Rights," Joseph DesJardins and John McCall, *Journal of Business Ethics* 4 (1985). We should emphasize that our concern is with the *moral* rights of privacy for employees and not with any specific or prospective *legal* rights. . . .

2. "Privacy, Polygraphs, and Work," George Brenkert, *Journal of Business and Professional Ethics,* vol. 1, no. 1 (Fall 1981). For a more general discussion of privacy in the workplace see "Privacy in Employment" by Joseph DesJardins, in *Moral Rights in the Workplace,* edited by Gertrude Ezorsky (SUNY Press, 1987). A good resource for philosophical work on privacy can be found in "Recent Work on the Concept of Privacy" by W. A. Parent, in *American Philosophical Quarterly,* vol. 20 (Oct. 1983), 341–358.

3. *U.S. News and World Report,* 22 Aug. 1983; *Newsweek,* 6 May 1983.

4. Obviously we are speaking here of harms that go beyond the simple economic harm that results from unsatisfactory job performance. These economic harms are discussed in the first argument above. Further, we ignore such "harms" as providing bad role models for adolescents, harms often used to justify drug tests for professional athletes. We think it unreasonable to hold an individual responsible for the image he or she provides to others.

Review and Discussion Questions

1. DesJardins and Duska consider two arguments intended to show that knowledge of drug use is job-relevant information. What are their reasons for rejecting the first argument and what are the limitations of the second argument? Are you persuaded by their reasoning?

2. Do you agree that the crucial question regarding drug testing in employment is whether the information sought is job relevant? Are there other reasons for drug testing that don't turn on this issue?

3. What, if any, procedural limitations should be placed on drug testing in those cases in which it is justified? Are DesJardins and Duska right to maintain that the illegality of drug use is irrelevant?

4. How voluntary do you think employee consent to drug testing really is?

5. What steps do you think employers should take to deal with the problem of employee drug use?

Reading ■

WORK, PRIVACY, AND AUTONOMY

RICHARD L. LIPPKE

Lippke argues that privacy is valuable because of its importance for human autonomy. Rejecting analyses of privacy in the workplace that focus on whether information is "job relevant" as this is defined by the work contract, Lippke sets the question of workplace privacy in the broader context of the imbalance of power that actually exists between employers and employees. He contends that this power imbalance and the accompanying authoritarian organization of work already deprive employees of any significant input into the decisions that affect their working lives. As a result, information-gathering techniques like surveillance and drug testing are to be resisted as further eroding what little autonomy employees have left.

Employees today face what many believe are unjustified assaults on their privacy. At present, the most well-known and controversial such assault is the urine test. Estimates are that about 30% of the Fortune 500 companies in the United States require a urine test as part of the employment application process. Proponents of such testing warn of the dangers of rampant drug use and abuse in our society. They insist on the need to safeguard co-worker and consumer health and safety, and the need to maintain productivity. Opponents of testing conjure up images of Orwell's *1984*—of large and powerful institutions run amok, forcing innocent people to urinate while under the intense (and let us hope not prurient) supervision of official inspectors. Opponents lambast testing as an invasion of privacy and as a form of self-incrimination. Their most effective tactic has been to raise the specter of inaccurate tests; of persons unfairly scored with the scarlet letter of drug use.

Reprinted by permission of the author from *Public Affairs Quarterly* 3 (April 1989). Copyright © 1989 by *Public Affairs Quarterly*. Section titles added; some notes omitted.

Unfortunately, in the public debate over these issues there is little in the way of patient and careful analysis. . . . I will maintain that the philosophical defenses of employee privacy that have been offered are either incomplete or misguided. At times, they say too little about the value of privacy. Or, they offer suspect models of the employer/employee relationship. Or, they fail to convincingly show how we should deal with the conflict between privacy and other, competing values.

I will begin my analysis by arguing that privacy is valuable because of its relation to autonomy. For the purposes of this discussion, I will define autonomy as the capacity of persons to make rationally reflective choices about their ends and activities. All areas of persons' lives are assumed to be fit subjects for the exercise of their autonomy. Unless the relation between privacy and autonomy is kept clearly in view, we will not be able to establish the need for restrictions on the information employers may gather or on the means they may use. More importantly, I will argue that we must examine the privacy issue in the context of an understanding of how the contemporary organization of work in the United States affects the autonomy of workers. Simply put, workers in the U.S. face myriad assaults to their autonomy. I will show how failure to recognize this and to incorporate it into philosophical analyses of employee privacy inevitably weakens the case that can be made on behalf of employees. I will argue that when the reality of work is ignored, workers are more likely to be blamed for behavior that arguably stems (at least in part) from the system of private property rights in productive resources that deprives them of control over their working lives. . . .

THE VALUE OF PRIVACY

There are difficulties in defining what privacy is. However, I do not think we need to be detained by them.[1] Generally, there is a consensus that it involves two things: (1) control over some information about ourselves; and (2) some control over who can experience or observe us. In the abstract, it is hard to further specify how much control privacy involves and over what types of information it ranges. This is because whether any given piece of information about me is private in relation to someone else depends on the type of relationship I have to that individual. What is private in relation to my spouse is very different from what is private in relation to an employer or working associate.

Joseph Kupfer has recently offered a compelling analysis of the value of privacy.[2] Two of the ways in which privacy is valuable are especially relevant to the employer/employee relationship, so I will concentrate on them. First, Kupfer argues that privacy plays an essential role in individuals coming to have an "autonomous self-concept," that is, a concept of themselves as in control of their own lives:

> An autonomous self-concept requires identifying with a particular body whose thoughts, purposes, and actions are subject to one's control. . . . [A]utonomy requires awareness of control over one's relation to others, including their access to us. . . . [P]rivacy contributes to the formation and persistence of autonomous individuals by providing them with control over whether or not their physical and psychological existence becomes part of another's experience.[3]

Kupfer does not argue that privacy is intrinsically good. He argues that it is causally related to the formation and maintenance of an autonomous self-concept. An autonomous self-concept is, in turn, a necessary condition of the basic good of autonomy. In other words, unless individuals conceive of themselves as able to determine their own courses of action, their own life-plans, they cannot be autonomous. If individuals are to develop and maintain an autonomous self-concept, others must grant them control over information about themselves and control over who can experience them and when. Kupfer offers some empirical evidence to substantiate the claim that lack of privacy defeats the formation and maintenance of an autonomous self-concept.

As Kupfer notes, the most autonomous person is one who evaluates his deepest convictions, or the most fundamental aspects of his life-plan. Privacy is essential to individuals having the concept that they can do this. It allows them to engage in this self-scrutiny without intrusion and distraction. When the most intimate aspects of their lives are up for scrutiny, individuals are vulnerable to ridicule or manipulation by others. It is vitally important for them to be able to remove themselves from observation and criticism by those they feel they cannot trust.

A second way in which privacy is valuable is that individuals subjected to invasions of their privacy seem less likely to conceive of themselves as *worthy* of autonomy:

> Privacy is a trusting way others treat us, resulting in a conception of ourselves as worth being trusted. In contrast, monitoring behavior or collecting data on us, projects a disvaluing of the self in question.[4]

Close, intrusive supervision and constant correction (or the threat of it) are inimical to individuals developing and maintaining a sense of themselves as worthy of autonomy. In contrast, social practices that respect privacy give the individual a chance to make mistakes or do wrong, and thus convey the message that the individual is worthy of acting autonomously. The sense that they are worthy of acting autonomously may, as Kupfer notes, increase the confidence of individuals in themselves, and so they may exercise their autonomy to an even greater extent. . . .

JOB RELEVANCE AND THE CONTRACTUAL MODEL

With this brief characterization of some of the ways in which privacy is valuable in hand, I turn first to consider the issues raised by the *content* of information that businesses might acquire about employees or prospective employees. Both George Brenkert and Joseph DesJardins offer arguments designed to restrict the types of information employers may justifiably gather about employees to information that is "job relevant." Both also construe the employer/employee relationship in contractual terms, relying, apparently, on the fact that the courts are increasingly viewing the relationship in that fashion.

DesJardins argues that the contractual model is a marked improvement over the old principal/agent model, where the moral and legal rights seemed to be largely on the side of the employer and the moral and legal duties on the side of the employee. The contractual model presumes the existence of a legal framework to enforce the contract. More importantly, "contracts also must be noncoercive, voluntary agreements between rational and free agents."[5] And, they must be free from fraud and deception.

DesJardins explores the implications of this model for the issue of privacy in the employment context. He argues that the employer is entitled to make sure that the contract is free from fraud and deception. The employer can legitimately acquire information about the prospective employee's job qualifications, work experience, educational background, and "other information relevant to the hiring decision."[6] Information is "relevant" if it has to do with determining whether or not the employee is capable of fulfilling her part of the contract. In a similar vein, Brenkert argues that the "job relevance" requirement limits the information sought "to that which is directly connected with the job description."[7] Brenkert admits that aspects of a person's social and moral character (for example, honesty, ability and willingness to cooperate with others) are job relevant. What both Brenkert and DesJardins want to rule out as job relevant is information about such things as a prospective employee's political or religious beliefs and practices, her sexual preferences, marital status, credit or other financial data, and the like. One of Brenkert's complaints about the use of polygraph tests is that they often involve asking employees for information that is *not* job relevant.

I am sympathetic with the idea of such content restrictions, but I believe the arguments of DesJardins and Brenkert are seriously flawed. In the first place, we should be wary of the contractual model of the employer/employee relationship. . . .

The danger in using this model is that it may lead us to ignore a crucial imbalance of power that exists in the marketplace. Individual employees rarely have bargaining power equal to that of their prospective employers. First, there are typically more potential employees available to firms than there are job openings available. Many jobs require little training or pre-existing expertise, and so workers can often be easily replaced. The threat that "there is always someone to take your place" is not an idle one for most workers. . . . Second, firms seem able to absorb underemployment more easily than workers can absorb unemployment. While firms need employees, they rarely need them as desperately as workers need jobs. As a result of these two factors, individual workers are rarely in a position to bargain on anything like equal terms with their prospective employers.

This imbalance of power renders most workers practically unable to resist the demands for information that precede and accompany employment offers, and makes all the more urgent the content restrictions DesJardins and Brenkert advocate. After all, what is the point of urging such restrictions if the wage-labor agreement is one between relative equals? Why not just leave the sorts of information to be exchanged up to the negotiations between employer and employee?

. . . My point is that the contractual model is very misleading if used as a way to conceive of the reality of work in the U.S. It suggests a type of equality that does not exist, and if its descriptive and normative functions are run together, it distorts our perception of where the balance of power lies in the relationship between workers and employers.

Leaving aside the problems with the contractual model, it does not seem that DesJardins and Brenkert help us to understand the moral basis for the content restrictions they advocate. The appeal to the notion of "job relevance" raises more questions than it answers. Lots of information both would prevent employers from obtaining is, arguably, job relevant. For instance, if all of my employees are politically and religiously conservative, knowing where prospective employees stand on these matters may very well be job relevant if my employees have to work closely together. After all, an atheist with socialist leanings may not get along at all with my employees and thereby disrupt productivity. Neither may a union supporter, a homosexual, or someone who is financially reckless or sexually promiscuous. I am not suggesting that we should cater to the prejudices of existing employees in making hiring decisions. What I am suggesting is that Brenkert's and DesJardins' arguments invoke a concept that is far from unproblematic.[8]

A DIFFERENT PERSPECTIVE

Even if the notion of "job relevance" was unproblematic, the argument would be incomplete. What we want is an argument that connects job relevance up with some moral value or values. In other words, why (morally speaking) limit employer access to only job relevant information? What is at stake in doing so?

If we turn back to the analysis of the value of privacy, the answer emerges. Suppose that employers are allowed to gather all of the sorts of information that the notion of "job relevance" is meant to exclude, and to use that information in making employment-related decisions. The result might be that business hiring and promotion decisions will wind up shaping people's lives in rather dramatic ways. Consider the likely chilling effects on employees. They may be reluctant to try out any new ideas or activities that may, at some future date, come back to haunt them. As we saw, privacy vitally contributes to our concept of ourselves as in control of our own lives. Part of this is that it protects our sense of self-determination by enabling us to engage in a "no holds barred" examination of all aspects of our lives. It allows us to experiment with different courses of our lives, if only in thought. These different courses may not be popular, especially to employers who are very conscious of the bottom line.

There is also the very real danger that all sorts of mistaken inferences about employee behavior will be made from access to such information. For instance, suppose that a polygraph test uncovers the fact that a person sometimes fantasizes about theft. It seems clear that a person who fantasizes about theft may be a long way from behaving as a thief. We do not understand the connections between the "inner workings" of people's minds and their behavior anywhere near well enough to allow employers to make such predictions in an accurate fashion.

In short, the content restrictions DesJardins and Brenkert favor are morally justified as ways of limiting the perceived power that businesses have over the lives of their employees. We should discourage invasions of privacy that will likely result in individuals narrowing the exploration and examination of their lives, or that will decrease their sense that they control and are responsible for their lives. In a work environment without such restrictions, and where employers are already in a position to impose their wills on employees in

other ways, it seems unlikely that employees will have as rich and lively a sense of their own autonomy. In turn, they will be less prone to exercise their autonomy.

It seems clear that many of the most controversial *means* of acquiring information about employees may provide employers with information that is, on any reasonable interpretation of the notion, job relevant. Surveillance to prevent theft or to maintain productivity provides such information. Urine tests will provide such information, though they will also provide information about off-the-job drug or alcohol use that is, less obviously, job relevant. Searches of employee desks or lockers, and even polygraph tests (where the questions are suitably restricted), will provide such information. Physical exams and skills tests will do so, though few have seen these as controversial.

Numerous writers have argued against the use of at least some of these means. One popular objection to some of these means is that they are so inaccurate. Polygraph tests, in particular, seem gravely defective in this way, and to a lesser extent, so do urine tests. The concern about accuracy is a concern about fairness, about the possibility of unfairly accusing individuals of actions they are innocent of. I think that the inaccuracy issue is a very serious one, but I do not believe we should base our case against such tests on it alone, or even primarily. The reason for this is simple: suppose through various technological developments such tests are made *very* accurate. Are we then to conclude that there is nothing objectionable about them? I think not. I will try to show that there are other objectionable features to such tests.

A second objection might be that such means of acquiring information are somehow too intrusive. It is important to ask what this means. Is it that such methods come too close to us, crossing some physical or psychological boundary that is morally significant? Administering the polygraph test does require that various devices be attached to our bodies, so maybe it is the actual physical contact that matters. It is hard to imagine anything more intrusive in this regard than a physical exam. Urine tests are not intrusive in this way, however, and neither are surveillance or forays through employee desks and lockers. Thus, physical contact does not seem to be a necessary condition of intrusiveness. It might be a sufficient condition, but we need to know precisely what is so objectionable about such contact . . . [especially] where the concern is with shielding individuals from physical harm. . . .

What all of these methods of acquiring information seem to have in common is that they are ways of checking on the things employees say about themselves or the ways employees present themselves. In this regard, I do not see how a urine test or surveillance is all that much different than the required disclosure of information about work experience or educational background. Perhaps some methods are more intrusive, as a matter of degree, than others. Employees are increasingly finding that not even their own bodies are safe havens, let alone their desks and lockers. At every turn, they are hounded by employer efforts to catch them speaking or acting in ways contrary to what are deemed the employer's interests.

The proliferation of these methods of acquiring contradicting information seems likely to have two sorts of effects on workers. First, all such methods implicitly remind the worker where the balance of power lies in the working world. Again, most workers are not in a position to refuse to cooperate with the use of such methods and workers are highly vulnerable to any negative employer reactions to the information so gleaned. The more a worker is checked on, tested, spied upon, and so on, the less likely she is to feel that she controls her own life in the working world. The aggregate and cumulative effects of many (by themselves seemingly innocent) attempts to check on workers might be an increased sense on the part of workers that the workplace is an oppressive environment. It is distressing that so many employees apparently submit to polygraph or urine tests without any reluctance. Can this be because they have already internalized the message that in the workplace their lives are not their own?

Second, random or across-the-board drug testing, or surveillance without "reasonable cause," implicitly tells employees that they are not trustworthy. It is important to keep in mind that in spite of statistics on the use of drugs by workers (esti-mates as high as one in six use drugs either on or off the job), the vast majority of workers are probably "clean" and honest. However, instead of there being a presumption that employees will act responsibly, the presumption behind the use of these methods of gathering information is that they cannot be trusted to act responsibly. Individuals who find themselves with a presumption of doubt against them may simply react with resentment. That is bad enough and a potential cost to employers. What is worse is the tendency such methods might have to undermine the employees' sense of trustworthiness, and therefore their sense that they are worthy of acting autonomously. Again, one valuable thing about privacy is that it affirms an individual's sense that she is worthy of autonomy. The more she lacks that sense, the more she is prone to tolerate invasions of her privacy, with the resulting debilitating effects on her autonomy.

THE ORGANIZATION OF WORK

In the abstract, concerns about the effects of such methods on employee autonomy might appear legitimate, but not of a sufficiently compelling nature to convince us that their use is wholly objectionable. If they are employed in a work environment that is otherwise supportive of employee autonomy, they might be only minor threats. Therefore, in order to strengthen the case against the use of such methods, it will help here to focus attention on how the organization of work in the U.S. *already* undermines the autonomy of most workers to an extraordinary extent.

As numerous critics of the organization of work in the U.S. have pointed out, the majority of workers are routinely subjected to a hierarchical, authoritarian management structure that deprives them of any significant input into the economic decisions directly affecting their working lives. Most have very little input into decisions about the organization of work at even the shop-floor level, let alone at levels above it. As Adina Schwartz argues, most workers are subjected to a division of labor where they are confined to increasingly narrowly defined tasks determined and supervised by others:

These routine jobs provide people with almost no opportunities for formulating aims, for deciding on means for achieving their ends, or for adjusting their goals and methods in light of experience.[9]

Work technology is decided by others, as are productivity quotas, criteria for evaluation, discipline procedures, and plant closings or employee lay-offs. Even the attitudes with which work is to be done are prescribed and pressures are put on workers to "be a loyal member of the team" or to "please the customer at all costs." . . .

Thus, each concession made to management's desire to gather information using the methods we have been discussing adds to an already impressive arsenal of weapons at its disposal for the assault on employee autonomy. The question is *not* whether we should endorse the use of methods that undermine employee autonomy in a setting where that autonomy is otherwise affirmed and nurtured. The question is whether we should endorse the use of methods that might further erode employee autonomy. For instance, random or across-the-board urine tests do not send a message to workers that they are untrustworthy in a context where their trustworthiness is normally affirmed. Instead, it sends a message that is likely repeated to workers in a thousand different ways throughout their working lives. A verdict wholly in favor of employees on all of the privacy issues we have been considering will, by itself, come nowhere near establishing working conditions supportive of employee autonomy.

Another way to put the preceding point about the organization of work in the U.S. is to say that property rights, with their supporting political-social institutions and practices, give some individuals a considerable amount of *power* over the lives of others. It is with this in mind that we should consider attempts to override the privacy of employees by appeals to the property rights of the owners and stockholders.

Proponents of gathering information about employees may admit that privacy is a value and that it is threatened by the means employers want to use to gather information. But, they will argue, the property rights of the owners and stockholders are valuable as well. They will rightly demand to be shown that the privacy rights of workers ought to prevail over these property rights. . . .

What this plausible-sounding argument ignores is how property rights in productive resources differ from privacy rights. The right to privacy is such that respecting it provides individuals with an increased sense of control (a necessary condition of autonomy) over their own lives. Respecting it does *not* provide individuals with increased control over the lives of others. Property rights as they exist in the U.S. are, as we have seen, not like this. They do give some power over the lives of others. And, importantly, a verdict in favor of the owners and stockholders will mean a further extension of that already considerable control.

Hence, the issue is not the rather abstract one of whether privacy rights are more or less important than property rights in relation to the autonomy of the bearers of those rights. Rather, since property rights as currently institutionalized give some power over the lives of others, the issue is whether to preserve or increase that power, *or* curtail it. Indeed, once the connection between property rights and power is revealed in this way, those rights become fit subjects for critical scrutiny. If we are concerned about the autonomy of workers, we can hardly ignore the existence of working conditions that systematically and pervasively undermine it.

A second reason for not allowing the issues to be framed simply in terms of conflicting rights is that this is likely to exonerate the existing organization of work from any blame for generating the employee behavior that is viewed as irresponsible. This irresponsible behavior is taken as a *given,* and various methods for collecting information about employees are proposed. The need to gather such information is implicitly attributed solely to defects in the character of employees. Those who seek to defend workers against invasions of their privacy are likely to be portrayed as condoning dishonesty, drug use, and the like. This portrayal is, of course, unfair, but it gains credence from the implicit assumption that such behaviors simply exist and must be countered. Thus, the debate about conflicting rights begins, and employers are all too easily depicted as the innocent victims of their unscrupulous, irresponsible, and ungrateful employees.

Many critics of the organization of work in the U.S. will argue that it is the character of that work itself which is a very significant factor in producing such "problem" behaviors. The research that exists in this area strongly suggests that this is a possibility we should not ignore.[10] It is surprising that in the popular and philosophical discussions of these issues, the following sorts of questions are so rarely asked: Why is it that employees show up drunk or drugged for work? Why is it that they shirk work and responsibility? Why is it that they lie about their credentials or exaggerate them? Why is it that they engage in theft or sabotage? When the question asked is whether the employee privacy that is violated in order to counter such behaviors outweighs or is outweighed by the right to property, the preceding sorts of questions are suppressed. Behaviors which may be symptomatic of a morally sick organization of work are viewed as the underlying cause of the conflict. Then, in a twist of bitter irony, the property rights in which that organization of work is anchored are brought in to beat back the challenge posed by the employees' privacy rights.

Appeals to co-worker health and safety, or to the health and safety of consumers and members of the general public, are also used to justify invasions of worker privacy. No one wants their airline pilot to be high on cocaine or their nuclear power plant operator to be blitzed on Jim Beam. Moreover, protecting people's health and safety does *not* ipso facto give them power over the lives of others. Health and safety are obviously essential conditions for the preservation and exercise of autonomy, perhaps more essential than privacy. So, it would seem that health and safety considerations ought to prevail over privacy considerations.

In response to this, I begin by noting that we should not isolate the issue of whether or not we can invade the privacy of workers to protect health and safety from the larger issue of the role of the current organization of work in generating dangerous behavior. The issue is not simply whether health and safety outweighs privacy, but also whether fundamental changes in the organization of work would lessen or eliminate the behavior that

makes overriding privacy seem so reasonable. It is hard to say whether and to what extent the means many would now use to gather information about employees would be used in a more democratically and humanely organized economy. Such an economy would eliminate or at least lessen the specter of unemployment, and so the felt need to lie about or exaggerate credentials in order to obtain work might be eliminated. Such an economy would give workers more real control over their working lives, and would eliminate the division between those who make decisions at work and those who simply implement the decisions of others. Such an economy would give workers more control over the products of their labor, and give them the power to discipline other workers. How such changes would affect employee morale, productivity, and the sense of responsibility for work performed are things we can only speculate about.

It seems likely that such changes will *not* eliminate all dangerous or destructive behavior on the part of workers. I do not wish to rule out, once and for all, the use of means of acquiring information that encroach on privacy. What I do want to suggest, in closing, is that in a more democratically and humanely organized economy, decisions about what measures to use and when to use them would not be made unilaterally by some people and then simply imposed on others. If we are going to respect the autonomy of persons, then we must give them input into decisions like this that vitally affect their lives.

Notes

1. For a useful discussion of the difficulties in defining privacy, see H. J. McCloskey, "Privacy and the Right to Privacy," *Philosophy,* vol. 55 (1980), pp. 17–38.

2. Joseph Kupfer, "Privacy, Autonomy, and Self-Concept," *American Philosophical Quarterly,* vol. 24 (1987), pp. 81–89. For a similar analysis, see Jeffrey H. Reiman, "Privacy, Intimacy, and Personhood," *Philosophy and Public Affairs,* vol. 6 (1976), pp. 26–44.

3. Kupfer, "Privacy, Autonomy, and Self-Concept," p. 82.

4. Ibid., p. 85.

5. Joseph R. DesJardins, "Privacy in Employment," in *Moral Rights in the Workplace,* Gertrude Ezorsky (ed.) (Albany: State University of New York Press, 1987), pp. 127–139, 131.

6. Ibid., p. 132.

7. George G. Brenkert, "Privacy, Polygraphs, and Work," in *Contemporary Issues in Business Ethics,* Joseph R. DesJardins and John J. McCall (eds.) (Belmont, CA: Wadsworth, 1985), pp. 227–237, 231.

8. Ibid., p. 231. Brenkert admits that the criterion of job relevance is "rather vague," yet proceeds to use it.

9. Adina Schwartz, "Meaningful Work," *Ethics,* vol. 92 (1982), pp. 634–646. Cf. also Edward Sankowski, "Freedom, Work, and the Scope of Democracy," *Ethics,* vol. 91 (1981), pp. 228–242.

10. See, for instance, *Work in America: Report of a Special Task Force to the Secretary of Health, Education, and Welfare* (Cambridge, MA: MIT Press, 1973); Harry Braverman, *Labor and Monopoly Capital: The Degradation of Work in the Twentieth Century* (New York: Monthly Review Press, 1974).

Review and Discussion Questions

1. Lippke maintains that privacy is valuable because of its relation to autonomy and (following Joseph Kupfer) highlights two ways in which privacy contributes to autonomy. Explain the connections between privacy and autonomy. Do you agree that autonomy is the reason privacy is valuable?

2. Relying on a contractual model of employer-employee relations, some writers like DesJardins and Duska use the concept of "job relevance" to restrict the information employers may justifiably gather about employees. What are Lippke's reasons for rejecting this approach? Are you persuaded by his arguments?

3. By contrast with the contractual model, what are Lippke's reasons both for opposing employers' acquiring certain sorts of information and for objecting to certain methods of gathering it?

4. Do you agree with Lippke that there is a grave imbalance in power between employers and employees and that the workplace is characterized by authoritarian management structures that deprive employees of much of their autonomy? What are the implications of viewing privacy rights in this context?

5. How does Lippke respond to the argument that the property rights of owners and stockholders should take precedence over the privacy rights of employees? Do you agree that the existing organization of work contributes significantly to problems like drug use and dishonesty?

Reading ────────────────■

WORKPLACE WARS: HOW MUCH SHOULD *I* BE REQUIRED TO MEET THE NEEDS OF *YOUR* CHILDREN?

CLAUDIA MILLS

Many companies these days are endeavoring to be more "family friendly," but this can be a burden on the childless employees who must sometimes take up the slack when, say, a parent has to leave work early to pick up children. In addition, some employees without children find it unfair that colleagues with children receive benefits that are denied to them. In this essay, Claudia Mills discusses the special needs of parents, what obligations these needs impose on others, and what workplace policies would be fair to employees both with and without children. Although she believes we all have an interest in the successful raising of the next generation, she contends that companies should, as far as possible, treat parents and nonparents alike.

Johnny's mom leaves work early to coach Johnny's soccer team; Katie's dad leaves work early to attend Katie's kindergarten graduation—while other, childless (or, alternatively, childfree) workers stay late to pick up the slack. Johnny's mom and Katie's dad both receive, as part of their benefit packages, health insurance for Johnny and Katie, as well as the opportunity to contribute to a tax-free child-care account—benefits not available to colleagues without children. While many applaud such company efforts to assist working parents, struggling under a dual burden of employment and parenthood, recently a chorus of voices has been raised to challenge "family-friendly" policies, charging that

Reprinted by permission from *Philosophy & Public Policy Quarterly* 21 (Winter 2001). References omitted.

they are friendly to families at the expense of unfairness to fellow workers without children.

Are the special needs of parents ones we should be seeking to meet? If so, who is this "we"—the government, employers, fellow workers? What policies in the workplace are most fair to parents and non-parents alike?

RESPONSIBILITIES, CHOICES, AND NEEDS

One first answer here, which I hear from some of my most environmentally conscious friends, is that the rest of us should bear no responsibility whatsoever for parents' special needs, because people shouldn't be becoming parents in the first place. In a world as crowded as ours, and as environmentally threatened, people should not be having children at all. Admittedly, those in Western, developed nations are not currently reproducing at greater than replacement rates; nonetheless, it is these children who have the heaviest and most destructive "ecological footprint." One of my friends, environmentally outraged, refused to speak to his own brother after his third nephew was born! Few of us subscribe to this draconian environmental ethic, however. Children provide such a great part of the good of life that it seems unreasonable to expect people to forgo the central life experience of parenthood in exchange for environmental benefits that are speculative and diffuse.

On the other end of the spectrum, it is claimed that the continued production of children is a positive good for all of us, and parents are thus to be congratulated, and heartily and humbly assisted in their endeavor. According to this view, those who do not have children, far from being paragons of environmental virtue, are parasites on those who do. Sylvia Ann Hewlett, chairman of the National Parenting Association, is quoted in the *Denver Rocky Mountain News* as saying, "Children are 100 percent of the future and we are all stakeholders in their future because they are the folks who will be paying our Social Security. If you are a childless adult you are kind of a free rider on the effort of raising children." But this view as well seems overstated. Collectively we may need and want *some* people to be having children, but we hardly feel the more, the better. And most of those who have children don't approach the having of children in this light, as a duty grimly assumed for the benefit of humankind generally.

We are left, then, with a middle position. Having children, I claim, is a morally permissible but not morally mandatory choice that persons make to enrich their own lives. This would seem to support the view that the consequences of this choice—the increased needs that parenthood brings—should be regarded by and large as the responsibility of the parents alone. After all, if they didn't want to assume those burdens, they could have refrained from having children. We see a similar reaction in other areas of life in which special needs flow from voluntary choices rather than from the vagaries of chance and the uncertainties of fortune. We question whether we should be collectively providing medical care for those whose medical problems arise from poor lifestyle choices: smoking, overeating, risky sexual behaviors. Moving closer to our current topic, some question whether welfare payments should be provided to poor mothers who repeatedly bear children out of wedlock.

However, even as we question the provision of assistance in such cases, by and large we do continue to provide it, and to feel morally uncomfortable with the refusal to provide it. Our response to need, we hope, is not in the first place dictated by a detached judgment regarding the cause of that need; we aspire to be more open-hearted than that. However, as the need in question becomes chronic rather than acute, and poses a less dire threat to life and health, we rethink our willingness to offer aid. We would rescue a child drowning in a pond, however she came to be floundering there; we don't feel the same way about repeatedly picking up our neighbor's child from day care, when he *could* leave work on time but chooses to stay late. In the latter case, we may wonder whether we have left the realm of "needs" behind altogether.

Yet it may be a mistake to press too heavily on the voluntariness of the choice to bear and raise children. While this is indeed a choice we make, it seems to be misrepresented as a (mere) "lifestyle choice." Having children is such a central part of a full human life, something Aristotle felt comfortable including as a fundamental element in *eudaimonia*, human flourishing. While some—and perhaps a growing number—obviously define flourishing for themselves differently, it is hardly eccentric to view a full human life as including children of one's own (biological or adopted) to love and care for. Life without children seems importantly similar, in my view, to life without sex. There are those who live a full and joyous life without sex; yet most of us don't feel that sex is something we can simply ask people to renounce, as the price of absolving themselves of responsibility for any future offspring (although some of us do). So, while we can consider the bearing and raising of children as a choice, it is not a choice which most people feel blithely free to take or leave, especially given heavy societal pressures and expectations to reproduce.

It is not clear how relevant this concession is, however, to the question we are pursuing here. For even if we accept that parents' special needs don't flow from choices we can reasonably ask them to forgo, we may be wary of workplace policies which place too much weight on the meeting of particular, personal needs. To be blunt, "To each according to his needs" is not, contrary to what many Americans in a recent opinion poll reported believing, a creed enshrined in the American Constitution. While I will argue below that allocation according to need *is* an important principle at the level of government policy, in the workplace other competing principles—such as allocation according to effort, or to accomplishment—command greater allegiance.

In the case of meeting parental need, it would seem strikingly unfair to most of us to pay parents more than non-parents for the same work, on the grounds that they have greater income requirements. In the past considerations such as this provided the rationale for paying men higher salaries (as family "breadwinners") than women without dependents. It is not only the sexism here that troubles us, but also the unfairness of giving greater pay to one employee than to another for the same contribution.

If we move toward the other extreme, however, of disregarding need, we can arrive at some seemingly ludicrous results. Should one worker complain that another, who suffers a heart attack, receives considerably greater benefits from his company-provided health insurance policy than she does from hers? Lisa Benenson, editor of *Working Mother* magazine, is quoted in the *New York Times* as asking, "If the person at the desk next to you gets cancer, do you think of them as 'earning' more because their health dollar costs are higher?" However, the health insurance case is a special one, which can't be generalized too far. The whole idea of health insurance is based on a commitment to risk-sharing; if we were just going to pay for our own health-care needs, unwilling to take a chance on having to pay for anybody else's, we wouldn't have gotten health insurance in the first place. We recognize that health insurance is in some respects a lottery, in which we may emerge as either winners or losers.

A better example to test our willingness to match benefits to needs might be: Suppose a company provides each employee with three days of bereavement leave annually, as needed. Would it make sense to allow the non-bereaved to use this leave to enjoy summer barbecues or time at the spa? Here, while intuitions may differ, this doesn't seem to me absurd. As we shall see below, many employers are moving in precisely this direction, of providing an extensive and variable menu of benefits from which both parents and non-parents can choose at will. Of course, what employers are willing and financially able to provide for all may fall considerably short of what employees in special circumstances need. But here it may be unreasonable for the needy to expect their plight to be addressed by their employer rather than by a general societal safety net.

My conclusion so far, then, is that greater parental need is an insecure foundation for greater parental benefits—partly because the need flows from a voluntary choice (although one that is hardly trivial or eccentric), partly because we are only moderately willing to apportion workplace benefits according to need, in any case.

A more promising approach, I suggest, proceeds as follows. Whatever we decide about the choice to have children, and our appropriate response to the needs generated by it, nobody benefits when children are not raised well. It may or may not be in my interest that you have children; but it is definitely in my interest that your children, once here

to share the planet with me, grow up to be as happy, loving, good, and decent as possible. This is one kind of argument that supports the provision of free public education to all children, financed by the contributions of taxpaying parents and non-parents alike. What good does it do anyone to have children growing up uneducated? And, we can also ask, what good does it do anyone to have children growing up with poor parenting? So even if we understand the choice to have children as one that implies the responsibility to assume at least some of the additional burdens involved in raising these children, we all—parents and non-parents alike—have a stake in seeing these children raised well. We all share an interest in the optimal raising of our future citizens, neighbors, colleagues, and friends.

Now, this argument appeals to the enlightened self-interest of non-parents, regarding the raising of other people's children. It may therefore seem to fall short of grounding actual moral obligations. What if someone were to listen to the argument just offered, and shrug and say, "Maybe I'm being foolishly shortsighted in not wanting to assist you with the raising of your children, but, frankly I just don't care"? Here my response is that one of the deepest problems of political philosophy is to establish actual obligations on the part of those who profess not to care about the collective benefits to be generated by collective cooperation: those who don't want to pay their share for national defense, or environmental protection, or other public goods. It is simply not feasible to permit individuals to opt out at will on the provision of collective benefits, while still remaining full-fledged citizens and members of our common life. Moreover, I argue that it is morally imperative (and not merely optional) for us to ensure that all persons' *basic* needs are met, simply out of respect for basic human rights. Thus, we all bear some responsibility for meeting all children's most basic needs (for food, shelter, health care, and education), not as a duty owed to these children's parents, but as a duty owed to the children, as our fellow human beings, themselves. However, current workplace policies aim beyond the bare meeting of basic, universal human needs, toward facilitating good, rather than just minimally adequate, parenting.

Now, the appeal to the widely shared benefits of optimal child rearing can take us only so far. Raising happy, healthy children is an important societal goal, but it is not our only societal goal. Indeed, raising happy, healthy children is not even the only goal of those children's parents, who presumably continue to care about other aspects of their lives as well: their work, their marriages, their contributions to the larger community. So we need now to consider actual policy proposals regarding the treatment of parents and non-parents in the workplace, and in the community beyond.

HOW FAR DO WE GO?

If we recognize compelling reasons to provide at least some assistance to parents in child rearing, what does this mean in practice? Who should be assisting parents, and how? There is currently a wide range of options possible. The federal government provides tax breaks for parents by giving a $2,800 tax deduction for each dependent in a family, as well as an additional dependent-care credit (up to $4,800), and has recently added a $500 per child tax credit. There are calls for greater governmental subsidization of day care, and for stricter governmental regulation of day care. Employers can provide more or less "family-friendly" policies, ranging from the provision of health insurance benefits for family members, to tax-free dependent-care accounts, to on-site, company-sponsored day care, to flextime and other ways of structuring a more accommodating workplace. And fellow workers and neighbors also lend various amounts of informal assistance: staying late when working parents need to be at home, watching children when working parents need to be at work.

Note that some family-friendly policies make it easier for parents *not* to work (by easing the financial burden imposed by children, and so reducing the need for parents to generate additional income); some make it easier for parents *to* work (by, for example, providing high-quality, affordable day care). Which kind of policies we favor will depend on our other views about how children are best raised: by stay-at-home parents or by working parents. I will not enter that debate here, except to say that, just

as children are an important part of a flourishing, full human life, so is work. Just as I am reluctant to ask workers to forgo being parents, so am I reluctant to ask parents to forgo being workers. I do happen to think it is beneficial for children to see both male and female parents as making some (paid or unpaid) contribution to the world beyond the home. But even if I didn't, I would not want to insist that parents—or any of the rest of us—are required to do *everything possible* to raise the *best possible* children. I will return to this issue below.

At this point, our question is, given the desirability of some family-friendly policies, who should bear the cost of putting family-friendly policies in place? I want to argue that it is best if this cost is shared as widely as possible, by all members of society. For the good in question—the raising of healthy, happy children—is a public good, equally shared by all. Thus, it is preferable, in my view, to provide family benefits through general governmental revenues. This would include tax deductions for dependents (I would limit this to deductions for *two* children, to address the environmental concerns raised above), deductions for child care as a legitimate business expense, and (in an ideal society) provision of welfare services and health care to all children, as to all persons generally.

I find it more problematic when differential benefits are provided to parents not by the government, but by employers (and more problematic still when working parents, through their own informal arrangements, simply impose a greater share of work on childless workers). Here it does seem to me that the provision of differential benefits to working parents violates our strong, long-standing commitment to the principle of equal pay for equal work. Elinor Burkett, author of *The Baby Boon: How Family-Friendly America Cheats the Childless,* says (in a *Denver Post* article), "If compensation packages given to parents are worth $10,000 more than those given to non-parents, then we're compensating parents for their fertility and not their work."

Thus I would argue for company policies that, as far as possible, treat parents and non-parents alike, by extending to all the benefits needed primarily by parents. This would mean offering a mix-and-match menu of benefits from which all workers could choose: health insurance for dependents, additional vacation time, flextime, and so forth. The case for uniform (but more generous) benefits goes like this. Employees have many needs, beyond the need to care for small children. As we move through the cycle of life, the need to care for growing children is replaced by the need to care for aging parents (though some, in the so-called "sandwich generation," may face both needs simultaneously). Employees who struggle with poor health would welcome a less strenuous schedule. Benefits such as flextime and enhanced personal leave (e.g., the typical European worker receives six weeks of annual leave, to our two weeks) would greatly enrich the lives of all workers, parents and non-parents alike. Many commentators have observed the extent to which the early twenty-first century workplace deforms and degrades human life. Juliet Schor, in *The Overworked American,* argues that leisure time has declined steeply for Americans in the past three decades. We work longer for less satisfaction, neglecting other passions and interests. It would be in the interest of all of us to adopt, as Jerome Segal has recently argued, a more graceful and humane pace of life. Theda Skocpol, Professor of Government and Sociology at Harvard, suggests that the solution to the workplace wars lies in looking for "ways to modify working conditions to facilitate both family and community involvements by everyone. In that way, contributions by parents can be considered one of a range of ways in which people engage in caring work and civic involvements." Even now some employers allow, and encourage, their employees to do a certain amount of community service on company time; employers could offer employees a choice of release time for *either* community service *or* family commitments.

Extending this idea still further, we might suggest that government offer tax benefits to its citizens for a range of important and life-enhancing activities: for dependent care generally, rather than child care more narrowly (as is the case with most of the deductions in the current tax code); for continuing education; and even for various other rewarding activities. The core idea here is to permit,

and indeed to promote, the seeking of our own flourishing in our own chosen way.

HAVING IT ALL

Would uniformly more benign workplace (and tax) policies solve the conflict between working parents and non-parents?

It may seem that uniform policies here would do violence to Aristotle's famous injunction to treat likes alike, and unlikes differently. Working parents may still complain that uniform policies would continue to leave them significantly disadvantaged at the end of the day. They have the same health stresses of their own as non-parents, the same obligations to elderly parents, the same need for a more graceful and humane pace of life. Plus, they have *kids.* So they need financial support and release time to meet parental obligations in addition to what they need just to *live.* Moreover, in our society at the present time, this double burden (triple burden? quadruple burden?) is especially likely to fall on women, who still assume a disproportionate share of childcare and other domestic responsibilities.

Here, though, is where I think working parents go too far. Part of maturity, indeed part of living gracefully, is to accept that all resources, including life itself, are finite. Quite simply, the time I spend doing x will be time I will not spend doing y. It would be unreasonable for parents to expect to face no consequences whatsoever for their choice to become parents. While the gendered inequities here trouble me deeply—mothers generally face greater consequences for their choice to become mothers than fathers do for their choice to become fathers—I don't think the best way to address these is to introduce further divisive inequities between parents and non-parents.

While I cannot document this, I suspect that some of the most bitter conflicts with working parents comes from those who consciously chose not to have children so as to pursue other valued objectives. Workers who are not currently parents, but were in the past, may be able to sympathize with working parents, even as they may mourn that certain benefits were not in place when they were struggling to balance home and work. (Of course, some are not: "I struggled without affordable day care; you should have to struggle, too.") Workers who are not currently parents, but will be someday, have a clear interest in seeing family-friendly policies put firmly in place, though this may not be an interest they are able fully to recognize (many of us have stories of friends who made a comically abrupt turn-around here on the day they discovered *they* were about to become parents). Those unable to have children may have less sympathy for working parents' laments: they would give anything to be able to assume such a double "burden." And those who made the decision not to have children just so that they could concentrate on professional success, or a strong marital relationship, or other interests, may well think: I made my choice and I'm living with it; why can't you live with yours?

A memory from my adolescent years comes to mind here. In the days before backpacks, I would limp home every day from school under the groaning weight of a huge armful of heavy textbooks. My best friend Debbie skipped and scampered beside me, unencumbered with any books whatsoever. Finally, one especially hot and weary afternoon, I asked her if she might want to help me out by carrying a few of my books. Her answer stayed with me for the next thirty years. "Claudia," Debbie told me, "if *I* wanted to carry home textbooks, *I'd* carry home textbooks, and *I'd* study, and *I'd* get good grades, but I don't want to carry home textbooks, so I don't." Her message was clear: if I wanted the good grades so badly, I would have to carry the weight of books that went with it.

To learn to live with our choices, and the inescapable limits they impose on us, is to give up the pipe dream of having it all. Yet one of the cruel paradoxes of our time is that just as parents are entering the work force in record numbers, the expectations for what counts as adequate parenting are also increasing. The less time parents have to give to parenting, the more we have come to expect of them as parents. Recent years have seen a staggering proliferation of extracurricular activities for children, all of which require parental chauffeuring, zealous attendance at games, endless recogni-

tion ceremonies. We not only have to be dutiful soccer moms, cheering at every soccer game, but, with children playing in two sports simultaneously, and studying two musical instruments, we have to cheer at every soccer game *and* every swim meet and every piano recital *and* every violin recital, as well as coach their Destination Imagination teams and plan extravaganzas for Vacation Bible School. We have seen the rise of what has been called "hyper-parenting"; we have taken too seriously the goal of *optimal* child rearing, as opposed simply to good parenting.

Now, it is admittedly difficult for individuals to act alone to buck societal trends. Working parents do feel intense pressures today—both to parent as if they were not workers, and to work as if they were not parents. But the sad, or perhaps not so sad, perhaps liberating and joyous, truth is that this can't be done. The sooner we accept this truth, the better it will be for us as workers, as parents, as human beings.

A rich and full life is a great good. I for one do not want to force people to choose between work and parenthood; and we all share some responsibility for meeting children's basic needs and assisting parents in raising tomorrow's citizens. It is best when this responsibility is met by broadly shared tax policies and governmental programs, and by workplace policies that offer a more humane and graceful way of working to parents and non-parents alike. But working parents also need to be realistic and non-hubristic, to accept the limitations of time and life, and experience the distinctive joy that such acceptance can bring.

Review and Discussion Questions

1. Do family-friendly workplace policies sometimes impose a burden on childless people? Is it unfair for corporations to provide special benefits for employees with children and thus spend more money on them than they do on employees without children?

2. Mills seeks a middle way between the view that producing children is a positive social good that we should all support and the view that it

is an environmentally irresponsible choice. Explain. Is the decision to have children simply a "lifestyle choice"?

3. Assess the argument that because parents choose to have children, they are not entitled to any special benefits or consideration in the workplace. Are you persuaded by her argument that it is in the enlightened self-interest of all of us to support the raising of healthy, happy children? What implications, if any, does this argument have for the workplace?

4. Explain why Mills finds it "problematic when differential benefits are provided to parents . . . by employers." Do you agree or disagree with her reasoning? Should companies try to treat

parents and nonparents alike, or should they take into account the special needs of parents?

5. Are the income-tax breaks that parents receive fair or unfair? Mills apparently favors the government's providing special benefits to people with families. If so, why don't corporations have a similar social responsibility?

6. Is it in the self-interest of corporations to adopt family-friendly workplace policies? What policies do you think companies should adopt with regard to maternity/paternity leave, release time for family matters, and day care? Would it ever be appropriate to pay an employee more because of his or her family responsibilities?

Reading ──────────■

PARTICIPATION IN EMPLOYMENT

JOHN J. MCCALL

After distinguishing different types of worker participation, John J. McCall presents five moral reasons that argue in favor of strong worker participation in the codetermination of policy. All of these reasons derive from a need to protect centrally important human goods. McCall contends that, in practice, protection for these goods is most effective when there are strong forms of employee participation. McCall also considers some traditional arguments against participation, none of which, he concludes, are of sufficient weight for rejecting it.

Until recently, worker participation in corporate decision making was a topic largely ignored in Ameri-

can management training and practice. Even in recent years, the attention usually given to worker participation by management theory has been confined to small-scale experiments aimed at increasing labor productivity. Little, if any, attention has been given to the possibility that there is a moral basis for extending a right to participation to all workers.

Numerous explanations for this lack of attention are possible. One is that management sees worker participation as a threat to its power and status. Another explanation may be found in a pervasive ideology underlying our patterns of industrial organization. The ruling theory of corporate property distinguishes sharply between the decision-making rights of ownership and its management representatives on the one hand, and employee duties of loyalty and obedience on the other. The justification for that distinction lies partly in a view of the rights of property owners to control their goods and partly in a perception that nonmanagement employees are technically unequipped to make intelligent policy decisions. The perceived threat to power and this dominant ideology of employment provide for strong resistance even to a discussion of broad worker participation in corporate decisions. But perhaps as strong a source of this resis-

Reprinted by permission from Joseph R. DesJardins and John J. McCall, eds., *Contemporary Issues in Business Ethics*, 4th ed. (Belmont, Calif.: Wadsworth, 2000). Some notes omitted.

tance comes from a confusion about the possible meanings of and moral justifications for worker participation. The primary aim of this essay is to clarify those meanings and justifications. If the essay is successful, it might also suggest that the above sources of resistance to participation should be abandoned.

What people refer to when they use the term "participation" varies widely. We can get a better grasp of that variation in meaning if we recognize that it is a function of variety in both the potential issues available for participatory decisions and the potential mechanisms for that decision making. The potential issues for participation can be divided into three broad and not perfectly distinct categories. First, employees could participate in decisions involving shop-floor operations. Characteristic shop-floor issues are the schedule of employee work hours, assembly line speed, and the distribution of work assignments. Second, employees could participate in decisions that have been the traditional prerogative of middle management. Issues here are hiring or discharge decisions, grievance procedures, evaluations of workers or supervisors, the distribution of merit wage increases, etc. Finally, employees might participate in traditional board-level decisions about investment, product diversification, pricing or output levels, and the like. Simply put, employee participation might refer to participation in decision making over issues that arise at any or all levels of corporate policy.

The mechanisms for participation vary as widely as do the potential issues. These participatory mechanisms vary both in terms of their location within or outside the corporation and in terms of the actual power they possess. For instance, some see employees participating in the shaping of corporate policy by individual acceptance or rejection of employment offers and by collective bargaining through union membership. These mechanisms are essentially external to the particular business institution. Internal mechanisms for participation in corporate policy making include employee stock ownership plans, "quality circle" consulting groups, and bodies that extend employees partial or total effective control of the enterprise. Employee participation through stock ownership might exist ei-

ther through union pension fund holdings or through individual employee profit sharing plans.

Internal participation can also exist in ways more directly related to the day-to-day functioning of the corporation. For example, quality circle participation is a recent adaptation of some Japanese approaches to the management of human resources. Employees in these quality circles are invited to participate in round-table discussions of corporate concerns such as improving productivity. It is important to note that these quality circle groups are advisory only; their function within the corporation is consultative and they have no actual authority to implement decisions.

Distinct from these advisory bodies are those mechanisms by which employees share in the actual power to make corporate policy. Among the mechanisms for such partial effective control are worker committees with authority to govern selected aspects of the work environment or worker representatives on the traditional organs of authority. An example of the former would be an employee-run grievance board; an example of the latter received significant notice in the United States when United Auto Workers' President Douglas Fraser assumed a seat on Chrysler's Board of Directors. Either of these mechanisms provides for only partial control, since one has a highly defined area of responsibility and the other provides employees with only one voice among many.

A final form of participation provides employees with full control of the operations of the corporation. Examples of this extensive participation are rare in North America, although some midwest farm and northwest lumber cooperatives are organized in this way.

. . . This brief survey should indicate that discussions of employee participation must be pursued with care, since arguments criticizing or supporting participation might be sufficient grounds for drawing conclusions about one form of participation but not sufficient grounds for conclusions about other forms. That caution brings us to the second major aim of this essay—the clarification of moral arguments in favor of broad extensions of worker rights to participate in corporate decisions. Five justifications, or arguments, for participation will be sketched. Comments about the issues of mechanisms required by each justification will follow each argument sketch.

ARGUMENT 1

The first . . . justification for employee participation . . . takes its cue from the fundamental objective of any morality—the impartial promotion of human welfare. That requirement of impartiality can be understood as a requirement that we try to guarantee a fair hearing for the interests of every person in decisions concerning policies that centrally affect their lives. Certainly, many decisions at work can have a great impact on the lives of employees. For instance, an employee's privacy and health, both mental and physical, can easily be threatened in his or her working life. Morality, then, requires that there be some attempt to guarantee fair treatment for workers and their interests. We might attempt to institutionalize that guarantee through government regulation of business practices. However, regulation, while helpful to some degree, is often an insufficient guarantee of fair treatment. It is insufficient for the following reasons:

1. Regulation, when it does represent the interests of workers, often does so imprecisely because it is by nature indirect and paternalistic.

2. Business can frequently circumvent the intent of regulations by accepting fines for violations or by judicious use of regulatory appeal mechanisms.

3. Perhaps most importantly, corporate interests can emasculate the content of proposed legislation or regulation through powerful lobbying efforts.

So it seems that an effective guarantee that worker interests are represented fairly requires at least some mechanisms additional to regulation.

We might avoid many of the difficulties of legislation and regulation if workers were allowed to represent their interests more directly whenever crucial corporate decisions are made. Thus, a fair hearing for workers' interests might have a more effective institutional guarantee where workers have available some mechanisms for participa-

tion in those decisions. In practice, then, morality's demand for impartiality presumptively may require worker input in the shaping of corporate policies. . . .

Clearly, if worker interests are to be guaranteed as much fair treatment as possible, the participatory mechanisms must have actual power to influence corporate decisions. For while workers might receive fair treatment even where they lack such power, possession of real power more effectively institutionalizes a *guarantee* of fairness. Thus, internal participatory mechanisms that serve in a purely advisory capacity (e.g., quality circle groups) are obviously insufficient vehicles for meeting the fairness demands of morality.

Less obvious are the weaknesses of individual contract negotiations, union membership, and stock ownership as devices for guaranteeing fairness. None of these devices, in practice, can provide enough power to protect fair treatment for workers. Individual contract decisions often find the prospective employee in a very poor bargaining position. The amount of effective power possessed through union membership varies with the changing state of the economy and with changes in particular industrial technologies. In addition, the majority of workers are not unionized; the declining proportion of union membership in the total work force now stands at about one-fifth. Stock ownership plans provide employees very little leverage on corporate decisions because, commonly, only small percentages of stock are held by workers. Moreover, all three of these participation mechanisms most often have little direct power over the important operating decisions which affect worker interests. . . .

Thus, a serious moral concern for fairness, a concern central to any moral perspective, presumptively requires that mechanisms for employee participation provide workers with at least partial effective control of the enterprise. And since decisions that have important consequences for the welfare of workers are made at every level of the corporation, employees ought to participate on issues from the shop floor to the board room. Moreover, since a balanced and impartial consideration of all interests is more probable when opposing parties have roughly equal institutional power, employees deserve more than token representation in the firm's decision-making structure. Rather, they should possess an amount of authority that realistically enables them to resist policies that unfairly damage their interests. This first moral argument, then, provides strong presumptive support for the right of employees to co-determine corporate policy.

ARGUMENT 2

The second moral argument . . . derives from points that . . . are similar to those of the preceding argument. Any acceptable moral theory must recognize the inherent value and dignity of the human person. One traditional basis for that belief in the dignity of the person derives from the fact that persons are agents capable of free and rational deliberation. We move towards respect for the dignity of the person when we protect individuals from humanly alterable interferences that jeopardize important human goods and when we allow them, equally, as much freedom from other interferences as possible. Persons with this freedom from interference are able to direct the courses of their own lives without threat of external control or coercion. (Such a view of persons provides for the moral superiority of self-determining, democratic systems of government over oppressive or totalitarian regimes.)

This moral commitment to the dignity of persons as autonomous agents has significant implications for corporate organization. Most of our adult lives are spent at our places of employment. If we possess no real control over that portion of our lives because we are denied the power to participate in forming corporate policy, then at work we are not autonomous agents. Instead we are merely anonymous and replaceable elements in the production process, elements with a moral standing little different from that of the inanimate machinery we operate. . . . The moral importance of autonomy in respecting the dignity of persons should make us critical of these traditional patterns of work and should move us in the direction of more employee participation. However, since autonomy is understood as an ability to control one's activities, the preferred mechanisms of participation should allow

employees real control at work. Thus, a commitment to the autonomy and the dignity of persons, just as a commitment to fairness, appears to require that workers have the ability to co-determine policy that directs important corporate activity.

ARGUMENT 3

These first two arguments for broad worker participation rights have ended in an explicit requirement that workers have real and actual power over corporate policy. The final three arguments focus not on actual power but on the worker's *perception* of his or her ability to influence policy. All of these last arguments concern the potential for negative consequences created when workers see themselves as having little control over their working lives.

The third argument warns that workers who believe themselves powerless will lose the important psychological good of self-respect. Moral philosophers have contended that since all persons should be treated with dignity, all persons consequently deserve the conditions that generally contribute to a sense of their own dignity or self-worth. Psychologists tell us that a person's sense of self is to a large degree conditioned by the institutional relationships she has and the responses from others that she receives in those relationships. A person will have a stronger sense of her own worth and will develop a deeper sense of self-respect when her social interactions allow her to exercise her capacities in complex and interesting activities and when they reflect her status as an autonomous human being. Of course, in contemporary America the development of the division of labor and of hierarchical authority structures leaves little room for the recognition of the worker's autonomy or for the ordinary worker to exercise capacities in complex ways. The consequence of such work organization is the well-documented worker burnout and alienation; workers disassociate themselves from a major portion of their lives, often with the psychological consequence of a sense of their own unimportance. Contemporary American patterns of work, then, often fail to provide individuals with those conditions that foster a strong sense of self-respect; instead, they more often undermine self-respect. Numerous studies have indicated that a reversal of these trends is possible where workers are provided greater opportunities for exercising judgment and for influencing workplace activities.

If we take seriously a demand for the universal provision of the conditions of self-respect, we ought to increase opportunities for satisfying work by allowing workers to participate in corporate policy decisions. It would seem, however, that this argument for worker participation need not conclude that workers be given actual power. All that the argument requires is that a worker's *sense* of self-respect be strengthened, and that is at least a possible consequence of participation in an advisory capacity. In fact, worker satisfaction has been shown to increase somewhat when employees are involved in Japanese-style quality circles that offer suggestions for improving production. Nor does it appear that the self-respect argument requires that workers be able to influence all aspects of corporate activity, since an increased sense of one's own significance could be had through participation only on immediate shop-floor issues.

However, we must be careful to estimate the long-range effects on worker alienation and self-respect of these less extensive forms of participation. Some evidence indicates that, over time, workers can grow more dissatisfied and alienated than ever if they perceive the participatory program as without real power or as simply a management attempt to manipulate workers for increased productivity.[1] We should consider, then, that a concern for long-run and substantial increases in self-respect might require workers to exercise some actual authority, of a more than token amount, over the workplace.

ARGUMENT 4

The fourth argument supporting participation also takes its cue from the studies that show repetitive work without control over one's activities causes worker alienation. The specific consequence that this argument focuses on, however, is not a lessening of self-respect but a potential threat to the mental and physical health of workers. Certainly, everyone is now aware that alienated individuals suffer from more mental disturbances and more stress-related physical illnesses. Workers who are

satisfied because they feel able to contribute to corporate policy are held to suffer from less alienation. Since mental and physical health are undoubtedly very central human goods, there seems strong presumptive moral reason for minimizing any negative effects on them that institutional organizations might have. Since broader powers apparently help to minimize such effects, we again have an argument for an expansion of worker rights to participate in corporate decisions.

As with the self-respect argument, however, the issues and mechanisms of participation that this requires are unclear. It could be that negative health effects are minimized in the short run through advisory bodies of participation. On the other hand, minimizing threats to mental or physical well-being in the long run might require more actual authority. Which sorts of mechanisms help most is a question only further empirical research can answer. However, since we have already seen presumptive reasons for actual power to co-determine policy from the first two arguments and since that power can have positive effects on self-respect and health, we perhaps have reasons for preferring the stronger forms of participation if we are presented with a choice between alternatives.

ARGUMENT 5

The fifth argument for worker participation also derives from the purported negative consequences of hierarchical and authoritarian organizations of work. This argument, however, focuses on broader social consequences—the danger to our democratic political structures if workers are not allowed to participate in corporate decisions.

Many political theorists are alarmed by contemporary voter apathy. They worry that with that apathy the political process will be democratic in name only, and that the actual business of government will be controlled by powerful and private economic interests. To reverse this trend that threatens democratic government demands that individual citizens become more involved in the political process. However, increased individual involvement is seen as unlikely unless citizens believe themselves to have political power. But an initial increased sense of one's own political power does not seem possible from involvement in the large macroscopic political institutions of contemporary government. Rather, involvement in smaller, more local and immediate social activities will nurture a sense of political efficacy. Since so much time and attention is devoted to one's work life, the place of employment appears a prime candidate for that training in democracy necessary for development of civic involvement. In fact, powerless and alienated workers can bring their sense of powerlessness home and offer their children lessons in the futility of involvement. Allowing those lessons to continue would only exacerbate the threat to vital democratic institutions. This fifth argument, then, sees participation at work as a necessary condition for the existence of a healthy and lasting system of democracy where citizens have the confidence to engage in self-determining political activities.

Again, since this argument focuses on the worker's perception of his or her own power, it provides presumptive support for those mechanisms that would increase both that sense of power and the tendency for political activity. Just what mechanisms these are can be open to argument. However, as before, if workers feel that their participatory mechanisms lack power, there is the danger that they will become even more cynical about their ability to influence political decisions. And since we have already seen arguments supporting participation with actual power to co-determine policy, there should be a presumption in favor of using mechanisms with real power.

SOURCES OF RESISTANCE

We have, then, five significant reasons for extending to workers a broad right to co-determine corporate policy. Now, in order to determine whether the presumption in favor of worker participation can be overridden, we need only to consider some of the common reasons for resisting this employee right to participate. Common sources of resistance to worker participation are that managers perceive it as a threat to their own status or power, that owners feel entitled to the sole control of their prop-

erty, and that ordinary employees are believed incompetent to make corporate decisions. We shall consider briefly each of these sources of resistance in turn. Our evaluation of these claims will show them to be unacceptable sources of resistance when measured against the above moral reasons in favor of broad participation.

First, in order for management's perception that participation threatens its power to count as an acceptable moral reason for resistance, management power must have some moral basis of its own. According to even traditional conservative theories of corporate property, management has no basic moral right of its own to control the corporation. Rather, management's authority stems from its position as an agent of the economic interests of shareholders, who are seen as the ultimate bearers of a right to use, control, or dispose of property. On the traditional theory, then, management can find a legitimate moral reason for resisting participation only if it can show that schemes of employee participation are real threats to the economic interests of shareholders. . . .

Does participation damage the interests of ownership in a morally unacceptable way? To answer this question, we need to consider what interests ownership has and to what benefits property ownership should entitle one. In the process of confronting these issues, we will also see reasons for suspicion about claims that workers are not capable of participating in the intelligent setting of corporate policy.

In legally incorporated businesses, shareholders commonly have a monetary return on their investment as their principal desire. Moreover, corporate property owners generally have surrendered their interest in day-to-day control of the corporation. The usual owner interest, then, concerns the profitability of the business. Worker participation does not pose a serious threat to this interest in monetary return. Evidence shows that worker participation schemes often improve the economic condition of the business by increasing the interest, motivation, and productivity of employees.[2] In addition, corporations seeking qualified and motivated workers in the future might, out of self-interest, have to construct mechanisms for participation to satisfy the demands of a more slowly growing but more highly educated entry-level labor force. And even in those cases where experiments at worker participation have not succeeded, the failures can often be explained by shortcomings of the particular program that are not generic to all forms of participation. In fact, some of those with experience in constructing participatory work schemes believe that employees can be trained to operate most efficiently with expanded responsibilities.[3] When programs are designed carefully and when time is invested in training both former managers and employees, the competence of workers has not been seen as a crucial reason behind examples of participation's lack of success. Thus, in light of both the marked economic successes of broader worker participation programs and the apparent absence of any *generic* threats to profitability (such as employee incompetence), the economic interests of owners do not appear to provide a substantial basis for a justified resistance to an employee right to participate in corporate decision making.

Some might object, however, that corporate property owners have other interests at stake. Many see a right to control one's goods as fundamental to the concept of property ownership, for example. Thus, they might claim that shareholders have, because of their property ownership, rights to retain control of the business enterprise even if they fail to exercise those rights on a day-to-day basis. This right to control one's property would effectively eliminate the possibility of an employee right to co-determine policy.

There are two reasons, however, to question whether a right to control property can provide a moral basis for denying workers a right to participate in corporate decisions. First, corporate property owners have been granted by society a limit on their legal liability for their property. If a legally incorporated business is sued, owners stand to lose only the value of their investment; an owner of an unincorporated business can lose personal property beyond the value of the business. Part of the motivation behind making this legal limit on liability available was that society would thereby encourage investment activity that would increase the welfare of its members.[4] It is not unreasonable to suggest that this justification for the special legal privilege requires that corporations concern themselves with the welfare of persons within the society in exchange for limited liability. Society, then, places limits on the extent to which owners can direct the use of their corporate property. For example, society can require that corporations concern themselves with the environmental health effects of their waste disposal policies. Failure to require such concern is tantamount to allowing some to profit from harms to others while preventing those others from obtaining reasonable compensation for grievous harms. However, if the legal limitation on liability requires corporations to have some moral concern for the welfare of others, it can also require corporations to protect the welfare of its employees. We have already seen, though, that morally serious goods are at stake when employees are unable to participate significantly in corporate decisions. Thus, if in exchange for limited liability the control of the corporation is to be limited by a concern for others, then the shareholders' interest in controlling corporate property could be limited to allow for an employee right to participate.

A second reason for rejecting the claim that an ownership right to control prohibits employee participation looks not on the legal privileges associated with corporate property but on the very concept of property itself. . . . It is certainly true that property ownership is meaningless without some rights to control the goods owned. It is equally true, however, that no morally acceptable system of property rights can allow unlimited rights to control the goods owned. You, for example, are not allowed to do just anything you please with your car; you cannot have a right to drive it through my front porch. We accept similar restrictions on the control of business property; we prohibit people from selling untested and potentially dangerous drugs that they produce. The point of these examples is to illustrate that control of property, corporate or not, has to be limited by weighing the constraints on owners against the significance of the human goods that would be jeopardized in the absence of the constraints. Acceptable institutions of property rights, then, must mesh with a society's moral concern for protecting the fundamental human goods of all its members.

We have seen in the first part of this essay that there are significant reasons for thinking that important moral values are linked to a worker's ability to participate in corporate decision making. If control of property, personal or corporate, is to override these moral concerns, we need to be presented with an argument showing what more central goods would be jeopardized if employees were granted strong participation rights. The burden of proof, then, is on those who want to deny an employee right to co-determine corporate policy. They must show that an owner's interest in broad control of corporate policy can stand as an interest worthy of protection as a moral right even when such protection would threaten the dignity, fair treatment, self-respect, and health of workers, as well as the continued viability of a democratic polity with an actively self-determining citizenship.

SUMMARY

To summarize: We have seen that there are various understandings of worker participation. The difference between these various understandings is a function of the workplace issues addressed and the participatory mechanisms that address them. We have also seen sketches of five arguments that purport to show a moral presumption in favor of strong worker participation in the form of an ability to actually co-determine policy. We have seen, further, that some traditional sources of resistance to worker participation (a threat to management or owner prerogatives of control, a belief in the incompetence of workers, a fear that profits will suffer) are either not supported by the evidence or are incapable of sustaining a moral basis for rejecting participation. The provisional conclusion we should draw, then, is that our society ought to move vigorously in the direction of a broader authority for all workers in their places of employment.

Notes

1. Cf. Daniel Zwerdling, *Workplace Democracy* (New York: Harper & Row, 1980).

2. Additional evidence is found in the experiences of the small but highly publicized Volvo experiments and of Donnelly Mirrors, Inc. Interviews with heads of both Volvo and Donnelly can be found in *Harvard Business Review,* 55:4 (1977) and 55:1 (1977), respectively. In West Germany, co-determination is mandated by law in some major industries that have been highly competitive with their American counterparts.

3. The Donnelly interview, *op cit.,* and Nancy Foy and Herman Gadon, "Worker Participation: Contrasts in Three Countries," *Harvard Business Review,* v. 54, no. 3 (1976).

4. Cf. W. Michael Hoffman and James Fisher, "Corporate Responsibility: Property and Liability," in *Ethical Theory and Business,* 1st ed., T. Beauchamp and N. Bowie, eds. (Englewood Cliffs, N.J.: Prentice Hall, 1979), pp. 187–196.

Review and Discussion Questions

1. What are the different forms that employee participation can take? Which do you see as the most valuable forms? In your experience, how extensive is employee participation today?

2. McCall argues for participation in terms of the values of fair treatment, human dignity, self-respect, physical and mental health, and the promotion of a democratic society. Explain how each of these values, according to him, supports the case for participation. Are you persuaded by his reasoning?

3. On what grounds does management typically resist worker participation? How sound are its reasons for doing so? Does participation violate the rights of the owners of corporate property?

4. Is worker participation compatible with the efficient functioning of a free-enterprise system?

5. Do you think that more extensive worker participation would make companies more socially responsible? Do you agree with McCall's conclusion "that our society ought to move vigorously in the direction of a broader authority for all workers in their places of employment"?

Further Reading for Chapter 7

Douglas Birsch, "The Universal Drug Testing of Employees," *Business and Professional Ethics Journal* 14 (Fall 1995), **Michael Cranford**, "Drug Testing and the Right to Privacy," *Journal of Business Ethics* 17 (November 1998), and **John R. Rowan,** "Limitations on the Moral Permissibility of Employee Drug Testing," *Business and Professional Ethics Journal* 19 (Summer 2000) examine the ethics of drug testing employees.

Gertrude Ezorsky, ed., *Moral Rights in the Workplace* (Albany: State University of New York Press, 1987) is a good collection of articles on the right to meaningful work, occupational health and safety, employee privacy, unions, industrial flight, and related topics.

Ben Hamper, *Rivethead* (New York: Warner Books, 1992) is a riotous look at life on a GM assembly line.

Sylvia Ann Hewlett, "Executive Women and the Myth of Having It All," *Harvard Business Review* 80 (April 2002) discusses the factors that prevent successful career women from having children.

 InfoTrac College Edition: For further information or to conduct research, please go to www.infotrac-college.com.

John Kaler, "Understanding Participation," *Journal of Business Ethics* 21 (September 2000) discusses different types of employee participation while **John J. McCall,** "Employee Voice in Corporate Governance," *Business Ethics Quarterly* 11 (January 2001) argues for a strong employee right to co-determine corporate policy.

Scott O. Lilienfeld, "Do 'Honesty' Tests Really Measure Honesty?" *Skeptical Inquirer* 18 (Fall 1993) is a critique of honesty exams.

Robert Mayer, "Is There a Right to Workplace Democracy?" *Social Theory and Practice* 26 (Summer 2000) argues on nonlibertarian grounds against such a right.

Adam D. Moore, "Employee Monitoring and Computer Technology." *Business Ethics Quarterly* 10 (July 2000) discusses the tension between privacy and evaluative surveillance.

Ira Sprotzer and **Ilene V. Goldberg**, "Fetal Protection: Law, Ethics, and Corporate Policy," *Journal of Business Ethics* 11 (October 1992) analyzes fetal protection policies and suggests some practical guidelines.

(Consult also the readings suggested at the end of Chapter 6.)

8

Moral Choices Facing Employees

When his eldest daughter asked him, "Why don't you just do what they want?" George Betancourt wasn't sure how he should answer. Betancourt was a senior engineer at Northeast Utilities, which operates five nuclear plants in New England, and all he had done was to speak up and express his professional judgment. Now Northeast wanted him to shut up. First, Northeast's human-resources officer had called him in. After complaining that Betancourt wasn't being a "team player," she described to him the company's termination policies. Three weeks later, Betancourt was informed he was being reassigned. "We'd like to help you, George," Eric DeBarba, vice president of technical services, told him. "But you've got to start thinking company."[1]

George Galatis was the Northeast engineer on whose behalf George Betancourt had spoken up. Galatis had discovered what he considered to be a glaring safety problem at Northeast's Millstone No. 1 nuclear power plant. In an effort to save downtime (and hence money) during the refueling process, the plant's procedures routinely violated federal guidelines and pushed its spent-fuel pool well beyond its design capacity. For eighteen months, Galatis's supervisors denied the problem existed and refused to report it to the Nuclear Regulatory Commission (NRC). Northeast brought in a series of outside experts to

prove Galatis wrong, but the consultants ended up agreeing with him. Within the company, Betancourt backed up Galatis's safety concerns. When Northeast finally began to acknowledge a possible problem, it didn't move fast enough to satisfy Galatis. Two years after having initially raised his safety concerns, he finally took the case directly to the NRC, only to learn that it had known about the unsafe procedures for years. He also discovered evidence that suggested collusion between Northeast and NRC officials to subordinate safety to profitability.

As a result of going to the NRC, Galatis says he experienced "subtle forms of harassment, retaliation, and intimidation." He wasn't just being paranoid. Two dozen Millstone No. 1 employees claimed they were fired or demoted for raising safety concerns. Some of his colleagues sided with the company, however, accusing Galatis of aiding antinuclear activists and trying to take away their livelihood. But Galatis didn't stop. He hired a lawyer who specializes in representing whistle blowers and kept after the NRC. With the lawyer's help, the public spotlight was focused on Millstone No. 1. Local politicians began asking questions. Even though the NRC ignored Galatis, it ended up validating his concerns, and Millstone No. 1 was shut down. Citing chronic safety concerns, employee harassment, and a "historic emphasis on cost savings vs.

performance," the NRC also put Northeast's other two Millstone plants on its high-scrutiny "watch list." And a new NRC head vowed to shake up the regulatory body itself.

Galatis and Betancourt managed to hang on to their jobs, but their careers are at a standstill. "The two Georges had better watch their backs," says one engineer. "Up at Northeast, they've got long memories." A disillusioned Galatis says, "If I had it to do over again, I wouldn't."

For someone in the shoes of George Galatis or George Betancourt, two general issues come up. First is a question of where an employee's overall moral duty lies. For a professional engineer to go public with documented safety concerns may seem to be a more straightforward moral decision than that faced by an employee who suspects irregularities, unsafe procedures, or wrongdoing in an area unrelated to his or her own job. In that case, the employee may possibly have conflicting moral obligations. Furthermore, if an employee reports irregularities to the appropriate authority, the employee must then decide whether he or she is morally obligated to pursue the matter further. Again other moral considerations come into play.

Second, once they have decided that they ought to blow the whistle, employees must face the possible negative consequences. Galatis and Betancourt are skilled, mature, and respected professionals, with established records and good credentials; in terms of employment options, they may have less to risk than do potential whistle blowers who are just starting their careers or who have restricted job options or heavy financial obligations. Nor is this simply a tug of war between moral duty and self-interest. Most moral theorists would agree that depending on the circumstances, certain personal sacrifices might be so great that we cannot reasonably be morally obliged to make them.

These two themes—determining one's moral responsibility amid a welter of conflicting demands and paying the personal costs that can be involved in living up to one's obligations—recur throughout this chapter. In particular, this chapter looks at the following topics:

1. The obligations employees have to the firm, company loyalty, and the problem of conflicts of interest

2. Illegitimate use of one's official position for private gain, through insider trading or access to proprietary data

3. Domestic and foreign bribery and the factors to consider in determining the morality of giving and receiving gifts in a business context

4. The obligations employees have to third parties and the considerations they should weigh in cases of conflicting moral duties or divided loyalties

5. What whistle blowing is and the factors relevant to evaluating its morality

6. The problem of how considerations of self-interest are to be weighed by an employee facing a tough moral choice

OBLIGATIONS TO THE FIRM

When you accept employment, you generally agree to perform certain tasks, usually during certain specified hours, in exchange for financial remuneration. Whether it is oral or written, implicit or explicit, a contract governs your employment relationship and provides the basic framework for understanding the reciprocal obligations between you and your employer. Your employment contract determines what you are supposed to do or accomplish for your employer, and it may cover a variety of other matters from parking privileges to your dress and deportment while carrying out your responsibilities. The terms of your employment contract may be specific and detailed or vague and open-ended.

Loyalty to the Company

Because you are hired to work for your employer, you have an obligation, when acting on behalf of the organization, to promote your employer's interests. Insofar as you are acting as an agent of your employer, the traditional law of agency places you under a legal obligation to act loyally and in good faith and to carry out all lawful instructions. But it would be morally benighted to view employees simply as agents of their employers or to expect them to subordinate entirely their autonomy and private lives to the organization. Morality requires neither blind loyalty nor total submission to the organization.

Some writers, however, have gone to the opposite extreme, denying that employees have any obligation of loyalty to the company, even a prima facie obligation, "because companies are not the kind of things that are properly objects of loyalty." Why not? Because a business firm functions to make money, the argument goes, self-interest is all that binds it together. But "loyalty depends on ties that demand self-sacrifice with no expectation of reward."[2] From this perspective, then, one can owe loyalty to family, friends, or country, but not to a corporation. Employees simply work to get paid, and they are misguided if they see themselves as owing loyalty to the company.

However, the notion of company loyalty is commonplace, and most people find it a coherent and legitimate concept. For the many employees who willingly make sacrifices for the organization above and beyond their job descriptions, loyalty is a real and important value. Indeed, it is not clear how well any business or organization could function without employee loyalty, and certainly most companies want more than minimal time and effort from their employees. Arguably, some obligations of loyalty simply come with the job—for example, the obligation to warn the organization of danger, the obligation to act in a way that protects its legitimate interests, and the obligation to cooperate actively in the furtherance of legitimate corporate goals.[3]

To be sure, many businesses demand more than this in the name of loyalty. They may expect employees to defend the company if it is maligned, to work overtime when the company needs it, to accept a transfer if necessary for the good of the organization, or to demonstrate their loyalty in countless other ways. Displaying loyalty in these ways certainly seems morally permissible, even if it is not morally required.[4] In addition, employees, like other individuals, can come to identify with the groups they are part of, accepting group goals and norms as their own. Some moral theorists believe not only that loyalty to the group can become an important value for the individual employee, but also that in the appropriate circumstances the process of group identification can create an additional obligation of loyalty that the employee would not otherwise have.[5]

Conflicts of Interest

Of course, even the most loyal employees can find that their interests collide with those of the organization. You want to dress one way, the organization requires you to dress another way; you'd prefer to show up for work at noon, the company expects you to be present at 8 A.M.; you'd like to receive $75,000 for your services, the organization pays you a fraction of that figure. The reward, autonomy, and self-fulfillment that workers seek aren't always compatible with the worker productivity that the organization desires. Whatever the matter in question, the perspectives of employee and employer can differ.

Sometimes this clash of goals and desires can take the serious form of a *conflict of interest*. In an organization, a conflict of interest arises when employees at any level have private interests that are substantial enough to interfere with their job duties; that is, when their private interests lead them, or might reasonably be expected to lead them, to make decisions or act in ways that are detrimental to their employer's interests.

As we have seen, the work contract is the primary source of an organization's right to expect employees to act on its behalf in a way that is unprejudiced by their personal interests. In general, if the contents of the work agreement are legal and if the employee freely consents to them, then he or she is under an obligation to fulfill the terms of the agreement. Implicit in any work contract is the assumption that employees will not sacrifice the interests of the organization for personal advantage. Of course, individuals may seek to benefit from being employed with a certain business or organization, but in discharging their contractual employment duties, employees should not subordinate the welfare of the organization for their own gain.

When the situation is such that the employee's private interests run counter to the interests of his or her employer, a conflict of interest exists. Sometimes these private interests may lead an employee to sacrifice the interests of his or her employer. For example, Bart Williams, sales manager for Leisure Sports World, gives all his firm's promotional work to Impact Advertising because its chief officer is Bart's brother-in-law. As a result, Leisure Sports World pays about 15 percent more in advertising costs than it would if its work went to another agency. Here Bart has allowed his decisions as an employee to be influenced by his personal interests, to the detriment of Leisure Sports World. Note that Williams's interest is not financial; a conflict of interest can take various forms.

Suppose that Bart Williams does not throw all of his company's promotional work to his brother-in-law; rather, he gives the firm's business to his brother-in-law only when he sincerely believes that doing so is best for Leisure Sports World. Nevertheless, a conflict of interest can still be said to exist. Because of his brother-in-law, Bart Williams still has a private interest in his business dealings for Leisure Sports World that could possibly lead him to act against the interests of the company. In other words, there is a danger that Bart's judgment may not be as objective as it should be.

Conflicts of interest are morally worrisome not only when an employee acts to the detriment of the organization but also when the employee's private interests are significant enough that they could tempt the employee to do so. That's why alarm bells went off when *Business Week* disclosed that two members of the audit committee at Qwest Communications, which was already under fire for its dubious accounting practices, directed companies with million-dollar contracts with Qwest, thus raising questions about their ability to exercise independent judg-

ment.[6] By definition, to have a conflict of interest is to be in a morally risky situation; that is why employees should avoid such situations. But deciding when the employee's private interests in a business transaction are substantial enough for the situation to constitute a conflict of interest can be difficult. Equally difficult can be deciding what employees should do when they find themselves with a conflict of interest. The answers to these questions probably need to be determined on a case-by-case basis.

Financial Investments. Conflicts of interest may exist when employees have financial investments in suppliers, customers, or distributors with whom their organizations do business. For example, Monica Walters, purchasing agent for Trans-Con Trucking, owns a substantial amount of stock with Timberline Paper. When ordering office supplies, Walters buys exclusively through a Timberline affiliate, even though she could get the identical supplies cheaper from another supplier. In this case, Walters has acted against Trans-Con's interests. But even if Walters never advantages herself this way, a conflict of interest still exists.

It's impossible to say how much of a financial investment is necessary for a serious conflict of interest to exist. Ordinarily it is acceptable to hold a small percentage of stock in a publicly held supplier that is listed on the stock exchange. Some organizations state what percentage of outstanding stock their members may own— usually up to 10 percent. Companies may also restrict the percentage of the employee's total investment funds that are involved in an investment. Some corporations even require key officers to make a full disclosure of all outside interests or of other relationships that could cloud their judgment or adversely affect their ability to promote the organization's interests. Organizational policy goes a long way toward determining the morally permissible limits of outside investments because it reflects the firm's specific needs and interests. Because such a policy can affect the financial well-being of those who fall under it, however, it should be subjected to the same kind of free and open negotiations that any form of compensation is.

ABUSE OF OFFICIAL POSITION

The use of one's official position for personal gain always raises moral concerns and questions because of the risk that one will thereby violate one's obligations to the firm or organization. Examples range from using subordinates for non-organization-related work to abusing a position of trust within an organization to enhance one's own financial leverage and holdings. Executives who use corporate funds for private purposes like health club memberships, extravagant parties, vacation travel, or remodeling their homes are guilty of this, as are CEOs like Bernard J. Ebbers of WorldCom, John Legere of Global Crossing, or L. Dennis Kozlowski of Tyco International, who used their high positions to borrow huge amounts of money at below market rates—in Ebbers's case over $400 million—from the companies they worked for.[7]

Insider Trading

One common way of abusing one's official position is through insider trading. *Insider trading* refers to the use of significant facts that have not yet been made public and are likely to affect stock prices. For example, as soon as he learned that the Food and Drug Administration was not going to approve his company's highly touted cancer drug Erbitux, Dr. Sam Waksal, the former CEO of ImClone Systems, knew its stock would plummet. Before the FDA's decision was made public, however, Waksal quickly but quietly sold his stock in the company and told his father and one of his daughters to do so as well. He is also alleged to have passed the word on to his friend, Martha Stewart, who dumped her ImClone stock the day before the FDA announced its decision.[8] One doesn't have to profit personally to cross the line, however. For example, the wife of the president and chief executive of Genentech was charged with insider trading for providing confidential information to her brother. Before the biotechnology firm was partly acquired by another company, she told her brother that "some good things were about to happen" to the company and suggested that he buy a few thousand dollars' worth of stock, even if he had to borrow the funds. She also advised him to keep the purchase secret and make it in the name of a "trustworthy" friend.[9]

Inside traders ordinarily defend their actions by claiming that they don't injure anyone. It's true that trading by insiders on the basis of nonpublic information seldom directly injures anyone. But moral concerns arise from indirect injury, as well as from direct. As one author puts it, "What causes injury or loss to outsiders is not what the insiders knew or did; rather it is what [the outsiders] themselves did not know. It is their own lack of knowledge which exposes them to risk of loss or denies then an opportunity to make a profit."[10] Case in point: the famous Texas Gulf Sulphur stock case.

When test drilling by Texas Gulf indicated a rich ore body near Timmins, Ontario, some officials at Texas Gulf attempted to play down the potential worth of the Timmins property in a press release by describing it as only a prospect. But four days later a second press release termed the Timmins property a major discovery. In the interim, inside investors made a handsome personal profit through stock purchases. At the same time, stockholders who unloaded stock based on the first press release or who sold the stock short, anticipating its price would fall, lost money.

The Securities and Exchange Commission (SEC), which is charged with policing the stock market, subsequently charged that a group of insiders—including Texas Gulf directors, officers, and employees—had violated the disclosure section of the Securities Exchange Act of 1934 by purchasing stock in the company while withholding information about the rich ore strike the company had made. The courts upheld the charge, finding that the first press release was "misleading to the reasonable investor using due care."[11] As a result, the courts not only ordered the insiders to pay into a special court-administered account all profits they made but also ordered them to repay profits made by outsiders whom they had tipped. The courts then used this account to compensate persons who had lost money by selling their Texas Gulf Sulphur stock on the basis of the first press release. This incident illustrates how indirect injury can result from insider dealings and the legal risks that insiders run in trading on inside information.

To be sure, insider dealings raise intriguing questions. When can employees buy and sell securities in their own companies? How much information must they disclose to stockholders about the firm's plans, outlooks, and prospects? When must this information be disclosed? There's also the question, Who is considered an insider? Corporate executives, directors, officers, and other key employees are certainly insiders. But what about outsiders whom a company temporarily employs, such as accountants, lawyers, and contractors? Or what about those who just happen upon inside information?

In its effort to police the marketplace, the SEC has interpreted "insider" in a broad sense to mean anyone who buys or sells stock based on nonpublic information—whether or not the person is a corporate officer or otherwise linked to the company whose stock is being bought or sold. However, in 1980 the U.S. Supreme Court challenged the SEC's broad conception of insider trading in the case of Vincent Chiarella, a financial printer who traded on information he culled from documents passing through his shop. The Court ruled that Chiarella was not an insider with fiduciary responsibilities and thus had not violated the Securities Exchange Act. The Court reinforced its decision three years later when it reversed the conviction of securities analyst Raymond Dirks, who advised several of his clients to dump their shares in a company that he was about to blow the whistle on for fraud. In so ruling, the Court held that there is nothing improper about an outsider's using information, as long as the information is not obtained from an insider who breaches a legal duty to the corporation's shareholders for personal gain or to show favor to friends.

Since then the SEC has developed a new tactic, arguing that people who trade on confidential information but are not traditional company insiders are guilty of insider trading if they have "misappropriated" sensitive information. Although some appellate courts had rejected the SEC's approach, in 1997 the Supreme Court endorsed the misappropriation theory of insider trading in *U.S. v. O'Hagan,* thus upholding one of the SEC's main legal weapons against insider trading. In this case, James O'Hagan, a lawyer, had reaped a $4.3 million profit after learning that a company represented by his law firm was planning a hostile takeover of another company. O'Hagan had not worked on the case himself, but he had—the Court ruled—misappropriated confidential information belonging to his firm and its client. Writing for the majority, Justice Ruth Bader Ginsburg stressed that the Court's decision reflected the "animating purpose" of the Securities and Exchange Act, namely, "to insure honest securities markets and thereby promote investor confidence."[12]

Arthur Levitt, Jr., chairman of the Securities and Exchange Commission at the time, applauds the Court's decision, stating that it "reaffirms the SEC's effort to make the stock market fair to all people, whether you're a Wall Street veteran or a Main Street newcomer."[13] Law professor Henry Manne, however, sees nothing inherently wrong with insider trading and thinks the SEC should stay totally out of the insider-trading field. "The use of insider information should be governed by private contractual relationships," he believes, such as those between corporations and their personnel or between a law firm and its members.[14]

At the core of this disagreement are two opposed perspectives on what makes the market work. Levitt and like-minded analysts contend that the marketplace can work only if it is perceived as being honest and offering equal investment opportunity. Insider trading, they argue, makes that impossible. Those who think like Manne believe that permitting insiders to trade is good for the market because it accelerates the flow of information to other shareholders and investors. As a result, information is more quickly reflected in stock prices, which is healthy for the market. They also believe that permitting insider trading can benefit a company by providing employees an incentive to invent new products, put together deals, or otherwise create new information that will increase the value of a company's stock.

Philosophy professor Jennifer Mills Moore agrees with Manne that it is difficult to prove that insider trading harms ordinary investors or to show that there is something unfair about it. However, she argues that insider trading is wrong because it undermines the fiduciary relationship, which is central to business management. Employees have a duty to act in the interests of the firm and its shareholders, but many ways of profiting from insider information do not benefit the company at all—indeed, they may seriously damage its interests.[15]

The information that employees garner within the company is not always the kind that affects stock prices. Sometimes the information concerns highly sensitive data related to company research, technology, product development, and so on. How employees treat such secret or classified data can also raise important moral issues.

Proprietary Data

Companies guard information that can affect their competitive standing with all the zealousness of a bulldog guarding a ham bone. Take Procter & Gamble, for example. Having patented the baking technique of its Duncan Hines brand of homemade-style chocolate chip cookies a few years ago, it then sued three rival food chains, charging them with using the patented process to make "infringing cookies." P&G further claimed that these companies had spied at a sales presentation and at cookie plants. One company allegedly even flew a spy plane over a P&G plant under construction. One of the defendants, Frito-Lay, admitted to sending a worker to photograph the outside of a Duncan Hines bakery. But it denied telling the man's college-age son to walk into the plant and ask for some unbaked cookie dough—which the enterprising youth did, and got. Frito-Lay insisted that it destroyed both the pictures and the dough without scrutinizing either and formally apologized to P&G. It also countersued P&G for trying to eliminate competition.[16]

When novel information is patented or copyrighted, it is legally protected but not secret. Others may have access to the information, but they are forbidden to use it (without permission) for the life of the patent or copyright. When a company patents a process, as Kleenex did with pop-up tissues, for example, the company has a monopoly on that process. Until the patent expires, no other firm may compete in the production of pop-up facial tissues. Although on the face of it this rule violates the ideal of a free market and would appear to slow the spread of new processes and technology, patents and copyrights are generally defended on the ground that without them technological innovation would be hampered. Individuals and companies would not be willing to invest in the development of a new process if other firms could then immediately exploit any new invention without having themselves invested in developing it.

Although patent law is complicated and patents are not easy to acquire, what it means for something to be patented is well defined legally. By contrast, the concept of a *trade secret* is broad and imprecise. The standard legal definition says that a trade secret is "any formula, pattern, device, or compilation of information which is used in one's business and which gives him an opportunity to obtain an advantage over competitors who do not know or use it."[17] Virtually any information that is not generally known (or whose utility is not recognized) is eligible for classification as a trade secret, as long as such information is valuable to its possessor and is treated confidentially. Most states have laws against the theft of trade secrets, and the Economic Espionage Act of 1996 makes it a federal crime. Nevertheless, trade secrets do not enjoy the same protection as patented information. The formula for Coca-Cola, for instance, is secret but not patented. No competitor has yet succeeded in figuring it out by "reverse engineering," but if your company managed to do so, then it would be entitled to use the formula itself.

There are at least three arguments for legally protecting trade secrets: (1) trade secrets are the intellectual property of the company; (2) the theft of trade secrets is unfair competition; and (3) employees who disclose trade secrets violate the confidentiality owed to their employers.[18] In individual cases, what constitutes intellectual property, unfair competition, or a violation of confidentiality can often be controversial. But clearly one of the biggest challenges facing an organization can be to prevent its trade secrets and proprietary data from being misused by its own employees.

This is an especially troublesome problem in high-tech firms, in which employees who are privy to sensitive information are especially prone to job hopping. (For example, the average job tenure of an executive in the software industry is a scant twenty-two months.[19]) Two factors conspire to make this a morally complicated problem: (1) the individual's right to seek new employment and (2) the difficulty of separating trade secrets from the technical knowledge, experience, and skill that are part of the employee's own intellect and talents.

A classic case involved Donald Wohlgemuth, who worked in the spacesuit department of B. F. Goodrich in Akron, Ohio.[20] Eventually Wohlgemuth became general manager of the spacesuit division and learned Goodrich's highly classified spacesuit technology for the Apollo flights. Shortly thereafter, Wohlgemuth, desiring a higher salary, joined Goodrich's competitor, International Latex Corporation in Dover, Delaware, as manager of engineering for the industrial area that included making spacesuits in competition with Goodrich. Goodrich protested by seeking an order restraining Wohlgemuth from working for Latex or for any other company in the space field. The Court of Appeals of Ohio denied Goodrich's

request for an injunction, respecting Wohlgemuth's right to choose his employer, but it did provide an injunction restraining Wohlgemuth from revealing Goodrich's trade secrets.

Cases like Wohlgemuth's are fundamentally different from those involving insider trading, for they pit a firm's right to protect its secrets against an employee's right to seek employment wherever he or she chooses. As a result, the moral dilemmas that arise in proprietary-data cases are not easily resolved. For one thing, the trade secrets that companies seek to protect have often become an integral part of the departing employee's total capabilities. They may, for instance, manifest themselves simply in a subconscious or intuitive sense of what will or will not work in the laboratory. Wohlgemuth's total intellectual capacity included the information, experience, and technical skills acquired at his former workplace. Goodrich might be justified in claiming much of Wohlgemuth's intellectual capacity as its corporate property, but it is difficult to see how he could divest himself of it.

One can also ask whether Wohlgemuth acted morally in leaving Goodrich for a competitor, the legality of his action notwithstanding. Wohlgemuth certainly thought so. When asked by Goodrich management whether he considered his action moral, he replied, "Loyalty and ethics have their price, and International Latex has paid the price."

BRIBES AND KICKBACKS

A *bribe* is a remuneration for the performance of an act that's inconsistent with the work contract or the nature of the work one has been hired to perform. The remuneration can be money, gifts, entertainment, or preferential treatment.

A typical but blatant case was that of Norman Rothberg, an accountant working at ZZZZ Best Carpet Cleaning Company in the Los Angeles area. When he learned that ZZZZ Best had falsified accounts on insurance restoration jobs, he gave the information to the accounting firm of Ernst & Whinney, which was overseeing ZZZZ Best's planned multimillion-dollar acquisition of another carpet-cleaning chain. When an investigation began, Rothberg accepted $17,000 from ZZZZ Best officials to back off from his initial reports.[21]

Rothberg's conduct was wrong because he accepted money in exchange for violating his responsibilities as an accountant. By contrast, a server who accepts a gratuity for providing good service to a restaurant customer is not accepting a bribe, for she is not violating her duties. However, the situation would be different if she took money in exchange for not charging the customer for the drinks he ordered. Of course, bribery can occur in more subtle forms than in the Rothberg case. For instance, in exchange for a "sympathetic reading of the books," a company gives a state auditor a trip to Hawaii. Or a sporting goods company provides the child of one of its retailers with free summer camp in exchange for preferred display space for its products. In both instances, individuals have received payments inconsistent with their job contract or the nature of the work they are expected to perform.

Bribery sometimes takes the form of *kickbacks*, a practice that involves a percentage payment to a person able to influence or control a source of income. Thus, Alice Farnsworth, sales representative for Sisyphus Books, offers a book-selection committee member a percentage of the handsome commission she stands to make if a Sisyphus civics text is adopted. The money the committee member receives for the preferred consideration is a kickback. A flagrant case of kickbacks involved American executives of the Honda Motor Company. For years they pocketed millions in bribes and kickbacks from local car dealers; in return, the dealers received permission to open lucrative dealerships and had no trouble obtaining models (such as the Acura) that were in scarce supply and could be sold at a large profit.[22]

The Foreign Corrupt Practices Act

Bribery is generally illegal in the United States, but U.S. companies have a history of paying off foreign officials for business favors. Such acts were declared illegal in the Foreign Corrupt Practices Act (FCPA) of 1977, which was passed in the wake of the discovery that nearly 400 U.S. companies had made such payments over several years amounting to about $300 million. Egregious within this sordid pattern of international bribery was Lockheed Aircraft Corporation's $22 million in secret payoffs to foreign politicians to get aircraft contracts. Lest one understate the effects of such bribery, it is worth noting that revelations of Lockheed bribes in Japan caused a government crisis there and that in Holland Prince Bernhard was forced to resign his government duties after admitting that he took a $1 million payoff from Lockheed. Gulf Oil also admitted to making secret payments to foreign politicians—specifically, $4 million to the ruling political party in South Korea to firm up its investments there. Exxon confirmed that it paid $59 million to Italian politicians to promote its business objectives in that country. And only after the suicide of United Brands chairman Eli Black did an SEC investigation reveal that the company had paid a $1.25 million bribe to a Honduran official to win a reduction in that country's business export tax.

The FCPA provides stiff fines and prison sentences for corporate officials engaging in bribery overseas and requires corporations to establish strict accounting and auditing controls to guard against the creation of slush funds from which bribes can be paid. The FCPA does not, however, prohibit "grease payments" to the employees of foreign governments who have primarily clerical or ministerial responsibilities. These payments are sometimes necessary to ensure that the recipients carry out their normal job duties. On the other hand, the FCPA makes no distinction between bribery and extortion. A company is extorted by a foreign official if, for instance, the official threatens to violate the company's rights, perhaps by closing down a plant on some legal pretext, unless the official is paid off.

One company caught violating the FCPA was Ashland Oil. Under its then-CEO Orin Atkins, Ashland had agreed to pay an entity controlled by an Omani government official approximately

$29 million for a majority interest in Midlands Chrome, Inc., a price far higher than it was worth, for the purpose of obtaining crude oil at a highly favorable price. When Atkins proposed the acquisition of Midlands Chrome to his board of directors, he said that although the acquisition was a high-risk project, it "had the potential for being more than offset by a potential crude oil contract." Midlands Chrome did not in fact prove particularly profitable, but the Omani government awarded Ashland a contract for 20,000 barrels a day for one year at a three-dollar-per-barrel discount from the regular selling price—a discount worth $21.9 million.[23]

The Case Against Overseas Bribery

The FCPA has been weakened by amendments that expand the exemption for grease payments and offer corporations more defenses against prosecution. In 1998, however, the law was extended to include bribery by foreign firms on American territory, and, thanks to the Federal Sentencing Guidelines, penalties are now stiffer than those originally specified by the FCPA. Few companies, though, are charged with violating the law—the Justice Department brings an average of only 1.5 cases per year, the SEC even fewer.[24] Nevertheless, critics of the FCPA insist that it puts American corporations at a competitive disadvantage in relation to foreign firms whose governments permit them to bribe. They assert that the law has resulted in lost exports for the United States.

However, competition is not always a factor in foreign bribes, as the United Brands case illustrates. In addition, studies show that before passage of the FCPA, when U.S. companies used bribery to beat out competitors, their competitors were usually other U.S. companies. As former Commerce Secretary Elliot Richardson reported to Congress, "in a multitude of cases—especially those involving the sale of military and commercial aircraft—payments have been made not to outcompete foreign competitors, but rather to gain a competitive edge over other U.S. manufacturers."[25] Furthermore, studies

show that the FCPA has been at most a minor disincentive to export expansion. Even in nations where the FCPA is alleged to have hurt American business, there has been no statistically discernible effect on U.S. market share. In fact, since passage of the FCPA, U.S. trade with bribe-prone countries has outpaced its trade with other countries.[26]

In 1997 the world's industrialized nations—the twenty-nine members of the Organization for Economic Cooperation and Development—formally agreed for the first time to a treaty that outlaws the bribing of foreign officials. This agreement makes it less likely that the FCPA will put American companies at a competitive disadvantage in the future. But even if the FCPA does handicap U.S. firms and cause them to lose exports, this fact would have to be carefully weighed against the ample documentary evidence of the serious harm done to individuals, companies, and governments as a result of systematic bribery overseas.

A frequently heard argument against the FCPA is that the law imposes U.S. standards on foreign countries and that bribery and payoffs are common business practices in other nations. But this argument is too glib, especially when it comes from those who don't really have a working knowledge of another culture. In some other nations, to be sure, bribery does seem more widespread than it is here, but that doesn't imply that bribery is considered morally acceptable even in those nations. (Drug dealing is not morally acceptable here, even though it is, unfortunately, widespread.) If other countries really did consider bribery and related practices to be morally acceptable, then presumably the people engaging in them would not mind having this fact publicized. But it is difficult to find a real-life example of foreign officials willing to let the public know they accept bribes.

Certainly the FCPA reflects our own moral standards, but those standards are not simply matters of taste (like clothing styles) or completely arbitrary (like our decision to drive on the right, whereas the British drive on the left). Good, objective arguments can be given against bribery and related corrupt practices because they are intended to induce people inside a business or other organization to make a decision that would not be justifiable according to normal business or other criteria. For example, by encouraging on nonmarket grounds the purchase of inferior goods or the payment of an exorbitant price, bribery can clearly injure a variety of legitimate interests—from stockholders to consumers, from taxpayers to other businesses. It subverts market competition by giving advantage in a way that is not directly or indirectly product related.

There is nothing "relative" about the damage that such corruption can do to a society. Studies show that the more corrupt a nation is, the less it invests and the slower its economic growth.[27] If we were to permit U.S. companies to engage in bribery overseas, we would be encouraging in other countries practices that we consider too harmful to tolerate at home. Moreover, even an occasional corporate bribe overseas can foster bribery and kickbacks at home and lead employees to subordinate the interest of the organization to their own private gain. Corruption is difficult to cordon off; once a company engages in it, corruption can easily spread throughout the organization.

The multiple impacts of bribery can be succinctly drawn out in one final case, which involved Bethlehem Steel Corporation, the nation's second-largest steel company. Bethlehem was fined $325,000 by a federal judge for bribery and other corrupt practices stretching over four years. Bethlehem admitted paying bribes to shipowners' representatives, including officers of the Colombian Navy. The bribes were paid to ensure that ships needing repairs would be steered into Bethlehem's eight shipyards. Thus, competitive bidding for the contracts was effectively eliminated, various members of the Colombian Navy were corrupted, and the Colombian government presumably ended up paying more for the repair work than it had to. Beyond this, Bethlehem generated more than $1.7 million for the payoffs by padding bills and skimming profits from legitimate shipyard repair work.

Thus, unsuspecting clients of Bethlehem were made to pay the bill for Bethlehem's bribery.

GIFTS AND ENTERTAINMENT

Business gifts and entertainment of clients and business associates are a familiar part of the business world. Still, both practices can raise conflict-of-interest problems and even border on bribery, but knowing where to draw the line is not always easy. One thing is clear: Those who cross that line, wittingly or not, can end up in big trouble. Ask the former General Services Administration (GSA) official who pleaded guilty to a criminal charge of accepting free lunches from a subsidiary of the BellSouth Corporation, which was seeking a telephone contract with the GSA.[28]

The federal government, in fact, now provides its procurement officers with two days' worth of lectures and case-study discussions on the ethics of government contracting. Procurement officers, for example, are taught that they may accept an invitation to speak before a trade association consisting of the contractors they buy from, but they must decline the fifty-dollar honorarium, whatever the topic of their talk. They must also refuse a ticket for their transportation to the meeting, although they may be permitted to accept lunch as a guest seated at the head of the table, if this is compatible with the policy of their particular agency.[29]

For people in the business world, the rules are not so cut and dried, but a number of considerations can help one determine the morality of giving and receiving gifts in a business situation.

1. *What is the value of the gift?* Is the gift of nominal value, or is it substantial enough to influence a business decision? Undoubtedly, definitions of "nominal" and "substantial" are open to interpretation and are often influenced by situational and cultural variables. Nevertheless, many organizations consider a gift worth twenty-five dollars or less given infrequently—perhaps once a year—only nominal, but anything larger or more frequent would constitute a substantial

gift. Although this standard won't fit all cases, it does indicate that accepting even a rather inexpensive gift might be deemed inappropriate.

2. *What is the purpose of the gift?* Dick Randall, a department store manager, accepts small gifts such as pocket calculators from an electronics firm. He insists that the transactions are harmless and that he doesn't intend to give the firm any preferential treatment in terms of advertising displays in the store. As long as the gift is not intended or received as a bribe and remains nominal, there doesn't appear to be any serious problem. But it would be important to ascertain the electronics firm's intention in giving the gift. Is it to influence how Randall lays out displays? Does Randall himself expect it as a palm-greasing device before he'll ensure that the firm receives equal promotional treatment? If so, extortion may be involved. Important to this question of purpose is a consideration of whether the gift is directly tied to an accepted business practice. For example, appointment books, calendars, or pens and pencils with the donor's name clearly imprinted on them serve to advertise a firm. Trips to Hawaii rarely serve this purpose.

3. *What are the circumstances under which the gift was given or received?* A gift given during the holiday season, for a store opening, or to signal other special events is circumstantially different from one unattached to any special event. Whether the gift was given openly or secretly should also be considered. An open gift, say, with the donor's name embossed on it, raises fewer questions than a gift known only to the donor and recipient.

4. *What is the position and sensitivity to influence of the person receiving the gift?* Is the person in a position to affect materially a business decision on behalf of the gift giver? In other words, could the recipient's opinion, influence, or decision result in preferential treatment for the donor? Another important point is whether the recipients have made it abundantly clear to the donors that they don't intend to allow the gift to influence their action one way or the other.

5. *What is the accepted business practice in the industry?* Is this the customary way of conducting this kind of business? Monetary gifts and tips are standard practice in numerous service industries. Their purpose is not only to reward good service but to ensure it again. But it's not customary to tip the head of the produce department in a supermarket so the person will put aside the best tomatoes for you. When gratuities are an integral part of customary business practice they are far less likely to pose moral questions.

6. *What is the company's policy?* Many firms explicitly forbid the practice of giving and receiving gifts to minimize even the suspicion that a conflict may exist. Kmart, for example, adopted such a policy, which it requires not only its managers, but also its vendors, suppliers, and real estate associates to sign, after one of its corporate directors was indicted for accepting kickbacks.[30] When such a policy exists, the giving or receiving of a gift would normally be wrong.

7. *What is the law?* Certain federal, state, or local government employees, for example, may be forbidden by law from receiving any gifts from firms with which they do business. When gift transactions violate the law, they are clearly unacceptable.

Related to gift giving is the practice of entertaining. Some companies distinguish entertainment from gifts as follows: If you can eat or drink it on the spot, it's entertainment. In general, entertainment should be interpreted more sympathetically than gifts because it usually occurs within the context of doing business in a social situation. Still, the morality of entertainment should be evaluated along the same lines as gifts—that is, with respect to value, purpose, circumstances, position and sensitivity to influence of the recipient, accepted business practice, company policy, and the law. In each case the ultimate moral judgment hinges largely on whether an objective party could reasonably suspect that the gift or entertainment might lead the recipient to sacrifice the interest of the firm for his or her personal gain.

OBLIGATIONS TO THIRD PARTIES

Consider the following situations:

A worker knows that a fellow worker occasionally sips whiskey on the job. Should she inform the boss?

A dishwasher knows that the restaurant's chef typically reheats three- or four-day-old food and serves it as fresh. When he informs the manager, he is told to forget it. What should the dishwasher do?

A consulting engineer discovers a defect in a structure that is about to be sold. If the owner will not disclose the defect to the potential purchaser, should the engineer do so?

A clerical worker learns that the personnel department has authorized hirings that violate the firm's anti-nepotism rules and neglect its affirmative action commitments. What should she do about it?

On a regular basis, a secretary is asked by her boss to lie to his wife about his whereabouts. "If my wife telephones," he tells her, "don't forget that 'I'm calling on a client.'" In fact, as the secretary well knows, the boss is having an affair with another woman. What should the secretary do?

Such cases are not unusual, but they are different from the ones previously considered in this chapter because they involve workers caught in the crossfire of competing ethical concerns and moral responsibilities. Should the employee ensure the welfare of the organization by reporting the fellow worker who drinks, or should she be loyal to her coworker and say nothing? Should the dishwasher go public with what he knows or should he simply forget the matter? Should the secretary carry out her boss's instructions, or should she tell his wife the truth? In each case the employee may experience conflicting obligations, diverging ideals, and divided loyalties.

Many of the difficult moral decisions that employees sometimes face involve such conflicts. How are they to be resolved? According to the procedure recommended in Chapter 2, our moral decisions should take into account our specific obligations, any important ideals that our actions would support or undermine, and, finally, the effects or consequences of the different options open to us. To begin with the latter consideration, remember that even staunch nonconsequentialists acknowledge that the likely results of our actions are relevant to their moral assessment and that we have some duty to promote human well-being. In general, the fuller our understanding of the possible results of the different actions we might take in the specific situation before us—that is, the better we understand the exact ramifications of the alternatives—the more likely we are to make a sound moral decision. Reflecting on the effects of these different courses of action can help us understand what ideals are at stake and determine the exact strength of the more specific obligations we have.

The impact of our actions on significant moral ideals is the second consideration to be weighed. Any serious moral decision should take into account the various ideals advanced or respected, ignored or hindered, by the alternative courses of conduct open to us. In addition, our moral choices are often strongly influenced by the personal weight we place on the different values at stake in a specific situation. Sometimes these values can point in different directions, as when our simultaneous commitment to professional excellence, personal integrity, and loyalty to friends pulls us in different ways.

Finally, any responsible moral decision must, of course, take into account the more specific obligations we have—in particular, those obligations that are a function of the particular relationships, roles, or circumstances we happen to be in. This chapter has already discussed the obligations employees have to the organization based on a freely negotiated work contract, and it is easy to see that employees have moral obligations arising from the business, professional, or organizational roles they have assumed. For example, teachers have an obligation to grade fairly, bartenders to refrain from overserving intoxicated customers, engineers to guarantee the safety of their projects, and accountants to certify that financial statements present data fairly and according to generally accepted accounting principles. Because of his or her role responsibilities, an auditor who suspects some irregularity has an obligation to get to the bottom of the matter, whereas an ordinary employee who has a hunch that something is not in order in another department probably would not have that responsibility.

Thus, employees have certain general duties to their employers, and because of the specific business, professional, or organizational responsibilities they have assumed, they may have other more precise role-based obligations. In addition, employees are human beings with moral responsibilities to friends, family, and coworkers—to those flesh-and-blood people with whom their lives are intertwined, both inside and outside the workplace. These ongoing relationships are the source of important moral obligations.

What about the obligations of employees to other parties or to society in general? In particular, what obligations do employees have to people with whom they have no relationship and for whom they have no specific professional, organizational, or other role responsibility? Here different moral theories may steer us in slightly different directions, but simply as a matter of ordinary commonsense morality it is clear that employees—like everyone else—have certain elementary duties to other people. Of particular significance are the obligations to avoid injuring others and to be truthful and fair.

When faced with a moral decision, then, employees should follow the two-step procedure set forth in Chapter 2: identify the relevant obligations, ideals, and effects and then try to decide where the emphasis should lie among these considerations. There is nothing mechanical about this process, but when we as employees weigh moral decisions, two simple things can help keep our deliberations free from the various rationalizations to which we are all prone. First, we can ask ourselves whether we would be willing to read an account of our actions in the newspaper. That is, when we have made our decisions, are the contemplated actions ones that we would be willing to defend publicly? Second, discussing a moral dilemma or ethical problem with a friend can often help us avoid bias and gain a better perspective. People by themselves, and especially when emotionally involved in a situation, sometimes focus unduly on one or two points, ignoring other relevant factors. Input from others can keep us from overlooking pertinent considerations, thus helping us make a better, more objective moral judgment.

As the preceding discussion mentioned, employees sometimes learn about the illegal or immoral actions of a supervisor or firm. When an employee tries to correct the situation within institutional channels and is thwarted, a central moral question emerges: Should the employee go public with the information? Should a worker who is ordered to do something illegal or immoral, or who knows of the illegal or immoral behavior of a supervisor or organization, inform the public?

Whistle Blowing

Morris H. Baslow, a forty-seven-year-old biologist and father of three, won't forget the day he dropped an envelope in the mail to Thomas B. Yost, an administrative law judge with the Environmental Protection Agency (EPA). For later that day, Baslow was fired from his job with Lawler, Matusky & Skelly, an engineering consulting firm that had been hired by Consolidated Edison of New York to help it blunt EPA demands. The EPA was insisting that the power company's generating plants on the Hudson River had to have cooling towers to protect fish from excessively warm water that it was discharging into the river.

Baslow claimed that the documents he sent showed that Con Ed and Lawler, Matusky & Skelly had knowingly submitted to the EPA invalid and misleading data, giving the false impression that the long-term effects of the utility's effluent on fish were negligible. On the basis of his own research, Baslow believed that the fish could be significantly harmed by the warm-water discharge. He said that for two years he tried to get his employers to listen, but they wouldn't.

Shortly after being fired, Baslow sent seventy-one company documents supporting his allegation to the EPA, the federal Energy Regulatory Commission, and the Justice Department. In the month following these disclosures, Baslow's employers accused him of stealing the documents and sued him for defamation. Baslow countersued, citing the Clean Water Act, which protects consultants from reprisals for reporting findings prejudicial to their employers and clients.

A year later, Lawler, Matusky & Skelly dropped all legal action against Baslow and gave him a cash settlement, reportedly of around $100,000. In return, Baslow wrote to the EPA and other government agencies, withdrawing his charges of wrongdoing and perjury but not recanting his own scientific conclusions. Asked why he finally accepted the cash payment, the unemployed Baslow said, "I've had to bear the brunt of this financially by myself. . . . I just wish somebody had listened to me six months ago."[31]

The Baslow case and scores more like it illustrate the ethical problem and personal risks facing employees who blow the whistle on what they perceive as organizational misconduct.

Whistle blowing refers to an employee act of informing the public about the illegal or immoral behavior of an employer or organization. One expert more fully defines whistle blowing as:

A practice in which employees who know that their company is engaged in activities that (a) cause unnecessary harm, (b) are in violation of human rights, (c) are illegal, (d) run counter to the defined purpose of the institution, or (e) are otherwise immoral inform the public or some governmental agency of those activities.[32]

Another business ethicist spells out the concept this way:

Whistle-blowing is the voluntary release of nonpublic information, as a moral protest, by a member or former member of an organization outside the normal channels of communication to an appropriate audience about illegal and/or immoral conduct in the organization or conduct in the organization that is opposed in some significant way to the public interest.[33]

These definitions limit the scope of what constitutes whistle blowing. Whistle blowing is something that can be done only by a (past or present) member of an organization. An investigative reporter, for example, who exposes corporate malfeasance is not a whistle blower. Nor is an employee who spreads gossip about in-house gaffes and indiscretions, thus abusing confidentiality and acting disloyally to colleagues and to the organization. By contrast, whistle blowing refers to exposing activities that are harmful, immoral, or contrary to the public interest or to the legitimate goals and purposes of the organization. It does not encompass sabotage or taking retaliatory action against the employer or firm, but it does require going outside normal channels. (This doesn't imply, however, that whistle blowing must be external. Most writers on the subject hold that there can also be internal whistle blowing, where disclosure of inappropriate conduct is made to someone inside the organization.)

Professor of philosophy Norman Bowie correctly points out that today's discussion of whistle blowing parallels the discussion of civil disobedience in the 1960s.[34] Just as civil disobedients of that time felt their duty to obey the law was overridden by other moral obligations, so the whistle blower overrides loyalty to colleagues and to the organization in order to serve the public interest. Coleen Rowley, for example, was a veteran FBI agent with twenty-one years of experience who had never worked for anyone else—indeed, she had wanted to be an agent ever since she was in fifth grade. When she decided to go public with evidence that her bosses had failed to follow up on information that might have thwarted the terrorist attacks of September 11, 2001, and were now misleading the public about what the FBI had known, her desire to do what was right took precedence over her lifelong love of the Bureau. Although whistle blowers like Rowley are often stigmatized as "disloyal," many of them see themselves as acting in the best interests of the organization.

Whistle blowing does, however, present dangers, as Professor Sissela Bok reminds us.[35] The whistle can be blown in error or malice, privacy invaded, and trust undermined. Not least, publicly accusing others of wrongdoing can be very destructive and brings with it an obligation to be fair to the persons accused. In addition, internal prying and mutual suspicion make it difficult for any organization to function. And, finally, one must bear in mind that whistle blowers are only human beings, not saints, and they can sometimes have their own self-serving agenda.[36]

In developing his analogy with civil disobedience, Professor Bowie proposes several conditions that must be met for an act of whistle blowing to be morally justified. These conditions may not be the last word on this controversial subject, but they do provide a good starting point for further debate over the morality of whistle blowing. According to Bowie, whistle blowing is morally justified only if:

1. *It is done from an appropriate moral motive.* For an act of whistle blowing to be justified, it must be motivated by a desire to expose unnecessary harm, illegal or immoral actions, or conduct counter to the public good or the defined purpose of the organization. Desire for attention or profit or the exercise of one's general tendency toward stirring up trouble is not a justification for whistle blowing.

Although, as Chapter 2 explained, the question of motive is an important one in Kantian ethics, not all moral theorists would agree with Bowie's first condition. Might not an employee be justified in blowing the whistle on serious wrongdoing by the employer, even if the employee's real motivation was the desire for revenge? Granted that the motivation was ignoble, the action itself might nonetheless have

been the morally right one. An action can still be morally justified, say some theorists, even when it is done for the wrong reason. Still, many people were troubled to learn that the whistle-blowing paralegal who provided anti-tobacco lawyers with crucial documents about a tobacco company's secret studies on the health dangers of cigarettes was paid more than $100,000 by the lawyers.[37]

2. *The whistle blower, except in special circumstances, has exhausted all internal channels for dissent before going public.* The duty of loyalty to the firm obligates workers to seek an internal remedy before informing the public of a misdeed. This is an important consideration, but in some cases the attempt to exhaust internal channels may result in dangerous delays or expose the would-be whistle blower to retaliation.

3. *The whistle blower has compelling evidence that wrongful actions have been ordered or have occurred.* Spelling out what constitutes "compelling evidence" is difficult, but employees can ask themselves whether the evidence is strong enough that any reasonable person in a similar situation would be convinced that the activity is illegal or immoral. Although this may not be a decisive guideline, the standard of what a reasonable person would believe is commonly invoked in other cases, such as deceptive advertising and negligence lawsuits.

4. *The whistle blower has acted after careful analysis of the danger: How serious is the moral violation? How immediate is the problem? Can the whistle blower point to specific misconduct?* These criteria focus on the nature of the wrongdoing. Owing loyalty to employers, employees should blow the whistle only for grave legal or moral matters. The greater the harm or the more serious the wrongdoing, the more likely is the whistle blowing to be justified. Indeed, in some circumstances, whistle blowing may not only be morally justified; it may be morally required. Additionally, employees should consider the time factor. The greater the time before the violation is to occur, the more likely the firm's own internal mechanisms will prevent it; and the more immediate a violation, the more justified the whistle blowing. Finally, the whistle blower must be specific. General allegations, such as that a company is "not operating in the best interests of the public" or is "systematically sabotaging the competition," won't do. Concrete examples are needed that can pass the other justificatory tests.

5. *The whistle blowing has some chance of success.* This criterion recognizes that the chances of remedying an immoral or illegal action are an important consideration. Sometimes the chances are good; other times they're slim. Probably most cases fall somewhere between these extremes. In general, whistle blowing that stands no chance of success is less justified than that with some chance of success. Even so, one may sometimes be justified in blowing the whistle when there is no chance of success. Sometimes merely drawing attention to an objectionable practice, although it may fail to improve the specific situation, encourages government and society to be more watchful of certain behavior. Still, given the potential harmful effects of whistle blowing, it seems fair to say that justification for whistle blowing increases with the chances of success.

THE QUESTION OF SELF-INTEREST

Conspicuously absent so far in the discussion of obligations to third parties and the special problem of whistle blowing has been any mention of the worker's own interests. And yet for many employees, protecting themselves or safeguarding their jobs is the primary factor in deciding whether to put third-party interests above those of the firm.

Concern with self-interest in cases that pit loyalty to the firm against obligations to third parties is altogether understandable and even warranted. After all, workers who subordinate the organization's interests to an outside party's expose themselves to charges of disloyalty, disciplinary action, freezes in job status, forced relocations, and even dismissal. Furthermore, even when an employee successfully blows the whistle, he or she can be blacklisted in an indus-

try. Given the potential harm to self and family that employees risk in honoring third-party obligations, it is perfectly legitimate to inquire about the weight considerations of self-interest should be given in resolving cases of conflicting obligations.

Sadly, there is no clear, unequivocal answer to this question. Moral theorists and society as a whole do distinguish between prudential reasons and moral reasons. "Prudential" (from the word *prudence*) refers here to considerations of self-interest; "moral" refers here to considerations of the interests of others and the demands of morality. Chapter 1 explained that it is possible for prudential and moral considerations to pull us in different directions. One way of looking at their relationship is this: If prudential concerns outweigh moral ones, then employees may do what is in their own best interest. If moral reasons override prudential ones, then workers should honor their obligations to others.

Consider the case of a cashier at a truck stop who is asked to write up phony chits so truckers can get a larger expense reimbursement from their employers than they really deserve. The cashier doesn't think this is right, so she complains to the manager. The manager explains that the restaurant is largely dependent on trucker business and that this is a good way to ensure it. The cashier is ordered to do the truckers' bidding and is thus being told to violate at least three duties owed to any outside party (in this case, the trucking firms): truth, noninjury, and fairness. Given these moral considerations, the cashier ought to refuse, and perhaps she should even report the conduct to the trucking companies.

But let's suppose that the cashier happens to be a recent divorcée with no formal education. She lacks occupational skills and stands little chance of getting another job in an economy that happens to be depressed—for months she was unemployed before landing her present position. With no other means of support, the consequences of job loss for her would be serious indeed. Now, given this scenario and given that the wrongdoing at issue is relatively minor, prudential concerns would probably take legitimate precedence over moral ones. In other words, the cashier would be justified in "going along," at least on a temporary basis.

Some moral theorists would agree with this conclusion but analyze the case somewhat differently. They think it is incorrect to say that in some circumstances we may permit prudential considerations to outweigh moral considerations. There is no neutral perspective outside both morality and self-interest from which one can make such a judgment. Furthermore, they would say that, by definition, nothing can outweigh the demands of morality.

Does that mean the cashier should refuse to do what her manager wants and, thus, lose her job? Not necessarily. Morality does not, these theorists contend, require us to make large sacrifices to right small wrongs. Writing up phony chits does violate some basic moral principles, and the cashier has some moral obligation not to go along with it. But morality does not, all things considered, require her—under the present circumstances—to take a course of action that would spell job loss. She should, however, take less drastic steps to end the practice (like continuing to talk to her boss and the truckers about it) and perhaps eventually find other work. Thus, according to this way of thinking, the cashier is not sacrificing morality to self-interest in "going along" for a while. The idea is that morality does not impose obligations on us without regard to their cost; it does not, under the present circumstances, demand an immediate resignation by the cashier.

Whichever way one looks at it, the question of balancing our moral obligations to others and our own self-interest is particularly relevant to whistle blowing. In situations in which whistle blowing threatens one's livelihood and career, prudential concerns may properly be taken into account in deciding what one should do, all things considered. This doesn't mean that if the worker blows the whistle despite compelling prudential reasons not to, he or she is not moral. On the contrary, such an action could be highly moral. (As Chapter 2 explained, ethical theorists term such actions "supererogatory," meaning

that they are, so to speak, above and beyond the call of duty.) On the other hand, when the moral concerns are great (for example, when the lives of others are at stake), elementary morality and personal integrity can require people to make substantial sacrifices.

A couple of further remarks are in order here. First, an evaluation of prudential reasons obviously is colored by one's temperament and perceptions of self-interest. Each of us has a tendency to magnify potential threats to our livelihood or career. Exaggerating the costs to ourselves of acting otherwise makes it easier to rationalize away the damage we are doing to others. In the business world, for instance, people talk about the survival of the firm as if it were literally a matter of life and death. Going out of business is the worst thing that can happen to a firm, but the people who make it up will live on and get other jobs. Keeping the company alive (let alone competitive or profitable) cannot justify seriously injuring innocent people.

Not only do we tend to exaggerate the importance of self-interested considerations, but also most of us have been socialized to heed authority. As a result, we are disinclined to question the orders of someone above us, especially when the authority is an employer or supervisor with power to influence our lives for better or worse. It's easy for us to assume that any boat rocking will be very harmful, even self-destructive.

It follows, then, that each of us has an obligation to perform a kind of character or personality audit. Do we follow authority blindly? Do we suffer from moral tunnel vision on the job? Do we mindlessly do what is demanded of us, oblivious to the impact of our cooperation and actions on outside parties? Have we given enough attention to our possible roles as accomplices in the immoral undoing of other individuals, businesses, and social institutions? Do we have a balanced view of our own interests versus those of others? Do we have substantial evidence for believing that our livelihoods are really threatened, or is that belief based more on an exaggeration of the facts? Have we been imaginative in trying to balance prudential and moral concerns? Have we sought to find some middle ground, or have we set up a false self-other dilemma in which our own interests and those of others are erroneously viewed as incompatible? These are just some of the questions that a personal inventory should include if we are to combat the all-too-human tendency to stack the deck in favor of prudential reasons whenever they are pitted against moral ones.

A second observation about the relationship between prudential and moral considerations concerns the welfare of society. In some cases, as we have seen, considerations of self-interest may mean one does not have an overriding moral obligation to blow the whistle; when that occurs, how can society be protected from wrongdoing? Is the welfare of society to be left to those few heroic souls willing to perform supererogatory actions? Perhaps the only reasonable solution is to restructure business and social institutions so such acts no longer carry such severe penalties.

Although a hodgepodge of legal precedents and state and federal legislation already affords some assistance to employees who blow the whistle, the Sarbanes-Oxley Act of 2002 marks an important advance. The act provides sweeping new legal protection for employees who report possible securities fraud, making it unlawful for companies to "discharge, demote, suspend, threaten, harass, or in any other manner discriminate against" them. Fired workers can sue, and they are guaranteed the right to a jury trial instead of having to endure months or years of administrative hearings. In addition, the Labor Department can order companies to rehire terminated whistle blowers with no court hearings whatsoever. Moreover, executives who retaliate against employees who report possible violations of *any* federal law now face imprisonment for up to ten years.

On the other hand, the law alone is not enough. Corporate attitudes need to change. In America, the *Economist* magazine writes, "it is almost always thought cheaper to fire whistle-blowers than to listen to them, despite years of legislation designed to achieve the opposite."[38]

Kris Kolesnik, director of the National Whistle-blower Center, is equally pessimistic. "No matter how many protections whistleblower laws have created over the years," he says, "the system always seems to defeat them."[39] In the long run, however, organizations benefit more from encouraging employees to come forward with their ethical concerns than they do from ignoring possible wrongdoing and retaliating against those who raise awkward queries. Openness and a receptive attitude toward moral questioning by employees give the organization a chance to take corrective action. This can save it money (by rooting out embezzlement, say, or forestalling litigation) or at least—as recent scandals make clear—help it to head off worse trouble when the problems bothering employees eventually leak out to the public.

To discharge their moral responsibilities and safeguard their own interests, companies need to develop explicit, proactive whistle-blowing policies. As a minimum, these policies should state that employees aware of possible wrongdoing have a responsibility to disclose that information; specific individuals or groups outside the chain of command should be designated to hear those concerns; employees who in good faith disclose perceived wrongdoing should be protected from adverse employment consequences; and there should be a fair and impartial investigative process.[40] In these ways, management can create organizational procedures and a corporate culture that make it less likely that employees will be forced to blow the whistle externally.

SUMMARY

1. The employment contract creates various obligations to one's employer. In addition, employees often feel loyalty to the organization. Conflicts of interest arise when employees have a personal interest in a transaction substantial enough that it does, or might reasonably be expected to, lead them to act against the interests of the organization.

2. When employees have financial investments in suppliers, customers, or distributors with whom the organization does business, conflicts of interest can arise. Company policy usually determines the permissible limits of such financial interests.

3. *Insider trading* refers to the use of significant facts that have not yet been made public and will likely affect stock prices. Insider trading seems unfair and can injure other investors. In practice, determining what counts as insider trading is not always easy, but it typically involves misappropriating sensitive information. Some writers defend insider trading as performing a necessary and desirable economic function.

4. *Proprietary data* refers to an organization's classified or secret information. Increasingly, problems arise as employees in high-tech occupations with access to sensitive information and trade secrets quit and take jobs with competitors. Proprietary-data issues pose a conflict between two legitimate rights: the right of employers to keep certain information secret and the right of individuals to work where they choose.

5. A *bribe* is payment in some form for an act that runs counter to the work contract or the nature of the work one has been hired to perform. The Foreign Corrupt Practices Act prohibits corporations from engaging in bribery overseas. Bribery generally involves injury to individuals, competitors, or political institutions and damage to the free-market system.

6. The following considerations are relevant in determining the moral acceptability of gift giving and receiving: the value of the gift, its purpose, the circumstances under which it is given, the position and sensitivity to influence of the person receiving the gift, accepted business practice, company policy, and what the law says.

7. Employees have duties to their employers, and they may also have more specific obligations based on the business or professional roles and responsibilities they have assumed. In addition, they have the same elementary moral obligations that all human beings have—including the obligation not to injure others and to be truthful and fair.

8. Balancing our obligations to employer or organization, to friends and coworkers, and to third parties outside the organization can create conflicts and divided loyalties. In resolving such moral conflicts, we must identify the relevant obligations, ideals, and effects and decide where the emphasis among them should lie.

9. *Whistle blowing* refers to an employee informing the public about the illegal or immoral behavior of an employer or organization.

10. An act of whistle blowing can be presumed to be morally justified if it is done from the appropriate moral motive; if the whistle blower, except in special circumstances, has exhausted internal channels before going public; if the whistle blower has compelling evidence; if the whistle blower has carefully analyzed the dangers; and if the whistle blowing has some chance of success.

11. Prudential considerations based on self-interest can conflict with moral considerations, which take into account the interests of others. Some sacrifices of self-interest would be so great that moral considerations must give way to prudential ones. But employees must avoid the temptation to exaggerate prudential concerns, thereby rationalizing away any individual moral responsibility to third parties. Legislation can protect whistle blowing so that it involves less personal sacrifice.

CASE 8.1

Changing Jobs and Changing Loyalties

Cynthia Martinez was thrilled when she first received the job offer from David Newhoff at Crytex Systems. She had long admired Crytex, both as an industry leader and as an ideal employer, and the position the company was offering her was perfect. "It's just what I've always wanted," she told her husband, Tom, as they uncorked a bottle of champagne. But as she and Tom talked, he raised a few questions that began to trouble her.

"What about the big project you're working on at Altrue right now? It'll take three months to see that through," Tom had reminded her. "The company has a lot riding on it, and you've always said that you're the driving force behind the project. If you bolt, Altrue is going to be in a real jam."

Cynthia explained that she had mentioned the project to David Newhoff. "He said he could understand I'd like to see it through, but Crytex needs someone right now. He gave me a couple of days to think it over, but it's my big chance."

Tom looked at her thoughtfully and responded, "But Newhoff doesn't quite get it. It's not just that you'd like to see it through. It's that you'd be letting your whole project team down. They probably couldn't do it without you, at least not the way it needs to be done. Besides, Cyn, remember what you said about that guy who quit the Altrue branch in Baltimore."

"That was different," Cynthia responded. "He took an existing account with him when he went to another firm. It was like ripping Altrue off. I'm not going to rip them off, but I don't figure I owe them anything extra. It's just business. You know perfectly well that if Altrue could save some money by laying me off, the company wouldn't hesitate."

"I think you're rationalizing," Tom said. "You've done well at Altrue, and the company has always treated you fairly. Anyway, the issue is what's right for you to do, not what the company would or wouldn't do. Crytex is Altrue's big competitor. It's like you're switching sides. Besides, it's not just a matter of loyalty to the company, but to the people you work with. I know we could use the extra money, and it would be a great step for you, but still . . ."

They continued to mull things over together, but the champagne no longer tasted quite as good. Fortunately, she and Tom never really argued about things they didn't see eye to eye on, and Tom wasn't the kind of guy who would try to tell her what she should or shouldn't do. But their conversation had started her wondering whether she really should accept that Crytex job she wanted so much.

Discussion Questions

1. What should Cynthia do? What ideals, obligations, and effects should she take into account when making her decision?

2. Would it be unprofessional of Cynthia to drop everything and move to Crytex? Would it show a lack of integrity? Could moving abruptly to Crytex have negative career consequences for her?

3. Is it morally wrong, morally permissible, or morally required for Cynthia to take the new job? Examine Cynthia's choice from a utilitarian point of view. How would Kant and Ross look at her situation?

4. What does loyalty to the company mean, and how important is it, morally? Under what circumstances, if any, do employees owe loyalty to their employers? When, if ever, do they owe loyalty to their coworkers?

CASE 8.2

Profiting on Columns
Prior to Publication

In the April 1995 issue of *Money* magazine, managing editor Frank Lalli wrote a column criticizing the magazine's rival, *Smart Money,* for permitting one of its writers to tout stocks in which he had a personal investment. Seven months later, Lalli's righteousness turned to embarrassment when *Business Week* reported that the SEC was investigating Dan Dorfman, *Money's* star columnist and syndicated stock tipster, based on reports of conflicts of interest and possible insider trading. *Money* subsequently dismissed Dorfman. Dorfman denies any wrongdoing, but the allegations against him bring to mind the controversial case of R. Foster Winans.

Along with their morning cup of coffee, readers of *The Wall Street Journal* got a shock one day when the paper announced that it had fired Winans, author of its highly influential stock market column, "Heard on the Street." This was immediately after the thirty-six-year-old business analyst admitted to federal investigators that he had leaked information about upcoming columns to associates who were then able to profit from the information by buying or selling stock.

A month later the SEC charged Winans with violating federal law by failing to disclose to readers that he had financial interests in the securities he wrote about. Winans, whose tips about columns prior to publication helped two stockbrokers net about half a million dollars, also was charged with personally profiting from the material.[41]

The basis of the charges was an SEC rule that prohibits anyone from omitting to state a material fact regarding the purchase or sale of securities. But the applicability of the SEC rule to the Winans case is unclear. Professor of journalism Gilbert Cranberg phrases the ambiguity this way: "Is the ownership by a reporter of stock in a company about which he writes a 'material fact' to readers sufficient to require disclosure, or must the reporter also intend to profit from the story?"[42] Ambiguous or not, the SEC's action has convinced some legal scholars that the media must disclose the financial holdings of their financial analysts.

Even before the Winans case, some publications had formulated explicit policies designed to leave no doubt in reporters' minds about the impropriety of trading on knowledge of stories. For example, the *Washington Post* requires that all its financial and business reporters submit to their editors a confidential statement outlining their stock holdings. *Post* policy prohibits writers from either writing about companies in which they have an interest or buying stock in companies they have written about. *The New York Times* has a similar policy, and *Forbes* magazine and the *Chicago Tribune* require editorial employees to divulge their corporate investments. Ralph Schulz, senior vice president at McGraw-Hill's publication unit, says his company has a conflict-of-interest policy based on the premise that "nobody who writes about a company ought to own stock in it."[43] *The Wall Street Journal's* three-and-a-half-page conflict-of-interest policy warns employees against trading in companies immediately before or after a *Journal* piece on that company. The policy reads in part:

> It is not enough to be incorruptible and act with honest motives. It is equally important to use good judgment and conduct one's outside activities so that no one—management, our editors, an SEC investigator with power of subpoena, or a political critic of the company— has any grounds for even raising the suspicion that an employee misused a position with the company.[44]

But such written policies remain the exception, as shown by an informal survey of the country's media conducted by *The Wall Street Journal.* Although many newspapers have formal dress codes, few have formal rules about stock trading. Moreover, few news executives show any concern about insider trading by noneditorial employees, although sensitive investigative reports generally are accessible to any employee in the newsroom.

The Wall Street Journal survey also reveals general indifference among media executives to stock trading by subjects of interviews, as in the case of G. D. Searle & Co. The SEC began investigating unusual activity in options on that company's stock just before the broadcast of a *CBS Evening News* report that raised questions about NutraSweet, Searle's new low-calorie sweetener. The SEC charged that an Arizona scientist interviewed by CBS for the report bought "put" options in Searle's NutraSweet before the story aired in order to profit when the stock tumbled as a result of negative comments by himself and others. "I honestly believe I had a right to do it," says the Arizona scientist. He adds, "I don't think it's unethical. It's the American way."[45] The scientist's lawyer and some CBS employees also were targets of the SEC investigation.

Dan Dorfman admits that his stories may affect the price of stocks, and by implication, shrewd subjects of interviews could stand to benefit on the stories. But he doesn't think there's anything he can do about that. "It's not my job to police," Dorfman says. "My job is to get information." John G. Craig, Jr., editor of the *Pittsburgh Post Gazette,* agrees. In his view, preventing sources from trading on an article "is an ethical responsibility a newspaper can't assume."[46] And yet James Michaels, the editor of *Forbes,* recalls once pulling a story when he learned that one of the sources had sold stock short, betting the article would have a negative impact. Likewise, *The Wall Street Journal* admits to killing stories when learning that investors were using their knowledge of them to wheel and deal on Wall Street.

In the case of R. Foster Winans, the government took a strong stand against such wheeling and dealing, with the Justice Department filing a sixty-one-count indictment for fraud and conspiracy against him and two alleged collaborators. Among other things, the indictment charged that Winans and his roommate speculated on stocks about to be mentioned in forthcoming columns. They made about a $4,500 profit on a $3,000 investment.[47] Although Winans described his role in these deals as "stupid" and "wrong," he denied he broke any law. After a long and technical legal battle, the U.S. Supreme Court upheld the Justice Department's contention that what he did was not just imprudent but criminal.

Professor Cranberg fears that the Winans case may ultimately make bad law. Although he thinks that the time has come for reporters and editors to report outside compensation and financial interests, he worries that the SEC and the courts may equate business-news reporters with investment advisers and, as a result, wield undue influence on the press.

Cranberg fears that such a development not only threatens freedom of the press but would have a chilling effect on press coverage of corporate America. "Not every problem has, or should have, a legal solution," Cranberg points out. "Most problems involving the press are best handled by voluntary measures. The way for the press to show that it can keep its house in order is to do it. More actions and less self-satisfied ridicule of concern about conflicts of interest would be signs that the press can and will."[48]

Michael Missal, a lawyer for the SEC, thinks such fears are unfounded. "We don't expect every journalist to disclose all financial relationships," he says. Instead, the government wishes to prevent profiteering on advance knowledge of stories. That, Missal says, is what the Winans case is all about.[49]

Discussion Questions

1. In your opinion, did Winans engage in insider trading? Did he do something wrong? Explain why or why not.

2. Did Winans violate some duty owed to his employer? What obligations, ideals, and effects should he have considered before acting as he did?

3. Do you believe that media financial analysts should disclose to their audience any financial interests they have in the securities they write about? Do you think they should be required to make such disclosures? If so, should the requirement take the form of an institutional policy, law, or both?

4. Does it make a difference to your assessment whether it is only the reporter who profits from prior knowledge of his or her financial story? Morally speaking, is it better or worse if the reporter does not profit but others do?

5. Do you think that McGraw-Hill's policy— that "nobody who writes about a company ought to own stock in it"—is fair? Or do you think it is an unreasonable encroachment on the employee's right to profit through investments?

6. Do you agree that the Arizona scientist had a right to trade on the information before it was broadcast?

7. What do you think Kant's position on insider trading would be? How would utilitarians look at it? What about libertarians?

8. Under what circumstances does a company have a right to know about the financial investments of its employees?

CASE 8.3

Two Who Made
Waves for the Navy

Zeke Storms, a fifty-two-year-old retired Navy chief, began his career as a whistle blower when he wrote Congressman Charles Pashayan to protest proposed cuts in the federal budget.[50] Storms had been employed as a civilian repairing flight simulators at the Lemoore Naval Air Base station near Fresno, California, since his retirement ten years before. Now he was suggesting that instead of supporting reductions in the Civil Service pay scale, Pashayan ought to take a closer look at Navy procurement practices. Enclosed in the letter was a list of spare parts showing that defense contractors were charging $435 for ordinary claw hammers and $100 or more for such electronic spare parts as diodes, transistors, and semiconductors, which cost less than $1 each. He also charged that the Navy purchased transistors at $100 each, which it could have obtained through the federal supply system for five cents apiece.

Storms's letter prompted Pashayan to query the Defense Department, which in turn kicked off an interservice investigation of military procurement practices. The Defense Department inspector general's office reported that the Navy had indeed failed to determine the most economical manner to acquire the spare parts Zeke Storms had listed.

It also suggested that the spare-parts-overcharge problem was more widespread than at first thought. The investigative body left no doubt that the Navy was wasting millions of dollars annually.

In the wake of this report, the Secretary of Defense ordered a tightening of procurement procedures to ensure the lowest price for spare parts. Meanwhile, Navy Secretary John Lehman ordered contractors at Lemoore to refund $160,000 in overcharges. He also gave Storms a $4,000 award.

But Storms wasn't about to lay down his muckrake. He suggested that Defense Department auditors review overpayment for jet-aircraft support equipment in the base shops. The auditors did and discovered overpayment of $482,000, most of it spent on four spectrum analyzers. Had the items been bought through the federal supply system, they would have cost $47,500.

Storms then discovered that the Navy had engaged private contractors to operate its flight simulators for a new aircraft. "I got mad," he says. "[The Navy] had spent $1 million training their own people to do the work, then they just scrapped that and turned the maintenance over to the contractor." The contractor in question apparently was demanding $785,000 to maintain the simulators, which worked out to about $100,000 per person per year. "I showed them that we [a team of Navy and Civil Service technicians] could do it for one-fourth that cost, so the contract was dropped to $411,000," says Storms.

That $411,000 was still higher than Storms believed the Navy had to pay, especially since the Navy had been maintaining its own simulators for two decades. So he took his case directly to Lehman, arguing that Office of Management and Budget (OMB) regulations required the Navy to do comparative cost studies to ensure the most cost-effective means. Lehman balked at Storms's proposal, saying that such studies would cost $45,000 each. That was too high a price to pay "to indulge Mr. Storms's eccentricities," the Secretary said in a letter to Congressman Pashayan.

Evidently deciding it was time to quiet the querulous Storms, Lehman then sent nine Navy brass to Lemoore. In the two-hour session that ensued, Storms did most of the talking. In the end, a commodore, four captains, two commanders, and two lieutenant commanders could do nothing to divert Storms from his course.

It was shortly thereafter that the ex-Navy chief did the "unpardonable." He accused Secretary Lehman and "his admirals" of lying. He said he had turned over to OMB officials Navy documents showing that Navy admirals willfully ignored requirements to do cost studies for private maintenance work. One of the documents included a message from Vice Admiral Robert F. Schoultz, the commander of naval forces in the Pacific. Addressing Admiral James D. Watkins, then commander of the Pacific Fleet, Schoultz wrote: "It is our intention to contract out all major training device maintenance. . . . [However] under the [contract] program our objective is hindered with cost studies that would yield inappropriate results." Schoultz's "inappropriate results" apparently was an allusion to the report by the fleet's top training officer, who estimated that the Navy's own people could do for $7 million the same work for which private contractors would charge $28 million.

In response to Storms, N. R. Lessard, officer in charge of the flight training groups for whom the ten-year Lemoore veteran was working, informed him that "your recent comments concerning senior Navy officials . . . constitute unacceptable employee conduct." To which Storms replied in a way most befitting a tobacco-chewing old salt: "[The Navy is] covering up, goddammit. I've got the facts, and they know it."

By contrast, Aaron Ahearn isn't an old salt, and he doesn't chew tobacco. But when the environmentally conscious, twenty-year-old sailor blew the whistle on the Navy's practice of dumping trash at sea, he made waves as big as Storms's.[51] Ahearn was a fireman's apprentice assigned to the scullery aboard the USS *Abraham Lincoln,* the world's largest nuclear-powered aircraft carrier. As part of his duties, Ahearn was supposed to dispose of the ship's garbage by tossing overboard up to 200 bags of plastic and other trash—some of it alleged to be toxic waste—every day. As a surfer who loves the ocean, Ahearn says that his conscience was troubled by what he had to do. He also reports seeing sailors dump broken desks, chairs, and computers into the ocean. When Ahearn's request for a change of assignment was denied, he jumped ship.

Environmentalists contend that plastic trash kills thousands of marine turtles, birds, and mammals annually and that it litters the beaches and wrecks boat propellers. Although private vessels can be fined up to $500,000 for dumping plastic debris, federal law specifically exempts the Navy. For its part, the Navy has always claimed that it can't avoid dumping plastic garbage because its ships house up to 5,500 sailors and spend months at sea.

Meanwhile, Ahearn, who had left the *Abraham Lincoln* on a weekend pass, went into hiding for two months, spending the time living with his girlfriend and surfing in the beach town of Santa Cruz, California. Eventually he decided to turn himself in. Before doing so, he received counseling from the Resource Center for Nonviolence and went to the media, saying his conscience would not allow him to pollute the ocean as ordered. He also announced that he wanted conscientious objector status on environmental grounds. Ahearn's story gained national coverage and focused pressure on the Navy to conform with international law governing plastic and trash disposal at sea. "What he did was commendable and brave," says Jil Zilligen of the Center for Marine Conservation in San Francisco. "I don't think many people realized this was going on at all."

Instead of battening down the hatches in response to the storm that Ahearn's allegations stirred up, the Navy announced that it would stop dumping plastic from all its surface ships and proposed a timetable for full compliance with the relevant international laws. What about Ahearn? Although environmental groups called him a hero, the Navy court-martialed him as a deserter who used his pollution allegations to cover up his unauthorized absence and as an excuse to leave the Navy. The ship's skipper, Navy Captain Ray Archer, contended that Ahearn told friends that he was going to jump ship to visit his girlfriend and would use his environmental concerns to justify it. And the Navy prosecutor, Lieutenant Tony Viera, said that Ahearn simply did not like his duty and needed to "grow up." The scullery is hot and sweaty, Viera remarked, and everybody hates working in it. But instead of sticking it out, Ahearn ran away and went surfing.

Ahearn and his attorney, Robert Rivkin, denied these charges, but the issue was never officially settled. In fact, at the court-martial, there was no mention at all of the environmental issues Ahearn had raised—except for the slogan "Pack Your Trash" tattooed across the back of his neck above the collar of his dress white Navy uniform. Instead, as part of a plea bargain, Ahearn pleaded guilty to unauthorized absence and to missing a ship's movement and was fined five hundred dollars and sentenced to thirty-five days in the brig. "Overall," commented his attorney, "it was a pretty good deal. It is a fair and reasonable sentence for what he did." Vicki Nichols, executive director of Save Our Shores, a marine conservation group, added, "I can't imagine that the Navy would ever admit a sailor who went AWOL has had any positive impact. But he did."

Discussion Questions

1. Do you think Storms and Ahearn qualify as whistle blowers? What do you think their motives were?

2. Examine Storms's and Ahearn's actions from the perspective of Bowie's criteria for justified whistle blowing. Are those criteria satisfied in both cases? Are Bowie's criteria themselves satisfactory?

3. What specific obligations, ideals, and effects should have been considered before either man became a whistle blower?

4. Based on the details provided, would you consider Storms morally justified in having gone public with his information? Was Ahearn's conduct justified? Explain.

5. If you believe Storms's whistle blowing was permissible, do you also believe that it was morally required of him? What about Ahearn's? Would someone in Storms's position have been justified in subordinating moral reasons to prudential concerns and thus in remaining silent? Explain.

6. Should whistle blowers be protected by law? How feasible would such a law be? Identify the advantages and disadvantages of such a law.

7. The Federal False Claims Act awards whistle blowers a portion of any money recovered by the government as a result of legal action against companies that overcharge it. Will such a law have good results, or will it encourage irresponsible whistle blowing?

CASE 8.4

The Housing Allowance

Wilson Mutambara grew up in the slums outside Stanley, capital of the sub-Saharan African country of Rambia.[52] Through talent, hard work, and luck he made it through secondary school and won a scholarship to study in the United States. He eventually received an MBA and went to work for NewCom, a cellular telephone service. After three years in the company's Atlanta office, Wilson was given an opportunity to return to Rambia, where NewCom was setting up a local cellular service. Eager to be home, Wilson Mutambara couldn't say yes fast enough.

NewCom provides its employees in Rambia with a monthly allowance of up to $2,000 for rent, utilities, and servants. By Western standards, most of the housing in Stanley is poor quality, and many of its neighborhoods are unsafe. By providing the allowance, NewCom's intention is to see that its employees live in areas that are safe and convenient and that they live in a style that is appropriate to the company's image.

To claim their housing allowance, NewCom's employees in Rambia are supposed to turn in receipts, and every month Wilson Mutambara turned in an itemized statement for $2,000 from his landlord. Nobody at NewCom thought it was unusual that Wilson never entertained his coworkers at home. After all, he worked long hours and traveled frequently on business. However, after Wilson had been in Rambia for about fifteen months, one of his coworkers, Dale Garman, was chatting with a Rambian customer, who referred in passing to Wilson as a person living in Old Town. Garman knew Old Town was one of the slums outside Stanley, but he kept his surprise to himself and decided not to mention this information to anyone else until he could independently confirm it. This wasn't difficult for him to do. Wilson was indeed living in Old Town in the home of some relatives. The house itself couldn't have rented for more than $300, even if Wilson had the whole place to himself, which he clearly didn't.

Dale reported what he had learned to Wilson's supervisor, Barbara Weston.

When Weston confronted him about the matter, Wilson admitted that the place did rent for a "little less" than $2,000, but he vigorously defended his action this way: "Every other NewCom employee in Rambia receives $2,000 a month. If I live economically, why should I be penalized? I should receive the same as everyone else." In response, Weston pointed out that NewCom wanted to guarantee that its employees had safe, high-quality housing that was in keeping with the image that the company wanted to project. Wilson's housing arrangements were "unseemly," she said, and not in keeping with his professional standing. Moreover, they reflected poorly on the company. To this, Wilson Mutambara retorted: "I'm not just a NewCom employee; I'm also a Rambian. It's not unsafe for me to live in this neighborhood, and it's insulting to be told that the area I grew up in is 'unseemly' or inappropriate for a company employee."

Barbara Weston pointed out that the monthly receipts he submitted had been falsified. "Yes," he admitted, "but that's common practice in Rambia. Nobody thinks twice about it." However, she pressed the point, arguing that he had a duty to NewCom, which he had violated. As the discussion continued, Mutambara became less confident and more and more distraught. Finally, on the verge of tears, he pleaded, "Barbara, you just don't understand what's expected of me as a Rambian or the pressure I'm under. I save every penny I have to pay school fees for eight nieces and nephews. I owe it to my family to try to give those children the same chance I had. My relatives would never understand my living in a big house instead of helping them. I'm just doing what I have to do."

Discussion Questions

1. Did Wilson Mutambara act wrongly? Explain why or why not. Assess each of the arguments

he gives in his own defense. What other courses of action were open to him? What would you have done in his place?

2. Was Dale Garman right to confirm the information he had received and to report the matter? Was it morally required of him to do so?

3. What should Barbara Weston and NewCom do? Should Wilson be ordered to move out of Old Town and into more appropriate housing?

Should he be terminated for having falsified his housing receipts? If not, should he be punished in some other way?

4. Is NewCom unfairly imposing its own ethnocentric values on Wilson Mutambara? Is the company's housing policy fair and reasonable? Is it culturally biased?

CASE 8.5

Ethically Dubious Conduct

Brenda Franklin has worked at Allied Tech for nearly eight years. It's a large company, but she likes it and enjoys the friendly work environment. When she tacked her list onto the bulletin board outside her office, she didn't intend to make things less friendly. In fact, she didn't expect her list to attract much attention at all.

It had all started the week before when she joined a group of coworkers for their weekly lunch get-together, where they always talked about all sorts of things. This time they had gotten into a long political discussion, with several people at the table going on at great length about dishonesty, conflicts of interest, and shady dealings among politicians and corporate leaders. "If this country is going to get on the right track, we need people whose integrity is above reproach," Harry Benton had said to nods of approval around the table, followed by a further round of complaints about corruption and corner-cutting by the powerful.

Brenda hadn't said much at the time, but she thought she sniffed a whiff of hypocrisy. Later that night, after pondering the group's discussion, she typed up her list of "Ethically Dubious Employee Conduct." The next day she posted it outside her door.

Harry Benton was the first one to stick his head in the office. "My, my, aren't we smug?" was all he said before he disappeared. Later that morning, her

friend Karen dropped by. "You don't really think it's immoral to take a pad of paper home, do you?" she asked. Brenda said no, but she didn't think one could just take it for granted that it was okay to take company property. She and Karen chatted more about the list. On and off that week, almost everyone she spoke with alluded to the list or commented on some of its items. They didn't object to her posting it, although they seemed to think it was a little strange. One day outside the building, however, an employee she knew only by sight asked Brenda sarcastically whether she was planning on turning people in for "moral violations." Brenda ignored him.

Now she was anticipating her group's weekly lunch. She had little doubt about what the topic of discussion would be, as she again glanced over her list:

Ethically Dubious Employee Conduct

1. Taking office supplies home for your personal use.

2. Using the telephone for personal, long-distance phone calls.

3. Making personal copies on the office machine.

4. Charging the postage on your personal mail to the company.

5. Making nonbusiness trips in a company car.

6. On a company business trip: staying in the most expensive hotel, taking taxis when you could walk, including wine as food on your expense tab, taking your spouse along at company expense.

7. Using your office computer to shop online, trade stocks, view pornography, or email friends on company time.

8. Calling in sick when you need personal time.

9. Taking half the afternoon off, when you're supposedly on business outside the office.

10. Directing company business to vendors who are friends or relatives.

11. Providing preferential service to corporate customers who have taken you out to lunch.

Discussion Questions

1. Review each item on Brenda's list and assess the conduct in question. Do you find it morally acceptable, morally unacceptable, or somewhere in between? Explain.

2. Examine Brenda's list from both the utilitarian and Kantian perspectives. What arguments can be given for and against the conduct on her list? Is the rightness or wrongness of some items a matter of degree? Can an action (such as taking a pad of paper) be both trivial and wrong?

3. Someone might argue that some of the things listed as ethically dubious are really employee entitlements. Assess this contention.

4. How would you respond to the argument that if the company doesn't do anything to stop the conduct on Brenda's list, then it has only itself to blame? What about the argument that none of the things on the list is wrong unless the company has an explicit rule against it?

5. What obligations do employees have to their employers? Do companies have moral rights that employees can violate? What moral difference, if any, is there between taking something that belongs to an individual and taking something that belongs to a company?

6. What, if anything, can we learn about an employee's character based on whether he or she does or does not do the things on Brenda's list? Would you admire someone who scrupulously avoids doing any of these ethically dubious things?

7. What should Brenda do when she finds a fellow employee engaging in what she considers ethically dubious conduct?

Notes to Chapter 8

1. See "Nuclear Warriors," *Time*, March 4, 1996, 47–54, from which the details that follow are taken.

2. Ronald Duska, "Whistleblowing and Employee Loyalty," in Tom L. Beauchamp and Norman E. Bowie, eds., *Ethical Theory and Business*, 6th ed. (Upper Saddle River, N.J.: Prentice Hall, 2001), 328.

3. John H. Fielder, "Organizational Loyalty," *Business and Professional Ethics Journal* 11 (Spring 1992): 87.

4. Richard T. De George, *Business Ethics*, 5th ed. (Upper Saddle River, N.J.: Prentice Hall, 1999), 413.

5. Fielder, "Organizational Loyalty," 80–84.

6. "A Case of Conflicts at Qwest," *Business Week*, April 22, 2002, 37.

7. "Loans to Corporate Officers Unlikely to Cease Soon," *Wall Street Journal*, July 2, 2002, A8.

8 "Insider Trading Alleged," *San Jose Mercury News*, June 13, 2002, 3C.

9. Douglas Frantz, "Genentech Chief's Wife Settles SEC's Insider Trading Charges," *Los Angeles Times*, November 21, 1990, D1.

10. John A. C. Hetherington, "Corporate Social Responsibility, Stockholders, and the Law," *Journal of Contemporary Business* (Winter 1973): 51.

11. "Texas Gulf Ruled to Lack Diligence in Minerals Case," *Wall Street Journal* (Midwest Edition), February 9, 1970, 1.

12. "Supreme Court Upholds S.E.C.'s Theory of Insider Trading," *New York Times*, June 26, 1997, C1.

13. Ibid.

14. "SEC, Professor Split on Insider Trades," *Wall Street Journal,* March 2, 1984, 8.

15. Jennifer Moore, "What Is Really Unethical About Insider Trading?" *Journal of Business Ethics* 9 (March 1990). Reprinted at the end of this chapter.

16. See "Cookie Cloak and Dagger," *Time,* September 10, 1984, 44; and "The Harm of Patents," *Economist,* August 22, 1992, 17.

17. Sissela Bok, *Secrets* (New York: Vintage, 1983), 136.

18. John R. Boatright, *Ethics and the Conduct of Business,* 4th ed. (Upper Saddle River, N.J.: Prentice Hall, 2003), 128–136.

19. Rory J. O'Connor, "Trade-Secrets Case Casts Chill," *San Jose Mercury News,* March 7, 1993, 1A.

20. See Michael S. Baram, "Trade Secrets: What Price Loyalty?" *Harvard Business Review* 46 (November–December 1968).

21. Kim Murphy, "Accountant for ZZZZ Best Convicted of Fraud," *Los Angeles Times,* December 20, 1988, II-1.

22. "Prosecutors Link Honda Fraud Cases to U.S. Executives," *New York Times,* March 15, 1994, A1.

23. Bill Shaw, "Foreign Corrupt Practices Act: A Legal and Moral Analysis," *Journal of Business Ethics* 7 (October 1988): 789–790.

24. "Special Report: Bribery and Business," *Economist,* March 2, 2002, 64.

25. Norman C. Miller, "U.S. Business Overseas: Back to Bribery?" *Wall Street Journal,* April 30, 1981, 22.

26. Bartley A. Brennan, "The Foreign Corrupt Practices Act Amendments of 1988: 'Death' of a Law," *North Carolina Journal of International Law and Commerce Regulation* 15 (1990): 229–247; Wesley Cragg and William Woof, "The U.S. Foreign Corrupt Practices Act: A Study of Its Effectiveness," *Business and Society Review* 107 (Spring 2002): 99.

27. "A Global War Against Bribery," *Economist,* January 16, 1999, 22–23; "The Worm That Never Dies," *Economist,* March 2, 2002, 12.

28. Calvin Sims, "Ex-U.S. Official Admits Guilt on Phone Contract," *New York Times,* May 24, 1989, C2.

29. David Johnston, "Boning Up on New Ethics of Procurement," *New York Times,* May 24, 1989, A16.

30. "New Kmart Code Bans Gifts, Bribes," *San Jose Mercury News,* April 12, 1996, 6C.

31. "Speaking Up Gets Biologist into Big Fight," *Wall Street Journal,* November 26, 1980, sec. 2, 25.

32. Ronald F. Duska, "Whistleblowing," in R. Edward Freeman and Patricia H. Werhane, eds., *The Blackwell Encyclopedic Dictionary of Business Ethics* (Oxford: Blackwell, 1998), 654.

33. Boatright, *Ethics and the Conduct of Business,* 106.

34. Norman Bowie, *Business Ethics* (Englewood Cliffs, N.J.: Prentice Hall, 1982), 142.

35. Bok, *Secrets,* Chapter 14.

36. Dan Seligman, "Blowing Whistles, Blowing Smoke," *Forbes,* September 6, 1999.

37. "Tobacco Whistle-Blower Acknowledges He's Paid," *New York Times,* May 1, 1996, A12.

38. "Peep and Weep," *Economist,* January 12, 2002, 56.

39. Ibid.

40. Tim Barnett, "Why *Your* Company Should Have a Whistleblowing Policy," *SAM Advanced Management Journal* 57 (Autumn 1992); cf. Boatright, *Ethics and the Conduct of Business,* 118–119.

41. For further details on Winans and his associates, see John Boatright, ed., *Cases in Ethics and the Conduct of Business* (Englewood Cliffs, N.J.: Prentice Hall, 1995), 44–56.

42. Gilbert Cranberg, "*Wall Street Journal* Case Could Bring Overreaction," *Los Angeles Times,* June 4, 1984, II-5.

43. See "Media Policies Vary on Preventing Employees and Others from Profiting on Knowledge of Future Business Stories," *Wall Street Journal,* March 2, 1984, 8.

44. Ibid.

45. "Market Leaks: Illegal Insider Trading Seems to Be on Rise," *Wall Street Journal,* March 2, 1984, 8.

46. "Media Policies," *Wall Street Journal,* 8.

47. See "Impropriety or Criminality?" *Time,* September 10, 1984, 45.

48. Cranberg, "Case Could Bring Overreaction," II-5.

49. "Impropriety or Criminality?" *Time,* 43.

50. The facts and quotations about Storms come from Ronald B. Taylor, "Making Waves: Whistle Blower Keeps Heat on Navy in Revealing Waste of Millions of Dollars," *Los Angeles Times,* June 26, 1984.

51. The discussion that follows is based on news stories in the *Santa Cruz Sentinel,* August 14 and 17, 1993, and the *San Jose Mercury News,* August 17, 1993.

52. This case study was inspired by one in *Across the Board* 36 (January 1999).

Reading ────────────■

FOUR CONCEPTS OF LOYALTY

DAVID E. SOLES

Loyalty is an ambiguous concept, and discussions of company loyalty and of whether employees owe loyalty to their employers are frequently hampered by the absence of a shared understanding of the meaning of loyalty. In this essay, David E. Soles explains and critically assesses four different concepts of loyalty: the idealist account, the commonsense conception, loyalties as norms, and the minimalist account. Each has different implications for business ethics.

Loyalty has figured prominently in recent discussions of business ethics and there seems to be a general consensus that loyalty is to be ranked among the virtues of a good employee. That employees have obligations of loyalty to their employers is largely assumed without question within the business community; the major concern there is how to strengthen and retain the bonds of loyalty.[1] It is not only representatives of business interests, however, who maintain that employees have obligations of loyalty to their employers; such a view is popular among philosophers writing on business ethics. Norman Bowie, for instance, articulates the majority opinion when he asserts that, "[o]ne of the chief duties of an employee is loyalty to an employer."[2] Though prevalent, this view has been challenged by a few distinguished philosophers like Richard De George who maintains that "[o]ne has no general, moral obligation of loyalty to one's employer, even though employers would like to have loyal employees."[3]

In the absence of a shared, fairly precise understanding of loyalty, it is very difficult, perhaps impossible, to adjudicate between the competing positions advocated by Bowie and De George. Yet it is just such an agreed-upon and precise conception of loyalty that is missing from current discussions. Participants appear to be employing vague and very different conceptions of loyalty and, thus, talking at cross purposes. My objective in this essay is to examine some of the different conceptions of loyalty embedded in current discussions and assess the relevance of each to employer/employee relations. In three of the cases I conclude that the notion of loyalty is such that we have no reason for saying that employees have general obligations of loyalty. In the fourth case, the notion of loyalty is sufficiently attenuated to warrant the advocacy of employee loyalty; it is so attenuated, however, that such advocacy cannot bear the weight placed upon it.

THE IDEALIST ACCOUNT

The first view of loyalty may be called an idealist account because of the close resemblance it bears to the position developed by the American idealist, Josiah Royce. According to Royce, loyalty is

> [t]he willing and practical and thorough-going devotion of a person to a cause. A man is loyal when, first, he has some *cause* to which he is loyal; secondly, he *willingly* and *thoroughly* devotes himself to this cause; and when, thirdly, he expresses his devotion in some *sustained and practical way*, by acting steadily in the service of his cause. Instances of loyalty are: The devotion of a patriot to his country, when this devotion leads him to actually live and perhaps to die for his country; the devotion of a martyr to his religion; the devotion of a ship's captain to the requirements of his office when, after a disaster, he works steadily for his ship and for the saving of the ship's company until the last possible service is accomplished, so that he is the last man to leave the ship, and is ready if need be to go down with his ship.[4]

As Royce realizes, each of the aspects of his analysis requires further elucidation. To begin with the object of loyalty: that to which one is loyal must be something objective, external to the individual, and possessed of its own inherent value; "[i]t does not get its value merely from your being pleased with it. You believe, on the contrary, that you love it just because of its own value, which it has by itself, even if you die" (19).

Reprinted by permission of the author from *The International Journal of Applied Philosophy* 8 (Summer 1993).

By saying that loyalty requires *willing* devotion, Royce is maintaining that loyalty must be freely given; while obedience can be demanded, loyalty cannot. In part, this follows from Royce's thesis that loyalty entails devotion: devotion is a mental state not reducible to behavior, and while behavior can be demanded, mental states cannot. But while loyalty may entail devotion, devotion is never sufficient for loyalty: "[l]oyalty is never mere emotion. Adoration and affection may go with loyalty, but can never alone constitute loyalty" (18).

This follows from the claim that loyalty is practical—to be loyal is to serve a cause. Furthermore, this service is thorough-going and sustained; a loyal person does whatever is necessary to promote the cause, "ready to live or die as the cause directs" (18).

This idealist conception of loyalty is germane to discussions of business ethics in the following way. If this is the accepted conception of loyalty and if it can be established that employees ought to be loyal to their employers, then the stringent obligations sometimes placed upon employees in the name of loyalty would be perfectly justified. A loyal employee would be one thoroughly dedicated to serving the interests of his principal, ready to live or die as directed, and to say that employees should be loyal would be to advocate such dedication. It is instructive to consider some examples of the sorts of obligations this conception of loyalty could require of a loyal employee. A loyal employee would always be willing to place the interests of the principal before purely private interests, even in matters unrelated to employment; a loyal employee would be willing to sacrifice the interests of uninvolved third parties or even society at large, if doing so served the employer's interest; a loyal employee would never advocate or vote for social policies or legislation that might damage the interests of the employer; a loyal employee would never publicly criticize or oppose the actions of the employer; a loyal employee would never consider leaving the employer. That something akin to the idealist conception of loyalty is operative in some quarters is evidenced by the frequent endorsements of these claims.

Lest it be thought that I am constructing a straw man here, consider the following case which Marcia Baron discusses in *The Moral Status of Loyalty*.

In a 1973 CBS report on Phillips Petroleum, Inc., one of its chief executives was asked to describe what sort of qualities his company looks for in prospective employees. He responded without hesitation that above all else, what Phillips wants and needs is loyalty on the part of its employees. A loyal employee, he elaborated, would buy only Phillips products. . . . Moreover, a loyal employee would vote in local, state, and national elections in whatever way was most conducive to the growth and flourishing of Phillips. And, of course, a loyal employee would never leave Phillips unless it was absolutely unavoidable. To reduce the likelihood of that happening, prospective employees were screened to make sure their respective wives did not have careers which might conflict with lifelong loyalty to Phillips.[5]

Is it true that employees have an obligation to so thoroughly dedicate themselves to the interests of their employers and, if so, what are the grounds of that obligation? One might begin to address this question by asking a more general question: is there any reason to so thoroughly dedicate oneself to any one thing?

Royce has an answer to this latter question, but it is one which will provide little comfort for those who advocate idealistic loyalty to employers. According to him, such dedication is demanded by the human predicament, for human beings are incapable of finding any meaning or significance to their lives within themselves. . . .

Thus, on Royce's account, because human life can be made meaningful and significant only through the total dedication of that life to the service of some external cause, loyalty becomes the highest moral virtue. One should totally dedicate oneself to the service to some cause because such dedication is necessary to make one's life meaningful.

There are, of course, myriad problems with such an account. . . . For the moment we can grant Royce his dubious views about human nature, for there is a more serious problem confronting the idealist account; its thorough-going, total dedication to a cause requires an abdication of moral autonomy that can be neither demanded nor given.

It is morally irresponsible to be willing to perform any conceivable action that would further the interests of one's chosen cause; one must always reserve the option of saying that one can no longer serve a cause if it requires the performance of certain sorts of actions. . . .

Royce . . . is right about one thing. If loyalty requires such total, thorough-going dedication to a cause, there are very few things worthy of loyalty; furthermore, since the interests of any two causes could conceivably come into conflict, one can be loyal to only one object. Therefore, it is incumbent upon each person to ensure that the object of his loyalty is of the highest inherent worth.

It is very unlikely that business institutions qualify as objects of the most inherent worth. To begin with, business institutions are instrumentally, not inherently, valuable; they are valued because they are means for providing goods and services which are valued. If we no longer cared for those goods and services or if we found better ways to obtain them, the institutions which provide them would lose much of their value. Furthermore, not all business institutions possess instrumental value: some produce more harm than good by manufacturing dangerous, inferior products, polluting the environment, engaging in illegal business practices, etc. But whether instrumentally good or evil, a business institution is not the sort of thing worthy of loyalty in the idealist sense.

In summary, if the idealist conception of loyalty were accepted as our working notion of loyalty, and if it could be established that employees ought to be loyal to their employers, then the demands placed upon employees in the name of loyalty would be justified: employees would have an obligation to place the interests of their employers before all other interests. However, it is not clear that we should accept this as our working conception of loyalty and, more importantly, even if we did, we must conclude that business institutions could not be appropriate objects of loyalty.

THE COMMON SENSE CONCEPTION

The common sense view of loyalty more satisfactorily captures the everyday conception of loyalty with which most of us are familiar. Most of us are untroubled by statements to the effect that someone is a loyal fan of the Kansas City Royals, a loyal member of the Republican party, or loyal to her alma mater, and when we hear such claims we are not inclined to suppose that the person is totally dedicated to the cause, "willing to live or die as the cause directs."

A version of the common sense view of loyalty has been formulated by Andrew Oldenquist in "Loyalties."[6] According to Oldenquist,

> . . . [w]hen I have a loyalty to something I have somehow come to view it as *mine*. It is an object of non-instrumental value to me in virtue (but not only in virtue) of its being mine, and I am disposed to feel pride when it prospers, shame when it declines, and anger or indignation when it is harmed. In general, people care about the objects of their loyalties, and they acknowledge obligations that they would not acknowledge were it not for their loyalties. (175)
>
> . . . [L]oyalty is positive and is primarily characterized by esteem and concern for the common good of one's group. (177)

On this view, there are three essential features of loyalty. First, loyalty entails having a positive attitude towards the objects of one's loyalty; a loyalty is to "an object of non-instrumental value," people "care about" the objects of their loyalties. Second, loyalty entails a disposition to serve the interests of the object to which one is loyal; loyal persons "acknowledge obligations that they would not acknowledge were it not for their loyalties." Third, both the concern and the obligations are rooted in the individual's belief that he stands in some personal relationship to the object of his loyalty; to have a loyalty to something is to somehow come to view it as one's own.

The first thing to note about this conception of loyalty is that it is not sufficient to distinguish loyalty from many other virtues.[7] While caring, acknowledging obligations, and feeling a personal relationship may be necessary features of loyalty, they also are necessary features of virtues such as love and friendship and may even characterize the relationship between some professionals and their patients, clients, students, etc. Many dedicated teachers consider their students to be objects of non-instrumental value, care about them, acknowledge supererogatory obligations, and both the concern and the obligations stem from the fact that these students are their students. Similar remarks may be made about doctors, nurses, lawyers, social workers, etc. To characterize their attitude as one of loyalty seems to be stretching the common sense notion of loyalty too far. . . .

In conflating loyalty with other, distinct, virtues, Oldenquist has failed to provide the promised analysis of loyalty. Nevertheless, while this common sense account should not be construed as providing a definition of "loyalty" in terms of necessary and sufficient conditions, it may be acceptable as a rough characterization of some essential features of loyalty. Loyalty, like friendship, love, and professional interest, entails concern, obligations, and a feeling of personal identification with the object of one's loyalty. The questions that need to be asked, then, are: (1) does one have any obligation to have such attitudes to one's employer, and (2) does the having of such attitudes justify always acting in the interests of the object of one's loyalty?

Beginning with the first question, on the common sense account, the mere fact that one happens to have been born in a particular country, happens to have attended a particular school, or happens to work for a particular institution is not sufficient for saying that one should be loyal to it. Oldenquist makes this point in maintaining that ". . . a loyalist doesn't value something simply because it is his. It must have features which make it worth having, and it could deteriorate to the extent that shame ultimately kills his loyalty" (178). On this conception of loyalty, one should bestow one's loyalty only on those objects which are worthy of it and loyalty bestowed upon some nations, schools or institutions would be misguided.

Furthermore, if this is our working conception of loyalty, no one has an obligation to be loyal to anything; to suppose that one has an obligation to be loyal to anything is to make a fundamental category mistake. On this view, being loyal entails having certain sorts of attitudes; to be loyal to an object one must care about it. But while persons can have moral obligations to perform certain actions and while certain attitudes may be morally desirable or indesirable, we do not have moral obligations to have certain attitudes and beliefs. Just as no one has an obligation to have feelings of love or friendship to another, no one has an obligation to have feelings of loyalty to anything. Thus, one can have no obligation to be loyal to her nation, school, or employer even if they are worthy of loyalty.

Turning to the second question, does loyalty require one to always act in the interest of that to which one is loyal? It is often suggested that loyalty is inconsistent with certain sorts of actions, for example, whistleblowing is alleged to be incompatible with loyalty. Sissela Bok, for instance, sets up the dichotomy this way.

> . . . [T]he whistleblower hopes to stop the game; but since he is neither referee nor coach, and since he blows the whistle on his own team, his act is seen as a violation of loyalty. In holding his position, he has assumed certain obligations to his colleagues and clients. He may even have subscribed to a loyalty oath or a promise of confidentiality. Loyalty to colleagues and clients comes to be pitted against loyalty to the public interest, to those who may be injured unless the revelation is made.
>
> *Not only is loyalty violated in whistleblowing,* hierarchy as well is often opposed. . . . If the facts warrant whistleblowing, how can the second element—*breach of loyalty*—be minimized?[8] (my italics)

On the common sense conception, this is a very misleading way of presenting the problem for it implies that whistleblowing is a breach of loyalty, that one cannot both be loyal to an institution and blow the whistle on it. But, on the common sense view, this is surely wrong; one can view an institution as one's own, care deeply about it, assume obligations towards it, and still publicly and strenuously oppose what one takes to be unethical or illegal actions on its part. This is a feature of loyalty explicitly recognized in British politics as "the loyal opposition."

Setting up a dichotomy between loyalty and whistleblowing is not merely a misleading way to present the problem of whistleblowing, it is dangerous. Loyalty is generally perceived as a virtue and disloyalty is perceived as a vice. To say that loyalty demands a certain action is to give a prima facie reason for performing that action and to label a particular action as disloyal is to give a prima facie reason for not performing that action. Under those conditions, potential whistleblowers are encouraged to construe themselves as choosing between performing a wrong act themselves (being disloyal) or remaining silent about the performance of wrongs committed by others. When presented this way, it is not surprising that many individuals choose silence. But if whistleblowing is not construed as an instance of disloyalty, the whole complexion of the problem changes. If loyalty does not require acquiescence in wrong doing, the refusal to remain silent about known wrongs cannot be construed as an ipso facto instance of disloyalty.

Acceptance of the common sense view of loyalty, thus, would justify two conclusions both of which are anathema to many discussions of business and professional ethics. First, it is simply a mistake to suppose that individuals have an obligation to be loyal to their employers and second, loyalty is compatible with strenuously opposing actions of one's employer.

LOYALTIES AS NORMS

While he does not appear to be aware that he is doing so, Oldenquist formulates a second conception of loyalty radically different from his common sense account. According to this second view, "loyalties are norms that define the domains within which we accept the moral machinery of universalizable reasons and relevant differences" (182); alternatively, "loyalties define moral communities or domains within which we are willing to universalize moral judgments, treat equals equally, protect the common good, and in other ways adopt the familiar machinery of impersonal morality. . . . A loyalty defines a moral community in terms of a conception of a common good and a special commitment to the members of the group who share this good" (177). This seems to be incompatible with the common sense account Oldenquist formulates. Attitudes, definitions and norms are different sorts of things. If loyalty is an attitude as the common sense account maintains, then it is neither a norm nor a definition.

Perhaps the confusion here is merely verbal. Perhaps Oldenquist's claim is something like this: the class of objects to which one is loyal is delineated by, or co-extensive with, the moral communities or domains "within which we are willing to universalize moral judgments, treat equals equally, protect the common good, and in other ways adopt the familiar machinery of impersonal morality." On this reading, loyalty is not literally a norm which

defines a moral community; rather, one has attitudes of loyalty towards the moral community determined by the norms.

There are two ways of interpreting this talk of loyalty to the moral community: (1) we might have feelings of loyalty to each of the members of the community defined by the norm, or (2) we might have feelings of loyalty to the community, but not necessarily to each of its members. Either alternative faces serious difficulties.

Beginning with the first interpretation, if loyalty is characterized by positive feelings of esteem and concern, a disposition to feel pride when the object of loyalty prospers, shame when it declines, and anger or hurt when it is harmed, then the moral community defined by the norms and the objects of one's loyalty might not be co-extensive. One might, for instance, define the moral community as rational, sentient beings; this would define the domain within which we are willing to universalize moral judgments, etc. One might not, however, have positive feelings of concern, esteem, etc. for all the members of this community. In that case, the community of objects to which one is loyal would not be coextensive with the moral community.

The second interpretation would avoid this conclusion by arguing that on the above example one is loyal to the class of rational sentient beings, not individual rational sentient beings; that communities and not individuals are the proper objects of loyalty. That this might be Oldenquist's position is implied by statements such as the following.

> A loyalty defines a moral community in terms of a conception of a common good and a special commitment to the members of the group who share this good. The members, along with certain conventional, institutional structures, and often a geographical location, together constitute the community that is the object of my loyalty. (177)

On this account, then, one is loyal to communities and to be loyal to a community just is to "adopt the familiar procedures of impersonal morality" in one's dealings with members of that community. Thus, according to Oldenquist, a Kantian who maintains that rationality is an end in itself is advocating loyalty to the class of rational beings (179) and a utilitarian who maintains that the happiness of all human beings is to count equally is advocating loyalty to the class of human beings (180–181). But to come to this conclusion is to trivialize talk of loyalty: as a moral category, loyalty has become vacuous, it no longer draws any moral distinctions.

If any moral norm to which one is committed defines a moral community to which one is loyal, then loyalty can never come into conflict with any other moral standard. Suppose that I am loyal to the institution where I am employed; it is a community towards which I have positive attitudes, I have assumed special obligations to promote its interests, I treat the members of that community according to the procedures of impersonal morality, recognizing universalizable reasons, and relevant differences, etc. Suppose that I am also committed to the principle that rational beings should always be treated as ends in themselves. Suppose, finally, that I come to perceive certain policies pursued by my institution as being grossly exploitive and am torn between a desire to protect the institution and an obligation to act on my moral principles. In choosing what course of action to pursue, it would be natural to describe myself as choosing between considerations of loyalty to the institution and some other principle of morality.

On Oldenquist's view, however, the choice is merely one between a wide and a narrow loyalty; on the one hand I am loyal to the institution and on the other hand I am loyal to the moral community defined by the norm. If any moral standard which I accept defines a moral community to which I am loyal, then loyalty can never come into conflict with any other moral standard, there can only be conflicts between wide and narrow loyalties. At precisely that point loyalty becomes a vacuous, trivial moral notion.

Furthermore, to say that loyalty is a norm does not answer any ethical questions nor provide moral guidance. . . . In particular, characterizing loyalties as norms which define moral communities provides no guidance in ascertaining whether we should be loyal to our employers nor does it provide any insight into what loyalty would demand should we decide that loyalty is appropriate. Consequently, such an analysis is useless for deciding the interest-

ing questions about loyalty that arise in the context of business and professional ethics.

THE MINIMALIST ACCOUNT

There is a fourth conception of loyalty which maintains that a loyal individual is one who meets reasonable expectations of trust; to be loyal just is to discharge one's obligations and responsibilities conscientiously. Such an attenuated view of loyalty does not demand positive feelings of affection, devotion, or respect nor does it expect one to perform supererogatory actions in promoting the interests of the object of one's loyalty. At most, loyalty demands that one act in a way that does not betray reasonable expectations of trust.

The Restatement of the Law of Agency is subject to a minimalist interpretation.[9] That Restatement maintains that a loyal agent has a duty ". . . to act solely for the benefit of the principal in all matters connected with his agency" (387). This claim that the agent is to act solely for the benefit of the principal is qualified in several important respects by the Restatement. First, an agent may act against the interests of his principal when doing so is necessary for the protection of his own interests or those of others (387b). Second, an agent has no obligation to perform acts which are illegal or unethical and ". . . in determining whether or not the orders of the principal are reasonable . . . business or professional ethics . . . are considered" (385-1a). Third, an agent is not "prevented from acting in good faith outside his employment in a manner which injuriously affects his principal's business" (387b). Finally, "[a]n agent is privileged to reveal information confidentially acquired . . . in the protection of a superior interest of himself or of a third person. Thus, if the confidential information is to the effect that the principal is committing or is about to commit a crime, the agent is under no duty not to reveal it" (395f).

Like most documents, the Restatement of Agency is subject to competing interpretations. As Blumberg has noted, the Restatement

> . . . is drafted in terms of economic activity, economic motivation, and economic advantage and formulates duties of loyalty and obedience for the agent to prevent the

agent's own economic interest from impairing his judgment, zeal, or single-minded devotion to the furtherance of his principal's economic interests. The reference in section 395, Comment f permitting the agent to disclose confidential information concerning a criminal act committed or planned by the principal is the sole exception to a system of analysis that is otherwise exclusively concerned with matters relating to the economic position of the parties.[10] . . .

As Blumberg rightly emphasizes, the Restatement is concerned almost exclusively with conflicts of economic interests; nevertheless, if interpreted liberally, the Restatement can be quite useful in responding to the broader issues. The discussion of criminal activity at 395f could be treated as an example of a case where the revelation of confidential material is justified by the need to protect a superior interest; it need not be read as limiting the revelation of confidential material to cases involving criminal activity. By the same token, 387b could be interpreted as maintaining that an agent is justified in acting against the interests of the principal when doing so is necessary to protect important noneconomic interests of himself or others. Interpreted thusly, either 395f or 387b could be appealed to in justifying the claim that loyalty is consistent with acting against the interests of one's employer.

On the minimalist account, loyalty would not entail a willingness to participate in, condone or remain silent about illegal activities. It would not entail willingness to participate in unethical conduct if doing so promoted the interests of one's principal. It would be compatible with acting against the interests of one's employer, even revealing confidential information, if doing so were necessary to protect important interests of the public. Finally, contrary to the opinion of the Phillips executive, loyalty would be compatible with voting in ways not conducive to the growth and flourishing of one's principal and even compatible with seeking employment elsewhere. In this minimalist sense, simply meeting reasonable expectations of trust is sufficient for loyalty.

This, of course, raises the issue of what responsibilities it is reasonable for employers to entrust to employees. Many of these are defined and clearly stipulated in job descriptions, contracts, and codes of professional ethics and many more are informally recognized as standard acceptable practices within a profession; and, while there are bound to be grey areas and points of disagreement, there are some activities which loyalty does not enjoin.

If the minimalist conception of loyalty is accepted, it seems clear that employees ought to be loyal to their employers. That, however, merely amounts to the claim that they ought to meet reasonable, legitimate expectations of trust; it does not impose upon them the sorts of obligations that often are urged in the name of loyalty.

CONCLUSION

Much of the confusion and disagreement infecting discussions of the role of loyalty in business and professional ethics has been engendered by equivocation and ambiguity in the concept itself. This essay has briefly considered four different conceptions of loyalty and examined some of the implications of each. If the idealist conception of loyalty is accepted, loyalty to one's employer would demand the sort of behavior sometimes advocated in its name. It is not clear, however, that this account should be accepted and, if we do accept it, employers would not be appropriate objects of loyalty. If the common sense conception of loyalty is accepted, two conclusions follow: first, since loyalty is supererogatory, no one has an obligation to feel loyal to anything; second, loyalty, in this sense, does not entail placing the interests of one's principal before all other considerations and, in fact, is compatible with opposing some of the interests of one's principal. The third conception, which maintains that the adoption of any norm regulating conduct generates a loyalty, trivializes the notion of loyalty to the point where it is useless for guiding conduct. Finally, on the minimalist conception, one can justify saying that employees ought to be loyal to their employers; the minimalist view is sufficiently attenuated, however, that such a claim does not amount to much.

Notes

1. See, for example, R. Rowan, "Rekindling Corporate Loyalty," *Fortune*, Fall, 1981, or P. C. Lederer, "Management's

Right to Loyalty of Supervisors," *Labor Law Review,* Fall, 1981, or "The End of Corporate Loyalty?" *Business Week,* Aug. 4, 1986.

2. Norman Bowie, *Business Ethics,* Prentice Hall, Inc., Englewood Cliffs, New Jersey, 1982, p. 13.

3. Richard De George, *Business Ethics,* MacMillan, New York, 1982, p. 154.

4. Josiah Royce, *The Philosophy of Loyalty,* The MacMillan Co., New York, 1916, pp. 16–17. Subsequent references to this work are provided as page numbers in the text.

5. Marcia Baron, *The Moral Status of Loyalty,* Kendal Hunt, Dubuque, Iowa, 1984, p. 1.

6. Andrew Oldenquist, "Loyalties," *The Journal of Philosophy,* April, 1982, pp. 173–193. Subsequent references to this work are provided as page numbers in the text.

7. This should not be construed as a criticism of Oldenquist. His objective seems to be to advocate loyalty, not explicate the conception.

8. Sissela Bok, "Whistleblowing and Professional Responsibility," *New York University Education Quarterly,* Vol. II, 4 (1980), 2–7. Reprinted in Beauchamp and Bowie, *Ethical Theory and Business,* 2nd ed., Prentice Hall, Inc., Englewood Cliffs, New Jersey, pp. 261–269.

9. *Restatement of the Law, Second, Agency,* Vol. 2, American Law Institute Publishers, St. Paul, Minn., 1958.

10. Phillip J. Blumberg, "Corporate Responsibility and the Employee's Duty of Loyalty and Obedience," in Beauchamp and Bowie, *Ethical Theory and Business,* Prentice Hall, Inc., Englewood Cliffs, New Jersey, 1979, pp. 309–310.

Review and Discussion Questions

1. Explain the key features of each of the four concepts of loyalty that Soles discusses. What do you see as the strong and weak points of each? Are there aspects of loyalty that all four concepts overlook?

2. What do you think is the best way to define loyalty? Is loyalty only a feeling, or is it a source of moral obligation? When and under what conditions do we owe loyalty?

3. Examine the following two questions from the perspective of each of the four concepts of loyalty; then give your own answer: (a) Do employees owe loyalty to their employers? (b) What does loyalty to one's employer require?

4. What are you loyal to? What determines your loyalties? Is loyalty important? Does it give meaning to our existence? Is it a necessary component of the moral life?

Reading ———————— ■

WHAT IS REALLY UNETHICAL ABOUT INSIDER TRADING?

JENNIFER MOORE

In this article Jennifer Moore examines the principal ethical arguments against insider trading: the claim that the practice is unfair, the claim that it involves a "misappropriation" of information, and the claim that it harms ordinary investors. She concludes that each of these arguments has serious deficiencies and that none of them suffices to outlaw insider trading. Instead, she argues that the real reason for prohibiting insider trading is that it undermines the fiduciary relationship that lies at the heart of business management.

This essay is divided into two parts. In the first part, I examine critically the principal ethical arguments against insider trading. The arguments fall into three main classes: arguments based on fairness, arguments based on property rights in information, and arguments based on harm to ordinary investors or the market as a whole. Each of these arguments, I contend, has some serious deficiencies. No one of them by itself provides a sufficient reason for outlawing insider trading. This does not mean, however, that there are no reasons for prohibiting the practice. Once we have cleared away the inadequate arguments, other, more cogent reasons for outlawing insider trading come to light. In the second part of the essay, I set out what I take to be the real reasons for laws against insider trading.

The term *insider trading* needs some preliminary clarification. Both the SEC and the courts have strongly resisted pressure to define the notion clearly. In 1961, the SEC stated that corporate in-

Journal of Business Ethics 9 (March 1990). Copyright © 1990 by D. Reidel Publishing Co. Reprinted by permission of Kluwer Academic Publishers. Some notes omitted.

siders—such as officers or directors—in possession of material, non-public information were required to disclose that information or to refrain from trading. But this "disclose or refrain" rule has since been extended to persons other than corporate insiders. People who get information from insiders ("tippees"), and those who become "temporary insiders" in the course of some work they perform for the company, can acquire the duty of insiders in some cases. Financial printers and newspaper columnists, not "insiders" in the technical sense, have also been found guilty of insider trading. Increasingly, the term *insider* has come to refer to the kind of information a person possesses rather than to the status of the person who trades on that information. My use of the term will reflect this ambiguity. In this essay, an "insider trader" is someone who trades in material, nonpublic information—not necessarily a corporate insider.

I. ETHICAL ARGUMENTS AGAINST INSIDER TRADING

Fairness

Probably the most common reason given for thinking that insider trading is unethical is that it is "unfair." For proponents of the fairness argument, the key feature of insider trading is the disparity of information between the two parties to the transaction. Trading should take place on a "level playing field," they argue, and disparities in information tilt the field toward one player and away from the other. There are two versions of the fairness argument: the first argues that insider trading is unfair because the two parties do not have *equal* information; the second argues that insider trading is unfair because the two parties do not have equal *access* to information. Let us look at the two versions one at a time.

According to the equal information argument, insider trading is unfair because one party to the transaction lacks information the other party has, and is thus at a disadvantage. Although this is a very strict notion of fairness, it has its proponents, and hints of this view appear in some of the judicial opinions. One proponent of the equal information argument is Saul Levmore, who claims that "fairness is achieved when insiders and outsiders are in equal positions. That is, a system is fair if we would not expect one group to envy the position of the other." As thus defined, Levmore claims, fairness "reflects the 'golden rule' of impersonal behavior—treating others as we would ourselves."[1] If Levmore is correct, then not just insider trading, but *all* transactions in which there is a disparity of information are unfair, and thus unethical. But this claim seems overly broad. An example will help to illustrate some of the problems with it.

Suppose I am touring Vermont and come across an antique blanket chest in the barn of a farmer, a chest I know will bring $2,500 back in the city. I offer to buy it for $75, and the farmer agrees. If he had known how much I could get for it back home, he probably would have asked a higher price—but I failed to disclose this information. I have profited from an informational advantage. Have I been unethical? My suspicion is that most people would say I have not. While knowing how much I could sell the chest for in the city is in the interest of the farmer, I am not morally obligated to reveal it. I am not morally obligated to tell those who deal with me *everything* that it would be in their interest to know. . . .

In general, it is only when I owe a *duty* to the other party that I am legally required to reveal all information that is in his interest. In such a situation, the other party believes that I am looking out for his interests, and I deceive him if I do not do so. Failure to disclose is deceptive in this instance because of the relationship of trust and dependence between the parties. But this suggests that trading on inside information is wrong, *not* because it violates a general notion of fairness, but because a breach of fiduciary duty is involved. Cases of insider trading in which no fiduciary duty of this kind is breached would not be unethical. . . .

The "equal information" version of the fairness argument seems to me to fail. However, it could be argued that insider trading is unfair because the insider has information that is not *accessible* to the ordinary investor. For proponents of this second type of fairness argument, it is not the insider's information advantage that counts, but the fact that

this advantage is "unerodable," one that cannot be overcome by the hard work and ingenuity of the ordinary investor. No matter how hard the latter works, he is unable to acquire non-public information, because this information is protected by law.[2]

This type of fairness argument seems more promising, since it allows people to profit from informational advantages of their own making, but not from advantages that are built into the system. Proponents of this "equal access" argument would probably find my deal with the Vermont farmer unobjectionable, because information about antiques is not in principle unavailable to the farmer. The problem with the argument is that the notion of "equal access" is not very clear. What does it mean for two people to have equal access to information?

Suppose my pipes are leaking and I call a plumber to fix them. He charges me for the job, and benefits by the informational advantage he has over me. Most of us would not find this transaction unethical. True, I don't have "equal access" to the information needed to fix my pipes in any real sense, but I could have had this information had I chosen to become a plumber. The disparity of information in this case is simply something that is built into the fact that people choose to specialize in different areas. But just as I could have chosen to become a plumber, I could have chosen to become a corporate insider with access to legally protected information. . . .

One might argue that I have easier access to a plumber's information than I do to an insider trader's, since there are lots of plumbers from whom I can buy the information I seek. The fact that insiders have a strong incentive to keep their information to themselves is a serious objection to insider trading. But if insider trading were made legal, insiders could profit not only from trading on their information, but also on selling it to willing buyers. Proponents of the practice argue that a brisk market in information would soon develop—indeed, it might be argued that such a market already exists, though in illegal and clandestine form.[3] . . .

The most interesting thing about the fairness argument is not that it provides a compelling reason to outlaw insider trading, but that it leads to issues we cannot settle on the basis of an abstract concept of fairness alone. The claim that parties to a transaction should have equal information, or equal access to information, inevitably raises questions about how informational advantages are (or should be) acquired, and when people are entitled to use them for profit. . . .

Property Rights in Information

As economists and legal scholars have recognized, information is a valuable thing, and it is possible to view it as a type of property. We already treat certain types of information as property: trade secrets, inventions, and so on—and protect them by law. Proponents of the property rights argument claim that material, non-public information is also a kind of property, and that insider trading is wrong because it involves a violation of property rights.

If inside information is a kind of property, whose property is it? How does information come to belong to one person rather than another? This is a very complex question, because information differs in many ways from other, more tangible sorts of property. But one influential argument is that information belongs to the people who discover, originate or "create" it. As Bill Shaw put it in a recent article, "the originator of the information (the individual or corporation that spent hard-earned bucks producing it) owns and controls this asset just as it does other proprietary goods."[4] Thus, if a firm agrees to a deal, invents a new product, or discovers new natural resources, it has a property right in that information and is entitled to exclusive use of it for its own profit.

It is important to note that it is the firm itself (and/or its shareholders), and not the individual employees of the firm, who have property rights in the information. To be sure, it is always certain individuals in the firm who put together the deal, invent the product, or discover the resources. But they are able to do this only because they are backed by the power and authority of the firm. The employees of the firm—managers, officers, directors—are not entitled to the information any more than they are entitled to corporate trade secrets or patents on products that they develop for the firm. It is the firm that makes it possible to create the information and that makes the information valuable once it has been created. As Victor Brudney puts it,

The insiders have acquired the information at the expense of the enterprise, and for the purpose of conducting the business for the collective good of all the stockholders, entirely apart from personal benefits from trading in its securities. There is no reason for them to be entitled to trade for their own benefit on the basis of such information. . . .[5]

If this analysis is correct, then it suggests that insider trading is wrong because it is a form of theft. It is not exactly like theft, because the person who uses inside information does not deprive the company of the use of the information. But he does deprive the company of the *sole* use of the information, which is itself an asset. The insider trader "misappropriates," as the law puts it, information that belongs to the company and uses it in a way in which it was not intended—for personal profit. It is not surprising that this "misappropriation theory" has begun to take hold in the courts, and has become one of the predominant rationales in prosecuting insider trading cases. In *U.S. v. Newman*, a case involving investment bankers and securities traders, for example, the court stated:

> In *U.S. v. Chiarella*, Chief Justice Burger . . . said that the defendant "misappropriated"—stole to put it bluntly—"valuable nonpublic information entrusted to him in the utmost confidence." That characterization aptly describes the conduct of the connivers in the instant case. . . . By sullying the reputations of [their] employers as safe repositories of client confidences, appellee and his cohorts defrauded those employers as surely as if they took their money.[6]

The misappropriation theory also played a major role in the prosecution of R. Foster Winans, a *Wall Street Journal* reporter who traded on and leaked to others the contents of his "Heard on the Street" column.[7]

This theory is quite persuasive, as far as it goes. But it is not enough to show that insider trading is always unethical or that it should be illegal. If insider information is really the property of the firm that produces it, then using that property is wrong *only when the firm prohibits it.* If the firm does not prohibit insider trading, it seems perfectly acceptable.* Most companies do in fact forbid insider

---

*Unless there is some other reason for forbidding it, such as that it harms others. See [the following section].

trading. But it is not clear whether they do so because they don't want their employees using corporate property for profit or simply because it is illegal. Proponents of insider trading point out that most corporations did not prohibit insider trading until recently, when it became a prime concern of enforcement agencies. . . .

A crucial factor here would be the shareholders' agreement to allow insider information. Shareholders may not wish to allow trading on inside information because they may wish the employees of the company to be devoted simply to advancing shareholder interests. We will return to this point below. But if shareholders did allow it, it would seem to be permissible. Still others argue that shareholders would not need to "agree" in any way other than to be told this information when they were buying the stock. If they did not want to hold stock in a company whose employees were permitted to trade in inside information, they would not buy that stock. Hence they could be said to have "agreed."

Manne and other proponents of insider trading have suggested a number of reasons why "shareholders would voluntarily enter into contractual arrangements with insiders giving them property rights in valuable information."[8] Their principal argument is that permitting insider trading would serve as an incentive to create more information—put together more deals, invent more new products, or make more discoveries. Such an incentive, they argue, would create more profit for shareholders in the long run. Assigning employees the right to trade on inside information could take the place of more traditional (and expensive) elements in the employee's compensation package. Rather than giving out end of the year bonuses, for example, firms could allow employees to put together their own bonuses by cashing in on inside information, thus saving the company money. In addition, proponents argue, insider trading would improve the efficiency of the market. We will return to these claims below.

If inside information really is a form of corporate property, firms may assign employees the right to trade on it if they choose to do so. The only reason for not permitting firms to allow employees to trade on their information would be that doing so causes harm to other investors or to society at large. Although our society values property rights very highly, they are not absolute. We do not hesitate to restrict property rights if their exercise causes significant harm to others. The permissibility of insider trading, then, ultimately seems to depend on whether the practice is harmful.

Harm

There are two principal harm-based arguments against insider trading. The first claims that the practice is harmful to ordinary investors who engage in trades with insiders; the second claims that insider trading erodes investors' confidence in the market, causing them to pull out of the market and harming the market as a whole. I will address the two arguments in turn.

Although proponents of insider trading often refer to it as a "victimless crime," implying that no one is harmed by it, it is not difficult to think of examples of transactions with insiders in which ordinary investors are made worse off. Suppose I have placed an order with my broker to sell my shares in Megalith Co., currently trading at $50 a share, at $60 or above. An insider knows that Behemoth Inc. is going to announce a tender offer for Megalith shares in two days, and has begun to buy large amounts of stock in anticipation of the gains. Because of his market activity, Megalith stock rises to $65 a share and my order is triggered. If he had refrained from trading, the price would have risen steeply two days later, and I would have been able to sell my shares for $80. Because the insider traded, I failed to realize the gains that I otherwise would have made.

But there are other examples of transactions in which ordinary investors *benefit* from insider trading. Suppose I tell my broker to sell my shares in Acme Corp., currently trading at $45, if the price drops to $40 or lower. An insider knows of an enormous class action suit to be brought against Acme in two days. He sells his shares, lowering the price to $38 and triggering my sale. When the suit is made public two days later, the share price plunges to $25. If the insider had abstained from trading, I would have lost far more than I did. Here, the insider has protected me from loss. . . .

The truth about an ordinary investor's gains and losses from trading with insiders seems to be not that insider trading is never harmful, but that it is not systematically or consistently harmful. Insider trading is not a "victimless crime," as its proponents claim, but it is often difficult to tell exactly who the victims are and to what extent they have been victimized. The stipulation of the law to "disclose *or* abstain" from trading makes determining victims even more complex. While some investors are harmed by the insider's trade, to others the insider's actions make no difference at all; what harms them is simply *not having complete information* about the stock in question. Forbidding insider trading will not prevent these harms. Investors who neither buy nor sell, or who buy or sell for reasons independent of share price, fall into this category.

Permitting insider trading would undoubtedly make the securities market *riskier* for ordinary investors. Even proponents of the practice seem to agree with this claim. But if insider trading were permitted openly, they argue, investors would compensate for the extra riskiness by demanding a discount in share price.[9] . . . If insider trading were permitted, in short, we could expect a general drop in share prices, but no net harm to investors would result. Moreover, improved efficiency would result in a bigger pie for everyone. These are empirical claims, and I am not equipped to determine if they are true. If they are, however, they would defuse one of the most important objections to insider trading, and provide a powerful argument for leaving the control of inside information up to individual corporations.

The second harm-based argument claims that permitting insider trading would cause ordinary investors to lose confidence in the market and cease to invest there, thus harming the market as a whole. As former SEC Chairman John Shad puts it, "if people get the impression that they're playing against a marked deck, they're simply not going to be willing to invest."[10] Since capital markets play a crucial role in allocating resources in our economy, this objection is a very serious one.

The weakness of the argument is that it turns almost exclusively on the *feelings* or *perceptions* of ordinary investors, and does not address the question of whether these perceptions are justified. If

permitting insider trading really does harm ordinary investors, then this "loss of confidence" argument becomes a compelling reason for outlawing insider trading. But if, as many claim, the practice does not harm ordinary investors, then the sensible course of action is to educate the investors, not to outlaw insider trading. It is irrational to cater to the feelings of ordinary investors if those feelings are not justified. We ought not to outlaw perfectly permissible actions just because some people feel (unjustifiably) disadvantaged by them. More research is needed to determine the actual impact of insider trading on the ordinary investor.[11]

II. IS THERE ANYTHING WRONG WITH INSIDER TRADING?

My contention has been that the principal ethical arguments against insider trading do not, by themselves, suffice to show that the practice is unethical and should be illegal. The strongest arguments are those that turn on the notion of a fiduciary duty to act in the interest of shareholders, or on the idea of inside information as company "property." But in both arguments, the impermissibility of insider trading depends on a contractual understanding among the company, its shareholders, and its employees. In both cases, a modification of this understanding could change the moral status of insider trading.

Does this mean that there is nothing wrong with insider trading? No. If insider trading is unethical, it is so *in the context* of the relationship among the firm, its shareholders, and its employees. It is possible to change this context in a way that makes the practice permissible. But *should* the context be changed? I will argue that it should not. Because it threatens the fiduciary relationship that is central to business management, I believe, permitting insider trading is in the interest neither of the firm, its shareholders, nor society at large.

Fiduciary relationships are relationships of trust and dependence in which one party acts in the interest of another. They appear in many contexts, but are absolutely essential to conducting business in a complex society. Fiduciary relationships allow parties with different resources, skills, and information to cooperate in productive activity. Shareholders who wish to invest in a business, for example, but who cannot or do not wish to run it themselves, hire others to manage it for them. Managers, directors, and to some extent, other employees, become fiduciaries for the firms they manage and for the shareholders of those firms.

The fiduciary relationship is one of moral and legal obligation. Fiduciaries, that is, are bound to act in the interests of those who depend on them even if these interests do not coincide with their own. Typically, however, fiduciary relationships are constructed as far as possible so that the interests of the fiduciaries and the parties for whom they act *do* coincide. Where the interests of the two parties compete or conflict, the fiduciary relationship is threatened. . . .

Significantly, proponents of insider trading do not dispute the importance of the fiduciary relationship. Rather, they argue that permitting insider trading would *increase* the likelihood that employees will act in the interest of shareholders and their firms.[12] We have already touched on the main argument for this claim. Manne and others contend that assigning employees the right to trade on inside information would provide a powerful incentive for creative and entrepreneurial activity. It would encourage new inventions, creative deals, and efficient new management practices, thus increasing the profits, strength, and overall competitiveness of the firm. Manne goes so far as to argue that permission to trade on insider information is the only appropriate way to compensate entrepreneurial activity, and warns: "[I]f no way to reward the entrepreneur within a corporation exists, he will tend to disappear from the corporate scene."[13] The entrepreneur makes an invaluable contribution to the firm and its shareholders, and his disappearance would no doubt cause serious harm.

If permitting insider trading is to work in the way proponents suggest, however, there must be a direct and consistent link between the profits reaped by insider traders and the performance that benefits the firm. It is not at all clear that this is the case—indeed, there is evidence that the opposite is true. There appear to be many ways to profit from inside information that do not benefit the firm at all. I mention four possibilities below. Two of these (2 and 3) are simply ways in which insider traders can profit without ben-

efiting the firm, suggesting that permitting insider trading is a poor incentive for performance and fails firmly to link the interests of managers, directors and employees to those of the corporation as a whole. The others (1 and 4) are actually harmful to the corporation, setting up conflicts of interest and actively undermining the fiduciary relationship.

1. Proponents of insider trading tend to speak as if all information were positive. "Information," in the proponents' lexicon, always concerns a creative new deal, a new, efficient way of conducting business, or a new product. If this were true, allowing trades on inside information might provide an incentive to work even harder for the good of the company. But information can also concern *bad* news—a large lawsuit, an unsafe or poor quality product, or lower-than-expected performance. Such negative information can be just as valuable to the insider trader as positive information. If the freedom to trade on positive information encourages acts that are beneficial to the firm, then by the same reasoning the freedom to trade on negative information would encourage harmful acts. At the very least, permitting employees to profit from harms to the company decreases the incentive to avoid such harms. Permission to trade on negative inside information gives rise to inevitable conflicts of interest. Proponents of insider trading have not satisfactorily answered this objection.[14]

2. Proponents of insider trading also assume that the easiest way to profit on inside information is to "create" it. But it is not at all clear that this is true. Putting together a deal, inventing a new product, and other productive activities that add value to the firm usually require a significant investment of time and energy. For the well-placed employee, it would be far easier to start a rumor that the company has a new product or is about to announce a deal than to sit down and produce either one—and it would be just as profitable for the employee. If permitting insider trading provides an incentive for the productive "creation" of information, it seems to provide an even greater incentive for the nonproductive "invention" of information, or stock manipulation. The invention of information is in the interest neither of the firm nor of society at large.

3. Even if negative or false information did not pose problems, the incentive argument for insider trading overlooks the difficulties posed by "free riders"—those who do not actually contribute to the creation of the information, but who are nevertheless aware of it and can profit by trading on it. . . . Unless those who do not contribute can be excluded from trading on it, there will be no incentive to produce the desired information; it will not get created at all.

4. Finally, allowing trading on inside information would tend to deflect employees' attention from the day-to-day business of running the company and focus it on major changes, positive or negative, that lead to large insider trading profits. This might not be true if one could profit by inside information about the day-to-day efficiency of the operation, a continuous tradition of product quality, or a consistently lean operating budget. But these things do not generate the kind of information on which insider traders can reap large profits. Insider profits come from dramatic changes, from "news"—not from steady, long-term performance. If the firm and its shareholders have a genuine interest in such performance, then permitting insider trading creates a conflict of interest for insiders. The ability to trade on inside information is also likely to influence the types of information officers announce to the public, and the timing of such announcements, making it less likely that the information and its timing is optimal for the firm. And the problems of false or negative information remain.[15]

If the arguments given above are correct, permitting insider trading does not increase the likelihood that insiders will act in the interest of the firm and its shareholders. In some cases, it actually causes conflicts of interest, undermining the fiduciary relationship essential to managing the corporation. This claim, in turn, gives corporations good reason to prohibit the practice. But insider trading remains primarily a private matter among corporations, shareholders, and employees. It is appropriate to ask why, given this fact about insider trading, the practice should be *illegal*. If it is primarily corporate and shareholder interests that are threatened by insider trading, why not let corporations themselves bear the burden of enforcement? Why involve the SEC? There are two possible reasons for continuing to support laws against insider trading. The first is that even if they wish to prohibit insider trading, individual corporations do not have the resources to do so effectively. The second is that society itself has a stake in the fiduciary relationship. . . .

The notion of the fiduciary duty owed by managers and other employees to the firm and its shareholders has a long and venerable history in our society. Nearly all of our important activities require some sort of cooperation, trust, or reliance on others, and the ability of one person to act in the interest of another—as a fiduciary—is central to this cooperation. The role of managers as fiduciaries for firms and shareholders is grounded in the property rights of shareholders. They are the owners of the firm, and bear the residual risks, and hence have a right to have it managed in their interest. The fiduciary relationship also contributes to efficiency, since it encourages those who are willing to take risks to place their resources in the hands of those who have the expertise to maximize their usefulness. While this "shareholder theory" of the firm has often been challenged in recent years, this has been primarily by people who argue that the fiduciary concept should be widened to include other "stakeholders" in the firm. I have heard no one argue that the notion of managers' fiduciary duties should be eliminated entirely, and that managers should begin working primarily for themselves.

III. CONCLUSION

I have argued that the real reason for prohibiting insider trading is that it erodes the fiduciary relationship that lies at the heart of our business organizations. The more frequently heard moral arguments based on fairness, property rights in information, and harm to ordinary investors are not compelling. Of these, the fairness arguments seem to me the least persuasive. The claim that a trader must reveal everything that it is in the interest of another party to know seems to hold up only when the other is someone to whom he owes a fiduciary duty. But this is not really a "fairness" argument at all. Similarly, the "misappropriation" theory is only persuasive if we can offer reasons for corporations not to assign the right to trade on inside information to their employees. I have found these in the fact that permitting insider trading threatens the fiduciary relationship. I do believe that lifting the ban against insider trading would cause harms to shareholders, corporations, and society at large. But again, these harms stem primarily from the cracks in the fiduciary relationship caused by permitting insider trading, rather than from actual trades with insiders. Violation of fiduciary duty, in short, is at the center of insider trading offenses.

Notes

1. Saul Levmore, "Securities and Secrets: Insider Trading and the Law of Contracts," 68 *Virginia Law Review* 117.

2. The equal access argument is perhaps best stated by Victor Brudney in his influential article, "Insiders, Outsiders, and Informational Advantages Under the Federal Securities Laws," 93 *Harvard Law Review* 322.

3. Manne, *Insider Trading and the Stock Market* (Free Press, New York, 1966), p. 75.

4. Bill Shaw, "Should Insider Trading Be Outside the Law?" *Business and Society Review* 66, p. 34. See also Macey, "From Fairness to Contract: The New Direction of the Rules Against Insider Trading," 13 *Hofstra Law Review* 9 (1984).

5. Brudney, "Insiders, Outsiders, and Informational Advantages," 344.

6. *U.S. v. Newman,* 664 F. 2d 17.

7. *U.S. v. Winans,* 612 F. Supp. 827. The Supreme Court upheld Winans' conviction, but was evenly split on the misappropriation theory. As a consequence, the Supreme Court has still not truly endorsed the theory, although several lower court decisions have been based on it. . . .

8. Carlton and Fischel, "The Regulation of Insider Trading," 35 *Stanford Law Review* 857. See also Manne, *Insider Trading and the Stock Market.*

9. Kenneth Scott, "Insider Trading: Rule 10b-5, Disclosure and Corporate Privacy," 9 *Journal of Legal Studies* 808.

10. "Disputes Arise Over Value of Laws on Insider Trading," *The Wall Street Journal,* November 17, 1986, p. 28.

11. One area that needs more attention is the impact of insider trading on the markets (and ordinary investors) of countries that permit the practice. Proponents of insider trading are fond of pointing out that insider trading has been legal in many overseas markets for years, without the dire effects predicted by opponents of the practice. Opponents reply that these markets are not as fair or efficient as U.S. markets, or that they do not play as important a role in the allocation of capital.

12. See Frank Easterbrook, "Insider Trading as an Agency Problem," *Principals and Agents: The Structure of Business* (Cambridge, MA: Harvard University Press, 1985). I speak here as if the interests of the firm and its shareholders are identical, even though this is sometimes not the case.

13. Manne, *Insider Trading and the Stock Market,* p. 129.

14. Manne is aware of the "bad news" objection, but he glosses over it by claiming that bad news is not as likely as good news to provide large gains for insider traders. *Insider Trading and the Stock Market,* p. 102.

15. There are ways to avoid many of these objections. For example, Manne has suggested "isolating" non-contributors so that they cannot trade on the information produced by others. Companies could also forbid trading on "negative" information. The problem is that these piecemeal restrictions seem very costly—more costly than simply prohibiting insider trading as we do now. In addition, each restriction brings us farther and farther away from what proponents of the practice actually want: unrestricted insider trading.

Review and Discussion Questions

1. Do you agree with Moore's criticism of the fairness argument, or is there something unethical about transactions between parties that lack equal information or equal access to information?

2. If insider trading were legal, then it would be up to individual companies and their shareholders to decide whether to permit it. Would it be in their interest to do so?

3. Critics of insider trading argue that it harms ordinary investors and that permitting it would cause them to lose confidence in the market. Is Moore right to reject these arguments?

4. What are fiduciary relationships, and what is their role in business? Would insider trading undermine such relationships, as Moore argues? Is this a sufficient reason for outlawing insider trading?

5. Are there any arguments against or for insider trading that Moore has overlooked or paid insufficient attention to? Do you believe that insider trading is wrong? Should it remain illegal?

Reading ———————————— ■

FOREIGN CORRUPT PRACTICES: HOW TO DEAL WITH FOREIGN FORMS OF BRIBERY

JEFF FADIMAN

Americans who travel on business to other lands frequently find themselves trying to do business against a backdrop of cultural patterns and expectations that they do not fully understand. How should businesspeople deal with customs that conflict with their own sense of ethics and our nation's laws? In this essay, professor of global marketing Jeff Fadiman discusses bribery in non-Western countries—the reasons for it, the different kinds one can encounter, and how it is done. Because in many non-Western countries turning one's back on all requests for payoffs can be commercial suicide, Fadiman recommends that Americans play the local bribery game—but with our own rules.

INTRODUCTION TO "CORRUPTION"

Some years ago I wrote a "Traveler's Guide to Gifts and Bribes" for *Harvard Business Review* that described my own introduction to overseas bribery. It began with a Kenyan colleague's request for 1,000 shillings as his *zawadi* (gift) and an eight-band radio to bring home for his *chai* (tea). Both *chai* and *zawadi* can be Swahili terms for payoff. His request came after negotiations that settled details of a business venture. The sum he sought was small, but the radio added insult to my injury. Outwardly, I smiled. Inside, my stomach churned. As an American, I settle money questions before contracts are signed. Moreover, I equate bribery with crime. My reaction was standard U.S.A. "I'm American," I

Copyright © 2001 Jeffrey A. Fadiman. Reprinted by permission of the author. Notes omitted.

said. "I don't pay bribes." Then I walked away—from both my colleague and the deal.

As time passed, other Americans told me similar tales. Some had been bribed; some asked to bribe others. Some agreed. Some evaded. Some refused. None had felt comfortable. Nor would most other Americans. To briefly illustrate, consider your personal comfort level in these situations.

Ghana: You enter customs to clear a consignment of goods. You note high stacks of forms, strewn loosely on a single table. The clerk admits your papers will be "difficult" to find, raises his eyebrows, and awaits your reply.

Peru: To establish an office, you require a license. A government official informs you that the process has encountered "unanticipated difficulties" that may cause "indefinite delay." He awaits your reply.

China: Your firm, a major U.S. department store, has ordered high-quality Chinese-made garments for the fall fashion season. A provincial official explains that their trucks have encountered "unexpected problems" in moving the shipment to port; thus he cannot predict the arrival date. Your season is at risk. He awaits your reply.

United States: You testify before the Securities and Exchange Commission regarding alleged violations of the Foreign Corrupt Practices Act (FCPA). How would you defend your response to each "difficulty"? How well would each explanation satisfy U.S. law? How well would they satisfy you?

THREE AMERICAN DILEMMAS

Situations like these provide Americans with three dilemmas. The first is legal, since much of our discomfort is due to U.S. law. We are all too aware that the FCPA forbids U.S. companies to offer foreign "officials" funds to influence them in obtaining or retaining business. The act also prohibits indirect payments, since firms may not offer funds to third parties while "knowing or having reason to know" they will be used for those purposes. Small payments that persuade lower-level foreign officials to perform their routine, lawful duties are allowed, but the law sets no border between what is legal and illegal. This uncertainty has also acted as a restraint. In short, since 1977 the FCPA has effectively forbidden U.S. citizens to bribe. . . . U.S. firms face a world in which our trading partners can bribe, but we cannot.

The second dilemma stems from U.S. ethics. We receive most of life's essential goods and services without experiencing either preferential treatment or overt discrimination. We thus categorize bribery (even in our dictionaries) as a payment used to obtain something illegal. Thus, most of us dislike the very thought of paying bribes. Payoffs do occur in U.S. business, but (unlike in many other countries) they are not the norm, and thus are almost universally condemned. Americans abroad reflect these feelings. Most see themselves as personally honest, professionally ethical, and willing to do business under law, both U.S. and foreign. They also realize that foreign governments have formal laws against private payoff. In consequence, few U.S. firms want to make illegal payments of any kind to anyone.

However, U.S. law and ethics combine to generate a third dilemma, this one both global and commercial. We are a small minority in a world that sanctions payoff. What should we do when key foreign contacts declare that bribes are prerequisite to business? Once overseas, for example, most Americans realize that non-Westerners who solicit bribes are simply following the rules of their respective homelands. However, many of these rules are similar within most homelands. Asians, Africans, Arabs, Latins, and Eastern Europeans share certain common payoff patterns that we can recognize in almost all non-Western nations. That leaves us with two related problems. One is to research their rules; the next is to adjust ours, to the point where *we* can operate in ways that meet the legal, ethical, and commercial requirements of both sides.

WHY DO THEY BRIBE?

While businesspeople bribe for many reasons, three seem particularly relevant to Americans who deal with non-Western variants of payoff. Non-Western cultures have a communal dimension that we often ignore. Within these regions, people define themselves in two distinct ways, once as individuals and again as members of communal groups

(extended family, clan, caste, sect, etc.). Each identity (individual, communal) creates specific obligations, reinforced by centuries of tradition. At least three of the communal obligations provide reasons for what we consider bribery.

1. *Meet extended family needs.* Payoff requests may be justified by the obligation to meet the financial needs of members within one's communal group, however broadly defined. In these cultures an individual lives symbolically within a series of concentric circles. The smallest—that closest to him—consists of blood kin, his immediate and extended family. The second is composed of kin by marriage. Outer circles consist of increasingly "fictional" kin, regarded as "brothers" ("uncles," etc.) because they share some portion of his past (age-mates, schoolmates, army comrades, etc.). Zaire's President Mobuto, for instance, claimed 3,000 blood relations and perhaps 5,000 others as "kin." Collectively, members of these varied circles make up an extended family that we may deem fictional but they see as real.

Collective tradition requires each family member to aid all kin (both real and fictional) in need. Thus, any relative can ask a favor, sure it will be granted to the extent allowed by custom. In consequence, a wage earner may respond to dozens (or hundreds) of requests from kinsfolk, each of whom may ask for funds in times of joy (to feast) or crisis (to cope). Similarly, job holders must also share earned income among workplace superiors (who may also be kin, whether fictional or real). When they seek work, applicants pay hirers to consider them. When they receive it, part of each wage moves "up" to supervisors—even as other parts move "down" to extended family.

As a result, many non-Western officials live in a nightmarish netherworld of high status and shared poverty. Egyptian customs officers earn $25 per month. Liberian counterparts earn 50 cents per month, when paid. Mexican police net $65, after payoffs to superiors, fees to rent patrol cars, uniforms, weapons, bullets, and a "rich" patrol zone. *In nations where hirees* know *all earnings must be shared, they do not seek posts as a source of wages, but as platforms from which to freelance routine services for fees*. Thus, when U.S. business personnel appear, payoff requests begin.

2. *Exchange favors/forge relationships*. A second reason to seek bribes is to offer favors in return. In these cultures, the promise of a future favor can often replace wages as a basis of economic security. If a supervisor hires a subordinate to perform a service, then pays a fee, the transaction is complete; no further relationship is required. However, if the subordinate rejects the fee and does the work as a favor, he creates a sense of obligation in the hirer and thus a potential relationship. In the future, he may ask this employer for a favor. Feeling under obligation, the employer may grant it, then ask a second favor in turn. The subordinate, placed under obligation in his turn, may once more grant it without asking payment. Thus, sequential favors launch relationships. Over time, the ebb and flow of favors should benefit both hirer and hiree, to the point where their relationship evolves from acquaintance to alliance to a fictional kinship that both find very real.

This "future favor exchange" is a key business tool in all non-Western nations. Japanese call it "inner duty." Kenyans create "relationship." Chinese seek "connections." Zulu call it "humanness"; Filipinos, "inner obligation." Each system of this type assumes that any person under obligation to another enters a relationship in which each prior favor must be repaid on request. Each repayment transfers the sense of obligation to the other side. The "good feelings" that spring from doing favors for each other create the trust prerequisite for doing business. Thus, when we appear—in need of business favors—exchanging current (U.S.) funds for future (on-site) favors appears a logical prerequisite for commercial relationship.

3. *Seek patronage, protection, security*. Payoff requests can finally be justified by the need to generate patronage. Americans derive security from their belief in the rule of law. Where such rule is lacking (or crumbling) security can also come from creating connections with those who have power, thus gaining their protection. "In America," one informant declared, "things are easy to get. You just buy them. In Congo, they are scarce. We cannot just buy what is not there. Thus, those who need big

things must ask 'big men' (those with power) to get them. To get their attention, we present gifts—before, during, and after a transaction. In turn, they provide for and thus protect us. They are our fathers. By giving to them, we store for ourselves."

This "big man" pattern can also apply when seeking business opportunities. Consider a Ghanian tradition called "sharing the goats," from an earlier era where goats were used as currency. An Akan/Kwi proverb, *Obiya dedee wu nea ejumamu* ("Everyone eats at his work"), tells listeners that one's post should be used to enrich one's person. Thus, a businessman seeking to launch a venture will offer the official the "first goat" (money) before even making his request. He does this both to establish himself as petitioner and the official as authority, thereby publicly launching an unequal relationship. He will offer additional "goats" as the venture progresses (to reinforce this public image) and a final one, in gratitude, at its completion. More important, he will contribute further gifts and services ("goats") forever after, thereby periodically reaffirming his dependent status should he need further favors.

We see each step in this process as bribery. Most non-Western colleagues do not. Rather, they see each "goat" as reaffirming tradition and thus displaying commercial wisdom. Thus, when we appear in search of business, some non-Western contacts seek our patronage. Others hope we seek theirs. Both groups simply want us to behave as custom commands. By "sharing goats," we signal that we seek relationships.

THEIR SIDE/OUR SIDE: WHO MUST "PLAY"?

For most of us, bribery begins at foreign borders. For convenience, consider it a game, complete with stages, rules, and players. As passengers disembark and divide into the conventional orderly lines for citizens and visitors, they are also separating into players and nonplayers. By passing through customs, they enter onto a foreign playing field, and some must begin to play the payoff game.

Players: These include all who must play (i.e., bribe). They have no option. Generally, this means all host nationals returning home as well as former nationals who have immigrated abroad, regardless of current citizenship. It can also include their grown children, born in the United States. Former Vietnamese, for instance, returning to their homeland, find they must deal with problems of payoff. Whether Vietnamese citizens, U.S. immigrants, or American born, they are still Vietnamese at the border. In consequence, few reenter Vietnam without negotiating supplementary fees.

Non-players: These include most U.S. tourists. In general, first-time visitors are placed outside the foreign system. Knowing neither the language nor the culture, they clearly cannot know the rules regarding bribes. Thus, foreign nationals approaching them for extra payments could generate both anger and embarrassment, leading to mutual loss of personal and professional dignity. Consequently, they are often simply let alone.

Future players: This is not true, however, for future players, U.S. businesspeople who cross the foreign border with sufficient frequency to gradually become known. In this case, a gradually increasing mastery of host nation languages and customs works against them. The more effectively they penetrate the culture, the more likely they will be asked to play as their contacts, commercial value, and knowledge of the game expand.

Once across the border, we must decide who will most likely solicit bribes. To anticipate them, we must learn how payoffs operate at various social levels as well as which players within each class are most likely to approach. To illustrate, consider three social groups who might solicit U.S. business personnel.

Clerks (service class): This level includes all commercial and government personnel with whom Americans must make initial contacts, including employees in immigration, banks, firms, security units (police, etc.), and government departments. Since risk of punishment is low among this class of players, direct requests for cash are common. Notwithstanding, fear of public accusation leads clerks to use synonyms when suggesting extra fees. Many reflect concerns with food. Thus when soliciting bribes, Congolese and Moroccans ask for "children's beans." Kenyans and Indonesians refer

to coffee money. Mexicans and Colombians speak of the "bite." Liberians ask for cold water. Chinese mention steamed buns and cigarettes, while Thai offer to "add value to your hot water" (i.e., make it tea). Other nations use similar terms. Americans should learn them, both to recognize the initial signal for a payoff and realize that the lower a petitioner's social class, the more direct (and cash oriented) his petition will be, and the less he will hope for a long-term relationship.

Officials (middle class): This group includes every administrator with whom we might logically do business. We refer to them as "bureaucrats" or "officials" and mean those who hold routine decision-making posts within commercial or government departments. These are the people who stand symbolically behind the clerks. They are middle class, hence more discreet. Their requests for payoff will be both larger in scope and more indirect in manner. Since bribery is formally illegal, direct discussion of it is both a social insult and commercial threat. In consequence, one side or both may use a go-between.

Executives (upper class): This includes executives in non-Western ministries, agencies, or corporations, who are often linked to long-established, wealthy families. The higher a key player's social class, the greater his need to preserve dignity—thus the more indirect, convoluted, and complex the bribery process may become. At this level, the number of people involved on both sides may expand exponentially. Colombians refer to the process as "twisted pastry" (*roscas*), to describe the intertwined commercial, social, professional, and military links among the families that make up that nation's upper class. Thus, to forge a "satisfying" financial arrangement at this level requires extensive contacts.

Among executives, the primary goal of both sides may go beyond cash transfer to developing long-term relationships. Latin informants suggest this type of (illicit) interaction should be handled with stylized flair, like a theater piece in which each partner knows what role to play. Asians claim it should be based on shared traditions, in which each side knows the others' expectations. Africans feel that mutual trust eliminates the need to negotiate, since both parties will know what to do. From a U.S. perspective, however, all three statements suggest the existence of a lengthy and complex sequence of unspoken rules by which the game is played. We should research them.

WHO STARTS, AND HOW

Clerks (silent signals): No nation makes bribery legal. Thus, nowhere is it prudent to openly ask for or offer a bribe. As a result, most non-Western clerical/service personnel prefer potential clients (including U.S. business clients) to introduce the topic, thus reducing risks to themselves. If the client fails to act appropriately, however, and especially if (by virtue of being foreign) he or she does not know how to begin, personnel at this level will try to indirectly provide guidance, beginning by sending silent signals.

In Nigeria and Thailand, for instance, commercial and government clerks deliberately stack huge piles of paper in appropriate positions along tables and desks, as "silent" signals of how busy they are. In Zaire, postal workers pile incoming mail on post office floors rather than sorting and placing it in postal boxes. When patrons appear, they let the setting silently signal appropriate behavior. In China, inspectors visit businesses and hang coats up on hangers while accepting tea. The hanging coat serves as an unspoken signal to fill the pockets with cash. In each case, the signal simply asks potential clients to take the next step.

Client expresses commercial need: If clients know both the signal and the rules, they then approach the topic. The least sophisticated method (most used by Westerners) is a direct request for a specific service. Alternately, Mexicans and Colombians may politely mention how busy the officials must be, then express commercial needs in non-specific terms. Thai and Vietnamese, perhaps more ceremoniously, may (1) do the same, (2) describe their own potential difficulties should these needs not be met, (3) ask the functionary's advice, (4) express willingness to follow it, and (5) display gratitude in advance. In every case, the purpose is to signal an initial willingness to consider payoff by vaguely expressing a commercial need.

Officials (difficulty = delay): An official may respond by citing "unspecified difficulties" that may cause "indefinite delay." These two verbal signals particularly disturb Americans because they clash with our desire for precision with regard to data. At this point, however, Americans often seek specific reasons for delay as well as equally specific (higher level) decision makers to resolve it. Sometimes these first reactions lead officials to deliberately delay decisions by referring them to supervisors. Alternately, they may accuse us of noncompliance with either real or fictional regulations. Others simply point in silence to the sheer volume of work piled on their desks and raise their eyebrows. In every case, such responses are simply second signals asking if we wish to carry on. We need only realize they are sent.

Client asks advice: Ideally, the potential client should respond to hints of difficulty and delay by asking the official for advice and/or offering to help. This can be done directly ("How can you facilitate . . . ," "How can I facilitate . . .") or indirectly. Sometimes, this is done through local proverbs (India: "Give and take is part of life, how . . ." Hungary: "Time is money to us all. Can you advise . . ."). Most often, the official may just agree to see what can be done. This is the first signal. If the client then responds with gratitude, agreement is reached.

HOW MUCH SHOULD WE PAY?

Standard rates? If asked to bribe, how much should we offer? What is appropriate? foolish? correct? Many Americans feel there are no rules and that petitioners charge what the market will bear. This may not be true. Several informants insist that rates in their nations are standardized by local custom. Egyptians and Indians, for example, contend that ethical behavior is central to clerical and middle-class *bakshish* (bribery). Officials know the rules and follow them. Thai and Filipinos also argue that those who violate traditional guidelines are criticized by coworkers and clientele alike. In Russia, payoff rates have standardized to the point where the daily newspaper *Komsomolskaya Pravda* was able to compile a Moscow price list of commercial bribes for 1993.

Other informants also feel that custom regulates payoff requests, at least at lower social levels, except where society itself breaks down. Thus, where payoff expectations seem limited, they are clearly predictable. However, double, triple, and multiple standards may also be applied. Vietnamese, for instance, suggest one "range" of possible rates for host nationals, a second for ex-nationals, and a third for foreigners. Within each range, payments may be further segmented and thus standardized by homeland (foreigners), home region (nationals, ex-nationals), and smaller factors such as age, sex, apparent wealth, and intensity of (client's) commercial need.

Still more subtle graduations may also be set by local custom. One Thai national, seeking permits to begin a business, paid just enough extra to have her application placed near the top of an appropriate pile. Contented, she explained that she knew she could not afford to "reach the top" but paid what was required to "avoid the middle." Asked how she knew this, she replied that it was common knowledge. Asked how foreigners could learn this type of knowledge, she suggested they ask.

HOW TO PAY

Avoid public payoff: Public payoffs are often commercially counterproductive. Despite our U.S. preference for direct and open business interaction, no bribe should be offered, accepted, nor transferred overtly. If you are solicited in public, politely decline and deal with competitors. To offer a payment where others can watch may violate local tradition, anger a potential recipient's coworkers, and expose him/her to possible blackmail or even arrest. In short, it momentarily strips the non-Western contact of both personal and professional dignity. In consequence, the recipient may strike back, magnifying the originally "unspecified" difficulties mentioned earlier into specific and significant violations of law.

Use paper camouflage: A more prudent (and more non-Western) method of transferring supplementary payments is to use "paper camouflage." In simple form, this can be done by slipping funds between two documents, then passing them to the official. Filipino and Peruvian informants suggest these not be stapled, bound, or taped, lest officials

even momentarily lose face in struggling to remove the contents. Indeed, many take pride in an ability to remove money so quickly and skillfully no coworker knows it takes place. A more common method is placing cash in an envelope. This is given the official with the instruction that he "read the documents as time allows," thus creating the illusion that both sides are conducting business. . . .

Add verbal camouflage: "Paper camouflage" should be accompanied by "verbal camouflage," meant both to conceal the transaction from listeners and create good feelings (and thus potential bonds) between giver and recipient. Thus "children's beans," "tea money," "steamed buns," and the like must never be given either in silence or with obvious bad grace. Rather, at the most basic level, a payoff must be given with verbal good wishes, often linked to directions as to how the funds may be used. Thus, Indians, Nigerians, and Thai may ask recipients to "use the documents (within the envelope) to educate your children." A giver may also include a business card to signal that future commercial interaction and thus a possible relationship are being solicited. The recipient signals agreement by returning his own. . . .

Executive Variants

Executive (upper class) bribery differs from clerical and mid-level variants mainly in scope. The wealthier the players, the more lavish their actions. The higher their social level, the greater their need to preserve reputations. Thus, though some methods of operation approximate those of the clerical class, their complexity, geographic scale, and time frame expand. Consider four differences most relevant to Americans.

Use multiple go-betweens: Clerks often seek bribes directly. Officials may use a go-between. Executives may utilize an entire network of subordinates, one for each decision maker. The higher the principal's social class, the more middlemen/women may be required. Thus, where Americans lack preestablished relationships with key decision makers, appropriate go-betweens may prove useful in making contacts at higher social levels.

In many non-Western nations, go-betweens fill a respected commercial niche. Their work is to bring key commercial players together, then help them form mutually useful relationships. In Congo, for example, where they are known as *musalisi,* go-betweens are commercial generalists. In contrast, Japan's *nakodo* specialize in narrowly defined commercial fields. Professional go-betweens emerge in countries where business is conducted through informal primary relationships rather than formal, written rules. The fees they ask are not considered bribes, but fair compensation for service rendered. . . .

Social camouflage: Executive payoff patterns also differ from working-class transactions in their use of social camouflage. Whereas clerical and (much) mid-level bribery often occurs in offices, elitist arrangements most often begin within elegant social settings. However, exclusive restaurants, nightclubs, golf courses, and the like do not serve as settings for currency exchange, but as places for potential principals (or their go-betweens) to grow acquainted, to the point where allegedly illicit financial arrangement can eventually be discussed. This may occur in a single evening but will more likely take place over weeks, as several similar occasions may be needed to create a climate appropriate to the sensitivity of financial discussion that may occur. . . .

Verbal ambiguity: Even after such a climate is created, discussion remains indirect and deliberately vague. No overt mention of a money transfer is made by either principal. Rather, each side indulges in ambiguities, so artfully rendered as to leave no doubt as to their double meanings. At their core, however, these are no different than the comparatively direct discussions that occur at clerical levels, in that:

- The client indicates commercial need.
- The official postulates potential difficulties, indefinite delay.
- The client asks advice, or offers aid.
- The official promises to see what can be done.

Thereafter, conversation on the topic stops. Other subjects are introduced, to permit both sides to reflect on the risks and rewards involved in what has covertly been decided. The evening may end with nothing resolved. Nonetheless, both sides will have achieved their goals—shared experiences, deeper acquaintance, and thus creation of a climate within which further interaction can occur.

Expanded use of space and time: Consider the U.S. businessman who offers these statistics on getting contracts in China:

> To get a small contract, say $20,000 . . . it's a couple of dinners out. . . . For a $250,000 contract, it's a familiarization trip for the official to the States. A contract of a million and above? Then, we're talking about getting a visa for the guy's son.

Can it be argued that this man is unaware of an entire dimension in non-Western business? Among executives, the scope of a payoff not only expands with regard to spending, but also space and time. At this level, the relationship's duration becomes increasingly significant to both sides. The more time taken in the presentation of a monetary favor, the more highly the presenter will be valued. Thus, the "gift" of membership in an exclusive U.S. club may require annual payment of required fees for many years. It is the long-term obligation that gives the gift its value. A U.S. college scholarship—made available for key decision makers' kin—can take years to complete; however, the receiving family may cherish the giver for a generation.

These deliberate expansions of the gift-and-favor process provide the most significant difference between lower- and upper-class patterns of bribery. The former wish to complete a single transaction with sufficient mutual goodwill to create the climate for another. The latter wish to gradually weave both sides into a web of lifelong mutual obligation that will form the basis for commercial trust. To do so takes time. Thus American executives should be particularly selective when choosing elite foreign colleagues. At this level, each relationship they offer may be meant to last a lifetime.

"PLAY" IN THEIR GAME?

No one forces us to bribe. If asked, why should we comply? Again, informants provide several reasons of commercial interest to Americans:

Gain commercial influence: One reason to consider non-Western forms of bribery is to acquire both an immediate and long-range commercial edge. Clearly, this can be achieved by gaining short-term influence over a potentially useful individual within a commercial setting, since a properly presented gift will place him under an initial sense of obligation. Over time, this can be nurtured into a longer-range relationship within which both sides exert influence on one another in ways each finds commercially useful.

Establish commercial reliability: As foreign strangers in a foreign land, we may be labeled high risk. Non-Westerners often find us untrustworthy, simply because we do not play by local rules. Thus, no one knows how an American will behave once commercial interaction has begun. This applies particularly to bribery. An Equadorian CEO once told me that he could never trust a man he couldn't bribe. "How else," he asked, "could I influence him?" A Hungarian contends that if you (the foreigner) accept the bribe, you will probably provide a favor in return, and thus can be trusted. Consequently, when you need a favor, you receive it. If not, you don't. Other informants agree, essentially arguing that one way to establish credibility in foreign commerce is to play by foreign rules, including payoff rules.

Avoid commercial ostracism: Conversely, refusing to bribe may damage your firm's commercial reputation in an unexpected way. The word may spread that you are "honest" (unbribable). A Budapest informant described the impact of this process on a U.S. business acquaintance. The American refused to either bribe or be bribed. The Hungarians who dealt with him decided that if he was "unbribable," he was unpredictable, thus "untrustworthy." Since bribery was both illegal and unavoidable within their system, to deal with him might actually create commercial risk, should he expose what they perceived as normal business methods to Hungarian law. In consequence, they chose to exclude him from the collective dimension of local Hungarian commerce. The American's commercial reputation ensured that his commercial efforts were ignored.

Save commercial time: Many informants argue that bribery saves time. A payoff can gain you special consideration. It can acquire commercial permission. It can hasten commercial action. Indians and Indonesians argue that officials control your commercial time by virtue of their post. You pay to avoid a deliberate imposition of delay. On occasion, the extent of this delay staggers U.S. imaginations. Vietnamese and Thai informants declare that payoffs create a "climate" wherein the official acts to save the foreign applicant "commercial time," which in these nations can be "ten years." To avoid this, Thai argue that "money cuts paper" (i.e., regulations).

Potential payoff, however, must also be evaluated in terms of human feelings. An official may equate rejection of what to him will seem a routine bribery request with rejection of relationship. He will thus do nothing to facilitate your project. That lack of action may indefinitely postpone it. Reexamine, for example, the situation of the U.S. department store in China. The project CEO had ordered quality garments for their fashion season, paid fair prices, but failed to develop long-range gifts-and-favors relationships with key decision makers in an appropriate ministry. In consequence, when an official informed him the trucks to transport the shipment from factory to port had met "unexpected difficulties," the American assumed the problems were mechanical and offered U.S. mechanics to "fix the trucks." This compounded his problems, for in fact, they were human. The deputy minister's message was simply an invitation to enter the system. The CEO's response was a rejection.

Make commercial connections: Recall that many non-Western traders conduct business along extended family networks, composed of kinsmen, colleagues, and comrades. To use an electrical analogy, each individual within a network is "wired" to all others by an intangible web of prior gifts and favors. Intermittent gifts and minor favors ensure all wiring remains in repair. Thus, should one person "switch on" someone in the system by seeking a favor, human electricity will flow. In crisis, he need contact just those individuals needed to help surmount it. They can contact him in turn. Ideally, each crisis strengthens the entire system. However, all members must stay wired in, since other extended families have competing systems of their own.

On first arrival, commercial Americans lack access to these systems, and indeed may not know they exist. Swahili describe such outsiders as *wageni* (strangers), meaning those with neither (local) friends nor kin. Japanese call them *gai koku jin* (outside-country-men), meaning those who lack all (Japanese) connections. Namibia's Xhoi-San simply call them "predators." Other non-Western nations use similar terms. Invariably, the unspoken implication is that such people should be shunned.

Thus, we face two options on first entering such settings. One is to ignore these competing systems altogether, thus risk remaining on the periphery of on-site commercial interaction. Another is to tap, selectively, into those commercial groups that seem most relevant to our venture, then learn to operate within them. In areas where connections seem prerequisite to commerce, we should develop them. Non-Westerners argue that what we see as bribery is, in fact, a useful method to accomplish this, by signaling foreign decision makers that we seek not just brief connections but relationships that lead to future business.

Avoid commercial retaliation: We must also realize there are penalties for staying off the playing field. By rejecting an offer to enter the system, we risk generating both private embarrassment and public loss of face. This loss is felt with equal intensity by a traffic policeman, customs clerk, corporate administrator, junior minister, or anyone else who requests what funds he feels are due to him in exchange for future favors he will do for you. Thus, when refused, each one may wish to retaliate. . . .

PLAY THEIR GAME? USE OUR RULES!

Naked bribery—exchanging U.S. currency for commercial favors—is the least subtle and most inconsiderate form of payment available to American business. Naked bribery ignores non-Western commercial traditions that idealize subtlety, gradualism, and long-term ties through an *exchange* of gifts and favors. Among Americans, naked bribery actively promotes ill will, thereby eroding rather than forging relationships. The same applies to Americans who trade abroad. There as here, *the more money you give, the less the recipients will like you and the less you will like them.* Surely, we can play

in foreign payoff games while using other rules—U.S. rules that satisfy our sense of ethics and our law. Consider the following.

Rule 1: Adjust Our U.S. Mindset

Why not begin by adjusting our American mindset? Consider, for instance, our U.S. view of non-Western target markets. Rather than labeling them as "less developed" or "corrupt," why not mentally equate them with Adam Smith's classic free market—a countrywide shopping mall, where every imaginable service is now for sale? This specifically includes those so-called "routine services" (customs clearance, application forms, commercial permits) that we Americans subconsciously expect either for free or fixed/fair prices, since U.S. officials receive fixed/fair wages to provide them. Since non-Western officials do not receive such fees, they will solicit them from us. Moreover, they will use at least five rules that differ markedly from ours:

- No fixed prices; each fee is negotiable.
- No contracts; each deal is based on trust.
- Buyer pays in advance; service comes after.
- Terms of agreement may change on the way.
- Twin goals: make profit, forge ties.

Why not adjust our pre-payoff mindset to these Third World realities?

Next, why not adjust our view of non-Western payoff requests? Why not research them—like any other business problem—before launching an initial venture? Each inquiry you make will provide a contact who may offer opportunities to enter the system in ways that satisfy you both. Examine the economic context within which each request appears—such as the actual wages available to officials who solicit you or the degree to which existing poverty is shared. Analyze the social context, such as the degree of kinship within each foreign firm. Analyze the legal context: Do those you work with have protection under law, or must they seek it from the rich and powerful? Now consider the payoff requests: Are they attempts at extortion or bids for relationship?

Rule 2: Deflect Cash Requests

Shield strategy: Why not develop a deflection strategy? Is everyone who solicits us interested only in private enrichment? How artfully can we deflect each solicitor away from an initial focus on cash payment and toward more attractive alternatives? *One useful first step might be to use the FCPA as a "commercial shield," which we need only raise to deflect requests for money payoff.* Unlike our foreign competitors, we need only state that U.S. law forbids such payoffs then ask if we could be of service in some other way. Look long range. Could we not offer uniquely U.S. services or opportunities or contacts? How could our firm enhance the business of a key non-Western contact over decades? Could he do the same for us? Would we then have a Third World–style relationship, and would that satisfy the FCPA?

Go-between strategy: Go-betweens can serve as on-site educators, deflecting requests for cash payoff before they are asked. Locate them by developing contacts with U.S.-based foreign nationals who are prominent both in their homeland and your commercial niche. Let these lead you to equally respected contacts—well connected to their own extended families—within the target market you intend to enter.

Nurture both professional and personal relationships with potential go-betweens, to the point where trust develops. Meet FCPA concerns by paying reasonable, well-documented fees for the service they provide. Do not ask them to arrange cash payoffs. Some U.S. firms skirt the law's intent by hiring foreign agents, then feigning ignorance of how they bribe. Why clash with FCPA concerns about indirect payment? Instead, use well-briefed go-betweens to educate potential foreign colleagues about your commercial limitations, including those imposed by the FCPA. Simultaneously, ask them to educate you about the limitations placed upon these same potential colleagues and anyone else with whom you might wish to do business.

Patron strategy: Thereafter, seek links with powerful on-site commercial allies. There are still too many countries in which Americans have no recourse to law. If you are not connected, in such regions, you are not protected. If you are not protected, you are fair game for that type of bribery we call exploitation. Therefore, as both your project and on-site expertise expand, consider asking go-betweens to aid you, over time, to develop relationships with a visible, established, and respected "commercial family" operating prominently in your field. Within their network, nurture contact with a patron to whom you can turn for advice in resolving local business problems (such as contract noncompliance) in local ways.

Rule 3: Counterbribe, American Style

An American proverb states that the best defense is a counterattack. Why not counterbribe, using methods that meet both U.S. and foreign norms? Why not use our uniquely American commercial strengths (access to capital, technology, marketing expertise, etc.) to create degrees of foreign commercial dependence on U.S. products, projects, and firms?

Goods strategy: Consider, for example, a Western firm's experience in 1970s Zaire—a time when the economy had decayed so badly that even ranking civil servants went unpaid. In consequence, key Zairois officials approached the firm's CEO requesting current funds for future favors. Instead, he responded by "donating" surplus goods for resale in black markets, thus enabling the officials to continue in their posts. Over time, they grew increasingly dependent on the firm's largesse, thus increasingly willing to provide commercial favors in their turn. By transforming the payoff from currency to saleable goods, the CEO created a gradually expanding degree of commercial dependence among its solicitors. In essence, they ended by working for him.

Status strategy: Counterbribery may also mean transforming cash requests into commercial status. Consider the experience of a U.S. firm in Java, which sought to buy rural acreage on which to site a factory. When numerous peasant owners refused to sell at any price, the firm worked through Indonesian officials to send them on the *hadj* (pilgrimage) to Mecca. Sending the *hadji* (pilgrims) added 10 percent to the purchase price for the land. However, the firm initially transformed a situation that normally would engender payoff requests by providing both religious and social status to virtually everyone involved.

Assume, hypothetically, that it repeats the process, financing a pilgrimage each year for both its most reliable employees and the oldest, most venerable men in surrounding communities. Would that not create both commercial and religious dependence among both groups? For the firm, that might mean a protected work site, contented workforce, and respect from the surrounding population. It might also lead to widespread local purchase of its products. Could *any* of these be achieved with cash bribes?

Service strategy: Counterbribery can also mean transforming payoff requests into commercial service. Key non-Western decision makers can be provided training and equipment in specific services they need but cannot provide—or sometimes even imagine. One U.S. informant deflected payoff requests in this way while investigating opportunities in Eastern Europe. Initially, his potential venture partners sought only bribes and capital. Refusing (citing the FCPA), he counteroffered expertise in marketing, only to realize that the very concept of demand creation lay outside their previous (communist) experience.

He responded by transforming their cash requests into services intended to develop their dependence on his firm. Initially, he provided his new colleagues with computers, then with training as to how they could be used in marketing. Periodically, he intensified the process by upgrading the equipment as well as selectively introducing them to U.S. marketing experts who reinforced his views. Gradually, as their professional dependence on computers deepened, their commercial dependence on U.S. marketing methods intensified, as did their personal dependence on my informant.

These strategies do not exhaust the list. Project heads could easily devise new options, each meant to simultaneously enhance commercial opportunity (for "them"), create commercial dependence (on "us"), and avoid the giveaway of U.S. funds. The FCPA provides us with a priceless opportunity: to gain an on-site reputation for providing services instead of bribes. As our legal dilemma dissolves, home offices may respond more favorably to overseas requests for funds. Turning private payments into public service should meet congressional, corporate, and even personal U.S. moral norms, thus easing our ethical dilemma. Finally, we can even resolve our commercial dilemma. Not only can we learn the rules of foreign payoff games, but how to modify them so that we can play.

Review and Discussion Questions

1. Explain the three reasons for foreign bribery that Fadiman discusses. Do most Americans look at bribery from a culturally biased perspective, or is Fadiman too tolerant of foreign corruption?

2. Fadiman lists several reasons why it may be in the commercial interest of Americans to play the bribery game. Should they do it? Does playing the bribery game make good business sense? Is it morally right?

3. Explain the three rules Fadiman proposes for dealing with bribery. Do they resolve the business and ethical dilemmas that U.S. businesspeople may face overseas?

4. Critics of the FCPA claim that it puts American companies at a competitive disadvantage by forbidding them to bribe foreign officials. Do you agree or disagree? Is the FCPA a good law? Should it be repealed?

5. Americans view bribery as immoral. But if bribery is an accepted practice in a foreign country, is it still immoral? Explain your answer. Why do we consider bribery wrong in the first place?

Reading————————■

SOME PARADOXES OF WHISTLEBLOWING

MICHAEL DAVIS

In this essay, Michael Davis challenges the standard the-
ory of justified whistle blowing, arguing that it gives rise
to three paradoxes—the paradox of burden, the paradox
of missing harm, and the paradox of failure. In its place he
advocates what he calls the complicity theory. *In contrast*
to the standard theory, which focuses on the whistle
blower's obligation to prevent harm, the complicity theory
justifies whistle blowing on the basis of the whistle
blower's obligation to avoid complicity in wrongdoing.
Davis tests his theory against a classic case of whistle
blowing, Roger Boisjoly's testimony before the commission
investigating the Challenger *disaster. (A senior engineer at*
Morton-Thiokol, Boisjoly had recommended that the
space shuttle Challenger *not be launched because the tem-*
perature at the launch site had fallen below the safety
range for the O-ring seals in the rocket boosters. Top man-
agement overrode the recommendation, and the next day,
shortly after being launched, the Challenger *exploded,*
killing its seven crew members.)

INTRODUCTION

By "paradox" I mean an apparent—and, in this
case, real—inconsistency between theory (our systematic understanding of whistleblowing) and the
facts (what we actually know, or think we know,
about whistleblowing). What concerns me is not a
few anomalies, the exceptions that test a rule, but a
flood of exceptions that seems to swamp the rule.

This essay has four parts. The first states the standard theory of whistleblowing. The second argues
that the standard theory is paradoxical, that it is inconsistent with what we know about whistleblowers. The third part sketches what seems to me a less

From *Business and Professional Ethics Journal* 15 (Spring 1996).
Reprinted by permission of the author. Some notes omitted.

paradoxical theory of whistleblowing. The fourth
tests the new theory against one classic case of
whistleblowing, Roger Boisjoly's testimony before
the presidential commission investigating the *Challenger* disaster ("the Rogers Commission"). I use
that case because the chief facts are both uncontro-
versial enough and well-known enough to make detailed exposition unnecessary. For the same reason,
I also use that case to illustrate various claims about
whistleblowing throughout the essay.

JUSTIFICATION AND WHISTLEBLOWING

The standard theory is not about whistleblowing,
as such, but about justified whistleblowing—and
rightly so. Whether this or that is, or is not, whistleblowing is a question for lexicographers. For the
rest of us, mere moral agents, the question is—
when, if ever, is whistleblowing justified?

We may distinguish three (related) senses in
which an act may be "justified." First, an act may be
something morality permits. Many acts, for example, eating fruit at lunch, are morally justified in this
weak sense. They are (all things considered) morally
all right, though some of the alternatives are morally
all right too. Second, acts may be morally justified
in a stronger sense. Not only is doing them morally
all right, but doing anything else instead is morally
wrong. These acts are *morally* required. Third,
some acts, though only morally justified in the
weaker sense, are still required all things considered. That is, they are mandatory because of some
non-moral consideration. They are *rationally* (but
not morally) required.

I shall be concerned here only with *moral* justification, that is, with what morality permits or requires. I shall have nothing to say about when other
considerations, for example, individual prudence
or social policy, make (morally permissible) whistleblowing something reason requires.

Generally, we do not *need* to justify an act unless we have reason to think it wrong (whether
morally wrong or wrong in some other way). So, for
example, I do not need to justify eating fruit for
lunch today, though I would if I were allergic to
fruit or had been keeping a fast. We also do not

need a justification if we believe the act in question wrong. We do not need a justification because, insofar as an act is wrong, justification is impossible. The point of justification is to show to be right an act the rightness of which has been put in (reasonable) doubt. Insofar as we believe the act wrong, we can only condemn or excuse it. To condemn it is simply to declare it wrong. To excuse it is to show that, while the act was wrong, the doer had good reason to do it, could not help doing it, or for some other reason should not suffer the response otherwise reserved for such a wrongdoer.

Most acts, though permitted or required by morality, need no justification. There is no reason to think them wrong. Their justification is too plain for words. Why then is whistleblowing so problematic that we need *theories* of its justification? What reason do we have to think whistleblowing might be morally wrong?

Whistleblowing always involves revealing information that would not ordinarily be revealed. But there is nothing morally problematic about that; after all, revealing information not ordinarily revealed is one function of science. Whistleblowing always involves, in addition, an actual (or at least declared) intention to prevent something bad that would otherwise occur. There is nothing morally problematic in that either. That may well be the chief use of information.

What seems to make whistleblowing morally problematic is its organizational context. A mere individual cannot blow the whistle (in any interesting sense); only a member of an organization, whether a current or a former member, can do so. Indeed, he can only blow the whistle on his own organization (or some part of it). So, for example, a police officer who makes public information about a burglary ring, though a member of an organization, does not blow the whistle on the burglary ring (in any interesting sense). He simply alerts the public. Even if he came by the information working undercover in the ring, his revelation could not be whistleblowing. While secret agents, spies, and other infiltrators need a moral justification for what they do, the justification they need differs from that which whistleblowers need. Infiltrators gain their information under false

pretenses. They need a justification for that deception. Whistleblowers generally do not gain their information under false pretenses.

What if, instead of being a police officer, the revealer of information about the burglary ring were an ordinary member of the ring? Would such an informer be a (justified) whistleblower? I think not. The burglary ring is a criminal organization. The whistleblower's organization never is, though it may occasionally engage in criminal activity (knowingly or inadvertently). So, even a burglar, who, having a change of heart, volunteers information about his ring to the police or the newspaper, does not need to justify his act in the way the whistleblower does. Helping to destroy a criminal organization by revealing its secrets is morally much less problematic than whistleblowing.

What then is morally problematic about the whistleblower's organizational context? The whistleblower cannot blow the whistle using just any information obtained in virtue of membership in the organization. A clerk in Accounts who, happening upon evidence of serious wrongdoing while visiting a friend in Quality Control, is not a whistleblower just because she passes the information to a friend at the *Tribune*. She is more like a self-appointed spy. She seems to differ from the whistleblower, or at least from clear cases of the whistleblower, precisely in her relation to the information in question. To be a whistleblower is to reveal information with which one is *entrusted*.

But it is more than that. The whistleblower does not reveal the information to save his own skin (for example, to avoid perjury under oath). He has no excuse for revealing what his organization does not want revealed. Instead, he claims to be doing what he should be doing. If he cannot honestly make that claim—if, that is, he does not have that intention—his revelation is not whistleblowing (and so, not justified as whistleblowing), but something analogous, much as pulling a child from the water is not a rescue, even if it saves the child's life, when the "rescuer" merely believes herself to be salvaging old clothes. What makes whistleblowing morally problematic, if anything does, is this high-minded but unexcused misuse of one's position in a generally law-abiding, morally decent organization, an organization that *prima facie* deserves the whistleblower's loyalty (as a burglary ring does not).

The whistleblower must reveal information the organization does not want revealed. But, in any actual organization, "what the organization wants" will be contested, with various individuals or groups asking to be taken as speaking for the organization. Who, for example, did what Thiokol wanted the night before the *Challenger* exploded? In retrospect, it is obvious that the three vice presidents, Lund, Kilminster, and Mason, did not do what Thiokol wanted—or, at least, what it would have wanted. At the time, however, they had authority to speak for the company—the conglomerate Morton-Thiokol headquartered in Chicago—while the protesting engineers, including Boisjoly, did not. Yet, even before the explosion, was it obvious that the three were doing what the company wanted? To be a whistleblower, one must, I think, at least temporarily lose an argument about what the organization wants. The whistleblower is disloyal only in a sense—the sense the winners of the internal argument get to dictate. What can justify such disloyalty?

THE STANDARD THEORY

According to the theory now more or less standard,[1] such disloyalty is morally permissible when:

(S1)   The organization to which the would-be whistleblower belongs will, through its product or policy, do serious considerable harm to the public (whether to users of its product, to innocent bystanders, or to the public at large);

(S2)   The would-be whistleblower has identified that threat of harm, reported it to her immediate superior, making clear both the threat itself and the objection to it, and concluded that the superior will do nothing effective; and

(S3)   The would-be whistleblower has exhausted other internal procedures within the organization (for example, by going up the organizational ladder as far as allowed)—or at least made use of as many internal procedures

as the danger to others and her own safety make reasonable.

Whistleblowing is morally required (according to the standard theory) when, in addition:

(S4)   The would-be whistleblower has (or has accessible) evidence that would convince a reasonable, impartial observer that her view of the threat is correct; and

(S5)   The would-be whistleblower has good reason to believe that revealing the threat will (probably) prevent the harm at reasonable cost (all things considered).

Why is whistleblowing morally required when these five conditions are met? According to the standard theory, whistleblowing is morally required, when it is required at all, because "people have a moral obligation to prevent serious harm to others if they can do so with little cost to themselves."[2] In other words, whistleblowing meeting all five conditions is a form of "minimally decent Samaritanism" (a doing of what morality requires) rather than "good Samaritanism" (going well beyond the moral minimum). . . .

THREE PARADOXES

That's the standard theory—where are the paradoxes? The first paradox I want to call attention to concerns a commonplace of the whistleblowing literature. Whistleblowers are not minimally decent Samaritans. If they are Samaritans at all, they are good Samaritans. They always act at considerable risk to career, and generally, at considerable risk to their financial security and personal relations.[3]

In this respect, as in many others, Roger Boisjoly is typical. Boisjoly blew the whistle on his employer, Thiokol; he volunteered information, in public testimony before the Rogers Commission, that Thiokol did not want him to volunteer. As often happens, both his employer and many who relied on it for employment reacted hostilely. Boisjoly had to say goodbye to the company town, to old friends and neighbors, and to building rockets; he had to start a new career at an age when most people are preparing for retirement.

Since whistleblowing is generally costly to the whistleblower in some large way as this, the standard theory's minimally decent Samaritanism provides *no* justification for the central cases of whistleblowing.[4] That is the first paradox, what we might call "the paradox of burden."

The second paradox concerns the prevention of "harm." On the standard theory, the would-be whistleblower must seek to prevent "serious and considerable harm" in order for the whistleblowing to be even morally permissible. There seems to be a good deal of play in the term *harm*. The harm in question can be physical (such as death or disease), financial (such as loss of or damage to property), and perhaps even psychological (such as fear or mental illness). But there is a limit to how much the standard theory can stretch "harm." Beyond that limit are "harms" like injustice, deception, and waste. As morally important as injustice, deception, and waste can be, they do not seem to constitute the "serious and considerable harm" that can require someone to become even a minimally decent Samaritan.

Yet, many cases of whistleblowing, perhaps most, are not about preventing serious and considerable physical, financial, or psychological harm. For example, when Boisjoly spoke up the evening before the *Challenger* exploded, the lives of seven astronauts sat in the balance. Speaking up then was about preventing serious and considerable physical, financial, and psychological harm—but it was not whistleblowing. Boisjoly was then serving his employer, not betraying a trust (even on the employer's understanding of that trust); he was calling his superiors' attention to what he thought they should take into account in their decision and not publicly revealing confidential information. The whistleblowing came after the explosion, in testimony before the Rogers Commission. By then, the seven astronauts were beyond help, the shuttle program was suspended, and any further threat of physical, financial, or psychological harm to the "public" was—after discounting for time—negligible. Boisjoly had little reason to believe his testimony would make a significant difference in the booster's redesign, in safety procedures in the shuttle program, or even in reawakening concern

for safety among NASA employees and contractors. The *Challenger*'s explosion was much more likely to do that than anything Boisjoly could do. What Boisjoly could do in his testimony, what I think he tried to do, was prevent falsification of the record.

Falsification of the record is, of course, harm in a sense, especially a record as historically important as that which the Rogers Commission was to produce. But falsification is harm only in a sense that almost empties "harm" of its distinctive meaning, leaving it more or less equivalent to "moral wrong." The proponents of the standard theory mean more by "harm" than that. De George, for example, explicitly says that a threat justifying whistleblowing must be to "life or health."[5] The standard theory is strikingly more narrow in its grounds of justification than many examples of justified whistleblowing suggest it should be. That is the second paradox, the "paradox of missing harm."

The third paradox is related to the second. Insofar as whistleblowers are understood as people out to prevent harm, not just to prevent moral wrong, their chances of success are not good. Whistleblowers generally do not prevent much harm. In this too, Boisjoly is typical. As he has said many times, the situation at Thiokol is now much as it was before the disaster. Insofar as we can identify cause and effect, even now we have little reason to believe that— whatever his actual intention—Boisjoly's testimony actually prevented any harm (beyond the moral harm of falsification). So, if whistleblowers must have, as the standard theory says (S5), (beyond the moral wrong of falsification) "good reason to believe that revealing the threat will (probably) prevent the harm," then the history of whistleblowing virtually rules out the moral justification of whistleblowing. That is certainly paradoxical in a theory purporting to state sufficient conditions for the central cases of justified whistleblowing. Let us call this "the paradox of failure."

A COMPLICITY THEORY

As I look down the roll of whistleblowers, I do not see anyone who, like the clerk from Accounts, just happened upon key documents in a cover-up.[6]

Few, if any, whistleblowers are mere third-parties like the good Samaritan. They are generally deeply involved in the activity they reveal. This involvement suggests that we might better understand what justifies (most) whistleblowing if we understand the whistleblower's obligation to derive from *complicity* in wrongdoing rather than from the ability to prevent harm.

Any complicity theory of justified whistleblowing has two obvious advantages over the standard theory. One is that (moral) complicity itself presupposes (moral) wrongdoing, not harm. So, a complicity justification automatically avoids the paradox of missing harm, fitting the facts of whistleblowing better than a theory which, like the standard one, emphasizes prevention of harm.

That is one obvious advantage of a complicity theory. The second advantage is that complicity invokes a more demanding obligation than the ability to prevent harm does. We are morally obliged to avoid doing moral wrongs. When, despite our best efforts, we nonetheless find ourselves engaged in some wrong, we have an obligation to do what we reasonably can to set things right. If, for example, I cause a traffic accident, I have a moral (and legal) obligation to call help, stay at the scene until help arrives, and render first aid (if I know how), even at substantial cost to myself and those to whom I owe my time, and even with little likelihood that anything I do will help much. Just as a complicity theory avoids the paradox of missing harm, it also avoids the paradox of burden.

What about the third paradox, the paradox of failure? I shall come to that, but only after remedying one disadvantage of the complicity theory. That disadvantage is obvious—we do not yet have such a theory, not even a sketch. Here, then, is the place to offer a sketch of such a theory.

Complicity Theory. You are morally required to reveal what you know to the public (or to a suitable agent or representative of it) when:

(C1) what you will reveal derives from your work for an organization;

(C2) you are a voluntary member of that organization;

(C3) you believe that the organization, though legitimate, is engaged in serious moral wrongdoing;

(C4) you believe that your work for that organization will contribute (more or less directly) to the wrong if (but *not* only if) you do not publicly reveal what you know;

(C5) you are justified in beliefs C3 and C4; and

(C6) beliefs C3 and C4 are true.

The complicity theory differs from the standard theory in several ways worth pointing out here. The first is that, according to C1, what the whistleblower reveals must derive from his work for the organization. This condition distinguishes the whistleblower from the spy (and the clerk in Accounts). The spy seeks out information in order to reveal it; the whistleblower learns it as a proper part of doing the job the organization has assigned him. The standard theory, in contrast, has nothing to say about how the whistleblower comes to know of the threat she reveals (S2). For the standard theory, spies are just another kind of whistleblower.

A second way in which the complicity theory differs from the standard theory is that the complicity theory (C2) explicitly requires the whistleblower to be a *voluntary* participant in the organization in question. Whistleblowing is not—according to the complicity theory—an activity in which slaves, prisoners, or other involuntary participants in an organization engage. In this way, the complicity theory makes explicit something implicit in the standard theory. The whistleblowers of the standard theory are generally "employees." Employees are voluntary participants in the organization employing them.

What explains this difference in explicitness? For the Samaritanism of the standard theory, the voluntariness of employment is extrinsic. What is crucial is the ability to prevent harm. For the complicity theory, however, the voluntariness is crucial. The obligations deriving from complicity seem to vary with the voluntariness of our participation in the wrongdoing. Consider, for example, a teller who helps a gang rob her bank because they have threatened to kill her if she does not; she does not have the same obligation to break off her association with the gang as someone who has freely joined it. The voluntariness of employment means that the would-be whistleblower's complicity will be more like that of one of the gang than like that of the conscripted teller.

A third way in which the complicity theory differs from the standard theory is that the complicity theory (C3) requires moral wrong, not harm, for justification. The wrong need not be a new event (as a harm must be if it is to be *prevented*). It might, for example, consist in no more than silence about facts necessary to correct a serious injustice.

The complicity theory (C3) does, however, follow the standard theory in requiring that the predicate of whistleblowing be "serious." Under the complicity theory, minor wrongdoing can no more justify whistleblowing than can minor harm under the standard theory. While organizational loyalty cannot forbid whistleblowing, it does forbid "tattling," that is, revealing minor wrongdoing.

A fourth way in which the complicity theory differs from the standard theory, the most important, is that the complicity theory (C4) requires that the whistleblower believe that her work will have contributed to the wrong in question if she does nothing, but it does *not* require that she believe that her revelation will prevent (or undo) the wrong. The complicity theory does not require any belief about what the whistleblowing can accomplish (beyond ending complicity in the wrong in question). The whistleblower reveals what she knows in order to prevent complicity in the wrong, not to prevent the wrong as such. She can prevent complicity (if there is any to prevent) simply by publicly revealing what she knows. The revelation itself breaks the bond of complicity, the secret partnership in wrongdoing, that makes her an accomplice in her organization's wrongdoing. The complicity theory thus avoids the third paradox, the paradox of failure, just as it avoided the other two.

The fifth difference between the complicity theory and the standard theory is closely related to the fourth. Because publicly revealing what one knows breaks the bond of complicity, the complicity theory does not require the whistleblower to have enough evidence to convince others of the wrong in question. Convincing others, or just being able to convince them, is not, as such, an element in the justification of whistleblowing.

The complicity theory does, however, require (C5) that the whistleblower be (epistemically) justified in believing both that his organization is engaged in wrongdoing and that he will contribute to that wrong unless he blows the whistle. Such (epistemic) justification may require substantial physical evidence (as the standard theory says) or just a good sense of how things work. The complicity theory does not share the standard theory's substantial evidential demand (S4).

In one respect, however, the complicity theory clearly requires more of the whistleblower than the standard theory does. The complicity theory's C6— combined with C5—requires not only that the whistleblower be *justified* in her beliefs about the organization's wrongdoing and her part in it, but also that she be *right* about them. If she is wrong about either the wrongdoing or her complicity, her revelation will not be justified whistleblowing. This consequence of C6 is, I think, not as surprising as it may seem. If the would-be whistleblower is wrong only about her own complicity, her revelation of actual wrongdoing will, being otherwise justified, merely fail to be justified *as whistleblowing* (much as a failed rescue, though justified as an attempt, cannot be justified as a rescue). If, however, she is wrong about the wrongdoing itself, her situation is more serious. Her belief that wrong is being done, though fully justified on the evidence available to her, cannot justify her disloyalty. All her justified belief can do is *excuse* her disloyalty. Insofar as she acted with good intentions and while exercising reasonable care, she is a victim of bad luck. Such bad luck will leave her with an obligation to apologize, to correct the record (for example, by publicly recanting the charges she publicly made), and otherwise to set things right.

The complicity theory says nothing on at least one matter about which the standard theory says much—going through channels before publicly revealing what one knows. But the two theories do not differ as much as this difference in emphasis suggests. If going through channels would suffice to prevent (or undo) the wrong, then it cannot be true (as C4 and C6 together require) that the would-be whistleblower's work will contribute to the wrong if she does not publicly reveal what she knows. Where, however, going through channels would *not* prevent (or undo) the wrong, there is no need to go through channels. Condition C4's if-clause will be satisfied. For the complicity theory, going through channels is a way of finding out what the organization will do, not an independent requirement of justification. That, I think, is also how the standard theory understands it.[7]

A last difference between the two theories worth mention here is that the complicity theory is only a theory of morally required whistleblowing while the standard theory claims as well to define circumstances when whistleblowing is morally permissible but not morally required. This difference is another advantage that the complicity theory has over the standard theory. The standard theory, as we saw, has trouble making good on its claim to explain how whistleblowing can be morally permissible without being morally required.

TESTING THE THEORY

Let us now test the theory against Boisjoly's testimony before the Rogers Commission. Recall that under the standard theory any justification of that testimony seemed to fail for at least three reasons: First, Boisjoly could not testify without substantial cost to himself and Thiokol (to whom he owed loyalty). Second, there was no serious and substantial harm his testimony could prevent. And, third, he had little reason to believe that, even if he could identify a serious and considerable harm to prevent, his testimony had a significant chance of preventing it.

Since few doubt that Boisjoly's testimony before the Rogers Commission constitutes justified whistleblowing, if anything does, we should welcome a theory that—unlike the standard one—justifies that testimony as whistleblowing. The complicity theory sketched above does that:

(C1)   Boisjoly's testimony consisted almost entirely of information derived from his work on booster rockets at Thiokol.

(C2)   Boisjoly was a voluntary member of Thiokol.

(C3)   Boisjoly believed Thiokol, a legitimate organization, was attempting to mislead its client, the government, about the causes of a deadly accident. Attempting to do that certainly seems a serious moral wrong.

(C4)   On the evening before the *Challenger* exploded, Boisjoly gave up objecting to the launch once his superiors, including the three Thiokol vice presidents, had made it clear that they were no longer willing to listen to him. He also had a part in preparing those superiors to testify intelligently before the Rogers Commission concerning the booster's fatal field joint. Boisjoly believed that Thiokol would use his failure to offer his own interpretation of his retreat into silence the night before the launch, and the knowledge that he had imparted to his superiors, to contribute to the attempt to mislead Thiokol's client.

(C5)   The evidence justifying beliefs C3 and C4 consisted of comments of various officers of Thiokol, what Boisjoly had seen at Thiokol over the years, and what he learned about the rocket business over a long career. I find this evidence sufficient to justify his belief both that his organization was engaged in wrongdoing and that his work was implicated.

(C6)   Here we reach a paradox of *knowledge*. Since belief is knowledge if, but only if, it is *both* justified *and* true, we cannot *show* that we know anything. All we can show is that a belief is now justified and that we have no reason to expect anything to turn up later to prove it false. The evidence now available still justifies Boisjoly's belief both about what Thiokol was attempting and about what would have been his part in the attempt. Since new evidence is unlikely, his testimony seems to satisfy C6 just as it satisfied the complicity theory's other five conditions.

Since the complicity theory explains why Boisjoly's testimony before the Rogers Commission was morally required whistleblowing, it has passed its first test, a test the standard theory failed.

Notes

1. Throughout this essay, I take the standard theory to be Richard T. De George's version in *Business Ethics*, 3rd Edition (New York: Macmillan, 1990), pp. 200–214 (amended only insofar as necessary to include non-businesses as well as businesses). Why treat De George's theory as standard? There are two reasons: first, it seems the most commonly cited; and second, people offering alternatives generally treat it as the one to be replaced. The only obvious competitor, Norman Bowie's account, is distinguishable from De George's on no point relevant here. See Bowie's *Business Ethics* (Englewood Cliffs, NJ: Prentice Hall, 1982), p. 143.

2. De George, *op. cit.* . . .

3. For an explanation of why whistleblowing is inevitably a high risk undertaking, see my "Avoiding the Tragedy of Whistleblowing," *Business and Professional Ethics Journal,* Vol. 8, No. 4 (1989): 3–19.

4. Indeed, I am tempted to go further and claim that, where an informant takes little or no risk, we are unlikely to describe her as a whistleblower at all. So, for example, I would say that using an internal or external "hot-line" is whistleblowing only when it is risky. We are, in other words, likely to consider using a hot-line as disloyalty (that is, as "going out of channels") only if the organization (or some part of it) is likely to respond with considerable hostility to its use.

5. De George, p. 210: "The notion of *serious* harm might be expanded to include serious financial harm, and kinds of harm other than death and serious threats to health and body. But as we noted earlier, we shall restrict ourselves here to products and practices that produce or threaten serious harm or danger to life and health."

6. See Myron Peretz Glazer and Penina Migdal Glazer, *The Whistleblowers: Exposing Corruption in Government and Industry* (New York: Basic Books, 1989) for a good list of whistleblowers (with detailed description of each); for an older list (with descriptions), see Alan F. Westin, *Whistleblowing! Loyalty and Dissent in the Corporation* (New York: McGraw-Hill, 1981).

7. Compare De George, p. 211: "By reporting one's concern to one's immediate superior or other appropriate person, one preserves and observes the regular practices of firms, which on the whole promote their order and efficiency; this fulfills one's obligation of minimizing harm, and *it precludes precipitous whistle blowing*" (italics mine).

Review and Discussion Questions

1. What makes whistle blowing morally problematic—that is, why does it need to be justified? According to Davis, why isn't the police officer, the criminal informant, or the clerk who happens upon evidence of wrongdoing in another department a whistle blower?

2. According to the standard theory, when is whistle blowing morally permissible and when is it morally required? Do you see any problems with conditions S1 through S5?

3. Explain the three paradoxes that Davis claims the standard theory gives rise to. If you were a defender of the standard theory, how might you respond to Davis's arguments?

4. Explain Davis's complicity theory. What are the most important differences between it and the standard theory? Is Davis's theory of justified whistle blowing an improvement over the standard theory? Explain why or why not.

5. Does the example of Roger Boisjoly fit the complicity theory better than it does the standard theory? If it does, is that a good argument for the complicity theory? Can you think of any examples of whistle blowing that favor the standard theory over the complicity theory?

6. Are there any aspects of whistle blowing that Davis's theory neglects or fails to do full justice to?

Further Reading for Chapter 8

Sissela Bok, *Secrets* (New York: Vintage, 1983) includes insightful writing on trade secrets and patents in Chapter 10 and on whistle blowing in Chapter 14.

Thomas L. Carson, "Conflicts of Interest," *Journal of Business Ethics* (May 1994) analyzes the concept and discusses the wrongness of conflicts of interest. Also useful is **Michael Davis**, "Conflict of Interest Revisited," *Business and Professional Ethics Journal* 12 (Winter 1993).

Natalie Dandekar, "Can Whistleblowing Be Fully Legitimated? A Theoretical Discussion," *Business and Professional Ethics Journal* 10 (Fall 1990), **Mike W. Martin**, "Whistleblowing: Professionalism, Personal Life, and Shared Responsibility for Safety in Engineering," *Business and Professional Ethics Journal* 11 (Summer 1992), and **C. Fred Alford,** "Whistleblowers and the Narrative of Ethics," *Journal of Social Philosophy* 32 (Fall 2001) are good studies of the moral complexity of whistle blowing.

Tibor Machan, "What Is Morally Right with Insider Trading," *Public Affairs Quarterly* 10 (April 1996) is a succinct libertarian defense of insider trading.

Brian Schrag, "The Moral Significance of Employee Loyalty," *Business Ethics Quarterly* 11 (January 2001) discusses the meaning of loyalty and whether it is good for either the employee or employer.

Martin Snoeyenbos, **Robert Almeder**, and **James Humber**, eds., *Business Ethics,* 3rd ed. (Buffalo: Prometheus, 2001), Part 3, provides essays and cases on conflict of interest, gifts and payoffs, patents, and trade secrets.

 InfoTrac College Edition: For further information or to conduct research, please go to www.infotrac-college.com.

9

Job Discrimination

When Notre Dame opened its 2002 football season, its team was led by a new coach, Tyrone Willingham. Nothing surprising about that, one might think; after all, colleges are always hiring and firing coaches. But Coach Willingham's arrival was newsworthy simply because he's African American. That makes him Notre Dame's first black coach in any sport, and it makes the Fighting Irish the only top-flight football team in the nation with a black coach. Indeed, looking at all Division 1-A schools, one finds only four black head football coaches. That's less than 3 percent of the total, even though half of all 1-A players are black.[1]

What explains this imbalance? Experts suggest several answers. At many universities, football is the biggest moneymaking sport, and search committees may fear that boosters and alumni will donate less if the team has a black coach. Another reason is that black men are often passed over for decision-making positions early in their athletic careers. Relatively few blacks play quarterback, for instance, and black assistant coaches may be relegated to recruiting or smoothing out race relations rather than calling plays. In addition, young black athletes may pursue careers in which they have seen their role models succeed—going on to the pros, in particular, instead of becoming a coach.

Finally, most commentators agree that the "old boys' network" among athletic directors

and coaches is part of the problem. "I don't see the problem as being the same as it was 30 or 40 years ago, when people said they didn't want a 'Negro' around," says Allen L. Sach, director of sports management at the University of New Haven. "It's more systematic than it is overt." Athletic directors, naturally enough, tend to look to people they know to fill coaching positions, and only 4 percent of the former are ethnic minorities, according to the Center for the Study of Sport in Society at Northeastern University. "Athletic directors, to the extent that they're white, generally have contacts who are also white, and they use those contacts as they engage in searches at the informal level," says sociologist Jay Oakley of the University of Colorado at Colorado Springs.

It's no secret that Willingham wasn't Notre Dame's first choice. It had initially hired George O'Leary, who resigned five days later when it became known that he had lied on his résumé about his academic and athletic background. In discussing the appointment, Notre Dame Athletic Director Kevin White explained that he had been charmed by O'Leary's Irish-American background and his rah-rah style. O'Leary was like "something out of central casting," White said. In other words, the flamboyant O'Leary fit White's stereotype about what a Notre Dame coach should look like. Sports columnist Mark Purdy writes that White's remark "basically confirms that athletic directors—at Notre Dame and too many other places—really do look for middle-aged white guys as the top choices for the top jobs. And that's depressing." It's to Notre Dame's credit, however, that after the O'Leary debacle, it took a second look at Willingham and, putting aside racial preconceptions and "central casting" stereotypes, went for a coach with a proven track record, one whose integrity, drive, and quiet competence more than make up for any lack of flamboyance.

Most people oppose racial or sexual bias and reject job discrimination as immoral. But, as the paucity of minority coaches reveals, explicit prejudice and overt discrimination are just part of the problem. Even open-minded people may operate on implicit assumptions that work to the disadvantage of women and minorities, and many who believe themselves to be unprejudiced harbor unconscious racist or sexist attitudes.

Stanford law professor Charles R. Lawrence III, for instance, recalls his college days as a token black presence in a white world. Companions would say to him, "I don't think of you as a Negro." Their conscious intent was benign and complimentary. The speaker was saying, "I think of you as a normal human being, just like me."

> But he was not conscious of the underlying implications of his words. What did this mean about most Negroes? Were they not normal human beings? . . . To say that one does not think of a Negro as a Negro is to say that one thinks of him as something else. The statement is made in the context of the real world, and implicit in it is a comparison to some norm. In this case the norm is whiteness. The white liberal's unconscious thought . . . is, "I think of you as different from other Negroes, as more like white people."[2]

In other cases unconscious racist stereotypes, which are normally repressed, slip out, as when sportscaster Howard Cosell, carried away by the excitement of the game, referred to an African-American football player as a "little monkey" or when Nancy Reagan told a public gathering that she wished her husband could be there to "see all these beautiful white people."[3]

Slavery in our country resulted in a long legacy of legally institutionalized racism and socioeconomic subordination of African Americans and other minorities. That history, and centuries of discrimination against women, lie behind the racially and sexually prejudiced attitudes so prevalent in the United States. We must bear that history and those attitudes in mind as we explore the area of job discrimination. In particular, this chapter examines the following topics:

1. The meaning of job discrimination and its different forms

2. The statistical and attitudinal evidence of discrimination

3. The historical and legal context of affirmative action

4. The moral arguments for and against affirmative action

5. The doctrine of comparable worth and the controversy over it

6. The problem of sexual harassment in employment—what it is, what forms it takes, what the law says about it, and why it's wrong

THE MEANING OF JOB DISCRIMINATION

According to Professor Manuel G. Velasquez, to discriminate in employment is to make an adverse decision against employees or job applicants based on their membership in a certain group.[4] Determining whether discrimination occurs in employment depends on three basic facts: (1) whether the decision is a function of an employee's or job applicant's membership in a certain group, rather than individual merit; (2) whether the decision is based on prejudice, false stereotypes, or the assumption that the group is in some way inferior and thus deserving of unequal treatment; and (3) whether the decision in some way harms those it's aimed at. Because most discrimination in the American workplace has traditionally been aimed at women and at minorities such as African Americans and Hispanics, the following discussion focuses on these groups.

Job discrimination can take different forms.[5] Individuals can intentionally discriminate out of personal prejudice or on the basis of stereotypes. An example is the executive at Rent-A-Center, the nation's largest rent-to-own furniture and home appliance company, who purposely disregarded job applications from women because he believed that they "should be home taking care of their husbands and children."[6] On the other hand, individuals may discriminate because they unthinkingly or unconsciously accept traditional practices or biased stereotypes. For example, if this Rent-A-Center executive had acted without being aware of the bias underlying his decisions, his actions would fall into this category.

Institutions can also discriminate. Sometimes they do so explicitly and intentionally—for example, employment agencies that screen out African Americans, Latinos, older workers, and others at the request of their corporate clients[7] or the Shoney's restaurants that color coded job applications to separate blacks from whites and that directed blacks, if hired, into kitchen jobs so they would not be seen from the dining room.[8] On the other hand, the routine operating procedures of a company may reflect stereotypes and prejudiced practices that it is not fully aware of. For example, for years the FBI routinely transferred its Hispanic agents around the country on temporary, low-level assignments where a knowledge of Spanish was needed; the agents functioned as little more than assistants to non-Hispanic colleagues. Hispanic agents dubbed this the "taco circuit" and claimed that it adversely affected their opportunities for promotion. A federal court agreed with them that the practice is indeed discriminatory.[9]

In addition, institutional practices that appear neutral and nondiscriminatory may harm members of groups that are traditionally discriminated against. When membership in an all-white craft union, for instance, requires nomination by those who are already members, racial exclusion is likely to result even if the motivation of those who do the nominating is purely nepotistic and results from no racially motivated ill will or stereotyping. Similarly, when USAir had a special backdoor hiring channel for pilots recommended by employees or friends of the company, only white pilots were ever hired this way.[10] Although the policy may look racially neutral, its outcome was biased. Institutional procedures like these may not involve job discrimination in the narrow sense, but they clearly work to the disadvantage of women and minority groups, denying them full equality of opportunity.

From a variety of moral perspectives there are compelling moral arguments against job discrimination on racial or sexual grounds. Discrimination involves false assumptions about the inferiority of a certain group and harms individual members of that group, so utilitarians would reject it because of its ill effects on total human welfare. Kantians would clearly repudiate it as failing to respect people as ends in themselves. Universalizing the maxim underlying discriminatory practices is virtually impossible. No people who now discriminate would be willing to accept such treatment themselves. Discrimination on grounds of sex or race also violates people's basic moral rights and mocks the ideal of human moral equality. Furthermore, such discrimination is unjust. To use Rawls's theory as an illustration, parties in the original position would clearly choose for themselves the principle of equal opportunity.

On the other hand, there are no respectable arguments in favor of racial and sexual discrimination. Whatever racist or sexist attitudes people might actually have, no one today is prepared to defend job discrimination publicly, any more than someone would publicly defend slavery or the repeal of the Nineteenth Amendment (which gave women the right to vote). This attitude toward job discrimination is reflected in legal and political efforts to develop programs to root out job discrimination and ameliorate the results of past discrimination.

Before looking at the relevant legal history and the controversies surrounding various anti-discrimination measures, this chapter examines the relative positions of whites and minorities and of males and females in the American workplace to see what they reveal about ongoing discrimination.

EVIDENCE OF DISCRIMINATION

When investigators sent equally qualified young white and black men—all of them articulate and conventionally dressed—to apply for entry-level jobs in Chicago and Washington, D.C., the results clearly showed racial discrimination against young African-American men.[11] And a study has shown that if you work for the federal government, you're more likely to be fired if you're black—regardless of your job status, experience, or education. In fact, race is more important in predicting who gets fired than job-performance ratings or even prior disciplinary history.[12] Job discrimination certainly exists, but determining how widespread it is isn't easy. However, when (1) statistics indicate that women and minorities play an unequal role in the work world and (2) endemic attitudes, practices, and policies are biased in ways that seem to account for the skewed statistics, then there is good reason to believe that job discrimination is a pervasive problem.

Statistical Evidence

According to government data, the median wealth of white households is ten times that of black households—$47,080 versus $4,500. And 29 percent of African-American households, but only 9 percent of all white households, are reported as having no wealth at all, meaning that they own no assets or that their liabilities exceed their assets.[13] Racial minorities bear the brunt of poverty in our nation. African Americans are about three times more likely to be poor than whites. Whereas one out of every ten white Americans is poor, one out of every four or five African Americans and Hispanics is poor. Today a black child has nearly one chance in three of being born into poverty.[14]

Thus, it is not too surprising that whereas white Americans have, according to U.N. figures, the highest standard of living in the world,

African Americans come in thirty-first and Hispanics thirty-fifth.[15] The median income of African-American families is only two-thirds that of white households; Hispanic family income is about 72 percent.[16]

Unemployment hits racial minorities hard, because they are often last hired and first fired. Unemployment among African Americans is in general twice as high as that of whites. Of every three minority workers, one is employed irregularly or has given up looking for work, and one in three is engaged primarily in a job that pays less than a living wage. Official unemployment figures for inner-city African-American youths exceed 40 percent, but the actual figures are thought to be much higher.

About 40 percent of working African Americans hold white-collar jobs, up from 11 percent in 1960. But black and other minority workers still find themselves clustered in low-paying, low-prestige, dead-end work. U.S. government statistics reveal clearly the extent to which the most desirable occupations (in management and administration, professional and technical jobs, sales, and crafts) are dominated by whites; blacks, Hispanics, and other ethnic minorities are relegated to less desirable jobs (in manual labor, service, and farmwork).[17] African Americans make up 10.1 percent of the workforce, but 21 percent of the janitors, 27.2 percent of the hotel maids and housemen, 31.2 percent of the nursing aides, and 23.5 percent of the security guards. In contrast, only 2.1 percent of the architects, 1.5 percent of the dentists and commercial pilots, and 0.7 percent of the geologists are black.[18] According to the Department of Labor, blacks account for only 6.1 percent of U.S. managers.[19]

Women, too, are clustered in poorer-paying jobs—the so-called pink-collar occupations. They tend to work as librarians, nurses, elementary schoolteachers, salesclerks, secretaries, bank tellers, and waitresses, jobs that generally pay less than traditionally male occupations such as electrician, plumber, auto mechanic, shipping clerk, or truck driver. It's not surprising, then, that 80 percent of working women earn less than $25,000 per year, although two-fifths of them are the sole head of a household.[20] In the real world of work, the top-paying occupations have been, and to a large extent continue to be, almost exclusively male preserves. For example, 98.5 percent of dental hygienists, but only 18.7 percent of dentists, are women.[21] Although women hold 43 percent of executive, administrative, and managerial positions, they account for less than 5 percent of the top executive positions nationwide.[22]

Even when women do the same work as men, they make less money. In fact, according to a General Accounting Office report, released in 2002, since 1995 the pay difference between full-time female managers and their male counterparts has increased in seven of the ten industries that collectively employ 71 percent of all female workers.[23] For example, in entertainment and recreation female managers now earn only 62 cents for each dollar earned by males; in finance, insurance, and real estate, it's 68 cents, and in retail trade, 65 cents. In education and in hospital and medical services, women managers have done better. Their earnings have increased to 91 and 85 percent, respectively, of what men make. The across-the-board wage gap between men and women shrank during the 1980s, but has since leveled off, with women who work full time continuing to take home, on average, less than 75 percent of what men make.[24] And one-third of the women polled in a recent survey complained that they do not receive equal pay at their current jobs.[25]

To be sure, in recent decades both women and minorities have made inroads into white-collar and professional ranks, but few have made it to the very top of their professions—as a glance at the companies that make up the *Fortune* 500 confirms. Only five of those companies have a female CEO. And when he took charge of Fannie Mae in 1999, Franklin Raines became the first African American to lead a *Fortune* 500 company. Now there are two more.

Attitudinal Evidence

Although some would disagree, statistics alone do not conclusively establish discrimination be-

cause one can always argue that other things account for the disparities in income and positions between men and women and between whites and other races. The U.S. Supreme Court, in fact, has stated that "no matter how stark the numerical disparity of the employer's work force," statistical evidence by itself does not prove discrimination.[26] But when widespread attitudes and institutional practices and policies are taken into account, they point to discrimination as the cause of the statistical disparities.

Take the case of Bari-Ellen Roberts. She left an $80,000-a-year job at Chase Manhattan Bank to join Texaco's finance department after a white friend, whose husband worked for the company, assured her that "Texaco's changing" and that the company was "looking for blacks." Her new job was closer to home and held the promise of overseas assignments, but her friend was mistaken about Texaco's having changed. Soon after she arrived, Roberts found herself subjected to demeaning racial comments from colleagues and superiors (for example, one referred to her as a "little colored girl"). They couldn't understand why Roberts found such remarks offensive. A report on diversity that she and some other black employees were asked to prepare was summarily dismissed with the comment "the next thing you know we'll have Black Panthers running down the halls." And a supervisor downgraded her performance record because he thought she was "uppity."[27]

Fed up with a "plague of racial insults" and "egregious acts of bigotry," she and several other black employees filed a discrimination suit citing "the poisonous racial atmosphere" at Texaco. Texaco settled the suit for $141 million in retroactive raises after the news media got a hold of a tape recording of an executive strategy session at Texaco. In the meeting, one official referred to black employees as "black jelly beans," saying, "This diversity thing, you know how all the black jelly beans stick together." To which another responded, "That's funny. All the black jelly beans seem to be stuck at the bottom of the bag." One of Roberts's supervisors said, "I can't punch her [Roberts] in the face, so I play mind games with her." The executives were also heard agreeing to shred incriminating personnel records.

Consider also the case of Elizabeth Hishon, who went to work for King & Spaulding, a big Atlanta law firm. Customarily, associates like Hishon are given a period of time to either make partner or seek another job. So when Hishon had not attained partner status after seven years, she was terminated. Hishon, however, claimed that her failure to become a partner was due to the law firm's sexism, and she filed a suit seeking monetary damages under Title VII of the Civil Rights Act of 1964, which prohibits sexual and racial discrimination at work. A federal district court held that the rights guaranteed by Title VII do not apply to the selection of partners in a law firm, but the Supreme Court overturned that ruling in a unanimous decision that held that women can bring sex-discrimination suits against law firms that unfairly deny them promotions to partner. In the meantime, however, Elizabeth Hishon had settled out of court with King & Spaulding, and the case never went to trial.

In November 1990, Nancy O'Mara Ezold became the first woman to win a sex-discrimination trial against a law firm in a partnership decision. A few days later, in a case in which the Supreme Court had already found sex discrimination, a federal appeals judge ruled that Price Waterhouse, the accounting firm, must give a partnership and back pay to Ann Hopkins, against whom it had discriminated. And in 2002 the Equal Employment Opportunity Commission filed its first sex-discrimination lawsuit against a major Wall Street firm, alleging that Morgan Stanley fired Allison Schieffelin, one of its top bond dealers, for complaining about pay discrimination. These cases have had a significant impact on partnerships and professional firms nationwide, causing pay and promotional practices to be reevaluated, not only in law and accounting firms, but also in advertising agencies, brokerage houses, architectural concerns, and engineering firms.

Of particular interest here are the discriminatory attitudes and policies revealed by these cases. In the Ezold case, the judge found that the prominent Philadelphia law firm for which she had worked had applied tougher standards to women seeking partnerships than to men. Ezold said, "It wasn't just that similarly situated men were treated better than me, which is the double-standard idea. Another thing that came out of the trial was that in the year preceding the partnership decision, [the firm] assigned me to less complex cases and to fewer partners than it did men, so that I was denied the exposure that was critical to the partnership decision."[28]

In Ann Hopkins's case, sex stereotyping was at the root of the discrimination. Though she was considered an outstanding worker, Price Waterhouse denied her the position because she was allegedly an abrasive and overbearing manager. Coworkers referred to her as "macho," advised her to go to charm school, and intimated that she was overcompensating for being a woman. One partner in the firm even told her that she should "walk more femininely, talk more femininely, dress more femininely, wear makeup, have her hair styled, and wear jewelry." Hopkins argued, and the Court agreed, that comments like these revealed an underlying sexism at the firm and that her strident manner and occasional cursing would have been overlooked if she had been a man.[29] The same issue comes up in the Schieffelin case, who was viewed by her firm as insubordinate, verbally abusive, and "physically threatening."

As for the Hishon decision, the case is noteworthy because the defendants expressed no specific complaints about Hishon's work. They apparently denied her a partnership based on a general feeling that "she just didn't fit in." In the words of another woman who had been an associate at King & Spaulding, "If you can't discuss the Virginia–North Carolina basketball game, you're an outcast."[30] Her pithy comment speaks volumes about how deep-seated attitudes operate against women and minorities in the workplace.

A woman entering males' turf can find herself uncomfortably measured according to the predominant male value system. Here's how Florence Blair, a twenty-five-year-old African American, described working as a civil engineer at Corning Glass Works:

> As a minority woman, you are just so different from everyone else you encounter. . . . I went through a long period of isolation. . . . When I came here, I didn't have a lot in common with the white males I was working with. I didn't play golf, I didn't drink beer, I didn't hunt. All these things I had no frame of reference to.
>
> You need to do your job on a certain technical level, but a lot of things you do on the job come down to socializing and how well you mesh with people. Sometimes I look at my role as making people feel comfortable with me.
>
> Sometimes it's disheartening. You think why do I have to spend all of my time and my energy making them feel comfortable with me when they're not reciprocating?[31]

Surveys support the evidence of these cases. Over the years, they have indicated that sex stereotyping and sexist assumptions are widespread in business.[32] Male managers frequently assume that women place family demands above work considerations; that they lack the necessary drive to succeed in business; that they take negative feedback personally rather than professionally; and that they are too emotional to be good managers. Myths, stereotypes, false preconceptions, and hostile attitudes victimize both women and minorities in the world of work, leading to decisions that disadvantage them in the areas of employee selection, promotion, and career development.

For example, a survey shows that three out of four whites believe that African Americans and Hispanics are more likely than whites to prefer living on welfare, and a majority of whites also believe that African Americans and Hispanics are more likely to be lazy, unpatriotic, and prone to violence.[33] Another survey, this time of Ivy League graduates, class of 1957, also illustrates the prevalence of racial stereotypes and assumptions.[34] For these men, "dumb" came to mind when they thought of African Americans. Only 36 percent of the Princeton class, 47 percent of the Yale class, and 55 percent of the Harvard men agreed with the statement "Blacks are as intelligent as whites." These are graduates of three leading universities who are now at an age typical of those holding senior corporate positions. In discussing this survey, Edward W. Jones, Jr., writes:

> All people possess stereotypes, which act like shorthand to avoid mental overload. . . . Most of the time stereotypes are mere shadow images rooted in one's history and deep in the subconscious. But they are very powerful. For example, in controlled experiments the mere insertion of the word black into a sentence has resulted in people changing their responses to a statement.
>
> One reason for the power of stereotypes is their circularity. People seek to confirm their expectations and resist contradictory evidence, so we cling to beliefs and stereotypes that become self-fulfilling. If, for example, a white administrator makes a mistake, his boss is likely to tell him, "That's OK. Everybody's entitled to one goof." If, however, a black counterpart commits the same error, the boss thinks, "I knew he couldn't do it. The guy is incompetent." The stereotype reinforces itself.[35]

Taken together, the statistics and the personal and institutional attitudes, assumptions and practices provide powerful evidence of intractable discrimination against women and minorities in the American workplace. Recognizing the existence of such discrimination and believing for a variety of reasons that it is wrong, we have as a nation passed laws to provide equality of opportunity to women and minorities. Such laws expressly forbid discrimination in recruitment, screening, promotion, compensation, and firing. But anti-discrimination laws do not address the present-day effects of past discrimination. To remedy the effects of past discrimination and counteract visceral racism and sexism, some companies and institutions have adopted stronger and more controversial affirmative action measures.

AFFIRMATIVE ACTION: THE LEGAL CONTEXT

In 1954 the Supreme Court decided in the case of *Brown v. Board of Education* that racially segregated schooling is unconstitutional. In doing so, the Court conclusively rejected the older doctrine that "separate but equal" facilities are legally permissible. Not only were segregated facilities in the South unequal, the Court found, but the very idea of separation of the races, based as it was on a belief in black racial inferiority, inherently led to unequal treatment. That famous decision helped launch the civil rights movement in this country. One fruit of that movement was a series of federal laws and orders that attempt to implement the right of each person to equal treatment in employment.

The changes began in 1961, when President John F. Kennedy signed Executive Order 10925, which decreed that federal contractors should "take affirmative action to ensure that applicants are employed without regard to their race, creed, color, or national origin." In 1963, the Equal Pay Act was passed by Congress. Aimed especially at wage discrimination against women, it guaranteed the right to equal pay for equal work. That was followed by the Civil Rights Act of 1964 (which was later amended by the Equal Employment Opportunity Act of 1972). It prohibits all forms of discrimination based on race, color, sex, religion, or national origin. Title VII, the most important section of the act, prohibits discrimination in employment. It says:

> It shall be an unlawful employment practice for an employer (1) to fail or refuse to hire or to discharge any individual, or otherwise discriminate against any individual with respect to his compensation, terms, conditions, or privileges of employment, because of such individual's race, color, religion, sex, or national origin; or (2) to limit, segregate, or classify his employees or applicants for employment in any way that would deprive or

tend to deprive any individual of employment opportunities or otherwise adversely affect his status as an employee, because of such individual's race, color, religion, sex, or national origin.

The Civil Rights Act of 1964 applies to all employers, both public and private, with fifteen or more employees. In 1967 the Age Discrimination in Employment Act was passed (amended in 1978), and in 1990 the Americans with Disabilities Act extended to people with disabilities the same rights to equal employment opportunities that the Civil Rights Act of 1964 guarantees to women and minorities. In addition, several acts and executive orders regulate government contractors and subcontractors and require equal opportunities for veterans. All of these acts are enforced through the Equal Employment Opportunity Commission (EEOC).

By the late 1960s and early 1970s, companies contracting with the federal government (first in construction and then generally) were required to develop *affirmative action programs,* designed to correct imbalances in employment that exist directly as a result of past discrimination. These programs corresponded with the courts' recognition that job discrimination can exist even in the absence of conscious intent to discriminate.[36] Affirmative action riders were added, with various degrees of specificity, into a large number of federal programs. Many state and local bodies adopted comparable requirements.

What do affirmative action programs involve? The EEOC lists general guidelines as steps to affirmative action. Under these steps, firms must issue a written equal-employment policy and an affirmative action commitment. They must appoint a top official with responsibility and authority to direct and implement their program and to publicize their policy and affirmative action commitment. In addition, firms must survey current female and minority employment by department and job classification. Whenever underrepresentation of these groups is evident, firms must develop goals and timetables to improve in each area of underrepresentation. They then must develop specific programs to achieve these goals, establish an internal audit system to monitor them, and evaluate progress in each aspect of the program. Finally, companies must develop supportive in-house and community programs to combat discrimination.

We saw earlier that Texaco was forced to pay its black employees $141 million, the largest race-discrimination settlement in history, because the company had discriminated against qualified African Americans by refusing to promote them or pay them comparable salaries. It had also retaliated against those who asserted their civil rights. Other firms are guilty of ignoring the spirit of equal employment opportunity even if they don't violate the letter of the law. For example, some companies forbid their employees from speaking Spanish among themselves even when their jobs do not require English proficiency or dealing with the public;[37] others, such as the Florida-based Publix grocery chain, have not tried to expand employment opportunities for women or minorities.[38] Yet today most large corporations not only accept the necessity of affirmative action but also find that the bottom line benefits when they make themselves more diverse. Because four-fifths of those entering the workforce today are women, minorities, or immigrants, affirmative action expands the pool of talent from which corporations can recruit. It also allows them to reach out to a demographically wider customer base and makes them better able to compete both in the global marketplace and in an increasingly multicultural environment at home. United Parcel Service, for example, credits its commitment to diversity for its high customer-satisfaction ratings, and Nicole Barde, a network manager at Intel Corporation, says, "We view diversity as one of our major competitive advantages. It allows us to understand global markets and the needs of our customers."[39]

However, in recent years political opposition to affirmative action, especially to government affirmative action programs, has grown greater than ever. Critics of affirmative action charge that it means, in practice, illegal quotas, preferential treatment of African Americans and women, and even reverse discrimination against white men. In the 1960s and early 1970s, federal courts dismissed legal challenges to affirmative action, and in 1972 Congress gave it increased legislative validity by passing the Equal Employment Opportunity Act. Eventually, however, the Supreme Court had to address the question. Although its decisions determine the law of the land with regard to affirmative action, the Court's rulings have not always been as simple and straightforward as one might wish.

The Supreme Court's Position

The U.S. Supreme Court's first major ruling on affirmative action was in 1978, in the case of *Bakke v. Regents of the University of California*. Allan Bakke, a white man, applied for admission to the medical school at the University of California at Davis. Only a tiny percentage of doctors are not white. To help remedy this situation, Davis's affirmative action program set aside for minority students 16 out of its 100 entrance places. If qualified minority students could not be found, those places were not to be filled. In addition to the special admissions process, minority students were free to compete through the regular admissions process for the unrestricted 84 positions. When Bakke was refused admission, he sued the University of California, contending that it had discriminated against him in violation of both the 1964 Civil Rights Act and the Constitution. He argued that he would have won admission if those 16 places had not been withdrawn from open competition and reserved for minority students. Bakke's grades, placement-test scores, and so on were higher than those of several minority students who were admitted. The university did not deny this but defended its program as legally permissible and socially necessary affirmative action.

Bakke won his case, although it was a close, 5 to 4 decision. Four justices sided with the University of California at Davis; four found that Davis's program was illegal in light of the 1964 Civil Rights Act; and one justice (Lewis Powell) held that even though the program did not violate that act, it was invalid on constitutional grounds. In announcing the judgment of the Court, Powell's opinion rejected explicit racial criteria setting rigid quotas and excluding non-preferred groups from competition. At the same time he held that the selection process can take race and ethnic origin into account as one factor and pointed to Harvard's admission program as a model. In such a program, "race or ethnic background may be deemed a 'plus' in a particular applicant's file, yet it does not insulate the individual from comparison with all other candidates for the available seats." Powell also granted that numerical goals may be permissible when the institution in question has illegally discriminated in the past.

A year later, in *United Steelworkers of America v. Weber,* the Supreme Court took up the issue again—but in a different situation and with a different verdict. At Kaiser Aluminum's Gramercy, Louisiana, plant, only 5 out of 273 skilled craft workers were black, although the local workforce was 39 percent black. Kaiser therefore entered into a collective bargaining agreement with the United Steelworkers that contained a plan "to eliminate conspicuous racial imbalances" in Kaiser's skilled craft positions. Kaiser agreed to set up a training program to qualify its own workers for craft positions and to choose trainees from the existing workforce on the basis of seniority, except that 50 percent of the positions would be reserved for African Americans until their percentage in these jobs approximated the percentage of African Americans in the local workforce.

Brian Weber, a young semiskilled worker at Kaiser, was one of several whites who had failed to gain admission to the training program for skilled craft positions, despite having more seniority than the most senior African-American trainee. Weber sued, arguing that he had been discriminated against on the basis of his race. This time the Supreme Court upheld the affirmative action program in a 5 to 2 decision. In delivering the Court's opinion, Justice William Brennan made clear that legal prohibition of racial discrimination does not prevent "private, voluntary, race-conscious affirmative action plans." He wrote:

We need not today define in detail the line of demarcation between permissible and impermissible affirmative action plans. It suffices to hold that the challenged Kaiser-USWA affirmative action plan falls on the permissible side of the line. The purposes of the plan mirror those of the [Civil Rights] statute. Both were designed to break down old patterns of racial segregation and hierarchy. Both were structured to "open employment opportunities for Negroes in occupations which have been traditionally closed to them." . . .

At the same time, the plan does not unnecessarily trammel the interest of the white employees. . . . Moreover, the plan is a temporary measure . . . simply to eliminate a manifest racial imbalance.

In 1984, however, the Supreme Court upheld seniority over affirmative action in *Memphis Firefighters v. Stotts.* The city of Memphis, Tennessee, began hiring African Americans as firefighters only in 1955. Between 1950 and 1976, the fire department hired 1,683 whites but only 94 blacks. A class-action suit was filed in 1977, charging the city with racial discrimination in hiring and promoting firefighters, and in 1980 the city signed a consent decree with the Justice Department. While not admitting it had engaged in racial discrimination, the city agreed to attempt to give 50 percent of new jobs and 20 percent of promotions to African Americans. Under the plan, the percentage of black firefighters rose from 4.0 to 11.5 percent.

When financial difficulties forced the city to lay off firefighters, it followed the seniority rules negotiated with the union. Last hired were to be let go first. Fearing that the progress black firefighters had made would be quickly lost, Carl Stotts, who had brought the original suit, asked a federal district court to protect blacks from layoffs. It did, and seventy-two whites, but only eight African Americans, were laid off or demoted.

The Supreme Court reversed the district court's ruling, holding that seniority systems are racially neutral and that the city may not lay off white workers to save the jobs of black workers with less seniority. Speaking for the majority, Justice Byron White wrote, "It is inappropriate to deny an innocent employee the benefits of his seniority . . . to provide a remedy in a [case] such as this." A court can award competitive seniority to an individual African American only when he or she has been the actual victim of illegal discrimination.

The principle of affirmative action was, however, upheld again in 1987, this time in a case concerning women. In *Johnson v. Transportation Agency,* the Supreme Court affirmed that considerations of sex were permissible as one factor in promoting Diane Joyce, a female county employee, to the position of road dispatcher over an equally qualified male employee, Paul Johnson. In summing up the Court's position, Justice Brennan stated that the promotion of Joyce "was made pursuant to an affirmative action plan that represents a moderate, flexible, case-by-case approach to effecting a gradual improvement in the representation of minorities and women in the Agency's work force."

As these cases show, the Supreme Court has approached affirmative action cautiously, basing its position on the relatively specific details of each case. Nevertheless, until 1989 a solid majority of the Court upheld the general principle of affirmative action. Since then, however, the Court has handed down a series of legal rulings generally considered antagonistic to affirmative action, with the result that the overall legal status of affirmative action has become less clear.

In *City of Richmond v. Croson,* the Court invalidated a Richmond, Virginia, law that channeled 30 percent of public-works funds to minority-owned construction companies (see Case 9.1). In another case, it reversed an eighteen-year-old precedent and removed from employers the burden of proving that job requirements that tend to screen out minorities or women are a business necessity; rather, plaintiffs must prove that such requirements are not necessities. And the Court has made it easier for white men to challenge court-approved consent decrees in which employers undertake programs to hire and promote African Americans, even when the plan was approved years earlier.[40]

In 1995 in *Adarand Constructors v. Pena,* the Supreme Court examined a federal program that provided financial incentives for contractors to hire "socially or economically disadvantaged" subcontractors. In her majority opinion in the 5 to 4 decision, Justice Sandra Day O'Connor affirmed the principle that "federal racial classification, like those of a State, must serve a compelling government interest, and must be narrowly tailored to further that interest." Accordingly, all government action based on race should be subjected to "the strictest judicial scrutiny" to ensure that no individual's right to equal protection has been violated. The Court then sent the case back to a lower court for rehearing.[41]

In addition to O'Connor's majority opinion, however, five other justices wrote opinions in the *Adarand* case, and these reveal a range of perspectives on affirmative action. For instance, Justice David Souter criticized the Court for departing from past practice, reminding his colleagues that it is well established "that constitutional authority to remedy past discrimination is not limited to the power to forbid its continuation, but extends to eliminating those effects that would otherwise persist and skew the operation of public systems even in the absence of current intent to practice any discrimination."

In his dissenting opinion, Justice John Paul Stevens also defended the general principle of affirmative action:

> There is no moral or constitutional equivalence between a policy that is designed to perpetuate a caste system and one that seeks to eradicate racial subordination. . . .
>
> A decision by representatives of the majority to discriminate against the members of a minority race is fundamentally different from those same representatives' decision to impose incidental costs on the majority of their constituents in order to provide a benefit to a disadvantaged minority. Indeed, as I have previously argued, the former is virtually always repugnant to the principles of a free and democratic society, whereas the latter is, in some circumstances, entirely consistent with the ideal of equality.

However, Justice Clarence Thomas explicitly challenged Stevens's position. In an opinion concurring with the majority's judgment, he asserted that

> there is a "moral and constitutional equivalence" between laws designed to subjugate a race and those that distribute benefits on the basis of race in order to foster some current notion of equality. Government cannot make us equal; it can only recognize, respect, and protect us as equal before the law. . . .
>
> In my mind, government-sponsored racial discrimination based on benign prejudice is just as noxious as discrimination inspired by malicious prejudice. In each instance, it is racial discrimination, plain and simple.

The upshot of recent judicial developments relative to affirmative action is not clear, tangled up as the rulings are in details, legal technicalities, and split opinions. Furthermore, Congress has intervened, passing the Civil Rights Act of 1991. Initially intended to overturn several of the Court's decisions hostile to affirmative action, the language of the act ended up so watered down and poorly written that it is subject to very different interpretations. The legal future is difficult to predict. Some observers believe that the Supreme Court may reverse itself directly and outlaw moderate and flexible affirmative action programs across the board; others believe this is unlikely. But even if they are right, the Court is increasingly antagonistic to job-discrimination suits and more clearly attuned than ever to what it perceives to be excesses in the cause of affirmative action.

AFFIRMATIVE ACTION: THE MORAL ISSUES

Understanding the Supreme Court's evolving position on affirmative action is important, because the Court sets the legal context in which business operates and lets employers know what they are and are not legally permitted to do. But legal decisions by themselves do not exhaust the relevant moral issues. Employers—as well as women, minorities, and white men—want to know whether affirmative action programs are

morally right. Indeed, it is a safe bet that the Supreme Court's own decisions are influenced not just by technical legal questions but also by how the justices answer this moral question.

Before evaluating arguments for and against affirmative action, one needs to know what is being debated. "Affirmative action" here means programs taking the race or sex of employees or job candidates into account as part of an effort to correct imbalances in employment that exist as a result of past discrimination, either in the company itself or in the larger society. To keep the discussion relevant, it is limited to affirmative action programs that might reasonably be expected to be upheld by the Supreme Court. Excluded are programs that establish rigid, permanent quotas or that hire and promote unqualified persons. Included are programs that hire or promote a woman or African American who might not otherwise, according to established but fair criteria, be the best-qualified candidate.

A word about terminology: Critics of affirmative action often label it "reverse discrimination," but this term is misleading. According to the definition offered earlier, job discrimination involves prejudice, inaccurate stereotypes, or the assumption that a certain group is inferior and deserves unequal treatment. No such forces are at work in the affirmative action cases already discussed. Those who designed the programs that worked to the disadvantage of Allan Bakke, Brian Weber, and Paul Johnson did not do so because they were biased against white men and believed them inferior and deserving of less respect than other human beings. Those who designed the programs in question were themselves white men.

Arguments for Affirmative Action

1. *Compensatory justice demands affirmative action programs.*

POINT: "As groups, women and minorities have historically been discriminated against, often viciously. As individuals and as a nation, we can't ignore the sins of our fathers and mothers. In fact, we have an obligation to do something to help repair the wrongs of the past. Affirmative action in employment is one sound way to do this."

COUNTERPOINT: "People today can't be expected to atone for the sins of the past. We're not responsible for them, and in any case, we wouldn't be compensating those who rightly deserve it. Young African Americans and women coming for their first job have never suffered employment discrimination. Their parents and grandparents may deserve compensation, but why should today's candidates receive any special consideration? No one should discriminate against them, of course, but they should have to compete openly and on their merits, just like everybody else."

2. *Affirmative action is necessary to permit fairer competition.*

POINT: "Even if young blacks and young women today have not themselves suffered job discrimination, blacks in particular have suffered all the disadvantages of growing up in families that have been affected by discrimination. In our racist society, they have suffered from inferior schools and poor environment. In addition, as victims of society's prejudiced attitudes, young blacks and young women have been hampered by a lack of self-confidence and self-respect. Taking race and sex into account makes job competition fairer by keeping white men from having a competitive edge that they don't really deserve."

COUNTERPOINT: "Your point is better when applied to blacks than to women, it seems to me, but I'm still not persuaded. You overlook the fact that there are a lot of disadvantaged whites out there, too. Is an employer going to have to investigate everyone's life history to see who had to overcome the most obstacles? I think an employer has a right to seek the best-qualified candidate without trying to make life fair for everybody. And isn't the best-qualified person entitled to get the job or the promotion?"

3. *Affirmative action is necessary to break the cycle that keeps minorities and women locked into low-paying, low-prestige jobs.*

POINT: "You advocate neutral, nondiscriminatory employment practices, as if we could just ignore our whole history of racial and sexual discrimination. Statistics show that African Americans in particular have been trapped in a socioeconomically subordinate position. If we want to break that pattern and eventually heal the racial rifts in our country, we've got to adopt vigorous affirmative action programs that push more African Americans into middle-class jobs. Even assuming racism were dead in our society, with mere nondiscrimination alone it would take a hundred years or more for blacks to equalize their position."

COUNTERPOINT: "You ignore the fact that affirmative action has its costs, too. You talk about healing the racial rifts in our country, but affirmative action programs make everybody more racially conscious. They also cause resentment and frustration among white men. Many African Americans and women also resent being advanced on grounds other than merit. Finally, if you hire and promote people faster and further than they merit, you're only asking for problems."

Arguments Against Affirmative Action

1. *Affirmative action injures white men and violates their rights.*

POINT: "Even moderate affirmative action programs injure the white men who are made to bear their brunt. Other people design the programs, but it is Allan Bakke, Brian Weber, Paul Johnson, and others like them, who find their career opportunities hampered. Moreover, such programs violate the right of white men to be treated as individuals and to have racial or sexual considerations not affect employment decisions."

COUNTERPOINT: "I'm not sure Bakke, Weber, and Johnson have the rights you are talking about. Racial and sexual considerations are often relevant to employment decisions. Jobs and medical school slots are scarce resources, and society may distribute these in a way that furthers its legitimate ends—like breaking the cycle of poverty for minorities. I admit that with affirmative action programs white men do not have as many advantages as they did before, and I'm against extreme programs that disregard their interests altogether. But their interests have to be balanced against society's interest in promoting these programs."

2. *Affirmative action itself violates the principle of equality.*

POINT: "Affirmative action programs are intended to enhance racial and sexual equality, but you can't do that by treating people unequally. If equality is the goal, it must be the means, too. With the affirmative action programs, you use racial and sexual considerations—but that is the very thing that has caused so much harm in the past and that affirmative action itself is hoping to get rid of."

COUNTERPOINT: "I admit that it is distasteful to have to take racial and sexual considerations into account when dealing with individuals in employment situations. I wish we didn't have to. But the unfortunate reality is that in the real world racial and sexual factors go a long way toward determining what life prospects an individual has. We can't wish that reality away by pretending the world is colorblind when it is not. Formal, colorblind equality has to be infringed now if we are ever to achieve real, meaningful racial and sexual equality."

3. *Nondiscrimination will achieve our social goals; stronger affirmative action is unnecessary.*

POINT: "The 1964 Civil Rights Act unequivocally outlaws job discrimination, and numerous employees and job candidates have won discrimination cases before the EEOC or in court. We need to insist on rigorous enforcement of the law. Also, employers should continue to recruit in a way that attracts minority applicants and to make sure that their screening and review practices do not involve any implicit racist or sexist assumptions. And they should monitor their internal procedures and the behavior of their white male employees to root out any discriminatory behavior. Stronger affirmative action measures, in particular taking race or sex into account in employment matters, are unnecessary. They only bring undesirable results."

COUNTERPOINT: "Without affirmative action, progress often stops. The percentage of minorities and women employed by those subject to federal affirmative action requirements has risen much higher than it has elsewhere. Take the example of Alabama. In the late 1960s, a federal court found that only 27 out of the state's 3,000 clerical and managerial employees were African American. Federal Judge Frank Johnson ordered extensive recruiting of blacks, as well as the hiring of the few specifically identified blacks who could prove they were victims of discrimination. Nothing happened. Another suit was filed, this time just against the state police, and this time a 50 percent hiring quota was imposed, until blacks reached 25 percent of the force. Today Alabama has the most thoroughly integrated state police force in the country."[42]

The debate over affirmative action is not the only controversy connected with job discrimination. Two other issues, both primarily concerning women, have been the topic of recent moral, legal, and political discussion: the issue of comparable worth and the problem of sexual harassment on the job.

COMPARABLE WORTH

Louise Peterson was a licensed practical nurse at Western State Hospital in Tacoma, Washington. For supervising the daily care of sixty men convicted of sex crimes, she was paid $192 a month less than the hospital's groundskeepers and $700 a month less than men doing work similar to hers at Washington State prisons. Convinced of the inequity of the state's pay scale, Peterson filed a suit claiming that she and other women were being discriminated against because men of similar skills and training and with similar responsibilities were being paid significantly more. A federal judge found Washington guilty of sex discrimination and ordered the state to reimburse its female employees a whopping $838 million in back pay.

Prodded by this and by its biggest public employee union, the state of Washington began a program intended to raise the pay for government jobs typically considered "women's work." Even though the program had flaws,[43] it helped raise to national prominence the doctrine of comparable worth and signaled a dramatic escalation in women's fight for equal employment rights.

In essence, the doctrine of *comparable worth* holds that women and men should be paid on the same scale, not just for doing the same or equivalent jobs, but for doing different jobs of equal skill, effort, and responsibility. One legal-affairs expert says, "The issue pits against each other two cherished American values: the ethic of nondiscrimination versus the free enterprise system."[44]

Advocates of comparable worth point to the substantial statistical evidence demonstrating that women are in more low-paying jobs than men. They also note the consistent relationship between the percentage of women in an occupation and the salary of that occupation: The more women dominate an occupation, the less it pays. Comparable-worth advocates contend that women have been shunted into a small number of pink-collar occupations and that a biased and discriminatory wage system has kept their pay below that of male occupations requiring a comparable degree of skill, education, responsibility, and so on. For example, studies have shown that legal secretaries and instrument-repair technicians hold jobs with the same relative value for a company in terms of accountability, know-how, and problem-solving skill. Yet legal secretaries, who are almost all women, earn an average of $9,432 less than instrument-repair technicians, who are generally men.[45]

As comparable-worth advocates see it, justice demands that women receive equal pay for doing work of comparable value. Jobs should be objectively evaluated in terms of the education, skills, and experience required and in terms of responsibilities, working conditions, and other relevant factors. Equivalent jobs should receive equivalent salaries, even if discriminatory job markets would otherwise put them on different pay scales. Some comparable-worth advocates further argue that when women have not received equivalent pay for jobs of comparable worth, justice requires that employers pay them reparation damages for the money they have lost. That would be expensive. But whether pay adjustments are retroactive or not, all comparable-worth programs envision adjusting the salary schedules of women upward rather than the pay of men downward.

Opponents of comparable worth insist that women, desiring flexible schedules and less taxing jobs, have freely chosen lower-paying occupations and thus are not entitled to any readjustment in pay scales. Phyllis Schlafly, for one, calls comparable worth "basically a conspiracy theory of jobs. . . . It asserts that, first, a massive societal male conspiracy has segregated or ghetto-ized women into particular occupations by excluding them from others; and then, second, devalued the women's job by paying them lower wages than other occupations held primarily by men." She adds: "Not a shred of evidence has been produced to prove those assumptions. For two decades at least women have been free to go into any occupation. . . . But most women continue to choose traditional, rather than non-traditional, jobs. This is their own free choice. Nobody makes them do it."[46]

Others who are sympathetic to the concept of comparable worth worry about its implementation. How are different jobs to be evaluated and compared, they wonder. "How do you determine the intrinsic value of one job and then compare it to another?" asks Linda Chavez, former staff director of the Commission on Civil Rights. She points out that "for 200 years, this has been done by the free marketplace. It's as good an alternative as those being suggested by comparable-worth advocates. I'm not sure the legislative bodies or courts can do any better."[47] Even if judgments of comparability are possible, opponents worry about the cost: Revising salaries could cost a medium-sized company millions of dollars in annual pay increases and increased pension benefits.

Advocates of comparable worth respond to these criticisms by pointing not only to statistical evidence demonstrating the inequity of pay scales but also to massive research documenting the reality of visceral sexism in the workplace and to the hundreds of legal cases involving workplace discrimination against women. They argue that it is not by accident or free choice that women find themselves in jobs paying less than men doing similar work. They have been victimized by a combination of institutional discrimination and a socialization process that has directed them to "female jobs." Moreover, proponents of comparable worth reject the argument that implementing comparable worth would be prohibitively expensive. They point to Minnesota, for example, which phased in a comparable-worth program over several years so the state incurred an expense of only about 1 percent a year. But the core of their argument remains an appeal to fairness and equity, which, they insist, cannot be sacrificed on the altar of economy.

The comparable-worth issue continues to engender legal controversy. The federal courts have not explicitly accepted the doctrine of comparable worth, even when they've rendered legal decisions that seem to support it. One form of job discrimination against women that the courts agree about, however, is sexual harassment.

SEXUAL HARASSMENT

Many men find the term *sexual harassment* amusing and have a difficult time taking it seriously. "It wouldn't bother me," they feel certain. "In fact," they chuckle, "I wouldn't mind being harassed a little more often." Others shrug it off, saying, "What's the big deal? You know what the world is like. Men and women, love and sex, they make it go 'round. Only uptight women are going to complain about sexual advances." But for millions of working women, the reality of sexual harassment is not something to be shrugged off. For them it is no laughing matter.

The courts agree. Sexual-harassment claims have emerged in the past two decades as a potent force in the effort to eliminate sex discrimination. These claims fall primarily under Title VII of the Civil Rights Act, which in certain circumstances imposes liability on employers for the discriminatory acts of their employees—including sexual harassment. The Supreme Court has joined a number of federal district and appeals courts in holding that sexual harassment violates the Civil Rights Act because it is based on the sex of the individual.[48] In short, sexual harassment is illegal.

It is also expensive and—unfortunately—widespread. A survey by *Working Woman* magazine revealed that 90 percent of the companies that make up the *Fortune* 500 have received complaints of sexual harassment.[49] One expert has estimated that the average cost to these firms of each sexual harassment complaint is $200,000—even if it doesn't go to court.[50] And this figure doesn't include the costs incurred when employees quit their jobs because of harassment, take leaves of absence, or stay at their jobs but become less productive. Since the early 1990s, the number of complaints of sexual harassment in the workplace filed annually with the EEOC or state and local authorities has increased by 50 percent—to over 15,000 a year.[51]

According to the Supreme Court, men, as well as women, can be victims of sexual harassment.[52] The focus here is on women, however, because they are the ones who suffer most from it. The U.S. Merit Systems Protection Board found that 42 percent of all female employees of the federal government had been sexually harassed; a study of private employers found that 62 percent of the women surveyed had been harassed in the office. And nine-tenths of the 9,000 women who responded to a questionnaire in *Redbook* magazine reported sexual harassment on the job.[53]

We are all familiar with the stereotype of construction workers who whistle and make lewd comments about women who walk by. But the truth is that all types of men in all sorts of occupations have been reported as harassers. Survey after survey, for example, reveals that high percentages of female professors and female students have encountered some form of sexual harassment from a person in authority at least once while they were in the university.

Critics may find it odd that sexual harassment is viewed by the courts as a kind of sex discrimination. If an infatuated supervisor harasses only the female employee who is the object of his desire, is his misconduct really best understood as discrimination against women? He does not bother women in general, just this particular individual. In viewing sexual harassment as a violation of the 1964 Civil Rights Act, however, the courts are rightly acknowledging that such behavior, and the larger social patterns that reinforce it, rest on male attitudes and assumptions that work against women.

Accepting this viewpoint still leaves puzzles, however. Assume that the infatuated supervisor is a woman and the employee a man. Are we to interpret this situation as sex discrimination, considering that it does not take place against a social backdrop of exploitation and discrimination against men? Or imagine a bisexual employer who sexually harasses both male and female employees. Because he discriminates against neither sex, is there no sexual harassment?

These conceptual puzzles have to do with the law's interpretation of sexual harassment as a kind of sex discrimination. Practically speaking, this interpretation has benefited women and brought them better and fairer treatment on the job, but it clearly has its limits. Legally speaking, the most important aspect of sexual harassment may be that it represents discrimination, but it is doubtful that discrimination is morally the worst aspect of sexual harassment. Morally, there is much more to be said about the wrongness of sexual harassment.*

What exactly is sexual harassment? The Equal Employment Opportunity Commission says that it is "unwelcome sexual advances, requests for sexual favors, and other verbal or physical conduct of a sexual nature." Catherine A. MacKinnon, author of *Sexual Harassment of Working Women,* describes sexual harassment as "sexual attention imposed on someone who is not in a position to refuse it." Alan K. Campbell, director of the Federal Office of Personnel Management, defines it as "deliberate or repeated unsolicited verbal comments, gestures, or physical contact of a sexual nature which are unwelcome."[54] Here is one useful legal definition of sexual harassment, which reflects the way most courts understand it:

> Unwelcome sexual advances, requests for sexual favors, and other verbal or physical conduct of a sexual nature constitute sexual harassment when (1) submission to such conduct is made either explicitly or implicitly a term or condition of an individual's employment, (2) submission to or rejection of such conduct by an individual is used as the basis for employment decisions affecting such individual, or (3) such conduct has the purpose or effect of substantially interfering with an individual's work performance or creating an intimidating, hostile, or offensive working environment.[55]

This definition helps us distinguish three different types of sexual harassment. Sexual threats are the first type—in its crudest form, "You'd better agree to sleep with me if you want to keep your job." The immorality of such threats seems clear. In threatening harm, they are coercive and violate the rights of the person threatened, certainly depriving him or her of equal treatment on the job. Obviously such threats can be seriously psychologically damaging and are hence wrong.

Sexual offers are the second type: "If you sleep with me, I'm sure I can help you advance more quickly in the firm." Often such offers harbor an implied threat, and unlike with genuine offers, the employee may risk something by turning them down. Larry May and John Hughes have argued that such offers by a male employer to a female employee put her in a worse position than she was before and, hence, are coercive.

---

*By analogy, compare the fact that often the only grounds on which the federal government can put a murderer on trial is on the charge of having violated the civil rights of his or her victim. The charge of violating the victim's civil rights doesn't get to the heart of the murderer's wrongdoing, even if it is the only legally relevant issue.

Even sexual offers without hint of retaliation, they suggest, change the female employee's working environment in an undesirable way.[56] In the case of both threats and offers, the employer is attempting to exploit the power imbalance between him and the employee.

The third category—hostile work environment—is the broadest, but it may be the most important because it is so pervasive. Sexual harassment includes behavior of a sexual nature that is distressing to women and interferes with their ability to perform on the job, even when the behavior is not an attempt to pressure the woman for sexual favors. Sexual innuendos; leering or ogling at a woman; sexist remarks about women's bodies, clothing, or sexual activities; the posting of pictures of nude women; and unnecessary touching, patting, or other physical conduct can all constitute sexual harassment. Such behavior is humiliating and degrading to its victim. It interferes with her peace of mind and undermines her work performance.

Neither the wrongness nor the illegality of sexual harassment requires that the harassing conduct be by the employee's supervisor. This is particularly relevant in the third category, in which the harassment a woman endures may come from coworkers. Firms, however, are responsible for providing a work environment in which an employee is free from harassment, and they can be sued for damages if they fail to do so. Different courts have reached different decisions on the question of whether supervisory personnel must be notified or made aware of sexual harassment by employees before the firm can be found legally liable. One can nevertheless safely say that, morally speaking, a company needs to be alert to the possibility of sexual harassment by its employees and take reasonable steps to guard against it.

Legally, a woman is not required to prove that she was psychologically damaged or unable to work in order to establish sexual harassment. On the other hand, an isolated or occasional sexist remark or innuendo does not constitute harassment. Harassment of the third type requires that the objectionable behavior be persis-

tent. The same holds for racial slurs and epithets. An ethnic joke by itself does not constitute discriminatory harassment, but a concerted pattern of "excessive and opprobrious" racially derogatory remarks and related abuse does violate the law.[57]

Human beings are sexual creatures, and when men and women work together, there may be sexual undertones to their interactions. Women as well as men can appreciate, with the right persons and at the appropriate times, sexual references, sex-related humor, and physical contact with members of the opposite sex. Flirting, too, is often appreciated by both parties. It is not necessary that a serious and professional work environment be entirely free from sexuality, nor is this an achievable goal.

When, then, is behavior objectionable or offensive enough to constitute harassment? What one person views as innocent fun or a friendly overture may be seen as objectionable and degrading by another. Comments that one woman appreciates or enjoys may be distressing to another. Who can decide what is right? In the case of sexual harassment, who determines what is objectionable or offensive?

To answer this question, the courts ask what the hypothetical "reasonable woman" would find offensive. What matters morally, however, is to respect each person's choices and wishes. Even if the other women in the office like it when the boss gives them a little hug, it would still be wrong to hug the one woman who is made uncomfortable. If the behavior is unwanted—that is, if the woman doesn't like it—then persisting in it is wrong. The fact that objectionable behavior must be persistent and repeated to be sexual harassment allows for the possibility that people can honestly misread coworkers' signals or misjudge their likely response to a sexual innuendo, a joke, or a friendly pat. That may be excusable; what is not excusable is persisting in the behavior once you know it is unwelcome.

Practically speaking, what should a female employee do if she encounters sexual harassment? First, she must make it clear that the behavior is unwanted. This may be more difficult to do than it sounds, because most of us like to please others and do not want to be thought to be prudes or to lack a sense of humor. The employee may wish to be tactful and even pleasant in rejecting behavior she finds inappropriate, especially if she thinks the offending party is well intentioned. But in any case, she has to make her feelings known clearly and unequivocally. Second, if the behavior persists, she should try to document it by keeping a record of what has occurred, who was involved, and when it happened. If others have witnessed some of the incidents, then that will help her document her case.

The third thing the female employee must do when faced with sexual harassment is to complain to the appropriate supervisor, sticking to the facts and presenting her allegations as objectively as possible. She should do this immediately in the case of sexual threats or offers by supervisors; in the case of inappropriate behavior by coworkers, she should generally wait to see if it persists despite telling the offending party that she objects. If complaining to her immediate supervisor does not bring quick action, then she must try whatever other channel is available to her in the organization—the grievance committee, for example, or the chief executive's office.

Fourth, if internal complaints do not bring results, then the employee should seriously consider seeing a lawyer and learning in detail what legal options are available. Many women try to ignore sexual harassment, but the evidence suggests that in most cases it continues or grows worse. When sexual threats or offers are involved, a significant number of victims are subject to unwarranted reprimands, increased work loads, or other reprisals. The employee must remember, too, that she has both a moral and a legal right to work in an environment free from sexual harassment.

SUMMARY

1. Discrimination in employment involves adverse decisions against employees or job applicants based on their membership in a group that is an object of prejudice or viewed as inferior or deserving of unequal treatment. Discrimination can be intentional or unintentional, institutional or individual.

2. Statistics, together with evidence of deep-seated attitudes and institutional practices and policies, point to racial and sexual discrimination in the workplace.

3. The Civil Rights Act of 1964 forbids discrimination in employment on the basis of race, color, sex, religion, and national origin. In the late 1960s and early 1970s, many companies developed affirmative action programs to correct racial imbalances existing as a result of past discrimination. Critics charge that in practice affirmative action has often meant preferential treatment of women and minorities and even reverse discrimination against white men.

4. The Supreme Court has adopted a case-by-case approach to affirmative action. Although recent decisions make the legal future less certain, in a series of rulings over the years a majority of the Court has upheld the general principle of affirmative action, as long as such programs are moderate and flexible. Race can legitimately be taken into account in employment-related decisions, but only as one among several factors. Affirmative action programs that rely on rigid and unreasonable quotas or that impose excessive hardship on present employees are illegal.

5. The moral issues surrounding affirmative action are controversial. Its defenders argue that compensatory justice demands affirmative action programs; affirmative action is necessary to permit fairer competition; and affirmative action is necessary to break the cycle that keeps minorities and women locked into poor-paying, low-prestige jobs.

6. Critics of affirmative action argue that affirmative action injures white men and violates their rights; affirmative action itself violates the principle of equality; and non-discrimination (without affirmative action) will suffice to achieve our social goals.

7. The doctrine of comparable worth holds that women and men should be paid on the same scale for doing different jobs of equal skill, effort, and responsibility.

8. Advocates of comparable worth say that women have been forced into low-paying jobs and justice requires that women receive equal pay for doing jobs of equal worth. Some contend further that monetary reparations are due to women who in the past have not received equal pay for doing jobs of equal value.

9. Opponents of comparable worth claim that women have freely chosen their occupations and are not entitled to compensation. They contend that only the market can and should determine the value of different jobs. Revising pay scales would also be expensive.

10. Sexual harassment is widespread. It includes unwelcome sexual advances and other conduct of a sexual nature in which submission to such conduct is a basis for employment decisions or such conduct substantially interferes with an individual's work performance. Sexual harassment is a kind of discrimination and is illegal.

11. Employees encountering sexually harassing behavior from coworkers should make it clear that the behavior is unwanted. If it persists, harassed employees should document the behavior and report it to the appropriate person or office in the organization. In the case of sexual threats or offers from supervisors, they should do this immediately. If internal channels are ineffective, employees should seek legal advice.

CASE 9.1

Minority Set-Asides

Richmond, Virginia, is the former capital of the Confederacy. It's not the sort of place one would normally associate with controversial efforts at affirmative action. But aware of its legacy of racial discrimination and wanting to do something about it, the Richmond City Council adopted what it called the Minority Business Utilization Plan—a plan that eventually brought it before the Supreme Court.

The plan, which the council adopted by a 5 to 2 vote after a public hearing, required contractors to whom the city awarded construction contracts to subcontract at least 30 percent of the dollar amount of their contracts to Minority Business Enterprises (MBEs). A business was defined as an MBE if minority group members controlled at least 51 percent of it. There was no geographical limit, however; a minority-owned business from anywhere in the United States could qualify as an MBE subcontrac-

tor. (The 30 percent set-aside did not apply to construction contracts that were awarded to minority contractors in the first place.)

Proponents of the set-aside provision relied on a study that indicated that whereas the general population of Richmond was 50 percent African American, only 0.67 percent of the city's construction contracts had been awarded to minority businesses. Councilperson Marsh, a proponent of the ordinance, made the following statement:

> I have been practicing law in this community since 1961, and I am familiar with the practices in the construction industry in this area, in the state, and around the nation. And I can say without equivocation, that the general conduct of the construction industry . . . is one in which race discrimination and exclusion on the basis of race is widespread.

Opponents, on the other hand, questioned both the wisdom and the legality of the ordinance. They argued that the disparity between minorities in the population of Richmond and the low number of contracts awarded to MBEs did not prove racial discrimination in the construction industry. They also questioned whether there were enough MBEs in the Richmond area to satisfy the 30 percent requirement.

The city's plan was in effect for five years until it expired on June 30, 1988. During that time, though, the plan was challenged in the courts. A federal district court upheld the set-aside ordinance, stating that the city council's "findings [were] sufficient to ensure that, in adopting the Plan, it was remedying the present effects of past discrimination in the construction industry." However, the case was appealed to the Supreme Court, which ruled in *City of Richmond v. Croson* that the Richmond plan was in violation of the equal protection clause of the Fourteenth Amendment.[58] In delivering the opinion of the majority of the Court, Justice O'Connor argued that Richmond had not supported its plan with sufficient evidence of past discrimination in the city's construction industry:

A generalized assertion that there has been past discrimination in an entire industry provides no guidance for a legislative body to determine the precise scope of the injury it seeks to remedy. It "has no logical stopping point." . . . "Relief" for such an ill-defined wrong could extend until the percentage of public contracts awarded to MBEs in Richmond mirrored the percentage of minorities in the population as a whole.

[The City of Richmond] argues that it is attempting to remedy various forms of past discrimination that are alleged to be responsible for the small number of minority businesses in the local contracting industry. . . . While there is no doubt that the sorry history of both private and public discrimination in this country has contributed to a lack of opportunities for black entrepreneurs, this observation, standing alone, cannot justify a rigid quota in the awarding of public contracts in Richmond, Virginia. Like the claim that discrimination in primary and secondary schooling justifies a rigid racial preference in medical school admissions, an

amorphous claim that there has been past discrimination cannot justify the use of an unyielding racial quota.

It is sheer speculation how many minority firms there would be in Richmond absent past societal discrimination, just as it was sheer speculation how many minority medical students would have been admitted to the medical school at Davis absent past discrimination in educational opportunities. Defining these sorts of injuries as "identified discrimination" would give local governments license to create a patchwork of racial preferences based on statistical generalizations about any particular field of endeavor.

These defects are readily apparent in this case. The 30% quota cannot in any realistic sense be tied to any injury suffered by anyone. . . .

In sum, none of the evidence presented by the city points to any identified discrimination in the Richmond construction industry. We, therefore, hold that the city has failed to demonstrate a compelling interest in apportioning public contracting opportunities on the basis of race. To accept Richmond's claim that past societal discrimination alone can serve as the basis for rigid racial preference would be to open the door to competing claims for "remedial relief" for every disadvantaged group. The dream of a Nation of equal citizens in a society where race is irrelevant to personal opportunity and achievement would be lost in a mosaic of shifting preferences based on inherently unmeasurable claims of past wrongs. . . . We think such a result would be contrary to both the letter and spirit of a constitutional provision whose central command is equality.

But the Court's decision was not unanimous, and Justice Thurgood Marshall was joined by Justices Brennan and Harry Blackmun in dissenting vigorously to the opinion of the majority. Justice Marshall wrote:

The essence of the majority's position is that Richmond has failed to . . . prove that past discrimination has impeded minorities from joining or participating fully in Richmond's construction contracting industry. I find deep irony in second-guessing Richmond's judgment on this point. As much as any municipality in the

United States, Richmond knows what racial discrimination is; a century of decisions by this and other federal courts has richly documented the city's disgraceful history of public and private racial discrimination. In any event, the Richmond City Council *has* supported its determination that minorities have been wrongly excluded from local construction contracting. Its proof includes statistics showing that minority-owned businesses have received virtually no city contracting dollars; . . . testimony by municipal officials that discrimination has been widespread in the local construction industry; and . . . federal studies . . . which showed that pervasive discrimination in the Nation's tight-knit construction industry had operated to exclude minorities from public contracting. These are precisely the types of statistical and testimonial evidence which, until today, this Court has credited in cases approving of race-conscious measures designed to remedy past discrimination.

Discussion Questions

1. What was the Richmond City Council trying to accomplish with its Minority Business Utilization Plan? If you had been a member of the council, would you have voted for the plan?

2. What are the pros and cons of a minority set-aside plan like Richmond's? Will it have good consequences? Does it infringe on anyone's

rights? What conflicting moral principles, ideals, and values are at stake?

3. Do you believe that there was sufficient evidence of racial discrimination to justify the city's plan? Who is right about this—Justice O'Connor or Justice Marshall?

4. Justice O'Connor and the majority of the Court seem to believe that there must be some specific, identifiable individuals who have been discriminated against before race-conscious measures can be adopted to remedy past discrimination. Do you agree that affirmative action measures must meet this standard?

5. In light of the fact that no federal statute specifically bars racial discrimination in private domestic commercial transactions between two business firms, and given the evidence that racism is an obstacle to African-American business success,[59] what obligation, if any, does state, local, or federal government have to assist minority-owned companies?

6. What measures could Richmond have taken that would have increased opportunities for minority business but would not have involved racial quotas? Would such measures be as effective as the original plan?

CASE 9.2

Hoop Dreams

In basketball, talent plus hard work equals success. That's an equation that holds true for women as well as men, and in recent years, dedicated female athletes have raised women's basketball to new heights and won the allegiance of many new fans.[60]

But what about their coaches? Do any obstacles stand between them and their dreams? Marianne Stanley didn't think so when she began coaching women's basketball for the University of Southern California, where she earned $64,000 a year—a fair sum, one might think, but less than half that of her counterpart, George Raveling, who coached the men's team. True, Raveling had been coaching for thirty-one years, had been an assistant on the U.S. Olympic team, and was twice named coach of the year. But Stanley was no slouch. She had been a head coach for sixteen years and won three national championships. In her last two years at USC, she had win-loss records of 23–8 and 22–7, which compared favorably with Raveling's 19–10 and 24–6.

So when her initial four-year contract expired, Marianne Stanley sought pay parity with Raveling. Stanley knew that Raveling was also earning tens of thousands of dollars in perks, but she was willing to overlook that and settle for an equal base salary of $135,000. Instead, USC offered Stanley a three-year contract starting at $88,000 and increasing to $100,000. When she rejected that offer, USC countered with a one-year contract for $96,000. Stanley declined the offer and left USC, her hoop dreams diminished, although she later began coaching at UC Berkeley, where her salary was equivalent to that of the men's coach.

For his part, George Raveling didn't mind Stanley's making as much money as he did. But he understood why USC paid him more. He was, after all, a hot property, and if USC was going to prevent his being lured away by some other university trying to boost its basketball program, then it had to pay him a high salary. By contrast, Marianne Stanley didn't have any other job offers.

Too bad, one might say, but that's how the market works in a capitalist society. But what if the market itself is discriminatory? Defenders of comparable worth argue that it is and that coaches like Stanley can't negotiate for comparable salaries because women's basketball isn't valued as highly as men's. And it's college administrators, they argue, who are to blame for that. As one feminist puts it:

> The women didn't get the advertising and marketing dollars. They didn't get the PR. Then when fans weren't showing up, the TV stations weren't carrying the games and other universities weren't fighting over the best coaches, administrators told the women that, because they and their sport didn't draw as much attention as men, they shouldn't be paid as much.

In response, defenders of USC deny that it or any other university is responsible for the fact that men's sports are big revenue earners and women's are not. The higher pay for those who coach men simply reflects that social and cultural reality, which is something college administrators have no control over. If someone like Marianne Stanley wants to enter the big leagues, then she should coach men.

Update:

Sadly, sometimes even those who have fought against discrimination can discriminate against others. In 2002 Sharrona Alexander, formerly an assistant women's basketball coach at UC Berkeley, filed suit against the university, alleging that head coach Marianne Stanley told her to get an abortion or lose her job. Stanley denies the abortion allegation, but admits that she did ask Alexander to resign because of her pregnancy. Either way, a champion of women's rights was guilty of trampling on someone else's hoop dreams. Ironically, Stanley herself played college basketball when she was pregnant (returning to practice eleven days after her daughter was born) and went on, single and with a toddler, to coach Old Dominion University to three national championships. Moreover, some sports commentators believe that, far from being a handicap, motherhood can give a coach an edge in recruiting because the parents of prospective recruits prefer their daughters to be coached by women who, when they say that they treat their teams as family, know what they are talking about. In addition, Arizona State coach Charli Turner Thorne says, because "you're taking young ladies at a very formative time, you have to play the parent role." She adds, "There's absolutely no doubt [motherhood] makes me a better coach."

Discussion Questions

1. The doctrine of comparable worth holds that men and women should be paid the same wage for doing jobs of equal skill, effort, and responsibility. Were Marianne Stanley and George Raveling doing work of comparable value?

2. Was Stanley treated unfairly or in some way discriminated against? Should USC have offered to pay her more?

3. Why do sports played by men tend to be more popular and generate more revenue than sports played by women? Are female athletes—and their coaches—disadvantaged? Are they discriminated against? If so, who is responsible for this discrimination, and do colleges and universities have an obligation to do something about it?

4. Should universities like USC base their coaching salaries entirely on market considerations? Or should they pay the coaches of men's and women's sports comparable salaries based on experience, skill, and performance?

5. Respond to the argument that because men are free to coach women's teams and women to coach men's teams, there is nothing discriminatory in the fact that one job pays more than the other.

6. Was Sharrona Alexander's pregnancy likely to have adversely affected her coaching performance? If so, was Marianne Stanley wrong to ask her to resign? How should Stanley have handled the situation?

CASE 9.3

Raising the Ante

Having spearheaded the women's cause on behalf of equal pay for jobs of equal value, Phyllis Warren was elated when the board decided to readjust salaries. Its decision meant Phyllis and the other women employed by the crafts firm would receive pay equivalent to men doing comparable jobs. But in a larger sense it constituted an admission of guilt on the part of the board, acknowledgment of a history blemished by sexual discrimination.

In the euphoria that followed the board's decision, neither Phyllis nor any of the other activists thought much about the implied admission of female exploitation. But some weeks later, Herm Leggett, a sales dispatcher, half-jokingly suggested to Phyllis over lunch that she shouldn't stop with equal pay now. Phyllis asked Herm what he meant.

"Back pay," Herm said without hesitation. "If they're readjusting salaries for women," he explained, "they obviously know that salaries are out of line and have been for some time." Then he asked her pointedly, "How long you been here, Phyl?" Eleven years, she told him. "If those statistics you folks were passing around last month are accurate," Herm said, "then I'd say you've been losing about $2,000 a year, or $22,000 over eleven years." Then he added with a laugh, "Not counting interest, of course."

"Why not?" Phyllis thought. Why shouldn't she and other women who'd suffered past inequities be reimbursed?

That night Phyllis called a few of the other women and suggested that they press the board for back pay. Some said they were satisfied and didn't think they should force the issue. Others thought the firm had been fair in readjusting the salary schedule, and they were willing to let bygones be bygones. Still others thought that any further efforts might, in fact, roll back the board's favorable decision. Yet a nucleus agreed that workers who had been unfairly treated in the past ought to receive compensation. They decided, however, that because their ranks were divided, they shouldn't

wage as intense an in-house campaign as previously but instead take the issue directly to the board, while it might still be inhaling deeply the fresh air of social responsibility.

The following Wednesday, Phyllis and four other women presented their case to the board, intentionally giving the impression that they enjoyed as much support from other workers as they had the last time they appeared before it. Although this wasn't true, Phyllis suggested it as an effective strategic ploy.

Phyllis's presentation had hardly ended when board members began making their feelings known. One called her proposal "industrial blackmail." "No sooner do we try to right an injustice," he said testily, "than you take our good faith and threaten to beat us over the head with it unless we comply with your request."

Another member just as vigorously argued that the current board couldn't be held accountable for the actions, policies, and decisions of previous boards. "Sure," he said, "we're empowered to alter policies as we see fit and as conditions change to chart new directions. And we've done that. But to expect us to bear the full financial liability of decisions we never made is totally unrealistic—and unfair."

Still another member wondered where it would all end. "If we agree," he asked, "will you then suggest we should track down all those women who ever worked for us and provide them compensation?" Phyllis said no, but the board should readjust retirement benefits for those affected.

At this point the board asked Phyllis if she had any idea what her proposal would cost the firm. "Whatever it is, it's a small price to pay for righting wrong," she said firmly.

"But is it a small price to pay for severely damaging our profit picture?" one of the members asked. Then he added, "I needn't remind you that our profit outlook directly affects what we can offer our current employees in terms of salary and fringe benefits. It directly affects our ability to revise our salary schedule." Finally, he asked Phyllis whether she'd accept the board's reducing everyone's current compensation to meet what Phyllis termed the board's "obligation to the past."

Despite its decided opposition to Phyllis's proposal, the board agreed to consider it and render a decision at its next meeting. As a final broadside, Phyllis hinted that, if the board didn't comply with the committee's request, the committee was prepared to pursue legal action.

Discussion Questions

1. If you were a board member, how would you vote? Why?

2. What moral principles are involved in this case?

3. Do you think Phyllis Warren was unfair in taking advantage of the board's implied admission of salary discrimination on the basis of sex? Why?

4. Do you think Phyllis was wrong in giving the board the impression that her proposal enjoyed broad support? Why?

5. If the board rejects the committee's request, do you think the committee ought to sue? Give reasons.

CASE 9.4

Consenting to Sexual Harassment

In the case of *Vinson v. Taylor*, heard before the federal district court for the District of Columbia, Mechelle Vinson alleged that Sidney Taylor, her supervisor at Capital City Federal Savings and Loan, had sexually harassed her.[61] But the facts of the case were contested. In court Vinson testified that about a year after she began working at the bank, Taylor asked her to have sexual relations with him. She claimed that Taylor said she "owed" him because he had obtained the job for her.

Although she turned down Taylor at first, she eventually became involved with him. She and Taylor engaged in sexual relations, both during and after business hours, in the remaining three years she worked at the bank. The encounters included intercourse in a bank vault and in a storage area in the bank basement. Vinson also testified that Taylor often actually "assaulted or raped" her. She contended that she was forced to submit to Taylor or jeopardize her employment.

Taylor, for his part, denied the allegations. He testified that he had never had sex with Vinson. On the contrary, he alleged that Vinson had made advances toward him and that he had declined them. He contended that Vinson had brought the charges against him to "get even" because of a work-related dispute.

In its ruling on the case, the court held that if Vinson and Taylor had engaged in a sexual relationship, that relationship was voluntary on the part of Vinson and was not employment related. The court also held that Capital City Federal Savings and Loan did not have "notice" of the alleged harassment and was therefore not liable. Although Taylor was Vinson's supervisor, the court reasoned that notice to him was not notice to the bank.

Vinson appealed the case, and the Court of Appeals held that the district court had erred in three ways. First, the district court had overlooked the fact that there are two possible kinds of sexual harassment. Writing for the majority, Chief Judge

Spottswood Robinson distinguished cases in which the victim's continued employment or promotion is conditioned on giving in to sexual demands and those cases in which the victim must tolerate a "substantially discriminatory work environment." The lower court had failed to consider Vinson's case as possible harassment of the second kind.

Second, the higher court also overruled the district court's finding that because Vinson voluntarily engaged in a sexual relationship with Taylor, she was not a victim of sexual harassment. Voluntariness on Vinson's part had "no bearing," the judge wrote, on "whether Taylor made Vinson's toleration of sexual harassment a condition of her employment." Third, the Court of Appeals held that any discriminatory activity by a supervisor is attributable to the employer, regardless of whether the employer had specific notice.

In his dissent to the decision by the Court of Appeals, Judge Robert Bork rejected the majority's claim that "voluntariness" did not automatically rule out harassment. He argued that this position would have the result of depriving the accused person of any defense, because he could no longer establish that the supposed victim was really "a willing participant." Judge Bork contended further that an employer should not be held vicariously liable for a supervisor's acts that it didn't know about.

Eventually the case arrived at the Supreme Court, which upheld the majority verdict of the Court of Appeals, stating that:

> [T]he fact that sex-related conduct was "voluntary," in the sense that the complainant was not forced to participate against her will, is not a defense to a sexual harassment suit brought under Title VII. The gravamen of any sexual harassment claim is that the alleged sexual advances were "unwelcome." . . . The correct inquiry is whether respondent by her conduct indicated that the alleged sexual advances were unwelcome, not whether her actual participation in sexual intercourse was voluntary.

The Court, however, declined to provide a definite ruling on employer liability for sexual harassment.

It did, however, reject the Court of Appeals's position that employers are strictly liable for the acts of their supervisors, regardless of the particular circumstances.[62]

Discussion Questions

1. According to her own testimony, Vinson acquiesced to Taylor's sexual demands. In this sense her behavior was "voluntary." Does the voluntariness of her behavior mean that she had "consented" to Taylor's advances? Does it mean that they were "welcome"? Do you agree that Vinson's acquiescence shows there was no sexual harassment? Which court was right about this? Defend your position.

2. In your opinion, under what circumstances would acquiescence be a defense to charges of sexual harassment? When would it not be a defense? Can you formulate a general rule for deciding such cases?

3. Assuming the truth of Vinson's version of the case, should her employer, Capital City Federal Savings and Loan, be held liable for sexual harassment it was not aware of? Should the employer have been aware of it? Does the fact that Taylor was a supervisor make a difference? In general, when should an employer be liable for harassment?

4. What steps do you think Vinson should have taken when Taylor first pressed her for sex? Should she be blamed for having given in to him? Assuming that there was sexual harassment despite her acquiescence, does her going along with Taylor make her partly responsible or mitigate Taylor's wrongdoing?

5. In court, Vinson's allegations were countered by Taylor's version of the facts. Will there always be a "your word against mine" problem in sexual harassment cases? What could Vinson have done to strengthen her case?

CASE 9.5

Facial Discrimination

Scene: A conference room of a branch office of Allied Products, Inc., where Tom, Frank, and Alice have been interviewing college students for summer internships.

Tom: Did you see that last candidate? Jeez, was he sorry looking.

Frank: Too ugly to work here, that's for sure. And those thick glasses didn't help. Still, he wasn't as ugly as that young woman you hired last summer. What was her name . . . Allison? Boy, she was enormous, and remember that hair of hers. It wasn't surprising we had to let her go.

Alice: Come on, Frank. Don't be so hung up on looks. That last guy seemed to know his stuff, and he certainly was enthusiastic about working for Allied.

Frank: Hey, don't get me wrong, Alice. I know you don't have to be beautiful to work for Allied—after all, look at Tom here. Still, with a face like that guy's, you got to wonder.

Tom: Wisecracks aside, Alice, Frank's got a point. Studies show that it's natural for people to discriminate on the basis of looks. I've read that even babies will look at a pretty face longer than an ugly face.

Alice: I know that. Studies also show that people attribute positive characteristics to people they find attractive and that they treat unattractive people worse than other people in lots of ways. Strangers are less likely to do small favors for unattractive people than they are for attractive people, and even parents and teachers have lower expectations for ugly, fat, or odd-looking children. But what this really boils down to is implicit discrimination.

Tom: That's what I'm saying. It's natural. Besides, it's not illegal to discriminate on the basis of appearance.

Frank: That's right. You wouldn't want us to hire somebody with green hair and rings in his nose and put him out at the front desk, would you? This is a business, not a freak show.

Alice: Hey, slow down, guys. First, it may be natural and it may even be legal to favor good-looking people, but that doesn't make it right. And second, I'm not talking about grooming or dress. It's your choice to dye your hair and decorate your face, and if you don't fit in because of that, that's your fault. But the guy we talked to today didn't choose to be ugly, so why hold it against him?

Frank: I suppose next you'll be telling us that we should have kept Allison on last summer just because she was fat.

Alice: No, I'm not saying you have to give preferential treatment to overweight people. But I think that nobody in the office cut her any slack. If she'd been normal size, things would have worked out okay, but people took one look at her and prejudged her to be a loser. You know, Frank, some courts have held that discrimination against the obese violates the Americans with Disabilities Act.

Tom: That's only if it's a medical condition.

Frank: Yeah, Allison's only problem was that she liked to eat.

Alice: You don't know that. You don't know anything about her.

Frank: I suppose her hair was a medical condition, too.

Tom: Okay, you two, take it easy. Seriously, though, Alice, a number of our interns have to interact with the public, and people can be put off by having to deal with ugly people, fat people, or even very short people. So why aren't an employee's looks a job-relevant issue?

Alice: No, I think that as long as the person is clean and well groomed, then the public shouldn't be put off by having to deal with someone who is unattractive or unusual looking. It's unreasonable.

Tom: That's what you say. But what if the public is "unreasonable"? What if they prefer companies with attractive or at least normal-looking employees?

Alice: It's still irrelevant. It's the same as if a company had customers who didn't like dealing with blacks. That's no reason for it not to hire blacks.

Tom: Yeah, I can see that.

Frank: Okay, but what about this ugly guy? Do we have to offer him an internship?

Discussion Questions

1. How frequently are people discriminated against on the basis of their looks? Is it a serious problem in job situations?

2. Assess the argument that there is nothing wrong with "facial discrimination"—that it simply reflects the fact that human beings are naturally attracted to, or repelled by, other human beings on the basis of their physical characteristics.

3. Under what circumstances is physical attractiveness a job-related employment criterion? Is it relevant to being a salesperson, a flight attendant, or a receptionist?

4. What arguments can be given for and against a law preventing job discrimination on the basis of immutable aspects of one's appearance?

5. Assess the argument that because fat, ugly, or strange-looking people have it tougher throughout their lives than do attractive people, we should give them preferential treatment whenever we can—for example, in job situations—to make up for the disadvantages they've suffered and to help level the playing field.

6. Are businesses morally obligated to try to prevent or reduce appearance discrimination in the workplace? What steps can they take?

Notes to Chapter 9

1. This and the following three paragraphs are based on Edward Wong, "The Mystery of the Missing Minority Coaches," *New York Times*, January 6, 2002, sec. 4, 5; Mark Purdy, "Riley Seems Right for Stanford, and That's Just the Problem," *San Jose Mercury News*, January 6, 2002, 1D; and Ann Killion, "Willingham Kept Dreams Quiet, Then Played His Hand Wisely," *San Jose Mercury News*, January 3, 2002, 1D.

2. Charles R. Lawrence III, "The Id, the Ego, and Equal Protection: Reckoning with Unconscious Racism," *Stanford Law Review* 39 (January 1987): 318, 340.

3. Ibid., 339–340.

4. Manuel G. Velasquez, *Business Ethics*, 5th ed. (Upper Saddle River, N.J.: Prentice Hall, 2002), 389.

5. Ibid., 390.

6. "A Texas-Size Case of Discrimination?" *Business Week*, March 18, 2002, 14.

7. "Screening Out Minority Workers," *San Francisco Chronicle*, December 5, 1990, A1.

8. "Restaurant Chain Must Pay $105 Million for Racial Bias," *San Jose Mercury News*, February 5, 1993, 14A.

9. Philip Shenon, "Judge Finds F.B.I. Is Discriminatory," *New York Times*, October 1, 1988, 1.

10. Tom L. Beauchamp and Norman E. Bowie, *Ethical Theory and Business*, 4th ed. (Englewood Cliffs, N.J.: Prentice Hall, 1993), 437.

11. Gertrude Ezorsky, *Racism and Justice: The Case for Affirmative Action* (Ithaca, N.Y.: Cornell University Press, 1991), 27. See also Velasquez, *Business Ethics*, 388–389.

12. "Black Staff Fired More, Study Finds," *San Jose Mercury News*, October 20, 1994, C1.

13. "Black-White Income Inequalities," *New York Times*, February 17, 1998, A22, and Robert Pear, "Rich Got Richer in 80s; Others Held Even," *New York Times*, January 11, 1991, A1.

14. U.S. Bureau of the Census, *Statistical Abstract of the United States 2001* (Washington, D.C.: U.S. Government Printing Office, 2002), Tables 679, 680.

15. "90% of World Lacks Full Rights, U.N. Says," *San Jose Mercury News,* May 16, 1993, 14A.

16. *Statistical Abstract,* Table 661; "Latinos' Wages Falling Behind," *Santa Cruz Sentinel,* May 23, 2002, A1.

17. *Statistical Abstract,* Table 593.

18. Andrew Hacker, "The Blacks and Clinton," *New York Review of Books,* January 28, 1993, 13.

19. *Personnel Journal,* February 1994, 16.

20. "Equal Pay Top Issue for Women," *San Francisco Chronicle,* September 5, 1997, A8; Julianne Malveaux, "On the Economy," *San Francisco Examiner,* April 13, 1997, B2.

21. *Statistical Abstract,* Table 753.

22. Susan J. Wells, "A Female Executive Is Hard to Find," *HR Magazine,* June 2001, 42.

23. "Women Losing Ground on Pay," *San Jose Mercury News,* January 24, 2002, 1C, and Toddi Gutner, "How to Shrink the Pay Gap," *Business Week,* June 24, 2002, 151.

24. Lisa Girion, "Wage Gap Continues to Vex Women," *Los Angeles Times,* February 11, 2001, W1.

25. "Equal Pay Top Issue for Women."

26. *Wards Cove Packing Co., Inc. v. Atonio,* 109 S. Ct. 2115 (1989).

27. This paragraph and the next are based on Andrew Hacker, "Grand Illusion," *New York Review of Books,* June 11, 1998, 28–29.

28. Tamar Lewin, "Sex Bias Found in Awarding of Partnerships at Law Firm," *New York Times,* November 30, 1990, B14.

29. "Judge Orders Partnership in a Bias Case," *Wall Street Journal,* December 5, 1990, B6; *Price Waterhouse v. Hopkins,* 109 S. Ct. 1775 (1989).

30. Ellen Goodman, "Women Gain a Better Shot at the Top Rungs," *Los Angeles Times,* May 29, 1984, II-45.

31. Lee Dembart, "Science: Still Few Chances for Women," *Los Angeles Times,* March 7, 1984, 1. See also "An Outsider's View of the Corporate World," *San Francisco Chronicle,* October 27, 1997, B2.

32. Benson Roxen and Thomas H. Jerdee, "Sex Stereotyping in the Executive Suite," *Harvard Business Review* 52 (May–June 1974); Crystal L. Owen and William D. Todor, "Attitudes Toward Women as Managers: Still the Same," *Business Horizons* 36 (March–April 1993).

33. "Racial Stereotypes Still Persist Among Whites, Survey Finds," *San Francisco Chronicle,* January 9, 1991, A10.

34. Edward W. Jones, Jr., "Black Managers: The Dream Deferred," *Harvard Business Review* 64 (May–June 1986): 84.

35. Jones, "Black Managers," 88.

36. See *Griggs v. Duke Power Co.,* 401 U.S. 424 (1971), and *Wards Cove Packing Co., Inc. v. Atonio,* 109 S. Ct. 2115 (1989) at 2115, in which the Court reiterates that Title VII can be violated by "not only overt discrimination but also practices that are fair in form but discriminatory in practice."

37. "Language Rights," *ACLU News* (San Francisco), March–April 1994, 7; "But Some Entry-Level Workers Still Face Difficulties," *San Francisco Chronicle,* April 7, 1997, B1.

38. "Revolt at the Deli Counter," *Business Week,* April 1, 1996, 32.

39. "Business Affirmative on Diversity," *San Jose Mercury News,* August 24, 1995, 3B. See also "A Strong Prejudice," *Economist,* June 17, 1995, 69.

40. *Wards Cove Packing Co., Inc. v. Atonio* (1989) and *Martin v. Wilks* (1989).

41. *Adarand Constructors, Inc. v. Pena,* 115 S. Ct. 2097 (1995).

42. Herman Schwartz, "Affirmative Action," in Gertrude Ezorsky, ed., *Moral Rights in the Workplace* (Albany: State University of New York Press, 1987), 276.

43. Peter Kilborn, "Comparable-Worth Pay Plan Creates Unseen Woe for State," *Denver Post,* June 3, 1990, 3A.

44. Nina Totenberg, "Why Women Earn Less," *Parade Magazine,* June 10, 1984, 5.

45. Velasquez, *Business Ethics,* 427.

46. Caroline E. Mayer, "The Comparable Pay Debate," *Washington Post National Weekly Edition,* August 6, 1984, 9.

47. Ibid.

48. *Meritor Savings Bank v. Vinson* (1986); *Harris v. Forklift Systems* (1993).

49. Ronnia Sandroff, "Sexual Harassment in the *Fortune* 500," *Working Woman,* December 1988, 69.

50. Anne B. Fisher, "Sexual Harassment: What to Do?" *Fortune,* August 1993, 85.

51. *www.eeoc.gov/stats/harass.html* (February 22, 2002); cf. "Women in Suits," *Economist,* March 2, 2002, 60–61.

52. *Oncale v. Sundowner Offshore Service* (1998).

53. Mary Jo Shaney, "Perceptions of Harm: The Consent Defense in Sexual Harassment Cases," *Iowa Law Review* 71 (May 1986): 1112n; and "Is Sexual Harassment Still on the Job?" *Business and Society Review* 67 (Fall 1988): 5, 8.

54. Shaney, "Perceptions of Harm," 1109.

55. Ibid.

56. Larry May and John C. Hughes, "Sexual Harassment," in Ezorsky, ed., *Moral Rights.*

57. Terry L. Leap and Larry R. Smeltzer, "Racial Remarks in the Workplace: Humor or Harassment?" *Harvard Business Review* 62 (November–December 1984).

58. *City of Richmond v. J. A. Croson Co.,* 109 S. Ct. 706 (1989).

59. Robert E. Suggs, "Rethinking Minority Business Development Strategies," *Harvard Civil Rights–Civil Liberties Law Review* 25 (Winter 1990); and Brent Bowers, "Black Owners Fight

Obstacles to Get Orders," *Wall Street Journal,* November 16, 1990, B1.

60. This case study is based on Joan Ryan, "Playing Field Is Still Not Level," *San Francisco Chronicle,* June 13, 1999, "Sunday," 1, and Ann Killion, "Belief That Coach Can't Be Pregnant Outdated," *San Jose Mercury News,* September 17, 2002, 1A.

61. See Shaney, "Perceptions of Harm," for the relevant legal citations and a presentation of the facts of this case.

62. *Meritor Savings Bank v. Vinson,* 106 S. Ct. 2399 (1986).

Reading ──────────■

A DEFENSE OF PROGRAMS OF PREFERENTIAL TREATMENT

RICHARD WASSERSTROM

Many critics of programs of preferential treatment for women and minorities argue that, even if such programs are effective, they are unfair or unjust. One common objection to them is that if it was wrong to take race or sex into account in the past when African Americans and women were excluded, then it is wrong to take race or sex into account now. A second objection is that preferential treatment programs are wrong because they do not base hiring or other decisions on an individual's qualifications. In this essay, Professor Richard Wasserstrom responds to these two criticisms of preferential treatment programs, arguing that such programs are not unjust or objectionable in the way that the discrimination they seek to remedy is.

Many justifications of programs of preferential treatment depend upon the claim that in one respect or another such programs have good consequences or that they are effective means by which to bring about some desirable end, e.g., an integrated, equalitarian society. I mean by "programs of preferential treatment" to refer to programs such as

Reprinted with permission from *National Forum: The Phi Kappa Phi Journal,* Volume LVIII, Number 1 (Winter 1978).

those at issue in the *Bakke* case—programs which set aside a certain number of places (for example, in a law school) as to which members of minority groups (for example, persons who are nonwhite or female) who possess certain minimum qualifications (in terms of grades and test scores) may be preferred for admission to those places over some members of the majority group who possess higher qualifications (in terms of grades and test scores).

Many criticisms of programs of preferential treatment claim that such programs, even if effective, are unjustifiable because they are in some important sense unfair or unjust. In this essay I present a limited defense of such programs by showing that two of the chief arguments offered for the unfairness or injustice of these programs do not work in the way or to the degree supposed by critics of these programs.

The first argument is this. Opponents of preferential treatment programs sometimes assert that proponents of these programs are guilty of intellectual inconsistency, if not racism or sexism. For, as is now readily acknowledged, at times past employers, universities, and many other social institutions did have racial or sexual quotas (when they did not practice overt racial or sexual exclusion), and many of those who were most concerned to bring about the eradication of those racial or sexual quotas are now untroubled by the new programs which reinstitute them. And this, it is claimed, is inconsistent. If it was wrong to take race or sex into account when blacks and women were the objects of racial and sexual policies and practices of exclusion, then it is wrong to take race or sex into account when the objects of the policies have their race or sex reversed. Simple considerations of intellectual consistency—of what it means to give racism or sexism as a reason for condemning these social policies and practices—require that what was a good reason then is still a good reason now.

The problem with this argument is that despite appearances, there is no inconsistency involved in holding both views. Even if contemporary preferential treatment programs which contain quotas are wrong, they are not wrong for the reasons that made quotas against blacks and women pernicious. The reason why is that the social realities do make an enormous difference. The fundamental evil of programs that discriminated against blacks or women was that these programs were a part of a larger social universe which systematically maintained a network of institutions which unjustifiably concentrated power, authority, and goods in the hands of white male individuals, and which systematically consigned blacks and women to subordinate positions in the society.

Whatever may be wrong with today's affirmative action programs and quota systems, it should be clear that the evil, if any, is just not the same. Racial and sexual minorities do not constitute the dominant social group. Nor is the conception of who is a fully developed member of the moral and social community one of an individual who is either female or black. Quotas which prefer women or blacks do not add to an already relatively overabundant supply of resources and opportunities at the disposal of members of these groups in the way in which the quotas of the past did maintain and augment the overabundant supply of resources and opportunities already available to white males.

The same point can be made in a somewhat different way. Sometimes people say that what was wrong, for example, with the system of racial discrimination in the South was that it took an irrelevant characteristic, namely race, and used it systematically to allocate social benefits and burdens of various sorts. The defect was the irrelevance of the characteristic used—race—for that meant that individuals ended up being treated in a manner that was arbitrary and capricious.

I do not think that was the central flaw at all. Take, for instance, the most hideous of the practices, human slavery. The primary thing that was wrong with the institution was not that the particular individuals who were assigned the place of slaves were assigned there arbitrarily because the assignment was made in virtue of an irrelevant characteristic, their race. Rather, it seems to me that the primary thing that was and is wrong with slavery is the practice itself—the fact of some individuals being able to own other individuals and all that goes with that practice. It would not matter by what criterion individuals were assigned; human slavery would still be wrong. And the same can be said for most if not all of the other discrete practices and institutions which comprised the system of racial discrimination even after human slavery was abolished. The practices were unjustifiable—they were oppressive—and they would have been so no matter how the assignment of victims had been made. What made it worse, still, was that the institutions and the supporting ideology all interlocked to create a system of human oppression whose effects on those living under it were as devastating as they were unjustifiable.

Again, if there is anything wrong with the programs of preferential treatment that have begun to flourish within the past ten years, it should be evident that the social realities in respect to the distribution of resources and opportunities make the difference. Apart from everything else, there is simply no way in which all of these programs taken together could plausibly be viewed as capable of relegating white males to the kind of genuinely oppressive status characteristically bestowed upon women and blacks by the dominant social institutions and ideology.

The second objection is that preferential treatment programs are wrong because they take race or sex into account rather than the only thing that does matter—that is, an individual's qualifications. What all such programs have in common and what makes them all objectionable, so this argument goes, is that they ignore the persons who are more qualified by bestowing a preference on those who are less qualified in virtue of their being either black or female.

There are, I think, a number of things wrong with this objection based on qualifications, and not the least of them is that we do not live in a society in which there is even the serious pretense of a qualification requirement for many jobs of substantial power and authority. Would anyone claim, for example, that the persons who comprise the judiciary are there because they are the most qualified lawyers or the most qualified persons to be judges? Would anyone claim that Henry Ford II is the head of the Ford Motor Company because he is the most qualified person for the job? Part of what is wrong with even talking about qualifications and merit is that the argument derives some of its force from the erroneous notion that we would have a meritocracy were it not for programs of preferential treatment. In fact, the higher one goes in terms of prestige, power and the like, the less qualifications seem ever to be decisive. It is only for certain jobs and certain places that qualifications are used to do more than establish the possession of certain minimum competencies.

But difficulties such as these to one side, there are theoretical difficulties as well which cut much more deeply into the argument about qualifications. To begin with, it is important to see that there is a serious inconsistency present if the person who favors "pure qualifications" does so on the ground that the most qualified ought to be selected because this promotes maximum efficiency. Let us suppose that the argument is that if we have the most qualified performing the relevant tasks we will get those tasks done in the most economical and efficient manner. There is nothing wrong in principle with arguments based upon the good consequences that will flow from maintaining a social practice in a certain way. But it is inconsistent for the opponent of preferential treatment to attach much weight to qualifications on this ground, because it was an analogous appeal to the good consequences that the opponent of preferential treatment thought was wrong in the first place. That is to say, if the chief thing to be said in favor of strict qualifications and preferring the most qualified is that it is the most efficient way of getting things done, then we are right back to an assessment of the different consequences that will flow from different programs, and we are far removed from the considerations of justice or fairness that were thought to weigh so heavily against these programs.

It is important to note, too, that qualifications—at least in the educational context—are often not connected at all closely with any plausible conception of social effectiveness. To admit the most qualified students to law school, for example—given the way qualifications are now determined—is primarily to admit those who have the greatest chance of scoring the highest grades at law school. This says little about efficiency except perhaps that these students are the easiest for the faculty to teach. However, since we know so little about what constitutes being a good, or even successful, lawyer, and even less about the correlation between being a very good law student and being a very good lawyer, we can hardly claim very confidently that the legal system will operate most effectively if we admit only the most qualified students to law school.

To be at all decisive, the argument for qualifications must be that those who are the most qualified deserve to receive the benefits (the job, the place in law school, etc.) because they are the most qualified. The introduction of the concept of desert now makes it an objection as to justice or fairness of the sort promised by the original criticism of the programs. But now the problem is that there is no reason to think that there is any strong sense of "desert" in which it is correct that the most qualified deserve anything.

Let us consider more closely one case, that of preferential treatment in respect to admission to college or graduate school. There is a logical gap in the inference from the claim that a person is most qualified to perform a task, e.g., to be a good student, to the conclusion that he or she deserves to be admitted as a student. Of course, those who deserve to be admitted should be admitted. But why do the most qualified deserve anything? There is simply no necessary connection between academic merit (in the sense of being the most qualified) and deserving to be a member of a student body. Suppose, for instance, there is only one tennis court in the community. Is it clear that the two best tennis players ought to be the ones permitted to use it?

Why not those who were there first? Or those who will enjoy playing the most? Or those who are the worst and, therefore, need the greatest opportunity to practice? Or those who have the chance to play least frequently?

We might, of course, have a rule that says that the best tennis players get to use the court before the others. Under such a rule the best players would deserve the court more than the poorer ones. But that is just to push the inquiry back one stage. Is there any reason to think that we ought to have a rule giving good tennis players such a preference? Indeed, the arguments that might be given for or against such a rule are many and varied. And few if any of the arguments that might support the rule would depend upon a connection between ability and desert.

Someone might reply, however, that the most able students deserve to be admitted to the university because all of their earlier schooling was a kind of competition, with university admission being the prize awarded to the winners. They deserve to be admitted because that is what the rule of the competition provides. In addition, it might be argued, it would be unfair now to exclude them in favor of others, given the reasonable expectations they developed about the way in which their industry and performance would be rewarded. Minority-admission programs, which inevitably prefer some who are less qualified over some who are more qualified, all possess this flaw.

There are several problems with this argument. The most substantial of them is that it is an empirically implausible picture of our social world. Most of what are regarded as the decisive characteristics for higher education have a great deal to do with things over which the individual has neither control nor responsibility: such things as home environment, socioeconomic class of parents, and, of course, the quality of the primary and secondary schools attended. Since individuals do not deserve having had any of these things vis-à-vis other individuals, they do not, for the most part, deserve their qualifications. And since they do not deserve their abilities they do not in any strong sense deserve to be admitted because of their abilities.

To be sure, if there has been a rule which connects, say, performance at high school with admis-

sion to college, then there is a weak sense in which those who do well at high school deserve, for that reason alone, to be admitted to college. In addition, if persons have built up or relied upon their reasonable expectations concerning performance and admission, they have a claim to be admitted on this ground as well. But it is certainly not obvious that these claims of desert are any stronger or more compelling than the competing claims based upon the needs or advantages to women or blacks from programs of preferential treatment. And as I have indicated, all rule-based claims of desert are very weak unless and until the rule which creates the claim is itself shown to be a justified one. Unless one has a strong preference for the status quo, and unless one can defend that preference, the practice within a system of allocating places in a certain way does not go very far at all in showing that that is the right or the just way to allocate those places in the future.

A proponent of programs of preferential treatment is not at all committed to the view that qualifications ought to be wholly irrelevant. He or she can agree that, given the existing structure of any institution, there is probably some minimal set of qualifications without which one cannot participate meaningfully within the institution. In addition, it can be granted that the qualifications of those involved will affect the way the institution works and the way it affects others in the society. And the consequences will vary depending upon the particular institution. But all of this only establishes that qualifications, in this sense, are relevant, not that they are decisive. This is wholly consistent with the claim that race or sex should today also be relevant when it comes to matters such as admission to college or law school. And that is all that any preferential treatment program—even one with the kind of quota used in the *Bakke* case—has ever tried to do.

I have not attempted to establish that programs of preferential treatment are right and desirable. There are empirical issues concerning the consequences of these programs that I have not discussed, and certainly not settled. Nor, for that matter, have I considered the argument that justice may permit, if not require, these programs as a way to provide compensation or reparation for injuries suffered in the recent as well as distant past, or as a way to remove benefits that are undeservedly enjoyed by those of the dominant group. What I have tried to do is show that it is wrong to think that programs of preferential treatment are objectionable in the centrally important sense in which many past and present discriminatory features of our society have been and are racist and sexist. The social realities as to power and opportunity do make a fundamental difference. It is also wrong to think that programs of preferential treatment are in any strong sense either unjust or unprincipled. The case for programs of preferential treatment could, therefore, plausibly rest both on the view that such programs are not unfair to white males (except in the weak, rule-dependent sense described above) and on the view that it is unfair to continue the present set of unjust—often racist and sexist—institutions that comprise the social reality. And the case for these programs could rest as well on the proposition that, given the distribution of power and influence in the United States today, such programs may reasonably be viewed as potentially valuable, effective means by which to achieve admirable and significant social ideals of equality and integration.

Review and Discussion Questions

1. Do you agree with Wasserstrom that there is nothing inconsistent about programs of preferential treatment?

2. How does Wasserstrom respond to the argument that such programs are to be rejected because they ignore an individual's qualifications? What about the related argument that the most able candidates deserve to be admitted? Are you persuaded by his reasoning?

3. Are there any important arguments against preferential treatment programs that Wasserstrom has neglected?

4. What goals do such programs seek to achieve and how effective are they in achieving them? Do preferential treatment programs have any negative consequences?

5. Assuming that Wasserstrom is right that preferential treatment programs are not unjust, does justice require us to adopt such programs?

Reading———————————————■

Making Sense of Sexual Harassment Law

Andrew Altman

Only a little more than twenty years old, the body of law concerning sexual harassment is still evolving. In this essay, Andrew Altman explicates and reformulates some of its key aspects. He begins with an analysis of the two broad types of sexual harassment—quid-pro-quo harassment and hostile environment harassment—and shows how they involve violations of the right to fair employment opportunity. Altman then discusses two unsettled areas of sexual harassment law. The first is sexual favoritism—that is, whether the rights of coworkers are violated when another employee receives a job benefit in return for sexual favors. The second is whether in sexual harassment cases the law should replace the traditional "reasonable person" standard with the "reasonable woman" standard.

I: INTRODUCTION

. . . Under current U.S. law, sexual harassment claims may be brought under Title VII of the Civil Rights Act of 1964, state fair employment practice laws, local ordinances, or under a tort claim. My main concern will be with Title VII. . . . Title VII prohibits discrimination on account of race, color, religion, sex, or national origin in the terms, conditions, or privileges of employment. The courts have held that sexual harassment is a form of sex discrimination and thus a violation of Title VII.[1]

Current doctrine distinguishes between two broad types of sexual harassment: quid-pro-quo and hostile environment. In the context of the workplace, quid-pro-quo harassment (QPQH) consists

Reprinted from *Philosophy and Public Affairs* 25 (Winter 1996). Copyright © 1996 by Princeton University Press. Reprinted by permission of Princeton University Press. Section titles added, and some notes omitted.

of unwelcome sexual advances, demands, or propositions acceptance of which is made a condition of obtaining some employment-related benefit or avoiding some employment-related harm. Hostile environment harassment (HEH) consists of unwelcome sexual conduct that unreasonably interferes with work performance or creates a sufficiently hostile or offensive work environment.

In this article, I undertake an explication, refinement, and defense of the existing law of sexual harassment. . . .

II: HOSTILE ENVIRONMENT HARASSMENT

HEH is best understood as speech or conduct that (a) is addressed to or oriented toward an employee's sexuality and (b) amounts to a material and unreasonable interference with her job performance.[2] By "sexuality" I mean a person's sexual desires, attitudes, and activities. It is not to be conceptually equated with "sex" as used in the phrase "sex discrimination." Persons can be discriminated against on the basis of their sex even if the treatment they receive is not addressed to their sexuality. Conceptually speaking, this is an elementary point, but it is one that is repeatedly misunderstood by courts and commentators.

"Material interference" with job performance should be broadly construed so that it includes cases in which the harassment creates obstacles or burdens that make it more difficult for the victim to maintain her job performance and prospects, even if she is successful in overcoming those difficulties. Moreover, "material interference" should cover harassing actions that harm the victim's occupational prospects by diminishing the regard in which she is held by her coworkers or supervisors.

One key issue to resolve in specifying the meaning of "unreasonable interference" is whether the standard of reasonableness should be gender-neutral or gendered. That question will be taken up in Section V. For now, the point is that the law should include a reasonableness standard of some kind, because employers should not be held liable if an employee's work performance suffers from remarks or conduct that would not have interfered with the work of a reasonable employee. The law justifiably expects employees to be reasonable and denies them legal means to shift to their employer costs they incur as a consequence of their own unreasonableness.

Acts of HEH are typically part of the broader class of social acts I will call "put-downs." Specific kinds of put-down include demeaning, degrading, debasing, and humiliating. There are significant differences here. For instance, humiliating a person is a more brutal put-down than demeaning her in that it can be reasonably expected to cause overwhelming shame. And some kinds of put-down, such as degradation and debasement, carry the implication that the victim is to be treated as less than a full human.

Prototypical put-downs are communicative acts targeting some specific person(s) and having the following features: The acts are reasonably construed as affirming that the target's status is subordinate to that of the agent's and as communicating that affirmation to her, and it is reasonable to expect that the acts will be found objectionable by the targeted person and cause her unwarranted distress or harm.

In a typical case of actionable HEH, the harassing conduct amounts to a put-down addressed in some way to the employee's sexuality, and the interference it creates with the employee's job performance is unreasonable precisely because of its character as a put-down. This is not to say that all workplace put-downs addressed to a person's sexuality should count as actionable HEH. For example, in some instances, an unrepeated and relatively mild sexual put-down would have only a vanishing effect on a reasonable employee's job performance and should not be actionable. To hold otherwise is to take an overly protective view of those who are put down. One can hardly go through life without being at the wrong end of many put-downs, and it is reasonable for the law to expect that people will have developed some "protective hide" to ward them off and get on with their lives.

Yet, actionable HEH usually does involve sexually demeaning or degrading the victim, and perhaps it almost always does when the victim is a woman and the perpetrator a man. That is because

male-on-female harassment is reasonably seen as reflecting and reinforcing a demeaning view of women that relegates them to second-class status in the workplace. On that view, it is enough for male workers that they do their job, but when it comes to female workers, they must also serve as the objects of the sexual attentions of the males.

However, it would be going too far to include as part of the very definition of HEH that it is sexually demeaning or involves some other kind of sexual put-down. We should leave conceptual space for cases in which there is a material and unreasonable interference with job performance, even though the victim does not construe (and it is not reasonable to construe) the harassing behavior as a put-down. In such cases, the behavior would be reasonably found to be very annoying and disruptive of work activities without being seen as demeaning.

It might be argued that the requirement of material and unreasonable interference sets too strict a standard for judging HEH lawsuits and that sexual conduct or remarks directed at an employee should be actionable even if they do not rise to that level. The Supreme Court has adopted this position in its most recent sexual harassment ruling, *Harris* v. *Forklift Systems*.[3] The Court held that if a work environment is sufficiently hostile or abusive, as judged by a reasonable person, then there may be a violation of Title VII's guarantee of workplace equality. Several variables must be taken into account in determining whether an environment is sufficiently hostile: unreasonable interference with job performance (or prospects) is one variable, but others include the frequency and the severity of the discriminatory conduct. The Court says that all variables need to be weighed and that sufficiently severe and frequent harassment violates the law's requirement of equality, even if there is no unreasonable interference with job performance.

The problem with the Court's position is that judging whether sexually demeaning conduct is "sufficiently" severe and pervasive requires some purpose or standard with respect to which the threshold of sufficiency is drawn. The Court would have the judgment made in terms of a standard of equality of treatment. But if "equality" is taken strictly to refer to any difference in treatment, then any sexually demeaning conduct violates equality and the whole idea of a threshold of sufficiency becomes misguided. And if it is not taken strictly, then we still need to know the purpose or standard in terms of which to specify the threshold.

The way out of this dilemma is to define the boundaries of HEH in light of the strongest justification for regarding HEH as a form of sex discrimination under Title VII, *viz.*, that it unjustly places persons—predominantly women—at a disadvantage in the workplace. That disadvantage consists of interference with their performance and prospects on the job, and the limits of HEH should be specified in terms of such interference. The severity and frequency of harassment are certainly relevant variables in a given case, but they are relevant to whether there has been unreasonable interference with a person's job, not to whether some free-floating concept of sufficiency has been satisfied.

The Court may have been concerned about cases in which each individual act of harassment at a certain workplace was, by itself, insufficient to create an unreasonable interference with the work of a female employee, but, in the aggregate, the acts created a very hostile environment for her. Yet, nothing in the idea of unreasonable and material interference is inconsistent with considering in the aggregate the harassing acts that occur at a particular workplace. If the aggregate effects are sufficient to create an unreasonable and material interference with her work, then the employee should have a cause of action. If the aggregate effects do not reach that threshold, then the law should conclude that there has been no actionable harassment.

Current doctrine requires that acts be "unwelcome" in order to count as actionable HEH. Roughly put, an unwelcome act is one that the targeted person finds objectionable and would have preferred not to have occurred. Courts have sometimes used the unwelcomeness requirement to put the burden on the plaintiff of establishing that she found objectionable the alleged acts of HEH. But this placement of the burden of proof cannot be justified, in light of the best understanding of HEH. Remarks or actions that interfere with work performance—especially when

reasonably construed as demeaning or degrading—should be presumed to be unwelcome by those at whom they are directed. The unstated and unwarranted premise behind judicial judgments to the contrary is that women are generally at work, not simply to do their jobs, but to find mates and are rather indiscriminate in their receptiveness to male advances.

Notwithstanding some court opinions, it should not be necessary for a plaintiff to have expressed to the perpetrator—or to anyone else—her objection to his sexual remarks, if the remarks are, prima facie, reasonably construed as demeaning or degrading. The law should expect persons to understand how others may reasonably construe what they do or say and to adjust their behavior accordingly. In order to avoid liability on the ground that his actions were not unwelcome, an employee who makes remarks to a coworker that are, prima facie, reasonably construed as sexually demeaning should be required to show that he had sufficient reason to think that the coworker would not in fact object to them. In short, along with the presumption of unwelcomeness goes the defendant's burden of showing that he reasonably believed his behavior to be not unwelcome.

Courts have also used the unwelcomeness requirement to license inquiry into the plaintiff's style of dress and workplace demeanor. There are cases in which this kind of inquiry has rested on demeaning and unwarranted assumptions about women. For example, contrary to the Supreme Court's claim, the way a woman dresses is not "obviously relevant" in determining whether she welcomed sexual behavior directed at her by a boss or coworker.[4] The assumption of its relevance rests on the unwarranted and sexist view that women who dress in ways that men find attractive are likely to be indiscriminately inviting men to direct sexual remarks and behavior toward them.

Some feminist critics of existing doctrine have suggested that the unwelcomeness requirement be jettisoned entirely. For example, Susan Estrich argues that the requirement perpetuates sexist assumptions about women and is "gratuitously punitive" because it allows the defendant to shift the focus of the case from him to the plaintiff and to invoke sexist views in portraying the plaintiff as "unworthy of respect or decency."[5] If the defendant's conduct could be reasonably construed as sexually demeaning or degrading, Estrich claims, then he should not be allowed to escape liability by refocusing the case on the plaintiff.

However, Estrich's argument as it stands is not entirely convincing, because it ignores the relevance of considerations of welcomeness to the question of whether the defendant's behavior was, all things considered, unreasonable or not. Acts of touching, e.g., may count as unreasonable interference when they are not welcome, since they can sometimes be reasonably construed as demeaning under those conditions. But such acts may not be unreasonable if the plaintiff had good grounds for thinking that the defendant welcomed them. To exclude automatically any inquiry into welcomeness would eliminate consideration of an aspect of the action-context that bears importantly on the meaning of the defendant's behavior. In short, it seems that the unwelcomeness requirement should be folded into the unreasonableness condition and not jettisoned as Estrich recommends. . . .

III: QUID–PRO–QUO HARASSMENT

Like HEH, QPQH is addressed to its victim as a sexual being and uses her sexuality against her. But unlike HEH, the perpetrator of QPQH seeks to gain sexual favors from his victim, and he attempts to do so by taking advantage of the authority he has over her in the hierarchy of the workplace. It is commonly held that such efforts by the harasser amount to coercion of the employee and that the coercive character of QPQH shows why statutory prohibitions on it are justified.

The concept of coercion has been subject to much philosophical controversy over the past few decades. Central to the controversy has been the question of whether there is an essential normative element to the concept. It is not necessary to settle that question for the purpose of explicating and defending the law of sexual harassment. However, it is necessary to explain why it should be illegal for a supervisor to say to a subordinate, "Have sex with me and I'll give you a promotion," but not illegal to say, "Land the IBM contract and I'll give you a promotion."

Many people would answer that the difference between the two statements is that the former is coercive and the latter is not. But the answer is incomplete unless it is elaborated in a way that explains how that difference provides grounds for having a legal ban on the one statement but not the other. Such an explanation would necessarily involve a normative claim about what is wrong with a supervisor's making one statement but not the other. For the purposes of the law, it makes no difference whether this normative element is folded into the concept of coercion or treated as separate. Either way, a constructive interpretation of the law needs to explain why we are justified in making it illegal for a supervisor to say, "Have sex with me and I'll give you a promotion."

So why are we so justified? My suggestion is this: Such statements violate the employee's right against having employment-related benefits (or burdens) accorded her on the basis of her willingness to perform sexual favors for her supervisor or employer. Such a right can be seen as an aspect of the more general right to fair employment opportunity and . . . an implication of the right to equal consideration. In contrast, fair employment opportunity clearly does not involve any claim against having job benefits or burdens made contingent on success in job-related activities.

Although the rules against HEH and QPQH both protect the right of fair employment opportunity, they do it in somewhat different ways. The ban on HEH protects against sexually oriented remarks or behaviors that unreasonably interfere with job performance. The ban on QPQH protects against efforts of the employer to extend the scope of his authority to include the sexual activities of the employee. There is some overlap, since one way of unreasonably interfering with job performance is by trying to extend one's authority into the domain of the employee's sexual behavior. And courts have recognized this by allowing evidence of such conduct by employers into cases that charge HEH. But demands or requests by an employer for sexual favors in return for employment benefits are not at all necessary for actionable HEH. In fact, the perpetrator in a case of HEH need not even be the employer or anyone with the authority to give or withhold employment benefits: A coworker with no more workplace authority than the victim can be liable for HEH.

As with HEH, current doctrine requires that conduct be "unwelcome" in order to count as QPQH: A plaintiff who did not find a sexual proposition unwelcome at the time it was made was not the victim of actionable harassment. Courts have done little to clarify the meaning of "unwelcome" in this context other than to suggest that it involves more than whether or not the employee acceded to the sexual proposition. A woman may accede solely out of fear of losing her job, for example, in which case current doctrine would count the sexual proposition as an unwelcome one. Beyond that, the meaning of the unwelcomeness requirement and its rationale have been left rather unclear.

The requirement should be understood in terms of an employee's waiver of her right against having job benefits or burdens accorded her on the basis of her compliance with the boss's sexual demands or propositions. There should be a strong presumption that employees have not waived that right, and the law should require that, prior to extending a proposition of sex in return for a job benefit, employers have good reason, based on the employee's words and actions, to think that she has waived her right. In cases where the employer does not have such reasons, courts should judge the employer's sexual proposition to have been unwelcome, even if the employee acceded to it. On the other hand, in cases where the prior words and actions of the employee made it reasonable for the employer to think that she had waived her right, courts should judge the employer's sexual proposition to have been not unwelcome.

The application of the unwelcomeness requirement in the context of a QPQH case carries with it all of the pitfalls noted previously in connection with HEH cases: Sexist assumptions can easily distort the determination of whether the requirement has been met. And courts have virtually invited the use of such assumptions by ruling, for example, that a woman's style of dress is a relevant consideration. However much these pitfalls may argue for eliminating the unwelcomeness requirement, it is a firmly entrenched part of doctrine. The best feasible approach, then, may be to insist on the strong presumption that employees have not waived their right to keep their sexual activities beyond the scope of their employer's authority and to criticize courts when they permit sexist assumptions to be introduced by defendants in an effort to overcome that presumption.

IV: SEXUAL FAVORITISM

One of the unsettled areas of law related to sexual harassment doctrine concerns "sexual favoritism," the act of an employer or supervisor in giving a job benefit to an employee in return for her willingness to perform sexual favors for him. Of course, if the initial sexual proposition came from the employer and was unwelcome to the employee, then we have a case of QPQH. But whether or not the proposition was unwelcome or even came from the employer, we can still ask whether other employees who are in competition for that job benefit have had their legal rights violated by the employer's action. The developing doctrine of sexual favoritism addresses that question.[6]

In cases of sexual favoritism, the employer is using sexual criteria for decisions distributing the benefits and burdens of employment. Even though the plaintiff in such a case has not been propositioned by her boss, her opportunities on the job have been determined, in part, by the boss's sexual desire for another employee. The boss has not violated the plaintiff's right against having job benefits and burdens distributed to her according to her compliance with the boss's sexual propositions or demands. But the more general right of fair employment opportunity has been violated in a way that is very similar to cases of QPQH: in both sorts of cases, irrelevant sexual criteria play a role in determining the plaintiff's employment prospects. In the case of QPQH, the criterion is the plaintiff's willingness to accede to the employer's sexual propositions. In the case of favoritism, it is another employee's willingness to accede to his sexual wishes.

Yet, however wrong favoritism is, the question remains whether it makes sense to regard it as a form of sex discrimination under Title VII. In order to answer that question, let us first consider the differential gender-effects of favoritism and then a gender-neutral account of those effects.

At first glance, it may seem that women as a group actually benefit from sexual favoritism. After all, such favoritism gives women a route to advancement that men typically lack. But such a view of the matter does not look seriously enough at the implications of two important premises on which the view rests: (1) Men occupy positions of workplace authority in far greater percentages than do women, and (2) men are much more inclined than women to use their power in the workplace to seek sexual favors from employees of the opposite sex.

These premises explain why women rather than men tend to be the ones at whom sexual favoritism is directed. But once we jettison the sexist assumption that women typically welcome the prospect of trading sex for job benefits, the two premises also point to the conclusion that women as a group suffer greater disadvantage than do men from the existence of sexual favoritism.

First, it is inevitable that in many instances of favoritism the boss's sexual proposition will be unwelcome to the woman, thus amounting to QPQH. And even where bosses would not retaliate against an employee for refusing, it will often be the case that she reasonably fears retaliation and so complies with the unwelcome proposition. Assuming that most women at whom sexual favoritism is directed do not wish to trade sex for job benefits, the female "beneficiaries" of sexual favoritism will typically and reasonably feel themselves forced into sexual relations they would prefer not to have. Finally, sexual favoritism helps to reinforce social beliefs that demean women and perpetuate workplace discrimination against them, such as the belief that women typically "sleep" their way to the top, or that they are generally less competent at their jobs than men are.

It is also possible to describe the systemic effects of sexual favoritism in gender-neutral terms and to justify a prohibition on favoritism on the grounds that it unfairly disadvantages persons on account of an irrelevant characteristic of theirs, *viz.*, their sex. On those grounds, men who are harmed by sexual favoritism should also have a good cause of action. But the gender-neutral justification would be only part of the strongest case for barring favoritism. As with HEH and QPQH, the strongest justification for banning sexual favoritism and regarding it as a form of sex discrimination would incorporate both the gender-neutral account and the claim that the effect of favoritism is to place women as a group at a systemic disadvantage relative to men in the workplace.

V: REASONABLE PERSON OR REASONABLE WOMAN?

One of the most controverted aspects of sexual harassment law at present concerns the sort of reasonableness test that should be used in setting out the legal criteria for HEH. Roughly put, the question is whether the law should use an ungendered, "reasonable person" standard or a gendered approach in which the "reasonable woman" is the standard for cases with a female plaintiff and the "reasonable man" for cases with a male one. Most courts—including the Supreme Court—have endorsed the reasonable-person standard, though there are commentators and judges who defend the gendered ones.

Advocates of a gendered approach make the very plausible claim that men and women do not employ the same interpretive grid when presented with sex-related behavior in the workplace. The kinds of acts that men tend to construe as innocuous or perhaps flattering when directed toward them, women tend to construe as demeaning or threatening when they are the targets. And, of course, a man might construe his own behavior toward a woman as a case of flattery, where she would understand it as demeaning or threatening to her. Defenders of a gendered approach argue that, when women are the plaintiffs, the law should judge their claim by the interpretive grid in terms of which women generally view sexual behavior in the workplace.

Let us assume for the sake of argument that the thesis about the (partial) disjunction of male and female interpretive grids is roughly accurate as a generalization about the tendencies of men and women to understand sexually related behavior in the workplace. What sort of reasonableness standard should the law of sexual harassment then incorporate?

Under the premise of disjoint interpretive grids, it seems clear that a gendered approach fits better than an ungendered one with one of the principal justifying aims of the ban on sexual harassment, *viz.*, to counteract the unfair and systemic disadvantage in the workplace that falls disproportionately on women. An ungendered standard would have the inevitable consequence that some instances of harassment directed at women that are reasonably construed by them as demeaning would fail to count as actionable. While such a consequence would not entirely defeat the law's efforts to combat the disadvantage women face in the workplace, it would not be as well-adapted to meeting that purpose as a gendered approach.

However, some may argue that a gendered approach violates fundamental principles of legal fairness by treating male workers less favorably than similarly situated female ones: A woman complainant in an HEH lawsuit could win her case, even though a man who complained of the same sort of behavior directed at him would lose. Moreover, male employees—at least heterosexual ones—would be held to stricter standards than heterosexual female ones. Since the reasonable man will presumably put up with more serious sexual put-downs without it materially affecting his work than the reasonable woman would put up with, male workers will have less latitude in making sexual remarks to their female coworkers than female employees will have in their remarks to their male coworkers.

In defending its use of a gendered approach, the Court of Appeals in *Ellison* v. *Brady* denied that it was holding men and women to different standards and claimed that it was treating them equally.[7] But the court's denial might mislead. Under a gendered approach, women who direct sexual remarks at men will not be held to as strict a standard of conduct as

men who direct such remarks at women. This does not mean that the court in *Ellison* was wrong in claiming that a gendered approach treats the sexes equally. Rather, it means that the court needed to make explicit the thesis underlying that claim: Given the premise of disjoint interpretive grids, equal protection from the harm of sexually derogatory remarks and behavior requires that different standards be used depending on the sex of the victim.

However, such a thesis leads directly to a common criticism of the gendered approach, *viz.*, that it harms women by reinforcing the stereotype of women as the weaker sex in need of special protection from the law. Such a stereotype, it is pointed out, supports the second-class status to which traditionalists would relegate women.

Nonetheless, the criticism is typically formulated in an ambiguous way. It might be an argument about what sort of justification can be offered for a gendered approach. Alternatively, it might be an argument about the causal effects that the use of such an approach has on how women are perceived by society.

On the first reading, the criticism would claim that a gendered approach can only be justified on the premise that women are the weaker sex, properly relegated to second-class social standing. But such a claim is mistaken. The justification for a gendered approach is not that women are the weaker sex in any overall way or in any sense that entails or assumes they should have second-class status. Rather the justification rests on the premises that there are certain specific ways in which women are systemically disadvantaged by the sexual behavior of men in the workplace and that those disadvantages are tied to the fact that women are more prone than men to interpret sexual behavior in the workplace directed at them as threatening and demeaning.

Such a justification does not entail or presuppose that women are "weaker than men" in any way that implies the justifiability of a second-class status. Quite the contrary, the presupposition is that women have a moral right to equal employment opportunities with men and that a gendered approach is needed to protect that right.

On a second reading, the criticism of the gendered approach makes the empirical-causal claim that its use would reinforce the traditional view of women as unfit to be the social equals of men. Such a claim cannot be dismissed a priori, especially if people are prone to mistakenly believe that the first version of the stereotype argument is right, i.e., if they think that a gendered approach can only be justified on the premise that women are the weaker sex in some morally significant way. That belief might lead some people to conclude that the law is endorsing the traditional "weaker sex" view of women, which could in turn reinforce that view in society.

Yet, any reinforcement of the traditional view must be weighed against the additional gains that women would make in the workplace as a result of a gendered standard. If—as I have argued—a gendered approach is more effective at combating the systemic disadvantage women face in the workplace, then the use of the approach would mean more women working more effectively and holding more positions of authority in the workplace. Such consequences would help weaken the traditional view of women. And it is not unreasonable to suppose that how women fare in the day-to-day activities of the workplace will ultimately weigh more heavily in social perceptions of them than how a certain, relatively esoteric legal policy is interpreted.

Moreover, how a policy is interpreted is in part a function of what people think the arguments for it are. It is possible to mitigate, even if not eliminate, the tendency of a gendered approach to reinforce the traditional view if courts and commentators clearly articulate that the argument for the approach rests squarely on a conception of the moral equality of the sexes that is incompatible with traditional views of gender.

VI: CONCLUSION

The law of sexual harassment is barely two decades old. It is still finding its way toward a clear and persuasive formulation. Judges and theorists have made a reasonable start, and current doctrine is, in broad outline, quite defensible. Yet, confusion remains about certain aspects of the law. It has been the aim of this essay to resolve some of that confusion in a way that systematically explicates the legal doctrine and provides the best justification for it.

Notes

1. This understanding of sexual harassment was affirmed by the Supreme Court in *Meritor Savings Bank* v. *Vinson* 477 U.S. 57 (1986).

2. Existing law also makes actionable harassing conduct addressed to an employee's race, religion, or nationality, among other factors, and courts largely reasoned their way to making sexual harassment in the workplace actionable by analogy with racial harassment, whose illegality was part of the settled law before sexual harassment doctrine took shape. . . .

3. *Harris* v. *Forklift Systems* 114 S. Ct. 367 (1993).

4. *Meritor Savings Bank* v. *Vinson* 477 U.S. 57, 69 (1986).

5. Susan Estrich, "Sex at Work," *Stanford Law Review* 43 (1991): 833.

6. Some court decisions hold that sexual favoritism is actionable under Title VII, and the regulations of the Equal Employment Opportunity Commission (EEOC) support those holdings. But other court decisions seem to take the opposite view, and even the EEOC regulations make important exceptions for certain cases. Compare *King* v. *Palmer* 778 F.2d 878 (D.C. Cir. 1985) with *DeCintio* v. *Westchester County Medical Center* 807 F.2d 304 (2nd Cir. 1986). Also see "EEOC: Policy Guide on Employer Liability for Sexual Favoritism under Title VII," in Alba Conte, *Sexual Harassment in the Workplace,* vol. 2 (New York, N.Y.: John Wiley and Sons, 1994), pp. 365–70.

7. *Ellison* v. *Brady* 924 F.2d 872, 879 (9th Cir. 1991).

Review and Discussion Questions

1. Altman argues that typically HEH is sexually demeaning or involves some kind of sexual put-down. Do you agree? Can there be sexually harassing behavior that is not demeaning?

2. Altman maintains that HEH requires "material and unreasonable interference with job performance." How should that phrase be interpreted? How does Altman's position differ from that of the Supreme Court in *Harris v. Forklift Systems*? In your view, does sexual harassment require that the acts be "unwelcome" by the woman? Why do some feminists recommend that the "unwelcomeness" requirement be jettisoned?

3. With reference to the moral principles and theories you have studied, explain what is morally wrong about QPQH. Is the law justified in making it illegal for a supervisor to say, "Have sex with me and I'll give you a promotion" but

not illegal to say, "Land the IBM contract and I'll give you a promotion"? Explain why or why not.

4. Suppose a supervisor rewards an employee for sexual favors. Does this violate the rights of other employees? Does any favoritism by a private employer violate the rights of other workers? Should sexual favoritism be seen as a form of sex discrimination?

5. Are men and women likely to differ over whether certain kinds of workplace conduct constitute sexual harassment? If so, should the law replace the traditional "reasonable person" standard with the "reasonable woman" standard in sexual harassment cases?

Reading ———————————— ■

HOMOSEXUALITY, PREJUDICE, AND DISCRIMINATION
RICHARD D. MOHR

The Civil Rights Act and other federal legislation forbid job discrimination on the basis of race, color, sex, age, religion, national origin, or disability—but not on the basis of sexual orientation. Although some cities and a handful of states prohibit sexual-orientation discrimination, in 1996 the U.S. Senate specifically voted not to outlaw job discrimination against homosexuals. In this essay, Richard D. Mohr describes the discrimination that homosexuals suffer, both on and off the job. Mohr attacks some of the myths and stereotypes surrounding homosexuality and rebuts the contention that it is immoral or unnatural. He argues that civil rights legislation should be extended to protect lesbians and gay men from private-sector discrimination because doing so will permit them to enter the mainstream, thus enriching society and confirming our commitment to human rights.

From *A More Perfect Union* by Richard D. Mohr. © 1994 by Richard D. Mohr. Reprinted by permission of Beacon Press, Boston. Section headings added.

STEREOTYPES

Who are gays anyway? Though the number of gays in America is hotly disputed, studies agree that gays are distributed through every stripe and stratum of Americans. Who are homosexuals? They are your friends, your minister, your teacher, your bankteller, your doctor, your mailcarrier, your officemate, your roommate, your congressional representative, your sibling, parent, and spouse. They are we. We are everywhere, virtually all ordinary, virtually all unknown.

Ignorance about gays, however, has not stopped people's minds from being filled with stereotypes about gays. Society holds two oddly contradictory groups of anti-gay stereotypes. One revolves around an individual's allegedly confused gender identity: lesbians are females who want to be, or at least look and act like, men—bulldykes, diesel dykes; while gay men are males who want to be, or at least look and act like, women—queens, fairies, nances, limpwrists, nellies, sissies, aunties. These stereotypes of mismatches between biological sex and socially defined gender provide the materials through which lesbians and gay men become the butts of ethniclike jokes. These stereotypes and jokes, though derisive, basically view lesbians and gay men as ridiculous. . . .

The other set of stereotypes revolves around gays as a pervasive sinister conspiratorial threat. The core stereotype here is that of the gay person—especially the gay man—as child molester, and more generally as sex-crazed maniac. Homosexuality here is viewed as a vampirelike corruptive contagion. These stereotypes carry with them fears of the very destruction of family and civilization itself. Now, that which is essentially ridiculous can hardly have such a staggering effect. Something must be afoot.

Clarifying the nature of stereotypes can help make sense of this incoherent amalgam. Stereotypes are not simply false generalizations from a skewed sample of cases examined. Admittedly, false generalizing plays some part in the stereotypes society holds about gays and other groups. If, for instance, one takes as one's sample gay men who are in psychiatric hospitals or prisons, as was done in nearly all early investigations, not surprisingly one will probably find them to be of a crazed or criminal cast. Such false generalizations, though, simply confirm beliefs already held on independent grounds, ones that likely led the investigator to the prison and psychiatric ward to begin with. Evelyn Hooker, who in the late 1950s carried out the first rigorous studies of non-clinical gay men, found that psychiatrists, when presented with case files including all the standard diagnostic psychological profiles—but omitting indications of sexual orientation—were unable to distinguish gay files from non-gay ones, even though they believed gay men to be crazy. These studies proved a profound embarrassment to the psychiatric establishment, which has profited throughout the century by attempting to "cure" allegedly insane gays. The studies led eventually to the decision by the American Psychiatric Association in 1973 to drop homosexuality from its registry of mental illnesses. Nevertheless, the stereotype of gays as "sick" continues to thrive in the mind of America.

False generalizations help maintain stereotypes; they do not form them. As the history of Hooker's discoveries shows, stereotypes have a life beyond facts; their origin lies in a culture's ideology—the general system of beliefs by which it lives—and they are sustained across generations by diverse cultural transmissions, including slang and jokes, which usually don't even purport to have a scientific basis. Stereotypes, then, are not the products of bad science, but reflections of society's conception of itself.

Understanding this much, it is easy to see how stereotypes about gays as gender-confused reinforce still powerful gender roles in American society. What these stereotypes presume about gays and condemn is the notion that freely choosing one's social roles independently of one's biological sex might threaten many guiding social divisions, both domestic and commercial. Blurred would be the socially sex-linked distinctions between breadwinner and homemaker, boss and secretary, doctor and nurse, protector and protected, even God and His world. The accusations "fag" and "dyke" serve in significant part to keep women in their place and to prevent men from breaking ranks and ceding away theirs.

The stereotypes of gays as destroyers of civilization function to displace (possibly irresolvable) social problems from their actual source to a remote and (society hopes) manageable one. For example, the stereotype of the gay person as child molester functions to give the traditionally defined family unit a false sheen of innocence. It keeps the unit from being examined too closely for incest, child abuse, wife-battering, and the terrorizing of women and children by a father's constant threats. The stereotype teaches that the problems of the family are not internal to it, but external.

If this account of stereotypes holds, society has been profoundly immoral. For its treatment of gays is a grand-scale rationalization, a moral sleight-of-hand. The problem is not that society's usual standards of evidence and procedure in decision making have been misapplied to gays, rather when it comes to gays, the standards themselves have simply been ruled out of court and disregarded in favor of mechanisms that encourage unexamined fear and hatred.

DISCRIMINATION AGAINST GAYS

Partly because lots of people suppose they don't know any gay people and partly through the maintaining of stereotypes, society at large is unaware of the many ways in which gays are subject to discrimination in consequence of widespread fear and hatred. Contributing to this social ignorance of discrimination is the difficulty for gay people, as an invisible minority, even to complain of discrimination. If one is gay, the act of registering a complaint suddenly targets oneself as a stigmatized person, and so, especially in the absence of any protection against discrimination, simply invites additional discrimination. So, discrimination against gays, like rape, goes seriously underreported. Even so, known discrimination is massive.

Annual studies by the National Gay and Lesbian Task Force have consistently found that over 90 percent of gay men and lesbians have been victims of violence or harassment in some form on the basis of their sexual orientation. Greater than one in five gay men and nearly one in ten lesbians have been punched, hit, or kicked; a quarter of all gays have had objects thrown at them; a third have been chased; a third have been sexually harassed, and 14 percent have been spit on, all just for being perceived to be gay. . . .

Gays are also subject to widespread discrimination in employment. Governments are leading offenders here. They do a lot of discriminating themselves, require that others do it, and set precedents favoring discrimination in the private sector. First and foremost, the armed forces discriminate against lesbians and gay men. The federal government has also denied gay men and lesbians employment in the CIA, FBI, and the National Security Agency—and continues to defend such discrimination in the courts. The government refuses to give security clearances to gays and so forces the country's considerable private sector military and aerospace contractors to fire employees known to be gay and to avoid hiring those perceived to be gay. State and local governments regularly fire gay teachers, policemen, firemen, social workers, and anyone who has contact with the public. Further, state licensing laws (though frequently honored only in the breach) officially bar gays from a vast array of occupations and professions—everything from doctors, lawyers, accountants, and nurses to hairdressers, morticians, even used-car dealers.

Gays are subject to discrimination in a wide variety of other ways, including private-sector employment, public accommodations, housing, insurance of all types, custody, adoption, and zoning regulations that bar "singles" or "non-related" couples from living together. A 1988 study by the Congressional Office of Technology Assessment found that a third of America's insurance compa-nies openly admit that they discriminate against lesbians and gay men. In nearly half the states, same-sex sexual behavior is illegal.

Legal sanctions, discrimination, and the absorption by gays of society's hatred all interact to impede and, for some, block altogether the ability of gay men and lesbians to create and maintain significant personal relations with loved ones. Every facet of life is affected by discrimination. Only the most compelling reasons could possibly justify it.

BUT ISN'T HOMOSEXUALITY IMMORAL?

Many people suppose society's treatment of gays is justified because they think gays are extremely immoral. To evaluate this claim, different senses of "moral" must be distinguished. Sometimes "morality" means the values generally held by members of a society—its mores, norms, and customs. On this understanding, gays certainly are not moral: lots of people hate them, and social customs are designed to register widespread disapproval of gays. The problem here is that this sense of morality is merely a descriptive one. Every society has this kind of morality—even Nazi society, which had racism and mob rule as central features of its "morality" understood in this sense. Before one can use the notion of morality to praise or condemn behavior, what is needed is a sense of morality that is prescriptive or normative.

As the Nazi example makes clear, the fact that a belief or claim is descriptively moral does not entail that it is normatively moral. A lot of people in a society saying that something is good, even over aeons, does not make it so. The rejection of the long history of the socially approved and state-enforced institution of slavery is another good example of this principle at work. Slavery would be wrong even if nearly everyone liked it. So consistency and fairness require that one abandon the belief that gays are immoral simply because most people dislike or disapprove of gays.

Furthermore, recent historical and anthropological research has shown that opinion about gays has been by no means universally negative. It has varied widely even within the larger part of the Christian era and even within the Church itself. There are even current societies—most notably in Papua New Guinea—where compulsory homosexual behavior is integral to the rites of male maturity. Within the last thirty years, American society has undergone a grand turnabout from deeply ingrained, nearly total condemnation to nearly total acceptance on two emotionally charged "moral" or "family" issues—contraception and divorce. Society holds its current descriptive morality of gays not because it has to, but because it chooses to.

Clearly popular opinion and custom are not enough to ground moral condemnation of homosexuality. Religious arguments are also frequently used to condemn homosexuality. Such arguments usually proceed along two lines. One claims that the condemnation is a direct revelation of God, usually through the Bible. The other sees condemnation in God's plan as manifested in nature; homosexuality (it is claimed) is "contrary to nature."

One of the more remarkable discoveries of recent gay research is that the Bible may not be as univocal in its condemnation of homosexuality as many have believed. Christ never mentions homosexuality. Recent interpreters of the Old Testament have pointed out that the story of Lot at Sodom is probably intended to condemn inhospitality rather than homosexuality. Further, some of the Old Testament condemnations of homosexuality seem simply to be ways of tarring those of the Israelites' opponents who happen to accept homosexual practices when the Israelites themselves did not. If so, the condemnation is merely a quirk of history and rhetoric rather than a moral precept.

What does seem clear is that those who regularly cite the Bible to condemn an activity like homosexual sex do so by reading it selectively. Do clergy who cite what they take to be condemnations of homosexuality in Leviticus maintain in their lives all the hygienic, dietary, and marital laws of Leviticus? If they cite the story of Lot at Sodom to condemn homosexuality, do they also cite the story of Lot in the Cave to condone incestuous rape? It seems then not that the Bible is being used to ground condemnations of homosexuality as much as society's dislike of homosexuality is being used to interpret the Bible.

Even if a consistent portrait of condemnation could be gleaned from the Bible, what social sig-

nificance should it be given? One of the guiding principles of society, enshrined in the Constitution as a check against the government, is that decisions affecting social policy are not made on religious grounds. The Religious Right has been successful in thwarting sodomy law reform, in defunding gay safe-sex literature and gay art, and in blocking the introduction of gay materials into school curriculums. If the real ground of the alleged immorality invoked by governments to discriminate against gays is religious (as it seems to be in these cases), then one of the major commitments of our nation is violated. Religious belief is a fine guide around which a person might organize his own life, but an awful instrument around which to organize someone else's life.

BUT ISN'T HOMOSEXUALITY UNNATURAL?

In the second kind of religious argument, people try to justify society's treatment of gays by saying they are unnatural. Though the accusation of unnaturalness looks whimsical, it is usually hurled against homosexuality with venom of forethought. It carries a high emotional charge, usually expressing disgust and evincing queasiness. Probably it is nothing but an emotional charge. For people get equally disgusted and queasy at all sorts of things which are perfectly natural and which could hardly be fit subjects for moral condemnation. Two typical examples in current American culture are some people's responses to mothers breastfeeding in public and to women who do not shave body hair. Similarly people fling the term "unnatural" at gays in the same breath and with the same force as when they call gays "sick" and "gross." When people have strong emotional reactions, as they do in these cases, without being able to give good reasons for them, they can hardly be thought of as operating morally, but more likely as obsessed and manic.

When "nature" is taken in technical rather than ordinary usages, it also cannot ground a charge of homosexual immorality. When unnatural means "by artifice" or "made by humans," it can be pointed out that virtually everything that is good about life is unnatural in this sense. The chief feature that distinguishes people from other animals is people's very ability to make over the world to meet their needs and desires. Indeed people's well-being depends upon these departures from nature. On this understanding of human nature and the natural, homosexuality is perfectly unobjectionable; it is simply a means by which some people adapt nature to fulfill their desires and needs.

Another technical sense of natural is that something is natural and so, good, if it fulfills some function in nature. On this view, homosexuality is unnatural because it violates the function of genitals, which is to make babies. One problem with this view is that lots of bodily parts have lots of functions and just because some one activity can be fulfilled by only one organ (say, the mouth for eating), this activity does not condemn other functions of the organ as immoral (say, the mouth for talking, licking stamps, or blowing bubbles). So the possible use of the genitals to produce children does not, without more, condemn the use of the genitals for other purposes, say, achieving ecstasy and intimacy.

The notion of function seemed like it might ground moral authority, but instead it turns out that moral authority is needed to define "proper function." If God is the moral authority, we are back to square one—holding others accountable to our own religious beliefs.

Finally, people sometimes attempt to establish authority for a moral obligation to use bodily parts in a certain fashion simply by claiming that moral laws are natural laws and vice versa. On this account, inanimate objects and plants are good in that they follow natural laws by necessity, animals follow them by instinct, and persons follow them by a rational will. People are special in that they must first discover the laws that govern them. Now, even if one believes the view—dubious in the post-Newtonian, post-Darwinian world—that natural laws in the usual sense ($e=mc^2$, for instance) have some moral content, it is not at all clear how one is to discover the laws in nature that apply to people.

On the one hand, if one looks to people themselves for a model—and looks hard enough—one finds amazing variety, including homosexual relations as a social ideal (as in upper-class fifth-century Athens) and even as socially mandatory (as

in some Melanesian initiation rites today). When one looks to people, one is simply unable to strip away the layers of social custom, history, and taboo in order to see what's really there to any degree more specific than that people are the creatures that make over their world and are capable of abstract thought. That this is so should raise doubts that neutral principles are to be found in human nature that will condemn homosexuality.

On the other hand, if one looks to nature apart from people for models, the possibilities are staggering. There are fish that change sex over their lifetimes: should we "follow nature" and be operative transsexuals? Orangutans, genetically our next of kin, live completely solitary lives without social organization of any kind among adults: ought we to "follow nature" and be hermits? There are many species where only two members per generation reproduce: shall we be bees? The search in nature for people's purpose far from finding sure models for action is likely to leave one morally rudderless.

SEXUAL ORIENTATION AND CHOICE

But (it might also be asked) aren't gays willfully the way they are? It is widely conceded that if sexual orientation is something over which an individual—for whatever reason—has virtually no control, then discrimination against gays is presumptively wrong, as it is against racial and ethnic classes.

Attempts to answer the question whether or not sexual orientation is something that is reasonably thought to be within one's own control usually appeal simply to various claims of the biological or "mental" sciences. But the ensuing debate over genes, hormones, hypothalamuses, twins, early childhood development, and the like is as unnecessary as it is currently inconclusive. All that is needed to answer the question is to look at the actual experience of lesbians and gay men in current society, and it becomes fairly clear that sexual orientation is not likely a matter of choice.

On the one hand, the "choice" of the gender of a sexual partner does not seem to express a trivial desire which might as easily be fulfilled by a simple substitution of the desired object. Picking the gender of a sex partner is decidedly dissimilar, that is, to such activities as picking a flavor of ice cream. If an ice cream parlor is out of one's flavor, one simply picks another. And if people were persecuted, threatened with jail terms, shattered careers, loss of family and housing, and the like for eating, say, Rocky Road ice cream, no one would ever eat it. Everyone would pick another easily available flavor. That gay people abide in being gay even in the face of persecution suggests that being gay is not a matter of easy choice.

On the other hand, even if establishing a sexual orientation is not like making a relatively trivial choice, perhaps it is like making the central and serious life choices by which individuals try to establish themselves as being of some type or having some occupation. Again, if one examines gay experience, this seems not to be the general case. For one virtually never sees anyone setting out to become a homosexual, in the way one does see people setting out to become doctors, lawyers, and bricklayers. One does not find gays-to-be picking some end—"At some point in the future, I want to become a homosexual"—and then setting about planning and acquiring the ways and means to that end, in the way one does see people deciding that they want to become lawyers, and then sees them plan what courses to take and what sort of temperaments, habits, and skills to develop in order to become lawyers. Typically, gays-to-be simply find themselves having homosexual encounters and yet, at least initially, resisting quite strongly the identification of being homosexual. Such a person even very likely resists having such encounters, but ends up having them anyway. Only with time, luck, and great personal effort, but sometimes never, does the person gradually come to accept her or his orientation, to view it as a given material condition of life, coming as all materials do with certain capacities and limitations. The person begins to act in accordance with his or her orientation and its capacities, seeing its actualization as a requisite for an integrated personality and as a central component of personal well-being. As a result, the experience of coming out to oneself has for gays the basic structure of a discovery, not the structure of a choice. And far from signaling immorality, coming out to others affords one of the few remaining opportunities in ever more bureaucratic, technological, and socialistic societies to manifest courage.

CIVIL RIGHTS

Current federal civil rights law bars private-sector discrimination in housing, employment, and public accommodations on the basis of race, national origin, ethnicity, gender, religion, age, and disability, but not sexual orientation. Where city councils and state legislatures have passed protections for gay men and lesbians, the protections have been under concerted and frequently successful attack through referendum initiatives. . . . [But there are strong] moral arguments for protecting lesbians and gay men from private-sector discrimination.

Even though civil rights legislation restricts somewhat the workings of free enterprise, it promotes other core American values that far outweigh this slight loss of entrepreneurial freedom. These values are self-respect, self-sufficiency, general prosperity, and individual flourishing.

No one in American society can have much self-respect or maintain a solid sense of self, if she is, in major ways affecting herself, subject to whimsical and arbitrary actions of others. Work, entertainment, and housing are major modes through which people identify themselves to themselves. Indeed in modern culture, work and housing rank just after personal relationships and perhaps (for some) religion, as the chief means by which people identify themselves to themselves. A large but largely unrecognized part of the misery of unemployment is not merely poverty and social embarrassment, but also a sense of loss of that by which one defined oneself, a loss which many people also experience upon retirement, even when their income and social esteem are left intact. People thrown out of work frequently compare this loss to the loss of a family member, especially to the loss of a child. Here the comparison is not simply to the intensity of the emotion caused by the loss, but to the nature of the loss: what was lost was a central means by which one constituted one's image of oneself.

Work is also the chief means by which people in America identify themselves to others. Indeed in America, one's job is tantamount to one's social identity. Socially one finds out who a person is by finding out what she or he does. At social gatherings, like parties, asking after a person's employment is typically the first substantive inquiry one makes of a person to whom one has been introduced. America is a nation of doers. When job discrimination is directed at lesbians and gay men, say, as a child care worker or museum director, it is a way of branding them as essentially un-American, as alien. It is a chief mode of expatriation from the national experience. . . .

In a nonsocialist, noncommunist society like America, there is a general expectation that each person is primarily responsible for meeting his or her own basic needs and that the government becomes an active provider only when all else fails. It is largely noncontroversial that people ought to have their basic needs met. For meeting basic needs is a necessary condition for anyone being able to carry out a life plan. If government aims at enhancing the conditions in which people are able to carry out their life plans, then enhancing the conditions in which basic needs are met will be a high government priority, all the more so if the means to this end themselves avoid greatly coercing people's life plans.

Current civil rights legislation tries to unclog channels between an individual's efforts and the fulfillment of the individual's needs. For it is chiefly through employment, in conjunction with access to certain public accommodations and housing, that people acquire the things they need to assure their continued biological existence—food, shelter, and clothing. Importantly, these are also the chief means by which people satisfy those various culturally relative needs which maintain them as credible players in the ongoing social, political, and economic "games" of the society into which they are born—say, needs for transportation and access to information. Civil rights legislation then helps people discharge their presumptive obligation to meet through their own devices their basic biological needs and other conditions required for human agency.

If gays were barred only from buying rocks at Tiffany's, eating truffles at "21," and holding seats on the Board of Trade, their inclusion in civil rights laws on the ground that such laws help meet needs would not be very compelling. And indeed America holds a stereotype of gays, especially gay men, as wealthy, frivolous, selfish, conspicuous consumers. Based on

this stereotype, some people claim that gays are not in need of civil rights protections. But the stereotype is false. One of the surprising findings of Alfred Kinsey's 1948 study of male sexuality was that more male homosexual behavior occurs among the economically disadvantaged and among the uneducated than among the wealthy and college educated. And it is generally acknowledged that lesbians on average fall well below the national average for income, if for no other reason than that women are so far below the national average for income. . . .

Extending civil rights protection to gay men and lesbians is also justified as promoting general prosperity. Such legislation tends to increase the production of goods and services for society as a whole. It does so in three ways.

First, by eliminating extraneous factors in employment decisions, such legislation promotes an optimal fit between a worker's capacities and the tasks of her prospective work. Both the worker and her employer are advantaged because a worker is most productive when her talents and the requirements of her job mesh. Across the business community as a whole, such legislation further enhances the prospects that talent does not go wasting and that job vacancies are not filled by second bests.

In response to prospective discrimination, gays are prone to take jobs which only partially use their talents. Many gays take dead-end jobs; they do so in order to avoid reviews which might reveal their minority status and result in their dismissal. Many gay men and lesbians go into small business because big business will not have them. In turn, many small businesses or dead-end occupations, like being a florist, hairdresser, male nurse, female trucker or construction worker, have in society's mind become so closely associated with homosexuality that nongays who might otherwise go into these lines of employment do not do so out of fear that they will be socially branded as gay. In these circumstances, the talents of people—both gay and nongay—are simply wasted both to themselves and to society. Rights for gays are good for everyone.

Second, human resources are wasted if one's energies are constantly diverted and devoured by fear of arbitrary dismissal. The cost of life in the closet is not small, for the closet permeates and largely consumes the life of its occupant. In the absence of civil rights legislation for gays, society is simply wasting the human resources which are expended in the day-to-day anxiety—the web of lies, the constant worry—that attends leading a life of systematic disguise as a condition for continued employment.

Third, employment makes up a large part of what happiness is. To a large extent, happiness is job satisfaction. When one's employment is of a favorable sort, one finds a delight in its very execution—quite independently of any object which the job generates, whether product or wage. People whose work on its own is rich enough and interesting enough to count as a personal flourishing, people, for instance, employed in human services, academics, and other professionals, and people whose jobs entail a large element of craft, like editors and artisans, are indeed likely to view job satisfaction as a major constituent of happiness and rank it high both qualitatively and quantitatively among the sources of happiness. And even people who are forced by necessity or misfortune to take up employment which does not use their talents, or which is virtually mechanical, or positively dangerous, or which has other conditions that make the workplace hateful—even these people are likely to recognize that the workplace, if properly arranged, would be a locus of happiness, and this recognition of opportunity missed is part of the frustration which accompanies jobs which are necessarily unsatisfying to perform. Permitting discriminatory hiring practices reduces happiness generally by barring access to one of its main sources. . . .

CONCLUSION

If discrimination ceased, gay men and lesbians would enter the mainstream of the human community openly and with self-respect. The energies that the typical gay person wastes in the anxiety of leading a day-to-day existence of systematic disguise would be released for use in personal flourishing. From this release would be generated the many benefits that accrue to a society when its individual members thrive.

Society would be richer for acknowledging another aspect of human diversity. Families with gay members would develop relations based on truth and trust rather than lies and fear. And the heterosexual majority would be better off for knowing that they are no longer trampling their gay friends and neighbors.

Finally and perhaps paradoxically, in extending to gays the rights and benefits it has reserved for its dominant culture, America would confirm its deeply held vision of itself as a morally progressing nation, a nation itself advancing and serving as a beacon for others—especially with regard to human rights. The words with which our national pledge ends—"with liberty and justice for all"—are not a description of the present, but a call for the future. America is a nation given to a prophetic political rhetoric which acknowledges that morality is not arbitrary and that justice is not merely the expression of the current collective will. It is this vision that led the black civil rights movement to its successes. Those senators and representatives who opposed that movement and its centerpiece, the 1964 Civil Rights Act, on obscurantist grounds, but who lived long enough and were noble enough, came in time to express their heartfelt regret and shame at what they had done. It is to be hoped and someday to be expected that those who now grasp at anything to oppose the extension of that which is best about America to gays will one day feel the same.

Review and Discussion Questions

1. What are the two chief types of antigay stereotypes? Is Mohr correct in contending that antigay stereotypes are a means of reinforcing gender roles in society? What do you think explains violence against, and harassment of, homosexuals?

2. That something is descriptively moral (or immoral) does not make it normatively moral (or immoral). What is the relevance of this point to homosexuality?

3. How does Mohr respond to the argument that homosexuality is unnatural because it violates the function of the genitals, which is to produce babies? Why does Mohr believe that sexual orientation is not a matter of choice? How is this point relevant to the issue of discrimination?

Are there moral arguments against homosexuality that Mohr has overlooked or not done justice to?

4. What arguments does Mohr give in favor of legislation banning job discrimination against homosexuals? Do you find them persuasive? Can any arguments be given against extending civil rights legislation to protect homosexuals?

5. For a period in the early 1990s, the Cracker Barrel Old Country Store, a restaurant and gift-shop chain in the Southeast, adopted a policy of firing homosexual employees and refusing to hire homosexuals. Supposedly based

on the company's commitment to "traditional American values" and the "perceived values of [its] customers," Cracker Barrel's policy violated no laws. Critically assess its policy both from a business point of view and from the moral point of view. If a private employer believes that homosexuality is immoral, is it wrong of the employer to choose not to hire homosexuals?

6. Do companies have a moral obligation to discourage antigay sentiment among their employees? How might they do so?

Further Reading for Chapter 9

Affirmative Action
Steven M. Cahn, ed., *The Affirmative Action Debate* (New York: Routledge, 1995) and **George E. Curry**, ed., *The Affirmative Action Debate* (Reading, Mass.: Addison-Wesley, 1996) offer a selection of essays both for and against affirmative action. The second book has a wider range of authors than the first, which is more philosophical.

Gertrude Ezorsky, *Racism and Justice: The Case for Affirmative Action* (Ithaca, N.Y.: Cornell University Press, 1991) provides a succinct, well-informed defense. **Louis P. Pojman,** "The Case Against Affirmative Action," in William H. Shaw, ed., *Social and Personal Ethics,* 4th ed. (Belmont, Calif.: Wadsworth, 2002) is a robust critique.

How Race Is Lived in America (New York: Henry Holt, 2001) is a collection of personal narratives and conversations, produced by the *New York Times,* that probes race relations today from various individual perspectives.

Comparable Worth
Laura Pincus and **Bill Shaw**, "Comparable Worth: An Economic and Ethical Analysis," *Journal of Business Ethics* 17 (April 1998) presents opposing views on adopting comparable worth as a public policy.

Helen Remick and **Ronnie J. Steinberg**, "Comparable Worth and Wage Discrimination," and **Robert L. Simon**, "Comparable Pay for Comparable Work?" in Tom L. Beauchamp and Norman E. Bowie, eds., *Ethical Theory*

and Business, 4th ed. (Englewood Cliffs, N.J.: Prentice Hall, 1993) provide a clear and thorough introduction to the comparable worth debate.

Sexual Harassment
Karen A. Crain and **Kenneth A. Heischmidt**, "Implementing Business Ethics: Sexual Harassment," *Journal of Business Ethics* 14 (April 1995) is a useful essay that discusses what actions companies should take.

Linda LeMoncheck and **Mane Hajdin**, *Sexual Harassment: A Debate* (Totowa, N.J.: Rowman & Littlefield, 1997) probes the philosophical and ethical issues. Also relevant are **M. J. Booker,** "Can Sexual Harassment Be Salvaged?" *Journal of Business Ethics* 17 (August 1998); **Vrinda Dalmiya,** "Why Is Sexual Harassment Wrong?" *Journal of Social Philosophy* 30 (Spring 1999); and **Linda L. Peterson,** "The Reasonableness of the Reasonable Woman Standard," *Public Affairs Quarterly* 13 (April 1999).

Workplace Discrimination
John Chandler, "Mandatory Retirement and Justice," *Social Theory and Practice* 22 (Spring 1996) argues against viewing mandatory retirement as unjust age discrimination.

D. W. Haslett, "Workplace Discrimination, Good Cause, and Color Blindness," *Journal of Value Inquiry* 36 (March 2002) provides a helpful theory of what constitutes unethical discrimination in the workplace.

Elizabeth Kristen, "Addressing the Problem of Weight Discrimination in Employment," *California Law Review* 90 (January 2002) argues that job discrimination against the overweight is a serious problem that the law should address.

 InfoTrac College Edition: For further information or to conduct research, please go to www.infotrac-college.com.

Part Four

Business and Society

10

Consumers

T he "Marlboro man" has long mesmerized people around the world, and few can deny the glamour of the ruggedly good-looking Marlboro cowboy, with boots, hat, chaps—and, of course, a cigarette in his mouth. Product of one of the most successful advertising campaigns in history, the Marlboro man revolutionized the image of Marlboro cigarettes, making it the best-selling brand in the United States. Few people remember, however, that the actor who originally portrayed the Marlboro man died of lung cancer as a result of smoking.

Everybody, of course, knows that smoking is hazardous to one's health—everyone, that is, but the tobacco industry. It continues, publicly at least, to deny any cause-and-effect relationship between smoking and disease, even though a smoker has ten times the chance of getting lung cancer and twice the chance of developing heart disease that a nonsmoker has. According to the Centers for Disease Control and Prevention (CDC), smoking remains the leading cause of preventable deaths in the United States and is responsible for 16 percent of all deaths nationwide. Although the percentage of Americans who smoke is dropping, the absolute number of smokers—and smoking's death toll—remains as high as ever. More than 440,000 Americans die each year of tobacco-related causes, at an annual price tag of $75 billion in medical expenditures and another $80 billion in indirect costs.[1]

In the mid-1990s forty-six state governments came together to sue the big tobacco companies, demanding compensation for the money that the states have had to spend on health problems caused by smoking. The suit was settled in 1998 for $206 billion. Among other things, the agreement requires tobacco firms to accept a tax hike on their products, to finance anti-smoking commercials, to cease tobacco-product placement in films and television shows, and to end outdoor tobacco advertisements. As a result, cigarette billboards came down across the country, including a famous 64-foot-high Marlboro man that loomed for years over Sunset Strip in Los Angeles.

Virtually no other consumer good compares to cigarettes in terms of individual injury and social cost. Because of this, during the Clinton administration the Food and Drug Administration (FDA) began laying plans to regulate the sale of cigarettes more closely. Because 90 percent of all smokers get hooked before age twenty-one, the FDA's prime interest was to discourage young people from taking up cigarettes in the first place. In 2000, however, the Supreme Court ruled that the FDA lacks jurisdiction over tobacco. This victory for cigarette manufacturers hasn't, of course, prevented smokers from suing them for injuries allegedly caused by their deadly habit. Despite the warnings that have been required on cigarette packs and ads since 1966, many smokers—or their estates—contend that they were addicted and couldn't stop. Some of these lawsuits are large class-action suits involving dozens of law firms with the collective resources to take on the big tobacco companies. In July 2000 in one of these lawsuits a Miami jury awarded the plaintiffs a record-breaking $144.8 billion in punitive damages, a verdict that the big tobacco companies are fighting to overturn.

These lawsuits have produced evidence that the tobacco companies suppressed research results establishing that cigarette smoke contains carcinogens and that nicotine is addictive. Industry documents have come to light that also show that the companies view cigarettes as nicotine dispensers and carefully manipulate the dose provided by their different brands. Even so-called low-tar and low-nicotine cigarettes, marketed as "light" or "ultra-light," have been designed so that addicted smokers can inhale just as much nicotine as they always have.[2]

Cigarettes are an especially dangerous product, and their manufacture, marketing, advertising, and sale raise a number of acute questions relevant to the consumer issues discussed in this chapter. For instance, what are the responsibilities to consumers of companies that sell potentially or (in the case of cigarettes) inherently harmful products? To what extent do manufacturers abuse advertising? When is advertising deceptive? Can advertisers create or at least stimulate desires for products that consumers would not otherwise want or would not otherwise want as much? How, if at all, should advertising be restricted?

Are consumers sufficiently well informed about the products they buy? Are they misled by deceptive labeling and packaging? In general, how far should society go in controlling the claims of advertisers, in regulating product packaging and labels, in monitoring product quality and price, and in upholding explicit standards of reliability and safety? What are the moral responsibilities of businesses in these matters? In a market-oriented economic system, how do we balance the interests of business with the rights of consumers? How do we promote social well-being while still respecting the choices of individuals?

These are among the issues probed in this chapter—in particular:

1. Product safety—the legal and moral responsibilities of manufacturers and the pros and cons of government regulations designed to protect consumers

2. The responsibilities of business to consumers concerning product quality, prices, labeling, and packaging

3. Deceptive and morally questionable techniques used in advertising

4. The choice between the "reasonable" consumer and "ignorant" consumer standards as the basis for identifying deceptive advertisements

5. Advertising and children

6. The social desirability of advertising in general—is it a positive feature of our economic system? Does it manipulate, or merely respond to, consumer needs?

PRODUCT SAFETY

Business's responsibility for understanding and providing for consumer needs derives from the fact that citizen-consumers depend on business to satisfy their needs. This dependence is particularly true in our highly technological society, characterized as it is by a complex economy, intense specialization, and urban concentration. These conditions contrast with those prevailing in the United States when the country was primarily agrarian, composed of people who could satisfy most of their own needs. Today, however, we rely on others to provide the wherewithal for our survival and prosperity. We rarely make our own clothing, supply our own fuel, manufacture our own tools, or construct our own homes, and our food is more likely to come from thousands of miles away than from our own gardens.

The increasing complexity of today's economy and the growing dependence of consumers on business for their survival and enrichment have heightened business's responsibilities to consumers—particularly in the area of product safety. From toys to tools, consumers use products believing that they won't be harmed or injured by them. Because consumers lack the technical expertise to judge many of the sophisticated products that are necessary for contemporary life, they must rely primarily on the conscientious efforts of business to ensure consumer safety.

Unfortunately, statistics indicate that the faith consumers place in manufacturers is often misplaced. Every year millions of Americans require medical treatment from product-related accidents. For example, in a typical year yard and garden equipment sends 76,000 consumers to hospital emergency rooms while personal use items cause 161,000 people to seek emergency care, toys 191,000 people, and packaging and containers for household products 298,000 people.[3] Consumer products also electrocute approximately 200 people annually.[4]

The Legal Liability of Manufacturers

If any of us is injured by a defective product, we can sue the manufacturer of that product. We take this legal fact for granted, but it wasn't always true. Before the landmark case of *MacPherson v. Buick Motor Car* in 1916, injured consumers could recover damages only from the retailer of the defective product—that is, from the party with whom they had actually done business. That made sense in a bygone day of small-scale, local capitalism. If the shoes you bought from the local shoemaker were defective, then your complaint was against him. By contrast, when a wheel fell off Donald MacPherson's Buick, the firm he had bought the Buick from hadn't actually made it.

Legal policy before *MacPherson* based a manufacturer's liability for damage caused by a defective product on the contractual relationship between it and the purchaser. Their contractual relationship is simply the sale—that is, the exchange of money for a commodity of a certain description. But that contractual relationship is an important source of moral and legal responsibilities for the producer. It obligates business firms to provide customers with a product that lives up to the claims the firm makes about the product. Those claims shape customers' expectations about what they are buying and lead them to enter into the contract in the first place. The question in *MacPherson,* however, was whether a manufacturer's liability for defective products was limited to those with whom it had a direct contractual relationship.

The New York Court of Appeals's *MacPherson* decision recognized the twentieth-century economic reality of large manufacturing concerns and national systems of product distribution. Among other things, local retailers are not as likely as large manufacturers to be able to bear financial responsibility for defective products that injure others. One can also see the court moving in *MacPherson* to a "due-care" theory of the manufacturer's duties to consumers. *Due care* is the idea that consumers and sellers do not meet as equals and that the consumer's interests are particularly vulnerable to being harmed by the manufacturer, who has knowledge and expertise the consumer does not have.[5] MacPherson, for instance, was in no position to have discovered the defective wheel before the Buick was purchased. According to the due-care view, then, manufacturers have an obligation, above and beyond any contract, to exercise due care to prevent the consumer from being injured by defective products.

As the concept of due care spread, legal policy moved decisively beyond the old doctrine of *caveat emptor,* which was seldom the guiding principle by the time of *MacPherson* anyway. *Caveat emptor* means "let the buyer beware," and today we associate it with an era of patent medicines and outrageously false product claims. Although legally the doctrine of "let the buyer beware" was never upheld across the board, it still symbolizes a period in which consumers themselves had a greater legal responsibility to accept the consequences of their product choices.

Consumers at that time were held to the ideal of being knowledgeable, shrewd, and skeptical. It was their free choice whether to buy a certain product. Accordingly, they were expected to take the claims of manufacturers and salespeople with a grain of salt, to inspect any potential purchase carefully, to rely on their own judgment, and to accept any ill results of their decision to use a given product. In the first part of the twentieth century, however, the courts repudiated this doctrine, largely on grounds of its unrealistic assumptions about consumer knowledge, competence, and behavior.

Despite *MacPherson*'s support for the due-care theory and for a broader view of manufacturer's liability, the case still left the burden on the injured consumer to prove that the manufacturer had been negligent. Not only might such an assertion be difficult to prove, but also a product might be dangerously defective despite the manufacturer's having taken reasonable steps to avoid such a defect.

Two important cases changed this situation. In the 1960 New Jersey case *Henningsen v. Bloomfield Motors* and in the 1963 California case *Greenman v. Yuba Power Products,* injured consumers were awarded damages without having to prove that the manufacturers of the defective products were negligent. Consumers, the courts ruled, have a right to expect that the products they purchase are reasonably safe when used in the intended way. On the basis of these and hundreds of subsequent cases, the "strict liability" approach to product safety has come to dominate legal thinking.

The doctrine of *strict product liability* holds that the manufacturer of a product has legal responsibilities to compensate the user of that product for injuries suffered because the product's defective condition made it unreasonably dangerous, even though the manufacturer has not been negligent in permitting that defect to occur. Under this doctrine a judgment for the recovery of damages could conceivably be won even if the manufacturer adhered to strict quality-control procedures. Strict liability, however, is not absolute liability. The manufacturer is not responsible for any injury whatsoever that might befall the consumer. The product must be defective, and the consumer always has the responsibility to exercise care.

Strict product liability is not without its critics, however. They contend that the doctrine is unfair. If a firm has exercised due care and taken reasonable precautions to avoid or eliminate foreseeable dangerous defects, they argue, then it should not be held liable for defects that are not its fault—that is, for defects that happen despite its best efforts to guard against them. To hold the firm liable anyway seems unjust.

The argument for strict liability is basically utilitarian. Its advocates contend, first, that only such a policy leads firms to bend over backward to guarantee product safety. Because they know that they will be held liable for injurious defects no matter what, they make every effort to enhance safety. Second, proponents of strict liability contend that the manufacturer is best able to bear the cost of injuries due to defects. Naturally, firms raise the price of their products to cover their legal costs (or pay for liability insurance). Defenders of strict liability do not disapprove of this. They see it as a perfectly reasonable way of spreading the cost of injuries among all consumers of the product, rather than letting it fall on a single individual—a kind of insurance scheme.

Protecting the Public

These developments in product liability law set the general framework within which manufacturers must operate today. In addition, a number of government agencies have become involved in regulating product safety. Congress created one of the most important of these agencies in 1972 when it passed the Consumer Product Safety Act. This act empowers the Consumer Product Safety Commission to protect the public "against unreasonable risks of injury associated with consumer products." The three-member commission sets standards for products, bans products presenting undue risk of injury, and in general polices the entire consumer-product marketing process from manufacture to final sale.

In undertaking its policing function, the commission aids consumers in evaluating product safety, develops uniform standards, gathers data, conducts research, and coordinates local, state, and federal product safety laws and enforcement. The commission's jurisdiction extends to more than 15,000 products, and it has the power to require recalls, public warnings, and refunds. Exceptionally risky products can be seized and condemned by court order. Rather than stressing punitive action, however, the commission emphasizes developing new standards and redesigning products to accommodate possible consumer misuse. It is less concerned with assigning liability than with avoiding injuries in the first place.

Despite the obvious public benefits of safety regulations, critics worry about the economic costs. New safety standards add millions of dollars to the cumulative price tag of goods like power lawn mowers. Recalls, too, can be expensive. BMW's 2002 recall of 17,000 7 Series sedans to check problematic electronic fuel pumps set the company back $3 million—a large sum, one might think, but only a tiny fraction of the $200–$300 million Ford spent six years earlier to recall 8.7 million vehicles with fire-prone ignition switches. And the estimated cost of Firestone's 2000 recall of 6.5 million tires it had made for Ford Explorers—the largest product recall in the United States since the Tylenol scare of 1982—surpasses that.

In addition, consumers sometimes reject mandated safety technology. In 1974, for example, Congress legislated an interlock system that would require drivers to fasten their seat belts before their cars could move. A public outcry forced lawmakers to rescind the law.

Safety regulations may also prevent individuals from choosing to purchase a riskier, though less expensive, product. Take the notorious Ford Pinto with its unsafe gas tank, for example. In 1978, after all the negative publicity, scores of lawsuits, and the trial of Ford Motor Company for reckless homicide, the sale of Pintos fell dramatically. Consumers evidently preferred a safer car for comparable money. However, when the state of Oregon took all the Pintos out of its fleet and sold them, at least one dealer reported brisk sales of the turned-in Pintos at their low, second-hand price.[6] Some consumers were willing to accept the risks of a Pinto if the price was right.

Economists worry about the inefficiencies of preventing individuals from balancing safety against price. Philosophers worry about interfering with people's freedom of choice. Take automobile safety again. Because smaller cars provide less protection than larger ones, people in small cars are less likely to survive accidents. Bigger, safer cars are more expensive, however, and many would prefer to spend less on their cars despite the increased risk. If only those cars that were as safe as, say, a Mercedes-Benz were allowed on the market, then there would be fewer deaths on the highways. But then fewer people could afford cars.

This example touches on the larger controversy over *legal paternalism,* which is the doctrine that the law may justifiably be used to restrict the freedom of individuals for their own good. No one doubts that laws justifiably restrict people from harming other people, but a sizable number of moral theorists deny that laws should attempt to prevent people from running risks that affect only themselves. Requiring your car to have brakes protects others; without brakes, you are more likely to run over a pedestrian. On the other hand, requiring you to wear a seat belt when you drive affects only you. Antipaternalists would protest that your being forced to wear a seat belt despite your wishes fails to respect your moral autonomy. Nonetheless, in the past hundred years a growing number of paternalistic laws have been enacted.

Paternalism is a large issue that can't be done justice here, but in regard to safety regulations, three comments are in order. First, the safety of some products or some features of products (such as a car's brakes) affects not just the consumer who purchases the product but third parties as well. Regulating these products or product features can be defended on nonpaternalistic grounds. Second, antipaternalism gains plausibility from the view that individuals know their own interests better than anyone else and that they are fully informed and able to advance those interests. But in the increasingly complex consumer world, this assumption is often doubtful. Whenever citizens lack knowledge and are unable to make intelligent comparisons and safety judgments, they may find it in their collective self-interest to set minimal safety standards. Such standards are particularly justifiable when few, if any, reasonable persons would want a product that did not satisfy those standards.

Finally, the controversy over legal paternalism pits the values of individual freedom and autonomy against social welfare. Requiring people to wear seat belts may infringe the former but saves thousands of lives each year. We may simply have to acknowledge that clash of values and be willing to make trade-offs. This doesn't imply a defense of paternalism across the board. Arguably, some paternalistic regulations infringe autonomy more than laws about seat belts do but bring less gain in social welfare. In the end, one may have to examine paternalistic product safety legislation case by case and weigh the conflicting values and likely results.

How Effective Is Regulation?

There is no doubt that in some cases regulation interferes with rather than safeguards consumer interests. Take, for example, the matter of drug regulation. In the late 1960s the Food and Drug Administration (FDA), with considerable fanfare, banned the sweetener cyclamate. Several years later, scientific bodies around the world determined that cyclamate was safe, and Abbott Laboratories, makers of cyclamate, asked the FDA to rescind the ban. The FDA refused, so Abbott took it to court. In doing so, it uncovered compelling evidence of the FDA's abuse of both regulatory process and scientific method, as well as a massive attempt at a cover-up. In particular, Abbott put into the record damning affidavits from a meeting between the FDA commissioner and corporate executives: The commissioner conceded that cyclamate was safe but would remain banned for political reasons. Abbott also forced the agency to turn over internal memos and other documents in which qualified FDA staffers admitted without reservation that cycla-

mate was safe and that superiors merely saw no point in permitting it back on the market.

In this instance, the interests of the consuming public do not seem to have been served. But regulations often prod business to recognize and act on its responsibilities to consumers. Sometimes even without applying the force of law, agencies can effectively safeguard the health and safety of consumers. A good example concerns the connection between certain kinds of tampons and the sometimes fatal disease called toxic shock syndrome.

In May 1980 the CDC published the first report characterizing many new cases of toxic shock affecting menstruating women. In June the CDC asked tampon makers for market information, partly because a reporter in Los Angeles had suggested that tampons might be involved. A subsequent CDC study confirmed a correlation between toxic shock and tampon use but deemed the rate of incidence too low to recommend that women stop using tampons. But in studying cases of toxic shock contracted in July and August, the CDC found that women with toxic shock were more than twice as likely as a similar group of healthy women to have used Procter & Gamble's Rely, which had garnered about one-quarter of the tampon market.

From the moment that the CDC's second report became public, Procter & Gamble tried to shore up its defense of Rely. Despite many denials about its product's complicity in toxic shock, it couldn't stem the flood of bad publicity. Knowing that Procter & Gamble was sensitive to bad publicity and aware of its own mandate to protect the public health, the FDA, the regulatory agency charged with acting on CDC findings, deliberately used the media as a weapon to drive Rely off the market. In the words of Wayne L. Pines, an associate FDA commissioner at the time: "Throughout the series of events, we made sure the press was notified so as to keep the story alive. We wanted to saturate the market with information on Rely. We deliberately delayed issuing press releases for a day to maximize the media impact. There was quite a concerted and deliberate effort to keep a steady flow of information before the public."[7]

The upshot: On September 23, 1980, Procter & Gamble voluntarily agreed to withdraw Rely from the market.

Because Procter & Gamble remained convinced that Rely was a safe product, it's fair to surmise that it would not have withdrawn the product without agency pressure. After all, there was no laboratory evidence implicating highly absorbent tampons in the incidence of toxic shock until over a year later. Had the FDA not acted as it did and had Procter & Gamble continued to sell the product, many women undoubtedly would have suffered and even died between September 1980 and December 1981, when incontrovertible clinical evidence became available.

Do regulations, then, help business meet its responsibility to consumers? Judging from these cases, the answer is generally yes but sometimes no. Nonetheless, the prevailing view today among businesspeople favors self-regulation. Such a view certainly is in keeping with the tenets of classical capitalism and is arguably an attractive ideal. However, self-regulation can easily become an instrument for subordinating consumer interests to profit making when the two goals clash. Under the guise of self-regulation, businesses may end up ignoring or minimizing responsibility to consumers.

Consider the auto industry, which has a long history of fighting against safety regulations. For example, it successfully lobbied the federal government to delay the requirement that new cars be equipped with air bags or automatic seat belts. Each year of the delay saved the industry millions of dollars. But the price paid by consumers was high: According to the National Highway Traffic Safety Administration, passive restraint devices reduce highway deaths by nearly 15,000 a year.[8]

When the law finally required passive restraint systems in new vehicles, Chrysler Motors became (in 1989) the first U.S. auto manufacturer to install driver-side air bags in all its new models. Only five years earlier, Chrysler chairman Lee Iacocca had boasted in his autobiography of fighting against air bags since their invention in the mid-1960s. In 1971, he and Henry Ford II (then the top executives at Ford) met secretly with President Richard Nixon to persuade him to kill a pending Department of Transportation regulation requiring air bags in every new car sold in the United States.[9] Had air bags been made standard equipment in 1974, more than 70,000 deaths and many times that number of severe injuries would have been avoided.

As car buyers have become better informed, automobile manufacturers are rethinking Iacocca's old bromide, "Safety doesn't sell." But even if safety does sometimes sell, for an industry to wait for marketplace demand before increasing safety standards can be irresponsible. Antilock brakes, to pick another example, save lives because they greatly improve a car's ability to stop short without skidding. Although the technology has been around for years, antilock brakes are still not required on new vehicles. Luxury cars have them, but antilock brakes will remain an expensive option until regulations require them as standard new-car equipment, thus bringing down their cost through manufacturing economies of scale. If society always waited for marketplace demand before insisting on public health and safety regulations, then pasteurization of milk and sprinkler systems to suppress fires in public places would still be "options."[10]

The Responsibilities of Business

Simply obeying laws and regulations does not exhaust the moral responsibilities of business in the area of consumer safety. The Consumer Product Safety Commission, for example, requires toy manufacturers to analyze their products for choking hazards, and it bans toys that small children can choke on. By contrast, no agency conducts safety testing of, or otherwise regulates or monitors, candy for its potential to choke children—even though these days many more children choke to death on candy, particularly little gel candies, than they do on toys.[11] However, this regulatory asymmetry between toy manufacturers and candy manufacturers marks no significant difference in their moral obligations. Regardless of what the law does or doesn't require, candy manufacturers have as great a responsibility as toy manufacturers do to minimize choking deaths.

When it comes to product safety, the exact nature of business's moral responsibilities is difficult to specify in general, because much depends on the particular product or service being provided. But abiding by the following steps would do much to help business behave morally with respect to consumer safety:

1. *Business should give safety the priority warranted by the product.* This injunction is important because businesses often base safety considerations strictly on cost. If the margin of safety can be increased without significantly insulting budgetary considerations, fine; if not, then safety questions are shelved.

Cost cannot be ignored, of course, but neither can two other factors. One is the seriousness of the injury the product can cause. For example, because lawn mowers can cause serious injury, their safety is of the utmost importance. The second factor to consider is the frequency of occurrence. How often is a particular product involved in an accident? Car crashes, for instance, are the leading killer of Americans under age thirty-five. When a product scores high on both the seriousness and frequency tests, it warrants the highest priority as a potential safety hazard.

2. *Business should abandon the misconception that accidents occur exclusively as a result of product misuse and that it is thereby absolved of all responsibility.* At one time such a belief may have been valid, but in using today's highly sophisticated products, even people who follow product instructions explicitly sometimes still suffer injuries. In any case, the point is that the company shares responsibility for product safety with the consumer. Rather than insisting that consumers' abuse of product leads to most accidents and injuries, firms would probably accomplish more by carefully pointing out how their products can be used safely.

A Pennsylvania court has endorsed this perspective. It awarded $11.3 million in damages to a twenty-year-old Philadelphia woman who was accidentally shot in the head when a handgun owned by her neighbor went off. The court decided the shop that had sold the weapon should pay 30 percent of the damages, because it had provided the buyer with no demonstration or written instructions for safe use of the gun.[12]

Both manufacturers and retailers have an obligation to try to anticipate and minimize the ways their products can cause harm, whether or not those products are misused. For example, a four-year-old girl was seriously injured when she stood on an oven door to peek into a pot on top of the stove and her weight caused the stove to tip over. A manufacturer can reasonably foresee that a cook might place a heavy roasting pan on the oven door. If doing so caused the stove to tip over, a court would almost certainly find the stove's design defective. But should the manufacturer have foreseen the use of the door not as a shelf but as a stepstool? The courts ruled that it should have.

If a product poses a serious potential threat, a company may need to take extraordinary measures to ensure continued safe use of it. Determining the extent to which the company must go, however, isn't an easy task. Sometimes a firm's moral responsibility for ensuring safety doesn't reach much beyond the sale of the product. Other times it may extend further. Consider, for example, a company that produces heavy machinery. Workers using its products could easily fall into bad habits. Some would argue, therefore, that the company has an obligation to follow up the sale of such a product, perhaps by visiting firms using its machinery to see if they've adopted dangerous shortcuts.

3. *Business must monitor the manufacturing process itself.* Frequently firms fail to control key variables during the manufacturing process, resulting in product defects. Companies should periodically review working conditions and the competence of key personnel. At the design stage of the process, they need to predict ways the product might fail and the consequences of such failure. For production, companies ordinarily can select materials that have been pretested or certified as flawless. If a company fails to do this, then we must question its commitment to safety. Similar questions arise when companies do not make use of available research about product safety. To answer some questions a company may have to generate its own research. However, independent research groups ensure impartial and disinterested analysis and are usually more reliable than in-house studies.

Testing should be rigorous and simulate the toughest conditions. Tests shouldn't assume that the product will be used in just the way the manufacturer intends it to be used. Even established products should be tested. The courts have repeatedly held that a trouble-free history does not justify the assumption that the product is free of defects.[13]

When a product moves into production, it is often changed in various ways. These changes should be documented and referred to some appropriate party, such as a safety engineer, for analysis. The firm must be scrupulous about coordinating department activities so manufacturing specifications are not changed without determining any potential dangers related to these changes.

4. *When a product is ready to be marketed, companies should have their product safety staff review their market strategy and advertising for potential safety problems.* This step is necessary because both product positioning and advertising influence how a product is used, which in turn affects the likelihood of safety problems. For example, the low-cost, appealing Suzuki Samurai was marketed to young adults. Because young drivers have comparatively little driving experience and a propensity to take risks behind the wheel, they are more likely to encounter those handling situations in which the Samurai was dangerously prone to roll over. Another example is a feeder auger manufacturer whose promotional brochure states that "even a child can do your feeding." The brochure had a photograph of the auger with its safety cover removed to show the auger's inner workings. When a young boy was injured while using the feeder auger with the safety cover removed, a jury found the promotional brochure misleading with respect to operating conditions and product safety.[14]

5. *When a product reaches the marketplace, firms should make available to consumers written information about the product's performance.* This information should include operating instructions, the product's safety features, conditions that will cause it to fail, a complete list of the ways the product can be used, and a cautionary list of the ways it should not be used. Warnings must be specific.

But no matter how specific they are, warnings are of little value if a consumer cannot read them. St. Joseph Aspirin for Children is marketed in Spanish-speaking areas and is advertised in the Spanish-language media. But you have to know English to read the crucial warning: "Children and teenagers should not use this medicine for chicken pox or flu symptoms before a doctor is consulted about Reye's Syndrome, a rare but serious illness reported to be associated with aspirin." Because his mother speaks only Spanish and couldn't read the label on the St. Joseph's box, little Jorge Ramirez of Modesto, California, contracted Reye's Syndrome. Today, he is blind, quadriplegic, and mentally impaired.[15]

6. *Companies should investigate consumer complaints.* This process encourages firms to deal fairly with consumers and to use the most effective source of product improvement: the opinions of those who use it.

Even if firms seriously attended to these safety considerations, they couldn't guarantee an absolutely safe product. Some hazards invariably attach to certain products, heroic efforts notwithstanding. But business must acknowledge and discharge its responsibilities in this area. Morally speaking, no one's asking for an accident- and injury-proof product, only that a manufacturer do everything reasonable to approach that ideal.

Cigarette fires illustrate the shortcomings of the tobacco industry in this respect. According to government estimates, about 1,500 Americans are killed each year in cigarette fires, making cigarettes the country's leading cause of fatal fires. Cigarette fires are responsible for 7,000 serious injuries per year and for property damage of $400 million annually. For years, however, research has shown that small design changes in cigarettes would make them less likely to ignite furniture and bedding, and lawmakers in a number of states have called for legislation to set a fire-resistance standard for cigarettes. But only in January 2000 did a tobacco company announce that it would introduce a cigarette designed to stop burning if the smoker forgets to puff.[16]

Unfortunately, there are numerous examples of companies and entire industries that play fast and loose with safety, resisting product improvements and dodging responsibility for consumer injury. But many companies do respond quickly to perceived or suspected hazards. Consider two examples of successful companies that place a premium on product safety.[17]

J.C. Penney and Burning Radios. Back in the early 1960s, a few of the radios sold by J.C. Penney were reported to have caught fire in customers' homes. J.C. Penney tested the radios and discovered a defective resistor in a few of them—less than 1 percent. Nonetheless, J.C. Penney informed the manufacturer, withdrew the entire line of radios, ran national ads informing the public of the danger, and offered immediate refunds. "This was before the Consumer Product Safety Commission even existed," said J.C. Penney vice chairman Robert Gill. "I guess some people might have thought we were crazy, and said that liability insurance was specifically designed to take care of such problems. But we felt we just could not sell that kind of product."

Johnson Wax and Fluorocarbons. In the mid-1970s, environmentalists became seriously alarmed at the possibility that fluorocarbons released from aerosol cans were depleting the earth's thin and fragile ozone layer. The media rapidly picked up the story, but virtually all manufacturers of aerosol cans denounced the scientific findings and stood by their products. The exception was Johnson Wax. The company acknowledged that the scientific questions were difficult to resolve, but it took seriously consumer concern about ozone depletion. Years before the FDA ban, Johnson Wax withdrew all its fluorocarbon products worldwide. "We picked up a lot of flak from other manufacturers," recalled company chairman Samuel Johnson, "and we lost business in some areas, but I don't have any question we were right. . . . Our belief is that as long as you can make do without a potentially hazardous material, why not do without it?"

OTHER AREAS OF BUSINESS RESPONSIBILITY

Product safety is naturally a dominant concern of consumers. No one wants to be injured by the products he or she uses. But safety is far from the only interest of consumers. The past forty years have seen a general increase in consumer awareness and an ever stronger consumer advocacy movement. One chief consumer issue has been advertising and its possible abuse, which will be discussed in subsequent sections. Three other areas of business responsibility— product quality, pricing, and packaging and labeling—are equally important and are taken equally seriously by the consumer movement.

Product Quality

The demand for high-quality products is closely related to a number of themes mentioned in the discussion of safety. Most people would agree that business bears a general responsibility to ensure that the quality of a product measures up to the claims made about it and to reasonable consumer expectations. They would undoubtedly see this responsibility as deriving primarily from the consumer's basic right to get what he or she pays for.

Although high product quality can also be in a company's interest, sometimes business shirks this responsibility. For example, in 1973 new car bumpers had to withstand a 5-mile-per-hour collision with no damage. Ten years later, the auto industry succeeded in getting this quality standard lowered: The speed was cut in half, and damage to the bumpers themselves was no longer taken into account. Or consider the bottled water industry. Most people who buy bottled water do so because they believe that it is purer and safer than tap water. Not so, reports the Natural Resources Defense Council, which recently tested 103 brands and found that one-third of them, including some of the best-known brands, contained contaminants that exceeded state or federal standards. These results do not mean that bottled water is dangerous, but they do suggest that consumers are not getting the product quality they're paying for.[18]

One way that business assumes responsibilities to consumers for product quality and reliability is through *warranties,* which are obligations to purchasers that sellers assume. People generally speak of two kinds of warranties, express and implied. *Express warranties* are the claims that sellers explicitly state—for example, that a product is "shrinkproof" or will require no maintenance for two years. The moral concern, of course, is whether a product lives up to its billing. Express warranties include assertions about the product's character, assurances of product durability, and other statements on warranty cards, labels, wrappers, and packages or in the advertising of the product. Many companies offer detailed warranties that are very specific about what defects they cover. Few go as far as L. L. Bean does with its "100% guarantee," which allows customers to return any purchase at any time for a full refund if it proves unsatisfactory.

Implied warranties include the claim, implicit in any sale, that a product is fit for its ordinary, intended use. The law calls this the implied warranty of *merchantability.* It's not a promise that the product will be perfect; rather, it's a guarantee that it will be of passable quality or suitable for the ordinary purpose for which it is used. Implied warranties can also be more specific—for example, when the seller knows that a buyer has a particular purpose in mind and is relying on the seller's superior skill or judgment to furnish goods adequate for that purpose.

The concept of an implied warranty is relevant to the case of Kodak's instant cameras. When Polaroid won a patent violation judgment against Kodak, Kodak was forced not only to stop selling its instant cameras but also to compensate previous purchasers, who could no longer obtain film for their cameras. These purchasers had relied on the implicit claim that Kodak would not suddenly make its products obsolete.[19]

With or without warranties, however, consumers today are more militant than ever in their insistence on product quality and on getting exactly what they paid for. For example, when Ira Gore learned that his new $40,000 car had been damaged and repainted before he took delivery, he sued BMW for having reduced his car's value by $4,000 and sought punitive damages based on the fact that BMW had sold 983 such "refinished" cars over a ten-year period. An Alabama jury agreed with Gore. It viewed the practice as consumer fraud and awarded him $4 million in punitive damages—not bad recompense for an injury to his car that it had cost BMW only $601.78 to fix. The Alabama Supreme Court subsequently cut the award in half, and in 1996 the U.S. Supreme Court ordered Alabama to lower it still further, holding that $2 million is "grossly excessive" punishment for the minor economic injury Gore had suffered.[20] Although the Court's precedent-setting ruling cheered many corporations, it left no doubt that punitive damages are appropriate in product-quality cases like this. The only question is whether they are excessive.

Prices

Have you ever wondered why a product sells at three for a dollar or is priced at $2.99 rather than simply $3.00? Or why a product that retails for $3.80 on Monday is selling for $4.10 on Friday? The answer may have little to do with the conventional determinants of product price such as overhead, operating expenses, and the costs of materials and labor. More and more frequently, purely psychological factors enter into the price-setting equation.

For example, why would a retailer price T-shirts at $9.88 instead of $9.99? "When people see $9.99, they say, 'That's $10,'" explains the general sales manager of one company. "But $9.88 isn't $10. It's just psychological."[21] Similar psychological considerations are at work when airlines advertise one-way fares that are available only with the purchase of a round-trip ticket for twice the price.

For many consumers, higher prices mean better products, so manufacturers arbitrarily raise the price of a product to give the impression of superior quality or exclusivity. But as often as not, the price is higher than the product's extra quality. For example, a few years ago Proctor-Silex's most expensive fabric iron sold for $54.95, a price $5 higher than the company's next most expensive. Its wholesale price was $26.98 against $24.20, a difference of only $2.78. Moreover, the extra cost of producing the top model was less than $1 for a light that signaled when the iron was ready.[22]

Manufacturers trade on human psychology when they sell substantially identical products at different prices. For example, Heublein raised the price of its Popov brand vodka from about $3.80 to $4.10 a fifth without altering the vodka that went into the fifth. Why the price increase? Heublein sales representatives believed that consumers wanted a variety of vodka prices to choose from. Apparently they were right: Even though Popov lost 1 percent of its market share, it increased its profits by 30 percent. Applying its theory further, Heublein offers vodka drinkers an even more expensive vodka: Smirnoff. Analysts insist that there is no qualitative difference among vodkas made in the United States.[23] In this case, the use of psychological pricing is closely related to the problem of pricing branded products higher than generic products that are otherwise indistinguishable. Consumers pay more assuming that the brand name or the higher price implies a better product.

Sometimes consumers are misled by prices that conceal a product's true cost. The price of tires, for example, frequently excludes balancing, mounting, and extended warranties. And manufacturers often disguise price increases by reducing the quality or quantity of the product—downsizing a pound of coffee to 13 ounces, for example, or shrinking a candy bar but not its price. Another ethically dubious practice is printing on packages a suggested retail price that is substantially higher than what retailers are known to charge. When retailers mark a new, lower price over the "suggested price," customers receive the false impression that the item is selling below its usual price. Retailers themselves are on questionable ethical ground when they use special pricing codes or fail to post a price on or near products, thus hindering consumers from easily comparing prices. And too many electronic scanners these days ring up prices incorrectly. One study found an error rate of 9 percent, with most mistakes favoring the stores; other studies place the error rate at 2 to 15 percent depending on the store and the type of merchandise. Whether store managers are deliberately padding their profits or whether sloppy practices are the problem, overcharging is costing consumers more than $1 billion a year.[24]

Promotional pricing can also be manipulative. Department stores today sell more products at "sale" prices—over 60 percent of their volume—and are marking them down more than ever before. But their initial markup has also increased.[25] A recent survey of San Francisco area furniture stores illustrates how misleading sale prices can be. While one retailer was advertising a Henredon sofa, model no. 8670, at an "original price" of $2,320, on sale for $2,170, and another small retailer had it on sale for $2,476, or 20 percent off an original price of $3,095, a major department store was offering the same sofa, with the same "E-grade" upholstery, for $2,500, "35 percent off" the "original price" of $4,000.[26]

Many practical consumers think of these pricing practices as more of a nuisance or irritant that they must live with than as something morally objectionable. But tricky or manipulative pricing does raise moral questions—not least about business's view of itself and its role in the community—that businesspeople and ethical theorists are now beginning to take seriously.

Price Fixing. Much more attention has been devoted to price fixing, which despite its prevalence is widely recognized as a violation of the rules of the game in a market system whose ideal is open and fair price competition. For example, in 1997 a federal judge found Toys "R" Us guilty of conspiring to keep prices for Barbie, Mr. Potato Head, and other popular toys artificially high. The retail giant used its market clout to force Mattel, Hasbro, and other major toymakers not to sell their toys to warehouse clubs like Sam's Club and Price Costco. Toys "R" Us threatened not to buy any toy that a manufacturer sold to a cost-cutting competitor, and it would use the acquiescence of one toymaker to force other manufacturers to go along.[27]

Often, of course, it is the manufacturer, not the retailer, that engages in price fixing. For example, Panasonic was found guilty of pressuring retailers such as Circuit City, Kmart, and Montgomery Ward into selling its products at the company's suggested retail price and not at a discount. Although manufacturers often suggest prices to their retailers, the retailers are supposed to be free to set their own prices, depending on the profit they foresee in the market. Any agreement between a manufacturer and a retailer to fix a price is illegal. Panasonic sales executives, however, badgered stores that did not honor the manufacturer's minimum prices and threatened to stop doing business with retailers that didn't comply. Until one large New York retailer finally complained to the New York State Attorney General's office, not only did the stores and chains go along, but they also reported uncooperative competitors to Panasonic.[28]

When a few companies gain control of a market, they are often in a position to force consumers to pay artificially high prices. To take a notorious example, in 1960 General Electric, Westinghouse, and twenty-seven other companies producing electrical equipment were found guilty of fixing prices in that billion-dollar industry. The companies were made to pay about $2 million in fines and many more millions to their corporate victims.[29] Given the oligopolistic nature of the electrical equipment market, consumers could not reasonably be said to have had the option to take their business elsewhere and thus drive down prices. (In fact, until it was exposed, they had no reason to believe they were being victimized by price fixing.) More recently, federal and state investigators have established that executives at the nation's largest national and regional dairy companies have conspired—sometimes for decades—to rig bids on milk products sold to schools and military bases. Forty-three companies, among them Borden, Pet, Dean, and Flav-O-Rich, have been convicted of price fixing and bid rigging.[30]

Of course, controlling prices need not be done so blatantly. Firms in an oligopoly can tacitly agree to remain uncompetitive with one another, thereby avoiding losses that might result from price-cutting competition. They can then play "follow the leader": Let the lead firm in the market raise its prices, and then the rest follow suit. The result is a laundered form of price fixing.

Even without tacit price fixing, the firms that dominate a field often implicitly agree not to compete in terms of price. Nobody, they say to themselves, wants a price war, as if price competition were a threat to our market system rather than its lifeblood. Familiar rivals such as Pepsi and Coca-Cola or McDonald's and Burger King usually prefer to compete in terms of image and jingles rather than price.

From the moral point of view, prices, like wages, should be just or fair. Merchants cannot morally charge whatever they want or whatever the market will bear any more than employers can pay workers whatever they (the employers) wish or can get away with. In particular, price gouging is widely viewed as unethical, although what exactly constitutes price gouging is often debated. Is it unethical for a hardware store to boost the price of snow shovels from $15 to $20 after a large snowstorm, for a car dealer to mark up the price of a popular car model that is in short supply, or for a gas station to raise the price of its current stock of gasoline because the wholesale price is scheduled to go up? Is it unfair for the big oil companies to set the wholesale price of gasoline 10 to 19 cents a gallon higher in San Francisco than in Los Angeles because average household income is greater there?[31]

It's not enough to say that a fair price exists when a merchant makes a reasonable profit after expenses, for we can still ask what "a reasonable profit" is. In the end, the question "What is a fair price?" probably defies a precise answer. Still, one can approach an answer by assessing the factors on which the price is based and the process used to determine it. Certainly factors such as the costs of material and production, operating and marketing expenses, and profit margin are relevant to price setting. One can also ask whether a seller's pricing practices treat buyers as ends in themselves or try to exploit them. Also relevant is whether it would be good for our socioeconomic system as a whole if a particular pricing practice were widespread or generally followed.

In a market-oriented society, of course, consumer choice is a key variable affecting price. Product price, in other words, reflects in part the consuming public's judgment of the relative value of the article. This judgment is formed in the open market in a free interplay between sellers and buyers. However, for this process to function satisfactorily, buyers must be in a position to exercise informed consent. As discussed in Chapter 7, informed consent calls for deliberation and free choice, which require in turn that buyers understand all significant relevant facts about the goods and services they are purchasing. But consumers are at least sometimes, perhaps often, denied informed consent. They do not always receive the clear, accurate, and complete information about product quality and price that they need to make prudent choices.

Labeling and Packaging

Business's general responsibility to provide clear, accurate, and adequate information un-

doubtedly applies to product labeling and packaging. The reason is that, despite the billions of dollars spent annually on advertising, a product's label and package remain the consumer's primary source of product information. Often, however, labels and packages do not tell consumers what they need to know, or even what exactly they are getting. For example, only in 1997 did the Liggett tobacco company introduce cartons that list the ingredients in its L&M cigarettes—a first among tobacco companies.* Yet even when product labels provide pertinent information, they are often difficult to understand or even misleading, and what they omit may be more important than what they say. For example, nothing is more misleading than environmental labeling. Manufacturers label products "biodegradable," "environmentally safe," or "recyclable" without defining these terms or providing any scientific evidence to back them up.

Consumers have long been equally baffled by food labels such as "light" or "97 percent fat-free," but the Food and Drug Administration has recently come to their aid. The FDA's labeling requirements now oblige manufacturers of packaged food to provide standardized nutritional information that is clearer, more specific, and of greater benefit to health-conscious consumers. Although the FDA relaxed many of its rules in the 1980s and required only voluntary compliance, recently it has been getting tougher. For example, it has cracked down on grain and vegetable cooking oils that label themselves "cholesterol-free." Although it is true that only animal products or by-products contain cholesterol, cooking oils are often replete with saturated vegetable fats and hydrogenated oils, which the body converts into cholesterol. The FDA has also gone after Procter & Gamble for

---

*In addition to tobacco, L&M cigarettes contain molasses, patchouli oil, high fructose corn syrup, sugar, natural and artificial licorice flavor, artificial milk chocolate and natural chocolate flavor, phenylacetic acid, glycerol, propylene glycol, isovaleric acid, hexanoic acid, 3-methylpentanoic acid, valerian root extract, vanilla extract, and cedarwood oil.

changing the name of its orange juice from "Citrus Hill Select" to "Citrus Hill Fresh Choice" in violation of the FDA's 1963 ban on using the word *fresh* to describe processed orange juice. Although labeled "pure, squeezed, 100% orange juice," Citrus Hill is in fact made by adding water to concentrated orange juice, pulp, and "orange essence."

A particularly blatant example of label abuse is Sebastiani Vineyards' wine product, Domaine Chardonnay. "Chardonnay" has a high level of name recognition and a positive reputation among wine consumers. Unfortunately for them, however, there isn't a drop of chardonnay in Domaine Chardonnay, which is a blend of chenin blanc, sauvignon blanc, French colombard, riesling, and other grapes. After a public outcry when the wine was introduced, the Bureau of Alcohol, Tobacco, and Firearms required the company to redesign its label, which now has a large "DC" and a small "Domaine Chardonnay" at the bottom. Many people, however, continue to feel that letting Sebastiani use the name of a grape varietal as a brand name is a travesty of labeling law—even if Sebastiani decides in the future to include a little chardonnay in the wine mixture.

The question of misleading labels takes an interesting twist in the case of companies that choose to omit their corporate logo from products. For example, a brand called Cascadian Farm sells organic breakfast cereal, but from looking at the box you can't tell that it's actually made by General Mills. That's because General Mills is aiming the cereal at buyers who tend to eschew the brands of the big conglomerates. Similarly, you can't guess from reading the label of Blue Moon beer that it comes from Adolph Coors Company, and the label of Red Dog beer identifies its maker as Plank Road Brewery although it is really produced by Miller Brewing Company. This practice is spreading as big food and drink makers buy up the little brands that populate organic food stores or create their own "natural" products and boutique brands.[32]

In addition to misleading labels, package shape can trick consumers by exploiting certain optical illusions. Tall and narrow cereal boxes look larger than short, squat ones that actually contain more cereal; shampoo bottles often have pinched waists to give the illusion of quantity; fruits are packed in large quantities of syrup; and dry foods often come in tins or cartons stuffed with cardboard. Package terms such as *large, extra large, jumbo, economy size,* and *value pack* frequently confuse or mislead shoppers about what they are buying and how good a deal they are getting. Although in theory unit pricing helps shoppers to compare the relative prices of items, in practice the spread of bar codes thwarts their ability to do so. By eliminating price tags from packages, bar codes make it harder for time-pressed buyers to recall specific prices for individual items.

This is part of the explanation of why many retailers are able to sell "economy size" items for a higher per unit price than their smaller counterparts. These "quantity surcharges" are a much wider spread phenomenon than most people realize. For example, at 3.7 ounces the candy bar that Snickers calls "The Big One" is nearly twice the size of the familiar 2.07-ounce bar, which runs about 50 cents. But when priced at 99 cents—which it was at a store visited by the *Wall Street Journal*—The Big One costs 11 percent more. At another store the gallon jug of Ocean Spray cranberry juice—so big it had a special handle on it—cost 41 cents more than two half-gallon bottles. Although consumers frequently compare prices between brands, they generally neglect to make intra-brand comparisons because they take it for granted that the larger the volume, the better the deal. "You assume 'bigger' is a better deal," says Tom Pirko, president of a beverage and food consulting company, "and that gives marketers an open door to take advantage of people."[33] Because quantity surcharges exploit a common consumer error, the practice raises at least two moral questions: Can it be justified as a conscious pricing policy, and can retailers ethically remain silent about its existence?[34]

In general, the moral issues involved in packaging and labeling, as in marketing as a whole, relate primarily to truth telling and consumer exploitation. Sound moral conduct in this matter must rest on a strong desire to provide consumers with clear and usable information about the price, quality, and quantity of a product so they can make intelligent comparisons and choices. When marketers are interested primarily in selling a product and only secondarily in providing relevant information, then morally questionable practices are bound to follow. Those responsible for labeling and packaging would be well advised to consider at least the following questions, a negative answer to any of which could signal a moral problem: Is there anything about the packaging that is likely to mislead consumers? Have we clearly and specifically identified the exact nature of the product in an appropriate part of the label? Is the net quantity prominently displayed? Is it readily understandable to those wishing to compare prices? Are ingredients listed so they can be readily recognized and understood? Have we indicated and represented the percentage of the contents that is filler, such as the bone in a piece of meat?

These questions represent only some that a morally responsible businessperson might ask. In addition, we must not forget people whose health necessitates certain dietary restrictions. They often have great difficulty determining what products they can safely purchase.

DECEPTION AND UNFAIRNESS IN ADVERTISING

We tend to take advertising for granted, yet sociologically and economically it is enormously important. Ads dominate our environment. Famous ones become part of our culture; their jingles dance in our heads, and their images haunt our dreams and shape our tastes. Advertising is also big business. Coca-Cola, for example, shells out $1.3 billion a year on advertising, Philip Morris spends $1.9 billion, Ford $2.2 billion, General Motors $3.2 billion, and Procter & Gamble a whopping $4.7 billion.[35] As a whole, advertisers in the United States spend annually more than $233 billion on all forms of media advertising.[36]

That works out to about $800 for every person in the country.

When people are asked what advertising does, their first thought is often that it provides consumers with information about goods and services. In fact, advertising conveys very little information. Nor are most ads intended to do so. Except for classified ads (by amateurs!) and newspaper ads reporting supermarket prices, very few advertisements offer any information of genuine use to the consumer. (Those wanting useful product information must go to a magazine like *Consumer Reports,* which publishes objective and comparative studies of various products.) Instead, advertisements offer us jingles, rhymes, and attractive images.

The goal of advertising, of course, is to persuade us to buy the products that are being touted. Providing objective and comparative product information may be one way to do this. But it is not the only way, and judging from ads these days—which frequently say nothing at all about the product's qualities—it is not a very common way. The similarity among many competing products may be the explanation. One writer identifies the effort to distinguish among basically identical products as the "ethical, as well as economic, crux of the [advertising] industry"; another refers to it as the "persistent, underlying bad faith" of much American advertising.[37]

Deceptive Techniques

Because advertisers are trying to persuade people to buy their products and because straight product information is not necessarily the best way to do this, there is a natural temptation to obfuscate, misrepresent, or even lie. In an attempt to persuade, advertisers are prone to exploit ambiguity, conceal facts, exaggerate, and use psychological appeals.

Ambiguity. When ads are ambiguous, they can be deceiving. For example, the Continental Baking Company was charged with such ambiguity by the Federal Trade Commission (FTC). In advertising its Profile bread, Continental implied that eating the bread would lead to weight loss. The fact was that Profile had about the same number of calories per ounce as other breads; each slice contained seven fewer calories but only because it was sliced thinner than most breads. Continental issued a corrective advertisement.

Ambiguous ads can mislead the consumer. The Profile ad is a good example. A large number of people interpreted that ad to mean that eating Profile bread would lead to weight loss.[38] Likewise, for years consumers inferred from its advertisements that Listerine mouthwash effectively fought bacteria and sore throats. Not so; accordingly, the FTC ordered Listerine to run a multimillion-dollar disclaimer. And when Sara Lee began promoting its Light Classics desserts, the implicit implication was that "light" meant the products contained fewer calories than other Sara Lee desserts. When pressed by investigators to support this implied claim, Sara Lee contended that "light" referred only to the texture of the product.[39] In cases like these, advertisers and manufacturers invariably deny that they intended consumers to draw false inferences, but sometimes the ambiguity is such that a reasonable person wouldn't infer anything else.

Aiding and abetting ambiguity is the use of "weasel" words, words used to evade or retreat from a direct or forthright statement. Consider the weasel word *help.* "Help" means "aid" or "assist" and nothing else. Yet as one author has observed, "'help' is the one single word which, in all the annals of advertising, has done the most to say something that couldn't be said."[40] Because the word *help* is used to qualify, almost anything can be said after it. Thus we're exposed to ads for products that "help us keep young," "help prevent cavities," "help keep our houses germ-free." Consider for a moment how many times a day you hear or read phrases like these: helps stop, helps prevent, helps fight, helps overcome, helps you feel, helps you look. And, of course, *help* is hardly the only weasel word. *Like, virtual* or *virtually, can be, up to* (as in "provides relief up to eight hours"), *as much as* (as in "saves as much as one gallon of gas"),

and numerous other weasel words are used to imply what can't be said. Sometimes weasel words deprive the message of any meaning whatsoever, as when *up to* and *more* come together in "save up to 40 to 50 percent and more."

The fact that ads are open to interpretation doesn't exonerate advertisers from the obligation to provide clear information. Indeed, this fact intensifies their responsibility, because the danger of misleading through ambiguity increases as the ad is subject to interpretation. At stake are not only people's money but also their health, loyalties, and expectations. The potential harm a misleading ad can cause is great, not to mention its cavalier treatment of the truth. For these reasons ambiguity in ads is of serious moral concern.

Concealed Facts. When advertisers conceal facts, they suppress information that is unflattering to their products. That is, they neglect to mention or distract consumers' attention away from information, knowledge of which would probably make their products less desirable.

Shell, for example, used to advertise that its gasoline had "platformate" but neglected to mention that all other brands did too. Similarly, subway ads for the Bowery Bank in New York touted the fact that it is "federally insured," but then so is almost every bank in the country. And Kraft advertised its Philadelphia Cream Cheese as having "half the calories of butter," but didn't tell consumers that it is also high in fat. When peanut butter makers advertise their products as cholesterol free, they omit the fact that only animal products contain cholesterol and that peanut butter is rich in fat. Weight Watchers tells consumers that its frozen meals are without butter, chicken fat, or tropical oils but not that they are high in salt. Caverject promotes itself as an alternative to Viagra as a treatment for male impotence. Its ads say that "Caverject can help you and your partner enjoy renewed spontaneity and sexual satisfaction." But they don't say that Caverject is a prescription medicine that must be injected with a needle inserted directly into the penis.

Ads that promise savings for dialing long distance with a 10-10 number rarely mention the hidden costs that often make these services more expensive than the discount plan offered by one's regular long-distance carrier. Indeed, many of the most popular dial-around numbers are subsidiaries of the large carriers. For example, AT&T owns Lucky Dog (10-10-343), although you won't find that information on any Lucky Dog ads. As a result, some customers who dial a 10-10 number end up using their own long-distance carrier—and paying a higher rate to boot.

Likewise, advertisements for painkillers routinely conceal relevant information. For years, Bayer aspirin advertised that it contained "the ingredient that doctors recommend most." What is that ingredient? Aspirin. The advertising claim that "last year hospitals dispensed ten times as much Tylenol as the next four brands combined" does not disclose the fact that Johnson & Johnson supplies hospitals with Tylenol at a cost well below what consumers pay. Interestingly, American Home Products sued Johnson & Johnson on the grounds that the Tylenol ad falsely implies that it is more effective than competing products. But at the same time, American Home Products was advertising its Anacin-3 by claiming that "hospitals recommended acetaminophen, the aspirin-free pain reliever in Anacin-3, more than any other pain reliever"—without telling consumers that the acetaminophen hospitals recommend is, in fact, Tylenol.

Concealment of relevant facts and information can exploit people by misleading them; it also undermines truth telling. Unfortunately, truth rarely seems foremost in the minds of advertisers. For example, Coors continued to advertise its beer as brewed from "Rocky Mountain spring water" even after it opened plants outside Colorado that use local water. And Perrier advertised its bottled water as having bubbled up from underground springs decades after it had begun pumping the water up from the ground through a pipe and combining it with processed gas.

As one advertising-industry insider writes: "Inside the agency the basic approach is hardly conducive to truth telling. The usual thinking in forming a campaign is first what can we say, true or not, that will sell the product best? The second consideration is, how can we say it effectively and get away with it so that (1) people who buy won't feel let down by too big a promise that doesn't come true, and (2) the ads will avoid quick and certain censure by the FTC."[41] This observation shows the common tendency to equate what's legal with what's moral. It's precisely this outlook that leads to advertising behavior of dubious morality.

Examples of ads that conceal important facts are legion. An old Colgate-Palmolive ad for its Rapid Shave Cream used sandpaper to demonstrate the cream's effect on tough beards. Colgate concealed the fact that the "sandpaper" in the ad was actually Plexiglas and that actual sandpaper had to be soaked in Rapid Shave for about eighty minutes before it came off in a stroke. A few years ago, Campbell vegetable soup ads showed pictures of a thick, rich brew calculated to whet even a gourmet's appetite. What the ads didn't show were clear glass marbles deposited in that bowl to give the soup the appearance of solidity. More recently, a television ad for Volvo showed a row of cars being crushed by a bigwheel truck, with only a Volvo remaining intact. What the ad neglected to say was that the Volvo had been reinforced and the other cars weakened.

Then there's the subject of feminine deodorant sprays (FDS), currently an industry worth in excess of $55 million. FDS ads fail to mention not only that such products in most cases are unnecessary but also that they frequently produce unwanted side effects: itching, burning, blistering, and urinary infections. An FDA "caution" now appears on these products.

If business has an obligation to provide clear, accurate, and adequate information, we must wonder if it meets this charge when it hides facts relevant to the consumer's purchase of a product. Concealing information raises serious moral concerns relative to truth telling and consumer exploitation. When consumers are deprived of comprehensive knowledge about a product, their choices are constricted and distorted.

If pushed further, the moral demand for full information challenges almost all advertising. Even the best advertisements never point out the negative features of their products or that there is no substantive difference between the product being advertised and its competitors, as is often the case. In this sense, they could be accused of concealing relevant information. Most advertisers would be shocked at the suggestion that honesty requires an objective presentation of the pros and cons of their products, and in fact consumers don't expect advertisers or salespeople to be impartial. Nevertheless, it is not clear why this moral value should not be relevant to assessing advertising. And it can be noted that retail salespeople, despite a sometimes negative reputation, often do approach this level of candor—at least when they are fortunate enough to sell a genuinely good and competitive product or when they do not work on commission.

Exaggeration. Advertisers can mislead through exaggeration—that is, by making claims unsupported by evidence. For example, claims that a pain reliever provides "extra pain relief" or is "50 percent stronger than aspirin," that it "upsets the stomach less frequently" or is "superior to any other nonprescription painkiller on the market" contradict evidence that all analgesics are effective to the same degree.[42] Manufacturers of vitamins and other dietary supplements are notorious for exaggerating the possible benefits of their products. Some drug companies do the same. Ads for Propecia tell men, "Starting today, you need not face the fear of more hair loss." But while Propecia can slow hair loss, it doesn't necessarily stop it.

Nabisco's advertising of its 100 percent bran cereal as being "flavored with two naturally sweet fruit juices" is typical of exaggerated product claims. Although fig juice and prune juice have indeed been added to the product, they are its least significant ingredients in terms of weight; the primary sweetener is sugar. As in this case, exaggeration often goes hand in hand with concealed information. Until stopped by legal action, General Electric advertised its 90-watt Energy Choice bulb as an energy-saving replacement for a conventional 100-watt bulb. But there is nothing special about the GE bulb; it simply produces fewer lumens than a 100-watt bulb. Trident chewing gum, to take another example, has long advertised that it helps fight cavities, but its ads (which describe Trident as a "dental instrument") clearly exaggerate the benefits of chewing Trident. Chewing gum can indeed help dislodge debris on dental enamel, but so can eating an apple or rinsing one's mouth with water. And the sugar substitute used by Trident (sorbitol) can indirectly promote tooth decay: It nurtures the normally harmless bacteria that sugar activates into decay-producing microorganisms.

"Anti-aging" skin-care products are one of the fastest-growing segments of the cosmetic industry, partly because the baby boom generation is getting older. Some companies misleadingly portray their products as "repairing cells" or skin layers below the surface rather than having only an external effect. Part of the labeling for Avon's Bioadvance Beauty Recovery System, for example, claimed that it "actually helps reverse many signs of facial aging in six weeks . . . helps revitalize and invigorate your skin's regenerative system," while Alfin Fragrances asserted that its anti-aging skin cream makes skin "function as if it were young again."[43]

The line between deliberate deception and so-called *puffery* is not always clear. Puffery is the supposedly harmless use of superlatives and subjective praise in advertisements. Thus advertisers frequently boast of the merits of their products by using words such as *best, finest,* or *most,* or phrases and slogans like *king of beers, breakfast of champions,* or *the ultimate driving machine.* In most instances, puffery appears innocuous, but sometimes it's downright misleading, as in the Dial soap ad that claimed Dial was "the most effective deodorant soap you can buy." When asked to substantiate that claim, the Armour-Dial company insisted that it was not claiming product superiority; all it meant was that Dial soap was as effective as any other soap.

The law permits puffery on the grounds that it doesn't deceive people. University of Wisconsin professor Ivan L. Preston, however, argues that puffery shouldn't be immune from regulation. Why? Because the public is often taken in by it. Consider the following pieces of puffery: "State Farm is all you need to know about life insurance," "Ford has a better idea," and "It's the real thing [Coca-Cola]." Although these statements may seem like meaningless verbal posturing, in one survey 22 percent of those sampled thought the first claim was "completely true" while 36 percent considered it "partly true." The second claim was judged "completely true" by 26 percent and "partly true" by 42 percent while 35 percent believed the third claim was "completely true" and 29 percent "partly true."[44] Moreover, argues Preston, if puffery didn't work, salespeople and advertisers wouldn't use it.[45]

Psychological Appeals. A psychological appeal is one that aims to persuade by appealing primarily to human emotional needs and not to reason. This is potentially the area of greatest moral concern in advertising. An automobile ad that presents the product surrounded by people who look wealthy and successful appeals to our need and desire for status. A life insurance ad that portrays a destitute family woefully struggling in the aftermath of a provider's death tries to persuade through pity and fear. Reliance on such devices, although not unethical per se, raises moral concerns because rarely do such products fully deliver what the ads promise.

Ads that rely extensively on pitches to power, prestige, sex, masculinity, femininity, acceptance, approval, and the like aim to sell more than a product. They are peddling psychological

satisfaction. Perhaps the best example is the increasingly explicit and pervasive use of sexual pitches in ads:

Scene:	An artist's skylit studio. A young man lies nude, the bedsheets in disarray. He awakens to find a tender note on his pillow. The phone rings and he gets up to answer it.
Woman's Voice:	You snore.
Artist (smiling):	And you always steal the covers.

More cozy patter between the two. Then a husky-voiced announcer intones: "Paco Rabanne. A cologne for men. What is remembered is up to you."[46]

Although sex has always been used to sell products, it has never before been used as explicitly in advertising as it is today—as the nudes in the ads for Calvin Klein products demonstrate. And the sexual pitches are by no means confined to products like cologne or clothes. The California Avocado Commission supplemented its "Love Food from California" recipe ads with a campaign featuring a leggy actress sprawled across two pages of some eighteen national magazines to promote the avocado's nutritional value. The copy line reads: "Would this body lie to you?" Similarly, Dannon yogurt ran ads featuring a bikini-clad beauty and this message: "More nonsense is written on dieting than any other subject—except possibly sex."

Some students of marketing claim that ads like these appeal to the subconscious mind of both marketer and consumer. Purdue University psychologist and marketing consultant Jacob Jacoby contends that marketers, like everyone else, carry around sexual symbols in their subconscious that, intentionally or not, they use in ads. A case in point: the Newport cigarette "Alive with Pleasure" campaign. One campaign ad featured a woman riding the handlebars of a bicycle driven by a man. The main strut of the bike wheel stands vertically beneath her body. In Jacoby's view, such symbolism needs no interpretation.

Author Wilson Bryan Key, who has extensively researched the topic of subconscious marketing appeals, claims that many ads take a subliminal form. *Subliminal advertising* is advertising that communicates at a level beneath our conscious awareness, where, some psychologists claim, the vast reservoir of human motivation primarily resides. Most marketing people would deny that such advertising occurs. Key disagrees. Indeed, he goes so far as to claim: "It is virtually impossible to pick up a newspaper or magazine, turn on a radio or television set, read a promotional pamphlet or the telephone book, or shop through a supermarket without having your subconscious purposely massaged by some monstrously clever artist, photographer, writer, or technician."[47]

Concern with the serious nature of psychological appeals appears to have motivated the California Wine Institute to adopt an advertising code of standards. The following restrictions are included:

> No wine ad shall present persons engaged in activities with appeal particularly to minors. Among those excluded: amateur or professional sports figures, celebrities, or cowboys; rock stars, race car drivers.
> No wine ad shall exploit the human form or "feature provocative or enticing poses or be demeaning to any individual."
> No wine ad shall portray wine in a setting where food is not presented.
> No wine ad shall present wine in "quantities inappropriate to the situation."
> No wine ad shall portray wine as similar to another type of beverage or product such as milk, soda, or candy.
> No wine ad shall associate wine with personal performance, social attainment, achievement, wealth, or the attainment of adulthood.
> No wine ad shall show automobiles in a way that one could construe their conjunction.

In adopting such a rigorous code of advertising ethics, the California Wine Institute rightly acknowledged the subtle implications and psychological nuances that affect the message that an ad communicates.

The Federal Trade Commission's Role

The Federal Trade Commission was originally created in 1914 as an antitrust weapon, but its mandate was expanded to include protecting consumers against deceptive advertising and fraudulent commercial practices. Although the FTC is not the only regulatory body monitoring advertisements, it is mainly thanks to the FTC that today we are spared the most blatant abuses of advertising.

One important question running through the FTC's history is relevant to all efforts to prohibit deceptive advertising: whether the FTC (or any other regulatory body) is obligated to protect only reasonable, intelligent consumers who conduct themselves sensibly in the marketplace, or whether it should also protect ignorant consumers who are careless or gullible in their purchases?[48] If the FTC uses the reasonable-consumer standard, then it should prohibit only advertising claims that would deceive reasonable people. People who are more gullible or less bright than average and are taken in as a result would be unprotected. On the other hand, if the FTC uses the ignorant-consumer standard and prohibits an advertisement that misleads anyone, no matter how ill informed and naive, then it will handle a lot more cases and restrict advertising much more. But in spending its time and resources on such cases, it is not clear that the FTC will be proceeding in response to a substantial public interest, as it is legally charged with doing.

The reasonable-person standard was traditional in a variety of areas of the law long before the FTC was established. If you are sued for negligence, you can successfully defend yourself if you can establish that you behaved as a hypothetical reasonable person would have behaved under like circumstances. On the other hand, in the law of misrepresentation, when you as a deceived consumer sue a seller on grounds that you were misled, then—assuming the deception is not proved to be intentional—you must establish that you were acting reasonably in relying on the false representation. If a reasonable person would not have been misled in like circumstances, then you will not win your case. Ads that make physically impossible or obviously exaggerated claims would thus escape legal liability under the reasonable-person standard.

One decisive case in the legal transition away from the reasonable-person standard in matters of advertising, sales, and marketing was *FTC v. Standard Education* in 1937.[49] In this case an encyclopedia company was charged by the FTC with a number of deceptive and misleading practices. The company's agents told potential customers that their names had been specially selected and that the encyclopedia they were being offered was being given away free as part of an advertising plan in return for use of their name for advertising purposes and in testimonials. The customer was only required to pay $69.50 for a series of looseleaf update volumes. Potential buyers were not told that both books and supplements regularly sold for $69.50.

In deciding the case, the U.S. Supreme Court considered the view of the appellate court, which had earlier dismissed the FTC's case. Writing for the appellate court, Judge Learned Hand had declared that the FTC was occupying itself with "trivial niceties" that only "divert attention from substantial evils." "We cannot take seriously the suggestion," he wrote, "that a man who is buying a set of books and a ten years' 'extension service,' will be fatuous enough to be misled by the mere statement that the first are given away, and that he is paying only for the second." The Supreme Court itself, however, looked at the matter in a different light and held for the FTC and against Standard Education.

First, it noted that the practice had successfully deceived numerous victims, apparently including teachers, doctors, and college professors. But instead of resting its decision on the claim that a reasonable person might have been deceived, it advocated a change of standard to something like the ignorant-consumer standard:

The fact that a false statement may be obviously false to those who are trained and experienced does not change its character, nor take away its power to deceive others less experienced. There is no duty resting upon a citizen to suspect the honesty of those with whom he transacts business. Laws are made to protect the trusting as well as the suspicious. The best element of business has long since decided that honesty should govern competitive enterprises, and that the rule of *caveat emptor* should not be relied upon to reward fraud and deception.

The decision in *FTC v. Standard Education,* as Ivan L. Preston notes, led the FTC to apply the ignorant-person standard liberally, even in cases in which there was no intent to deceive. In the 1940s the FTC challenged ads in some cases in which it is difficult to believe that anyone could possibly have been deceived. For example, it issued a complaint against Bristol-Myers's Ipana toothpaste on the grounds that its "smile of beauty" slogan would lead some to believe that Ipana toothpaste would straighten their teeth. Eventually, however, the FTC abandoned the ignorant-consumer standard in its extreme form and stopped trying to protect everybody from everything that might possibly deceive them. It now follows the "modified" ignorant-consumer standard and protects consumers from ads that mislead significant numbers of people, whether those people acted reasonably or not.[50]

Still, deciding what is likely to be misleading to a significant number of consumers is not necessarily easy. Consider these advertising claims, which are contested by some as deceptive: that Kraft Cheez Whiz is real cheese; that Chicken McNuggets are made from "whole breasts and thighs" (when they allegedly contain processed chicken skin as well and are fried in highly saturated beef fat); that ibuprofen causes stomach irritation (as Tylenol's ads seem to imply). Is Sprint's "dime-a-minute" ad campaign deceptive when a minute-and-a-half telephone call is rounded up to twenty cents? Was it deceptive of Diet Coke to proclaim that it was sweetened "now with NutraSweet," even though the product also contained saccharin? Under legal pressure, Diet Coke changed its ads to read "NutraSweet blend." Is that free of any misleading implications?

Ads Directed at Children

The FTC has always looked after one special group of consumers without regard to how reasonable they are: children. Still, several consumer groups think the FTC has not done enough, and they advocate even stricter controls over advertisements that reach children.

Advertising to children is big business. Every year children between ages four and twelve earn or receive $20.3 billion and spend approximately $17.4 billion of it on such items as snacks, candy, and toys. And this figure doesn't begin to take into account the billions of adult purchases for gifts, clothes, and groceries that are influenced by children.[51] In recent years advertising aimed specifically at children has grown exponentially. Advertisers now spend more than $1.5 billion a year on ads for children, and there are more and more venues for such ads—with new magazines, Web sites, and entire television channels aimed at children.[52]

Furthermore, it's no longer just cereal, candy, and toys that are being advertised. Advertisers of other products are wooing children in an effort to create customers for the future. As Jackie Pate of Delta Air Lines puts it, "By building brand loyalty in children today, they'll be the adult passengers of the future." Ann Moore, Chairman and CEO of Time Inc., which publishes *Sports Illustrated for Kids,* adds, "We believe children make brand decisions that will carry into their adult lives."[53] Although the magazine attracts mostly eight- to fourteen-year-old boys as readers, a recent issue featured a two-page spread for the Chevy Venture minivan.

Of course, advertisers admit that it's not just future consumers they want. "We're relying on the kid to pester the mom to buy the product, rather than going straight to the mom," says Barbara A. Martino of Grey Advertising. And Karen Francis, brand manager for the Chevy Venture,

reports that even she was surprised how often parents tell her that their kids played a tie-breaking role in deciding which car to buy. Naturally, advertisers argue that parents still have ultimate control over what gets purchased and what doesn't. But is the strategy of selling to parents by convincing the children a fair one? As one parent complains, "Brand awareness has been an incredibly abusive experience—the relentless requests to go to McDonald's [or] to see movies that are inappropriate for six-year-olds [but] that are advertised on kids' shows."

Television and advertising play a large role in most children's lives. At age seven a typical child sees 20,000 television commercials a year, and children remember what they see. For example, most of them can recognize the Budweiser frogs and recite the beer's slogan. The problem is that children, particularly young children, are naïve and gullible and thus particularly vulnerable to advertisers' enticements. Consider, for example, ads in which children are shown, after eating a certain cereal, to have enough power to lift large playhouses. No adult would be misled by that ad, but children lack experience and independent judgment. This provides at least a prima facie case for protecting them.

"Kids are the most pure consumers you could have," says one advertising expert. "They tend to interpret your ad literally. They are infinitely open." This problem is growing greater because the line between children's shows and the commercials that come with them is fading away. Children's entertainment features characters whose licensed images are stamped on toys, sheets, clothes, and food. Moreover, at the same time that movies and television shows are ever more tightly linked to the selling of toys and other items, commercials are becoming more like entertainment. Is it any wonder that many children perceive little difference between ads and television shows? As one nine-year-old sees it, the only distinction is that "commercials are shorter."

Advertising to children obviously raises the question of children's special susceptibilities and how far we need to go to protect them from possible manipulation. It also leads to the larger question of the nature and desirability of advertising's role in today's media-dominated society, which is our next topic.

THE DEBATE OVER ADVERTISING

The controversy over advertising does not end with the issue of deceptive techniques and unfair advertising practices. Advertising provides little usable information to consumers. Advertisements almost always conceal relevant negative facts about their products, and they are frequently based on subtle appeals to psychological needs, which the products they peddle are unlikely to satisfy. These realities are the basis for some critics' wholesale repudiation of advertising on moral grounds. They also desire a less commercially polluted environment, one that does not continually reinforce materialistic values.

Consumer Needs

Some defenders of advertising take these points in stride. They concede that images of glamour, sex, or adventure sell products, but they argue that these images are what we, the consumers, want. We don't want just blue jeans; we want romance or sophistication or status with our blue jeans. By connecting products with important emotions and feelings, advertisements can also satisfy our deeper needs and wants. As one advertising executive puts it:

> Advertising can show a consumer how a baby powder helps affirm her role as a nurturing mother—Johnson & Johnson's "The Language of Love." Or it can show a teenager how a soft drink helps assert his or her emerging independence—Pepsi's "The Choice of a New Generation."[54]

Harvard business professor Theodore Levitt has drawn an analogy between advertising and art. Both take liberties with reality, both deal in symbolic communication, and neither is interested in literal truth or in pure functionality. Rather, both art and advertising help us repackage the otherwise crude, drab, and generally oppressive reality that surrounds us. They create "illusions, symbols, and implications that promise more." They help us modify, transform, embellish, enrich, and reconstruct the world around us. "Without distortion, embellishment, and elaboration," Levitt writes, "life would be drab, dull, anguished, and at its existential worst." Advertising helps satisfy this legitimate human need. Its handsome packages and imaginative promises produce that "elevation of the spirit" that we want and need. Embellishment and distortion are therefore among advertising's socially desirable purposes. To criticize advertising on these counts, Levitt argues, is to overlook the real needs and values of human beings.[55]

Levitt's critics contend that even if advertising appeals to the same deep needs that art does, advertising promises satisfaction of those needs in the products it sells, and that promise is rarely kept. At the end of the day, blue jeans are still just blue jeans, and your love life will be unaffected by which soap you shower with. The imaginative, symbolic, and artistic content of advertising, which Levitt sees as answering real human needs, is viewed by critics as manipulating, distorting, and even creating those needs.

In his influential books *The Affluent Society* and *The New Industrial State,* John Kenneth Galbraith has criticized advertising on just this point. Galbraith argues that the process of production today, with its expensive marketing campaigns, subtle advertising techniques, and sophisticated sales strategies, creates the very wants it then satisfies. Producers, that is, create both the goods and the demand for those goods. If a new breakfast cereal or detergent were so much wanted, Galbraith reasons, why must so much money be spent trying to get the consumer to buy it? He thinks it is obvious that "wants can be synthesized by advertising, catalyzed by salesmanship, and shaped by" discreet manipulations.

Accordingly, Galbraith rejects the economist's traditional faith in "consumer sovereignty": the idea that consumers should and do control the market through their purchases. Rather than independent consumer demand shaping production, as classical economic theory says it does, nowadays it is the other way around. Galbraith dubs this the "dependence effect": "As a society becomes increasingly affluent, wants are increasingly created by the process by which they are satisfied."[56]

One consequence, Galbraith thinks, is that our system of production cannot be defended on the ground that it is satisfying urgent or important wants. We can't defend production as satisfying wants if the production process itself creates those wants. "In the absence of the massive and artful persuasion that accompanies the management of demand," Galbraith argues,

> increasing abundance might well have reduced the interest of people in acquiring more goods. They would not have felt the need for multiplying the artifacts—autos, appliances, detergents, cosmetics—by which they were surrounded.[57]

Another consequence is our general preoccupation with material consumption. In particular, Galbraith claims, our pursuit of private goods, continually reinforced by advertising, leads us to neglect public goods and services. We need better schools, parks, artistic and recreational facilities; safer and cleaner cities and air; more efficient, less crowded transportation systems. We are rich in the private production and use of goods, Galbraith thinks, and starved in public services. Our preoccupation with private consumption leads us to overlook opportunities for enjoyment that could be provided more efficiently by public production.

Galbraith's critics have concentrated their fire on a couple of points. First, Galbraith never shows that advertising has the power he attributes to it. Despite heavy advertising, most new products fail to win a permanent place in the hearts of consumers. Advertising campaigns like that for Listerine in the 1920s, which successfully created the problem of "halitosis" in order to sell the new idea of "mouthwash," are rare.* Although it is true that we are inundated with ads, experiments suggest we no longer care much

about them. Each of us sees an average of 1,600 advertisements a day, notices around 1,200 of them, and responds favorably or unfavorably to only about 12. We also appear to pay more attention to ads for products that we already have.[58]

Second, critics have attacked Galbraith's assumption that the needs supposedly created by advertisers and producers are, as a result, "false" or "artificial" needs and therefore less worthy of satisfaction. Human needs, they stress, are always socially influenced and are never static. How are we to distinguish between "genuine" and "artificial" wants, and why should the latter be thought less important? Ads might produce a want that we would not otherwise have had without that want being in any way objectionable.

Although conclusive evidence is unavailable, critics of advertising continue to worry about its power to influence our lives and shape our culture and civilization. Even if producers cannot create wants out of whole cloth, many worry that advertising can manipulate our existing desires—that it can stimulate certain desires, both at the expense of other, nonconsumer-oriented desires and out of proportion to the likely satisfaction that fulfillment of those desires will bring.

Market Economics

Defenders of advertising are largely untroubled by these worries. They see advertising as an aspect of free competition in a competitive market, which ultimately works to the benefit of all. But this simple free-market defense of advertising has weaknesses. First, advertising doesn't fit too well into the economist's model of the free market. Economists can prove, if we grant them enough assumptions, that free-market buying and selling lead to optimal results.* One of these assumptions is that everyone has full and complete information, on the basis of which they then buy and sell. But if this were so, advertising would be pointless.

---

*Given that the saliva in one's mouth is completely replenished every fifteen minutes or so anyway, no mouthwash can have an effect longer than that.

*Technically, they lead to *Pareto optimality,* which means that no one person can be made better off without making someone else worse off.

One might argue that advertising moves us closer to the ideal of full information, but there is good reason to doubt this. Even if we put aside the question of whether ads can create, shape, or manipulate wants, they do seem to enhance brand loyalty, which generally works to thwart price competition. A true brand-name consumer is willing to pay more for a product that is otherwise indistinguishable from its competitors. He or she buys a certain beer despite being unable to taste the difference between it and other beers.

More generally, critics of advertising stand the invisible-hand argument on its head. The goal of advertisers is to sell you products and to make money, not to maximize your well-being. Rational demonstration of how a product will in fact enhance your well-being is not the only way advertisers can successfully persuade you to buy their products. Indeed, it is far from the most common technique. Critics charge, accordingly, that there is no reason to think that advertising even tends to maximize the well-being of consumers.

Defenders of advertising may claim that, nonetheless, advertising is necessary for economic growth, which benefits us all. The truth of this claim, however, is open to debate. Critics maintain that advertising is a waste of resources and serves only to raise the price of advertised goods. Like Galbraith, they may also contend that advertising in general reinforces mindless consumerism. It corrupts our civilization and misdirects our society's economic effort toward private consumption and away from the public realm. The never-ending pursuit of material goods may also divert us as a society from the pursuit of a substantially shorter workday.[59]

Free Speech and the Media

Two final issues should be briefly noted. Defenders of advertising claim that, despite criticisms, advertising enjoys protection under the First Amendment as a form of speech. Legally this claim probably requires qualification, especially in regard to radio and television, for which one must have a license to broadcast. Banning cigarette advertisements from television, for instance, did not run contrary to the Constitution. More important, even if we concede advertisers the legal right to free speech, not every exercise of that legal right is morally justifiable. If advertisements in general or of a certain type or for certain products were shown to have undesirable social consequences, or if certain sorts of ads relied on objectionable or nonrational persuasive techniques, then there would be a strong moral argument against such advertisements regardless of their legal status.

Advertising subsidizes the media, and that is a positive but far from conclusive consideration in its favor. This is not the place to launch a discussion of the defects of American television. But the very fact that it is free results in far more consumption than would otherwise be the case and probably, as many think, far more than is good for us. Although satellite and cable television have improved things, the mediocrity of much American television fare is hardly accidental. The networks need large audiences. Obviously they can't run everyone's favorite type of program, because people's tastes differ, so they seek to reach a common denominator. If viewers instead of advertisers paid for each show they watched, things would be different.[60]

SUMMARY

1. The complexity of today's economy and the dependence of consumers on business increase business's responsibility for product safety.

2. The legal liability of manufacturers for injuries caused by defective products has evolved over the years. Today the courts have moved to the doctrine of *strict liability,* which holds the manufacturer of a product responsible for injuries suffered as a result of defects in the product, regardless of whether the manufacturer was negligent.

3. Government agencies, such as the Consumer Product Safety Commission, have broad powers to regulate product safety.

Critics contend that these regulations are costly and that they prevent individuals from choosing to purchase a riskier but less expensive product. This argument touches on the controversy over *legal paternalism,* the doctrine that the law may justifiably be used to restrict the freedom of individuals for their own good.

4. Although there are exceptions, regulations generally help ensure that business meets its responsibilities to consumers. Businesspeople, however, tend to favor self-regulation and government deregulation.

5. To increase safety, companies need to give safety the priority necessitated by the product, abandon the misconception that accidents are solely the result of consumer misuse, monitor closely the manufacturing process, review the safety implications of their marketing and advertising strategies, provide consumers with full information about product performance, and investigate consumer complaints. Some successful companies already put a premium on safety.

6. Business also has other obligations to consumers: Product quality must live up to express and implied warranties; prices should be just, and business should refrain from manipulative pricing and the use of price fixing to avoid competition; and product labeling and packaging should provide clear, accurate, and adequate information.

7. Advertising tries to persuade people to buy products. Ambiguity, the concealment of relevant facts, exaggeration, and psychological appeals are among the morally dubious techniques that advertisers use.

8. The Federal Trade Commission protects us from blatantly deceptive advertising. But it is debatable whether the FTC should ban only advertising that is likely to deceive reasonable people or whether it should protect careless or gullible consumers as well. The FTC now seeks to prohibit advertising that misleads a significant number of consumers, regardless of whether it was reasonable for them to have been misled.

9. Advertising to children is big business, but children are particularly susceptible to the blandishments of advertising. Advertisers contend that parents still control what gets purchased and what doesn't. However, critics doubt the fairness of selling to parents by appealing to children.

10. Defenders of advertising view its imaginative, symbolic, and artistic content as answering real human needs. Critics maintain that advertising manipulates those needs or even creates artificial ones. John Kenneth Galbraith contends that today the same process that produces products also produces the demand for those products (the dependence effect). Galbraith argues, controversially, that advertising encourages a preoccupation with material goods and leads us to favor private consumption at the expense of public goods.

11. Defenders of advertising see it as a necessary and desirable aspect of competition in a free-market system, a protected form of free speech, and a useful sponsor of the media, in particular television. Critics challenge all three claims.

CASE 10.1

Breast Implants

In the last few decades, silicone has become a crucial industrial product, playing a role in the manufacture of thousands of products, from lubricants to adhesive labels to Silly Putty. One of its medical uses, however, has been controversial—namely, as the gel used for breast implants. Dow Corning, which was founded in 1943 to produce silicones for commercial purposes, invented mammary prostheses in the 1960s. Since then a million American women have had bags of silicone gel implanted in their breasts. For many of them, silicone implants are part of reconstructive surgery after breast cancer or other operations. However, by 1990 four out of five implants were for the cosmetic augmentation of normal, healthy breasts—a procedure that became increasingly popular in the 1980s as celebrities such as Cher and Jenny Jones spoke openly of their surgically enhanced breasts.

Today, however, what used to be a common elective operation is rarely performed.[61] The reason dates from the 1980s, when women with silicone breast implants first began reporting certain patterns of illness. There were stories of ruptured or leaky bags, although the estimates of the proportion of women affected ranged from 1–5 percent to 32 percent. And there were allegations that the silicone implants were responsible for various autoimmune disorders—such as rheumatoid arthritis, lupus erythematosus, and scleroderma—in which the body's immune system attacks its own connective tissue. Then, in 1991, a jury heard the case of Mariann Hopkins, who claimed that her implants had ruptured and released silicone gel, causing severe joint and muscle pain, weight loss, and fatigue. On the basis of documents suggesting that Dow Corning knew of the dangers of leaky bags, a San Francisco jury found the company guilty of negligence and fraud and awarded Hopkins $7.3 million.

When Dow Corning first sold breast implants in 1965, they were subject to no specific government regulations. In 1978 the Food and Drug Administration classified them as "Class II" devices, meaning that they did not need testing to remain on the market. In 1989, however, as worries about the dangers of silicone implants increased, the FDA reclassified them as "Class III" devices and in 1991 required all manufacturers to submit safety and effectiveness data. Although some FDA staff members were scathingly critical of the poor and inconclusive documentation submitted by the manufacturers, the FDA's advisory panel ruled that the implants were not a major threat to health. Based on public need, it voted to keep them on the market.

After the Hopkins case, however, David A. Kessler, the FDA's new chairman, called for a moratorium on breast implants. He asked doctors to stop performing the operation, but told women who had already had the operation not to have the bags removed. Still, the moratorium terrified the women who had had breast implants, a few of whom tried in desperation to carve them out themselves, and it galvanized a political movement led by women who were upset about having been used, yet again, as guinea pigs for an unsafe medical procedure. For them, it was just one more episode in a long history of the mistreatment of women by a medical, scientific, and industrial establishment that refused to treat them as persons and take their needs seriously. The FDA moratorium also galvanized the legal forces marshaled against the manufacturers of silicone bags. By 1994, some 20,000 lawsuits had been filed against Dow Corning alone. Entrepreneurial lawyers organized most of these actions into a few large class-action suits so that their pooled legal resources would be more than a match for the manufacturers.

Meanwhile, Kessler instructed the FDA's advisory panel to restudy the breast implant question. Presented with a series of anecdotal reports about diseases that are not rare, the panel complained about the lack of hard scientific data. From the scientific point of view, the problem was how to distinguish coincidence from causation. For example, if connective-tissue disease strikes 1 percent of all women and if 1 million women have implants, then statistically one should expect that 10,000 women will have both implants and connective-tissue disease. So if a woman develops the disease, can it correctly be said that it was caused by her breast implants? Moreover, not only does silicone appear to be chemically inert, but silicone from a ruptured breast implant will remain trapped inside a fibrous capsule of scar tissue. Nevertheless, the panel recommended that silicone be used only for reconstruction and that cosmetic breast augmentation be done only with saline packs.

At this point the gulf between science, on the one hand, and the FDA and public opinion, on the other, began to widen further. A Mayo Clinic study published in the prestigious *New England Journal of Medicine* in June 1994 showed that there was no difference between women with breast implants and other women with respect to incidence of connective-tissue disease; by the summer of 1995 two larger studies had confirmed the Mayo Clinic's report. On top of this, the FBI and other investigators exposed several labs that were selling to lawyers and victims fraudulent test results purporting to show the presence of silicone in the blood of women with breast implants.

Lawyers and other advocates for the women with implants repudiate these studies, contending that the women have a new disease. To this contention scientists respond that the description of the symptoms of this supposed disease keeps changing. Some say it looks like fibromyalgia, which is included in their studies. Many feminist activist groups distrust science; they believe that we should pay less attention to statistics and medical studies and greater attention to the women who have suffered. These women know what their bodies have been through, and they are convinced that their implants are responsible. This reasoning, and the skepticism toward science and statistics that it represents, has swayed jurors. After Dow Corning filed bankruptcy in 1995, which brought to a halt the lawsuits against it, new lawsuits were filed against its parent company, Dow Chemical. The first of these resulted in a $14.1 million verdict against the company, despite the lack of scientific evidence. Disregarding the studies in the *New England Journal of Medicine*,

the jurors were convinced that this particular plaintiff's suffering somehow stemmed from her Dow-manufactured breast implant.

As a result of the suit, Dow Chemical may close its whole medical division. Although the FDA admits that there is no evidence that breast implants are dangerous, it has not permitted the manufacturers to reenter the market, arguing that the companies that manufacture the implants have not adequately proved their safety. If the companies want to sell silicone implants in the future, they must resubmit applications to the FDA and demonstrate the safety of their products to the FDA's satisfaction. Given the legal situation, none of the companies intends to do so.

Update:

In June 1999, women who said their silicone breast implants made them ill agreed to settle their claims against Dow Corning for $3.2 billion. The settlement is part of its bankruptcy reorganization plan and is similar to a settlement entered into earlier by 3M, Bristol-Myers Squibb, and other manufacturers of breast implants. By now, however, more than twenty reputable scientific studies have been conducted on implant safety. Three European governments have convened scientific panels. The American College of Rheumatology, the American Academy of Neurology, the Institute of Medicine, and the American Medical Association have all published reviews of the evidence, as has an independent scientific panel appointed by a federal court. The conclusion is unanimous and unequivocal: There is no evidence that breast implants cause disease of any kind.[62]

Discussion Questions

1. What does the breast implant controversy reveal about society's attitudes toward product safety, about the legal liability of manufacturers, and about the role of regulatory agencies like the FDA in protecting consumers? Is our society too cautious about product safety or not cautious enough?

2. Was the FDA justified in placing a moratorium on breast implants? Is the agency right to have

effectively halted cosmetic breast implants by requiring manufacturers to resubmit their silicone prostheses for approval? Is the agency too concerned with public opinion? Should it pay greater attention to scientific evidence or to the individual women who have suffered?

3. Was it irresponsible of the manufacturers of breast implants to have marketed them without first conclusively proving they were safe? If you were on the jury, would you have found Dow Corning or its parent company liable for the illnesses suffered by women who have had breast implants?

4. On safety matters, should the FDA or any regulatory agency err on the side of overprotection or underprotection? Is the FDA's stance

on breast implants fair to the women who would like breast augmentation but cannot now get it? Some people disapprove of cosmetic augmentation or believe it to be a frivolous operation. Do you think that attitudes like this played a role in the controversy over the safety of breast implants?

5. Some argue that in the case of new drugs or medical procedures in which the dangers are uncertain, consumers should be free to decide for themselves whether they wish to run the health risks associated with these products or services. Assess this argument.

CASE 10.2

Hot Coffee at McDonald's

To aficionados of the bean, there's nothing like a piping-hot cup of java to get the day off to a good start, and nothing more insipid than lukewarm coffee. That's what McDonald's thought, anyway—until it learned differently, the hard and expensive way, when seventy-nine-year-old Stella Liebeck successfully sued the company after she was burned by a spilled cup of hot coffee that she'd bought at the drive-through window of her local McDonald's. The jury awarded her $160,000 in compensatory damages and a whopping $2.7 million in punitive damages. After the trial judge reduced the punitive damages to $480,000, she and McDonald's settled out of court for an undisclosed sum.[63]

Unlike most other lawsuits, news of the hot-coffee verdict received nationwide attention, most of it unfavorable. To many ordinary people, the case epitomized the excesses of a legal system out of control. If hot coffee is dangerous, what's next: soft drinks that are too cold? To conservatives, the case represented the all-too-familiar failure of consumers to take responsibility for their own conduct,

to blame business rather than themselves for their injuries. More policy-oriented pundits used the case as an occasion to call for reform of product liability law—in particular, to make winning frivolous suits more difficult and to restrict the punitive awards that juries can hand down.

However, those who examined the facts more closely learned that the Liebeck case was more complicated than it first appeared. For one thing, Liebeck suffered third-degree burns on her thighs and buttocks that were serious enough to require skin grafting and leave permanent scars. After her injury, she initially requested $10,000 for medical expenses and an additional amount for pain and suffering. When McDonald's refused, she went to court, asking for $300,000. Lawyers for the company argued in response that McDonald's coffee was not unreasonably hot and that Liebeck was responsible for her own injuries.

The jury saw it differently, however. First, McDonald's served its coffee at 185 degrees Fahrenheit, significantly hotter than home-brewed coffee.

The jury was persuaded that coffee at that temperature is both undrinkable and more dangerous than a reasonable consumer would expect. Second, before Liebeck's accident, the company had received over 700 complaints about burns from its coffee. In response to the complaints, McDonald's had in fact put a warning label on its cups and designed a tighter-fitting lid for them. Ironically, the new lid was part of the problem in the Liebeck case because she had held the coffee cup between her legs in an effort to pry it open.

Although the jury found that Liebeck was 20 percent responsible for her injuries, it also concluded that McDonald's had not done enough to warn consumers. The jury's $2.7 million punitive-damage award was intended, jurors later said, to send a message to fast-food chains. Although the judge reduced the award—equivalent to only about two days' worth of coffee sales for McDonald's—he called McDonald's conduct "willful, wanton, reckless, and callous."

Discussion Questions

1. Is hot coffee so dangerous, as the jury thought? Should a reasonable consumer be expected to know that coffee can burn and to have assumed this risk? Is a warning label sufficient? Is our society too protective of consumers these days, or not protective enough?

2. In serving hot coffee, did McDonald's act in a morally responsible way? What ideals, obligations, and effects should it have taken into consideration?

3. McDonald's claims that most consumers would prefer to have their coffee too hot than not hot enough. After all, if it's too hot, they can always wait a minute before drinking it. Suppose this is true; how does it affect McDonald's responsibilities? Given that McDonald's serves millions of cups of coffee every week, how important are a few hundred complaints about its coffee being too hot?

4. Was Liebeck only 20 percent responsible for her injuries? Do you agree with the amount of compensatory and punitive damages that the jury awarded her? If not, what would have been a fairer monetary award?

5. Should juries be permitted to award punitive damages in product liability cases? If so, should there be a limit to what they can award? Is it right for a jury to award punitive damages against one company in order to send a message to a whole industry?

CASE 10.3

Sniffing Glue
Could Snuff Profits

Harvey Benjamin Fuller founded the H. B. Fuller Company in 1887. Originally a one-man wallpaper-paste shop, H. B. Fuller is now a leading manufacturer of industrial glues, coatings, and paints, with operations worldwide. The company's 10,000 different varieties of glue hold together everything from cars to cigarettes to disposable diapers. However, some of its customers don't use Fuller's glues in the way they are intended to be used.

That's particularly the case in Central America, where Fuller derives 27 percent of its profits and where tens of thousands of homeless children sniff some sort of glue. Addicted to glue's intoxicating but dangerous fumes, these unfortunate children are called *resistoleros* after Fuller's Resistol brand. Child-welfare advocates have urged the company to add a noxious oil to its glue to discourage abusers, but the company has resisted, either because it might reduce the glue's effectiveness or because it will irritate legitimate users.[64]

Either way, the issue is irritating H. B. Fuller, which has been recognized by various awards, honors, and socially conscious mutual funds as a company with a conscience. Fuller's mission statement says that it "will conduct business legally and ethically, support the activities of its employees in their communities and be a responsible corporate citizen." The St. Paul–based company gives 5 percent of its profits to charity; it has committed itself to safe environmental practices worldwide (practices that are "often more stringent than local government standards," the company says); and it has even endowed a chair in business ethics at the University of Minnesota. Now Fuller must contend with dissident stockholders inside, and demonstrators outside, its annual meetings.

The glue-sniffing issue is not a new one. In 1969 the Testor Corporation added a noxious ingredient to its hobby glue to discourage abuse, and in 1994 Henkel, a German chemical company that competes with Fuller, stopped making certain toxic glues in Central America. However, Fuller seems to have been singled out for criticism not only because its brand dominates Central America but also because—in the eyes of its critics, anyway—the company has not lived up to its own good-citizen image. Timothy Smith, executive director of the Interfaith Center for Corporate Responsibility, believes that companies with a reputation as good corporate citizens are more vulnerable to attack. "But as I see it," he says, "the hazard is not in acting in a socially responsible way. The hazard is in over-marketing yourself as a saint."

Saintly or not, the company has made matters worse for itself by its handling of the issue. In 1992 H. B. Fuller's board of directors acknowledged that "illegal distribution was continuing" and that "a suitable replacement product would not be available in the near future." Accordingly, it voted to stop selling Resistol adhesives in Central America. "We simply don't believe it is the right decision to keep our solvent product on the market," a company spokesman said.

The Coalition on Resistoleros and other corporate gadflies were ecstatic, but their jubilation turned to anger when they learned a few months later that Fuller had not in fact stopped selling Resistol in Central America, and did not intend to. True, Fuller no longer sold glue to retailers and small-scale users in Honduras and Guatemala, but it continued to sell large tubs and barrels of it to industrial customers in those countries and to a broader list of commercial and industrial users in neighboring countries.

The company says that it has not only restricted distribution but also taken other steps to stop the abuse of its product. It has altered Resistol's formula, replacing the sweet-smelling but highly toxic solvent toluene with the slightly less toxic chemical cyclohexane. In addition, the company has tried—

without success, it says—to develop a nonintoxicating water-based glue, and it contributes to community programs for homeless children in Central America. But the company's critics disparage these actions as mere image polishing. Bruce Harris, director of Latin American programs for Covenant House, a nonprofit child-welfare advocate, asserts that Resistol is still readily available to children in Nicaragua and El Salvador and, to a lesser extent, in Costa Rica. "If they are genuinely concerned about the children," he asks, "why haven't they pulled out of all the countries—as their board mandated?"

Discussion Questions

1. What are H. B. Fuller's moral obligations in this case? What ideas, effects, and consequences are at stake? Have any moral rights been violated? What would a utilitarian recommend? A Kantian?

2. What specifically should H. B. Fuller do about Resistol? Are the critics right that the steps the company has taken so far are mere image polishing? Is the company's only moral option to

withdraw from the Central American market altogether?

3. When, if ever, is a company morally responsible for harm done by the blatant misuse of a perfectly legitimate and socially useful product? Does it make a difference whether the abusers are adults or children? Is it relevant that other companies market similar products?

4. Tobacco companies have a strong financial interest in cultivating future smokers, and although they deny doing so, they consciously market their product to make it attractive to young people. Contrast their conduct with that of H. B. Fuller.

5. Given H. B. Fuller's conduct in other matters, would you judge it to be a morally responsible company, all things considered? Are companies that pride themselves on being morally responsible likely to be held to a higher standard than other companies? If so, is this fair?

CASE 10.4

Warning: The Following Ad
May Contain a Subliminal Message

There's nothing like the smell of a new car, right? Well, there is, and it comes in a can—a product called Velvet Touch, which is an aerosol fountain of youth for any moribund old clunker. With a blast or two of this vehicular elixir, you can instantly give an auto that smells like a stockyard a "new-car scent."

Marvin Ivy, president of the National Independent Auto Dealers Association, disapproves of using such products to sell used cars. "I think you'll deceive the public," he says. "That car could have 60,000 miles on it and smell like hell."[65]

Joseph Eikenberg, owner of Aero Motors, doesn't know what hell smells like, but his nose knows the lingering fetor left in cars by dogs and smokers. And the Baltimore car dealer thinks it's okay to use the artificial odor to combat them.

Researchers have shown that one's sense of smell affects one's attitude toward shopping,[66] so it is no surprise that used-car dealerships aren't the only businesses using synthetic scents. Have you ever been strolling through a shopping mall and been seduced by the mouthwatering aroma of a freshly baked chocolate chip cookie? If so, the source of your temptation may not have been a cookie at all but one of the many scents made and packaged by International Flavors & Fragrances. IF&F infuses into aerosol cans the palate-pleasing scents of such foods as fresh pizza, hot apple pie, nongreasy french fries, and, to be sure, the once inimitable chocolate chip cookie. Sniffing profits in the scents wafting from IF&F's olfactory factory, many merchants are time-releasing the odors into the walkways of shopping malls. They hope shoppers will find the aromas so tempting that they will succumb to their urge to splurge.

IF&F's success comes as no surprise to Minnesota Mining and Manufacturing (3M), which provides most of the music we hear in commercial buildings. "We have been told [by retailers] that it will increase impulse purchases," says Donald Conlin, project manager at 3M.[67] The specially arranged music is also supposed to reduce absenteeism, worker turnover, and customer complaints, as well as increase sales volume and profit.

Hal C. Becker, president of Behavioral Engineering Corporation, claims that what people don't consciously hear can be as influential as what they do. He has developed a subliminal message machine being marketed as "Dr. Becker's Black Box." (It sells for $9,180 or leases for $4,800 a year.) The messages and recipients vary. A Louisiana supermarket beams to workers and shoppers the inaudible message, "I will not steal. If I steal I go to jail." The owner of the supermarket is thrilled with the results. Before buying the device, he claims, pilferage used to run about $4,500 over six months and cashier shortages about $125 a week. Now the pilferage is down to $1,300 and the shortages to less than $10. In a Buffalo, New York, real estate management concern, salespeople hear tapes saying, "I love my job" and "I am the greatest salesman." According to the company's president, revenue has risen 35 percent despite a drop in advertising.[68]

Many of Becker's customers don't want to be identified for fear that the American Civil Liberties Union (ACLU) will sue them. Apparently their fears have some merit.

"The potential for abuse is enormous," says Barbara Shack, executive director of the New York branch of the ACLU. "If it is a distortion of sound and camouflaged so the receiver isn't aware and can influence his behavior, it's tantamount to brainwashing and ought to be prohibited by legislation." Adds Jack Novik, the ACLU's national staff counsel: "We are very skeptical and suspicious of anything that imposes outside control on behavior."[69]

Some academicians consider the "black box" no more than a money machine for Becker. Professor of business Jay Russo points to the inconclusiveness of studies in subliminal suggestions. "It's an open issue," he says. "It won't die, but every time you do research it disappears like sand through your hands."[70]

Don't tell that to Wilson Key, though. Since *Subliminal Seduction* (1972), his first book, Key has been the center of the controversy over alleged widespread use of subliminals in advertising. He has been both praised as a trenchant critic of the mass media and criticized as a "kook" and "paranoid" for suggesting that ads are glutted with subliminally suggestive graphics. Although invisible to anyone not looking for them, such graphics can manipulate the beholder. Key has compiled a massive collection of ads that he claims present shockingly erotic images disguised as something innocuous.

"The strange-but-true part is that messages might actually affect us under certain conditions," says professor of communications Phillip Bozek. "Research suggests that our minds can register and begin to process information we didn't clearly hear or see, and that subliminal techniques can suggest to us images or phrases which we may later think we conceived ourselves, and which we are therefore less likely to resist. A subliminal message could urge a consumer to go ahead and buy something after all, and he or she might never suspect the subtle prodding."[71] Bozek sees ample evidence of the commercial use of subliminals.

So does one California legislator, who sponsored a bill that would require broadcasters to warn the public of subliminally embedded communications. The bill would not outlaw subliminal communications but would require consumer warnings when "sounds" and "visual images" are "conveyed to people" but are "not immediately and consequently perceptible" to normal seeing and hearing faculties.

Discussion Questions

1. How effective do you think subliminal communication is? Of what examples of subliminal communication have you become aware?

2. What moral issues are raised by the use of subliminal communication? What rights, if any, are at stake? What moral factors must be taken into account by a company considering using subliminal communication?

3. How would a utilitarian assess the use of subliminals in advertising?

4. Do you think the end or purpose for which a subliminal message is used affects its morality? For example, what if the Surgeon General used subliminals on television to get people to stop smoking?

5. Professor Bozek, for one, draws a distinction between electronic and printed subliminals. You need special equipment to pick out electronic subliminals, but you can see printed subliminals unassisted if you know how to look for them. This distinction leads Bozek to conclude that government should regulate electronically transmitted subliminals, whereas education should inform us about print subliminals. Do you agree? Or do you think both should be regulated? Or neither?

CASE 10.5

Closing the Deal

Now that she had to, Jean McGuire wasn't sure she could. Not that she didn't understand what to do. Wright Boazman, sales director for Sunrise Land Developers, had made the step clear enough when he described a variety of effective "deal-closing techniques."

As Wright explained it, very often people actually want to buy a lot but suffer at the last minute from self-doubt and uncertainty. The inexperienced salesperson can misinterpret this hesitation as a lack of interest in a property. "But," as Wright pointed out, "in most cases it's just an expression of the normal reservations we all show when the time comes to sign our names on the dotted line."

In Wright's view, the job of a land salesperson was "to help the prospect make the decision to buy." He didn't mean to suggest that salespeople should misrepresent a piece of property or in any way mislead people about what they were purchasing. "Law prohibits this," he pointed out, "and personally I find such behavior repugnant. What I'm talking about is helping them buy a lot that they genuinely want and that you're convinced will be compatible with their needs and interests." For Wright Boazman, salespeople should serve as motivators, people who can provide whatever impulse was needed for prospects to close the deal.

In Wright's experience, one of the most effective closing techniques was what he termed "the other party." It goes something like this.

Suppose someone like Jean McGuire had a hot prospect, someone who was exhibiting real interest in a lot but who was having trouble deciding. To motivate the prospect into buying, Jean ought to tell the person that she wasn't even sure the lot was still available because a number of other salespeople were showing the same lot, and they could already have closed a deal on it. As Wright put it, "This first ploy generally has the effect of increasing the prospect's interest in the property, and more important to us, in closing the deal pronto."

Next Jean should say something like, "Why don't we go back to the office, and I'll call headquarters to find out the status of the lot?" Wright indicated that such a suggestion ordinarily "whets their appetite" even more. In addition, it turns prospects away from wondering whether they should purchase the land and toward hoping that it's still available.

When they return to the office, Jean should make a call in the presence of the prospect. The call, of course, would not be to "headquarters" but to a private office only yards from where she and the prospect sit. Wright or someone else would receive the call, and Jean should fake a conversation about the property's availability, punctuating her comments with contagious excitement about its desirability. When she hangs up, she should breathe a sigh of relief that the lot's still available—but barely. At any minute, Jean should explain anxiously, the lot could be "green-tagged," meaning that headquarters is expecting a call from another salesperson who's about to close a deal and will remove the lot from open stock. (An effective variation of this, Wright pointed out, would have Jean abruptly excuse herself on hanging up and dart over to another sales representative with whom she'd engage in a heated, although staged, debate about the availability of the property—loud enough, of course, for the prospect to hear. The intended effect, according to Wright, would be to place the prospect in a "now or never" frame of mind.)

When Jean first heard about this and other closing techniques, she felt uneasy. Even though the property was everything it was represented to be and the law allowed purchasers ten days to change their minds after closing a deal, she instinctively objected to the use of psychological manipulation. Nevertheless, Jean never expressed her reservations to anyone, primarily because she didn't want to endanger her job. She desperately needed it owing to the recent death of her husband, which had left her as the sole supporter of herself and three young children. Besides, Jean had convinced herself that she could deal with closures more respectably than Wright and other salespeople might. But the truth was that, after six months of selling land for Sunrise, Jean's sales lagged far behind those of the other sales representatives. Whether she liked it or not, Jean had to admit she was losing a considerable number of sales because she couldn't close. And she couldn't close because, in Wright Boazman's words, she lacked technique. She wasn't using the psychological closing devices that he and others had found so successful.

Now as she drove back to the office with two hot prospects in hand, she wondered what to do.

Discussion Questions

1. Do you disapprove of this sales tactic, or is it a legitimate business technique? How might it be morally defended?

2. Suppose you knew either that the prospect would eventually decide to buy the property anyway or that it would genuinely be in the prospect's interest to buy it. Would that affect your moral assessment of this closing technique? Do customers have any grounds for complaining about this closing technique if the law allows them ten days to change their minds?

3. What ideals, obligations, and effects must Jean consider? What interests and rights of the customer are at stake?

4. What weight should Jean give to self-interest in her deliberations? What do you think she should do? What would you do?

5. What rule, if any, would a rule utilitarian encourage realtors in this situation to follow? What should the realtors' professional code of ethics say about closing techniques?

CASE 10.6

The Skateboard Scare

The skateboard craze had been slow to reach River City, but when it arrived, it was big—big enough to have salvaged Colin Brewster's sport shop, which only a few months before had been barely scraping by. Skateboards had changed that. In fact, skateboard business was so brisk that Brewster could hardly keep them in stock. But storm clouds loomed on the horizon.

Just last week members of a concerned River City consumer committee visited his shop. They informed Brewster that they had ample evidence to prove that skateboards present a real and immediate hazard to consumer safety. Brewster conceded that the group surely provided enough statistical support; the number of broken bones and concussions that had resulted directly and indirectly from accidents involving skateboards was shocking. But he thought the group's position was fundamentally unsound because, as he told them, "It's not the skateboards that are unsafe but how people use them."

Committee members weren't impressed with Brewster's distinction. They likened it to saying automobile manufacturers shouldn't be conscious of consumer safety because it's not the automobiles that are unsafe but how we drive them. Brewster objected that automobiles present an entirely different problem, because a number of things could be done to ensure their safer use. "But what can you do about a skateboard?" he asked them. "Besides, I don't manufacture them, I just sell them."

The committee pointed out that other groups were attacking the problem on the manufacturing level. What they expected of Brewster was some responsible management of the problem at the local retail level. They pointed out that recently Brewster had run a series of local television ads portraying young but accomplished skateboarders performing fancy flips and turns. The ad implied that anyone could easily accomplish such feats. Only yesterday one parent had told the committee of her child's breaking an arm attempting such

gymnastics after having purchased a skateboard from Brewster. "Obviously," Brewster countered, "the woman has an irresponsible kid whose activities she should monitor, not me." He pointed out that his ad was not intended to imply that anyone could or should do those tricks, no more than an ad showing a car traveling at high speeds while doing stunts implies that one should drive that way.

The committee disagreed. They said Brewster not only should discontinue such misleading advertising but also should actively publicize the potential dangers of skateboarding. Specifically, the committee wanted him to display prominently beside his skateboard stock the statistical data testifying to its hazards. Furthermore, he should make sure anyone buying a skateboard reads this material before the purchase.

Brewster argued that the committee's demands were unreasonable. "Do you have any idea what effect that would have on sales?" he asked them.

Committee members readily admitted that they were less interested in his sales than in their children's safety. Brewster told them that in this matter their children's safety was their responsibility, not his. But the committee was adamant. Members told Brewster that they'd be back in a week to find out what positive steps, if any, he'd taken to correct the problem. In the event he'd done nothing, they indicated they were prepared to picket his shop.

Discussion Questions

1. With whom do you agree—Brewster or the committee? Why?

2. Would you criticize Brewster's advertisements? Do you think the demand that he publicize the dangers of skateboarding is reasonable?

3. What responsibilities, if any, do retailers have to ensure consumer safety? Compare the responsibilities of manufacturers, skateboarders, and parents.

4. What steps could Brewster take to promote skateboard safety?

5. Identify the ideals, obligations, and effects that Brewster should consider in reaching his deci-sion. Which of the considerations do you think is most important?

■

Notes to Chapter 10

1. See the CDC's Web site, *www.cdc.gov/tobacco/issue.htm* (September 1, 2002).

2. "Low-Tar Duplicity," *New York Times,* December 3, 2001, A22.

3. U.S. Bureau of the Census, *Statistical Abstract of the United States 2001* (Washington, D.C.: U.S. Government Printing Office, 2001), Table 179. See the Consumer Product Safety Commission's regular reports on toy-related deaths and injuries at *www.cpsc.gov.*

4. The Consumer Product Safety Commission reports regularly on electrocutions associated with consumer products. See *www.cpsc.gov.*

5. Manuel G. Velasquez, *Business Ethics,* 5th ed. (Upper Saddle River, N.J.: Prentice Hall, 2002), 348–350.

6. Richard T. De George, "Ethical Responsibilities of Engineers in Large Organizations," *Business and Professional Ethics Journal* 1 (Fall 1981).

7. Dean Rothbart and John A. Prestbo, "Taking Rely Off Market Costs Procter & Gamble a Week of Agonizing," *Wall Street Journal,* November 3, 1980, 1.

8. See *www.nhtsa.dot.gov/airbags/factsheets/numbers.html* (September 1, 2002).

9. Dan Oldenburg, "Chrysler's Reversal in Airbag Debate," *San Francisco Chronicle,* August 23, 1989, in "Business Briefing," 9.

10. Benjamin Kelley, "How the Auto Industry Sets Roadblocks to Safety," *Business and Society Review* 83 (Fall 1992): 51.

11. "Dangerous Candies," *San Jose Mercury News,* June 13, 2002, 1A.

12. Milo Geyelin, "Gun Dealer Is Held Liable in Accident for Not Teaching Customer Safe Use," *Wall Street Journal,* June 6, 1989, B10.

13. Marisa Manley, "Products Liability: You're More Exposed Than You Think," *Harvard Business Review* 65 (September–October 1987): 28–29.

14. Melvyn A. J. Menezes, "Ethical Issues in Product Policy," in N. Craig Smith and John A. Quelch, eds., *Ethics in Marketing* (Homewood, Ill.: Irwin, 1993), 286.

15. "Child Contracts Reye's Syndrome," *ACLU News* (San Francisco), July–August 1993, 1.

16. Terry Ann Halbert, "The Fire-Safe Cigarette: The Other Tobacco War," *Business and Society Review* 102–103 (1998): 25–36 and J. Jennings Moss, "Smoke, But No Fire" (January 11, 2000), available at *www.abcnews.go.com*

17. These are taken from Tad Tuleja, *Beyond the Bottom Line* (New York: Penguin, 1987), 77–78.

18. *New York Times,* March 31, 1999, A16, and *San Francisco Chronicle,* March 31, 1999, A1.

19. Smith and Quelch, *Ethics in Marketing,* 337–339.

20. "For First Time, Justices Reject Punitive Awards," *New York Times,* May 21, 1996, C1.

21. Jeffrey H. Birnbaum, "Pricing of Product Is Still an Art, Often Having Little Link to Costs," *Wall Street Journal,* November 25, 1981, sec. 2, 29.

22. Ibid.

23. Ibid.

24. "Scanners That Err at Checkout Counter," *International Herald Tribune,* June 13, 1994, 3, and "Store Scanners in the Crosshairs," *San Francisco Chronicle,* April 5, 1997, A15.

25. Smith and Quelch, *Ethics in Marketing,* 405–406.

26. Ibid., 407.

27. *San Francisco Chronicle,* October 1, 1997, A3.

28. Constance L. Hays, "Panasonic to Return $16 Million to Consumers," *New York Times,* January 19, 1989, A1.

29. For a thorough look at this case, see M. David Ermann and Richard J. Lundman, *Corporate Deviance* (New York: Holt, Rinehart & Winston, 1982), Chapter 5.

30. "Price-Fixing Probe Nets Dairy Giants," *San Jose Mercury News,* May 23, 1993, 8A.

31. *San Francisco Chronicle,* May 9, 1997, A1.

32. Kevin Helliker, "In Natural Foods, a Big Name's No Big Help," *Wall Street Journal,* June 6, 2002, B1.

33. Michael J. McCarthy, "Taking the Value Out of Value-Sized," *Wall Street Journal,* August 14, 2002, D1. See also Omprakash K. Gupta and Anna S. Rominger, "Blind Man's Bluff: The Ethics of Quantity Surcharges," *Journal of Business Ethics* 15 (1996): 1299–1312.

34. Gupta and Rominger, "Blind Man's Bluff."

35. See International Advertising Resource Center, a Web site of Louisa Ha, professor of telecommunications at Bowling Green State University, at www.bgsu.edu/departments/tcom/faculty/ha/intlad1.html (August 2, 2002).

36. Hairong Li, "Advertising Media," in *Encyclopedia of Advertising* (Chicago: Fitzroy Dearborn, 2002).

37. Roger Draper, "The Faithless Shepherd," *New York Review of Books,* June 26, 1986, 17.

38. See "Mea Culpa, Sort Of," *Newsweek,* September 27, 1971, 98.

39. *Business and Society Review* 67 (Fall 1988): 27.

40. Paul Stevens, "Weasel Words: God's Little Helpers," in Paul A. Eschhol, Alfred A. Rosa, and Virginia P. Clark, eds., *Language Awareness* (New York: St. Martin's Press, 1974), 156.

41. Samm Sinclair Baker, *The Permissible Lie* (New York: World Publishing, 1968), 16.

42. See the *Washington Post*'s health supplement, January 8, 1994.

43. Ann Hagedorn, "FDA Cracks Down on Cosmetic Firms' Age-Treatment Drugs," *Wall Street Journal,* April 27, 1987.

44. Ivan L. Preston, *The Great American Blow-Up: Puffery in Advertising and Selling,* rev. ed. (Madison, Wis.: University of Wisconsin Press, 1996), 181.

45. Preston, *Great American Blow-Up,* 24.

46. Gail Bronson, "Sexual Pitches in Ads Become More Explicit and Pervasive," *Wall Street Journal,* November 18, 1980, 1.

47. Wilson Bryan Key, *Subliminal Seduction* (New York: New American Library, 1973), 11.

48. Preston, *Great American Blow-Up,* 113–123.

49. 302 U.S. 112 (1937).

50. Preston, *Great American Blow-Up,* 122–123.

51. "Advertisers Gear Their Pitches to the Group with Pull: Kids," *Santa Cruz Sentinel,* April 28, 1996, D2.

52. "Hey Kid, Buy This," *Business Week,* June 30, 1997, 63. Except as otherwise noted, the following four paragraphs are based on this article.

53. Lisa J. Moore, "The Littlest Consumers," *San Francisco Chronicle,* January 13, 1991, in "This World," 8.

54. Randall Rothenberg, "Executives Defending Their Craft," *New York Times,* May 22, 1989, C7.

55. Theodore Levitt, "The Morality (?) of Advertising," *Harvard Business Review* 48 (July–August 1970): 84–92.

56. John Kenneth Galbraith, *The Affluent Society,* 3rd ed. (New York: Houghton Mifflin, 1976), 131.

57. John Kenneth Galbraith, *The New Industrial State* (New York: Signet, 1967), 219.

58. Draper, "The Faithless Shepherd," 16.

59. See Al Gini, "Work, Identity, and Self: How We Are Formed by the Work We Do," *Journal of Business Ethics* 17 (May 1998): 711.

60. For a discussion of this, see "All by the Numbers," *Economist,* December 20, 1986.

61. This case study is based on the *Frontline* program "Breast Implants on Trial," aired on PBS, February 27, 1996. For background details, see Anne T. Lawrence, "Dow Corning and the Silicone Breast Implant Controversy," in John R. Boatright, ed., *Cases in Ethics and the Conduct of Business* (Englewood Cliffs, N.J.: Prentice Hall, 1995).

62. See "Talk of the Town," *New Yorker,* January 11, 1999, 23–24, and *New York Times,* July 11 and November 10, 1998, and June 2, June 29, and December 2, 1999.

63. This case study is based on one in Joseph R. DesJardins and John J. McCall, eds., *Contemporary Issues in Business Ethics,* 4th ed. (Belmont, Calif.: Wadsworth, 2000), 345–346.

64. This case study is based on Diana B. Henriques, "Black Mark for a 'Good Citizen,'" *New York Times,* November 26, 1995, sec. 3, 1.

65. "Sight, Smell, Sound: They're All Arms in Retailers' Arsenal," *Wall Street Journal,* April 17, 1979, 1.

66. "Can You Smell a Sale?" *San Jose Mercury News,* January 12, 1996, 16A.

67. "Words Whispered to Subconscious Supposed to Deter Theft, Fainting," *Wall Street Journal,* November 25, 1980, 26.

68. Ibid.

69. "Sight, Smell, Sound," *Wall Street Journal,* 1.

70. Ibid., 1, 27.

71. "Letters to Editor," *Bakersfield Californian,* June 3, 1983, 5.

Reading ————————■

THE ETHICS
OF SALES

THOMAS L. CARSON

*In this essay, Thomas L. Carson, professor of philosophy
at Loyola University of Chicago, examines the moral
obligations of salespeople. After explaining and criticizing
David Holley's well-known account of the ethics of sales,
Carson puts forward his own theory, which identifies four
moral duties of salespeople. Carson contends that his theory provides intuitively plausible results in concrete cases,
that it avoids the weaknesses of Holley's approach, and
that it explains why different kinds of salespeople have
different kinds of duties to their customers. He goes on to
argue that the most plausible version of the Golden Rule
supports his theory. He concludes by discussing several
examples that illustrate and clarify his theory.*

SALES

The ethics of sales is an important, but neglected,
topic in business ethics. Approximately 10 percent
of the U.S. work force is involved in sales. In addition, most of us occasionally sell major holdings
such as used cars and real estate. Because sales
were long governed by the principle of *caveat emptor*, discussions of the ethics of sales usually focus
on the ethics of withholding information and the
question "What sort of information is a salesperson
obligated to reveal to customers?" One of the best
treatments of this topic is David Holley's paper "A
Moral Evaluation of Sales Practices." In this essay,
I explain Holley's theory, propose several criticisms,
and formulate what I take to be a more plausible
theory about the duties of salespeople. My theory
avoids the objections I raise against Holley and
yields intuitively plausible results when applied to
cases. I also defend my theory by appeal to the
golden rule and offer a defense of the version of
the golden rule to which I appeal.

Copyright © 2002 Thomas L. Carson. Reprinted by permission.

PRELIMINARIES: A CONCEPTUAL ROADMAP

We need to distinguish between lying, deception,
withholding information, and concealing information. Roughly, deception is intentionally causing
someone to have false beliefs. Standard dictionary
definitions of lying say that a lie is a false statement
intended to deceive others. The *Oxford English
Dictionary* (1989) defines a lie as: "a false statement made with the intent to deceive." *Webster's*
(1963) gives the following definition of the verb *lie:*
"to make an untrue statement with intent to deceive." (We might want to add a third condition to
this definition and say that in order for a false statement to be a lie, the person who makes it must
know or believe that it is false. The third condition
makes a difference in cases in which someone attempts to deceive another person by means of a
false statement that he mistakenly believes to be
true. Nothing in the present essay turns on this
issue.) Lying arguably requires the intent to deceive others—I express my doubts about this in
Carson (1988)—but lies that don't succeed in causing others to have false beliefs are not instances of
deception. The word *deception* implies success in
causing others to have false beliefs, but lying is
often unsuccessful in causing deception. A further
difference between lying and deception is that,
while a lie must be a false statement, deception
needn't involve false statements; true statements
can be deceptive and many forms of deception do
not involve making statements of any sort. Thus,
many instances of deception do not constitute
lying. Withholding information does not constitute
deception. It is not a case of *causing* someone to
have false beliefs; it is merely a case of failing to
correct false beliefs or incomplete information. On
the other hand, actively concealing information
usually constitutes deception.

THE COMMON LAW PRINCIPLE OF <u>CAVEAT EMPTOR</u>

According to the common law principle of *caveat
emptor*, sellers are not required to inform prospective buyers about the properties of the goods they
sell. Under *caveat emptor*, sales and contracts to

sell are legally enforceable even if the seller fails to inform the buyer of serious defects in the goods that are sold. Buyers themselves are responsible for determining the quality of the goods they purchase. In addition, English common law sometimes called for the enforcement of sales in cases in which sellers made false or misleading statements about the goods they sold (Atiyah 464–65).

Currently, all U.S. states operate under the Uniform Commercial Code of 1968. Section 2-313 of the code defines the notion of sellers' warranties (Preston 52). The code provides that all factual affirmations or statements about the goods being sold are warranties. This means that sales are not valid or legally enforceable if the seller makes false statements about the goods s/he is selling. The American legal system has developed the concept of an "implied" (as opposed to an express or explicit) warranty. Implied warranties are a significant limitation on the principle of *caveat emptor.* According to the Uniform Commercial Code, any transaction carries with it the following implied warranties: 1) that the seller owns the goods he is selling and 2) that the goods are "merchantable," i.e., suitable for the purposes for which they are sold (Preston 56–57). Many local ordinances require that people who sell real estate inform buyers about all known serious defects of the property they sell. These ordinances are also a significant limitation on the traditional principle of *caveat emptor.*

Deceptive sales practices also fall under the purview of the Federal Trade Commission (FTC). The FTC prohibits deceptive sales practices— practices likely to materially mislead reasonable consumers (FTC Statement 1983).

Many salespeople take complying with the law to be an acceptable moral standard for their conduct and claim that they have no moral duty to provide buyers with information about the goods they sell, except for that information which the law requires for an enforceable sale.

HOLLEY'S THEORY

Holley's theory is based on his concept of a "voluntary" or "mutually beneficial" market exchange (Holley uses the terms *voluntary exchange* and *mu-* *tually beneficial exchange* interchangeably). He says that a voluntary exchange occurs "only if" the following conditions are met (Holley takes his conditions to be *necessary* conditions for an acceptable exchange):

1. Both buyer and seller understand what they are giving up and what they are receiving in return.

2. Neither buyer nor seller is compelled to enter into the exchange as a result of coercion, severely restricted alternatives, or other constraints on the ability to choose.

3. Both buyer and seller are able at the time of the exchange to make rational judgments about its costs and benefits. (Holley 463)

These three conditions admit of degrees of satisfaction. An ideal exchange is an exchange involving people who are fully informed, fully rational, and "enter into the exchange entirely of their own volition" (Holley 464). The conditions for an ideal exchange are seldom, if ever, met in practice. However, Holley claims that it is still possible to have an "acceptable exchange" if the parties are "adequately informed, rational, and free from compulsion."

According to Holley, "the primary duty of salespeople to customers is to avoid undermining the conditions of an acceptable exchange." He makes it clear that, on his view, acts of omission (as well as acts of commission) can undermine the conditions of an acceptable exchange (Holley 464).

Because of the complexity of many goods and services, customers often lack information necessary for an acceptable exchange. Careful examination of products will not necessarily reveal problems or defects. According to Holley, *caveat emptor* is not acceptable as a moral principle, because customers often lack information necessary for an acceptable exchange. In such cases, salespeople are morally obligated to give information to the buyer. The question then is: *What kind of information* do salespeople need to provide buyers in order to ensure that the buyer is adequately informed? Holley attempts to answer this question in the following passage in which he appeals to the golden rule:

Determining exactly how much information needs to be provided is not always clear-cut. We must in general rely on our assessments of what a reasonable person would want to know. As a practical guide, a salesperson might consider, "What would I want to know, if I were considering buying this product?" (Holley 467)

This principle is very demanding, perhaps more demanding than Holley realizes. Presumably, most reasonable people would *want* to know *a great deal* about the things they are thinking of buying. They might want to know *everything* relevant to the decision whether or not to buy something (more on this point shortly).

CRITICISMS OF HOLLEY

First, when time does not permit it, a salesperson cannot be morally obligated to provide all information necessary to ensure that the customer is adequately informed (all the information that a reasonable person would *want* to know if she were in the buyer's position). In many cases, reasonable customers would *want* to know a great deal of information. Often salespeople simply don't have the time to give all customers all the information Holley deems necessary for an acceptable exchange. Salespeople don't always know all the information that the buyer needs for an acceptable exchange. It cannot be a person's duty to do what is impossible—the statement that someone *ought* to do a certain act implies that she *can* do that act. Further, in many cases, salespeople don't know enough about the buyer's state of knowledge to know what information the buyer needs in order to be adequately informed. A salesperson might know that the buyer needs certain information in order to be adequately informed but not know whether or not the buyer possesses that information. One might reply that salespeople *should* know all the information necessary for an adequate exchange. However, on examination, this is not a plausible view. A salesperson in a large retail store cannot be expected to be knowledgeable about every product he sells. Often, it is impossible for realtors and used car salesmen to know much about the condition of the houses and cars they sell or the likelihood that they will need expensive repairs.

Second, Holley's theory implies that a salesperson in a store would be obligated to inform customers that a particular piece of merchandise in her store sells for less at a competing store if she knows this to be the case. (Presumably, she would *want* to know where she can get it for the lowest price, were she herself considering buying the product.) Not only do salespeople have no duty to provide this kind of information, (ordinarily) it would be wrong for them to do so.

Third, Holley's theory seems to yield unacceptable consequences in cases in which the buyer's alternatives are severely constrained. Suppose that a person with a very modest income attempts to buy a house in a small town. Her options are severely constrained, since there is only one house for sale in her price range. According to Holley, there can't be an acceptable exchange in such cases, because condition number 2 is not satisfied. However, it's not clear what he thinks sellers ought to do in such cases. The seller can't be expected to remove these constraints by giving the buyer money or building more homes in town. Holley's view seems to imply that it would be wrong for anyone to sell or rent housing to such a person. This result is unacceptable.

TOWARD A MORE PLAUSIBLE THEORY ABOUT THE ETHICS OF SALES

I believe that salespeople have the following moral duties regarding the disclosure of information when dealing with *rational adult consumers* (cases involving children or adults who are not fully rational raise special problems that I will not try to deal with here):

1. Salespeople should provide buyers with safety warnings and precautions about the goods they sell. (Sometimes it is enough for salespeople to call attention to written warnings and precautions that come with the goods and services in question. These warnings are unnecessary if the buyers already understand the dangers or precautions in question.)

2. Salespeople should refrain from lying and deception in their dealings with customers.

3. As much as their knowledge and time constraints permit, salespeople should fully answer

questions about the products and services they sell. They should answer questions forthrightly and not evade questions or withhold information that has been asked for (even if this makes it less likely that they will make a successful sale). Salespeople are obligated to answer questions about the goods and services they sell. However, they are justified in refusing to answer questions that would require them to reveal information about what their competitors are selling. They are not obligated to answer questions about competing goods and services or give information about other sellers.

4. Salespeople should not try to "steer" customers toward purchases that they have reason to think will prove to be harmful to customers (financial harm counts) or that customers will come to regret.

These are *prima facie* duties that can conflict with other duties and are sometimes overridden by other duties. A *prima facie* duty is one's actual duty, other things being equal; it is an actual duty in the absence of conflicting duties of greater or equal importance. For example, my *prima facie* duty to keep promises is my actual duty in the absence of conflicting duties of equal or greater importance. The above is a *minimal list* of the duties of salespeople concerning the disclosure of information. I believe that the following are also *prima facie* duties of salespeople, but I am much less certain that these principles can be justified:

5. Salespeople should not sell customers goods or services they have reason to think will prove to be harmful to customers or that the customers will come to regret later, without giving the customers their reasons for thinking that this is the case. (This duty does not hold if the seller has good reasons to think that the customer already possesses the information in question.)

6. Salespeople should not sell items they know to be defective or of poor quality without alerting customers to this. (This duty does not hold if the buyer can be reasonably expected to know about the poor quality of what he is buying.)

I have what I take to be strong arguments for 1–4, but I'm not so sure that I can justify 5 and 6. I believe that reasonable people can disagree about 5 and 6. (I have very little to say about 5 and 6 in the present essay. See Carson [2001] for a discussion of arguments for 5 and 6.)

There are some important connections between duties 2, 4, and 6. Lying and deception in sales are not confined to lying to or deceiving customers about the goods one sells. Many salespeople misrepresent their own motives to customers/clients. Almost all salespeople invite the trust of customers/clients and claim, implicitly or explicitly, to be acting in the interests of customers/clients. Salespeople often ask customers to defer to their judgment about what is best for them. For most salespeople, gaining the trust of customers or clients is essential for success. Many salespeople are *not* interested in helping customers in the way they represent themselves as being. A salesperson who misrepresents her motives, and intentions to customers violates rule 2. This simultaneous inviting and betrayal of trust is a kind of treachery. In ordinary cases, rules against lying and deception alone prohibit salespeople from steering customers toward goods or services they have reason to think will be bad for them. It is difficult to steer someone in this way without lying or deception, e.g., saying that you believe that a certain product is best for someone when you don't believe this to be the case. Similar remarks apply to selling defective goods. Often, it is impossible to do this without lying to or deceiving customers. In practice, most or many violations of rules 4 and 6 are also violations of rule 2.

A JUSTIFICATION FOR MY THEORY

Rules 1–4 yield intuitively plausible results in concrete cases and avoid all of the objections I raised against Holley. They can also be justified by appeal to the golden rule.

Taken together, rules 1–4 give us an intuitively plausible theory about the duties of salespeople regarding the disclosure of information; they give more acceptable results in actual cases than Holley's theory. They can account for cases in which the conduct of salespeople seems clearly wrong, e.g., cases of lying, deception, and steering customers into harmful decisions. Unlike Holley's theory, rules 1–4 do not make unreasonable demands on salespeople. They don't require that salespeople provide information that they don't have or spend more time with customers than they can spend. Nor do they require salespeople to divulge information about the virtues of what their competitors are selling.

In addition, my theory explains why different kinds of salespeople have different kinds of duties to their customers. For example, ordinarily, realtors have a duty to provide much more information to customers than sales clerks who sell inexpensive items in gift stores. My theory explains this difference in terms of the following:

1. the realtor's greater knowledge and expertise;

2. the much greater amount of time the realtor can devote to the customer;

3. the greater importance of the purchase of a home than the purchase of a small gift and the greater potential for harm or benefit to the buyer; and (in some cases)

4. implicit or explicit claims by the realtor to be acting on behalf of prospective home buyers (clerks in stores rarely make such claims).

The Golden Rule

I think that the golden rule is most plausibly construed as a consistency principle (those who violate the golden rule are guilty of inconsistency). The following version of the golden rule can be justified:

> GR. Consistency requires that if you think that it would be morally permissible for someone to do a certain act to another person, then you must consent to someone else doing the same act to you in relevantly similar circumstances.

How the Golden Rule Supports My Theory

Given this version of the golden rule, any rational and consistent moral judge who makes judgments about the moral obligations of salespeople will have to accept rules 1–4 as *prima facie* duties. Consider each duty in turn:

1. All of us have reason to fear the hazards about us in the world; we depend on others to warn us of those hazards. Few people would survive to adulthood were it not for the warnings of others about such things as oncoming cars, live electric wires, and approaching tornadoes. No one who values her own life can honestly say that she is willing to have others fail to warn her of dangers.

2. Like everyone else, a salesperson needs correct information in order to act effectively to achieve her goals and advance her interests. She is not willing to act on the basis of false beliefs. Consequently, she is not willing to have others deceive her or lie to her about matters relevant to her decisions in the marketplace. She is not willing to have members of other professions (such as law and medicine) make it a policy to deceive her or lie to her whenever they can gain financially from doing so.

3. Salespeople have questions about the goods and services they themselves buy. They can't say that they are willing to have others evade or refuse to answer those questions. We want our questions to be answered by salespeople or else we wouldn't ask them. We are not willing to have salespeople evade or refrain from answering our questions. (Digression. Rule 3 permits salespeople to refuse to answer questions that would force them to provide information about their competitors. Why should we say *this*? Why not say instead that salespeople are obligated to answer *all questions* that customers ask? The answer is as follows: A salesperson's actions affect *both* her customers and her employer. In applying the golden rule to this issue she can't simply ask what kind of information she would want were she in the customer's position [Holley poses the question in just this way]. Rule 3 can probably be improved upon, but it is a decent first approximation. A disinterested person who was not trying to give preference to the interests of salespeople, employers, or customers could endorse 3 as a policy for salespeople to follow. We can and must recognize the legitimacy of employers' demands for loyalty. The role of being an advocate or agent for someone who is selling things is legitimate within certain bounds— almost all of us are willing to have real estate agents work for us. A rational person could consent to the idea that everyone follow principles such as rule 3.)

4. All of us are capable of being manipulated by others into doing things that harm us, especially in cases in which others are more knowledgeable than we are. No one can consent to the idea that other people (or salespeople) should manipulate us into doing things that harm us whenever doing so is to their own advantage. Salespeople who claim that it would be permissible for them to make it a policy to deceive customers, fail to warn them about dangers, evade their questions, or manipulate them into doing things that are harmful to them whenever doing so is advantageous to them are inconsistent because they are not willing to have others do the same to them. They must allow that 1–4 are *prima facie* moral duties.

Rules 1–4 are only *prima facie* duties. The golden rule can account for the cases in which 1–4 are overridden by other more important duties. For example, we would be willing to have other people violate rules 1–4 if doing so were necessary in order to save the life of an innocent person. In practice, violating 1, 2, 3, or 4 is permissible only in very rare cases. The financial interests of salespeople seldom justify violations of 1, 2, 3, or 4. The fact that a salesperson can make more money by violating 1, 2, 3, or 4 would not justify her in violating any of these unless she has very pressing financial obligations that she cannot meet otherwise. Often, salespeople need to meet certain minimum sales quotas to avoid being fired. Suppose that a salesperson needs to make it a policy to violate 1–4 in order to met her sales quotas and keep her job. Would this justify her in violating 1–4? *Possibly.* But, in order for this to be the case, the following conditions would have to be met: a) she has important moral obligations such as feeding and housing her family that require her to be employed (needing money to keep one's family in an expensive house or take them to Disney World wouldn't justify violating 1–4); and b) she can't find another job that would enable her to meet her obligations without violating 1–4 (or other equally important duties). Those salespeople who can't keep their jobs or make an adequate income without violating 1–4 should seek other lines of employment.

A DEFENSE OF THE VERSION OF THE GOLDEN RULE EMPLOYED EARLIER

My argument is as follows:

1. Consistency requires that if you think that it would be morally permissible for someone to do a certain act to another person, then you must grant that it would be morally permissible for someone to do that same act to you in relevantly similar circumstances.

2. Consistency requires that if you think that it would be morally permissible for someone to do a certain act to you in certain circumstances, then you must *consent* to him/her doing that act to you in those circumstances.

Therefore,

> GR. Consistency requires that if you think that it would be morally permissible for someone to do a certain act to another person, then you must consent (not object to) someone doing the same act to you in relevantly similar circumstances. (You are inconsistent if you think that it would be morally permissible for someone to do a certain act to another person, but do not consent to someone doing the same act to you in relevantly similar circumstances.) (This argument follows the argument given by Gensler 89–90.)

This argument is valid, i.e., the conclusion follows from the premises, and both its premises are true. Both premises are consistency requirements. Premise 1 addresses questions about the consistency of a person's different moral beliefs. Premise 2 addresses questions about whether a person's moral beliefs are consistent with her attitudes and actions. Our attitudes and actions can be either consistent or inconsistent with the moral judgments we accept.

Premise 1

Premise 1 follows from, or is a narrower version of, the universalizability principle (UP). The UP can be stated as follows:

Consistency requires that, if one makes a moral judgment about a particular case, then one must make the same moral judgment about any similar case, unless there is a morally relevant difference between the cases.

Premise 1 is a principle of consistency for judgments about the moral permissibility of actions. The UP, by contrast, is a principle of consistency for *any kind of moral judgment,* including judgments about what things are good and bad.

Premise 2

How shall we understand what is meant by "consenting to" something? For our present purposes, we should not take consenting to something to be the same as desiring it or trying to bring it about. My thinking that it is morally permissible for you to beat me at chess does not commit me to desiring that you beat me, nor does it commit me to playing so as to allow you to beat me. Consenting to an action is more like not objecting to it, not criticizing, or not resenting the other person for doing it. If I think that it is permissible for you to beat me at chess then I cannot object to your beating me. I am inconsistent if I object to your doing something that I take to be morally permissible. If I claim that it is permissible for someone to do something to another person, then, on pain of inconsistency, I cannot object if someone else does the same thing to me in relevantly similar circumstances. The gist of my application of the golden rule to sales is that since we *do object* to salespeople doing such things as lying to us, deceiving us, and failing to answer our questions, we cannot consistently say that it is morally permissible for them to *do* these things.

EXAMPLES

I will discuss several cases to illustrate and clarify my theory.

Example A

I am selling a used car that I know has bad brakes; this is one of the reasons I am selling the car. You don't ask me any questions about the car, and I sell it to you without informing you of the problem with the brakes.

Example B

I am selling a used car that starts poorly in cold weather. You arrange to look at the car early in the morning on a very cold day. I don't own a garage so the car is out in the cold. With difficulty, I start it up and drive it for thirty minutes shortly before you look at it and then cover the car with snow to make it seem as if it hasn't been driven. The engine is still hot when you come and the car starts up immediately. You then purchase the car, remarking that you need a car that starts well in the cold to get to work, since you don't have a garage.

Example C

While working as a salesperson, I feign a friendly concern for a customer's interests. I say, "I will try to help you find the product that is best suited for your needs. I don't want you to spend any more money than you need to. Take as much time as you need." The customer believes me, but she is deceived. In fact, I couldn't care less about her welfare. I only want to sell her the highest priced item I can as quickly as I can. I don't like the customer; indeed, I am contemptuous of her.

In example A, I violate rule 1 and put the buyer and other motorists, passengers, and pedestrians at risk. In example B, I violate rules 2 and 5. In example C, I violate rule 2. In the absence of conflicting obligations that are at least as important as the rules I violate, my actions in cases A–C are morally wrong.

Example D: A Longer Case (an Actual Case)

In 1980, I received a one-year fellowship from The National Endowment for the Humanities. The fellowship paid for my salary, but not my fringe benefits. Someone in the benefits office of my university told me that I had the option of continuing my health insurance through the university if I paid for the premiums out of my own pocket. I told the benefits person that this was a lousy deal and that I could do better by going to a private insurance company. I went to the office of Prudential Insurance agent Mr. A. O. "Ed" Mokarem. I told him that I was looking for a one-year medical insurance policy to cover me during the period of the fellowship and that I planned to resume my university policy when I returned to teaching. (The university provided this policy free of charge to all faculty who were teaching.) He showed me a comparable Prudential policy that cost about half as much as the university's policy. He explained the policy to me. I asked him to fill out the forms so that I could purchase the policy. He then told me that there was a potential problem I should consider. He said roughly the following:

> You will want to return to your free university policy next year when you return to teaching. The Prudential policy is a one-year terminal policy. If you develop any serious medical problems during the next year, Prudential will probably consider you "uninsurable" and will not be willing to sell you health insurance in the future. If you buy the Prudential policy, you may encounter the same problems with your university policy. Since you will be dropping this policy *voluntarily*, they will have the right to underwrite your application for re-enrollment. If you develop a serious health problem during the next year, their underwriting decision could be "Total Rejection," imposing some waivers and/or exclusions, or (at best) subjecting your coverage to the "pre-existing conditions clause," which would not cover any pre-existing conditions until you have been covered under the new policy for at least a year.

If I left my current health insurance for a year, I risked developing a costly medical condition for which no one would be willing to insure me. That would have been a very foolish risk to take. So, I thanked him very much and, swallowing my pride, went back to renew my health insurance coverage through the university. I never bought any insurance from Mr. Mokarem and never had occasion to send him any business.

I have discussed this case with numerous classes through the years. It usually generates a lively discussion. Most of my students do not think that Mr. Mokarem was morally obligated to do what he did, but they don't think that what he did was wrong either—they regard his actions as supererogatory or above and beyond the call of duty.

My View About Example D On my theory, this is a difficult case to assess. If rules 1–4 are a salesperson's only duties concerning the disclosure of information, then Mr. Mokarem was not obligated to inform me as he did. (In this case, the information in question was information about a *competing product*—the university's health insurance policy.) If rule 5 is a *prima facie* duty of salespeople, then (assuming that he had no conflicting moral duties of greater or equal importance) it was his duty, all things considered, to inform me as he did. Since I am uncertain that 5 can be justified, I'm not sure whether or not Mr. Mokarem was obligated to do what he did or whether his actions were supererogatory. This case illustrates part of what is at stake in the question of whether rule 5 is a *prima facie* duty of salespeople.

Acknowledgments

This essay is a revised and abridged version of material from two earlier essays, "Deception and Withholding Information in Sales," *Business Ethics Quarterly* 11 (2001): 275–306, and "Ethical Issues in Selling and Advertising," *The Blackwell Guide to Business Ethics*, ed. Norman Bowie (Oxford: Blackwell, 2002), 186–205. Many thanks to Ivan Preston for his very generous and helpful advice and criticisms. Everyone interested in these topics should read his work.

References

Atiyah, P. S. (1979) *The Rise and Fall of Freedom of Contract*. Oxford: The Clarendon Press.

Carson, Thomas. (1988) "On the definition of lying: a reply to Jones and revisions." *Journal of Business Ethics*, 7: 509–14.

Carson, Thomas. (2001) "Deception and withholding information in sales." *Business Ethics Quarterly* 11: 275–306.

FTC policy statement on deception. (1983—still current) Available on the Web at: http://www.ftc.gov/bcp/guides/guides.htm then click on FTC Policy Statement on Deception.

Gensler, Harry. (1986) "A Kantian argument against abortion." *Philosophical Studies* 49: 83–98.

Holley, David. (1993) "A moral evaluation of sales practices." In Tom Beauchamp and Norman Bowie, eds., *Ethical Theory and Business*, fourth edition, 462–72. Englewood Cliffs, NJ: Prentice Hall.

Preston, Ivan. (1975) *The Great American Blow-Up: Puffery in Advertising and Selling.* Madison: University of Wisconsin Press, 1975.

Review and Discussion Questions

1. What's the difference between lying and deception? According to Carson, does withholding information constitute deception? What about concealing information?

2. What is the principle of *caveat emptor*? What is *merchantability*?

3. Holley writes that salespeople are required to avoid undermining the conditions of an acceptable exchange. What three conditions are necessary for an "acceptable exchange"?

4. Assess the three criticisms that Carson makes of Holley's theory. Do you find them persuasive?

5. According to Carson, what four duties do salespeople have? Explain how the Golden Rule supports these duties. Is Carson's interpretation of the Golden Rule the best way of understanding it? In your view, is the Golden Rule a basic principle of ethics? Explain why or why not. What implications does the Golden Rule have for salespeople?

6. Do Carson's duties 1 through 4 provide a more plausible account of the ethics of sales than Holley's theory does? Explain why or why not. Do you agree that the actions in examples A, B, and C are morally wrong?

7. Carson believes that he makes a strong case for duties 1 through 4, but that reasonable people can disagree about duties 5 and 6. In your view, do salespeople have duties 5 and 6? In example D, was Mr. Mokarem morally obligated to do what he did?

8. Do salespeople ever face ethical issues that Carson's theory doesn't answer? If so, give an example.

9. Have you encountered unethical conduct by a salesperson? Is such conduct widespread, or do most salespeople try to behave ethically? When salespeople do act unethically, what explains this, and what can be done about it?

Reading ———————————— ■

THE INCONCLUSIVE ETHICAL CASE AGAINST MANIPULATIVE ADVERTISING

MICHAEL J. PHILLIPS

Critics of advertising maintain that it manipulates our needs and fears, increasing our propensity to consume and swaying our individual purchasing decisions. Granting for the sake of argument that the critics of advertising are correct about its effectiveness, Michael J. Phillips, professor emeritus of business administration at Indiana University, assesses four possible attacks on manipulative advertising, each from a different ethical perspective: (1) that manipulative advertising has negative consequences for utility, (2) that it undermines personal autonomy, (3) that it violates Kant's categorical imperative, and (4) that it weakens the personal virtue of its practitioners and victims. After considering one final, partial defense of manipulative advertising, he concludes that although the practice is morally problematic, there is room for doubt about its badness and no completely definite basis for condemning it.

This essay explores the ethical implications of [the] perception that advertisers successfully "exploit and manipulate the vast range of human fears and needs." It begins by defining its sense of the term *manipulative advertising.* Then the essay asserts for purposes of argument that manipulative advertising actually works. Specifically, I make two controversial assumptions about such advertising: (1) that it plays a major role in increasing the general propensity to consume, and (2) that it powerfully influences individual consumer purchase decisions. With the deck thus stacked against manipulative advertising,

From *Business and Professional Ethics Journal* 13 (Winter 1994). Reprinted by permission of the author.

the essay goes on to inquire whether either assumption justifies its condemnation, by considering four ethical criticisms of manipulative advertising. Ethically, I conclude, manipulative advertising is a most problematic practice. If probabilistic assertions are valid in ethics, then the odds strongly favor the conclusion that manipulative advertising is wrong. Nevertheless, there still is room for doubt about its badness. Like the apparently easy kill that continually slips out of the hunter's sights, manipulative advertising evades the clean strike that would justify its condemnation for once and all.

WHAT IS MANIPULATIVE ADVERTISING?

. . . What, then, is manipulative advertising? . . . I define "manipulative advertising" as advertising that tries to favorably alter consumers' perceptions of the advertised product by appeals to factors other than the product's physical attributes and functional performance. There is no sharp line between such advertising and advertising that is nonmanipulative; even purely informative ads are unlikely to feature unattractive people and depressing surroundings. Nor is it clear what proportion of American advertising can fairly be classed as manipulative. Suffice it to say that that proportion almost certainly is significant. As we will see, advertising's critics sometimes seem to think that all of it is manipulative.

Perhaps the most common example of manipulative advertising is a technique John Waide (1987, 73–74) calls "associative advertising." Advertisers using this technique try to favorably influence consumer perceptions of a product by associating it with a nonmarket good (e.g., contentment, sex, vigor, power, status, friendship, or family) that the product ordinarily cannot supply on its own. By purchasing the product, their ads suggest, the consumer somehow will get the nonmarket good. Michael Schudson describes this familiar form of advertising as follows: "The ads say, typically, 'buy me and you will overcome the anxieties I have just reminded you about' or 'buy me and you will enjoy life' or 'buy me and be recognized as a successful person' or 'buy me and everything will be easier for you' or 'come spend a few dollars and share in this society of freedom, choice, novelty, and abundance'" (1986, 6). Through such linkages between product and nonmarket good, associative advertising seeks to increase the product's perceived value and thus to induce its purchase. Because these linkages (e.g., the connection between beer and attractive women) generally make little sense, such advertising is far removed from rational persuasion.

THE EFFECTS OF MANIPULATIVE ADVERTISING: WHAT THE CRITICS THINK

In the previous section, I tried to describe manipulative advertising in terms of sellers' *efforts,* rather than their actual accomplishments. But does manipulative advertising successfully influence consumers? As might be expected, advertising's critics generally answer this question in the affirmative. Perhaps the best-known example is chapter XI of John Kenneth Galbraith's *The Affluent Society,* where he described his well-known dependence effect.

Galbraith's dependence effect might be described as the way the process of consumer goods production creates and satisfies consumer wants (1958, 158). "That wants are, in fact, the fruit of production," he intoned, "will now be denied by few serious scholars" (154). In part, these wants result from emulation, as increased production means increased consumption for some, followed by even more consumption as others follow suit (154–55). But advertising and salesmanship provide an even more direct link between production and consumer wants. Those practices, Galbraith says:

> [C]annot be reconciled with the notion of independently determined desires, for their central function is to create desires. . . . This is accomplished by the producer of goods or at his behest. A broad empirical relationship exists between what is spent on production of consumers' goods and what is spent in synthesizing the desires for that production. A new consumer product must be introduced with a suitable advertising campaign to arouse an interest in it. The path for an expansion of output must be paved by a suitable expansion in the advertising budget. Outlays for the manufacturing of a product are not more important in the strategy of modern business

enterprise than outlays for the manufacturing of demand for the product. (155–56)

. . . To Galbraith, therefore, advertising in general is manipulative. In *The Affluent Society,* it apparently worked mainly to promote aggregate demand, rather than to shift demand from one brand to another. Many of advertising's critics follow Galbraith's lead by stressing how it socializes people to embrace consumerist values. . . .

From all this, it is a short step to the notion that advertising plays a major role in shaping and sustaining the modern society of material abundance. Implicitly, at least, some accounts of this kind liken society to a huge machine whose aim is the conversion of natural resources into consumer products. For the machine to work properly, its human components must be motivated to play their role in producing those products. This can be accomplished by: (1) implanting in people an intense desire for consumer goods, and (2) requiring that they do productive work to get the money to buy those goods. . . . Galbraith suggested that these social imperatives of production and consumption make the worker/consumer resemble a squirrel who races full-tilt to keep abreast of a wheel propelled by his own efforts (1958, 154, 159).

Although they naturally evaluate the matter differently, business leaders often second the argument that advertising is essential to prosperity. In . . . an exchange on advertising expenditures by the fast-food industry, William H. Genge, the chairman of Ketchum Communications' board, wrote:

> I regard the many millions of dollars spent by fast-food companies (and other retailers as well) as healthy and necessary stimulation of the consumption that makes our economy the most dynamic and productive in the world.
>
> Some people talk as though large advertising budgets are wasteful and nonproductive. It just takes one simple question to put that down. The question is: Where does the money go? The answer is: It provides jobs and livelihoods for hundreds of thousands of people—not only in the advertising and communications sector but for all the people employed by fast-food companies and, indeed, all marketing organizations. (1985, 58–59)

"So," Genge concluded, "large advertising expenditures are not a misallocation of economic resources. They are, in fact, an essential allocation and the driving force behind consumption, job creation, and prosperity" (59).

Advertising that is sufficiently manipulative to create a consumer society also might be able to determine consumers' individual purchase decisions. Most often, I suppose, these would be brand choices within a particular product category, although advertising might also steer people toward certain products and away from others. . . .

ASSUMPTIONS AND PLAN OF ATTACK

As we have just seen, many critics of advertising say that it socializes people to a life of consumption. And some regard it as a strong influence on individual brand or product decisions. However, these beliefs are not universally shared. Some students of advertising doubt that ads do much to dictate individual brand choices. And even if advertising strongly influences consumer decisions, it does not follow that any specific ad invariably compels the purchase of the product it touts. The reason is that a particular product advertisement is only one of many factors—especially competing advertisements—influencing consumers (Hayek 1961, 347). For the same general reason, it is difficult to assess advertising's role in making people lifetime consumers. . . .

Despite such difficulties, this essay assumes for the sake of argument that manipulative advertising really works. Thus, I assume that such advertising strongly influences individual purchase decisions, and that it plays a major role in producing consumerist attitudes among the populace. In neither case, however, do I wish to specify all the links in the causal chain through which manipulative advertising does its work. In particular, I make no assumptions about the personal traits that render consumers responsive to manipulative advertising. Later in the essay, for example, I consider the possibility that manipulative advertising succeeds because consumers want and need it.

Operating under the assumptions just stated, I now consider four possible ethical attacks on manipulative advertising. These are the claims that such advertising: (1) has negative consequences for utility, (2) undermines personal autonomy, (3) violates Kant's categorical imperative, and (4) weakens the personal virtue of its practitioners and its victims. I also consider one qualified defense of manipulative advertising: that even though no moral person would choose it were he writing on a clean slate, by now its elimination would be worse than its continuance.

For each attack on manipulative advertising, I assume the validity of the relevant moral value or ethical theory, thus precluding defenses of manipulative advertising that attack the value or theory itself. . . .

UTILITARIANISM

As just stated, this essay assumes that advertising can manipulate people in two distinct ways: (1) by socializing them to embrace consumerist values, and (2) by dictating individual purchase decisions. One important utilitarian criticism of manipulative advertising seems mainly to involve the first of these effects. Another implicates the second effect. . . . I now discuss each of these utilitarian attacks in turn. Throughout, I explicitly or implicitly compare my assumed world in which manipulative advertising exists and is effective with a world in which all advertising is merely informative.

The Implications of the Dependence Effect

The Affluent Society marked Galbraith's arrival as a critic of consumer society and its works. For his critique to be persuasive, he had to counter the argument that America's enormous production of consumer goods is justified because people want, enjoy, and demand them. This required that he undermine at least two widespread beliefs: (1) that consumer desires are genuinely autonomous, and (2) that they produce significant satisfactions. As we saw earlier, he attacked the first assumption by maintaining that consumer wants are created by the productive process through which they are satisfied, with advertising serving as the main generator of those wants. This argument would have enabled Galbraith to contend that advertising is bad because it denies autonomy, but he seemed not to emphasize that point. Instead, he maintained that the satisfaction of advertising-induced desires generates little additional utility. His argument was that if advertising is needed to arouse consumer wants, they cannot be too strong. "The fact that wants can be synthesized by advertising, catalyzed by salesmanship, and shaped by the discreet manipulations of the persuaders shows that they are not very urgent. A man who is hungry need never be told of his need for food" (1958, 158).

As a result, Galbraith continued, one cannot assume that the increased production characterizing the modern affluent society generates corresponding increases in utility. Instead, as he summarizes the matter:

> [O]ur concern for goods . . . does not arise in spontaneous consumer need. Rather, the dependence effect means that it grows out of the process of production itself. If production is to increase, the wants must be effectively contrived. In the absence of the contrivance the increase would not occur. This is not true of all goods, but that it is true of a substantial part is sufficient. It means that since the demand for this part would not exist, were it not contrived, its utility or urgency, ex contrivance, is zero. If we regard this production as marginal, we may say that the marginal utility of present aggregate output, ex advertising and salesmanship, is zero. (160)

Because wants must be contrived for production to increase, on Galbraith's assumptions production would be lower were advertising completely informative. Since on those assumptions that contrived production generates little additional utility, however, the loss would not be much felt. Indeed, with resources shifted away from advertising and consumption and toward activities that improve the quality of our lives, overall utility might well grow in manipulative advertising's absence.

Galbraith's basic argument was that because consumer wants are contrived, they are not urgent; and that because they are not urgent, their satisfaction does not generate much utility. One way to attack his argument is to maintain that consumer desires really do arise from within the individual, but my two assumptions foreclose that possibility here. Another is to follow the lead established by Friedrich Hayek's 1961 critique of Galbraith's dependence ef-

fect. To Hayek, Galbraith's argument involves a massive non sequitur: the attempt to reason from a desire's origin outside the individual to its unimportance (1961, 346–47). If that assertion were valid, he thought, it would follow that "the whole cultural achievement of man is not important" (346).

> Surely an individual's want for literature is not original with himself in the sense that he would experience it if literature were not produced. Does this mean that the production of literature cannot be defended as satisfying a want because it is only the production which provokes the demand? In this, as in the case of all cultural needs, it is unquestionably, in Professor Galbraith's words, "the process of satisfying the wants that creates the wants." (347)

Presumably, the same general point applies to utility-maximization. Just because product desire A originated within Cal Consumer while product desire B came his way through manipulative advertising, it does not follow that satisfying desire A would give him more utility than satisfying desire B. Indeed, as we will see presently, the opposite may be true.

The Frustration of Rational Interbrand Choices

The second major utilitarian objection to manipulative advertising concerns its power to distort consumer choices among brands and products. As R. M. Hare once observed:

> [T]he market economy is only defensible if it really does . . . lead to the maximum satisfaction of the preferences of the public. And it will not do this if it is distorted by various well-known undesirable practices. . . . By bringing it about that people decide on their purchases . . . after being deceived or in other ways manipulated, fraudulent advertisers impair the wisdom of the choices that the public makes and so distort the market in such a way that it does not function to maximize preference-satisfactions. (Hare 1984, 27–28)

For example, now suppose that Cal Consumer's preferences would find their optimum satisfaction in Product A. Intoxicated by Product B's manipulative advertising, Cal instead buys that product, which satisfies his original preferences less well than Product A. If Cal would have bought Product A in a regime where advertising is purely informative, presumably B's manipulative advertising cost him some utility.

The previous argument, however, might fail if manipulative advertising gives consumers satisfactions that they would not otherwise obtain from their purchases. In that event, the utility lost when manipulative advertising causes consumers to choose the wrong product for their needs must be weighed against the utility consumers gain from such advertising. Due to the inherent uncertainty of utility calculations, it may be unclear which effect would predominate. Sometimes, though, the gains could outweigh the losses: that is, manipulative advertising could generate more utility than purely informative advertising.

But how can "manipulated" desires and purchases generate more utility than their "rational" counterparts? One answer emerges from the dark masterpiece of the literature on manipulative advertising—Theodore Levitt's 1970 contribution to the *Harvard Business Review*. Levitt's main thesis is that "embellishment and distortion are among advertising's legitimate and socially desirable purposes" (Levitt 1970, 85). His determinedly nonlinear argument for that conclusion may be regarded as proceeding through several steps. The first is his assertion that when seen without illusions, human life is a poor thing. Natural reality, Levitt insists, is "crudely fashioned"; "crude, drab, and generally oppressive"; and "drab, dull, [and] anguished" (86, 90). For this reason, people try to transcend it whenever they can. "Everyone everywhere wants to modify, transform, embellish, enrich, and reconstruct the world around him—to introduce into an otherwise harsh or bland existence some sort of purposeful and distorting alleviation" (87). People do so mainly through artistic endeavor, but also through advertising. "[W]e use art, architecture, literature, and the rest, and advertising as well, to shield ourselves, in advance of experience, from the stark and plain reality in which we are fated to live" (90). Thus, "[m]any of the so-called distortions of advertising, product design, and packaging may be viewed as a paradigm of the many responses that man makes to the conditions of survival in the environment" (90).

From all this, it follows that consumers demand more than "pure operating functionality" from the products they buy (89). As Charles Revson of Revlon, Inc. once said: "In the factory we make cosmetics; in the store we sell hope" (85). Thus, "[i]t is not cosmetic chemicals women want, but the seductive charm promised by the alluring symbols with which these chemicals have been surrounded—hence the rich and exotic packages in which they are sold, and the suggestive advertising with which they are promoted" (85). In other words, consumers demand an expanded notion of functionality which includes "'non-mechanical' utilities," and do so to "help . . . solve a problem of life" (89). Therefore, "the product" they buy includes not only narrowly functional attributes, but also the emotional or affective content produced by its packaging and advertising. "The promises and images which imaginative ads and sculptured packages induce in us are as much the product as the physical materials themselves. . . . [T]hese ads and packagings describe the product's fullness for us; in our minds, the product becomes a complex abstraction which is . . . the conception of a perfection which has not yet been experienced" (89–90). . . .

To Levitt, therefore, we do not merely buy a physical product, but also a set of positive feelings connected with it by advertising. If his argument is sound, those feelings give us extra utility above and beyond the utility we get from the product's performance of its functions. This extra utility might well outweigh the utility we lose because manipulative advertising has made us buy a product that is suboptimum in purely functional terms and that we would not have bought were advertising only informative.

Is Levitt's argument sound? Although his description may not apply to all people, or even to most, it hardly seems ridiculous. People who object to Levitt's contention that human life is crude, drab, and dull should recall that he is speaking of a human life we infrequently experience—human life absent the embellishments all civilizations try to give it. If his contention is correct, the need to transcend our natural condition is an obvious motive for those embellishments. John Waide, however, insists that our need for embellishment can be satisfied without manipulative advertising—through, for example, ideals, fantasies, heroes, and dreams (Waide 1987, 76). But why assume this? If the need for comforting illusions is strong and pervasive, why should embellishment not extend to the products people buy?

Bigger problems, however, arise from Levitt's assumption that consumers are aware of advertising's illusions. If people know that advertising lies, how can they derive much psychic benefit—i.e., much utility—from its embellishments? Worse yet, products tend not to deliver on manipulative advertising's promises of sex, status, security, and the like. When this is so, how can such advertising deliver much utility to the consumers it controls (cf. Waide 1987, 75)? Indeed, the gap between manipulative advertising's implicit promises and its actual performance may lead to frustrated expectations and significant *dis*utility.

Recall, however, that for Levitt consumers want and need to be manipulated because life without advertising's illusions is too much to bear. If so, it is unlikely that everyone would be *continuously* aware of advertising's illusions and the low chance of their realization. Only intermittently, in other words, would people assume a tough-minded, rational-actor mentality toward advertising. On other occasions, some would effectively suspend disbelief in advertising's embellishments. Although they might retain latent knowledge of those illusions, that knowledge would not be constantly present to their consciousness. And when the illusions rule, they could generate real satisfactions.

Are these assumptions about consumers realistic ones? To me, they are plausible as applied to some people some of the time. . . . There . . . is nothing ridiculous in assuming that people gain utility by accepting advertising's illusions, while retaining some latent and/or intermittent knowledge of their condition. . . .

AUTONOMY

All things considered, the utilitarian arguments against manipulative advertising are unimpressive. Indeed, utilitarianism might even support that practice. Galbraith claimed that little utility is generated when we satisfy contrived wants. But the connection between a desire's origin outside the individual and the low utility resulting from its satisfaction is unclear. At first glance, it appears that manipulative

advertising robs consumers of utility by inducing them to buy functionally suboptimal products. But while this may be true, the resulting utility losses arguably are counterbalanced by the utility people gain from manipulative advertising. . . .

The Autonomy–Related Objection to Manipulative Advertising

To some people, however, the preceding points may say more about utilitarianism's deficiencies than about manipulative advertising's worth. One standard criticism of utilitarianism emphasizes its indifference to the moral quality of the means by which utility is maximized. Thus, even if manipulative advertising increases consumers' utility, it is bad because it does so by suppressing their ability to make intelligent, self-directed product choices on the basis of their own values and interests. In a word, manipulative advertising now seems objectionable because it denies personal *autonomy*.

Among the many strands within the notion of autonomy, one of the most common equates it with self-government or self-determination. According to Steven Lukes, for example, autonomy is "self-direction"; the autonomous person's "thought and action are his own, and [are] not determined by agencies or causes outside his control" (Lukes 1973, 52). At the social level, Lukes adds, an individual is autonomous "to the degree to which he subjects the pressures and norms with which he is confronted to conscious and critical evaluation, and forms intentions and reaches practical decisions as the result of independent and rational reflection" (52).

If manipulative advertising has the effects this essay assumes, it apparently denies autonomy to the individuals it successfully controls. On this essay's assumptions, people become consumers and make product choices precisely through "agencies and causes outside [their] control," and not through "conscious and critical evaluation" or "independent and rational reflection." To Lippke [1990], moreover, advertising also has an "implicit content" that further suppresses autonomy. Among other things, this implicit content causes people to accept emotionalized, superficial, and oversimplified claims; desire ease and gratification rather than austerity and self-restraint;

let advertisers dictate the meaning of the good life; defer to their peers; and think that consumer products are a means for acquiring life's nonmaterial goods (44–47). People so constituted are unlikely to be independent, self-governing agents who subject all social pressures to an internal critique. Nor is it likely that they would have much resistance to manipulative appeals to buy particular products.

Are Consumers Autonomous on Levitt's Assumptions?

On Levitt's assumptions, however, perhaps consumers do act autonomously when they submit to manipulative advertising. If Levitt is correct: (1) manipulative advertising works much as its critics say that it works; because (2) consumers suspend disbelief in its claims and embrace its illusions; because (3) they want, need, and demand those illusions to cope with human existence; while (4) nonetheless knowing on some level that those illusions indeed are illusions. In sum, one might say, advertising manipulates consumers because they knowingly and rationally want to be manipulated. That is, they half-consciously sacrifice their autonomy for reasons that make some sense on Levitt's assumptions about human life. In still other words, they more or less autonomously relinquish their autonomy. . . .

Levitt's argument, however, appears to concern only individual purchase decisions, and not advertising's assumed ability to socialize people to accept consumerism and reject autonomy. But his argument is broad enough to explain this second process. On Levitt's assumptions, people would more or less knowingly embrace consumerism because unfiltered reality is too much to bear, and would reject autonomy in favor of Lippke's "implicit content" because autonomy offers too little payoff at too much cost. If those assumptions are accurate, moreover, people arguably have sound reasons for behaving in these ways. . . .

THE CATEGORICAL IMPERATIVE

One problem with some of the claims discussed thus far is that they present difficult empirical issues. This is plainly true of Levitt's claims. It also is true of Gal-

braith's assertion that because advertising-induced wants originate outside the individual, they have low urgency and therefore generate little utility when they are satisfied. The same can be said of Hayek's response to Galbraith. Given these problems, maybe manipulative advertising is best addressed by ethical theories whose conclusions do not depend on empirical matters such as consumer psychology, or on manipulation's consequences for utility. Kant's categorical imperative is an obvious candidate.

R. M. Hare made two Kantian arguments against manipulative advertising. "Kantians will say . . . that to manipulate people is not to treat them as ends—certainly not as autonomous legislating members of a kingdom of ends. . . . But even apart from that it is something that we prefer not to happen to us and therefore shall not will it as a universal maxim" (Hare 1984, 28). His reference, of course, was to the two major formulations of Kant's categorical imperative. The first, which comes in several versions, underlies Hare's second argument. The version employed here goes as follows: "Act only on that maxim through which you can at the same time will that it should become a universal law" (Kant 1964, 88). According to the second major formulation of the imperative, one must "[a]ct in such a way that you always treat humanity, whether in your own person or in the person of any other, never simply as a means, but always at the same time as an end" (96).

Under either formulation of the imperative, it seems, manipulative advertising stands condemned. Under the first formulation, it seems difficult to identify a maxim that would: (1) clearly justify manipulative advertising, and (2) be universalized by any advertiser. Consider, for example, the following possibility: "In order to induce purchases and make money, business people can use advertising tactics that undermine the rational evaluation and choice of products by associating them with desired states to which they have little or no real relation." Presumably, no one would will the maxim's universalization, because to do so is to waive any moral objection to manipulative advertising aimed at oneself. Manipulative advertising apparently fares even worse under the second statement of the categorical imperative. As James Rachels has noted, under this formulation "we may never *manipulate* people, or *use* people, to achieve our purposes" (Rachels 1993, 129). Instead, we should respect their rational nature by giving them the information that will enable them to make informed, autonomous decisions (Rachels 1993, 129–30). As the term *manipulative advertising* suggests, businesses that employ it to generate sales obviously try to use people as means to their own ends, and do so precisely by undermining their rationality and their ability to make informed, autonomous decisions.

Even in the Kantian realm, however, empirical concerns intrude. Suppose again that Levitt is right in claiming that people want and need manipulative advertising. Given this assumption, the relevant maxim becomes something like the following: "In order to induce purchases and make money, people can use manipulative advertising tactics that undermine the rational evaluation and choice of products and services, but only when such advertising tactics liberate consumers from their dark, stark, and depressing natural existence." Although I cannot speak for everyone (or for Kant), I might will this maxim's universalization if I found Levitt's conception of the human condition at all plausible. This illustrates a common criticism of the first formulation of the categorical imperative: that one can manipulate the imperative to get the results one wishes by framing the maxim appropriately.

Even if Levitt's account is perfectly accurate, however, the second major statement of the imperative still creates problems for manipulative advertising. Here, the question seems to boil down to the following: are firms that employ manipulative advertising using a consumer merely as a means to their own ends and therefore violating the imperative if the consumer, in effect, needs and wants to be manipulated? If, as I suggested earlier, the suspension of disbelief required for one to accept manipulative advertising may be more or less reasonable, then advertisers conceivably *are* respecting consumers' rationality by providing them with product-related illusions. . . .

VIRTUE ETHICS

Earlier I depicted Galbraith as a utilitarian, but other moral aspirations probably were at work within *The Affluent Society*. The book opened with the following quotation from Alfred Marshall: "The economist, like everyone else, must concern himself with the ultimate aims of man." Galbraith's conviction that consumerism does not rank high among those aims pervades much of his writing, and almost certainly informed his critique of advertising. However, the ethical values and theories previously considered in this essay do not state and enjoin the desirable substantive conditions of human life. . . .

Waide's alternative to such approaches is to examine "the virtues and vices at stake" in manipulative advertising (1987, 73), and to see "what kind of lives are sustained" by it (77). Stanley Benn sounds the same note when he suggests that the key question about advertising is whether it promotes "a valuable kind of life," with this determination depending on "some objective assessment of what constitutes excellence in human beings" (1967, 273). Because manipulative advertising encourages advertisers to ignore the well-being of their targets and encourages those targets to neglect the cultivation of nonmarket goods, Waide concludes that it makes us less virtuous persons and therefore is morally objectionable (1987, 74–75). Many other critics of advertising make the same general point. . . . Heilbroner called advertising "perhaps the single most value-destroying activity of a business civilization," due to the "subversive influence of the relentless effort to persuade people to change their lifeways, not out of any knowledge of, or deeply held convictions about, the 'good life,' but merely to sell whatever article or service is being pandered" (1976, 113–14). His main specific complaint is that by offering a constant stream of half-truths and deceptions, advertising makes "cynics of us all" (114). Virginia Held makes a related point when she criticizes advertising for undermining intellectual and artistic integrity (1984, 64–66).

To Christopher Lasch, on the other hand, advertising's greatest evil may be its tendency to leave consumers "perpetually unsatisfied, restless, anxious, and bored" (1978, 72). . . . One suspects that Lasch might reject advertising's consequences as inherently bad even if they did mark an increase in utility. The same probably holds for most of advertising's cultural critics. As a group, Michael Schudson remarks, they see "the emergence of a consumer culture as a devolution of manners, morals and even manhood, from a work-oriented production ethic of the past to the consumption, 'lifestyle'-obsessed, ethic-less pursuits of the present" (1986, 6–7).

Uniting all these varied criticisms of advertising is the notion that it promotes substantive behaviors, experiences, and states of character which are inherently undesirable, and that it is morally objectionable for this reason. . . . This essay assumes that manipulative advertising both creates a consumer culture and strongly influences individual purchase decisions. Its main means for accomplishing the second aim (and perhaps the first) is to associate the product with such nonmarket goods as sex, status, and power. On those assumptions, manipulative advertising almost certainly undermines such standard virtues as honesty and benevolence in its practitioners, and arguably dilutes its targets' moderation, reasonableness, self-control, self-discipline, and self-reliance (Rachels 1993, 163 [listing these virtues]). . . .

MANIPULATIVE ADVERTISING'S LAST DEFENSE

All things considered, virtue ethics appears to be the best basis for attacking manipulative advertising. In particular, it seems to dispose of a defense that has plagued our other three attacks on such advertising: Levitt's claim that people want and need advertising's illusions and therefore more or less knowingly and willingly embrace it. Like our other bases for attacking manipulative advertising, however, virtue ethics is not assumed to be an absolute. This might mean that the claims of virtue would have to give way if human beings simply could not endure without advertising's illusions or if its psychic satisfactions give people enormous amounts of utility.

In any event, there is yet another possible defense of manipulative advertising. This defense is mainly utilitarian, but it also implicates my other three ethical criteria to some degree. It arises because by hypothesis all my criteria must be weighed against competing moral claims. The defense does

not so much challenge the assertion that manipulative advertising is bad, as argue that it is the lesser of two evils.

Throughout this essay, I have assumed for the sake of argument that manipulative advertising's critics are correct in their assessment of its effects. As we have seen, these people usually maintain that manipulative advertising plays an important role in socializing people to consume. This means that on the critics' view of things, manipulative advertising is central to the functioning of modern consumer society. But if manipulative advertising is central to the system's operation, how safely can it be condemned? Assuming that the condemnation is effective, manipulative advertising disappears, and all advertising becomes informative, people gradually would be weaned from their consumerist ways. This is likely to create social instability, with a more authoritarian form of government the likely end result. That, in turn, could well mean an environment in which aggregate utility is lower than it is today, human autonomy and rational nature are less respected, and/or the virtues less recognized.

One set of reasons for these conclusions is largely economic. If people become less consumerist as manipulative advertising leaves the scene, aggregate demand and economic output should decline. At first glance, this would seem to be of little consequence because by hypothesis people would value material things less. The problem is that the economic losses probably will be unevenly distributed: for example, some businesses will fail and some will not, and some people will lose their jobs while others stay employed. These inequalities are a potential source of social instability. Both to redress them and to preserve order, government is likely to intervene. This may involve a significant increase in outright governmental coercion. . . .

To my knowledge, Waide is the only business ethicist to raise these kinds of problems, and he finds himself without a solution to them. Because "[i]t seems unlikely that [manipulative] advertising will end suddenly," however, Waide is "confident that we will have the time and the imagination to adapt our economy to do without it" (1987, 77). Although I suspect that Waide is too optimistic, I have no solution to the dilemma either. Thus, I am left with the unsatisfactory conclusion that while various moral arguments may provide sound bases for attacking manipulative advertising, prudential considerations dictate that none of them be pressed too vigorously. Manipulative advertising's ultimate justification, in other words, may be its status as a necessary evil.

CONCLUDING REMARKS

For all the preceding reasons, it seems that there is no completely definitive basis for condemning manipulative advertising. But this obviously is not to say that the practice is morally unproblematic. Of my four suggested attacks on the practice, virtue ethics seems the strongest, with Kantianism a close second, autonomy third, and utilitarianism last. Indeed, utilitarianism may even support manipulative advertising. The main reason is that the practice's three most important defenses—Levitt's argument, the assertion that there is little connection between a want's origin outside the individual and the benefit resulting from its satisfaction, and manipulative advertising's centrality to our economic system—are more or less utilitarian in nature.

Except perhaps for hard-core utilitarians, therefore, manipulative advertising actually works. Specifically, I assumed that such advertising is a morally dubious practice. However, this conclusion may depend heavily on a critical assumption made earlier: that manipulative advertising: (1) socializes people to adopt a consumerist lifestyle, and (2) strongly influences individual purchase decisions. But what happens if, by and large, each assumption is untrue?

On first impressions, at least, it appears that if manipulative advertising is inefficacious, utilitarianism, autonomy, and virtue ethics largely cease to be bases for criticizing it. . . .

However, Kantian objections to manipulative advertising might well remain even if it is inefficacious. On that assumption, admittedly, perhaps one would will the universalization of a maxim permitting such advertising. If manipulative advertising simply fails to work, moreover, maybe it does not treat consumers merely as means to advertisers' ends. But such arguments ignore the strong anti-consequentialism of Kant's ethics, which arguably

renders advertising's ineffectiveness irrelevant. More importantly, those arguments ignore Kant's stress on the motives with which people should act. The only thing that is unqualifiedly good, Kant says, is a good will; and the good will is good not because of what it accomplishes, but simply because it wills the good (Kant 1964, 61–62). Even if manipulative advertising is unsuccessful, advertisers presumably try to make it work. Unless they believe that their efforts would benefit consumers in the end, it is unlikely that they are acting with a good will when they devise and employ their stratagems.

At a first cut, therefore, it seems that if manipulative advertising is ineffective, the only significant ethical objections to it are Kantian. (To these we might add the money wasted on the practice, as well as its effect on the virtue of its practitioners.) For those inclined to ignore Kantian objections, therefore, it seems that manipulative advertising's rightness or wrongness depends less on ethical theory than on empirical questions within the purview of the social sciences. . . . As the preceding discussion suggests, the most important such question is the extent to which manipulative advertising actually affects purchase decisions and socializes people to consume. Even if manipulative advertising actually has those effects, other more or less empirical issues would remain. These include the validity of Levitt's arguments, Galbraith's asserted connection between a desire's origin outside the individual and the low utility resulting from its satisfaction, and manipulative advertising's contribution to gross domestic product. All these questions, I submit, are unlikely to be answered any time soon. . . .

References

Benn, S. (1967) "Freedom and persuasion." *The Australasian Journal of Philosophy* 45: 259–75.

Galbraith, J. K. (1958) *The Affluent Society* (Boston: Houghton Mifflin).

Genge, W. (1985) "Ads stimulate the economy." *Business and Society Review* 1, no. 55: 58–59.

Hare, R. M. (1984) "Commentary." *Business and Professional Ethics Journal* 3, nos. 3 & 4: 23–28.

Hayek, F. A. (1961) "The *non sequitur* of the 'dependence effect.'" *Southern Economic Journal* 27: 346–48.

Heilbroner, R. (1976) *Business Civilization in Decline* (New York: W. W. Norton).

Held, V. (1984) "Advertising and program content." *Business and Professional Ethics Journal* 3, nos. 3 & 4: 61–76.

Kant, I. (1964) *Groundwork of the Metaphysic of Morals* (New York: Harper Torchbook, H. J. Paton tr.).

Lasch, C. (1978) *The Culture of Narcissism: American Life in An Age of Diminishing Expectations* (New York: W. W. Norton).

Levitt, T. (1970). "The morality (?) of advertising." *Harvard Business Review* (July–August): 84–92.

Lippke, R. (1990) "Advertising and the social conditions of autonomy." *Business and Professional Ethics Journal* 8, no. 4: 35–58.

Lukes, S. (1973) *Individualism* (Oxford: Basil Blackwell).

Rachels, J. (1993) *The Elements of Moral Philosophy* (New York: McGraw-Hill, 2nd ed.).

Schudson, M. (1986). *Advertising, the Uneasy Persuasion: Its Dubious Impact on American Society* (New York: Basic Books, 2nd ed.).

Waide, J. (1987) "The making of self and world in advertising." *Journal of Business Ethics* 6, no. 2: 73–79.

Review and Discussion Questions

1. What is "manipulative advertising"? What is "associative advertising"? Give examples of advertisements that you consider manipulative. Does advertising socialize people to a life of consumption? To what extent does it influence or even dictate our individual brand and product choices?

2. Assess Galbraith's contention that because advertising induces or creates consumer wants, those wants are not urgent and their satisfaction does not generate much utility.

3. Is Levitt correct that consumers need and want the illusions of advertising? Is it true that as consumers we are buying not only a physical product, but also a set of positive feelings connected with it by advertising? Do you agree with Levitt that "embellishment and distortion are among advertising's legitimate and socially desirable purposes"? Do the promises and images of advertising bring us genuine satisfaction?

4. Hare advances two Kantian arguments against manipulative advertising (based on different ways of formulating Kant's categorical imperative). What are they?

5. Assuming that manipulative advertising is effective, does it undermine one's autonomy? Does it promote undesirable behaviors and character traits, as the virtue-ethics critique alleges?

6. Assess the argument that manipulative advertising is a necessary evil because it is central to the continued functioning of our socioeconomic system. In your view, does advertising play a positive or negative role in our society?

7. Is manipulative advertising wrong? What do you see as the strongest ethical argument against it? Suppose manipulative advertising doesn't work. Would it still be wrong?

Further Reading for Chapter 10

Robert L. Arrington, "Advertising and Behavior Control," *Journal of Business Ethics* 1 (February 1982); **John Waide**, "The Making of Self and World in Advertising," *Journal of Business Ethics* 6 (February 1987); **Roger Crisp**, "Persuasive Advertising, Autonomy, and the Creation of Desire," *Journal of Business Ethics* 6 (July 1987); **Richard L. Lippke**, "Advertising and the Social Conditions of Autonomy," *Business and Professional Ethics Journal* 8 (Winter 1989); and **Andrew Gustafson**, "Advertising's Impact on Morality in Society: Influencing Habits and Desires of Consumers," *Business and Society Review* 106 (Fall 2001) are valuable, philosophical discussions of advertising.

Joseph R. DesJardins and **John J. McCall**, eds., *Contemporary Issues in Business Ethics,* 4th ed. (Belmont, Calif.: Wadsworth, 2000) contains important and useful essays on product liability, consumer regulation, advertising and free speech, subliminal advertising, and advertising to children, among other issues.

David M. Holley, "A Moral Evaluation of Sales Practices," *Business and Professional Ethics Journal* 5 (Fall 1987) is a seminal discussion of the ethics of sales. Holley revisits the subject in "Information Disclosure in Sales," *Journal of Business Ethics* 17 (April 1998) and replies to Thomas L. Carson in "Alternative Approaches to Applied Ethics: A Response to Carson's Critique," *Business Ethics Quarterly* 12 (January 2002).

Gene R. Laczniak and **Patrick E. Murphy,** *Ethical Marketing Decisions* (Boston: Allyn and Bacon, 1993) is an informative survey of a wide range of issues in marketing ethics.

Juliet Schor, *Do Americans Shop Too Much?* (Boston: Beacon Press, 2000) is a provocative essay on contemporary consumerism, followed by nine responses to Schor by other writers.

N. Craig Smith and **John A. Quelch,** *Ethics in Marketing* (Homewood, Ill.: Irwin, 1993) contains informative essays and case studies on all aspects of marketing ethics.

Manuel G. Velasquez, *Business Ethics,* 5th ed. (Upper Saddle River, N.J.: Prentice Hall, 2002), and **John R. Boatright,** *Ethics and the Conduct of Business,* 4th ed. (Upper Saddle River, N.J.: Prentice Hall, 2003) provide good discussions of consumer issues.

InfoTrac College Edition: For further information or to conduct research, please go to www.infotrac-college.com.

11

The Environment

In feeding, clothing, and sheltering ourselves and in manufacturing and consuming countless different kinds of products, human beings have scarred the globe, contaminated the natural environment, and gobbled up the earth's resources. The effects of this environmental recklessness are now coming home to roost. Our rivers and lakes are dirty, and our air is unclean. The planet is warming, its protective ozone fraying. Lush forests are disappearing, and with them countless species of plants and animals. As our numbers have multiplied, half the world's wetlands have disappeared. Eighty percent of its grasslands now suffer from soil degradation; 20 percent of its drylands are in danger of turning into deserts, and groundwater is seriously depleted. As a result, the earth is losing its capacity to continue to provide the goods we need, threatening our economic well-being and ultimately our survival—so concludes a mammoth United Nations Assessment of global ecosystems.[1]

The environment is a huge topic, but as one expert remarks, "the concerns of environmental ethics might begin with the food on our plate."[2] This is because with fertilizers, herbicides, and pesticides, agriculture uses hundreds of chemicals in crop production. Although chemically intensive agriculture has yielded many benefits, it is hard on the environment—both in terms of what it consumes and in its impact on the surrounding ecosystem. In addition to the ecological price we pay for what we eat, there is the risk of chemical residues left in food.

In the United States pesticide use has doubled in the past thirty years and poses a greater danger than most people realize.[3] Because of exposure to pesticides, many fish and birds in the Great Lakes region have lost their ability to reproduce. After a pesticide spilled into Florida's Lake Apopka, alligators were born with half-sized penises. When laboratory rats were fed DDT, they developed genital abnormalities. Now researchers believe that by mimicking estrogen and testosterone, the chemicals in pesticides may threaten human reproduction by disrupting the endocrine system that regulates it. These "endocrine disrupters" may explain certain disturbing reproductive problems now being seen in human beings: a rise in breast cancer rates, a drop in sperm count, and an increase in the incidence of testicular cancer.[4] The pesticide problem is even more alarming when we consider children. Because they have smaller bodies and different eating patterns than adults, children's exposure to carcinogens and neurotoxins can be hundreds of times what is safe for them.[5] Yet until recently, the Environmental Protection Agency (EPA) set the legal limits on the amount of pesticide residues allowed to remain on food with adults in mind.

The contaminants that infiltrate the food chain can also spread into our water. Toxic chemicals used in farming can and do run off into underground reservoirs, a major source of drinking water. In 1972, Congress passed the Clean Water Act, which proclaimed the goal of eliminating all water pollution by 1985. Since Congress acted, billions have been spent on pollution control. Some streams and lakes have improved; others have gotten worse. On average, though, according to government figures, water quality hasn't changed much.

Pollutants also contaminate the air we breathe, despoiling vegetation and crops, corroding construction materials, and threatening our lives and health. Although precise figures are impossible to obtain, there is little doubt that air pollution is responsible for thousands of deaths and millions of sick days every year because of air-related ailments such as asthma, emphysema, and lung cancer. Moreover, pregnant women living in regions with high levels of air pollution are up to three times more likely to give birth to children with serious heart defects.[6] According to a congressional survey of toxic air pollution, 2.4 billion pounds of hazardous pollutants are emitted into the air each year, including tons of toxic chemicals that can cause cancer and damage the nervous system.[7] These figures don't include emissions of nontoxic substances such as sulfur and nitrogen oxides that are a major source of acid rain and of the smog that blankets so many U.S. cities. And the figures also omit fine-particle pollution—dust, soot, smoke, and tiny droplets of acid—a form of air pollution that the EPA began to regulate only in 1997. Yet recent studies conclude that fine-particle pollution causes 15,000 premature deaths every year.[8]

Thanks to the groundbreaking Clean Air Act of 1970, our air is better than it would otherwise have been, and by some measures it is better than it was thirty years ago. In particular, by banning lead as a fuel additive in gasoline, the act has reduced its presence in the air by nearly 90 percent. And the Clean Air Act Amendments of 1990 require new measures to be taken to fight smog, acid rain, and toxic emissions. But the fact remains: More than three decades after Congress first set a strict deadline for reducing air pollution to safe levels, the air in more than fifty U.S. cities remains a health risk.

Related to the problem of atmospheric pollution is the issue of global warming. After years of study and debate, there is now a scientific consensus that human activity is indeed heating up the planet.[9] As we burn coal, oil, and gasoline for heat, electricity, and transportation, carbon dioxide (CO_2) is released into the atmosphere, trapping excess energy from the sun and warming the globe—the so-called greenhouse effect. The evidence of global warming is all around us. The past decade has been the hottest on record; in the Northern Hemisphere, spring now comes, on average, a week earlier than it used to. Storms have become more intense and weather patterns more erratic. Only by drastically reducing the consumption of fossil fuels can we hope to slow down this trend and stabilize the climate at current levels of disruption.

Surprisingly, one of the largest sources of pollution is not all that exotic—namely, the animals we raise for food. In fact, the ecological costs of producing beef, poultry, and pork are second only to the manufacture and use of cars and light trucks. In addition to the electrical energy, fuel, fertilizer, and pesticides consumed by the meat industry is the manure problem. Mega-farms with tens or hundreds of thousands of animals have replaced factories as the biggest polluters of America's waterways. The United States generates 1.4 billion tons of animal manure every year—130 times more than the annual production of human waste. This waste wasn't a problem when small farms crisscrossed the nation, and farmers used the manure as fertilizer. But giant farms with 100,000 hogs or a million chickens all defecating in the same place seriously damage the environment.[10]

Nuclear wastes, of course, are in a class by themselves. Significant danger arises from even the small amounts that are released into the atmosphere during normal operation of a nuclear power plant or in mining, processing, or transporting nuclear fuels. A nuclear-plant accident would, of course, have frightening consequences, as the 1986 disaster at Chernobyl, Ukraine, brought vividly home to the world. Illnesses caused by the fallout from Chernobyl are still emerging, over fifteen years later.[11] In addition, the disposal of nuclear wastes has to worry anyone who is sensitive to the legacy we leave future generations. Will the nuclear wastes we bury today return to haunt us tomorrow?

It is little wonder, then, that considerable attention has focused on business's and industry's responsibility for preserving the integrity of our natural environment. This chapter explores some of the moral dilemmas posed for business by our environmental relationships—not just the problem of pollution but also the ethical issues posed by the depletion of natural resources and by our treatment of animals. The chapter's purpose is not to argue that the environmental problems facing us are serious and that industry has greatly contributed to them. Few people today doubt this. Rather, this chapter is largely concerned with a more practical question: Given the problems of environmental degradation, of resource depletion, and of the abuse of animals for commercial purposes, what are business's responsibilities? Specifically, this chapter examines:

1. The meaning and significance of *ecology*

2. The traditional business attitudes toward the environment that have encouraged environmental degradation and resource depletion

3. The moral problems underlying business's abuse of the environment—in particular, the question of externalities, the problem of free riders, and the right to a livable environment

4. The costs of environmental protection and the question of who should pay them

5. Three methods—regulations, incentives, and pricing mechanisms—for allocating the costs of environmental protection

6. Some of the deeper and not fully resolved questions of environmental ethics: What

obligations do we have to future generations? Does nature have value in itself? Is our commercial exploitation of animals immoral?

BUSINESS AND ECOLOGY

To deal intelligently with the question of business's responsibilities for the environment, one must realize that as business uses energy and materials, discharges waste, and produces products and services, it is functioning within an ecological system. *Ecology* refers to the science of the interrelationships among organisms and their environments. The operative term is "interrelationships," implying that an interdependence exists among all entities in the environment. In particular, we must not forget that human beings are part of nature and thus intricately connected with and interrelated to the natural environment.

In speaking about ecological matters, ecologists frequently use the term *ecosystem*, which refers to a total ecological community, both living and nonliving. Webs of interdependency structure ecosystems. Predators and prey, producers and consumers, hosts and parasites are linked together, creating interlocking mechanisms—checks and balances—that stabilize the system.

An ordinary example of an ecosystem is a pond. It consists of a complex web of animal and vegetable life. Suppose that the area where the pond is located experiences a prolonged period of drought, or that someone begins to fish in the pond regularly, or that during a period of excessive rainfall, plant pesticides begin to spill into it. Under any of these circumstances, changes will occur in the relationships among the pond's constituent components. Damage to a particular form of plant life may mean that fewer fish can live in the pond; a particular species might even disappear. A change in the pond's ecosystem may also affect other ecosystems. Because of water contamination, for example, a herd of deer that live nearby may have to go elsewhere for water; their presence there may reduce the berry crop which had previously supported other animals. The point is that in considering any ecosystem, one must remember its complex and interrelated nature and the intricate network of interdependencies that bind it to other ecosystems.

Every living organism affects its environment, yet *Homo sapiens* possesses the power to upset dramatically the stability of natural ecosystems. In particular, many human commercial activities (for example, using pesticides and establishing oil fields) have unpredictable and disruptive consequences for ecosystems. For example, farmers in the Midwest use nitrogen fertilizer liberally. Excess nitrogen runs off their fields and finds its way into the Mississippi River and eventually into the Gulf of Mexico. There, in what has historically been the nation's best shrimping grounds, it has created what is known as the dead zone, where the water is devoid of life to about 10 feet below the surface. This dead zone has now grown to about 8,500 square miles, an area the size of New Jersey.[12]

On the other hand, tampering with ecosystems does not always have injurious effects. Sometimes unforeseen benefits result, as was true years ago when oil and gas drilling expanded into the Gulf. Much to everyone's surprise, the operational docks, pipes, and platforms provided a better place for lower forms of life to attach themselves than the silt-laden sea ever did. This in turn increased the fish catch in the area. But even in fortuitous instances like this, environmental intrusions affect the integrity of ecosystems. And that's the point. Because an ecosystem represents a delicate balance of interrelated entities and because ecosystems are interlocked, an intrusion into one will affect its integrity and the integrity of others. And we are not usually so lucky in the results. Dr. Paul Ehrlich, one of the best-known exponents of ecological awareness, has put the matter succinctly. "There are a number of ecological rules it would be wise for people to remember," Ehrlich has written. "One of them is that there is no such thing as a free lunch. Another is that when we change something into something

else, the new thing is usually more dangerous than what we had originally."[13]

In its role as the major instrument of production in our society, business must intrude into ecosystems. Yet not all intrusions or all kinds of intrusions are justifiable. In fact, precisely because of the interrelated nature of ecosystems and because intrusions generally produce serious unfavorable effects, business must scrupulously avoid actions, practices, and policies that have an undue impact on the environment. There's ample documentation to show that business traditionally has been remiss in both recognizing and adequately discharging its obligations in this regard. We needn't spend time retelling the sorry tale, but it does seem worthwhile to isolate some business attitudes that have been responsible for this indifference.

Business's Traditional Attitudes Toward the Environment

Several related attitudes, prevalent in our society in general and in business in particular, have led to or increased our environmental problems. One of these is the tendency to view the natural world as a "free and unlimited good"—that is, as something we can exploit, even squander, without regard to the future. Writer John Steinbeck once reflected on this attitude:

> I have often wondered at the savagery and thoughtlessness with which our early settlers approached this rich continent. They came at it as though it were an enemy, which of course it was. They burned the forests and changed the rainfall; they swept the buffalo from the plains, blasted the streams, set fire to the grass, and ran a reckless scythe through the virgin and noble timber. Perhaps they felt that it was limitless and could never be exhausted and that a man could move on to new wonders endlessly. Certainly there are many examples to the contrary, but to a large extent the early people pillaged the country as though they hated it, as though they held it temporarily and might be driven off at any time.

This tendency toward irresponsibility persists in very many of us today; our rivers are poisoned by reckless dumping of sewage and toxic industrial wastes, the air of our cities is filthy and dangerous to breathe from the belching of uncontrolled products from combustion of coal, coke, oil, and gasoline. Our towns are girdled with wreckage and debris of our toys—our automobiles and our packaged pleasures. Through uninhibited spraying against one enemy we have destroyed the natural balances our survival requires. All these evils can and must be overcome if America and Americans are to survive; but many of us conduct ourselves as our ancestors did, stealing from the future for our clear and present profit.[14]

Traditionally, business has considered the environment to be a free, virtually limitless good. In other words, air, water, land, and other natural resources from coal to beavers (trapped almost to extinction for their pelts in the nineteenth century) were seen as available for business to use as it saw fit. In this context, pollution and the depletion of natural resources are two aspects of the same problem: Both involve using up natural resources that are limited. Pollution uses up clean air and water, just as extraction uses up the minerals or oil in the ground. The belief that both sorts of resources are unlimited and free promotes wasteful consumption of them.

Garrett Hardin describes the consequences of this attitude in his modern parable, "The Tragedy of the Commons." Hardin asks us to imagine villagers who allow their animals to graze in the commons, the collectively shared village pasture. Even though it is in the interest of each to permit his or her animals to graze without limit on the public land, the result of each doing so is that the commons is soon overgrazed, making it of no further grazing value to anyone.[15]

Today the international fishing industry exemplifies Hardin's point: Overfishing by ships armed with advanced technology is dramatically reducing the world's stock of fish, threatening to undermine the whole industry.[16] But the moral of Hardin's story is perfectly general: When it comes to "the commons"—that is, to public or communal goods like air, water, and wilderness—problems arise as the result of individuals' and companies' following their own self-interest. Each believes that his or her own use of the commons has only a negligible effect, but the cumulative result can be the gradual destruction of the public domain, which makes everyone worse off. In the tragedy of the commons we have the reverse of Adam Smith's invisible hand: Each person's pursuit of self-interest makes everyone worse off.

The tragedy of the commons also illustrates the more general point that there can be a difference between the private costs and the social costs of a business activity. Chapter 5 discussed this issue when it described what economists call "externalities," but it is worth reviewing the point in the present context.

Suppose a paper mill only partially treats the chemical wastes it releases into a lake that's used for fishing and recreational activities, thus saving on production costs. If the amount of effluent is great enough to reduce the fishing productivity of the lake, then while the mill's customers pay a lower price for its paper than they otherwise would, other people end up paying a higher price for fish. Moreover, the pollution may make the lake unfit for recreational activities such as swimming or for use as a source of potable water. The result is that other people and the public generally pay the cost of the mill's inadequate water-treatment system. Economists term this disparity between private industrial costs and public social costs a *spillover* or *externality*. In viewing things strictly in terms of private industrial costs, business overlooks spillover. This is an economic problem because the price of the paper does not reflect the true cost of producing it. Paper is underpriced and overproduced, thus leading to a misallocation of resources. This is also a moral problem because the purchasers of paper are not paying its full cost. Instead, part of the cost of producing paper is being unfairly imposed on other people.

In sum, then, spillovers or externalities, pursuit of private interest at the expense of the commons, and a view of the environment as a free good that can be consumed without limit have combined with an ignorance of ecology and of the often fragile interconnections and interdependencies of the natural world to create the serious environmental problems facing us today.

THE ETHICS OF ENVIRONMENTAL PROTECTION

Much of what we do to reduce, eliminate, or avoid pollution and the depletion of scarce natural resources is in our collective self-interest. Many measures that we take—for example, recycling our cans or installing catalytic converters in our cars—are steps that benefit all of us, collectively and individually: Our air is more breathable and our landscapes less cluttered with garbage. But even if such measures benefit each and every one of us, there will still be a temptation to shirk individual responsibilities and be a "free rider." The individual person or company may rationalize that the little bit it adds to the total pollution problem doesn't make any difference. The firm benefits from the efforts of others to prevent pollution but "rides for free" by not making the same effort itself.

The unfairness here is obvious. Likewise, as explained in the previous section, the failure of companies to "internalize" their environmental "externalities" spells unfairness. Others are forced to pick up the tab when companies do not pay all the environmental costs involved in producing their own products. As mentioned in Chapter 5, those who adopt the broader view of corporate social responsibility emphasize that business and the rest of society have an implicit social contract. This contract reflects what society hopes to achieve by allowing business to operate; it sets the "rules of the game" governing business activity. Companies that try to be free riders in environmental matters or who refuse to address the spillover or external costs of their business activity violate this contract.

So far this chapter has emphasized that we need to view the environment differently if we are to improve our quality of life and even to

continue to exist. And it has just stressed how the failure of an individual or business to play its part is unfair. Some moral theorists, like William T. Blackstone, have gone further to argue that each of us has a human right to a livable environment. "Each person," Blackstone argues, "has this right *qua* being human and because a livable environment is essential for one to fulfill his human capacities."[17] This right has emerged, he contends, as a result of changing environmental conditions, which affect the very possibility of human life as well as the possibility of realizing other human rights.

Recognition of a right to a livable environment would strengthen further the ethical reasons for business to respect the integrity of the natural world. In addition, recognition of this moral right could, Blackstone suggests, form a sound basis for establishing a legal right to a livable environment through legislation and even, perhaps, through a constitutional amendment or an environmental bill of rights. An official recognition of such rights would enhance our ability to go after polluters and other abusers of the natural environment.

Acknowledging a human right to a livable environment, however, does not solve many of the difficult problems facing us. In the effort to conserve irreplaceable resources, to protect the environment from further degradation, and to restore it to its former quality, we are still faced with difficult choices, each with its economic and moral costs. The next section focuses on pollution control, but most of the points apply equally to other problems of environmental protection, as well as to the conservation of scarce resources.

The Costs of Pollution Control

It is easy to say that we should do whatever it takes to improve the environment. Before this answer has any operational worth, however, we must consider a number of things. One is the quality of environment that we want. This can vary from an environment restored to its pristine state to one minimally improved over its current condition. Then there's the question of precisely what is necessary to bring about the kind of environment we want. In some cases we may lack the technological capacity to restore the environment. Finally, an important concern in any determination of what should be done to improve the environment is a calculation of what it will cost.

To draw out this point, we must consider a major technique for determining the total costs of environmental improvement. *Cost-benefit analysis* is a device used to determine whether it's worthwhile to incur a particular cost—for instance, the cost of employing a particular pollution-control device. The general approach is to evaluate a project's direct and indirect costs and benefits, the difference being the net result for society. Suppose that the estimated environmental damage of operating a particular plant is $1 million per year, that closing the plant would have dire economic consequences for the community, and that the only technique that would permit the plant to operate in an environmentally nondamaging way would cost $6 million per year. In this case, cost-benefit analysis would rule against requiring the plant to introduce the new technique.* If the cost of the technique had been only $800,000, however, cost-benefit analysis would have favored it.

Cost-benefit analysis can quickly get very complicated. For example, in determining whether it would be worthwhile to initiate more stringent air-pollution standards for a particular industry, a multitude of factors must be considered. Possible costs might include lower corporate profits, higher prices for consumers, unfavorable effects on employment, and adverse consequences for the nation's balance of payments. On the side of anticipated benefits, a reduction in airborne particulates over urban areas would reduce illness and premature death from bronchitis, lung cancer, and other respiratory diseases by some de-

terminate percentage. The increase in life expectancy would have to be estimated along with projected savings in medical costs and increases in productivity. In addition, diminished industrial discharges would mean reduced property and crop damage from air pollution, and that would save more money.

This example suggests the extreme difficulty of making reliable estimates of actual costs and benefits, of putting price tags on the different effects of the policy being considered. Any empirical prediction in a case like this is bound to be controversial. This problem is compounded by the fact that decision makers are unlikely to know for certain all future results of the policy being studied. Not only is estimating the likelihood of its various possible effects difficult, but some future effects may be entirely unanticipated.

The new discipline of ecological economics is attempting to expand further the boundaries of environmental cost-benefit analysis by calculating the value of an ecosystem in terms of what it would cost to provide the benefits and services it now furnishes us—for example, the worth of a wetland in terms of the cost of constructing structures that provide the same flood control and storm protection that natural wetlands do.[18] Although conventional economists dismiss the idea of equating the value of something with its replacement cost rather than with what people are willing to pay for it, ecological economists respond that traditional market pricing fails to capture the nonmarketed externalities that nature provides, such as the nutrients that a forest recycles. In one study, for example, ecological economists established that a mangrove swamp in Thailand was worth 72 percent more when left intact to provide timber, charcoal, fish, and storm protection than when converted to a fish farm. "In every case we looked at," states Cambridge University biologist Andrew Balmford, "the loss of nature's services outweighed the benefits of development, often by large amounts."[19]

Even putting aside the debate over ecological economics, cost-benefit analyses of rival environmental policies will frequently prove

---

*Cost-benefit analysis would not, however, prevent other strategies for getting the plant to internalize this externality. It could be taxed $1 million or be required to reimburse those who suffer the $1 million loss.

controversial because they inevitably involve making value judgments about nonmonetary costs and benefits. Costs relative to time, effort, and discomfort can and must be introduced. Benefits can take even more numerous forms: health, convenience, comfort, enjoyment, leisure, self-fulfillment, freedom from odor, enhanced beauty, and so on. Benefits are especially difficult to calculate in environmental matters because they often take an aesthetic form. Some environmentalists, for example, may campaign for the preservation of a remote forest visited annually by only a handful of stalwart backpackers, whereas developers wish to convert it into a more accessible and frequented ski resort. Should the forest be preserved or should it be converted into a ski resort? Conflicting value judgments are at stake.

With the assistance of an economics consulting firm, the U.S. Department of the Interior has asked Americans how much they are willing to shell out for environmental restoration. For instance, what would each consent to pay to restore the ecological balance of the Grand Canyon, even if few of them will actually see or truly understand the improvements: Ten cents a month? A dollar a month? Ten dollars a month? The Interior Department used this technique to justify reintroducing wolves into parts of Montana, Wyoming, and Idaho—a controversial move opposed by some taxpayers, ranchers, and consumers of beef. Some environmentalists applaud this attempt to calculate what economists call "non-use value," but others fear that the attempt to put a monetary price tag on ecosystems belittles the values they champion.[20]

An evaluation of costs and benefits is unavoidably wed to value judgments—to assessments of worth and the ranking of values. Although a cost-effectiveness analysis may be necessary for determining the soundness of an environmental-preservation measure or a pollution-control project, it seems inevitable that any assessment of costs and benefits will be subject to various factual uncertainties and significantly influenced by the values one holds.

Who Should Pay the Costs?

The price of pursuing the nation's ecological goals is high. An EPA estimate puts the total cost of regulatory programs from 1970 to 1990 at $1.4 trillion, and the cost for the ten-year period ending in 2000 at $1.6 trillion (in constant dollars).[21] Of course, the losses to polluters are often the gains of those paid to clean up or prevent the pollution. Indeed, restoring the environment could become the biggest economic enterprise of our times, a huge source of jobs, profits, and poverty alleviation.[22] Still, environmental protection and restoration do not come cheap, and determining who should pay the necessary costs raises a tough question of social justice. Two popular answers to this question currently circulate: that those responsible for causing the pollution ought to pay, and that those who stand to benefit from protection and restoration should pick up the tab.

Those Responsible. The claim that those responsible for causing the pollution ought to pay the costs of pollution control and environmental restoration seems eminently fair until one asks a simple question. Just who is responsible for the pollution? Who are the polluters? Many people argue that big business is the chief polluter and therefore ought to bear the lion's share of the costs of environmental protection and restoration. Moreover, a policy of making polluters pick up the tab would probably have the desirable social effect of shifting income from the richer to the poorer and thus providing for a more equitable distribution of wealth. In the minds of some persons, the question of who should pay the bill is connected with the fair and just distribution of wealth.

Although business probably has benefited financially more than any other group from treating the environment as a free good, not all corporate wealth or even most of it has resulted directly from doing so. Moreover, consumers themselves have benefited enormously by not having to pay higher costs for products. In fact, some would argue that consumers are primarily to blame for pollution because they create the demand for the products whose production impairs the environment. Therefore, it is the consumer, not business, who should pay to protect and restore the environment. In this way, the argument goes, social costs are not unfairly passed on to those who have not incurred them.

However, both versions of the polluter-should-pay-the-bill thesis, one attributing primary responsibility for pollution to big business, the other to consumers, largely ignore the manifold, deep-rooted causes of environmental degradation.

Two important causes of pollution have been a growing population and its increasing concentration in urban areas. In 1900, Americans numbered 76.2 million; now at the beginning of the twenty-first century our population has more than tripled, to approximately 281.5 million. An increasingly urbanized nation, we are a long way from the rural, agriculturally oriented society we once were. Today, for example, the number of college students is more than three times the entire U.S. farm population. More than 70 million Americans live in our ten largest metropolitan areas, and nearly half the country lives in metropolitan areas with populations of a million or more. This tremendous population growth and equally staggering level of urbanization have brought with them an ever-increasing demand for goods and services, natural resources, energy, and industrial production. And these in turn have increased air, water, space, and noise pollution.

Another root cause of environmental problems is rising affluence. As people get more money to spend, they buy and consume more tangible goods, discard them more quickly, and produce more waste, all of which hasten degradation of the environment. Americans today produce 60 percent more garbage per capita than we did thirty years ago, almost 1,600 pounds per person per year.[23] We own more than 216 million motor vehicles[24]—far and away the world record—and are only making matters worse by our growing preference for big, gas-guzzling pickups, minivans, and sports utility vehicles, which emit significantly more carbon dioxide (a principal cause of global warming) and nitrogen oxides (the main source of smog) than ordinary passenger cars do.

Thus, the enemy in the war against environmental abuse turns out to be all of us. No solution to the question of who should pay the costs of pollution control can ignore this fact.

Those Who Would Benefit. A second popular reply to the payment problem is that those who will benefit from environmental improvement should pay the costs.

The trouble with this argument is that every individual, rich or poor, and every institution, large or small, stands to profit from environmental improvement, albeit not to the same degree. As a result, the claim that those who will benefit should pay the costs is not satisfactory, because everyone is touched by pollution. If, on the other hand, this position means that individuals and groups should pay to the degree that they will benefit, then one must wonder how this could possibly be determined. For example, changing the operation of the Glen Canyon Dam has raised electricity bills in the West, but it has reduced ecological damage to the Grand Canyon. Who benefits the most—local residents, visitors to the Grand Canyon, all who value this national resource—and how much should they pay?[25] But perhaps the most serious objection to this thesis is that it seems to leave out responsibility as a legitimate criterion.

Any equitable solution to the problem of who should pay the bill of environmental cleanup should take into account responsibility as well as benefit. The preceding analysis suggests that we all share the blame for pollution and collectively stand to benefit from environmental improvement. This doesn't mean, however, that individual entities cannot be isolated as chronic and flagrant polluters. DuPont's eighty-five facilities, for example, release more than a million pounds of toxic material per day, making it the largest single emitter of hazardous chemicals, and GM releases three times more toxics than either Ford or Chrysler.[26] The EPA lists Dow Chemical as the potentially responsible party in forty-five Superfund toxic waste sites.[27] And it remains true that certain individuals will benefit more than others from environmental controls. For example, residents of the Los Angeles basin gain more from stringently enforced auto-emission-control standards than those living in a remote corner of Wyoming.

Still, the point is that a fair and just program for assigning costs begins with a recognition that we all bear responsibility for environmental problems and that we all stand to benefit from correcting them. But even if we agree that it is only fair that everyone share the cost of environmental improvement, we can still wonder about how the bill ought to be paid. What would be the fairest and most effective way of handling those costs?

COST ALLOCATION

Most would probably agree that environmental pollution cannot be stopped unless business and government work together. The main proposals for revitalizing the environment conceptualize government as initiating programs that will prod business into responsible action. The moral question that concerns us, then, is the fairest way of allocating costs for environmental revitalization.

Three approaches have gained the most attention: the use of regulations, incentives, and pricing mechanisms. Although similar in some respects, they carry different assumptions about the roles of government and business, as well as about what's fair and just. Each approach has distinct advantages and weaknesses; each raises some questions of social justice.

Regulations

The regulatory approach makes use of direct public regulation and control in determining how the pollution bill is paid. State and federal legislation, and regulations formulated by agencies such as the EPA, set environmental standards, which are then applied and enforced by those agencies, other regulatory bodies, and the courts. An emissions standard that, for example, prohibits industrial smokestacks from releasing more than a certain percentage of particulate matter would require plants exceeding that standard to comply with it by installing an appropriate pollution-control device.

A clear advantage to such a regulatory approach is that standards would be legally enforceable. Firms not meeting them could be fined or even shut down. Also, from the view of morality, such standards are fair in that they apply to all industries in the same way. There are, however, distinct disadvantages in this approach.

First, pollution statutes and regulations generally require polluters to use the strongest feasible means of pollution control. But that requires the EPA or some other regulatory body to investigate pollution-control technologies and economic conditions in each industry to find the best technology that companies can afford. Such studies may require tens of thousands of pages of documentation, and legal proceedings may be necessary before the courts give final approval to the regulation. Moreover, expecting the EPA to master the economics and technology of dozens of industries, from petrochemicals to steel to electric utilities, may be unreasonable. It is bound to make mistakes, asking more from some companies than they can ultimately achieve while letting others off too lightly.[28]

Second, there's the question of both the equity and the economic sense of requiring compliance with universal standards, without regard for the idiosyncratic nature of each industry or the particular circumstances of individual firms. Is it reasonable to force two companies that cause very different amounts of environmental damage to spend the same amount on pollution abatement? In one case, the courts required two paper mills on the West Coast to install expensive pollution-control equipment, even though their emissions were diluted effectively by the Pacific Ocean. It took a special act of Congress to rescue the mills.[29]

Although universal environmental standards are fair in the sense that they apply to all equally, this very fact raises questions about their effectiveness. In attempting to legislate realistic and reliable standards for all, will government so dilute the standards that they become ineffectual? Or consider areas where the environment is cleaner than government standards. In such cases, should an industry be allowed to pollute up to the maximum of the standard? The Supreme Court thinks not. In a case brought before it by the Sierra Club, the Court ruled that states with relatively clean air must prohibit industries from producing significant air pollution even when EPA standards are not violated. In this case a firm is being forced to pay the costs of meeting an environmental standard that, in one sense, is sterner than what competitors must meet elsewhere.

Regulation can also take away an industry's incentive to do more than the minimum required by law. No polluter has any incentive to discharge less muck than regulations allow. No entrepreneur has an incentive to devise technology that will bring pollution levels below the registered maximum. Moreover, firms have an incentive not to let the EPA know they can pollute less. Under the regulatory approach, a government agency may have the desire to regulate pollution but lack the information to do it efficiently. The position of industry is reversed: It may have the information and the technology but no desire to use it.[30]

Finally, there's the problem of displacement costs resulting from industrial relocation or shutdown due to environmental regulations. For example, Youngstown Sheet and Tube Company moved its corporate headquarters and some production lines to the Chicago area, thus eliminating 500 jobs in Youngstown and causing serious economic problems in nearby communities. One of the reasons for the transfer was the need to implement water-pollution controls, which depleted vital capital. Consider also the marginal firms that would fail while attempting to meet the costs of such standards. When air-pollution regulations were applied to a sixty-year-old cement plant in San Juan Bautista, California, the plant had to close because it was too obsolete

to meet the standard economically. The shutdown seriously injured the economy of the little town, which had been primarily supported by the cement plant.[31]

On the other hand, if regulations are tougher for new entrants to an industry than for existing firms, as they often are, then new investment may be discouraged—even if newer plants would be cleaner than older ones. For example, a clause in the Clean Air Act exempts old coal plants from complying with current emissions rules. As a result, much of America's electricity is produced by coal plants that are over thirty years old and far dirtier than newer plants would be.[32] Clearly, then, a regulatory approach to environmental improvement, while having advantages, also raises serious questions.

Incentives

A widely supported approach to the problem of cost allocation for environmental improvement is government investment, subsidy, and general economic incentive.

The government might give a firm a tax incentive for the purchase and use of pollution-control equipment, or it might offer matching grants to companies that install such devices. In its "33/50 Program," the EPA asked 600 industrial facilities to reduce voluntarily their discharges of seventeen toxic contaminants, first by 33 percent, then by 50 percent. The incentive for firms to commit to the reductions was simply the public relations opportunities afforded by EPA press releases and outstanding performance awards—along with, perhaps, the firms' desire to stave off future regulatory action.[33] The advantage of an incentive approach is that it minimizes government interference in business and encourages voluntary action rather than coercing compliance, as in the case of regulation. By allowing firms to move at their own pace, it avoids the evident unfairness to firms that cannot meet regulatory standards and must either relocate or fail. In addition, whereas regulated standards can encourage minimum legal compliance, an incentive approach provides an economic reason for going beyond minimal compliance. Firms have a financial inducement to do more than just meet EPA standards.

But incentives are not without disadvantages that bear moral overtones. First, as an essentially voluntary device, an incentive program is likely to be slow. Environmental problems that cry out for a solution may continue to fester. Incentive programs may allow urgently needed action to be postponed. In addition, government incentive programs often amount to a subsidy for polluters, with polluting firms being paid not to pollute. Although this approach may sometimes address the economics of pollution more effectively than the regulatory approach, it nonetheless raises questions about the justice of benefiting not the victims of pollution but some of the egregious polluters. This problem grows darker when one realizes that, as indirect government expenditures, incentives rarely involve close government scrutiny. Thus, a firm might be able to manipulate the total costs of antipollution equipment within a nest of other business expenditures reported in tax returns. Not only is the government thereby defrauded, but it is also left without any realistic way of determining the cost-effectiveness payoff of its incentive program.[34]

Pricing Mechanisms

A third approach to the cost-allocation problem involves programs designed to charge firms for the amount of pollution they produce. This could take the form of pricing mechanisms, or effluent charges, which spell out the cost for a specific kind of pollution in a specific area at a specific time. The prices would vary from place to place and from time to time and would be tied to the amount of damage caused. For example, during the summer months in the Los Angeles basin, a firm might pay much higher charges for fly ash emitted into the environment than it would during the winter months. Whatever the set of prices, they would apply equally to every producer of a given type of pollution at the same time and place. The more a firm pollutes, the more it pays.

One advantage in this approach is that it places the cost of pollution control on the polluters. Pricing mechanisms or effluent charges would penalize, not compensate, industrial polluters. For many persons this is inherently fairer than a program that compensates polluters.

Also, because costs are internalized, firms would be encouraged to do more than meet the minimal requirements established under a strict regulatory policy. Under this approach a firm, in theory, could be charged for any amount of pollution and not just incur legal penalties whenever it exceeded an EPA standard. In effect, pollution costs become production costs.

Pollution Permits. Instead of imposing a tax or a fee on the pollutants released into the environment, the government could charge companies for pollution permits. Or it could auction off a limited number of permits. An even more market-oriented strategy is to give companies permits to discharge a limited amount of pollution and then to allow them to buy and sell the right to emit pollutants. With pollution permits, companies with low pollution levels can make money by selling their pollution rights to companies with poorer controls. Thus, each firm can estimate the relative costs of continuing to pollute as opposed to investing in cleaner procedures. The government can also set the precise amount of pollution it is prepared to allow and, by lowering the amount permitted over time, can reduce or even eliminate it.

The EPA successfully experimented with this strategy in the 1970s when it gave oil refineries two years to reduce the allowable lead content in gasoline. Refineries received quotas on lead, which they could then trade with one another. Later, the 1990 Clean Air Act Amendments adopted this approach with respect to the sulfur dioxide (SO_2) emissions of electric utilities. Although controversial at the time—the power industry insisted the SO_2 cuts were prohibitively costly while environmental groups derided the measure as a sham—the scheme has surpassed its initial objectives and at a far lower cost than expected.[35]

Although pricing mechanisms and pollution permits may not work in all situations and for all environmental problems, economists generally favor using them wherever possible. However, they trouble many environmentalists. For one thing, the price tag for polluting seems arbitrary. How will effluent charges or permit prices be set? What is a fair price? Any decision seems bound to reflect debatable economic and value judgments. Moreover, environmentalists dislike the underlying principle of pricing mechanisms and pollution permits and view with suspicion anything that sounds like a license to pollute. They resent the implication that companies have a right to pollute and reject the notion that companies should be able to make money by selling this right to other firms. In fact, Michael J. Sandel, professor of government at Harvard, argues that it's immoral to buy the right to pollute. "Turning pollution into a commodity to be bought and sold removes the moral stigma that is properly associated with it," he says.[36]

In sum, although each of these approaches to cost allocation has decided advantages, none is without its weak points. Because there appears to be no single, ideal approach to all our environmental problems, a combination of regulation, incentive, effluent charges, and permits is probably called for. Any such combination must take into account not only effectiveness but also fairness to those who will have to foot the bill. Fairness in turn calls for input from all sectors of society, a deliberate commitment on the part of all parties to work in concert, a sizable measure of good faith, and perhaps above all else a heightened sense of social justice. This is no mean challenge.

Still, environmental protection is not always a static trade-off, with a fixed economic price to be paid for the gains we want. One reason is that higher environmental standards and properly designed regulatory programs can pressure corporations to invest capital in newer, state-of-the-art manufacturing technology; this both reduces pollution and enhances productive efficiency. In addition, international data in a range of industrial sectors show that innovation can minimize or even eliminate the costs of conforming to tougher environmental standards by increasing productivity, lowering total costs, and improving product quality.[37] The reason is that pollution is evidence of economic waste. The discharge of scrap, chemical wastes, toxic substances, or energy in the form of pollution is a sign that resources have been used inefficiently.

Consider some examples.[38] Environmental regulations forced Dow Chemical to redesign the production process at its complex in California to avoid storing chemical waste in evaporation ponds. Not only did the new process reduce waste, but the company found that it could reuse part of it as raw material in other parts of the plant. For a cost of $250,000 Dow is now saving $2.4 million each year. Likewise, when new environmental standards forced 3M to reduce the volume of solvents to be disposed of, the company found a way to avoid the use of solvents altogether, which yielded it an annual savings of more than $200,000. Most distillers of coal tar opposed regulations requiring them to reduce benzene emissions; they thought the only solution was to cover tar storage tanks with costly gas blankets. But Aristech Chemical Corporation found a way to remove benzene from tar in the first processing step. Instead of a cost increase, the company saved itself $3.3 million.

A broad array of economists, led by Nobel laureates Kenneth J. Arrow and Robert M. Solow, have urged that with regard to global warming, measures to reduce greenhouse gas emissions need not harm the economy and "may in fact improve U.S. productivity in the long run." This is because many innovative, energy-efficient technologies are just waiting for the right financial incentives to enter the market. And in many of these fields, U.S. industry is the leader.[39]

DELVING DEEPER INTO ENVIRONMENTAL ETHICS

So far the discussion of environmental ethics has focused on business's obligation to understand its environmental responsibilities, to acknowledge and internalize its externalities (or spillovers), and to avoid free riding. It has stressed the extent to which environmental protection is in our collective self-interest, and it has looked at the operational and moral dilemmas involved in dealing with the costs of pollution.

The subject of environmental ethics can be pursued more deeply than this, and many moral theorists would advocate doing so. In particular, they would insist that we also consider our obligations to those who live outside our society. The United States has 6 percent of the world's population but uses 30 percent of the world's refined oil. Similar figures hold for other non-renewable natural resources. Moreover, the United States must depend on foreign nations to supply its needs.

The average amount of energy consumed per year by a person in the United States is 3.4 times that of the average Hungarian, 5.5 times that of a Chilean, 14.4 times that of a Chinese, and 29.6 times that of someone in India.[40] The birth of a baby in the United States imposes more than a hundred times the stress on the world's resources as a birth in, say, Bangladesh. Babies from Bangladesh do not grow up to own automobiles and air conditioners or to eat huge quantities of grain-fed beef. Their lifestyles do not require large inputs of minerals and energy, and they do not undermine the planet's life-support capacity.[41]

Tropical rain forests are of special concern. They are the earth's richest, oldest, and most complex ecosystems. Tropical forests are major reservoirs of biodiversity, home to 40 to 50 percent of all types of living things—as many as 5 million species of plants, animals, and insects. At least 50 million acres of tropical rain forest are destroyed each year, or 100 acres every minute. And already half the globe's original rain forest has disappeared. Tropical forests are often cleared in an attempt to provide farms for growing Third World populations, but the affluence of people in rich nations like the United States is responsible for much forest destruction. Central American forests are cleared in part for pasture land to make pet food and convenience food slightly cheaper in the United States. In Papua, New Guinea, forests are destroyed to supply cardboard packaging for Japanese electronic products. Thus, an affluent American living thousands of miles away can cause more tropical forest destruction than a poor person living within the forest itself.[42]

Our bloated levels of consumption, our dependence on foreign resources to satisfy our needs, and the impact of both on the economies and environments of other nations raise a variety of moral and political issues. This section mentions briefly just two of those problems.

First is the question of how the continued availability of foreign resources is to be secured. Will our need for resources outside our territory lead us to dominate other lands, politically and economically, particularly in the Middle East, Asia, and Latin America? To do so is morally risky, because political and economic domination almost always involves violations of the rights and interests of the dominated population, as well as of our own moral ideals and values.

Second is the question of whether any nation has a right to consume the world's irreplaceable resources at a rate so grossly out of proportion to the size of its population. Of course, we pay to consume resources like oil that other nations own, but in the view of many the fact that other nations acquiesce in our disproportionate consumption of resources does not resolve the moral problem of our doing so. Are we respecting the needs and interests of both our present co-inhabitants on this planet and the future generations who will live on Earth? This question is particularly burning now that scientists believe that human demand for natural resources has outstripped the biosphere's regenerative capacity.[43]

Obligations to Future Generations

Almost everybody feels intuitively that it would be wrong to empty the globe of resources and to irreparably contaminate the environment that we pass on to future generations. Certainly there is a danger that we will do both of these things.

But the question of what moral obligations we have to future generations is surprisingly difficult, and discussion among philosophers has not resolved all the important theoretical issues.

Even though most of us agree that it would be immoral to make the world uninhabitable for future people, can we talk meaningfully of those future generations having a right that we not do this? After all, our remote descendants are not yet alive and thus cannot claim a right to a livable environment. In fact, since these generations do not yet exist, they cannot at present, it seems, be said to have any interests at all. How can they then have rights?

Professor of philosophy Joel Feinberg argues, however, that whatever future human beings turn out to be like, they will have interests that we can affect, for better or worse, right now. Even though we do not know who the future people will be, we do know that they will have interests and what the general nature of those interests will be. This is enough, he contends, both to talk coherently about their having rights and to impose a duty on us not to leave ecological time bombs for them.

Feinberg concedes that it doesn't make sense to talk about future people having a right to be born. The child that you could conceive tonight, if you felt like it, cannot intelligibly be said to have a right to be born. Thus, the rights of future generations are "contingent," says Feinberg, on those future people coming into existence. But this qualification does not affect his main contention: "The interests that [future people] are sure to have when they come into being . . . cry out for protection from invasions that can take place now."[44]

Even if we are persuaded that future generations have rights, we still do not know exactly what those rights are or how they are to be balanced against the interests and rights of present people. If we substantially injure future generations to gain some small benefit for ourselves, we are being as selfish and shortsighted as we would be by hurting other people today for some slight advantage for ourselves. Normally, however, if the benefits of some environmental policy outweigh the costs, then a strong case can be made for adopting the policy. But what if it is the present generation that receives the benefits and future generations that pay the costs? Would it be unfair of us to adopt such a policy? Would doing so violate the rights of future people?

An additional puzzle is raised by the fact that policies we adopt will affect who is born in the future. Imagine that we must choose between two environmental policies, one of which would cause a slightly higher standard of living over the next century. Given the effects of those policies on the details of our lives, over time it would increasingly be true that people would marry different people under one policy than they would under the other. And even within the same marriages, children would increasingly be conceived at different times:

> Some of the people who are later born would owe their existence to our choice of one of the two policies. If we had chosen the other policy, these particular people would never have existed. And the proportion of those later born who owe their existence to our choice would, like ripples in a pool, steadily grow. We can plausibly assume that, after three centuries, there would be no one living in our community who would have been born whichever policy we chose.*

This reasoning suggests that subsequent generations cannot complain about an environmental policy choice we make today that causes them to have fewer opportunities and a lower standard of living. If we had made a different choice, then those people would not have existed at all. On the other hand, it can be claimed that we act immorally in causing people to exist whose rights to equal opportunity and an equally high standard of living cannot be fulfilled. But if those future people knew the facts, would they regret that we acted as we did?[45]

---

*Derek Parfit, *Reasons and Persons* (New York: Oxford University Press, 1986), 361. Parfit adds: "It may help to think about this question: How many of us could truly claim, 'Even if railways and motor cars had never been invented, I would still have been born'?"

Perhaps it is mistaken to focus on the rights and interests of future people as individuals. Annette Baier argues that the important thing is to "recognize our obligations to consider the good of the continuing human community."[46] This stance suggests adopting a utilitarian perspective and seeking to maximize total human happiness through time. But a utilitarian approach is also not without problems. If our concern is with total happiness, we may be required to increase greatly the earth's population. Even if individuals on an overcrowded earth do not have much happiness, there may still be more total happiness than there would be if we followed a population-control policy that resulted in fewer but better-off people. This distasteful conclusion has led some utilitarians to modify their theory and maintain that with regard to population policy we should aim for the highest average happiness rather than the highest total happiness. But this, too, is problematic because in theory one could, it seems, increase average happiness by eliminating unhappy people.

John Rawls has suggested another approach to the question of our obligations to future generations, an approach that reflects his general theory of justice (which was discussed in Chapter 3). He suggests that the members of each generation put themselves in the "original position." Then, without knowing what generation they belong to, they could decide what would be a just way of distributing resources between consecutive generations. They would have to balance how much they are willing to sacrifice for their descendants against how much they wish to inherit from their predecessors. In other words, the device of the original position and veil of ignorance might be used to determine our obligations to future generations—in particular, how much each generation should save for use by those who inherit the earth from it.[47]

The Value of Nature

A more radical approach to environmental ethics goes beyond the question of our obligations to future generations. It challenges the human-centered approach adopted so far. Implicit in the discussion has been the assumption that preservation of the environment is good solely because it is good for human beings. This reflects a characteristic human attitude that nature has no intrinsic value, that it has value only because people value it. If human nature were different and none of us cared about the beauty of, say, the Grand Canyon, then it would be without value.

Many writers on environmental issues do not recognize their anthropocentric, or human-oriented, bias. William F. Baxter is one who does. In discussing his approach to the pollution problem, Baxter mentions the fact that the use of DDT in food production is causing damage to the penguin population. He writes:

> My criteria are oriented to people, not penguins. Damage to penguins, or sugar pines, or geological marvels is, without more, simply irrelevant. . . . Penguins are important because people enjoy seeing them walk about rocks. . . . In short, my observations about environmental problems will be people-oriented. . . . I have no interest in preserving penguins for their own sake. . . .
>
> I reject the proposition that we *ought* to respect the "balance of nature" or to "preserve the environment" unless the reason for doing so, express or implied, is the benefit of man.[48]

Contrast Baxter's position with what Holmes Rolston III calls the "naturalistic ethic." Advocates of a naturalistic ethic contend, contrary to Baxter's view, "that some natural objects, such as whooping cranes, are morally considerable in their own right, apart from human interests, or that some ecosystems, perhaps the Great Smokies, have intrinsic values, such as aesthetic beauty, from which we derive a duty to respect these landscapes."[49] Human beings may value a mountain for a variety of reasons—because they can hike it, build ski lifts on it, mine the ore deep inside it, or simply because they like looking at it. According to a naturalistic ethic, however, the value of the mountain is not simply a function of these human interests. Nature can have value in and of itself, apart from human beings.

Some defenders of a naturalistic ethic contend that we have a particularly strong obligation to preserve species from extinction. This attitude, shared by many, was one of the factors behind the controversial legal efforts to prevent construction of the Tellico Dam on the Little Tennessee River in order to save the only known population of snail darters. But do species really have value above and beyond the individuals that make them up? Scientists have formally identified 1.8 million species (including, for example, 6,700 kinds of starfish, 12,000 species of earthworm, and 400,000 types of beetle), and recent studies suggest that the number of species inhabiting the planet may be much, much higher—with perhaps as many as 30 million kinds of insects alone. Species are always coming into and going out of existence.[50] How valuable is this diversity of species, and how far are we morally required to go in maintaining it?

Adopting a naturalistic ethic would definitely alter our way of looking at nature and our understanding of our moral obligations to preserve and respect the natural environment. Many philosophers doubt, however, that nature has intrinsic value or that we can be said to have moral duties to nature. Having interests is a precondition, they would contend, of something's having rights or of our having moral duties to that thing. Natural objects, however, have no interests. Can a rock meaningfully be said to have an interest in not being eroded or in not being smashed into smaller pieces?

Plants and trees are different from rocks and streams. They are alive, and we can talk intelligibly about what is good or bad for a tree, plant, or vegetable. They can flourish or do poorly. Nonetheless, philosophers who discuss moral rights generally hold that this is not enough for plants to be said to have rights. To have rights, a thing must have genuine interests, and to have interests, most theorists contend, a thing must have beliefs and desires. Vegetative life, however, lacks any cognitive awareness. Claims to the contrary are biologically unsupportable.

Even if the plant world lacks rights, can it still have intrinsic value? Can we still have a moral obligation to respect that world and not abuse it? Or are the only morally relevant values the various interests of human beings and other sentient creatures? These are difficult questions. Among philosophers there is no consensus on how to answer them.

Our Treatment of Animals

Above a certain level of complexity, animals do have at least rudimentary cognitive awareness. No owner of a cat or dog doubts that his pet has beliefs and desires. Accordingly, a number of philosophers have recently defended the claim that animals can have rights. Because they have genuine interests, animals can have genuine moral rights—despite the fact that they cannot claim their rights, that they cannot speak, that we cannot reason with them, and that they themselves lack a moral sense. Animals, it is more and more widely contended, do not have to be equal to human beings to have certain moral rights that we must respect.

Rather than talking about animals' rights, utilitarians would stress that higher animals are sentient—that is, that they are capable of feeling pain. Accordingly, there can be no justifiable reason for excluding their pleasures and pains from the overall utilitarian calculus. As Jeremy Bentham, one of the founders of utilitarianism, put it: "The question is not, Can they *reason*? nor, Can they *talk*? but, Can they *suffer*?"[51] Our actions have effects on animals, and these consequences cannot be ignored. When one is deciding, then, what the morally right course of action is, the pleasures and pains of animals must be taken into account too.

Business affects the welfare of animals very substantially. One way is through experimentation and the testing of products on animals. Critics such as Peter Singer contend that the vast majority of experimentation and testing cannot be justified on moral grounds. Consider the "LD 50" test, which until recently was the standard method of testing new foodstuffs. The object of the test is to find the dosage level at which 50 percent of the test animals die. Nearly all test animals become very sick before finally succumbing or surviving. When the substance is harmless, huge doses must be forced down the animals, until in some cases the sheer volume kills them.[52]

In principle, utilitarians are willing to permit testing and experimentation on animals, provided the overall results justify their pain and suffering. Not only is this proviso frequently ignored, but human beings typically disregard altogether the price the animals must pay. Consider the actions of the pharmaceutical firm Merck Sharp and Dohme, which sought to import chimpanzees to test a vaccine for hepatitis B. Chimps are an endangered species and highly intelligent. Capturing juvenile chimps requires shooting the mother. One analyst assessed the situation this way:

> The world has a growing population of 4 billion people and a dwindling population of some 50,000 chimpanzees. Since the vaccine seems unusually innocuous, and since the disease is only rarely fatal, it would perhaps be more just if the larger population could find some way of solving its problem that was not to the detriment of the smaller.[53]

Business's largest and most devastating impact on animals, however, is through the production of animal-related products—in particular, meat. Many of us still think of our chicken and beef as coming from something like the idyllic farms pictured in storybooks, where the animals roam contentedly and play with the farmer's children. But meat and egg production is big business, and today most of the animal products we eat are from factory farms. In 1921, the largest commercial egg farm had a flock of 2,000 hens that ran loose in a large pasture; today the largest commercial flock contains 2.5 million birds, and 80 percent of the 440 million laying hens are housed in 3 percent of the known chicken farms. These birds live in small multitiered wire cages.[54]

Laying hens that are stuffed into tiny cages with several other chickens now produce over 95 percent of our eggs. In these cages, hens are unable to satisfy such fundamental behavioral needs as stretching their wings, perching, walking, scratching, and nest building. Unsuited for wire cages, they suffer foot damage, feather loss, and other injuries. Birds are "debeaked" to prevent pecking injuries and cannibalism from overcrowding.[55]

Of the 95 million hogs born each year in the United States, 80 percent spend their lives in intensive confinement. Piglets are weaned after only three weeks and placed in bare wire cages or tiny cement pens. Once they reach 50 pounds, they are moved into bare 6-foot stalls with concrete-slatted floors. Veal calves have even worse lives. To produce gourmet "milk-fed" veal, newborn calves are taken from their mothers and chained in crates measuring only 22 inches by 54 inches. Here they spend their entire lives. To prevent muscle development and speed weight gain, the calves are allowed absolutely no exercise; they are unable even to turn around or lie down. Their special diet of growth stimulators and antibiotics causes chronic diarrhea, and the withholding of iron to make their meat light-colored makes them anemic. The calves are kept in total darkness to reduce restlessness.[56]

The individuals involved in the meat and animal-products industries are not brutal, but the desire to cut business costs and to economize routinely leads to treatment of animals that can only be described as cruel. Philosopher and animal-rights advocate Tom Regan describes their treatment this way:

> In increasing numbers, animals are being brought in off the land and raised indoors, in unnatural, crowded conditions—raised "intensively," to use the jargon of the animal industry. . . . The inhabitants of these "farms" are kept in cages, or stalls, or pens . . . living out their abbreviated lives in a technologically created and sustained environment: automated feeding, automated watering, automated light cycles, automated waste removal, automated what-not. And the crowding: as many as 9 hens in cages that measure 18 by 24 inches; veal calves confined to 22 inch wide stalls; hogs similarly confined, sometimes in tiers of cages, two, three, four rows high. Could any impartial, morally sensitive person view what goes on in a factory farm with benign approval?[57]

When it comes to the protection of animals, England has stricter laws than the United States. Consider, then, the following proposals for protecting commercially farmed animals, which were turned down by the British government as being too idealistic and unrealistic: (1) Any animal should have room to turn around. (2) A dry bed should be provided for all stock. (3) Palatable roughage must be readily available to all calves after one week of age. (4) Cages for poultry should be large enough for a bird to be able to stretch one wing at a time.[58]

Moral vegetarians are people who reject the eating of meat on moral grounds. Their argument is simple and powerful: The raising of animals for meat, especially with modern factory farming, sacrifices the most important and basic interests of animals simply to satisfy human tastes. Americans eat, per capita, a phenomenal amount of meat, by some estimates more than twice as much as we ate in the 1950s. Chicken production alone is now five times what it was in 1960. Many people eat meat three times a day. Our preference for a Big Mac over a soybean burger is only a matter of taste and culture, but it accounts for many of the 100,000 cows we slaughter every day.[59] The extra pleasure we believe we get from eating the hamburger cannot justify the price the animals must pay.

Would it be wrong to eat animals that were raised humanely, like those that run around freely and happily in children's picture books of farms? Unlike the lives of animals that we do in fact eat, the lives of such humanely raised animals, before being abruptly terminated, are not painful ones. Some philosophers would contend that it is permissible to raise animals for food if their lives are, on balance, positive. Other moral theorists challenge this view, contending that at least higher animals have a right to life and should not be killed.

This debate raises important philosophical issues; but it is also rather hypothetical. Given economic reality, mass production of meat at affordable prices dictates factory farming. The important moral issue, then, is the real suffering and unhappy lives that billions of creatures experience on the way to our dinner tables. This aspect of environmental ethics is often overlooked, but it raises profound and challenging questions for business and consumers alike.

SUMMARY

1. Business functions within a global ecological system. Because of the interrelated nature of ecosystems, and because intrusion into ecosystems frequently creates unfavorable effects, business must be sensitive to its impacts on the physical environment.

2. Traditionally, business has regarded the natural world as a free and unlimited good. Pollution and resource depletion are examples of situations in which each person's pursuit of self-interest can make everyone worse off (the "tragedy of the commons"). Business must be sensitive to possible disparities between its private economic costs and the social costs of its activities (the problem of externalities or spillovers).

3. Companies that attempt to be free riders in environmental matters or that refuse to address the external costs of their business activities behave unfairly. Some philosophers maintain, further, that each person has a human right to a livable environment.

4. Pollution control has a price, and trade-offs must be made. But weighing costs and benefits involves controversial factual assessments and value judgments. Any equitable solution to the problem of who should pay must recognize that all of us in some way contribute to the problem and benefit from correcting it.

5. Cost allocation requires a combination of regulations, incentives, and charges or permits for polluting. Such an approach must not only consider what is effective but must also seek a fair assignment of costs.

6. A broader view of environmental ethics considers our obligations to those in other societies and to future generations. Some philosophers argue that we must respect the

right of future generations to inherit an environment that is not seriously damaged, but talk of the rights of future people raises puzzles.

7. Philosophers disagree about whether nature has intrinsic value. Some, adopting a human-oriented point of view, contend that the environment is valuable only because human beings value it. Those adopting a naturalistic ethic believe that the value of nature is not simply a function of human interests.

8. Through experimentation, testing, and the production of animal products, business has a very substantial impact on the welfare of animals. The meat and animal-products industries rely on factory-farming techniques, which many describe as cruel and horrible. Because of these conditions, moral vegetarians argue that meat eating is wrong.

CASE 11.1

Hazardous Homes in Herculaneum

Twenty-five miles or so outside of St. Louis, Missouri, lies little Herculaneum, a town of only 2,369 people. Looming over the town's economy and the local environment is the Doe Run Company's lead-smelter, which dates back to 1892 and is the largest in the United States. For over twenty years now federal and state regulators have been after the company for polluting. In 1991 they required Doe Run to replace the topsoil in the gardens of about ninety houses in the vicinity of its smelter. In 2001 a study found that 24 percent of the children under six living within a mile of the company's plant had dangerously high levels of lead in their blood. As a result, Doe Run has agreed to clean up the site and has started installing new pollution-control devices to prevent further contamination.[60]

In the meantime, however, environmental investigators have found lead levels as high as 300,000 parts per million on a road used by the plant's trucks. Because of the health hazard that lead contamination poses, the state government and the company want to move local residents temporarily from their homes, replace the topsoil in their lawns and gardens, and clean their houses of lead dust. The state has put up signs warning residents of Herculaneum not to let children play outside, and

the federal government is helping out by advising people to alter their diets to resist lead poisoning (the gist: don't drink tea but eat more liver, eggs, whole-grain bread, and ice cream). Not so surprisingly, many residents of Herculaneum find this sort of assistance insulting. Instead, they want the federal government to step in, declare Herculaneum a Superfund cleanup site, and use federal funds to buy up the whole town. The Environmental Protection Agency (EPA), however, believes that adding Herculaneum to the long list of places seeking a Superfund buyout will only delay a solution.

The EPA is right not to exaggerate the speed with which Superfund projects move. When Congress created Superfund in 1980, sponsors of the legislation believed that the program could mop up the nation's worst toxic dumps and other dangerously polluted sites within five years and do so for a relatively modest $1.6 billion, to be covered by sales taxes on chemical and petroleum-based products. Superfund was authorized to recover its costs from the polluters themselves and to use this money to pay for future cleanup efforts. In this way, Superfund would become self-financing, with industry, not the taxpayers, picking up the tab. But the hopes of Superfund's sponsors have yet to be realized.

Congress has repeatedly had to pour money into the program to keep it going; there are continual complaints about inefficient, top-heavy administration, and to date only a portion of the country's most environmentally damaged sites have been restored.

Moreover, Superfund has grown increasingly and staggeringly expensive. Its cleanup efforts have become mired in lawsuits, with the resulting litigation costs climbing to the stars. The problem, many observers believe, goes back to the initial Superfund legislation, which permits the EPA to penalize companies for dumping and polluting that was not illegal at the time it occurred. In addition, it makes individual polluters liable for the entire cleanup costs of toxic sites that may have been used by many other firms. Not only do corporations dislike these liability principles; they find it less expensive to resist the EPA in court than to pay up. "From the individual corporation's perspective," says David Morell, a toxic removal consultant and an expert on Superfund's history, "lawyers' bills are still cheaper than paying for an entire cleanup." And he adds: "The longer you can stall—and convince yourself that you may never have to pay at all—the more the legal fees seem like a bargain."

As a result, a flood of lawsuits has slowed Superfund's cleanup efforts to a crawl while the costs of those efforts have ballooned. "The idea [behind Superfund]," Morell says, "was supposed to be 'shovels first and litigation later.' Instead, it has become 'litigation first and shovels never.'" Many experts agree that Superfund has become a financial black hole. Legal fees, transaction costs, and administrative overhead associated with its cleanup projects are projected to exceed $200 billion. Others put the bill as high as $2,000 per person—paid in price increases on countless everyday chemical and petroleum-based products. And this sum doesn't pay for the removal of hazardous wastes; it covers only litigation-related costs.

According to critics, Congress had done little to solve the problems with Superfund, except to keep digging deeper into the national coffers to keep it going. However, in 2001 Congress did exempt small businesses from Superfund liability if they contributed only a relatively small amount of hazardous waste to a targeted site, and it required the EPA to consider a company's ability to pay when negotiating a settlement. For its part, the EPA contends that it is making good progress. It reports that 760 of the 1,509 toxic waste sites now designated as National Priorities List Sites have been cleaned up and that work has started on over 400 more. Still, every day of delay increases the cleanup costs as waste from untreated sites seeps into the groundwater and increases the size of the polluted area. "These sites are not like fine wine," John O'Connor, director of the National Campaign Against Toxic Hazards, has explained. "They get worse with age, and they get more difficult and costly to clean up."

Meanwhile back in Herculaneum, the state of Missouri and Doe Run have come up with a plan to purchase the homes of twenty-six families who live within a half mile of the plant and have children under six years old and then later to buy up another 134 homes in the same area. Although the plan is voluntary, residents are questioning it for several reasons. First, two schools are within the half-mile zone. What is to be done with them? Second, the plan does nothing for the rest of Herculaneum, where contamination, though less dangerous, is still serious. And finally there is no guarantee that the company will give the homeowners more than the fair market value of their homes—which is, unfortunately, practically nothing. Residents want pre-contamination prices.

Discussion Questions

1. Identify the values and describe the attitudes that have contributed to pollution problems like those at Herculaneum. How would you feel if you lived in Herculaneum?

2. Do individuals inside the company, now or in the past, bear responsibility for causing the environmental damage at Herculaneum, or is it only the company as a whole? Is that responsibility shared by anyone outside the company? Should families who moved to Herculaneum have known better?

3. Who should pay the costs of cleaning up Herculaneum—the company? The town? The state? The federal government? What if the cost of restoring Herculaneum exceeds Doe

Run's resources? In general, whose responsibility is it to clean up the country's hazardous pollution sites and waste dumps?

4. What exactly should be done for residents living near the smelter? Are they entitled to receive the original cost of their homes from either the government or Doe Run? What about the rest of the town—should Superfund purchase all of it?

5. Is it fair for Superfund to fine polluters for dumping or polluting that was legal at the

time? Is it fair that each individual polluter have full liability for cleaning up environmental damage to which others may have also contributed? How might Superfund be made to work better?

6. With regard to pollution in general and the disposal of toxic wastes in particular, what are the obligations of individual manufacturers and of society as a whole to future generations?

CASE 11.2

Poverty and Pollution

It is called Brazil's "valley of death," and it may be the most polluted place on Earth. It lies about an hour's drive south of São Paulo, where the land suddenly drops 2,000 feet to a coastal plain. More than 100,000 people live in the valley, along with a variety of industrial plants that discharge thousands of tons of pollutants into the air every day. A reporter for *National Geographic* recalls that within an hour of his arrival in the valley, his chest began aching as the polluted air inflamed his bronchial tubes and restricted his breathing.[61]

The air in the valley is loaded with toxins—among them benzene, a known carcinogen. One in ten of the area's factory workers has a low white-blood cell count, a possible precursor to leukemia. Infant mortality is 10 percent higher here than in the region as a whole. Out of 40,000 urban residents in the valley municipality of Cubatão, nearly 13,000 cases of respiratory disease were reported in a recent year.

Few of the local inhabitants complain, however. For them, the fumes smell of jobs. They also distrust bids to buy their property by local industry, which wants to expand, as well as government efforts to relocate them to free homesites on a landfill. One young mother says, "Yes, the children are often ill and sometimes can barely breathe. We want to live in another place, but we cannot afford to."

A university professor of public health, Dr. Oswaldo Campos, views the dirty air in Cubatão simply as the result of economic priorities. "Some say it is the price of progress," Campos comments, "but is it? Look who pays the price—the poor."[62]

Maybe the poor do pay the price of pollution, but there are those who believe that they should have more of it. One of them is Lawrence Summers, who was chief economist of the World Bank and subsequently Secretary of the U.S. Treasury, and is now president of Harvard University. He has argued that the bank should encourage the migration of dirty, polluting industries to the poorer, less-developed countries.[63] Why? First, Summers reasons, the costs of health-impairing pollution depend on the earnings forgone from increased injury and death. So polluting should be done in the countries with the lowest costs—that is, with the lowest wages. "The economic logic behind dumping a load of toxic waste in the lowest-wage country," he writes, "is impeccable."

Second, because pollution costs rise disproportionately as pollution increases, it makes sense to shift pollution from already dirty places such as Los Angeles to clean ones like the relatively underpopulated countries in Africa, whose air Summers describes as "vastly *under*-polluted." Third, people value a clean environment more as their incomes rise. If other things are equal, costs fall if pollution moves from affluent places to less affluent places.

Critics charge that Summers views the world through "the distorting prism of market economics" and that his ideas are "a recipe for ruin." Not only do the critics want "greener" development in the Third World, but also they are outraged by Summers's assumption that the value of a life—or of increases or decreases in life expectancy—can be measured in terms of per capita income. This premise implies that an American's life is worth that of a hundred Kenyans and that society should value an extra year of life for a middle-level manager more than it values an extra year for a blue-collar, production-line worker.

Some economists, however, believe that Summers's ideas are basically on the right track. They emphasize that environmental policy always involves trade-offs and that therefore we should seek a balance between costs and benefits. As a matter of fact, the greatest cause of misery in the Third World is poverty. If environmental controls slow growth, then fewer people will be lifted out of poverty by economic development. For this reason, they argue, the richer countries should not impose their standards of environmental protection on poorer nations.

But even if economic growth is the cure for poverty, other economists now believe that sound environmental policy is necessary for durable growth, or at least that growth and environmental protection may not be incompatible. First, environmental damage can undermine economic productivity, and the health effects of pollution on a country's workforce reduce output. Second, poverty itself is an important cause of environmental damage because people living at subsistence levels are unable to invest in environmental protection. Finally, if economic growth and development are defined broadly enough, then enhanced environmental quality is part and parcel of the improvement in welfare that development must bring. For example, 1 billion people in developing countries lack access to clean water while 1.7 billion suffer from inadequate sanitation. Economic development for them means improving their environment. Still, rich and poor countries tend to have different environmental concerns: Environmentalists in affluent nations worry about protecting endangered species, preserving biological diversity, saving the ozone, and preventing climate change, whereas their counterparts in poorer countries are more concerned with dirty air, dirty water, soil erosion, and deforestation.

Update:

According to a World Bank report, environmental conditions have improved in Cubatão, where, thanks to state action and an aroused population, pollution is no worse today than in other medium-sized industrial cities in Brazil. True, it's no paradise, but some days you can see the sun, children are healthier, and fish are returning to the river (though their tissues are laced with toxic metals).[64]

Discussion Questions

1. What attitudes and values on the part of business and others lead to the creation of areas like the "valley of death"?

2. Should the Third World have more pollution, as Lawrence Summers argues? Assess his argument that dirty industries should move to poorer and less-polluted areas.

3. Some say, "Pollution is the price of progress." Is this assertion correct? What is meant by "progress"? Who in fact pays the price? Explain both the moral and economic issues raised by the assertion. What are the connections between economic progress and development, on one hand, and pollution controls and environmental protection, on the other?

4. Do human beings have a moral right to a livable environment? To a nonpolluted environment? It might be argued that if people in the "valley of death" don't complain and don't wish to move, then they accept the risks of living there and the polluters are not violating their rights. Assess this argument.

5. Assess the argument that people in the Third World should learn from the errors of the West and seek development without pollution. Should there be uniform, global environmental standards, or should pollution control standards be lower for less-developed countries?

CASE 11.3

Rewrapping the Big Mac

Consumers don't much like campaigns that promote corporate donations to environmental groups and causes. Take, for example, the Minute Maid advertisements that urged consumers to send in 75 cents and a proof-of-purchase seal, after which the company would "help keep America growing and beautiful" by matching each donation with equal money and planting a redwood seedling. When only a few thousand donations came in, Minute Maid's redwood campaign sputtered embarrassingly to a halt. Worse yet from the company's point of view, it was soon caught up in a flap with environmentalists who publicly pointed out that Minute Maid's juice cartons were not recyclable.

Researchers, in fact, have established the not-so-surprising fact that Americans quite sensibly prefer companies to clean up their own environmental problems before trying to hitch their names and products to the green bandwagon.[65] Perhaps an appreciation of this fact was behind McDonald's decision to do away with its famous "clamshell"-style, polystyrene foam hamburger boxes and switch to paper packaging. This decision came as a surprise to industry observers because only a week earlier the company had been preparing to respond to public pressure for a cleaner environment by announcing that it would extend its limited plastics-recycling program to all of its 8,500 restaurants.

The company continues to insist that its foam packaging was environmentally sound. But "our customers just don't feel good about it," said Edward H. Rensi, the president of McDonald's U.S.A. "So we're changing." McDonald's, which has gone beyond selling hamburgers to become a kind of national institution, knew that the last thing it needed was to have schoolchildren told that its products were damaging society. As one commentator put it, "If it appeared to be putting profit over the environment by stubbornly staying with a material widely regarded as detrimental to the environment, the company risked alienating many of the same younger customers who avoided buying tuna caught by methods that kill dolphins." "Customer demands are changing," adds a design firm executive. "In the past, convenience was the most important attribute of a package. Now there is a new need: to be sensitive to the environment."

One person who helped drive this message home to Rensi was Frederic D. Krupp, executive director of the Environmental Defense Fund. When he learned that McDonald's had decided to stick with recycling, he called Rensi personally to air his objections. Krupp let McDonald's know that the Environmental Defense Fund was prepared to oppose publicly the recycling program if the company went ahead with it. Krupp and the Fund are not against recycling, but they felt that the benefit of a switch in materials was greater. "The hierarchy is this: reduce, reuse, and recycle," Krupp says, adding that "the new packaging has 90 percent less bulk than foam." Krupp also argued that switching to paper would save McDonald's money, something Rensi now says the company already knew.

In any case, Krupp's intervention prompted a top-level management review and, after years of defending the use of foam, a swift reversal of policy. So swift, in fact, that Allen Hershkowitz, a senior scientist with the Natural Resources Defense Council, says, "This is a case for the business schools. The decision was made in the last 72 hours. You get the impression they do something and then try to figure out what it means."

Although some applaud the plastic-to-paper decision as proof that corporations and environmentalists can work together, others, especially those in the polystyrene packaging industry, resent what they see as McDonald's caving in to the ill-considered demands of the environmental lobby. "This came as a shock to us," reports R. Jerry Johnson, president of the polystyrene packagers' trade association. "We have been working for ten years with these guys on recycling." Joseph W. Bow, president of the Foodservice and Packaging Institute, adds, "This is a big deal to us because of the fact that

McDonald's bowed to public pressure. We want to see a free economy where materials are used based on their advantages, not on the wishes of powerful groups."

In terms of design, there's no question that the old foam carton was a packaging success. Not only did it protect the hamburger, but its revolutionary design allowed it to latch itself; all an employee had to do was shove it shut. And it was ideal for maintaining the hamburger at an appropriate temperature; even McDonald's concedes that paper packaging is not as good as foam at retaining heat. The company's critics see the pressure on McDonald's simply as an environmentalist attack on a major symbol of the throwaway, fast-food lifestyle. "This is not about polystyrene," says John Giroux, president of the Amoco subsidiary that supplied foam packaging to McDonald's, noting that the material is widely used throughout the food industry—for example, in egg cartons, which have not come under attack. Other commentators join him, seeing the pressure on McDonald's as one more ill-informed, middle-class enthusiasm of the environmental movement. And some environmentalists agree.

"Using a lot more paper means a lot more pollution," points out Jan Beyea, a scientist at the National Audubon Society. "It is a mistake to make plastic the great satan and paper the great saint." For one thing, polystyrene can be recycled, whereas McDonald's new paper packaging cannot because of its multilayered construction. Furthermore, the production of paper packaging requires significantly more energy than polystyrene manufacture, and it produces more atmospheric emissions and waterborne wastes.

Ironically, McDonald's introduced its clamshell foam box in 1975, replacing its earlier paper packaging, in part because of environmental concerns. At the time, an independent study by the Stanford Research Institute had reported: "There appears to be no supportable basis for any claim that paper-related products are superior from an environmental standpoint to plastic-related ones, including polystyrene.

The weight of existing evidence indicates that the favorable true environmental balance, if any, would be in the direction of the plastic-related product." Chuck Ebeling, director of Communications for McDonald's, acknowledges that the foam boxes were considered environmentally innovative. "There was a lot of concern about paper [then]," he says. "Getting out of paper was considered a real progressive move."

Discussion Questions

1. Describe the factors that prompted McDonald's decision. Why do you think it reversed its longstanding policy so quickly? To what extent was the company motivated by a genuine concern for the environment and to what extent by self-interest?

2. Do you agree with the decision? Was it an environmentally sound one? Should the issue have been studied further? What do you make of the fact[66] that McDonald's continues to use polystyrene foam boxes overseas?

3. What were McDonald's moral obligations in this case? How should we address the problem of fast-food packaging, waste, and recycling?

4. Was the pressure applied by the Environmental Defense Fund and other environmentalists a good thing, or was it, as Johnson and Bow intimate, an illegitimate intrusion into a business decision? Does such pressure cause environmental issues to be oversimplified, or is it necessary to ensure that companies behave responsibly toward the environment?

5. Critics of the decision claim that environmentalists focused on McDonald's because the company symbolizes a throwaway, fast-food culture that they don't like, and not because its cartons were particularly damaging to the environment. Do you agree?

CASE 11.4

The Fordasaurus

Before Ford publicly unveiled the biggest sport-utility vehicle ever, the Sierra Club ran a contest for the best name and marketing slogan for it. Among the entries were "Fordasaurus, powerful enough to pass anything on the highway except a gas station" and "Ford Saddam, the truck that will put America between Iraq and a hard place." But the winner was "Ford Valdez: Have you driven a tanker lately?"[67]

Ford, which decided to name the nine-passenger vehicle the Excursion, was not amused. Sales of sport-utility vehicles (SUVs) exploded in the 1990s, going up nearly sixfold, and the company sees itself as simply responding to consumer demand for ever larger models. Although most SUVs never leave the pavement, their drivers like knowing their vehicles can go anywhere and do anything. They also like their SUVs to be big. The Excursion is now the largest passenger vehicle on the road, putting Ford far ahead of its rivals in the competition to build the biggest and baddest SUV. The Excursion weighs 8,500 pounds, equivalent to two mid-sized sedans or three Honda Civics. It is more than 6½ feet wide, nearly 7 feet high, and almost 19 feet long—too big to fit comfortably into some garages or into a single parking space.

Although the Excursion is expensive ($40,000 to $50,000 when loaded with options), it is, like other SUVs, profitable to build. Because Ford based the Excursion on the chassis of its Super Duty truck, the company was able to develop the vehicle for a relatively modest investment of about $500 million. With sales of 50,000 to 60,000 per year, Ford earns about $20,000 per vehicle.

Most SUVs are classified as light trucks. Under current rules, they are allowed to emit up to several times more smog-causing gases per mile than automobiles. In 1999, the Clinton administration proposed tighter emissions restrictions on new passenger cars, restrictions that new vehicles in the light-truck category would also have to meet by 2009. However, these rules would not affect the Excursion, which is heavy enough to be classified as a medium-duty truck.

Ford says that the Excursion, with its 44-gallon gas tank, gets 10 to 15 miles per gallon, and that its emission of pollutants is 43 percent below the maximum for its class. By weight, about 85 percent of the vehicle is recyclable, and 20 percent of it comes from recycled metals and plastics. The company thus believes that the Excursion is in keeping with the philosophy of William Clay Ford, Jr. When he became chairman in September 1998, he vowed to make Ford "the world's most environmentally friendly auto maker." He added, however, that "what we do to help the environment must succeed as a business proposition. A zero-emission vehicle that sits unsold on a dealer's lot is not reducing pollution."

The company, however, has failed to win environmentalists to its side. They believe that with the Excursion, the Ford Company is a long way from producing an environmentally friendly product. Daniel Becker of the Sierra Club points out that in the course of an average lifetime of 120,000 miles, each Excursion will emit 130 tons of carbon dioxide, the principal cause of global warming. "It's just bad for the environment any way you look at it," he says. John DeCicco of the American Council for an Energy-Efficient Economy agrees. He worries further that the Excursion is clearing the way for bigger and bigger vehicles. "This is the antithesis of green leadership."

Stung by criticism of the Excursion, William Clay Ford, Jr., has vowed to make the company a more responsible environmental citizen. Worried that if automobile producers don't clean up their act, they will become as vilified as cigarette companies, in August 2000 Ford promised it would improve the fuel economy of its SUVs by 25 percent over the next five years, smugly inviting other automakers to follow its green leadership. To this GM responded that it was the real green leader and "will still be in five years, or 10 years, or for that matter 20 years. End of story." When they aren't bragging about their greenness, however, both companies continue to lobby Congress to forbid the Department of Transportation from studying fuel economy increases.[68]

Update:
According to media reports, yet to be confirmed by Ford, the company is planning on phasing out the Excursion after 2004.

Discussion Questions

1. Are environmentalists right to be concerned about the environmental impact of SUVs? How do you explain the growing demand for ever larger passenger vehicles?

2. In developing and producing the Excursion, is the Ford Motor Company sacrificing the environment to profits, or is it acting in a socially responsible way by making the Excursion rela-

tively energy efficient for its vehicle class? If you had been on the board of directors, would you have voted for the project? Why/why not? Do Ford's stockholders have a right to insist that it produce the most profitable vehicles it legally can, regardless of their environmental impact?

3. Assess William Clay Ford's claim that he wants to make his company the "world's most environmentally friendly automaker"? What are the environmental responsibilities of automakers?

4. Is Ford Motor Company simply responding to consumer demand for large vehicles, or is it helping to shape and encourage that demand?

5. Should there be tighter pollution restrictions on SUVs? Should the government try to discourage the production and use of SUVs?

CASE 11.5

The Fight over the Redwoods

Dense forests of coastal redwood trees once covered 2.2 million acres of southern Oregon and northern California. Today, only about 86,000 acres of virgin redwood forest remain. Most of this is in public parks and preserves, but about 6,000 acres of old-growth forest are privately owned—nearly all of it by the Pacific Lumber Company, headquartered in San Francisco.

Founded in 1869, Pacific Lumber owns 220,000 acres of the world's most productive timberland, including the old-growth redwoods. For years the family-run company was a model of social responsibility and environmental awareness. Pacific Lumber paid its employees well, supported them in bad times, funded their pensions, and provided college scholarships for their children. It sold or donated nearly 20,000 acres of forest to the public, and instead of

indiscriminate clear-cutting, the company logged its forests carefully and selectively. Throughout its history, the company harvested only about 2 percent of its trees annually, roughly equivalent to their growth rate. After other timber firms had logged all their old-growth stands, Pacific Lumber had a virtual monopoly on the highly durable lumber that comes from the heart of centuries-old redwood trees.[69]

Because Pacific Lumber was debt free and resource rich, its potential value drew attention on Wall Street, where the firm of Drexel Burnham Lambert suspected that the company was undervalued—and thus ripe for raiding. In 1985 Drexel hired a timber consultant to fly over Pacific Lumber's timberland to estimate its worth. With junk-bond financing arranged by its in-house expert, Michael Milken, Drexel assisted Charles Hurwitz, a Texas tycoon, and his firm, Maxxam, Inc., to take over Pacific Lumber for $900 million. After initially resisting the leveraged buyout, the timber company's directors eventually acquiesced, and by the end of the year Hurwitz and Maxxam had control of Pacific Lumber. At the time, Hurwitz was primary owner of United Financial Group, the parent company of United Savings Association of Texas. In exchange for Milken's raising the money for the takeover of Pacific Lumber, Hurwitz had United Savings purchase huge amounts of risky junk bonds from Drexel. Three years later, the savings and loan failed, and taxpayers were stuck with a bill for $1.6 billion.

The takeover of Pacific Lumber left Maxxam with nearly $900 million in high-interest debt. To meet the interest payments, Maxxam terminated Pacific Lumber's pension plan and replaced it with annuities purchased from an insurance company owned by Hurwitz. Worse still, Maxxam tripled the rate of logging on Pacific Lumber's lands, and it was soon clear that Hurwitz intended to log the now-famous Headwaters forest, a 3,000-acre grove of virgin redwoods—the largest single stand of redwoods still in private hands. The value of the grove is astronomical: Milled into lumber, some of the trees are worth $100,000 each.

The potential lumber may be worth a fortune to Hurwitz, but environmentalists consider the Headwaters grove to be priceless as it is, and they have stepped in to do battle with Hurwitz. They see the Headwaters forest with its 500- to 2,000-year-old trees as an intricate ecosystem that took millions of years to evolve, a web of animals and plants that depend not just on living trees but also on dead, fallen redwoods that provide wildlife habitat and reduce soil erosion. Some of these activists—including Darryl Cherney, a member of the environmental group Earth First!—have devoted their lives to stopping Hurwitz.

Earth First! is not a mainstream conservation organization; it has a reputation for destroying billboards, sabotaging bulldozers and lumber trucks, and spiking trees with nails that chew up the blades of saws. "Hurwitz is a latter-day robber baron," says Cherney. "The only thing that's negotiable . . . is the length of his jail sentence."

Other environmental organizations have opposed Hurwitz in court. The Sierra Club Legal Defense Fund and the Environmental Protection Information Center have filed sixteen lawsuits against Pacific Lumber, giving the company's legal experts a run for their money. One of these suits bore fruit in 1995, when a judge blocked the company's plan to harvest timber in a smaller old-growth forest known as Owl Creek Grove. The legal reason was protection of the marbled murrelet, a bird about the size of a thrush, which breeds in the forest and is close to extinction. The judge also noted that "after the logging of an old-growth forest, the original cathedral-like columns of trees do not regenerate for a period of 200 years."

Pacific Lumber appealed the Owl Creek decision, but the ruling was upheld a year later. However, at the same time, the company won the right to appeal to another court to be allowed to harvest timber in the larger Headwaters forest. Meanwhile, both conservationists and a number of public officials are making strenuous efforts to acquire Headwaters and nine other surrounding redwood groves of about 200 acres each from Hurwitz. Although Hurwitz continues to fight both environmentalists and the government in court, he has quietly taken some steps to facilitate a sale, both through an indirect public relations campaign and by refinancing his takeover debt so that if the grove is sold, the proceeds would flow to Maxxam free and clear. Hurwitz has never named a price, but his deputies claim that the U.S. Forest Service has appraised the Headwaters forest at $500 million.

Some environmentalists balk at paying Hurwitz what amounts to ransom. They point to the fact that several government agencies, including the Federal Deposit Insurance Corporation, have filed suit against Hurwitz; they want $250 million from Hurwitz and $500 million from United Financial Group for their role in the $1.6 billion crash of United Savings. The environmentalists argue that Hurwitz should be forced to swap the forest in exchange for being forgiven the federal government's claims against him: The public gets Headwaters; Hurwitz gets off. Hurwitz, however, says that the lawsuits are without merit and denies any wrongdoing in the failure of the savings and loan.

Other environmentalists worry that too much attention is being directed toward saving the 3,000-acre Headwaters grove while leaving Pacific Lumber free to log the rest of its land with abandon. They are less concerned about the murrelets in particular or even the redwoods themselves; rather, what disturbs them is the dismantling of an ancient and intricate ecosystem—an irreplaceable temperate rain forest, home to some 160 species of plants and animals. Their aim is to build a new style of forestry based on values other than board feet of lumber and dollars of profit. They seek sustainable forest management and a new resource ethic devoted to rebuilding and maintaining habitats for coho salmon, the murrelet, the weasel-like fisher, and the northern spotted owl. As a first step, these conservationists call for protection, not just of the 3,000 Headwaters acres, but for an area nearly twenty times that amount, called the Headwaters Forest Complex. This tract includes all the ancient redwoods that Hurwitz owns and large areas of previously logged forest. "We have a vision that's bigger than Headwaters," says Cecelia Lanman of the Environmental Protection Information Center.

Her vision is definitely more sweeping than that of the Pacific Lumber workers in Scotia, California, a village containing 272 company-owned homes. Because Hurwitz has instituted stepped-up logging, which has meant more jobs, his employees tend to side with him, not the environmentalists. Workers say that Hurwitz has reinvested more than $100 million in modernizing his mills and has kept up the tradition of paying college scholarships for their children. The environmentalists are the real threat, says one employee. "You've got a group of people who hate Mr. Hurwitz, and they're using the Endangered Species Act and anything they can to hurt him. And we're caught in the middle."

Update:

In March 1999, Hurwitz signed a deal that a federal team led by Senator Dianne Feinstein and Deputy Interior Secretary John Garamendi had begun negotiating with him several years earlier.[70] In exchange for a 7,500-acre tract that includes the Headwaters grove and 2,500 additional acres of old-growth forest, the U.S. government and the state of California agreed to pay Pacific Lumber $480 million. The agreement also bans logging for fifty years on 8,000 other acres of company land in order to safeguard the murrelet, and it sets up buffer zones to protect the river habitats of endangered coho salmon and steelhead trout. A Habitat Protection Plan regulates how and where Pacific Lumber harvests timber on the rest of its land. However, because Hurwitz transferred the $868 million debt that still remains from his original hostile takeover of Pacific Lumber from Maxxam to Pacific Lumber itself, the company will need to log as much as it can to make its interest payments.

Feinstein and Garamendi defended the deal as the best that they could get, and President Clinton and California Governor Gray Davis called the pact that saved Headwaters "historic." But Darryl Cherney and other activists have criticized the agreement as a sellout. They would like to see Pacific Lumber more closely regulated, claiming that the company still engages in overharvesting, clearcutting instead of thinning, and various other poor logging practices. They also note that for 10,000 acres the government is paying Hurwitz half of what he originally spent for the entire company with its 220,000 acres of timberland.

Pacific Lumber, for its part, contends that state and federal agencies are so rigidly enforcing the habitat conservation plan that it can't cut enough lumber to keeps its mills running, and in late 2001 it closed down Scotia's 104-year-old mill. "We are being strangled by the operating restraints," said Robert Manne, current president of Pacific Lumber, which are "not working to meet the company and its employees' economic needs." To this complaint, conservationists and governmental officials respond that Pacific Lumber, which will continue to operate two smaller and much newer mills in neighboring towns, is scapegoating them for problems stemming from falling timber prices and the company's depletion of its old-growth redwood groves by clear-cutting. According to Paul Mason, president of a local environmental organization, "The lumber market is right in the tank, and that takes a bite out of your profit margin. The company has been operating at an unsustainable level for a number of years."

Discussion Questions

1. Does an ancient redwood forest have value other than its economic one as potential lumber? If so, what is this value, and how is it to be weighed against the interests of a company like Maxxam? Are redwoods more important than jobs?

2. Is it morally permissible for private owners to do as they wish with the timberland they own? Explain why or why not. What's your assessment of Hurwitz? Is he a robber baron or a socially responsible businessperson, or something in between?

3. Are mainstream environmentalists right to try to thwart Hurwitz, or are they simply trying to impose their values on others? Does a radical group like Earth First! that engages in sabotage go too far, or do its ends justify its means?

4. Do we have a moral obligation to save old redwood forests? Can a forest have either moral or legal rights? Does an old-growth forest have value in and of itself, or is its value only a function of human interests? How valuable is a small, but endangered species such as the murrelet?

5. Before its takeover by Hurwitz, did Pacific Lumber neglect its obligations to its stockholders by not logging at a faster rate? What would be a morally responsible policy for a timber company to follow? Do we need a new environmental resource ethic?

6. How would you respond to the argument that there is no need to try to save the Headwaters (or any other private) forest because there are already tens of thousands of acres of old-growth redwood forest in parks and preserves?

7. Is the deal that the U.S. government and the state of California struck with Pacific Lumber a fair and reasonable one? Are taxpayers having to pay too much, as environmentalists think? Is Pacific Lumber being squeezed too hard? What about Scotia and its laid-off workers?

Notes to Chapter 11

1. Eugene Linden, "Condition Critical," *Time* (Special Edition), April/May 2000, 19, 20.

2. Tom Regan, ed., *Earthbound: Introductory Essays in Environmental Ethics* (New York: Random House, 1984), 3.

3. See John Wargo, *Our Children's Toxic Legacy: How Science and Law Fail to Protect Us from Pesticides* (New Haven, Conn.: Yale University Press, 1996).

4. "From *Silent Spring* to Barren Spring?" *Business Week,* March 18, 1996, 42.

5. "Kids Need More Protection from Chemicals," *Los Angeles Times,* January 28, 1999, B9.

6. "Study Links Air Pollution, Heart Defects in Newborns," *San Jose Mercury News,* December 31, 2002, 17A.

7. "U.S. Reveals How Much Industry Pollutes the Air," *San Francisco Chronicle,* March 23, 1989, A1.

8. "Clinton Sharply Tightens Air Pollution Regulations," *New York Times,* June 26, 1997, A1.

9. See Michael D. Lemonick, "How to Prevent a Meltdown," *Time* (Special Edition), 61; Bill McKibben, "Acquaintance of the Earth," *New York Review of Books,* May 25, 2000, 48–49; and "Special Report: Global Warming," *Time,* April 23, 2001, 46–55.

10. Ken Silverstein, "Meat Factories," *Sierra,* January–February 1999; "Group's Surprising Beef with Meat Industry," *San Francisco Chronicle,* April 27, 1999; A1; and "Big Farms Making a Mess of U.S. Waters, Cities Say," *New York Times,* February 10, 2002, sec. 1, 20.

11. "Chernobyl Still Has a Future," *San Jose Mercury News,* April 13, 1996, 15A.

12. "The Dead Zone," *Economist,* August 24, 2002, 26.

13. "*Playboy* Interview: Dr. Paul Ehrlich," *Playboy,* August 1970, 56.

14. John Steinbeck, *America and Americans* (New York: Viking Press, 1966), 127.

15. Garrett Hardin, "The Tragedy of the Commons," *Science* 162 (December 13, 1968): 1243–1248.

16. "The Tragedy of the Oceans," *Economist,* March 19, 1994, 21–24; John McQuaid, "Reaching the Limit," *San Francisco Examiner,* July 7, 1996, A10; Linden, "Condition Critical," 18.

17. William T. Blackstone, "Ethics and Ecology," in William T. Blackstone, ed., *Philosophy and Environmental Crisis* (Athens: University of Georgia Press, 1974).

18. Sharon Begley, "Furry Math? Market Has Failed to Capture the True Value of Nature," *Wall Street Journal,* August 9, 2002, B1.

19. Ibid.

20. "Would You Pay More to Let Nature Thrive?" *San Jose Mercury News,* October 4, 1994, 1A.

21. James Lis and Kenneth Chilton, "Limits of Pollution Prevention," *Society* 30 (March–April 1993): 50.

22. Mark Hertsgaard, "A Global Green Deal," *Time* (Special Edition), 82–83.

23. *Business Horizons* 39 (January–February 1996): 67; *Time* (Special Edition), 87; "Waste Not," *San Francisco Chronicle,* July 9, 2000, "Sunday," 1.

24. U.S. Bureau of the Census, *Statistical Abstract of the United States 2001* (Washington, D.C.: U.S. Government Printing Office, 2002), Table 1084.

25. "Would You Pay More?" *San Jose Mercury News.*

26. *Business and Society Review* 84 (Winter 1993): 22–23.

27. Molly Ivins, "America's Corporate Hall of Shame," *San Francisco Chronicle,* April 9, 1999, A23.

28. "Grime and Punishment," *New Republic,* February 20, 1989, 7.

29. Ibid.

30. Ibid., 8.

31. Keith Davis and Robert L. Blomstein, *Business and Society* (New York: McGraw-Hill, 1978), 440.

32. "Environmental Enemy No. 1," *Economist,* July 6, 2002, 11.

33. Lis and Chilton, "Limits of Pollution Prevention," 53.

34. See George Steiner, *Business and Society* (New York: Random House, 1973), 247.

35. "How Many Planets? A Survey of the Global Environment," *Economist,* July 6, 2002, 16.

36. Michael J. Sandel, "It's Immoral to Buy the Right to Pollute," *New York Times,* December 15, 1997, A19.

37. Michael E. Porter and Claas van der Linde, "Green and Competitive: Ending the Stalemate," *Harvard Business Review* 73 (September–October 1995): 120, 122, 125; Hertsgaard, "A Global Green Deal."

38. Porter and van der Linde, "Green and Competitive," 125–126, 128–129.

39. "Yes, Global Warming," *International Herald Tribune,* February 2, 1997, 8; Hertsgaard, "A Global Green Deal."

40. U.S Bureau of the Census, *Statistical Abstract of the United States 2001,* Table 1369.

41. Paul R. Ehrlich and Anne H. Ehrlich, "Population, Plenty, and Poverty," *National Geographic,* December 1988, 917.

42. Ibid.

43. Mathis Wackernagel et al., "Tracking the Ecological Overshoot of the Human Economy," *Proceedings of the National Academy of Sciences* 99 (June 27, 2002): 9266.

44. Joel Feinberg, "The Rights of Animals and Unborn Generations," in Tom L. Beauchamp and Norman E. Bowie, eds.,

Ethical Theory and Business, 2nd ed. (Englewood Cliffs, N.J.: Prentice Hall, 1983), 435.

45. Derek Parfit, *Reasons and Persons* (New York: Oxford University Press, 1986), 365.

46. Annette Baier, "The Rights of Past and Future Persons," in Joseph R. DesJardins and John J. McCall, eds., *Contemporary Issues in Business Ethics* (Belmont, Calif.: Wadsworth, 1985), 501; and Robert Elliot, "The Rights of Future People," *Journal of Applied Philosophy* 6 (1989).

47. See John Rawls, *A Theory of Justice* (Cambridge: Harvard University Press, 1971), 284–293.

48. William F. Baxter, *People or Penguins: The Case for Optimal Pollution* (New York: Columbia University Press, 1974), Chapter 1.

49. Holmes Rolston III, "Just Environmental Business," in Tom Regan, ed., *Just Business: New Introductory Essays in Business Ethics* (New York: Random House, 1984), 325.

50. See W. Wayt Gibbs, "On the Termination of Species," *Scientific American,* November 2001.

51. Jeremy Bentham, *An Introduction to the Principles of Morals and Legislation* (1789), Chapter 17, sec. 2.

52. Peter Singer, "Animal Liberation," *New York Review of Books,* April 5, 1973.

53. Quoted by Rolston, "Just Environmental Business," 340.

54. Tom L. Beauchamp, *Case Studies in Business, Society, and Ethics* (Englewood Cliffs, N.J.: Prentice Hall, 1983), 118–119.

55. Bradley S. Miller, "The Dangers of Factory Farming," *Business and Society Review* 65 (Spring 1988): 44; "What Humans Owe to Animals," *Economist,* August 19, 1995, 11.

56. Miller, "Dangers of Factory Farming," 43, 44.

57. Tom Regan, "Ethical Vegetarianism and Commercial Animal Farming," in Richard A. Wasserstrom, ed., *Today's Moral Problems,* 3rd ed. (New York: Macmillan, 1985), 463–464. See also "Also a Part of Creation," *Economist,* August 19, 1995, 19.

58. Singer, "Animal Liberation."

59. Jeremy Rifkin, "Hold Your Nose at the Steak House," *International Herald Tribune,* March 25, 1992, 4.

60. This case study is based on "At War with a Lead-Smelter," *Economist,* April 6, 2002, 30; front-page reports on Superfund in the *San Francisco Chronicle,* May 29 and May 30, 1991; and Michael Wines, "Waste Dumps Untouched, Survey Says," *Los Angeles Times,* September 7, 1984, I-5. See also *www.epa.gov/superfund.*

61. See Noel Grove, "Air: An Atmosphere of Uncertainty," *National Geographic,* April 1987.

62. Ibid.

63. The following paragraphs are based on "Let Them Eat Pollution," *Economist,* February 8, 1992, 66; "Pollution and the Poor," *Economist,* February 15, 1992, 18; "Economics Brief: A Greener Bank," *Economist,* May 23, 1992, 79; and "A Great Leap Forward," *Economist,* May 11, 2002.

64. David R. Wheeler, *Greening Industry,* (New York: Oxford University Press, 1999), Chapter 5.

65. " 'Green' Ads Can Make Consumer See Red," *Wall Street Journal,* December 5, 1990, B4. The rest of this case study is based on "Packaging and Public Image" and "A Symbol of America's Fast-Food Culture," *New York Times,* November 2, 1990, and Warren T. Brookes, "How McDonald's Caved in to Environmental Yuppies," *San Francisco Chronicle,* December 11, 1990, C3. See also "Plastic Finds Friend in Canadian Chemist," *San Francisco Chronicle,* February 2, 1991, A6, and "Management Brief: Food for Thought," *Economist,* August 29, 1992, 64–66.

66. Eric Schlosser, *Fast Food Nation* (New York: HarperCollins, 2000), 268–269.

67. This case study is based on Donald W. Nauss, "Ford About to Unveil 4 Tons of Controversy," *Los Angeles Times,* March 11, 1999, A1.

68. Margot Roosevelt, "How Green Was My SUV," *Time* (overseas edition), August 14, 2000, 34.

69. The primary source for this case study is Elliot Diringer, "Cutting a Deal on Redwoods," *San Francisco Chronicle,* September 4, 1996, A1.

70. This update is based on news stories in *San Francisco Chronicle,* March 3, 1999, A1; *New York Times,* March 3, 1999, A1, and March 6, 1999, A7; *Economist,* March 6, 1999, 30; and *San Jose Mercury News,* December 8, 2001, 21A.

Reading ■

THE PLACE OF NONHUMANS IN ENVIRONMENTAL ISSUES

PETER SINGER

Peter Singer's writings have catalyzed the debate over our treatment of animals. In the following essay, he argues that the effects of our environmental actions on nonhumans should figure directly in our deliberations about what we ought to do. Because animals can feel pleasure and pain and have the capacity for subjective experience, they can therefore be said to have interests, interests we must not ignore. Singer contends that we must extend the moral principle of "equal consideration of interests" to include the interests of nonhumans, and he sketches the

The first five sections of this essay are reprinted from Peter Singer, "Not for Humans Only: The Place of Nonhumans in Environmental Ethics," in K. E. Goodpaster and K. M. Sayre, eds., *Ethics and Problems of the 21st Century* (Notre Dame, Ind.: University of Notre Dame Press, 1979). Reprinted by permission. The final section is reprinted by permission from Peter Singer, "All Animals Are Equal," *Philosophic Exchange,* vol. 1, no. 5 (Summer 1974). Copyright © 1974 the Center for Philosophic Exchange. (Section headings have been added.)

implications of our doing so—including the necessity of abandoning our present practice of rearing and killing other animals for food.

I. HUMANS AND NONHUMANS

When we humans change the environment in which we live, we often harm ourselves. If we discharge cadmium into a bay and eat shellfish from that bay, we become ill and may die. When our industries and automobiles pour noxious fumes into the atmosphere, we find a displeasing smell in the air, the long-term results of which may be every bit as deadly as cadmium poisoning. The harm that humans do the environment, however, does not rebound solely, or even chiefly, on humans. It is nonhumans who bear the most direct burden of human interference with nature.

By "nonhumans" I mean to refer to all living things other than human beings, though for reasons to be given later, it is with nonhuman animals, rather than plants, that I am chiefly concerned. It is also important, in the context of environmental issues, to note that living things may be regarded either collectively or as individuals. In debates about the environment the most important way of regarding living things collectively has been to regard them as species. Thus, when environmentalists worry about the future of the blue whale, they usually are thinking of the blue whale as a species, rather than of individual blue whales. But this is not, of course, the only way in which one can think of blue whales, or other animals, and one of the topics I shall discuss is whether we should be concerned about what we are doing to the environment primarily insofar as it threatens entire species of nonhumans, or primarily insofar as it affects individual nonhuman animals.

The general question, then, is how the effects of our actions on the environment of nonhuman beings should figure in our deliberations about what we ought to do. There is an unlimited variety of contexts in which this issue could arise. To take just one: Suppose that it is considered necessary to build a new power station, and there are two sites, A and B, under consideration. In most respects the sites are equally suitable, but building the power station on site A would be more expensive because the greater depth of shifting soil at that site will require deeper foundations; on the other hand, to build on site B will destroy a favored breeding ground for thousands of wildfowl. Should the presence of the wildfowl enter into the decision as to where to build? And if so, in what manner should it enter, and how heavily should it weigh?

In a case like this the effects of our actions on nonhuman animals could be taken into account in two quite different ways: directly, giving the lives and welfare of nonhuman animals an intrinsic significance which must count in any moral calculation; or indirectly, so that the effects of our actions on nonhumans are morally significant only if they have consequences for humans. . . .

II. SPECIESISM

The view that the effects of our actions on other animals have no direct moral significance is not as likely to be openly advocated today as it was in the past; yet it is likely to be accepted implicitly and acted upon. When planners perform cost-benefit studies on new projects, the costs and benefits are costs and benefits for human beings only. This does not mean that the impact of [a] power station or highway on wildlife is ignored altogether, but it is included only indirectly. That a new reservoir would drown a valley teeming with wildlife is taken into account only under some such heading as the value of the facili-

ties for recreation that the valley affords. In calculating this value, the cost-benefit study will be neutral between forms of recreation like hunting and shooting and those like bird watching and bush walking—in fact hunting and shooting are likely to contribute more to the benefit side of the calculations because larger sums of money are spent on them, and they therefore benefit manufacturers and retailers of firearms as well as the hunters and shooters themselves. The suffering experienced by the animals whose habitat is flooded is not reckoned into the costs of the operation; nor is the recreational value obtained by the hunters and shooters offset by the cost to the animals that their recreation involves.

Despite its venerable origin, the view that the effects of our actions on nonhuman animals have no intrinsic moral significance can be shown to be arbitrary and morally indefensible. If a being suffers, the fact that it is not a member of our own species cannot be a moral reason for failing to take its suffering into account. This becomes obvious if we consider the analogous attempt by white slave-owners to deny consideration to the interests of blacks. These white racists limited their moral concern to their own race, so the suffering of a black did not have the same moral significance as the suffering of a white. We now recognize that in doing so they were making an arbitrary distinction, and that the existence of suffering, rather than the race of the sufferer, is what is really morally significant. The point remains true if "species" is substituted for "race." The logic of racism and the logic of the position we have been discussing, which I have elsewhere referred to as "speciesism," are indistinguishable; and if we reject the former then consistency demands that we reject the latter too.[1]

It should be clearly understood that the rejection of speciesism does not imply that the different species are in fact equal in respect of such characteristics as intelligence, physical strength, ability to communicate, capacity to suffer, ability to damage the environment, or anything else. After all, the moral principle of human equality cannot be taken as implying that all humans are equal in these respects either—if it did, we would have to give up the idea of human equality. That one being is more intelligent than another does not entitle him to enslave, exploit, or disregard the interests of the less intelligent being. The moral basis of equality among humans is not equality in fact, but the principle of equal consideration of interests, and it is this principle that, in consistency, must be extended to any nonhumans who have interests.

III. NONHUMANS HAVE INTERESTS

There may be some doubt about whether any nonhuman beings have interests. This doubt may arise because of uncertainty about what it is to have an interest, or because of uncertainty about the nature of some nonhuman beings. So far as the concept of "interest" is the cause of doubt, I take the view that only a being with subjective experiences, such as the experience of pleasure or the experience of pain, can have interests in the full sense of the term; and that any being with such experiences does have at least one interest, namely, the interest in experiencing pleasure and avoiding pain. Thus consciousness, or the capacity for subjective experience, is both a necessary and a sufficient condition for having an interest. While there may be a loose sense of the term in which we can say that it is in the interests of a tree to be watered, this attenuated sense of the term is not the sense covered by the principle of equal consideration of interests. All we mean when we say that it is in the interests of a tree to be watered is that the tree needs water if it is to continue to live and grow normally; if we regard this as evidence that the tree has interests, we might almost as well say that it is in the interests of a car to be lubricated regularly because the car needs lubrication if it is to run properly. In neither case can we really mean (unless we impute consciousness to trees or cars) that the tree or car has any preference about the matter.

The remaining doubt about whether nonhuman beings have interests is, then, a doubt about whether nonhuman beings have subjective experiences like the experience of pain. I have argued elsewhere that the commonsense view that birds and mammals feel pain is well founded,[2] but more serious doubts arise as we move down the evolutionary scale. Vertebrate animals have nervous systems broadly similar to our own and behave in ways that resemble our own pain behavior when subjected to stimuli that we would find painful; so the inference that vertebrates are capable of feeling pain is a reasonable one, though not as strong as it is if limited to mammals and birds. When we go beyond vertebrates to insects, crustaceans, mollusks and so on, the existence of subjective states becomes more dubious, and with very simple organisms it is difficult to believe that they could be conscious. As for plants, though there have been sensational claims that plants are not only conscious, but even psychic, there is no hard evidence that supports even the more modest claim.[3]

The boundary of beings who may be taken as having interests is therefore not an abrupt boundary, but a broad range in which the assumption that the being has interests shifts from being so strong as to be virtually certain to being so weak as to be highly improbable. The principle of equal consideration of interests must be applied with this in mind, so that where there is a clash between a virtually certain interest and a highly doubtful one, it is the virtually certain interest that ought to prevail.

In this manner our moral concern ought to extend to all beings who have interests. . . .

IV. EQUAL CONSIDERATION OF INTERESTS

Giving equal consideration to the interests of two different beings does not mean treating them alike or holding their lives to be of equal value. We may recognize that the interests of one being are greater than those of another, and equal consideration will then lead us to sacrifice the being with lesser interests, if one or the other must be sacrificed. For instance, if for some reason a choice has to be made between saving the life of a normal human being and that of a dog, we might well decide to save the human because he, with his greater awareness of what is going to happen, will suffer more before he dies; we may also take into account the likelihood that it is the family and friends of the human who will suffer more; and finally, it would be the human who had the greater potential for future happiness. This decision would be in accordance with the principle of equal consideration of interests, for the interests of the dog get the same consideration as those of the human, and the loss to the dog is not discounted because the dog is not a member of our species. The outcome is as it is because the balance of interests favors the human. In a different situation—say, if the human were grossly mentally defective and without family or anyone else who would grieve for it—the balance of interests might favor the nonhuman.[4]

The more positive side of the principle of equal consideration is this: where interests are equal, they must be given equal weight. So where human and nonhuman animals share an interest—as in the case of the interest in avoiding physical pain—we must give as much weight to violations of the interest of the nonhumans as we do to similar violations of the human's interest. This does not mean, of course, that it is as bad to hit a horse with a stick as it is to hit a human being, for the same blow would cause less pain to the animal with the tougher skin. The principle holds between similar amounts of felt pain, and what this is will vary from case to case.

It may be objected that we cannot tell exactly how much pain another animal is suffering, and that therefore the principle is impossible to apply. While I do not deny the difficulty and even, so far as precise measurement is concerned, the impossibility of comparing the subjective experiences of members of different species, I do not think that the problem is different in kind from the problem of comparing the subjective experiences of two members of our own species. Yet this is something we do all the time, for instance when we judge that a wealthy person will suffer less by being taxed at a higher rate than a poor person will gain from the welfare benefits paid for by the tax; or when we decide to take our two children to the beach instead of to a fair, because although the older one would prefer the fair, the younger one has a stronger preference the other way. These comparisons may be very rough, but since there is nothing better, we must use them; it would be irrational to refuse to do so simply because they are rough. Moreover, rough as they are, there are many situations in which we can be reasonably sure which way the balance of interests lies. While a difference of species may make compar-

isons rougher still, the basic problem is the same, and the comparisons are still often good enough to use, in the absence of anything more precise. . . .

V. EXAMPLES

We can now draw at least one conclusion as to how the existence of nonhuman living things should enter into our deliberations about actions affecting the environment: Where our actions are likely to make animals suffer, that suffering must count in our deliberations, and it should count equally with a like amount of suffering by human beings, insofar as rough comparisons can be made.

The difficulty of making the required comparison will mean that the application of this conclusion is controversial in many cases, but there will be some situations in which it is clear enough. Take, for instance, the wholesale poisoning of animals that is euphemistically known as "pest control." The authorities who conduct these campaigns give no consideration to the suffering they inflict on the "pests," and invariably use the method of slaughter they believe to be cheapest and most effective. The result is that hundreds of millions of rabbits have died agonizing deaths from the artificially introduced disease, myxomatosis, or from poisons like "ten-eighty"; coyotes and other wild dogs have died painfully from cyanide poisoning; and all manner of wild animals have endured days of thirst, hunger, and fear with a mangled limb caught in a leg-hold trap.[5] Granting, for the sake of argument, the necessity for pest control—though this has rightly been questioned—the fact remains that no serious attempts have been made to introduce alternative means of control and thereby reduce the incalculable amount of suffering caused by present methods. It would not, presumably, be beyond modern science to produce a substance which, when eaten by rabbits or coyotes, produced sterility instead of a drawn-out death. Such methods might be more expensive, but can anyone doubt that if a similar amount of human suffering were at stake, the expense would be borne?

Another clear instance in which the principle of equal consideration of interests would indicate methods different from those presently used is in the timber industry. There are two basic methods of obtaining timber from forests. One is to cut only selected mature or dead trees, leaving the forest substantially intact. The other, known as clear-cutting, involves chopping down everything that grows in a given area, and then reseeding. Obviously when a large area is clear-cut, wild animals find their whole living area destroyed in a few days, whereas selected felling makes a relatively minor disturbance. But clear-cutting is cheaper, and timber companies therefore use this method and will continue to do so unless forced to do otherwise.[6] . . .

VI. THE MEAT INDUSTRY

For the great majority of human beings, especially in urban, industrialized societies, the most direct form of contact with members of other species is at meal-times: We eat them. In doing so we treat them purely as means to our ends. We regard their life and well-being as subordinate to our taste for a particular kind of dish. I say "taste" deliberately—this is purely a matter of pleasing our palate. There can be no defenses of eating flesh in terms of satisfying nutritional needs, since it has been established beyond doubt that we could satisfy our need for protein and other essential nutrients far more efficiently with a diet that replaced animal flesh by soy beans, or products derived from soy beans, and other high-protein vegetable products.

It is not merely the act of killing that indicates what we are ready to do to other species in order to gratify our tastes. The suffering we inflict on the animals while they are alive is perhaps an even clearer indication of our speciesism than the fact that we are prepared to kill them.[7] In order to have meat on the table at a price that people can afford, our society tolerates methods of meat production that confine sentient animals in cramped, unsuitable conditions for the entire durations of their lives. Animals are treated like machines that convert fodder into flesh, and any innovation that results in a higher "conversion ratio" is liable to be adopted. As one authority on the subject has said, "cruelty is acknowledged only when profitability ceases."[8] So hens are crowded four or five to a cage

with a floor area of twenty inches by eighteen inches, or around the size of a single page of the *New York Times*. The cages have wire floors, since this reduces cleaning costs, though wire is unsuitable for the hens' feet; the floors slope, since this makes the eggs roll down for easy collection, although this makes it difficult for the hens to rest comfortably. In these conditions all the birds' natural instincts are thwarted: They cannot stretch their wings fully, walk freely, dust-bathe, scratch the ground, or build a nest. Although they have never known other conditions, observers have noticed that the birds vainly try to perform these actions. Frustrated at their inability to do so, they often develop what farmers call "vices," and peck each other to death. To prevent this, the beaks of young birds are often cut off.

This kind of treatment is not limited to poultry. Pigs are now also being reared in cages inside sheds. These animals are comparable to dogs in intelligence, and need a varied, stimulating environment if they are not to suffer from stress and boredom. Anyone who kept a dog in the way in which pigs are frequently kept would be liable to prosecution, in England at least, but because our interest in exploiting pigs is greater than our interest in exploiting dogs, we object to cruelty to dogs while consuming the produce of cruelty to pigs. Of the other animals, the condition of veal calves is perhaps worst of all, since these animals are so closely confined that they cannot even turn around or get up and lie down freely. In this way they do not develop unpalatable muscle. They are also made anemic and kept short of roughage, to keep their flesh pale, since white veal fetches a higher price; as a result they develop a craving for iron and roughage, and have been observed to gnaw wood off the sides of their stalls, and lick greedily at any rusty hinge that is within reach.

Since, as I have said, none of these practices cater to anything more than our pleasures of taste, our practice of rearing and killing other animals in order to eat them is a clear instance of the sacrifice of the most important interests of other beings in order to satisfy trivial interests of our own. To avoid speciesism we must stop this practice, and each of us has a moral obligation to cease supporting the practice. Our custom is all the support that the meat industry needs. The decision to cease giving it that support may be difficult, but it is no more difficult than it would have been for a white Southerner to go against the traditions of his society and free his slaves; if we do not change our dietary habits, how can we censure those slaveholders who would not change their own way of living?

Notes

1. For a fuller statement of this argument, see my *Animal Liberation* (New York: A New York Review Book, 1975), especially Ch. 1.

2. Ibid.

3. See, for instance, the comments by Arthur Galston in *Natural History*, 83, no. 3 (March 1974): 18, on the "evidence" cited in such books as *The Secret Life of Plants*.

4. Singer, *Animal Liberation*, pp. 20–23.

5. See J. Olsen, *Slaughter the Animals, Poison the Earth* (New York: Simon and Schuster, 1971), especially pp. 153–164.

6. See R. and V. Routley, *The Fight for the Forests* (Canberra: Australian National University Press, 1974); for a thoroughly documented indictment of clear-cutting in America, see *Time*, May 17, 1976.

7. Although one might think that killing a being is obviously the ultimate wrong one can do to it, I think that the infliction of suffering is a clearer indication of speciesism because it might be argued that at least part of what is wrong with killing a human is that most humans are conscious of their existence over time, and have desires and purposes that extend into the future—see, for instance, M. Tooley, "Abortion and Infanticide," *Philosophy and Public Affairs,* vol. 2,

no. 1 (1972). Of course, if one took this view one would have to hold—as Tooley does—that killing a human infant or mental defective is not in itself wrong, and is less serious than killing certain higher mammals that probably do have a sense of their own existence over time.

8. Ruth Harrison, *Animal Machines* (Stuart, London, 1964). This book provides an eye-opening account of intensive farming methods for those unfamiliar with the subject.

Review and Discussion Questions

1. Describe the human practices that most clearly demonstrate speciesism.

2. Do you agree that animals have interests that human beings must take into account? If so, which animals and what interests? What about plants?

3. What does the principle of "equal consideration of interests" imply for our treatment of animals? What does it not imply?

4. Give examples of how adherence to the principle of equal consideration would change our conduct. What are the principle's implications for business?

5. Singer rejects "our practice of rearing and killing other animals in order to eat them." Explain why. How might a critic respond to his argument? Can meat eating be morally justified?

Reading ────────────── ■

PEOPLE OR PENGUINS

WILLIAM F. BAXTER

In contrast to Peter Singer and many environmentalists, William F. Baxter defends a human-centered, cost-benefit approach to environmental issues. According to him the impact of our actions on, for example, penguins, sugar pines, or geological marvels is irrelevant except insofar as it affects human interests. Baxter argues that this is the only realistic approach to take and that, in any case, what is good for humans is in many respects good for plant and animal life as well. He also rejects the claim that we have an obligation to respect the "balance of nature" or to "preserve the environment." No natural or morally correct state of nature exists, and even pollution is only defined by reference to the needs of human beings. For Baxter, the goal is not pure air and water but the "optimal state of pollution"—that is, the level of pollution that yields the greatest amount of human satisfaction.

I start with the modest proposition that, in dealing with pollution, or indeed with any problem, it is helpful to know what one is attempting to accomplish. Agreement on how and whether to pursue a particular objective, such as pollution control, is not possible unless some more general objective has been identified and stated with reasonable precision. We talk loosely of having clean air and clean water, of preserving our wilderness areas, and so forth. But none of these is a sufficiently general objective: each is more accurately viewed as a means rather than as an end.

With regard to clean air, for example, one may ask, "how clean?" and "what does clean mean?" It is even reasonable to ask, "Why have clean air?" Each of these questions is an implicit demand that

a more general community goal be stated—a goal sufficiently general in its scope and enjoying sufficiently general assent among the community of actors that such "why" questions no longer seem admissible with respect to that goal.

If, for example, one states as a goal the proposition that "every person should be free to do whatever he wishes in contexts where his actions do not interfere with the interests of other human beings," the speaker is unlikely to be met with a response of "why?" The goal may be criticized as uncertain in its implications or difficult to implement, but it is so basic a tenet of our civilization—it reflects a cultural value so broadly shared, at least in the abstract—that the question of "why" is seen as impertinent or imponderable or both. . . .

Without any expectation of obtaining unanimous consent to them, let me set forth four goals that I generally use as ultimate testing criteria in attempting to frame solutions to problems of human organization. My position regarding pollution stems from these four criteria. . . .

My criteria are as follows:

1. The spheres of freedom criterion stated [two paragraphs] above.

2. Waste is a bad thing. The dominant feature of human existence is scarcity—our available resources, our aggregate labors, and our skill in employing both have always been, and will continue for some time to be, inadequate to yield to every man all the tangible and intangible satisfactions he would like to have. Hence, none of those resources, or labors, or skills, should be wasted—that is, employed so as to yield less than they might yield in human satisfactions.

3. Every human being should be regarded as an end rather than as a means to be used for the betterment of another. Each should be afforded dignity and regarded as having an absolute claim to an even-handed application of such rules as the community may adopt for its governance.

4. Both the incentive and the opportunity to improve his share of satisfactions should be preserved to every individual. Preservation of

Reprinted by permission from William F. Baxter, *People or Penguins: The Case for Optimal Pollution.* Copyright © 1974 Columbia University Press.

incentive is dictated by the "no-waste" criterion and enjoins against the continuous, totally egalitarian redistribution of satisfactions, or wealth; but subject to that constraint, everyone should receive, by continuous redistribution if necessary, some minimal share of aggregate wealth so as to avoid a level of privation from which the opportunity to improve his situation becomes illusory.

The relationship of these highly general goals to the more specific environmental issues at hand may not be readily apparent, and I am not yet ready to demonstrate their pervasive implications. Recently scientists have informed us that use of DDT in food production is causing damage to the penguin population. For the present purposes let us accept that assertion as an indisputable scientific fact. The scientific fact is often asserted as if the correct implication—that we must stop agricultural use of DDT—followed from the mere statement of fact of penguin damage. But plainly it does not follow if my criteria are employed.

My criteria are oriented to people, not penguins. Damage to penguins, or sugar pines, or geological marvels is, without more, simply irrelevant. One must go further, by my criteria, and say: Penguins are important because people enjoy seeing them walk about rocks; and furthermore, the well-being of people would be less impaired by halting use of DDT than by giving up penguins. In short, my observations about environmental problems will be people-oriented, as are my criteria. I have no interest in preserving penguins for their own sake.

It may be said by way of objection to this position that it is very selfish of people to act as if each person represented one unit of importance and nothing else was of any importance. It is undeniably selfish. Nevertheless I think it is the only tenable starting place for analysis for several reasons. First, no other position corresponds to the way most people really think and act—i.e., corresponds to reality.

Second, this attitude does not portend any massive destruction of nonhuman flora and fauna, for people depend on them in many obvious ways, and

they will be preserved because and to the degree that humans do depend on them.

Third, what is good for humans is, in many respects, good for penguins and pine trees—clean air for example. So that humans are, in these respects, surrogates for plant and animal life.

Fourth, I do not know how we could administer any other system. Our decisions are either private or collective. Insofar as Mr. Jones is free to act privately, he may give such preferences as he wishes to other forms of life: he may feed birds in winter and do with less himself, and he may even decline to resist an advancing polar bear on the ground that the bear's appetite is more important than those portions of himself that the bear may choose to eat. In short my basic premise does not rule out private altruism to competing life-forms. It does rule out, however, Mr. Jones' inclination to feed Mr. Smith to the bear, however hungry the bear, however despicable Mr. Smith.

Insofar as we act collectively, on the other hand, only humans can be afforded an opportunity to participate in the collective decisions. Penguins cannot vote now and are unlikely subjects for the franchise—pine trees more unlikely still. Again each individual is free to cast his vote so as to benefit sugar pines if that is his inclination. But many of the more extreme assertions that one hears from some conservationists amount to tacit assertions that they are specially appointed representatives of sugar pines, and hence that their preferences should be weighted more heavily than the preferences of other humans who do not enjoy equal rapport with "nature." The simplistic assertion that agricultural use of DDT must stop at once because it is harmful to penguins is of that type.

Fifth, if polar bears or pine trees or penguins, like men, are to be regarded as ends rather than means, if they are to count in our calculus of social organization, someone must tell me how much each one counts, and someone must tell me how these life-forms are to be permitted to express their preferences, for I do not know either answer. If the answer is that certain people are to hold their proxies, then I want to know how those proxy-holders are to be selected: self-appointment does not seem workable to me.

Sixth, and by way of summary of all the foregoing, let me point out that the set of environmental issues under discussion—although they raise very complex technical questions of how to achieve any objective—ultimately raise a normative question: what *ought* we to do? Questions of *ought* are unique to the human mind and world—they are meaningless as applied to a nonhuman situation.

I reject the proposition that we *ought* to respect the "balance of nature" or to "preserve the environment" unless the reason for doing so, express or implied, is the benefit of man.

I reject the idea that there is a "right" or "morally correct" state of nature to which we should return. The word "nature" has no normative connotation. Was it "right" or "wrong" for the earth's crust to heave in contortion and create mountains and seas? Was it "right" for the first amphibian to crawl up out of the primordial ooze? Was it "wrong" for plants to reproduce themselves and alter the atmospheric composition in favor of oxygen? For animals to alter the atmosphere in favor of carbon dioxide both by breathing oxygen and eating plants? No answers can be given to these questions because they are meaningless questions.

All this may seem obvious to the point of being tedious, but much of the present controversy over environment and pollution rests on tacit normative assumptions about just such nonnormative phenomena: that it is "wrong" to impair penguins with DDT, but not to slaughter cattle for prime rib roasts. That it is wrong to kill stands of sugar pines with industrial fumes, but not to cut sugar pines and build housing for the poor. Every man is entitled to his own preferred definition of Walden Pond, but there is no definition that has any moral superiority over another, except by reference to the selfish needs of the human race.

From the fact that there is no normative definition of the natural state, it follows that there is no normative definition of clean air or pure water— hence no definition of polluted air—or of pollution—except by reference to the needs of man. The "right" composition of the atmosphere is one which has some dust in it and some lead in it and some hydrogen sulfide in it—just those amounts that attend a sensibly organized society thoughtfully and knowledgeably pursuing the greatest possible satisfaction for its human members.

The first and most fundamental step toward solution of our environmental problems is a clear recognition that our objective is not pure air or water but rather some optimal state of pollution. That step immediately suggests the question: How do we define and attain the level of pollution that will yield the maximum possible amount of human satisfaction?

Low levels of pollution contribute to human satisfaction but so do food and shelter and education and music. To attain ever lower levels of pollution, we must pay the cost of having less of these other things. I contrast that view of the cost of pollution control with the more popular statement that pollution control will "cost" very large numbers of dollars. The popular statement is true in some senses, false in others; sorting out the true and false senses is of some importance. The first step in that sorting process is to achieve a clear understanding of the difference between dollars and resources. Resources are the wealth of our nation; dollars are merely claim checks upon those resources. Resources are of vital importance; dollars are comparatively trivial.

Four categories of resources are sufficient for our purposes: at any given time a nation, or a planet if you prefer, has a stock of labor, of technological skill, of capital goods, and of natural resources (such as mineral deposits, timber, water, land, etc.). These resources can be used in various combinations to yield goods and services of all kinds—in some limited quantity. The quantity will be larger if they are combined efficiently, smaller if combined inefficiently. But in either event the resource stock is limited, the goods and services that they can be made to yield are limited; even the most efficient use of them will yield less than our population, in the aggregate, would like to have.

If one considers building a new dam, it is appropriate to say that it will be costly in the sense that it will require x hours of labor, y tons of steel and concrete, and z amount of capital goods. If these resources are devoted to the dam, then they cannot be used to build hospitals, fishing rigs, schools, or electric can openers. That is the meaningful sense in which the dam is costly.

Quite apart from the very important question of how wisely we can combine our resources to produce goods and services is the very different question of how they get distributed—who gets how many goods? Dollars constitute the claim checks which are distributed among people and which control their share of national output. Dollars are nearly valueless pieces of paper except to the extent that they do represent claim checks to some fraction of the output of goods and services. Viewed as claim checks, all the dollars outstanding during any period of time are worth, in the aggregate, the goods and services that are available to be claimed with them during that period—neither more nor less.

It is far easier to increase the supply of dollars than to increase the production of goods and services—printing dollars is easy. But printing more dollars doesn't help because each dollar then simply becomes a claim to fewer goods, i.e., becomes worth less.

The point is this: many people fall into error upon hearing the statement that the decision to build a dam, or to clean up a river, will cost $X million. It is regrettably easy to say: "It's only money. This is a wealthy country, and we have lots of money." But you cannot build a dam or clean a river with $X million—unless you also have a match, you can't even make a fire. One builds a dam or cleans a river by diverting labor and steel and trucks and factories from making one kind of goods to making another. The cost in dollars is merely a shorthand way of describing the extent of the diversion necessary. If we build a dam for $X million, then we must recognize that we will have $X million less housing and food and medical care and electric can openers as a result.

Similarly, the costs of controlling pollution are best expressed in terms of the other goods we will have to give up to do the job. This is not to say the job should not be done. Badly as we need more housing, more medical care, and more can openers, and more symphony orchestras, we could do with somewhat less of them, in my judgement at least, in exchange for somewhat cleaner air and rivers. But that is the nature of the trade-off, and analysis of the problem is advanced if that unpleasant reality is kept in mind. Once the trade-off relationship is clearly perceived, it is possible to state in a very general way what the optimal level of pollution is. I would state it as follows:

People enjoy watching penguins. They enjoy relatively clean air and smog-free vistas. Their health is improved by relatively clean water and air. Each of these benefits is a type of good or service. As a society we would be well advised to give up one washing machine if the resources that would have gone into that washing machine can yield greater human satisfaction when diverted into pollution control. We should give up one hospital if the resources thereby freed would yield more human satisfaction when devoted to elimination of noise in our cities. And so on, trade-off by trade-off, we should divert our productive capacities from the production of existing goods and services to the production of a cleaner, quieter, more pastoral nation up to—and no further than—the point at which we value more highly the next washing machine or hospital that we would have to do without than we value the next unit of environmental improvement that the diverted resources would create.

Now this proposition seems to me unassailable but so general and abstract as to be unhelpful—at least unadministerable in the form stated. It assumes we can measure in some way the incremental units of human satisfaction yielded by very different types of goods. The proposition must remain a pious abstraction until I can explain how this measurement process can occur. . . . But I insist that the proposition stated describes the result for which we should be striving—and again, that it is always useful to know what your target is even if your weapons are too crude to score a bull's eye.

Review and Discussion Questions

1. What are the practical implications of Baxter's human-centered, cost-benefit approach to environmental issues? How sympathetic are you to his approach? What do you see as its strong points? Its weak points?

2. Assess each of Baxter's six reasons for claiming that his is the best starting point for examining environmental issues.

3. What exactly does Baxter mean by saying the "questions of *ought* are unique to the human mind and world—they are meaningless as applied to a nonhuman situation"? Does the fact that only human beings are moral agents imply that human beings can have moral responsibilities only to other human beings?

4. Is Baxter right in arguing that there is no right or wrong level of pollution independent of human needs?

5. How does Peter Singer's perspective contrast with Baxter's? How would he reply to Baxter's arguments?

6. Does the idea of an optimal level of pollution make sense? If so, how do we determine that level? Is it possible to calculate it or to reach agreement on trade-offs between environmental goods and other goods?

Reading ■

BUSINESS AND ENVIRONMENTAL ETHICS

W. MICHAEL HOFFMAN

W. Michael Hoffman argues that business has an obligation to protect the environment beyond what the law requires and that it must creatively find ways to become part of the solution to our environmental problems. Protecting the environment can be compatible with profitability, but there is a risk, Hoffman argues, in wooing business to the environmental cause solely on the basis of self-interest. Likewise, even though enlightened human self-interest may dictate environmental preservation and protection, Hoffman—in contrast to Baxter— advocates approaching environmental ethics from a biocentric, rather than human-centered, perspective.

Albert Gore said, "The fact that we face an ecological crisis without any precedent in historic times is no longer a matter of any dispute worthy of recognition."[1] The question, he continued, is not whether there is a problem, but how we will address it. This will be the focal point for a public policy debate which . . .must clarify such fundamental questions as: (1) What obligation does business have to help with our environmental crisis? (2) What is the proper relationship between business and government, especially when faced with a social problem of the magnitude of the environmental crisis? And (3) what rationale should be used for making and justifying decisions to protect the environment? Corporations, and society in general for that matter, have yet to answer these questions satisfactorily. In the first section of this essay I will briefly address the first two questions. In the final two sections I will say a few things about the third question.

I.

. . . Norman Bowie [has] offered some answers to the first two questions.

> Business does not have an obligation to protect the environment over and above what is required by law; however, it does have a moral obligation to avoid intervening in the political arena in order to defeat or weaken environmental legislation.[2]

I disagree with Bowie on both counts.

Bowie's first point is very Friedmanesque.[3] The social responsibility of business is to produce goods and services and to make profit for its shareholders, while playing within the rules of the market game. These rules, including those to protect the

From *Business Ethics Quarterly* 1 (April 1991). Copyright © 1991 *Business Ethics Quarterly*. Reprinted by permission. Some notes omitted.

environment, are set by the government and the courts. To do more than is required by these rules is, according to this position, unfair to business. In order to perform its proper function, every business must respond to the market and operate in the same arena as its competitors. As Bowie puts this:

> An injunction to assist in solving societal problems [including depletion of natural resources and pollution] makes impossible demands on a corporation because, at the practical level, it ignores the impact that such activities have on profit.[4]

If, as Bowie claims, consumers are not willing to respond to the cost and use of environmentally friendly products and actions, then it is not the responsibility of business to respond or correct such market failure.

Bowie's second point is a radical departure from this classical position in contending that business should not lobby against the government's process to set environmental regulations. To quote Bowie:

> Far too many corporations try to have their cake and eat it too. They argue that it is the job of government to correct for market failure and then they use their influence and money to defeat or water down regulations designed to conserve and protect the environment.[5]

Bowie only recommends this abstinence of corporate lobbying in the case of environmental regulations. He is particularly concerned that politicians, ever mindful of their reelection status, are already reluctant to pass environmental legislation which has huge immediate costs and in most cases very long-term benefits. This makes the obligations of business to refrain from opposing such legislation a justified special case.

I can understand why Bowie argues these points. He seems to be responding to two extreme approaches, both of which are inappropriate. Let me illustrate these extremes by the following two stories.

. . . Harvard Business School Professor George Cabot Lodge told of a friend who owned a paper company on the banks of a New England stream. On the first Earth Day in 1970, his friend was converted to the cause of environmental protection. He became determined to stop his company's pollution of the stream, and marched off to put his new-found religion into action. Later, Lodge learned his friend went broke, so he went to investigate. Radiating a kind of ethical purity, the friend told Lodge that he spent millions to stop the pollution and thus could no longer compete with other firms that did not follow his example. So the company went under, 500 people lost their jobs, and the stream remained polluted.

When Lodge asked why his friend hadn't sought help from the state or federal government for stricter standards for everyone, the man replied that was not the American way, that government should not interfere with business activity, and that private enterprise could do the job alone. In fact, he felt it was the social responsibility of business to solve environmental problems, so he was proud that he had set an example for others to follow.

The second story portrays another extreme. A few years ago "Sixty Minutes" interviewed a manager of a chemical company that was discharging effluent into a river in upstate New York. At the time, the dumping was legal, though a bill to prevent it was pending in Congress. The manager remarked that he hoped the bill would pass, and that he certainly would support it as a responsible citizen. However, he also said he approved of his company's efforts to defeat the bill and of the firm's policy of dumping wastes in the meantime. After all, isn't the proper role of business to make as much profit as possible within the bounds of law? Making the laws—setting the rules of the game—is the role of government, not business. While wearing his business hat the manager had a job to do, even if it meant doing something that he strongly opposed as a private citizen.

Both stories reveal incorrect answers to the questions posed earlier, the proof of which is found in the fact that neither the New England stream nor the New York river was made any cleaner. Bowie's points are intended to block these two extremes. But to avoid these extremes, as Bowie does, misses the real managerial and ethical failure of the stories. Although the paper company owner and the chemical company manager had radically different views of the ethical responsibilities of business, both saw business and government performing separate roles, and neither felt that business ought to cooperate with government to solve environmental problems.

If the business ethics movement has led us anywhere in the past fifteen years, it is to the position that business has an ethical responsibility to become a more active partner in dealing with social concerns. Business must creatively find ways to become a part of solutions, rather than being a part of problems. Corporations can and must develop a conscience, as Ken Goodpaster and others have argued—and this includes an environmental conscience.[6] Corporations should not isolate themselves from participation in solving our environmental problems, leaving it up to others to find the answers and to tell them what not to do.

Corporations have special knowledge, expertise, and resources which are invaluable in dealing with the environmental crisis. Society needs the ethical vision and cooperation of all its players to solve its most urgent problems, especially one that involves the very survival of the planet itself. Business must work with government to find appropriate solutions. It should lobby for good environmental legislation and lobby against bad legislation, rather than isolating itself from the legislative process as Bowie suggests. It should not be ethically quixotic and try to go it alone, as our paper company owner tried to do, nor should it be ethically inauthentic and fight against what it believes to be environmentally sound policy, as our chemical company manager tried to do. Instead business must develop and demonstrate moral leadership.

There are examples of corporations demonstrating such leadership, even when this has been a risk to their self-interest. In the area of environmental moral leadership one might cite DuPont's discontinuing its Freon products, a $750-million-a-year business, because of their possible negative effects on the ozone layer, and Procter and Gamble's manufacture of concentrated fabric softener and detergents that require less packaging. But some might argue, as Bowie does, that the real burden for environmental change lies with consumers, not with corporations. If we as consumers are willing to accept the harm done to the environment by favoring environmentally unfriendly products, corporations have no moral obligation to change so long as they obey environmental law. This is even more the case, so the argument goes, if corporations must take risks or sacrifice profits to do so. . . .

Activities that affect the environment should not be left up to what we, acting as consumers, are willing to tolerate or accept. To do this would be to use a market-based method of reasoning to decide on an issue which should be determined instead on the basis of our ethical responsibilities as a member of a social community.

Furthermore, consumers don't make the products, provide the services, or enact the legislation which can be either environmentally friendly or unfriendly. Grassroots boycotts and lobbying efforts are important, but we also need leadership and mutual cooperation from business and government in setting forth ethical environmental policy. Even Bowie admits that perhaps business has a responsibility to educate the public and promote environmentally responsible behavior. But I am suggesting that corporate moral leadership goes far beyond public educational campaigns. It requires moral vision, commitment, and courage, and involves risk and sacrifice. I think business is capable of such a challenge. Some are even engaging in such a challenge. Certainly the business ethics movement should do nothing short of encouraging such leadership. I feel morality demands such leadership.

II.

If business has an ethical responsibility to the environment that goes beyond obeying environmental law, what criterion should be used to guide and justify such action? Many corporations are making environmentally friendly decisions where they see there are profits to be made by doing so. They are wrapping themselves in green where they see a green bottom line as a consequence. This rationale is also being used as a strategy by environmentalists to encourage more businesses to become environmentally conscientious. . . . The highly respected Worldwatch Institute published an article by one of its senior researchers entitled "Doing Well by Doing Good" which gives numerous examples of corporations improving their pocketbooks by improving the environment. It concludes by saying that "fortunately, businesses that work to preserve the environment can also make a buck."[7]

In a recent Public Broadcast Corporation documentary entitled "Profit the Earth," several efforts are depicted of what is called the "new environmentalism," which induces corporations to do things for the environment by appealing to their self-interest. The Environmental Defense Fund is shown encouraging agribusiness in Southern California to irrigate more efficiently and profit by selling the water saved to the city of Los Angeles. This in turn will help save Mono Lake. EDF is also shown lobbying for emissions trading that would allow utility companies that are under their emission allotments to sell their "pollution rights" to those companies that are over their allotments. This is for the purpose of reducing acid rain. Thus, the frequent strategy of the new environmentalists is to get business to help solve environmental problems by finding profitable or virtually costless ways for them to participate. They feel that compromise, not confrontation, is the only way to save the earth. By using the tools of the free enterprise system, they are in search of win-win solutions, believing that such solutions are necessary to take us beyond what we have so far been able to achieve.

I am not opposed to these efforts; in most cases I think they should be encouraged. There is certainly nothing wrong with making money while protecting the environment, just as there is nothing wrong with feeling good about doing one's duty. But if business is adopting or being encouraged to adopt the view that good environmentalism is good business, then I think this poses a danger for the environmental ethics movement—a danger which has an analogy in the business ethics movement.

As we all know, the position that good ethics is good business is being used more and more by corporate executives to justify the building of ethics into their companies and by business ethics consultants to gain new clients. For example, the Business Roundtable's *Corporate Ethics* report states:

> The corporate community should continue to refine and renew efforts to improve performance and manage change effectively through programs in corporate ethics. . . . [C]orporate ethics is a strategic key to survival and profitability in this era of fierce competitiveness in a global economy.[8]

And, for instance, the book *The Power of Ethical Management* by Kenneth Blanchard and Norman Vincent Peale states in big red letters on the cover jacket that "Integrity Pays! You Don't Have to Cheat to Win." The blurb on the inside cover promises that the book "gives hard-hitting, practical, *ethical* strategies that build profits, productivity, and long-term success." Whoever would have guessed that business ethics could deliver all that! In such ways business ethics gets marketed as the newest cure for what ails corporate America.

Is the rationale that good ethics is good business a proper one for business ethics? I think not. One thing that the study of ethics has taught us over the past 2,500 years is that being ethical may on occasion require that we place the interests of others ahead of or at least on par with our own interests. And this implies that the ethical thing to do, the morally right thing to do, may not be in our own self-interest. What happens when the right thing is not the best thing for the business?

Although in most cases good ethics may be good business, it should not be advanced as the only or even the main reason for doing business ethically. When the crunch comes, when ethics conflicts with the firm's interests, any ethics program that has not already faced up to this possibility is doomed to fail because it will undercut the rationale of the program itself. We should promote business ethics, not because good ethics is good business, but because we are morally required to adopt the moral point of view in all our dealings—and business is no exception. In business, as in all other human endeavors, we must be prepared to pay the costs of ethical behavior.

There is a similar danger in the environmental movement with corporations choosing or being wooed to be environmentally friendly on the grounds that it will be in their self-interest. There is the risk of participating in the movement for the wrong reasons. But what does it matter if business cooperates for reasons other than the right reasons, as long as it cooperates? It matters if business believes or is led to believe that it only has a duty to be environmentally conscientious in those cases where such actions either require no sacrifice or actually make a profit. And I am afraid this is exactly what is happening. I suppose it wouldn't matter if the environmental cooperation of business was only needed in those cases where it was also in business's self-interest. But this is surely not the case, unless one begins to really reach and talk about that amorphous concept "long-term" self-interest. Moreover, long-term interests, I suspect, are not what corporations or the new environmentalists have in mind in using self-interest as a reason for environmental action.

I am not saying we should abandon attempts to entice corporations into being ethical, both environmentally and in other ways, by pointing out and providing opportunities where good ethics is good business. And there are many places where such attempts fit well in both the business and environmental ethics movements. But we must be careful not to cast this as the proper guideline for business's ethical responsibility. Because when it is discovered that many ethical actions are not necessarily good for business, at least in the short run, then the rationale based on self-interest will come up morally short, and both ethical movements will be seen as deceptive and shallow.

III.

What is the proper rationale for responsible business action toward the environment? A minimalist principle is to refrain from causing or prevent the causing of unwarranted harm, because failure to do so would violate certain moral rights not to be harmed. There is, of course, much debate over what harms are indeed unwarranted due to conflict of rights and questions about whether some harms are offset by certain benefits. Norm Bowie, for example, uses the harm principle, but contends that business does not violate it as long as it obeys environmental law. Robert Frederick, on the other hand, convincingly argues that the harm principle morally requires business to find ways to prevent certain harm it causes even if such harm violates no environmental law.[9]

However, Frederick's analysis of the harm principle is largely cast in terms of harm caused to human beings and the violation of rights of human beings. Even when he hints at the possible moral obligation to protect the environment when no one is caused unwarranted harm, he does so by suggesting that we look to what we, as human beings, value. This is very much in keeping with a humanistic position of environmental ethics which claims that only human beings have rights or moral standing because only human beings have intrinsic value. We may have duties with regard to nonhuman things (penguins, trees, islands, etc.) but only if such duties are derivative from duties we have toward human beings. Nonhuman things are valuable only if valued by human beings.

Such a position is in contrast to a naturalistic view of environmental ethics which holds that natural things other than human beings are intrinsically valuable and have, therefore, moral standing. Some naturalistic environmentalists only include other sentient animals in the framework of being deserving of moral consideration; others include all things that are alive or are an integral part of an ecosystem. This latter view is sometimes called a biocentric environmental ethic as opposed to the homocentric view which sees all moral claims in terms of human beings and their interests. Some characterize these two views as deep versus shallow ecology.

The literature on these two positions is vast and the debate is ongoing. The conflict between them goes to the heart of environmental ethics and is crucial to our making of environmental policy and to our perception of moral duties to the environment, including business's. I strongly favor the biocentric view. And although this is not the place to try to adequately argue for it, let me unfurl its banner for just a moment.

A version of R. Routley's "last man" example[10] might go something like this: Suppose you were the last surviving human being and were soon to die from nuclear poisoning, as all other human and sentient animals have died before you. Suppose also that it is within your power to destroy all remaining life, or to make it simpler, the last tree which could continue to flourish and propagate if left alone. Furthermore, you will not suffer if you do not destroy it. Would you do anything wrong by cutting it down? The deeper ecological view would say yes because you would be destroying something that has value in and of itself, thus making the world a poorer place.

It might be argued that the only reason we may find the tree valuable is because human beings generally find trees of value either practically or aesthetically, rather than the atoms or molecules they might turn into if changed from their present form. The issue is whether the tree has value only in its relation to human beings or whether it has a value deserving of moral consideration inherent in itself in its present form. The biocentric position holds that when we find something wrong with destroying the tree, as we should, we do so because we are responding to an intrinsic value in the natural object, not to a value we give to it. This is a view that argues against a humanistic environmental ethic and urges us to channel our moral obligations accordingly.

Why should one believe that nonhuman living things or natural objects forming integral parts of ecosystems have intrinsic value? One can respond to this question by pointing out the serious weaknesses and problems of human chauvinism.[11] More complete responses lay out a framework of concepts and beliefs which provides a coherent picture of the biocentric view with human beings as a part of a more holistic value system. . . . In the final analysis, environmental biocentrism is adopted or not depending on whether it is seen to provide a deeper, richer, and more ethically compelling view of the nature of things.

If this deeper ecological position is correct, then it ought to be reflected in the environmental movement. Unfortunately, for the most part, I do not think this is being done, and there is a price to be paid for not doing so. Moreover, I fear that even those who are of the biocentric persuasion are using homocentric language and strategies to bring business and other major players into the movement because they do not think they will be successful otherwise. They are afraid, and undoubtedly for good reason, that the large part of society, including business, will not be moved by arguments regarding the intrinsic value and rights of natural things. It is difficult enough to get business to recognize and act on their responsibilities to human beings and things of human interest. . . .

A major concern in using the homocentric view to formulate policy and law is that nonhuman nature will not receive the moral consideration it deserves. It might be argued, however, that by appealing to the interests and rights of human beings, in most cases nature as a whole will be protected. That is, if we are concerned about a wilderness area, we can argue that its survival is important to future generations who will otherwise be deprived of contact with its unique wildlife. We can also argue that it is important to the aesthetic pleasure of certain individuals or that, if it is destroyed, other recreational areas will become overcrowded. . . .

In most cases, what is in the best interests of human beings may also be in the best interests of the rest of nature. After all, we are in our present environmental crisis in large part because we have not been ecologically intelligent about what is in our own interest—just as business has encountered much trouble because it has failed to see its interest in being ethically sensitive. But if the environmental movement relies only on arguments based on human interests, then it perpetuates the danger of making environmental policy and law on the basis of our strong inclination to fulfill our immediate self-interests, on the basis of our consumer viewpoints, on the basis of our willingness to pay. There will always be a tendency to allow our short-term interests to eclipse our long-term interests and the long-term interest of humanity itself. Without some grounding in a deeper environmental ethic with obligations to nonhuman natural things, then the temptation to view our own interests in disastrously short-term ways is that much more encouraged. The biocentric view helps to block this temptation.

Furthermore, there are many cases where what is in human interest is not in the interest of other natural things. Examples range from killing leopards for stylish coats to destroying a forest to build a golf course. I am not convinced that homocentric arguments, even those based on long-term human interests, have much force in protecting the interests of such natural things. Attempts to make these interests coincide might be made, but the point is that from a homocentric point of view the leopard and the forest have no morally relevant interests to consider. It is simply fortuitous if nonhuman natural interests coincide with human interests, and are thereby valued and protected. Let us take an example from the work of Christopher Stone. Suppose a stream has been polluted by a business. From a homocentric point of view, which serves as the basis for our legal system, we can only correct the problem through finding some harm done to human beings who use the stream. Reparation for such harm might involve cessation of the pollution and restoration of the stream, but it is also possible that the business might settle with the people by paying them for their damages and continue to pollute the stream. Homocentrism provides no way for the stream to be made whole again unless it is in the interests of human beings to do so. In short it is possible for human beings to sell out the stream.[12] . . .

Finally, perhaps the greatest danger that biocentric environmentalists run in using homocentric strategies to further the movement is the loss of the very insight that grounded their ethical concern in the first place. This is nicely put by Lawrence Tribe:

> What the environmentalist may not perceive is that, by couching his claim in terms of human self-interest—by articulating environmental goals wholly in terms of human needs and preferences—he may be helping to legitimate a system of discourse which so structures human thought and feeling as to erode, over the long run, the very sense of obligation which provided the initial impetus for his own protective efforts.[13]

Business ethicists run a similar risk in couching their claims in terms of business self-interest.

The environmental movement must find ways to incorporate and protect the intrinsic value of animal and plant life and even other natural objects that are integral parts of ecosystems. This must be done without constantly reducing such values to human interests. This will, of course, be difficult, because our conceptual ideology and ethical persuasion are so dominantly homocentric; however, if we are committed to a deeper biocentric ethic, then it is vital that we try to find appropriate ways to promote it. Environmental impact statements should make explicit reference to nonhuman natural values. Legal rights for nonhuman natural things, along the lines of Christopher Stone's proposal, should be sought. And naturalistic ethical guidelines, such as those suggested by Holmes Rolston,

should be set forth for business to follow when its activities impact upon ecosystems.[14]

At the heart of the business ethics movement is its reaction to the mistaken belief that business only has responsibilities to a narrow set of its stakeholders, namely its stockholders. Crucial to the environmental ethics movement is its reaction to the mistaken belief that only human beings and human interests are deserving of our moral consideration. I suspect that the beginnings of both movements can be traced to these respective moral insights. Certainly the significance of both movements lies in their search for a broader and deeper moral perspective. If business and environmental ethicists begin to rely solely on promotional strategies of self-interest, such as good ethics is good business, and of human interest, such as homocentrism, then they face the danger of cutting off the very roots of their ethical efforts.

Notes

1. Albert Gore, "What Is Wrong with Us?" *Time* (January 2, 1989), 66.

2. Norman Bowie, "Morality, Money, and Motor Cars," *Business, Ethics, and the Environment: The Public Policy Debate,* edited by W. Michael Hoffman, Robert Frederick, and Edward S. Petry, Jr. (New York: Quorum Books, 1990), p. 89.

3. See Milton Friedman, "The Social Responsibility of Business Is to Increase Its Profits," *The New York Times Magazine* (September 13, 1970).

4. Bowie, p. 91.

5. Bowie, p. 94.

6. Kenneth E. Goodpaster, "Can a Corporation Have an Environmental Conscience?" *The Corporation, Ethics, and the Environment,* edited by W. Michael Hoffman, Robert Frederick, and Edward S. Petry, Jr. (New York: Quorum Books, 1990).

7. Cynthia Pollock Shea, "Doing Well by Doing Good," *WorldWatch* (November/December, 1989), p. 30.

8. *Corporate Ethics: A Prime Business Asset,* a report by The Business Roundtable, February, 1988, p. 4.

9. Robert Frederick, "Individual Rights and Environmental Protection," presented at the Annual Society for Business Ethics Conference in San Francisco, August 10 and 11, 1990.

10. Richard Routley and Val Routley, "Human Chauvinism and Environmental Ethics," *Environmental Philosophy,* Monograph Series, No. 2, edited by Don Mannison,

Michael McRobbie, and Richard Routley (Australian National University, 1980), pp. 121ff.

11. See Paul W. Taylor, "The Ethics of Respect for Nature," found in *People, Penguins, and Plastic Trees,* edited by Donald VanDeVeer and Christine Pierce (Belmont, Calif.: Wadsworth, 1986), pp. 178–183. Also see R. and V. Routley, "Against the Inevitability of Human Chauvinism," found in *Ethics and the Problems of the 21st Century,* edited by K. E. Goodpaster and K. M. Sayre (Notre Dame: University of Notre Dame Press, 1979), pp. 36–59.

12. Christopher D. Stone, "Should Trees Have Standing?— Toward Legal Rights for Natural Objects," *Southern California Law Review* 45 (1972).

13. Lawrence H. Tribe, "Ways Not to Think About Plastic Trees: New Foundations for Environmental Law," found in *People, Penguins, and Plastic Trees,* p. 257.

14. Holmes Rolston III, *Environmental Ethics* (Philadelphia: Temple University Press, 1988), pp. 301–313.

Review and Discussion Questions

1. What is Norman Bowie's position, and what are the two extreme approaches that Hoffman sees him as trying to avoid? On what grounds does Hoffman reject Bowie's stance?

2. Why is Hoffman critical of the position that "good ethics is good business"? How is his argument relevant to the effort to get corporations to be more environmentally responsible?

3. Explain the difference between a homocentric and a biocentric approach to environmental ethics. Why does Hoffman favor a biocentric approach? Compare his perspective to Baxter's. Whose position do you find more persuasive and why?

4. If what is in the best interests of human beings is usually what is in the best interests of the rest of nature, why does Hoffman think it is bad for the environmental movement to rely on arguments based on human interests?

5. With regard to preserving and protecting the environment, who has the most important role to play—government, individual consumers, or business?

Further Reading for Chapter 11

Robin Attfield, *The Ethics of Environmental Concern,* 2nd ed. (Athens: University of Georgia Press, 1991) and **Holmes Rolston III**, *Philosophy Gone Wild: Environmental Ethics* (Buffalo, N.Y.: Prometheus, 1990) are good introductions to environmental ethics.

Dale Jamieson, ed., *A Companion to Environmental Ethics* (Malden, Mass.: Blackwell, 2001) is a valuable, although philosophically advanced, reference work.

Daniel J. Kevles, "Endangered Environmentalists," *New York Review of Books,* February 20, 1997, is an informative but succinct account of the many environmental problems we face.

Lisa H. Newton and **Catherine K. Dillingham**, *Watersheds: Classic Cases in Environmental Ethics,* 3rd ed. (Belmont, Calif.: Wadsworth, 2002) offers ten detailed and insightful environmental case studies.

Joel Reichart and **Patricia H. Werhane,** eds., *Environmental Challenges to Business* (Bowling Green, Ohio: Philosophy Documentation Center, 2000) collects new and insightful essays on business and the environment by prominent business ethicists.

Mark Sagoff, *The Economy of Earth* (New York: Cambridge University Press, 1990) is an informed discussion of environmental policy.

Peter Singer, *Animal Liberation,* 2nd ed. (New York: Random House, 1990) is a seminal work advocating a radical change in our treatment of animals.

James Sterba, ed., *Earth Ethics: Introductory Readings in Animal Rights and Environmental Ethics,* 2nd ed. (Upper Saddle River, N.J.: Prentice Hall, 2000) is an excellent, wide-ranging collection of essays, representing different environmental and philosophical approaches.

Timothy S. Yoder, "Corporate Responsibility and the Environment," *Business and Society Review* 106 (Fall 2001) takes up the topic of corporate responsibility for environmental malfeasance.

 InfoTrac College Edition: For further information or to conduct research, please go to www.infotrac-college.com.

Index ∎